June 6–9, 2017
Bucharest, Romania

Association for
Computing Machinery

Advancing Computing as a Science & Profession

ICMR'17

Proceedings of the 2017 ACM
International Conference on Multimedia Retrieval

Sponsored by:

ACM SIGMM

Supported by:

Vodafone, Tencent, HERE, Google,
Politehnica University of Bucharest, & University of Trento

Association for
Computing Machinery

Advancing Computing as a Science & Profession

The Association for Computing Machinery
2 Penn Plaza, Suite 701
New York, New York 10121-0701

Notice to Past Authors of ACM-Published Articles
ACM intends to create a complete electronic archive of all articles and/or other material previously published by ACM. If you have written a work that has been previously published by ACM in any journal or conference proceedings prior to 1978, or any SIG Newsletter at any time, and you do NOT want this work to appear in the ACM Digital Library, please inform permissions@acm.org, stating the title of the work, the author(s), and where and when published.

ISBN: 978-1-4503-4701-3 (Digital)

ISBN: 978-1-4503-5600-8 (Print)

Additional copies may be ordered prepaid from:

ACM Order Department
PO Box 30777
New York, NY 10087-0777, USA

Phone: 1-800-342-6626 (USA and Canada)
+1-212-626-0500 (Global)
Fax: +1-212-944-1318
E-mail: acmhelp@acm.org
Hours of Operation: 8:30 am – 4:30 pm ET

ICMR 2017 Chairs' Welcome

It is our great pleasure to welcome you to the *2017 ACM International Conference on Multimedia Retrieval* (*ICMR 2017*). This year's conference continues a 17-year tradition of being the premier forum for presentation of research results and experience reports on core topics in multimedia retrieval, as well as the broader set of topics that must be addressed to ensure that multimedia retrieval technologies are of practical use in real-world use cases. Special emphasis was placed on topics related to large-scale indexing, user interaction, exploiting diverse and multimodal data, and domain-specific challenges. This annual international conference, combines the long-standing experience of the former ACM CIVR (International Conference on Image and Video Retrieval) and ACM MIR (International Conference on Multimedia Information Retrieval) series, and was set up in 2011 to highlight the state of the art in multimedia (e.g., text, image, video, audio, sensor data, and 3D) retrieval.

This year's edition has attracted submissions from all over the world: Asia, Canada, Australia, Africa, Europe, and the United States. In total, it received 178 valid submissions, which were reviewed by the program committee. For the classic research paper tracks, out of 95 full paper submissions, 33 were accepted — 20 for full oral presentation and 13 for spotlight oral presentation (acceptance rate of 34%; full oral paper acceptance rate of 21%) — and, out of 35 short paper submissions, 13 were accepted (acceptance rate of 37%).

Next to full and short paper tracks, the conference includes a diversity of other tracks: open-source software (acceptance rate of 80%), technical demonstrations (acceptance rate of 85%), brave new ideas papers (acceptance rate of 75%), doctoral symposium papers (acceptance rate of 80%), and special session papers (acceptance rate of 66%). In addition to the tracks of the main conference, two workshops are offered: "Wearable MultiMedia" and "Multimedia Forensics and Security".

The conference program is complemented by a full day of tutorials on "Video Indexing, Search, Detection, and Description", keynote talks given by world-class researchers ("Searching for a thing", Arnold W.M. Smeulders & Ran Tao, and "Making cultural visits with a smart mate", Alberto Del Bimbo), industry keynote talks given by leading companies ("With 5G Approaching, How will Audio/Video Technology that Serves 800 Million QQ Users Bring Forth New Ideas", Xiaozheng Huang, Tencent, China, "Information Retrieval from Multi-Sensor Data for Enriching Location Services at HERE Technologies", Matei Stroilă, HERE, USA, and "Intelligently Connecting People with Information", Changhu Wang, Toutiao AI Lab, China) and a panel session on "Indicators of Innovation and Signs of Success: Recognizing which multimedia information retrieval research is most valuable to industry".

Putting together *ICMR'17* was a large team effort. We first thank the many authors for providing the technical and interactive content of the program. We would like to acknowledge, with appreciation, the high quality of the submissions. We are grateful to the many program committee members who worked hard in recruiting, reviewing, and organizing their sessions. We are especially grateful to our webmaster for creating and maintaining the conference website (http://www.icmr2017.ro/).

We thank University Politehnica of Bucharest, Electronica 2000 Foundation, and University of Trento for their precious logistical and financial support. We thank our official sponsors, ACM and SIGMM, for their sustained help and for providing the student grants. We thank all our industrial supporters: Tencent, Vodafone, Google, and HERE for their valuable contribution.

We hope that you will find the conference informative and stimulating, and the venue — city of Bucharest and in particular the University Politehnica of Bucharest — to be an exciting place to interact with your fellow researchers and practitioners from all around the world.

Bogdan Ionescu
General Chair
University Politehnica of Bucharest,
Romania

Nicu Sebe
General Chair
University of Trento,
Italy

Jiashi Feng
Program Chair
National University of Singapore,
Singapore

Martha Larson
Program Chair
Radboud University Nijmegen & TU Delft,
The Netherlands

Rainer Lienhart
Program Chair
University of Augsburg,
Germany

Cees Snoek
Program Chair
University of Amsterdam &
Qualcomm Research Netherlands,
The Netherlands

Table of Contents

Special Oral Beyond Semantics: Multimodal Understanding of Subjective Properties

Session Chair: Miriam Redi *(Bell Labs Cambridge)*

Oral Brave New Ideas

Session Chair: Chong-Wah Ngo *(City University of Hong Kong)*

Oral Open Software

Session Chair: Mathias Lux *(Alpen-Adria-University Klagenfurt)*

Oral Session 2: Multimedia Indexing (Oral Presentations)

Session Chair: Adrian Ulges *(RheinMain University of Applied Sciences)*

Posters

Session Chair: Petra Galuščáková *(Charles University)*

Demonstrations

Session Chair: Jaeyoung Choi *(Delft University of Technology & International Computer Science Institute)*

Oral Doctoral Symposium

Session Chair: Tomas Piatrik *(Queen Mary University of London)*

Industry Keynotes

Session Chair: Neil O'Hare *(Yahoo Research)*

2017 International Conference on Multimedia Retrieval Organization

General Chairs: Bogdan Ionescu *(University Politehnica of Bucharest, Romania)*
Nicu Sebe *(University of Trento, Italy)*

Program Chairs: Jiashi Feng *(National University of Singapore, Singapore)*
Martha Larson *(Radboud University & Delft University of Technology, Netherlands)*
Rainer Lienhart *(University of Augsburg, Germany)*
Cees Snoek *(University of Amsterdam & Qualcomm Research Netherlands, Netherlands)*

Industry and Practitioners Day Chairs: Alejandro Jaimes *(AiCure, USA)*
Liangliang Cao *(customerserviceAI.com, USA)*

Demonstrations Chairs: Xavier Anguera *(ELSA Corp, USA)*
Benoit Huet *(EURECOM, France)*

Open Software Session Chair: Mathias Lux *(Alpen-Adria-Universität Klagenfurt, Austria)*

Special Sessions Chairs: Henning Müller *(HES-SO, University of Applied Sciences Western Switzerland, Switzerland)*
Allan Hanbury *(Technische Universität Wien, Austria)*
Marius Leordeanu *(University Politehnica of Bucharest & Institute of Mathematics of the Romanian Academy, Romania)*

Brave New Ideas Chairs: David A. Shamma *(Centrum Wiskunde & Informatica (CWI), Netherlands)*
K. Selcuk Candan *(Arizona State University, USA)*

Workshop Chairs: Shin'ichi Satoh *(National Institute of Informatics, Japan)*
Jenny Benois-Pineau *(University of Bordeaux, France)*

Tutorials Chairs: Marco Cristani *(University of Verona, Italy)*
Alexis Joly *(INRIA, France)*

Doctoral Symposium Chairs: Yu-Gang Jiang *(Fudan University, China)*
Tomas Piatrik *(Queen Mary University of London, United Kingdom)*

Panels Chairs: Ansgar Scherp *(Kiel University, Germany)*
Yi Yang *(University of Technology Sydney, Australia)*

Publicity Chairs: Horia Cucu *(University Politehnica of Bucharest, Romania)*
Bernard Merialdo *(EURECOM, France)*

Sponsorship Chair: Andi Buzo *(Infineon Technologies & University Politehnica of Bucharest, Romania)*

Proceedings Chairs: Erwin M. Bakker *(Leiden University, Netherlands)*
Zhigang Ma *(Carnegie Mellon University, USA)*
Ionuţ Mironică *(University Politehnica of Bucharest, Romania)*

Special Session Organizers: Xavier Alameda-Pineda *(INRIA Grenoble, France)*
Shih-Fu Chang *(Columbia University, USA)*
Claire-Helene Demarty *(Technicolor, France)*
Ngoc Q. K. Duong *(Technicolor, France)*
Maria Eskevich *(Radboud University, Netherlands)*
Benoit Huet *(EURECOM, France)*
Gareth Jones *(Dublin City University, Ireland)*
Roeland Ordelman *(University of Twente, Netherlands)*
Miriam Redi *(Bell Labs Cambridge, United Kingdom)*
Nicu Sebe *(University of Trento, Italy)*
Mats Sjöberg *(University of Helsinki, Finland)*
Mohammad Soleymani *(University of Geneva, Switzerland)*

Workshop Organizers: Stefano Alletto *(University of Modena and Reggio Emilia, Italy)*
Andrea Ferracani *(University of Florence, Italy)*
Vasilis Katos *(Bournemouth University, United Kingdom)*
Federico Pernici *(University of Florence, Italy)*
Anderson de Rezende Rocha *(University of Campinas, Brazil)*
Yoichi Sato *(University of Tokyo, Japan)*
Ioannis Tsampoulatidis *(Information Technologies Institute, CERTH, Greece)*
Stefanos Vrochidis *(Information Technologies Institute, CERTH, Greece)*
Markos Zampoglou *(Information Technologies Institute, CERTH, Greece)*

Local Organizing Committee: Şeila Abdulamit *(University Politehnica of Bucharest, Romania)*
Mihai-Gabriel Constantin *(University Politehnica of Bucharest, Romania)*
Mihai Dogariu *(University Politehnica of Bucharest, Romania)*
Liviu-Daniel Ştefan *(University Politehnica of Bucharest, Romania)*

Website Chair: Bogdan Boteanu (*University Politehnica of Bucharest, Romania)*

Program Committee: Esra Açar *(Technische Universität Berlin, Germany)*
Laurent Amsaleg *(CNRS-IRISA, France)*
Claudio Baecchi *(University of Florence, Italy)*
Werner Bailer *(JOANNEUM RESEARCH, Austria)*
Lamberto Ballan *(University of Padua, Italy)*
Olfa Ben-Ahmed *(EURECOM, France)*
Marco Bertini *(University of Florence, Italy)*
Damian Borth *(German Research Center for Artificial Intelligence (DFKI), Germany)*
Hervé Bredin *(CNRS, LIMSI, University of Paris-Saclay, France)*
K. Selcuk Candan *(Arizona State University, USA)*
Axel Carlier *(University of Toulouse, France)*
Pablo Cesar *(Centrum Wiskunde & Informatica (CWI), Netherlands)*
Vincent Charvillat *(IRIT-ENSEEIHT, France)*
Savvas Chatzichristofis *(Neapolis University Pafos, Cyprus)*
Jingjing Chen *(City University of Hong Kong, China)*
Kuan-Ta Chen *(Academia Sinica, Taiwan)*
Yan-Ying Chen *(National Taiwan University, Taiwan)*
Wen-Huang Cheng *(Academia Sinica, Taiwan)*
Jaeyoung Choi *(Delft University of Technology, Netherlands & International Computer Science Institute, USA)*
Matthew Cooper *(FX Palo Alto Laboratory, USA)*
Wei-Ta Chu *(National Chung Cheng University, Taiwan)*
Yung-Yu Chuang *(National Taiwan University, Taiwan)*
Qi Dai *(Fudan University, China)*
Maaike de Boer *(TNO / Radboud University, Netherlands)*
Alberto Del Bimbo *(University of Florence, Italy)*
Emmanuel Dellandrea *(LIRIS-Ecole Centrale de Lyon, France)*
Andreas Dengel *(German Research Center for Artificial Intelligence (DFKI), Germany)*
Hamdi Dibeklioglu *(Delft University of Technology, Netherlands)*
Ajay Divakaran *(SRI International, USA)*
Jana Eggink *(BBC, United Kingdom)*
Maria Eskevich *(Radboud University, Netherlands)*
Ralph Ewerth *(German National Library of Science & Technology and L3S Research Center, Germany)*
Jianping Fan *(University of North Carolina Charlotte, USA)*
Quanfu Fan *(IBM, USA)*
Gerald Friedland *(Lawrence Livermore National Laboratory and University of California, Berkeley, USA)*
Chuang Gan *(Tsinghua University, China)*
Efstratios Gavves *(University of Amsterdam, Netherlands)*
Xavier Giro-i-Nieto *(Universitat Politècnica de Catalunya (UPC), Spain)*
Nikolaos Gkalelis *(Information Technologies Institute, CERTH, Greece)*
Guillaume Gravier *(CNRS-IRISA, France)*
Carsten Griwodz *(Simula Research Laboratory, Norway)*
William Grosky *(University of Michigan, USA)*
Cathal Gurrin *(Dublin City University, Ireland)*

Program Committee (continued):

Michael Gygli *(ETH Zurich, Switzerland & Gifs.com, USA)*
Jonathon Hare *(University of Southampton, United Kingdom)*
Claudia Hauff *(Delft University of Technology, Netherlands)*
Andreas Henrich *(University of Bamberg, Germany)*
Djoerd Hiemstra *(University of Twente, Netherlands)*
Richang Hong *(Hefei University of Technology, China)*
Frank Hopfgartner *(University of Glasgow, United Kingdom)*
Timothy Hospedales *(University of Edinburgh, United Kingdom)*
Qingming Huang *(University of Chinese Academy of Sciences, China)*
Ichiro Ide *(Nagoya University, Japan)*
Alejandro Jaimes *(AiCure, USA)*
Yu-Gang Jiang *(Fudan University, China)*
Sagar Joglekar *(King's College London, United Kingdom)*
Alexis Joly *(INRIA, France)*
Gareth Jones *(Dublin City University, Ireland)*
Joemon Jose *(University of Glasgow, United Kingdom)*
Brendan Jou *(Google Research, USA)*
Mohan Kankanhalli *(National University of Singapore, Singapore)*
John Kender *(Columbia University, USA)*
Lyndon Kennedy *(Futurewei Technologies, USA)*
Ewa Kijak *(Université de Rennes 1- IRISA, France)*
Peter Knees *(Technische Universität Wien, Austria)*
Yiannis Kompatsiaris *(Information Technologies Institute, CERTH, Greece)*
Patrick Le Callet *(Nantes University, France)*
Olivier Le Meur *(University of Rennes 1, France)*
Hyowon Lee *(Singapore University of Technology and Design, Singapore)*
Bruno Lepri *(Fondazione Bruno Kessler, Italy)*
Michael S. Lew *(Leiden University, Netherlands)*
Xirong Li *(Renmin University of China, China)*
Xuelong Li *(Chinese Academy Of Sciences, China)*
Cynthia Liem *(Delft University of Technology, Netherlands)*
Joo-Hwee Lim *(Institute for Infocomm Research (I2R) A*STAR, Singapore)*
Yen-Liang Lin *(National Taiwan University, Taiwan)*
Dong Liu *(Columbia University, USA)*
Guojun Lu *(Federation University Australia, Australia)*
Mathias Lux *(Alpen-Adria-Universität Klagenfurt, Austria)*
Joao Magalhaes *(Universidade Nova de Lisboa, Portugal)*
Yasushi Makihara *(Osaka University, Japan)*
Oge Marques *(Florida Atlantic University, USA)*
Kevin McGuinness *(Dublin City University, Ireland)*
Tao Mei *(Microsoft Research, China)*
Britta Meixner *(Centrum Wiskunde & Informatica (CWI), Netherlands)*
Thomas Mensink *(University of Amsterdam, Netherlands)*
Bernard Merialdo *(EURECOM, France)*
Michele Merler *(IBM Research, USA)*
Pascal Mettes *(University of Amsterdam, Netherlands)*
Vasileios Mezaris *(Information Technologies Institute, CERTH, Greece)*
Daniel Moreira *(University of Notre Dame, USA)*

Program Committee (continued):

Henning Müller *(HES-SO, Switzerland)*
Venkatesh N. Murthy *(University of Massachusetts, Amherst, USA)*
Chong-Wah Ngo *(City University of Hong Kong, Hong Kong)*
Liqiang Nie *(National University of Singapore, Singapore)*
Naoko Nitta *(Osaka University, Japan)*
Noel E. O'Connor *(Dublin City University, Ireland)*
Vincent Oria *(New Jersey Institute of Technology, USA)*
Sharath Pankanti *(IBM Research, USA)*
Symeon *(Papadopoulos, Information Technologies Institute, CERTH, Greece)*
Nikolaos Pappas *(Idiap Research Institute, Switzerland)*
Yuxin Peng *(Peking University, China)*
Andrea Pilzer *(University of Trento, Italy)*
Lorenzo Porzi *(Universitat Politècnica de Catalunya (UPC), Spain)*
Balakrishnan Prabhakaran *(University of Texas at Dallas, USA)*
Georges Quénot *(Laboratoire d'Informatique de Grenoble, CNRS, France)*
Miriam Redi *(Bell Labs Cambridge, United Kingdom)*
Haoyu Ren *(Samsung, USA)*
Elisa Ricci *(University of Perugia, Italy)*
Michael Riegler *(Simula Research Laboratory and University of Oslo, Norway)*
Samuel Rota Bulò *(Fondazione Bruno Kessler, Italy)*
Peter M. Roth *(Graz University of Technology, Austria)*
Stevan Rudinac *(University of Amsterdam, Netherlands)*
Mohammed Abdel-Megeed M. Salem *(Ain Shams University, Egypt)*
Darshan Santani *(Idiap Research Institute/Ecole Polytechnique Federale de Lausanne (EPFL), Switzerland)*
Maria Luisa Sapino *(University of Turin, Italy)*
Shin'ichi Satoh *(National Institute of Informatics, Japan)*
Markus Schedl *(Johannes Kepler University Linz, Austria)*
Rossano Schifanella *(University of Turin, Italy)*
Klaus Schöffmann *(Alpen-Adria-Universität Klagenfurt, Austria)*
Lorenzo Seidenari *(University of Florence, Italy)*
Fumin Shen *(University of Electronic Science and Technology of China, China)*
Koichi Shinoda *(Tokyo Institute of Technology, Japan)*
Lidan Shou (*Zhejiang University, China)*
Chiao-Fe Shu *(IBM Research, USA)*
Mei-Ling Shyu *(University of Miami, USA)*
Carlos N. Silla Jr. *(Pontifical Catholic University of Parana (PUCPR), Brazil)*
Mats Sjöberg *(University of Helsinki, Finland)*
Malcolm Slaney *(Google Research, USA)*
Alan F. Smeaton *(Dublin City University, Ireland)*
John Smith *(IBM Research, USA)*
Mohammad Soleymani *(University of Geneva, Switzerland)*
Thomas Steiner *(Google, Germany)*
Chen Sun *(Google, USA)*
Mengfan Tang *(University of California, Irvine, USA)*

Program Committee (continued):

Bart Thomee *(Google, USA)*
Qi Tian *(The University of Texas at San Antonio, USA)*
Christian Timmerer *(Alpen-Adria-Universität Klagenfurt, Austria)*
Mercan Topkara *(Teachers Pay Teachers, USA)*
Theodora Tsikrika *(Information Technologies Institute, CERTH, Greece)*
Rosario Uceda-Sosa *(IBM Research, USA)*
Tiberio Uricchio *(University of Florence, Italy)*
Remco Veltkamp *(Utrecht University, Netherlands)*
Stefanos Vrochidis *(Information Technologies Institute, CERTH, Greece)*
Xiangyu Wang *(National University of Singapore, Singapore)*
Yan Wang *(Microsoft, USA)*
Yilin Wang *(Arizona State University, USA)*
Christian Wartena *(Hannover University of Applied Sciences and Arts, Germany)*
Marcel Worring *(University of Amsterdam, Netherlands)*
Xiao Wu *(Southwest Jiaotong University, China)*
Dan Xu *(University of Trento, Italy)*
Changsheng Xu *(Chinese Academy of Sciences, China)*
Keiji Yanai *(University of Electro-Communications, Tokyo, Japan)*
Yi-Hsuan Yang *(Academia Sinica, Taiwan)*
Guangnan Ye *(IBM Research, USA)*
Jun Yu *(Xiamen University, China)*
Maia Zaharieva *(Technische Universität Wien, Austria)*
Gloria Zen *(University of Trento, Italy)*
Zheng-Jun Zha *(Chinese Academy of Sciences, China)*
Xiao Zhang *(University of Denver, USA)*
Xiangdong Zhou *(Fudan University, China)*
Xiaofang Zhou *(University of Queensland, Australia)*

Workshop reviewers: Irene Amerini *(University of Florence, Italy)*
Fernanda Andaló *(Institute of Computing, University of Campinas, Brazil)*
Sandra Avila *(Institute of Computing, University of Campinas, Brazil)*
Mauro Barni *(University of Siena, Italy)*
Jenny Benois-Pineau *(University of Bordeaux, France)*
Paolo Bestagini *(Politecnico di Milano, Italy)*
Alejandro Betancourt *(University of Eindhoven, Netherlands)*
Giulia Boato *(University of Trento, Italy)*
Roberto Caldelli *(CNIT-University of Florence, Italy)*
Tiago Carvalho *(Institute of Computing, University of Campinas, Brazil)*
Adam Czajka *(University of Notre Dame, USA)*
Touraj Ebrahimi *(Ecole Polytechnique Federale de Lausanne (EPFL), Switzerland)*
Pasquale Ferrara *(University of Florence, Italy)*
Alexandre Ferreira *(Institute of Computing, University of Campinas, Brazil)*
Francisco Florez-Rovuelta *(University of Alicante, Spain)*
Helen Gibson *(Sheffield Hallam University, United Kingdom)*
Daniel Henriques Moreira *(Institute of Computing, University of Campinas, Brazil)*
Chryssanthi Iakovidou *(Information Technologies Institute, CERTH, Greece)*
Ramesh Jain *(University of California, Irvine, USA)*
George Kalpakis *(Information Technologies Institute, CERTH, Greece)*
Dimitris Kavallieros *(Center for Security Studies-KEMEA, Greece)*
Giuseppe Lisanti *(University of Florence, Italy)*
Walterio Mayol-Cuevas *(University Bristol, United Kingdom)*
Symeon Papadopoulos *(Information Technologies Institute, CERTH, Greece)*
Iraklis Paraskakis *(South East European Reserach Centre, Greece)*
Cecilia Pasquini *(Universität Innsbruck, Austria)*
William Puech *(Université de Montpellier, France)*
Alessia De Rosa *(University of Florence, Italy)*
William Schwartz *(Federal University of Minas Gerais, Brazil)*
Giuseppe Serra *(University of Udine, Italy)*
Nikolai Stoianov *(Defence Institute "Prof. Tsvetan Lazarov", Bulgaria)*
Theodora Tsikrika *(Information Technologies Institute, CERTH, Greece)*
Stefano Tubaro *(Politecnico di Milano, Italy)*
Luisa Verdoliva *(University of Naples Federico II, Italy)*
Ryo Yonetani *(University of Tokyo, Japan)*

Additional reviewers: Konstantinos Avgerinakis *(Information Technologies Institute, CERTH, Greece)*
Federico Bartoli *(University of Florence, Italy)*
Federico Becattini *(University of Florence, Italy)*
Alexia Briassouli *(Information Technologies Institute, CERTH, Greece)*
Lisa Brown *(IBM Research Center, USA)*
Elisavet Chatzilari *(Information Technologies Institute, CERTH, Greece)*
Szu-Yu Chou *(National Taiwan University, Taiwan)*
Simone Ercoli *(University of Florence, Italy)*
Lei Feng *(Zhejiang University, China)*
Claudio Ferrar *(University of Florence, Italy)*
Teddy Furon *(INRIA, France)*
Leonardo Galteri *(University of Florence, Italy)*
Ilias Gialampoukidis *(Information Technologies Institute, CERTH, Greece)*
Xiaoling Gu *(Zhejiang University, China)*
Meina Kan *(Chinese Academy of Sciences, China)*
Mert Kilickaya *(University of Amsterdam, Netherlands)*
Jaehun Kim *(Delft University of Technology, Netherlands)*
Huan Li *(Zhejiang University, China)*
Jie Lin *(Institute for Infocomm Research (I2R) A*STAR, Singapore)*
Dimitris Liparas *(Information Technologies Institute, CERTH, Greece)*
Jen-Yu Liu *(National Taiwan University, Taiwan)*
Martin Memmel *(German Research Center for Artificial Intelligence (DFKI), Germany)*
André Mourão *(Universidade Nova de Lisboa, Portugal)*
Eric Müller *(German National Library of Science and Technology, Germany)*
Christian Otto *(German National Library of Science and Technology, Germany)*
Jeroen Peperkamp *(Delft University of Technology, Netherlands)*
Georgios Rizos *(Information Technologies Institute, CERTH, Greece)*
David Semedo *(Universidade Nova de Lisboa, Portugal)*
Giuseppe Serra *(University of Udine, Italy)*
Xiaobo Shen *(Nanjing University of Science and Technology, China)*
Matthias Springstein *(German National Library of Science and Technology, Germany)*
Eleftherios Spyromitros-Xioufis *(Information Technologies Institute, CERTH, Greece)*
Shangxuan Tian *(National University of Singapore, Singapore)*
Francesco Turchini *(University of Florence, Italy)*
Arwa Wali *(New Jersey Institute of Technology, USA)*
Xiang Wang *(National University of Singapore, Singapore)*
Ming-Chi Yen *(National Taiwan University, Taiwan)*
Mengmi Zhang *(National University of Singapore, Singapore)*
Zeyu Zhao *(Simon Fraser University, Canada)*

2017 International Conference on Multimedia Retrieval Sponsors & Supporters

Sponsors:

acm Association for Computing Machinery

SIGMM

Supporters:

vodafone

Tencent 腾讯

here

Google

Institutional supporters:

POLITEHNICA UNIVERSITATEA DIN BUCUREȘTI UPB 1818

UNIVERSITAS ATHESINA STUDIORUM

UNIVERSITY OF TRENTO - Italy

Searching for A Thing

Arnold W.M. Smeulders
a.w.m.smeulders@uva.nl

Ran Tao
r.tao@uva.nl

ABSTRACT

For humans, one picture usually suffices to identify an object of search. *I am looking for this little girl, have you seen her?* or *Do you have such another one?* are two ways to specify a target even to someone who has never seen the object of search before. Searching from one example in digital multimedia retrieval is a hard problem. From the one example one needs to derive an accurate estimate of all accidental variations in the target picture as well as the structural variation of the target in all other potential pictures. From the one example one needs to derive an accurate estimate of all accidental variations the target instance might have.

We argue that with only one reliable example, locality is at the core of the instance search algorithms. What we need is to emphasize locality at all steps in the algorithm [1]. For each image in the dataset, first one needs to gather evidence from a local area in the image and compare the evidence from that region with the target. Then one needs to search in feature space in the region around the feature points of the target for evidence in the current local region to explain all evidence in view. And, finally one needs to emphasize the similarity function to give preference to evidence which is close to appearances of the target. With this emphasis on locality one is especially successful when searching for flat 2D geometrically rigid layouts like logos and buildings. It also holds for scene recognition, who are effectively flat and one-sided as well due to their large depth.

To generalize to searching for rigid 3D-objects from one example image the variability in view point variations is so big that one needs to learn about other viewpoints in general. General knowledge can come from known object-types, which will limit the search to objects of the same type, prior to verifying in the resulting local neighborhood for instances of the one given example [2]. Then, also the attributes within the category need to be similar to the attributes of the target. We have learned viewpoint invariant attributes from clean shoe images automatically, that is without labelling the attributes a priori [2]. Most of these attributes appear to correspond to components of shoes such as high heels, boots, open toes and so on. With the offline-learned viewpoint-invariant category type and subtype (attributes) classification, the search for the target in the wild is surprisingly successful from one example [2].

To generalize further, there is no other route than first learning the variances and invariances off-line. Where in [1] objects are essentially 2D-flat, and in [2] objects are rigid 3D, the next boundary to cross is searching for articulated objects. Then, non-rigid objects are a hurdle yet to take, followed by searching for objects for which the category or attributes have not been seen before. Current research is on learning more about object variations in general [3].

Searching things from one example is not over yet, but there is a reward waiting in the sense that one example search is useful in other branches of retrieval.

KEYWORDS

Instance search; content based image retrieval

ACM Reference format:

Arnold W.M. Smeulders, Ran Tao. Int Conf Multimedia Retrieval 2017.

ACM ISBN 978-1-4503-4701-3/17/06.
http://dx.doi.org/10.1145/3078971.3079006

REFERENCES

[1] R Tao, E Gavves, CGM Snoek, and AWM Smeulders, Locality in generic instance search from one example. In CVPR, 2014.
[2] R Tao, AWM Smeulders, and SF Chang, Attributes and categories for generic instance search from one example. In CVPR, 2015.
[3] R Tao, E Gavves, and AWM Smeulders, Siamese instance search for tracking. In CVPR, 2016.

Making a Cultural Visit with a Smart Mate*

Keynote Talk Abstract†

Alberto Del Bimbo
Dipartimento di Ingegneria dell'Informazione
Università di Firenze, Italy
alberto.delbimbo@unifi.it

ABSTRACT

Digital and mobile technologies have become increasingly popular to support and improve the quality of experience during cultural visits. The portability of the device, the daily adaptation of most people to its usage, the easy access to information and the opportunity of interactive augmented reality have been key factors of this popularity. We believe that computer vision may help to improve such quality of experience, by making the mobile device smarter and capable of inferring the visitor interests directly from his/her behavior, so triggering the delivery of the appropriate information at the right time without any specific user actions. At MICC University of Florence, we have developed two prototypes of *smart audio guides*, respectively for indoor and outdoor cultural visits, that exploit the availability of multi-core CPUs and GPUs on mobile devices and computer vision to feed information according to the interests of the visitor, in a non intrusive and natural way. In the first one [L. Seidenari et al., 2017], the YOLO network [J. Redmon et al. 2016] is used to distinguish between artworks and people in the camera view. If an artwork is detected, it predicts a specific artwork label. The artwork's description is hence given in audio in the visitor's language. In the second one, the GPS coordinates are used to search Google Places and obtain the interest points closeby. To determine what landmark the visitor is actually looking at, the actual view of the camera is matched against the Google Street Map database using SIFT features. Matched views are classified as either artwork or background and for artworks, descriptions are obtained from Wikipedia. Both prototypes were conceived as a *smart mate* for visits in museums and outdoor sites or cities of art, respectively. In both prototypes, voice activity detection provides hints about what is happening in the surrounding context of the visitor and triggers the audio description only when the visitor is not talking with the accompanying persons. They were developed on NVIDIA Jetson TK1 and deployed on a NVIDIA Shield K1 Tablet, run in real time and were tested in real contexts in a musum and the city of Florence.

ICMR '17, June 06-09, 2017, Bucharest, Romania

ACM ISBN 978-1-4503-4701-3/17/06.
http://dx.doi.org/10.1145/3078971.3079005

BIOGRAPHY

Prof. Del Bimbo is the *Director* of MICC–Media Integration and Communication Center of the University of Firenze, where he was also the *Deputy-Rector* for Research and Innovation and the *Director* of the Dept. of Systems and Computer Science, and the *President* of the Foundation for Research and Innovation. His research is in computer vision, multimedia content indexing and retrieval, as well as multimodal interactivity. He is the author of over 350 publications in journals and conferences. He has been the coordinator of many research and industrial projects at the international and national level. He was the *Program Chair* of ICPR 2016, and ICPR 2012, and ACM Multimedia 2008, and the *General Chair* of the ECCV 2012, ICMR 2011, ACM Multimedia 2010, and IEEE ICMCS 1999. He is the *Editor in Chief* of ACM TOMM journal, and *Associate Editor* of MTAP and PAAA journals. He was *Associate Editor* of IEEE TPAMI and IEEE TMM and also served as the *Guest Editor* of many Special Issues in highly ranked journals. Prof. Del Bimbo is *IAPR Fellow, ACM disinguished Scientist* and is the recipient of the *2016 ACM SIGMM Award* for *Outstanding Technical Contributions to Multimedia Computing, Communications and Applications*.

ACKNOWLEDGMENTS

I acknowledge L. Seidenari, C. Baecchi, T. Uricchio, A. Ferracani, M. Bertini, G. Taverriti and S. Lombini and H. Haderaj who in different times and intensity have contributed to the development of the idea and to the different releases of this research.

Video Indexing, Search, Detection, and Description with Focus on TRECVID

George Awad
National Institute of Standards and Technology
Gaithersburg, Maryland 20899, USA
gawad@nist.gov

Duy-Dinh Le
University of Information Technology,
Vietnam National University HCMC
Ho Chi Minh City, Vietnam
duyld@uit.edu.vn

Chong-Wah Ngo
Department of Computer Science,
City University of Hong Kong
Hong Kong, China
cscwngo@cityu.edu.hk

Vinh-Tiep Nguyen
University of Science, Vietnam
National University HCMC
Ho Chi Minh City, Vietnam
nvtiep@fit.hcmus.edu.vn

Georges Quénot
Univ. Grenoble Alpes
CNRS, Grenoble INP, LIG
F-38000 Grenoble, France
Georges.Quenot@imag.fr

Cees Snoek
University of Amsterdam
Amsterdam, The Netherlands
cgmsnoek@uva.nl

Shin'ichi Satoh
National Institute of Informatics
Japan
satoh@nii.ac.jp

ABSTRACT

There has been a tremendous growth in video data the last decade. People are using mobile phones and tablets to take, share or watch videos more than ever before. Video cameras are around us almost everywhere in the public domain (e.g. stores, streets, public facilities, ...etc). Efficient and effective retrieval methods are critically needed in different applications. The goal of TRECVID is to encourage research in content-based video retrieval by providing large test collections, uniform scoring procedures, and a forum for organizations interested in comparing their results. In this tutorial, we present and discuss some of the most important and fundamental content-based video retrieval problems such as recognizing predefined visual concepts, searching in videos for complex ad-hoc user queries, searching by image/video examples in a video dataset to retrieve specific objects, persons, or locations, detecting events, and finally bridging the gap between vision and language by looking into how can systems automatically describe videos in a natural language. A review of the state of the art, current challenges, and future directions along with pointers to useful resources will be presented by different regular TRECVID participating teams. Each team will present one of the following tasks:

Semantic INdexing (SIN). The TRECVID SIN task [3] ran from 2010 to 2015 and evaluated methods and systems for automatic content-based video indexing. The task was defined as follows: given a test collection, a reference shot segmentation, and concept definitions, return for each target concept a list of at most 2000 shot IDs from the test collection ranked according to their likelihood of containing the target. This tutorial session will give an overview of the SIN task followed by the description of two main approaches, a "classical" one based on engineered features, classification and fusion, and a deep learning-based one [4]. A baseline implementation built by the LIG team and the IRIM group will be introduced and shared.

Zero-example (0Ex) Video Search (AVS). The TRECVID AVS task models the end user search use-case, who is looking for segments of video containing persons, objects, activities, locations, etc. and combinations of the former. Zero-example (0Ex) is basically text-to-video search, where queries are described in text and no visual example is given. Such search paradigm depends heavily on the scale and accuracy of concept classifiers in interpreting the semantic content of videos. The general idea is to annotate and index videos with concepts during offline processing, and then retrieve videos with relevant concepts matching query description [12, 13]. 0Ex video search started since the very beginning of TRECVid in year 2003, growing from around twenty concepts to currently more than ten thousands of classifiers. The queries also evolved from finding a specific thing (e.g., find shots of an airplane taking off) to detecting a complex and generic events (e.g., wedding shower) [18], while dataset size has expanded yearly from less than 200 hours to more than 5,000 hours of videos [17]. This tutorial session will give an overview of the AVS task [1] and 0Ex search paradigm, with topics in development of concept classifiers, indexing and feature pooling, query processing and concept selection, and video recounting. Interesting problems to be discussed include how to determine the number of concepts for query answering, and how to identify query-relevant fragments for feature pooling and video recounting. An overview of the methods used by AVS task participants in 2016 will be presented and a 0Ex baseline system, with a few thousands of concept classifiers (from SIN, ImageNet concept banks) and built on Multimedia Event Detection (MED) and AVS datasets, will be introduced and shared in public domain.

ICMR '17, June 6–9, 2017, Bucharest, Romania
 ACM ISBN 978-1-4503-4701-3/17/06.
DOI: http://dx.doi.org/10.1145/3078971.3079044

Instance Search (INS). The TRECVID INS task [2] aims at exploring technologies that efficiently and effectively search and retrieve specific objects from videos by given visual examples. The task is especially focusing on finding "instances" of object, person, or location, unlike finding objects of specified classes as in the case of the SIN task or ad-hoc video search. This tutorial section will give an overview of the INS task followed by a standard pipeline including short list result generation by bag of visual word technique [20], handling of geometric information and context, efficiency management such as inverted index, and so on [11, 19]. A baseline implementation built by NII team will be introduced and shared.

Multimedia Event Detection (MED). This session will highlight recent research towards detection of events, like 'working on a woodworking project' and 'winning a race without a vehicle', when video examples to learn from are scarce or even completely absent. In the first part of the session we consider the scenario where in the order of ten to hundred examples are available. We provide an overview of supervised classification approaches to event detection, relying on shallow and deep feature encodings, as well as semantic encodings atop of convolutional neural networks predicting concepts and attributes [9]. As events become more and more specific, it is unrealistic to assume that ample examples to learn from will be commonly available [15, 16]. That is why we turn our attention to retrieval approaches in the second part. The key to event recognition when examples are absent is to have a lingual video representation. Once the video is represented in a textual form, standard retrieval metrics can be used. We cover video representation learning algorithms that emphasize on concepts, social tags or semantic embeddings [7, 10, 14]. We will detail how these representations allow for accurate event retrieval and are also able to translate and summarize events in video content, even in the absence of training examples.

Video to Text (VTT). This tutorial session considers the challenge of matching or generating a sentence to a video. The major challenge in video to text matching is that the query and the retrieval set instances belong to different domains, so they are not directly comparable. Videos are represented by audiovisual feature vectors which have a different intrinsic dimensionality, meaning, and distribution than the textual feature vectors used for the sentences. As a solution, many works aim to align the two feature spaces so they become comparable. We will discuss solutions based on low-level, mid-level and high-level alignment for video to text matching [5, 6, 8]. The goal of video to text generation is to automatically assign a caption to a video. We will cover state-of-the-art approaches relying on recurrent neural networks atop a deep convolutional network, and highlight recent innovations inside and outside the network architectures. Examples will be illustrated in the context of the new TRECVID video to text (VTT) pilot task.

CCS CONCEPTS

• **Information systems → Information retrieval;**

KEYWORDS

TRECVID, Semantic Indexing, Multimedia Event Detection, Video Search, Instance Search, Video Description

ACM Reference format:
George Awad, Duy-Dinh Le, Chong-Wah Ngo, Vinh-Tiep Nguyen, Georges Quénot, Cees Snoek, and Shin'ichi Satoh. 2017. Video Indexing, Search, Detection, and Description with Focus on TRECVID. In *Proceedings of ICMR '17, June 6–9, 2017, Bucharest, Romania, ,* 2 pages.
DOI: http://dx.doi.org/10.1145/3078971.3079044

REFERENCES

[1] George Awad, Jonathan Fiscus, Martial Michel, David Joy, Wessel Kraaij, Alan F Smeaton, Georges Quénot, Maria Eskevich, Robin Aly, and Roeland Ordelman. 2016. Trecvid 2016: Evaluating video search, video event detection, localization, and hyperlinking. In *Proceedings of TRECVID*, Vol. 2016.
[2] George Awad, Wessel Kraaij, Paul Over, and ShinâĂŹichi Satoh. 2017. Instance search retrospective with focus on TRECVID. *International Journal of Multimedia Information Retrieval* 6, 1 (2017), 1–29.
[3] George Awad, Cees GM Snoek, Alan F Smeaton, and Georges Quénot. 2016. [Invited Paper] TRECVid Semantic Indexing of Video: A 6-Year Retrospective. *ITE Transactions on Media Technology and Applications* 4, 3 (2016), 187–208.
[4] Mateusz Budnik, Efrain-Leonardo Gutierrez-Gomez, Bahjat Safadi, Denis Pellerin, and Georges Quénot. 2016. Learned features versus engineered features for multimedia indexing. *Multimedia Tools and Applications* (2016), 1–18.
[5] Jianfeng Dong, Xirong Li, Weiyu Lan, Yujia Huo, and Cees GM Snoek. 2016. Early Embedding and Late Reranking for Video Captioning. In *Proceedings of the 2016 ACM on Multimedia Conference*. ACM, 1082–1086.
[6] Jianfeng Dong, Xirong Li, and Cees GM Snoek. 2016. Word2VisualVec: Image and Video to Sentence Matching by Visual Feature Prediction. In *ArXive*.
[7] Amirhossein Habibian, Thomas Mensink, and Cees GM Snoek. 2014. Videostory: A new multimedia embedding for few-example recognition and translation of events. In *Proceedings of the 22nd ACM international conference on Multimedia*. ACM, 17–26.
[8] Amirhossein Habibian, Thomas Mensink, and Cees GM Snoek. 2015. Discovering semantic vocabularies for cross-media retrieval. In *Proceedings of the 5th ACM on International Conference on Multimedia Retrieval*. ACM, 131–138.
[9] Amirhossein Habibian, Thomas Mensink, and Cees GM Snoek. 2017. Video2vec Embeddings Recognize Events when Examples are Scarce. *IEEE Transactions on Pattern Analysis and Machine Intelligence* (2017).
[10] Amirhossein Habibian and Cees GM Snoek. 2014. Recommendations for recognizing video events by concept vocabularies. *Computer Vision and Image Understanding* 124 (2014), 110–122.
[11] Duy-Dinh Le, S. Phan, V. Nguyen, C. Zhu, D. M. Nguyen, T. D. Ngo, S. Kasamwattanarote, P. Sebastien, M. Tran, D. A. Duong, and Shin'ichi Satoh. 2014. National Institute of Informatics, Japan at TRECVID 2014. In *TRECVID*.
[12] Yi-Jie Lu, Phuong Anh Nguyen, Hao Zhang, and Chong-Wah Ngo. 2017. Concept-Based Interactive Search System. In *International Conference on Multimedia Modeling*. Springer, 463–468.
[13] Yi-Jie Lu, Hao Zhang, Maaike de Boer, and Chong-Wah Ngo. 2016. Event detection with zero example: select the right and suppress the wrong concepts. In *Proceedings of the 2016 ACM on International Conference on Multimedia Retrieval*. ACM, 127–134.
[14] Masoud Mazloom, Efstratios Gavves, and Cees GM Snoek. 2014. Conceptlets: Selective semantics for classifying video events. *IEEE Transactions on Multimedia* 16, 8 (2014), 2214–2228.
[15] Masoud Mazloom, Xirong Li, and Cees GM Snoek. 2016. Tagbook: A semantic video representation without supervision for event detection. *IEEE Transactions on Multimedia* 18, 7 (2016), 1378–1388.
[16] Pascal Mettes, Dennis C Koelma, and Cees GM Snoek. 2016. The imagenet shuffle: Reorganized pre-training for video event detection. In *Proceedings of the 2016 ACM on International Conference on Multimedia Retrieval*. ACM, 175–182.
[17] Xiao-Yong Wei, Yu-Gang Jiang, and Chong-Wah Ngo. 2011. Concept-driven multi-modality fusion for video search. *IEEE Transactions on Circuits and Systems for Video Technology* 21, 1 (2011), 62–73.
[18] Hao Zhang, Yi-Jie Lu, Maaike de Boer, Frank ter Haar, Zhaofan Qiu, Klamer Schutte, Wessel Kraaij, and Chong-Wah Ngo. 2015. VIREO-TNO@ TRECVID 2015: multimedia event detection. In *Proc. of TRECVID*.
[19] Cai-Zhi Zhu, Hervé Jégou, and Shin Ichi Satoh. 2013. Query-adaptive asymmetrical dissimilarities for visual object retrieval. In *Proceedings of the IEEE International Conference on Computer Vision*. 1705–1712.
[20] Cai-Zhi Zhu and Shin'ichi Satoh. 2012. Large vocabulary quantization for searching instances from videos. In *Proceedings of the 2nd ACM International Conference on Multimedia Retrieval*. ACM, 52.

Generating Video Descriptions with Topic Guidance

Shizhe Chen
Multimedia Computing Lab
School of Information
Renmin University of China
cszhe1@ruc.edu.cn

Jia Chen
Language Technologies Institute
School of Computer Science
Carnegie Mellon University
jiac@cs.cmu.edu

Qin Jin*
Multimedia Computing Lab
School of Information
Renmin University of China
qjin@ruc.edu.cn

Abstract

Generating video descriptions in natural language (a.k.a. video captioning) is a more challenging task than image captioning as the videos are intrinsically more complicated than images in two aspects. First, videos cover a broader range of topics, such as news, music, sports and so on. Second, multiple topics could coexist in the same video. In this paper, we propose a novel caption model, topic-guided model (TGM), to generate topic-oriented descriptions for videos in the wild via exploiting topic information. In addition to predefined topics, i.e., category tags crawled from the web, we also mine topics in a data-driven way based on training captions by an unsupervised topic mining model. We show that data-driven topics reflect a better topic schema than the predefined topics. As for testing video topic prediction, we treat the topic mining model as teacher to train the student, the topic prediction model, by utilizing the full multi-modalities in the video especially the speech modality. We propose a series of caption models to exploit topic guidance, including implicitly using the topics as input features to generate words related to the topic and explicitly modifying the weights in the decoder with topics to function as an ensemble of topic-aware language decoders. Our comprehensive experimental results on the current largest video caption dataset MSR-VTT prove the effectiveness of our topic-guided model, which significantly surpasses the winning performance in the 2016 MSR video to language challenge.

Keywords

Video Captioning; Data-driven Topics; Multi-modalities; Teacher-student Learning

1 Introduction

It is an ultimate goal of video understanding to automatically generate natural language descriptions of video contents. A wide range of applications can benefit from it such as assisting

*Corresponding author.

ICMR '17, June 6–9, 2017, Bucharest, Romania
 ACM ISBN 978-1-4503-4701-3/17/06...$15.00
DOI: http://dx.doi.org/10.1145/3078971.3079000

Speech Content: 50% of Canada's research Publications have co-authors from other countries this is double the world ...
Groundtruth Captions:
People in white lab coats working on a project.
A person using a laptop.
Canada has double the number co-authors than other countries.
This is a video about technology in Canada.

Speech Content: you can unlock a bus if you really want a driver...
Groundtruth Captions:
A gamer describes how to unlock a feature.
A guy is playing a pc video game.
A lego man with wings is picking a vehicle.
A man is describing a video game as he plays it.

Figure 1: Topic diversity across videos and within one video.

blind people, video editing, indexing, searching or sharing. Drawing on the recent success of image captioning [1–4], where a sentence is generated to describe the image content, more researchers are paying attention to the video captioning task to translate videos to natural language.

However, the open domain videos are quite diverse in topics which makes generating video descriptions more complicated than the image captioning. For various topics ranging from political news to edited movie trailers, the vocabularies and expression styles vary a lot in describing the video contents. For example, for political news videos, words from the political domain occur more frequently. Also political news descriptions are typically in the style of somebody reporting something, which are quite different from descriptions for other topics such as gaming, travel, movie, and animals etc. Besides the topic diversity across videos, even in the same video, its diversity in content and video structure can result in very different video descriptions capturing different topics in the video as shown in Figure 1. Therefore, the topic information is important to guide the caption model to generate better topic-oriented language expression.

In our previous study [5], we have utilized the predefined topics, the category tags crawled from video meta-data during data collection, to improve the captioning performance. However, the predefined topics are suboptimal for video

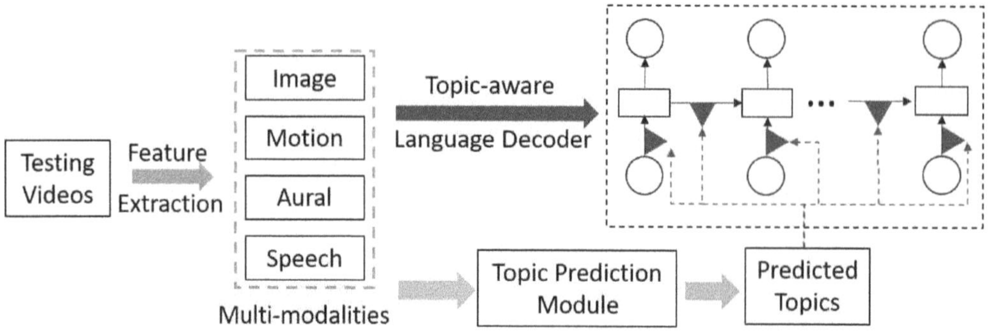

Figure 2: Framework of the proposed topic-guided model (TGM). We use the automatically mined topics as our topic guidance. For testing videos, multimodal features are utilized to predict the mined topics. Then the predicted topics are adopted in the topic-aware language decoder to generate topic-oriented video captions.

captioning because: 1) The crawled information contains labelling mistakes which harms the captioning performance; 2) The exclusive topic labels do not capture the topic diversity nature inside the video; 3) The predefined topic schema is not specially designed for the video captioning task, which may not reflect the topic distributions well. In this work, we propose the data-driven topics to deal with the drawbacks of predefined topics. We use the Latent Dirichlet Allocation (LDA) topic mining model to automatically generate topics from the annotated video captions in training set.

In order to use the mined topic information in the captioning task, two questions need to be addressed: 1) how to obtain the topics automatically for testing videos; and 2) how to effectively employ the topic information to model the difference of sentence descriptions in different video topics.

For the first question, we take a teacher-student learning perspective [6] to train the data-driven topic prediction model. The LDA topic mining model is viewed as the teacher to guide the student topic prediction model to learn. A video generally contains multiple modalities including image, motion, aural and speech modalities. Image modality provides rich information for understanding the video's semantic contents such as object and scene. The motion modality presents actions of the objects and the temporal structure of videos. Aural and speech modalities provide additional information for understanding semantic topics from the sound perspective. Hence, we build one general topic prediction model that utilizes all the four modalities and another topic prediction model dedicated to speech modality as its feature representation is different from other modalities.

For the second question, we propose a novel topic-guided model (TGM) to employ the predicted topics, which is based on the encoder-decoder framework [7]. The TGM functions as an ensemble of topic-aware language decoders to learn specific vocabularies and expressions for various video topics. We also compare the TGM with a series of caption models that we propose in this paper to exploit the topic information, including topic concatenation in encoder (TCE), topic concatenation in decoder (TCD), topic embedding addition/multiplication in decoder (TEAD/TEMD). These compared models implicitly use topics to change the input features of the encoder or decoder, while our proposed TGM explicitly modifies the weights in the decoder according to the predicted topics to capture the sentence distributions within the topic more effectively. The framework of the overall system for testing videos is shown in Figure 2. Experimental results on the MSR-VTT dataset demonstrate the effectiveness of our proposed method, which can generate more comprehensive and accurate video descriptions.

In summary, our contributions in this work include: 1) we show that the data-driven topics are more suitable as the topic representation for video captioning than the predefined topics, e.g. the category tags, with respect to the topic accuracy and schema; 2) to the best of our knowledge, we are the first to use the full multi-modalities especially the speech modality to successfully boost the video captioning performance; and 3) the proposed topic-guided model can exploit the topic information more effectively to generate better topic-oriented video descriptions.

The rest of the paper is organized as follows: Section 2 introduces the related work. Section 3 compares the predefined and the data-driven topics. Our proposed topic-guided model is described in Section 4. Section 5 presents experimental results and analysis. Section 6 draws some conclusions.

2 Related Works

There are mainly two directions in previous image/video captioning works. The first is to build rule based systems, which first detect words by object or action recognition and then generate sentences with predefined language constrains. For example, Lebret et al. [1] predict phrases with a bilinear model and generate descriptions using simple syntax statistics. Rohrbach et al. [8] use the Conditional Random Field to learn object and activity labels from the video. Such systems suffer from the expression accuracy and flexibility.

More recently, researches have been focusing on the second direction of encoder-decoder framework [7] which generates sentences based on image/video features in an end-to-end manner. For example, Vinyals et al. [2] utilize the LSTM to generate sentences with CNN features extracted from the image. Venugopalan et al. [9] transfer knowledge from image caption models with the encoder to perform mean pooling over frame CNN features for video captioning. Pan et al. [10] explicitly embed the sentences and the videos into a common space in addition to the video description generation.

There are also works considering to employ semantic concepts in the encoder-decoder framework. For example, Wu et al. [11] directly generate image captions based on the detected semantic concepts. You et al. [4] propose to selectively attend to concept proposals in the decoder. Gan et al. [12] propose the semantic compositional networks (SCN) which works as an ensemble of concept-dependent language decoder. Our topic-guided model is inspired by SCN but with different aims of producing topic-oriented descriptions to address the topic diversity in video captioning. The reasons of using topics rather than semantic concepts are as follows: 1) There are much more objects in a video than in an image but many of them might be irrelevant to the video description. 2) The topics contain more additional information than semantic objects such as from the motion, aural and speech modalities; and 3) The prediction accuracy is very important for the model as shown in [12]. The topic classification is much easier than object classification.

For video captioning, various video topics result in quite diverse expressions compared with image captioning. Previous works have explored generating descriptions for narrow-domain videos such as YouCook [13] and TACoS [14], whose vocabularies and expressions are similar in the dataset. However, for open-domain videos with various topics such as the MSR-VTT dataset [15], Jin et al. [5] exploit the predefined video categories in the encoder and significantly improve the captioning performance, which results in their winning of the MSR video to language challenge [16]. In our work, we further analyze the qualities of the predefined categories and propose to mine topics in a data-driven approach that leads to better accuracy and topic schema.

Multi-modality nature is also emphasized in video captioning. For the motion modality in videos, Yao et al. [17] explore the temporal structure with local C3D features and global temporal attention mechanism. Venugopalan et al. [18] propose the sequence to sequence structure which utilizes the LSTM as encoder to capture the temporal dynamics of videos. Pan et al. [19] further propose the hierarchical RNN encoder as well as the temporal-spatial attention. Aural modality has also been explored for video captioning. Jin et al. [5, 20] and Ramanishka et al. [21] integrate the visual and aural features in the encoder by early fusion and show that the multimodal fusion was beneficial to improve captioning performance. In our work, we consider more modalities in videos especially for the use of speech content modality.

3 Predefined vs. Data-driven Topics

Our previous study [5] has shown that using predefined topics such as category tags can significantly boost video captioning performance. In this section, we analyze the qualities of these predefined topics, and propose a data-driven approach to develop better topics for the captioning task.

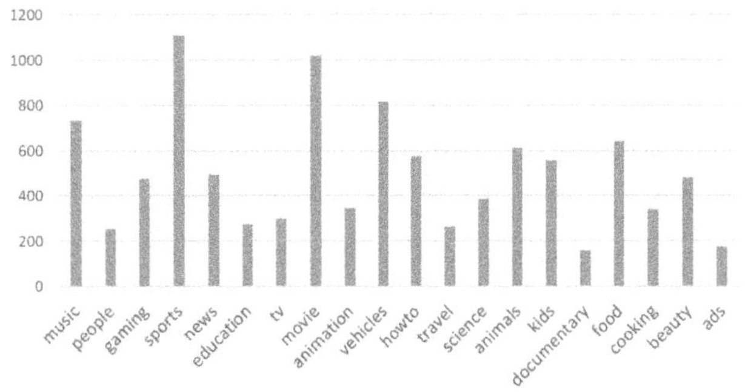

Figure 3: The number of video clips for the 20 predefined video categories of MSR-VTT dataset.

Figure 4: Examples of inaccurate category tags in MSR-VTT dataset. The word in black is the original category tag and the red is the more appropriate tag.

3.1 Predefined Topics: Category Tags

Each video clip in the MSR-VTT dataset contains a predefined category tag derived from the meta-data of the video. The distribution of the category tags is shown in Figure 3. The predefined category tags reflect the variety of the video topics, but there are mainly three disadvantages of them:

(1) Inaccurate category labels: The predefined category labels contain a certain amount of labelling mistakes as shown in the examples in Figure 4, which greatly harm the captioning performance.

(2) Exclusive topic distributions: The users can only assign one of the category labels. Such one-hot topic representation cannot reflect the topic diversity inside the video.

(3) Suboptimal topic schema: a) Ambiguous category definition. For example, the 'people' category is too general to classify. b) Overlap between different categories. For example, the 'food' and 'cooking' categories cover almost similar videos. c) Large mixed categories. Some categories contain much more videos than others and are mixed with

Table 1: Examples of some data-driven topics with their representative words and their co-occurrence with predefined category tags.

topic id	#videos	co-occurrence with predefined categories	representative words
1	182	music:43%, people:21%	people dancing group girls dance women music video dances
3	281	music:50%	stage man playing singing band performing song guitar music
13	439	food:63%, cooking:29%	food cooking kitchen dish person bowl ingredients pan preparing
8	864	news:15%, edu:14%, sci:13%	man talking talks guy speaking person sitting giving camera

many subclasses. d) Indirect connection with captioning task. The category tags are defined to organize videos in the wild, they are not specifically defined for video captioning.

Therefore, although the predefined category tags have benefited video captioning a lot, there is still much room for improvement by defining a better topic schema to represent the diversity of videos for the video captioning task.

3.2 Data-driven Topics

In order to overcome the drawbacks of the predefined category tags, we propose a data-driven way to generate a more suitable set of video topics. The human generated groundtruth captions provide us with rich and accurate annotations about the videos, which also reflect a more task-related topic distributions of the videos. Thus, we propose to mine topics from the groundtruth video captions in the training set. We note that it requires no additional labelling effort on the dataset.

We observe that the multiple human generated groundtruth captions sometimes do not agree with each other even for the same video. For example, Figure 1 shows an example video and its groundtruth captions which describe the video from different aspects including detailed frame contents, speech contents and general video contents. Such example indicates that a video usually contains several topics, which are reflected in its multiple diverse groundtruth captions. The above observation aligns with the generation process of Latent Dirichlet Allocation (LDA) model [22]:
1. the model first draws a topic index $z_{di} \sim Multinomial(\theta_d)$ from the video, where $\theta_d \sim Dirichlet(\alpha), d = 1, ..., D$.
2. the model draws the observed word $w_{ij} \sim Multinomial(\beta_{z_{di}})$ from the selected topic, where $\beta_k \sim Dirichlet(\eta), k = 1...K$.
Here, we group the multiple groundtruth captions of a video into one document to mine latent topics from the training data. Stopwords are removed and the the bag-of-words representation is used as our document feature.

3.3 Relation between Predefined Topics and Data-driven Topics

We study the relation between the predefined topics and data-driven topics based on their co-occurrence in videos. For each video in the training set, we have its corresponding predefined category tag and the data-driven topic distribution calculated from the LDA model. To simplify the calculation of co-occurrence, we assign each video with the most likely topic. Table 1 shows co-occurrence between some predefined categories and data-driven topics. We can see that some predefined categories are split into different topics. For example, the music category is mainly separated into topic 1 of dancing and topic 3 of singing. Some content similar categories are combined together as one topic, i.e. topic 13 consisting of food and cooking categories. And categories that are different but express similar content are also merged. For example, news, educations and science categories are merged into one as most of the descriptions under these categories are "somebody is talking about something". In summary, it shows that the data-driven topics are quite promising and reflect video content distributions better than predefined categories.

4 Topic Guidance Model

In this section, we provide our solutions for the following two problems: 1) how to automatically predict topics for testing videos with multi-modalities; 2) how to maximize the effects of the topic information for caption generation.

4.1 Multimodal Features

We extract features from image, motion, aural and speech modalities to fully represent the content of videos.

Image modality: The image modality reflects the static content of videos. We extract activations from the penultimate layers of the inception-resnet [23] pre-trained on the ImageNet as image object features, and the penultimate layers of the resnet [24] pre-trained on the places365 [25] as image scene features, the dimensionality of which are 1536 and 2048 respectively.

Motion modality: The motion modality captures the local temporal motion. We extract features from the C3D model [26] pre-trained on the Sports-1M dataset. We extract activations from the last 3D convolution layer and max-pooling them along the spatial dimension (width and height) to obtain video features with dimensionality of 512. We then applied l_2-norm on the C3D features.

Aural modality: Aural modality is complementary to visual modalities, especially for distinguishing scenes or events. We extract the Mel-Frequency Cepstral Coefficients (MFCCs) [27] as the basic low-level descriptors. Two encoding strategies, Bag-of-Audio-Words [28] and Fisher Vector [29], are used to aggregate MFCC frames into one video-level feature vector, with dimensionality of 1024 and 624 respectively.

Speech modality: Speech modality provides semantic topics and content details of the video. We use the IBM Watson API [30] for speech recognition. Since the backgrounds of the videos are noisy, we clean the speech transcriptions by removing transcriptions with less than 10 words and out-of-vocabulary words based on the training caption vocabulary.

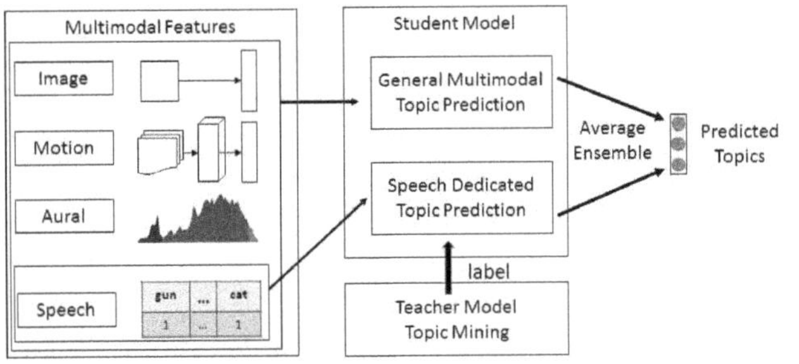

Figure 5: The framework for topic prediction. We treat the problem from a teacher-student perspective. The teacher topic mining model is used to guide the two student topic prediction models to learn based on general multi-modalilties and speech modality respectively.

Only about half portion of the videos contain speech transcriptions afterwards and a certain amount of transcription errors still exist in the transcriptions. We use the bag-of-words representation as the speech modality feature.

4.2 Topic Prediction

For predefined topics, i.e. category tag, we train a standard one hidden layer neural network with cross-entropy loss to predict. The inputs of this neural network are the multimodal features as described in the section 4.1.

For data-driven topics, as there is no direct topic class label, we leverage the topic distribution generated from the topic mining LDA model in section 3.2. We take a teacher-student learning perspective [6] to train the data-driven topic prediction model. To be specific, the topic mining LDA model is viewed as the teacher and the topic prediction model is viewed as the student. The teacher, topic mining model, is trained in unsupervised style and it generates label, i.e. topic, to guide the student, topic prediction model, to learn. First, we design two topic prediction models: one is general for all multimodal features and the other one is dedicated to speech modality features. Then, we ensemble predictions from these two models by averaging to get the final prediction.

General Multimodal Topic Prediction Model: This model is designed to predict topic from the video content using all the multimodal features. In the teacher-student perspective, the student model usually learns the output distribution on labels, i.e. dark knowledge [31], rather than output label from the teacher model. Following this way, we choose to use KL-divergence as our loss function. The formulation of KL-divergence is as follows:

$$D_{KL}(P||Q) = \sum_{k=1}^{K} P_k log \frac{P_k}{Q_k} \tag{1}$$

where P, Q are the probability distributions of the mined topics and predicted topics respectively. The $D_{KL}(P||Q)$ is differentiable and thus can be optimized via back-propagation.

Speech Dedicated Topic Prediction Model: As speech modality is very informative but not always available in videos, we build a dedicate topic prediction model using speech features. Different from other modality features, the speech text feature is of high dimensionality with noises and is sparse. Instead of using the same architecture of the general multimodal topic prediction model, we design a very different architecture for the speech dedicated topic prediction model. We make a simple choice of the architecture: reusing the topic mining model for topic prediction on speech text features. As the representation of speech text features is the same as that of features used in the topic mining model, we don't need to reinvent the wheel.

As to the problem of missing modalities, we only use videos that contain the corresponding speech modality in the speech dedicated topic prediction model. In general multimodal topic prediction model, the features of missing modalities are padded as zeros. In ensembling, predictions of the missing modalities are not considered in the average process.

4.3 Caption Models with Topic Guidance

Suppose we have multiple video-sentence pairs (V, y) in video captioning dataset, where $\mathrm{y} = \{w_1, \ldots, w_{N_w}\}$ is the sentence with N_w words. Assume the multimodal features of the video are $m_1, \ldots, m_{N_m}$, where N_m is the number of modalities, the multimodal encoder is a neural network that fuses the multimodal features into a dense video representation x as follows:

$$\mathrm{x} = W_e[m_1; \ldots; m_{N_m}] + b_e \tag{2}$$

where W_e, b_e are the parameters in the encoder and $[\cdot]$ denotes the feature concatenation. Since the captioning output is the sequential words, we utilize the LSTM [32] recurrent neural networks as our language decoder:

$$h_t = f(h_{t-1}, w_{t-1}; \theta_d) \text{ for } t = 1, \ldots, N_w \tag{3}$$

where f is the LSTM update function, h_t is the state of LSTM and θ_d is the parameter in LSTM. We initialize h_0 as x to condition on the video representation and w_0 as the sentence start symbol. Then the probability of the correct word conditioned on the video content and previous words can be expressed as:

$$\Pr(w_t|\mathrm{x}, w_0, \ldots, w_{t-1}) = \mathrm{Softmax}(W_d h_t + b_d) \tag{4}$$

where W_d, b_d are parameters. The objective function is to maximize the log likelihood of the correct description:

$$\log \Pr(\mathrm{y}|\mathrm{x}) = \sum_{t=1}^{N_w} \log \Pr(w_t|\mathrm{x}, w_0, \ldots, w_{t-1}) \tag{5}$$

We denote the predicted topics in Section 4.2 as $\mathrm{z} \in \mathbb{R}^K$, where K is the number of topics. In order to effectively exploit the topics z for video captioning, we propose the novel topic-guided model (TGM), and a series of simple yet strong caption models with topic guidance for comparison, called TCE, TCD and TEAD/TEMD for short. Detailed descriptions of these models are as follows.

Topic Concatenation in Encoder (TCE): We fuse the topic distribution z together with multimodal features in the encoder as the topic-aware video representation x:

$$\mathrm{x} = W_e([m_1; \ldots; m_{N_m}; \mathrm{z}]) + b_e \tag{6}$$

The LSTM decoder then generates video description conditioning on the new topic-aware representation x.

Topic Concatenation in Decoder (TCD): In the TCE model, the topic information only occurs at the first step in the decoder, which could easily make the topic guidance "drift away". To enhance the topic guidance, we concatenate the topic distribution z with the word embedding w_{t-1} as the input to the LSTM every step, which is similar to the gLSTM proposed in [33]:

$$h_t = f(h_{t-1}, [w_{t-1}; \mathrm{z}]; \theta_d) \tag{7}$$

The extra input of topic z can guide the language decoder to generate words related to the topic in every step.

Topic Embedding Addition/Multiplication in Decoder (TEAD/TEMD): To generate a more comparable representation for the topic representation z compared to the word embedding, we embed each topic into a latent vector space with the same dimensionality as the word embedding:

$$\mathrm{z}_e = W_z \mathrm{z} + b_z \tag{8}$$

where W_z, b_z are topic embedding parameters. We perform addition or multiplication on the topic embedding and word embedding to generate the topic-aware input feature for the language decoder every step, which are expressed as:

$$\text{TEAD}: \; h_t = f(h_{t-1}, w_{t-1} \oplus \mathrm{z}_e; \theta_d) \tag{9}$$

$$\text{TEMD}: \; h_t = f(h_{t-1}, w_{t-1} \odot \mathrm{z}_e; \theta_d) \tag{10}$$

where $\oplus, \odot$ are element-wise addition and multiplication respectively.

Topic-Guided Model (TGM): The above TCD and TEAD/TEMD models only implicitly using the topic information as the global guidance, which modify the inputs to the language decoder in every step and cannot take into account of the overall expressions within the topic. Inspired by Gan et al. [12], therefore, we further propose the topic-guided model (TGM) that explicitly functions as an ensemble of topic-aware language decoders to capture different sentence distributions for each topic. The structure of the TGM is shown in the right side in Figure 2, which can automatically modify the weight matrices in LSTM according to the topic distribution z.

Let us take one of weight matrices in the LSTM as an example, and other parameters in LSTM cell are alike. We define weight $W_\tau \in \mathbb{R}^{n_h \times n_w \times K}$, where n_h is the number of hidden units and n_w is the dimension of word embedding. The W_τ can be viewed as the ensemble of K topic-specific LSTM weight matrices. The topic-related weight matrix $W(\mathrm{z}) \in \mathbb{R}^{n_h \times n_w}$ can be specified as

$$W(\mathrm{z}) = \sum_{k=1}^{K} \mathrm{z}_k W_\tau[k] \tag{11}$$

where z_k is the k-th topic in z; $W_\tau[k]$ denote the k-th matrix of W_τ. In this way, the video topic z can automatically generate its corresponding LSTM decoders to produce the topic-oriented video descriptions. However, the parameters are increasing with K which may result in over-fitting easily. So the ideas in [34] are used to share parameters by factorizing $W(\mathrm{z})$ as follows:

$$W(\mathrm{z}) = W_a \cdot diag(W_b \mathrm{z}) \cdot W_c \tag{12}$$

where $W_a \in \mathbb{R}^{n_h \times n_f}$, $W_b \in \mathbb{R}^{n_f \times K}$ and $W_c \in \mathbb{R}^{n_f \times n_w}$. n_f is the number of factors. W_a and W_c are shared among all topics, while W_b can be viewed as the latent topic embedding.

5 Experiments

5.1 Experimental Setup

Dataset: The MSR-VTT corpus [15] is currently the largest video to language dataset with a wide variety of video contents. It consists of 10,000 video clips with 20 human generated captions per clip. Each video also contains a predefined category tag, which is one of the 20 popular video categories in web videos. Following the standard data split, we use 6,513 videos for training, 497 videos for validation and the remained 2,990 for testing.

Data Preprocessing: We convert all descriptions to lower case and remove all the punctuations. We add begin-of-sentence tag <BOS> and end-of-sentence tag <EOS> to our vocabulary. Words which appear more than twice are selected, resulting in a vocabulary of size 10,868. The maximum length of a generated caption is set to be 30.

Training Settings: We empirically set the feed forward neural networks for topic prediction to have one hidden layer with 512 units. The dimension of LSTM hidden size is set to be 512. The output weights to predict the words are the transpose of the input word embedding matrix. We apply dropout with rate of 0.5 on the input and output of LSTM and use ADAM algorithm [35] with learning rate of 10^{-4}. Beam search with beam width of 5 is used to generate sentences during testing process. The baseline system is the vanilla encoder-decoder framework with multimodal features (we call it the multimodal baseline)[1].

Evaluation Metrics: We evaluate the caption results comprehensively on all major metrics, including BLEU [36], METEOR [37], ROUGE-L [38] and CIDEr [39].

5.2 Evaluation

Table 2 presents captioning performances on testing set with predefined category tags and the data-driven topics using their corresponding best caption model with topic guidance. We can see that the different topic guidances (the second to forth rows) all greatly improve the performance of the multimodal baseline (the first row). Since the data-driven topics on testing set are predicted as shown in Figure 5, we also use the predicted category tags for a fair comparison.

[1] In our experiments, we find that the dimensionality of the features to the encoder should not be too high in order to avoid over-fitting, so only the image object, video motion, and aural features are used as input to the encoder.

Table 2: Captioning performance of the predefined categories and data-driven topics using the best caption model with topic guidance. The acronyms B, M, R, C denote BLEU@4, METEOR, ROUGE-L and CIDEr respectively.

	B	M	R	C
multimodal	0.4211	0.2872	0.6170	0.4608
pred category TGM	0.4276	0.2885	0.6167	0.4754
pred topic TGM	**0.4397**	**0.2921**	0.6234	**0.4970**
category TCE	0.4343	0.2921	**0.6249**	0.4890

Table 3: Captioning performance comparison among caption models with topic guidance (using the predicted data-driven topics). The acronyms B, M, R, C denote BLEU@4, METEOR, ROUGE-L and CIDEr respectively.

	B	M	R	C
pred topic TCE	0.4353	0.2916	0.6226	0.4783
pred topic TCD	0.4246	0.2861	0.6171	0.4714
pred topic TEAD	0.4333	0.2893	0.6221	0.4765
pred topic TEMD	0.4304	0.2884	0.6207	0.4694
pred topic TGM	**0.4397**	**0.2921**	**0.6234**	**0.4970**
v2t_navigator [5]	0.4080	0.2820	0.6090	0.4480

The guidance from predicted data-driven topics outperforms that from the predicted category tags on all four evaluation metrics, and the Student's t-test shows the improvement is significant with p-value< 0.002. Even compared with the category tags assigned by video uploaders, the predicted data-driven topics also slightly boost the captioning performance on multiple metrics with the Student's t-test p-value< 0.01 on BLEU@4 and CIDEr metrics, which shows the performance gain is robust. These results suggest that the data-driven topics are more suitable as the topic representation than predefined topics for video captioning.

To demonstrate the effectiveness of the proposed topic-guided model (TGM), we further compare the TGM with other caption models with topic guidance. As shown in Table 3, the TGM achieves the best performance among all the caption models on all four metrics especially for the CIDEr score. It suggests that modifying the weights of the decoder according to the topic distributions can employ the topic guidance more effectively to generate better topic-oriented descriptions. Our proposed TGM model also achieves better performance than the winning performance in 2016 MSR video to language challenge [5], where we use multimodal features and select best models by the predefined categories.

Figure 6 presents some examples in the testing set. In addition to more accurate video descriptions, the TGM can also generate more novel concepts such as the llama. Our statistics on the generated sentence show that the number of unique caption words generated by TGM is 397, while it is 360 by the multimodal baseline model.

multimodal: a group of people are dancing.
category TCE: a group of people are playing basketball.
pred topic TGM: a group of people are wrestling.

multimodal: a group of people are sitting on the grass.
category TCE : a group of people are playing with a horse.
pred topic TGM: a group of llamas are running in a field.

Figure 6: Examples on testing set to demonstrate the effectiveness of the TGM.

Table 4: Captioning performance of predicted topics and the annotated topics. The acronyms B, M, R, C denote BLEU@4, METEOR, ROUGE-L and CIDEr respectively.

	B	M	R	C
pred topic TGM	0.4397	0.2921	0.6234	0.4970
anno topic TGM	**0.4548**	**0.3009**	**0.6339**	**0.5418**

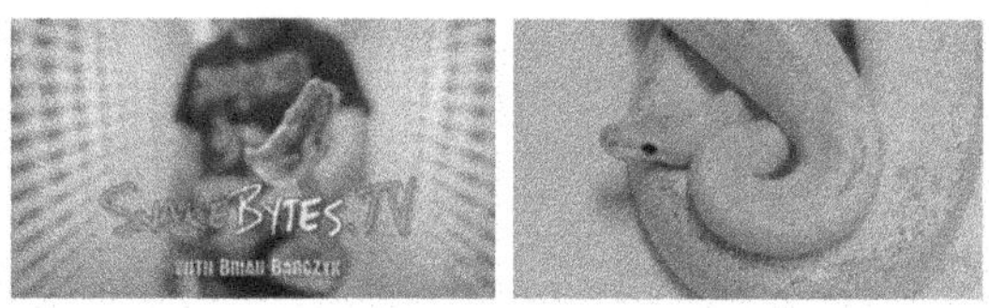

Pred topic: a man is showing how to make a dish.
Anno topic: a man is talking about a snake.
GT: a man is talking about pigments showing a white snake.

Pred topic: there is a man in a suit is talking to a woman.
Anno topic: a man in black shirt is presenting the latest news.
GT: a person is showing information on the screen.

Figure 7: Examples on testing set. Pred topic and anno topic denote using the predicted and annotated topics in the topic-guided model. GT is a random groundtruth caption sentence.

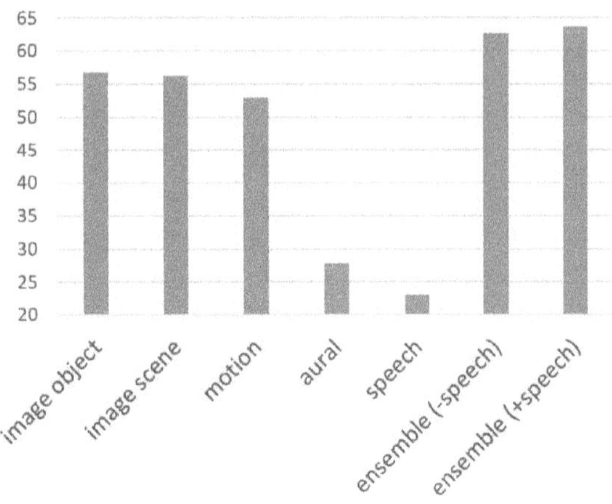

Figure 8: Accuracy of topic prediction with different modalities and ensembles. (-speech) and (+speech) means ensemble without and with speech modality.

5.3 Ablation Experiments

Interactive Caption with Manually Annotated Topic: Our model offers the flexibility of manually assigned topics to the video. It means that we could interactively annotate the topics for testing videos based on relevance between video contents and the representative words in topics to generate better captions. Results in Table 4 and examples in Figure 7 presents the captioning performance with the annotated topics. Both show that with more accurate topic information the captioning performance can be further improved.

Influence of Multi-Modalities: As an implicit evaluation, we can evaluate the topic prediction performance with the annotated topics on testing set. The prediction accuracies with different modalities are shown in Figure 8. The performance of the aural and speech modality are evaluated only on videos containing the corresponding modality. Though the aural modality alone do not perform well, the ensemble of aural with image and motion modalities improves the prediction significantly with an absolute 6% boost. By further using the speech modality predictions, the accuracy is improved from 62.61% to 63.65% on testing set.

To explicitly explore the usefulness of speech modality in video captioning, we use two kinds of predicted topics which are obtained by the fusion with or without the predictions from speech modality. Results are presented in Table 5. We can see that the captioning performance achieves large gain in all metrics although the speech modality gets only 1.04% absolute prediction accuracy improvement as mentioned above. It mainly results from the similar topic probability distributions using the shared topic mining model for speech modality. So the speech modality is quite useful to generate topic proposals and thus boost the captioning performance.

Influence of the Number of Topics: We also explore the performance of TGM with different numbers of topics. As shown in Table 6, the number of topics 20 achieves the best performance, which is the balance between the topic prediction performance and the topic guidance performance. When there is fewer number of topics, the accuracy of topic prediction is higher but it provides less guidance to generate video descriptions. When there is more number of topics, though the topic guidance becomes strong, the captioning performance suffers from the low topic prediction accuracy. Since the more the topics are the more the topics resemble semantic concepts, it suggests that using a small number of topics is enough for the video captioning task and are superior to the large number of detected concepts.

Table 5: Captioning performance with or without using speech modality for topic prediction. The acronyms B, M, R, C denote BLEU@4, METEOR, ROUGE-L and CIDEr respectively.

	B	M	R	C
w/o speech	0.4266	0.2910	0.6192	0.4874
with speech	**0.4397**	**0.2921**	**0.6234**	**0.4970**

Table 6: Captioning performance with different numbers of topics. The acronyms B, M, R, C denote BLEU@4, METEOR, ROUGE-L and CIDEr respectively.

#topics	B	M	R	C
10	0.4258	0.2889	0.6196	0.4789
20	**0.4397**	**0.2921**	**0.6234**	**0.4970**
30	0.4229	0.2901	0.6169	0.4799

6 Conclusions

Descriptions of videos with diverse topics vary a lot in vocabularies and expression styles. In this paper, we propose a novel topic-guided model to deal with the topic diversity nature of videos. It can generate better topic related descriptions for videos in various topics. Our experimental results show that the topic information is very useful to guide the caption model for more topic appropriate description generation and topics automatically mined in data-driven way are superior to the predefined topics as the topic guidance. Multimodal features especially the speech modality features are vital to predict topics for testing videos. Our proposed topic-guided model which functions as an ensemble of topic-aware language decoders can utilize the topic information more effectively than other caption models. It significantly improves the multimodal baseline performance on the current largest video caption dataset MSR-VTT, outperforming the winning performance in the 2016 MSR video to language challenge. In the future work, we will continue to improve the topic prediction performance and jointly learn the topic representation and caption generation end-to-end.

7 Acknowledgments

This work is supported by National Key Research and Development Plan under Grant No. 2016YFB1001202.

References

[1] Rémi Lebret, Pedro H. O. Pinheiro, and Ronan Collobert. Phrase-based image captioning. In *ICML*, pages 2085–2094, 2015.

[2] Oriol Vinyals, Alexander Toshev, Samy Bengio, and Dumitru Erhan. Show and tell: A neural image caption generator. In *CVPR*, pages 3156–3164, 2015.

[3] Kelvin Xu, Jimmy Ba, Ryan Kiros, Kyunghyun Cho, Aaron Courville, Ruslan Salakhutdinov, Richard S Zemel, and Yoshua Bengio. Show, attend and tell: Neural image caption generation with visual attention. *arXiv:1502.03044*, 2(3):5, 2015.

[4] Quanzeng You, Hailin Jin, Zhaowen Wang, Chen Fang, and Jiebo Luo. Image captioning with semantic attention. *arXiv:1603.03925*, 2016.

[5] Qin Jin, Jia Chen, Shizhe Chen, Yifan Xiong, and Alexander Hauptmann. Describing videos using multi-modal fusion. In *ACM*, pages 1087–1091, 2016.

[6] Lei Jimmy Ba and Rich Caruana. Do deep nets really need to be deep? *NIPS*, pages 2654–2662, 2013.

[7] Dzmitry Bahdanau, Kyunghyun Cho, and Yoshua Bengio. Neural machine translation by jointly learning to align and translate. *arXiv:1409.0473*, 2014.

[8] Marcus Rohrbach, Wei Qiu, Ivan Titov, Stefan Thater, Manfred Pinkal, and Bernt Schiele. Translating video content to natural language descriptions. In *ICCV*, pages 433–440, 2013.

[9] Subhashini Venugopalan, Huijuan Xu, Jeff Donahue, Marcus Rohrbach, Raymond Mooney, and Kate Saenko. Translating videos to natural language using deep recurrent neural networks. *Computer Science*, 2014.

[10] Yingwei Pan, Tao Mei, Ting Yao, Houqiang Li, and Yong Rui. Jointly modeling embedding and translation to bridge video and language. In *CVPR*, pages 4594–4602, 2016.

[11] Qi Wu, Chunhua Shen, Lingqiao Liu, Anthony Dick, and Anton van den Hengel. What value do explicit high level concepts have in vision to language problems? In *Proceedings of the IEEE Conference on Computer Vision and Pattern Recognition*, pages 203–212, 2016.

[12] Zhe Gan, Chuang Gan, Xiaodong He, Yunchen Pu, Kenneth Tran, Jianfeng Gao, Lawrence Carin, and Li Deng. Semantic compositional networks for visual captioning. In *CVPR*, 2017.

[13] Pradipto Das, Chenliang Xu, Richard F. Doell, and Jason J. Corso. A thousand frames in just a few words: Lingual description of videos through latent topics and sparse object stitching. In *CVPR*, pages 2634–2641, 2013.

[14] Michaela Regneri, Marcus Rohrbach, Dominikus Wetzel, Stefan Thater, Bernt Schiele, and Manfred Pinkal. Grounding action descriptions in videos. *TACL*, 1:25–36, 2013.

[15] Jun Xu, Tao Mei, Ting Yao, and Yong Rui. Msr-vtt: A large video description dataset for bridging video and language. In *CVPR*, 2016.

[16] Msr video to language challenge. *http://www.acmmm.org/2016/wp-content/uploads/2016/04/ACMMM16_GC_MSR_Video_to_Language_Updated.pdf*.

[17] Li Yao, Atousa Torabi, Kyunghyun Cho, Nicolas Ballas, Christopher J. Pal, Hugo Larochelle, and Aaron C. Courville. Describing videos by exploiting temporal structure. In *ICCV*, pages 4507–4515, 2015.

[18] Subhashini Venugopalan, Marcus Rohrbach, Jeffrey Donahue, Raymond Mooney, Trevor Darrell, and Kate Saenko. Sequence to sequence-video to text. In *ICCV*, pages 4534–4542, 2015.

[19] Pingbo Pan, Zhongwen Xu, Yi Yang, Fei Wu, and Yueting Zhuang. Hierarchical recurrent neural encoder for video representation with application to captioning. *arXiv:1511.03476*, 2015.

[20] Qin Jin and Junwei Liang. Video description generation using audio and visual cues. In *ICMR*, pages 239–242. ACM, 2016.

[21] Vasili Ramanishka, Abir Das, Dong Huk Park, Subhashini Venugopalan, Lisa Anne Hendricks, Marcus Rohrbach, and Kate Saenko. Multimodal video description. In *Proceedings of the 2016 ACM on Multimedia Conference*, pages 1092–1096. ACM, 2016.

[22] David M. Blei, Andrew Y. Ng, and Michael I. Jordan. Latent dirichlet allocation. *Journal of Machine Learning Research*, 3:993–1022, 2003.

[23] Christian Szegedy, Sergey Ioffe, Vincent Vanhoucke, and Alex Alemi. Inception-v4, inception-resnet and the impact of residual connections on learning. 2016.

[24] Kaiming He, Xiangyu Zhang, Shaoqing Ren, and Jian Sun. Deep residual learning for image recognition. In *CVPR*, pages 770–778, 2016.

[25] Bolei Zhou, Aditya Khosla, Agata Lapedriza, Antonio Torralba, and Aude Oliva. Places: An image database for deep scene understanding. *arXiv:1610.02055*, 2016.

[26] Du Tran, Lubomir Bourdev, Rob Fergus, Lorenzo Torresani, and Manohar Paluri. Learning spatiotemporal features with 3d convolutional networks. In *ICCV*, pages 4489–4497. IEEE, 2015.

[27] Steven Davis and Paul Mermelstein. Comparison of parametric representations for monosyllabic word recognition in continuously spoken sentences. *IEEE transactions on acoustics, speech, and signal processing*, 28(4):357–366, 1980.

[28] Stephanie Pancoast and Murat Akbacak. Softening quantization in bag-of-audio-words. In *ICASSP*, pages 1370–1374. IEEE, 2014.

[29] Jorge Sánchez, Florent Perronnin, Thomas Mensink, and Jakob Verbeek. Image classification with the fisher vector: Theory and practice. *International journal of computer vision*, 105(3):222–245, 2013.

[30] Ibm watson speech to text api. http://www.ibm.com/watson/developercloud/speech-to-text.html.

[31] Geoffrey Hinton, Oriol Vinyals, and Jeff Dean. Distilling the knowledge in a neural network. *Computer Science*, 14(7):38–39, 2015.

[32] Sepp Hochreiter and Jürgen Schmidhuber. Long short-term memory. *Neural computation*, 9(8):1735–1780, 1997.

[33] Xu Jia, Efstratios Gavves, Basura Fernando, and Tinne Tuytelaars. Guiding the long-short term memory model for image caption generation. In *Proceedings of the IEEE International Conference on Computer Vision*, pages 2407–2415, 2015.

[34] R Memisevic and G Hinton. Unsupervised learning of image transformations. In *CVPR*, pages 1–8, 2007.

[35] Diederik Kingma and Jimmy Ba. Adam: A method for stochastic optimization. *arXiv preprint arXiv:1412.6980*, 2014.

[36] Kishore Papineni, Salim Roukos, Todd Ward, and Wei-Jing Zhu. Bleu: a method for automatic evaluation of machine translation. In *Proceedings of the 40th annual meeting on association for computational linguistics*, pages 311–318. Association for Computational Linguistics, 2002.

[37] Michael Denkowski and Alon Lavie. Meteor universal: Language specific translation evaluation for any target language. In *In Proceedings of the Ninth Workshop on Statistical Machine Translation*. Citeseer, 2014.

[38] Chin-Yew Lin. Rouge: A package for automatic evaluation of summaries. In *Text summarization branches out: Proceedings of the ACL-04 workshop*, volume 8. Barcelona, Spain, 2004.

[39] Ramakrishna Vedantam, C Lawrence Zitnick, and Devi Parikh. Cider: Consensus-based image description evaluation. In *CVPR*, pages 4566–4575, 2015.

Estimating the Information Gap between Textual and Visual Representations

Christian Henning[◇]
[◇]Leibniz Universität Hannover
Institute of Distributed Systems, and
L3S Research Center
Hannover, Germany
christian.henning@tib.eu

Ralph Ewerth[◇,★]
[★]German National Library of Science & Technology (TIB)
Department of Research and Development
Research Group Visual Analytics
Hannover, Germany
ralph.ewerth@tib.eu

ABSTRACT

Photos, drawings, figures, etc. supplement textual information in various kinds of media, for example, in web news or scientific publications. In this respect, the intended effect of an image can be quite different, e.g., providing additional information, focusing on certain details of surrounding text, or simply being a general illustration of a topic. As a consequence, the semantic correlation between information of different modalities can vary noticeably, too. Moreover, cross-modal interrelations are often hard to describe in a precise way. The variety of possible interrelations of textual and graphical information and the question, how they can be described and automatically estimated have not been addressed yet by previous work. In this paper, we present several contributions to close this gap. First, we introduce two measures to describe cross-modal interrelations: cross-modal mutual information (CMI) and semantic correlation (SC). Second, a novel approach relying on deep learning is suggested to estimate CMI and SC of textual and visual information. Third, three diverse datasets are leveraged to learn an appropriate deep neural network model for the demanding task. The system has been evaluated on a challenging test set and the experimental results demonstrate the feasibility of the approach.

CCS CONCEPTS

• **Computing methodologies → Artificial intelligence**; *Natural language processing*; *Computer vision*; Information extraction; Natural language generation; Computer vision tasks; Computer vision representations;

KEYWORDS

Text-image relations; multimodal embeddings; deep learning.

ACM Reference format:
Christian Henning[◇] and Ralph Ewerth[◇,★]. 2017. Estimating the Information Gap between Textual and Visual Representations. In *Proceedings of ICMR '17, June 6–9, 2017, Bucharest, Romania*, , 9 pages.
DOI: http://dx.doi.org/10.1145/3078971.3078991

Christian Henning[◇] and Ralph Ewerth[◇,★]

1 INTRODUCTION

"A picture is worth a thousand words." This insight is often utilized to enhance, for instance, textual information in documents, where photos, graphics, diagrams are inserted to supplement textual information. But a bunch of other cross-modal interrelations exists. For example, supplementing a video sequence with music, overlaid speech, and/or overlaid text is very common. In the early stage of (silent) movies, text inserts were used to complement visual scene content with additional text information. Interestingly, in the very early stage of film, text inserts (intertitles) were even used to inform the audience about what will happen in the subsequent shot. This, however, changed soon and intertitles were used in a much more creative and complementary way[1]. Talks in lectures or scientific presentations are complemented with slides[2] which themselves often consist of a mixture of textual, visual, and audio-visual information. Also in the field of software engineering visual representations are exploited, e.g., via specialized diagrams based on the Unified Modeling Language, to describe and understand complex software architectures. These examples hint at the power – but also at the complexity – of combining two or more modalities to convey information in a more appropriate or more understandable way. In this respect, this paper focuses on describing and measuring interrelations of textual and visual information, in short, image-text relations.

In general, two or more different modalities can be used to convey information in a better way. On the other hand, an additional modality (or communication channel) does not always provide an improvement by means of information gain. It can be observed that complementary information is often added for aesthetic reasons or as a visual anchor, e.g., in Web news. For example, textual and visual information is often more related to one another in scientific documents than it is in Web news (cp. Figure 1), we will get back to that later. But how can we describe precisely which and how much information is shared by a text and a related image? How can we describe if the visual information emphasizes an aspect of the text or vice versa, and how can we measure by which means textual and visual information are used complementary?

In recent years, Natural Language Processing (NLP) and Computer Vision (CV) have been employed and combined to tackle interesting challenges that are somewhat related to these questions, for instance, automatic image captioning or multimodal document retrieval. Increasing computational power and deep learning have

[1]In fact, during the first Academy Awards ceremony in 1929, an Oscar was awarded for *Best Writing – Title Cards*, but there was never again an award for intertitles.
[2]Though their usefulness might be questionable in some cases.

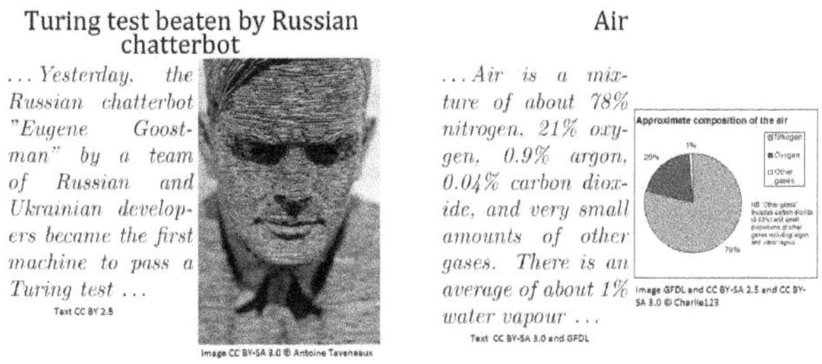

(a) News articles are often loosely tied to their co-occurring image.

(b) Encyclopedia articles are typically mainly concerned about the content of an enclosed image.

Figure 1: Examples of image-text pairs with low (a)[3] and high (b)[4] semantic correlation.

enabled impressive systems such as NeuralTalk2 [12] that generates image descriptions in real-time. However, the focus of these approaches is to generate *precise descriptions* of the scene content that is depicted in an image, whereas they do not aim at providing complementary information. Some approaches investigate the interrelations of text and images, but they simply assume that an image is always semantically related to its surrounding text [23, 27]. For the latter, it is easy to find examples showing that this is clearly not true, for example, by simply exploring today's online news in the World Wide Web. On the other hand, automatic recognition of image-text interrelations and correlations in terms of quantity (how much information is shared) and quality (how much meaning is shared) would open up new possibilities to address a variety of interesting challenges and applications: For example, news retrieval can be optimized by selecting articles that include images that show *specific* aspects for a topic or providing a diverse result set, respectively.

In this paper, we present two main contributions that aim at illuminating the gap between – as well as relations of – textual and visual information[5]. First, two measures are introduced that describe different aspects of image-text interrelations: Cross-modal Mutual Information (CMI) and Semantic Correlation (SC). *Cross-modal Mutual Information* captures the amount of information that is shared, while *Semantic Correlation* measures how much meaning is shared among text and image. In Section 3, it is explained and derived why two complementary measures are required to describe image-text relations. As a second main contribution, we present a novel deep learning framework to automatically estimate image-text interrelations by means of CMI and SC. This deep learning framework consists of an autoencoder that exploits a multimodal embedding in order to gather a compact representation of a multimodal document, i.e., a text (document) plus an image in our case. The network uses the popular *InceptionV3* [19] model to encode images. The overall encoding architecture is based on the *Neural Image Caption Generator* from Google [20], which we have extended by an hierarchical text encoding that enables the comprehension of sentences as entities appearing in the context of a variable-sized text. The compact multimodal embedding representation is finally used to train a classifier in order to infer CMI as well as SC. Experimental results demonstrate the feasibility of the approach on a challenging test set including Web news and Wikipedia pages.

The remainder of the paper is structured as follows. Related work is presented in Section 2. Section 3 motivates, introduces and explains in detail the two measures CMI and SC for describing image-text relations. Subsequently, the deep learning architecture for automatically estimating image-text relations is explained in Section 4. The experimental results are presented in Section 5, while Section 6 concludes the paper and outlines areas for future work.

2 RELATED WORK

Many researchers have moved their focus onto tasks involving multiple modalities, especially for tasks laying on the edge of Natural Language Processing and Computer Vision. One interesting idea is to think of the syntax and semantics of images and texts, respectively, being arranged in a hidden latent space, where both modalities can be projected to a multimodal embedding space [7, 8, 11–14, 20, 24].

The approach which proved to be most promising involves deep neural networks to generate the embedding space. A more fine-grained approach has been proposed by Karpathy and Li [12] and Karpathy et al. [11]. They intentionally assimilate decompositions of their representations (in addition to the full input) and ensure that those match up in the embedding space as well.

Vinyals et al. [20] use a simpler approach, motivated by recent advances in statistical machine translation [21]. They generate image captions by transforming an image to a compact representation (a fixed embedding) via deep CNNs (convolutional neural networks) and then using an RNN (recurrent neural network), conditioned on the image and all previously predicted words, to produce sentences. Their system is trained in an end-to-end fashion, such that any detail and context can be revealed by the hidden structure.

A general advantage of multimodal embeddings is that they can be used in a number of applications, e.g., for image-sentence retrieval tasks by using ranking algorithms or for text generation by training a network above the embedding space. Ngiam et al. [16] show that multimodal embeddings learned via autoencoders can even enhance results on tasks that do not obviously incorporate more than one modality.

Some approaches also consider the generation of more realistic image captions, thus captions that do not state what is visually obvious, and aim to build a bridge that connects an image with its context. Ramisa et al. [18] report on various tasks on collected news articles including caption generation. Also Feng and Lapata [6] suggest an approach to generate *context-aware* captions on another news corpora. However, current captioning results in this field are poor, which may come from the loose relation between an article text and its image. Beside caption generation, they also propose a method to extract a sentence from the article text that can serve as a legitimate image caption. But in general it is doubtable that co-occurring text provides appropriate captions.

[3]Source: https://en.wikinews.org/wiki/Turing_test_beaten_by_Russian_chatterbot (Accessed: 2/3/17)
[4]Source: https://simple.wikipedia.org/wiki/Air (Accessed: 2/3/17)
[5]It is assumed that image and text are jointly placed *on purpose*.

There is a variety of other applications involving or leveraging multiple modalities (e.g., question answering [22]). For instance, Izadinia et al. [10] show that pure NLP tasks, i.e., paraphrase detection, can benefit from learning semantic correspondences of visual similar scenes.

While a larger number of proposals is exploiting more than one modality, only few works concentrate on a closer investigation of the relation between co-occurring image-text pairs and how to utilize this relation. Yanai and Barnard [25] are trying to estimate the uncertainty of how an image region will be affected by a concept using an entropy measure. Here, they directly want to estimate the *visualness* of adjectives. For instance, the word *dark* is considered to be more visual than the word *religious*, simply because there is less variability in how an image region can be modified by an associated concept such as *dark* compared to a concept, that does not as easily reveal its influence (e.g., a *religious* image region might still depict anything from churches to ancient vases).

There are also some attempts to model semantic correlation between images and texts [23, 26, 27]. Xue et al. [23] propose an approach to estimate semantic correlation by aligning the semantics of visual and textual blobs (local image regions and words) . In order to assign blobs to a document of another modality, they have to make the assumption that co-occurring image-text pairs do express the same semantics. This assumption allows them to transfer a distribution of hidden topics learned among entities from one modality to another one, such that, e.g., visual blobs can be assigned to a textual document. In this case, the assumption is true since they are utilizing an image tagging dataset, i.e., each image is tagged with words that have a high semantic relevance with respect to that image.

3 IMAGE-TEXT RELATIONS

As the analysis of related work reveals, different levels of semantic image-text interrelations have not been investigated yet. In this section, we provide an analysis of important aspects of image-text interrelations and derive two measures to appropriately capture their characteristics. In particular, we are interested in the question in which way visual and textual data complement one another. Humans are involved at both sides of the communication channel: Humans intentionally add visual information to text (or vice versa) in order to supplement additional (normally complementary) information, and humans perceive and interpret such kind of bi-modal information. Of course, the intended effect is not always achieved and depends on many aspects (e.g., knowledge of creator and viewer etc.). Human knowledge about textual facts and depicted visual content plays a vital role in this process of communication. Before we introduce two measures to describe image-text interrelations, we discuss some examples of image-text pairs that share different kinds of information.

3.1 Examples for Image-Text Relations

The understanding of the image-text interrelations requires an analysis of 1.) what can be expressed by either of those modalities and 2.) how humans perceive and evaluate their co-occurrence.

Figure 2 shows the rare case, that a text and an image actually have the same information content. If each entity of one modality would have a corresponding entity in the other modality that exactly contains the same information, then one might claim either one of the modalities is obsolete. However, it is easier for humans to perceive attributes such as shape and color from an image, whereas the exact size is easier to read from a text. In fact, human capabilities of judging absolute measures of a visual object's length, size, area without any additional supporting information is rather limited. Hence, a certain modality can make the same information more difficult (or easier) to perceive. This leads to a natural usage where the depicted information shall complement one another such that each modality depicts partially unique information, that is easier to read from compared to other modalities.

A gray circle with a diameter of 1cm.

Figure 2: Example of a text and an image that convey the same information.

Moreover, some kind of information cannot be encoded in one modality as succinctly and precisely as in another one. For instance, the sentence

Ada Lovelace was born in 1815.

has no proper representation in an image without using text. An image that aims to convey the same information would necessarily express a lot of redundant additional information, such as events unique to the year 1815. The same applies for the reverse direction. There is neither a text that precisely describes the shape of a certain maple leaf nor its texture. Both observations lead to the conclusion that each modality plays an essential role to convey certain kinds of information by either addressing strengths or avoiding weaknesses of human visual perception.

Interrelations of images and texts can be understood as the alignment of concepts. Again, we consider an example:

A family of four is sitting at a table having a warm meal. They are all talking vividly about their day.

The sentence equally fits to the images in Figure 3a and 3c, respectively. But when relating the sentence to Figure 3b, where the family is expressing a sad mood, this is intuitively perceived as a contradiction (or in other words: a negative correlation). The contradiction of concepts is that a sad mood normally is not aligned with a vivid conversation as we know from our own experience. However, the reason for human intuition when judging the interrelation of such co-occurrences is often not obvious nor easily expressible. More precisely, the alignments that define the interrelation are hidden. To some extent, this is similar to the problem of paraphrase detection, where humans are easily able to judge whether sentences express the same meaning but struggle to deliver a sensible and consistent reasoning for that claim in terms of syntactic and semantic justifications. While the annotation in the case of paraphrase detection is clear, it is not obvious how to quantify or rate the relation of image-text pairs as they usually do not represent the same meaning as outlined above. Moreover, they complement one another such that a good annotation would take into account the rationale or purpose of their co-occurrence.

(a) Happy facial expressions.

(b) Sad facial expressions.

(c) Color of plates has changed.

Figure 3: The images (b) and (c) only differ in a certain concept from the image (a). The effect of the modification depends on the textual context.

3.2 Measures for Image-Text Relations

Three major goals are associated with the proposed measures for describing image-text relations. First, the measures should be easily explainable to humans, in particular for annotation and retrieval processes. Second, the descriptions, i.e., labels, for a given image-text pair should be easily inferable and disagreements between annotators should be avoided as far as possible. Third, the descriptions should be expressive, i.e., revealing distinguishable and high-quality relations. This goal enlarges the pool of possible future applications.

Judging several distinct aspects of complex inter-modal relations is easier than estimating a single score or classifying them into certain categories. This claim assumes that a one-dimensional categorization that meets the previously stated goals is not easily inferable. Therefore, we suggest to judge inter-modal relations based on two measurements, namely *Cross-modal Mutual Information* and *Semantic Correlation*.

Cross-modal Mutual Information (CMI) focuses solely on the mutual presence of concepts. Note, that the outlined measurement of *Cross-modal Mutual Information* is not equivalent to the term of mutual information in information theory. In order to better phrase its purpose, we take over the idea of *visualness* of concepts introduced in [2, 25] as explained in Section 2. Image captioning samples are a prominent example for high CMI for two reasons. First, the text exclusively focuses on the image content[6], thus only a few concepts are depicted solely in the image. Second, the shared concepts are highly visual, meaning that they have clearly defined representations in both modalities. On the other hand, image-text pairs occurring in news articles are usually characterized by a rather loose intersection in terms of information content. For instance, an article about austerity politics associated with an image depicting a piggy bank shares only one concept *"saving money"*. Hence, the amount of shared concepts is low, but also the visualness of the concept is low. A concept that has low visualness (e.g., "spring", "saving money", "religious") tolerates an immense variety among possible visual representations. The detection of concepts with low visualness is particularly difficult as it requires extensive background knowledge. However, visualness alone is not a sufficient measure to judge the salience of a concept. Even highly visual concepts might represent negligible details depending on the context. Hence, the annotator has to estimate the amount of shared concepts as well as their influence and importance.

Cross-modal Mutual Information solely does not sufficiently describe inter-modal relations. Irrespective of the amount of shared concepts, the appearance of only one pair of contradicting concepts might lead to an unfitting or disturbing image-text relation. Therefore, we propose a second measure called ***Semantic Correlation***, which aims to reveal how much meaning a text and an image share. This measure aims to mimic human intuition with respect to the sophisticated ability to detect matching pairs by considering context and regardless of the amount of shared information. A negative score shall indicate that the co-occurrence of an image and a text disturbs the comprehension of the depicted information, whereas a positive score eases the transfer of knowledge. The measure can be illustrated as follows. If two entities do not have any concepts in common, they are considered as unrelated (no correlation). If concepts appear that contradict one another, the correlation shall be estimated as negative. Depending on the relevance of the contradicting concepts, the negative correlation might be low or high. For instance, a color might be wrongly stated in the text. If this incorrectly referred object does only play a minor/negligible role compared to the overall content, the comprehension task is only insignificantly perturbed and even positive correlation can be assigned. We suggest to use an interval of [0,1] for CMI and [-1, 1] for SC, respectively, and refer to the description of our annotation process in Section 4.4.

4 ESTIMATING IMAGE-TEXT RELATIONS

In this section, we describe in detail the proposed deep learning framework for automatically estimating image-text interrelations. The framework consists of two main components, an autoencoder and a classifier.

The overall goal of this work is to develop a system that mimics human intuition when judging the interrelation of co-occurring images and texts. Therefore, it is essential that the system is able to comprehend individual modalities and to correctly evaluate their coexistence. Our main incentive is that humans use and comprehend several modalities to convey information that complements one another. This insight has been already stated by others (e.g., [1]), but it has been weakly addressed by related work as outlined in Section 2. There are two reasons for that. First, it is very difficult to model human intuition that includes visual perception as well as complex cognitive processes. Second, immense computational power is necessary to process a sufficient amount of data to learn appropriate models to achieve at least a basic understanding of the world, which is necessary when considering multimodal documents from unconstrained domains.

The human learning process is twofold: supervised and unsupervised. We are observing the world and draw our own conclusions, but we get also directed and corrected by the people surrounding us. For instance, if we observe *elephants*, we are capable of extracting

[6] This would also allow us to view the CMI relation of captioning samples as an inclusion, since the text does not express concepts that are not covered by the image.

prominent features (shape, trunk, skin color, etc) and generalize all elephants into a single concept without supervision. However, someone has to tell us that these mammals are called *"elephants"*. Hence, the overwhelming majority – but also the apparently more complicated – part of the learning task is done fully unsupervised. Nonetheless, this insight is encouraging since it allows us to train a complex system with just a small fraction of supervised training data or intervention, respectively. Still, annotated training data is necessary to direct the learning process such that the semantic outcome is aligned with our understanding of the world.

4.1 The Autoencoder Network Structure

As it has been highlighted during the description of our measurements (CMI and SC), extensive knowledge about the world is required to quantify the co-occurrence of images and texts. More precisely, concepts have to be generalized within and across modalities. For instance, synonyms and paraphrases in sentences and texts, respectively, have to be identified as well as objects and actions in images. The generalized concepts within modalities have to be mapped to a multimodal representation.

A supervised scheme would require an infeasible amount of annotated data – representing as many constellations of image-text relations as possible – to accomplish this goal. Therefore, we propose to learn this ability via an unsupervised learning scheme. One obvious proper realization of this learning scheme would be through GANs (generative adversarial networks) [9], as they are uniquely capable of learning the semantics rather than the syntax of the input space. For instance, Radford et al. [17] have shown that GANs allow vector arithmetics on images similar to word embeddings. However, since we intend to directly learn feature vectors, we decided to use an autoencoder architecture instead. The encoder network compresses the input to a low-dimensional representation that contains less redundant information. Subsequently, a decoder network decompresses this intermediate representation back to the original input encoding. The intermediate representation can be considered as a feature vector that describes the complete input in a vector space of lower dimension. To achieve this, the encoder has to generalize concepts (e.g. objects, shapes, or poses in images) that are available in the input data.

As a point of departure, we use the implementation of Vinyals et al. [20] to build our own model. Figure 4a depicts the autoencoder. Image-text pairs are mapped to an intermediate feature representation, called article embedding $\mathbf{a}_e$. The decoding network tries to restore the initial input from this embedding $\mathbf{a}_e$. To encode images, we leverage *InceptionV3* [19] followed by a fully-connected layer (FC) to generate a final image embedding. All FC and LSTM (long short-term memory) layers in our networks use dropout for regularization. Texts are embedded in a hierarchical LSTM network that considers a sentence as a sequence of words and a text as a sequence of sentences. To generate a proper initialization of word embeddings, a *Word2Vec* model [15] has been trained prior to the autoencoder training. The network can basically adjust to dynamically sized sentences and text, respectively (although sentences are constrained by a maximum length). The hierarchical structure enables a more natural way of text processing since it allows us to consider sentences as self-contained entities. Furthermore, it is

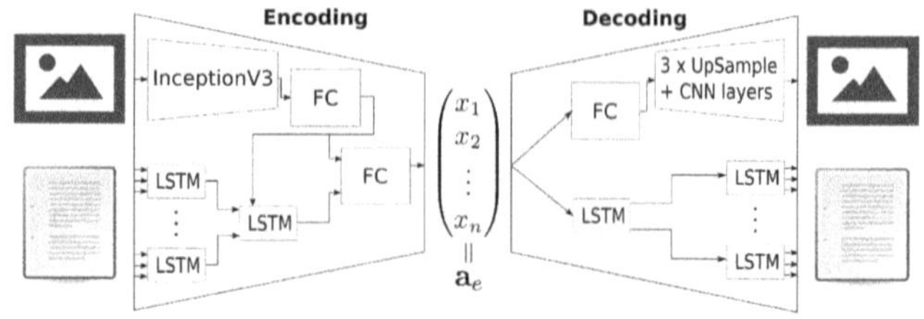

(a) The autoencoder encodes an image-text pair into a compact representation. Subsequently, a decoder network tries to restore the original image-text pair.

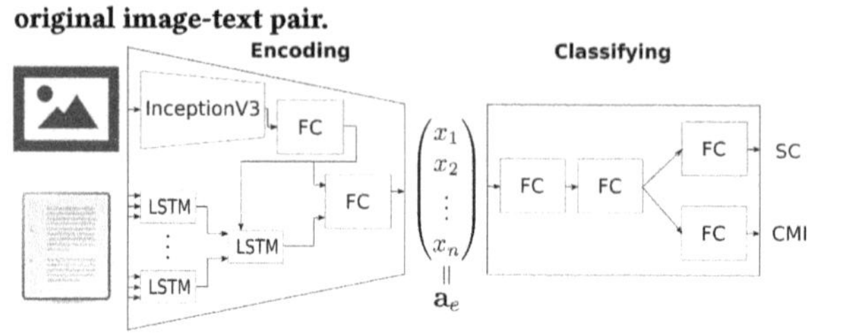

(b) The classifier uses the encoding architecture from the autoencoder to map an input pair to a multimodal embedding. A multi-class classifier on top of that embedding quantifies the image-text relation.

Figure 4: The simplified architectures of the autoencoder (a) and classifier (b).

doubtable that a single LSTM layer can process a text as a plain sequence of tokens, as it is more difficult to maintain long-term dependencies if the input sequence becomes too long. The last output that is generated by an LSTM layer for a given input sequence is considered as a sentence or text embedding, respectively. To generate the text embedding, the first input to the LSTM layer is the image embedding in order to emulate a natural article processing (reading the text under consideration of the enclosed image). After the whole text has been processed, the image is reconsidered due to a further FC layer, that produces the final article embedding $\mathbf{a}_e$.

Ideally, $\mathbf{a}_e$ can be decompressed by the decoder network without loss of information compared to the original input. The basic architecture of the decoder network is depicted on the right side of Figure 4a. The decoder is split into two networks that receive $\mathbf{a}_e$ as input.

The upper part of the decoding network represents the image decoding. The image decoder computes a thumbnail via a fully-connected layer to extract visual information from $\mathbf{a}_e$. This thumbnail is then gradually up-sampled and refined through a series of CNN layers until the size of the input image is reached. More precisely, the network consists of three up-sample layers, each followed by a convolutional layer. The up-sample layers use nearest neighbor interpolation to increase the input size. The consecutive CNN layers are using 32, 8, and 3 feature maps, respectively. A squared-error loss evaluates the prediction compared to the input image.

The lower part of the decoding network depicts the text decoder. The text decoding architecture is reverse to the text encoding architecture. An LSTM layer generates a sequence of predicted sentence embeddings. Therefore, at each time step it takes the article embedding $\mathbf{a}_e$ as input in addition to its previous state. Analogously, predicted sentence embeddings are decoded into tokens. The text decoding network does not allow dynamically sized predictions. The same restriction applies for the number of tokens in predicted sentences.

To estimate the quality of the predicted token embeddings, they have to be retranslated to words of the vocabulary. This is done by computing the cosine similarity between the predicted word embedding and all embeddings of words in the vocabulary. A softmax layer followed by a cross-entropy loss is used to compare the token predictions with the input text.

4.2 The Classifier Network Structure

The classifier combines the already accomplished achievements. Therefore, annotated samples are mapped to a feature representation via an encoder network, which has been learned by the autoencoder. Subsequently, a classifier network (left-hand side of Figure 4b) tries to infer CMI and SC labels for the sample. Recall, that the feature representation ideally contains all the information comprised by the input entities, as the features were trained with the ability to restore this input from them. Hence, the feature representation can be viewed as machine-readable representation of the sample, that hopefully allows an elementary concept matching even for non-visual concepts.

The encoding network is initialized via a pre-trained autoencoder model. In the best case, the encoder network does not require further weight modifications. Remember, that we justify a small annotated dataset with the unsupervised learning of strong feature representations. So, the supervised process is only needed to learn the relatively small classifier network on top of a complex encoder network. The encoded sample $\mathbf{a}_e$ is processed by a series of two fully-connected layers, that shall reveal the hidden alignments between textual and visual concepts. Subsequently, two separate fully-connected units are computing the final MI and SC prediction, respectively. As an alternative, we will also evaluate a SVM (Support Vector Machine) implementation [4] for classification.

4.3 Datasets

To meet the claims with respect to comprehending complex intermodal relations and to appropriately train the autoencoder and classifier, a diverse training database is needed. This database should sufficiently encode knowledge about the world, represent natural co-occurrences and enable the understanding of the semantics of images and text. For this purpose, we have leveraged three different datasets.

The first dataset shall enable the system to learn a translation of salient information from one modality to another. Therefore, the image captioning dataset MS COCO [3] is used, since such a dataset uniquely represents alignments of highly visual concepts between both modalities. The BBC news article set from [5] is used as an example corpus of particularly complicated image-text relations, since their content is typically loosely correlated and the meaning of their co-occurrence usually hard to infer. In most cases, there are neither direct references in the text to the image content nor is their semantic correlation easily inferable. Even humans do often need the provided caption to understand why the image fits to its article.

In addition, a dataset of encyclopedia articles is included in order to incorporate knowledge about the world. An online-encyclopedia such as Wikipedia is a powerful knowledge base that at the same time is structured and sufficiently trustworthy. Wikipedia contains general knowledge about the world and its entities, but also specialized knowledge about individuals, historic as well as recent events, or even proprietary products. However, many articles are not or at least difficult to understand for someone who is outside the subject area. Therefore, we have decided to use Simple English Wikipedia[7] (SimpleWiki) instead of the more extensive but also more complex English Wikipedia. SimpleWiki is the same as the normal Wikipedia, except that it aims to convey complex matters with simple textual descriptions. Such an encyclopedia dataset is necessary, since the understanding of relations between different modalities often requires background knowledge. We have created an encyclopedia dataset, that we call *SimpleWiki* dataset, by downloading articles from SimpleWiki and generating image-text pairs. We allow all occurring image types, such as photos, charts, maps, and drawings. An image is either matched with the text of its enclosed section or with the text of the full article in case when the image is associated with the summary. Currently, our SimpleWiki dataset consists of 2, 999 image-text pairs.

4.4 The Annotation Process

Annotations have been gathered for subsets of all three datasets described in section 4.3. Although we basically allow real-valued data for both measures, we have simplified the annotation process and used only five different levels for each. The distribution of labels is shown in Table 1 and 2). In addition to judging *Cross-modal Mutual Information* and *Semantic Correlation*, text snippets were marked that can be considered as specifically relevant given the current image and to select the image type of the depicted image (e.g., photograph, map, chart, etc.).

In total, **761** annotations have been generated for the BBC News (205) and SimpleWiki (556) dataset by one of the authors. We have defined detailed label descriptions and examples in order to precisely judge the intermodal relation in the desired and a reproducible manner. The exact distribution of image types among those datasets shows that our overall dataset is still biased towards photos, because 71% of the SimpleWiki and 97% of the news samples are photos. In future work, this imbalance may be addressed by incorporating scientific articles into the dataset.

Since the MS COCO dataset has a homogeneous image-text-relation type by means of our measures, we have assigned high CMI and SC values to the 100 samples taken from this dataset. This step has been undertaken to reduce a strong label imbalance among CMI labels, since in natural image-text co-occurrences the text normally does not state obvious visual facts. To prevent the system from overfitting by learning the length of the text (an image caption is always a single sentence), we have concatenated a random subset of all 5 provided reference captions to generate an image-text pair.

[7] https://simple.wikipedia.org

Label	0	0.25	0.5	0.75	1.0
Meaning	$T \cap I = \emptyset$	$T \cap I \neq \emptyset$			
# Samples	44	157	466	52	107

Table 1: Distribution of CMI labels in the newly annotated dataset.

Label	-1.0	-0.5	0.0	0.5	1.0
# Samples	7	31	109	138	541

Table 2: Distribution of SC labels in the newly annotated dataset.

The final distributions of *Cross-modal Mutual Information* and *Semantic Correlation* labels are shown in Table 1 and Table 2, respectively. As stated in the previous section, most image-text pairs share concepts of both types, abstract (e.g., spring) or highly visual. This is the reason why there are more sublevels between 0 and 1 for CMI. In the annotation process, the amount of shared concepts has to be rated from label 0 (no intersection) to label 1 (large intersection) based on definitions for each case. Some samples have been marked as invalid, because the automatic retrieval of SimpleWiki samples has led to meaningless text extractions in rare cases. Altogether, 826 pairs have been sampled to generate a dataset for the classification scenario.

However, our initial claim, that the semantic correlation of co-occurring image-text pairs is not necessarily high, has been verified. News articles in our dataset have an average *Semantic Correlation* of 0.15, whereas SimpleWiki articles have an average SC of 0.88.

5 EXPERIMENTAL RESULTS

In this section, experimental results are presented for the proposed approach relying on a deep learning architecture to judge image-text relations. All experiments have been conducted using the system explained in Section 4, the dataset described in Section 4.3, and the annotated subset explained in Section 4.4, respectively.

5.1 Experimental Setup

Autoencoder (AE) and classifier (CL) are using stochastic gradient descent (SGD) with mini-batches and an initial learning rate of 0.1. The learning rate is halved every time a complete sweep through the training set has been accomplished. A mini batch consists of 16 image-text pairs. Note, that all samples within a batch are padded to have the same size as the largest sample. To further reduce this maximum size, texts have been truncated during preprocessing. We have found out that a maximum text size of 50 sentences and a maximum sentence length of 40 tokens yielded a manageable memory utilization per batch. This restriction does not severely distort the sample texts since only a few samples are affected by this measure.

In order to be included in the vocabulary, a word has to appear at least 10 times in the AE training set. Furthermore, a dictionary has been used to translate words from British English to American English for all samples taken from the *BBC News Database*. In this way, the vocabulary could be reduced from its original size of 59, 349 tokens to a final size of 12, 591.

Figure 5: Example input-output image pairs of the trained autoencoder. These are randomly chosen unseen samples, i.e., they have not been seen during training.

The complete AE dataset is decomposed into three parts. 202, 654 samples have been generated from the MS COCO validation set (all image-caption pairs). In addition, all 3, 361 image-text pairs from the BBC News Corpora and 2, 999 image-text pairs from the SimpleWiki dataset have been included. From this randomly shuffled corpus, samples have been selected to generate a disjoint split of 190, 202 training and 6, 270 validation samples[8]. The image encoding network has been initialized with weights of a pre-trained *InceptionV3* model. Initial word embedding estimates have been taken from a *Word2Vec* implementation that was trained among the whole text contained in the dataset.

As outlined in Section 4.4, the CL dataset consists of 826 samples. The dataset has been divided in a training set consisting of 734 samples and a test set consisting of 92 samples. The CL encoding network has been initialized with the weights learned during AE training. Both systems use 300-dimensional word embeddings, 600-dimensional sentence and image embeddings, as well as 2400-dimensional article embeddings. Input images are scaled to size 300 × 300.

5.2 Performance of the Autoencoder

The capabilities of the AE are depicted in Figure 5. To make a qualitative statement about its performance, we measure the perplexity. During training, the image perplexity has decreased by 16.6% and the text perplexity by 5.5%, respectively.

As it can be seen, the AE is capable to store the global image contours in the extremely dense intermediate image embedding.

[8]The remaining samples are allocated for future usage.

Experiment	Accuracy CMI	Accuracy SC
CL	**0.6953**	**0.7344**
$\mathbb{E}_{\text{CL}}^{\text{no }AE}$	0.5625	0.6562
$\mathbb{E}_{\text{SVM}}^{AE}$	0.6875	0.7125
$\mathbb{E}_{\text{RAND}}^{MF}$	0.5642	0.6550

Table 3: The overall accuracy of predicting the correct CMI and SC labels that has been achieved in our experiments. The first row contains the results of the trained CL model.

Small architectural improvements may be sufficient to represent the salient semantics, such that the decoded image can be interpreted without the need of knowing the original input.

However, the text encoding has not been as successful yet. This may be due to the careful engineering of the utilized *InceptionV3* model which has no counterpart in the text decoding network. Yet, it can be assumed that the AE architecture is suited for feature learning and especially for conceptualization.

5.3 Performance of the Classifier

The encoder network of the CL has been initialized with the AE weights from the previous section. The article embeddings generated with the AE encoder do not fully contain the salient semantics yet. Therefore, the encoder network for article embeddings and the classifying network (Figure 4b) have been trained jointly in the supervised learning process. To minimize the risk of overfitting in this setting, we omitted one intermediate FC layer of the classifying network in Figure 4b. Furthermore, we stated the prediction of CMI and SC as multiclass problems using a cross-entropy loss.

In addition, the following systems have been setup as reference baselines for comparison:

- $\mathbb{E}_{\text{CL}}^{\text{no }AE}$: The trained classifier CL is used, but with randomly initialized weights in the encoder network, i.e., pre-trained AE is not used.
- $\mathbb{E}_{\text{SVM}}^{AE}$: A multiclass SVM [4], trained with the feature vectors of article embeddings $\mathbf{a}_e$ that have been generated by the trained AE model from Section 5.2[9].
- $\mathbb{E}_{\text{RAND}}^{MF}$: A random baseline, i.e., a "classifier" that simply outputs the most frequent label.

The accuracy achieved in all the previously described experiments is depicted in Table 3. The experimental results show that the deep learning architecture is basically able to predict image-text relations by means of CMI and SC. In both cases, the deep learning system outperforms the SVM approach. The results also reveal that the proposed pipeline consisting of an unsupervised pre-training and supervised refinement is necessary. Without the initialization of pre-trained weights, the classifier does not even outperform the random baseline.

6 CONCLUSIONS

In this paper, we have presented a novel approach to estimate the relations of co-occurring image-text pairs. Based on an analysis by which means interrelations can differ, we have derived two measures to describe image-text relations: Cross-modal Mutual Information and Semantic Correlation. Furthermore, we have proposed a deep learning architecture that consists of both an unsupervised as well as a supervised learning component. The purpose of the unsupervised autoencoder is to achieve a compact representation of multimodal image-text relations while at the same time minimizing the supervision efforts, i.e., reducing the number of required training samples. A deep neural classifier was trained using the autoencoder representation. In addition, we constructed several baseline systems to highlight the strengths of the designed system. The baseline systems have been consistently outperformed by the proposed deep learning system. Moreover, we highlighted the necessity of the full learning pipeline, consisting of unsupervised concept clustering and supervised concept-relation learning. Hence, the feasibility of the proposed deep learning system has been demonstrated for the challenging task of estimating image-text relations.

In future work, we are planning to improve the intermediate autoencoder representation by using a more sophisticated network structure. An expressive article embedding may enable an alternative fully unsupervised approach that involves an estimate of the pointwise mutual information of two entities. Since probability estimates drawn from the initial modality representations are presumably not expressive enough, they can be computed from the feature distribution in article embeddings. Hopefully, this approach will resolve currently existing shortcomings due to insufficient size of annotated training data. Finally, we will improve the annotation process by employing a group of annotators and investigating in detail the level of subjective judgments by means of inter-coder agreement.

[9] A suitable value for *weight-decay* has been found via grid search.

REFERENCES

[1] Kobus Barnard, Pinar Duygulu, David Forsyth, Nando de Freitas, David Blei, and Michael Jordan. 2003. Matching Words and Pictures. *Journal of Machine Learning Research* 3, 2 (2003), 1107–1135.

[2] Kobus Barnard and Keiji Yanai. 2006. Mutual Information of Words and Pictures. *Information Theory and Applications* 2 (2006), 5 pages.

[3] Xinlei Chen, Hao Fang, Tsung-Yi Lin, Ramakrishna Vedantam, Saurabh Gupta, Piotr Dollár, and Lawrence Zitnick. 2015. Microsoft COCO Captions: Data Collection and Evaluation Server. *arXiv* (2015), 7 pages. http://arxiv.org/abs/1504.00325

[4] Koby Crammer and Yoram Singer. 2002. On the Algorithmic Implementation of Multiclass Kernel-based Vector Machines. *Journal of Machine Learning Research* 2, 12 (2002), 265–292.

[5] Yansong Feng and Mirella Lapata. 2008. Automatic Image Annotation Using Auxiliary Text Information. *Proceedings of Association for Computational Linguistics* 8 (2008), 272–280.

[6] Yansong Feng and Mirella Lapata. 2013. Automatic Caption Generation for News Images. *IEEE Transactions on Pattern Analysis and Machine Intelligence* 35, 4 (2013), 797–812.

[7] Andrea Frome, Greg Corrado, Jon Shlens, Samy Bengio, Jeff Dean, Marc' Aurelio Ranzato, and Tomas Mikolov. 2013. DeViSE: A Deep Visual-Semantic Embedding Model. *Proceedings of Neural Information Processing Systems* 26 (2013), 2121–2129.

[8] Yunchao Gong, Liwei Wang, Micah Hodosh, Julia Hockenmaier, and Svetlana Lazebnik. 2014. Improving Image-Sentence Embeddings Using Large Weakly Annotated Photo Collections. *Proceedings of European Conference on Computer Vision* 13 (2014), 529–545.

[9] Ian Goodfellow, Jean Pouget-Abadie, Mehdi Mirza, Bing Xu, David Warde-Farley, Sherjil Ozair, Aaron Courville, and Yoshua Bengio. 2014. Generative Adversarial Nets. *Proceedings of Neural Information Processing Systems* 26 (2014), 2672–2680.

[10] Hamid Izadinia, Fereshteh Sadeghi, Santosh Divvala, Hannaneh Hajishirzi, Yejin Choi, and Ali Farhadi. 2015. Segment-Phrase Table for Semantic Segmentation, Visual Entailment and Paraphrasing. *Proceedings of the IEEE International*

Conference on Computer Vision (2015), 10–18.
[11] Andrej Karpathy, Armand Joulin, and Fei-Fei Li. 2014. Deep Fragment Embeddings for Bidirectional Image Sentence Mapping. *arXiv* (2014), 9 pages. http://arxiv.org/abs/1406.5679
[12] Andrej Karpathy and Fei-Fei Li. 2014. Deep Visual-Semantic Alignments for Generating Image Descriptions. *arXiv* (2014), 17 pages. http://arxiv.org/abs/1412.2306
[13] Wei Liu and Xiaoou Tang. 2005. Learning an Image-word Embedding for Image Auto-annotation on the Nonlinear Latent Space. *Proceedings of ACM International Conference on Multimedia* 13 (2005), 451–454.
[14] Junhua Mao, Wei Xu, Yi Yang, Jiang Wang, and Alan Yuille. 2014. Explain Images with Multimodal Recurrent Neural Networks. *arXiv* (2014), 9 pages. http://arxiv.org/abs/1410.1090
[15] Tomas Mikolov, Ilya Sutskever, Kai Chen, Greg Corrado, and Jeff Dean. 2013. Distributed Representations of Words and Phrases and their Compositionality. *Proceedings of Neural Information Processing Systems* 26 (2013), 3111–3119.
[16] Jiquan Ngiam, Aditya Khosla, Mingyu Kim, Juhan Nam, Honglak Lee, and Andrew Ng. 2011. Multimodal Deep Learning. *Proceedings of International Conference on Machine Learning* 28 (2011), 689–696.
[17] Alec Radford, Luke Metz, and Soumith Chintala. 2015. Unsupervised Representation Learning with Deep Convolutional Generative Adversarial Networks. *arXiv* (2015), 16 pages. https://arxiv.org/abs/1511.06434
[18] Arnau Ramisa, Fei Yan, Francesc Moreno-Noguer, and Krystian Mikolajczyk. 2016. Breakingnews: Article Annotation by Image and Text Processing. *arXiv* (2016), 21 pages. http://arxiv.org/abs/1603.07141
[19] Christian Szegedy, Vincent Vanhoucke, Sergey Ioffe, Jonathon Shlens, and Zbigniew Wojna. 2015. Rethinking the Inception Architecture for Computer Vision. *arXiv* (2015), 10 pages. http://arxiv.org/abs/1512.00567
[20] Oriol Vinyals, Alexander Toshev, Samy Bengio, and Dumitru Erhan. 2014. Show and Tell: A Neural Image Caption Generator. *arXiv* (2014), 9 pages. http://arxiv.org/abs/1411.4555
[21] Oriol Vinyals, Alexander Toshev, Samy Bengio, and Dumitru Erhan. 2016. Show and Tell: Lessons Learned from the 2015 MSCOCO Image Captioning Challenge. *IEEE Transactions on Pattern Analysis and Machine Intelligence* 39, 4 (2016), 652–663.
[22] Qi Wu, Chunhua Shen, Lingqiao Liu, Anthony Dick, and Anton van den Hengel. 2016. What Value do Explicit High Level Concepts have in Vision to Language Problems? *Proceedings of the IEEE Conference on Computer Vision and Pattern Recognition* (2016), 203–212.
[23] Jiao Xue, Youtian Du, and Hanbing Shui. 2015. Semantic Correlation Mining between Images and Texts with Global Semantics and Local Mapping. *Proceedings of International Conference on Multimedia Modeling* 8936 (2015), 427–435.
[24] Fei Yan and Krystian Mikolajczyk. 2015. Deep Correlation for Matching Images and Text. *Proceedings of the IEEE Conference on Computer Vision and Pattern Recognition* (2015), 3441–3450.
[25] Keiji Yanai and Kobus Barnard. 2005. Image Region Entropy: A Measure of Visualness of Web Images Associated with one Concept. *Proceedings of the annual ACM international conference on Multimedia* 13 (2005), 419–422.
[26] Yi Zhang, Jeff Schneider, and Artur Dubrawski. 2008. Learning the Semantic Correlation: An Alternative Way to Gain from Unlabeled Text. *Proceedings of the International Conference on Neural Information Processing Systems* 21 (2008), 1945–1952.
[27] Yue-Ting Zhuang, Yi Yang, and Fei Wu. 2008. Mining Semantic Correlation of Heterogeneous Multimedia Data for Cross-Media Retrieval. *IEEE Transactions on Multimedia* 10, 2 (2008), 221–229.

MSRC: Multimodal Spatial Regression with Semantic Context for Phrase Grounding

Kan Chen
University of Southern California
kanchen@usc.edu

Rama Kovvuri
University of Southern California
nkovvuri@usc.edu

Jiyang Gao
University of Southern California
jiyangga@usc.edu

Ram Nevatia
University of Southern California
nevatia@usc.edu

ABSTRACT

Given an image and a natural language query phrase, a grounding system localizes the mentioned objects in the image according to the query's specifications. State-of-the-art methods address the problem by ranking a set of proposal bounding boxes according to the query's semantics, which makes them dependent on the performance of proposal generation systems. Besides, query phrases in one sentence may be semantically related in one sentence and can provide useful cues to ground objects. We propose a novel Multimodal Spatial Regression with semantic Context (MSRC) system which not only predicts the location of ground truth based on proposal bounding boxes, but also refines prediction results by penalizing similarities of different queries coming from same sentences. The advantages of MSRC are twofold: first, it removes the limitation of performance from proposal generation algorithms by using a spatial regression network. Second, MSRC not only encodes the semantics of a query phrase, but also deals with its relation with other queries in the same sentence (*i.e.*, context) by a context refinement network. Experiments show MSRC system provides a significant improvement in accuracy on two popular datasets: Flickr30K Entities and Refer-it Game, with 6.64% and 5.28% increase over the state-of-the-arts respectively.

CCS CONCEPTS

•**Computing methodologies** →**Visual content-based indexing and retrieval;** *Information extraction;* Scene understanding;

KEYWORDS

phrase grounding; spatial regression; multimodal; context

ACM Reference format:
Kan Chen, Rama Kovvuri, Jiyang Gao, and Ram Nevatia. 2017. MSRC: Multimodal Spatial Regression with Semantic Context for Phrase Grounding. In *Proceedings of ICMR '17, June 6–9, 2017, Bucharest, Romania, ,* 9 pages.
DOI: http://dx.doi.org/10.1145/3078971.3078976

ICMR '17, June 6–9, 2017, Bucharest, Romania

DOI: http://dx.doi.org/10.1145/3078971.3078976

1 INTRODUCTION

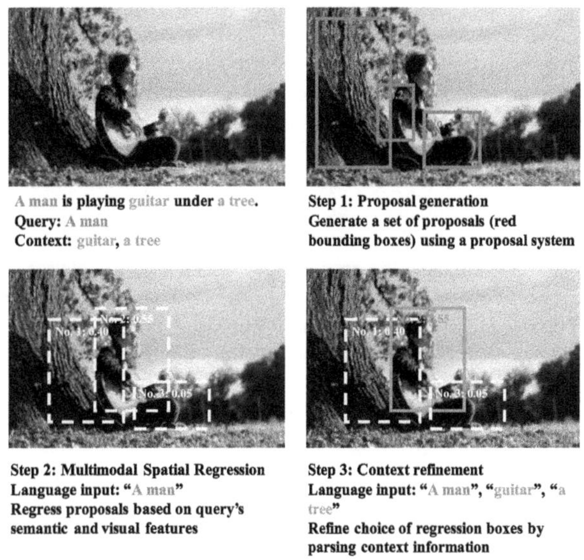

Figure 1: Multimodal Spatial Regression with semantic Context (MSRC) system regresses each proposal based on query's semantics and visual features. Besides, MSRC takes advantage of context cues to filter out confusing candidates and refine regression results. (Each regression box's ID corresponds to proposal box's ID, with confidence on the top-left corner.)

Given an image and a natural language query phrase, phrase grounding attempts to localize the mentioned objects in the image according to the query's specification. It can be utilized in many daily life applications, such as electronic entertainment, early education, security surveillance, *etc.* Solution to this problem can be an important building block for image-language related tasks, such as image captioning [1, 6, 14], visual question answering [2, 3, 7] and image retrieval [10, 24].

Phrase grounding is a challenging problem in reasoning language queries and transferring their semantics to localize object in visual contents. To address this problem, typically a set of proposal bounding boxes are first generated as candidates by some proposal generation system. The main difficulties then lie in how to correlate language input and proposals' features and how to localize objects after learning such multimodal correlation. State-of-the-art methods address the first difficulty by treating phrase grounding as a ranking problem, and learn a multimodal subspace where relevance between visual and language inputs are measurable and then rank proposals according to the relevance of query's specification. Among these, Phrase-Region CCA [23] and SCRC [13] models learn a subspace using Canonical Correlation Analysis (CCA) and a Recurrent Neural Network (RNN) respectively. GroundeR [27] adopts an attention network, which learns a latent subspace to attend on related proposals given different queries via phrase reconstruction.

These methods are bounded by two limitations. First, when the proposal generation system fails to provide good proposals which overlap the object mentioned by the query with a large region (Fig. 1), these proposal-based models are unable to localize the correct object; as a result, there exists a performance upper bound from proposal generation systems. Second, these grounding systems consider query phrases as unrelated to each other; however, sometimes different queries for the same image are semantically related. For example, we observe query phrases for the same images are usually correlated in same image-related captions in Flickr30K Entities [23] dataset. Intuitively, given a query phrase, other phrases from the same sentence, which are the query's context, can provide useful cues for grounding the correct objects. As shown in Fig. 1, with the context "the tree", the grounding system should be able to infer the current query "a man" does not refer to the tree object in the image, even though the proposal of tree also has high confidence; and the context "guitar" can provide hints for the system to find "a man" near the object "guitar".

To address the aforementioned two issues, we propose a Multimodal Spatial Regression with semantic Context (MSRC) deep network. MSRC system is composed of two parts: a Spatial Regression Network (SRN) and a Context Refinement Network (CRN). SRN applies a bi-directional LSTM to encode the query and takes each proposal's feature as visual information. It learns to predict the probability of each proposal being related to query, and regresses each proposal to the mentioned object's location via a joint projection in a multimodal subspace. SRN is robust to performance of proposal generation program, because when proposal does not overlap much with the mentioned object in the query, SRN can regress the proposal to best fit the mentioned object. CRN takes a pair of queries from the same sentence and jointly predicts proposals' probability of being relevant to each query. Based on the assumption that different queries in the same sentence refer to different objects, CRN adopts a joint prediction loss, which penalizes the probabilities of confusing proposal candidates. The final prediction of MSRC is by a late fusion of SRN decision and CRN decision, which takes advantages of both spatial regression results and context information.

We evaluate the MSRC system on two popular phrase grounding datasets: Flickr30K Entities [23] and Refer-it Game [15] datasets. Flickr30K Entities contains more than 30K images associated with 5 captions for each image. There are 244K query phrases referring to 276K manually annotated bounding boxes of objects in images. Every query phrase comes from some image related caption. Refer-it Game has 130K query phrases, referring to 96K objects, which are annotated for 19K images of natural scenes. We adopt ratio of phrases which are successfully grounded by MSRC as metric. Experiments show that MSRC system has more than 6% improvement in Flickr30K Entities and 5% improvement in Refer-it Game datasets, indicating the effectiveness of our approach.

Our contributions are two fold: First, we propose a spatial regression approach in multimodal space, which relieves performance limitation from proposal generation systems. Second, we encode context information with query phrase by adopting a joint prediction loss during training stage, which helps filter out confusing candidates during grounding. In the following paper, we first discuss related work in phrase grounding problem in Sec. 2. More details about MSRC system are presented in Sec. 3. Finally, experiments of MSRC system and related results are provided and analyzed in Sec. 4.

2 RELATED WORK

Language grounding. Language grounding is a hot topic in both computer vision and natural language processing communities. To parse the semantic information from queries, Krishnamurthy *et al.* [19] and Matuszek *et al.* [21] introduce joint learning models to parse knowledge in language sentences and apply models on scene understanding, attribute classification and geographical question answering. Recently, Wang *et al.* [30] propose a structured system to match phrase and deal with the "partial match coreference" relation in queries to boost performance. To correlate visual contents with language embeddings, Karpathy *et al.* [17] propose to align sentence fragments and image regions in a subspace, and replace the dependency tree with a bi-directional RNN in [1]. Plummer *et al.* [23] apply a Canonical Correlation Analysis (CCA) model to ground object in images. Based on these methods, Hu *et al.* [13] propose a hierarchy of RNNs to retrieve objects given a query. Rohrbach *et al.* [27] learn to attend on mentioned object via phrase reconstruction in the unsupervised scenario. These methods learn the correlation between language and visual modalities, and are effective when a proposal system generates good candidate proposals. However, their performances are dependent on the proposal system's upper bound. As a result, these methods are unable to localize the mentioned object when there are no proposals overlapping much with it.

Spatial regression. Spatial regression is successfully applied in object detection. Fast R-CNN [8] first introduces regression loss in object detection. Based on this, Ren *et al.* [26] adopt a Region Proposal Network (RPN) which further improves the accuracy in proposal regression. Redmon *et al.* [25] regress image in grid level and merge regressed grids using the non-max suppression algorithm, which efficiently improves the detection speed. Liu *et al.* [20] integrate proposal generation in a single network and discretize the output into a set of bounding boxes with default sizes over different ratios and scales of feature maps, which further improve the accuracy and speed of detection. Inspired by the success of regression in object detection, MSRC system applies a spatial regression network in phrase grounding problem, which is robust to different proposal generation algorithms and improves the performance of grounding.

Semantic context encoding. Context brings useful information and is successfully applied in image-sentence referring and object detection problems. Kantorov *et al.* [16] propose a ContextLocNet which encodes region proposals and context around regions

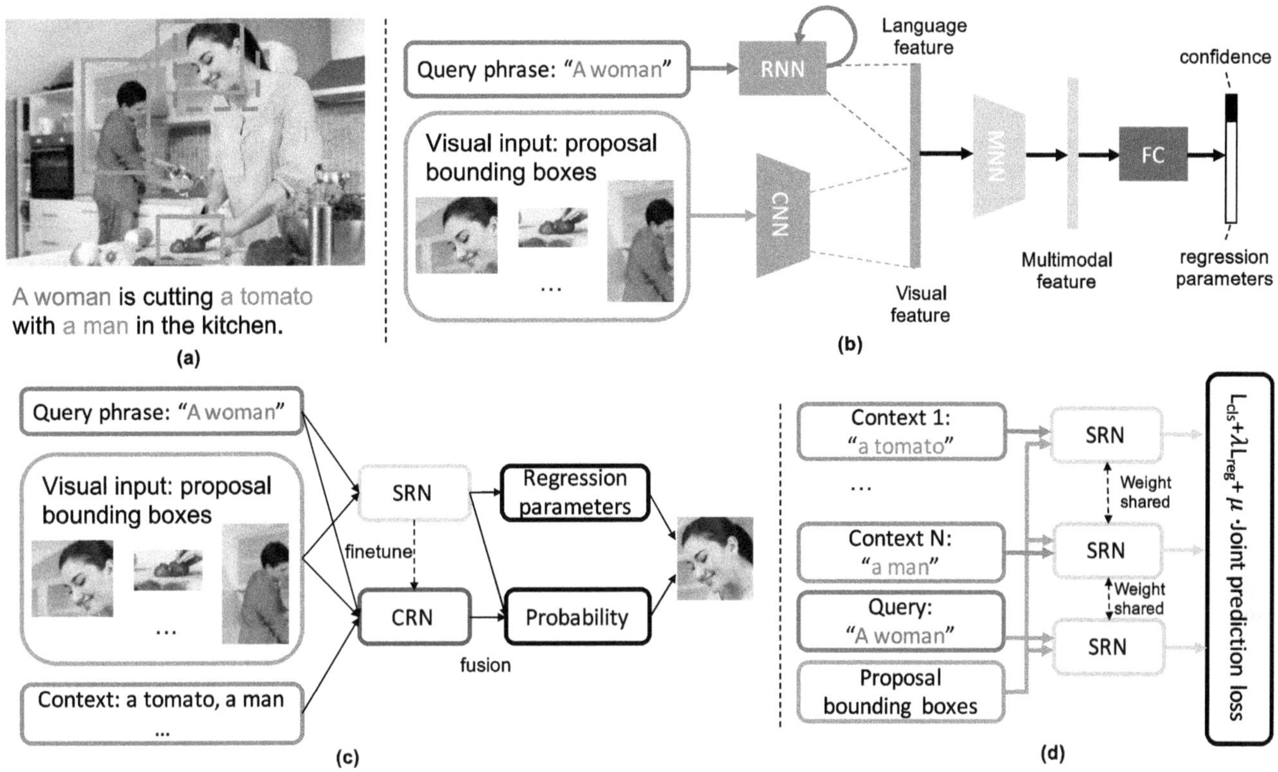

Figure 2: Structure of MSRC system. (a) An example image and query phrases: For query "A woman" (blue text), queries in red text are considered as its context, which are further utilized by CRN. Input image is represented as a set of proposal bounding boxes (green), and the ground truth for the query is the red box. (b) Structure of SRN: SRN takes proposals and query phrase as inputs. Multimodal features are encoded by a Multimodal Neural Network (MNN). SRN predicts each proposal's probability of being related to the query as well as regression parameters to localize the mentioned object. (c) Framework of MSRC: A SRN is first trained and utilized to finetune CRN later. CRN refines probability predicted by SRN via encoding context information. (d): Structure of CRN: Each (language, proposal set) pair has a SRN to predict confidence. All SRNs share weights during training. We propose a joint prediction loss to encode context information.

using context-aware models, and achieve the state-of-the-art performance on PASCAL VOC 2007 dataset [5]. Nagaraja *et al.* [22] introduce a Multiple Instance Learning (MIL) approach to the object referring problem, which learns to rank query regions among context regions in images to boost performance. Yu *et al.* [31] jointly predict all query regions in one image, and encode context information by sharing information between CNNs and RNNs, which achieves the state-of-the-art performance in referring task. MSRC system is inspired by the success of using context information. However, it considers language phrases rather than visual contents as context information, and applies a context refinement network on grounding problem.

3 MSRC SYSTEM

Multimodal Spatial Regression with semantic Context (MSRC) system contains two parts: a Spatial Regression Network (SRN) and a Context Refinement Network (CRN). We first introduce the framework of MSRC followed by structures of SRN and CRN. Then we provide more details about training and grounding of MSRC system.

3.1 Framework

The visual input of SRN and CRN is a set of N proposal bounding boxes $\{r_i\}$ generated from an input image I. Each proposal r_i is represented as the visual feature $\mathbf{x}_i \in \mathbb{R}^{d_v}$ extracted by a pre-trained Convolutional Neural Network (CNN), where d_v is the visual feature's dimension. The language input of SRN is a query phrase q, while CRN takes q and its context phrases $\{p_i^q\}$ parsed from the same sentence as inputs. We adopt a Bi-directional LSTM [12] to encode semantics of query q and its context $\{p_i^q\}$, which are denoted as $\mathbf{q} \in \mathbb{R}^{d_l}$ and $\mathbf{p}_i^q \in \mathbb{R}^{d_l}$ respectively, where d_l is the language embedding vector's dimension. In this paper, we select query phrases from the same image description of query $\mathbf{q}$ as its context phrases $\{\mathbf{p}_i^q\}$.

Given $\{\mathbf{x}_i\}$ and $\mathbf{q}$, SRN predicts a probability distribution over the N proposals as well as each proposal's regression parameters to infer the location of object mentioned by the query phrase q. The objective is defined as:

$$\arg\min_{\theta_s} \sum_{\mathbf{q}} \left[L_{cls}^s(\{x_i\}, \mathbf{q}) + \lambda L_{reg}^s(\{\mathbf{x}_i\}, \mathbf{q}) \right] \quad (1)$$

where θ_s is the parameters of SRN. L^s_{cls} is a cross entropy function adopted for multiclass classification task. L^s_{reg} is a regression loss function, weighted by a hyper parameter λ, whose details are in Sec. 3.2

To further refine the grounding results, we propose a CRN to generate a more accurate probability distribution over the N proposals via encoding context information. CRN is based on an assumption: different phrases in one sentence refer to different objects in one image, which is always true in Flickr30K Entities dataset [23]. Given N proposals' visual features $\{\mathbf{x}_i\}$, language features of query q and M context phrases $\{p^q_j\}$, the objective of CRN is defined as:

$$\arg\min_{\theta_c} \sum_{\mathrm{q}} \left[L^c_{cls} + \lambda L^c_{reg} + \mu J(\{\mathbf{x}_i\}, \mathrm{q}, \{\mathbf{p}^q_j\})\right] \tag{2}$$

where θ_c is the parameters of CRN and μ, λ are hyper parameters. L^c_{cls} and L^c_{reg} are similar to L^s_{cls} and L^s_{reg} in Eq. (1). We propose a novel joint prediction loss function J, penalizing prediction results which match the semantic of context phrases $\{p^q_i\}$. With this term, CRN penalizes the probabilities of proposals referred by context queries in the same sentence.

We first train SRN and then finetune CRN based on the trained weights of SRN. During evaluation, we fuse the predicted probabilities from both SRN and CRN, and regress the proposal with maximum probability according to the regression parameters predicted by SRN, with more details in Sec. 3.4.

3.2 Spatial Regression Network (SRN)

As shown in Fig. 2, SRN concatenates language embedding vector q with each of the proposal's visual feature $\mathbf{x}_i$. It then applies a network to generate multimodal features $\{\mathbf{v}^q_i\} \in \mathbb{R}^m$ for each of the $\langle q, r_i\rangle$ pair in a m-dimensional subspace (We term the network as MNN). The multimodal feature $\mathbf{v}^q_i$ is calculated as:

$$\mathbf{v}^q_i = \varphi(\mathbf{W}_m(\mathrm{q}||\mathbf{x}_i) + \mathbf{b}_m) \tag{3}$$

where $\mathbf{W}_m \in \mathbb{R}^{(d_l+d_v)\times m}, \mathbf{b}_m \in \mathbb{R}^m$ are projection parameters of MNN. $\varphi(.)$ is a non-linear activation function. "||" denotes a concatenation operator. We also replace MNN with a Multimodal Compact Bilinear Pooling layer in [7] to evaluate performances of different multimodal features, with more details discussed in Sec. 4.

Given the multimodal feature $\mathbf{v}^q_i$, SRN predicts a 5D vector $\mathbf{s}^p_i \in \mathbb{R}^5$ for each proposal r_i via a linear projection (superscript "p" denotes prediction).

$$\mathbf{s}^p_i = \mathbf{W}_s \mathbf{v}^q_i + \mathbf{b}_s \tag{4}$$

where $\mathbf{W}_s \in \mathbb{R}^{d\times 5}$ and $\mathbf{b}_s \in \mathbb{R}^5$ are projection weight and bias to be optimized. The first element in $\mathbf{s}^p_i$ indicates the confidence of r_i being related to input query q's semantics. We denote $\{\mathbf{s}^{p'}_i\}$ as the probability distribution of $\{r_i\}$ after we feed $\{\mathbf{s}^p_i[0]\}$ to a softmax function. During training, we choose the positive label of proposal as the one which overlaps most with ground truth and with Intersection of Union (IoU)> 0.5. Thus, the classification loss is calculated as:

$$L^s_{cls}(\{\mathbf{x}_i\}, \mathrm{q}) = -\log(\mathbf{s}^{p'}_{i^*}[0]) \tag{5}$$

where i^* is positive proposal's index in the proposal set.

The next four elements of $\mathbf{s}^p_i$ record the regression information based on current location of r_i, which are defined as:

$$\begin{aligned} \mathbf{s}^p_i[1] &= (x_{pred} - x_{r_i})/w_{r_i} \\ \mathbf{s}^p_i[2] &= (y_{pred} - y_{r_i})/h_{r_i} \\ \mathbf{s}^p_i[3] &= \log(w_{pred}/w_{r_i}) \\ \mathbf{s}^p_i[4] &= \log(h_{pred}/h_{r_i}) \end{aligned} \tag{6}$$

where $[x_{pred}, y_{pred}, w_{pred}, h_{pred}]$ are the predicted regressed bounding box's center x, y coordinates, width and height. Similarly, $[x_{r_i}, y_{r_i}, w_{r_i}, h_{r_i}]$ is the location information of r_i.

Each proposal's ground truth regression data $\mathbf{s}^q_i \in \mathbb{R}^4$ is calculated in the same way as Eq.(6), by replacing $[x_{pred}, y_{pred}, w_{pred}, h_{pred}]$ with the ground truth bounding box's location information. The regression loss for SRN is:

$$L^s_{reg}(\{\mathbf{x}_i\}, \mathrm{q}) = \frac{1}{4N}\sum_{i=1}^{N}\sum_{j=0}^{3} f\left(\left|\mathbf{s}^p_i[j+1] - \mathbf{s}^q_i[j]\right|\right) \tag{7}$$

where $f(.)$ is the smooth L1 loss function: $f(x) = 0.5x^2(x < 1)$, and $f(x) = |x| - 0.5(x \geq 1)$.

3.3 Context Refinement Network (CRN)

CRN is built on an assumption: different query phrases in one sentence usually refer to different objects in the same image, which is common in Flickr30K Entities dataset [23]. Based on this assumption, CRN penalizes prediction results which match context's semantics during training. In this way, CRN maximizes probabilities of proposals referred by queries rather than context from same sentences.

CRN takes proposals' visual features $\{\mathbf{x}_i\}$, embedding vector q of query q, and M context phrases' embedding vectors $\{\mathbf{p}^q_j\}$ as inputs. As shown in Fig. 2, for each query or its context phrase, CRN builds an SRN-like structure to process language embedding and visual features, which share weights with each other during training. We denote the output of SRN for pair $\langle \mathrm{q}, \{\mathbf{x}_i\}\rangle$ as $\{\mathbf{t}^q_i\}$ and for pair $\langle \mathrm{p}_j, \{\mathbf{x}_i\}\rangle$ as $\{\mathbf{t}^{p_j}_i\}$. Besides, we denote the proposal set S_q as the proposals which overlap with ground truth with IoU> 0.5. The cross-entropy loss and regression loss in Eq. (2) are calculated in the same way as Eq. (5) and Eq. (7), while the last term in Eq. (2) is calculated as:

$$J(\{\mathbf{x}_i\}, \mathrm{q}, \{\mathbf{p}^q_j\}) = -\sum_{j=1}^{M}\sum_{i=1}^{N} \delta(i \in S_q)\log(\mathbf{t}^{p_j\prime}_i[0]) \tag{8}$$

where $\mathbf{t}^{p_j\prime}_i[0]$ is the softmax normalized probability generated from $\{\mathbf{t}^{p_j}_i[0]\}$. $\delta(.)$ is an indicator function to judge whether current label matches query q's semantic. If yes, then CRN penalizes these results, because the proposal should belong to context phrase rather than input query.

3.4 Training & Phrase grounding of MSRC

The number of context training samples is much smaller than that of single query phrases. To compensate for this, we first train the SRN using single queries with image proposals, and then we finetune the CRN by introducing context training samples and initialize CRN structure by the pre-trained SRN. We use the Adam algorithm [18] to optimize the deep learning framework, and adopt the rectified linear unit (ReLU) as the non-linear activation function.

During phrase grounding stage, if an input query q has T_q context phrases in the same sentence, SRN first predicts a probability distribution $\{\text{Pr}_{srn}(i)\}$ over the proposals as well as each proposal's regression parameters $\{\text{Reg}_{srn}(i)\}$. Then CRN receives a triplet $\langle q, \{r_i\}, p_j^q \rangle$ successively and predicts a probability distribution over the proposals $\{\text{Pr}_{crn}(i|p_j^q)\}$. MSRC system gives the final prediction result as:

$$\text{Box}^* = \text{Regression}(\text{Reg}_{srn}(i^*), r_i), \text{where}$$
$$i^* = \arg\max_i \left(\text{Pr}_{srn}(i) + \frac{\tau}{T_q} \sum_{j=1}^{T_q} \text{Pr}_{crn}(i|p_j^q) \right) \quad (9)$$

τ is a hyper parameter. Regression(.) denotes the regression operation based on the input bounding box and regression parameters.

4 EXPERIMENTS

We evaluate MSRC system on Flickr30K Entities [23] and Refer-it Game datasets [15] for phrase grounding.

4.1 Datasets

Flickr30K Entities [23] contains 31,783 images, with 29783, 1000, 1000 images for training, validation and testing respectively. Each image is associated with 5 captions. There are 559,767 query phrases extracted from these captions referring to 276K manually annotated bounding boxes in images. The vocabulary size of queries is 17,150. The maximum length of query phrases is 19 words.

Refer-it Game [15] contains 19,894 images of natural scenes. There are 96,654 distinct objects in these images. Each of them is referred to by 1-3 query phrases (130,525 in total). The vocabulary size of queries is 8800, and the maximum length of query phrases is 19 words.

4.2 Experiment Setup

Proposal generation. We choose Selective Search [29] to generate proposals for Flickr30K Entities and Edge Box [32] to generate proposals for Refer-it Game, which are the same settings as in GroundeR [27] for fair comparison.

Visual feature extraction. We choose a VGG network [28] pre-trained on ImageNet [4] to extract each proposal bounding box's visual feature, which is denoted as "VGG_{cls}", for both Flickr30K Entities and Refer-it Game datasets. Besides, we apply a VGG network finetuned by Fast-RCNN [8] on PASCAL VOC 2007 [5] dataset to extract visual features for Flickr30K Entities, which are denoted as "VGG_{det}".

To predict regression parameters, we need to include spatial information from each proposal. For Flickr30K Entities, we augment each proposal's visual feature with its spatial information $[x_{tl}/W, y_{tl}/H, x_{br}/W, y_{br}/H, wh/WH]$ defined in [31]. We denote these augmented features as "VGG_{cls}-SPAT1" and "VGG_{det}-SPAT1" for "VGG_{cls}" and "VGG_{det}" respectively, each being a 4101D ($d_v = 4101$) vector. For Refer-it Game dataset, we augment each proposal's visual feature with its spatial information $[x_{min}, y_{min}, x_{max}, y_{max}, x_{center}, y_{center}, w_{box}, h_{box}]$ defined in [13]. We denote the augmented visual features as "VGG_{cls}-SPAT2", which are 4104D ($d_v = 4104$) vectors.

Approach	Accuracy (%)
Compared approaches	
SCRC [13]	27.80
Wang *et al.* [30]	42.08
GroundeR (VGG_{cls}) [27]	41.56
GroundeR (VGG_{det}) [27]	47.70
MCB [7]	48.69
CCA embedding [23]	50.89
Spatial regression models	
MCB+Reg (VGG_{det}-SPAT1)	51.01
MNN+Reg (VGG_{cls}-SPAT1)	51.18
MNN+Reg (VGG_{det}-SPAT1)	55.99
Context models	
CRN (MNN+Reg(VGG_{det}-SPAT1))	56.31
MSRC Full	**57.53**

Table 1: Different models' performance on Flickr30K Entities. CRN is finetuned based on MNN with Regression layer and take VGG_{det}-SPAT1 as input visual features

Language encoding. We encode query's information by a Bi-directional LSTM [12]. We choose the last hidden state from the LSTM as output **q** (dimension $d_l = 1000$), which is same as in [27].

Model initialization. We initialize the convolution layers with the MSRA method [11] and initialize the fully-connected layers with the Xavier method [9]. We introduce batch normalization layers after projecting visual features and language features, which is the same setting as in [27]. During training, we set batch size to be 40, and learning rate to be 0.0005.

Metric. We adopt the accuracy as an evaluation metric, defined to be the ratio of phrases for which the regressed box overlaps with the ground-truth box by more than 50% IoU.

Compared approaches. We choose GroundeR [27], CCA embedding [23], MCB [7] and the approach proposed by Wang *et al.* [30] for comparison, which all achieve state-of-the-art performances in image grounding problem. For GroundeR [27], we focus on its supervised learning scenario, which achieves the best performance among different scenarios.

4.3 Performance on Flickr30K Entities

SRN model. During training, we set the Multimodal Neural Network (MNN) output dimension as 128 ($m = 128$), which is same as [27]. By using the VGG_{cls}-SPAT1 features, we achieve 51.18% accuracy. Compared to GroundeR (VGG_{cls}), SRN achieves 9.62% increase in accuracy. Compared to VGG_{cls}, VGG_{det} focuses on object detection task, which is more suitable for object localization. By using the VGG_{det} feature for each proposal, we further improve the performance to 55.99%. We also substitute the MNN with a Multimodal Compact Bilinear pooling (MCB) layer in SRN, which is the model MCB+Reg in Table 1. Experiment shows MCB+Reg has 2.32% increase compared to MCB [7] model.

Phrase Type	people	clothing	body parts	animals	vehicles	instruments	scene	other
GroundeR (VGG_{cls}) [27]	53.80	34.04	7.27	49.23	58.75	22.84	52.07	24.13
GroundeR (VGG_{det}) [27]	61.00	38.12	10.33	62.55	68.75	36.42	58.18	29.08
Wang *et al.* [30]	57.89	34.61	15.87	55.98	52.25	23.46	34.22	26.23
CCA embedding [23]	64.73	46.88	17.21	65.83	68.75	**37.65**	51.39	31.77
SRN: MCB+Reg (VGG_{det}-SPAT1)	62.75	43.67	14.91	65.44	65.25	24.74	64.10	34.62
SRN: MNN+Reg (VGG_{det}-SPAT1)	67.38	47.57	20.11	73.75	72.44	29.34	63.68	37.88
CRN: MNN+Reg (VGG_{det}-SPAT1)	68.24	47.98	20.11	73.94	73.66	29.34	66.00	38.32
MSRC Full	**69.57**	**48.01**	**20.11**	**73.97**	**75.32**	29.34	**66.17**	**39.01**

Table 2: Phrase grounding performances in different phrase types defined in Flickr30K Entities. Accuracy is in percentage.

Multimodal dimension m	64	128	256	512	1024
MNN+Reg	51.21	**55.99**	54.59	55.31	55.97

Table 3: SRN MNN+Reg (VGG_{det}-SPAT1) model's performance (accuracy in %) under different dimension of multimodal subspace (weight of regression loss $\lambda = 1.0$).

Regression weight λ	0.5	1.0	2.0	4.0	10.0
MNN+Reg	54.04	**55.99**	55.68	55.32	54.12

Table 4: SRN MNN+Reg (VGG_{det}-SPAT1) model's performance (accuracy in %) under different weight λ of regression loss in Eq. 1 (multimodal subspace dimension $m = 128$).

We test different output dimensions of MNN, which is discussed in later section (Table 3). Experiments show that MNN+Reg achieves the best performance among models taking single query phrase as language input, with 8.29% improvement compared to GroundeR [27], and 5.1% to state-of-the-art approach [23].

CRN model. We finetune CRN based on the MNN+Reg SRN, and take VGG_{det}-SPAT1 as input. In training and testing stage, we treat other query phrases from the same caption of the input query phrase as context. We set the input number of context phrases for CRN to be 1 ($M = 1$) and the weight of joint prediction loss $\mu = 1.0$. There is slight improvement (0.32%) increase in accuracy.

MSRC System. For MSRC model's prediction, we fuse CRN's probability as well as SRN's probability, select the proposal with maximum probability and then regress the proposal according to the regression parameters predicted by SRN. We set the weights $\tau = 1.0$ in Eq. (9). The MSRC Full model achieves best performance on Flickr30K Entities (57.53%), with 6.64% increase compared to [23].

Since Flickr30K Entities provides the phrase type for each query, we further compare the detailed phrase localization results. In Table 2, we observe similar boosts in performance by adopting SRN, CRN and fusion by MSRC as in Table 1. However, different models' strengths are different. CCA embedding [23] model is strong in localizing "instruments" while GroundeR [27] is better in localizing "scenes". By using SRN, we observe that the regression network achieves increase in accuracy compared to GroundeR model (VGG_{det}). Typically, there is a large increase in performance of localizing "animals" and "body parts" (with increase of 24% and 13% respectively). By using CRN, we observe that the increase in "scene" is the largest. In the final fusion stage, MSRC Full model achieves more than 6.5%, 5.88%, 2.9% increase in accuracy in all categories (except "instrument" for CCA embedding [23]) compared to GroundeR [27], Wang *et al.* [30] and CCA embedding [23] respectively.

Dimension of multimodal subspace in SRN. To find the relation between SRN's performance and multimodal subspace's dimension, we train and test SRN (MNN+Reg) in five different multimodal subspace dimensions, which are $m = 64, 128, 256, 512, 1024$. The performances are recorded in Table 3. From the results, we observe SRN has lower performance when multimodal subspace has a smaller dimension, which may be caused by lack of trainable parameters to exhibit the model's expressive power. When multimodal subspace has larger dimensions, the performance fluctuates in a small scale, which reflects that SRN is insensitive to multimodal subspace's dimension when m is large.

Weight of regression loss. During training, SRN's loss in Eq. 1 is classification loss plus a weighted regression loss. We test different weights, with $\lambda = 0.5, 1.0, 2.0, 4.0$ to combine regression loss with classification loss. The results are shown in Table 4. From the results, we observe that the hyper parameter λ does not have a big influence on SRN if L^s_{cls} and L^s_{reg} are in the similar range. When λ is large, SRN loses useful information contained in the classification part which helps SRN choose a good proposal to regress. Thus, when $\lambda = 10.0$, we observe a decrease in performance.

4.4 Performance on Refer-it Game

SRN only. Based on Refer-it Game dataset's structure, there is no context information labeled, because there are no image captions for each image. Hence, we only evaluate SRN's performance on Refer-it Game dataset. In testing stage, we choose the proposal with maximum probability predicted only by SRN. This is equal to setting $\tau = 0$ in Eq. (9).

Comparison of different approaches on Refer-it Game dataset is shown in Table 5. From the results, we observe MCB does not have good performance as MNN. This is likely due to MCB needs to maintain a large output dimension to exhibit the model's expressive power. Refer-it Game does not have as much data as Flickr30K Entities. Thus, the training procedure may overfit in early stage. After using regression network, SRN with MCB (MCB+Reg) has comparable performance with GroundeR [27]. By using MNN (MNN+Reg),

Approach	Accuracy (%)
Compared approaches	
SCRC [13]	17.93
GroundeR (VGG_{cls}-SPAT2) [27]	26.93
Spatial Regression models	
MCB+Reg (VGG_{cls}-SPAT2)	26.54
MNN+Reg (VGG_{cls}-SPAT2)	**32.21**

Table 5: Different models' performance on Refer-it Game. Since there is no context information annotated, we only evaluate SRN models

Multimodal dimension m	64	128	256	512
MNN+Reg	30.72	**32.21**	30.89	31.65

Table 6: SRN MNN+Reg (VGG_{cls}-SPAT2) model's performance (accuracy in %) under different dimension of multimodal subspace on Refer-it Game dataset. We fix weight of regression loss $\lambda = 1.0$.

Regression weight λ	0.5	1.0	2.0	4.0	10.0
MNN+Reg	31.65	**32.21**	31.56	31.69	32.04

Table 7: SRN MNN+Reg (VGG_{cls}-SPAT2) model's performance (accuracy in %) under different co-efficient λ of regression loss in Eq. 1. We fix multimodal subspace dimension $m = 128$.

SRN achieves the highest performance, with 5.28% improvement compared to the state-of-the-art method.

Dimension of multimodal subspace in SRN. Similar to Flickr30K Entities, we train and test SRN (MNN+Reg) in four different multimodal subspace dimensions, which are $m = 64, 128, 256, 512$. The performances are recorded in Table 6. From the results, we observe SRN has some fluctuation in accuracy. Overall it is insensitive to multimodal subspace dimension m, which is similar to Table 3.

Weight of regression loss. We test different values of λ in Eq. (1). The results are shown in Table 7. From the results, we find that when λ is small, SRN's performance is low, because classification part is mostly involved in training. When λ becomes large, SRN's performance fluctuates and achieves the best at $\lambda = 1.0$, which is similar to results in Table 4.

4.5 Qualitative results

We visualize some phrase grounding results of Flickr30K Entities and Refer-it Game datasets (Fig. 3). For Flickr30K Entities, we show an image and its caption as well as the queries in the caption. For each query, we visualize the ground truth box, the selected proposal box by MSRC system and the regressed bounding box based on the regression parameters predicted by SRN. Since there is no context information in Refer-it Game, we visualize query and its ground truth, with selected proposal and regressed box predicted by SRN.

We observe MSRC achieves good performance in grounding people and clothing, which is consistent with results in Table 2. However, when the query is not clear with no context information, MSRC may ground reasonably incorrect objects (Fig. 3).

5 CONCLUSION

We proposed a novel Multimodal Spatial Regression with semantic Context (MSRC) system, which focuses on phrase grounding problem. Given a query and query-related context information, MSRC system applies a Spatial Regression Network (SRN) to predict the mentioned object's location based on the proposal bounding box with the highest probability. Besides, MSRC system applies a Context Refinement Network (CRN) to refine the results by encoding context information and adopting a novel joint prediction loss during training stage. MSRC system not only relieves the performance limitation brought from proposal generation system, but also takes advantage of context information to filter out confusing candidates. MSRC system has a significant improvement in performance compared to state-of-the-arts, with 6.64% and 5.28% increase in accuracy on Flickr30K Entities [23] and Refer-it Game [15] datasets respectively.

6 ACKNOWLEDGEMENTS

This paper is based, in part, on research sponsored by the Air Force Research Laboratory and the Defense Advanced Research Projects Agency under agreement number FA8750-16-2-0204. The U.S. Government is authorized to reproduce and distribute reprints for Governmental purposes notwithstanding any copyright notation thereon. The views and conclusions contained herein are those of the authors and should not be interpreted as necessarily representing the official policies or endorsements, either expressed or implied, of the Air Force Research Laboratory and the Defense Advanced Research Projects Agency or the U.S. Government.

REFERENCES

[1] K. Andrej and F.-F. Li. 2015. Deep visual-semantic alignments for generating image descriptions. In *CVPR*.

[2] S. Antol, A. Agrawal, J. Lu, M. Mitchell, D. Batra, C Lawrence Z., and D. Parikh. 2015. VQA: Visual question answering. In *ICCV*.

[3] K. Chen, J. Wang, L.-C. Chen, H. Gao, W. Xu, and R. Nevatia. 2015. ABC-CNN: An attention based convolutional neural network for visual question answering. *arXiv preprint arXiv:1511.05960* (2015).

[4] J. Deng, W. Dong, R. Socher, L.-J. Li, K. Li, and F.-F Li. 2009. Imagenet: A large-scale hierarchical image database. In *CVPR*.

[5] M. Everingham, L. Van Gool, C. K. I. Williams, J. Winn, and A. Zisserman. 2010. The PASCAL Visual Object Classes Challenge. In *IJCV*.

[6] H. Fang, S. Gupta, F. Iandola, R. K. Srivastava, L. Deng, P. Dollár, J. Gao, X. He, M. Mitchell, J. C Platt, and others. 2015. From captions to visual concepts and back. In *CVPR*.

[7] A. Fukui, D. H Park, D. Yang, A. Rohrbach, T. Darrell, and M. Rohrbach. 2016. Multimodal compact bilinear pooling for visual question answering and visual grounding. *EMNLP* (2016).

[8] R. Girshick. 2015. Fast R-CNN. In *ICCV*.

[9] X. Glorot and Y. Bengio. 2010. Understanding the difficulty of training deep feedforward neural networks.. In *Aistats*.

[10] A. Gordo, J. Almazán, J. Revaud, and D. Larlus. 2016. Deep image retrieval: Learning global representations for image search. In *ECCV*.

[11] K. He, X. Zhang, S. Ren, and J. Sun. 2015. Delving deep into rectifiers: Surpassing human-level performance on imagenet classification. In *CVPR*.

[12] S. Hochreiter and J. Schmidhuber. 1997. Long short-term memory. *Neural computation* (1997).

[13] R. Hu, H. Xu, M. Rohrbach, J. Feng, K. Saenko, and T. Darrell. 2016. Natural language object retrieval. In *CVPR*.

[14] J. Justin, K. Andrej, and F.-F. Li. 2016. Densecap: Fully convolutional localization networks for dense captioning. In *CVPR*.

[15] Sahar K., Vicente O., Mark M., and Tamara L. B. 2014. ReferIt Game: Referring to Objects in Photographs of Natural Scenes. In *EMNLP*.

Figure 3: Some phrase grounding results generated by MSRC system in Flickr30K and Refer-it Game datasets. We visualize ground truth bounding box, selected proposal box and regressed bounding box in blue, green and red respectively. First three rows are phrase grounding results in Flickr30K Entities dataset. First column is input image and query phrases coming from the same image caption. The 2nd – 4th columns correspond to different queries and grounding results. Forth row contains grounding results in Refer-it Game dataset. For different queries, MSRC system is able to localize objects in same images. However, when query is not clear without further context information, MSRC system may ground wrong objects (image in row four, column four).

[16] V. Kantorov, M. Oquab, M. Cho, and I. Laptev. 2016. Contextlocnet: Context-aware deep network models for weakly supervised localization. In *ECCV*.

[17] A. Karpathy, A. Joulin, and F.-F. Li. 2014. Deep fragment embeddings for bidirectional image sentence mapping. In *NIPS*.

[18] D. Kingma and J. Ba. 2014. Adam: A method for stochastic optimization. *arXiv preprint arXiv:1412.6980* (2014).

[19] J. Krishnamurthy and T. Kollar. 2013. Jointly learning to parse and perceive: Connecting natural language to the physical world. *TACL* (2013).

[20] W. Liu, D. Anguelov, D. Erhan, C. Szegedy, S. Reed, C.-Y. Fu, and A. C. Berg. 2016. SSD: Single shot multibox detector. In *ECCV*.

[21] C. Matuszek, N. FitzGerald, L. Zettlemoyer, L. Bo, and D. Fox. 2012. A joint model of language and perception for grounded attribute learning. *ICML* (2012).

[22] V. K Nagaraja, V. I Morariu, and L. S Davis. 2016. Modeling context between objects for referring expression understanding. In *ECCV*.

[23] B. A Plummer, L. Wang, C. M Cervantes, J. C Caicedo, J. Hockenmaier, and S. Lazebnik. 2016. Flickr30k Entities: Collecting region-to-phrase correspondences for richer image-to-sentence models. In *IJCV*.

[24] F. Radenović, G. Tolias, and O. Chum. 2016. CNN image retrieval learns from BoW: Unsupervised fine-tuning with hard examples. In *ECCV*.

[25] J. Redmon, S. Divvala, R. Girshick, and A. Farhadi. 2016. You only look once: Unified, real-time object detection. In *CVPR*.

[26] S. Ren, K. He, R. Girshick, and J. Sun. 2015. Faster r-cnn: Towards real-time object detection with region proposal networks. In *NIPS*.

[27] A. Rohrbach, M. Rohrbach, R. Hu, T. Darrell, and B. Schiele. 2016. Grounding of textual phrases in images by reconstruction. In *ECCV*.

[28] K. Simonyan and A. Zisserman. 2014. Very Deep Convolutional Networks for Large-Scale Image Recognition. *CoRR* (2014).

[29] J. R. Uijlings, Koen E. Van D. S., T. Gevers, and A. W. Smeulders. 2013. Selective search for object recognition. *IJCV* (2013).

[30] M. Wang, M. Azab, N. Kojima, R. Mihalcea, and J. Deng. 2016. Structured matching for phrase localization. In *ECCV*.

[31] L. Yu, P. Poirson, S. Yang, A. C Berg, and T. L Berg. 2016. Modeling context in referring expressions. In *ECCV*.

[32] C. L. Zitnick and P. Dollár. 2014. Edge boxes: Locating object proposals from edges. In *ECCV*.

Leveraging Multi-modal Prior Knowledge for Large-scale Concept Learning in Noisy Web Data

Junwei Liang
Carnegie Mellon University
junweil@cs.cmu.edu

Lu Jiang
Carnegie Mellon University
lujiang@cs.cmu.edu

Deyu Meng
Xi'an Jiaotong University
dymeng@mail.xjtu.edu.cn

Alexander Hauptmann
Carnegie Mellon University
alex@cs.cmu.edu

ABSTRACT

Learning video concept detectors automatically from the big but noisy web data with no additional manual annotations is a novel but challenging area in the multimedia and the machine learning community. A considerable amount of videos on the web is associated with rich but noisy contextual information, such as the title and other multi-modal information, which provides weak annotations or labels about the video content. To tackle the problem of large-scale noisy learning, We propose a novel method called Multi-modal WEbly-Labeled Learning (WELL-MM), which is established on the state-of-the-art machine learning algorithm inspired by the learning process of human. WELL-MM introduces a novel multi-modal approach to incorporate meaningful prior knowledge called curriculum from the noisy web videos. We empirically study the curriculum constructed from the multi-modal features of the Internet videos and images. The comprehensive experimental results on FCVID and YFCC100M demonstrate that WELL-MM outperforms state-of-the-art studies by a statically significant margin on learning concepts from noisy web video data. In addition, the results also verify that WELL-MM is robust to the level of noisiness in the video data. Notably, WELL-MM trained on sufficient noisy web labels is able to achieve a better accuracy to supervised learning methods trained on the clean manually labeled data.

KEYWORDS

Video Understanding; Prior Knowledge; Web Label; Big Data; Webly-supervised Learning; Noisy Data; Concept Detection

ACM Reference format:
Junwei Liang, Lu Jiang, Deyu Meng, and Alexander Hauptmann. 2017. Leveraging Multi-modal Prior Knowledge for Large-scale Concept Learning in Noisy Web Data. In *Proceedings of ICMR '17, June 6–9, 2017, Bucharest, Romania*, , 9 pages.
DOI: http://dx.doi.org/10.1145/3078971.3079003

DOI: http://dx.doi.org/10.1145/3078971.3079003

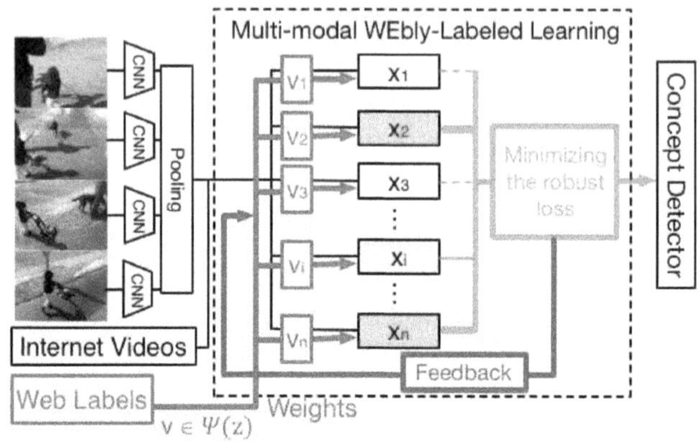

Figure 1: Overview of Multi-modal WEbly-Labeled Learning (WELL-MM). The algorithm jointly models the prior knowledge extracted from web labels and the current learned model at each iteration to overcome the noise labels. $\{x_i\}_{i=1}^n$ are input samples and their current weights are determined by $\{v_i\}_{i=1}^n$. Colored samples are the samples with nonzero weights at the current iteration. The blue line indicates the feedback from the previous objective function value.

1 INTRODUCTION

Millions of videos are being uploaded to the Internet every day. These videos capture different aspects of multimedia content about our daily lives. Automatically categorizing videos into concepts, such as people, actions, objects, etc., is an important topic. Recently many studies have been proposed to tackle the problem of concept learning [1, 6, 10, 14, 21, 23, 29, 30].

Many datasets acquire the clean concept labels via annotators. These datasets include ImageNet [10], TRECVID MED [36] and FCVID [22]. Collecting such datasets requires significant human effort, which is particularly expensive for video data. As a result, the labeled video collection is usually much smaller than the image collection. For example, FCVID [22], only contains about 0.09 million labels on 239 concept classes, much less than the 14 million labels on over 20,000 classes in the image collection ImageNet [10]. On the other hand, state-of-the-art concept models utilize deep neural networks [23, 46], which need more data to train. However, training only on manually labeled clean data seem insufficient for large-scale concept learning.

Images or videos on the web often contain rich contextual information, such as their titles or descriptions. We can infer the label by the metadata. Figure 2 shows an example of a video with inferred concept label "walking a dog". In this paper, we call the samples with inferred labels *weakly labeled* or *webly labeled*. The webly-labeled data are easy to collect and thus usually orders-of-magnitude larger than manually-labeled data. However, the web labels are very noisy and have both low accuracy and low recall.

Concept learning over weakly labeled data becomes popular as it allows for large-scale learning on big data. However, these methods have only focused on utilizing a single text modality to model the noisy labels [4, 8, 13, 14, 27]. For example, in Figure 2, the textual metadata is useful but also contain lots of noises. In fact, the video is of multiple modalities and our intuition is that the inference obtained from multiple modalities is more reliable than that from a single text modality. For example, we can more confident to say this video is about "walk a dog" if we spot the text in the title, hear the words "good boy" in the speech, and see a dog in some key frames. To this end, we can leverage the prior knowledge in automatically extracted multi-modal features from the video content such as pre-trained still image detectors, automatic speech recognition and optical character recognition. In some cases when videos have little textual metadata, multi-modal knowledge become the only useful clues in concept learning.

Recent studies on weakly labeled concept learning show promising results. However, since existing approaches only focuses on a single modality, two important questions have yet: 1) what are the important multi-modal prior knowledge, except textual metadata, for modeling noisy labels? 2) how to integrate the multiple modalities into concept learning in a theoretically sound manner?

In this paper, to utilize multi-modal prior knowledge for concept learning, we propose a learning framework called **Multi-modal WEbly-Labeled Learning (WELL-MM)**. The learning framework is motivated by human learning, in which the learner starts from learning easier aspects of a concept, and then gradually take more complex examples into the learning process[3, 20, 25]. Specifically. WELL-MM learns a concept detector iteratively from first using a few samples with more confident labels, then gradually incorporate more samples with noisier labels. Figure 1 shows the overview of the proposed framework. The algorithm integrates multi-modal prior knowledge, which is derived from the multi-modal video and image features, into the dynamic learning procedure. The idea of curriculum and self-paced learning paradigm has been proved to be efficient to deal with noise and outliers [8, 18, 25]. Our proposed method is the first to generalize the learning paradigm to leverage multi-modal prior knowledge into concept learning. Experimental results show that multi-modal prior knowledge is important in concept learning over noisy data. The proposed WELL-MM outperforms other weakly labeled learning methods on three real-world large-scale datasets, and obtains the state-of-the-art results with recent deep learning models.

The contribution of this paper is threefold. First, we propose a novel solution to address the problem of weakly labeled data learning through a general framework that considers multi-modal prior knowledge. We show that the proposed WELL-MM not only outperforms state-of-the-art learning methods on noisy labels, but also, notably, achieves comparable results with models trained using

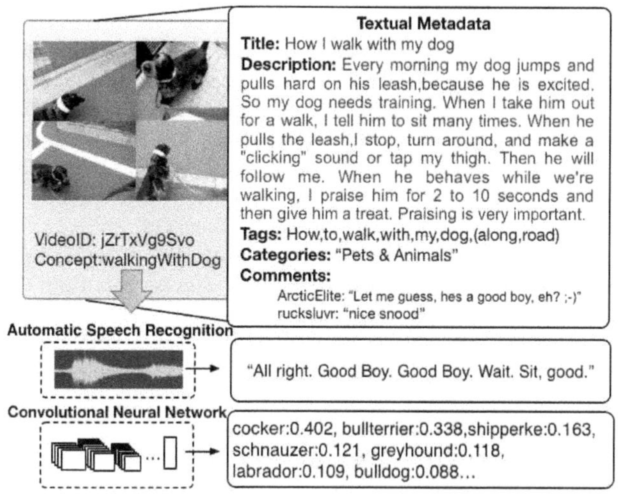

Figure 2: Multi-modal prior knowledge from web video.

manual annotation on one of the video dataset. Second, we provide valuable insights by empirically investigating different multi-modal prior knowledge for modeling noisy labels. Experiments validate that by incorporating multi-modal information, our method is robust against certain levels of noisiness. Finally, the efficacy and the scalability have been demonstrated on three public large-scale benchmarks, which include datasets on both Internet videos and images. The promising results suggest that detectors trained on sufficient weakly labeled videos may outperform detectors trained on existing manually labeled datasets.

2 RELATED WORK

Curriculum and Self-paced Learning: Recently a learning paradigm called *curriculum learning* (CL) was proposed by Bengio et al., in which a model is learned by gradually incorporating from easy to complex samples in training so as to increase the entropy of training samples [3]. A curriculum determines a sequence of training samples and is often derived by predetermined heuristics in particular problems. For example, Chen et al. designed a curriculum where images with clean backgrounds are learned before the images with noisy backgrounds [8], i.e. their method first builds a feature representation by a Convolutional Neural Network (CNN) on images with clean background and then they fine tune the models on images with noisy background. In [41], the authors approached grammar induction, where the curriculum is derived in terms of the length of a sentence. Because the number of possible solutions grows exponentially with the length of the sentence, and short sentences are easier and thus should be learned earlier.

The heuristic knowledge in a problem often proves to be useful. However, the curriculum design may lead to inconsistency between the fixed curriculum and the dynamically learned models. That is, the curriculum is predetermined a prior and cannot be adjusted accordingly, taking into account the feedback about the learner. To alleviate the issue of CL, Kumar et al. designed a learning paradigm, called *self-paced learning* (SPL) [25]. SPL embeds curriculum design as a regularizer into the learning objective. Compared with CL,

SPL exhibits two advantages: first, it jointly optimizes the learning objective with the curriculum, and thus the curriculum and the learned model are consistent under the same optimization problem; second, the learning is controlled by a regularizer which is independent of the loss function in specific problems. This theory has been successfully applied to various applications, such as matrix factorization [48], action/event detection [19], domain adaption [44], tracking [43] and segmentation [26], reranking [18], etc.

Learning Detectors in Web Data: Many recent studies have been proposed to utilize a large amount of noisy data from the Internet. For example, [35] proposed a Never-Ending Language Learning (NELL) paradigm and built adaptive learners that make use of the web data by learning different types of knowledge and beliefs continuously. In the image domain, existing methods try to tackle the problem of constructing qualified training sets based on the search results of text or image search engines [9, 11, 30, 47]. For example, NEIL [9] followed the idea of NELL and learned from web images to form a large collection of concept detectors iteratively via a semi-supervised fashion. By combining the classifiers and the inter-concept relationships it learned, NEIL can be used for scene classification and object detection task. [11] introduced a webly-supervised visual concept learning method that automatically learns a large amount of models for a wide range of variations within visual concepts. They discovered concept variances through the vocabulary of online books, and then downloaded images based on text-search from the web to train object detection and localization models. [30] presented a weakly-supervised method called Baby Learning for object detection from a few training images and videos. They first embed the prior knowledge into a pre-trained CNN. When given very few samples for a new concept, a simple detector is constructed to discover much more training instances from the online weakly labeled videos. As more training samples are selected, the concept detector keeps refining until a mature detector is formed. [47] proposed a noise estimation method for training convolutional neural network with large-scale e-commerce images. Another recent work in image domain [8] proposed a webly supervised learning of Convolutional Neural Network. They utilized easy images from search engine like Google to bootstrap a first-stage network and then used noisier images from photo-sharing websites like Flickr to train an enhanced model.

In video domain, only a few studies [12, 16, 46] have been proposed for noisy data learning since training robust video concept detectors is more challenging than the problem in the image domain. [12] tackled visual event detection problem by using SVM based domain adaptation method in web video data. [16] described a fast automatic video retrieval method using web images. Given a targeted concept, compact representations of web images obtained from search engines like Google, Flickr are calculated and matched to compact features of videos. Such method can be utilized without any pre-defined concepts. [46] discussed a method that exploits the YouTube API to train large-scale video concept detectors on YouTube. The method utilized a calibration process and hard negative mining to train a second order mixture of experts model in order to discover correlations within the labels.

Most of the existing methods are heuristic approaches as it is unclear what objective is being optimized on the noisy data. Moreover, results obtained from the web search results is just one approach to acquire prior knowledge or curriculum. To the best of our knowledge, there have been no systematical studies on exploiting the multi-modal prior knowledge in video concept learning on noisy data. Since search engine algorithm is changing rapidly, it is unclear that how noisy the web labels are and how the level of noisiness in the data will affect performance. In this paper, we proposed a theoretically justified method with a clear framework for curriculum constructing and model learning. We also empirically demonstrate its superior performance over representative existing methods and systemically verify that WELL-MM is robust against the level of noisiness of the video data.

3 MULTI-MODAL WEBLY-LABELED LEARNING (WELL-MM)

3.1 Problem Description

In this paper, following [46], we consider a concept detector as a classifier and our goal is to train concept detectors from webly-labeled video data without any manually annotated labels. Given a collection of training samples with noisy labels, we do not make any assumption over the underlying noise distribution. Formally, we represent the training set as $\mathcal{D} = \{(\mathbf{x}_i, \mathbf{z}_i, \tilde{\mathbf{y}}_i)\}_{i=1}^{n}$, where $\{\mathbf{x}_1, \cdots, \mathbf{x}_n\}$ are the d-dimensional features of the training set, and $\{\mathbf{z}_1, \cdots, \mathbf{z}_n\}$ represent each sample's corresponding noisy web labels. We assume that the noisy labels are given. The noisy web labels are often automatically inferred using the sample's textual metadata provided by its uploader, or from other modalities such as pre-trained convolutional neural network over still images[7], Automatic Speech Recognition [37], or Optical character recognition [40]. For example, for instance, a video might have a noisy label "cat" as its title and speech both contain the word cat. The $\tilde{\mathbf{y}}_i \subset \mathcal{Y}$ is the inferred concept label set for the ith observed sample based on its noisy web label, and $\mathcal{Y}$ denotes the full set of target concepts. In our experiment, to simplify the problem, we employ one-versus-all strategy for multi-class classification, and discuss our method in the context of binary classification over the noisy web labels.

3.2 Model

3.2.1 Objective Function. In this section, we propose a model called Multi-modal WEbly-Labeled Learning (WELL-MM) to leverage multi-modal prior knowledge for weakly labeled data. Formally, given the training set $\mathcal{D}$ mentioned previously, Let $L(\tilde{y}_i, g(\mathbf{x}_i, \mathbf{w}))$,denote the loss function which calculates the cost between the inferred label $\tilde{y}_i$ and the estimated label given by the decision function $g(\mathbf{x}_i, \mathbf{w})$. Here $\mathbf{w}$ represents the model parameters. Our objective function is to jointly learn the model parameter $\mathbf{w}$ and the latent weight variable $\mathbf{v} = [v_1, \cdots, v_n]^T$ by:

$$\min_{\mathbf{w}, \mathbf{v} \in [0,1]^n} \mathbb{E}(\mathbf{w}, \mathbf{v}; \lambda, \Psi) = \sum_{i=1}^{n} v_i L(\tilde{y}_i, g(\mathbf{x}_i, \mathbf{w})) + f(\mathbf{v}; \lambda), \quad \text{subject to } \mathbf{v} \in \Psi \tag{1}$$

where the latent weight variable $\mathbf{v} = [v_1, \cdots, v_n]^T$ represents the inferred labels' confidence, and thus reflects the learning sequence of samples. In order to learn concept detectors in noisy data, we utilize the self-paced regularizer f [20] to control the learning process, where f is expect to assign greater weights to samples with

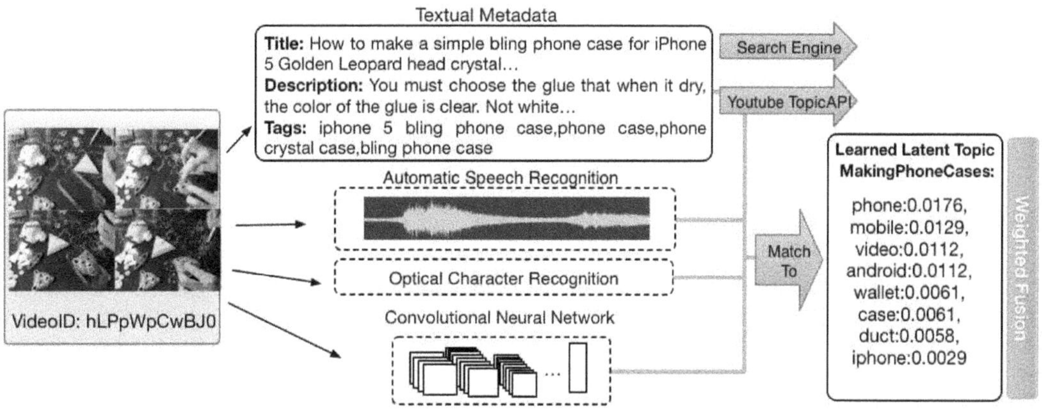

Figure 3: Curriculum Extraction Example. We automatically extract information using meaningful prior knowledge from several modalities and fuse them to get curriculum for WELL-MM. Our method makes use of text, speech, visual cues while common methods like search engine only extract textual information.

confident labels. For simplicity, we consider the linear regularizer Eq. (3) proposed in [20]:

$$f(\mathbf{v};\lambda) = \frac{1}{2}\lambda\sum_{i=1}^{n}(v_i^2 - 2v_i), \tag{2}$$

$\lambda \in (0,1)$ is a hyper-parameter that controls the pace of model training, which resembles the "age" of the model. We set λ to be small at the beginning and only samples of with small loss will be considered in training. As λ grows, more samples with larger loss will be gradually included. As stated in related studies [28, 33], the self-paced in Eq. (3) corresponds to a robust loss function. The robust loss in our problem tends to depress samples with noisy labels or outliers and thus may be instrumental in avoiding bad local minima.

In order to utilize the rich contextual information in the noisy data, we embed the multi-modal prior knowledge derived from the web labels $\mathbf{z}$ into a convex curriculum region Ψ for the latent weight variables. The shape of the region weakly implies the learning sequence, where favored samples have larger expected values. Generally, Ψ can be represented by $\Psi = \{\mathbf{v} \mid c(\mathbf{v}, \mathbf{a}) \le b\}$, where $\mathbf{a} = [a_1, \cdots, a_n]$ is the parameters of the region. In this paper, we use a linear constraint to form the curriculum region [20]:

$$\Psi = \{\mathbf{v} \mid \sum_{i=1}^{n} a_i v_i \le b\} \tag{3}$$

The curriculum region is introduced to leverage the prior knowledge about the noisy labels and, as demonstrated in our experiments, is a crucial factor in weakly labeled data learning. We use multi-modal information to derive the probabilities of samples being positive of a class and if the probabilities are below a threshold (in our experiments it is set at zero) the samples will be consider as negatives. We assign value to a_i in correlated to samples 's probabilities being in the class, and b is set to 1. We use curriculum as a warm start in training, and set μ to zero after the first iteration. Since we empirically observed that curriculum constraints mostly benefit the first few iterations. We will discuss how to derive the multi-modal curriculum in details in the following section.

Eq. (1) is difficult to minimize over big data due to the constraints. In this paper, we propose to relax the constraints by introducing a Lagrange multiplier μ. The objective function then becomes:

$$\min_{\mathbf{w},\mathbf{v}\in[0,1]^n} \mathbb{E}(\mathbf{w},\mathbf{v};\lambda,\mathbf{a},b,\mu) =$$

$$\sum_{i=1}^{n} v_i L(\tilde{y}_i, g(\mathbf{x}_i,\mathbf{w})) + \frac{1}{2}\lambda\sum_{i=1}^{n}(v_i^2 - 2v_i) + \mu(\sum_{i=1}^{n} a_i v_i - b), \tag{4}$$
$$\text{subject to } \mu \ge 0$$

The proposed Eq. (4) has two benefits over Eq. (1). First it enables the large-scale training on noisy data. This is important because as our experiments show that training on noisy data can outperform training on manually labeled data only when the noisy data are orders-of-magnitude larger. Second, it may tolerate the noise introduced in the curriculum region.

3.2.2 Multi-modal Curriculum. In this section we discuss the details on how to construct the curriculum region Ψ. Ψ is a feasible region that embeds the multi-modal prior knowledge extracted from the webly-labeled data as shown in Figure. 3. It geometrically corresponds to a convex feasible space for the latent weight variable. Given a set of training samples $\mathbf{X} = \{\mathbf{x}_i\}_{i=1}^n$ with corresponding noisy labels $\mathbf{Z} = \{\mathbf{z}_i\}_{i=1}^n$, we want to extract the learning curriculum based on how related the training samples are to the target classes, which is modeled by the probability of the samples being the inferred class label (since we don't have the actual label in webly learning). The training samples with a greater value of probability mean that they are more confident to belong to the true class and should be learned earlier. Similar to Information Retrieval theory [31], here we use random variable $\mathbf{z}$ to represent the noisy web labels, $\mathbf{y}$ to represent the label classes, and the curriculum for a sample is then determined by:

$$\mathbf{P}(\mathbf{z} \mid \mathbf{y}) = \mathbf{P}(\mathbf{y} \mid \mathbf{z})\mathbf{P}(\mathbf{z})/\mathbf{P}(\mathbf{y}) \tag{5}$$

Since $\mathbf{P}(\mathbf{y})$ is the same for all samples, it can be regarded as a constant. The prior probability of a web video $\mathbf{P}(\mathbf{z})$ can be implemented with the duration, the view count and comments about the video. In this paper we treat the prior as uniform so it can be ignored as well. Therefore, we calculate the curriculum simply based on $\mathbf{P}(\mathbf{y} \mid \mathbf{z})$, the probability of the sample being class $\tilde{y}_i$ given the noisy label. Since we want to incorporate the multi-modal prior information, we calculate the curriculum from:

$$\mathbf{P}(\mathbf{y} \mid \mathbf{z}) \propto \sum_{m} \theta_m \mathbf{P}(\mathbf{y} \mid \mathbf{z_m}) \tag{6}$$

We use random variable z_m to represent the m-th modality of the noisy labels for a sample and θ_m is the predetermined weight for modality m. In this paper, other than the textual metadata, we also utilize other modalities such as Automatic Speech Recognition (ASR) [37], Optical Character Recognition (OCR) [40] and basic image detector pre-trained on still images [38] (in this paper we use VGG net [39], extract keyframe-level image classification results and average them to get video-level results). Therefore the total number of the modalities is 4. We compare common ways to extract curriculum from web data for concept learning to the proposed novel method that utilizes state-of-the-art topic modeling techniques in natural language processing.

In the following methods (Word Hard Matching and Latent Topic with Word Embedding), we first extract bag-of-words features from different modalities for each video and then match them using specific matching methods to the concept words to get the probabilities in Eq. (6) as shown in Figure 3.

Word Hard Matching We build curriculum directly using exact word matching or stemmed word matching between the textual metadata of the noisy videos to the targeted concept names. This is the same method as stated in Webly Labeled Learning [28]. Noted that this method only utilizes one modality.

YouTubeTopicAPI The YouTube topic API is utilized to search for videos that are related to the concept words. The topic API uses textual information of the uploaded videos to obtain related topics of the videos from Freebase. This is the method used in [46].

SearchEngine The curriculum is built using the search result from a text-based search engine [32]. It is similar to related web-search based methods.

Ours We build the curriculum based on the latent topic we learned from the noisy label. We incorporate Latent Dirichlet Allocation (LDA) [5] to determine how each noisy labeled video is related to each target concept. The intuition is that each web video consists of mixtures of topics (concepts), and each topic is characterized by a distribution of words. We impose asymmetric priors over the word distribution so that each learned topic will be seeded with particular words in our target concept. For example, a topic will be seeded with words "make, phone, cases" for the target concept "MakingPhoneCases". we use the online variational inference algorithm from [17]. An example of the learned latent topic word distribution is shown on the right in Figure 3. We then match noisy labels from each modality $\mathbf{z_{im}}$ to the latent topic word distribution using word embedding soft matching [34]. The word embedding is pre-trained using Google News data.

Figure 3 shows an example of the noisy web video data and how the curriculum is extracted with different methods. Our method can utilize information from different modalities while common methods like search engine only consider textual information. We compare the performance of different ways of curriculum design by training detectors directly in Section 4.

3.3 Algorithm

As proven in recent studies [25, 33], Eq. (1) is a biconvex optimization problem. We utilize the alternative convex search algorithm (ACS) [2] to optimize Eq. (1) following [20, 25]. Algorithm 1 takes the input of the training set, an instantiated self-paced regularizer and the curriculum constraint function; it outputs an optimal model parameter $\mathbf{w}$. it derives the curriculum region from multi-modal noisy labels $\mathbf{Z} \in \mathbb{R}^{m \times n}$ and forms the curriculum constraint function. Then, it initializes the latent weight variables in the feasible region. In the while loop, the algorithm alternates between two steps until it finally converges: In step 4 given the most recent $\mathbf{v}^*$, the algorithm learns the optimal model parameters; In step 5, we fix the $\mathbf{w}^*$ and the algorithm learns the optimal weights $\mathbf{v}^*$ for each sample. Starting in the beginning, the model grows from learning with easy (less noisy) samples with a small model "age". The model "age" is gradually increased so that the model can incorporate more noisy samples in the training and become more robust over time. Step 4 can be implemented by existing off-the-shelf supervised learning methods such as the Support Vector Machine or back propagation. Gradient-based methods can be used to solve the convex optimization problem in Step 5. According to [15], the alternative search in Algorithm 1 converges as the objective function is monotonically decreasing and is bounded from below.

Algorithm 1: Multi-modal WEbly-Labeled Learning

input : Input dataset $\mathcal{D} = \{\mathbf{X}, \mathbf{Z}, \tilde{\mathbf{Y}}\}$, self-paced function f and a curriculum constraint function c
output: Model parameter $\mathbf{w}$

1 Derive curriculum region from $\mathbf{Z} \in \mathbb{R}^{m \times n}$ into $\mathbf{a}, b$;
2 Initialize $\mathbf{v}^*$, λ in the curriculum region;
3 **while** *not converged* **do**
4   Update $\mathbf{w}^* = \arg\min_{\mathbf{w}} \mathbb{E}(\mathbf{w}, \mathbf{v}^*; \lambda, \mathbf{a}, b)$;
5   Update $\mathbf{v}^* = \arg\min_{\mathbf{v}} \mathbb{E}(\mathbf{w}^*, \mathbf{v}; \lambda, \mathbf{a}, b)$;
6   **if** *λ is small* **then** increase λ by the step size;
7 **end**
8 **return** $\mathbf{w}^*$

4 EXPERIMENTS

In this section, we evaluate our method WELL-MM for learning video detectors on noisy labeled data. We first conduct our method on noisy learning in image domain. The efficacy of our methods are mainly verified on two major public benchmarks: FCVID and YFCC100M, where FCVID is by far one of the biggest manually annotated video dataset [22], and the YFCC100M dataset is the largest multimedia benchmark [45].

4.1 Experimental Setup

Datasets, Features and Evaluation Metrics Previous studies on noisy learning in image domain have been focusing on noise estimation [42, 47]. We compare our method with them on the synthesized noisy dataset CIFAR-10 generated using code from [47]. We report accuracy on each setting along with the results reported in papers [42, 47] experimented on the same dataset.

Fudan-columbia Video Dataset (FCVID) contains 91,223 YouTube videos (4,232 hours) from 239 categories. It covers a wide range of concepts like activities, objects, scenes, sports, DIY, etc. Detailed descriptions of the benchmark can be found in [22]. Each video is manually labeled to one or more categories. In our experiments, we do not use the manual labels in training, but instead we automatically generate the web labels according to the concept name appearance in the video metadata. The manual labels are used only in testing to evaluate our and the baseline methods. Following [22], the standard train/test split is used. The second set is YFCC100M [45] which contains about 800,000 videos on Yahoo! Flickr with metadata such as the title, tags, the uploader, etc. There are no manual labels on this set and we automatically generate the curriculum from the metadata in a similar way. Since there are no annotations, we train the concept detectors on the most 101 frequent latent topics found in the metadata. There are totally 47,397 webly labeled videos on the 101 concepts for training.

On FCVID, as the manual labels are available, the performance is evaluated in terms of the precision of the top 5 and 10 ranked videos (P@5 and P@10) and mean Average Precision (mAP) of 239 concepts. On YFCC100M, since there are no manual labels, for evaluation, we apply the detectors to a third public video collection called TRECVID MED which includes 32,000 Internet videos [36]. We apply the detectors trained on YFCC100M to the TRECVID videos and manually annotate the top 10 detected videos returned by each method for 101 concepts.

Implementation Details We build our method on top of a pre-trained convolutional neural network as the low-level features (VGG network [39], except in the image experiment we use AlexNet [24] as in [47]). We extract the key-frame level features and create a video feature by the average pooling. The same features are used across different methods on each dataset. The concept detectors are trained based on a hinge loss cost function by SVM. Algorithm 1 is used to train the concept models iteratively and the λ stops increasing after 100 iterations. At each iteration, we apply a dropout of 0.5 when sampling negative samples. We automatically generate curriculum labels based on the video metadata, ASR, OCR and VGG net 1,000 classification results using latent topic modeling with word embedding matching as shown in Section 3.

Baselines in video domain experiment The proposed method is compared against the following five baseline methods which cover both the classical and the recent representative learning algorithms on webly-labeled data. *BatchTrain* trains a single SVM model using all samples in the multi-modal curriculum built with our method as described in section 3.2.2. *Self-Paced Learning (SPL)* is a classical method where the curriculum is generated by the learner itself [25]. *BabyLearning* is a recent method that simulates baby learning by starting with few training samples and fine-tuning using more weakly labeled videos crawled from the search engine [30]. *GoogleHNM* is a hard negative mining method proposed by Google [46]. It utilizes hard negative mining to train a second order mixture of experts model according to the video's YouTube topics. *FastImage* [16] is a video retrieval method that utilizes web images from search engine to match to the video with re-ranking. *WELL-MM* is the proposed method. The hyper-parameters of all methods including the baseline methods are tuned on the same validation set. On FCVID, the set is a standard development set with manual labels randomly selected from 10% of the training set (No training was done using ground truth labels) whereas on YFCC100M it is also a 10% proportion of noisy training set.

Table 1: Comparison of different curriculum using the BatchTrain learning method.

Method	P@5	P@10	mAP
WordHardMatching	0.782	0.763	0.469
YouTubeTopicAPI	0.587	0.563	0.315
SearchEngine	0.723	0.713	0.413
WordEmbedding	0.790	0.774	0.462
LatentTopic	0.731	0.716	0.409
WELL-MM	**0.838**	**0.820**	**0.486**

4.2 Experiments on FCVID

Curriculum Comparison As discussed in Section 3.2.2, we compare different ways to build curriculum for noisy label learning. Here we also compare their effectiveness by training concept detectors directly using the curriculum labels. The batch train model is used for all generated curriculum labels. In Table 1 we show the batch trained models' precision at 5, 10 and mean average precision on the test set of FCVID. For WELL-MM, we extract curriculum from different modalities as shown in Section 3.2.2, and combine them using linear weights. The weights are hyper-parameters that are tuned on the validation set, and the optimal weights for textual metadata, ASR, image classification and OCR results are 1.0, 0.5, 0.5 and 0.05, respectively. This attempt to combining curriculum from different modalities serves as a pilot study. However, experiments show that such simple linear weighting is already effective with WELL-MM. Further research in this direction is left for future work. We also compare WELL-MM with using only latent topic modeling and word embedding soft matching. Results show that the curriculum generated by combining latent topic modeling and word embedding using multi-modal prior knowledge is the most accurate, which indicates our claim of exploiting multi-modal information is beneficial.

Baseline Comparison Table 2 compares the precision and mAP of different methods where the best results are highlighted. As we see, the proposed WELL-MM significantly outperforms all baseline methods, with statistically significant difference at p-level of 0.05. Comparing SPL with BatchTrain, it shows that the self-paced learning model over-fits to the noise without prior knowledge and performs worse than the simple BatchTrain model. Comparing WELL-MM with SPL and BatchTrain, the effect of incorporating multi-modal curriculum makes a significant difference in terms of performance, which suggests the importance of prior knowledge and preventing over-fitting in webly learning. The promising experimental results substantiate the efficacy of the proposed method.

Robustness to Noise Comparison In this comparison we manually control the noise level of the curriculum in order to systematically verify how our methods would perform with respect to the noise level within the web data. To this end, we randomly select video samples with ground truth labels for each concept, so that

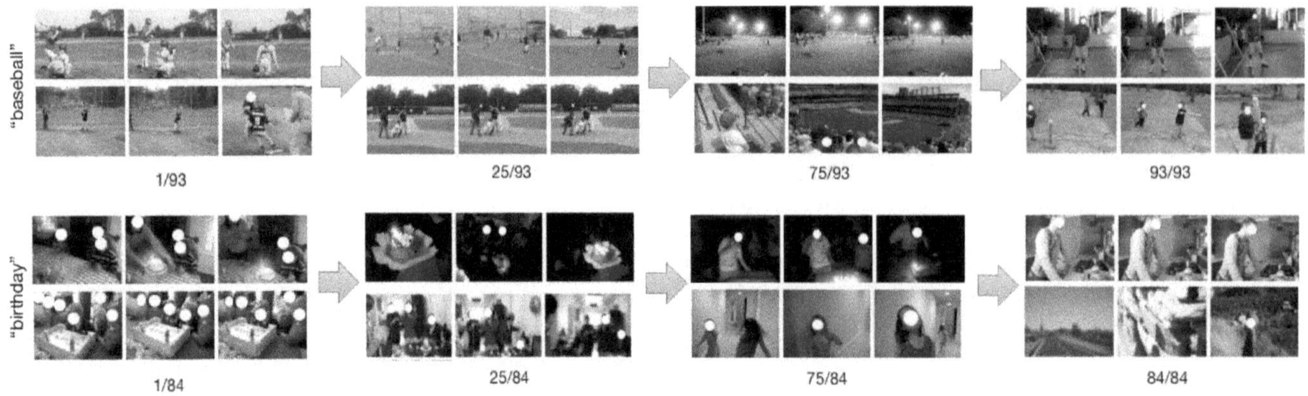

Figure 4: Illustration of representative videos selected by WELL-MM at different iterations

Table 2: Baseline comparison on FCVID

Method	P@5	P@10	mAP
BatchTrain	0.838	0.820	0.486
FastImage [16]	-	-	0.284
SPL [26]	0.793	0.754	0.414
GoogleHNM [46]	0.781	0.757	0.472
BabyLearning [30]	0.834	0.817	0.496
WELL-MM	**0.918**	**0.906**	**0.615**

the noise level of the curriculum labels are set at 20%, 40%, 60%, 80% and we fix the recall of all the labels. We then train WELL-MM using such curriculum and test them on the FCVID testing set. We also compare WELL-MM to three other methods with the same curriculum, among them *GoogleHNM* is a recent method to train video concept detector with large-scale data. We exclude *BabyLearning*, which relies on the returned results by the search engine, since in this experiment the curriculum is fixed. As shown in Table 3, as the noise level of the curriculum grows, WELL-MM maintains its performance while other methods drop significantly. Specifically, when the noise level of curriculum increased from 60% to 80%, other methods' mAP drops 46.5% on average while WELL-MM's mAP only drops 19.1% relatively. It shows that WELL-MM is robust against different level of noise, which shows great potential in larger scale webly-labeled learning as the dataset gets bigger, the noisier it may become.

Table 3: WELL-MM performance with curriculum consisting of multiple artificial noise levels.

Method \ Noise Level	20%	40%	60%	80%
BatchTrain	0.592	0.538	0.463	0.232
SPL	0.586	0.515	0.396	0.184
GoogleHNM	0.602	0.552	0.477	0.304
WELL-MM	**0.673**	**0.646**	**0.613**	**0.496**

Noisy Dataset Size Comparison To investigate the potential of concept learning on webly-labeled video data, we apply the methods on different sizes of subsets of the data. Specifically, we randomly split the FCVID training set into several subsets of 200, 500, 1,000, and 2,000 hours of videos, and train the models on each subset without using manual annotations. The models are then tested on the same test set. Table 4 lists the average results of each type of subsets. As we see, the accuracy of WELL-MM on webly-labeled data increases along with the growth of the size of noisy data while other webly learning methods' performance tend to be saturated.

Comparing to the methods trained using ground truth, In Table 4, WELL-MM trained using the whole dataset (2000 hours) outperforms Static CNN (trained using manual labels) using around 1400 hours of data and rDNN-F (trained using manual labels with three features) trained using around 450h of data. And since the incremental performance increase of WELL-MM is close to linear, we conclude that with sufficient webly-labeled videos (which are not hard to obtain) WELL-MM will be able to outperform the rDNN-F trained using 2000h of data, which is currently the largest manual labeled dataset.

Table 4: MAP comparison of models trained using web labels and ground-truth labels on different subsets of FCVID. The methods marked by * are trained using human annotated labels.

Method \ Dataset Size	200h	500h	1000h	2000h
BatchTrain	0.364	0.422	0.452	0.486
SPL [26]	0.327	0.379	0.403	0.414
GoogleHNM [46]	0.361	0.421	0.451	0.472
BabyLearning [30]	0.390	0.447	0.481	0.496
WELL-MM	0.487	0.554	0.595	0.615
Static CNN[22]*	0.485	0.561	0.604	0.638
rDNN-F[22]*	0.550	0.620	0.650	0.754

4.3 Experiments on CIFAR-10

Following [47], we generate synthesized noisy training data with a noise level of 30%, 40% and 50% on CIFAR-10 dataset. The models

Table 5: Experimental results on CIFAR-10

Methods \ Noise Level	30%	40%	50%
Noisy-CNN [42]	0.697	0.667	0.634
Massive-Learning [47]	0.698	0.668	0.630
WELL-MM	**0.709**	**0.700**	**0.682**

are trained on noisy data and tested on clean data. Classification Accuracy is reported. Our method doesn't assume any kind of noise distribution, while Noisy-CNN [42] assumes the noise distribution depends on classes and Massive-Learning [47] assumes it also depends on the image content. We show the experimental results in Table 5. The results show that WELL-MM outperforms the other methods at all noise levels. More interestingly, as the noise level rises from 30% to 50%, the performance of Massive-Learning [47] drops about 9.8%, while WELL-MM only drops 3.8%. It shows that WELL-MM can also effectively learn robust concept detectors in image domain.

4.4 Experiments on YFCC100M

In the experiments on YFCC100M, we train 101 concept detectors on YFCC100M and test them on the TRECVID MED dataset which includes 32,000 Internet videos. Since there are no manual labels, to evaluate the performance, we manually annotate the top 10 videos in the test set and report their precisions in Table 6. The MED evaluation is done by four annotators and the final results are averaged from all annotations. The Fleiss' Kappa value for these four annotators is 0.64. A similar pattern can be observed where the comparisons substantiate the rationality of the proposed webly learning framework. Besides, the promising results on the largest multimedia set YFCC100M verify the scalability of the proposed method.

Table 6: Baseline comparison on YFCC100M

Method	P@3	P@5	P@10
BatchTrain	0.535	0.513	0.487
SPL [26]	0.485	0.463	0.454
GoogleHNM [46]	0.541	0.525	0.500
BabyLearning [30]	0.548	0.519	0.466
WELL-MM	**0.667**	**0.663**	**0.649**

4.5 Qualitative Analysis

In this section we show training examples of WELL-MM. In Figure 4, we demonstrate the positive samples that WELL select at different stage of training the concept "baseball" and "birthday". For the concept "baseball", at the early stage (1/93, 25/93), WELL-MM selects easier and clearer samples such as the ones with camera directly pointing at the playground, while at the later stage (75/93, 93/93) WELL-MM starts to train with harder samples with different lighting conditions and untypical samples for the concept. For the concept "birthday", as we see, at later stage of the training, complex samples for birthday event like a video with two girl singing birthday song (75/84) and a video of celebrating birthday during hiking (84/84) are included in the training, while at the early stage, only typical "birthday" videos with birthday cake and candles are included.

5 CONCLUSIONS

In this paper, we proposed a novel method called WELL-MM for webly labeled video data learning. WELL-MM extracts multi-modal informative knowledge from noisy weakly labeled video data from the web through a general framework and achieves the best performance only using webly-labeled data on two major video datasets. The comprehensive experimental results demonstrate that WELL-MM outperforms state-of-the-art studies by a statically significant margin on learning concepts from noisy web video data. In addition, the results also verify that WELL-MM is robust to the level of noisiness in the video data. The result suggests that with more webly-labeled data, which is not hard to obtain, WELL-MM can potentially outperform models trained on any existing manually-labeled data.

ACKNOWLEDGEMENTS

This work was based in part on work supported by the National Science Foundation (NSF) under grant number IIS-1251187. Any opinions, findings, and conclusions or recommendations expressed in this material are those of the author(s) and do not necessarily reflect the views of the National Science Foundation.

REFERENCES

[1] Sami Abu-El-Haija, Nisarg Kothari, Joonseok Lee, Paul Natsev, George Toderici, Balakrishnan Varadarajan, and Sudheendra Vijayanarasimhan. 2016. Youtube-8m: A large-scale video classification benchmark. *arXiv preprint arXiv:1609.08675* (2016).
[2] Mokhtar S Bazaraa, Hanif D Sherali, and Chitharanjan M Shetty. 2013. *Nonlinear programming: theory and algorithms.* John Wiley & Sons.
[3] Yoshua Bengio, Jérôme Louradour, Ronan Collobert, and Jason Weston. 2009. Curriculum learning. In *ICML*.
[4] Alessandro Bergamo and Lorenzo Torresani. 2010. Exploiting weakly-labeled web images to improve object classification: a domain adaptation approach. In *NIPS*.
[5] David M Blei, Andrew Y Ng, and Michael I Jordan. 2003. Latent dirichlet allocation. *the Journal of machine Learning research* 3 (2003), 993–1022.
[6] Shih-Fu Chang, Dan Ellis, Wei Jiang, Keansub Lee, Akira Yanagawa, Alexander C Loui, and Jiebo Luo. 2007. Large-scale multimodal semantic concept detection for consumer video. In *Proceedings of the international workshop on Workshop on multimedia information retrieval*.
[7] Ken Chatfield, Karen Simonyan, Andrea Vedaldi, and Andrew Zisserman. 2014. Return of the devil in the details: Delving deep into convolutional nets. In *BMVC*.
[8] Xinlei Chen and Abhinav Gupta. 2015. Webly supervised learning of convolutional networks. In *ICCV*.
[9] Xinlei Chen, Abhinav Shrivastava, and Abhinav Gupta. 2013. Neil: Extracting visual knowledge from web data. In *Proceedings of the IEEE International Conference on Computer Vision*.
[10] Jia Deng, Wei Dong, Richard Socher, Li-Jia Li, Kai Li, and Li Fei-Fei. 2009. Imagenet: A large-scale hierarchical image database. In *CVPR*.
[11] Santosh K Divvala, Alireza Farhadi, and Carlos Guestrin. 2014. Learning everything about anything: Webly-supervised visual concept learning. In *CVPR*.
[12] Lixin Duan, Dong Xu, IW-H Tsang, and Jiebo Luo. 2012. Visual event recognition in videos by learning from web data. *Pattern Analysis and Machine Intelligence, IEEE Transactions on* 34, 9 (2012), 1667–1680.
[13] Robert Fergus, Li Fei-Fei, Pietro Perona, and Andrew Zisserman. 2005. Learning object categories from Google's image search. In *ICCV*.
[14] Pierre Garrigues, Sachin Farfade, Hamid Izadinia, Kofi Boakye, and Yannis Kalantidis. 2016. Tag Prediction at Flickr: a View from the Darkroom. *arXiv preprint arXiv:1612.01922* (2016).
[15] Jochen Gorski, Frank Pfeuffer, and Kathrin Klamroth. 2007. Biconvex sets and optimization with biconvex functions: a survey and extensions. *Mathematical Methods of Operations Research* 66, 3 (2007), 373–407.

[16] Xintong Han, Bharat Singh, Vlad I Morariu, and Larry S Davis. 2015. Fast Automatic Video Retrieval using Web Images. *arXiv preprint arXiv:1512.03384* (2015).

[17] Matthew Hoffman, Francis R Bach, and David M Blei. 2010. Online learning for latent dirichlet allocation. In *advances in neural information processing systems*. 856–864.

[18] Lu Jiang, Deyu Meng, Teruko Mitamura, and Alexander G Hauptmann. 2014. Easy Samples First: Self-paced Reranking for Zero-Example Multimedia Search. In *MM*.

[19] Lu Jiang, Deyu Meng, Shoou-I Yu, Zhenzhong Lan, Shiguang Shan, and Alexander Hauptmann. 2014. Self-Paced Learning with Diversity. In *NIPS*.

[20] Lu Jiang, Deyu Meng, Qian Zhao, Shiguang Shan, and Alexander G Hauptmann. 2015. Self-paced curriculum learning. In *AAAI*.

[21] Lu Jiang, Shoou-I Yu, Deyu Meng, Yi Yang, Teruko Mitamura, and Alexander G Hauptmann. 2015. Fast and accurate content-based semantic search in 100m internet videos. In *Proceedings of the 23rd ACM international conference on Multimedia*.

[22] Yu-Gang Jiang, Zuxuan Wu, Jun Wang, Xiangyang Xue, and Shih-Fu Chang. 2015. Exploiting Feature and Class Relationships in Video Categorization with Regularized Deep Neural Networks. *arXiv preprint arXiv:1502.07209* (2015).

[23] Andrej Karpathy, George Toderici, Sachin Shetty, Tommy Leung, Rahul Sukthankar, and Li Fei-Fei. 2014. Large-scale video classification with convolutional neural networks. In *CVPR*.

[24] Alex Krizhevsky, Ilya Sutskever, and Geoffrey E Hinton. 2012. Imagenet classification with deep convolutional neural networks. In *Advances in neural information processing systems*. 1097–1105.

[25] M Pawan Kumar, Benjamin Packer, and Daphne Koller. 2010. Self-paced learning for latent variable models. In *NIPS*.

[26] M Pawan Kumar, Haithem Turki, Dan Preston, and Daphne Koller. 2011. Learning specific-class segmentation from diverse data. In *ICCV*.

[27] Li-Jia Li and Li Fei-Fei. 2010. Optimol: automatic online picture collection via incremental model learning. *International journal of computer vision* 88, 2 (2010), 147–168.

[28] Junwei Liang, Lu Jiang, Deyu Meng, and Alexander Hauptmann. 2016. Learning to Detect Concepts from Webly-Labeled Video Data. In *IJCAI*.

[29] Junwei Liang, Qin Jin, Xixi He, Gang Yang, Jieping Xu, and Xirong Li. 2014. Semantic Concept Annotation of Consumer Videos at Frame-Level Using Audio. In *Pacific Rim Conference on Multimedia*. Springer, 113–122.

[30] Xiaodan Liang, Si Liu, Yunchao Wei, Luoqi Liu, Liang Lin, and Shuicheng Yan. 2015. Towards computational baby learning: A weakly-supervised approach for object detection. In *ICCV*.

[31] Christopher D Manning, Prabhakar Raghavan, and others. *Introduction to information retrieval*. Vol. 1.

[32] Michael McCandless, Erik Hatcher, and Otis Gospodnetic. 2010. *Lucene in Action: Covers Apache Lucene 3.0*. Manning Publications Co.

[33] Deyu Meng and Qian Zhao. 2015. What Objective Does Self-paced Learning Indeed Optimize? *arXiv preprint arXiv:1511.06049* (2015).

[34] Tomas Mikolov, Ilya Sutskever, Kai Chen, Greg S Corrado, and Jeff Dean. 2013. Distributed representations of words and phrases and their compositionality. In *Advances in neural information processing systems*. 3111–3119.

[35] T Mitchell, W Cohen, E Hruschka, P Talukdar, J Betteridge, A Carlson, B Dalvi, M Gardner, B Kisiel, J Krishnamurthy, and others. 2015. Never-Ending Learning. In *AAAI*.

[36] Paul Over, Jon Fiscus, Greg Sanders, David Joy, Martial Michel, George Awad, Alan Smeaton, Wessel Kraaij, and Georges Quénot. 2014. Trecvid 2014–an overview of the goals, tasks, data, evaluation mechanisms and metrics. In *Proceedings of TRECVID*. 52.

[37] Daniel Povey, Arnab Ghoshal, Gilles Boulianne, Lukáš Burget, Ondřej Glembek, Nagendra Goel, Mirko Hannemann, Petr Motlíček, Yanmin Qian, Petr Schwarz, and others. 2011. The Kaldi speech recognition toolkit. (2011).

[38] Olga Russakovsky, Jia Deng, Hao Su, Jonathan Krause, Sanjeev Satheesh, Sean Ma, Zhiheng Huang, Andrej Karpathy, Aditya Khosla, Michael Bernstein, Alexander C. Berg, and Li Fei-Fei. 2015. ImageNet Large Scale Visual Recognition Challenge. *International Journal of Computer Vision (IJCV)* 115, 3 (2015), 211–252.

[39] Karen Simonyan and Andrew Zisserman. 2014. Very deep convolutional networks for large-scale image recognition. *arXiv preprint arXiv:1409.1556* (2014).

[40] Ray Smith. 2007. An overview of the Tesseract OCR engine. In *icdar*. IEEE, 629–633.

[41] Valentin I Spitkovsky, Hiyan Alshawi, and Daniel Jurafsky. 2009. Baby Steps: How fiLess is Morefi in unsupervised dependency parsing. *NIPS GRLL* (2009).

[42] Sainbayar Sukhbaatar, Joan Bruna, Manohar Paluri, Lubomir Bourdev, and Rob Fergus. 2014. Training convolutional networks with noisy labels. *arXiv preprint arXiv:1406.2080* (2014).

[43] James Steven Supancic and Deva Ramanan. 2013. Self-paced learning for long-term tracking. In *CVPR*.

[44] Kevin Tang, Vignesh Ramanathan, Li Fei-Fei, and Daphne Koller. 2012. Shifting weights: Adapting object detectors from image to video. In *NIPS*.

[45] Bart Thomee, David A. Shamma, Gerald Friedland, Benjamin Elizalde, Karl Ni, Douglas Poland, Damian Borth, and Li-Jia Li. 2015. The New Data and New Challenges in Multimedia Research. *arXiv preprint arXiv:1503.01817* (2015).

[46] Balakrishnan Varadarajan, George Toderici, Sudheendra Vijayanarasimhan, and Apostol Natsev. 2015. Efficient Large Scale Video Classification. *arXiv preprint arXiv:1505.06250* (2015).

[47] Tong Xiao, Tian Xia, Yi Yang, Chang Huang, and Xiaogang Wang. 2015. Learning from massive noisy labeled data for image classification. In *Proceedings of the IEEE Conference on Computer Vision and Pattern Recognition*.

[48] Qian Zhao, Deyu Meng, Lu Jiang, Qi Xie, Zongben Xu, and Alexander G Hauptmann. 2015. Self-Paced Learning for Matrix Factorization.. In *AAAI*.

Transductive Visual-Semantic Embedding for Zero-shot Learning

Xing Xu
Center for Future Media & School of Computer Science and Engineering
University of Electronic Science and Technology of China
Chengdu, China
xing.xu@uestc.edu.cn

Fumin Shen
Center for Future Media & School of Computer Science and Engineering
University of Electronic Science and Technology of China
Chengdu, China
fumin.shen@gmail.com

Yang Yang
Center for Future Media & School of Computer Science and Engineering
University of Electronic Science and Technology of China
Chengdu, China
dlyyang@gmail.com

Jie Shao
Center for Future Media & School of Computer Science and Engineering
University of Electronic Science and Technology of China
Chengdu, China
shaojie@uestc.edu.cn

Zi Huang
School of Information Technology & Electrical Engineering
The University of Queensland
Brisbane, Australia
huang@itee.uq.edu.au

ABSTRACT

Zero-shot learning (ZSL) aims to bridge the knowledge transfer via available semantic representations (e.g., attributes) between labeled source instances of seen classes and unlabelled target instances of unseen classes. Most existing ZSL approaches achieve this by learning a projection from the visual feature space to the semantic representation space based on the source instances, and directly applying it to the target instances. However, the intrinsic manifold structures residing in both semantic representations and visual features are not effectively incorporated into the learned projection function. Moreover, these methods may suffer from the inherent projection shift problem, due to the disjointness between seen and unseen classes. To overcome these drawbacks, we propose a novel framework termed transductive visual-semantic embedding (TVSE) for ZSL. In specific, TVSE first learns a latent embedding space to incorporate the manifold structures in both labeled source instances and unlabeled target instances under the transductive setting. In the learned space, each instance is viewed as a mixture of seen class scores. TVSE then effectively constructs the relational mapping between seen and unseen classes using the available semantic representations, and applies it to map the seen class scores of the target instances to their predictions of unseen classes. Extensive experiments on four benchmark datasets demonstrate that the proposed TVSE achieves competitive performance compared with the state-of-the-arts for zero-shot recognition and retrieval tasks.

CCS CONCEPTS

• **Computing methodologies → Transfer learning**; *Supervised learning by classification*;

KEYWORDS

Zero-shot learning; transductive learning; matrix factorization; manifold learning

ACM Reference format:
Xing Xu, Fumin Shen, Yang Yang, Jie Shao, and Zi Huang. 2017. Transductive Visual-Semantic Embedding for Zero-shot Learning. In *Proceedings of ICMR '17, Bucharest, Romania, June 6–9, 2017*, 9 pages.
DOI: http://dx.doi.org/10.1145/3078971.3078977

DOI: http://dx.doi.org/10.1145/3078971.3078977

1 INTRODUCTION

Conventional visual recognition systems usually require a lot of manually labeled training data to achieve good classification accuracy, typically several thousand images for each class to be learned. Due to the ever increasing number of available images and categories to be recognized, it becomes infeasible to label images for each possible class. In the real-world setting, it would be desirable for visual recognition systems to be able to recognize instances of those rare classes, while demanding minimum human efforts and labeled examples. Zero-shot learning (ZSL) [13, 15] has long been believed to hold the key to the above problem of recognition a new object class without ever seeing a visual instance.

In ZSL, two sets of instances with disjoint classes are considered: labeled source instances of seen classes, and unlabeled target instances to be classified in new classes that have never been seen before. ZSL requires to extract the knowledge from the source set and to transfer that knowledge to the target set. This is often achieved by mapping both seen and unseen classes to a semantic embedding space where each class label/name is represented as a high dimensional vector. A commonly adopted semantic representation space is constructed based on the available semantic representations of classes including binary vectors of visual attributes [13, 16] and continuous word vectors [7, 20] encoding linguistic context. For example, the class "polar bear" can be represented as a binary attribute vector indicating that it is "while", "has fur" and "eat fish". Given a semantic embedding space, most existing approaches [1, 14, 27] for ZSL first learns a projection function that maps the low-level visual features to the semantic representations of seen classes from the source set by traditional classification or regression models. The learned projection function is then applied to the target set to map each target instance into the same embedding space. Finally, the classification of these target instances can be obtained by distance/similarity matching to the semantic representations of unseen classes.

However, two inherent problems exist in these projection based ZSL approaches. The first one is that the intrinsic manifold structure residing in the available semantic representations of classes is not well explored when learning the projection function. Indeed, the semantically related classes generally lie in the same manifold and the manifold structure is rational to be associated with the visual features of the corresponding classes. The second problem is the inherent projection shift problem, which has also been addressed in [9, 30]. The source and target sets may have different data distribution due to the disjoint classes that are semantically unrelated. Therefore, using the projection function learned between the visual features and the semantic representations of seen classes in the source set, are prone to unknown bias when predicting unseen classes in the target set.

In this paper, we propose to tackle the aforementioned problems by developing a novel framework termed Transductive Visual-Semantic Embedding (TVSE). The flowchart of the proposed TVSE is illustrated in Figure 1. Different from the works [10, 30] that directly model the manifold structures based on the available semantic representations of classes, TVSE turns to learning a common latent embedding space, where each instance of both source and target sets is viewed as a mixture of seen classes scores. The latent embedding space is learned by performing collective matrix factorization with graph regularization on both source and target instances under the transductive setting, ensuring the coherent manifold structures of visual features and classes are effectively incorporated for knowledge transfer. For example, the instances in the same class form a cluster in the embedding space, and the clusters of the semantically related classes (e.g, "Lazuli_Bunting" and "Painted_Bunting") are nearer in the space. Furthermore, to overcome the issue of inherent projection shift, an effective scheme is developed for TVSE to construct the relational mapping between seen and unseen classes based on the available semantic representations of classes. For example, the relation between a seen class (e.g., "Lazuli_Bunting") and all the unseen classes can be obtained based on the relational mapping. Finally, the seen class proportions of the target instances can be mapped to their predictions of unseen classes.

The main contributions of our work are three-folds: 1) We propose a novel framework termed TVSE for zero-shot learning. TVSE utilizes collective matrix factorization technique with graph regularization to learn a latent embedding space, where the valuable manifold structures of both visual features and classes are effectively modeled. 2) We also develop a scheme in TVSE to effectively construct the relational mapping between the seen and unseen classes. 3) TVSE can overcome the inherent drawbacks in previous projection based ZSL approaches. We conduct extensive experiments on four widely used benchmark datasets on zero-shot recognition task, showing that TVSE achieves competitive performance compared with the state-of-the-arts for zero-shot recognition and retrieval tasks.

The remainder of the paper is organized as follows. In the next section, we briefly review the related methods for ZSL. Then, we introduce our proposed framework, followed by experimental results with comprehensive analysis on four benchmark datasets. Finally, we draw the conclusion.

2 RELATED WORK

Recently, ZSL has received a growing amount of attention [8, 11, 15, 18, 22, 31, 32, 35]. Existing ZSL methods differ in two aspects: 1) the available semantic representations used and 2) how the knowledge is transferred from the seen classes to the unseen classes.

The available semantic representations of classes typically include visual attributes and semantic word vectors. As an appealing source of information, attributes (binary or continuous) describe common properties of object classes and can be acquired from domain experts or crowd-sourcing techniques. However, the attributes need to be manually annotated, which is of high cost and limited to large-scale recognition. As an alternative to visual attributes, the methods based on semantic word vectors have gained popularity. In this case, a word space is extracted from linguistic knowledge bases, e.g., Wikipedia by independent natural language processing model [19]. Then each class's textual name can be represented by a continuous vector using the language model. Importantly, regardless of the available semantic representations used, most existing methods focus on how to best learn the projections. However, they may fail to explore the manifold structures residing in the semantic representations of classes and to associate these valuable structures to the visual features of the

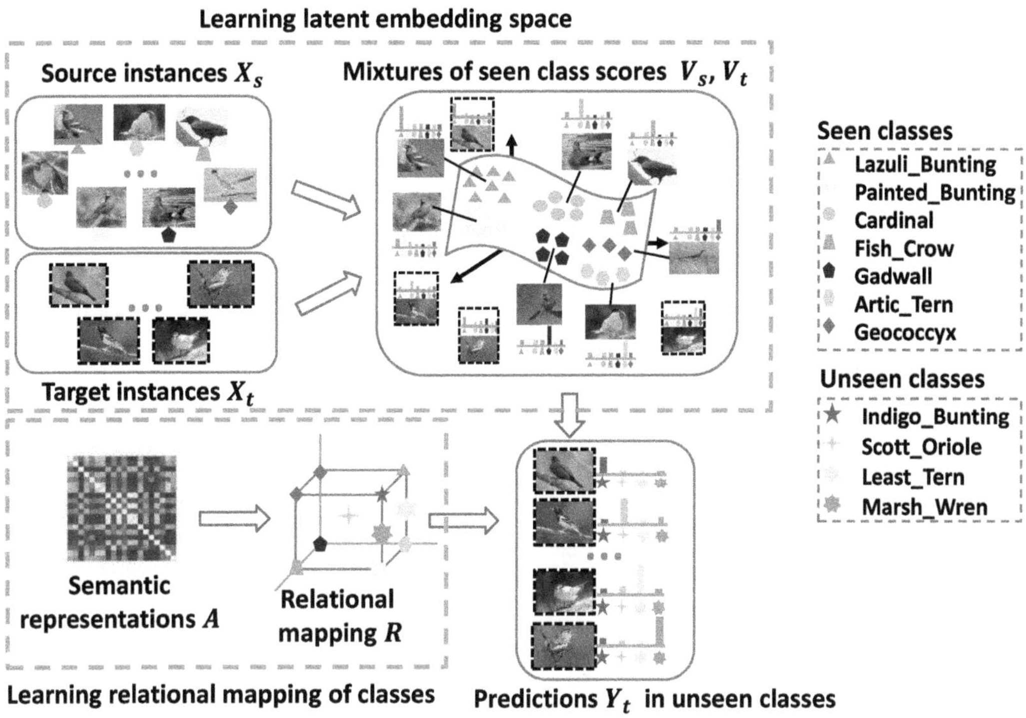

Figure 1: The general flowchart of the proposed TVSE on CUB [29] dataset. TVSE represents each instance in both source and target set are represented by a mixture of seen class scores by learning a latent embedding space under the transductive setting. It then maps the seen class scores of the target instances (in black dot rectangles) to their predictions of unseen classes via the relational mapping built from the available semantic representations.

instances in both source and target sets. In our work, we propose to learn a latent embedding space under the transductive setting to explore the manifold structures of both source and target instances. In addition, different from previous transductive ZSL approaches [9, 24] that employ generative model or graph-based label propagation scheme, the manifold structures in both source and target instances are explored via an advanced technique of collective matrix factorization with graph regularization.

To bridge the knowledge transfer between seen and unseen classes, according to the discussion in [10], existing ZSL methods can be grouped into two categories: classification based and projection based. The projection based methods [1, 7, 31, 34] directly embed the visual feature vectors into a semantic embedding space defined by the available semantic representations via learning a projection function. Such a function is learned from the labeled source instances containing seen classes only. By applying the same visual feature embedding process on the target instances, the predictions of unseen classes can be obtained directly by nearest neighbor matching or its variants [14]. In contrast, the classification based methods [13, 21] rely on learning a n-way discrete classifier for the seen classes using the visual features of the instances in the source set. The classifier is then used to compute the visual similarity between an instance of unseen classes in the target set to those of seen classes in the source set. The semantic relatedness between the seen and unseen classes is modeled by the distance between their available semantic representations. Indeed, our work has the characteristics of both categories. Specifically, compared with the projection based methods, we learn a latent embedding space which directly associates the relations between visual features and seen classes. Similar to the classification based ones, in our work, each instance in both source and target sets can be viewed as a mixture of seen classes scores, and we also model the semantic relatedness between seen and unseen classes by weighted graph, rather than the distance matching.

3 TRANSDUCTIVE VISUAL-SEMANTIC EMBEDDING

3.1 Problem Statement

Suppose we have c_s seen classes with n_s labeled instances in source set $D_s = \{\mathbf{X}_s, \mathbf{Y}_s\}$, and c_t unseen classes with n_t unlabeled instances in target set $D_t = \{\mathbf{X}_t, \mathbf{Y}_t\}$. The indices of the source and target sets are $\mathcal{I} = \{s, t\}$. Let $\mathbf{X}_\pi = [\mathbf{x}^\pi_{*1}, ..., \mathbf{x}^\pi_{*n_\pi}] \in \mathbb{R}^{m \times n_\pi}$ denote the m-dimensional visual feature vectors of source and target instances with $\mathbf{x}^\pi_{*i}$ being the ith instances in $\mathcal{D}_\pi$, $\pi \in \mathcal{I}$. Class labels of the instances in $\mathcal{D}_\pi$ are denoted as $\mathbf{Y}_\pi = [\mathbf{y}^\pi_{1*}, ..., \mathbf{y}^\pi_{n_\pi *}] \in \mathbb{R}^{c_\pi \times n_\pi}$, where $\mathbf{y}^\pi_{i*}$ is the one-hot vector for the ith instance in D_π. Note that the instances in D_s and D_t have disjoint class labels, i.e. $\mathbf{Y}_s \cap \mathbf{Y}_t = \emptyset$. In addition, the available semantic representations (e.g., attributes) of classes in D_π are denoted as $\mathbf{A}_\pi = [\mathbf{a}_1, ..., \mathbf{a}_{n_\pi}] \in \mathbb{R}^{d \times n_\pi}$, where $\mathbf{a}_i$ represents an d-dimensional binary/continuous vector for the ith class. The problem of zero-shot learning (ZSL) is to estimate $\mathbf{Y}_t$ given $\mathbf{X}_t$ and $\mathbf{A}_t$.

To this end, our proposed *Transductive Visual-Semantic Embedding* (TVSE) is to learn a common latent embedding space underlying both source and target sets as the bridge for smooth knowledge transfer. One one hand, the learned latent embedding space is expected to overcome the limitations of the available semantic representations to incorporate the intrinsic manifold structures (visual features and classes) that are coherent in both source and target sets. One the other hand, it is also desired to tackle the problem of the inherent projection shift during knowledge transfer from the source instances to the target instances.

3.2 The Proposed Framework

To achieve the goal of TVSE, we propose an algorithm that utilizes collective matrix factorization technique combining with graph regularization under the transductive setting. We then construct the relational mapping between seen and unseen classes through the weight graph method.

3.2.1 Learning the latent embedding space. We assume that a latent embedding space connects the visual features and the seen classes in the source set $\mathcal{D}_s$. Besides, under the transductive setting, the target set $\mathcal{D}_t$ is also taken into account during learning the latent embedding space. Thus, the connection between the visual features in $\mathcal{D}_t$ and the seen classes in $\mathcal{D}_s$ is also constructed. To ensure smooth knowledge transfer from $\mathcal{D}_s$ to $\mathcal{D}_t$, the latent embedding space is required to be shared between the two sets, and each instance in each set can be represented by a mixture of latent factors in the embedding space. These latent factors can be obtained by applying collective matrix factorization [17] on the visual feature matrices $\mathbf{X}_s$ and $\mathbf{X}_t$ jointly, to minimize the reconstruction loss

$$\mathcal{L} = \|\mathbf{X}_s - \mathbf{U}_s\mathbf{H}\mathbf{V}_s^\top\|^2 + \|\mathbf{X}_t - \mathbf{U}_t\mathbf{H}\mathbf{V}_t^\top\|^2, \\ = \sum_{\pi \in \mathcal{I}} \|\mathbf{X}_\pi - \mathbf{U}_\pi\mathbf{H}\mathbf{V}_\pi^\top\|^2, \quad (1)$$

where $\|\cdot\|^2$ is the Frobenius norm of a matrix. In Eq. 1, $\mathbf{U}_\pi = [\mathbf{u}^\pi_{*1}, ..., \mathbf{u}^\pi_{*k}] \in \mathbb{R}^{m \times k}$ with each $\mathbf{u}_{*i}$ representing a visual feature cluster. $\mathbf{V}_\pi = [\mathbf{v}^\pi_{*1}, ..., \mathbf{v}^\pi_{*c_s}] \in \mathbb{R}^{n_s \times c_s}$ with each $\mathbf{v}_i$ being the mixture of seen class scores. $\mathbf{H} \in \mathbb{R}^{k \times c_s}$ denotes the latent factors residing in the seen classes, and it also builds the associations between the feature clusters $\mathbf{U}_\pi$ of each set $\mathcal{D}_\pi$ and their mixtures of seen class scores $\mathbf{V}_\pi$. Different from the previous work [25] that considers the available semantic representations $\mathbf{A}_s$ of seen classes explicitly as the latent factors, here $\mathbf{H}$ is learned from both the source instances of seen classes and the unlabeled target instances. Therefore, $\mathbf{H}$ is more effective to incorporate informative associations between visual features in each set and the seen classes.

Given the seen class information $\mathbf{Y}_s$ for instances in $\mathcal{D}_s$, we enforce $\mathbf{V}_s \equiv \mathbf{Y}_s$ as in [17] to make the latent embedding space effectively bridge the connection between the visual features and seen classes. Through the connection, the instances in $\mathcal{D}_t$ can also be appropriately represented by mixtures of seen class scores ($\mathbf{V}_t$) in the latent embedding space, with the knowledge from $\mathbf{Y}_s$ in $\mathcal{D}_s$ being smoothly transferred to the $\mathbf{V}_t$ in $\mathcal{D}_s$.

3.2.2 Modeling the manifold structures of instances. For ZSL, it is expected that the geometric structures in the labeled source instances can be preserved for smooth transfer procedure. Specifically, if two instances $\mathbf{x}_i, \mathbf{x}_j$ in each dataset D_π are close the visual feature space, then their class label should also be close. This assumption can be reflected in their mixtures of seen class scores $\mathbf{v}_i$, $\mathbf{v}_j$ in the latent embedding space. Inspired by [4], the geometric structure can be modeled by a nearest neighbor graph in the instance space. Consider an instance graph G^I_π with n_I vertices with each representing an instance in set D_π. Then the pairwise similarity matrix can be defined as

$$(\mathbf{W}^I_\pi)_{ij} = \begin{cases} cos(\mathbf{x}^\pi_{*i}, \mathbf{x}^\pi_{*j}), & if\ \mathbf{x}^\pi_{*i} \in N_p(x^\pi_{*j})\ or\ \mathbf{x}^\pi_{*j} \in N_p(x^\pi_{*i}) \\ 0, & otherwise \end{cases} \quad (2)$$

where $N_p(x)$ denotes the top-p nearest neighbors of the ith instance $\mathbf{x}^\pi_{*i}$. By defining $\mathbf{Q}^I_\pi = diag(\sum_i (\mathbf{W}^I_\pi)_{ij})$, then preserving the visual feature manifold structure in D_π is derived to minimize the instance graph regularizer

$$R^I_\pi = \frac{1}{2}\sum_{ij} \|\mathbf{v}_i - \mathbf{v}_j\|^2 (\mathbf{W}^I_\pi)_{ij} = tr(\mathbf{V}_\pi^\top(\mathbf{Q}^I_\pi - \mathbf{W}^I_\pi)\mathbf{V}_\pi) \quad (3)$$

Furthermore, from the aspect of features, each dimension of the features is sampled from a distribution supported by another low-dimensional manifold. Therefore, we construct a feature graph G^F_π with n_F vertices each representing a feature in set D_π as

$$(\mathbf{W}^F_\pi)_{ij} = \begin{cases} cos(\mathbf{x}^\pi_{i*}, \mathbf{x}^\pi_{j*}), & if\ \mathbf{x}^\pi_{i*} \in N_p(\mathbf{x}^\pi_{j*})\ or\ \mathbf{x}^\pi_{j*} \in N_p(\mathbf{x}^\pi_{i*}) \\ 0, & otherwise, \end{cases} \quad (4)$$

where $N_p(\mathbf{x}^\pi_{i*})$ denotes the top-p nearest neighbors of the ith dimension of feature in $\mathbf{x}^\pi_{i*}$. Let $\mathbf{Q}^F_\pi = diag(\sum_i (\mathbf{W}^F_\pi)_{ij})$, preserving the geometric structure in each dataset D_π further includes minimizing the feature graph regularizer

$$R^F_\pi = \frac{1}{2}\sum_{ij} \|\mathbf{u}_i - \mathbf{u}_j\|^2 (\mathbf{W}^F_\pi)_{ij} = tr(\mathbf{U}_\pi^\top(\mathbf{Q}^F_\pi - \mathbf{W}^F_\pi)\mathbf{U}_\pi) \quad (5)$$

Clearly, the graph regularizer defined in Eq. 3 and Eq. 5 can preserve the coherent manifold structures for each dataset during the latent embedding space learning procedure. Therefore, we can incorporate the two regularization terms into Eq. 1 to reach the final optimization problem as

$$\min_{\mathbf{U}_\pi,\mathbf{H},\mathbf{V}_\pi\geq 0} \mathcal{O} = \mathcal{L} + \sum_{\pi\in\mathcal{I}}(\lambda R_\pi^I + \mu R_\pi^F),$$
$$s.t.\ \mathbf{U}_\pi^\top \mathbf{1}_m = \mathbf{1}_k,\ \mathbf{V}_\pi^\top \mathbf{1}_{n_\pi} = \mathbf{1}_{c_s},\ \forall \pi \in \mathcal{I} \tag{6}$$

where λ, μ are regularization coefficients, and $\mathbf{1}_\Delta$, $\Delta \in \{m, k, c_s\}$ is the vector of ones. The ℓ_1 normalization constraints on each column of $\mathbf{U}_s$ and $\mathbf{V}_s$ are used to make the optimization well-defined. With the optimization results, for instances in the target set $\mathcal{D}_t$, their mixtures of seen classes scores $\mathbf{V}_t$ can be obtained.

Next, we discuss how to map $\mathbf{V}_t$ of the target instances to their predictions of unseen classes, which relies on the mapping between the seen and unseen classes.

3.2.3 Constructing the relational mapping of classes. Inspired by [5, 33, 34], we assume that each seen class can be represented as a combination of all unseen classes based on their semantic representations $\mathbf{A}_\pi = [\mathbf{a}_1, ..., \mathbf{a}_{n_\pi}]$. In order to effectively incorporate the intra-class relationship, we further transform the semantic representation of each class via kernel mapping, e.g., the simple linear kernel, where $\mathbf{\Phi}_\pi = [\boldsymbol{\phi}_1, ..., \boldsymbol{\phi}_{c_\pi}] \in \mathbb{R}^{c_\pi \times c_s}$ with $\boldsymbol{\phi}_i$ denoting the kernelized version of $\mathbf{a}_i$.

Given each $\boldsymbol{\phi}_i$ of a seen class, we propose a parameterized optimization problem inspired by the weight graph method [5], which minimizing the reconstruction error of each $\boldsymbol{\phi}_i$ based on the kernelized semantic representations of all unseen classes as follows:

$$\min \gamma\|\mathbf{R}\|^2 + \sum_{i=1}^{c_s} \|\boldsymbol{\phi}_s^i - \sum_{j=1}^{c_t} \boldsymbol{\phi}_t^j r_{ij}\|^2, \tag{7}$$

where $\gamma \geq 0$ is the regularization parameter, $\|\cdot\|^2$ denotes the ℓ_2 norm of a vector, and $\mathbf{R} = \{r_{ij}\} \in \mathbb{R}^{c_s \times c_t}$ describes the relational mapping matrix that contains the pairwise weight value for pairwise classes. Eq. 7 can be solved using standard quadratic programming as in [5].

3.2.4 Prediction for Target Dataset. For an instance $\mathbf{x}_{*,i}^t$ in the target dataset $\mathcal{D}_t$, given its mixture of seen class scores $\mathbf{v}_{i*}^t$, we can infer the prediction for $\mathbf{x}_{*,i}^t$ by

$$\mathbf{y}_{*,i}^t = argmax_j(\mathbf{v}_{i*}^t \mathbf{R})_j, \tag{8}$$

where $\mathbf{v}_{i*}^t R$ indicates the mixture of unseen class scores for $\mathbf{x}_{*,i}^t$ through the relational mapping $\mathbf{R}$ from the mixture of seen classes $\mathbf{v}_{i*}^t$. The operation $argmax(\cdot)$ selects the unseen class with the highest score as the prediction.

3.3 Optimization

We now discuss the solution to the optimization problem in Eq. 1. As the original formulation in Eq. 1 belongs to the constrained optimization problem, we add Lagrange functions for the parameters $\mathbf{U}_\pi$ and $\mathbf{V}_\pi$ with nonnegative

Algorithm 1 TVSE for Zero Shot Learning.

Input: Matrices $\mathbf{X}_\pi$, $\mathbf{A}_\pi$ and $\mathbf{Y}_s$, parameters k, p, λ, γ;
Output: Predictions $\mathbf{Y}_t$ for instances in target dataset $\mathcal{D}_t$.

1: Normalize $\mathbf{X}_\pi$ with ℓ_2 normalization and build graphs G_π^I and G_π^F.
2: Initialize $\mathbf{U}_\pi$, $\mathbf{H}$ as random positive matrix respectively, $\mathbf{V}_s$ as $\mathbf{Y}_s$, $\mathbf{V}_t$ by ridge regression trained on $\{\mathbf{X}_s, \mathbf{Y}_s\}$.
3: **repeat**
4: Update $\mathbf{U}_\pi$, $\mathbf{V}_\pi$ and $\mathbf{H}$ by Eq. 10 $\sim$ Eq. 12.
5: Set $\mathbf{V}_s = \mathbf{Y}_s$ and normalize each column of $\mathbf{U}_\pi$ and $\mathbf{V}_\pi$ by ℓ_1 normalization.
6: **until** Objective function of Eq. 1 converges.
7: Compute $\mathbf{R}$ in Eq. 7 by quadratic programming.
8: Compute $\mathbf{Y}_t$ given $\{\mathbf{V}_t, \mathbf{R}\}$ by Eq. 8.

and L1 normalization constraints to Eq. 1 as

$$\hat{\mathcal{L}} = \mathcal{O} + \sum_{\pi\in\mathcal{I}} tr(\Omega_\pi(\mathbf{U}_\pi^\top \mathbf{1}_m - \mathbf{1}_k)(\mathbf{U}_\pi^\top \mathbf{1}_m - \mathbf{1}_k)^\top)$$
$$+ \sum_{\pi\in\mathcal{I}} tr(\Theta_\pi(\mathbf{V}_\pi^\top \mathbf{1}_{n_\pi} - \mathbf{1}_{c_s})(\mathbf{V}_\pi^\top \mathbf{1}_{n_\pi} - \mathbf{1}_{c_s})^\top), \tag{9}$$

where $\Omega_\pi \in \mathbb{R}^{k\times k}$, $\Theta_\pi \in \mathbb{R}^{c\times c}$ are the Lagrange multipliers for the two constraints with respect to $\mathbf{U}_\pi$ and $\mathbf{V}_\pi$. We iteratively optimize one variable and derive its updating rule while fixing the remaining ones. The procedure will monotonically decrease the objective function in Eq. 9 until convergence. Similar as the derivations in [17], the updating rules for each variable in $\{\mathbf{U}_\pi, \mathbf{V}_\pi\}$ can be achieved by using the Karush-Kuhn-Tucker (KKT) complementarity condition [3] and setting their derivations to zero, which leads to the following updating formula respectively:

$$\mathbf{U}_\pi \leftarrow \mathbf{U}_\pi \circ \sqrt{\frac{\mathbf{X}_\pi\mathbf{V}_\pi\mathbf{H}^\top + \lambda\mathbf{W}_\pi^I\mathbf{U}_\pi}{\mathbf{U}_\pi\mathbf{H}\mathbf{V}_\pi^\top\mathbf{V}_\pi\mathbf{H}^\top + \lambda\mathbf{Q}_\pi^I\mathbf{U}_\pi}}, \tag{10}$$

$$\mathbf{V}_\pi \leftarrow \mathbf{V}_\pi \circ \sqrt{\frac{\mathbf{X}_\pi^\top\mathbf{U}_\pi\mathbf{H} + \mu\mathbf{W}_\pi^F\mathbf{V}_\pi}{\mathbf{V}_\pi\mathbf{H}^\top\mathbf{U}_\pi^\top\mathbf{U}_\pi\mathbf{H} + \mu\mathbf{Q}_\pi^F\mathbf{V}_\pi}}, \tag{11}$$

where $\circ$ denotes the element-wise operations for the matrix computation. For variable H without constraints, we can also derive the close-form updating rule for it, as:

$$\mathbf{H} \leftarrow \mathbf{H} \circ \sqrt{\frac{\sum_{\pi\in\mathcal{I}}\mathbf{U}_\pi^\top\mathbf{X}_\pi\mathbf{V}_\pi}{\sum_{\pi\in\mathcal{I}}\mathbf{U}_\pi^\top\mathbf{U}_\pi\mathbf{H}\mathbf{V}_\pi^\top\mathbf{V}_\pi}}. \tag{12}$$

The parameter learning and prediction procedures for the proposed TVSE is summarized in Algorithm 1. The time complexity of TVSE consists of solving Eq. 1 and Eq. 7. Typically, optimizing Eq. 1 costs complexity of $\mathcal{O}(\sum_{\pi\in\mathcal{I}}(kmn_\pi^2 T + mn_\pi^2 + m^2 n_\pi)$, where T is the is the number of iterations. For Eq. 1, it requires about $\mathcal{O}(c_s^3)$ time. As $c_s \ll n_\pi$, the time complexity of TVSE is quadratic to the numbers of the source and target instances. We will release our implementation code for public usage.

4 EXPERIMENTS

4.1 Experimental Setup

Datasets. We evaluate our work on four benchmark ZSL datasets: 1) Animals with Attributes (AwA) [13], 2) Caltech UCSD Birds (CUB) [29], 3) aPascal-aYahoo (aPY) [6] and 4) SUN Attribute (SUN) [23], for zero-shot recognition problem. They consist of images belonging to coarse-grained or fine-grained categories in different scopes, such as animals, vehicles and natural scenes. Table 1 summarizes the statistics in each dataset. In our experiments, we utilize the same experimental settings as [34], including the splits of source/target images and seen/unseen classes. Regarding the available semantic representations of classes, we use the provided attributes of each dataset. For AwA and aPY datasets, we directly utilize the provided class-level attribute vector of continuous value. For CUB and SUN datasets which have binary attribute vector image-level, we take the mean of attribute vectors of all images from the same classes to generate class-level attribute vector.

Table 1: General statistics of the four datasets used in the experiments, where "*/*" in columns "Images" and "Classes" stands for the number of source/target images and seen/unseen classes, respectively.

Datasets	Images	Attributes	Classes
AwA	24,295 / 6,180	85	40 / 10
CUB	8,855 / 2,933	312	150 / 50
aPY	12,695 / 2,644	64	20 / 12
SUN	14,140 / 200	102	707 / 10

Features. For all the datasets, we utilize the deep features extracted from popular CNN architecture. It has been shown that the deep features work remarkably better than the low-level features as they lead to good intra-class separation [2]. Specifically, we use the CNN features originally provided in [34], which are extracted from the 4,096 dimensional top-layer hidden unit activations (fc7) in VGG (very-deep-19) [26] network. Similar CNN features have already been used in previous works [2, 34, 35] for zero-shot recognition.

Settings. We use classification accuracy as the evaluation criteria, as it has been widely adopted in the literature. The proposed TVSE involves five parameters: the regularization coefficients λ, μ and γ, the number of feature cluster k, the number of nearest neighbors p. When compared with other approaches, we empirically set $\{\lambda, \mu, \gamma, k, p\}$ to $1, 100, 100, 4, 16$ for TVSE through all the experiments. We report the averaged results over five runs with the optimal parameters chosen on each dataset. In the coming section, we make a detailed analysis on parameter sensitivity which shows that TVSE is able to achieve stable performance with a wide range of parameter values. All the experiments are conducted on a desktop machine which has 4-core 3.3GHz CPUs with 16GB RAM.

4.2 Main Results

4.2.1 Results on Zero-shot Recognition. To make comprehensive comparison for the recognition task on the four datasets, we compare the proposed TVSE against various state-of-the-art alternatives: 1) the inductive methods, i.e., DAP [13], ALE [1], ESZSL [25], SSE-ReLU [34], JSLE [35] and SynC-struct [5]; 2) the transductive methods, i.e., UDA-ZSL [12] and TMV-HLP [9]; 3) the integrated methods, i.e., three extensions based on SP-ZSR [36].

Table 2 shows the overall classification accuracy of the different methods on the four datasets. It can be observed that: 1) The proposed TVSE clearly outperforms the best inductive methods such as JSLE and SynC-struct by a large margin. The main advantage of TVSE compared with the inductive methods is that it can incorporate the data of both seen and unseen classes during the learning procedure, hence overcomes the test-time projection shift between seen and unseen classes. 2) TVSE also significantly outperforms the other transductive methods UDA-ZSL and TMV-HLP, e.g, 10.9% on AwA and 13.4% on CUB. It indicates the superiority of TVSE on exploring the data structures of both seen and unseen classes via modelling their manifold structures. In addition, compared with the projection based method TMV-HLP, TVSE provides a new perspective to learn a more effective latent embedding space under the transductive setting. 3) TVSE achieves competitive recognition performance against the integrated methods based on SP-ZSR. Specifically, compared with TVSE, the performance of these integrated methods depends on the specific inductive method used and the specific dataset. For example, TVSE obtains better accuracy scores than those of ESZSL + SP-ZSR on aPY and AwA, while performs on par with JSLE + SP-ZSR and BL-ZSL + SP-ZSR on these two datasets. In contrast, TVSE performs inferior to ESZSL + SP-ZSR while obtains better results than JSLE + SP-ZSR and BL-ZSL + SP-ZSR on SUN. 4) While these integrated methods boost the already learned recognition models by the inductive methods such as ESZSL, JSLE and BL-ZSL, the proposed TVSE directly learns promising recognition model more effectively. Thus it indicates that TVSE is promising to account for the test-time projection shift problem as the SP-ZSR does.

4.2.2 Results on Zero-shot Retrieval. In the retrieval task, a semantic embedding vector of an unseen class is used as a query to retrieve top matched test images. The performance is measured by mean average precision (mAP). As the retrieval task is not widely evaluated in prior studies, in this work we provide a comprehensive comparison with the state-of-the-art methods including the inductive methods SSE-ReLU, JSLE and SynC-struct; and the integrated methods based on SP-ZSR.

Table 3 summarizes the overall retrieval results in terms of mAP for all datasets. We can see that our TVSE obtains mAP score of 79.8% compared to the result (51.1%) with a large margin from the best inductive method of SynC-struct. It thus again validates the superiority of our TVSE

Table 2: Comparison of classification accuracy (%) for zero-shot recognition task on the four datasets, in the form of mean±standard deviation, and "-" means no result reported. The best results on each dataset are highlighted in bold font.

Method	aPY	AwA	CUB	SUN	Average
DAP [13]	38.2	57.2	-	72.0	
ALE [1]	-	61.9	40.3	-	-
ESZSL [25]	24.22±2.89	75.32±2.28	-	82.10±0.32	-
SSE-ReLU [34]	46.23±0.53	76.33±0.83	30.41±0.20	82.50±1.32	58.91
JSLE [35]	50.35±2.97	79.12±0.53	41.78±0.52	83.83±0.29	63.77
SynC-struct [5]	48.88±0.77	78.57±3.25	50.32±1.14	81.53±0.54	64.82
UDA-ZSL [12]	-	75.6	40.2	-	-
TMV-HLP [9]	-	80.5	47.9	-	-
ESZSL + SP-ZSR [36]	37.5	84.3	-	89.5	-
JSLE + SP-ZSR [36]	62.19±4.65	**92.08±0.14**	**55.34±0.77**	86.12±0.99	73.93
BL-ZSL + SP-ZSR [36]	**69.74±3.47**	92.06±0.18	53.26±1.04	86.01±1.32	**75.27**
TSVE	66.21±1.02	89.28±0.45	53.87±1.96	**88.05±1.46**	74.35

on learning more effective projection under the transductive setting. Furthermore, our TVSE also outperforms the integrated methods ESZSL + SP-ZSR and BL-ZSL + SP-ZSR, and obtains comparative mAP score (79.8%) against that of JSLE + SP-ZSR (80.0%). The competitive performance of TVSE in retrieval is due to the useful manifold structure explored in the test instances, which enhances the learned projection to better match the test instances to the semantic embeddings of unseen classes. Visualized retrieval examples are in the Suppl.

Table 3: Retrieval performance comparison (%) in terms of mAP. The best results on each dataset are highlighted in bold font.

Method	aPY	AwA	CUB	SUN	Ave.
SSE-ReLU [34]	14.1	42.6	3.7	44.6	26.2
JSLE [35]	32.7	66.5	23.9	76.5	49.9
SynC-struct [5]	30.4	65.4	34.3	74.3	51.1
ESZSL + SP-ZSR [36]	37.5	84.3	-	89.5	-
JSLE + SP-ZSR [36]	70.7	**94.0**	**63.2**	92.1	**80.0**
BL-ZSL + SP-ZSR [36]	**74.1**	92.0	58.8	91.2	75.3
TVSE	72.3	92.4	60.9	**93.0**	79.6

4.3 Detailed Analysis on TVSE

4.3.1 Effects of the Latent Embedding Space. To better understand the proposed TVSE on recognizing the target instances of unseen classes, we employ t-SNE [28] to visualize their CNN features (X_t) and mixtures of seen class scores V_t of the visual feature space and the learned latent embedding space, respectively. The four sub-figures in Figure 2 illustrate the visualized distributions of the two spaces on AwA and CUB datasets. On AwA dataset, in Figure 2 (a) the CNN features seem to form separate clusters for the 10 unseen classes with some overlaps, which is useful for recognition. The gaps between each class are much clearer in Figure 2 (b), which indicates TVSE well explores the manifold structures of the target instance under the transductive setting. In contrast, on CUB dataset, in Figure 2 (c) the CNN features are heavily overlapped for the 50 unseen classes due to the much finer granularity in the classes. Nevertheless, TVSE still appears to learn more separable embeddings as seen in Figure 2 (d), where the embeddings appear to be more cluttered with smaller intra-class gaps and overlaps.

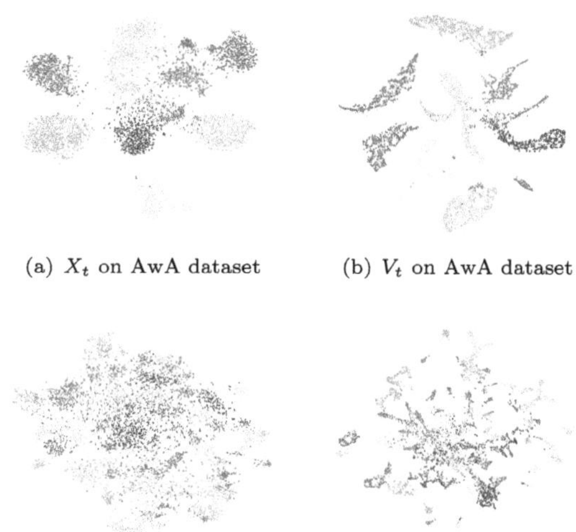

(a) X_t on AwA dataset (b) V_t on AwA dataset

(c) X_t on CUB dataset (d) V_t on CUB dataset

Figure 2: t-SNE visualization comparison of X_t in the visual feature space and V_t in the latent embedding space on the AwA and CUB datasets.

4.3.2 Parameter Sensitivity. To study the parameter sensitivity of TVSE, we tune one parameter at each time while fixing the others to their optimal values. Due to the space limit, we only report the performance variations with four parameters λ, γ, k and p except for μ, since μ plays the same role as λ. Figure 3 (a) shows the accuracy under varying values of λ. We can observe that TVSE achieves steady performance when λ spans over a wide range in $[10, 1000]$. In contrast, TVSE is not very sensitive to γ as shown in Figure 3 (b), which implies that the proposed scheme for relational mapping of classes in TVSE is robust. Moreover, due to the intrinsic manifold structures in the different dataset, the optimal values of k and p vary depending on the specific dataset. In general, TVSE can obtain considerable performance when $k \in [4, 16]$ and $p \in [16, 32]$.

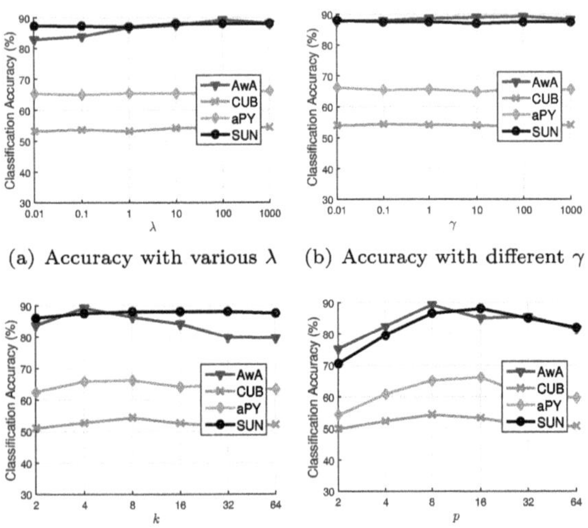

(a) Accuracy with various λ (b) Accuracy with different γ

(c) Accuracy with different k (d) Accuracy with different p

Figure 3: Parameter sensitivity of TVSE on the four datasets.

4.3.3 Run Time Comparison. In this subsection, we evaluate the efficiency of TVSE in comparison with several baseline methods. We record the training time costs for all methods with their best performance obtained. Table 4 shows the training and test time for all methods on AwA. Firstly, we can observe that the training time cost for different method is various. In particular, the inductive methods JSLE and SynC-struct cost much more time to train the models and to conduct prediction on test-data than SSE-ReLU due to the heavy load of computing the structured loss term of pairwise instances during optimizing and prediction. Thus it implies that they may not be suitable for large-scale data. Secondly, it can be learned that the transductive method TMV-HLP and the integrated methods based on SP-ZSR generally need more time for joint learning and prediction than the inductive methods. Though our TVSE also forms the learning and prediction procedures jointly, it requires much less time than TMV-HLP and the integrated methods based on SP-ZSR. Note that it even runs faster than the inductive method SynC-struct. As TVSE needs to calculate the affine matrix (manifold information) of the test instances and iteratively updates the prediction result, it is essential for TVSE to achieve superior prediction performance to TMV-HLP and SynC-struct. Therefore, TVSE can learns the prediction model with acceptable running time and comparative performance.

Table 4: Comparison of the running time (in seconds) on AwA.

Method	Training	Test
SSE-ReLU [34]	114.1	0.7
JSLE [35]	332.7	6.9
SynC-struct [5]	500.5	9.4
TMV-HLP [9]	745.2	
ESZSL + SP-ZSR [36]	619.5	
JSLE + SP-ZSR [36]	869.3	
TVSE	376.4	

5 CONCLUSION

In this paper, we proposed a novel transductive visual-semantic embedding (TVSE) framework for zero-shot learning. Different from most existing ZSL approaches, TVSE resolves the inherent projection shift problem by learning a latent embedding space using labeled source instances and unlabeled target instances under the transductive setting. We employed collective matrix factorization with graph regularization to incorporate the manifold structures of instances in the latent embedding space. Then we developed a scheme for TVSE to construct the relational mapping between seen and unseen classes, which maps the representations of the target instances in the latent embedding space to their predictions of unseen classes. We compared TVSE against several state-of-the-art approaches over four widely used benchmark datasets, and the extensive evaluations validate the advantages and show the promising capability of TVSE over these alternatives on the zero-shot recognition and retrieval tasks.

ACKNOWLEDGMENTS

This work was supported in part by the National Natural Science Foundation of China under Project 61602089, Project 61502081, Project 61572108, Project 61632007, and the Fundamental Research Funds for the Central Universities under Project ZYGX2014Z007, Project ZYGX2015J055, Project ZYGX2016KYQD114.

REFERENCES

[1] Zeynep Akata, Florent Perronnin, Zaïd Harchaoui, and Cordelia Schmid. 2013. Label-Embedding for Attribute-Based Classification. In *CVPR*. 819–826.

[2] Zeynep Akata, Scott E. Reed, Daniel Walter, Honglak Lee, and Bernt Schiele. 2015. Evaluation of output embeddings for fine-grained image classification. In *CVPR*. 2927–2936.

[3] Stephen Boyd and Lieven Vandenberghe. 2004. *Convex Optimization*.

[4] Deng Cai, Xiaofei He, Xuanhui Wang, Hujun Bao, and Jiawei Han. 2009. Locality Preserving Nonnegative Matrix Factorization. In *IJCAI*. 1010–1015.

[5] Soravit Changpinyo, Wei-Lun Chao, Boqing Gong, and Fei Sha. 2016. Synthesized Classifiers for Zero-Shot Learning. In *CVPR*. 580–587.

[6] Ali Farhadi, Ian Endres, Derek Hoiem, and David A. Forsyth. 2009. Describing objects by their attributes. In *CVPR*. 1778–1785.

[7] Andrea Frome, Gregory S. Corrado, Jonathon Shlens, Samy Bengio, Jeffrey Dean, Marc'Aurelio Ranzato, and Tomas Mikolov. 2013. DeViSE: A Deep Visual-Semantic Embedding Model. In *NIPS*. 2121–2129.

[8] Yanwei Fu, Timothy M. Hospedales, Tao Xiang, Zhen-Yong Fu, and Shaogang Gong. 2014. Transductive Multi-view Embedding for Zero-Shot Recognition and Annotation. In *ECCV*. 584–599.

[9] Yanwei Fu, Timothy M. Hospedales, Tao Xiang, and Shaogang Gong. 2015. Transductive Multi-View Zero-Shot Learning. *IEEE Trans. Pattern Anal. Mach. Intell.* 37, 11 (2015), 2332–2345.

[10] Zhen-Yong Fu, Tao A. Xiang, Elyor Kodirov, and Shaogang Gong. 2015. Zero-shot object recognition by semantic manifold distance. In *CVPR*. 2635–2644.

[11] Chuang Gan, Tianbao Yang, and Boqing Gong. 2016. Learning Attributes Equals Multi-Source Domain Generalization. In *CVPR*. 87–97.

[12] Elyor Kodirov, Tao Xiang, Zhen-Yong Fu, and Shaogang Gong. 2015. Unsupervised Domain Adaptation for Zero-Shot Learning. In *ICCV*. 2452–2460.

[13] Christoph H. Lampert, Hannes Nickisch, and Stefan Harmeling. 2009. Learning to detect unseen object classes by between-class attribute transfer. In *CVPR*. 951–958.

[14] Christoph H. Lampert, Hannes Nickisch, and Stefan Harmeling. 2014. Attribute-Based Classification for Zero-Shot Visual Object Categorization. *IEEE Trans. Pattern Anal. Mach. Intell.* 36, 3 (2014), 453–465.

[15] Hugo Larochelle, Dumitru Erhan, and Yoshua Bengio. 2008. Zero-data Learning of New Tasks. In *AAAI*. 646–651.

[16] Jingen Liu, Benjamin Kuipers, and Silvio Savarese. 2011. Recognizing human actions by attributes. In *CVPR*. 3337–3344.

[17] Mingsheng Long, Jianmin Wang, Guiguang Ding, Dou Shen, and Qiang Yang. 2012. Transfer Learning with Graph Co-Regularization. In *AAAI*.

[18] Thomas Mensink, Jakob Verbeek, Florent Perronnin, and Gabriela Csurka. 2012. Metric Learning for Large Scale Image Classification: Generalizing to New Classes at Near-Zero Cost. In *ECCV*. 488–501.

[19] Tomas Mikolov, Kai Chen, Greg Corrado, and Jeffrey Dean. 2013. Efficient Estimation of Word Representations in Vector Space. *CoRR* abs/1301.3781 (2013).

[20] Tomas Mikolov, Ilya Sutskever, Kai Chen, Gregory S. Corrado, and Jeffrey Dean. 2013. Distributed Representations of Words and Phrases and their Compositionality. In *NIPS*. 3111–3119.

[21] Mohammad Norouzi, Tomas Mikolov, Samy Bengio, Yoram Singer, Jonathon Shlens, Andrea Frome, Greg Corrado, and Jeffrey Dean. 2013. Zero-Shot Learning by Convex Combination of Semantic Embeddings. *NIPS* (2013), 410–418.

[22] Mark Palatucci, Dean Pomerleau, Geoffrey E. Hinton, and Tom M. Mitchell. 2009. Zero-shot Learning with Semantic Output Codes. In *NIPS*. 1410–1418.

[23] Genevieve Patterson, Chen Xu, Hang Su, and James Hays. 2014. The SUN Attribute Database: Beyond Categories for Deeper Scene Understanding. *International Journal of Computer Vision* 108, 1-2 (2014), 59–81.

[24] Marcus Rohrbach, Sandra Ebert, and Bernt Schiele. 2013. Transfer Learning in a Transductive Setting. In *NIPS*. 46–54.

[25] Bernardino Romera-Paredes and Philip H. S. Torr. 2015. An embarrassingly simple approach to zero-shot learning. In *ICML*. 2152–2161.

[26] Karen Simonyan and Andrew Zisserman. 2014. Very Deep Convolutional Networks for Large-Scale Image Recognition. *CoRR* abs/1409.1556 (2014).

[27] Richard Socher, Milind Ganjoo, Christopher D. Manning, and Andrew Y. Ng. 2013. Zero-Shot Learning Through Cross-Modal Transfer. In *NIPS*. 935–943.

[28] Laurens van der Maaten and Geoffrey E. Hinton. 2008. Visualizing High-Dimensional Data Using t-SNE. *Journal of Machine Learning Research* 9 (2008), 2579–2605.

[29] C. Wah, S. Branson, P. Welinder, P. Perona, and S. Belongie. 2011. *The Caltech-UCSD Birds-200-2011 Dataset*. Technical Report CNS-TR-2011-001. California Institute of Technology.

[30] Donghui Wang, Yanan Li, Yuetan Lin, and Yueting Zhuang. 2016. Relational Knowledge Transfer for Zero-Shot Learning. In *AAAI*. 2145–2151.

[31] Xing Xu, Fumin Shen, Yang Yang, Dongxiang Zhang, Heng Tao Shen, and Jingkuan Song. 2017. Matrix Tri-Factorization with Manifold Regularizations for Zero-shot Learning. In *CVPR*.

[32] Yang Yang, Yadan Luo, Weilun Chen, Fumin Shen, Jie Shao, and Heng Tao Shen. 2016. Zero-Shot Hashing via Transferring Supervised Knowledge. In *ACM MM*. 1286–1295.

[33] Shan You, Chang Xu, Yunhe Wang, Chao Xu, and Dacheng Tao. 2016. Streaming Label Learning for Modeling Labels on the Fly. (2016). arXiv:arXiv:1604.05449

[34] Ziming Zhang and Venkatesh Saligrama. 2015. Zero-Shot Learning via Semantic Similarity Embedding. In *ICCV*. 4166–4174.

[35] Ziming Zhang and Venkatesh Saligrama. 2016. Zero-Shot Learning via Joint Latent Similarity Embedding. In *CVPR*. 2124–2132.

[36] Ziming Zhang and Venkatesh Saligrama. 2016. Zero-Shot Recognition via Structured Prediction. In *ECCV*. 533–548.

3D Facial Video Retrieval and Management for Decision Support in Speech and Language Therapy

Ricardo Carrapiço[1], Isabel Guimarães[2], Margarida Grilo[2], Sofia Cavaco[1] and João Magalhães[1]
[1]NOVA LINCS, Computer Science Dept., Universidade NOVA Lisboa
[2]Escola Superior de Saúde do Alcoitão
Lisbon, Portugal
r.carrapico@campus.fct.unl.pt,iguimaraes@essa.pt,margarida.grilo@essa.pt
scavaco@fct.unl.pt,jm.magalhaes@fct.unl.pt

ABSTRACT

3D video is introducing great changes in many health related areas. The realism of such information provides health professionals with strong evidence analysis tools to facilitate clinical decision processes. Speech and language therapy aims to help subjects in correcting several disorders. The assessment of the patient by the speech and language therapist (SLT), requires several visual and audio analysis procedures that can interfere with the patient's production of speech. In this context, the main contribution of this paper is a 3D video system to improve health information management processes in speech and language therapy. The 3D video retrieval and management system supports multimodal health records and provides the SLTs with tools to support their work in many ways: (i) it allows SLTs to easily maintain a database of patients' orofacial and speech exercises; (ii) supports three-dimensional orofacial measurement and analysis in a non-intrusive way; and (iii) search patient speech-exercises by similar facial characteristics, using facial image analysis techniques. The second contribution is a dataset with 3D videos of patients performing orofacial speech exercises. The whole system was evaluated successfully in a user study involving 22 SLTs. The user study illustrated the importance of the retrieval by similar orofacial speech exercise.

KEYWORDS

Speech and Language Therapy, Facial Anthropometry, Decision Tool, 3D Video Retrieval

ACM Reference format:
Ricardo Carrapiço[1], Isabel Guimarães[2], Margarida Grilo[2], Sofia Cavaco[1] and João Magalhães[1]. 2017. 3D Facial Video Retrieval and Management for Decision Support in Speech and Language Therapy. In *Proceedings of ICMR '17, Bucharest, Romania, June 06-09, 2017,* 8 pages.
DOI: http://dx.doi.org/10.1145/3078971.3078984

1 INTRODUCTION

Speech is a form of human communication that starts to develop during infancy. While young children typically produce many speech errors, as the child becomes older, many speech production errors are corrected without the need of a specialist's intervention. However, in many cases speech and language therapy is required for the treatment of communication related problems.

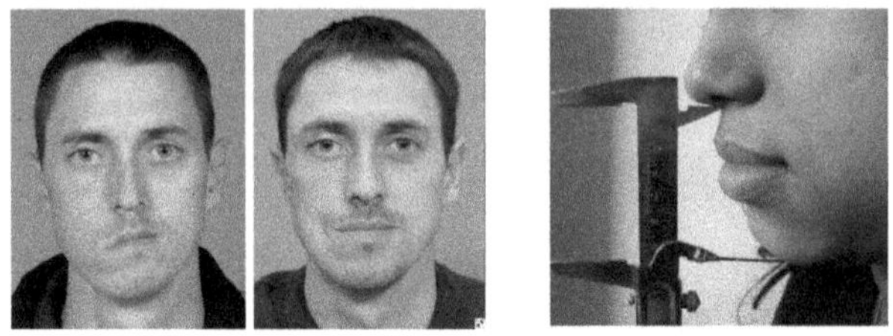

(a) (b)

Figure 1: (a) Facial paralysis is a disorder that requires specific exercises. (b) Close facial measurements with calipers (figure from [1]).

To assess the patients conditions, SLTs use several speech and language exercises. The assessment of the patient is mainly done by observation: the SLT decides if the patient is correctly producing speech sounds or not mostly based on normative data [10]. In addition to the exercises, SLTs also take measurements of the patient's face, in particular when assessing oral-motor disorders (figure 1a). The tools used by the SLT for assessment or during speech and language therapy can be quite intrusive which creates discomfort to the patient. As an example, figure 1b shows a caliper being used to take facial measurements. This is especially critical when applied to children, who may be impatient and may not understand the benefits of its use. For this reason, speech and language therapy could benefit from an improved acquisition and visualization of the therapy exercises information [11].

The work of an SLT is diverse and multidimensional, nevertheless interactive technologies and 3D video systems can be useful and helpful on several SLT's tasks. Serious games are an example of computational tools that have already introduced many successful changes [13, 14, 16]. Other tools are focused on health data to help both the SLT and the patient by providing the needed information for the SLT and by being almost transparent to the patient [11, 18–20]. The SLT relies in both speech and visual evidence to make the best clinical decision with respect to the best possible therapy [17]. By providing new sources of information or further improving the current ones, computer vision can help improving the quality and capability of speech and language disorders assessment.

This paper proposes a system that provides SLTs with state-of-the-art 3D video managament and retrieval methods to improve

DOI: http://dx.doi.org/10.1145/3078971.3078984

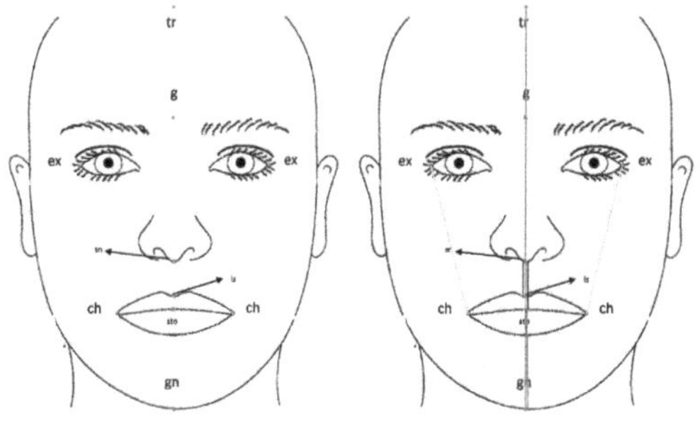

Figure 2: Facial anthropometry in speech and language therapy. (Figure from [3].) (a) Eight facial anthropometric points. (b) Seven anthropometric measurements.

health information management processes. Existing systems for speech and language therapy [11, 18] do not offer the same functionality as we propose in this paper. There are already speech repositories [11] but they do not integrate a 3D viewer. And the only tool that supports 3D [18] is focused on telemedicine and is not a video repository. Our 3D video retrieval and management system supports multimodal health records and provides the SLTs with tools to support their work in many ways: (i) it allows SLTs to easily maintain a database of their patients speech exercises; (ii) it supports three-dimensional orofacial measurement and analysis in a non-intrusive way; and (iii) it offers the possibility of searching patient speech-exercises by similar facial characteristics, using facial image analysis techniques.

The system is described in section 3. Section 4 describes a dataset of 3D videos with patients performing orofacial speech exercises. Section 5 reports the user study evaluation results.

2 RELATED WORK

Most of electronic health records (EHR) management systems are too generic and do not offer search or annotation functionalities for rich multimedia content. Current work in this direction only offers visualization of 3D synthetic models [20] or medical imaging [2]. Moreover, information retrieval methods with a ranking by relevance algorithm, are only now making way to such systems [19]. In our system, we propose two key advances over the state-of-the-art: the facial anthropometry of real patient's 3D digitized model, and the search for similar orofacial exercises.

Facial anthropometry consists of the measurements of the human face either in rest or in activity. In the particular case of speech and language therapy, facial anthropometry is related to seven specific anthropometric measurements between eight points of the face that are considered relevant (figure 2) [3]. Knowing these measurements, and their distance variations through time, allows the SLT to better assess the patients and measure their progress. There has been work in computational 3D facial anthropometry, including inference methods on 2D images [8], 3D face modeling with laser scans [15], inference on 3D images [21] and recent advances in the detection of facial landmarks [23] which already offer very good accuracy. Our system uses a semi-automated method, so as not to break the SLT trust on the system – we "suggest" some key landmarks and provide the SLT with the tools to mark further landmarks or adjust existing ones.

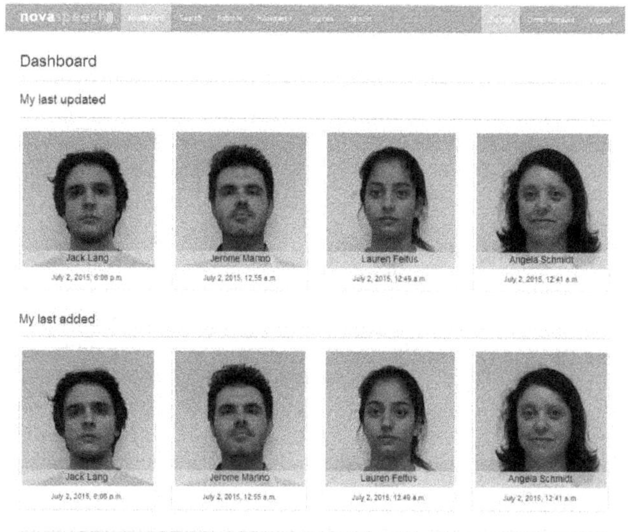

Figure 3: NOVASpeech is a system for storing, searching and visualizing video recordings of orofacial speech exercises.

Recent work in 3D shape retrieval [9, 22] relies on too strict measures to be used in speech and language therapy. The advances observed in the ImageCLEF Visceral track [12] concerning 3D image retrieval in the health domain already offer important metrics that can relax the similarity computation required by our problem. Closer to our setting is the work of Chen et al. [6] that aims at analysing 3D facial data to infer facial expressions. However, due to the specific facial characteristics we are looking for in our setting, we opted for not using 3D face features and instead explore multiple evidence from metadata fields, multiple visual descriptors and a wise diversity strategy that is focused on the SLT information needs.

3 THE NOVASPEECH FRAMEWORK

NOVASpeech is a web tool[1] that allows SLTs to easily maintain a database of their patients recorded therapy exercises (figure 3[2]). The tool is focused on having useful and easy to use features that will improve the SLT experience when evaluating patients. Apart from being used by individual SLTs, the tool can be used, for example, at health institutions, where the SLT works, as it allows multiple private user accounts. With each SLT having his/her own account, the patients information is private to each SLT (unless the SLT explicity gives access to his/her patients' data to his/her colleagues).

The exercises are captured while the patient performs the therapy exercises, without any interruptions, using only a Kinect camera and a computer (section 3.1). By being on the web, the SLT can access the patients information from anywhere, including home and without having to go through a software installation process.

[1] http://3dspeech.novasearch.org/

[2] All names and information shown in this paper are illustrative and do not correspond to real patients.

It suffices to have a web browser. Being a support tool for speech and language therapy, one important part of this experience is the **browsing and analysis** of the therapy exercises, which helps the SLT on assessing the patient's speech sounds or oral-motor disorder and on evaluating the patient's progression. For this reason, NOVASpeech offers different functionalities to improve this experience (section 3.2). To help the SLT on assessing different aspects of the disorder, the tool supports different types of data, which include audio, video, visible images and infrared images, and 3D models of the patients.

One of the major innovations of our work is the **visualization and annotation of the patient's exercises in 3D**, allowing a type of control and examination that was not possible before: the SLT can now rotate and move the patient's 3D model to observe from different perspectives (figure 4). This feature can be used for several purposes by the SLT and it is of particular interest for facial anthropometry, as it allows to take relevant anthropometric measurements without the need to use a caliper directly in the patient's face (more details in section 3.3). The second main functionality is the possibility of **searching** through the SLT's patients. NOVASpeech uses computer vision techniques to improve the SLT experience when using this fucntionality (section 3.4).

3.1 Patient data management

Generating and adding new information to NOVASpeech is one fundamental task that needs to be addressed. *How to record the data* and *how to add the recordings to the tool* are important questions that the SLT, not being a specialist in these matters, should not be worried about. To address these questions, we developed a tool called NOVASpeech Kinect Recorder that captures and saves the information generated by the Kinect Sensor. At the recording stage the files do not contain any metadata, like the patients name or type of exercise, but these can be inserted when the data is added to NOVASpeech.

NOVASpeech organizes the data according to the requirements from the SLTs. Each SLT has an account that holds all his/her patients. The patient entities have exercises, which are the recordings made by the SLT during the therapy session. Each recording consists of a sequence of frames (visible and infrared). These entities are all related in a way that leads to the SLT who inserted the data in the system.

SLTs have full access over their patients data. They can add, edit and delete the patients and exercises. This way SLTs have a tight control over what they have in NOVASpeech and can maintain a more dynamic experience by, for example, editing the notes of a patient to reflect his/her performance or motivation upon adding a new exercise to the therapy session.

The patient entity holds personal information (name, gender, age and photo). For privacy concerns, the patient's health information is stored as a separate entity and holds data related to oral habits, like onychophagia or chewing objects, nasal obstruction, orthodontic treatment, facial trauma and SLTs' free-text notes.

A speech exercise is a central data entity in our system. This entity, stores the type of exercise (rest or dynamic), the video frames and the audio file. A dynamic speech exercise can be an oral diadochokinesis training, (repetition of sounds like 'pa' or 'ma' to assess articulatory rate in speech production) or a labial training with stretching or protrusion of the lips. Like with the patient entity, each exercise also has a text-free notes field. Table 1 shows a summary of the fields for each data entity.

Patient details	Patient condition	S&L Exercise
Name	Oral habits	Rest
Gender	Nasal obstruction	Oral diadochokinesis
Age	Orthodontic treatment	Labial training
Photo	Facial trauma	Notes
	Others	

Table 1: Summary of data fields

3.2 Data navigation and examination

One main feature of NOVASpeech is the navigation and analysis of the therapy exercises. With each exercise being associated with a patient, the SLT first has to select the patient before having access to the exercise list (*Patients* option in the top menu of figure 3).

Upon selecting a patient, we are redirected to his/her page, which shows all the information that the system has about the patient, plus his/her exercise list. To easily navigate through this list, we added two features: a timeline representation of the exercises, and the possibility of applying filters to the list and timeline (figure 5). The timeline allows the SLT to inspect the sequence of exercises that the patient performed.

By selecting an exercise, the user is redirected to the exercise page (figure 6). Similar to the patient page, the exercise page has the patient information, so the SLT can maintain context of the patient's condition, and also the exercise data. The SLT is then offered with a visualization of the exercise audio signal and the corresponding video frames. With NOVASpeech the user can see the current frame plus the two preceding and following frames (figure 6.a). This way it is easier for the SLT to examine the differences on the patient face as the frames are in a timeline. It is also possible to navigate through this sequence manually, controlling it with the scrollbar. Every frame can be seen in more detail by clicking on it, opening the frame page.

The exercise is also composed of an audio track. To control the track we added an audio player with waveform support, so the SLT can visually identify the parts where the patient has emitted a sound (figure 6.c). The player allows selecting a region and playing only that portion of the audio. The audio player is connected to the sequence of frames in a way that playing the audio controls the progress of the sequence. There is also a slider that the SLT can use to control the sequence play speed, by making both the audio play and image transition slower or faster.

Finally, inspecting the frame allows the SLT to see the image in more detail. The frame page also has emphasis on frame navigation, by having a frame selector that allows a frame-by-frame displaying (figure 6.b). This way the SLT can see the differences between frames more easily. The SLT can also see the infrared image that the Kinect sensor captured, mapped onto a visible color space and choose to interact with the 3D model, as will be explained in the following section.

Figure 4: NOVASpeech 3D visualizer with a model being rotated.

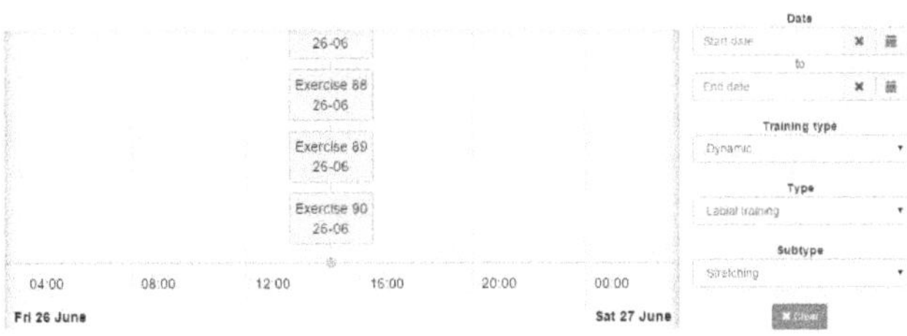

Figure 5: Timeline representation of the exercises and the corresponding exercise filters.

3.3 3D visualization and facial anthropometry

The NOVASpeech 3D visualizer uses the 3D point cloud of the video frame to form the 3D model of the patient. Exhibiting the patient's 3D model is a unique feature of NOVASpeech, as it allows non-intrusive facial anthropometry. The model can be moved and rotated, as seen in figure 4, similarly to an object on a scene with the origin being the Kinect camera position. It should be noted that the model shows a partial view of the patient face. This is because the camera is in front of the patient, thus not capturing side views of the patient's face. However, it is sufficient for speech and language therapy because the face is complete.

Seeing the patient from different perspectives is important and is something that before, was only possible by photographing the patient multiple times, requiring the patient to be still. This means that it cannot be done during a speech sound exercise, as asking the patient to stop or make a particular position can be unnatural and difficult, specially for patients with facial paralysis, where they cannot accurately control part of their face. Being able to examine a 3D model with only one capture and during an exercise opens new opportunities. One of such opportunities is, for example, rotating the model to inspect the gap between a patient lips, while he/she is producing speech sounds, without any sort of intrusion of the patients space.

Another important aspect of the 3D visualizer is the facial anthropometry. Double-clicking on the model marks a point and a total of two points can be marked at the same time, as exemplified in figure 7. Marking a point in three dimensions can be confusing. The approach we took is that the point has to exist in the point cloud (the model) for it to be marked. After selecting two points we obtain the three dimensional euclidean distance between them. This facial measurement is then associated to the patient exercise and kept as a record for later search or filtering. The annotation of points completely eliminates the need of a vernier caliper, as it allows measuring the patients face at any moment during the speech sound exercises, without any sort of contact with the patient.

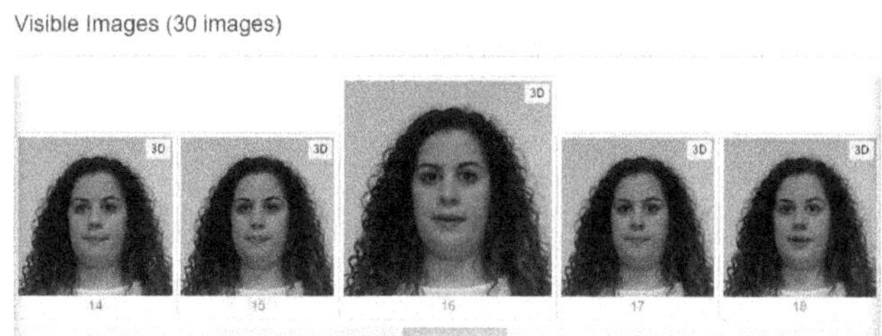

(a)

(b)

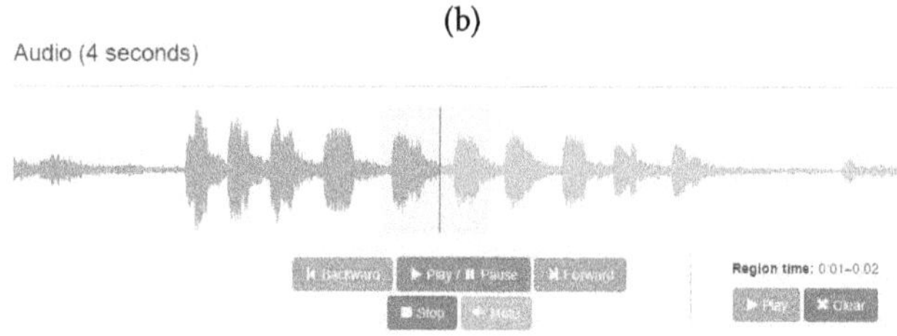

(c)

Figure 6: Exercise visualization: (a) video frame sequence (b) frame selector, and (c) audio player with a region selected.

3.4 Search for similar exercises

NOVASpeech's search mechanism allows SLTs to find exercises (restricted to the SLT's patients) that have similar facial anthropometrics. In addition, it allows choosing the facial anthropometry search type, by searching only the face's lower or middle third for visible images and the whole face for both visible and infrared images (figure 8). This functionality is particularly useful to the SLTs who can now more easily support their clinical decisions on evidence from past patient data.

To be searchable, an image needs to have annotations of where the eyes are. NOVASpeech provides an initial automatic detection of the eyes and the SLT can then adjust the position of the eyes on the query image. NOVASpeech's search mechanism compares the input image characteristics with the remaining images in the database, and then forms a rank based on the results. Due to the

Figure 7: NOVASpeech 3D visualizer with marked points for facial anthropometry

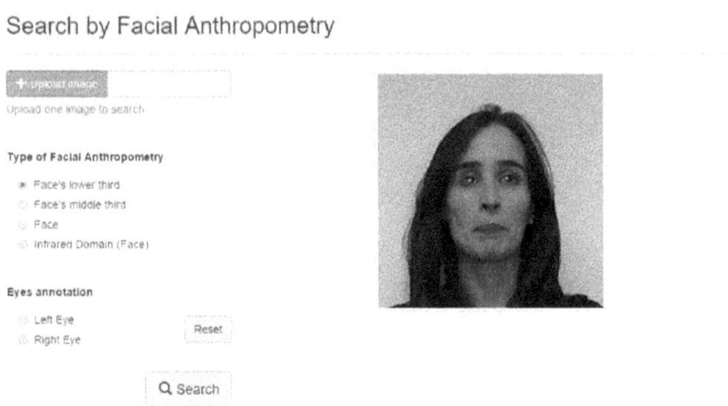

Figure 8: Facial anthropometry search

nature of the data organization in our setting, it makes more sense to rank exercises instead of single images. For this reason we opted to merge the images in their respective exercises. The rank fusion process is applied before the merging into exercises, and the result diversity is applied afterwards.

Ranking of face images. To robustly capture the different facial traits of the patient, we rely on several different image descriptors: Gabor filters, Local Binary Patterns, Color and Edge Directivity Descriptor [4] and Fuzzy Color and Texture Histogram [5].

For each type of image descriptor, we take the face image descriptor vector and compute the distance between the query and the indexed images. This creates one rank for each type of feature descriptor for all frames of all exercises that we have in our index.

Rank fusion. When there are several ranks that offer different views of the same data, we need to combine them into one single rank to present the search results to the end user. To accomplish this rank fusion we use reciprocal rank fusion (RRF) [7]. RRF is based on the fact that while highly-ranked images are important, lower-ranked images should not be penalized hardly. RRF assumes there is a set of images D to be ranked and a set of ranks R, each one corresponding to an visual feature. The score of each image is calculated by the following expression:

$$RRFScore(d \in D) = \sum_{r \in R} \frac{1}{k + pos_r(d)},$$

where $pos_r(d)$ is the position of image d in rank r, and k can be adjusted to diminish the difference between highly-ranked and lower-ranked images. As suggested by the Cormack et al. [7], we used $k = 60$.

Results diversity. Now that we have a single rank of all the images in the system, we need to compute the actual rank of the orofacial exercises. To generate the rank, it is important to obtain some diversity in the results so we do not end up with several results from the same person.

To increase the results diversity, we applied a logarithmic penalty to the score of each result in the rank. This approach was inspired by the inverse document frequency used in information retrieval and is as follows:

$$Score(r \in Rank) = log\left(\frac{1}{\#occurrences(r)}\right) + 1\,.$$

The expression was applied progressively through the rank instead of statically, i.e. instead of applying the same value to all the instances of that person. More specifically, the $\#occurrences(r)$ increases by one (starting at one) each time we see the occurrence of a person .

In summary, **rank fusion** enable us to combine the different features in a single rank and using **result diversity** made the rank less monotonous by allowing other patients to rank up (instead of returning only exercises from the patient in the query).

4 3D VIDEO OROFACIAL SPEECH DATA

Given the pioneering nature of this research, we created a new 3D depth video dataset for Speech and Language Therapy[3]. We recorded a total of 31 volunteers, 25 females and 6 males with an average age of ≈ 25 years. Most volunteers were graduate students. The volunteers were asked to do five different speech sound exercises while seated in front of a camera. These exercises were chosen as being good indicators of patient progress.

The whole process was designed and curated by two SLTs - the sequence of exercises and the recording instructions were provided by them. They were also present during the capture. The exercises are: (1) stretching the lips, (2) protrusion of the lips and repeatedly saying the sounds (3) "pa", (4)"ba" and (5) "ma". The patients were also recorded while in rest, doing a neutral face. Each one of the volunteers was recorded six times for a total of 186 recordings. Table 2 illustrates each exercise with an image of a 3D model from the dataset.

A Kinect 2.0 camera was used to capture 3D video, visible and infrared images, audio and field depth. The recordings were done with an application implemented in the scope of this work.

5 EVALUATION

In order to validate NOVASpeech, we performed a user study with volunteer student and professional SLTs. There were 22 volunteers with ages between 21 and 39 years who participated in the study. Their average age was ≈ 27 years. The study started with a short presentation of NOVASpeech, after which the volunteers tested and explored the tool. Afterwards they answered a survey regarding the experience.

The survey included some questions on personal data and work experience (such as the age, years of experience, and usage of computer tools for speech and language therapy) and questions about

[3] Available at: http://3dspeech.novasearch.org/

Exercise type					
In Rest	Stretching	Protusion	"pa"	"ba"	"ma"
				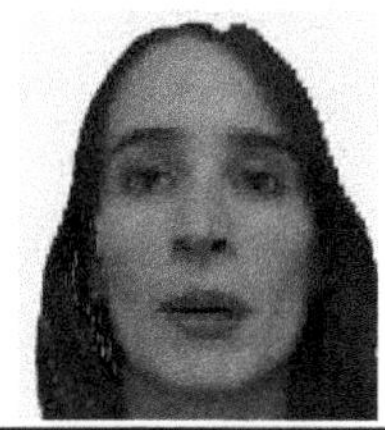	

Table 2: Example of the speech sound exercises in the dataset, illustrated with 3D images.

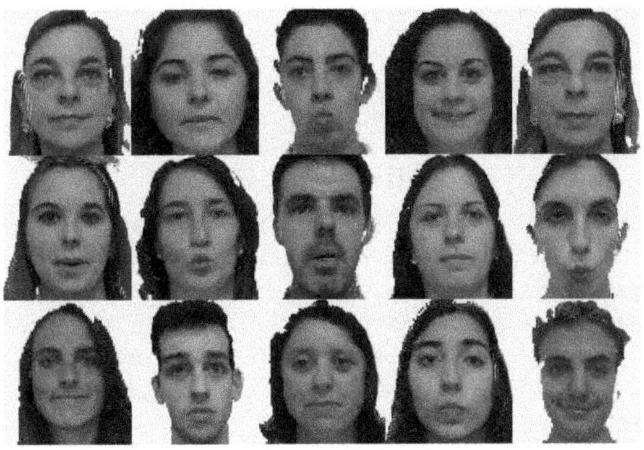

Figure 9: Example of the 3D models present in the NOVASpeech dataset.

NOVASpeech. The latter included questions about: (i) the visualization of speech and orofacial exercises, (ii) 3D facial anthropometry, (iii) search and (iv) general usability.

The survey showed that all volunteers were computer literate and had all the needed background to evaluate the tool. Their work experience was divided between no experience for students (36.4%), 1-5 years (27.2%) and 6-10 years of experience (36.4%). Also, all volunteers used computer tools to assist them during speech and language therapy sessions or to evaluate the speech sound productions of patients. They used computer games (85.7%), audio recording tools to record the speech exercises (71.4%) and tools to keep the patients data (66.7%).

5.1 Orofacial and speech exercise visualization

The user study included a set of questions to assess NOVASpeech exercise visualization features. These include the visualization of the exercise image sequence and inspection of frames (figure 6.a and b), the control of the playback speed, and the waveform visualization and audio player (figure 6.c).

NOVASpeech navigation and visualization of speech exercises had great acceptance. All volunteers considered useful to observe and analyze the orofacial dynamics across multiple simultaneous frames, as shown in figure 6.a. However, one volunteer considered that the images were too small for the type of observation he/she needs to perform.

An important feature to observe the orofacial exercises in detail is the control of the playback speed. Figure 10 shows that all volunteers considered slow motion useful for at least one purpose, but mostly for inspecting orofacial movements. Most participants considered that fast forward is also useful for analyzing the orofacial fatigue while producing speech sounds over a long period of time.

The audio player is an important component of NOVASpeech. Both its features, namely the waveform visualization and play of an audio region, also had great acceptance. All volunteers considered them beneficial. Moreover, one SLT mentioned that it could be useful to show the patient a normal rate of talk in the case of him/her speaking slower or faster than normal.

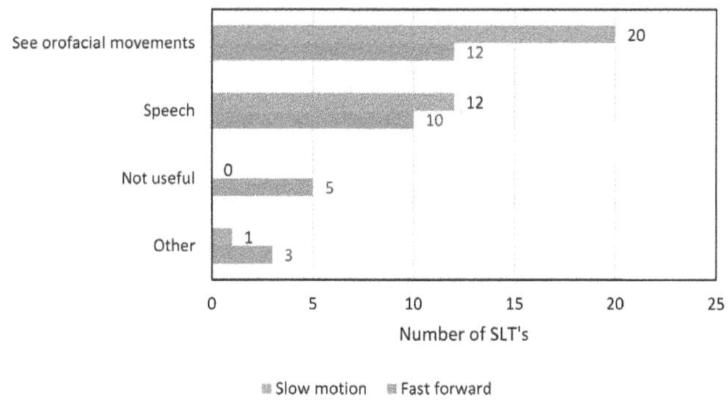

Figure 10: Orofacial speech exercise inspection with slow motion/fast forward

5.2 3D facial anthropometry assessment

As mentioned above, one of the main innovations of NOVASpeech is the set of features offered to navigate and inspect the 3D models of the patients, including the possibility of using the 3D models for facial anthropometry. The survey included questions to evaluate the usefulness of these features. The volunteers could rate the features with a 5-point Likert scale.

Figure 11 shows the results for the 3D visualization of exercises in rest and with motion (like stretching the lips, or speech exercises), where 1 corresponds to *not useful* and 5 corresponds to *very useful*. The results show that the 3D visualization is very useful for dynamic exercises, with 68.2% of the participants rating it at the maximum and no participant rating it below 3 (neutral). While the participants

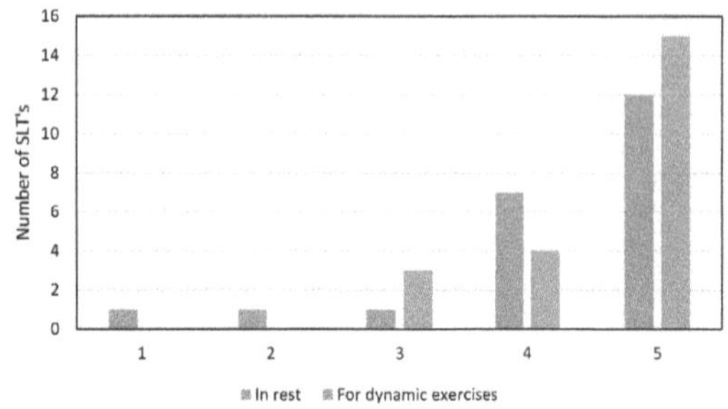

Figure 11: Utility of using the 3D visualizer

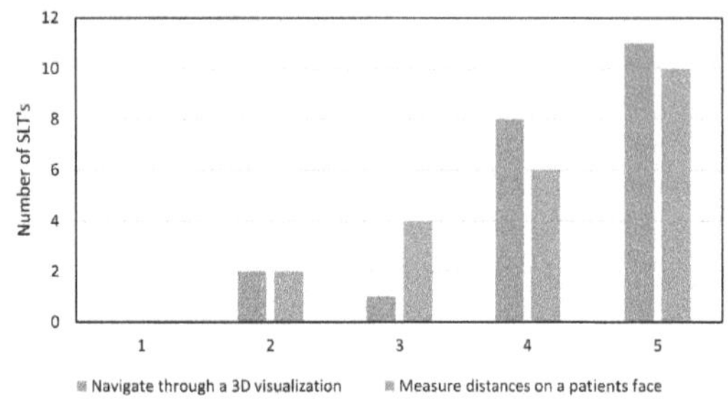

Figure 12: Usability of the 3D visualization and anthropometry

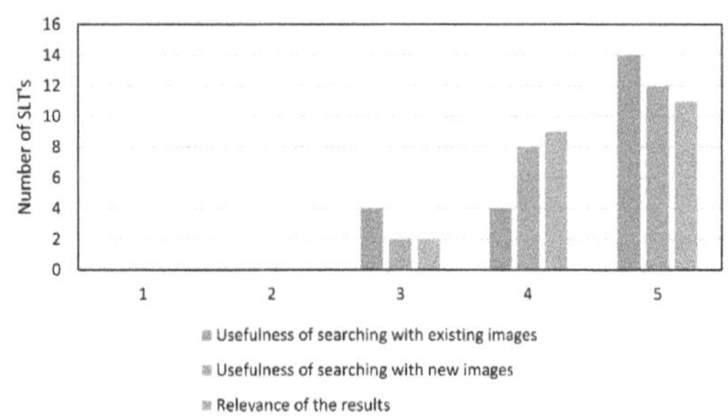

Figure 13: Usefulness of search and relevance of results

considered that the 3D visualization to examine the patient in rest was less useful, the classification was still high enough to allows us to conclude that it has its usefulness.

Most volunteers (86.3%) rated the navigation through the 3D models above 4 (figure 12), where 1 corresponds to the *very difficult* and 5 corresponds to the *very easy*. Also, most volunteers (95.5%) found the possibility of going through the 3D frames one by one very useful. This type of navigation allows the SLTs to see nearby frames almost instantly without losing context of the exercise.

Whilst most users rated measuring the distances for facial anthropometry above 4, for some users this feature was considered slightly less easy to use than navigating the 3D models (figure 12). While observing the volunteers exploring these features, we noticed that they had some initial difficulty manipulating the 3D frames, namely for rotating and zooming the frames. Nonetheless, it is also important to note that no participant thought that either task was very difficult to use. From these results and observations from the participant SLTs, we were able to conclude that while there is room

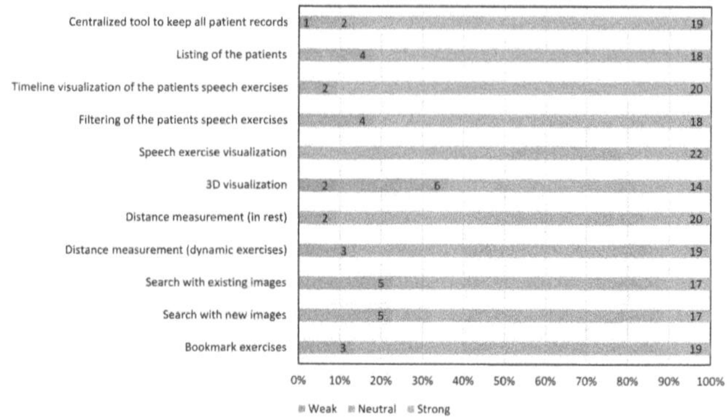

Figure 14: Usability evaluation of NOVASpeech

for improvement in the manipulation of the 3D frames, the SLTs were eager to use the system.

5.3 Search of similar exercises

Another key feature of NOVASpeech is the search of exercises by similarity to a query image. We asked the SLTs to rate the usefulness of searching with both imported images and images already in the dataset. Figure 13 shows the results obtained. With no votes under 3 in a scale of 1 to 5 (where 1 is *less useful* and 5 is *more useful*), it is clear that the SLTs consider both types of search as being similarly important and relevant.

We were also able to conclude that the search algorithm is able to retrieve relevant samples. Figure 13 shows that all volunteers rated the relevance of the retrieved samples above 3 (where 1 is *less relevant* and 5 is *more relevant*) and with an average rate of ≈ 4.41. When asked if they would use the search functionality, all participant gave a positive answer. These results allowed us to be certain of the quality of this feature as well as the utility it has in speech therapy.

5.4 Usability assessment

The survey included questions to evaluate NOVASpeech as a whole and assess its strong, neutral and weak points. Figure 14 shows which features the volunteers find that are the strongest and weakest characteristics of NOVASpeech. Speech exercise visualization is clearly the main functionality of NOVASpeech. General repository features for searching, managing, bookmarking, and filtering were all rated high by the volunteers. The results of the survey show that the tool is accessible to the end users as $\approx 82\%$ of the volunteers rated it 4 or 5 on a scale of 1 to 5 (with 5 being the easiest). However, we should not ignore the fact that two subjects voted 2 and other two subjects voted 3. It is important to make more tests and improve the areas where NOVASpeech is less accessible.

Among all the features, the 3D visualization was the one with less positive opinions. Observation showed us that controlling a 3D model is still an unusual experience, and requires some training. The volunteers were not used to that type of controls, leading them to feel that it is not as easy to use as the other features (section 5.2). Still, while the 3D visualization was rated as a strong feature by less participants than the other features, more than half of the participants (63.6%) rated it high. Also, it is interesting to note that the answers to this question contrast with the answers about the 3D anthropometric features, which was rated as a strong feature by 90.9% of the participants. The answers to these questions allowed us to conclude that all the implemented features provide important functionalities to the SLTs.

The last question was about the SLTs' interest in sharing patients' data with colleagues to help them in their decision process. Almost all the volunteers (91%) were interested in this functionality, which allowed us to understand that sharing data between SLTs is important.

6 CONCLUSIONS

We proposed NOVASpeech, a 3D video management and retrieval system directed to assist the SLTs. The system supports multimodal health records and provides several different features that were designed to contribute to speech and language therapy as a whole.

Apart from allowing SLTs to maintain a database of their patients' recorded therapy exercises, the tool provides visualization and navigation features that help SLTs on inspecting and analysing their patients' data. These features allow SLTs to more easily assess the patients' disorders and monitor their progress.

The major novelty of NOVASpeech is the visualization and annotation of the 3D models of patients' faces. To the best of our knowledge, this is the first tool for speech and language therapy that offers the possibility of visualizing and navigating 3D data, allowing a type of examination that was not possible before. Moreover, NOVASpeech allows to take facial measurements for facial anthropometry in a non-intrusive way. This is an innovation that has been received with enthusiasm by SLTs who experimented the tool.

Another significant feature offered by NOVASpeech is searching similar exercises. Given a query image, NOVASpeech returns data from recorded exercises that have similar facial anthropometrics. This feature allows SLTs to support their clinical decisions based on similar cases.

In order to assess the offered features, we run a user study with 22 volunteers. NOVASpeech was very well received by the participant SLTs, who showed interest in acquiring the tool. The results showed that most features were well designed and easy to use.

Finally, another significant contribution of our work is a 3D video dataset of orofacial speech exercises used for assessing the patients: (1) rest position, (2) stretching the lips, (3) protrusion of the lips, and repeatedly saying the sounds (4)"pa", (5) "ba" and (6) "ma". Overall, the set of features implemented by NOVASpeech and the characteristics of the dataset, introduce several new advances and materials that are unique in relation to the state-of-the-art.

ACKNOWLEDGEMENTS

This work has been partially funded by the CMU|Portugal research project BioVisualSpeech, reference CMUP-ERI/TIC/0033/2014 and by the project NOVA LINCS Ref. UID/CEC/04516/2013. We would like to thank Cátia Pedroso who was essential in guiding the recordings sessions and to all the volunteers at ESSA who participated in the 3D video recordings.

REFERENCES

[1] B. Basnet, P. Parajuli, R. Singh, P. Suwal, P. Shrestha, and D. Baral. An anthropometric study to evaluate the correlation between the occlusal vertical dimension and length of the thumb. volume 7, page 33–39. Dove Medical Press Limited, 2015.

[2] A. A. Bui, W. Hsu, C. Arnold, S. El-Saden, D. R. Aberle, and R. K. Taira. Imaging-based observational databases for clinical problem solving: the role of informatics. *Journal of the American Medical Informatics Association*, 20(6):1053–1058, 2013.

[3] D. Cattoni. O uso do paquímetro na avaliação da morfologia orofacial. *Revista Soc. Bras. Fonoaudiologia*, 11(1):52–58, 2006.

[4] S. a. Chatzichristofis and Y. S. Boutalis. CEDD: Color and edge directivity descriptor: A compact descriptor for image indexing and retrieval. In *Lecture Notes in Computer Science (including subseries Lecture Notes in Artificial Intelligence and Lecture Notes in Bioinformatics)*, volume 5008 LNCS, pages 312–322, 2008.

[5] S. a. Chatzichristofis and Y. S. Boutalis. FCTH: Fuzzy Color and texture histogram a low level feature for accurate image retrieval. *WIAMIS 2008 - Proceedings of the 9th International Workshop on Image Analysis for Multimedia Interactive Services*, pages 191–196, 2008.

[6] J. Chen, Y. Ariki, and T. Takiguchi. Robust facial expressions recognition using 3d average face and ameliorated adaboost. In *Proceedings of the 21st ACM international conference on Multimedia*, pages 661–664. ACM, 2013.

[7] G. V. Cormack, C. L. a. Clarke, and S. Buettcher. Reciprocal rank fusion outperforms condorcet and individual rank learning methods. *Proceedings of the 32nd international ACM SIGIR conference on Research and development in information retrieval - SIGIR '09*, page 758, 2009.

[8] D. DeCarlo, D. Metaxas, and M. Stone. An anthropometric face model using variational techniques. In *Proceedings of the 25th annual conference on Computer graphics and interactive techniques*, pages 67–74. ACM, 1998.

[9] T. Furuya and R. Ohbuchi. Diffusion-on-manifold aggregation of local features for shape-based 3d model retrieval. In *Proceedings of the 5th ACM on International Conference on Multimedia Retrieval*, pages 171–178. ACM, 2015.

[10] I. Guimarães, C. Birrento, C. Figueiredo, and C. Flores. *Manual do Teste de Articulação Verbal.* Oficina Didáctica, 2014.

[11] Intelligent Video Sollutions. Video Recording for Speech Therapy Training.

[12] O. A. Jiménez-del Toro, A. Hanbury, G. Langs, A. Foncubierta-Rodríguez, and H. Müller. Overview of the visceral retrieval benchmark 2015. In *Multimodal Retrieval in the Medical Domain*, pages 115–123. Springer, 2015.

[13] M. Lopes, J. a. Magalhães, and S. Cavaco. A voice-controlled serious game for the sustained vowel exercise. In *Proceedings of the 13th International Conference on Advances in Computer Entertainment Technology*, ACE2016, pages 32:1–32:6, New York, NY, USA, 2016. ACM.

[14] A. Mourão and J. a. Magalhães. Competitive affective gaming: Winning with a smile. In *Proceedings of the 21st ACM International Conference on Multimedia*, MM '13, pages 83–92, New York, NY, USA, 2013. ACM.

[15] K. F. O'Grady and M. Antonyshyn. Facial asymmetry: three-dimensional analysis using laser surface scanning. *Plastic and reconstructive surgery*, 104(4):928–937, 1999.

[16] M. A. Rahman, D. Hossain, A. M. Qamar, F. U. Rehman, A. H. Toonsi, M. Ahmed, A. El Saddik, and S. Basalamah. A low-cost serious game therapy environment with inverse kinematic feedback for children having physical disability. In *Proceedings of International Conference on Multimedia Retrieval*, page 529. ACM, 2014.

[17] R. R. Riely and A. Smith. Speech movements do not scale by orofacial structure size. *Journal of Applied Physiology*, 94(6):2119–2126, 2003.

[18] M. Stürmer, A. Maier, J. Penne, S. Soutschek, C. Schaller, R. Handschu, M. Scibor, and E. Nöth. 3D Tele-Medical Speech Therapy using Time-of-Flight Technology. pages 1500–1503. 2009.

[19] A. R. Tate, N. Beloff, B. Al-Radwan, J. Wickson, S. Puri, T. Williams, T. Van Staa, and A. Bleach. Exploiting the potential of large databases of electronic health records for research using rapid search algorithms and an intuitive query interface. *Journal of the American Medical Informatics Association*, 21(2):292–298, 2014.

[20] B. Temkin, E. Acosta, P. Hatfield, E. Onal, and A. Tong. Web-based three-dimensional virtual body structures: W3d-vbs. *Journal of the American Medical Informatics Association*, 9(5):425–436, 2002.

[21] S. M. Weinberg, S. Naidoo, D. P. Govier, R. A. Martin, A. A. Kane, and M. L. Marazita. Anthropometric precision and accuracy of digital three-dimensional photogrammetry: comparing the genex and 3dmd imaging systems with one another and with direct anthropometry. *Journal of Craniofacial Surgery*, 17(3):477–483, 2006.

[22] J. Xie, F. Zhu, G. Dai, and Y. Fang. Progressive shape-distribution-encoder for 3d shape retrieval. In *Proceedings of the 23rd Annual ACM Conference on Multimedia Conference*, pages 1167–1170. ACM, 2015.

[23] Z. Zhang, W. Zhang, J. Liu, and X. Tang. Facial landmark localization based on hierarchical pose regression with cascaded random ferns. In *Proceedings of the 21st ACM international conference on Multimedia*, pages 561–564. ACM, 2013.

Music-Guided Video Summarization using Quadratic Assignments

Thomas Mensink
University of Amsterdam
thomas.mensink@uva.nl

Thomas Jongstra
University of Amsterdam
jongstra@gmail.com

Pascal Mettes
University of Amsterdam
p.s.m.mettes@uva.nl

Cees G.M. Snoek
University of Amsterdam
cgmsnoek@uva.nl

ABSTRACT

This paper aims to automatically generate a summary of an unedited video, guided by an externally provided music-track. The tempo, energy and beats in the music determine the choices and cuts in the video summarization. To solve this challenging task, we model video summarization as a quadratic assignment problem. We assign frames to the summary, using rewards based on frame interestingness, plot coherency, audio-visual match, and cut properties. Experimentally we validate our approach on the SumMe dataset. The results show that our music guided summaries are more appealing, and even outperform the current state-of-the-art summarization methods when evaluated on the F1 measure of precision and recall.

CCS CONCEPTS

• **Information systems → Multimedia content creation**;

KEYWORDS

Video Summarisation, Quadratic Assignment Problem

ACM Reference format:
Thomas Mensink, Thomas Jongstra, Pascal Mettes, and Cees G.M. Snoek. 2017. Music-Guided Video Summarization using Quadratic Assignments. In *Proceedings of ICMR '17, June 6–9, 2017, Bucharest, Romania*, , 7 pages.
DOI: http://dx.doi.org/10.1145/3078971.3079024

1 INTRO

The goal of this paper is to create high-quality video summarizations, guided by an externally provided music-track. Consider for example that after a day of skiing with your GoPro camera, you reflect your mood by selecting a music-track and the computer will automatically create a video summary of your skiing day fitted on this specific music-track. Clearly a summary with classical music should have different dynamics, plots, and cuts than a summary based on funk music, even when the summaries are created from the same source video. Such an adaptive summarization method could be useful for creating video summarizations of social events by social media services or to personalize video summarizations.

ICMR '17, June 6–9, 2017, Bucharest, Romania

978-1-4503-4701-3/17/06…$15.00
DOI: http://dx.doi.org/10.1145/3078971.3079024

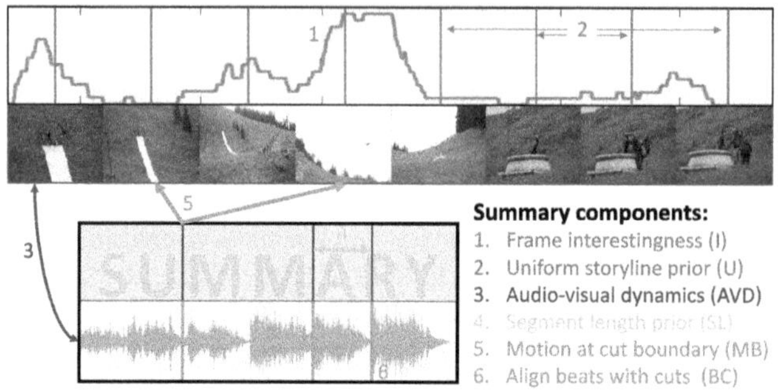

Figure 1: Illustration of key factors included in our model for automatically generating music-guided summaries.

The key key factors used in our music-guided summarization model are illustrated in Fig. 1. We are inspired by a large body of research focused on video summarization, either using only the visual source video [5, 8, 11, 13, 14, 19, 22], or combining multiple video modalities [4, 10, 12]. In contrast to these works, we aim to create a video summary fitted on a given music-track, which to the best of our knowledge has never been considered before.

1.1 Related work

Video summarization is often simplified to a frame interestingness problem [19], where interestingness can be measured using a variety of approaches, including object detections [11, 14], saliency [5, 8, 15], person detection [18], and landmark detection [13]. However, frame interestingness does not include any clues about the aesthetics of the summarization itself. Rather than relying exclusively on heterogeneous measures of interestingness for our video summarization, we emphasize on creating summaries, with a coherent plot and logical cuts.

Several works have previously incorporated coherency to make video summaries more viewer friendly. Such coherency can be performed by selecting sets of consecutive frames [5] or by adding temporal regularization [11]. The balance between interestingness and coherency, can be obtained using pre-segmentation methods [5], submodular optimization [6, 20] or recurrent neural networks [22]. Here, we propose a model that jointly incorporates interestingness, coherency, and which is capable of adjusting the summaries based on a user-provided music-track.

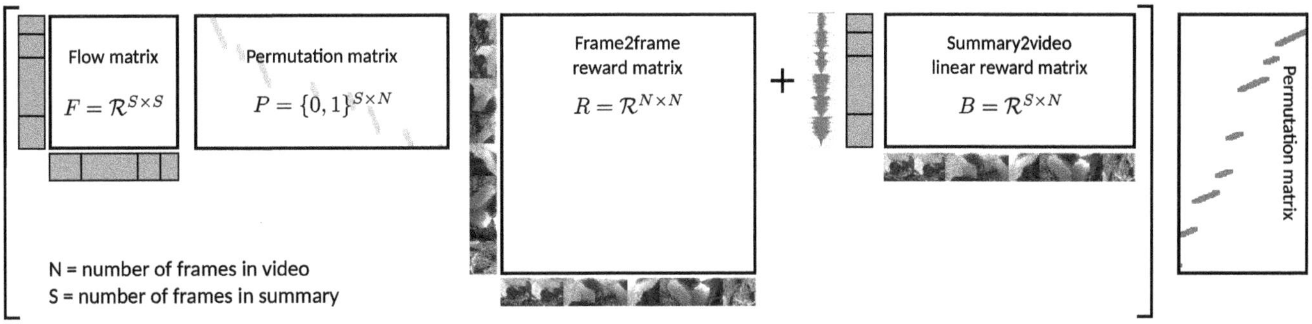

Figure 2: Overview of the Quadratic Assignment Problem formulation for audio-guided video summarization.

Beyond exploiting just the visual content of videos for summarization, a number of works have proposed to jointly model the visual and audio modalities of videos [4, 10, 12]. For example, in [10] features from the visual, audio, and textual (subtitles) modalities are used to highlight interesting frames. In this work, we have an orthogonal goal, namely to align the summarization of videos with an externally provided music-track. Aligning video with a music-track is important for viewer experience, as indicated by [21].

Existing computational models for video summarization can not incorporate music-guidance. For example pre-segmentation methods are unlikely to yield segments which match the music properties, indicating we need a frame-based model. In contrast to seeing summarization as a selection process [5, 6], we see it as an assignment problem. Where for each summary slot the most suitable frame from the source video is assigned. Therefore we model our approach using the classical Quadratic Assignment Problem.

1.2 Contributions

We make the following contributions:

- we propose to summarize videos based on joint audio-visual information from the original video and a user-provided music-track,
- we model interestingness, coherency, and audio-match of the summaries jointly as a Quadratic Assignment Problem,
- we introduce measures for matching the dynamics and the beats of the music-track to the summary.

We include experimental evaluation to show that our approach is competitive to state-of-the-art summarization methods and generates audio-visual summaries that are tailored to the user provided music-tracks.

2 AUDIO-GUIDED SUMMARIZATION AS A QUADRATIC ASSIGNMENT PROBLEM

We see video summarization as classical assignment problem, where to each summary location $s \in S$, the most suitable frame $n \in N$ from the source-video is assigned. The suitability (or reward) of the assignment depends on three major factors:

- the interestingness of the frame;
- the match between the music in the summary and the visuals of the specific frame;
- the match with the previous frame in the summary, to model a story-line, segments, and cuts.

While frame-relevance yields a selection problem, and the music-video match can be modeled as a linear assignment problem, to model the cost for the subsequent frames we need to resort to quadratic assignment problems (QAP). Originally introduced for allocating facilities to certain locations in 1957 by Koopmans and Beckman [9], the QAP suits our model for music-guided video summarization. It enables to start from the summary, without the need of any pre-segmentation which would limit the flexibility to adjust to a specific music-track.

The QAP is a permutation problem, which aims to find the permutation $P \in \mathcal{P}$ with the highest reward:

$$f_{\text{QAP}}(P) = \text{tr}\left(\left(FPR^{\top} + B\right)P^{\top}\right), \tag{1}$$

Where, F denotes the flow matrix defined over the slots in the summary, and R defines a reward matrix between the frames in the source video, the last term B is a linear summary-source reward matrix, see Fig. 2 for an overview. Note that our permutation $P \in \mathcal{P}$ also encompasses a selection, since the summary contains less frames than the original source video. Therefore for any valid permutation P holds: $\sum_{j=1}^{N} p_{ij} = 1$ and $\sum_{i=1}^{S} p_{ij} = 1$.

Below, we introduce 6 summary components to model the three major factors of a good summarization, mentioned above. These components include, frame interestingness (I), Uniformity of storyline (U), Audio-Video Dynamics (AVD), Segment Length (SL), Motion Boundaries (MB), and Beat Cuts (BC). Each of these component is modeled as an assignment problem, and our final model is a weighted combination of these c components:

$$f_{\text{AVsummary}}(P) = \sum_{c} w^{c} f_{\text{QAP}}^{c}(P). \tag{2}$$

In general, solving a QAP, or its ϵ-approximate solution, is a NP-hard problem [17], in Section 2.4 we discuss our search strategy.

2.1 Frame interestingness

The first factor is the interestingness of each frame, for which we learn a frame-based interestingness classifier, using the human selected summaries as positive examples and the remaining frames as negative examples. For each frame we extract a set of M features, and compute the interestingness score for frame k based on unary

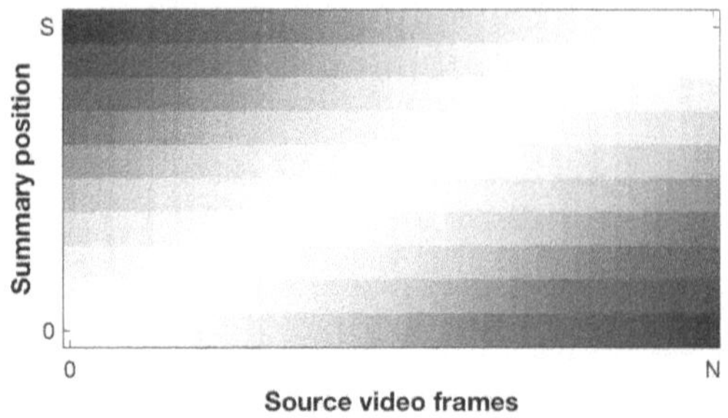

Figure 3: Illustration of the uniform reward B^{U}. Highest reward (white) obtained when following a uniform storyline.

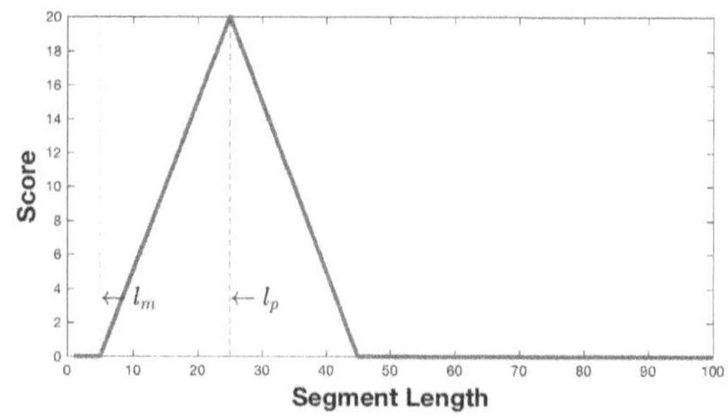

Figure 4: Illustration of *length prior*, given the segment length, the reward is based on l_m and l_p (5 and 25 in this fig).

and pairwise terms, following [5, 11] we use:

$$i^k = w_0 + \sum_{m=1}^{M} w_m\, x_m^k + \sum_{m=1}^{M} \sum_{n=m+1}^{M} w_{mn}\, x_m^k\, x_n^k, \tag{3}$$

where x_m^k denotes the score of the m-th feature of the k-th frame.

Maximizing the interestingness of a summary is in principle (just) a selection problem, to remain within the QAP formulation, we define the linear matrix B^{I} to have identical values for each location s, given a frame k, as follows:

$$B^{\mathrm{I}}_{sk} = i^k. \tag{4}$$

Uniform Storyline. Besides the frame interestingness factor, we also observe that the source videos tell a roughly temporal uniform coherent story. This was also observed in [6], and indicates that a priori a good summary samples frames uniformly from the source video. Such a uniform sampling reward can be modeled as the linear part of the QAP, measuring the distance between summary position s and its uniform sampled frame $\tilde{p}_s$ from the source video:

$$\tilde{p}_s = \tfrac{N}{S}\left(s - \tfrac{1}{2}\right), \tag{5}$$

$$B^{\mathrm{U}}(s,n) = 1 - \tfrac{1}{N^2}\left(\tilde{p}_s - n\right)^2, \tag{6}$$

where B^{U} is normalized between 1 (when $n = \tilde{p}_s$) and 0, illustrated in Fig. 3. This could be seen as a prior model to retain uniform temporal coherency of the source video.

2.2 Music-Video Match

The second factor is the match between the music-track in the summary and the visuals of the source video. In this paper we aim to let the summary follow the audio dynamics, and therefore that the music dynamics should be similar to visual dynamics. To determine the audio dynamics we compute the relative amplitude for each summary frame location: $\hat{a}^s = a^s - \frac{1}{S}\sum_{s'} a^{s'}$, where a^s is the amplitude at time s. For the video dynamics we compute the relative motion per frame: $\hat{f}^n = f^n - \frac{1}{N}\sum_{k'} f^{k'}$, where f^n indicates the motion in frame n, based on the computation of the optical flow. We use the following linear rewards:

$$B^{\mathrm{AVD}}(s,m) = 1 - \gamma\,|\hat{a}^s - \hat{f}^m|, \tag{7}$$

where γ is a constant normalizing all rewards between 0 and 1.

2.3 Subsequent Frames

The last factor is to model the relation between two subsequent frames in the summary. This is important given that our model does not use pre-segmentations of the video. Subsequent frames could either form a consecutive segment, or define a cut (jump). The final model should balance between the length of series of consecutive frames, the placing of the cuts based on the frame features and based on the alignment with the music-track, and to represent the story-line of the original video.

Segment length. First, we model the length of a segment, since too short segments results in many cuts and makes the summary chaotic, while too long segments make the summary boring. Therefore we include a score based on the segment length l:

$$s(l) = \max(0, l_p - |l - l_p| - l_m) \tag{8}$$

where l is the length of a segment, l_p the prior length, and l_m the minimum length, see Fig. 4 (top). In QAP formulation, this entails the following flow and reward matrices:

$$R^{\mathrm{SL}}(m,n) = \begin{cases} 2 \text{ if } n = m + l_p, & 2 \text{ if } m = n + l_p, \\ 1 \text{ if } n = m + 2l_p - l_m, & 1 \text{ if } m = n + 2l_p - l_m, \\ 1 \text{ if } n = m + l_m, \text{and} & 0 \text{ otherwise,} \end{cases} \tag{9}$$

$$F^{\mathrm{SL}}(s,t) = \delta(s = t + l_m) - \delta(s = t + l_p) + \delta(s = t + 2l_p - l_m) - \delta(s = t - l_m), \tag{10}$$

where the flow matrix F uses the Dirac delta function $\delta(\cdot)$, which returns 1 if and only if the condition is true. The complexity of these matrices originate to ensure that coincidental rewards are canceled, *e.g.* a jump of exactly l_p frames would normally add an additional reward for a good sequence, yet due to the jump this needs to be zeroed.

Motion boundaries. Besides the segment length, we also have an aesthetic view on cuts, namely, a cut should take place when there is a minimum of motion in the frames, see Fig. 5. This is included in the QAP, by using the following flow and reward matrices:

$$R^{\mathrm{MB}}(m,n) = \frac{-1}{2}\delta(m > n+1)\,(x_m^m + x_n^m), \tag{11}$$

$$F^{\mathrm{MB}}(s,t) = \delta(s = t+1), \tag{12}$$

where x^m denotes the estimated motion magnitude, based on the KLT tracker. The reward matrix uses negative rewards between

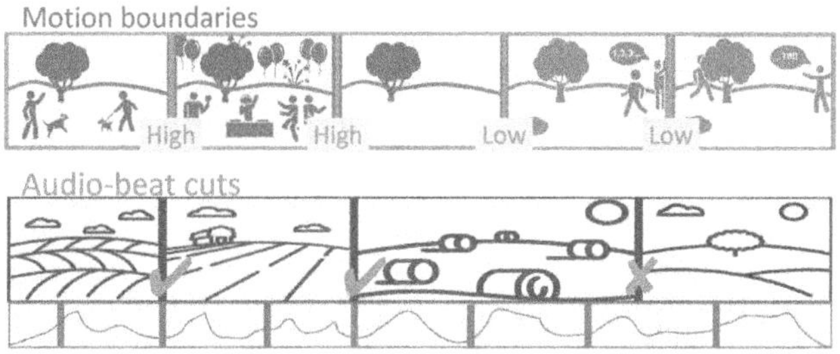

Figure 5: Illustration of *Motion boundaries* (top) and *Beat cuts* (bottom). Motion boundaries promote cuts between frames with low motion. Beat cuts promote cuts in the summary aligned with the music beat.

frames with high-motion. The flow matrix aggregates the motion magnitude scores for neighboring frames in the summary. This component is inspired by the pre-segmentation criterion used by [5].

Beat Cuts. A final consideration is the placement of cuts in the summary with respect to the music-track. We believe that cuts should be placed on the beat of the music, as illustrated in Fig. 5. Therefore we reward beat cuts with the following QAP:

$$R^{\text{BC}}(m, n) = \delta(m > n+1), \tag{13}$$

$$F^{\text{BC}}(s, t) = \delta(s = t+1)\ \delta(s \in \mathcal{B}), \tag{14}$$

where $\mathcal{B}$ denotes the set of summary slots matching a beat. The reward matrix returns a one, if and only if the frames in are not neighboring in the source video, and F aggregates these scores only when there is a beat.

2.4 Greedy search

The search space, for a summary of S frames, from a source video with N frames, is huge, even though we constraint the search space to a forward selection process only. Consider a 5 minute source video (N=9000) and a 30 seconds summary (S=900), for the first frame we can select (N-S) frames, the second frame is then selected from (N-f_1-S-1), *i.e.* pick any frame between the previous selected frame and the S-1 last frames, etc etc. This is in the order of $O(N!/(N-S)!)$, and yield zillions of possible permutations. As said before, for a general QAP (or its ϵ-approximate solution) there exist no efficiently optimal solution. Therefore we resort to a greedy search which selects one frame at the time.

Given a partial permutation P_g, consisting of the permutation of the first g summary frames, we add the next frame $p_{g+1} = t$. We select the best frame t, based on the current reward and an approximation of the (expected) future rewards. We approximate the future rewards of frame t, by evaluating Eq. (2) with the partial permutation when adding frames t, t+1, t+2, . . . consecutively to the summary, to the manifistation of the next 1 to 4 beats. This yields per frame t four scores, which we normalize for their different lengths, and we select the frame with the highest score. We call our approximation the *beat-look-ahead* score.

To further reduce the search we (1) require each segment to last at least one second, *i.e.* for a new segment the next 25 frames are also added, this is identical to adding a reward of $-\infty$ on segments shorter than $l_m = 25$; and (2) consider only frames in a small window around the previous selected frame, if $p_g = v$, then frame t is selected from $v + 1 \leq t \leq v + \frac{N}{5}$. This window size is based on preliminary experiments.

Figure 6: A frame from each of the 25 videos of SumMe [5].

3 EXPERIMENTS

In this section we experimentally validate our proposed methods. First, we describe the experimental setup. Then, we present *visual-only* summarization results to compare to recent work. Finally, we present the results of our music-guided video summarization.

3.1 Dataset and experimental setup

SumMe dataset [5]. For all experiments we use the recently introduced SumMe dataset, which contains 25 amateur-shot raw videos (40-400 seconds) covering holiday moments, events and sports. The videos are illustrated in Fig. 6. For each video, 15-18 human participants have been asked to create a video summary of 5-15% of the original length. The diversity of the videos and the availability of multiple annotations make the dataset perfectly suited for illustrating performance of our summarization methods.

Evaluation. To evaluate a video summarization we use the provided human summaries. First, we compute precision and recall of frames between a generated summary and a human summary, and use the F1-score to balance precision and recall. Gygli *et al.* [5, 6] observed that the human summaries are highly subjective, therefore we exclude the average F1 score and only report the highest F1 score between an automatically generated summary and any of the human summaries, we denote this as the **Best F1**. It rewards the generated summary if it matches closely to one of the human annotators, and allows to compare to other recent work [6, 22].

	Best F1	Recall	Precision
Random	16.8	17.5	16.6
Uniform	27.1	29.4	25.1
Gygli et. al. [5]	39.3	44.4	35.3
Gygli et. al. [6]	39.7	43.0	36.8
Single Frames*	34.7	38.4	33.5
Super Frames* [5]	36.4	40.4	34.2
QAP Model*	38.3	42.4	36.6

Table 1: Comparison to state-of-the-art. Methods indicated with * use the same features. Our QAP model allows to directly use frame-based interestingness prediction, without resorting to pre-segmentation methods

Interestingness Features. For the interestingness prediction, we use a subset of the features used in [5]. This is a collection of features modeling *attention*, using spatial and temporal salience [3, 7]; and modelling *aesthetics*, based on colourfulness, contrast, and distribution of edges [1, 8]. The other features used in [5], *a.o.* landmark detection and person detection, were not reproducible, and therefore not used in our experiments.

We extend this collection of features, with a high-level frame description based on ImageNet objects [2]. In order to do so, we extract per frame the penultimate layer of the deep network, provided by [16]. This is a 1024 dimensional feature, which we reduce to 64 dimensions using PCA, so that we can learn both the unary and pairwise terms in the interestingness prediction.

We learn the parameters w of Eq. (3), by random sampling 100 frames from each video in the dataset and train a predictor. The final model is an average over 50 repetitions of this training.

3.2 Visual-only Summaries

In this set of experiments we evaluate the performance of our proposed models and compare them to the current state-of-the-art.

Tuning summarization components. In a set of preliminary results, we tune the weights, used in Eq. (2), of each component. Starting with an equal weighting ($\forall c: w_c = 1$), we tune the components one by one. For each component, we use leave-one-out performance to vote for a specific parameter value, and the value with the highest number of votes is selected. Since parameters interact, repeating this search could result in different weight values. The obtained weights are: I = 1, MB = 2, SL = 1, and U = $\frac{1}{2}$.

Experimental results. The goal of this experiment is to see whether the QAP model is able to generate high quality summarizations without the need for pre-segmentation methods. We compare our QAP model with current state-of-the-art methods on this dataset and we add a model based on *Single Frame* interestingness predictions and on the *Super Frames* pre-segmentation used in [5]. The latter methods use exactly the same raw interestingness predictions, which makes them comparable.

The results are presented in Table 1. We observe that any of the computational methods outperform random or uniform segmentation. Furthermore we observe that our implementation of [5]

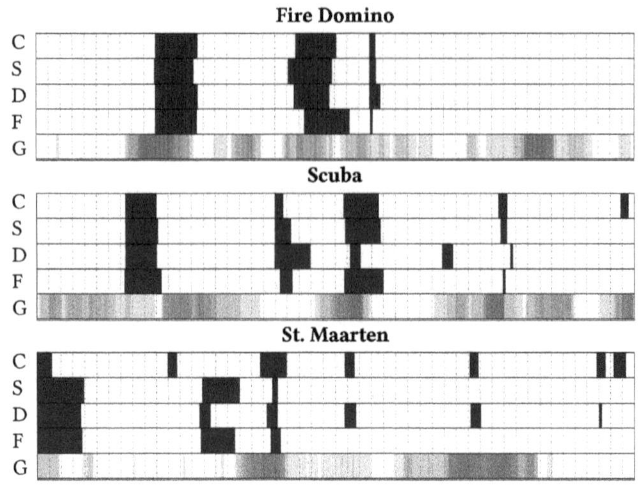

Figure 7: Illustration of summaries guided by different music styles. Selected frames are indicated in blue, the (average) human summary in red. Clearly our model combines frame interestingness with music properties (energy / beats), resulting in different summaries for different songs.

(denoted as Super Frames) scores about 3% worse compared to the published results, this is due to differences in the used features. Finally, when looking at models using the same features, we observe that adding structure to the single frame interestingness predictions is beneficial, given that super frames outperform single frames, and our QAP model outperforms both.

In Table 2, we show per video performance of our different models, *Single*, *Super Frames*, and *QAP*. We observe that in general, the performance of the QAP model is superior. However, we can see some outliers: the single model performs exceptionally well on the video "Playing ball" (75.8% vs 36.0% for QAP), the super frames on the video "Eiffel tower" (47.9% vs 30.6% for QAP), and the QAP model for the "Jumps" video (93.8% vs 41.0/35.7% for single/super frames). These large differences indicate that the relative importance of specific model components vary for some of these videos.

3.3 Music-Guided Summaries

In this set of experiments we validate our model for creating summaries guided by an externally provided soundtrack, we coin our method **QAP-AV**. For illustrating the influence of different styles, we use four songs of different genres: classical, swing, funk and downtempo. In the provided *supplementary material*, we show a composition of several summaries fitted on these music-tracks.

Weighing audio-visual summarization components. To determine the weights of the different components we resort to the same heuristic grid search as used for the visual-only method. We start from an equal weighting ($\forall c: w_c = 1$) of all components, and tune all weights based on the *swing* music-track, using leave-one-out voting based on the **Best F1** score. The obtained weights are: I = 5, MB = 2, SL = 5, U = 1, AVD= 5 and BC= 1.

Results. In Table 2, we show the results of the **QAP-AV** method evaluated for the four different music-tracks for each video. For comparison we have also included the visual-only QAP models.

		Visual only			**Music - Guided**				
		Single Frames	Super Frames [5]	QAP	Funk	Downtempo	Swing	Classical	*Best Song*
ego.	Base jumping	21.7	32.7	21.6	**31.0**	28.9	29.3	29.0	***31.0***
	Bike polo	37.5	39.2	39.0	**47.9**	47.7	45.7	46.3	***47.9***
	Scuba	39.3	56.5	37.2	**57.0**	44.4	55.7	56.7	***57.0***
	Valparaiso downhill	26.3	29.8	26.9	39.7	**43.1**	36.1	33.3	***43.1***
moving	Bearpark climbing	27.6	29.3	24.3	**33.0**	26.9	22.3	28.4	***33.0***
	Bus in rock tunnel	39.5	**46.1**	34.9	37.8	43.3	39.4	42.5	*43.3*
	Car rail crossing	**39.3**	30.6	31.0	22.0	23.4	20.0	23.8	*23.8*
	Cockpit landing	38.8	39.9	52.0	53.5	56.0	56.4	**56.8**	***56.8***
	Cooking	20.9	22.3	30.2	27.7	27.2	**36.6**	25.6	***36.6***
	Eiffel tower	42.3	**47.9**	30.6	42.1	40.8	42.4	43.9	*43.9*
	Excavators river crossing	22.6	23.3	**33.5**	29.0	28.9	28.9	28.8	*29.0*
	Jumps	41.0	35.7	**93.8**	70.8	71.5	71.5	72.9	*72.9*
	Kids playing in leaves	38.2	39.3	28.4	47.3	**50.3**	**50.3**	48.4	***50.3***
	Playing on water slide	44.0	44.0	35.3	24.2	48.3	**50.1**	**50.1**	***50.1***
	Saving dolphins	21.3	29.3	**46.9**	23.6	25.2	27.5	29.8	*29.8*
	St. Maarten Landing	37.9	26.7	39.6	28.1	**44.6**	26.2	42.3	***44.6***
	Statue of Liberty	22.7	**26.0**	24.4	25.0	22.2	22.6	16.7	*25.0*
	Uncut evening flight	19.3	20.4	**36.8**	33.3	33.8	34.6	33.3	*34.6*
	Paluma jump	25.0	21.9	**50.6**	36.3	35.8	37.6	30.5	*37.6*
	Playing ball	**75.8**	72.0	36.0	56.2	66.2	65.4	67.5	*67.5*
	Notre Dame	**28.6**	28.2	21.8	23.6	22.1	22.4	22.9	*23.6*
static	Air Force One	32.1	**36.2**	27.3	35.0	26.4	24.3	24.4	*35.0*
	Fire domino	40.8	44.2	49.7	62.2	67.2	69.7	**71.0**	***71.0***
	Car over camera	44.6	48.7	65.8	66.3	68.1	67.3	**70.6**	***70.6***
	Paintball	36.2	40.1	39.3	**48.9**	40.5	42.7	41.6	***48.9***
	Mean Best-F1	34.7	36.4	38.3	40.1	41.3	41.0	**41.5**	***44.3***
	Segment statistics								
	Avg. # of cuts	154.4	5.1	8.6	5.9	6.5	6.5	6.8	–
	On-beat cuts (%)	–	–	± 5*	89.8	94.4	99.4	95.9	–

Table 2: Per video results on the SumMe dataset using the Best F1 measure, comparing *visual-only* to *audio-guided* methods on 4 different audio-tracks. (*) Average on-beat cuts over all songs (for QAP). Surprisingly the audio-guided methods outperform the visual-only methods by up to 6% absolute performance when an oracle could provide the most suited audio-track per video.

First, we observe that our music-guided methods, surprisingly, obtain better results than any of visual-only methods, even better than the state-of-the-art summarization method of [6] (39.7%, see Table 1). Our results are also better than the recent work of [22], where 38.6% is reported using slightly different evaluation settings and on par with their method that uses extensive additional labeled data to train interestingness and hyper-parameters (41.8%). Further, the relatively stable average **Best F1** for the different music-tracks, indicate that the weighting of the components is not music-track specific per se. Still the large variation in performance between different models for a specific video, indicate that the relative importance of model components vary. Finally, when we compare statistics about the cuts in the video summary, it is apparent that the no-music QAP model generates more cuts, and have hardly any aligned with the audio (averaged over all songs), while the music guided model has almost all cuts aligned with music. In conclusion, the music guidance (in audio-visual match and beat cuts), enables to generate higher quality video summarizations.

In Fig. 7 we show the selection of frames for the QAP-AV model for different soundtracks for three different videos, and as reference show the average human summary selection. Video examples are included in the supplementary material.

4 CONCLUSION

In this paper we have introduced a model for music-guided video summarization, which we have modeled as a quadratic assignment problem (QAP). The QAP formulation allows to dynamically create video segments, match the music-dynamics, have boundaries with low motion, and with cuts (mostly) on the beat of a provided music-track. Experimentally we have validated our approach on the SumMe dataset, showing that our QAP model is on par with current state-of-the-art video summarization and that our music-guided models even outperform these. Probably the provided music track acts as an efficient regularizer for selecting more consistent segments. In conclusion our QAP model yields high quality summaries (in terms of F1), which are also more appealing to watch.

For future work, we aim to extend our method to exploit the audio track of the source video as input modality, to allow for repetitions (*e.g.* for the chorus of a song), and to include basic video effects (panning, crop, zoom, speed-up and slow-motion), the challenge is that these extensions require long temporal dependencies.

ACKNOWLEDGMENTS

This research is supported in part by the NWO VENI What&Where project and the STW STORY project.

REFERENCES

[1] R. Datta, D. Joshi, J. Li, and J. Wang. 2006. Studying Aesthetics in Photographic Images Using a Computational Approach. In *ECCV*.

[2] J. Deng, W. Dong, R. Socher, L.-J. Li, K. Li, and L. Fei-Fei. 2009. ImageNet: A Large-Scale Hierarchical Image Database. In *CVPR*.

[3] N. Ejaz, I. Mehmood, and S. W. Baik. 2013. Efficient visual attention based framework for extracting key frames from videos. *Signal Processing: Image Communication* 28, 1 (2013), 34–44.

[4] G. Evangelopoulos, A. Zlatintsi, A. Potamianos, P. Maragos, K. Rapantzikos, G. Skoumas, and Y. Avrithis. 2013. Multimodal Saliency and Fusion for Movie Summarization Based on Aural, Visual, and Textual Attention. *IEEE Trans. Multimedia* 15, 7 (2013), 1553–1568.

[5] M. Gygli, H. Grabner, H. Riemenschneider, and L. Van Gool. 2014. Creating summaries from user videos. In *ECCV*.

[6] M. Gygli, H. Grabner, and L. Van Gool. 2015. Video summarization by learning submodular mixtures of objectives. In *CVPR*.

[7] X. Hou, J. Harel, and C. Koch. 2012. Image signature: Highlighting sparse salient regions. *IEEE Trans. PAMI* 34, 1 (2012), 194–201.

[8] Y. Ke, X. Tang, and F. Jing. 2006. The Design of High-Level Features for Photo Quality Assessment. In *CVPR*.

[9] T. Koopmans and M. Beckmann. 1957. Assignment problems and the location of economic activities. *Econometrica* (1957), 53–76.

[10] P. Koutras, A. Zlatintsi, E. Iosif, A. Katsamanis, P. Maragos, and A. Potamianos. 2015. Predicting audio-visual salient events based on visual, audio and text modalities for movie summarization. In *ICIP*.

[11] Y. Lee, J. Ghosh, and K. Grauman. 2012. Discovering important people and objects for egocentric video summarization. In *CVPR*.

[12] Y. Li and B. Mérialdo. 2012. Video Summarization Based on Balanced AV-MMR. In *MMM*.

[13] F. Liu, Y. Niu, and M. Gleicher. 2009. Using Web Photos for Measuring Video Frame Interestingness.. In *IJCAI*.

[14] Z. Lu and K. Grauman. 2013. Story-driven summarization for egocentric video. In *CVPR*. 2714–2721.

[15] Y.-F. Ma, L. Lu, H.-J. Zhang, and M. Li. 2002. A user attention model for video summarization. In *ACM Multimedia*.

[16] P. Mettes, D. Koelma, and C. Snoek. 2016. The ImageNet Shuffle: Reorganized Pre-training for Video Event Detection. In *ICMR*.

[17] S. Sahni and T. Gonzalez. 1976. P-complete approximation problems. *J. ACM* 23, 3 (1976), 555–565.

[18] M. Smith and T. Kanade. 1998. Video skimming and characterization through the combination of image and language understanding. In *Workshop on Content-Based Access of Image and Video Database*.

[19] B. Truong and S. Venkatesh. 2007. Video abstraction: A systematic review and classification. *ACM TOMCAPP* (2007).

[20] J. Xu, L. Mukherjee, Y. Li, J. Warner, J. Rehg, and V. Singh. 2015. Gaze-enabled egocentric video summarization via constrained submodular maximization. In *CVPR*.

[21] J. You, U. Reiter, M Hannuksela, M. Gabbouj, and A. Perkis. 2010. Perceptual-based quality assessment for audio-visual services: A survey. *Signal Processing: Image Communication* 25, 7 (2010), 482–501.

[22] K. Zhang, W.-L Chao, F. Sha, and K. Grauman. 2016. Video Summarization with Long Short-Term Memory. In *ECCV*.

Insiders and Outsiders: Comparing Urban Impressions between Population Groups

Darshan Santani
Idiap Research Institute and EPFL
Switzerland
dsantani@idiap.ch

Salvador Ruiz-Correa
IPICYT
Mexico
salvador.ruiz@ipicyt.edu.mx

Daniel Gatica-Perez
Idiap Research Institute and EPFL
Switzerland
gatica@idiap.ch

ABSTRACT

There is a growing interest in social and urban computing to employ crowdsourcing as means to gather impressions of urban perception for indoor and outdoor environments. Previous studies have established that reliable estimates of urban perception can be obtained using online crowdsourcing systems, but implicitly assumed that the judgments provided by the crowd are not dependent on the background knowledge of the observer. In this paper, we investigate how the impressions of outdoor urban spaces judged by online crowd annotators, compare with the impressions elicited by the local inhabitants, along six physical and psychological labels. We focus our study in a developing city where understanding and characterization of these socio-urban perceptions is of societal importance. We found statistically significant differences between the two population groups. Locals perceived places to be more *dangerous* and *dirty*, when compared with online crowd workers; while online annotators judged places to be more *interesting* in comparison to locals. Our results highlight the importance of the degree of familiarity with urban spaces and background knowledge while rating urban perceptions, which is lacking in some of the existing work in urban computing.

CCS CONCEPTS

• **Information systems → Crowdsourcing**;

KEYWORDS

Urban Perception; Crowdsourcing; Mobile; Youth; Subjective Properties

ACM Reference format:
Darshan Santani, Salvador Ruiz-Correa, and Daniel Gatica-Perez. 2017. Insiders and Outsiders: Comparing Urban Impressions between Population Groups. In *Proceedings of ICMR '17, Bucharest, Romania, June 06–09, 2017 (ICMR'17)*, 7 pages.
DOI: http://dx.doi.org/10.1145/3078971.3079022

ICMR'17, June 06–09, 2017, Bucharest, Romania

ACM ISBN 978-1-4503-4701-3/17/06...$15.00
DOI: http://dx.doi.org/10.1145/3078971.3079022

1 INTRODUCTION

Online crowdsourcing platforms are regularly being used to conduct behavioral studies in computer and social science. In the context of urban computing, recent research has established the feasibility of obtaining impressions of urban scenes for both indoor and outdoor environments using crowdsourcing [6, 7, 9, 11, 13, 16]. In [9], the authors conducted a study to measure the perception of outdoor urban scenes on safety, class and uniqueness, based on images in four cities – two each in the US and Austria. In a similar study on urban perception, judgments from over 3,000 individuals were collected to examine visual cues that could correlate outdoor places in London with three dimensions (beauty, quietness, and happyness) [6]. A recent work [16] explored the connections between visual attributes of the built environment and safety perception and found that familiarity with the environment is associated with the perception of safety.

In addition to using online crowdsourcing platforms, there are numerous studies in the domain of urban planning which have used qualitative methods including questionnaires and interviews to quantify urban perception. In this domain, researchers have examined the relationship between the visual characteristics of the built environment and perceptual attributes [3, 5, 10], including the effect of time on urban perception [2, 4]. In contrast with these works, our current work focuses on the observer attributes i.e., who is observing as opposed to what the observer sees. In this paper, we investigate how the impressions of outdoor urban spaces judged by online crowd annotators, compares with the impressions elicited by the local inhabitants, along six physical and psychological labels. In other words, we empirically test the observer differences from the point of view of urban perception of six subjective attributes of outdoor environment. Our current study is closely related and builds upon our earlier research, where we presented a mobile crowdsourcing methodology to collect perceptions of urban awareness labels (dangerous, dirty, preserved, etc.) by local inhabitants of Guanajuato city in Mexico [7].

Most of the existing studies on urban visual perception have focused on collecting impressions by "external" observers, however an issue which remains open in the literature is whether these perceptions match with the perceptions of locals who live there. By locals, we refer to citizens familiar with the outdoor places, streets and terrain under study; by context, we explicitly mean the knowledge people possess by being a "local". In this study, our objective is to compare the perceived impressions of outdoor urban scenes between

(a) (b) (c) (d)

Figure 1: Sample images from the manually collected image corpus.

two population groups: local inhabitants and non-local online crowd workers. We investigate whether the background knowledge of the observers has an impact on the generated impressions, i.e., between city inhabitants who have a context of the places and the characteristics of the built environment, and external observers who might not.

To capture the perceptions of urban spaces, we rely on a method where images are used to form impressions. We gather images which describe urban scenes and city's built environment in their natural setting, e.g., images showing different neighborhoods, alleys and streets, touristic and historical sites. In most of the recent studies, urban perceptions were elicited using images obtained from Google Street View (GSV) [6, 9]. Even though GSV provides a scalable and automated way to collect images, it suffers from two limitations. First, the image database of GSV is not exhaustive in spatial coverage, which is particularly evident in developing countries. In our earlier work, we found that 58% of our images were either unavailable or erroneous in the GSV database for Guanajuato city [7]. Second, due to the way Google collects the street views (via cameras mounted on top of a vehicle), GSV does not always contains images of narrow streets and winding alleys, which is often the case in this city. Consequently, we rely on a set of manually collected images in our study. We acknowledge that our current image collection methodology is not scalable, but we plan to investigate alternate means to obtain representative and diverse images in a scalable manner, as part of future work.

Our contributions are two-fold. First, we designed and conducted a crowdsourcing study to gather impressions of local residents and non-local online crowd-workers along six physical and psychological labels (*dangerous*, *dirty*, *interesting*, etc.), based on images of outdoor places (Section 3). Second, we performed statistical analysis to compare the perceptual impressions of online crowd workers and local residents (Section 4). We found statistically significant differences between the population groups. As key findings, locals perceived places to be more *dangerous* and *dirty*, when compared with online annotators; while online annotators judged places to be more *interesting* in comparison to locals. As a potential application, we could imagine embedding our findings into existing online photo-sharing platforms (such as Flickr or Instagram), to enhance the view of a place by integrating "insiders" knowledge for "outsiders", who otherwise might not have access to these kinds of resources e.g., an American tourist planning for a Mexican holiday.

In summary, our current work attempts to empirically test the observer differences from the point of view of urban perception of subjective attributes. Our work highlights the importance of context, background knowledge, and prior beliefs in urban perception studies.

2 IMAGE CORPUS

We ground our analysis on an image corpus collected as part of our previous study [7]. The image corpus was collected in Guanajuato, a mid-size Mexican city with a population of around 170,000 people. One of the paper's authors and about 10 volunteers, who were also residents of Guanajuato, visited different parts of the city and captured images of outdoor urban sites using their mobile phones. City areas covered included different neighborhoods, historical city alleys and streets, central plaza, and touristic and historical sites. Most of the images were collected during early mornings and weekends. Volunteers were asked to capture images of urban scenes in their natural setting and not necessarily capture beautified images or apply some form of digital filters, as usually the case with images found on social media platforms, like Flickr or Instagram. As a result of this data collection, we obtained a set of 99 images which we analyze in this study. Figure 1 shows a sample of images from the corpus. All the images were geo-tagged. A map showing the spatial coverage of the images is shown in our previous study [7]. We refer the readers to [8, 13] for a detailed description of the mobile crowdsourcing methodology deployed to gather images.

3 METHODS

3.1 Selection of Labels

In order to select labels to characterize urban awareness for outdoor environments, we base our methodology on our earlier work [7], where we proposed a rating instrument consisting of six labels to characterize urban awareness, which are: *accessible*, *dangerous*, *dirty*, *interesting*, *preserved*, and *pretty* (see Table 1). Throughout the paper, we will use the term "urban awareness" to refer to these labels. For both the population groups, images served as stimuli to rate perceptions for the selected six urban awareness labels, along a seven-point Likert scale ranging from *strongly disagree* (1) to *strongly agree* (7).

We have chosen this list of labels for two reasons. First, these labels encompass the physical and psychological constructs evoked while describing the characteristics of the studied build environment. Second, Guanajuato is a historical city and a UNESCO world heritage site, with a vibrant tourism industry but it also faces various socio-urban and civic problems including crime, street gangs, prevalence of alcoholism and drugs in streets and alleys, dirty streets with garbage and non-artistic graffiti and murals. In addition to affecting the prosperity and safety of citizens, these issues also hurt the city's image as a tourist destination. As a result, it is essential to study and understand the role these perceptions play in Guanajuato city.

3.2 Crowdsourcing Impressions

MTurkers: To gather impressions of online annotators, we designed a crowdsourcing study online on Amazon's Mechanical Turk (AMT). We chose US-based "Master" annotators with at least 95% approval rate for historical HITs (Human Intelligence Tasks). In each HIT, workers were asked to view an image of an urban space, and then rate their perceptual impression based on what they saw, for six labels. Additionally, annotators were given the option to describe how the urban space made them feel (as free-form text). Workers were not given any information of the studied city, to reduce potential bias and stereotyping associated to the city identity. We collected 10 annotations for each image, resulting in a total of 990 responses. Every worker was reimbursed 0.10 USD per impression.

Locals: In addition to obtaining the image corpus, we also obtained the associated "local" annotations of the same corpus from our previous work [7]. Images were annotated by a separate group of volunteers, which was different from the one which collected the data. To collect the impressions, a website was designed to allow volunteers to submit their annotations. Unlike the AMT study, each image was annotated more than 10 times, but to enable a fair comparison across the population groups, we randomly sampled 10 impressions per image. As a result, we collected a total of 990 responses for 99 images. No financial incentives were provided to the volunteers for their participation. Volunteers were intrinsically motivated to contribute towards the study. Note that local annotators knew that the images being annotated, were taken in Guanajuato.

All the local annotators are high-school students aged 16–18 years old. 95% of them are born in Guanajuato city; while those who were not born in Guanajuato, have lived in Guanajuato for at least 8 years. 85% of the annotators currently live either in Guanajuato city or suburban areas close to the city (within aprrox. 6KM).

Labels	Locals		MTurkers	
	Mean±SD	ICC	Mean±SD	ICC
Accessible	4.16±1.16	0.69	4.13±1.29	0.81
Dangerous	4.43±0.91	0.63	3.19±1.20	0.83
Dirty	4.33±1.24	0.68	3.25±1.26	0.85
Interesting	3.55±1.23	0.70	4.14±1.10	0.63
Preserved	3.54±1.28	0.76	3.63±1.30	0.78
Pretty	3.47±1.38	0.80	3.25±1.36	0.83

Table 1: Means, standard deviations and $ICC(1, k)$ of annotation scores for each label and group.

4 RESULTS

4.1 Annotations Quality

We begin our analysis by assessing the reliability of annotations given by locals and MTurkers. We measure the inter-rater consensus by computing intraclass correlation (ICC) among ratings given by the worker pool. Our annotation procedure requires every place to be judged by k annotators randomly selected from a larger population of K workers. $ICC(1, 1)$ and $ICC(1, k)$ values, which respectively stand for single and average ICC measures [14], are computed for each label across all images.

Table 1 reports the $ICC(1, k)$ values for both groups (due to space constraints, we omit $ICC(1, 1)$ values.) We observe acceptable inter-rater consensus for most labels, with all values being statistically significant at p-value < 0.01. We notice that the inter-rater reliability for all labels is reasonably high (above 0.6) for both the groups. From Table 1, we find that label *pretty* (resp. *dirty*) achieved high agreement for locals (resp. MTurkers). Further, we find that for all labels (except *interesting*), the consensus between MTurkers is higher relative to locals. In other words, locals tend to disagree more for most of the urban awareness labels, when compared to online annotators.

4.2 Descriptive Statistics

As noted in Section 3.2, for each label and image, we collected 10 impressions. So, it becomes relevant to create a composite score for each image, given a label. To gather the individual ratings, we used an ordinal scale, which implicitly describes a ranking. It is known that the central tendency of an ordinal variable is better expressed as median [15]. Thus, we computed the median score for each label given the 10 responses per image. Given the median scores, we then computed the mean scores and standard deviations for each label using all 99 images for both groups.

Table 1 lists the descriptive statistics for each population group and label. At the level of individual annotations, minimum and maximum values are 1 and 7 respectively for each label and population group, indicating that the full scale was used by locals and MTurkers alike. The mean scores for majority of labels is below 4, which indicates a trend towards disagreement with the corresponding label. Recall that annotators were asked to label images along a seven-point Likert

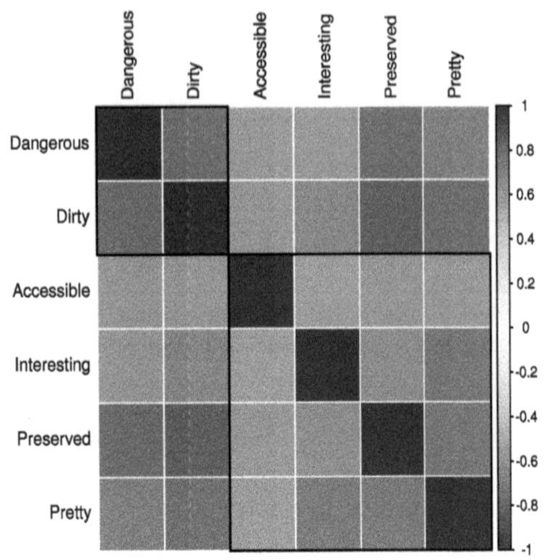

Figure 2: Plot showing the correlation matrix between all labels for MTurkers. Black rectangular borders indicate the two distinct clusters found in the correlation matrix. All cells are statistically significant at $p < 0.05$.

scale ranging from *strongly disagree* (1) to *strongly agree* (7). Based on the overall mean scores, locals annotators perceived images to be more *dangerous* and *dirty*, while MTurkers perceived them to be more *interesting*. A statistical analysis of these observed differences are presented later in Section 4.3.

It is natural to examine the relationship between the perceptual ratings and official government statistics, as in previous studies [9]. But, as is the case with most developing cities, due to a lack of publicly available data, a statistical analysis between these two sources, e.g. dangerous label ratings and crime rates of Guanajuato neighborhoods, was not feasible.

Correlation Analysis: To understand the statistical relationship between labels, we perform correlation analysis between all labels, for both the population groups. For both groups, we find that *accessible*, *interesting*, *preserved* and *pretty* labels are positively correlated, with pairwise correlations exceeding 0.7 (bottom-right rectangular box in Figure 2); furthermore *dangerous* and *dirty* labels are also positively correlated, with pairwise correlations exceeding 0.65 (top-left rectangular box in Figure 2). Figure 2 shows the correlation matrix between urban awareness labels for MTurkers. Similar matrix is obtained for locals, but we are not showing it due to space constraints. These findings corroborate earlier findings reported in the literature [13].

It is interesting to observe the correlation between the *dirty* and *dangerous* labels. Clearly, no causal relation can be inferred from here. Historically, some literature in urban sociology (now under much criticism) has postulated that the presence of physical disorder (garbage, grafitti, etc.) in urban environments might lead to social disorder (crime, fear) [18].

4.3 Comparing Impressions

Now we turn our attention towards comparing impressions between locals and MTurkers. From Table 1, we observe that mean values of perceptual ratings for all labels differ across both groups. To understand whether mean differences between groups for some of these labels are statistically significant, we perform the Tukey's honest significant difference (HSD) test. Tukey's HSD test is a statistical procedure to examine whether mean values are significantly different across groups [17]. We perform the Tukey HSD test to compute the pairwise comparisons of mean values between population groups for each label. Table 2 present the results. To complement Tukey's HSD statistics, we also show the plot comparing the distributions of perception ratings across both the population groups in Figure 3. Based on these statistics, we observe that:

(1) Images were perceived to be significantly more *dangerous* and *dirty* by locals when compared to MTurkers. When looking at the individual ratings, we found that 87% (resp. 81%) of images were rated by locals as more *dangerous* (resp. *dirty*) in comparison to MTurkers (Fig 3b and 3c).
(2) Images were perceived to be significantly more *interesting* by MTurkers than locals, a contrasting trend relative to the previous observation. 57% of images were rated on a higher *interesting* scale by MTurkers than locals, when looking at the individual ratings (Figure 3a).
(3) For the rest of the labels, the range of perceptions elicited are not statistically different between locals and MTurkers. Both groups found images to be equally *accessible*, *preserved* and *pretty*.

Discussion: The results presented above point towards a clear difference between groups across three dimensions. We believe that locals are using familiarity with the place, background information and prior beliefs, while judging places on being *dangerous* and *dirty*. Recall that locals knew that images were taken in Guanajuato city (Section 3.2). On the other hand, external observers viz. MTurkers form their impressions based on visual cues present in an image. For online annotations, we have used US-based MTurkers, so it is probable that they might not have seen these kinds of urban scenes or terrain in the past. This behavior is particularly evident in the way MTurkers judged places to be on a higher *interesting* scale compared to locals.

To further examine this behavior, we analyzed some of the comments made by MTurkers. Remarks such as "I want to wander through the street" and "This space gives me a sense of wonder, I feel as if i need to explore whats around the corner" were made on images which were rated significantly high on being *dangerous* by locals, but low by MTurkers. Additionally, comments like "This space makes me feel warm because of the brick and the ambiance" and "A picturesque backdrop to step into ancient history!" were given on images which were rated significantly high on being *interesting* by MTurkers, and vice-versa for locals. These comments further highlight the crucial role of background knowledge and beliefs in forming urban perceptions.

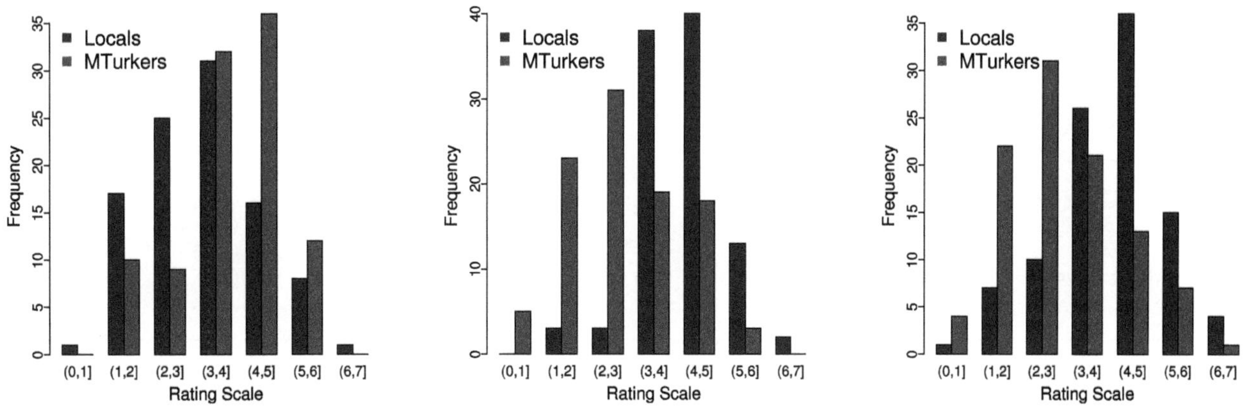

(a) Interesting (b) Dangerous (c) Dirty

Figure 3: Plots comparing the distributions of perception ratings for a) Interesting, b) Dangerous, and c) Dirty, for both locals and MTurkers.

Label	Group Pair	Mean Difference	p–value
Accessible	LO–MT	+0.03	0.89
Dangerous	LO–MT	+1.24	**0.00**
Dirty	LO–MT	+1.08	**0.00**
Interesting	LO–MT	−0.59	**5×10^{-3}**
Preserved	LO–MT	−0.09	0.62
Pretty	LO–MT	+0.22	0.24

Table 2: Tukey's HSD statistics. LO and MT respectively stands for locals and MTurkers. Values in bold are statistically significant at $p < 0.01$

4.4 Pair-wise Analysis

In the previous section, we have established that perceptual ratings differ between groups. Now in order to understand the variability of ratings for individual images, we examined the pair-wise ratings of each image between groups. We focus our pair-wise analysis on the statistically significant labels. Figure 4 shows the respective plots. If the perception ratings were similar between groups, most of the points would have fallen on the 45° line. On the contrary, we observe that a significant majority of points lie below the line for *dangerous* and *dirty* (Figure 4b and 4c), indicating that locals perceive these labels on a higher scale compared to MTurkers. Reverse trend is observed for *interesting* label (Figure 4a). These plots further validate our findings reported in Section 4.3.

Qualitative Analysis: In Figure 4, we observe that some of the images differ in ratings significantly. For some of the images, the perceptions between groups differ by more than three ordinal scales. Figure 5 shows two such images. One of the authors of our study is a local resident of Guanajuato, and we asked him to provide possible explanations to interpret some of these disparities.

Figure 5a (marked as I-1 in Figure 4a) depicts an image which was rated 2 (resp. 5.5) by locals (resp. MTurkers) on the *interesting* scale. The image shows a view taken from south to north. If one sees in the opposite direction, the street connects to the busiest street in Guanajuato, which is possibly the reason why local people have judged it as not very interesting; while, MTurkers found the view quite interesting as it conveys a picturesque town or as one of the MTurkers remarked: "This space makes me feel serene." The second image (Figure 5b) shows a street that is very close to a dangerous part of the city. It is not surprising that locals have rated it as 5 on the *dangerous* scale, while MTurkers only 2, as one would by just looking at the image. To the naked eye, the image does not look unsafe at all, which was corroborated by one of the MTurkers: "This area looks moderately well-off, though by no means wealthy; I feel that this area is relatively safe."

Further, it is interesting to observe the disparity in ratings for the *dirty* label. As shown in Figure 4c, for some of the images the difference in ratings between locals and MTurkers is high (by two or more ordinal scales). As with other labels, we want to examine the possible causes for the difference in ratings. We manually browsed few images, which are rated low by MTurkers and high by locals, and found those images to be relatively *clean* to our naked eyes. We show one such image in Figure 1c, which was rated 5 (resp. 2) by locals (resp. MTurkers) on the *dirty* scale. For this particular image, one of the MTurkers commented: "This space makes me feel relaxed, like I'm taking a stroll through a quaint European city on my way to brunch or lunch.", which corroborates with the ratings given by MTurkers. A plausible hypothesis to support this finding might be the expectations of locals (i.e., high-school students in our study) to be sensitive about the *dirty* issue. Being a youth resident, one has high expectations for his neighbourhood or the city to be clean and thus would rate the images of his city *dirty* on a higher scale, with the expectation that the urban spaces should be more cleaner than their status quo. On the contrary, one might also argue that since locals are used to seeing the place as is (i.e. being dirty or clean), there is no obvious reason to explain why they would rate images as more *dirtier* than external observers. We plan to investigate this issue in more depth, as part of future work.

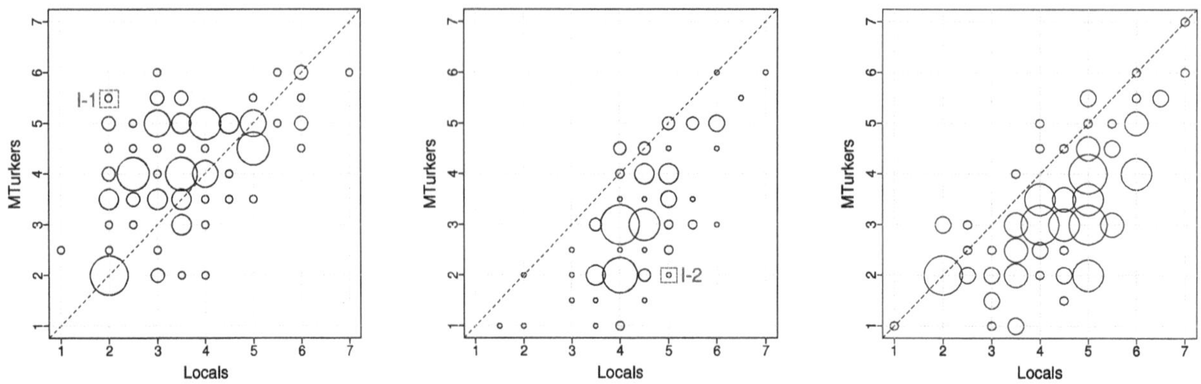

(a) Interesting (b) Dangerous (c) Dirty

Figure 4: Scatter plots showing the pair-wise annotator ratings by Locals and MTurkers for a) Interesting, b) Dangerous, and c) Dirty. Each dot corresponds to an image, with the size of the dots proportional to the number of images at a given rating pair. 45° line is also shown in all the plots. Two dots highlighted in the plots as I-1 and I-2 are enlarged in Figure 5a and 5b respectively.

5 LIMITATIONS AND FUTURE WORK

In this section, we address the three limitations of our work and outline potential future directions. As a first limitation, while comparing the observer differences, we did not control for observers' demographics attributes e.g., gender, age, ethnicity, education status, or familiarity with living or experiencing urban environments in developing countries. We will examine the effect of demographics differences on the perceptual ratings as part of future work. Moreover, we also plan to conduct an additional crowdsourcing study to explore the differences between youth populations of Mexico and other developed countries e.g., Switzerland. Second, in this paper we have examined the observer differences using 99 images. We plan to extend our analysis to include more images and annotations as well as extending the study to multiple cities. Third, due to the subjective nature of the labels, it is difficult to contextualize some of the findings reported in the paper. For some of the studied labels (e.g., *interesting*, *preserved*, *pretty*), there exist no ground truth or "gold standard". In order to contextualize some of the findings or evaluate the applications of the perception work, an interesting future analysis will be to gather impressions by domain experts (e.g., designers, architects, city planners), who are responsible for designing these urban spaces. This would facilitate creation of a "gold standard" for visual perception research of urban places.

In addition to addressing these limitations, an interesting future direction will be to perform visual content analysis by training a machine learning classifier to infer perceptual scores of different observer populations using automatically extracted visual cues, following recent work [1, 12].

6 CONCLUSION

In this paper, we investigated how the impressions of outdoor urban spaces judged by online annotators, compares with the impressions elicited by local residents, along six psychological labels. We focus our study in a developing city where understanding and characterization of these socio-urban perceptions is of societal importance. We found statistically significant differences between the two population groups. Locals perceived places to be more *dangerous* and *dirty*, when compared with non-local online annotators; while online annotators judged places to be more *interesting* in comparison to locals. Our findings can be potentially integrated with existing online photo-sharing platforms (Flickr, Instagram, etc.), to enhance the view of a place by using "insiders" knowledge for "outsiders". While our study was conducted using data collected from one city, it clearly shows that there is a need to better characterize the observers of crowdsourced urban perception studies as biases due to background knowledge and context are significant.

(a) I-1 (b) I-2

Figure 5: Images where the perceptual ratings differ significantly between local and MTurk population.

7 ACKNOWLEDGEMENTS

This work has been supported by the SNSF Youth@Night and EPFL-CODEV SenseCityVity projects. We thank all the members of the SenseCityVity collective. We also thank all the student volunteers for their participation and the school authorities of CECYTE for their support.

REFERENCES

[1] Abhimanyu Dubey, Nikhil Naik, Devi Parikh, Ramesh Raskar, and Cesar A Hidalgo. 2016. Deep Learning the City: Quantifying Urban Perception at a Global Scale. In *European Conference on Computer Vision (ECCV)*. Springer.

[2] Kazunori Hanyu. 1997. Visual Properties and Affective Appraisals in Residential Areas After Dark. *Journal of Environmental Psychology* (1997).

[3] Pall J. Lindal et al. 2013. Architectural Variation, Building Height, and the Restorative Quality of Urban Residential Streetscapes. *Journal of Environmental Psychology* (2013).

[4] Laura J. Loewen et al. 1993. Perceived Safety from Crime in the Urban Environment. *Journal of Environmental Psychology* (1993).

[5] Kate Painter. 1996. The Influence of Street Lighting Improvements on Crime, Fear and Pedestrian Street Use, After Dark. *Landscape and Urban Planning* (1996).

[6] Daniele Quercia, Neil Keith O'Hare, and Henriette Cramer. 2014. Aesthetic Capital: What Makes London Look Beautiful, Quiet, and Happy? *CSCW* (2014).

[7] Salvador Ruiz-Correa, Darshan Santani, and Daniel Gatica-Perez. 2014. The Young and the City: Crowdsourcing Urban Awareness in a Developing Country. In *Proceedings of the First International Conference on IoT in Urban Space (URB-IOT '14)*.

[8] S Ruiz-Correa et al. 2017. SenseCityVity: Mobile Crowdsourcing, Urban Awareness, and Collective Action in Mexico. *IEEE Pervasive Computing* (2017).

[9] Philip Salesses, Katja Schechtner, and Cesar A Hidalgo. 2013. The Collaborative Image of The City: Mapping the Inequality of Urban Perception. *PLoS ONE* (2013).

[10] Robert J Sampson and Stephen W. Raudenbush. 2004. Seeing Disorder: Neighborhood Atigma and the Social Construction of "Broken Windows". *Social Psychology Quarterly* (2004).

[11] Darshan Santani and Daniel Gatica-Perez. 2015. Loud and Trendy: Crowdsourcing Impressions of Social Ambiance in Popular Indoor Urban Places. In *Proceedings of the 23rd Annual ACM Conference on Multimedia Conference (MM '15)*. ACM.

[12] Darshan Santani, Rui Hu, and Daniel Gatica-Perez. 2016. InnerView: Learning Place Ambiance from Social Media Images. In *Proceedings of the 2016 ACM on Multimedia Conference (MM '16)*. ACM.

[13] Darshan Santani, Salvador Ruiz-Correa, and Daniel Gatica-Perez. 2015. Looking at Cities in Mexico with Crowds. In *Proceedings of the 2015 Annual Symposium on Computing for Development*. ACM.

[14] Patrick E Shrout and Joseph L Fleiss. 1979. Intraclass Correlations: Uses in Assessing Rater Reliability. *Psychological Bulletin* (1979).

[15] S. S. Stevens. 1946. On the Theory of Scales of Measurement. *Science* (1946).

[16] Martin Traunmueller, Paul Marshall, and Licia Capra. 2016. ... when you're a Stranger: Evaluating Safety Perceptions of (un)familiar Urban Places. In *Proceedings of the Second International Conference on IoT in Urban Space*. ACM.

[17] John W Tukey. 1991. The Philosophy of Multiple Comparisons. *Statist. Sci.* (1991).

[18] James Q Wilson et al. 1982. Broken Windows. *Atlantic Monthly* (1982).

Deep Sentiment Features of Context and Faces for Affective Video Analysis

Claudio Baecchi, Tiberio Uricchio, Marco Bertini and Alberto Del Bimbo
Media Integration and Communication Center, Università degli Studi di Firenze
{name.surname}@unifi.it

ABSTRACT

Given the huge quantity of hours of video available on video sharing platforms such as YouTube, Vimeo, etc. development of automatic tools that help users find videos that fit their interests has attracted the attention of both scientific and industrial communities. So far the majority of the works have addressed semantic analysis, to identify objects, scenes and events depicted in videos, but more recently affective analysis of videos has started to gain more attention. In this work we investigate the use of sentiment driven features to classify the induced sentiment of a video, i.e. the sentiment reaction of the user. Instead of using standard computer vision features such as CNN features or SIFT features trained to recognize objects and scenes, we exploit sentiment related features such as the ones provided by Deep-SentiBank [4], and features extracted from models that exploit deep networks trained on face expressions. We experiment on two recently introduced datasets: LIRIS-ACCEDE [2] and MEDIAEVAL-2015, that provide sentiment annotations of a large set of short videos. We show that our approach not only outperforms the current state-of-the-art in terms of valence and arousal classification accuracy, but it also uses a smaller number of features, requiring thus less video processing.

CCS CONCEPTS

• **Information systems → Sentiment analysis; Multimedia and multimodal retrieval**; • **Computing methodologies →** *Computer vision tasks*;

KEYWORDS

Sentiment analysis; video analysis; affect recognition

ACM Reference format:
Claudio Baecchi, Tiberio Uricchio, Marco Bertini and Alberto Del Bimbo. 2017. Deep Sentiment Features of Context and Faces for Affective Video Analysis. In *Proceedings of ICMR '17, June 6–9, 2017, Bucharest, Romania, ,* 6 pages.
DOI: http://dx.doi.org/10.1145/3078971.3079027

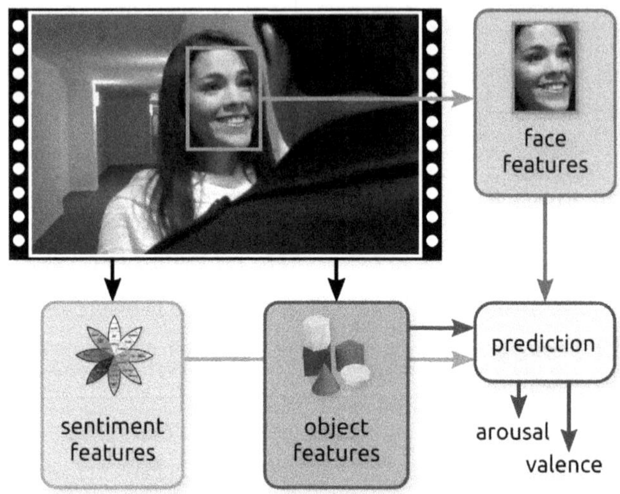

Figure 1: Overview of the proposed method. Prediction of arousal and valence of a video using visual sentiment features related to the context and to the facial expressions.

1 INTRODUCTION

In the last few years, popular social media platforms have enabled their users to upload an ever increasing amount of video content, that is shared and personally recommended. As a result, the retrieval of relevant content is becoming more and more difficult, due to the large scale quantity of data and the new need of personalizing the subjective experience of the user. Affective video content analysis, i.e. the process of automatically evince the induced sentiment in the viewer of a video, can be helpful in the process of personalizing the user experience. In fact, users can be attracted to videos that reflect their emotional status or look for some specific emotions.

Understanding the emotion induced by a video is useful in many applications, including the delivery of content personalized on the mood of the user [13], video indexing and recommendation [37], summarization [15] or emotional interfaces for impaired users [9].

The main difficulty of this task resides in the *semantic gap* that arises between the low level features and the human interpretation of a video [20]. This poses a set of unique challenges, requiring the abstraction of human concepts like emotion and affect. Typical semantic concept detection regards the recognition of visual concepts (e.g. "duck", "horse") that simply can be present or not in the visual content. In contrast, recognizing abstract concepts like affection, is difficult because, while they are still related to the visual stimuli, the human response is naturally subjective.

Therefore, a large attention from researchers has been dedicated to study features and their relations to the induction of emotions in viewers. They are often based on work on color in art [14], as well as the results of psychological experiments on emotional

ICMR '17, June 6–9, 2017, Bucharest, Romania
 ACM ISBN 978-1-4503-4701-3/17/06...$15.00
DOI: http://dx.doi.org/10.1145/3078971.3079027

response to color [31]. Works like [7, 8, 20] are all dedicated to explore different aspects of such features. These efforts have also been encouraged by the MediaEval community that proposed a competition on measuring the affective impact of movies in recent years [29]. On a different line of research, induction of emotions with face expressions are well known in psychological studies. Human faces are known to induce sentiments in people looking at them [32] and, moreover, basic emotions are constants among cultures [10]. Several works have proposed features for recognizing emotion in faces (e.g. [7, 33]), but optimal features for this task are still unclear.

In this work, we address the problem of predicting the sentiment induced on the audience, focusing on classifying the induced sentiment type (i.e. valence) and its strength (i.e. arousal). Figure 1 shows an overview of the proposed approach. We further advance the study of features for affect video recognition by evaluating recently introduced deep sentiment features and showing better performance than those obtainable with standard deep features derived from object classification. We consider the role of actors as an important element in conveying emotions to the viewer. By combining deep sentiment features with face descriptors, we obtain a performance improvement. Compared to previous work, we demonstrate state-of-the-art performance with an effective pipeline on such features, without the many other features usually exploited.

The paper is organized as follows: in Section 2 we describe relevant previous works in detail. In Section 3 we explain the importance of sentiment-related features and describe how we are going to make use of them, and then, in Section 4, we report the experimental results of the evaluation of these features on two recent datasets, also used in the MediaEval contest. Finally, in Section 5 we give our conclusions of the presented work.

2 RELATED WORK

Visual sentiment classification has received an increasing attention among the scientific community in the last few years. Studies have been extensively conducted on image analysis, as in SentiBank [3] and in its improved version Deep-SentiBank [4] that makes use of deep neural networks. They have been recently extended to the multi-lingual context [16] and to image+text sentiment analysis, as in [1, 34]. However, studies on video are still lacking. Video sentiment analysis is a wide task, encompassing different types of emotion understanding problems. The great majority of works revolve around studying the sentiment expressed by a speaking actor. These works focus on interpreting words, voice and expressions performed in the video. The Acted Facial Expressions in the Wild (AFEW) [6] dataset has been used in several emotion recognition challenges. It consists of 1,426 short sequences (with an average length of 2 seconds) extracted from movies, containing facial expressions, annotated with 6 emotions as identified by Ekman *et al.* [11], plus a neutral class. The baseline uses LBPTOP descriptors and SVR [7] while, typically, solutions that achieve the best results combine audio (e.g. MFCC) and video (e.g. CNN trained on faces) features; for instance, recurrent neural network (RNN) and 3D convolutional networks (C3D), specifically trained on faces, have been combined with audio features by Fan *et al.* [12]. Wöllmer *et al.* [33], try to understand the speaker's sentiment in on-line videos containing movie reviews by leveraging acoustic, visual and linguistic features. Rosas *et al.* [24] use a similar approach to classify the speaker's emotion in Spanish videos. Sentiment analysis is performed on both sentiment polarity and strength by Zadeh *et al.* [36], where they aim at mining opinions in YouTube videos.

Another type of sentiment analysis is the one performed on the audience, that, while watching a video, is induced different kind of emotions. Dumoulin *et al.* [8] have proposed a hierarchical approach for affect classification, using a combination of audio and visual features, including convolutional neural networks for content and sentiment recognition. The proposed method has been tested on the FilmStim dataset [26], that contains 70 movie excerpts annotated with 7 emotions. The task of categorizing the induced sentiment of videos has been thoroughly studied in the MediaEval 2015 challenge [29], extending a new large scale dataset called LIRIS-ACCEDE [2]. Here participants used computer vision features to classify induced emotions. For example, Mironica *et al.* [22] used ColorSIFT and AlexNet's FC6 descriptors. Seddati *et al.* [27] also took Optical Flow into consideration to improve the overall accuracy using motion information. Vlastelica *et al.* [21] used GIST features in combination with HOG and HOF features and AlexNet's FC7 descriptors. Trigeorgis *et al.* [30] used eGeMAPS audio features together with CNN features to improve the classification power of their model. Qi Dai *et al.* [5] also used audio features, specifically the MFCC descriptor, in conjunction with a set of CNN features, LSTM features and texture information. YunYi *et al.* [35] made also use of the Fisher Vector representation of various local spatial and temporal features. Vu Lam *et al.* [19], combining most of the previous features, provided the best classifier in the contest for sentiment classification. Zhu *et al.* [38] proposed to base affective video content analysis on the presence of an actor to identify the most important keyframes and then extract patch features of the scene using CNNs trained on ImageNet, and fusing with audio features such as MFCC. They do not consider a description of the facial expressions of the actors. The authors evaluate the performance of the method on LIRIS-ACCEDE dataset.

Our work addresses the problem of classifying the induced sentiment in the viewer in terms of valence and arousal. Differently from all these works that have used the LIRIS-ACCEDE dataset, we propose to use sentiment-oriented features in addition to the classical computer vision features. Inspired by the studies on sentiment induction from faces, we also specifically consider the emotion showed in faces of the actors, shown for example in close-up and medium shots. In particular we add visual sentiment features from Deep-SentiBank and combine it with descriptions of the facial expressions of the actors, using CNNs trained for face recognition, to better capture the details of the faces.

3 EXPLOITING SENTIMENT-RELATED FEATURES

Given a short video V, the task of affective video recognition is to classify the global valence and arousal of the sequence from its frames. We address the problem using a pipeline based on two steps, feature extraction and classification. We consider three types of features: *sentiment features*, *face features*, for which we consider faces extracted using a face detector, and *object features*. Each feature type is first treated independently. They are extracted from every

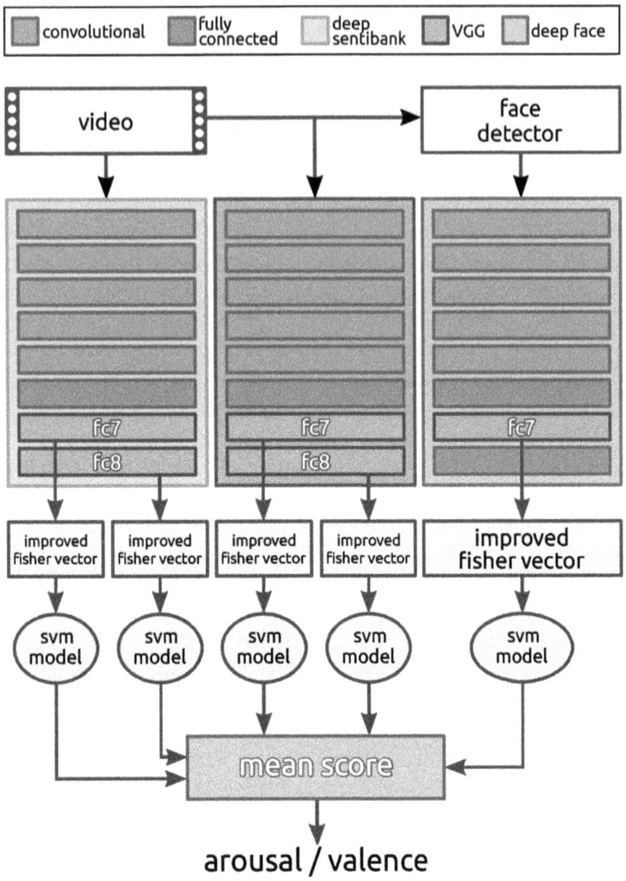

Figure 2: Pipeline of the proposed method. Each feature set is encoded separately into an IFV and a prediction is made by performing late fusion of any subset of the classifiers.

frame and singularly pooled into a global representations of the sequence. Each global representation is used to train a prediction model and lately combined with a late fusion approach. Figure 2 shows the complete pipeline, including each feature extraction and the final classification process.

Sentiment Features. In order to capture sentiment-related information we choose Deep-SentiBank [4] as sentiment related feature extractor. Deep-SentiBank is a deep convolutional neural network trained to discover Adjective-Noun Pairs (ANP) from images and its features can be used as statistical cues to detect emotions. We processed each video $V = \{f_1, f_2, \ldots, f_v\}$ composed of v frames and for each frame f_i we extracted both FC7 and FC8 descriptors from Deep-SentiBank, which we will refer to as Sent-FC7 and Sent-FC8, obtaining two sets of descriptors $D = \{d_1, d_2, \ldots, d_v\}$ and $R = \{r_1, r_2, \ldots, r_v\}$ respectively. To overcome the problem of handling video with different durations and to include the time information into the system, all Sent-FC7 and Sent-FC8 of a video are encoded into an Improved Fisher Vector (IFV) [25] representation $\mathcal{I}$ using a Fisher Encoding $\mathcal{F}$. Each feature type is treated separately to avoid mixing different contributions into a single representation. For each feature type d and r, we first performed an estimation of a Gaussian Mixture Model (GMM) using 32 components obtaining $\mathcal{G}_d$ and $\mathcal{G}_r$. These are then used to encode the features of a video obtaining a single descriptor, that is, $\mathcal{I}_D = \mathcal{F}(D, \mathcal{G}_d)$ and $\mathcal{I}_R = \mathcal{F}(R, \mathcal{G}_r)$.

Face Features. Face related features are extracted using a similar approach to sentiment features. Inspired by the work of Parkhi *et al.* [23] we trained an AlexNet network [18] on the Oxford face dataset provided in the same paper, structuring the problem as an N−classification task. The dataset is composed of 2.622 identities which are used to train the deep classifier. We will refer to this network as *deep face*. First we performed face detection using Dlib toolkit [17], extracting for each video a set $A = \{a_1, a_2, \ldots, a_v\}$ of faces. For videos where faces have been detected, similarly to Sent-FC7 and Sent-FC8, we first extracted FC7 descriptors from our *deep face* network for each face of a video, obtaining a set of descriptors $C = \{c_1, c_2, \ldots, c_v\}$, then we estimated a GMM using 32 components obtaining $\mathcal{G}_c$. This model is used to encode the features into an IFV, that is, $\mathcal{I}_C = \mathcal{F}(C, \mathcal{G}_c)$.

Object Features. Since the scene context and objects can be associated to sentiments, we also add object feature information. To this extent we employ features extracted using VGG-16 network [28], taking its FC7 and FC8 descriptors, that we will refer to as VGG-FC7 and VGG-FC8. Following the same procedure used for the visual sentiment features, we extract two sets of features $P = \{p_1, p_2, \ldots, p_v\}$ ans $Q = \{q_1, q_2, \ldots, q_v\}$, we encode them using two GMM $\mathcal{G}_p$ and $\mathcal{G}_q$, and finally we produce the IFV $\mathcal{I}_P$ and $\mathcal{I}_Q$.

Score Prediction. Sentiment prediction is performed separately per feature vector $\mathcal{I}$. We trained five linear SVM, one for each feature, producing five distinct models that can be grouped in three sets: two models for sentiment features; *ii)* one model for facial expression features; *iii)* two models for object features. By computing a separate model for every feature and performing late fusion on the classifier scores we are able to study every feature combination. This way it is possible to study the contribution of each feature, appreciating if one or more share the same information or give different types of contributions to the final prediction. In case a feature is not available for a video, such as in the case of videos where no faces have been detected, no contribution is given for that feature and the score is computed by averaging only the available ones. Prediction is performed distinctly for valence and arousal.

4 EXPERIMENTAL RESULTS

Here we report results of two experimental settings on sentiment annotated videos. First, we will show the effectiveness of single sentiment features for valence and arousal classification tasks. Then, we will report experiments on the combination of two and more features, showing that faces always give a positive contribution, supporting our hypothesis that actors' facial expressions are an important element in conveying emotions to the viewer.

4.1 Datasets

Each year the MediaEval Benchmarking Initiative [1] proposes a number of tasks to be addressed about a variety of multimedia topics. One of these is the affective impact of movies, first introduced in the

[1] https://www.multimediaeval.org/

Figure 3: LIRIS-ACCEDE sample frames: negative *(left)*, neutral *(center)*, positive *(right)*. First row *(top)* shows scene-related samples, second row *(bottom)* shows face-related ones.

MediaEval 2015 challenge [29], that proposes various sentiment-related tasks to be evaluated on a new common dataset, the LIRIS-ACCEDE dataset [2]. Examples of frames from the LIRIS-ACCEDE dataset are shown in Figure 3, we show examples for each class and highlight frames with and without faces with a strong sentiment value. This dataset is the first that directly addresses the problem of affect evaluation of viewers on movies taken from social media. It was in fact created using 160 movies taken from the Vimeo platform [2]. From these movies, 9,800 excerpts of around 10 seconds have been extracted and discretely classified for valence, arousal and violence. The dataset is divided into a training and a test set, both consisting of 4,900 excerpts.

All videos have been labeled using Amazon Mechanical Turk and fall in one of three categories: negative, neutral or positive for valence classification and calm, neutral or aroused for arousal classification. In the occasion of the MediaEval 2015 contest, the LIRIS-ACCEDE dataset has been enriched with 39 additional videos, annotated in the same manner, from which 1,100 new excerpts have been extracted. These videos, together with the original 9,800 form a new dataset composed by 10,900 videos, referred from now on as the MEDIAEVAL-2015 dataset. The excerpts are divided into two sets, a training set, composed of 6,144 elements from the LIRIS-ACCEDE dataset, and a test set, composed of the remaining 3,656 elements of the LIRIS-ACCEDE dataset and the new 1,100 excerpts introduced by the MEDIAEVAL 2015 challenge, for a total of 4,756 elements. While the valence score are well balanced, we note that arousal values are biased towards the class calm. To address this, we set SVM label weights proportional to the inverse ratio of the training examples for each class.

Following the metrics used in the MediaEval contest [29], we evaluate the performance in terms of accuracy, and compare the proposed method with several state-of-the-art methods.

4.2 Single Feature

To test the discriminative capacity of our features we first use each of them alone. Table 1 reports the results for the task of valence and arousal classification on the MEDIAEVAL-2015 dataset. Considering the Valence column, we observe that sentiment-based CNN features Sent-FC7 and Sent-FC8 have higher accuracy than those obtained from object-based features. This confirm the importance of using networks trained for the specific task at hand. Comparing our single-feature results *(top)* to the ones obtained during the MediaEval 2015 contest *(bottom)*, we can see that both results that make use of Deep-SentiBank features are very close, if not the same, to the state-of-the-art result, which is a remarkable outcome considering that Vu Lam [19] is using a combination of nine features whether our method is using only one feature.

Results for the task of arousal classification are reported in the last column of Table 1. Similarly to the valence classification task, we can observe that sentiment-based CNN features outperform object-based features, and obtain results that are comparable to several of the competing methods that use more features.

Results on the LIRIS-ACCEDE dataset only, to allow the comparison with the method of Zhu *et al.* [38], are reported in Table 2, showing behaviors similar to the MEDIAEVAL-2015 setting. We observe that Sent-FC7 and Sent-FC8 are slightly superior to the Faces feature for both valence and arousal, as seen also in Table 1. They all outperform [38], suggesting that our method, exploiting sentiment features and pooling on all frames, is more powerful than generic CNN features on few frames.

4.3 Feature Fusion

Following the trend of fusing multiple features to incorporate more information, we performed late fusion of all five features to prove that they contain different information. To this end we performed a late fusion of the scores of up to five classifiers, weighting them in equal manner. We performed all possible combinations of fusion between two of the three sentiment features and in the end we combined all the three sentiment features together to further improve the accuracy. Finally we combined sentiment feature with object-based features, using a total of five features. In the Valence column of Table 1 we report results for the related task using the MEDIAEVAL-2015 dataset. Figures reported in the *(middle)* part

[2] https://vimeo.com/

Data	Feature Type	Valence Accuracy	Arousal Accuracy
Single Features	Random	33.29%	33.91%
	VGG-FC7	40.16%	49.14%
	VGG-FC8	40.92%	49.33%
	Sent-FC7	42.14%	52.31%
	Sent-FC8	42.72%	52.29%
	Faces	40.37%	51.96%
Two Features	Sent-FC7 + Faces	43.67%	52.84%
	Sent-FC8 + Faces	44.24%	52.90%
	Sent-FC7 + Sent-FC8	43.50%	53.11%
Three Features	Sent-FC7 + Sent-FC8 + Faces	44.68%	54.52%
Five Features	VGG-FC7 + VGG-FC8 + Sent-FC7 + Sent-FC8 + Faces	**45.31%**	**55.98%**
Other Methods (Contest)	Mironica [22] *(3 features)*	36.10%	45.04%
	Seddati [27] *(1 features)*	37.20%	52.44%
	Vlastelica [21] *(5 features)*	38.50%	51.90%
	Trigeorgis [30] *(2 features)*	41.40%	55.72%
	Qi Dai [5] *(3 features)*	41.80%	48.80%
	YunYi [35] *(7 features)*	41.90%	55.93%
	Vu Lam [19] *(9 features)*	42.90%	55.91%

Table 1: Experimental results on the MEDIAEVAL-2015 dataset. *(top)* our results showing single-feature and feature-fusion accuracies; *(bottom)* other methods that participated in the MediaEval 2015 contest.

Data	Feature Type	Valence Accuracy	Arousal Accuracy
Single Features	Random	33.61%	33.92%
	VGG-FC7	41.04%	45.00%
	VGG-FC8	40.94%	44.43%
	Sent-FC7	42.16%	47.55%
	Sent-FC8	41.61%	47.12%
	Faces	40.24%	45.71%
Two Features	Sent-FC7 + Faces	44.53%	48.41%
	Sent-FC8 + Faces	42.40%	49.32%
	Sent-FC7 + Sent-FC8	43.16%	49.52%
Three Features	Sent-FC7 + Sent-FC8 + Faces	45.19%	52.24%
Five Features	VGG-FC7 + VGG-FC8 + Sent-FC7 + Sent-FC8 + Faces	**45.82%**	**53.11%**
Other Methods	Zhu [38] *(3 features)*	30.76%	30.95%

Table 2: Experimental results on the LIRIS-ACCEDE dataset. *(top)* our results showing single-feature and feature-fusion accuracies; *(bottom)* Zhu *et al.* [38].

show that using multiple features yields better results, and the more features we use the higher the improvement, demonstrating that different features contribute with different kind of information. Looking at the numbers, combining two features yield an improvement of 1.5% over our single feature model, obtaining a classification accuracy that surpasses the state-of-the-art result. Moreover, when combining all three sentiment features together the improvement goes up to 2.0%. Adding the two object-based features adds 0.6% performance. These results show that faces carry additional information, in fact adding face features always improves results. This can be also appreciated in Figure 4, where, for the valence task, we show some positive and negative examples of initially misclassified videos that are then correctly classified when face information is included in the method.

Similar considerations apply for the arousal task. Results are reported in the Arousal column of Table 1. In this case the combination of sentiment features improves over object-based features alone, but the gain over single sentiment features is very limited. It is necessary to also add object-based features to the sentiment ones to improve, albeit slightly, over competing methods.

Results on the LIRIS-ACCEDE dataset only are reported in Table 2. Again combining semantic features (*(top)*, lower part) is beneficial, obtaining improvements up to 2%. Similarly to the MEDIAEVAL-2015 dataset using the three sentiment-based features together with the two object-based features provides additional improvements that, in this case, are more pronounced also for the arousal task.

5 CONCLUSIONS

In this paper we proposed a novel approach to sentiment video analysis to classify induced arousal and valence of a video by exploiting sentiment-related features instead of using object related features only. We proposed to exploit sentiment-related features derived from the Deep-SentiBank network [4], together with features related to the actor face expression. To make use of the latter, we trained a neural network for face recognition on the Oxford face dataset. Features are extracted per-frame, and encoded into an Improved Fisher Vector for each feature. A classical linear SVM is used to learn a per-feature classifier, allowing us to perform late fusion on any combination of features. Experiments have been conducted on both the LIRIS-ACCEDE dataset [2], a collection of 9,800 movie excerpts with a variable duration of 8-12 seconds, and the MEDIAEVAL-2015 dataset, an extension of the previous dataset with an additional 1,100 excerpts. We first performed classification of single features, showing that they carry good classification power, then we performed multiple feature combinations by late fusing the classification scores, proving not only that different features give different contributions to the final classification, but also that including information about actor expressions always give a considerable improvement. Results show that with our strategy, using both sentiment related features and object features, we obtain better than state-of-the art results, outperforming the best current methods on both datasets for arousal and valence classification tasks by leveraging a smaller number of features.

ACKNOWLEDGMENTS

This work is partially supported by the MIUR "Social Museum and Smart Tourism" project (Grant No.: CTN01_00034_231545).

REFERENCES

[1] Claudio Baecchi, Tiberio Uricchio, Marco Bertini, and Alberto Del Bimbo. 2016. A multimodal feature learning approach for sentiment analysis of social network multimedia. *Multimedia Tools and Applications* 75, 5 (2016), 2507–2525.

[2] Yoann Baveye, Emmanuel Dellandrea, Christel Chamaret, and Liming Chen. 2015. LIRIS-ACCEDE: A video database for affective content analysis. *IEEE Transactions on Affective Computing* 6, 1 (2015), 43–55.

[3] Damian Borth, Tao Chen, Rongrong Ji, and Shih-Fu Chang. 2013. SentiBank: large-scale ontology and classifiers for detecting sentiment and emotions in visual content. In *Proc. of ACM MM.*

Figure 4: Examples of videos where face information is essential for correct classification. First row *(top)*: positive videos that were classified as negatives, second row *(bottom)*: frames of negative videos that were classified as positives.

[4] Tao Chen, Damian Borth, Trevor Darrell, and Shih-Fu Chang. 2014. DeepSentiBank: Visual sentiment concept classification with deep convolutional neural networks. *arXiv preprint arXiv:1410.8586* (2014).

[5] Qi Dai, Rui-Wei Zhao, Zuxuan Wu, Xi Wang, Zichen Gu, Wenhai Wu, and Yu-Gang Jiang. 2015. Fudan-Huawei at MediaEval 2015: Detecting Violent Scenes and Affective Impact in Movies with Deep Learning. In *Working Notes Proceedings of the MediaEval Workshop.*

[6] A. Dhall, R. Goecke, S. Lucey, and T. Gedeon. 2012. Collecting Large, Richly Annotated Facial-Expression Databases from Movies. *IEEE MultiMedia* 19, 3 (July 2012), 34–41.

[7] Abhinav Dhall, O.V. Ramana Murthy, Roland Goecke, Jyoti Joshi, and Tom Gedeon. 2015. Video and Image Based Emotion Recognition Challenges in the Wild: EmotiW 2015. In *Proc. of ACM ICMI.*

[8] Joël Dumoulin, Diana Affi, Elena Mugellini, Omar Abou Khaled, Marco Bertini, and Alberto Del Bimbo. 2015. Affect Recognition in a Realistic Movie Dataset Using a Hierarchical Approach. In *Proc. of ASM.* 6.

[9] Joël Dumoulin, Diana Affi, Elena Mugellini, Omar Abou Khaled, Marco Bertini, and Alberto Del Bimbo. 2015. Movie's Affect Communication Using Multisensory Modalities. In *Proc. of ACM MM.* 739–740. DOI : http://dx.doi.org/10.1145/2733373.2807965

[10] Paul Ekman and Wallace V Friesen. 1971. Constants across cultures in the face and emotion. *Journal of Personality and Social Psychology* 17, 2 (1971), 124.

[11] Paul Ekman, Wallace V. Friesen, Maureen O'Sullivan, Anthony Chan, Irene Diacoyanni-Tarlatzis, Karl Heider, Rainer Krause, William Ayhan LeCompte, Tom Pitcairn, Pio E. Ricci-Bitti, Klaus Scherer, Masatoshi Tomita, and Athanase Tzavaras. 1987. Universals and cultural differences in the judgments of facial expressions of emotion. *Journal of Personality and Social Psychology* 53, 4 (1987), 712–717.

[12] Yin Fan, Xiangju Lu, Dian Li, and Yuanliu Liu. 2016. Video-based Emotion Recognition Using CNN-RNN and C3D Hybrid Networks. In *Proc. of ACM ICMI.*

[13] Alan Hanjalic. 2006. Extracting moods from pictures and sounds: Towards truly personalized TV. *IEEE Signal Processing Magazine* 23, 2 (2006), 90–100.

[14] Johannes Itten. 1973. The Art of Color: The Subjective Experience and Objective Rationale of Color (trans. Ernest van Haagen). (1973).

[15] Hideo Joho, Joemon M Jose, Roberto Valenti, and Nicu Sebe. 2009. Exploiting facial expressions for affective video summarisation. In *Proc. of CIVR.*

[16] Brendan Jou, Tao Chen, Nikolaos Pappas, Miriam Redi, Mercan Topkara, and Shih-Fu Chang. 2015. Visual Affect Around the World: A Large-scale Multilingual Visual Sentiment Ontology. In *Proc. of ACM MM.*

[17] Davis E King. 2009. Dlib-ml: A machine learning toolkit. *J. Mach. Learning Research* 10 (2009), 1755–1758.

[18] Alex Krizhevsky, Ilya Sutskever, and Geoffrey E. Hinton. 2012. ImageNet Classification with Deep Convolutional Neural Networks. In *Proc. of NIPS.*

[19] Vu Lam, Sang Phan, Duy-Dinh Le, Shinichi Satoh, and Duc Anh Duong. 2015. NII-UIT at MediaEval 2015 Affective Impact of Movies Task. In *Working Notes Proceedings of the MediaEval Workshop.*

[20] Jana Machajdik and Allan Hanbury. 2010. Affective image classification using features inspired by psychology and art theory. In *Proc. of ACM MM.*

[21] P Marin Vlastelica, Sergey Hayrapetyan, Makarand Tapaswi, and Rainer Stiefelhagen. 2015. KIT at MediaEval 2015 – Evaluating Visual Cues for Affective Impact of Movies Task. In *Working Notes Proceedings of the MediaEval Workshop.*

[22] Ionut Mironica, Bogdan Ionescu, Mats Sjöberg, Markus Schedl, and Marcin Skowron. 2015. RFA at MediaEval 2015 Affective Impact of Movies Task: A Multimodal Approach. In *Working Notes Proceedings of the MediaEval Workshop.*

[23] O. M. Parkhi, A. Vedaldi, and A. Zisserman. 2015. Deep Face Recognition. In *Proc. of BMVC.*

[24] Veronica Rosas, Rada Mihalcea, and Louis-Philippe Morency. 2013. Multimodal sentiment analysis of Spanish online videos. *IEEE Intelligent Systems* 28, 3 (2013), 38–45.

[25] Jorge Sánchez, Florent Perronnin, Thomas Mensink, and Jakob Verbeek. 2013. Image classification with the fisher vector: Theory and practice. *International Journal of Computer Vision* 105, 3 (2013), 222–245.

[26] Alexandre Schaefer, Frédéric Nils, Xavier Sanchez, and Pierre Philippot. 2010. Assessing the effectiveness of a large database of emotion-eliciting films: A new tool for emotion researchers. *Cognition and Emotion* 24, 7 (2010), 1153–1172.

[27] Omar Seddati, Emre Kulah, Gueorgui Pironkov, Stéphane Dupont, Saïd Mahmoudi, and Thierry Dutoit. 2015. UMons at MediaEval 2015 Affective Impact of Movies Task including Violent Scenes Detection. In *Working Notes Proceedings of the MediaEval Workshop.*

[28] Karen Simonyan and Andrew Zisserman. 2014. Very deep convolutional networks for large-scale image recognition. *arXiv preprint arXiv:1409.1556* (2014).

[29] Mats Sjöberg, Yoann Baveye, Hanli Wang, Vu Lam Quang, Bogdan Ionescu, Emmanuel Dellandréa, Markus Schedl, Claire-Hélène Demarty, and Liming Chen. 2015. The MediaEval 2015 affective impact of movies task. In *Working Notes Proceedings of the MediaEval Workshop.*

[30] George Trigeorgis, Eduardo Coutinho, Fabien Ringeval, Erik Marchi, Stefanos Zafeiriou, and Björn Schuller. 2015. The ICL-TUM-PASSAU Approach for the MediaEval 2015 "Affective Impact of Movies" Task. In *Working Notes Proceedings of the MediaEval Workshop.*

[31] Patricia Valdez and Albert Mehrabian. 1994. Effects of color on emotions. *Journal of Experimental Psychology: General* 123, 4 (1994), 394.

[32] Barbara Wild, Michael Erb, Michael Eyb, Mathias Bartels, and Wolfgang Grodd. 2003. Why are smiles contagious? An fMRI study of the interaction between perception of facial affect and facial movements. *Psychiatry Research: Neuroimaging* 123, 1 (2003), 17–36.

[33] Martin Wöllmer, Felix Weninger, Tobias Knaup, Björn Schuller, Congkai Sun, Kenji Sagae, and Louis-Philippe Morency. 2013. Youtube movie reviews: Sentiment analysis in an audio-visual context. *IEEE Intelligent Systems* 28, 3 (2013), 46–53.

[34] Quanzeng You, Jiebo Luo, Hailin Jin, and Jianchao Yang. 2015. Joint Visual-Textual Sentiment Analysis with Deep Neural Networks. In *Proc. of ACM MM.*

[35] Gang Yu and Junsong Yuan. 2015. Fast action proposals for human action detection and search. In *Proc. of CVPR.*

[36] Amir Zadeh, Rowan Zellers, Eli Pincus, and Louis-Philippe Morency. 2016. Multimodal sentiment intensity analysis in videos: Facial gestures and verbal messages. *IEEE Intelligent Systems* 31, 6 (2016), 82–88.

[37] Sicheng Zhao, Hongxun Yao, Xiaoshuai Sun, Pengfei Xu, Xianming Liu, and Rongrong Ji. 2011. Video indexing and recommendation based on affective analysis of viewers. In *Proc. of ACM MM.*

[38] Yingying Zhu, Zhengbo Jiang, Jianfeng Peng, and Sheng-hua Zhong. 2016. Video Affective Content Analysis Based on Protagonist via Convolutional Neural Network. In *Proc. of PCM.*

Frame-Transformer Emotion Classification Network

Jiarui Gao[1], Yanwei Fu[2], Yu-Gang Jiang[1], and Xiangyang Xue[12*]
[1]School of Computer Science, Shanghai Key Laboratory of Intelligent Information Processing, Fudan University, China
[2]School of Data Science, Fudan University, China
{jrgao14,yanweifu,ygj,xyxue}@fudan.edu.cn

ABSTRACT

Emotional content is a key ingredient in user-generated videos. However, due to the emotions sparsely expressed in the user-generated video, it is very difficult to analayze emotions in videos. In this paper, we propose a new architecture–Frame-Transformer Emotion Classification Network (FT-EC-net) to solve three highly correlated emotion analysis tasks: emotion recognition, emotion attribution and emotion-oriented summarization. We also contribute a new dataset for emotion attribution task by annotating the ground-truth labels of attribution segments. A comprehensive set of experiments on two datasets demonstrate the effectiveness of our framework.

KEYWORDS

Video emotion recognition; video emotion attribution; video emotion-oriented summarization and spatial-transformer network

ACM Reference format:
Jiarui Gao[1], Yanwei Fu[2], Yu-Gang Jiang[1], and Xiangyang Xue[12]. 2017. Frame-Transformer Emotion Classification Network. In *Proceedings of ICMR '17, June 6–9, 2017, Bucharest, Romania,* , 6 pages.
DOI: http://dx.doi.org/10.1145/3078971.3079030

1 INTRODUCTION

The explosive growth of user-generated videos creates a great demand for computational understanding of visual media data. Great efforts and success have been made on the video content understanding, such as video actions and activities. Sentimental analysis on text data [10] and image data [4] have been studied recently. However, the ability to understand emotions from videos, to a large extent, remains an unaddressed problem, despite the fact that video content can convey strong emotional information to their viewers. Computational understanding of the emotions aroused by video content nevertheless has many real-world applications. For example, video recommendation services can benefit from matching users' interests with the emotions of video content.

The challenges of video emotion understanding come from three aspects. Firstly, the emotions are often sparsely expressed by a subset of the video, while the other parts of the video perform as the story context for video emotion. Secondly, there are several different types of emotions in one video, despite a single dominant emotion exists. It is essential to know, and yet difficult to answer which video segment contributes the most to the video's overall emotion, which is defined as video emotion attribution [24]. Thirdly, the user-generated videos are often captured in an uncontrolled environment and of high diverse content. The unconstrained space of objects, scenes, and events in user-generated videos, not only makes their content very complex to be analyzed; but also gets the user-generated videos more likely to suffer from the problems of occlusions of objects and illumination conditions than the commercial videos (e.g. movies, news and sports).

Previous efforts of understanding video emotion aim at solving the three tasks of emotion recognition, emotion attribution and emotion-oriented summarization, by either combining various of low-level and middle-level features [7]; or by using auxiliary image sentiment dataset to re-encode the features of video frames [23, 24]. These works still have to design a specific algorithm for each task, rather than a single framework solving all these three highly correlated tasks jointly.

In this paper, we propose our new architecture – Frame-Transformer Emotion Classification Network (FT-EC-net), which facilitates solving emotion recognition, emotion attribution and emotion-oriented summarization jointly. FT-EC-net is composed of FT-net and EC-net. Particularly, the FT-net is a variant of spatial transform networks (ST-net) [6]. It can learn to detect the emotional video segments; and thus facilitates both emotion attribution and emotion-oriented summarization. The EC-net is a classification network which further processes the results of FT-net for emotion recognition. Our architecture is thoroughly evaluated on Ekman6 and Emotion6 video dataset.

Contributions: (1) Our newly proposed FT-EC-net can solve the emotion recognition, emotion attribution and emotion-oriented summarization simultaneously. As a variant of ST-net, FT-net is firstly introduced in this paper to enable video emotion attribution and emotion-oriented summarization; (2) In establishing a good benchmark for emotion attribution task, we re-annotate the Ekman6 dataset with the most emotion-oriented segments which can be used as the ground-truth for emotion attribution task. (3) We also introduce a new evaluation metric to evaluate the video segments detected in attribution tasks.

2 RELATED WORK

Image and Video Emotion Recognition. Recently, inspired by the psychological theory, such as Ekman's six pan-cultural basic emotions and Plutchik's wheel of emotions, researchers have studied the problem of image emotion recognition extensively. Various features have been explored, such as the features inspired by psychology and art theory[15], and the shape features [13].

*Yanwei Fu is the corresponding authour.

ICMR '17, June 6–9, 2017, Bucharest, Romania
 ACM ISBN 978-1-4503-4701-3/17/06…$15.00
DOI: http://dx.doi.org/10.1145/3078971.3079030

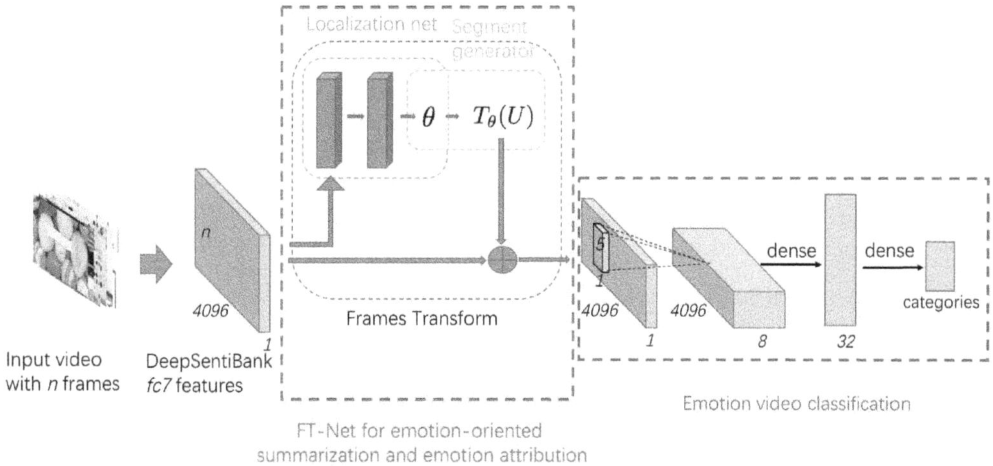

Figure 1: An overview of our framework. We use the DeepSentiBank to extract the features of each frame. With the extracted deep features, the localization network is thus regressed towards the parameters θ. The FT-EC-Net uses the extracted $fc7$ features as inputs, and is capable of emotion recognition (right part), emotion-oriented summarization and emotion attribution (middle part).

Recently with the renaissance of convolution neural networks, deep convolutional neural networks have been used for visual sentiment analysis [2, 25]. A large scale of visual sentiment dataset was proposed in Sentibank [2] and DeepSentiBank [4]. It contains a set of 1,533 adjective-noun pairs, such as "cute dog" and "happy wedding".

Video emotion recognition has been investigated recently and great progress has been made on extracting different types of features, such as the low-level visual and audio features, attribute features in [7] as well as the mid-level audio-visual features in [1]. Emotions have also been analyzed in GIF files [8] which can be taken as one type of short videos. The facial expressions have also been investigated on videos [5]. For a more recent survey, we refer to [21].

Most these existing works still formulate emotion understanding as a classification task. In our previous work [23, 24], we propose another two tasks – video emotion attribution and video emotion-oriented video summarization. Thus different from all previous works, we propose a new architecture that is able to solve these three tasks jointly.

Emotion attribution and emotion-oriented summarization. Video summarization has been explored for more than two decades [19] and the detailed review is beyond our scope. In general, the video summary has two forms, i.e., keyframes extraction and video skims; and to generate video summary, a set of features have been exploited, such as visual saliency[14], motion cues [12], mid-level features [20], and semantic recognition [22].

Recently, we [24] introduced the tasks of emotion-oriented summarization which aims at extracting video summarization according to more general video emotion content. Inspired by the task of semantic attribution in text analysis, [24] also defined the emotion attribution as attributing the video's overall emotion to its individual segments. However, [24] still treated the emotion recognition, summarization and attribution tasks as several separate tasks. Intrinsically, the emotion recognition can greatly help emotion attribution and emotion-oriented summarization; and the emotion-oriented summary can be selected from the results of emotion attribution. Thus, our framework is designed to solve these three tasks simultaneously.

Spatial transform networks. Spatial transform networks (ST-net) are firstly proposed in [6] for image classification. ST-Net provides the spatial transformation capabilities[6], which enables a wide variety of tasks such as co-localization [18], and spatial attention [17]. Our FT-net component is a variant of ST-net and it enables selectively learning to segment the emotional video segments.

3 FRAME-TRANSFORMER EMOTION CLASSIFICATION NETWORK

As illustrated in Fig. 1, this section introduces our framework which is composed of three parts: DeepSentibank, Frame-Transformer subnetwork (FT-net) and Emotion Classification subnetwork (EC-net).

Suppose we have n frames extracted from each video. The DeepSentiBank [4] is utilized to extract the features of each frame. It contains five convolutional layers and three fully-connected layers. Specifically, we use as features the $4096 - dim$ output of $fc7$ layer of DeepSentiBank. The DeepSentiBank is trained on 2089 Adjective Noun Pairs(ANPs) (such as "sad eyes") with 867919 images. In practice, a particular number of frames are equally sampled from each video to formulate the input of the network.

The FT-net aims at learning to detect emotional video segments. It has the localization sub-network regressing the transformer parameter θ and normalized segment generator of partitioning the video segments from the data stream generated by DeepSentiBank.

The segments generated by FT-net can be used for emotion attribution and emotion-oriented summarization.The EC-net is constructed for video emotion recognition, with one convolutional layer and two fully connected layers. We will explain each part in the following subsections.

3.1 FT-net

The FT-Net can be further processed into localization sub-network and normalized segment generator.

Localization sub-Network. It has two fully connected layers to further project the extracted features of each frame into a non-linear representation. The localization network in Fig. 1 aims at regressing the sampling parameter $\theta = [\theta_1, \theta_2]$ for normalized segment generator. The parameter θ is calculated through backpropagation from the EC-net; thus no supervision is provided to the localization network.

Normalized Segment Generator. To represent the specific output frames, we set x_i^t as the target coordinate of each frame in the regular output segment and x_i^s as the source input coordinate of each frame along the input frames n. The output segment S is formed by L frames, *i.e.*, $S = \left[x_i^t\right]_{i=1}^{L}$. The segment generator enables projecting the emotional frames (with coordinate x_i^t, $i = 1, \cdots, L$) to the corresponding source frames x_i^s by the 2D affine transformation,

$$x_i^s = \begin{bmatrix}\theta_1 & \theta_2\end{bmatrix} \begin{pmatrix} x_i^t \\ 1 \end{pmatrix} \tag{1}$$

where θ_1 is the scale parameter which controls the length ratio in the input video projected from output segments; and θ_2 is the translation parameter which indicates the offset of the segment over the video. The reason why the computation above is backward (from x_i^t to x_i^s) is that it enables the length of the source segment from the original video to be unfixed. But this network can only detect one main segment due to its structure. In practice, to avoid the numerical issues, the coordinates x_i^t and x_i^s are normalized to $(-1, 1)$ $(-1 \leq x_i^t, x_i^s \leq 1)$.

This parameter θ is computed through the localization subnetwork according to the same input features as it is applied, so the output segment S can be taken as the attribution results of the original video. We can further generate the summary by the attribution results.

3.2 EC-net

The output of normalized segment generator is further processed by classification sub-network.

One Convolutional layer has 8 convolutional filters with the size of 5×1. Intuitively, the $fc7$ features extracted by DeepSentiBank can be taken as a generic extractor for sentimental related features. Nevertheless, the FT-net does not have a principle way to model the contextual information among the consecutive frames, which however is extremely important for our task of emotion analysis. Thus this layer is utilized to compute contextual information among each feature channel.

Two fully connected layers have 32 neurons individually. The final softmax layer is followed to classify the emotions. Due to the difficulty of emotion analysis task, the fully connected layers are added to increase the non-linearity of the classification network.

Note that the convolutional layer follows the fully connected layers in DeepSentiBank and FT-net, which however do not have negative effects on learning the parameters of convolutional layers. (1) The DeepSentiBank is pre-trained beforehand and its parameters are fixed when we extract the $fc7$ features of frames. (2) The FT-net has two fully connected layers to regress the parameter θ in its localization subnetwork. Once the θ is learned to segment the input features, our convolutional layer still processes the data extracted by DeepSentiBank as shown in Fig. 1.

3.3 Our tasks

A very nice property of our network is that it can enable the emotion recognition, emotion attribution and emotion-oriented summarization simultaneously. Specifically,

Emotion recognition. The final softmax layer of EC-net is to identify the emotion. It thus outputs the likelihood of one video belonging to which type of emotion.

Emotion attribution. The video segments of high emotion scores, i.e. emotion attribution, can be directly computed by using the θ values computed by FT-net. With the well trained FT-EC-net and θ computed, the emotion attribution segment is computed as follows. Suppose the length of candidate video is l, the selected segment starts at t_s and ends at t_e;

$$t_s = \frac{l}{2} \cdot (\theta_2 - \theta_1 + 1) \tag{2}$$

$$t_e = \frac{l}{2} \cdot (\theta_1 + \theta_2 + 1) \tag{3}$$

The Eq (2) and Eq (3) are derived from Eq (1).

Emotion-oriented summarization. By utilizing the results of video attribution, the summary of video skims can be directly generated from the selected segments. We also uniformly sample the frames/video clips from selected segments as the keyframes summary/video skims.

4 EXPERIMENTS

4.1 Dataset

We conduct experiments on two video emotion datasets.

Emotion6 video dataset. Inspired by [6], we augment the Emotion6 dataset [16] and create Emotion6 video dataset as the testbed for our tasks. Emotion6 dataset consists of 6 basic emotions. Each image has been labelled with a distribution of all these emotions as well as one domaint emotion. To construct the dataset, we randomly crawled an auxiliary image dataset online which has no strong evoked emotions and uses as the noise set. The frames of each video are selected either from Emotion6 dataset with the dominant evoked emotion, or from the auxiliary image set. The corresponding emotion labels come from Emotion6 dataset.

Ekman6 dataset. Ekman6 dataset is firstly collected by [24]. It contains 6 different types of emotions; totally 1637 videos with around 220 videos per class. To further evaluate the tasks of emotion-oriented video summarization and attribution, all the videos are annotated with the most emotion-oriented segments. Specifically, for each video, three annotators are invited to label the key segments which contribute the most to the overall emotion label of this video. The overlapped segment labels beween two annotators are thus saved as ground-truth segments. Finally, we obtain $1-3$ emotion related segments of each video. In this paper, we employ as the evaluation the anger and surprise classes, which have most number of video instances. We will release these annotations upon the acceptance.

Features. DeepSentibank [4] is utilized to extract the features of the $fc7$ layer of each frame. DeepSentibank is initialized with the weights trained from ImageNet and fine-tuned on the Sentibank dataset.

4.2 Competitors

Our model is compared against the following models.
SVM by Majority Voting (SVM) . The $fc7$ features of Emotion6 training set are used to train a linear SVM classifier. The emotion scores can be thus predicted on each individual frame of testing videos. The final classification labels are voted majoritively; and the attribution/summarization results are obtained by selecting the segments with the highest emotion scores.
Image Transfer Encoding (ITE). Our model is compared with the state-of-the-art method – ITE [24]. Particularly, we use the same setting of ITE as [24]: we cluster 2000 centers from the emotion-rich auxiliary image dataset; and by using these 2000 centers as bins, we encode the frames of one video into video-level representation; a linear SVM model is trained to solve the emotion recognition task. The attribution/summarization can also be solved by selecting the frames that have the smallest distances to video-level representation.
Convolutional neural networks (CNN). In video emotion classification, our model is compared with convolutional neural networks. We remove the FT-net from our framework and get a pure CNN structure capable for emotion recognition task.

4.3 Settings and Evaluation

Emotion recognition. The predicted labels are compared against the ground truth labels to calculate the classification accuracy.
Emotion Attribution. We employ the evaluation metrics – mean Average Precision (mAP) for video detection [3].
Emotion-oriented summarization. User study is employed to quantitatively compare our results against the competitors.
Parameter Settings. We empirically set the initial value of ; We empirically set the bias of the second fully connected layer in localization network, which is also the value of $\theta = [0.2, 0]$, to be $[0.2, 0]$. The models are trained for 1000 epochs with the batch size of 40 on Emotion6 video dataset, and the batch size of 20 on Ekman6 dataset. Dropout is employed here on all fully connected layers and the ratio is set as 0.75. A softmax layer is utilized to calculate loss and Adam[9] is used to accelerate learning. Our codes are implemented on tensorflow. For each dataset, the model is repeatedly trained from 5 times to reduce the variance; and the averaged performance is reported. The codes are downloadable from https://github.com/kittenish/Frame-Transformer-Network.

Table 1: Emotion recognition results.

Dataset	Chance	SVM	ITE	CNN	Ours
Emotion6 video	16.7%	80.0%	77.5%	81.3%	**82.2%**
Ekman6	50.0%	60.1%	67.0%	74.0%	**74.4%**

Preprocessing of dataset. On Emotion6 video dataset, we uniformly sample 30 frames for each video. Due to the fact that videos in Ekman6 dataset are slightly longer, 100 frames are uniformly sampled from each video. Zero-value frames are added if the total frames of one video is less than 100 .

4.4 Results on Emotion Recognition

We perform the emotion recognition on two datasets. The results are reported in Tab. 1. We compare with SVM, ITE, and CNN methods. The experimental results show that our framework outperforms all the other baselines on both datasets. This validates the effectiveness of our methods.

We also observe that, (1) comparing with CNN methods, our model has 0.9 and 0.4 absolute percentage improvement thanks to the FT-net which can attribute the emotional segments. (2) The improvement of our model over ITE and SVM shows that by integrating the attribution results, our EC-net can get better emotion classification results. (3) The worst performance comes from SVM. This might be due to the fact that emotion is intrinsically sparsely expressed in the video; and thus the trained linear SVM classifier is not reliable to predict confident emotion scores of frames.

4.5 Results on Emotion Attribution

We conduct the experiments on emotion attribution. Specifically we compare with the methods of ITE and SVM. For SVM method, the emotion segments can be sampled from the longest majority-voted video emotion segments.

The mAP score is introduced here to evaluate the performance of emotion attribution[3]. To compare the mAP, we have to decide whether one video detection is true positive or not. In particular, we firstly calculate the overlap between the prediction of temporal video segment and the ground-truth segment. This overlap is measured by the temporal intersection over union ($tIou$) score of predicted and ground-truth segment. The prediction is marked as positive if the overlapping is greater than a threshold α. The mAP score can thus be computed.

We compare the emotion attribution results on the two classes of Ekman6 and Emotion6 video dataset in Fig. 2. We vary the threshold α on these two datasets. On Ekman6 dataset, our results are comparable or better than those of ITE method. This validates that our FT-net network can actually help identify the video segments that contribute the most to the overall emotion of one video. Furthermore, note that the good results of FT-net also benefit greatly from the recognition task of EC-net, since FT-net is basically learning to sample the video segments by the classification results. On the Emotion6 video dataset, our results still consistently outperform those of ITE method. On this dataset, we also notice that the SVM method has very good and stable performance; this is because our SVM classifier is exclusively trained on Emotion6 images. However,

Figure 2: Emotion attribution results. We report the mAP scores for each dataset.

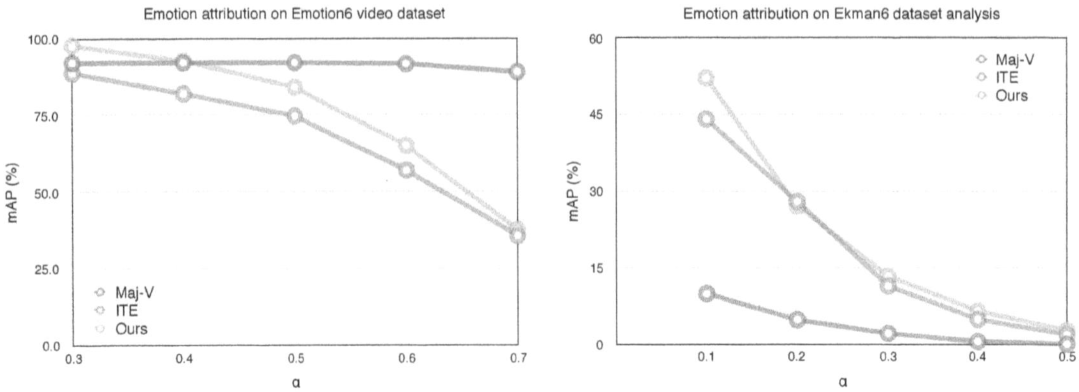

Figure 3: The qualitative results of emotion-oriented video summarization. We compare several baselines.

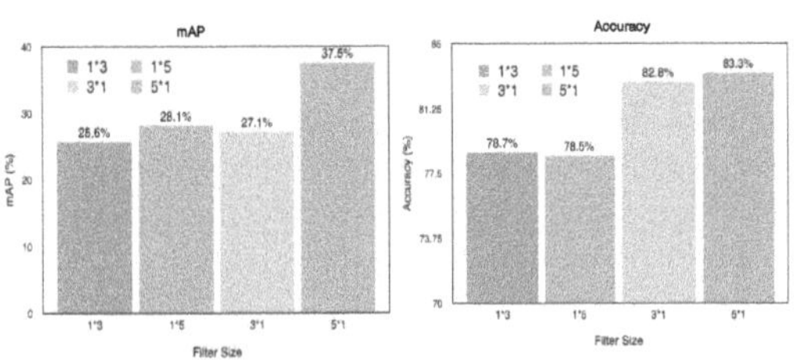

Figure 4: The classification accuracy and mAP scores of ablation study on the filter size of convolutional layer. We use $\alpha = 0.7$ to compute the mAP score.

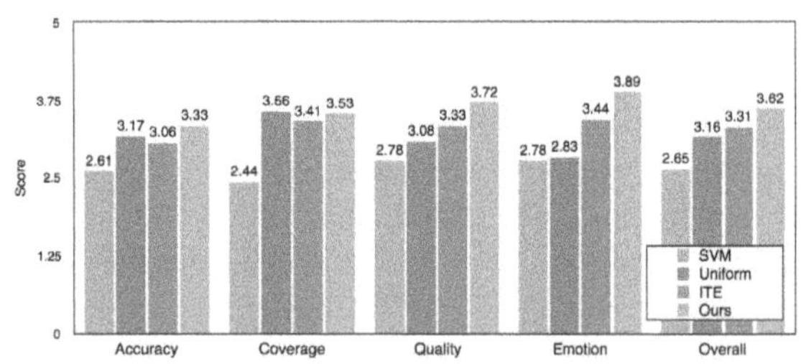

Figure 5: The qualitative results of emotion-oriented video summarization. "Overall" scores are the averaged sum of all the other four scores.

when we empirically validate training a SVM predictor which is weakly supervised on Ekman6 dataset, the performance is very poor.

4.6 Video Emotion-oriented Summarization

The emotion-oriented video summarization is evaluated finally. Several different baselines are compared against our results: (1) Uniform (Uni): uniformly sample the frames/clips from the videos; (2) SVM: the video is summarized by the scores of SVM prediction. The frames with top-6 scores of each label are selected in practice. (3) ITE: we use the method based on ITE [24] for video summarization. To make the results more comparable, the length of summary is fixed to the same length.

User study is utilized to evaluate the results of summarization. Five students kept unknown from our project participate in the study. We show the results of all methods to each participant who rate the quality of summary on five-point scale by answering the following four questions [24]: (1) Accuracy: whether the summary accurately describes the main content of original video?(2) Coverage: how much visual content has been covered in the summary?(3) Quality: how is the overall subjective quality of summary? (4) Emotion: how many percentage of the same emotion has been conveyed from original video?

The user-study results are shown in Fig. 5. Our framework achieves good performance on all the scores. This shows the good summary results that our model can generate. Figure 3 gives the qualitative illustration of the summary generated by different methods. The example is an "angry" video, which capture the process of an angry man smashing everything in the room. The Uniform and SVM methods are not good enough to grasp the video summary of angry emotion; and it makes the viewers think that the man is finding something. In contrast, both ITE and ours can help identify emotional segments. Especially, our summary has the shot of the man smashing the sofa with a hammer.

4.7 Ablation Study of the Convolutional Layer

The convolutional layer in EC-net performs the role of connecting FT-net and EC-net in our architecture. This layer processes the output of FT-net for the classification in EC-net. Previous work [11] used symmetric convolutional filters. In contrast, with the $fc7$ input features, our convolutional layer aims at modeling the contextual information within consecutive frames of each feature dimension. Considering the importance of the convolutional layer, we conduct the ablation study to verify different filter sizes of this layer. We compare the tasks of emotion recognition and emotion attribution with the filter sizes of 1×3, 1×5, 3×1, and 5×1 respectively on Emotion6 video dataset.

The results are reported in Fig.4. The results with the filter size of 5×1 can beat all the other choices on both classification accuracy and mAP score. This suggests that our choice of 5×1 filter size can successfully capture the contextual emotion information which can finally help both emotion classification and attribution tasks. In general, the convolutional filter sizes of 3×1 and 5×1 capture the information on the same feature channel (totally 4096 channels) along consecutive frames. In contrast, the filter sizes of 1×3 and 1×5 extract information from the same frame of neighboring feature channels, which however have limited contextual information usable for EC-net. That explains the low results of emotion recognition accuracy of filter sizes 1×3 and 1×5.

5 CONCLUSION

In this paper, we present a new architecture– Frame-Transformer Emotion Classification Network (FT-EC-net), which can solve the emotion recognition, emotion attribution and emotion-oriented summarization tasks simultaneously. A new labelled emotion attribution dataset is contributed. We also introduce an objective evaluation metric of emotion attribution task. The experiments on Emotion6 video and Ekman6 dataset have validated the effectiveness of our framework.

6 ACKNOWLEDGEMENT

This work was supported in part by three NSFC projects (#U1611461, #U1509206, #61572134) and a grant from STCSM, Shanghai, China (#16JC1420401), and Shanghai Sailing Program (17YF1427500).

REFERENCES

[1] Esra Acar, Frank Hopfgartner, and Sahin Albayrak. 2016. A comprehensive study on mid-level representation and ensemble learning for emotional analysis of video material. *Multimedia Tools and Applications* (2016), 1–29.
[2] Damian Borth, Rongrong Ji, Tao Chen, Thomas M. Breuel, and Shih-Fu Chang. 2013. Large-scale Visual Sentiment Ontology and Detectors using Adjective Noun Pairs. In *ACM MM*.
[3] Fabian Caba Heilbron, Victor Escorcia, Bernard Ghanem, and Juan Carlos Niebles. 2015. Activitynet: A large-scale video benchmark for human activity understanding. In *Proceedings of the IEEE Conference on Computer Vision and Pattern Recognition*. 961–970.
[4] Tao Chen, Damian Borth, Darrell, and Shih-Fu Chang. 2014. DeepSentiBank: Visual Sentiment Concept Classification with Deep Convolutional Neural Networks. *CoRR* (2014).
[5] Abhinav Dhall, Roland Goecke, Jyoti Joshi, Jesse Hoey, and Tom Gedeon. 2016. Emotiw 2016: Video and group-level emotion recognition challenges. In *Proceedings of the 18th ACM International Conference on Multimodal Interaction*. ACM, 427–432.
[6] Max Jaderberg, Karen Simonyan, Andrew Zisserman, and others. 2015. Spatial transformer networks. In *Advances in Neural Information Processing Systems*. 2017–2025.
[7] Yu-Gang Jiang, Baohan Xu, and Xiangyang Xue. 2014. Predicting Emotions in User-Generated Videos. In *AAAI*.
[8] Brendan Jou, Subhabrata Bhattacharya, and Shih-Fu Chang. 2014. Predicting Viewer Perceived Emotions in Animated GIFs. In *ACM MM*.
[9] Diederik Kingma and Jimmy Ba. 2014. Adam: A method for stochastic optimization. *arXiv preprint arXiv:1412.6980* (2014).
[10] Dimitrios Kotzias, Misha Denil, Phil Blunsom, and Nando de Freitas. 2014. Deep Multi-Instance Transfer Learning. *CoRR* (2014).
[11] Alex Krizhevsky, Ilya Sutskever, and Geoffrey E. Hinton. 2012. ImageNet Classification with Deep Convolutional Neural Networks. In *NIPS*.
[12] Jie-Ling Lai and Yang Yi. 2012. Key frame extraction based on visual attention model. *Journal of Visual Communication and Image Representation* 23, 1 (2012), 114–125.
[13] X. Lu, P. Suryanarayan, R. B. Adams, J. Li, M. G. Newman, and J. Z Wang. 2012. On shape and the computability of emotions. In *ACM MM*.
[14] Yu-Fei Ma, Lie Lu, Hong-Jiang Zhang, and Mingjing Li. 2002. A User Attention Model for Video Summarization. In *ACM MM*.
[15] J. Machajdik and A. Hanbury. 2010. Affective image classication using features inspired by psychology and art theory. In *ACM MM*.
[16] Kuan-Chuan Peng, Tsuhan Chen, Amir Sadovnik, and Andrew Gallagher. 2015. A Mixed Bag of Emotions: Model, Predict, and Transfer Emotion Distributions. In *CVPR*.
[17] Attend Show. 2015. Tell: Neural Image Caption Generation with Visual Attention. *Kelvin Xu et. al.. arXiv Pre-Print* (2015).
[18] Krishna Kumar Singh and Yong Jae Lee. 2016. End-to-end localization and ranking for relative attributes. In *European Conference on Computer Vision*. Springer, 753–769.
[19] Ba Tu Truong and Svetha Venkatesh. 2007. Video Abstraction: A Systematic Review and Classification. *ACM TOMM* 3, 1 (2007), 79–82.
[20] Meng Wang, R. Hong, Guangda Li, Zheng-Jun Zha, Shuicheng Yan, and Tat-Seng Chua. 2012. Event Driven Web Video Summarization by Tag Localization and Key-Shot Identification. *IEEE TMM* 14, 4 (2012), 975–985.
[21] S. Wang and Q. Ji. 2015. Video affective content analysis: a survey of state of the art methods. *IEEE TAC* PP, 99 (2015), 1–1. DOI:https://doi.org/10.1109/TAFFC.2015.2432791
[22] Xi Wang, Yu-Gang Jiang, Zhenhua Chai, Zichen Gu, Xinyu Du, and Dong Wang. 2014. Real-time summarization of user-generated videos based on semantic recognition. In *ACM MM*.
[23] Baohan Xu, Yanwei Fu, Yu gang Jiang, Boyang Li, and Leonid Sigal. 2016. Video Emotion Recognition with Transferred Deep Feature Encodings. In *ICMR*.
[24] Baohan Xu, Yanwei Fu, Yu gang Jiang, Boyang Li, and Leonid Sigal. 2017. Heterogeneous Knowledge Transfer in Video Emotion Recognition, Attribution and Summarization. *IEEE TAC* (2017).
[25] Quanzeng You, Jiebo Luo, Hailin Jin, and Jianchao Yang. 2015. Robust Image Sentiment Analysis Using Progressively Trained and Domain Transferred Deep Networks. In *AAAI*.

The Geo-Privacy Bonus of Popular Photo Enhancements

Jaeyoung Choi
Delft University of Technology
Netherlands
International Computer Science Institute, USA
j.choi@tudelft.nl

Martha Larson
Radboud University
Delft University of Technology
Netherlands
mlarson@science.ru.nl

Xinchao Li
Delft University of Technology
Netherlands
x.li-3@tudelft.nl

Kevin Li
University of California, Berkeley
USA
kevinli7@berkeley.edu

Gerald Friedland
Lawrence Livermore National Laboratory
University of California, Berkeley
USA
fractor@eecs.berkeley.edu

Alan Hanjalic
Delft University of Technology
Netherlands
a.hanjalic@tudelft.nl

ABSTRACT

Today's geo-location estimation approaches are able to infer the location of a target image using its visual content alone. These approaches typically exploit visual matching techniques, applied to a large collection of background images with known geo-locations. Users who are unaware that visual analysis and retrieval approaches can compromise their geo-privacy, unwittingly open themselves to risks of crime or other unintended consequences. This paper lays the groundwork for a new approach to geo-privacy of social images: Instead of requiring a change of user behavior, we start by investigating users' existing photo-sharing practices. We carry out a series of experiments using a large collection of social images to systematically analyze how photo editing practices impact the performance of geo-location estimation. We find that standard image enhancements, including filters and cropping, already serve as natural geo-privacy protectors. In our experiments, up to 19% of images whose location would otherwise be automatically predictable were unlocalizeable after enhancement. We conclude that it would be wrong to assume that geo-visual privacy is a lost cause in today's world of rapidly maturing machine learning. Instead, protecting users against the unwanted effects of pixel-based inference is a viable research field. A starting point is understanding the geo-privacy bonus of already established user behavior.

KEYWORDS

geo-privacy; geo-location estimation; usable privacy for multimedia retrieval

ACM ISBN 978-1-4503-4701-3/17/06...$15.00
DOI: http://dx.doi.org/10.1145/3078971.3080543

Figure 1: Geo-location Estimation can automatically infer the location of a target photo (a) shared online by a user if at least one visually matching, geo-tagged image, e.g., (b), a 'geo-propagator', exists in the background collection. However, widespread practices, such as enhancement filters (c) can serve to protect image geo-location information.

ACM Reference format:
Jaeyoung Choi, Martha Larson, Xinchao Li, Kevin Li, Gerald Friedland, and Alan Hanjalic. 2017. The Geo-Privacy Bonus of Popular Photo Enhancements. In *Proceedings of ICMR '17, June 6–9, 2017, Bucharest, Romania, ,* 9 pages.
DOI: http://dx.doi.org/10.1145/3078971.3080543

1 INTRODUCTION

As multimedia retrieval technologies improve, it is possible in an increasing number of cases to automatically infer the location at which a photo was taken on the basis of its visual content. Most work on Geo-location Estimation (GLE), emphasizes the usefulness of geo-coordinates in organizing photo collections, and improving multimedia retrieval, e.g., [16, 30, 31]. However, the success of GLE in supporting users in browsing and finding photos depends critically on our ability as a multimedia research community to understand and mitigate its risks.

Users unknowingly release information about their location when they share photos, thus surrendering control of their own geo-privacy, and making themselves vulnerable. Relatively harmless vulnerabilities include the annoyance of unwelcome targeted advertisement. Worse risks also exist, for example, users can expose themselves to criminal attack. Even users who are cautious with publicly sharing photos, are vulnerable if their photos are passed from friend to friend, or if they are stored in unencrypted form, and the storage is hacked.

The key points about GLE for social images that are relevant for this paper are illustrated by the examples in Fig. 1. The leftmost image is a photo that has been uploaded by a user to a popular photo sharing platform (Flickr), and whose geo-location is correctly predicted by our GLE approach, but not predictable after a filter is applied (rightmost image). This geo-privacy 'bonus' of filters is a form of privacy by obfuscation [5] applied to the visual domain. The main approach we apply in this paper, which uses geometric visual matching, represents the state of the art in GLE, and is described in detail later. We also train a deep convolutional neural network inspired by [31] for comparison but, as we will see, the resolution of geo-estimation is much higher for the visual-matching-based approach.

We emphasize that we are not trying to compare different GLE methods and claim that our approach is superior, nor are we trying to argue that our proposed photo taking or enhancing behavior will provide complete geo-privacy protection against current and future GLE systems. Instead, the purpose of this paper is to lay the foundation for a new line of research directed at supporting users in protecting themselves, given their own natural photo-taking and sharing behavior.

At this point, we introduce the core mechanism of our approach. Retrieval-based GLE makes use of a large background collection containing photos for which the geo-location is already known, for example, because the photos are accompanied by GPS coordinates or manually geo-tagged by the uploading user. Here, we use 8.5 million images. The target image is used to retrieve 'geo-propagators', visually matching images from the background collection. Geo-location prediction is accomplished by propagating the geo-coordinates of one or more geo-propagators to the target image.

In Fig. 1, the middle image is an example of a 'geo-propagator', one of the images used to infer the location of the target image (leftmost image). This image was taken by a different user, who either used a camera that recorded GPS coordinates, or provided the geo-location during upload. Note that retrieval-based GLE does not build a explicit model of a location, rather, a single photo uploaded by another user is sufficient to identify the geo-location at which the target photo was taken. In this example, the target photo and the geo-propagator clearly depict the same object/landmark. However, the visual match can also involve what could otherwise be considered unimportant background detail.

It is natural for the images (a) and (b) in Fig. 1 to be a cause for some alarm. The leftmost photograph was uploaded by a user, who most likely would assume that the location of the photo would be protected if he turned off the GPS of his cameras. As already mentioned, the unintended consequences range from annoying (e.g., for newly weds who were not planning to reveal their secret honeymoon destination) to downright dangerous (e.g., for a young mother targeted by a stalker). This alarm is the factor that triggered this paper. However, the basic insight that we build on is fundamentally a positive one: Users' photo taking and sharing behavior does not always lead to geo-privacy risks. If we can analyze natural behavior that protects privacy, then we take a step towards achieving our ultimate, long term goal, of developing multimedia technology that puts control over geo-privacy back into the hands of users.

The rightmost image (c) of Fig. 1 represents the widespread practice of filtering, which is naturally protective of geo-privacy. This image is comparable to image (a) from the user perspective. However, in contrast to (a), the location can *not* be correctly predicted via visual matching with images in the background collection. In the example, the "Toaster" Instagram filter has been applied. After application of the filter, the location of the image can no longer be correctly predicted by our GLE algorithm.

In short, this example points towards the existence of simple practices applied by users that naturally *geo-cloak* their images, i.e., prevent the locations of those images from being automatically predicted. The implication is that it is not necessary to introduce new, never-before-seen technologies in order to protect users' geo-privacy. Such technologies require user acceptance and widespread uptake before they can be effective. Rather, we can target new information retrieval technologies that build on behaviors that users naturally engage in, independently of privacy considerations. This paper represents a first step on the road to such technologies.

We take the position that GLE technology has both positive and negative implications for users. For this reason, we necessarily approach the topic of geo-privacy for social images, not with the goal of developing the ultimate privacy protecting algorithm, but rather, with the goal of attaining the *correct balance* between positive and unintended consequences. It is important to note that we are *not* asserting that every image must be geo-privacy protected/geo-cloaked. Indeed, there are many images taken and shared by users precisely for the reason of revealing geo-location, apparently to as many other people as possible. We do not propose that every picture of the Eiffel Tower or of the Taj Mahal should be enhanced to become visually distinctive. Rather, we strive to understand how users' behavior impacts geo-privacy because of its importance in situations where geo-location information is 'incidental' to images, and represents a potential, unintended geo-privacy leak. Because of the rate at which photos are taken and shared by users online the balance that we strive to achieve is necessarily a *dynamic balance*. A photo whose geo-location cannot be identified by our system today, might well be identifiable tomorrow, as more images are taken and added to the background collection. We address the dynamic balance by considering not only the geo-cloaking of individual images, but also the connection of how the ability of a given photo to compromise the geo-privacy of the user is related to the availability of other photos online.

The paper makes the following contributions:

- Danger of Geo-Location Estimation: Comparison of a state-of-the-art GLE system that uses image retrieval (visual-based matching) and a deep network-based classification approach.
- Image editing behavior: Experiments showing the way in which widespread image enhancements (e.g., filters and cropping) impact automatic GLE,
- Research challenges: Provide the motivation for a new line of research devoted to visual geo-privacy that protects

users against unwanted affects of visual retrieval by leveraging their own natural behavior.

In the next section, we provide additional motivation for the paper and also cover related work. Then, we present the results of our experiment-based analysis. We finish with an outlook on the challenges to be tackled in the future.

2 MOTIVATION AND RELATED WORK

In this section, we take a closer look at the background and motivation for our work, and discuss its relationship to existing work.

2.1 Image Privacy Classification

Studies on privacy-aware image classification [27, 33] try to provide a safeguarding mechanism that relies on the automatic classification of privacy-related images by image sharing platforms. Such an approach attempts to alleviate the limitations of privacy settings in social networks. Although this approach may provide some measure of improvement in users' privacy, there is no guarantee that an online social network platform will incorporate necessary solutions to provide adequate protection to its users. For this reason, privacy solutions must focus on the users' side and factors directly under the users' control.

2.2 The Importance of Geo-Privacy

Privacy involves the ability to control information about oneself, and, by extension, we define *geo-privacy* as the ability to control information about one's location, both in the past and in the future. As mentioned in the introduction, leaks of personal geo-information can be annoying. The literature, however, tends to cover the more dangerous consequences, especially the phenomena of 'cybercasing', burglars automatically harvesting information about potential victims online [13]. cybercasing [13], generally, out-of-town homeowners. Ready-or-Not[1] and PleaseRobMe[2] serve to illustrate the privacy implciations of location disclosure in online social networks. Further, the phenomenon of stalking has been connected to opportunity [25], and, as such, geo-information in the hands of the perpetrator renders the victim more vulnerable.

In the real world, there are no failsafe protections against burglars and stalkers. Instead, people protect themselves by trading off convenience with conventional protection measures. Our goal in seeking to protect geo-privacy is to increase the number of measures at users' disposal to protect themselves.

There are obvious parallels between concerns about automatic face detection algorithms compromising privacy [29], and geo-location estimation algorithms compromising privacy. However, geo-location estimation is potentially more pernicious, since users are likely unaware of conditions under which a GLE algorithm can automatically predict the locations of their images. The first 'GLE condition' is the visual distinctiveness of the image content. The visual elements that allow GLE to geo-locate the image in the first column of Fig. 1 range from fairly obvious to barely noticeable. The second 'GLE condition' is the presence of 'geo-propagators' in the background collection that are visually closer to the target image than images taken at other locations. Although a user may have a rough idea of the number of photographs taken at a given location, there is no way to guess the existence of visually similar locations. The impossibility of deciding whether the GLE conditions are satisfied, mean that users are, an can be expected to remain, easily susceptible to inadvertently leaking geo-information when sharing photos.

Two points characterize the nature of the negative impact that automatic GLE of social images poses to user geo-privacy. First, GLE is dangerous not because it is able to identify the location at which an image is taken, but rather because it is able to do so *automatically*. Automatic processing is fast, and makes it possible to mine large collections of social images in search of vulnerabilities, as with cybercasing, mentioned above. Second, automatic processing can potentially identify location in cases that would be challenging for a human observer. The number of people who can identify the location of the images in Fig. 1 is relatively small. The location can, however, be identified by anyone with access to GLE technology. The goal in protecting geo-privacy is not to completely eradicate evidence of location in social images, but rather to slow down or hold back the ability of GLE algorithms to automatically process large quantities of social images and extract location information. Users should retain control over whether or not their images are geo-locatable or not.

2.3 Social images and geo-location estimation

This paper takes the position that it is important to understand how user behavior impacts automatic geo-location estimation technology, since this technology opens users to risks that they may be unaware of. It should be noted that this is a nuanced stance—we do not claim that all automatic geo-location estimation is bad, rather that we need to understand the extent to which users can control whether or not it can be applied to their photos. In this subsection, we briefly review the work on geo-location estimation. This work has generally emphasized the positive side of image GLE, and the potential it has to serve users in browsing and finding images.

Although this paper is devoted to protecting users against the unintended consequences of visual GLE, we point out that ultimately researchers need to address the unintended consequences of multimodal (such as visual/text or visual/audio) GLE.

2.3.1 Visual-based geo-location estimation. Visual-approaches to automatic geo-location estimation can be divided into two types of approaches. The first type, geo-constrained GLE approaches, attempts to predict the geo-location given a relatively restricted range of candidate locations. The second type, global-scale GLE approaches, attempt to predict the geo-location of photos any where on the surface of the earth. For this purpose, visual retrieval techniques applied to a large background collection of geo-tagged images are exploited, as mentioned in the introduction.

The first type of approaches, geo-constrained GLE, has included city-scale landmark recognition [7], estimation of location in target images using geo-informative visual attributes learned from training images of cities [18] [12], and classification [14].

Compared to the effort that has been devoted to geo-constrained GLE, there has been relatively less work dedicated to predicting locations at global scale. A major contribution in this direction was the approach by Hays and Efros [16]. They deployed various

[1] app.teachingprivacy.org
[2] pleaserobme.com

global visual representations to model the visual scene similarity between images and employed the Mean Shift Clustering approach to estimate the location. Further contributions were made by the Placing Task of the MediaEval multimedia evaluation benchmark, which addressed the challenge of location estimation for social images [15].

Here, we focus on a state-of-the-art GLE system called Distinctive Visual Element Matching approach, which was proposed by Li et al. [21]. Given a query image, a geo-location is predicted based on the evidence collected from images that have sufficient visual similarity to the query image and are also geographically close. The use of such 'geo-visual neighborhoods' to predict allows DVEM to improve over two major classes of previous visual-based retrieval approaches, addressing the disadvantages of both 1-NM and clustering [16].

Google's PlaNet [31] is a deep convolutional neural network (CNN) approach that divides the surface of the globe into cells. The algorithm adapts cell size to the number of images in its training set that are labeled with geo-coordinates for a specific location location, i.e., a location that has more photos will be divided into finer cells. Each cell is considered a class, and is used to train a CNN classifier. Inspired by the result reported in [31], we trained a deep network and compared with the retrieval based approach by Li et al. [21].

2.3.2 Image augmentation for convolutional neural networks. A major factor in the recent success of deep convolutional neural networks has been the availability of vast quantities of data. Data augmentation, which effectively increases the amount of training data by imposing a variety of changes on the original data, has been shown to increase the classification accuracy of deep convolutional neural networks. The winners [32] of the 2016 ILSVRC scene classification challenge [26] used color augmentation, PCA jittering, random image interpolation, and crop sampling in their training. Upon first consideration, Instagram filters may appear to qualify as a perturbation that might improve the performance of GLE estimation if applied to the training data. However, our assumption is that the geo-privacy bonus effect arises because image enhancements constitute information loss, and for this reason we expect that adding filtered images to the training data will not deliver an improvement related to data augmentation, but rather will be detrimental to GLE performance.

2.4 Weakness of other geo-privacy approaches

Next we cover possible alternative approaches that could be taken to geo-privacy. We mention them here in order to highlight their weaknesses, and underline the importance of gaining insight into how users natural behavior can already serve to protect their privacy.

2.4.1 Image alteration for keypoint removal and re-injection. The forensics and image analysis communities have devoted quite a bit of effort to techniques that conceal images from SIFT-based image retrieval system by removing keypoints and forging in new keypoints [9, 10, 17]. These systems were studied in the context of copyright detection and explore the robustness of near duplicate detection systems. This work differs from our own in that social images uploaded by users are very diverse, and for this reason, the need to handle near-duplicates is not common in GLE. In [24], image obfuscation methods are proposed to protect privacy of users against threats caused by Internet bots that extract biometric and other features for data-linkage purposes.

There are two drawbacks to keypoint removal and re-injection technology for protecting user geo-privacy. First, these type of image alteration may add unwanted distortion and artifacts to the image. In contrast to our approach, such technology cannot take for granted that the aesthetics of the image will be preserved. Second, such technology requires users to add a separate step to their photo-taking and image enhancement practices. A certain number of users would likely adopt the technologies, but large-scale adoption would demand an unprecedented level of acceptance.

2.4.2 Human-based solutions. So-called 'human-based solutions' would require users to change their behavior in response to awareness of the risks of online photo sharing. Social networking and photo-sharing websites are increasingly offering the opportunities to share photos privately. Researchers studying user behavior with respect to photo privacy have found that users experience a strong desire to participate in social sharing, which exerts a force on them to accept problems resulting from lack of control over their identity and disclosures [4]. The difficulty that users experience in dealing with complicated privacy settings is uncovered by [20] As a result of these difficulties, users make the choice of easy (i.e., public) sharing over privacy protective measures when they get overloaded. People are worried that the photo will not be shared properly and this impact their decision to share privately [1]. Computer scientists have developed many mechanisms to protect users' privacy, such as encrypted email and messaging. However, users are slow to adopt such solutions for a range of reasons. We reject solutions that require users to radically change their behavior for the simple practical reason that any approach to geo-privacy that is not actively used by users is effectively worthless.

2.4.3 Strength of simplicity. Recently, appreciation has arisen for simple, practical, filter-based approaches in service of privacy protection. The movement, typified by [6], has been led by researchers investigating how private information in images can be protected from *human* viewers. In contrast, in this work we investigate approaches to protect image content from *algorithms.*

However, like these researchers we recognize the value of simple approaches that are easy to apply in practice. Additionally, we point out the recent work that has been carried out on deceiving image classifiers that use deep neural networks [23]. In the context of privacy preservation, deceiving a classifier means protecting the content of an image. Here, we compare both *classification* and *retrieval* approaches to infer image content. *Retrieval* approaches may ultimately prove more difficult to defeat, since they require minimally one correct match, rather than a set of classifier training data.

3 EXPERIMENTAL SETUP

In this section, we set the stage for our analysis of the interaction of automatic GLE technology with user behavior by describing the setup of our experiments.

3.1 Data set and evaluation

In order to ensure the validity and impact of our experimental results, we need a data set that is representative in scale for the state of the art in social image geo-location estimation. The data should also publicly be available, in order to make it possible for researchers who follow us to reproduce the experimental findings of this paper. We choose the MediaEval Placing Task 2013 Data Set [15][3], a Creative Commons licensed set of images gathered from Flickr, which fulfills both of these criteria. Our experiments consist of two parts, GLE matching, and result analysis, and call for the application of both commercial tools and manual analysis. In order to ensure that we do not surpass the bonds of the resources at our disposal, we concentrate our experiments on a set of target images (also called, 'query images') that were taken in a specific region, San Francisco, California. We choose our region to be highly dense, since in this way it can be considered representative of the state which many regions of the world can be projected to reach, as the number of images taken by users continues to grow in future years. The total number of background collection images is 8,539,050 and the target images is 2,006.

The results of our experiments are reported in terms of two different kinds of evaluation. First, the evaluation performance of the image GLE system. This is measured in terms of the percentage of photos whose geo-locations were correctly estimated with a given distance threshold (i.e., radius) of their ground truth location. The ground truth of the photos is the position at which the photographer was standing when the picture was taken. We use the geo-coordinates recorded by the GPS of the user's camera, or assigned by hand to the user during the process of uploading to Flickr. We focus on two distance thresholds: 100 meters and 1 kilometer, under the assumption these are relevant for privacy concerns. Second, we report the performance the results of our experiments in terms of *percent cloaked*. The percent cloaked is the proportion of the number of images that can be correctly geo-located with the original image, that can no longer be correctly geo-located once a specific 'enhancement', e.g., a filter, has been applied.

3.2 Visual geo-location estimation approach

Next we describe the GLE systems that were used for the experiments: DVEM, the search approach based on geometric visual-feature matching and a deep convolutional neural network based approach.

3.2.1 DVEM: Distinctive Visual Element Matching. Distinctive Visual Element Matching [21] is a search-based approach to the prediction of the geo-location of an image. This algorithm uses local image features (upright SIFT) for retrieval, and then creates geo-clusters in the list of image search results. It adopts the top ranked clusters and validates the visual match at the cluster level (rather than at the level of an individual image) using a geometric verification technique for object/scene matching. DVEM leverages the occurrence of visual elements that are discriminative for specific locations.

3.2.2 Deep Convolution Neural Network. As many neural network approaches are achieving the state of the art result in a variety of tasks, we also implemented a deep convolutional neural network for location estimation based on PlaNet [31]. The world map was partitioned into grids with respect to the density of the photos using Google's S2 library[4] with $t_1 = 5000$ (maximum number of photos per grid) and $t_2 = 50$ (minimum number of photos per grid). We employed the GoogleNet [28] model with pre-trained weights from Places365 Dataset [34]. We trained our model by fine-tuning the fully connected layer and the last inception module using AdaGrad [11] with a learning rate of 0.2 to minimize cross-entropy loss with L2 regularization with a regularization constant of 0.01. Training was stopped when training loss converged. Geo-location labels were naively assigned as the average latitude and longitude values of the training images in each grid.

4 GEO-LOCATABLE SOCIAL IMAGES

First, we discuss the overall performance of our image GLE systems. Figure 2 shows the performance of two visual geo-location estimation systems. DVEM is the visual-based matching (i.e., image retrieval) approach using upright-SIFT descriptors and DCNN represents the deep convolutional neural network approach. Each number represents the percentage of query images whose geo-locations are correctly estimated within the distance thresholds from the groundtruth. We see that, DVEM system outperforms the DCNN system, and is able to correctly estimate the location of nearly 18% of the photos in the test collection.

Note that although this is the first time that DVEM and DCNN results have been reported for a problem at this scale, the focus here is not on the image GLE algorithm itself, but rather on widespread user photo-taking and enhancement practices. For this reason, it is important that the DVEM algorithm is the state of the art, but we are not looking to improve it, but rather we are investigating the factors that negatively impact its performance. When compared to the ultimate target of image GLE, to correctly geo-locate 100% of social images, our advanced system, which can only geo-locate 18% of images seems rather unthreatening. Unfortunately, this feeling is a false sense of security. Recall from above, that geo-privacy is compromised by large scale mining of images that searches for vulnerable victims to target. For people who leak visual geo-information by mistake, the potential of 18% to translates into direct damage is something that the community needs to take seriously, given that in 7.40% of the cases, the information is exact to the 100 meters level. The current state of GLE technology is a strong motivator to start, as is our goal in this paper, on the large mission of understanding how control over visual geo-information can be put in the hands of the user.

5 IMPACT OF IMAGE ENHANCEMENT

In this section, we examine practices of image enhancement that are in widespread use among users who share photos online. We investigate how enhancement affects automatic GLE of individual photos, and also how enhancement practices scale up as they are used not just by individual users, but by many users contributing images to the background collection.

[3] http://www.st.ewi.tudelft.nl/~hauff/placingTask2013Data.html

[4] https://github.com/google/s2-geometry-library-java

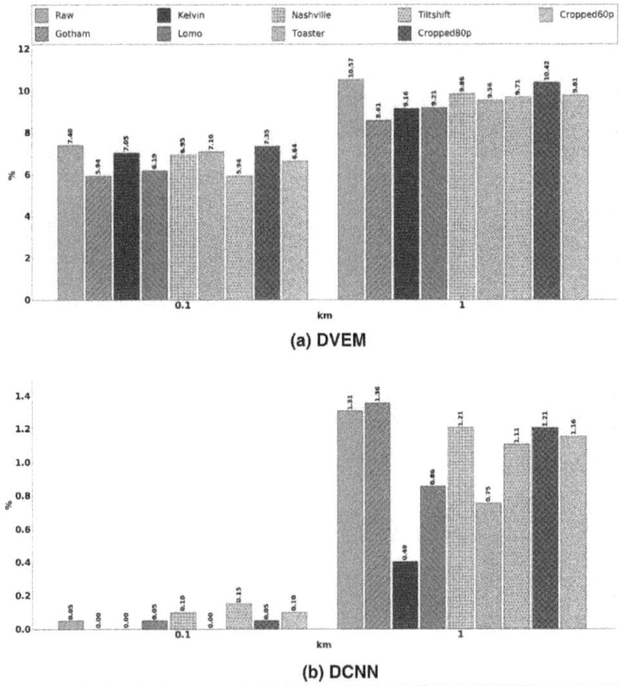

Figure 2: Two charts show the percentages of images correctly geo-located within an 100m and 1km radius from the groundtruth for the (a) DVEM and (b) DCNN approaches. Note that the accuracy (values of y-axis) of DCNN was much lower than DVEM and scale of y-axis is adjusted to show the effect of each photo enhancement.

5.1 Users' behavior and image enhancement

We define image enhancement as filters and other edits that people apply during or after image capture in order to heighten the attractiveness of the image. Specifically, we are interested in enhancements that are highly popular, since these best reflect widespread natural user behavior, which is the focus of our study. We focus on filters and features that are available to users on Instagram[5], one of the most widely used photo sharing/social networking services.

Perhaps the simplest thing that users do to make their images more attractive is cropping. Cropping is often used to cut out clutters in the image and helps the viewer to concentrate on the main subject. Images lose some of its contents along the edge lines when cropped. We are interested in cropping because of its potential to cut out incidental matches in background that could allow photos to be geo-located. Next, we are interested in tilt-shift. Tilt-shift photography manipulates focus and depth-of-field to yield photos that have selective focus, often mimicking a miniature model. Instagram provides a post-production fake tilt-shift feature. Unlike cropping, tilt-shifted image still retains all of the original pixels, although the areas outside the focus point becomes blurred. We are interested in tilt-shift because it is popular, and also because the blur potentially eliminates matches in background.

[5]https://instagram.com/

Figure 3: Image enhancements (popular on Instagram) use in our experiment. Center is the original image. Clockwise from top left: Gotham, Kelvin, Lomo, Toaster, Tiltshift, Crop40%, Crop20% and Nashville.

We focus a large number of experiments on filters. A filter is a preset recipe for adjusting various photographic settings (exposure, contrast, color balance, etc) of a photo to give it certain look and feel. Instagram offers a large number of filters that are carefully tailored, and provide users with a convenient means of enhancing the attractiveness of the photo, with no need for special skill [2]. We are interested in Instagram filters, since their popularity strongly suggests that users feel that they add value to images. Effectively, these filters represent a common practice already applied by users that potentially results in a loss of visual information in images, that can provide a geo-cloaking effect.

Instagram currently provides 40 filters for use. Among the popular filters are Kelvin, Lomo, Nashville, and Toaster. We have selected these filters for our study because they have a relatively strong influence on the original image, and for this reason provide a promising jumping-off point to study geo-cloaking effects. Although the Gotham filter has been discontinued by Instagram, we chose to also include it in our study, since effects are very dramatic with lots of contrast added. The following gives an overview of the filters. Figure 3 shows an example with each filters' effect.

- Gotham filter produces a black & white, high contrast image with bluish undertones.
- Kelvin filter applies a strong peach/orange overlay.
- Lomo filter boosts contrast, and applies vignette (i.e., reduction in brightness/saturation around the edges).
- Nashville filter gives a washed out 80s fashion photo feel with warmed up temperature, lowered contrast and increased exposure.
- Toaster filter features vivid colors with pink/orange glow out of the center.

To carry out the experiments we applied the enhancements to the target photos (i.e., test photos), and, for the final experiment, also to images in the background collection. Instagram filters were applied using ImageMagick[6] in a Python wrapper. Cropping was done using Smart Cropping service provided by Imagga[7]. The Imagga cropping API analyzes images in terms of composition, color and object localization, and attempts to crop in a way that the main subject material of interest remains in the photo. Cropping was applied to crop out 20% and 40% of the original image, respectively. The aspect ratio of the photo was preserved. The tilt-shift effect was applied with a simple Python script [22]. We took the center point of a cropped image generated by Smart Cropping as the focus point of the original image, and the y-axis value of the center point was used to apply linear tilt-shift.

5.2 Geo-cloaking effects of image enhancement

Our experiments revealed that our enhancement filters demonstrated a clear ability to protect the location of images from being automatically predicted by GLE. An overview of the geo-cloaking performance of the filters is provided in Table 1.

	Filter					Crop		Tilt
	GOT	KEL	LOM	NAS	TOA	20%	40%	shift
DVEM	19.04	9.80	14.3	6.45	7.28	12.9	1.12	8.40
DCNN	0	70.4	33.3	3.7	44.4	7.4	7.4	7.4

Table 1: Net geo-cloaking percentage for DVEM and DCNN: Ratio between the number of images that can be automatically geo-located after and before an enhancement has been applied. (Filters: GOTham, KELvin, LOMo, NAShville, TOAster. Crop 20% and 40% represents the percent of the image cropped.) Higher number shows more geo-cloaking effect. Note that these values are relative gain from the images that were correctly geo-located.

Figure 4: Example images whose locations are protected *after* enhancement. First column is the target image; second column is one of the 'geo-propagator' in the background collection; third column is the target protected with enhancement; fourth column is a close visual neighbor of the enhanced target (calculated with respect to a standard nearest neighbor visual matching in order to illustrate the effect). From top to bottom, the enhancements are: Toaster, Lomo, Kelvin, tilt-shift.

These results are worth exploring further, since they clearly show that users' natural behavior can serve to help protect them from geo-privacy leaks, without requiring them to adopt new, yet-unknown technology or applications, or radical changes in their current photo sharing practices. For both DVEM and DCNN approaches, many filters do impressively well.

These findings suggest that geo-location-specific information is being naturally removed from the photo, as the user filters the photo to enhance its attractiveness. Examples of the protective effect of enhancements at work are provided in Fig. 4.

A major insight we can gain from this chart is the the ability of enhancements to geo-cloak photos is comparable at both the 100m as well as the 1km level, although cloaking is slightly more effective at 100m.

5.3 Collective image enhancement patterns

Our experiments so far have yielded a quite satisfying insight—we have determined that the use of image enhancement filters can lead to the substantial reduction of the ability of a geo-estimation system to correctly predict the location of an image. However, an obvious question to ask is whether enhancements might lose their power to protect geo-privacy as the number of enhanced images in the background collection grows. Our final experiment takes a look at what happens to the ability of enhancements to block GLE location by the DCNN approach when training set images are themselves enhanced (original images augmented with enhanced images). In real life, there are two considerations that would impact how filtered images would accumulate in the set of images available creating the GLE system in a training set: first, the number of images that is filtered overall, and, second, the number of images that are filtered with a given type of filter. Here, we chose to focus on a scenario that constitutes a 'worse case' for geo-cloaking. In particular, we investigate the effects when the same enhancement is applied to both the target image and also to the training set images. We perform this experiment using the DCNN system and also report the result of a nearest neighbor based system [8] for comparison.

Table. 2 reports the percentages of enhanced target images that were geo-located when the background collection for nearest neighbor approach [8] consists of enhanced images and training set for DCNN includes both original and the enhanced images. Our hypothesis that filters introduce a loss of information for automatic GLE approaches is supported by the result shown here.

[6]http://www.imagemagick.org
[7]https://imagga.com/technology/smart-cropping-and-slicing.html

		BNN [8]	DCNN
Original	100m	1.51	0
Back. Collect.	1km	4.48	0.25
Enhanced	100m	1.33	0
Back. Collect.	1km	4.08	0.1

Table 2: Comparison of percentage of enhanced (Gotham filter) target images whose location is correctly predicted using the original collection, and using both the original collection and the images with enhancement. In both systems, including filtered images in the background collection (nearest neighbor approach [8]) or training set (DCNN) did not improve the performance.

Overall, the results of this experiment point to the conclusion that a growth in the use of filters will not reduce their ability to geo-cloak users' photos. In fact, enhancing the collection slightly reduces the ability of the GLE approach to correctly predict the location of images. With these results we are apparently observing that filters introduce a loss of that sort of information that is important in order for automatic GLE approaches to function optimally.

6 VISUAL GEO-PRIVACY CHALLENGES

We have argued in this paper that the current state of geo-location estimation technology warrants concern about the geo-privacy of users who take photos and share them online. The conditions under which the location of a photo can be automatically estimated depend both on the photo, and on the contents of the data available to use as the background collection or training set. Since these factors extend beyond what a user can be expected to be aware of, it is impossible for individual users to assess the risks to their own geo-privacy. Instead, they need support from technologies developed by multimedia information retrieval experts.

Our ultimate goal is to give users more control over geo-privacy by supporting them in preventing unintended leaks of geo-information while sharing photos online. Simple solutions, such as 'No-sharing', fail because of the immediacy of other concerns during the photo sharing process. Even if users share only privately, photos can fall into the wrong hands.

This paper has pointed out that although geo-privacy concerns are growing, the situation is not hopeless. Rather there are valuable insights that can be provided by research in the area of visual information retrieval. We have shown that users' own photo taking and image enhancement behavior actually has a contribution to make to protecting their privacy. We have systematically evaluated popular practices in image enhancement, and shown their impact on state-of-the-art geo-location estimation technology. Although certain Instagram filters are effective in helping to protect privacy, there is no silver bullet solution. Instead, more work is needed to understand the interactions of enhancements.

One part of the solution is obviously educating users, and a growing number of efforts are under way to actually teach users about social multimedia privacy [3]. However, an important part of the solution involves technical challenges.

Research dedicated, for example, to techniques that approximate the background collection, could take a step nearer to fitting the collection in memory, and thereby a step nearer to running a geo-privacy aware camera from a mobile phone. We envision such an application would also recommend to the user filters that add Instagram style enhancements, but that are specially chosen to protect geo-privacy. The key challenge of the geo-privacy aware camera is that it should fit seamlessly into currently widespread photographic practices, e.g., use of image enhancements.

Looking towards the future, there is much work to be done. The simplest, most pressing step to be taken is to avoid falling into the currently common language use, e.g., of [19], which refers to techniques that foil machine learning algorithms as 'attacks' independently of a well-specified use scenario. A neutral term such as 'cloaking' projects the positive importance of techniques, such as those that we have discussed in this paper, that inhibit automatic inference. Beyond geo-privacy there are numerous other application scenarios in which users might prefer to defeat machine learning inference to protect the information depicted in images that they share. If we are to create automatic inference systems using data that was generated by users, our first responsibility is to protect the interests of our users.

Moving forward in the longer term, it is critical that research focus both on improving performance of automatic geo-location estimation, but also on allowing users to protect themselves against it. The closer that geo-privacy protection can stay to people's own, already-existing, natural behavior, the greater the chance that it will be effective for the general user population in practice.

7 ACKNOWLEDGMENTS

Part of the experimentation for this work was carried out on the Dutch national e-infrastructure with the support of the SURF Foundation. It was also partially supported by a National Science Foundation Grant No. CNS 1514509 and a collaborative LDRD led by Lawrence Livermore National Laboratory (U.S. Dept. of Energy contract DE-AC52-07NA27344). Any findings and conclusions are the authors', and do not necessarily reflect the views of the funders.

REFERENCES

[1] Shane Ahern, Dean Eckles, Nathaniel S Good, Simon King, Mor Naaman, and Rahul Nair. 2007. Over-exposed?: privacy patterns and considerations in online and mobile photo sharing. In *Proceedings of the SIGCHI conference on Human factors in computing systems*. ACM, 357–366.
[2] Saeideh Bakhshi, David A Shamma, Lyndon Kennedy, and Eric Gilbert. 2015. Why We Filter Our Photos and How It Impacts Engagement. In *Proceedings of International Conference on Web and Social Media*. 12–21.
[3] Julia Bernd, Blanca Gordo, Jaeyoung Choi, Bryan Morgan, Nicholas Henderson, Serge Egelman, Daniel D Garcia, and Gerald Friedland. 2015. Teaching Privacy: Multimedia Making a Difference. *IEEE MultiMedia* 22, 1 (2015), 12–19.
[4] Andrew Besmer and Heather Richter Lipford. 2010. Moving beyond untagging: photo privacy in a tagged world. In *Proceedings of the SIGCHI Conference on Human Factors in Computing Systems*. ACM, 1563–1572.
[5] Finn Brunton and Helen Nissenbaum. 2015. *Obfuscation: A user's guide for privacy and protest*. MIT Press.
[6] Serdar Çiftçi, Pavel Korshunov, Ahmet Akyüz Oğuz, and Touradj Ebrahimi. 2015. Using False Colors to Protect Visual Privacy of Sensitive Content. In *SPIE Human Vision and Electronic Imaging*. 93941L–1–93941L–13.
[7] David M Chen, Georges Baatz, Kevin Köser, Sam S Tsai, Ramakrishna Vedantham, Timo Pylvänäinen, Kimmo Roimela, Xin Chen, Jeff Bach, Marc Pollefeys, and others. 2011. City-scale landmark identification on mobile devices. In *Proceedings of the IEEE Conference on Computer Vision and Pattern Recognition*. IEEE, 737–744.
[8] Jaeyoung Choi, Martha Larson, Xinchao Li, Gerald Friedland, and Alan Hanjalic. 2016. Where to be wary: The impact of widespread photo-taking and image

enhancement practices on users' geo-privacy. *arXiv preprint arXiv:1603.01335* (2016).

[9] Andrea Costanzo, Irene Amerini, Roberto Caldelli, and Mauro Barni. 2014. Forensic Analysis of SIFT Keypoint Removal and Injection. *IEEE Transactions on Information Forensics and Security* 9, 9 (July 2014), 1450–1464.

[10] Thanh-Toan Do, Ewa Kijak, Teddy Furon, and Laurent Amsaleg. 2010. Deluding Image Recognition in SIFT-based CBIR Systems. In *Proceedings of the ACM Workshop on Multimedia in Forensics, Security and Intelligence (MiFor '10)*. 7–12.

[11] Hazan E. Singer Y. Duchi, J. 2011. Adaptive Subgradient Methods for Online Learning and Stochastic Optimization. *JMLR* 12 (2011), 2121–2159.

[12] Quan Fang, Jitao Sang, and Changsheng Xu. 2013. GIANT: Geo-informative Attributes for Location Recognition and Exploration. In *Proceedings of the ACM International Conference on Multimedia (MM '13)*. 13–22.

[13] Gerald Friedland and Robin Sommer. 2010. Cybercasing the Joint: On the Privacy Implications of Geo-tagging. In *Proceedings of the 5th USENIX Conference on Hot Topics in Security (HotSec'10)*. 1–8.

[14] Petr Gronat, Guillaume Obozinski, Josef Sivic, and Tomas Pajdla. 2013. Learning and calibrating per-location classifiers for visual place recognition. In *Proceedings of the IEEE Conference on Computer Vision and Pattern Recognition*. 907–914.

[15] Claudia Hauff, Bart Thomee, and Michele Trevisiol. 2013. Working Notes for the Placing Task at MediaEval 2013. In *Working Notes Proceedings of the MediaEval 2013 Workshop*.

[16] James Hays and Alexei A Efros. 2008. IM2GPS: estimating geographic information from a single image. In *Proceedigns of the IEEE Conference on Computer Vision and Pattern Recognition*. IEEE, 1–8.

[17] Chao-Yung Hsu, Chun-Shien Lu, and Soo-Chang Pei. 2010. Secure and robust sift with resistance to chosen-plaintext attack. In *IEEE International Conference on Image Processing*. 997–1000.

[18] Yannis Kalantidis, Giorgos Tolias, Yannis Avrithis, Marios Phinikettos, Evaggelos Spyrou, Phivos Mylonas, and Stefanos Kollias. 2011. VIRaL: Visual Image Retrieval and Localization. *Multimedia Tools and Applications* 51, 2 (Jan. 2011), 555–592.

[19] Erica Klarreich. 2016. Learning Securely. *Commun. ACM* 59, 11 (Oct. 2016), 12–14.

[20] Bart P. Knijnenburg, Alfred Kobsa, and Hongxia Jin. 2013. Preference-based Location Sharing: Are More Privacy Options Really Better?. In *Proceedings of the ACM SIGCHI Conference on Human Factors in Computing Systems (CHI '13)*. 2667–2676.

[21] Xinchao Li, Martha A Larson, and Alan Hanjalic. 2016. Geo-distinctive Visual Element Matching for Location Estimation of Images. *arXiv preprint arXiv:1601.07884* (2016).

[22] matveyco. 2013. python-tilt-shift. https://github.com/matveyco/python-tilt-shift. (2013).

[23] Anh Nguyen, Jason Yosinski, and Jeff Clune. 2015. Deep Neural Networks Are Easily Fooled: High Confidence Predictions for Unrecognizable Images. In *Proceedings of the IEEE International Conference on Computer Vision and Pattern Recognition*.

[24] Andreas Poller, Martin Steinebach, and Huajian Liu. 2012. Robust Image Obfuscation for Privacy Protection in Web 2.0 Applications. In *IS&T/SPIE Electronic Imaging*. International Society for Optics and Photonics, 830304–830304.

[25] Bradford W. Reyns, Billy Henson, and Bonnie S. Fisher. 2012. Stalking in the Twilight Zone: Extent of Cyberstalking Victimization and Offending Among College Students. *Deviant Behavior* 31, 1 (2012), 1–25.

[26] Olga Russakovsky, Jia Deng, Hao Su, Jonathan Krause, Sanjeev Satheesh, Sean Ma, Zhiheng Huang, Andrej Karpathy, Aditya Khosla, Michael Bernstein, Alexander C. Berg, and Li Fei-Fei. 2015. ImageNet Large Scale Visual Recognition Challenge. *International Journal of Computer Vision (IJCV)* 115, 3 (2015), 211–252.

[27] Eleftherios Spyromitros-Xioufis, Symeon Papadopoulos, Adrian Popescu, and Yiannis Kompatsiaris. 2016. Personalized privacy-aware image classification. In *Proceedings of the ACM International Conference on Multimedia Retrieval*. ACM, 71–78.

[28] Christian Szegedy, Wei Liu, Yangqing Jia, Pierre Sermanet, Scott Reed, Dragomir Anguelov, Dumitru Erhan, Vincent Vanhoucke, and Andrew Rabinovich. 2015. Going Deeper with Convolutions. In *Proceedings of the IEEE Conference on Computer Vision and Pattern Recognition*. 1–9.

[29] Yaniv Taigman, Ming Yang, Marc'Aurelio Ranzato, and Lars Wolf. 2014. Deepface: Closing the gap to human-level performance in face verification. In *Proceedings of the IEEE Conference on Computer Vision and Pattern Recognition*. IEEE, 1701–1708.

[30] Michele Trevisiol, Hervé Jégou, Jonathan Delhumeau, and Guillaume Gravier. 2013. Retrieving geo-location of videos with a divide & conquer hierarchical multimodal approach. In *Proceedings of the ACM International Conference on Multimedia Retrieval*. ACM, 1–8.

[31] Tobias Weyand, Ilya Kostrikov, and James Philbin. 2016. PlaNet - Photo Geolocation with Convolutional Neural Networks. In *Proceedings of the European Conference on Computer Vision (ECCV)*.

[32] Shicai Yang. 2016. Towards Good Practices for Recognition and Detection. (2016). http://image-net.org/challenges/talks/2016/Hikvision_at_ImageNet_2016.pdf.

[33] Sergej Zerr, Stefan Siersdorfer, and Jonathon Hare. 2012. Picalert!: A System for Privacy-aware Image Classification and Retrieval. In *Proceedings of the ACM International Conference on Information and Knowledge Management*. ACM, 2710–2712.

[34] Bolei Zhou, Aditya Khosla, Agata Lapedriza, Antonio Torralba, and Aude Oliva. 2016. Places: An Image Database for Deep Scene Understanding. *arXiv preprint arXiv:1610.02055* (2016).

Light Curve Analysis From Kepler Spacecraft Collected Data

Eduardo Nigri
School of Computer Science
University of St Andrews
North Haugh
St Andrews, United Kingdom KY16 9SX
eduardonigri@dcc.ufmg.br

Ognjen Arandjelović
School of Computer Science
University of St Andrews
North Haugh
St Andrews, United Kingdom KY16 9SX
ognjen.arandjelovic@gmail.com

ABSTRACT

Although scarce, previous work on the application of machine learning and data mining techniques on large corpora of astronomical data has produced promising results. For example, on the task of detecting so-called *Kepler objects of interest* (KOIs), a range of different 'off the shelf' classifiers has demonstrated outstanding performance. These rather preliminary research efforts motivate further exploration of this data domain. In the present work we focus on the analysis of *threshold crossing events* (TCEs) extracted from photometric data acquired by the Kepler spacecraft. We show that the task of classifying TCEs as being effected by actual planetary transits as opposed to confounding astrophysical phenomena is significantly more challenging than that of KOI detection, with different classifiers exhibiting vastly different performances. Nevertheless, the best performing classifier type, the random forest, achieved excellent accuracy, correctly predicting in approximately 96% of the cases. Our results and analysis should illuminate further efforts into the development of more sophisticated, automatic techniques, and encourage additional work in the area.

CCS CONCEPTS

•Applied computing → Physical sciences and engineering; **•Computing methodologies →** *Artificial intelligence;* Machine learning;

KEYWORDS

Astronomy; Big Data; photometry; space; pattern recognition; random forests; support vector machines

ACM Reference format:
Eduardo Nigri and Ognjen Arandjelović. 2017. Light Curve Analysis From Kepler Spacecraft Collected Data. In *Proceedings of ICMR '17, Bucharest, Romania, June 06-09, 2017,* 6 pages.
DOI: http://dx.doi.org/10.1145/3078971.3080544

1 INTRODUCTION

Technological advances seen in recent years have had a profound effect on the shape of applied computing. Owing to improvements in hardware and the possibility to acquire [14], store [32], and transmit [20] large amounts of information cheaply, there has been a dramatic increase in the availability of highly heterogeneous data. Acting as a part of a positive feedback loop, the broad field of artificial intelligence has seen major breakthroughs and conceptual leaps. Machine learning, pattern recognition, data science, and data mining are just some of the sub-disciplines of artificial intelligence which have come into prominence in the age of so-called Big Data [33]. The wealth of available data is an opportunity for the development of data driven (and hence evidence driven) algorithms relying on minimal hand-crafting, which have the potential to perform in a manner free of various forms of bias that humans are prone to [10].

Unsurprisingly, much of the applied research attention has focused on domains which have tangible commercial benefit or which emotionally engage the general public. Personalized product recommendations [1] typify the former. A range of applications which fall under the broad umbrella of 'social administration', have also attracted significant efforts e.g. the use of social media to track and learn about different types of emergencies [15]. Public health monitoring is also an area of great interest both to governments and individuals [7, 26].

A major application domain of interest to modern artificial intelligence and computing in general is that of scientific research. Indeed, a great and increasing amount of science now relies on the analysis of large quantities of data [2, 6, 35]. Significant efforts in the realm of personalized medicine, for example in the analysis of large scale electronic health records [3, 30, 37] have already demonstrated highly promising results.. The highly multi-modal nature of such data [5] which may consist of 'conventional' or infrared images, depth information, physical measurements of different types, demographic information, and numerous other forms, as well as the domain specific semantic gap interlaced with the interpretation of the aforementioned information, all also present major research challenges. Notwithstanding the breadth of efforts touched upon above, there are many scientific areas in which the use of state of the art artificial intelligence remains little explored, arguably in no small part because they are (often incorrectly) seen as having limited practical relevance. Yet these disciplines often stand to gain enormously from the use of data science. Astronomy is but one of them. Indeed, astronomy has over time increasingly become driven by the analysis of vast amounts of data. Data collection efforts in the form of sky surveys and others, routinely collect astonishing amounts of data. At the very least for practical reasons this collection has to be accompanied with the development of sophisticated machine learning based algorithms capable of discarding irrelevant information, automatically searching (data mining) for new information, detecting data of interest etc. To date, efforts

978-1-4503-4701-3/17/06...$15.00
DOI: http://dx.doi.org/10.1145/3078971.3080544

towards this goal have been limited and only the most elementary techniques evaluated in pilot style experiments [16, 25, 28, 31]. Our goal in the present paper is twofold: (i) to verify independently the results reported in the existing literature, and (ii) to contribute to the understanding of the problem by comparing a greater number of classifiers than previous work.

2 TECHNICAL DETAIL

In this section we explain the types of features extracted from raw data collected by the Kepler mission, and the classification methodologies pursued in the experiments described in the present paper.

2.1 Background context

The Kepler mission was conceived by NASA to detect Earth like planets orbiting Sun like stars in the Milky Way galaxy [11]. One of the main goals of the mission is to find and determine the frequency of planets outside of the solar system (so-called exoplanets) in the habitable zone of their host stars. Such exoplanets would have temperatures that would allow liquid water to exist on their surface, which is one of the key necessary elements for making them suitable for life as we know it.

The Kepler spacecraft was launched in 2009 in an Earth-trailing heliocentric orbit. The single instrument carried by Kepler is a photometer which measures the brightness of the stars in its 115 deg^2 field-of-view [19]. Observations were sent to Earth on a monthly basis and grouped by quarters. Kepler observed a patch of the sky in the constellations of Cygnus and Lyra from May 2009 to May 2013. After losing a second reaction wheel in 2013, the spacecraft was re-purposed for the K2 mission [22].

The Kepler mission uses transit photometry to find exoplanets. As illustrated conceptually in Figure 1(a), when a planet transits in front of its host star, it blocks some of the light emitted by the star in the direction of the observer. This dip in brightness can be measured, and a periodicity in the observed dips serves as an indication of the existence of an exoplanet.

2.2 Input data and its pre-processing

As already noted in the previous section, the sole instrument onboard Kepler is a photometer – a camera, in effect – which directly senses incoming light brightness [23]. This raw data is then processed through a series of steps in order to extract features used in our experiments. Each of the steps in the pipeline will be described in more detail in Section 2.2.1. In broad terms, following the calibration of measurements a series of so-called *light curves* is created for each targeted star. Succinctly put, a light curve is a temporal characteristic variation in the brightness of a star. From light curves, an exoplanet can be detected by finding the associated periodic dips of brightness which correspond to the exoplanet's transit in front of the star from the point of view of Kepler's photometer. Sequences of transit like signals in the light curve are readily identified using multi-scale wavelet analysis and are referred to as *threshold crossing events* (TCEs). The pipeline is described in more detail next.

2.2.1 Data processing pipeline. Starting from raw photometric data sensed by charge-coupled device (CCD) detectors, the first step in the data processing pipeline involves pixel level calibration, as

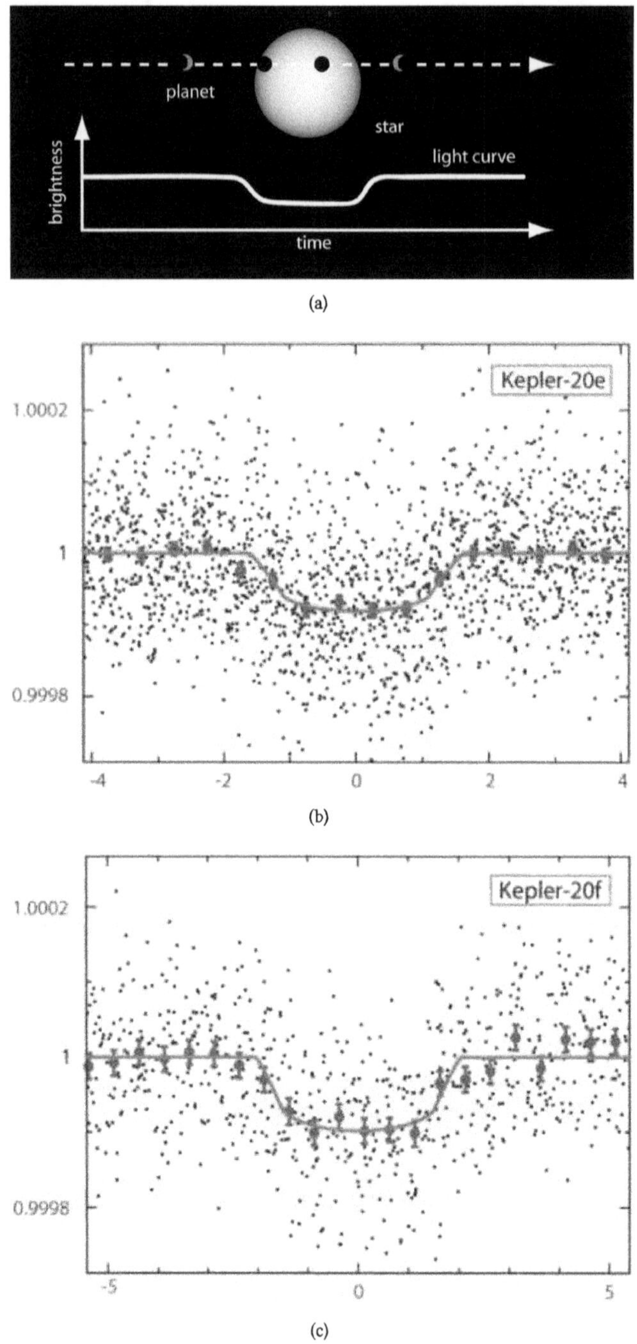

Figure 1: (a) Conceptual illustration of the extracted light curve distortion effected by a passing exoplanet. (b,c) Raw and statistically robust photometric measurements, and smooth, fitted light curves corresponding to transits of two Earth like exoplanets, Kepler-20e and Kepler-20f respectively. The horizontal axis shows time in hours relative to the time of mid-transit, and the vertical the relative flux.

shown in Figure 2. This step corrects for the effects of cosmic rays and variations in pixel sensitivity, and is performed in a standard manner for calibrating CCD data, performing corrections for bias, dark current, gain etc. Calibrated pixels are then used for photometric analysis which produces raw light curves, see Figure 1(b,c). This step too involves commonly used techniques from signal processing, such as background subtraction based on temporal averages, and robust estimation through the use of flux weighted centroids. Transiting planet detection is done next, resulting in the detection of threshold crossing events. As noted earlier, this is achieved by identifying kinks in raw light curves which also show periodicity across time. The last step in the pipeline involves what is commonly termed data validation. This is a model driven stage which results in the estimates of the relative radius of the planet, the associated period, epoch, orbit parameters, star density etc. The estimates are made by optimizing their values in a manner that fits a physical planet model.

As explained in the next section, each of the steps in the described pipeline is used for the extraction of possibly salient input features we used for KOI classification.

2.3 Extracted input features

Features used as input to the classification algorithms used in our experiments comprise the four sets used for KOI classification [31] (namely, transit fit parameters, threshold crossing event information, stellar parameters, and pixel based KOI vetting statistics – see Figure 2), TCE specific statistics, and an additional, derived feature. The derived feature was inspired by the work of McCauliff *et al.* [28] and it captures the similarity of a host star's TCEs . Its value was computed as the minimum absolute difference between periods of TCEs.

Gathering all features described above resulted in a feature set comprising 64 features in total. Two strategies were used to reduce the number of features: removing features with low variance and redundant features (showing high correlation with another feature). An empirical threshold of 1% of the mean value was used to prune features with low variance, resulting in the removal of 12 features. To measure the correlation between pairs of variables, we used the well known Pearson correlation coefficient, with values of 1 and -1 indicating perfect correlation and 0 no correlation at all. The threshold of 0.9 was adopted and the less significant feature of the pair, quantified by performing the analysis of variance, was removed. This process resulted in the final, reduced number of features of 44.

2.4 Classification methodologies

For our experiments we adopted the use of five different classification approaches. These were primarily selected on the basis of their widespread use, well understood behaviour, and promising performance in a variety of other classification tasks. Our goal was also to compare classifiers which are based on different assumptions on the relationship between different features, as well as classifiers which differ in terms of the functional forms of classification boundaries they can learn. The five compared classifiers are naïve Bayes [24], logistic regression [8], support vector machine [4], k-nearest neighbours [27], and random forest [13]. For completeness we summarize the key aspects of each next.

2.4.1 Naïve Bayes classification. Naïve Bayes classification applies the Bayes theorem by making the 'naïve' assumption of feature independence. Formally, given a set of n features $x_1, \ldots, x_n$, the associated pattern is deemed as belonging to the class y which satisfies the following condition:

$$y = \arg\max_j P(C_j) \prod_{i=1}^{n} p(x_i|C_j) \tag{1}$$

where $P(C_j)$ is the prior probability of the class C_j, and $p(x_i|C_j)$ the conditional probability of the feature x_i given class C_j (readily estimated from data using a supervised learning framework) [9].

2.4.2 Logistic regression. In logistic regression, the conditional probability of the dependent variable (class) y is modelled as a logit-transformed multiple linear regression of the explanatory variables (input features) $x_1, \ldots, x_n$:

$$P_{LR}(y = \pm 1|\mathbf{x}, \mathbf{w}) = \frac{1}{1 + e^{-y\mathbf{w}^T\mathbf{x}}}. \tag{2}$$

The model is trained (i.e. the weight parameter $\mathbf{w}$ learnt) by maximizing the likelihood of the model on the training data set, given by:

$$\prod_{i=1}^{2} Pr(y_i|\mathbf{x}_i, \mathbf{w}) = \prod_{i=1}^{2} \frac{1}{1 + e^{-y_i\mathbf{w}^T\mathbf{x}_i}}, \tag{3}$$

penalized by the complexity of the model:

$$\frac{1}{\sigma\sqrt{2\pi}} e^{-\frac{1}{2\sigma^2}\mathbf{w}^T\mathbf{w}}, \tag{4}$$

which can be restated as the minimization of the following regularized negative log-likelihood:

$$\mathfrak{L} = C \sum_{i=1}^{2} \log\left(1 + e^{-y_i\mathbf{w}^T\mathbf{x}_i}\right) + \mathbf{w}^T\mathbf{w}. \tag{5}$$

A coordinate descent approach described by Yu *et al.* [38] was used to minimize $\mathfrak{L}$.

2.4.3 Support vector machines. Support vector machines perform classification by constructing a series of class separating hyperplanes in a high dimensional (potentially infinitely dimensional) space into which the original input data is mapped [34]. For comprehensive detail of this regression technique the reader is referred to the original work by Vapnik [36]; herein we present a summary of the key ideas relevant to the present work.

In the context of support vector machines, the seemingly intractable task of mapping data into a very high dimensional space is achieved efficiently by performing the aforesaid mapping implicitly, rather than explicitly. This is done by employing the so-called *kernel trick* which ensures that dot products in the high dimensional space are readily computed using the variables in the original space. Given labelled training data (input vectors and the associated labels) in the form $\{(x_1, y_1), \ldots, (x_n, y_n)\}$, a support vector machine aims to find a mapping which minimizes the number of misclassified training instances, in a regularized fashion. As mentioned earlier,

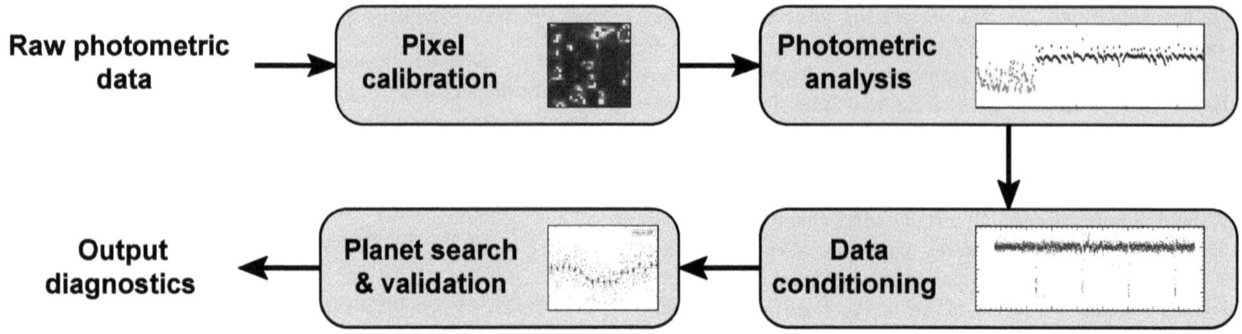

Figure 2: Feature extraction pipeline. Different sets of features, namely (1) transit fit parameters, (2) threshold crossing event information, (3) stellar parameters, and (4) pixel based KOI vetting statistics, are extracted at different stages in the pipeline.

an implicit mapping of input data $x \longrightarrow \Phi(x)$ is performed by employing a Mercer-admissible kernel [29] $k(x_i, x_j)$ which allows for the dot products between mapped data to be computed in the input space: $\Phi(x_i) \cdot \Phi(x_j) = k(x_i, x_j)$. The classification vector in the transformed, high dimensional space of the form

$$w = \sum_{i=1}^{n} c_i y_i \Phi(x_i) \tag{6}$$

is sought by minimizing

$$\sum_{i=1}^{n} c_i - \frac{1}{2} \sum_{i=1}^{n} \sum_{j=1}^{n} y_i c_i k(x_i, x_j) y_j c_j \tag{7}$$

subject to the constraints $\sum_{i=1}^{n} c_i y_i = 0$ and $0 \leq c_i \leq 1/(2n\lambda)$. The regularizing parameter λ penalizes prediction errors.

2.4.4 k-nearest neighbours. The k-nearest neighbour classifier classifies a novel pattern comprising features $x_1, \ldots, x_n$ to the class dominant in the set of k nearest neighbours to the input pattern (in the feature space) amongst the training patterns with known class memberships [17]. The usual distance metric used is the Euclidean distance which is adopted in the present paper too.

2.4.5 Random forests. Random forest classifiers fall under the broad umbrella of ensemble based learning methods [13]. They are simple to implement, fast in operation, and have proven to be extremely successful in a variety of domains [18, 21]. The key principle underlying the random forest approach comprises the construction of many "simple" decision trees in the training stage and the majority vote (mode) across them in the classification stage. Amongst other benefits, this voting strategy has the effect of correcting for the undesirable property of decision trees to overfit training data [39]. In the training stage random forests apply the general technique known as bagging [12] to individual trees in the ensemble. Bagging repeatedly selects a random sample with replacement from the training set and fits trees to these samples. Each tree is grown without any pruning. The number of trees in the ensemble is a free parameter which is readily learnt automatically using the so-called out-of-bag error [13]; this approach is adopted in the present work as well.

3 EXPERIMENTS

In this section we describe the experiments we conducted to evaluate the effectiveness of the classification approaches described in the previous section. We examine both the effect of each classification algorithm as well as that of different features extracted from raw data.

3.1 Source data

In our experiments we adopted the same training data set used by McCauliff *et al.* [28]. TCEs are labelled as corresponding to one of three classes, namely: (i) planet candidates (PCs), (ii) , astrophysical false positives (AFPs), and (iii) non-transiting phenomena (NTP). This training set was created by matching TCEs and KOIs of the first 12 quarters of the mission, which were manually vetted by the TCERT. Detailed information is available in the DR24 catalog. In summary, the training set contains 15737 TCEs of which 3600 are PCs, 9596 AFPs, and 2541 NTPs.

3.2 Results and discussion

We started our analysis by comparing the average classification accuracies achieved by different classification approaches. The average accuracy of naïve Bayes, logistic regression, SVM, and k-nearest neighbours approaches was computed using 10-fold cross-validation. The performance of the random forest based classifier was calculated using the widely used and so-called out-of-bag error [13].

A summary of our results is shown in Table 1. As the table readily shows, the two arguably simplest approaches, namely the the naïve Bayes and logistic regression based classifiers, performed very poorly indeed, making the correct classification decision in only about 25% of the cases. The support vector machine based approach performed significantly better, achieving a respectable accuracy of 72%. The k-nearest neighbour based classifier improved on this yet further, reaching the realm of practically useful and misclassifying in only 16% of the cases (it should be noted that for k-nearest neighbour classification we optimized for the value of k on the training set and the reported results are for the learnt

Table 1: The average accuracy achieved by each of the five classifier types adopted in our experiments.

Classification methodology	Average accuracy (%)
Naïve Bayes	24.8
Logistic regression	25.1
Support vector machine	72.0
k-nearest neighbours	83.8
Random forest	95.7

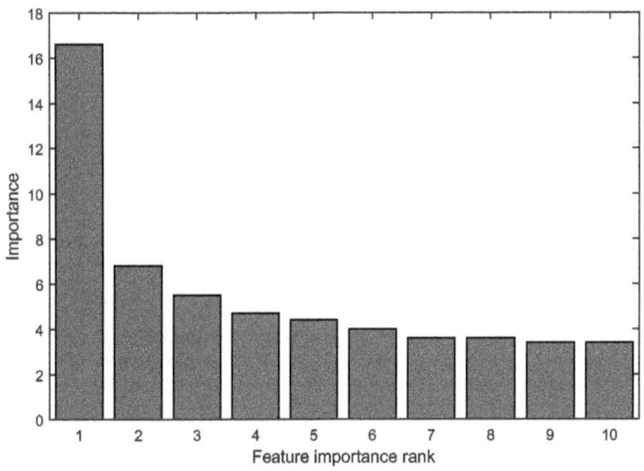

Figure 3: Relative importance of the top 10 most significant features in the context of the best performing classifier type: the random forest (see Table 1). Observe the stark dominance of the highest ranked feature, the *minimum period difference*.

optimum of $k = 4$). However, by far the best performance, and one very impressive in its own right, is that of the random forest based method which erred in only approximately 4% of the cases.

We also sought novel insight into the relative importances of different input features. Given the superior performance of the random forest based classifier we focused on this approach. A summary of our results is shown in Table 2. As the table shows, by far the most important feature was found to be the *minimum period difference*. It accounted for nearly 17% of the total importance, far exceeding the importance of the second most important feature (importance less than 7%). This feature importance distribution, illustrated further in Figure 3, is somewhat different from that previously reported on the task of KOI detection which was characterized by multiple significant features [31]. Another difference can be observed by comparing the importances of different feature types (i.e. sets), summarized in Section 2.3. While for KOI detection various transit properties accounted for half of the ten most important features, on the present task the transit, TCE, and pixel based feature sets were found to be equally represented by number in the top 10 significant features. In both cases the only top 10 ranked stellar parameter was the associated KOI count, albeit higher ranked in importance herein.

4 SUMMARY AND CONCLUSIONS

Motivated by promising results of previous research on the automation of laborious tasks in the processing of astronomical data, the present paper sought to assess the performance of several well-known classifier types in the classification of threshold crossing events detected from photometric data collected by the Kepler spacecraft. In particular, we were interested in distinguishing between events which are actually caused by planetary transits and those which are artefacts of confounding phenomena, using input features extracted from raw photometric data (images) using a multi-stage processing pipeline. Unlike on the problem of KOI classification, we found that different types of classifiers exhibited vastly different behaviours, their accuracies ranging from very low (25% for naïve Bayes) to outstandingly good (96% for random forests). This finding and our analysis should serve to encourage further work in this area. The primary focus of our future work will be on the use of raw Kepler images which would eliminate the need for the hand-crafted data pre-processing pipeline currently used to extract classifier input features.

ACKNOWLEDGEMENTS

The authors would like to thank CNPq-Brazil and the University of St Andrews for their kind support.

REFERENCES

[1] F. Abel, Q. Gao, G. J. Houben, and K. Tao. Analyzing user modeling on Twitter for personalized news recommendations. *In Proc. International Conference User Modeling, Adaptation and Personalization*, pages 1–12, 2011.

[2] V. Andrei and O. Arandjelović. Identification of promising research directions using machine learning aided medical literature analysis. *In Proc. International Conference of the IEEE Engineering in Medicine and Biology Society*, pages 2471–2474, 2016.

[3] O. Arandjelović. Discovering hospital admission patterns using models learnt from electronic hospital records. *Bioinformatics*, 31(24):3970–3976, 2015.

[4] O. Arandjelović. Learnt quasi-transitive similarity for retrieval from large collections of faces. *In Proc. IEEE Conference on Computer Vision and Pattern Recognition*, pages 4883–4892, 2016.

[5] O. Arandjelović. Weighted linear fusion of multimodal data – a reasonable baseline? *In Proc. ACM Conference on Multimedia*, pages 851–857, 2016.

[6] A. Beykikhoshk, O. Arandjelović, D. Phung, and S. Venkatesh. Hierarchical Dirichlet process for tracking complex topical structure evolution and its application to autism research literature. *In Proc. Pacific-Asia Conference on Knowledge Discovery and Data Mining*, 1:550–562, 2015.

[7] A. Beykikhoshk, O. Arandjelović, D. Phung, and S. Venkatesh. Overcoming data scarcity of Twitter: using tweets as bootstrap with application to autism-related topic content analysis. *In Proc. IEEE/ACM International Conference on Advances in Social Network Analysis and Mining*, pages 1354–1361, 2015.

[8] A. Beykikhoshk, O. Arandjelović, D. Phung, S. Venkatesh, and T. Caelli. Using Twitter to learn about the autism community. *Social Network Analysis and Mining*, 5(1):5–22, 2015.

[9] C. M. Bishop. *Pattern Recognition and Machine Learning*. Springer-Verlag, New York, USA, 2007.

[10] G. V. Bodenhausen, S. Gabriel, and M. Lineberger. Sadness and susceptibility to judgmental bias: The case of anchoring. *Psychological Science*, 11(4):320–323, 2000.

[11] W. J. Borucki, D. Koch, G. Basri, N. Batalha, and et al. Kepler planet-detection mission: introduction and first results. *Science*, 327(5968):977–980, 2010.

[12] L. Breiman. Bagging predictors. *Machine Learning*, 24(2):123–140, 1996.

[13] L. Breiman. Random forests. *Machine Learning*, 45(1):5–32, 2001.

[14] M. Chan, D. Estève, C. Escriba, and E. Campo. A review of smart homes?present state and future challenges. *Computer Methods and Programs in Biomedicine*, 91(1):55–81, 2008.

Table 2: Our findings regarding the relative importance of different features in the context of a random forest classifier. The *minimum period difference* stands out as by far the most discriminative feature in the set. Legend: † median absolute deviation (MAD), pixel response function (PRF), multiple quarters (MQ), multiple event statistic (MES), Kepler Input Catalog (KIC). See http://exoplanetarchive.ipac.caltech.edu/docs/API_tce_columns.html for comprehensive information.

Feature importance rank	Feature set	Feature description	Relative importance (%)
1	–	Minimum period difference	16.6
2	1	Chi-square (χ^2) 2	6.8
3	3	Number of associated KOIs	5.5
4	2	Bootstrap false alarm probability	4.7
5	2	Weak secondary MAD-MES†	4.4
6	1	Chi-square (χ^2) 1	4.0
7	2	Weak secondary min MES	3.6
8	1	Planet-star separation	3.6
9	4	PRF MQ(KIC)†	3.4
10	4	Flux-weighted offset significance	3.4

[15] C. Chew and G. Eysenbach. Pandemics in the age of Twitter: content analysis of Tweets during the 2009 H1N1 outbreak. *PLOS ONE*, 5(11):e14118, 2010.

[16] J. L. Coughlin, F. Mullally, S. E. Thompson, J. F. Rowe, C. J. Burke, D. W. Latham, N. M. Batalha, A. Ofir, B. L. Quarles, and C. E. Henze. Planetary candidates observed by Kepler. VII. The first fully uniform catalog based on the entire 48-month data set (Q1–Q17 DR24). *The Astrophysical Journal Supplement Series*, 224(1):12, 2016.

[17] P. Cunningham and S. J. Delany. k-nearest neighbour classifiers. *Multiple Classifier Systems*, pages 1–17, 2007.

[18] D. R. Cutler, T. C. Edwards, K. H. Beard, A. Cutler, K. T. Hess, J. Gibson, and J. J. Lawler. Random forests for classification in ecology. *Ecology*, 88(11):2783–2792, 2007.

[19] M. N. Fanelli, J. M. Jenkins, S. T. Bryson, E. V. Quintana, and et al. *Kepler Data Processing Handbook*. NASA Ames Research Center, 2011.

[20] G. Fettweis and S. Alamouti. 5G: personal mobile internet beyond what cellular did to telephony. *IEEE Communications Magazine*, 52(2):140–145, 2014.

[21] P. Ghosh and B. Manjunath. Robust simultaneous registration and segmentation with sparse error reconstruction. *IEEE Transactions on Pattern Analysis and Machine Intelligence*, 35(2):425–436, 2013.

[22] S. B. Howell, C. Sobeck, M. Haas, M. Still, and et al. The K2 mission: characterization and early results. *Publications of the Astronomical Society of the Pacific*, 126(938):398, 2014.

[23] J. M. Jenkins, D. A. Caldwell, H. Chandrasekaran, J. D. Twicken, and et al. Overview of the Kepler science processing pipeline. *The Astrophysical Journal Letters*, 713(2):L87, 2010.

[24] A. Jordan. On discriminative vs. generative classifiers: a comparison of logistic regression and naive Bayes. *Advances in Neural Information Processing Systems*, 14:841, 2002.

[25] R. S. J. Kim, J. V. Kepner, M. Postman, M. A. Strauss, and et al. Detecting clusters of galaxies in the sloan digital sky survey I: Monte Carlo comparison of cluster detection algorithms. *The Astronomical Journal*, 123(1):20..., 2002.

[26] J. Lin and D. Ryaboy. Scaling big data mining infrastructure: the Twitter experience. *ACM SIGKDD Explorations Newsletter*, 14(2):6–19, 2013.

[27] R. Martin and O. Arandjelović. Multiple-object tracking in cluttered and crowded public spaces. *In Proc. International Symposium on Visual Computing*, 3:89–98, 2010.

[28] S. D. McCauliff, J. M. Jenkins, J. Catanzarite, C. J. Burke, J. L. Coughlin, J. D. Twicken, P. Tenenbaum, S. Seader, J. Li, and M. Cote. Automatic classification of Kepler planetary transit candidates. *The Astrophysical Journal*, 806(1):6, 2015.

[29] J. Mercer. Functions of positive and negative type and their connection with the theory of integral equations. *Philosophical Transactions of the Royal Society A*, 209:415–446, 1909.

[30] P. M. Nadkarni. Drug safety surveillance using de-identified EMR and claims data: issues and challenges. *J Am Med Inform Assoc*, 17(6):671–674, 2010.

[31] E. Nigri and O. Arandjelović. Machine learning based detection of Kepler objects of interest. *In Proc. ICME Workshop on Emerging Multimedia Systems and Applications*, 2017.

[32] S. F. Oliveira, K. Fürlinger, and D. Kranzlmüller. Trends in computation, communication and storage and the consequences for data-intensive science. *In Proc. IEEE International Conference on Embedded Software and Systems & High Performance Computing and Communication*, pages 572–579, 2012.

[33] F. Provost and T. Fawcett. Data science and its relationship to big data and data-driven decision making. *Big Data*, 1(1):51–59, 2013.

[34] B. Schölkopf, A. Smola, and K. Müller. *Advances in Kernel Methods – SV Learning*, chapter Kernel principal component analysis., pages 327–352. MIT Press, Cambridge, MA, 1999.

[35] A. Szalay. Extreme data-intensive scientific computing. *Computing in Science & Engineering*, 13(6):34–41, 2011.

[36] V. Vapnik. *The Nature of Statistical Learning Theory*. Springer-Verlag, 1995.

[37] I. Vasiljeva and O. Arandjelović. Towards sophisticated learning from EHRs: increasing prediction specificity and accuracy using clinically meaningful risk criteria. *In Proc. International Conference of the IEEE Engineering in Medicine and Biology Society*, pages 2452–2455, 2016.

[38] H.-F. Yu, F.-L. Huang, and C.-J. Lin. Dual coordinate descent methods for logistic regression and maximum entropy models. *Machine Learning*, 85(1–2):41–75, 2011.

[39] B. Zadrozny and C. Elkan. Obtaining calibrated probability estimates from decision trees and naive Bayesian classifiers. *In Proc. IMLS International Conference on Machine Learning*, 1:609–616, 2001.

Health Multimedia: Lifestyle Recommendations Based on Diverse Observations

Nitish Nag
University of California, Irvine
Irvine, USA
nagn@uci.edu

Vaibhav Pandey
University of California, Irvine
Irvine, USA
vaibhap1@uci.edu

Ramesh Jain
University of California, Irvine
Irvine, USA
rcjain@uci.edu

ABSTRACT

Managing health lays the core foundation to enabling quality life experiences. Modern multimedia research has enhanced the quality of experiences in fields such as entertainment, social media, and advertising; yet lags in the health domain. We are developing an approach to leverage multimedia systems for human health. Health is primarily a product of our everyday lifestyle actions, yet we have minimal health guidance on making everyday choices. Recommendations are the key to modern content consumption and decisions. Cybernetic navigation principles that integrate health media sources can power dynamic recommendations to dramatically improve our health decisions. Cybernetic components give real-time feedback on health status, while the navigational approach plots health trajectory. These two principles coalesce data to enable personalized, predictive, and precise health knowledge that can contextually disseminate the right actions to keep individuals on a path to wellness.

KEYWORDS

cybernetics; navigation; quantified-self; objective-self; precision medicine; predictive health; prevention; event mining; context awareness; mobile health; persuasion; personalized

ACM Reference format:

Nitish Nag, Vaibhav Pandey, and Ramesh Jain. 2017. Health Multimedia: Lifestyle Recommendations Based on Diverse Observations. In *Proceedings of ICMR '17, Bucharest, Romania, June 06-09, 2017,* 8 pages. https://doi.org/http://dx.doi.org/10.1145/3078971.3080545

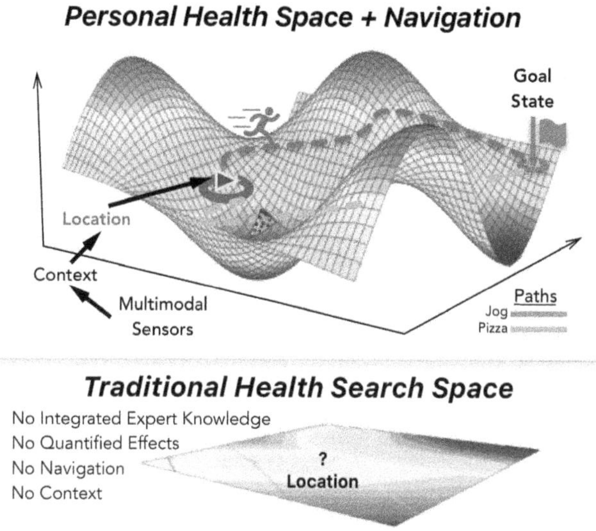

Figure 1: Increased dimensionality (both time and space) of personalized health space can provide actionable navigation towards health goals. As a simple example, although jogging may have a higher effort at the moment (hence the uphill initial slope), it informs the user how this action will reach the goal node. By having the pizza, it may be easier in the moment, but the user will have to climb out of a sink in the map to reach their goal.

1 INTRODUCTION

Inaccessibility and delayed dissemination of medical knowledge for lifestyle guidance persists in all health care systems, while global health burdens continue to rapidly rise. Health care is yearning for a major transformation, from reactive and hospital-centered to proactive prevention; from doctor-centered to patient-centered; from disease-centered to wellness promotion; and a shifting focus from temporary fixes to long-term solutions [23]. Commonly, physicians focus primarily on medical methods to manage health when a patient becomes ill. True health outcomes result from actions taken in every moment and place, not just medical intervention during sickness. Future advancements in health must continuously sense individual needs and rapidly provide the relevant resources so corrective actions ensure health stability.

Health is essentially a product of our genome and lifestyle [28]. Lifestyle is the primary controllable aspect of our health. Unfortunately, lifestyle associated diseases continue to lead the rapid rise of chronic diseases across the globe. Monitoring lifestyle factors has been difficult, and computational power with effective methods to address the needs of each individual have been limited. Trying to produce changes in routine lifestyle habits is also a tremendous psychological hurdle. Media platforms such as food analysis from images or accelerometer based activity sensors have started collecting data about lifestyle factors. These isolated efforts forgo the integration of other media sources and lack synchronization across time and space. Imagine how Google Maps on mobile phones alerts the driver of an upcoming turn. This is the product of real-time

ACM ISBN 978-1-4503-4701-3/17/06...$15.00
https://doi.org/http://dx.doi.org/10.1145/3078971.3080545

multimedia synchronization to power recommendations. Synergistic and synchronized *multimedia* technologies will play a major role in advancing progress to solve health issues.

Current health search systems place the burden of querying on the uninformed user, without understanding any health context. A new era of health multimedia will usher expert knowledge with computational power to drive dynamic recommendations, alleviating the user of querying for answers, and provide the right actions at the right time for users to best manage their health.

1.1 Navigation Systems

A fundamental basis of capturing actionable knowledge rests in maps. Physical maps represent spatial worlds, where as a textbook maps the knowledge of a certain domain. Search engines capture the knowledge of virtual structures. Traversing this spatio-temporal knowledge is the fundamental problem in navigation. We start from an initial node and usually wish to end up at a goal node (Figure 1). In the instance of health, we want to construct the health map of each individual based on knowledge from biological science, but also from sensors that capture the dynamic life history of the person (Figure 5). Multimedia health systems must elucidate the current location of an individual on their personal health map, highlight the optimal goal destination, and illuminate the path from the current status to the goal (Figure 1). Two *key* differences separate this new paradigm from traditional search. First, understanding the context of the individual from multimedia signals maps the location of the user in their health spectrum, similar to a GPS location of a car. Second, we must quantitatively model the effects of future actions on the user while calculating the ability of the user to execute a given action, similar to calculating the various routes and traffic for driving. Given the models of the car, roads, and traffic, we can predict when the car will arrive at the destination. Similarly, we need to be able to predict the course of an individuals health for future health systems.

1.2 Health Issues of the 21st Century

Our paper targets three significant problems in modern health care. First: Health systems largely react to problems, rather than avoiding problems through preventive measures. Second: Gold-standard medical practices depend on "evidence-based" medicine taken from population averages. A lack of individual contextual analysis results in compromised care and sub-optimal outcomes. Third: Access to medical guidance is limited due to poor information dissemination, and restricted physical time and space. When doctors give lifestyle suggestions to patients, they are hard to translate into everyday life decisions. Although the knowledge exists, it is not in an actionable form. Users also do not know what their context means in relation to how their choices are affecting their health (Figure 1). When a need or question arises for health advice, such as "What should I eat?" or "Should I take this medicine now or later?", there is a large delay to receive meaningful assistance. The difficulty of scaling physical systems, like hospitals and personnel, further limits high quality care. Each of these three issues are coated with a vast splattering of emerging media and data streams. Herein lies a great opportunity for multimedia systems.

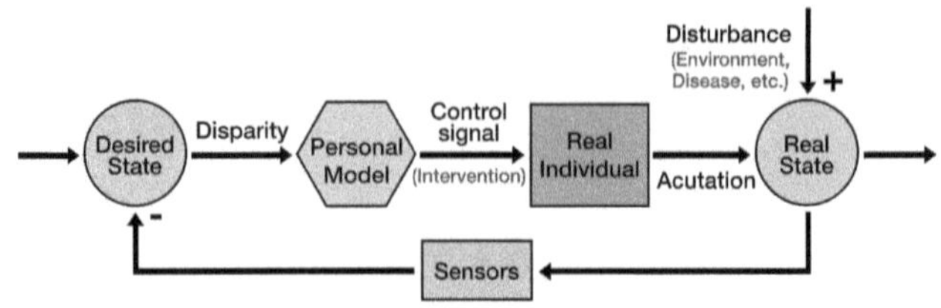

Figure 2: Cybernetic Control pairs the individual user and digital health assistance to enact real-world changes to optimize health.

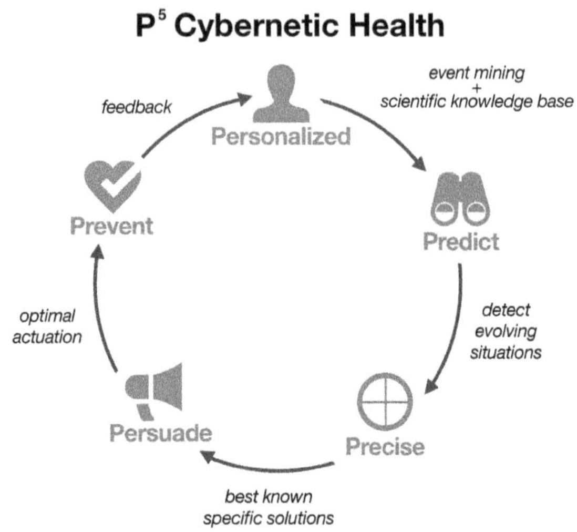

Figure 3: P5 Cybernetic Health coordinates the elements of personalized, predictive and precision medicine through persuasion techniques that result in disease prevention.

1.3 Cybernetic Principles

Cybernetic principles transformed the design of complex systems [32]. Continuous observations/measurements are a key component in closed loop feedback control systems. Airplanes, ovens, and other machines use these feedback loops to safely and efficiently operate. Imagine if the thermometer in an oven gave a reading once every year. How would the oven know to heat or turn off? The thermometer, heater, and other components of the oven must all be coordinated and continuously working for the machine to operate correctly. Similarly, the human body maintains homeostasis in a remarkable array of perturbations. Biological systems have an intricate play of real-time sensors and actuators within the body to do this. Cellular sensors collect personalized information based on the individual body changes. These signals affect outputs for corrective action. These cybernetic mechanisms keep the human body naturally stable (Figure 2).

Occasionally, this human system becomes unstable which results in deteriorating health. In the current medical ecosystem, there is a great delay between deterioration and detection, resulting in further destabilizing of the human biological system and degrading health. Our vision is to reduce this latency in health care through early detection, by continuously collecting sensor data that are specific to the individual, while enabling corrective actions to transform an unstable health condition back to full health stability. For example, anesthesiologists are beginning to develop closed-loop drug administration systems that will replace much of their own job during a surgery [22], and in type 1 diabetics, mechanical devices can replace the biological pancreas with a hormone pump and continuous glucose monitoring. Both of these examples are mechanical implementations of cybernetics for health. The next step needs to combine real world multimedia information sources into a virtual environment that patients can use to interact and understand their live health status.

Modern technology systems intimately link navigation and cybernetic systems. Airplane auto-pilot systems use navigational components to know the route, and mechanical cybernetic systems to help correct the course of travel en-route to the destination. This is only possible through perpetual monitoring and updates. Navigation systems, like Google Maps, became rapidly popular by providing expert knowledge with real-time personalized contextual information to guide travel. We believe this is the future of human health systems, and the time is ripe.

2 P5 CYBERNETIC HEALTH CONCEPT

Multimedia system integration into standard health practices paves a path for future leaps in addressing personalized and preventive health. Leading medical professionals have advocated for a deeper integration of technology into health care [27]. Future health care systems will intertwine lifestyle multimedia data with medical knowledge to develop a new paradigm that optimizes individual health. This is illustrated by research that shows patients make better lifestyle choices that would combat diabetes if given guidance [25]. Ultimately, transforming data and knowledge to actionable lifestyle choices is the most promising, effective, and attainable method to improve human health. We have developed a 5 component system to bring this vision to reality.

First, we use a multi-layer modeling system to understand how to build an increasingly accurate personalized model (Figure 5). Second, using this dynamic model connected with real time sensors allows us to predict evolving situations that an individual may encounter. Third, we use the predictions in conjunction with validated expert medical knowledge to give the most precise solutions to avoid emerging problems. Fourth, we effectively persuade the individual as an actuator in the system by optimizing their preferences, convenience, and specific health needs. Fifth, we give feedback on how the patient's actions have quantitatively affected their health. The realization of this personalized, predictive, precise, persuasive, and preventive system depends upon the coordination of available and future technologies. We call this above approach P5 Cybernetic Health (P5C) (Figure 3).

3 MULTIMEDIA RETRIEVAL IN THE P5C FRAMEWORK

Recommendations are the key to modern content consumption. Recommending effective lifestyle changes requires accurate models that represent the individual. This model will understand interactions

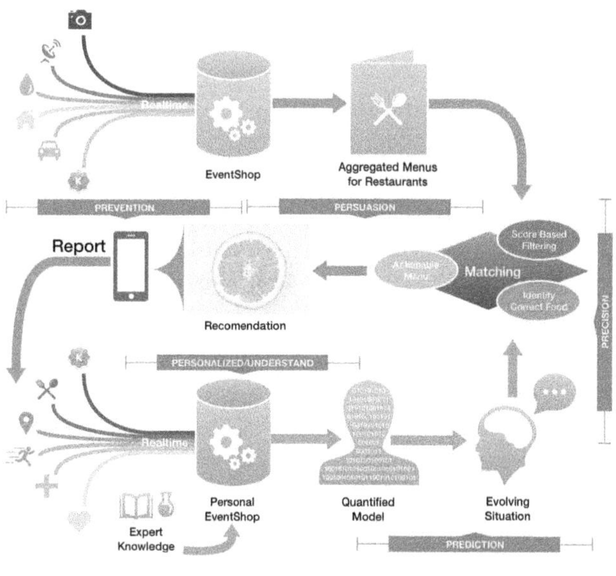

Figure 4: System Architecture of P5C: Quantified individual models allow for matching the individuals needs with the appropriate environmental resources to enable optimal recommendation systems.

of user events with various situations. Combining this understanding with live contextual situations establishes the real-time needs of the individual. We match these needs to accessible resources. These resources are presented as recommendations which move the person towards the optimal health state.

Multimedia work in this field has primarily focused on giving the user figures and statistics of past data. This is true for both hardware and software in personal health. Hardware such as the Fitbit, and health software like Apple's HealthKit only function to acquire and accumulate data. This does not fulfill the function of providing timely and personalized health advice in a predictive manner. Most importantly current digital health mechanisms are rudimentary in detecting context for each individual. Additionally, recommendation engines that are used in health applications ignore mechanisms to maintain retention and trust of the user. Users quickly get notification/alert fatigue from poor recommendations. To sustain users, applications must give users autonomy, cater to their desires and convenience, autonomously track data, while also informing them in an encouraging manner. Furthermore, many lifestyle data parameters are gathered through manual mechanisms. For example, popular nutrition tracking apps ask users to manually enter information, placing high burden on the user. This further causes a loss in user retention, while having poor fidelity of input values. Users desire low data entry burden, with high functionality to help reach their goals. All of these problems open vast opportunities for multimedia research and application.

Different components of P5C enable us to accomplish this task by creating a layered architecture where different layers are responsible for completing the cybernetic navigation of health (Figure 4).

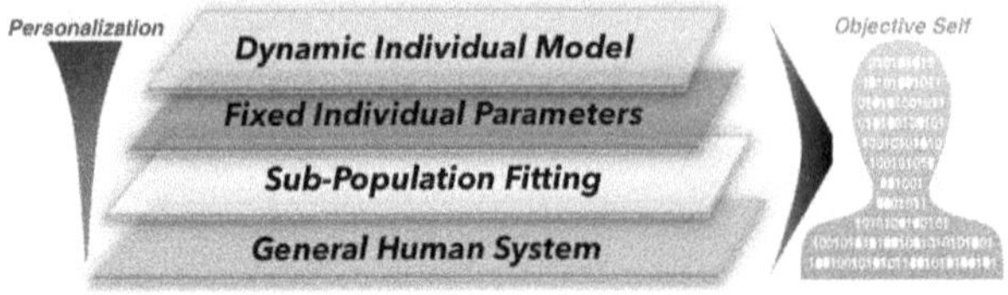

Figure 5: We integrate increasingly personalized knowledge layers derived from multimedia data fusion to build a comprehensive health map of each individual.

3.1 Personalized Model : Objective Self

An objective self threads all pieces of life data to make a true universal multimedia map of the human life. This becomes a hub for integrating sensors and methods to enhance the personal multimedia model. In the future, as computer science, medicine and other fields progress, there needs to be an effective method to combine these into increasingly high resolution health map layers.

The first step in making effective recommendations is maintaining a personicle, a complete and quantified log of the events in a person's life[14]. The personicle records all user activities on a time line and we can use this to model the user's current status. We refer to this model of the person as Objective Self, which allows us to determine the future state of the person based on the interactions between their current state and possible future events. Objective Self contains the user's current state along with their preferences. In our map analogy, this would represent the current location of the user and the topography of the map, which represent the user preferences for different types of events (Figure 1). High cost events are further away from the users preferences, while low cost events are aligned with their preferences. This cost is mapped by the slope of the health topography, with higher cost mapped as a higher slope (Figure 1). The Objective Self model of the person would allow us to find the quantitative effect of future events which are possible from the given state. Creation of Objective Self requires the integration of various life logs which are maintained as a part of the P5C system.

In health care applications, the most effective changes in a person's life can be brought about by inducing changes in controllable actions such as lifestyle, food habits, or environment. The emotional response of the user to different activities or events are relevant for letting us estimate the user's preferences. We maintain a log of the activities, dietary habits, environment, and emotional state of the user using primary sensors (such as mobile phones and wearables). Future health multimedia logging must be done passively without placing any overhead on the user or interfering with their usual activities.

Events in our daily lives and can be logged passively to create the activity log of a person [2, 6, 19, 20]. Personalized life log raw data is then extracted to semantic-level activities in real-time. These real-time semantic events allow for intuitive analysis of a dynamic human life. Realistic systems may never completely capture everything due to the lack of standard data formats and the complexity of life [24]. Therefore, the range of semantic activity also needs to be refined to a number of meaningful universal activities. Quantitative information of time, frequency, intensity, stress, enjoyment, and other affective states are most meaningful to medical researchers [17]. We currently target 17 standard semantic level activities including: socializing, relaxing, prayer, eating, exercising, home events(watching TV, preparing food, sleeping, housework), shopping, conversations, computer/e-mail/Internet usage, working, and commuting. We can extract additional information about events using existing expert systems and use these as features in the Objective Self models. For example, from an exercise event which represents jogging for 30 minutes, we can get the amount of calories and fat burned using expert systems such as Wolfram Alpha[33]. We can obtain similar features and measures for other activities as well and use expert systems to generate tags about the nature of these activities such as "strenuous" or "resting".

Nutritional intake can be captured by analysis of photos, transactions, or conversations of food to create a quantitative nutrition diary. Using pictures, open source deep-learning techniques by Google and Clarifai for food recognition in photos [4] can give us the semantic information about nutrition. Once we have the name of the dish and ingredients, we can look up the item in publicly available food databases such as USDA Food Composition Databases [30] and obtain the quantity of each nutritional group in the food item as well as features, tags, and relevant flavors related to the ingredients. Nutritional parameters for each person are then analyzed based on their personal health status [11, 34] to give them the most relevant food suggestions.

Environmental factors continuously affect the health of every individual. The ability to measure the local environment of each individual gives us insights into how they are being affected by factors the user is otherwise unaware of. Air and water pollution have been shown to increase the risk of asthma and diabetes [5] While public data regarding the quality of the environment is readily available, it is not incorporated and tracked at the individual level. We are using an open source software platform, called *EventShop* to ingest and assimilate different data streams [21, 26]. The real time synchronization of personal activities/events and the environmental factors allows P5C to respond to changing situations in a swift and effective manner.

The Objective Self could be viewed as the person's coordinates on a health map (the dimensions are represented by the health parameters which we are trying to estimate and optimize such as weight, blood glucose etc.), and the set of probable events obtained from the personicle represent the possible paths for the user. The desired state for the user can be represented in the same map, and the problem of reaching the goal node would be similar to finding the path with the least amount of work /resistance. In our analogy, the resistance is represented by the user's preferences and the prevalence of the event sequence in the personicle. It is possible that the shortest path to the destination may not be the best or the optimal path due to the terrain, similarly any event which has rarely appeared in a person's event history or is against their preferences is unlikely to be an actionable recommendation, even if it has the most positive impact on health. Thus in the precision layer of our system, we need to recommend an action by optimizing the health of the user under the constraints placed on them by their history and preferences. We can define the user's preferences by attaching tags with every event in the personicle, which are representative of the event's parameters. For instance, a food event may have tags related to the taste and ingredients of the dish as well as describing the image concepts obtained from deep learning based image recognition systems. Prevalence of a tag is an estimate of the user's preference of the event aspect represented by the particular tag. We can use use these preference scores to rank the set of possible events by matching the tags associated with the events and their respective preference scores.

It is vital that the system should allow for seamless integration of latest developments in AI and new sources of media in creating the Objective Self model. The event based processing model allows us to do that as long as we can convert the new source of data into an event stream, thus allowing us to adapt with changing modalities of data while preserving the existing infrastructure.

3.2 Prediction : Personalized Probability of Events

We have talked about viewing the recommendation problem as a navigation system, and how it is analogous to suggesting optimum routes considering terrain and distance. The first step in identifying the optimum path or activity, is to find out all the possible activities and estimating their influence on the health of the user so that we can identify desired activities. This is similar to comparing the available paths in the map and finding out the ones which bring us closer to our destination (Figure 1).

We use data driven analysis and pattern mining algorithms to find event patterns in a personicle and predict events that are most likely to appear next in the sequence. Event relationship operators formulate compound events and compute co-occurrences which are then tested with a new set of data [13, 15, 16]. This framework extends traditional complex event processing [3] significantly by including space, multiple event streams, with point and interval events to enable real world data analysis. Every event has a set of constraints as prerequisites which must be fulfilled for the event to occur. Given an environment, we filter out events whose prerequisites are not satisfied (meaning, they would not be executed). This gives us the set of next possible events based on the person's history. Based on how these events affect user's health, we recommend actions which induce a positive change.

Merged event streams in a personicle [14] produce a stream of time-indexed events, e.g., high fat meal eaten at 3pm Monday / 40 minutes of exercise at 2pm on Saturday / high blood glucose level at 5pm Thursday. Statistical models [12] are used to identify recurring patterns in a sequence of events. By fitting such models we can identify sequences of events that have high co occurrence with an adverse medical event, allowing prediction of health status in the future. Fitting the model to an individual's event stream data is a challenge that may require weeks of observations. Bayesian hierarchical models [10] can be used to leverage information from a population of users to give upfront meaningful analysis until the data from a single user is sufficient. This approach provides an intuitive data-determined degree of synergistic sharing between individual and population information. Parameters of models that fit separate individuals can be described by a population distribution where recurring patterns are shared while some remain unique to each individual [12].

We need to have a calibration period to train the models which can predict the effects of an event on the person's health. We need to create features which represent the inherent health aspects of the events, for example a food event may have features representing the nutritional content of the dish, and we may want to find an association between different dishes and the person's blood sugar levels. As described in the previous section, these features may come from deep learning and AI based systems or expert knowledge based systems and will be used to build models which can estimate the relevant health parameters. For example, in section 4, we talk about an application (HealthButler) for managing type II diabetes. In the calibration phase, the user may be required to measure their blood glucose levels at periodic intervals of time, we can use the features obtained for events (nutritional values, calories burned etc.) to build a model for estimating the change in health parameters (blood glucose level) due to these events. Once we have these models, we can use them to predict the effects of different events on the user's health to give healthy recommendations.

Aside from this, we can use the event history of the user to identify anomalies in their behavior. Some of these anomalies may represent medically significant behavior changes, for example if we can identify sudden mood shifts using an emotion log, there is a high likelihood of hyper or hypoglycemia. This activates the system to provide emergency relief services and information. We also use the personalized data to predict developing insulin resistance over time. An accumulation of low activity, high fat and sugar foods, with associated lethargy indicates the individual is not on track to improve their insulin sensitivity.

The prediction layer enables us to find the next set of events and how these may affect the user's health, the next step is to match these events with the user's preferences and obtain a ranked list of actionable items which the user is likely to follow.

3.3 Precision : Constraint Optimization with Knowledge and Context

A lack of data on personal lifestyle in relation to biomarkers has been a struggle in the quest to provide precise treatments for patients [31]. President Barack Obama also began the Precision Medicine Initiative to follow various cohorts of patients to understand what constitutes better treatments for different people [8]. Researchers are also trying to link genetic factors to diabetes outcomes, but they are confounded in their research due to a lack of quality lifestyle data [29].

By predicting the probability of physiologic events, we can send the most appropriate control signals to the user to take corrective action to maintain their health status before it starts becoming unstable. Algorithms should incorporate various factors such as the severity of adverse events along with the likelihood of occurrence. To prevent alarm fatigue, we dispatch the control signal only after the threshold of maintaining optimal health is crossed. Otherwise the control signal of actions are given as choices/recommendations to help guide the user towards better health goals. Precise diagnostic tools, medications and other medical interventions are also suggested to the physician as to reduce waste of resources and ensure better outcomes. Most importantly, giving the most precise treatment for an individual relies on the generation of actionable interventions [31].

Generating precise recommendations refers to filtering out and ranking the available events based on the context of the user and expert knowledge. Once the next set of possible events have been generated using event mining and the environment log, we can then match constraints placed on these events with the context of the user which is represented by their Objective Self. This includes matching the event parameters with the preferences of the user and using the appropriate domain knowledge. As mentioned earlier in section 3.1, the events have tags associated with them which are related to different aspects and parameters of the events. The Objective Self model stores the preferences of the users by assigning a weight to the tags which are present in the user's personicle and also can include the emotional response of a user to these events. Assigning a utility/preference score to these events by using a similarity metric (eg. Cosine similarity) to maximize recommendations for the events which align with user's preferences. Continuing our map analogy, this step is finding out the work required along the different routes (terrain is represented by the user's preferences), thus it gives us the most convenient route to reach our goal (Figure 1).

3.4 Persuasion : Enabling User Execution

The goal of our system is to induce gradual habit changes via suggestions which cater to user's preferences and push sustainable long-term positive habits and health. Executing this health navigation in the real world is only done when the user takes action on a given recommendation. Persuasive multimedia systems in advertising, social media, news, and other platforms are constantly under development to push people to take a certain action. Concepts from persuasive technology generate recommendations that are most suited for the individual[1, 9]. We use Fogg's Behavior Model [7] to optimize three factors which strongly determine behavior: motivation, ability and trigger.

Motivation captures the individual's willingness to follow through with a suggestion. The list of recommendations are ordered on the basis of the preferences of the user which are determined from Objective Self. This ensures that the recommended actions have the highest motivation weight.

Ability encompasses the resource availability in performing the suggested behavior. This factor is an interplay of the individual's environment and their intrinsic capability, and must ensure those constraints are met.

Triggers are instances of events that lead to accomplishment of a task[7]. These can be optimized by using the current spatio-temporal context of the user to filter the list of recommended actionable items. For example, a notification about healthy food options when the person is hungry. The efficacy of a trigger is maximized when it is generated according to the context of the user and the current situation. For example, a recommendation suggesting a cup of coffee may be very relevant at 9 AM but it is unlikely to be effective at 7 PM, even if the user prefers coffee and has no obvious constraints placed.

Thus by combining the right triggers with context, we can maximize the effectiveness of positive health actions.

3.5 Prevention : The Ultimate Goal

P5C systems prevent adverse outcomes through addressing several points. First, multimedia experiences (such as through an app) give direct feedback to quantitatively understand personal health status. Second, user ownership of their total integrated health multimedia data is key to empower patient participation in health and driving user engagement. Third, Multimedia systems can inform the individual of risks regarding their choices. In the USA, calories are printed on menus of large franchise restaurants by law. This allows consumers to have direct basic information on what they are consuming, but remains a rudimentary form of information dissemination. Similarly, the practice of having cancer warning signs on cigarette packages or labeling alcohol warnings for pregnant women are designed to inform the consumer of their choice. Future systems will use augmented reality systems to inform users in how real world items or actions will quantitatively affect their health. Systems derived from the P5C concept must focus on informing the user in a personalized fashion for *all* health related decisions. Ultimately, the prevention of deteriorating health conditions keeps the individual in the steady state of optimal health: original cybernetic goal.

4 HEALTHBUTLER APPLICATION

To illustrate the delivery of P5C, a type 2 diabetic named "Bruce Uberschweet", uses the HealthButler (HB) mobile app system to optimally manage his health condition. This will include analysis to better control blood sugar and reduce drug dependency through improved metabolism [18]. Bruce is looking for lunch on his commute to work on Monday and knows that HB always gives him the fastest access point to tasty and nutritious food. An intelligent recommendation engine takes into consideration his real-time personal tastes, logistical convenience, and current health needs (including blood sugar) to provide him a curated list of specific dishes that he can easily pre-order. He can also clearly see how each dish affects his diabetes so he can feel empowered to choose what is good for himself (Figure 8). After attending a wedding on Sunday, HB predicts a rising insulin resistance based on his life log data, and gives him immediate actions to take in order to address the worsening condition. It tells him when to take his blood sugar, gives him a clinical mono-filament test with a tutorial video that he can do at home, and simplifies booking an urgent appointment with his doctor to change his medication dose (Figure 8). These are two examples of how HB is actively engaged in predicting Bruce's health status from his health data (Figure 7), merging in with his daily life in an unobtrusive and useful way. Bruce can actively see how his external world and internal body are interacting through HB. Figure 6 shows the flow of information from the smart phone to the logs and how the raw media is converted to event streams and stored as logs.

5 RESEARCH OPPORTUNITIES

P5C paves new research pathways in which multimedia recommendation systems can take advantage of health data to benefit users.

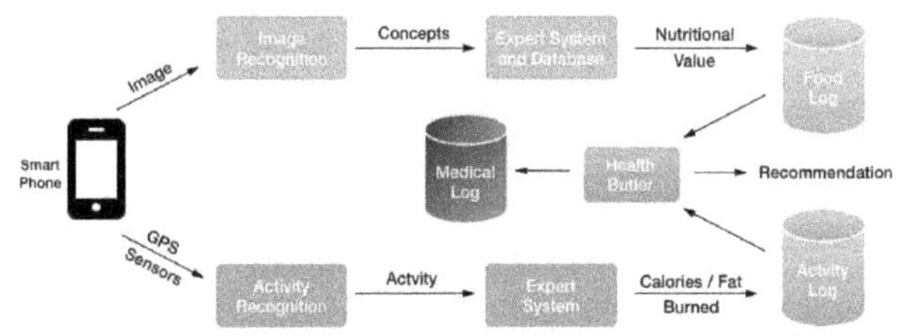

Figure 6: Flow of information in the Health Butler Application, with respect to activity and food event streams.

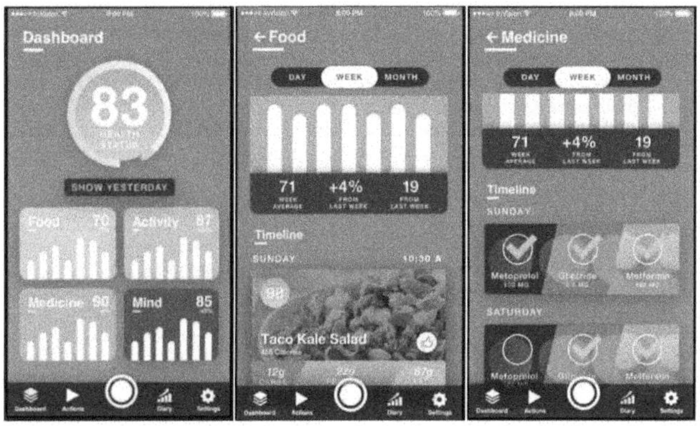

Figure 7: Left: Aggregate summary of health status Center: FoodSense Log. Right: MedicalSense Log.

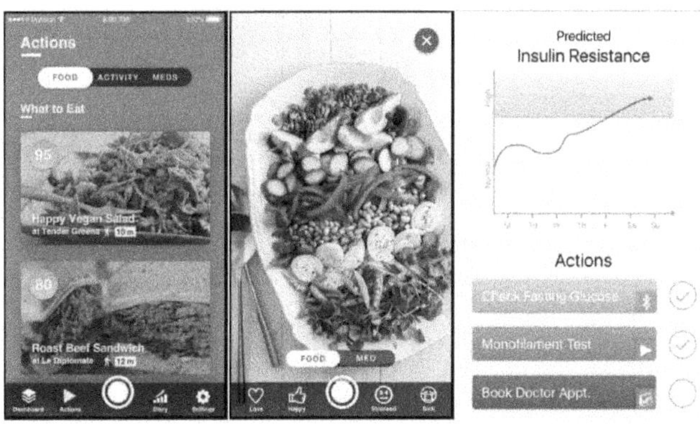

Figure 8: Left: Nutrition guidance is catered to the user's preferences, needs, and available resources. Center: Easy one-touch food and mood tracking. Right: real-time health status is shown, with direct actions to take for help.

These applications can range from acute, sub-acute, and chronic disease health management to preventive medicine (such as vaccines) and wellness. These opportunities also allow open more doors for collaborative efforts across various fields.

5.1 Diverse Multimedia/Multimodal Data

Health applications already use traditional multimedia data sources: text, images of different types, video, and audio. The more exciting and challenging part is the use of sensors that create data streams ranging from GPS and accelerometers to glucose measurements, heart-reate monitoring, blood oxygen level and many more. The list of different multimodal measurements will keep increasing. This offers a great opportunity to the multimedia research community to address time-sensitive data streams of diverse modality and combine their semantics to solve the most important problem for humans, health. Developing P5C to universally digest and synchronize various sensor data streams will continue to be important for human health and will be a rewarding challenge for multimedia technology.

5.2 Personal Logs and Relevant Applications

Life logs and related research areas have attracted multimedia researchers. Much activity in this area has remained limited to video sensors and determination of simple activities. As discussed above, now we need to associate everyday activities to different measurements related to behavior and health data obtained from diverse sensors. Such logs are essential for building models that will be used for personalization and prediction. Since we are dealing with diverse sensors, synchronization and semantics become a very important issue in analyzing these logs. Data is collected from different sensors at different frequencies. Synchronizing them requires the understanding of their semantics as well, which becomes a new challenge.

5.3 Multimodal Retrieval and Recommendation Approaches

Data from various streams need to be analyzed to detect events during the daily activities of a person. All these data streams will be stored 24/7 for the lifetime of a person. Since this data needs to be analyzed to build models of the person as well as to understand current events for predictive purposes, it is important to develop techniques for retrieving different events in these streams in context of various queries. Moreover, in most cases, the result of such queries is not limited to presenting those events, but to relate those events to personal models for predictions based on medical knowledge and provide appropriate actions as recommendations. As augmented and virtual reality platforms become more ubiquitous, future health multimedia systems can start overlaying health information directly on objects in our real world. For example, if there is a food dish with peanuts at the grocery story, it will be highlighted with a warning color in augmented reality glasses. Facebook and other companies are already working on general systems like this, but need health data to effectively power such a system. This is a new challenge for multimedia research where results from a retrieval are continuously converted to recommendations based on the situation of the user.

6 CONCLUSIONS

Cybernetic navigation principles lay the foundational bricks of building health systems that are responsive in keeping individuals at optimal health over the course of a lifetime. P5C is based on the most fundamental principles in cybernetics while incorporating the ability to seamlessly integrate both present and future technological advancements. The most important concept in this paper is how synergistic health multimedia fusion will fuel the recommendation engines of the future. These actionable recommendations enable the human actuator in cybernetic health to form a true closed-loop feedback system.

Real human health progress relies on an interdisciplinary effort between hospital clinicians, engineers, computer scientists, bio-science researchers amongst other fields. P5C systems will sow the seed of this interdisciplinary approach within future health systems will accelerate multimedia research progress into real systems that benefits patients.

REFERENCES

[1] S. M Arteaga, M. Kudeki, and A. Woodworth. 2009. Combating obesity trends in teenagers through persuasive mobile technology. *ACM SIGACCESS Accessibility and Computin* 94 (2009), 17–25.

[2] G. Biegel and V. Cahill. 2004. A framework for developing mobile, context-aware applications. In *Pervasive Computing and Communications, 2004. PerCom 2004. Proceedings of the Second IEEE Annual Conference on.* IEEE, 361–365.

[3] A. Buchmann and B. Koldehofe. 2009. Complex event processing. *IT-Information Technology Methoden und innovative Anwendungen der Informatik und Informationstechnik* 51, 5 (2009), 241–242.

[4] Clarifai 2017. Clarifai Food Recognition. (2017). http://blog.clarifai.com/.

[5] I. C Eze, M. Imboden, A. Kumar, A. von Eckardstein, D. Stolz, M. W Gerbase, N. Künzli, M. Pons, F. Kronenberg, C. Schindler, and others. 2016. Air pollution and diabetes association: Modification by type 2 diabetes genetic risk score. *Environment International* 94 (2016), 263–271.

[6] D. Ferreira, V. Kostakos, and A. K Dey. 2015. AWARE: mobile context instrumentation framework. *Frontiers in ICT* 2 (2015), 6.

[7] B. Fogg. 2009. A behavior model for persuasive design. *Proceedings of the 4th International Conference on Persuasive Technology - Persuasive '09* (2009), 40:1–-40:7.

[8] J. E Fradkin, M. C Hanlon, and G. P Rodgers. 2016. NIH Precision Medicine Initiative: Implications for Diabetes Research. *Diabetes Care* 39, 7 (2016).

[9] T. Fritz, E. M Huang, G. C Murphy, and T. Zimmermann. 2014. Persuasive Technology in the Real World: A Study of Long-Term Use of Activity Sensing Devices for Fitness. *Proceedings of the 32nd annual ACM conference on Human factors in computing systems - CHI '14* (2014), 487–496.

[10] A. Gelman, J. B Carlin, H. S Stern, and D. B Rubin. 2014. *Bayesian data analysis.* Vol. 2. Chapman & Hall/CRC Boca Raton, FL, USA.

[11] S. Goyal, P. Morita, G. F Lewis, C. Yu, E. Seto, and J. A Cafazzo. 2016. The Systematic Design of a Behavioural Mobile Health Application for the Self-Management of Type 2 Diabetes. *Canadian Journal of Diabetes* 40, 1 (2 2016), 95–104. https://doi.org/10.1016/j.jcjd.2015.06.007

[12] K. Heins and H. Stern. 2014. A Statistical Model for Event Sequence Data.. In *AISTATS.* 338–346.

[13] L. Jalali. 2016. Interactive Event-driven Knowledge Discovery from Data Streams. (2016).

[14] L. Jalali, D. Huo, H. Oh, M. Tang, S. Pongpaichet, and R. Jain. 2014. Personicle: Personal Chronicle of Life Events. In *Workshop on Personal Data Analytics in the Internet of Things (PDA@ IOT) at the 40th International Conference on Very Large Databases (VLDB), Hangzhou, China.*

[15] L. Jalali and R. Jain. 2015. Bringing deep causality to multimedia data streams. In *Proceedings of the 23rd ACM international conference on Multimedia.* ACM, 221–230.

[16] L. Jalali, H. Oh, R. Moazeni, and R. Jain. 2016. Human Behavior Analysis from Smartphone Data Streams. In *International Workshop on Human Behavior Understanding.* Springer, 68–85.

[17] D. Kahneman, A. B Krueger, D. A Schkade, N. Schwarz, and A. A Stone. 2004. A survey method for characterizing daily life experience: The day reconstruction method. *Science* 306, 5702 (2004), 1776–1780.

[18] R. W McGarrah, C. A Slentz, and W. E Kraus. 2016. The Effect of Vigorous- Versus Moderate-Intensity Aerobic Exercise on Insulin Action. *Current Cardiology Reports* 18, 12 (12 2016), 117.

[19] H Oh. 2015. *A Life Event Detection System Using Real Time Heterogeneous Context Monitoring and Formal Concept Analysis.* Master's thesis. University of California, Irvine, Irvine,CA.

[20] H. Oh, L. Jalali, and R. Jain. 2015. An intelligent notification system using context from real-time personal activity monitoring. In *Multimedia and Expo (ICME), 2015 IEEE International Conference on.* IEEE, 1–6.

[21] S. Pongpaichet, V. K Singh, M. Gao, and R. Jain. 2013. EventShop: recognizing situations in web data streams. In *Proceedings of the 22nd International Conference on World Wide Web.* ACM, 1359–1368.

[22] J. Rinehart and C. Canales. 2015. Closed-Loop Pharmacology in Anesthesia and Critical Care. *International Anesthesiology Clinics* 53, 2 (21 2015), 91–101.

[23] M. Sagner, A. McNeil, P. Puska, C. Auffray, N. D Price, L. Hood, C. J Lavie, Z. Han, Z. Chen, S. K. Brahmachari, and others. 2016. The P4 Health Spectrum âĂŞ A Predictive, Preventive, Personalized and Participatory Continuum for Promoting Healthspan. *Progress in Cardiovascular Diseases* (8 2016).

[24] A. J Sellen and S. Whittaker. 2010. Beyond total capture: a constructive critique of lifelogging. *Commun. ACM* 53, 5 (2010), 70–77.

[25] D. Sherifali, V. Viscardi, J Bai, and R M. U. Ali. 2016. Evaluating the Effect of a Diabetes Health Coach in Individuals with Type 2 Diabetes. *Canadian Journal of Diabetes* 40, 1 (2 2016), 84–94.

[26] M. Tang, P. Agrawal, and R. Jain. 2015. Habits vs environment: What really causes asthma?. In *Proceedings of the ACM Web Science Conference.* ACM, 30.

[27] E. Topol. 2015. *The patient will see you now: the future of medicine is in your hands.* Basic Books.

[28] E. J Topol. 2012. *The creative destruction of medicine: How the digital revolution will create better health care.* Basic Books.

[29] Type 2 Diabetes Genetics 2017. Type 2 Diabetes Genetics. (2017). http://www.type2diabetesgenetics.org/.

[30] USDA Food Composition Database 2017. USDA food database. (2017). https://ndb.nal.usda.gov/ndb/search/list.

[31] W. M. Valencia and H. Florez. 2017. How to prevent the microvascular complications of type 2 diabetes beyond glucose control. *BMJ (Clinical research ed.)* 356 (1 2017), i6505.

[32] N. Wiener. 1948. *Cybernetics: Control and communication in the animal and the machine.* Wiley New York.

[33] WolfromAlpha 2017. Wolfram Alpha. (2017). https://www.wolframalpha.com.

[34] F. G Wood, E. Alley, S. Baer, and R. Johnson. 2015. Interactive Multimedia Tailored to Improve Diabetes Self-Management. *The Nursing clinics of North America* 50, 3 (9 2015), 565–76.

An Unsupervised Distance Learning Framework for Multimedia Retrieval

Lucas Pascotti Valem and Daniel Carlos Guimarães Pedronette
Department of Statistics, Applied Math. and Computing, São Paulo State University (UNESP)
Rio Claro, Brazil
lucasvalem@rc.unesp.br,daniel@rc.unesp.br

ABSTRACT

Due to the increasing availability of image and multimedia collections, unsupervised post-processing methods, which are capable of improving the effectiveness of retrieval results without the need of user intervention, have become indispensable. This paper presents the *Unsupervised Distance Learning Framework* (UDLF), a software which enables an easy use and evaluation of unsupervised learning methods. The framework defines a broad model, allowing the implementation of different unsupervised methods and supporting diverse file formats for input and output. Seven different unsupervised methods are initially available in the framework. Executions and experiments can be easily defined by setting a configuration file. The framework also includes the evaluation of the retrieval results exporting visual output results, computing effectiveness and efficiency measures. The source-code is public available, such that anyone can freely access, use, change, and share the software under the terms of the GPLv2 license.

CCS CONCEPTS

• **Information systems → Multimedia and multimodal retrieval**;

KEYWORDS

content-based image retrieval; unsupervised learning; reranking; rank-aggregation

1 INTRODUCTION

The facilities in image acquisition and sharing available nowadays have been resulted in profound changes in human lifestyle. Mainly supported by the development of mobile devices, social networks, and cloud environments, visual content have become the mean of communication for a growing number of people. Considering the huge and increasing amount of image collections available, the development of automatic methods for analysing, indexing and searching the visual content became indispensable.

In this scenario, Content-Based Image Retrieval (CBIR) systems have been established as a central solution [7]. The main objective of such systems consists in retrieving relevant images ranked according to their similarity to a query input. Initially, the ranking tasks relied only in the comparison between images based on their low-level features. Therefore, for many years, the progress of CBIR systems have been mainly supported by the development of diverse visual features [2]. In order to provide a common and public available implementation of such features, open-source tools as LIRE [9] and Eva [20] have been proposed.

However, the retrieval model grounded on pairwise comparisons computed between feature vectors faces serious challenges. Such model analyzes similarity only in terms of pairs of images, ignoring the global relationships encoded in the dataset. More recently, various methods [1, 3–5, 14, 15, 17, 18, 21, 25–28] have focused on other stages of the retrieval process, post-processing the initial results in order to improve the retrieval effectiveness, without the need of user intervention. Generally, such methods compute unsupervised global affinity measures capable of considering the intrinsic manifold structure of datasets. Although such methods represent an indispensable tool for improving the retrieval results, few of them are public available and, when available, require specific software environments and input/output formats. In this scenario, a common tool capable of executing different methods under a unified environment is missing.

In this work, we introduce the *Unsupervised Distance Learning Framework* (UDLF), which provides a software environment to easily implement, use, and evaluate unsupervised post-processing methods. The framework defines a general model, allowing the implementation of different methods, based on distance measures or rank information. The user can easily select the method to be executed and set the respective parameters. Different file formats (for both input and output) are supported, and effectiveness and efficiency evaluation are also available. The framework includes the implementation of seven different unsupervised methods and is licensed under the terms of the GPLv2, such that it can be easily extended.

The paper is organized as follows: Section 2 presents the main aspects of the framework and describes the methods currently implemented; Section 3 describes the use of the framework and discusses some examples. Finally, Section 4 discusses the conclusions and presents possible future works.

ICMR '17, June 06-09, 2017, Bucharest, Romania

ACM ISBN 978-1-4503-4701-3/17/06...$15.00
https://doi.org/10.1145/3078971.3079017

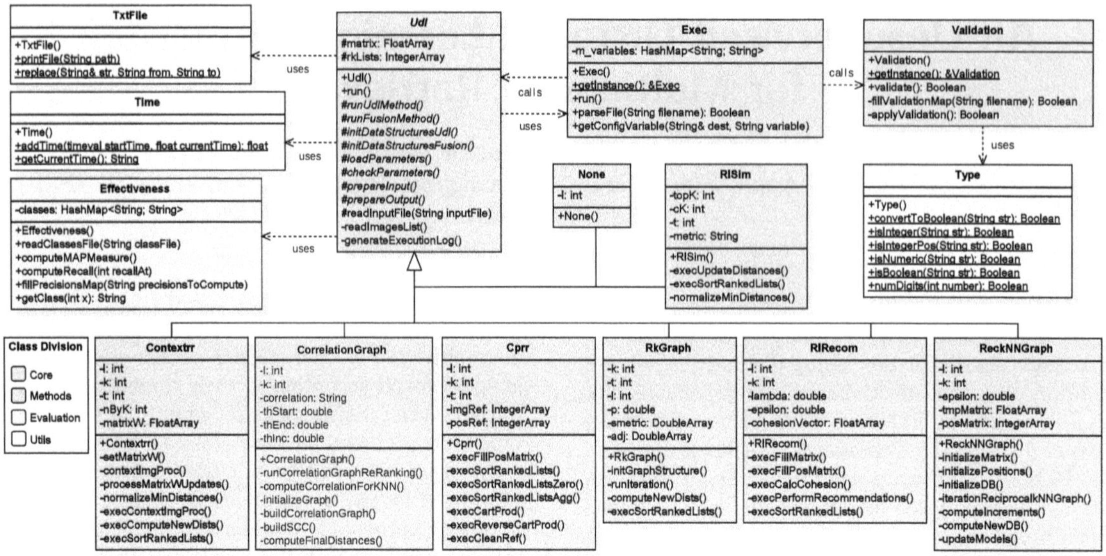

Figure 1: General organization of the UDLF proposed framework in a UML class diagram.

2 UDL FRAMEWORK

As discussed, several unsupervised post-processing methods have been proposed recently aiming at improving the effectiveness of multimedia retrieval tasks. However, the implementation of such methods are not always public available and, when provided, they do not follow any standard. In this way, any person interested in using such methods is required to understand the implementation, parameters configuration, and file formats for input and output. This process is necessary for each method, therefore limiting the widespread use of such relevant tools. This paper aims to fill this gap by introducing the *Unsupervised Distance Learning Framework* (UDLF). The main objective consists in providing a software environment which includes the follow requirements:

- **General and extensible model:** the framework defines a broadly unsupervised distance learning model, which can be used for implementing different methods. The framework was initially validated considering seven distinct methods (discussed in Section 2.2) and is ready to extensions.
- **Flexible input/output:** the retrieval results can be read and exported in different file formats, defined in terms of distance measures or ranking information.
- **Easy use and configuration:** the code is compiled once and different executions can be done just by changing file paths and parameter values in a configuration file, since no installation is required. This allows the user to easily perform experiments using different methods and datasets.
- **Evaluation:** in addition to the processed output files, the framework includes evaluation information considering both effectiveness and efficiency aspects. The framework reports measures as Precision, Recall and MAP (Mean Average Precision).

The framework is an open-source software licensed under the terms of GPLv2. The framework is public available[1], allowing anyone to access, use, and contribute with the code.

[1]https://github.com/UDLF/UDLF

2.1 Language and Organization

UDLF is designed trough a object-oriented paradigm and implemented using C++ 2011. The framework is independent of external libraries and portable among different operation systems. Figure 1 presents a UML class diagram, which illustrates the general organization of the framework, including the most important functions and attributes for each class. The colors represent directories in which the classes are divided, according to their role.

The execution flow starts from the `Core` classes, where `Exec` parses the configuration file reading the parameters values. The `Validation` class verifies if all the attributed values are lexically acceptable. Otherwise, they are set to the default values. All the classes of `Methods` are a generalization of `Udl`, an abstract class which establishes a protocol to implement new methods. Regarding the remaining classes, while `Utils` encompasses all static classes that have auxiliary purposes, `Evaluation` implements the necessary measures to evaluate the results. As can be seen, different effectiveness measures are currently implemented in the `Effectiness` class. To compute the efficiency, the `Time` class is used as an utility by the `Udl` class.

2.2 Distance Learning Methods

This section presents a briefly description of the unsupervised methods currently implemented in the framework.

- **Correlation Graph Manifold Learning [16]**: the algorithm builds a correlation graph for encoding the dataset similarity information. The dataset manifold is analysed through the graph and its strongly connected components, in order to compute a more effective distance measure.
- **Ranked List Graph Distance [12]**: the method represents each ranked list as a weighted sub-graph based on its top-k positions. Subsequently, the sub-graphs are combined in a single graph and the weight of the edges is used to increment the similarity scores between images.

• **RL-Sim*** **[11, 15]**: the algorithm is defined in terms of an iterative re-ranking method that computes a similarity score between images based on the similarity of their ranked lists. The algorithm is motivated by the conjecture that if two images are similar, their ranked lists should also be similar.

• **CPRR** **[22]**: the Cartesian Product of Ranking References (CPRR) algorithm applies the Cartesian product operations to kNN and reverse kNN sets aiming at considering the contextual information encoded in the ranked lists.

• **Manifold Reciprocal kNN Graph** **[19]**: the method builds a graph considering the reciprocal references in the top-k positions of the ranked lists. The method exploits the graph structure through scores in order to analyze the dataset manifold and compute new ranked lists.

• **RL-Recom** **[23]**: the algorithm exploits the concept of recommendations among ranked lists. The motivation is based on the conjecture that similarity information available in the ranked lists can be used to recommend images among themselves. In this scenario, a recommendation indicates a reduction in the distance measures.

• **ContextRR** **[13]**: the method uses context images, which are abstractions obtained from the ranked lists and distance measures to make an analysis of the dataset as a whole. Based on information extracted from context images, a more effective distance measure is computed.

3 FRAMEWORK USAGE

The framework usage is mainly based on the configuration file, which specifies all information about the execution: the desired task, method being used, dataset information, input and output files, evaluation settings, and other details. In this way, no recompilation is necessary, such that the user is able to perform a totally different execution just by changing the configuration file. The software considers only a single configuration file per execution, allowing the user to have distinct configuration files for different executions.

A command line interface, which varies according to the operating system, must be used to execute the software. When the binary is executed, a `config.ini` file is searched in the current directory. The user can also specify a different configuration file as a parameter: `./udlf my_conf.ini`. The next sub-sections briefly describe the structure of the configuration file and usage examples. More detailed information can be found at https://github.com/UDLF/UDLF/wiki.

3.1 Configuration File

The configuration file syntax is at the same time very simple and powerful. Basically, values are attributed to parameters using the expression: `PARAMETER = VALUE`. All the parameters are upper case and have words separated by _. If a nonexistent parameter is used, the attribution is ignored. If the attributed value is invalid, the parameter is set to its default value, defined in internal configuration files. Comments can be included using the character `#`, such that all the text after it is ignored.

Listing 1 shows an example of configuration file. The comments contain explanations about parameter meaning and its acceptable values (provided by the regular expressions). For a better organization, the parameters were separated into five different categories, which are described in the following.

Listing 1: Configuration file example.

```
0  #The comments follow the structure:
1  #PARAMETER = VALUE #(regular expression): Explanation about the parameter
2  #If a regular expression is not specified, any input string can be used
3  #To simplify the expressions, we adopt:
4  #TBool  = (TRUE|FALSE)
5  #TUInt  = (0-9)*
6  #TFloat = ["+"|"-"] [0-9]* ["."] [0-9]+
7
8  #CATEGORY 1. GENERAL CONFIGURATION
9  UDL_TASK = UDL #(UDL|FUSION): Selection of task to be executed
10 UDL_METHOD = CPRR #(NONE|CPRR|RLRECOM|RLSIM|CONTEXTRR|RECKNNGRAPH|RKGRAPH|
   CORGRAPH): Selection of method to be executed
11 #CATEGORY 2. INPUT FILE SETTINGS
12 SIZE_DATASET = 1400 #(TUint): Number of images in the dataset
13 INPUT_FILE_FORMAT = MATRIX #(MATRIX|RK): Format of input file
14 INPUT_MATRIX_TYPE = DIST #(DIST|SIM): Type of matrix file
15 INPUT_RK_FORMAT = NUM #(NUM|STR): Format of ranked list file
16 MATRIX_TO_RK_SORTING = HEAP #(HEAP|INSERTION): Convert matrix to rks
17 NUM_INPUT_FUSION_FILES = 2 #(TUint): Number of files for FUSION tasks
18 INPUT_FILES_FUSION_1 = input1.txt #Path of the first input file
19 INPUT_FILES_FUSION_2 = input2.txt #Path of the second input file
20 #INPUT_FILES_FUSION_* = input*.txt #Path of the *th input file
21 INPUT_FILE = input.txt #Path of the main input file (matrix/rks)
22 INPUT_FILE_LIST = list.txt #Path of the list file
23 INPUT_FILE_CLASSES = classes.txt #Path of the classes file
24 INPUT_IMAGES_PATH = images/ #Dataset images path
25 #CATEGORY 3. OUTPUT FILE SETTINGS
26 OUTPUT_FILE = TRUE #(TBool): Generate output file(s)
27 OUTPUT_FILE_FORMAT = MATRIX #(RK|MATRIX): Format of output file
28 OUTPUT_MATRIX_TYPE = DIST #(DIST|SIM): Type of matrix file to output
29 OUTPUT_RK_FORMAT = ALL #(NUM|STR|HTML|ALL): Output format for rks
30 OUTPUT_FILE_PATH = output #Path of the output file(s)
31 OUTPUT_HTML_RK_PER_FILE = 1 #(TUint): Number of rks for each html file
32 OUTPUT_HTML_RK_SIZE = 20 #(TUint): Number of images per ranked list
33 OUTPUT_HTML_RK_COLORS = TRUE #(TBool): Color borders around images
34 OUTPUT_HTML_RK_BEFORE_AFTER = TRUE #(TBool): Comparison of rks
35 #CATEGORY 4. EVALUATION SETTINGS
36 EFFICIENCY_EVAL = TRUE #(TBool): Enable efficiency evaluation
37 EFFECTIVENESS_EVAL = TRUE #(TBool): Enable effectiveness evaluation
38 EFFECTIVENESS_COMPUTE_PRECISIONS = TRUE #(TBool): Compute precisions
39 EFFECTIVENESS_COMPUTE_MAP = TRUE #(TBool): Compute MAP
40 EFFECTIVENESS_COMPUTE_RECALL = TRUE #(TBool): Compute recall
41 EFFECTIVENESS_RECALL_AT = 40 #(TUint): Position to compute recall
42 EFFECTIVENESS_PRECISIONS_TO_COMPUTE = 5, 20 #(TUint ["," TUint]*):
   Precisions to be computed (unsigned integers separated by commas)
43 #CATEGORY 5. METHOD PARAMETERS
44 PARAM_CPRR_L = 400 #(TUint): Size of ranked lists to consider
45 PARAM_CPRR_K = 20  #(TUint): Number of nearest neighbors
46 PARAM_CPRR_T = 2   #(TUint): Number of iterations
```

1. General configuration: the execution type and the method to be executed are defined in lines 9 and 10, respectively. For the execution types, the available options are re-ranking (traditional distance learning) and rank-aggregation (fusion distance learning). Regarding the methods, there is an option called `NONE`, which can be used to easily perform an execution to change file formats or evaluate files.

2. Input file settings: the main input files encode similarity information, generally provided by visual descriptors. The files are supported both in the ranked lists (numeric or string) or matrices (similarity or distance) format. Lines 13, 14, and 15 define the format to be used. While only one main input file is considered for `UDL` tasks (line 21), `FUSION` tasks consider two or more main input files (lines 17-20). Lines 22, 23 and 24 specify the list file, the classes file, and the images path (used to export visual results to `html`), respectively. The list file is always required because it offers the name of each image. However, the classes file is only necessary when effectiveness evaluation is enabled. Internally, the framework can convert matrices to ranked lists using the sorting method specified in line 16. Complete examples of input files for distinct datasets are available at https://github.com/UDLF/Datasets.

3. Output file settings: analogous to the input files, the output format can also be configured. Additionally, there is a feature for exporting ranked lists to `HTML` files, which provides visual results (customized in lines 31-34).

4. Evaluation settings: an evaluation report can be provided in the end of execution, containing information as the time elapsed (line 36) and effectiveness measures as Precision, Recall, and MAP (lines 38, 39 and 40, respectively). Recall and Precision measures can be computed considering different depths of the ranked lists (lines 41 and 42).

5. Method parameters: definition of parameters settings, according to the method being executed (CPRR [22] in this example, lines 44-46).

3.2 Input/Output File Formats

The framework input is composed by three files: list, classes and ranked lists (or matrix). The list file considers each line as an *identifier* for a dataset element, as shown in Listing 2. For the effectiveness evaluation, each image is associated to a class, information that is defined in the classes file using the expression: `image:class`. An example of a classes file is presented in Listing 3. Ranked lists can be represented in both numeric or string format. A string example is shown in Listing 4. Each line corresponds to a ranked list and the name of the images are separated by spaces. The output file is generated according to the same format.

Listing 2: List file.

```
apple1.png
apple2.png
bird1.png
bird2.png
bat1.png
bat2.png
```

Listing 3: Classes file.

```
apple1.png:apple
apple2.png:apple
bird1.png:bird
bird2.png:bird
bat1.png:bat
bat2.png:bat
```

Listing 4: Ranked list file example - string format.

```
apple1.png apple2.png bird1.png bat1.png bat2.png bird2.png
apple2.png apple1.png bird2.png bird1.png bat1.png bat2.png
bird1.png bird2.png bat2.png apple2.png apple1.png bat1.png
bird2.png bird1.png bat2.png apple1.png apple2.png bat1.png
bat1.png bat2.png apple1.png apple2.png bird2.png bird1.png
bat2.png apple1.png apple2.png bat1.png bird2.png bird1.png
```

3.3 Execution Reports and Visual Results

The framework also generates execution reports and visual retrieval results. Listing 5 shows an example of an execution report (`log.txt`) generated by the framework.

Listing 5: Example of `log.txt` file.

```
- GENERAL INFORMATION -
Task:              UDL
Method:            CPRR
Dataset Size:      1400
Image List File:   desc/lists/mpeg7.txt
Image Class File:  desc/classes/mpeg7.txt
Input File:        desc/matrices/mpeg7/cfd.txt
Input Format:      MATRIX DIST
Output File:       output/output
Output Format:     RK ALL
---------------------------------------
- METHOD PARAMETERS -
PARAM_CPRR_K = 20
PARAM_CPRR_L = 400
PARAM_CPRR_T = 2
---------------------------------------
- EVALUATION RESULTS -
* Efficiency: Total Time of the Algorithm Execution: 0.0438 s
* Effectiveness:
Before:
     P@20         0.7559
     Recall@40    0.8444
     MAP          0.8064
After:
     P@20         0.8979
     Recall@40    0.9477
     MAP          0.9215
Relative Gains:
     P@20         +18.7866%
     Recall@40    +12.2404%
     MAP          +14.2707%
---------------------------------------
Log generated at 2017/1/26 16:37:24
```

The report is organized in sections, providing various information about the framework execution. Firstly, general information about the input/output files are shown. Next, the parameters of the executed method are presented. Finally, effectiveness and efficiency measures are reported, including the effectiveness gains obtained.

Figure 2 presents visual examples of ranked lists exported from executions of the framework considering different image datasets (Corel5k [8], MPEG-7 [6], OxfordFlowers-17 [10] and Soccer [24], respectively). The query images are presented in green borders and wrong results in red borders. The first line represents the original retrieval results and the second line, the results after the algorithm execution.

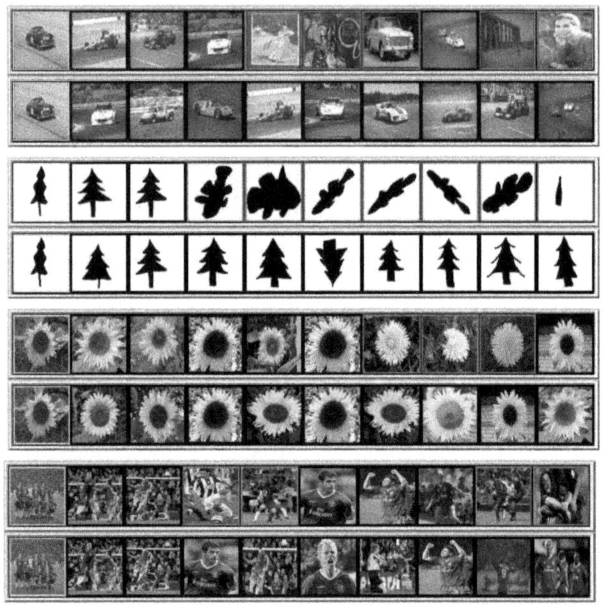

Figure 2: Visual examples showing the impact of distance learning on retrieval results.

4 CONCLUSIONS

In this work, we have presented UDLF, an open-source software that currently contains seven different unsupervised distance learning methods for multimedia retrieval. As future work, we intend to keep improving the software incorporating new features and other methods from different authors. We also intend to provide scripts, facilitating conversions between file formats and providing a visual interface to generate the configuration file. This facilitates the execution of experiments for users that do not want to use the command line. Aiming at maximizing the performance of the algorithms, parallel computing versions of the methods can also be implemented. We intend to provide more information about how the framework can be expanded, allowing the scientific community to contribute to the software.

5 ACKNOWLEDGMENTS

The authors are grateful to São Paulo Research Foundation - FAPESP (grants 2013/08645-0 and 2014/04220-8).

REFERENCES

[1] S. Bai and X. Bai. Sparse contextual activation for efficient visual re-ranking. *IEEE Transactions on Image Processing*, 25(3):1056–1069, March 2016.

[2] R. Datta, D. Joshi, J. Li, and J. Z. Wang. Image retrieval: Ideas, influences, and trends of the new age. *ACM Computing Surveys*, 40(2):5:1–5:60, 2008.

[3] M. Donoser and H. Bischof. Diffusion Processes for Retrieval Revisited. In *IEEE Conference on Computer Vision and Pattern Recognition (CVPR)*, pages 1320–1327, 2013.

[4] H. Jegou, C. Schmid, H. Harzallah, and J. Verbeek. Accurate image search using the contextual dissimilarity measure. *IEEE Transactions on Pattern Analysis and Machine Intelligence*, 32(1):2–11, 2010.

[5] J. Jiang, B. Wang, and Z. Tu. Unsupervised metric learning by self-smoothing operator. In *Internation Conference on Computer Vision (ICCV)*, pages 794–801, 2011.

[6] L. J. Latecki, R. Lakmper, and U. Eckhardt. Shape descriptors for non-rigid shapes with a single closed contour. In *CVPR*, pages 424–429, 2000.

[7] M. S. Lew, N. Sebe, C. Djeraba, and R. Jain. Content-based multimedia information retrieval: State of the art and challenges. *ACM Transactions on Multimedia Computing, Communications, and Applications*, 2(1):1–19, 2006.

[8] G.-H. Liu, L. Zhang, Y.-K. Hou, Z.-Y. Li, and J.-Y. Yang. Image retrieval based on multi-texton histogram. *Pattern Recogn.*, 43(7):2380–2389, July 2010.

[9] M. Lux. Content based image retrieval with LIRE. In *ACM Multimedia (MM'11)*, pages 735–738, 2011.

[10] M.-E. Nilsback and A. Zisserman. A visual vocabulary for flower classification. In *Proceedings of the IEEE Conference on Computer Vision and Pattern Recognition*, volume 2, pages 1447–1454, 2006.

[11] C. Y. Okada, D. C. G. a. Pedronette, and R. da S. Torres. Unsupervised distance learning by rank correlation measures for image retrieval. In *ACM International Conference on Multimedia Retrieval (ICMR'15)*, pages 331–338, 2015.

[12] D. C. G. Pedronette, J. Almeida, and R. da S. Torres. A graph-based ranked-list model for unsupervised distance learning on shape retrieval. *Pattern Recognition Letters*, 83, Part 3:357 – 367, 2016.

[13] D. C. G. Pedronette and R. da S. Torres. Exploiting contextual information for image re-ranking and rank aggregation. *International Journal of Multimedia Information Retrieval*, 1(2):115–128, 2012.

[14] D. C. G. Pedronette and R. da S. Torres. Exploiting pairwise recommendation and clustering strategies for image re-ranking. *Information Sciences*, 207:19–34, 2012.

[15] D. C. G. Pedronette and R. da S. Torres. Image re-ranking and rank aggregation based on similarity of ranked lists. *Pattern Recognition*, 46(8):2350–2360, 2013.

[16] D. C. G. Pedronette and R. da S. Torres. A correlation graph approach for unsupervised manifold learning in image retrieval tasks. *Neurocomputing*, 208:66 – 79, 2016.

[17] D. C. G. Pedronette and R. da S. Torres. Rank diffusion for context-based image retrieval. In *ACM International Conference on Multimedia Retrieval (ICMR'2016)*, 2016.

[18] D. C. G. Pedronette and R. da Silva Torres. A correlation graph approach for unsupervised manifold learning in image retrieval tasks. *Neurocomputing*, 208:66–79, 2016.

[19] D. C. G. Pedronette, O. A. Penatti, and R. da S. Torres. Unsupervised manifold learning using reciprocal knn graphs in image re-ranking and rank aggregation tasks. *Image and Vision Computing*, 32(2):120 – 130, 2014.

[20] O. A. Penatti and R. d. S. Torres. Eva: An evaluation tool for comparing descriptors in content-based image retrieval tasks. In *International Conference on Multimedia Information Retrieval*, MIR '10, pages 413–416, 2010.

[21] D. Qin, S. Gammeter, L. Bossard, T. Quack, and L. van Gool. Hello neighbor: Accurate object retrieval with k-reciprocal nearest neighbors. In *IEEE Conference on Computer Vision and Pattern Recognition (CVPR)*, pages 777 –784, 2011.

[22] L. P. Valem and D. C. G. Pedronette. Unsupervised similarity learning through cartesian product of ranking references for image retrieval tasks. *Conference on Graphics, Image and Patterns (SIBGRAPI)*, 2016.

[23] L. P. Valem, D. C. G. Pedronette, R. d. S. Torres, E. Borin, and J. Almeida. Effective, efficient, and scalable unsupervised distance learning in image retrieval tasks. *ACM International Conference on Multimedia Retrieval (ICMR)*, 2015.

[24] J. van de Weijer and C. Schmid. Coloring local feature extraction. In *European Conference on Computer Vision (ECCV)*, volume Part II, pages 334–348, 2006.

[25] J. Wang, Y. Li, X. Bai, Y. Zhang, C. Wang, and N. Tang. Learning context-sensitive similarity by shortest path propagation. *Pattern Recognition*, 44(10-11):2367–2374, 2011.

[26] X. Yang, X. Bai, L. J. Latecki, and Z. Tu. Improving shape retrieval by learning graph transduction. In *European Conference on Computer Vision (ECCV)*, volume 4, pages 788–801, 2008.

[27] X. Yang, S. Koknar-Tezel, and L. J. Latecki. Locally constrained diffusion process on locally densified distance spaces with applications to shape retrieval. In *IEEE Conference on Computer Vision and Pattern Recognition (CVPR)*, pages 357–364, 2009.

[28] X. Yang, L. Prasad, and L. Latecki. Affinity learning with diffusion on tensor product graph. *IEEE Trans. on Pattern Analysis and Machine Intelligence*, 35(1):28–38, 2013.

ClusterTag: Interactive Visualization, Clustering and Tagging Tool for Big Image Collections

Konstantin Pogorelov
Simula Research Laboratory, Norway
University of Oslo, Norway

Michael Riegler
Simula Research Laboratory, Norway
University of Oslo, Norway

Pål Halvorsen
Simula Research Laboratory, Norway
University of Oslo, Norway

Carsten Griwodz
Simula Research Laboratory, Norway
University of Oslo, Norway

ABSTRACT

Exploring and annotating collections of images without meta-data is a complex task which requires convenient ways of presenting datasets to a user. Visual analytics and information visualization can help users by providing interfaces, and in this paper, we present an open source application that allows users from any domain to use feature-based clustering of large image collections to perform explorative browsing and annotation. For this, we use various image feature extraction mechanisms, different unsupervised clustering algorithms and hierarchical image collection visualization. The performance of the presented open source software allows users to process and display thousands of images at the same time by utilizing heterogeneous resources such as GPUs and different optimization techniques.

CCS CONCEPTS

• **Information systems** → **Open source software**; **Multimedia databases**; **Clustering**; Data cleaning; • **Human-centered computing** → **Information visualization**; **Visualization toolkits**; • **Applied computing** → Annotation;

KEYWORDS

Clustering; Visualization; Annotation; Big Collections; Image Browsing; Open Source

ACM Reference format:
Konstantin Pogorelov, Michael Riegler, Pål Halvorsen, and Carsten Griwodz. 2017. ClusterTag: Interactive Visualization, Clustering and Tagging Tool for Big Image Collections. In *Proceedings of ICMR '17, Bucharest, Romania, June 6–9, 2017,* 5 pages.
https://doi.org/http://dx.doi.org/10.1145/3078971.3079018

This work is founded by the Norwegian FRINATEK project "EONS" (#231687).
Contact author's address: Konstantin Pogorelov, Simula Research Laboratory, Oslo, Norway, email: konstantin@simula.no .

ICMR '17, June 6–9, 2017, Bucharest, Romania

ACM ISBN 978-1-4503-4701-3/17/06...$15.00
https://doi.org/http://dx.doi.org/10.1145/3078971.3079018

1 INTRODUCTION

User-guided interactive exploration of big image collections is an important task in many scientific and applied domains. Examples include medical, satellite and industrial image analysis, security, social media and news analysis, and personal photos. Despite the many new and powerful automated image analysis and clustering softwares, the human eye remains the most important analytic instrument. Research on the topic of interactive image database visualization [8] confirms the importance of human-accessible representation in combination with image clustering, annotation and tagging. Existing image processing tools and frameworks demonstrate interesting and promising approaches, and they give wide opportunities for image browsing, content analysis and performing various data analytic tasks. However, there is a lack of tools that implement both fast and efficient image collection visualization together with image content analysis and annotation. In our previous research, we showed [11] the importance of interactive visualization and clustering for unsupervised knowledge discovery in the medical image analysis domain, and we developed the initial application for a medical scenario [6, 12].

To solve the visualization performance issue and provide an efficient solution for visualization and annotation, we continued the development of our tool. We made all necessary modifications and improvements to extend the tool to make it universal and usable for any use case involving interactive browsing, visual analysis and annotation of a large amount of image or video data. In this paper, we present our open source version of the ClusterTag application that we designed for interactive exploration and labeling of big image collections in conjunction with unsupervised image clustering, annotation and tagging.

The proposed software has four main benefits. First, it allows users to investigate and analyze vast collections of images by providing a configurable focus and context view based on similarity of frames. Second, it provides a focus and context view for annotation and tagging of the dataset, making it more accessible for complementary information systems. Third, it supports real-time, interactive viewing, analysis and modifications of the dataset, giving new opportunities for data analytics. Fourth, the tool structure is flexible and it can be easily adapted to different use cases and extended with new image processing algorithms.

In this paper, we first investigate the state of the art for visualization of big image collection. Next, we describe the clustering methodology, the structure of our system and the optimization approaches implemented in ClusterTag. Then, we describe the open source software project, its installation requirements, and provide the overall usage instructions. Finally, we discuss the contribution of the application and further work.

2 RELATED WORK

The problem of efficient visual representation of big collections of clustered data is well known. One of the first and most prominent implementations was the hyperbolic browser [3], with the visualization abstraction based on a hierarchy, i.e., a directed tree. A hyperbolic view on a hierarchical structure is best described with a fish eye view on a particular tree branch or leaf, with the rest being visible, but out of focus. A more recent implementation of this approach is presented in [1], where the authors employ a force-directed placement algorithm to display images on a large video wall, showing good performance for a dataset of limited size.

Another promising method for visualization is based on visual similarity of images. In this approach, a combination of automated image content analysis and image cluster visualization is used for building an easy-to-analyze plain representation of an image set. Treemap [14] and Semantic Image Browser (SIB) [15] implement efficient visualization and search in large image databases according to semantic content of images together with the ability to evaluate image annotations through interactive visual exploration of image collections. The disadvantage of Treemap is that it does not support interactive collection browsing. In contrast, SIB does support interactive browsing, but without support for a hierarchical collection structure, which is important for tag-based dataset creation. The approach presented in [7] adds a new visualization scheme that implements a representation of images as various 3D shapes, e.g., a cube or a cone, but without any analyzing, clustering and tagging abilities. The PhotoTOC project [5] uses clustering to create dataset overview and a detailed view representation by clustering images based on color histogram, and then present the clusters using medoids. So far, the PhotoTOC does not provide any collection manipulation functionality. In [13], images are displayed based on their distance with respect to texture features resulting in a 2D dense-visual-representation. Nevertheless, the visualization system does not support both hierarchical structures and multiple clusters within one collection.

Despite the good overall visual representation and easy browsing, methods based on hyperbolic tree visualization are only suitable for small image collections or strictly hierarchical collections with an emphasized tree-structure. For large structured image collections, e.g., in medical image analysis, a different visualization approach is required. Cluster-based image collection representation methods show good browsing capabilities and convenient dataset structure representation together with an additional featured analysis. Nevertheless, the performance of the current implementations of feature extraction, analysis and visualization in the existing frameworks is not good enough to be able to handle large databases containing thousands of images.

3 CLUSTERING

One of the main features of our ClusterTag application is interactivity with a visual collection representation, i.e., users interact with the images and the created or already defined clusters. Clustering, being a well-known technique in machine learning, is used to group entities based on a similarity metric. For instance, textual user comments can be clustered based on the nouns they contain, or images can be grouped based on image features (e.g., grouping those with similar colors).

To help the user in building clusters, we use WEKA[1] [2], a collection of algorithms for machine learning and data mining released as open source software under the GNU General Public License. Clustering algorithms provided by WEKA require the analytical abstraction of image contents. In our approach, we use global features describing image contents in terms of different overall attributes, such as sharpness, color distribution, histogram of brightness, etc. For feature extraction, we use Lucene Image Retrieval (LIRE)[2] [4], which supports extraction and comparison of multiple global and local features out-of-the-box, and allows integration of feature extractors in arbitrary applications. In the fusion between these two frameworks, LIRE is responsible for the feature extraction and processing. WEKA is responsible for unsupervised clustering of images based the extracted features. A detailed description of used global features, corresponding clustering algorithm and clustering performance metrics can be found in [12]. Both the WEKA and LIRE can be easily replaced by other machine learning or feature extraction libraries if desired.

4 VISUALIZATION

To be able to implement a visualization tool for thousands of images simultaneously in real-time and give the user the ability to interact with them, we developed an optimized and highly efficient visualization engine. It is written in Java and uses a number of libraries, enabling high-performance image processing and a real-time image cluster representation.

An overall structure of the software is depicted in figure 1. First, we perform an initial analysis of the image collection file structure. This is the only synchronous operation in the tool, and after it is completed, the user is able to start working with the collection. All other operations on the dataset are asynchronous and implemented as the background threads. The observed initial folder structure is then used in the user interface to draw the visual representations via a painter module. The painter reads the cluster hierarchical structure and interacts with the image in-memory database and the image cache in order to perform an optimized image preloading, rescaling and drawing. This is performed using the hardware accelerated image handler. The database interface performs the in-memory image database synchronization with an on-disk mirror copy. The folder structure update module is responsible for updating the collection's file structure on the disk after any modification done to the clusters by the user or by the clustering procedure.

For the image processing tasks, namely loading, saving, rescaling, rotating, masking operations and drawing on top of images, we use the Java bindings of the Open Source Computer Vision Library (OpenCV)[3]. The library provides large number of common and state-of-the-art functions for image processing, with possible acceleration

[1] http://www.cs.waikato.ac.nz/ml/weka/ Accessed: 2017-04-19
[2] http://www.lire-project.net/ Accessed: 2017-04-19
[3] http://opencv.org/ Accessed: 2017-04-19

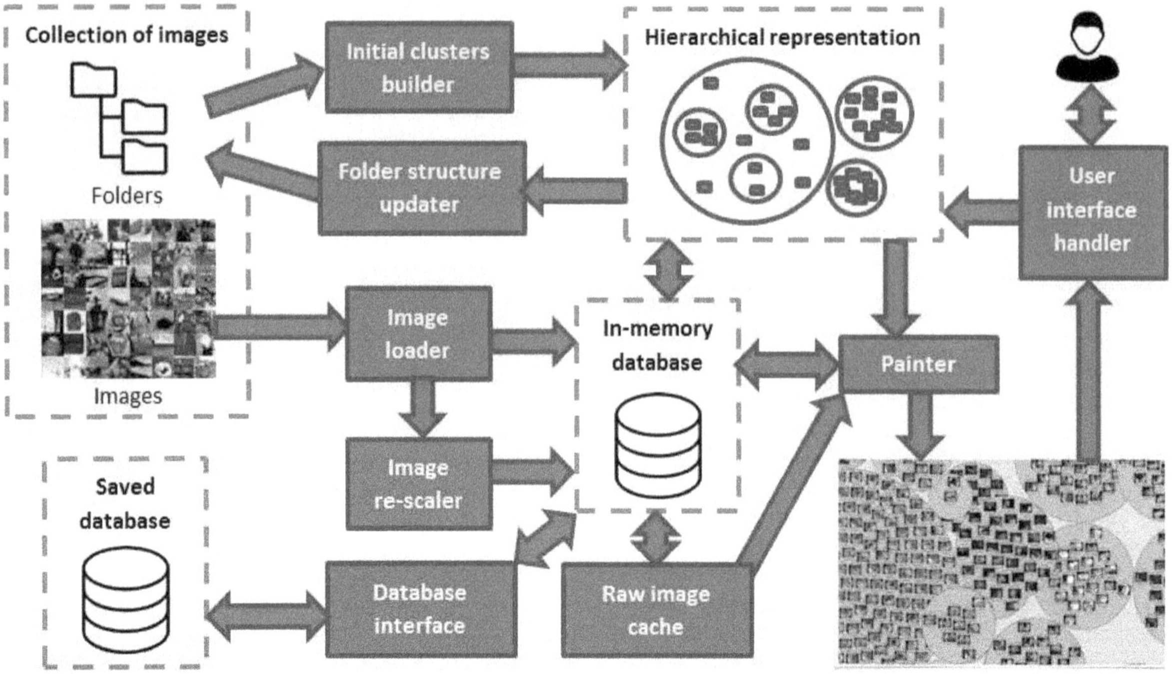

Figure 1: Structure of the visualization and user interface engine of the presented ClusterTag application. A number of caching and intermediate data processing routines are used to make it possible to perform real-time visualization and interaction with huge image collections.

on GPUs. The library is cross-platform and free for use under the open source BSD license.

Real-time drawing of hierarchical representation of the image clusters is implemented using the Lightweight Java Game Library (LWJGL)[4], an open source BSD licensed Java software library for video game developers. It exposes high performance cross-platform libraries, such as OpenGL, Vulkan, OpenAL and OpenCL, and provides a way to get access to high-performance computer resources from Java code.

Regardless of high drawing and image handling performance provided by the OpenCV and LWJGL libraries, several additional optimization techniques have been implemented in the ClusterTag application to allow real-time handling of large image collections. The most important are a database of ready-to-draw pre-processed images, raw image visual representation caching, adaptive image spatial resolution painting, interaction with partially processed collections, multi-threaded image processing and feature extraction (see figure 1 for an overview).

The database of pre-processed images is implemented as a custom binary record storage with a separate index, which allows dynamic database updates with effortless seeking and simultaneous retrieval of multiple records. This is useful for multi-threaded drawing and update of the collection's content at the same time.

The raw image visual representation cache is implemented using concurrent hash maps in conjunction with a custom memory management strategy and is designed to hold the last images used for visual-representation drawing in the memory. Caching is required due to inability to load all the images of the big collection into the system memory. The implemented raw image cache allows fast and smooth image collection browsing without putting the enormous task of image loading and decoding on the CPU.

Our painting engine uses multiple image scales to accelerate the visual-representation drawing. To determine the resolution of the scaled images, we divide the width and height of the original images by power-of-two numbers. The different scaled versions are used depending of the current zoom level of the image collection's field of view. This optimized painting scheme significantly increases the application frame rate, reduces the GPU load and decreases overall system load. All rescaled versions of the image are stored in the database of pre-processed images.

To solve the common slow loading problem of big data collections, we use multiple different techniques in several parts of the system. The main focus is put on the ability to start exploring the image collection as soon as possible regardless of the image pre-processing and feature extraction progress. In case of a newly opened collection, a visual representation becomes available immediately after the initial directory structure listing. Image loading, pre-processing and feature extraction are performed in the background while the user begins to explore the collection and performs fine tuning of the clustering parameters. The visual representation is updated at every screen redraw to reflect the current stage of the collection analysis. All resulting information is immediately stored in the database of pre-processed images and gives the opportunity to continue pre-processing and analyzing the collection at next application startup from the same point.

[4] http://lwjgl.org/ Accessed: 2017-04-19

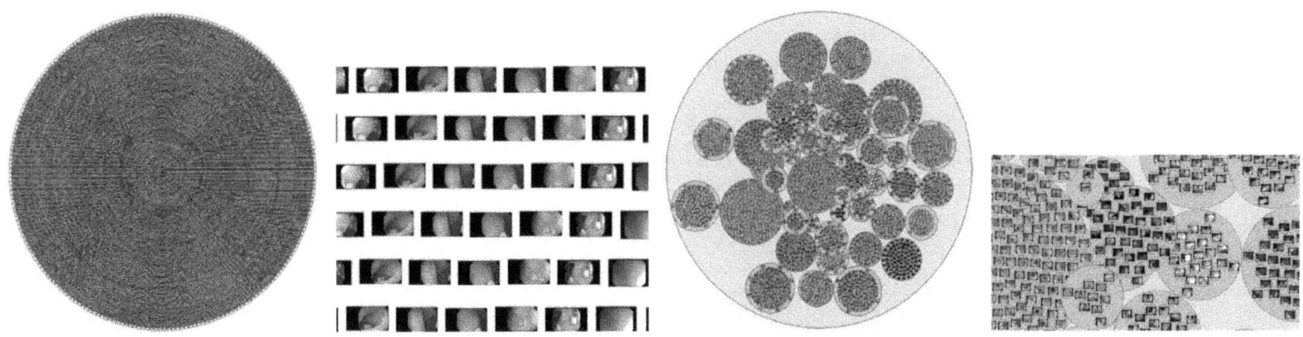

(a) Unsorted collection of images. (b) Zoomed view of the unsorted collection. (c) Clustered collection of images. (d) Zoomed view of the clustered collection.

Figure 2: Examples of visual representations of an image collection containing 36,476 unsorted medical images generated by the ClusterTag application. The initial view of the loaded collection shows all the images in one big cluster. After the clustering, using the JCD and Tamura global image features, the software generates a number of dense clusters representing visually similar images in the same clusters.

5 THE CLUSTERTAG PROJECT

The ClusterTag software is an open source project[5] and can be used, modified and distributed under GNU General Public License Version 3. The application has been tested successfully and used with large image collections containing up to 36,476 images [9, 10].

5.1 Installation

We have tested our software on the Linux, Mac OS X and Windows operating systems. ClusterTag has the following dependencies which have to be downloaded and installed before compilation of the ClusterTag source code: Oracle Java SE Development Kit 8, IntelliJ IDEA 2016.3.4, OpenCV 2.4.13, LIRE 0.9.5 and LWJGL 2.9.3. The detailed compilation and installation instructions can be found on the project's web-page.

5.2 Usage

Our open-source application combines content-based similarity, unsupervised classification and focus/context views to provide a way to easily explore, analyze and annotate a vast number of images or video frames. The application allows users to choose the folder containing the image collection. Immediately after listing the files of a new image collection, it appears in the main window as it was organized in folder structure, and the user can immediately start exploring the collection. Figure 2(a) shows a visualization of an unsorted collection of 36,476 medical images. The user can navigate through the collection's view using the mouse to move, zoom into and zoom out of the field of view (see figure 2(b)). To perform clustering, the user can select a desired clustering algorithm, its parameters and several different image features. If more than one feature is selected, they will be combined using early fusion. After selecting all the parameters, the user can apply clustering to the dataset creating the clusters. Figure 2(c) shows a visualization of the collection of medical images clustered using the JCD and Tamura global image features, which produce a number of dense clusters representing visually similar images in the same clusters. The zoomed view of the clustered collection is depicted in figure 2(d).

The cluster leaves are represented using the image that is closest to the cluster center, i.e., the cluster medoid. It is possible to interact with the view and the clusters by zooming and turning them in different angles. The user can select multiple images to perform grouping. Individual images and image groups can be dragged and dropped between different clusters. The corresponding changes to the file structure of the collection are made in the background. The user can double click on clusters, which opens the folder containing all images in the selected cluster. A right click on the clusters allows the user to see information like the cluster center and the purity of the cluster. Finally, the user can name/tag the clusters, which adds the tag to the name of the images in the cluster. The detailed usage instructions can be found on the project's web-page.

6 CONCLUSION

In this paper, we presented an open source application called ClusterTag which enables users and domain experts to explore, cluster, annotate and tag collections of thousands of images in real-time using an optimized and easy visual representation. We also presented an example of how to use the software with the dataset containing almost 37,000 medical images.

For future work, we plan to test the application with end users and domain experts. In particular, we will use the application to process an unannotated dataset of endoscopic images from two different Norwegian Hospitals that contains more than 200.000 images and 600 videos. The focus of this user study will be the usefulness of the visual representation, and the perceived complexity of the user interface, i.e., the selection of image features and clustering algorithms as well as performance of our visualization engine. The next development steps for this project will focus on efficient video handling, representation and processing, implementing a plug-in-like feature extraction and clusterisation subsystems, adding new clustering algorithms and unsupervised collection annotation based on preselected image sets.

REFERENCES

[1] Yi Gu, Chaoli Wang, Jun Ma, Robert J Nemiroff, and David L Kao. 2015. iGraph: a graph-based technique for visual analytics of image and text collections. In *Proc. of IS&T/SPIE Electronic Imaging*. 939708–939708.

[5] https://bitbucket.org/mpg_projects/clustertag Accessed: 2017-04-19

[2] Mark Hall, Eibe Frank, Geoffrey Holmes, Bernhard Pfahringer, Peter Reutemann, and Ian H Witten. 2009. The WEKA data mining software: an update. *ACM SIGKDD explorations newsletter* 11, 1 (2009), 10–18.

[3] John Lamping, Ramana Rao, and Peter Pirolli. 1995. A focus+ context technique based on hyperbolic geometry for visualizing large hierarchies. In *Proc. of ACM CHI.* 401–408.

[4] Mathias Lux, Michael Riegler, Pål Halvorsen, Konstantin Pogorelov, and Nektarios Anagnostopoulos. 2016. LIRE: open source visual information retrieval. In *Proc. of MMSys.* Article no. 30.

[5] John C Platt, Michal Czerwinski, and Brent A Field. 2003. PhotoTOC: Automatic clustering for browsing personal photographs. In *Proc. of ICICS-PAM.* 6–10.

[6] Konstantin Pogorelov, Michael Riegler, Pål Halvorsen, Peter Thelin Schmidt, Carsten Griwodz, Dag Johansen, Sigrun L. Eskeland, and Thomas de Lange. 2016. GPU-accelerated Real-time Gastrointestinal Diseases Detection. In *Proc. of CBMS.* 185–190.

[7] Marco Porta. 2006. Browsing large collections of images through unconventional visualization techniques. In *Proc. of AVI.* 440–444.

[8] Marco Porta. 2009. New visualization modes for effective image presentation. *International Journal of Image and Graphics* 9, 01 (2009), 27–49.

[9] Michael Riegler, Carsten Griwodz, Concetto Spampinato, Thomas de Lange, Sigrun L. Eskeland, Konstantin Pogorelov, Wallapak Tavanapong, Peter Thelin Schmidt, Cathal Gurrin, Dag Johansen, Håvard Johansen, and Pål Halvorsen. 2016. Multimedia and Medicine: Teammates for Better Disease Detection and Survival. In *Proc. of ACM MM.* 968–977.

[10] Michael Riegler, Konstantin Pogorelov, Sigrun Losada Eskeland, Peter Thelin Schmidt, Zeno Albisser, Dag Johansen, Carsten Griwodz, Pål Halvorsen, and Thomas de Lange. 2017. From Annotation to Computer Aided Diagnosis: Detailed Evaluation of a Medical Multimedia System. *Transactions on Multimedia Computing, Communications and Applications* 9, 4 (2017).

[11] Michael Riegler, Konstantin Pogorelov, Pål Halvorsen, Thomas de Lange, Carsten Griwodz, Peter Thelin Schmidt, Sigrun Losada Eskeland, and Dag Johansen. 2016. EIR - Efficient Computer Aided Diagnosis Framework for Gastrointestinal endoscopies. In *Proc. of CBMI.* 1–6.

[12] Michael Riegler, Konstantin Pogorelov, Mathias Lux, Pål Halvorsen, Carsten Griwodz, Thomas de Lange, and Sigrun Losada Eskeland. 2016. Explorative Hyperbolic-Tree-Based Clustering Tool for Unsupervised Knowledge Discovery. In *Proc. of CBMI.* 1–4.

[13] Ricardo S Torres, Celmar G Silva, Claudia B Medeiros, and Heloisa V Rocha. 2003. Visual structures for image browsing. In *Proc. of ACM CIKM.* 49–55.

[14] Chaoli Wang, John P Reese, Huan Zhang, Jun Tao, and Robert J Nemiroff. 2013. iMap: A stable layout for navigating large image collections with embedded search. In *Proc. of IS&T/SPIE Electronic Imaging.* 86540K–86540K.

[15] Jing Yang, Jianping Fan, Daniel Hubball, Yuli Gao, Hangzai Luo, William Ribarsky, and Matthew Ward. 2006. Semantic image browser: Bridging information visualization with automated intelligent image analysis. In *Proc. of IEEE VIS.* 191–198.

Scalable Hadoop-Based Pooled Time Series of Big Video Data from the Deep Web

Chris A. Mattmann[1,2], Madhav Sharan[1, 2]
{mattmann,msharan}@usc.edu

[1]Computer Science Department
University of Southern California
Los Angeles, CA 90089 USA

[2]Jet Propulsion Laboratory
California Institute of Technology
Pasadena, CA 91109 USA

ABSTRACT

We contribute a scalable, open source implementation [1] of the Pooled Time Series (PoT) algorithm from CVPR 2015. The algorithm is evaluated on approximately 6800 human trafficking (HT) videos collected from the deep and dark web, and on an open dataset: the Human Motion Database (HMDB). We describe PoT and our motivation for using it on larger data and the issues we encountered. Our new solution reimagines PoT as an Apache Hadoop-based algorithm. We demonstrate that our new Hadoop-based algorithm successfully identifies similar videos in the HT and HMDB datasets and we evaluate the algorithm qualitatively and quantitatively.

CCS CONCEPTS

•**Information systems** → **Information retrieval; Image search;** •**Applied computing** → *Computer forensics;*

KEYWORDS

pooled time series; hadoop; darpa; memex; video

1 INTRODUCTION

We have seen an increase in online video content used in "dark markets" that deal with illegal trade and sale of goods. In particular, working on the DARPA MEMEX [2] effort our team has worked in conjunction with law enforcement to mine videos on the web to help thwart human, weapons and arms trafficking, and trafficking of other products, such as counterfeit electronics. Multimedia content is a tool used by those selling their wares in these markets to remain hidden from traditional web searches and from bulk analysis - MEMEX is working to change this.

Our team collected a large video set from human-trafficking (HT) focused sites. The dataset - dubbed `HT video dataset` - is 26Gb in size and 6805 in number (including duplicates); 14.3 Gb and 3266 in number (without duplicates). All videos are in MP4 format with an average video size of 3.8MB, and at least 1Mb, and at most ~10Mb in the deduplicated set - in the set with duplicates the average size is 4Mb, the minimum size 1Mb and the maximum size ~10Mb. Total length of recording is ≈ 2250 hours with average length of recording = 19.8 seconds.

Law enforcement and other stakeholders have challenged us to reliably and at scale find similar videos in the `HT video dataset`. We used the Apache Tika system [3] initially for this task. Tika is an open source content detection and analysis system that automatically identifies a file's type; and automatically selects a relevant parser to extract text, metadata and language information from it. Tika supports multimedia metadata extraction such as EXIF metadata that is present in images and videos and that tells us scene, content editing, and authorship properties. Simply looking at the metadata is fast, reliable, and effective[4].

While metadata forensics were initially useful, it became necessary to perform actual video pixel (*gradient*) analysis in order to find similar videos. We also found *temporal* relationships and *motion* present in the videos were effective at relating them. Members of our team previously developed the Pooled Time Series (PoT) approach [5] that combines both oriented gradient (image differencing) and optical flow (image motion differencing) to realize such an approach. With PoT we identified relationships between victims; common scenes and housing (*gradient*); common movements such as dancing and/or derobing (*flow*); common clothing (*gradient*) and more.

PoT's existing implementation worked on up to 500 videos from the `HT video dataset`. We could analyze them in reasonable amounts of time (maximum: 2 days). However, as soon as we entered the realm of ~7000 videos, we were never able to get the PoT reference implementation in Java to complete. We discerned several causes: (1) *Out of Memory (OoM)* – Since PoT computes time-interval based descriptions and must pool and summarize those for motion and gradient difference over many video frames over many 1000s of videos, we constantly ran out of memory; (2) *Sequential Code* – PoT steps were sequentially implemented in Java. That is, first the histogram of oriented gradients (HoG) was computed; then histogram of optical flow (HoF) - each of these are very large matrices with N dimensional vectors for each video. Then the differences between HoG and HoF for each video and mean chi square is computed; and (3) *Instrumentation and Checkpointing* – PoT code lacked critical logging information.

While we added logging and checkpointing to PoT's code, OoM issues and sequential code prevented us from running PoT across the entire `HT video dataset`. As our team includes a member of the Apache Nutch committee that helped to build Apache Hadoop [6], we were inspired to develop a Hadoop-version of PoT that was parallel, and memory efficient. Hadoop is an open source

ICMR '17, June 6–9, 2017, Bucharest, Romania
© 2017 ACM. ACM ISBN 978-1-4503-4701-3/17/06...$15.00
DOI: http://dx.doi.org/10.1145/3078971.3079019

implementation of Google's Map Reduce [7] and Google File System (GFS) [8] for fast parallel data processing and highly reliable, available and redundant data on commodity clusters.

A roadmap for the paper follows. Sec. 2 describes the general steps of PoT motivating their conversion to Hadoop. Sec. 3 describes the steps of our `Hadoop-POT` algorithm and approach. We evaluate our approach in Sec. 4. Sec. 5 rounds out the paper.

2 POOLED TIME SERIES VIDEO SIMILARITY

Pooled Time Series (PoT) [5] is an algorithm that takes as input a set of N videos and generates as output an $N \times N$ matrix with the pair-wise similarities between each video $1...N$. The diagonals of the matrix are unused, as is half of the matrix since it contains duplicative information. The first step in computing PoT is generating two histograms: one histogram of oriented gradients (HoG) to identify object movements and one histogram of optical flow (HoF) to model relative motion between actor and viewer in a video.

To calculate raw similarity scores we generate all possible video pairs. If the initial video dataset size is N we end up with $\frac{N(N-1)}{2}$ pairs and an $N \times N$ sized matrix V where V_{ij} is the pair of videos v_i and v_j and $i, j \in [1, N]$. For each V_{ij} we assign a similarity score. The chi squared distance (CSD) between all the features of all the possible V_{ij} in V is calculated next. For each video $1...N$ we have two series histograms (HoF and HoG) and three pooling operators so for each video we have total of six features where feature f is denoted $f(s, p)$. After computing CSD, PoT computes the mean CSD (mCSD) for the whole video dataset. After mCSD is computed, PoT computes kernel distances (KD) for the dataset by calculating CSD for a given feature $f(s, p)$ between two videos. We then divide the CSD by its corresponding mCSD. Adding all the kernel distances for one video pair gives us the total distance between the pair.

The overall time complexity of the PoT algorithm is roughly $O(N^2)$. The main factor that influences complexity is the number of videos, all other factors like number of series and pooling operators are constant and chosen manually. In the `HT video dataset` there are nearly 24.5 million pairs. If both pairs have 800 frames with a 200 pixel representation in HoF and HoG we are processing 640, 000 raw values for each pair. This restricts PoT to a few hundred videos to complete in any meaningful amount of time - we ran it for nearly a week without completion on a 20 node Amazon cloud cluster, where each node was M3.xlarge, with 32Gb of RAM.

3 HADOOP POOLED TIME SERIES

Re-envisioning PoT as a Hadoop Map Reduce [6] job was an iterative process. We began by using a *list of video files* as the core data structure to be split and partitioned using Hadoop. Hadoop requires us to define the following constructs: (1) a *Split/Partition* function that will partition the video datasets into equally sized, independent jobs that can proceed in parallel; (2) a *Mapper* function, that, given a set of equally sized independent data from the split, will process that data, and produce some intermediate results; (3) a *Reducer* function, that takes the intermediate output from the *Mapper* jobs, and that combines them into final output results. Hadoop handles *Mapper* and *Reducer* job execution; re-execution in the case of failure; data input/output storage in a highly redundant and available filesystem, HDFS. Hadoop provides native capabilities to split datasets e.g., via hashing.

Since PoT is data-flow dependent e.g., HoF and HoG must be calculated *before* raw similarity score generation, then the raw similarity scores need to be computed *before* mean chi squared computation, and that mean chi square values must be present *before* the final kernel distance can be computed, we were unable to define a single Mapper and Reducer job to represent each of these steps. Instead, the best way to proceed was to define several sets of Map/Reduce tasks, representing each of the stages of the algorithm.

3.1 Implementation Considerations

We considered using the Hadoop Image Processing Interface (HIPI) [9], but instead chose to use core OpenCV since the early implementation of the sequential PoT algorithm was done using direct calls to OpenCV and we wanted to remain backwards compatible with the prior code as much as possible. We also looked at Xuggle [10] but its main focus was streaming video.

We realized early on that we could have separate Mapper/Reducer tasks for HoG and HoF, and that those largely could be done once, offline, and then kept in HDFS for future use in the other Mapper/Reducer task combinations. For example, once the HoF and HoG were generated for all videos, we could create a Reducer that could be used to compute similarities (initially raw), and also mean chi squared distance and kernel distance. We wanted to keep the output format for the matrix simple, so we chose a simple ASCII-text file to represent it, and also to take advantage of Hadoop HDFS and its native support for text files. HoF and HoG outputs were similarly stored as matrices in ASCII oriented text file formats (such as CSV), as were the output raw similarity scores and distances. The initial `Hadoop-PoT` design includes two jobs for HoF and HoG, one job for calculating mean distance (using the raw distances and mean chi squared) and another job for calculating similarity (using kernel distance).

3.2 **Hadoop-POT v1**

We have one job each for calculating HoF and HoG from videos. Each of these jobs takes a file path as parameter and uses OpenCV to calculate features. These features are saved as text files, **.of.txt* and **.hog.txt*.To compute similarity we generate a cartesian product of video set with itself. Consider that we are processing a video set of three videos. For this, we will generate pair like v_1v_2, v_1v_3, v_2v_3. These pair of video names are stored in a CSV file which is provided as input to both similarity calculating jobs. The first job calculates mean chi square distance for whole data set. It reads **.of.txt* and **.hog.txt* for each respective video pair and generates one output file having mean chi squared distance (mCSD). We calculate mCSD for each series and for each pooling operator which gives us $2 \times 3 = 6$ mean distances. Our *Mapper* jobs in this step calculate chi squared distances (CSD) for one pair and the associated *Reducer* job calculates the mean of all the distances. We create a second *Mapper* job that takes a pair of filenames as input and that then calculates similarity score using the kernel distance. The output of this job is a CSV file with a similarity score per video.

The original Hadoop-POT v1 design involved dumping the output results (CSVs, text files) of individual steps from HDFS to the local file system and then by copying those local file system results from the local file system to HDFS for the next stage. This was performed for the following reason - we initially had great difficulty getting the Java OpenCV APIs to read data from HDFS. Errors ranged from intermittent exceptions to I/O errors with Java itself. We later traced these to the implementation bindings in the Java OpenCV library and its API. Another flaw with our v1 implementation was that while dumping *video_name.of.txt* and *video_name.hog.txt* we saved `double` values in a text file. This caused both of our similarity jobs to read these files repeatedly $O(N^2)$ times and to, during the process, convert them from `string` values to `double` values for each value in the matrices. Considering previous example *Mapper* jobs had to convert 640, 000 values to `double` at a cost of about 1.5 seconds per file, scaling this up to 24 million jobs as required by `HT video dataset` would require more than a year of processing time which we did not have. We also realized that we were calculating features repeatedly for each pair instead of caching them.

Instead of text files, we decided that the next Hadoop-POT iteration should use better representations for matrices and vectors and that it should store *all of the values* for our video data set in a single file. Our initial approach of using a CSV with file paths pointing to the computed text files for HoF and HoG for each video masked the real input and its size was thus determined via a single file, rather than the actual total N video files present in the dataset. This led to a smaller input splits as Hadoop had no idea about the size of the real input. Input splits should contain values of features rather than path to features for fair input splits. Using less input splits underutilized the cluster and as a result, our Hadoop-POT v1 was quite slow.

Apart from input splits with this input structure we could not use Hadoop's distributed file processing effectively. Hadoop HDFS is made to deal with large files wherein which a file is broken into small splits and each split can be on a different machine. When a job is assigned to a container it is assigned to container that is running on same machine where the split is stored to reduce IO and contention. With input files being paths to features we were unable to use Hadoop's I/O data locality, and instead *Mapper* jobs read data from different nodes instead of those that contained the actual data from the split.

3.3 Redis and Hadoop-POT v2

Our Hadoop-POT v2 architecture converted `text` to `double` format for the values in our matrices by using a Redis cache server. Redis is an efficient, scalable key value based caching utility that operates in a client server fashion with automatic data typing. A client connects to a Redis server and then PUTS a key, value pair, where the key and value can be any typed data. Redis efficiently stores that key, value pair, providing a GET based interface to retrieve it later rapidly and efficiently. We built our v2 system using a Redis cache with the key being a single video file name and the value being computed feature vector. This reduced job execution time to milliseconds instead of 1.5 seconds per job as in the v1 architecture. However, in doing so, we introduced yet another component into

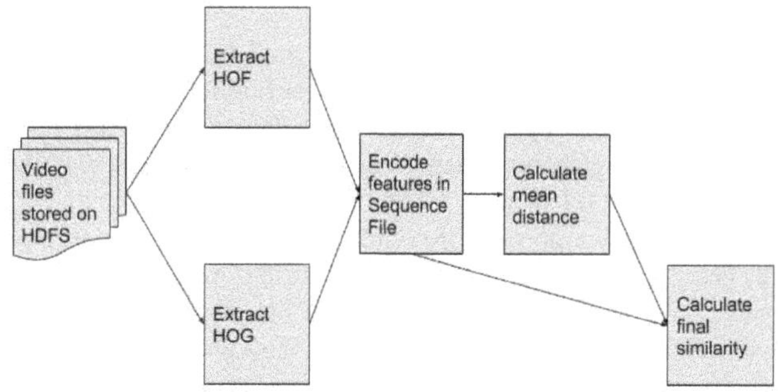

Figure 1: Our final Hadoop-PoT v3 architecture.

our architecture besides Hadoop and went around Hadoop's native support for similar data structures.

We also tried resource localization by archiving all the *video_name.of.txt* and *video_name.hog.txt* into one big zip file and passing that file as a cached archive in our Hadoop similarity jobs. This reduced time in reading the file for the very first time. We also experimented with different split sizes to increase resource utilization. Redis brought down computation time, but increased our system complexity.

3.4 Hadoop-POT-v3

Realizing that Hadoop provided native data structures for fast storage and retrieval of multiple objects, and structures that themselves were easily splittable and usable as input to *Mapper* jobs, and *Reducer* jobs, we eliminated the Redis component introduced in v2 of our architecture and replaced it with Hadoop `SequenceFiles`. `SequenceFiles` are a native Hadoop construct that allow easy combination and summarization of many small input files. Sequence files can be thought of as a zipped version of multiple files. As shown in Fig. 1 we take both features of one video and compute its PoT representation as a java object and serialize that object to bytes in v3 of our architecture. This serialized vector is stored as the value in sequence file, wherein which the key is the name of video file. We use this key later while outputting the overall PoT similarity CSV as output of the algorithm. This sequence file is also generated natively by our *Mapper* jobs and read natively by our *Reducer* jobs, removing any specialized code that we had present in v2 of our architecture.

The final step in our v3 architecture was computation of the Cartesian product on sequence files. We did this by overriding Hadoop's `RecordReader` and `FileInputFormat` classes. Our similarity jobs take generated `SequenceFiles` as input and use our own `CartesianInputFormat` which first permutes through splits and then permutes within a split to generate a pair of video features for our *Mapper jobs*.

4 EVALUATION

Quantitatively our Hadoop-POT v3 algorithm reduced the time necessary for each of our *Mapper* jobs to complete to $\approx$ 42 milliseconds evaluated on `HT video dataset` allowing the needed 24 million+ computations to be executable in a reasonable amount of time. This entire `HT video dataset` was processed using Hadoop-POT v3 on a 10 node cluster in Amazon using M3.xlarge instances with 32Gb memory each, and with EBS storage with 8 containers on each node in $\approx$ 26 hours. We used cached vector files for this run which takes $\approx$6.5 hours to generate from input videos in the `HT video dataset`. Complete quantitative evaluation for Hadoop-POT jobs is provided at [11].

Qualitatively evaluating our results involves multiple areas. Simply being able to compute PoT on the `HT video dataset` which we were unable to do using the previous PoT algorithm and implementation is a core contribution of our work. Without our `Hadoop-POT` v3 algorithm and its implementation, large video datasets cannot be run through the PoT algorithm and its previous sequential implementation. One of the satisfying results was identifying almost identical video pairs. Some videos had same content but they differed in their hash codes due to subtle differences. For example, Hadoop-POT was able to identify the same video clips of different length. In addition, the same videos with different resolutions (e.g., 800×600 versus 1024×768) were also easily identifiable using our method.

We also evaluated our algorithm by comparing how well it grouped videos that were identified as similar by automated tagging. We used the Inception-V3 model packaged with Google's Tensorflow [12] to label each video using video frame extraction and image tagging. We then leveraged the labels from Tensorflow to compare `Hadoop-POT` recall rates. We extracted the five most similar videos for all videos in the `HT video dataset` and grouped results by Tensorflow label. We observed that for the top $k = 20$ categories (e.g., beer, toilet, bikini, brassiere) that our algorithm could find related videos accurately and efficiently. Experimentations performed with another labeling toolkit, sklearn[13] and its DBSCAN [14] algorithm, produced similar observations.

To demonstrate that `Hadoop-POT` results were not specific to our own dataset, we evaluated it on the pre-annotated openly available HMDB - Human Motion Database [15]. HMDB is a large data set having 6.8 thousand annotated videos of 51 human motions. The dataset is 1.9Gb with the shortest video being 37KB and largest being 1.3 MB. The total duration of recording is $\approx$ 350 hours with mean length of a video equals 3.1 seconds. Actions include facial actions like laughing and talking and body movement like walking, climbing etc. HMDB includes object interaction e.g., smoking, kicking a ball, etc.

We ran `Hadoop-POT` on HMDB dataset and it took 26.85 hours to complete. The final size of the similarity matrix is $\approx 6800 \times 6800$ which is $\approx$23 million unique pairs of videos. We observed that for each video category in HMDB that the most similar category returned by `Hadoop-POT` is also the same. For example videos under category "golf" are most similar to videos under category "golf". We also see "walk" category to be most similar with other categories due to its uneven distribution. Nearly 10% of data set is "walk" videos as compared to 2% under equal division. The complete set of 49 labels we extracted/evaluated is at [11].

5 CONCLUSIONS AND FUTURE WORK

Several opportunities to improve `Hadoop-POT` exist. Videos exist in both datasets in which a person performed similar hand and head movements but that were not identified as similar. Intuition tells us in these examples that HoF and HoG were unable to effectively capture certain movements, e.g., patterns or shapes,and as such adding more descriptors would likely aid these situations. We will support more video features based on convoluted neural networks (CNN) as they have shown promise in detecting such motions.

We will also investigate: (1) removing banners at starting of a video; (2) dividing a video into a set of scenes as done in [16]; and (3) finding and extracting important parts of a video e.g., as in [17]. These steps will help in comparing videos of dissimilar length and removing unwanted parts from the video.

ACKNOWLEDGMENT

This work was supported by the DARPA XDATA/Memex/D3M programs. In addition, the NSF award numbers ICER-1639753, PLR-1348450 and PLR-144562 funded a portion of the work. Effort supported in part by JPL, managed by the California Institute of Technology on behalf of NASA. The authors would like to thank Soumya Ravi and Michael Joyce for working with Dr. Michael Ryoo on hardening his initial PoT implementation.

REFERENCES

[1] M. Sharan and C. Mattmann, "Hadoop pooled time series - github repository," 2016. [Online]. Available: https://github.com/USCDataScience/hadoop-pot/
[2] T. Fox-Brewster, "Memex in action: Watch darpa artificial intelligence search for crime on the fidark web.fi," 2015.
[3] C. Mattmann and J. Zitting, *Tika in action.* Manning Publications Co., 2011.
[4] V. Murdock, C. L. Clarke, J. Kamps, and J. Karlgren, "Second workshop on search and exploration of x-rated information (sexi'16): Wsdm workshop summary," in *Proceedings of the Ninth ACM International Conference on Web Search and Data Mining.* ACM, 2016, pp. 697–698.
[5] M. S. Ryoo, B. Rothrock, and L. Matthies, "Pooled motion features for first-person videos," in *IEEE Conference on Computer Vision and Pattern Recognition (CVPR)*, Boston, MA, June 2015.
[6] T. White, *Hadoop: The definitive guide.* " O'Reilly Media, Inc.", 2012.
[7] J. Dean and S. Ghemawat, "Mapreduce: simplified data processing on large clusters," *Communications of the ACM*, vol. 51, no. 1, pp. 107–113, 2008.
[8] S. Ghemawat, H. Gobioff, and S.-T. Leung, "The google file system," in *ACM SIGOPS operating systems review*, vol. 37, no. 5. ACM, 2003, pp. 29–43.
[9] C. Sweeney, L. Liu, S. Arietta, and J. Lawrence, "Hipi: a hadoop image processing interface for image-based mapreduce tasks."
[10] C.-R. Lan, H.-H. Lu, C.-W. Yi, and C.-C. Tseng, "A p2p hd live video streaming system," in *Multimedia Technology (ICMT), 2011 International Conference on.* IEEE, 2011, pp. 475–478.
[11] M. Sharan and C. Mattmann, "Hadoop pooled time series - github wiki," 2016. [Online]. Available: https://github.com/USCDataScience/hadoop-pot/wiki/Evaluation
[12] M. A. et al., "TensorFlow: Large-scale machine learning on heterogeneous systems," 2015, software available from tensorflow.org. [Online]. Available: http://tensorflow.org/
[13] F. e. a. Pedregosa, "Scikit-learn: Machine learning in Python," *Journal of Machine Learning Research*, vol. 12, pp. 2825–2830, 2011.
[14] M. Ester, H. peter Kriegel, J. Sander, and X. Xu, "A density-based algorithm for discovering clusters in large spatial databases with noise." AAAI Press, 1996, pp. 226–231.
[15] H. Kuehne, H. Jhuang, E. Garrote, T. Poggio, and T. Serre, "HMDB: a large video database for human motion recognition," in *Proceedings of the International Conference on Computer Vision (ICCV)*, 2011.
[16] Z. Rasheed and M. Shah, "Detection and representation of scenes in videos," *Trans. Multi.*, vol. 7, no. 6, pp. 1097–1105, Dec. 2005. [Online]. Available: http://dx.doi.org/10.1109/TMM.2005.858392
[17] C. Sun and R. Nevatia, "Discover: Discovering important segments for classification of video events and recounting," in *The IEEE Conference on Computer Vision and Pattern Recognition (CVPR)*, June 2014.

PACE: Prediction-based Annotation for Crowded Environments

Federico Bartoli, Giuseppe Lisanti, Lorenzo Seidenari, Alberto Del Bimbo
University of Florence

ABSTRACT

We present a new tool we have developed to ease the annotation of crowded environments, typical of visual surveillance datasets. Our tool is developed using HTML5 and Javascript and has two back-ends. A PHP based back-end implement the persistence using a relational database and manage the dynamic creation of pages and the authentication procedure. A python based REST server implement all the computer vision facilities to assist annotators. Our tool allows collaborative annotation of person identity, group membership, location, gaze and occluded parts. PACE supports multiple cameras and if calibration is provided the geometry is used to improve computer vision based assistance. We detail the whole interface comprising an administrative view that ease the setup of the system.

CCS CONCEPTS

• **Information systems** → *Web interfaces*; • **Computing methodologies** → *Computer vision tasks*;

GENERAL TERMS

ALGORITHMS

KEYWORDS

Annotation; Surveillance; Computer Vision

ACM Reference format:
Federico Bartoli, Giuseppe Lisanti, Lorenzo Seidenari, Alberto Del Bimbo. 2017. PACE: Prediction-based Annotation for Crowded Environments. In *Proceedings of ICMR '17, June 6–9, 2017, Bucharest, Romania*, , 4 pages.
DOI: http://dx.doi.org/10.1145/3078971.3079020

1 INTRODUCTION

Progress in machine learning and computer vision is partially driven by the availability of large scale annotated datasets [8, 9, 12]. An important computer vision task is human behavior understanding which also addresses group behavior understanding. Not much data is available to develop learning algorithms to solve this highly challenging task. Problems such as person-to-person interaction and collective behaviors have been recently addressed [1, 5, 6, 14].

This research was supported by "THE SOCIAL MUSEUM AND SMART TOURISM", MIUR project no. CTN01_00034_23154_SMST and by "TESEO", POR FESR 2014-2020, funded by Regione Toscana, project no. 3389.30072014.068000017.
Author's addresses: F. Bartoli, G. Lisanti, L. Seidenari and A. Del Bimbo are with the Media Integration and Communication Center, Università degli Studi di Firenze, Viale Morgagni 65, 50134 Firenze, Italia. Email: name.lastname@unifi.it.

ICMR '17, June 6–9, 2017, Bucharest, Romania
 ACM ISBN 978-1-4503-4701-3/17/06...$15.00
DOI: http://dx.doi.org/10.1145/3078971.3079020

Group behavior datasets often are collected from multiple surveillance cameras and depict crowded environments. Moreover social cues such as gaze are very relevant for interaction understanding. Since dataset annotation is extremely time consuming, collaborative distributed frame tagging is a must. Moreover supporting annotators with predictive algorithms, allowing a smooth transfer of labels from a frame to next one, is very desirable.

Thanks to the cooperation of the National Museum of Bargello of Florence and the project MNEMOSYNE we were able to collect several thousands of unannotated frames from four cameras. Part of this data has been released as the MuseumVisitors dataset [3] which we annotated using WATSS[4]. To keep up with the annotation of this evergrowing data we developed an improvement of WATSS incorporating computer vision based annotation propagation, that allows annotators to highly reduce the workload.

Our tool is web based, supports collaborative annotation and allows annotators to specify detailed information such as body and gaze orientation, identity and group membership.

2 RELATED TOOLS AND DATA

A thorough review of publicly available datasets can be found in our previous work [3, 4]. For the sake of space we do not review datasets in this paper. We now give a brief overview of existing open source annotation tools.

LabelMe [15] is a tool focused on scene annotation which also has web and mobile versions allowing collaborative work. This tool requires annotators to outline object polygons which is extremely useful for tasks such as segmentation and scene understanding but when a highly crowded environment of people has to be annotated with identity and gaze direction it is not suitable.

VIPER [13] and VATIC [16] are tools specifically devised for surveillance video annotation. VIPER is highly limited by the fact that only works as a desktop annotation thus making annotation of large dataset not scalable. VATIC is an online tool that also provide automatic prediction of annotation, but is focused on the annotation of articulated objects [17] and has some flexibility allowing attributes to be specified for every object.

In this work we build on WATSS [4], which was developed to cope with the aforementioned limitations. WATSS is a cooperative web-based tool which has similar annotation capabilities but does not provide predictive annotations and a timeline navigation. Our MuseumVisitors Dataset [3] was completely annotated using WATSS. Recently we used this data to develop a novel gaze estimation method [2]. During the annotation process we found out that to improve annotators efficiency some aid must be provided using computer vision. To the best of our knowledge VATIC is the only tool that provides such feature, however our method is geared towards multi-camera indoor visual surveillance and group behavior understanding while VATIC is a more generic tool missing some key features such as instance identity, group definition and gaze annotation.

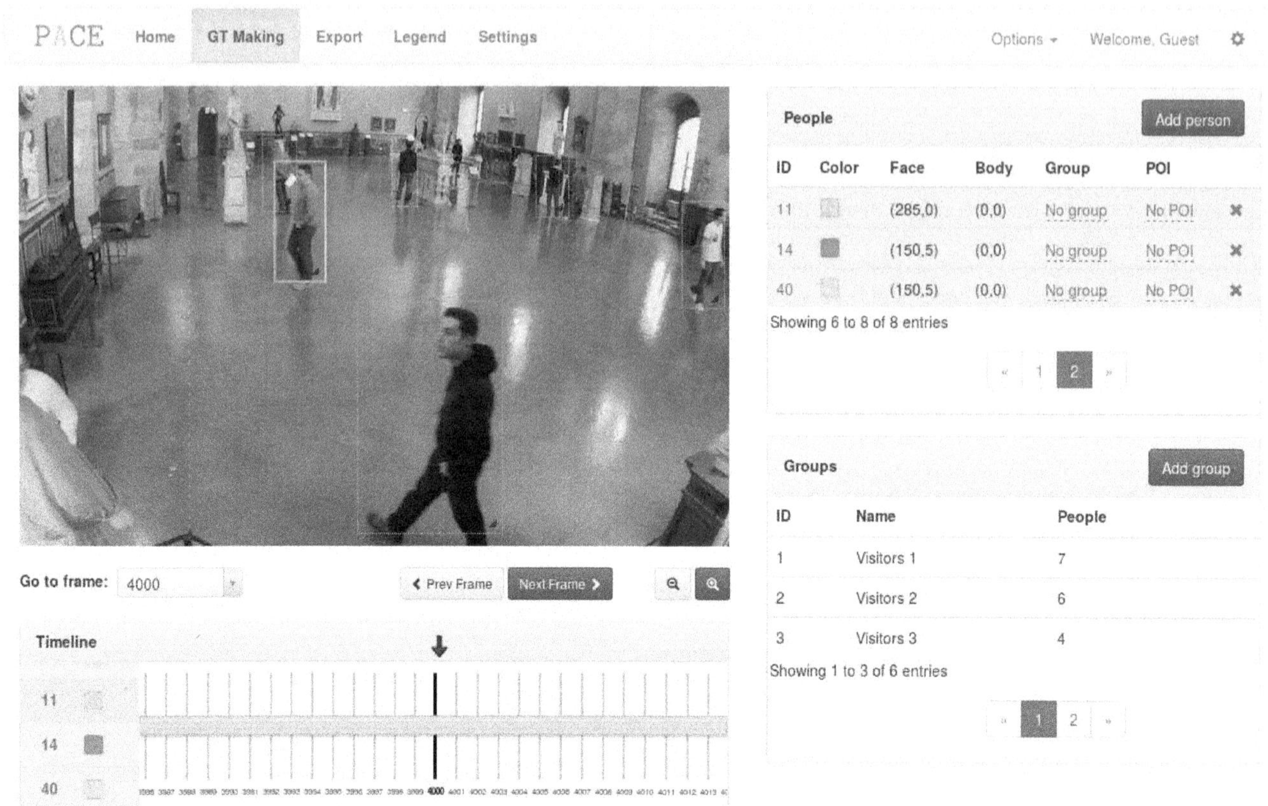

Figure 1: PACE annotation interface.

3 ANNOTATION TOOL

PACE is a web annotation tool for surveillance scenarios. The system allows annotating several information for the persons present in a frame, such as: the location (defined with a bounding box), the identity, the visible part of the body (through a second bounding box) and the orientations of both head and body. The annotation interface is shown in Figure 1.

3.1 Configuration interface

Installing a web application can be cumbersome, it often involves setting up many components such as the web server, the database and possibly other dependencies. In WATSS[4] these operation where all detailed in the documentation. At the first run, PACE will prompt the user with a setup wizard that will guide the administrative user to configure the system. This script will create the database table that will contain annotations, the configurations of every camera and users. Importing annotations previously exported from WATSS is also possible.

Moreover in PACE we added an administrative interface that checks database connection, allows to change the database password, change the camera calibration and manage users.

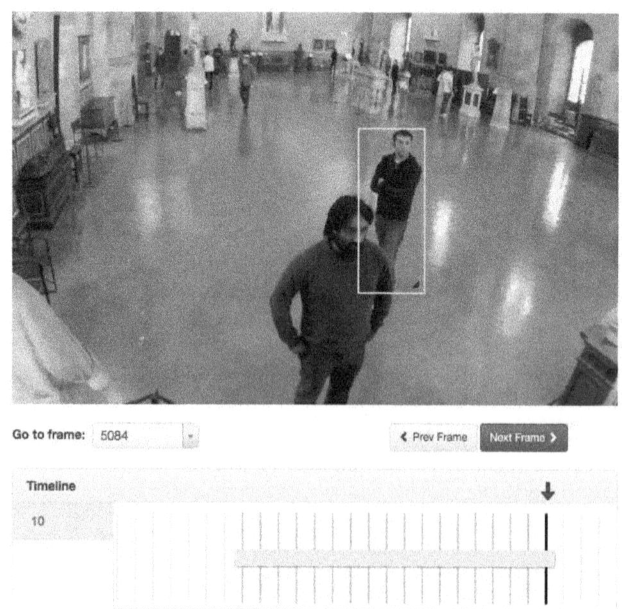

Figure 2: An example of frame with the timeline, showing the identity id (10) of the selected person (yellow bounding box).

Figure 3: Example of two predictions obtained using the drag and drop function of the timeline. First, three frame are manually annotated, then the prediction is exploited to automatically generate person annotation up to 5 and then 10 frames.

3.2 Annotation protocol

PACE annotation protocol requires a user to first select to *Add Person* by choosing between a set of possible existing identities or adding a new one. The bounding box is automatically scaled depending on the position on the ground plane if the calibration is provided and the *Geometry* option is enabled (more details in section 3.5). Two bounding boxes must be specified, the whole person bounding box and the visible area bounding box. Group identities and point of interests can be also added.

3.3 The web based annotation tool

PACE interface is derived from WATSS, it is roughly split in two sections. On the right end of the screen we have two tables summarizing the persons and groups already annotated for the given frame. The top toolbar allows to navigate to the Settings and Export page. The Options menu allows to enable or disable Geometry. A link to Legend provides access to a page reporting all keyboard shortcuts.

On the left, the frame to be annotated is shown in a zoomable canvas. Zooming is extremely useful to reduce the space occupied by the frame and to allow users annotating accurately also high resolution frames. Under the frame we show the timeline which facilitates the navigation between frames and also report a list of the annotated persons for that frame. If a person is selected a bar appear over the timeline showing the annotated interval for that person, see Figure 2. The timeline interface allows the annotator to propagate the current annotation easily. Dragging the bar forward in time will trigger the computer vision based prediction, propagating annotations as shown in Figure 3.

3.4 Annotation Propagation

To ease the annotation process we extended our previous solution [4] by integrating some computer vision techniques that are used jointly to automatically generate accurate bounding box predictions for a person in the scene. In particular, given a person and its annotations from frame $t-k$ up to the current frame t we propose to infer future locations up to frame $t+m$, by exploiting motion detection, person detection and tracking.

To perform motion detection we use the background subtraction method based on Mixture of Gaussians (MoG) [10]. To this end we first train a *background model* using 40 frames randomly chosen from the whole sequence. Then for each one of the m frames we extract the foreground mask and apply morphological operations to remove small regions and merge together the one that are close to each other. Regions are then replaced with a bounding box. Bounding boxes with an area lower than a given threshold (set to 500 pixels) are discarded. A person detector based on HOG [7] is also applied to each one of the m frames in order to extract another set of candidate regions. Figure 4 shows an example of the detections process.

Given a person the system predicts the position at the next frame $t+1$ using Kalman filtering [11]. Intersection over union scores are then computed between the Kalman prediction and the observations generated using both motion detection and pedestrian detection. The observation with the highest score is finally used to update the state of the Kalman filter and consequently the bounding box of the person. Some examples of this process are shown in Figure 5. If no valid observations are generated by both motion and pedestrian detection for that frame, the prediction of the Kalman filter is used as new bounding box.

3.5 Scene Geometry

The system also includes the possibility of specifying the geometry of the scene. In particular, through the configuration interface (see section 3.1) it is possible to specify for each camera the intrinsic parameter matrix K, the cross-ratio parameter μ and the projective homography H (between the camera view and the ground plane).

Once the calibration information are specified, the scale of a person in a given location $\mathbf{z}$ can be estimated as follows:

$$\mathbf{z}' = \mathsf{W}\,\mathbf{z}. \tag{1}$$

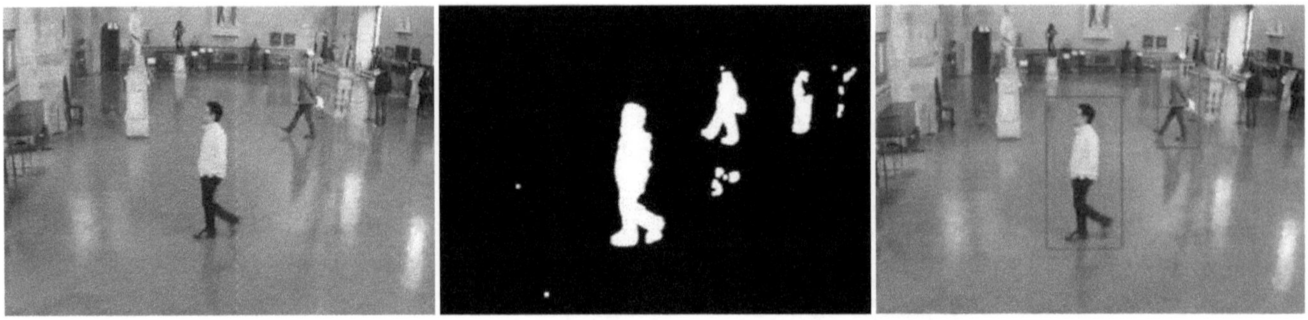

Figure 4: Detections extraction on a sample frame *(left)* using motion detection *(middle)* and pedestrian detection *(right)*.

Figure 5: Example of annotation prediction for two consecutive frames. Bounding box in the previous frame *(green solid line)*, bounding box generated using motion detection *(red solid line)*, bounding box obtained through pedestrian detection *(blue solid line)*, the position predicted with the Kalman filter *(orange circle)*.

being $\mathbf{z}'$ the position of the head of the person and $\mathtt{W}$ a planar homology, computed as:

$$\mathtt{W} = \mathtt{I} + (\mu - 1)\frac{\mathbf{v}_{\infty} \cdot \mathbf{l}_{\infty}^{T}}{\mathbf{v}_{\infty}^{T} \cdot \mathbf{l}_{\infty}}, \tag{2}$$

where $\mathbf{l}_{\infty}$ and $\mathbf{v}_{\infty}$ are respectively the vanishing line and the vanishing points, obtained as:

$$\mathbf{l}_{\infty} = \mathtt{H} \cdot [0, 0, 1]^{T}, \qquad \mathbf{v}_{\infty} = \mathtt{KK}^{T} \cdot \mathbf{l}_{\infty} \tag{3}$$

When a user adds a new annotation the system exploits scene geometry to automatically suggest a dimension of the bounding box that is coherent with its perspective, making the annotation process even faster and easier.

4 CONCLUSION

We presented PACE a web application to annotate multi-camera crowded environments typical of visual surveillance datasets. The tool source can be forked or downloaded from bitbucket at https://bitbucket.org/fbert/pace and is available under GPLv3 License. Differently from WATSS, we provided an easier setup, administrative features and more importantly predictive annotations based on a computer vision engine.

REFERENCES

[1] M.R. Amer, P. Lei, and S. Todorovic. Hirf: Hierarchical random field for collective activity recognition in videos. In *Proc of ECCV*, 2014.

[2] Federico Bartoli, Giuseppe Lisanti, Lorenzo Seidenari, and Alberto Del Bimbo. User interest profiling using tracking-free coarse gaze estimation. 2015.

[3] Federico Bartoli, Giuseppe Lisanti, Svebor Seidenari, Lorenzo Karaman, and Alberto Del Bimbo. Museumvisitors: a dataset for pedestrian and group detection, gaze estimation and behavior understanding. In *Proc. of CVPR Int.'l Workshop on Group And Crowd Behavior Analysis And Understanding*, 2015.

[4] Federico Bartoli, Lorenzo Seidenari, Giuseppe Lisanti, Svebor Karaman, and Alberto Del Bimbo. Watts: a web annotation tool for surveillance scenarios. In *ACM Multimedia*, 2015.

[5] L. Bazzani, V. Murino, and M. Cristani. Decentralized particle filter for joint individual-group tracking. In *Proc. of CVPR*, 2012.

[6] W. Choi and S. Savarese. A unified framework for multi-target tracking and collective activity recognition. In *Proc. of ECCV*, 2012.

[7] Navneet Dalal and Bill Triggs. Histograms of oriented gradients for human detection. In *Proc. of CVPR*, 2005.

[8] J. Deng, W. Dong, R. Socher, L.-J. Li, K. Li, and L. Fei-Fei. ImageNet: A Large-Scale Hierarchical Image Database. In *Proc. of CVPR*, 2009.

[9] Mark Everingham, Luc Van Gool, Christopher K. Williams, John Winn, and Andrew Zisserman. The pascal visual object classes (voc) challenge. *Int. J. Comput. Vision*, 88(2):303–338, June 2010.

[10] A. B. Godbehere, A. Matsukawa, and K. Goldberg. Visual tracking of human visitors under variable-lighting conditions for a responsive audio art installation. In *2012 American Control Conference (ACC)*, pages 4305–4312, June 2012.

[11] Rudolph Emil Kalman. A new approach to linear filtering and prediction problems. *Transactions of the ASME–Journal of Basic Engineering*, 82(Series D):35–45, 1960.

[12] Alex Krizhevsky, Ilya Sutskever, and Geoffrey E. Hinton. Imagenet classification with deep convolutional neural networks. In *Proc. of NIPS*. 2012.

[13] V.Y. Mariano, J. Min, J.-H. Park, R. Kasturi, D. Mihalcik, D. Doermann, and T. Drayer. Performance evaluation of object detection algorithms. international conference on pattern recognition. In *In Proc. of ICPR*, 2002.

[14] S. Pellegrini, A. Ess, K. Schindler, and L. Van Gool. You'll never walk alone: Modeling social behavior for multi-target tracking. In *Proc. of ICCV*, 2009.

[15] B. C. Russell, A. Torralba, K. P. Murphy, and W. T. Freeman. Labelme: a database and web-based tool for image annotation. *International Journal of Computer Vision*, 77:157–173, May 2008.

[16] Carl Vondrick, Donald Patterson, and Deva Ramanan. Efficiently scaling up crowdsourced video annotation. *International Journal of Computer Vision*, pages 1–21.

[17] Yi Yang and Deva Ramanan. Articulated pose estimation with flexible mixtures-of-parts. In *Computer Vision and Pattern Recognition (CVPR), 2011 IEEE Conference on*, pages 1385–1392. IEEE, 2011.

TEX-Nets: Binary Patterns Encoded Convolutional Neural Networks for Texture Recognition

Rao Muhammad Anwer
Department of Computer Science, Aalto University School of Science, Finland
rao.anwer@aalto.fi

Fahad Shahbaz Khan
Computer Vision Laboratory, Linköping University, Sweden
fahad.khan@liu.se

Joost van de Weijer
Computer Vision Centre Barcelona, Universitat Autonoma de Barcelona, Spain
joost@cvc.uab.es

Jorma Laaksonen
Department of Computer Science, Aalto University School of Science, Finland
jorma.laaksonen@aalto.fi

ABSTRACT

Recognizing materials and textures in realistic imaging conditions is a challenging computer vision problem. For many years, local features based orderless representations were a dominant approach for texture recognition. Recently deep local features, extracted from the intermediate layers of a Convolutional Neural Network (CNN), are used as filter banks. These dense local descriptors from a deep model, when encoded with Fisher Vectors, have shown to provide excellent results for texture recognition. The CNN models, employed in such approaches, take RGB patches as input and train on a large amount of labeled images. We show that CNN models, which we call TEX-Nets, trained using mapped coded images with explicit texture information provide complementary information to the standard deep models trained on RGB patches. We further investigate two deep architectures, namely early and late fusion, to combine the texture and color information. Experiments on benchmark texture datasets clearly demonstrate that TEX-Nets provide complementary information to standard RGB deep network. Our approach provides a large gain of 4.8%, 3.5%, 2.6% and 4.1% respectively in accuracy on the DTD, KTH-TIPS-2a, KTH-TIPS-2b and Texture-10 datasets, compared to the standard RGB network of the same architecture. Further, our final combination leads to consistent improvements over the state-of-the-art on all four datasets.

KEYWORDS

Convolutional Neural Networks, Texture Recognition, Local Binary Patterns

ACM Reference format:
Rao Muhammad Anwer, Fahad Shahbaz Khan, Joost van de Weijer, and Jorma Laaksonen. 2017. TEX-Nets: Binary Patterns Encoded Convolutional Neural Networks for Texture Recognition. In *Proceedings of ICMR '17, Bucharest,Romania, June 06-09,2017,* 8 pages.
DOI: http://dx.doi.org/10.1145/3078971.3079001

DOI: http://dx.doi.org/10.1145/3078971.3079001

1 INTRODUCTION

Texture classification is challenging problem where the task is to associate each texture image to its respective texture category. Recognizing textures play a crucial role in many applications, related to biomedical imaging, material recognition, document image analysis, biometrics and retrieval. Over the years, a variety of approaches have been proposed [31, 32, 53] for robust texture description in challenging imaging conditions, including blur, illumination, scale and rotation variations. Most texture description approaches are based on orderless distribution of local features leading to the development of several successful image classification models, including histograms of vector quantized filter responses [28], textons theory [29], bag-of-words [10] and later the Fisher Vector [40]. In this paper, we investigate the problem of learning robust texture description for texture classification.

One of the most successful texture description approaches is that of Local Binary Patterns (LBP) [38] and its variants. The standard LBP descriptor captures the spatial structure of a texture pattern by describing the pixel neighbourhood by its binary derivatives which are used to form a short local binary pattern code. The standard LBP descriptor was later extended to obtain multi-scale, rotation invariant and uniform representations. Later works have improved the performance of LBP by either combining its different variants [14] or fusing LBP with other texture descriptors and color [20]. Other than LBP and its variants, bag-of-words based representations employing a SIFT feature and Fisher Vector encoding scheme have also shown promising results for texture recognition [8].

Recently, Convolutional Neural Networks (CNNs) have shown significant performance gains in many computer vision applications, including texture recognition [9]. CNNs or deep networks comprise of several layers performing convolution and pooling operations followed by one or more fully connected (FC) layers. The deep networks are trained using raw image pixels (RGB) with a fixed input size and require large amounts of labeled training data (ImageNet [11]). Generally, deep feature based methods either employ end-to-end training or use raw activations from the FC layers as input to linear SVMs. Several recent works [9, 34] have demonstrated promising results by using convolutional layer activations instead of the FC layers. The multi-scale deep local features, extracted from the convolutional layers of CNNs, are then encoded with Fisher Vector to obtain a scale-invariant image representation. The combination of these Fisher Vector CNNs (FV-CNN) with FC layer activations (FC-CNN) currently holds the state-of-the-art for texture recognition [9].

As mentioned above, the *de facto* practice when training a CNN is to use RGB values of the image patch as an input to the network. Different to standard approaches, Levi and Hassner [30] propose to train CNNs on pre-processed texture coded images in addition to RGB for emotion recognition. The LBP codes are mapped to a 3D metric space by applying the approximation of the Earth Mover's Distance (EMD), resulting in a 3 channel image. An ensemble of CNN models are trained in their approach using RGB and LBP mapped coded images. A weighted average over the outputs of the network ensemble is then computed to obtain the score of an emotion class. Despite their success for emotion recognition, CNN models trained using texture coded images are yet to be investigated for the task of texture recognition. Further, different fusion strategies, to combine the RGB and explicit texture coded information is an open problem and therefore yet to be investigated in these networks. In this paper, we investigate the impact of mapped binary patterns encoded deep models for the problem of texture recognition. We evaluate these deep models by constructing both FV-CNN and FC-CNN based deep representations for texture classification.

The aforementioned texture coded mapped images can be combined with RGB in several ways. In the first strategy, termed here as late fusion, separate deep models can be trained using RGB and texture coded mapped images. The information from the two networks can then be combined by joining them either at the convolutional level or at the fully connected layers. Such a late fusion strategy is also commonly used in action recognition [7, 42] to combine appearance and motion information. In the second strategy, termed here as early fusion, a joint deep model is trained by aggregating the RGB and texture image channels as an input to the network. To the best of our knowledge, we are the first to investigate these two fusion approaches, to combine texture coded mapped images with RGB, in the context of texture classification.

Contributions: In this work, we investigate how to integrate one of the most popular hand-crafted texture descriptor, Local Binary Patterns (LBP), within deep learning architectures for texture recognition problem. We trained deep models, which we call TEX-Nets, on Local Binary Patterns (LBP) based coded images. First, as in [30], the unordered LBP code values are mapped to points in a 3D metric space by employing Multi Dimensional Scaling (MDS) using code-to-code dissimilarity scores based on approximated Earth Mover's Distance (EMD). We then investigate two TEX-Nets architectures, early and late fusion, to combine texture and color information. We further evaluate these deep models by constructing representations from the convolutional layer (FV-CNN) and FC layers (FC-CNN) of the deep networks.

Experiments are performed on four challenging texture datasets: DTD, KTH-TIPS-2a, KTH-TIPS-2b and Texture-10. Our results clearly suggest that TEX-Nets are complementary to standard deep model based on only RGB. Late fusion TEX-Net architecture provides significantly superior performance compared to both standard RGB and early fusion TEX-Nets. Moreover, we also perform experiments by combining different TEX-Net models. Our experiments show that the combination of different TEX-Net models lead to consistent improvements over the state-of-the-art in all datasets.

2 RELATED WORK

Here, we briefly review the Local Binary Patterns (LBP) and its variants for texture recognition together with deep feature learning.

Local Binary Patterns: In the field of texture recognition, local binary patterns (LBP) [38] is one of the most commonly used texture description approaches. Besides texture recognition, LBP based texture description has been applied to other vision tasks, including face recognition [45], object localization [51] and person detection [49]. The LBP descriptor works by thresholding intensity values of a pixel around its neighborhood. The threshold is computed from the intensity of each neighborhood's centre pixel. A circular symmetric neighborhood is employed by interpolating the locations not exactly at the center of a pixel. A variety of LBP variants have been proposed in literature, including Local Ternary Patterns [46], Local Binary Pattern Variance [16], Noise Tolerant Local Binary Patterns [13], Completed Local Binary Patterns [15], Extended Local Binary Patterns [35] and Rotation Invariant Local Phase Quantization [39]. In addition to the introduction of different LBP variants, the fusion of LBP descriptor with color features have also been investigated in previous studies [20, 37].

Deep Learning: In recent years Convolutional Neural Networks (CNNs) [26] have shown to provide excellent performance for many computer vision tasks. CNNs are generally trained using large amount of labeled training samples and take fixed sized RGB images as input to a series of convolution, normalization and pooling operations (termed as layers). The network typically ends with several fully-connected (FC) layers, used to extract features for recognition. Several attempts have been made to improve deep network architectures, including increasing the depth of the network by introducing additional convolutional layers [17, 43]. In addition to RGB based appearance networks, other modalities such as motion and depth have also been used to construct multi-cue deep networks for action recognition [42] and RGB-D object recognition [12].

Deep Learning for Texture Recognition: Recently, deep features have also been investigated for texture recognition. Bruna and Mallat [2] introduce wavelet convolutional scattering network (ScatNet), where no learning is required and convolutional filters are defined as wavelets. The work of [4] proposes deep network based on multistage principal component analysis (PCANet). The work of [9] proposes to use the convolutional layers of the deep networks as dense local descriptors encoded with Fisher Vector (FV-CNN) to obtain the final image representation. The employed deep networks in FV-CNN are pre-trained on ImageNet using RGB images as input. The use of convolutional layers allows the images to be of arbitrary resolution and was shown to generalize well to new data thereby mitigating the need of fine-tuning.

Differences to Our Approach: As discussed above, most existing hand-crafted approaches employ LBP and its variants for texture description. On the other hand, deep learning based approaches extract features from either the FC layer of the network or using the convolutional layers with Fisher Vector encoding. In such cases, the deep networks are pre-trained on ImageNet using *RGB images* as input. Our approach differs from the aforementioned state-of-the-art texture recognition method [9] in several aspects. Different to RGB based deep network methods [9], our approach is based on

Figure 1: On the left, visualization of filter weights from the RGB and TEX-Net model with only mapped coded texture information respectively. On the right, visualization of activations with highest energy from the conv3 layer of RGB (top row) and TEX-Net (bottom row) networks on an example texture image. The TEX-Net model is trained on the mapped coded images (visualized here in color), obtained by converting LBP codes into a 3D metric space.

learning deep models on Local Binary Patterns (LBP) coded images. Further, as in [30], the unordered LBP coded images values are mapped to points in a 3D metric space, resulting in a 3 channel mapped coded image. The work of [30] investigates the impact of the texture coded deep networks, in an ensemble fashion, for emotion recognition. Different to [30], we investigate learning deep networks with texture coded information for the problem of texture recognition. Additionally, we investigate two network architectures, early and late fusion, to combine the texture information (mapped coded images) with color (RGB). Finally, we construct both Fisher Vector encoded deep convolutional features (FV-CNN) and standard activations from the FC layer (FC-CNN) based image representations, from these models, for texture recognition.

3 BINARY PATTERNS ENCODED CONVOLUTIONAL NEURAL NETWORKS

Here, we describe the construction of binary patterns encoded CNN models. We start by describing mapped local binary patterns (LBP) codes to be used within the training of CNN models. We then describe two strategies to fuse the binary patterns encoded images, containing explicit texture information, with RGB. Finally, we present scale-coded deep texture representations with Fisher Vector encoding obtained from our TEX-Net models.

3.1 Mapped LBP Codes

As mentioned earlier, Local Binary Patterns (LBP) is one of the most successful approaches for texture description. LBP descriptor captures the local gray-scale distribution, obtained by thresholding the intensity values of pixels in a small block by the intensity value of its centre pixel. The resulting discrete distribution of LBP codes are binary numbers (lower than threshold (0) or higher than the threshold (1)). Generally, the LBP codes are computed over a 8 pixel neighborhood resulting in a binary string of eight-bit numbers between 0 and 255. However, LBP codes can be computed over any neighborhood size or to the number of sampling points. The final image representation is obtained by computing the histogram of LBP codes over an entire image region which normalizes for translation. The resulting representation is invariant to monotonic photometric transformations and further invariance with respect to rotation is achieved through rotation invariant mapping.

Integrating the strength of LBP descriptor within deep learning architectures, for texture recognition, is an open research problem. However, despite their success, LBP and its variants are not directly applicable as CNN inputs, due to the unordered nature of LBP code values. This is due to the convolution operation performed within CNN models. The convolution operation is equivalent to a weighted average of the input values, thereby unsuitable for the unordered LBP set. To counter this problem, Levi et. al [30] proposes to map the LBP codes to points in a 3D metric space using Multi Dimensional Scaling for emotion recognition. The resulting transformed LBP points enable to perform convolution operations while approximately preserving the original code-to-code distances. When considering the code similarity, both the number of different bit values and their locations need to be considered. The work of [30] propose to use Earth Mover's Distance (EMD) as a measure of the difference between two LBP codes. The proposed strategy accounts for differences in spatial locations of pixel codes. We refer to [30] for further details.

3.2 TEX-Nets Models for Texture Recognition

As discussed earlier, the de-facto standard when training CNN models is to use raw RGB pixels values of an image as input. These RGB based deep networks have achieved state-of-the-art results for texture recognition recently [9]. In this work, we investigate to what extent texture coded deep networks complement the standard RGB based CNN models. To this end, we train CNN models, referred as TEX-Nets, using the mapped LBP coded images (section 3.1) on the ImageNet ILSVRC-2012 dataset [11]. We employ the VGG-M architecture [5] which is similar to Zeiler and Fergus network [50]. The VGG-M network consists of five convolutional and three fully-connected layers. The network takes as input an image of 224×224 dimensions. The first convolutional layer employs smaller stride (1) and receptive field. The second convolutional layer uses a relatively larger stride (2 compared to 1). The number of convolution filters is 96 in the first convolutional layer, 256 in the second convolutional layer and 512 in the third and last convolutional layers. During training, the learning rate is set to 0.001, a weight decay of 0.0005 and momentum is set to 0.9.

Both RGB and mapped LBP coded images are likely to contain complementary information. We therefore further investigate two

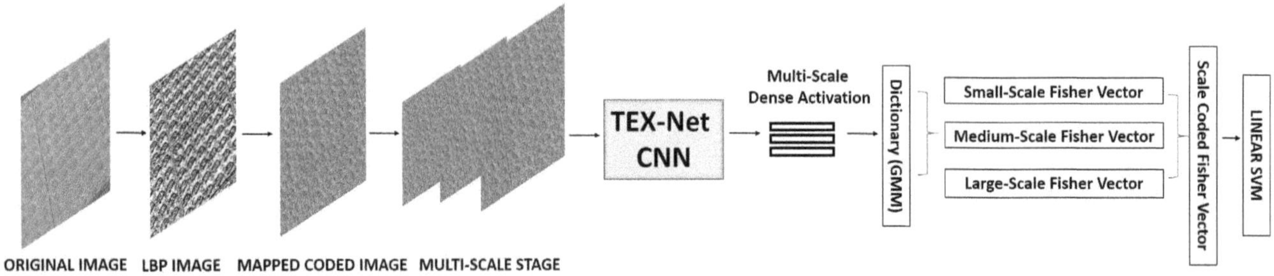

Figure 2: Overview of our scale coded deep texture representations. Here we use the TEX-Net model incorporating explicit texture information. The mapped coded images (visualized here in color) obtained by converting LBP codes (shown as grayscale values) into a 3D metric space.

different strategies to fuse the two sources (color and texture) of information.

Late Fusion: In this strategy, both standard (RGB) and texture coded networks are trained separately on the ImageNet dataset. The standard network takes RGB values as input. For texture coded network, LBP encoding is applied to each image. The LBP encoding converts intensity values in an image to one of the 256 LBP code values. The LBP code values are then mapped into a 3D metric space. The resulting 3 channel mapped coded images are then used as input to CNN models. Despite being efficient to compute, the mapped coded images still introduce a bottleneck if done on-the-fly. We therefore pre-compute the mapped coded images before training the deep network on ImageNet. Once separately trained, RGB and texture coded networks are combined by concatenating the activations from the FC layers of the two networks respectively. The stacked FC layer activations from the two networks are then used as features (FC-CNN) which are input to linear SVMs. Generally, activations from the second fully-connected (FC) layer of the network are used in image classification and texture recognition [9]. The two-stream late fusion strategy has been previously used in action recognition to combine spatial (RGB) and temporal (flow) information [7, 42]. Further, late fusion strategy has been previously shown to provide improved performance compared to early fusion, when combining multiple cues, for object recognition [24, 25], object detection [19], and action recognition [18, 23].

Early Fusion: As an alternative strategy, we also investigate combining RGB and texture coded images in an early fusion manner. In this strategy, RGB and 3 channel mapped coded texture images are stacked together resulting in a 6 channel image. As a result, the input to CNN is an image of $224 \times 224 \times 6$ dimensions. We also investigated converting the 3 channel mapped coded images into a single channel and combining it with the three RGB channels. In both networks, the filters are learned jointly on the RGB and texture coded images. In figure 1 we show the filters learned by training a network using the standard RGB and our mapped coded texture images. Additionally, we show the activations with the highest energy from the conv3 layer of the RGB (top row) and TEX-Net (bottom row) networks on an example texture image.

3.2.1 Scale Coded Deep Texture Representations. Recently, it has shown that deep convolutional features, extracted at multiple scales from the convolutional layers of CNNs, provide excellent results for texture recognition [9]. These dense deep convolutional features are used with Fisher Vector encoding scheme (FV-CNN) to obtain the final image representation. It was also shown that both FC-CNN and FV-CNN contain complementary information and their combination improves the overall texture recognition performance [9]. The use of activations from the convolutional layers mitigate the need of fine-tuning, while enabling the input images to be of any arbitrary resolution.

Despite extracting deep convolutional features at multiple scales, the final image representation in FV-CNN [9] is scale-invariant since all local deep features are pooled into a single Fisher Vector representation. Recently, Khan et. al [22] propose scale coding strategies to explicitly incorporate multi-scale information in the final image representation for human attribute and action recognition. One such strategy is absolute scale coding in which three scale partitions are constructed for small, medium and large scale features. The final image representation is obtained by concatenating the three scale partition based Fisher Encodings. In the work of [22] absolute scale coding was shown to provide superior results compared to FV-CNN. Therefore, in this work, we also investigate absolute scale coded based deep texture representations (here onwards referred as FV-CNN) with our TEX-Net models. In figure 2 we show the different stages of the construction of absolute scale coding based deep texture representations.

4 EXPERIMENTS

Here, we present the results of our experiments. We first provide a baseline comparison of texture coded CNN models with standard RGB based deep network. We then provide a comparison of our approach with state-of-the-art results reported in literature.

Datasets: We perform experiments on four challenging texture datasets: DTD, KTH-TIPS-2a, KTH-TIPS-2b and Texture-10. The DTD dataset consists of 5640 images from 47 texture classes, collected from the web. Each texture class consists of 120 images with the dataset equally divided into training, validation and test. The training and test splits are provided by the authors. The KTH-TIPS-2a dataset consists of 11 texture classes. The 4752 images are captured at 9 different scales, 3 poses and 4 different illumination conditions. Similar to previous works [3, 6, 41], average classification performance is reported over the 4 test runs. In each run, images from 1 sample are used for test while the images from the remaining 3 samples are used as a training. The KTH-TIPS-2b dataset consists of 11 texture categories. Here, all images from 1 sample are used for training while all the images from remaining 3 samples are used for testing in each test run. Lastly, the Texture-10

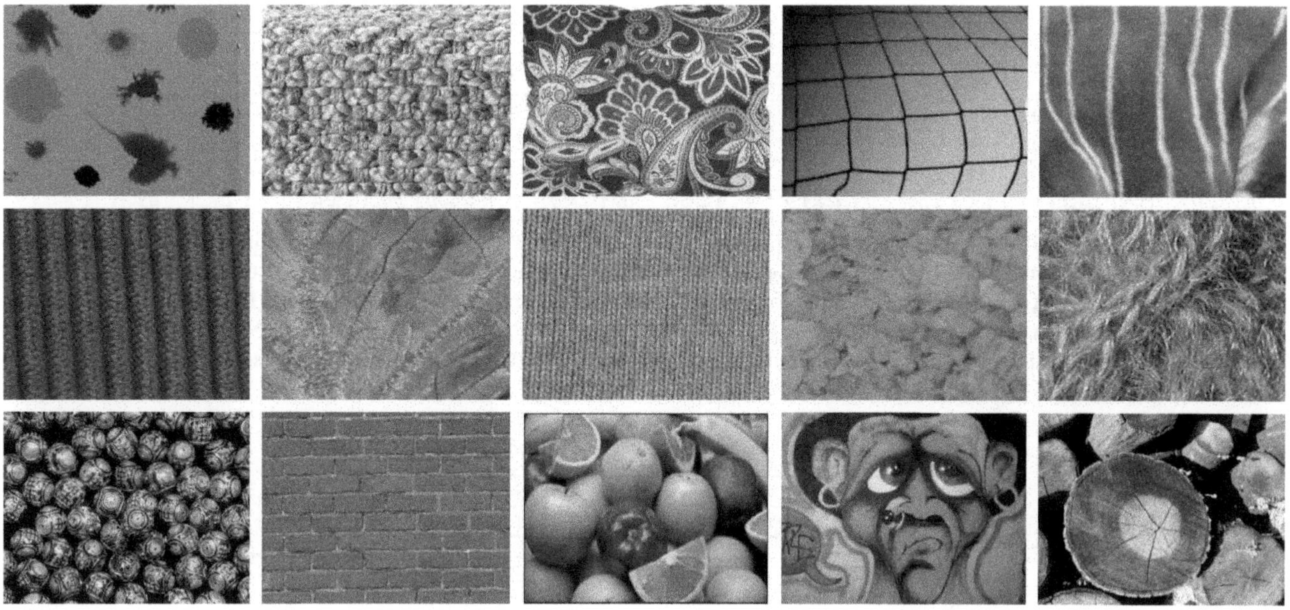

Figure 3: Example images from the four texture datasets: DTD, KTH-TIPS-2a, KTH-TIPS-2b and Texture-10 used in our experiments. The images show different challenges, including inter and intra-class variations, encountered when tackling the problem of texture recognition.

dataset consists of 400 images of 10 different texture categories. In figure 3 we show example images from the four texture datasets used in our experiments.

Experimental Setup: As mentioned earlier, we employ the VGG-M architecture and train the TEX-Net models, from scratch, using the Matconvnet library. All the networks are trained on ImageNet 2012 training set. The FC-CNN features are extracted from the FC7 (second last) layer of the network and are of 4096 dimensions. The FC-CNN features are L_2-normalised and input to a linear SVM classifier. To construct FV-CNN representations (section 3.2.1), we extract the convolutional features from the output of the last convolutional layer of the networks. The convolutional features are extracted after rescaling the image at 9 different scales $s \in \{0.5 + 0.1n \mid n = 0, 1, \dots, 8\}$. The resulting dense local features are of 512 dimensions. A visual vocabulary of 32 components is constructed using Gaussian Mixture Model (GMM) with diagonal covariances. The GMM model parameters are fit using the extracted dense local descriptors sampled over all scales on the training data. Finally, the local descriptors from each scale partition are encoded with Fisher Vector using the GMM vocabulary. The final image representation is obtained by concatenating the Fisher Vector representations of the three scale partitions. We employ VLFeat library to construct GMM and Fisher Vector encoding.

Evaluation Criteria: In all cases, the results are reported as average classification accuracy over all texture classes in a dataset. We employ one-versus-all SVMs with linear kernel. The category label from the classifier providing the highest confidence is assigned to the test instance. The overall classification results are obtained by calculating the average recognition score over all texture categories.

4.1 Baseline Comparison

We first provide a baseline comparison for both FC-CNN and FV-CNN based deep representations. We compare our models with the standard RGB based CNN approach and investigate if the TEX-Net models contain complementary information to standard RGB network. We also investigate both early and late fusion schemes for combining texture and RGB information. For fair comparison, we do not fine-tune any CNN model and use the same VGG-M network architecture together with the same set of parameters for all CNN models. Table 1 shows the baseline comparison on four texture datasets. On the DTD dataset, the FC-CNN representation from the standard RGB network obtains a mean accuracy of 63.4%. Our FC-CNN representation based on early fusion TEX-Net-EF-6ch model obtains 64.0% mean accuracy rate. The FC-CNN representation based on early fusion TEX-Net-EF-4ch model obtains 64.6% mean accuracy. The FC-CNN representation based on TEX-Net standard model provides a classification score of 55.9%. The best results are obtained when combining the FC-CNN representations from the standard RGB and mapped coded texture networks in a late fusion manner (TEX-Net-LF). This FC-CNN representation from the late fusion TEX-Net-LF model obtains 68.2% mean accuracy rate, while achieving a significant gain of 4.8% compared to the standard RGB network. Similarly, the FV-CNN representation from the standard RGB network obtains an average accuracy of 66.2%. Our late fusion based FV-CNN from the TEX-Net-LF model achieves the best results with mean recognition of 71.1%.

On the KTH-TIPS-2a dataset, the FC-CNN representation from the standard RGB network obtains a mean classification score of

	DTD		KTH-TIPS-2a		KTH-TIPS-2b		Texture-10	
	FC-CNN	FV-CNN	FC-CNN	FV-CNN	FC-CNN	FV-CNN	FC-CNN	FV-CNN
Standard RGB	63.4 ±0.7	66.2 ±1.2	81.8 ±5.1	82.2 ±5.6	72.9 ±2.1	74.1±3.1	87.3	87.5
TEX-Net Standard	55.9 ±1.1	59.6 ±1.2	68.6 ±5.3	69.5 ±5.8	60.2 ±2.9	64.3 ±4.1	81.7	81.8
TEX-Net-EF-6ch	64.0 ±0.8	66.8 ±1.4	82.6 ±5.5	83.1 ±5.5	73.6 ±2.6	76.1 ±3.8	89.1	89.0
TEX-Net-EF-4ch	64.6 ±0.9	67.5 ±1.1	83.4 ±5.3	83.9 ±5.8	73.8 ±2.7	76.2 ±3.6	89.3	89.2
TEX-Net-LF	**68.2 ±0.8**	**71.1 ±1.2**	**85.3 ±5.6**	**86.1 ±5.7**	**75.5 ±2.7**	**77.3 ±3.8**	**91.3**	**91.4**

Table 1: Baseline comparison (in %) of our approaches with the standard RGB network. We show comparison with our different TEX-Net models: based on only texture coded images (TEX-Net Standard), early fusion architecture combining the RGB and 3 mapped coded channels (TEX-Net-EF-6ch), early fusion architecture combining the RGB and a single mapped coded channel (TEX-Net-EF-6ch) and the late fusion architecture (TEX-Net-LF) combining standard RGB and TEX-Net standard networks. In all cases, our representations from TEX-Net-LF outperform the standard RGB network based representations.

	DTD	KTH-TIPS-2a	KTH-TIPS-2b	Texture-10
MRELBP [33]	44.9	-	69.0	–
CLBP [15]	42.6	-	64.2	64.3
ELBP [36]	39.9	-	64.8	73.8
CLBPHF [55]	50.2	-	68.1	76.1
LHS [41]	–	73.0	–	–
WLD [6]	–	56.4	–	–
CNLBP [21]	–	-	–	77.0
PM [21]	–	-	–	73.0
MWLD [6]	–	64.7	–	–
LQP [48]	–	64.2	–	–
LTP [46]	–	60.0	–	–
CMR [54]	–	69.4	–	–
LVCBP [27]	–	61.7	53.6	58.7
LEP [52]	38.7	-	63.1	–
LBP-HF [1]	–	-	54.6	–
CCTD [20]	–	82.7	70.6	82.0
TFT [47]	–	-	66.3	–
SM [44]	–	88.2	76.0	–
FV-CNN [9]	75.5	-	81.5	–
This paper	**76.3**	**88.3**	**82.4**	**96.9**

Table 2: Comparison (in %) of our final representation with the state-of-the-art. Our approach provides consistent improvement over the state-of-the-art on all four datasets.

81.8%. Among FC-CNN representations from the different TEX-Net models, the best results are obtained when combining the FC-CNN representations from the standard RGB and mapped coded texture networks in a late fusion manner (TEX-Net-LF). In case of FV-CNN representation from the standard RGB network, a mean accuracy of 82.2% is obtained. Late fusion based FV-CNN from the standard RGB and and mapped coded texture networks (TEX-Net-LF) achieves the best results with mean recognition of 86.1%. On the KTH-TIPS-2b dataset, a mean classification accuracy of 72.9% is achieved when using the FC-CNN representation from the standard RGB network. The two early fusion based TEX-Net models provide inferior performance compared to the late fusion based TEX-Net FC-CNN representation. In case of FV-CNN representation, the best results are again obtained with the late fusion TEX-Net model. Finally, on the Texture-10 dataset, both the FC-CNN and FV-CNN representations from the late fusion TEX-Net model (TEX-Net-LF) provide the best results and outperform the standard RGB network.

In summary, both early and late fusion based TEX-Net models improve the performance compared to only using the standard RGB network. For both FC-CNN and FV-CNN, the best results are obtained from the late fusion of explicit color and texture CNN models. A large improvement of 4.8%, 3.5%, 2.6% and 4.1% respectively is achieved by the late fusion of deep color and texture representations on the DTD, KTH-TIPS-2a, KTH-TIPS-2b and Texture-10 datasets, compared to the baseline.

4.2 Comparison with the State-of-the-art

As discussed above, the late fusion of deep color and texture representations provides superior performance. Here, we compare our approach with state-of-the-art methods in literature. Recently, the work of [9] proposed to combine FC-CNN and FV-CNN representation from the standard RGB Very deep network [43]. For fair comparison, we also employ the very deep RGB network (VGG-16) and combine it with our mapped coded TEX-Net in a late fusion fashion. Table 2 provides comparison of our final representation with state-of-the-art methods on four datasets. On the DTD dataset, the FV-CNN [9] provides mean accuracy of 75.5%. Our approach provides consistent improvements over the state-of-the-art on this dataset by achieving a mean recognition rate of 75.5%. On the KTH-TIPS-2a dataset, the local-high-order statistics based approach of [41] achieves a classification accuracy of 73.0%. The local color vector binary patterns based method [27] obtains a recognition rate of 61.7%. Our approach significantly improves the state-of-the-art by achieving a classification score of 88.3%.

On the KTH-TIPS-2b dataset, the extended LBP descriptor based approach [36] achieves an accuracy of 58.1%. The Fisher Vector and holistic based very deep representation (FV-CNN) obtains an accuracy of 81.5%. The approach combining of LBP and Fourier features [1] achieves an accuracy of 54.6%. The compact color and texture description method [20] combining color names and heterogenous texture representations achieves a classification score of 70.6%. Our approach improves the state-of-the-art and achieves a classification score of 82.4%. Finally, on the Texture-10 dataset, the compact color and heterogenous texture representation approach [20] provides a recognition accuracy of 82.0%. Our approach outperforms the CCTD approach [20] by achieving a classification score of 96.9%.

5 CONCLUSIONS

This paper investigated the integration of the popular hand-crafted texture descriptor, Local Binary Patterns (LBP), within deep learning architectures for texture recognition problem. We trained deep models on the mapped coded images obtained by converting LBP codes into a 3D metric space. We also investigated two TEX-Nets architectures, early and late fusion, to combine texture coded mapped images with RGB. Experiments on four challenging texture datasets clearly demonstrate that the late fusion architecture, fusing features from the standard RGB and mapped coded texture deep networks, significantly outperforms the standard RGB network. One interesting future direction will be to investigate fusion strategies at various intermediate layers of the two networks.

Acknowledgments: This work has been funded by the grant 251170 of the Academy of Finland, Projects TIN2013-41751- P, TIN2016-79717-R of the Spanish Ministry of Economy, Industry and Competitiveness, SSF through a grant for the project SymbiCloud, VR starting grant (2016-05543), through the Strategic Area for ICT research ELLIIT. The calculations were performed using computer resources within the Aalto University School of Science "Science-IT" project and NSC. We also acknowledge the support from Nvidia.

REFERENCES

[1] Timo Ahonen, Jiri Matas, Chu He, and Matti Pietikainen. 2009. Rotation Invariant Image Description with Local Binary Pattern Histogram Fourier Features. In *SCIA*.

[2] Joan Bruna and Stephane Mallat. 2013. Invariant Scattering Convolution Networks. *TSE* 35, 8 (2013), 1872–1886.

[3] Barbara Caputo, Eric Hayman, and P Mallikarjuna. 2005. Class-Specific Material Categorisation. In *ICCV*.

[4] Tsung-Han Chan, Kui Jia, Shenghua Gao, and Yi Ma. 2014. PCANet: A Simple Deep Learning Baseline for Image Classification? *TIP* 24, 12 (2014), 5017–5032.

[5] Ken Chatfield, Karen Simonyan, Andrea Vedaldi, and Andrew Zisserman. 2014. Return of the Devil in the Details: Delving Deep into Convolutional Nets. In *BMVC*.

[6] Jie Chen, Shiguang Shan, Chu He, Guoying Zhao, Matti Pietikainen, Xilin Chen, and Wen Gao. 2010. WLD: A Robust Local Image Descriptor. *PAMI* 32, 9 (2010), 1705–1720.

[7] Guilhem Cheron, Ivan Laptev, and Cordelia Schmid. 2015. P-CNN: Pose-Based CNN Features for Action Recognition. In *ICCV*.

[8] Mircea Cimpoi, Subhransu Maji, Iasonas Kokkinos, Sammy Mohamed, and Andrea Vedaldi. 2014. Describing Textures in the Wild. In *CVPR*.

[9] Mircea Cimpoi, Subhransu Maji, Iasonas Kokkinos, and Andrea Vedaldi. 2016. Deep Filter Banks for Texture Recognition, Description, and Segmentation. *IJCV* 118, 1 (2016), 65–94.

[10] G. Csurka, C. Bray, C. Dance, and L. Fan. 2004. Visual categorization with bags of keypoints. In *Workshop on Statistical Learning in Computer Vision, ECCV*.

[11] Jia Deng, Wei Dong, Richard Socher, Li-Jia Li, Kai Li, and Fei-Fei Li. 2009. ImageNet: A large-scale hierarchical image database. In Proc. CVPR.

[12] Andreas Eitel, Jost Tobias Springenberg, Luciano Spinello, Martin Riedmiller, and Wolfram Burgard. 2015. Multimodal Deep Learning for Robust RGB-D Object Recognition. In *IROS*.

[13] Abdolhossein Fathi and Ahmad Nilchi. 2012. Noise tolerant local binary pattern operator for efficient texture analysis. *PRL* 33, 9 (2012), 1093–1100.

[14] Yimo Guo, Guoying Zhao, and Matti Pietikainen. 2012. Discriminative features for texture description. *PR* 45, 10 (2012), 3834–3843.

[15] Zhenhua Guo, Lei Zhang, and David Zhang. 2010. A Completed Modeling of Local Binary Pattern Operator for Texture Classification. *TIP* 19, 6 (2010), 1657–1663.

[16] Zhenhua Guo, Lei Zhang, and David Zhang. 2010. Rotation invariant texture classification using LBP variance (LBPV) with global matching. *PR* 43, 3 (2010), 706–719.

[17] Kaiming He, Xiangyu Zhang, Shaoqing Ren, and Jian Sun. 2016. Deep Residual Learning for Image Recognition. In *CVPR*.

[18] Fahad Shahbaz Khan, Rao Muhammad Anwer, Joost van de Weijer, Andrew Bagdanov, Antonio Lopez, and Michael Felsberg. 2013. Coloring Action Recognition in Still Images. *IJCV* 105, 3 (2013), 205–221.

[19] Fahad Shahbaz Khan, Rao Muhammad Anwer, Joost van de Weijer, Andrew D. Bagdanov, Maria Vanrell, and Antonio M. Lopez. 2012. Color attributes for object detection. In *CVPR*.

[20] Fahad Shahbaz Khan, Rao Muhammad Anwer, Joost van de Weijer, Michael Felsberg, and Jorma Laaksonen. 2015. Compact color-texture description for texture classification. *PRL* 51 (2015), 16–22.

[21] Fahad Shahbaz Khan, Joost van de Weijer, Sadiq Ali, and Michael Felsberg. 2013. Evaluating the Impact of Color on Texture Recognition. In *CAIP*.

[22] Fahad Shahbaz Khan, Joost van de Weijer, Rao Muhammad Anwer, Andrew Bagdanov, Michael Felsberg, and Jorma Laaksonen. 2016. Scale Coding Bag of Deep Features for Human Attribute and Action Recognition. *arXiv preprint arXiv:1612.04884* (2016).

[23] Fahad Shahbaz Khan, Joost van de Weijer, Rao Muhammad Anwer, Michael Felsberg, and Carlo Gatta. 2014. Semantic Pyramids for Gender and Action Recognition. *TIP* 23, 8 (2014), ?3633–3645.

[24] Fahad Shahbaz Khan, Joost van de Weijer, and Maria Vanrell. 2009. Top-Down Color Attention for Object Recognition. In *ICCV*.

[25] Fahad Shahbaz Khan, Joost van de Weijer, and Maria Vanrell. 2012. Modulating Shape Features by Color Attention for Object Recognition. *IJCV* 98, 1 (2012), 49–64.

[26] Yann LeCun, Bernhard Boser, John Denker, Donnie Henderson, R Howard, Wayne Hubbard, and Lawrence Jackel. 1989. Handwritten Digit Recognition with a Back-Propagation Network. In *NIPS*.

[27] Seung Ho Lee, Jae Young Choi, Yong Man Ro, and Konstantinos Plataniotis. 2012. Local Color Vector Binary Patterns From Multichannel Face Images for Face Recognition. *TIP* 21, 4 (2012), 2347–2353.

[28] Thomas Leung and Jitendra Malik. 1996. Detecting, localizing and grouping repeated scene elements from an image. In *ECCV*.

[29] Thomas Leung and Jitendra Malik. 2001. Representing and Recognizing the Visual Appearance of Materials using Three-dimensional Textons. *IJCV* 43, 1 (2001), 29–44.

[30] Gil Levi and Tal Hassner. 2015. Emotion Recognition in the Wild via Convolutional Neural Networks and Mapped Binary Patterns. In *ICMI*.

[31] Li Liu, Paul Fieguth, Yulan Guo, Xiaogang Wang, and Matti Pietikainen. 2017. Local binary features for texture classification: Taxonomy and experimental study. *PR* 62 (2017), 135–160.

[32] Li Liu, Paul Fieguth, Xiaogang Wang, Matti Pietikainen, and Dewen Hu. 2016. Evaluation of LBP and Deep Texture Descriptors with a New Robustness Benchmark. In *ECCV*.

[33] Li Liu, Songyang Lao, Paul Fieguth, Yulan Guo, Xiaogang Wang, and Matti Pietikainen. 2016. Median Robust Extended Local Binary Pattern for Texture Classification. *TIP* 25, 3 (2016), 1368–1381.

[34] Lingqiao Liu, Chunhua Shen, and Anton van den Hengel. 2015. The Treasure beneath Convolutional Layers: Cross-convolutional-layer Pooling for Image Classification. In *CVPR*.

[35] Li Liu, Lingjun Zhao, Yunli Long, and Paul Fieguth. 2012. Extended local binary patterns for texture classification. *IMAVIS* 30, 2 (2012), 86–99.

[36] Li Liu, Lingjun Zhao, Yunli Long, Gangyao Kuang, and Paul Fieguth. 2012. Extended local binary patterns for texture classification. *IVC* 30, 2 (2012), 86–99.

[37] Topi Maenpaa and Matti Pietikainen. 2004. Classification with color and texture: jointly or separately? *PR* 37, 8 (2004), 1629–1640.

[38] Timo Ojala, Matti Pietikainen, and Topi Maenpaa. 2002. Multiresolution Gray-Scale and Rotation Invariant Texture Classification with Local Binary Patterns. *PAMI* 24, 7 (2002), 971–987.

[39] Ville Ojansivu, Esa Rahtu, and Janne Heikkila. 2009. Rotation Invariant Local Phase Quantization for Blur Insensitive Texture Analysis. In *ICPR*.

[40] Florent Perronnin and Christopher Dance. 2007. Fisher Kernels on Visual Vocabularies for Image Categorization. In *CVPR*.

[41] Gaurav Sharma, Sibt ul Hussain, and Frederic Jurie. 2012. Local Higher-Order Statistics (LHS) for Texture Categorization and Facial Analysis. In *ECCV*.

[42] Karen Simonyan and Andrew Zisserman. 2014. Two-Stream Convolutional Networks for Action Recognition in Videos. In *NIPS*.

[43] Karen Simonyan and Andrew Zisserman. 2015. Very Deep Convolutional Networks for Large-Scale Image Recognition. In *ICLR*.

[44] Milan Sulc and Jiri Matas. 2014. Fast Features Invariant to Rotation and Scale of Texture. In *ECCV Workshops*.

[45] Xiaoyang Tan and Bill Triggs. 2007. Fusing Gabor and LBP Feature Sets for Kernel-Based Face Recognition. In *AMFG*.

[46] Xiaoyang Tan and Bill Triggs. 2010. Enhanced Local Texture Feature Sets for Face Recognition Under Difficult Lighting Conditions. *TIP* 19, 9 (2010), 1635–1650.

[47] Radu Timofte and Luc Van Gool. 2012. A Training-free Classification Framework for Textures, Writers, and Materials. In *BMVC*.

[48] Sibt ul Hussain and Bill Triggs. 2012. Visual Recognition Using Local Quantized Patterns. In *ECCV*.

[49] Xiaoyu Wang, Tony Han, and Shuicheng Yan. 2009. An HOG-LBP Human Detector with Partial Occlusion Handling. In *ICCV*.

[50] Matthew Zeiler and Rob Fergus. 2014. Visualizing and Understanding Convolutional Networks. In *ECCV*.

[51] Junge Zhang, Kaiqi Huang, Yinan Yu, and Tieniu Tan. 2011. Boosted local structured HOG-LBP for object localization. In *CVPR*.

[52] Jun Zhang, Jimin Liang, and Heng Zhao. 2013. Local Energy Pattern for Texture Classification Using Self-Adaptive Quantization Thresholds. *TIP* 22, 1 (2013), 31–42.

[53] J. Zhang, M. Marszalek, S. Lazebnik, and C. Schmid. 2007. Local features and kernels for classification of texture and object catergories: A Comprehensive Study. *IJCV* 73, 2 (2007), 213–218.

[54] Jun Zhang, Heng Zhao, and Jimin Liang. 2013. Continuous rotation invariant local descriptors for texton dictionary-based texture classification. *CVIU* 117, 1 (2013), 56–75.

[55] Guoying Zhao, Timo Ahonen, Jiri Matas, and Matti Pietikainen. 2012. Rotation-Invariant Image and Video Description With Local Binary Pattern Features. *TIP* 21, 4 (2012), 1465–1477.

DeepHash for Image Instance Retrieval: Getting Regularization, Depth and Fine-Tuning Right

Jie Lin
Institute for Infocomm Research, Singapore
lin-j@i2r.a-star.edu.sg

Olivier Morère
Université Pierre et Marie Curie, Paris, France
olivier.morere@gmail.com

Antoine Veillard
Université Pierre et Marie Curie, Paris, France
antoine.veillard@gmail.com

Ling-Yu Duan
School of EE&CS, Peking University, China
lingyu@pku.edu.cn

Hanlin Goh
Institute for Infocomm Research, Singapore
gohhanlin@gmail.com

Vijay Chandrasekhar*
Institute for Infocomm Research / Nanyang Technological University, Singapore
vijay@i2r.a-star.edu.sg

ABSTRACT

This work focuses on representing very high-dimensional global image descriptors using very compact 64-1024 bit binary hashes for instance retrieval. We propose DeepHash: a hashing scheme based on deep networks. Key to making DeepHash work at extremely low bitrates are three important considerations – regularization, depth and fine-tuning – each requiring solutions specific to the hashing problem. In-depth evaluation shows that our scheme outperforms state-of-the-art methods over several benchmark datasets for both Fisher Vectors and Deep Convolutional Neural Network features, by up to 8.5% over other schemes. The retrieval performance with 256-bit hashes is close to that of the uncompressed floating point features – a remarkable 512× compression.

CCS CONCEPTS

•**Information systems → Image search;**

KEYWORDS

RBM; Hashing; Regularization; Siamese Network; Fisher Vectors; CNN; Image Instance Retrieval

1 INTRODUCTION

A compact binary image representation such as a 64-bit hash is a definite must for fast image retrieval. 64 bits provide more than enough capacity for any practical purposes, including internet-scale problems. In addition, a 64-bit hash is directly addressable in RAM and enables fast matching using Hamming distances.

State-of-the-art global image descriptors such as Fisher Vectors (FV) [40] and Deep Convolutional Neural Network (DCNN) features [27] allow for robust image matching. However, the dimensionality of such descriptors is typically very high: 8192 to 65536 floating point numbers for FVs[40] and 512 to 4096 for DCNNs [5, 4, 45]. Bringing such high-dimensional floating point representations down to a 64-bit hash is a considerable challenge.

Deep learning has achieved remarkable success in many visual tasks such as image classification [27, 43], image retrieval [5], face recognition [1, 44] and pose estimation [47]. Furthermore, specific architectures such as stacked restricted Boltzmann machines (RBM) are primarily known as powerful dimensionality reduction techniques [42].

We propose *DeepHash*, a deep binary hashing scheme that combines purpose-specific regularization with weakly-supervised fine-tuning. A thorough empirical evaluation on a number of publicly available data sets shows that DeepHash surpasses other state-of-the-art methods at bitrates from 1024 down to 64. This is due to the correct mix of regularization, depth and fine-tuning. This work represents a strong step towards the Holy Grail of a perfect 64-bit hash.

2 RELATED WORK AND CONTRIBUTIONS

Hashing schemes can be broadly categorized into unsupervised and supervised (including semi-supervised) schemes. Examples of unsupervised schemes are Iterative Quantization [17], Spectral Hashing [50], Restricted Boltzmann Machines [42], while some examples of state-of-the-art supervised schemes include Minimal Loss Hashing [39], Kernel-based Supervised Hashing [28], Ranking-based Supervised Hashing [49] and Column Generation Hashing [31]. Supervised hashing schemes are typically applied to the semantic retrieval problem. In this work, we are focused on instance retrieval: semantic retrieval is outside the scope of this work.

There is plenty of work on binary codes for descriptors like SIFT or GIST [17, 48, 30, 18, 50, 28, 34, 39, 46, 8, 9]. There is comparatively little work on hashing descriptors like Fisher Vectors (FV) which are two orders of magnitude higher in dimensionality. Perronnin et al. [40] propose ternary quantization of FV, quantizing each dimension to +1,-1 or 0. Perronnin et al. also explore Locality Sensitive Hashing [51] and Spectral Hashing [50]. Spectral Hashing

*J. Lin, O. Morère, A. Veillard and V. Chandrasekhar contributed equally to this work.

ICMR '17, June 6–9, 2017, Bucharest, Romania
© 2017 ACM. ACM ISBN 978-1-4503-4701-3/17/06...$15.00
DOI: http://dx.doi.org/10.1145/3078971.3078983

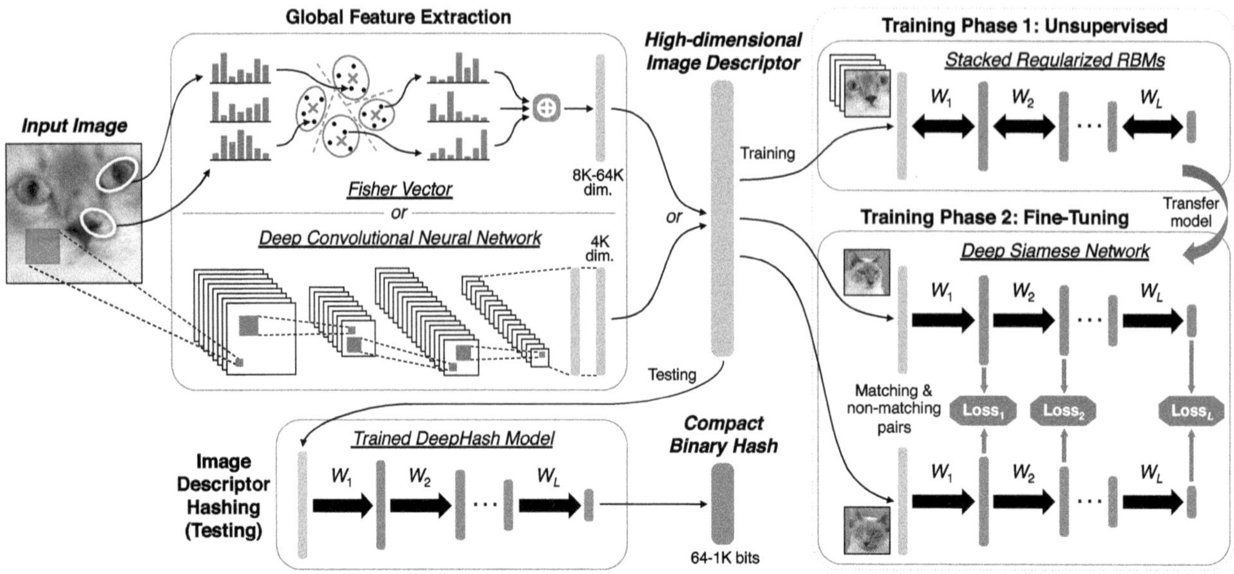

Figure 1: Our proposed hashing and model training pipeline. A high-dimensional global image descriptor, such as fisher vector and deep convolutional neural net feature, is extracted from an image. The trained DeepHash model transforms this image descriptor to a compact binary hash (between 64 to 1K bits), via a succession of L nonlinear feedforward projections. The DeepHash model is trained in two phases: a unsupervised pre-training phase and a weakly supervised fine-tuning phase. In phase 1, restricted Boltzmann machines (RBMs) are trained in a layer-wise manner and stacked into a deep network. In phase 2, matching and non-matching pairs are used to construct deep Siamese networks for parameter fine-tuning.

performs poorly at high rates, while LSH and simple ternary quantization need thousands of bits to achieve good performance. Gong et al. propose the popular Iterative Quantization (ITQ) scheme and apply it to GIST [17]. In subsequent work, Gong et al. [16] focus on generating very long codes for global descriptors, and the Bilinear Projection-based Binary Codes (BPBC) scheme requires tens of thousands of bits to match the performance of the uncompressed global descriptor. Jegou et al. propose Product Quantization (PQ) for obtaining compact representations [25]. While this produces compact descriptors, the resulting representation is not binary and cannot be compared with Hamming distances. As opposed to previous work, our focus is on generating extremely compact binary representations for FV and DCNN features in the 64 bits-1024 bits range.

In this paper, we propose *DeepHash* (Figure 1), a hashing scheme based on deep networks for high-dimensional global descriptors. The key to making the DeepHash scheme work at extremely low bitrates are three important considerations – regularization, depth and fine-tuning – each requiring solutions specific to the hashing problem.

- We pre-train a deep network using a RBM regularization scheme that is specifically adapted to the hashing problem. This enhances the efficiency of compact hashes, while achieving performance close to the uncompressed descriptor.
- Using stacked RBMs as a starting point, we fine-tune the model as a deep Siamese network. Critical improvements in the loss function lead to further improvements in retrieval results.
- DeepHash training is only required to be performed once on a single large independent training set. Through a thorough evaluation against state-of-the-art hashing schemes used for instance retrieval across a wide range of data sets with both DCNN and FV descriptors, we show that DeepHash outperforms other schemes (up 8.5%), particularly at low bit rates.

3 DEEPHASH

DeepHash is a hashing scheme based on a deep network to generate binary compact hashes for image instance retrieval (Figure 1).[1] Given a global image descriptor $\mathbf{z}^0$, a deep network performs a series of L layers of nonlinear projections to generate a compact hash $\mathbf{z}^L$. The model is trained in two phases: 1) greedy layer-wise unsupervised pre-training with hashing regularization and 2) weakly-supervised Siamese fine-tuning.

In the unsupervised phase, stacked restricted Boltzmann machines (RBMs) [22] are used to learn the initial parameters of the deep network. Each new layer in the network is trained to model the data distribution of the previous layer and is regularized specifically for hashing. A key feature is that this unsupervised pre-trained model is easily transferable. The unsupervised RBM parameters, which can be used to generate good hashes, can be further optimized with a fine-tuning phase. Fine-tuning is done through weak supervision by treating the deep model as a Siamese network [6]. Fine-tuning is also carried out an independent data set. In the rest

[1]DeepHash will be made publicly available on Caffe Model Zoo [26] (https://github.com/BVLC/caffe/wiki/Model-Zoo).

of this section, we will describe the details of the training process for our deep hashing scheme.

3.1 Stacked Reguarized RBMs

The deep network with L layers is initially pre-trained layer-by-layer from the bottom up through unsupervised learning, where each pair of successive layers ($\mathbf{z}^{l-1}$ and $\mathbf{z}^{l}$) is trained as an RBM building block. An RBM is an bipartite Markov random field with the input layer $\mathbf{z}^{l-1} \in \mathbb{R}^{I}$ connected to a latent layer $\mathbf{z}^{l} \in \mathbb{R}^{J}$ via a set of undirected weights $\mathbf{W}^{l} \in \mathbb{R}^{IJ}$. The input units z_i^{l-1} and latent units z_j^{l} are also parameterised by their corresponding biases c_i^{l-1} and b_j^{l}, respectively.

Binary RBMs. The first layer of the deep network takes a high-dimensional image descriptor as input. Previous works [40, 3] have shown that binarization of FV and DCNN features results in negligible loss in performance. For this work, binarization is done by component-wise mean thresholding for the inputs. We use binary latent units with sigmoid activation function, because binary output bits are desired for our hash. Binary RBMs are also faster and simpler to train as compared to continuous RBMs [20]. All layers in the deep network will consist of binary units and binary hashes can be extracted from all intermediate layers.

The units within a layer are conditionally independent pairwise. Therefore, the activation probabilities of one layer can be sampled by fixing the states of the other layer, and using distributions given by logistic functions for binary RBMs:

$$\mathbb{P}(z_j^l|\mathbf{z}^{l-1}) = 1/(1+\exp(-\mathbf{w}_j\mathbf{z}^{l-1} - b_j)), \quad (1)$$

$$\mathbb{P}(z_i^{l-1}|\mathbf{z}^{l}) = 1/(1+\exp(-\mathbf{w}_i^\top\mathbf{z}^{l} - c_i)). \quad (2)$$

As a result, alternating Gibbs sampling can be performed between the two layers. The sampled states are used to update the parameters $\{\mathbf{W}^l, \mathbf{b}^l, \mathbf{c}^{l-1}\}$ through minibatch gradient descent using the contrastive divergence algorithm [21] to approximate the maximum likelihood of the input distribution.

Given a trained RBM with fixed parameters and an input vector, a hash can be generated through a feedforward projection and thresholding Equation (1) at 0.5.

$$z_j^l = \begin{cases} 1, & \text{if } \mathbb{P}(z_i^{l-1}|\mathbf{z}^l) > 0.5 \\ 0, & \text{otherwise.} \end{cases} \quad (3)$$

Hashing Regularization. The unsupervised RBM is naively trained without considering the task, which in this case is image hashing. It is, however, important for the RBMs to project the data in a latent subspace that is suitable for hashing. One way to encourage the learning of suitable representations is to perform regularization, such as sparsity [29, 37, 15]. For classification, representations are encouraged to be very sparse to improve separability. For hashing, however, it is desirable to encourage the representation to make efficient use of the limited latent subspace.

For a given l and a minibatch of input instances $\mathbf{z}_\alpha^{l-1}$, we add a regularization term to the RBM optimization problem to encourage (a) half the bits to be active for a given hash, and (b) each bit value to be equiprobable across hashes:

$$\underset{\{\mathbf{W}^l, \mathbf{b}^l, \mathbf{c}^{l-1}\}}{\arg\min} -\sum_\alpha \log\Bigg(\sum_{\mathbf{z}_\alpha^l \in \mathcal{E}_\alpha} \mathbb{P}(\mathbf{z}_\alpha^{l-1}, \mathbf{z}_\alpha^l) + \lambda h(\mathcal{E}_\alpha)\Bigg), \quad (4)$$

where $\mathcal{E}_\alpha$ is the minibatch of sampled latent units for layer l and λ is the regularization constant.

We adapt the fine-grained regularization proposed in [15] to suit our hashing problem. For each instance $\mathbf{z}_\alpha^l$, the regularization term for binary units penalises each unit $z_{j\alpha}^l$ with the cross entropy loss with respect to a target activation $t_{j\alpha}^l$ based on a predefined distribution,

$$h(\mathcal{E}_\alpha) = -\sum_{\mathbf{z}_\alpha^l \in \mathcal{E}_\alpha} \sum_j t_{j\alpha}^l \log z_{j\alpha}^l + (1 - t_{j\alpha}^l)\log(1 - z_{j\alpha}^l). \quad (5)$$

Unlike [15], we choose the $t_{j\alpha}^l$ such that each $\{t_{j\alpha}^l\}_j$ for fixed α and each $\{t_{j\alpha}^l\}_\alpha$ for fixed j is distributed according to $\mathcal{U}(0,1)$. The uniform distribution is suitable for hashing high-dimensional vectors because the regularizer encourages the each latent unit to be active with a mean of 0.5, while avoiding activation saturation. The result is a space-filling effect in the latent subspace, where data is efficiently represented.

After RBM training, we further enforce space utilization by substituting the learned RBM bias by the data set mean $\langle \mathbf{w}_j \mathbf{z}^{l-1} \rangle$ of the linear projection preceding the logistic. Equation (3) is modified such that the final hash is centered around 0.5:

$$z_j^l = \begin{cases} 1, & \text{if } \mathbf{w}_j\mathbf{z}^{l-1} - \langle \mathbf{w}_j\mathbf{z}^{l-1} \rangle > 0 \\ 0, & \text{otherwise.} \end{cases} \quad (6)$$

Stacked RBMs. The set of global image descriptors lie in a complex manifold in a very high-dimensional feature space. Deeper networks have the potential to discover more complex nonlinear hash functions and improve image instance retrieval performance. Following [22], we stack multiple RBMs by training one layer at a time to create a deep network with several layers.

Each layer models the activation distribution of the previous layer and captures higher order correlations between those units. For the hashing problem, we are interested in low-rate points of 64, 256 and 1024 bits, which are typical operating points as discussed in Section 4. We progressively decrease the dimensionality of latent layers by a factor of 2^n per layer, where n is a tuneable parameter. For our final models, n is empirically selected for each layer resulting in variable network depth.

3.2 Deep Siamese Fine-Tuning

Retrieval results are driven by the structure of the local neighborhood around the query. The unsupervised training is followed by a fine-tuning step in order to improve the local structure of the embedding. The fine-tuning is performed with a learning architecture known as Siamese networks first introduced in [6]. The principle was later successfully applied to deep architectures for face identification [12] and shown to produce representations robust to various transformations in the input space [19]. The use of Siamese architectures in the context of image retrieval from DCNN features was recently suggested as a possible improvement to the state-of-the-art on the subject [5].

A Siamese network is a weakly-supervised scheme for learning a similarity measure from pairs of data instances labeled as matching or non-matching. In our adaptation of the concept, the weights of the trained RBM network are fine-tuned by learning a similarity measure at every intermediate layer in addition to the target space.

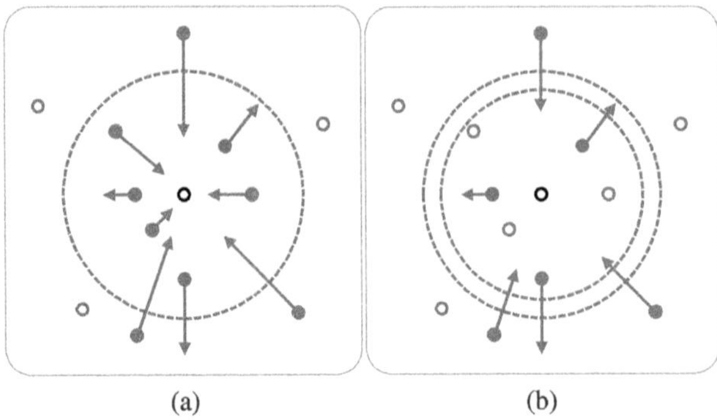

Figure 2: A sample point (black dot) with corresponding matching (red dots) and non-matching (blue dots) samples. The contrastive divergence loss used for fine-tuning can be interpreted as applying attractive forces between matching elements (red arrows) and repulsive forces between non-matching elements (blue arrows). (a) The loss function (7) proposed in [19] with a single margin parameter for non-matching pairs (blue circle). Matching elements are subject to attractive forces regardless of whether they are already close enough from each other which adversely affects fine-tuning. (b) Our proposed loss function (8) with an additional margin parameter affecting matching pairs reciprocally (red circle).

Given a pair of data $(\mathbf{z}_\alpha^0, \mathbf{z}_\beta^0)$, a contrastive loss $\mathcal{D}_l$ is defined for every layer l and the error is back propagated though gradient descent. Back propagation for the losses of individual layers ($l = 1..L$) is performed at the same time. Applying the loss function proposed by Handsell et al. in [19] yields:

$$\mathcal{D}_l(\mathbf{z}_\alpha^0, \mathbf{z}_\beta^0) = y\|\mathbf{z}_\alpha^l - \mathbf{z}_\beta^l\|_2^2 + (1-y)\max(m - \|\mathbf{z}_\alpha^l - \mathbf{z}_\beta^l\|_2^2, 0) \quad (7)$$

where $y = 1$ if $(\mathbf{z}_\alpha^0, \mathbf{z}_\beta^0)$ is a matching pair or $y = 0$ otherwise, and $m > 0$ is a margin parameter affecting non-matching pairs. As shown in Figure 2(a), the effect is to apply a contractive force between elements of any matching pairs and a repulsive force between elements of non-matching pairs which element-wise distance is shorter than $\sqrt{m}$.

However, experiment results in Figure 3 show that the loss function (7) causes a quick drop in retrieval results. Results with non-matching pairs alone suggest that the handling of matching pairs is responsible for the drop. The indefinite contraction of matching pairs well beyond what is necessary to distinguish them from non-matching elements is a damaging behaviour, specially in a fine-tuning context since the network is first globally optimized with a different objective. Figure 4 shows that any two elements, even matching, are always far apart in high dimension. As a solution, we propose a double-margin loss with an additional parameter affecting matching pairs:

$$\begin{aligned}\mathcal{D}_l(\mathbf{z}_\alpha^0, \mathbf{z}_\beta^0) =& y\max(\|\mathbf{z}_\alpha^l - \mathbf{z}_\beta^l\|_2^2 - m_1, 0)\\ &+ (1-y)\max(m_2 - \|\mathbf{z}_\alpha^l - \mathbf{z}_\beta^l\|_2^2, 0)\end{aligned} \quad (8)$$

As shown in Figure 2(b), the new loss can thus be interpreted as learning "local large-margin classifiers" (if $m_1 \leq m_2$) to distinguish between matching and non-matching elements. In practice, we found that the two margin parameters can be set equal ($m_1 = m_2 = m$) and tuned automatically from the statistical distribution of the sampled matching and non-matching pairs (Figure 4).

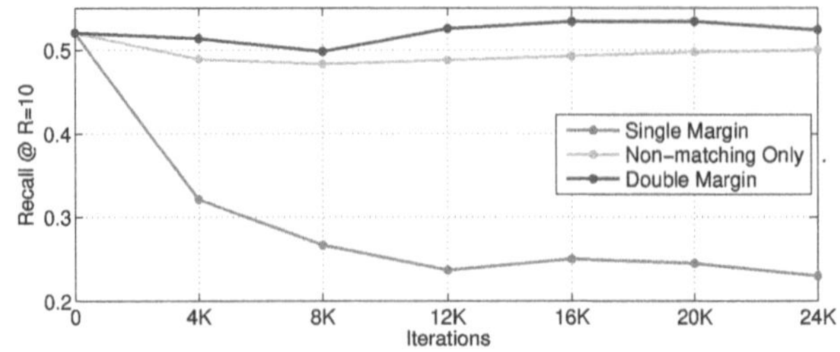

Figure 3: Recall @ R=10 on the *Holidays* data set (See Section 4.1 for a description of the data sets) over several iterations of Siamese fine-tuning. The recall rate quickly collapses when using the single margin loss function suggested by Hadsell et al. [19] while performance is better retained when only non-matching pairs are passed. The double-margin loss solves the problem. The network is a stacked RBM (8192-4096-2048-64) trained with Fisher descriptors on the *ImageNet* data set. Matching pairs are sampled from the *Yandex* data set. For every matching pair, a random non-matching element is chosen from the data set to form two non-matching pairs. There are 33 matching pairs and 66 corresponding non-matching pair with every iteration. The test set is the Holidays data set.

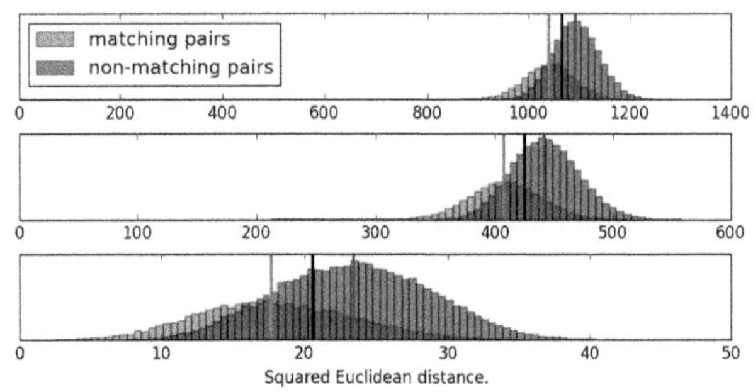

Figure 4: Histograms of squared Euclidean distances for 20,000 matching pairs and corresponding 40,000 non-matching pairs for an 8192-4096(top)-2048(middle)-64(bottom) stacked RBM network. The red and blue vertical lines indicate the median values for the matching and non-matching pairs respectively. The Siamese loss shared margin value m is systematically set to be the mean of the two values (black vertical lines).

4 EXPERIMENTAL RESULTS

4.1 Evaluation Framework

Global Descriptors. For the FV, we extract SIFT [35] features obtained from Difference-of-Gaussian (DoG) interest points. We use PCA to reduce dimensionality of the SIFT descriptor from 128 to 64 dimensions, which has shown to improve performance [24]. We use a Gaussian Mixture Model (GMM) with 128 centroids, resulting in 8192 dimensions each for first and second order statistics. Only the first-order statistics are retained in the global descriptor representation, as second-order statistics only results in a small improvement in performance [32]. The FV is L_2-normalized to unit-norm, after signed power normalization. We denote this configuration as the FV feature from here-on.

DCNN features are extracted using the open-source software Caffe [26] for AlexNet proposed for *ImageNet* classification in their seminal contribution [27]. For simplicity, we use the 4096-dimensional feature extracted from layer *fc6* (before softmax) for image retrieval, following [5]. We refer to this feature as the DCNN feature from here-on.

Training Data. Most schemes, including our proposed scheme, require a training step. We use the *ImageNet* data set for training, which consists of 1 million images from 1000 different image categories [13]. We randomly sample a subset of images from *ImageNet*. For the proposed deep Siamese fine-tuning scheme proposed, we use the 200K matching image pairs data set provided by *Yandex* in their recent work [5], consisting primarily of landmark images. For every matching pair, a random sample is picked to generate 2 corresponding non-matching pairs. This training set is independent of the query and database data described next.

Testing Data. We use 4 popular data sets for small scale experiments: *Oxford* (55 queries, 5062 database images) [41], *INRIA Holidays* (500 queries, 991 database images) [23], Stanford Mobile Visual Search *Graphics* (1500 queries, 1000 database images) [7, 2] and University of Kentucky Benchmark (UKB) (10200 queries, 10200 database images) [38]. For large-scale retrieval experiments, we present results on *Holidays* and *UKB* data sets, combined with the 1 million MIR-FLICKR distractor data set [36].

Comparisons. We compare several state-of-the-art schemes. Some have been proposed for lower dimensional vectors like SIFT and GIST, but we evaluate their performance on both FV and DCNN features.

- *ITQ* [17]. For the Iterative Quantization (ITQ) scheme, the authors propose signed binarization after applying two transforms: first the PCA matrix, followed by a rotation matrix, which minimizes the quantization error of mapping PCA-transformed data to the vertices of a zero-centered binary hypercube.
- *BPBC* [16]. Instead of the large PCA projection matrices used in [17], the authors apply bilinear projections, which require far less memory.
- *LSH* [51]. LSH is based on random unit-norm projections followed by signed binarization.
- *PQ* [25]. For FV and Product Quantization, we consider blocks of dimensions $D = 64, 256$ and 1024, and train $K = 256$ centroids for each block, resulting in $b = 64, 256$ and 1024 bit descriptors respectively. For DCNN, we consider blocks of dimensions $D = 32, 128$ and 1024, with $K = 256$ centroids, resulting in the same bitrates. Here, we do not apply Random Rotations, or PCA before applying PQ [25]. Such preprocessing can be applied to other schemes too. This is not a binary hashing scheme and only included for reference.

We ignore Spectral Hashing [50] due to its inferior performance on FV in [40].

4.2 DeepHash Experiments

Hashing Regularization. In Figure 6(a), we show the effect of applying regularization proposed in Section 3.1 on a single layer RBM 8192-b, for $b = 64, 256, 1024$. The *Holidays* data set and FV features are chosen. Hashing regularization improves performance significantly, ~10% absolute recall @ $R = 10$ at low-rate point $b = 64$. The performance gap increases as rate decreases. This is intuitive as the regularization pushes the network towards keeping half the bits alive and equiprobable (across hashes), with its effect being more pronounced at lower rates.

Depth. In Figure 6(b), we plot recall @ $R = 10$ for the *Holidays* data set and *FV* features, as depth is increased for a given rate point b. For $b = 1024$, we consider configurations 8192-1024, 8192-4096-1024, and 8192-4096-2048-1024 corresponding to depth 1, 2, 3 respectively. For rate points $b = 64$ and 256, similar configurations of varying depth are chosen. We observe that, with no regularization, recall improves as depth is increased for $b = 256$ and $b = 64$, with optimal depth of 3 and 4 respectively, beyond which performance drops. At higher rates of $b = 1024$ and beyond, increasing depth does not improve as performance saturates. For hashing, a sweet spot in performance for the depth parameter is observed for each rate point, as deeper networks can cause performance to drop due to loss of information over the layers. Similar trends are obtained for recall @ $R = 100$. Importantly, we observe that with the proposed regularization, we can achieve the same performance with lower depth at each rate point. This is critical, as lower the depth, the faster the hash generation, and lower the memory requirements.

Table 1: Retrieval results before and after Siamese fine-tuning, with corresponding differences. The stacked RBM network (8192-4096-2048-64) is trained with Fisher descriptors from the ImageNet data set. Fine-tuning consistently improves retrieval results at any bit-rate.

	Layer	Recall @ R=10			Recall @ R=100		
		bef.	aft.	diff.	bef.	aft.	diff.
Holidays	4096	70.83	73.67	**2.84**	89.92	91.40	**1.48**
	2048	67.74	71.12	**3.38**	88.77	92.04	**3.27**
	64	52.06	53.04	**0.98**	80.38	83.91	**3.53**
Oxford	4096	19.38	21.73	**2.35**	41.09	45.19	**4.10**
	2048	14.32	17.23	**2.91**	36.03	41.03	**5.00**
	64	10.69	12.01	**1.32**	23.75	29.99	**6.24**
UKB	4096	79.22	82.22	**3.00**	92.04	93.73	**1.69**
	2048	75.62	79.37	**3.75**	90.79	92.82	**2.03**
	64	47.94	49.25	**1.31**	73.02	73.94	**0.92**

Fine-Tuning. Table 1 provides detailed retrieval results for a 3-layer model before and after Siamese fine-tuning. The results show consistent improvements with every training data set and at any bit-rate with a global average difference of 2.78% (up to 6.24%). The difference is more significant at higher recall rates with an average of 2.43% @ R=10 compared to 3.13% @ R=100. They are however quite comparable when relative improvement rate is considered: 7.46% @ R=10 and 7.24% @ R=100 relatively.

We notice differences across test sets with improvements on the *Oxford* set being more pronounced. The *Yandex* data set used for fine-tuning is made with matching pairs of landmark structures which can explain the better performance of the *Oxford* data set made of buildings only. The systematic improvements on all sets are nevertheless evidence of the high transferability of both unsupervised training and semi-supervised fine-tuning.

Fast Optimization with ROC Experiments. The Stanford Mobile Visual Search (*SMVS*) data set [7] contains a list of 16,319 matching image pairs, comprising a wide range of object categories. We extract FV for matching and non-matching pairs from the *SMVS* data set, hash the data to different rate points, and compute the Receiver Operating Characteristic (ROC) curve. In Figure 5(a), we plot ROC Area Under Curve (AUC) for different schemes for the *SMVS* data set. In Figure 5(b) and 5(c), we plot recall @ 10 and MAP on the *Holidays* data set. The retrieval performance of a scheme at a given database size depends on the ROC curve at different

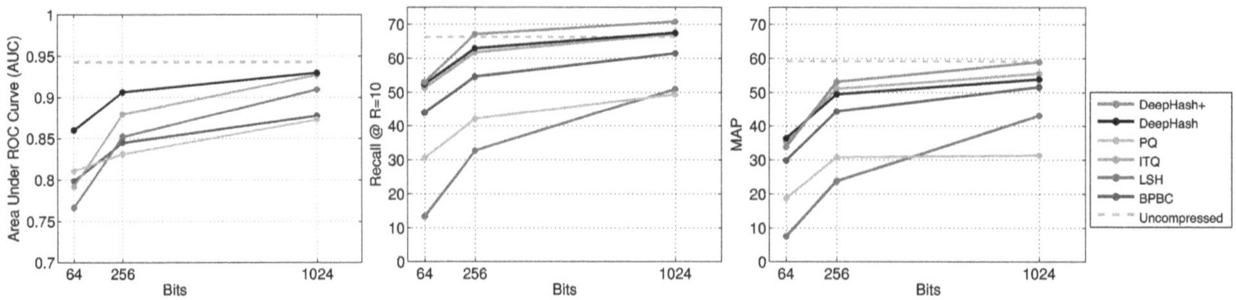

(a) (b) (c)

Figure 5: Comparing AUC, Recall and MAP performance of different schemes at varying b in (a),(b) and (c) respectively. ***Holidays*** **and FV are used for retrieval experiments, and** ***SMVS*** **for AUC. DeepHash outperforms all schemes. Also, the performance ordering of schemes is largely consistent between AUC results and retrieval results, both MAP and Recall. AUC can be used for fast optimization of parameters.**

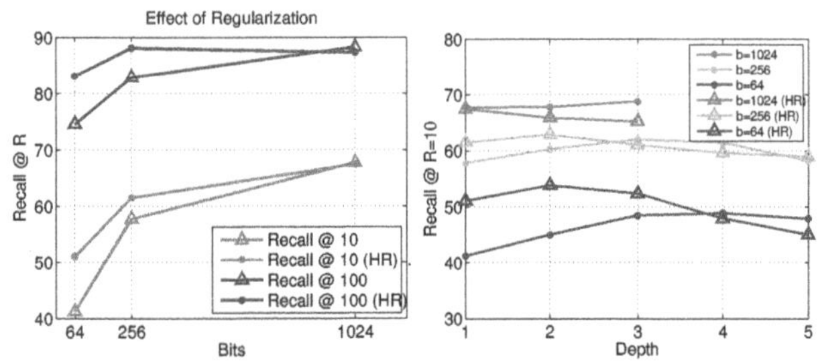

(a) (b)

Figure 6: Hashing FV for ***Holidays.*** **(HR) refers to schemes trained with hashing regularization. (a) Hashing regularization improves performance significantly for single layer models 8192-b as b is decreased. (b) Recall improves as depth is increased for lower rate points $b = 64$ and $b = 256$. With regularization, we can achieve the same or better recall at lower depth.**

TPR/FPR operating points, as shown in [11]. Low FPR points are important [11, 10]. We observe that the Area Under Curve (AUC) results predict well the performance ordering (MAP and Recall) of different schemes for retrieval experiments. The retrieval and AUC experiments are performed on very different data sets, but the AUC results generalize well, and are used for fast optimization of parameters.

DeepHash Parameters. For RBM learning, we set the learning rate to 0.001 for the weight and bias parameters, momentum to 0.9, and ran the training on 150,000 images from the *ImageNet* data set for a maximum 30 epochs. Binary descriptors for the first layer are generated by subtracting the mean for each data set. For each rate point, we consider a set of models with dimensionality progressively reduced by a factor of 2 from the starting representation for FV and DCNN respectively. The best model is chosen based on greedy optimization of AUC on the *SMVS* data set, which works well as seen in detailed experimental results of Section 4.3. The chosen architectures are described in Table 2. The depth of the network increases as hash size decreases. Each target setting requires several hours to train on a modern CPU.

Bits	FV	DCNN
1024	8192-1024	4096-1024
256	8192-4096-256	4096-2048-256
64	8192-4096-2048-64	4096-2048-1024-64

Table 2: DeepHash Architecture

4.3 Retrieval Experiments

We present retrieval results using FV and DCNN features in Figure 7 and Figure 8. For instance retrieval, it is important for the relevant image to be present in the first step of the pipeline, matching global descriptors, so that a Geometric Consistency Check (GCC) [14] step can find it subsequently. We present recall @ typical operating points, R = 100 and R = 1000 for small and large data sets respectively. For *UKB* small experiments, we plot 4× recall @ $R = 4$ to be consistent with the literature. We refer to hashes before and after fine-tuning as DeepHash and DeepHash+ respectively in all figures. We refer to deep hashes based on DCNN and FV features as DCNN-DeepHash and FV-DeepHash respectively.

Performance of DeepHash. For DCNN and FV features, the proposed DeepHash outperforms state-of-the-art schemes on most data sets. The statistics of FV and DCNN features are very different. FV are dense descriptors with zero blocks corresponding to centroids not visited, while deep DCNN features tend to be sparse. Our method works well for both types of features.

For the retrieval experiments in Figure 7, there is up to 7.4% improvement in absolute recall at $b = 64$ bits compared to the second performing scheme. Up to 8.5% improvement is seen at $b = 256$, which can be a practical rate point for many applications, as there is only a marginal drop in performance for DCNN features compared to uncompressed features. Similar trends are obtained for recall @ $R = 10$ and MAP, as seen by comparing *Holidays* results in Figure 5(b),(c) and Figure 7(a), with a higher gap for larger R. Consistent trends are also obtained for the large-scale retrieval results in Figure 8.

The performance ordering of other schemes depends on the bitrate and type of feature, while DeepHash is consistent across data sets. Compared to *ITQ* scheme which applies a single PCA transform, each output bit for DeepHash is generated by a series of

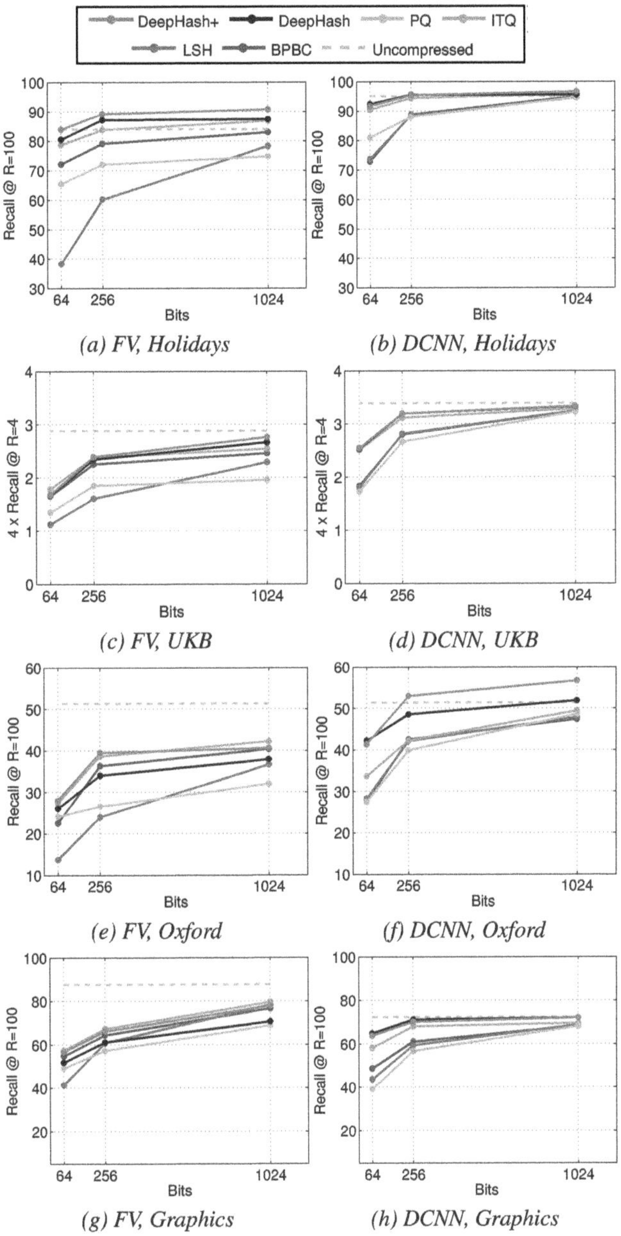

Figure 7: **Small-scale retrieval results.** ***DeepHash*** **outperforms other schemes by a significant margin.**

projections. The *PQ* scheme performs poorly at the low rates in consideration, as large blocks of the global descriptor are quantized with a small number of centroids, as previously observed in [16]. *LSH* performs poorly at low rates, but catches up given enough bits.

We observe a consistent improvement using Siamese fine-tuning, which learns more discriminative projections. The learnt projections generalize well, which is key for diverse retrieval tasks, thus showing the robustness of our proposed method.

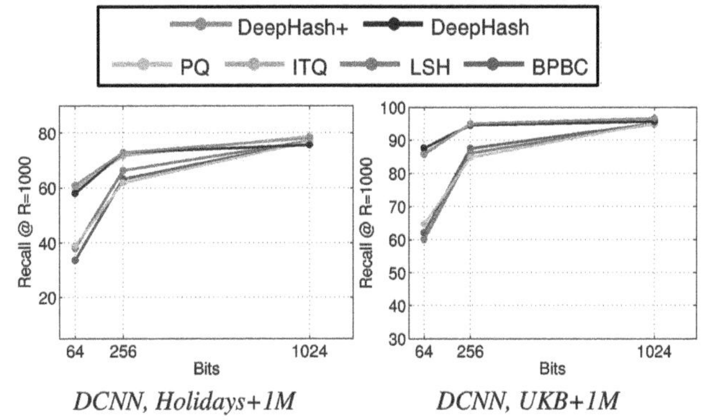

Figure 8: **Large-scale retrieval results (with 1M distractor images) for different compression schemes.** ***DeepHash*** **outperforms other schemes at most rate points and data sets.**

Comparing FV-DeepHash and DCNN-DeepHash. At a given rate point, DCNN-DeepHash outperforms FV-DeepHash hashes for all data sets except *Graphics* as seen by comparing across rows of Figure 7. At low rates, DCNN-DeepHash improves performance by more than 10% on some of the small data sets.

The results are data-set dependent. DCNN features are able to capture more complex low level features and have a lower starting dimensionality compared to FV. However, DCNN features have limited rotation and scale invariance, based on the level of data invariance seen at training time. FV, on the other hand, aggregate hand-crafted SIFT descriptors from scale and rotation invariant interest points, which results in a scale and rotation invariant representation. The *Graphics* data set has more objects with large variations in scale and rotation compared to the other data sets: this is one of the reasons, why peak performance of FV is higher than DCNN for *Graphics*.

Comparison to Uncompressed Descriptors. We compare the performance of DeepHash to the uncompressed descriptor in Figure 7. We obtain remarkable compression performance - at 256 bits for DCNN hashes, we only observe a marginal drop (a few%) compared to the uncompressed representation for retrieval on a wide range of data sets: a 512 × compression compared to a floating point representation, and 16 × compared to a binary representation. For FV, we can match the performance of the uncompressed descriptor with 1024 bits for *Holidays* and *UKB*, with a drop for *Graphics* and *Oxford*. At some rate points, DeepHash performs better than the uncompressed descriptor, which is probably due to quantization of noise in the uncompressed descriptor.

The instance retrieval hashing problem becomes increasingly difficult as we move towards a 64-bit hash. At 64 bits, there is a 5-10% drop in performance compared to 256 bits for DCNN features, while a drop is also observed for FV. For the million scale experiments, however, we observe a 10-20% drop in performance at 64 bits compared to 1024 bits for DCNN features.

Future Work. Improving performance further at very low-rate points like 64 bits for even larger databases is an interesting direction for future work. Studying mathematical models which relate hash size to performance for varying database size is also an exciting direction to pursue. Finally, in this work, we learnt compact hashes starting from a pre-trained DCNN model. Learning the hash directly from pixels in a DCNN framework might lead to further improvements [33].

5 CONCLUSIONS

A perfect image hashing scheme would convert a high-dimensional descriptor into a low-dimensional bit representation without losing retrieval performance. We believe that DeepHash, which focuses on achieving complex hash functions with deep learning, is a significant step in this direction. Our method is focused on a deep network which efficiently utilizes the binary subspace through hashing regularization and further fine-tuning using a Siamese training algorithm. Through a rigorous evaluation process, we show that our model performs well across various data sets, regardless of the type of image descriptors used, sparse or dense. The improvement over existing hashing schemes attests to the importance of regularization, depth and fine-tuning for hashing image descriptors.

6 ACKNOWLEDGMENTS

This work was partially supported by grants from National Natural Science Foundation of China (U1611461, 61661146005) and National Hightech R&D Program of China (2015AA016302).

REFERENCES

[1] DeepFace: Closing the Gap to Human-Level Performance in Face Verification. In *Conference on Computer Vision and Pattern Recognition (CVPR)*.

[2] *MPEG CDVS (Compact Descriptors for Visual Search) Benchmark. Stanford Digital Repository*. http://purl.stanford.edu/qy869qz5226.

[3] Pulkit Agrawal, Ross Girshick, and Jitendra Malik. Analyzing the performance of multilayer neural networks for object recognition. In *Proceedings of the European Conference on Computer Vision (ECCV)*, 2014.

[4] A. Babenko and V. Lempitsky. Aggregating local deep features for image retrieval. In *International Conference on Computer Vision (ICCV)*, 2015.

[5] Artem Babenko, Anton Slesarev, Alexandr Chigorin, and Victor Lempitsky. Neural Codes for Image Retrieval. In *Proceedings of European Conference on Computer Vision (ECCV)*, 2014.

[6] Jane Bromley, Isabelle Guyon, Yann Lecun, Eduard Sckinger, and Roopak Shah. Signature Verification using a "Siamese" Time Delay Neural Network. In *Advances in Neural Information Processing Systems (NIPS)*, 1994.

[7] V. Chandrasekhar, D.M.Chen, S.S.Tsai, N.M.Cheung, H.Chen, G.Takacs, Y.Reznik, R.Vedantham, R.Grzeszczuk, J.Back, and B.Girod. Stanford Mobile Visual Search Data Set. In *Proceedings of ACM Multimedia Systems Conference (MMSys), San Jose, California, February 2011*.

[8] V. Chandrasekhar, M. Makar, G. Takacs, D.M. Chen, S. S. Tsai, N. M. Cheung, R. Grzeszczuk, Y. Reznik, and B. Girod. Survey of SIFT Compression Schemes. In *Proceedings of International Mobile Multimedia Workshop (IMMW), IEEE International Conference on Pattern Recognition (ICPR)*, Istanbul, Turkey, August 2010.

[9] V. Chandrasekhar, G. Takacs, D. M. Chen, S. S. Tsai, R. Grzeszczuk, and B. Girod. CHoG: Compressed Histogram of Gradients - A Low Bit Rate Feature Descriptor. In *Proceedings of IEEE Conference on Computer Vision and Pattern Recognition (CVPR)*, pages 2504–2511, Miami, Florida, June 2009.

[10] D. M. Chen, S. S. Tsai, V. Chandrasekhar, G. Takacs, R. Vedantham, R. Grzeszczuk, and B. Girod. Residual Enhanced Visual Vector as a Compact Signature for Mobile Visual Search. In *Signal Processing, Elsevier, In Press*, June 2012.

[11] David M. Chen. Memory-Efficient Image Databases for Mobile Visual Search. *Ph.D. thesis, Department of Electrical Engineering, Stanford University*, April 2014.

[12] Sumit Chopra, Raia Hadsell, and Yann Lecun. Learning a similarity metric discriminatively, with application to face verification. In *Proceedings of IEEE Conference on Computer Vision and Pattern Recognition (CVPR)*, pages 539–546. IEEE Press, 2005.

[13] J. Deng, W. Dong, R. Socher, L.-J. Li, K. Li, and L. Fei-Fei. Imagenet: A large-scale hierarchical image database. In *IEEE Conference on Computer Vision and Pattern Recognition (CVPR)*, 2009.

[14] M. A. Fischler and R. C. Bolles. Random Sample Consensus: A Paradigm for Model Fitting with Applications to Image Analysis and Automated Cartography. *Communications of ACM*, 24(6):381–395, June 1981.

[15] Hanlin Goh, Nicolas Thome, Matthieu Cord, and Joo-Hwee Lim. Unsupervised and supervised visual codes with restricted Boltzmann machines. In *European Conference on Computer Vision (ECCV)*, 2012.

[16] Yunchao Gong, Sanjiv Kumar, Henry Rowley, and Svetlana Lazebnik. Learning Binary Codes for High-Dimensional Data Using Bilinear Projections. In *Proceedings of CVPR*, pages 484–491, 2013.

[17] Yunchao Gong and S. Lazebnik. Iterative Quantization: A Procrustean Approach to Learning Binary Codes. In *Proceedings of the 2011 IEEE Conference on Computer Vision and Pattern Recognition*, CVPR '11, pages 817–824, Washington, DC, USA, 2011.

[18] Kristen Grauman and Rob Fergus. Learning Binary Hash Codes for Large-Scale Image Search. In *Machine Learning for Computer Vision*, volume 411, pages 49–87. 2013.

[19] R. Hadsell, S. Chopra, and Y. LeCun. Dimensionality Reduction by Learning an Invariant Mapping. In *Proceedings of IEEE Conference on Computer Vision and Pattern Recognition*, volume 2, pages 1735–1742, 2006.

[20] Geoffrey Hinton. A Practical Guide to Training Restricted Boltzmann Machines. In *Neural Networks: Tricks of the Trade*, volume 7700 of *LNCS*, pages 599–619. Springer Berlin Heidelberg, 2012.

[21] Geoffrey E Hinton. Training products of experts by minimizing contrastive divergence. *Neural Computation*, 14(8):1771–1800, 2002.

[22] Geoffrey E. Hinton, Simon Osindero, and Yee-Whye Teh. A fast learning algorithm for deep belief networks. *Neural Computation*, 18(7):1527–1554, 2006.

[23] H. Jégou, M. Douze, and C. Schmid. Hamming Embedding and Weak Geometric Consistency for Large Scale Image Search. In *Proceedings of European Conference on Computer Vision (ECCV)*, pages 304–317, Berlin, Heidelberg, October 2008.

[24] H. Jégou, M. Douze, C. Schmid, and P. Perez. Aggregating Local Descriptors into a Compact Image Representation. In *Proceedings of IEEE Conference on Computer Vision and Pattern Recognition (CVPR)*, pages 3304–3311, San Francisco, CA, USA, June 2010.

[25] Hervé Jégou, Florent Perronnin, Matthijs Douze, Jorge Sánchez, Patrick Pérez, and Cordelia Schmid. Aggregating local image descriptors into compact codes. *IEEE Transactions on Pattern Analysis and Machine Intelligence*, 34(9):1704–1716, September 2012.

[26] Yangqing Jia, Evan Shelhamer, Jeff Donahue, Sergey Karayev, Jonathan Long, Ross Girshick, Sergio Guadarrama, and Trevor Darrell. Caffe: Convolutional architecture for fast feature embedding. *arXiv preprint arXiv:1408.5093*, 2014.

[27] Alex Krizhevsky, Ilya Sutskever, and Geoffrey E Hinton. Imagenet classification with deep convolutional neural networks. In *Advances in Neural Information Processing Systems (NIPS)*, 2012.

[28] Brian Kulis and Kristen Grauman. Kernelized Locality-Sensitive Hashing for Scalable Image Search. In *Proceedings of IEEE International Conference on Computer Vision (ICCV*, 2009.

[29] Honglak Lee, Chaitanya Ekanadham, and Andrew Ng. Sparse deep belief net model for visual area V2. In *Advances in Neural Information Processing Systems (NIPS)*, pages 873–880, 2008.

[30] Youngwoon Lee. Spherical Hashing. In *Proceedings of the 2012 IEEE Conference on Computer Vision and Pattern Recognition (CVPR)*, pages 2957–2964, Washington, DC, USA, 2012. IEEE Computer Society.

[31] Xi Li, Guosheng Lin, Chunhua Shen, Anton van den Hengel, and Anthony R. Dick. Learning Hash Functions Using Column Generation. In *Proceedings of ICML*, volume 28, pages 142–150, 2013.

[32] Jie Lin, Ling-Yu Duan, Tiejun Huang, and Wen Gao. Robust Fisher Codes for Large Scale Image Retrieval. In *Proceedings of International Conference on Acoustics and Signal Processing (ICASSP)*, 2013.

[33] K. Lin, J. Lu, C. Chen, and J. Zhou. Learning compact binary descriptors with unsupervised deep neural networks. In *IEEE Conference on Computer Vision and Pattern Recognition (CVPR)*, 2016.

[34] Wei Liu, Jun Wang, Rongrong Ji, Yu-Gang Jiang, and Shih-Fu Chang. Supervised Hashing with Kernels. In *Computer Vision and Pattern Recognition (CVPR)*, 2012.

[35] D. Lowe. Distinctive Image Features from Scale-invariant Keypoints. *International Journal of Computer Vision*, 60(2):91–110, November 2004.

[36] B. Thomee Mark J. Huiskes and Michael S. Lew. New Trends and Ideas in Visual Concept Detection: The MIR Flickr Retrieval Evaluation Initiative. In *Proceedings of the 2010 ACM International Conference on Multimedia Information Retrieval*, pages 527–536, New York, NY, USA, 2010.

[37] Vinod Nair and Geoffrey Hinton. 3D Object Recognition with Deep Belief Nets. In *Advances in Neural Information Processing Systems (NIPS)*, pages 1339–1347, 2009.

[38] D. Nistér and H. Stewénius. Scalable Recognition with a Vocabulary Tree. In *Proceedings of IEEE Conference on Computer Vision and Pattern Recognition (CVPR)*, pages 2161–2168, New York, USA, June 2006.

[39] Mohammad Norouzi and David Fleet. Minimal Loss Hashing for Compact Binary Codes. In *Proceedings of ICML*, pages 353–360, 2011.
[40] F. Perronnin, Y. Liu, J. Sanchez, and H. Poirier. Large-scale Image Retrieval with Compressed Fisher Vectors. In *Proceedings of IEEE Conference on Computer Vision and Pattern Recognition (CVPR)*, pages 3384–3391, San Francisco, CA, USA, June 2010.
[41] J. Philbin, O. Chum, M. Isard, J. Sivic, and A. Zisserman. Object Retrieval with Large Vocabularies and Fast Spatial Matching. In *Proceedings of CVPR*, pages 1–8, Minneapolis, Minnesota, June 2007.
[42] Ruslan Salakhutdinov, Andriy Mnih, and Geoffrey Hinton. Restricted Boltzmann Machines for Collaborative Filtering. In *Proceedings of the 24th International Conference on Machine Learning*, ICML '07, pages 791–798, New York, NY, USA, 2007. ACM.
[43] Karen Simonyan and Andrew Zisserman. Very deep convolutional networks for large-scale image recognition. *CoRR*, abs/1409.1556, 2014.
[44] Yi Sun, Xiaogang Wang, and Xiaoou Tang. Deep learning face representation from predicting 10,000 classes. June 2014.
[45] Giorgos Tolias, Ronan Sicre, and Hervé Jégou. Particular object retrieval with integral max-pooling of CNN activations. In *International Conference on Learning Representations (ICLR)*, 2016.
[46] A. Torralba, R. Fergus, and Y. Weiss. Small Codes and Large Image Databases for Recognition. In *Proceedings of IEEE Conference on Computer Vision and Pattern Recognition (CVPR)*, pages 1–8, Anchorage, Alaska, June 2008.
[47] Alexander Toshev and Christian Szegedy. Deeppose: Human pose estimation via deep neural networks. June 2014.
[48] Jun Wang, Sanjiv Kumar, and Shih-Fu Chang. Semi-Supervised Hashing for Scalable Image Retrieval. In *Proceedings of IEEE Computer Society Conference on Computer Vision and Pattern Recognition (CVPR)*, San Francisco, USA, June 2010.
[49] Jun Wang, Wei Liu, Andy X Sun, and Yu-Gang Jiang. Learning Hash Codes with Listwise Supervision. In *Proceedings of IEEE International Conference on Computer Vision, ICCV 2013, Sydney, Australia, December 1-8, 2013*, pages 3032–3039, 2013.
[50] Y. Weiss, A. Torralba, and R. Fergus. Spectral Hashing. In *Proceedings of Neural Information Processing Systems (NIPS)*, pages 1753–1760, Vancouver, BC, Canada, December 2008.
[51] C. Yeo, P. Ahammad, and K. Ramchandran. Rate-efficient Visual Correspondences using Random Projections. In *Proceedings of IEEE International Conference on Image Processing (ICIP)*, pages 217–220, San Diego, California, October 2008.

Balanced Search Space Partitioning for Distributed Media Redundant Indexing

André Mourão
NOVA LINCS
Faculdade de Ciências e Tecnologia
Universidade NOVA de Lisboa 2825-516 Caparica
a.mourao@campus.fct.unl.pt

João Magalhães
NOVA LINCS
Faculdade de Ciências e Tecnologia
Universidade NOVA de Lisboa 2825-516 Caparica
jmag@fct.unl.pt

ABSTRACT

This paper addresses the problem of balanced, redundant indexing of media information. Our goal is to partition and distribute the search index, taking advantage of the distributed systems properties: balanced load across nodes, redundancy on node down and efficient node usage under concurrent querying. We follow an information compression approach to solve this problem and propose to represent data with overcomplete codebooks, where each document is represented by only a few codewords and an indexing node is responsible for several codewords. Quantization algorithms are designed to fit the original data as best as possible, leading to bias towards codewords that fit the principal directions of data. In this paper, we propose the balanced KSVD (B-KSVD) algorithm, that distributes the allocation of data across a balanced number of codewords, according to the global distribution of data. Indexing experiments showed that B-KSVD can achieve 38% *1-recall* by inspecting only 1% of the full index, distributed over 10 partitions. Traditional methods based on k-means need to either use larger codebooks or to inspect a larger portion of the index to achieve the same retrieval performance.

KEYWORDS

Search space partitioning; Distributed search; High-dimensional indexing; Dictionary design; Clustering; Approximate nearest neighbor search

ACM Reference format:
André Mourão and João Magalhães. 2017. Balanced Search Space Partitioning for Distributed Media Redundant Indexing. In *Proceedings of ICMR '17, Bucharest, Romania, June 06-09, 2017,* 8 pages.
DOI: http://dx.doi.org/10.1145/3078971.3078999

1 INTRODUCTION

The goals of index partitioning algorithms are to distribute documents across nodes based on document similarity, to facilitate the efficient selection of retrieval resources, such that documents relevant to a query are concentrated across a few shards [22]. There are two main index partitioning strategies [9]:

- **horizontal** partition or **sharding**: divide documents across nodes;
- **vertical** or **term-based** partition: divide document features across multiple nodes.

In addition to dealing with high-dimensional data and its unknown underlying structure, these algorithms have the opportunity to take advantage of the characteristics of new distributed systems (e.g. cloud environments), parallel processing, hardware redundancy (i.e. index documents on more than one node), and ability to deploy additional nodes on-demand. Existing multimedia document distribution do not explore these characteristics, as document allocation policies are either random, e.g. [29], or based on existing partitions of single node algorithms, e.g. [6]. One of the works that goes towards our partitioning goals is by Ji et al. [20]. They tested *global* and *local* indexing partitioning techniques (*horizontal* and *vertical* partition respectively), based on Vocabulary Tree model quantization, and showed that vertical partitioning offers the best temporal performance on a distributed setting, without an increase in load imbalance.

Our goal in this paper is to study the impact of overcomplete data representations on the load balancing and retrieval performance of distributed indexes. Codebooks for overcomplete data representations are composed of a large number of codewords, each one corresponding to a partition of the search space. The overcomplete property of the codebook, means that the number of partitions/codewords is much higher than the original data dimensionality. Indexing is achieved by encoding each media vector as a linear combination of just a few codewords.

The main contribution of this paper is the balanced-KSVD algorithm (B-KSVD) that distributes the allocation of data across a balanced number of codewords. B-KSVD is a distributed indexing algorithm that computes a codebook with an overcomplete set of codewords that addresses a number of challenges. The first one, is the even distribution of data across codewords to achieve better load-balancing when allocating data to nodes. The second, is that documents should be assigned to partitions with documents that are also close in the original space. And third, because a vector is encoded with multiple codewords, each one corresponding to a space partition, data will be stored redundantly across multiple nodes (each node has the capacity to serve multiple codewords).

The proposed approach offers several advantages. An overcomplete balanced index means that concurrent queries will be answered by different subsets of nodes, reducing the bottleneck of

978-1-4503-4701-3/17/06...$15.00
DOI: http://dx.doi.org/10.1145/3078971.3078999

having all nodes answering all queries. (e.g. Figure 1 (b)). Furthermore, these properties mean that distributed indexes can still operate with good performance when a node fails. In other words, failure to inspect a partition (e.g. as a consequence of a node failure) will result in a performance decrease, instead of no results returned.

This paper is organized as follows: Section 2 details the related work in distributed media search and space partitioning. Section 3 details the formalization of overcomplete redundant partitioning and proposed solutions. Section 4 describes the experiments and section 5 in we discuss our conclusions.

2 RELATED WORK

The bulk of distributed multimodal retrieval comes from combining Map Reduce [13] with single node algorithms or from distributing the feature spaces across nodes [28]. When applied to CBMI [27, 29, 38], Map Reduce can be used to partition indexes horizontally. As Map Reduce requires Map and Reduce nodes to be data agnostic, indexes must either query all nodes for all queries [29], which does not meet our efficiency goal, or have all nodes accessing to the full index [27], which is limited by the time it takes to fetch the relevant index subset. Moise et al. [27] experiments also show that the overhead behind the Map and Reduce operations is considerable (e.g. copying data to Hadoop Distributed File Systems), as it is only optimized for massive batches of queries. Distributed tree-based systems have also been studied for horizontal index partitioning for CBMI [2, 6], but the effectiveness of sub-tree based index partitioning is reduced when the dimensionality of the vectors to index increases [36], meaning that more nodes need to be queried.

Effective partitioning of the search space is a key part of approximate nearest neighbour algorithms. It enables faster search by inspecting the subset of the index where there is a higher density of nearest neighbours. Recent algorithms in this area rely on Hamming embeddings or on codebooks learned from data.

Hamming embeddings. Binary hash techniques such as LSH (Locality Sensitive Hashing) [3], partition search space in a data independent way, according to a set of randomly generated hyperplanes. Each hash bit represents an hyperplane in the original feature space that divides it in two, assigning a value of zero or one related to the side in which the document is. Hash codes are generated by concatenating multiple of the values of these functions. The search space is partitioned horizontally, according to the document's hash: documents with similar hash codes have a high probability of being similar in the original space, hence should be stored on the same buckets. LSH spawn multiple techniques [11, 12, 32] that explore alternatives to hyperplane partitioning by applying other families of functions with different structures (e.g. grid).

Other works have focused on creating better hash functions, by exploring the structure of the data in original space. By leveraging on the distribution of documents in the original search space, data dependent hash functions [16, 24, 35, 37] can create better partitions for similarity search. Grauman and Fergus [15] authored a review of data dependent hash techniques.

Regression and codebook design. Sparse hashes are generated in a very high dimensional overcomplete space. Documents with more non-zero coefficients on the same hash positions have higher degrees of similarity than documents with no common non-zero coefficients. Effective partitioning is achieved by having only a very small subset of hashes with non-zero values. Lewicki and Sejnowski [23] show that the transformation of dense feature representations into a sparse high-dimensional representations achieves a high degree of compression, while preserving locality structure on the non-null coefficients.

Multiple techniques were developed to generate high dimensional sparse hashes. These techniques differ by the type of regulation applied to the hashes: l_0 penalty (e.g. OMP [31]), l_1 penalty (e.g. Lasso [34]), l_2 penalty (e.g. Ridge [17]) or a combination of the l_1 and l_2 penalties (e.g. Elasticnet [39]). OMP controls sparsity by greedily selecting the most correlated coefficient at each iteration with the current residual (l_0 pseudo-norm penalty). Lasso does sparse selection by applying the l_1 penalty, Ridge limits the coefficient magnitude by applying the l_2 penalty Elasticnet's penalty is a mixture of Lasso's l_1 penalties with Ridges l_2 penalties, having both the sparsity properties of l_1 penalty and the limited coefficient magnitude of the l_2 penalty.

Regression techniques use a codebook (or dictionary) as the basis of the transformation into the new space. Codebook computation algorithms such as K-SVD, select codewords that minimize reconstruction error. K-SVD [1] alternatively updates a codebook and the coefficients. Stochastic gradient descent techniques (e.g. [30]) update each example per iteration, to minimize reconstruction error. Cherian et al. [10] presented an index based on hashes created using l_1 regression and the Newton Descent for codebook learning. Borges et al. [8] presented an indexes based on sparse hashes created using l_0 regression and a codebook learned through K-SVD.

Quantization through clustering. Clustering techniques are one of the most used space partitioning techniques, with applications that range from image retrieval [26] to image indexing [18]. The search space is partitioned by generating a set of centroids, and vectors are assigned to the closest centroid according to a metric (e.g. euclidean distance). k-means, a popular clustering technique, aims to find the set of centroids that minimizes sum of squares within-cluster distances. Lloyd [25] proposed a local search solution that is still widely applied today. On the original formulations, the initial seed centroids are selected randomly from the training data, which may greatly increase the convergence time. k-means++ [4] is a centroid selection technique that estimates a good set of seed centroids, by analysing the distribution of the seed centroids and the training data distribution. Fuzzy c-means clustering/soft clustering [7] techniques extends the assignment of documents to multiple clusters, by keeping membership information of documents to clusters (e.g. ratio of the distance to the centroids). Clustering techniques such as DBSCAN [14], do not set the number of centroids as a parameter, focusing instead on the cluster density and points per cluster.

Clustering techniques are behind some of the best performing nearest neighbour search algorithms. Jégou et al. [18] proposed an index that divides the space into a set of Voronoi cells through k-means based vector quantization. Further works improve candidate distance computation [19], descriptor quantization [21] and more effective centroid evaluation [5]. Tavenard et al. [33] proposed a technique for balancing k-means cluster size, by shifting cluster boundaries into parallel boundaries. Their experiments showed less variability in the number of candidates retrieved per query.

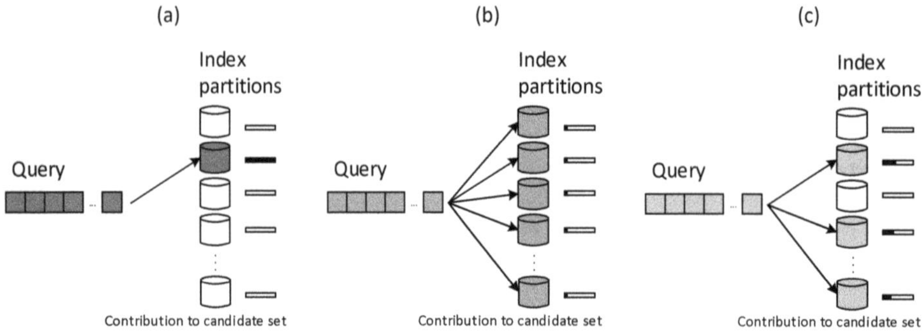

Figure 1: Examples of the querying process of multiple document partitioning policies: (a) single node indexing, (b) random indexing, (c) redundant overcomplete indexing

3 SPACE PARTITIONING CODEBOOKS

On the previous section, we described how indexing partitioning techniques are applied to distributed search. Figure 1 illustrates the assignment of queries to partitions for existing index partitioning techniques and for our proposed technique. Figure 1 (a) shows a single assignment technique, where each document is assigned to a single partition (e.g. [6]). Figure 1 (b) shows a random assignment technique, where documents are assigned to a single partition randomly, and queries are assigned to all partitions. This technique is applied on some Map-Reduce systems (e.g. [29]). Figure 1 (c) shows our proposal: a similarity-based, multiple assignment technique. Under this partitioning paradigm, each document is assigned to multiple partitions, based on similarity in the original feature space. Inspecting multiple partitions will result on a incremental increases in retrieval performance. Conversely, node failures will also result on incremental losses in retrieval performance, instead of returning no results (Figure 1 (a)). To create representations that fit this partitioning paradigm, partition methods must have the following properties:

- fixing **overcompleteness** of the codewords as a parameter, i.e. sparsity factor;
- give partition **membership information** (e.g. distance to centroid, reconstruction weight) to allow candidate selection inside partitions;
- **partitions** should group **similar documents** in the original space;
- generate **evenly sized** partitions.

Formally, consider the original vector $y \in \mathbb{R}^n$, a codeword $x \in \mathbb{R}^k$ and a sparsity coefficient s.

$$y \in \mathbb{R}^n \rightarrow x \in \mathbb{R}^k \quad \text{where } \|x\|_0 = s \text{ and } s \ll n \ll k. \tag{1}$$

Forcing sparsity to be equal to the sparsity factor s, instead of the general constraint of smaller or equal, ensures that each document will be placed exactly on s partitions. For a set of vectors $y_a, y_b, y_c \in Y \in \mathbb{R}^{m,n}$ and corresponding codewords $x_a, x_b, x_c \in X \in \mathbb{R}^{m,k}$, our goal is to generate codewords that respect the following property:

$$\|y_a - y_b\|_2 < \|y_a - y_c\|_2 \rightarrow \|x_a + x_b\|_0 < \|x_a + x_c\|_0 \tag{2}$$

In other words, vectors that are close in the original space have non-zero coefficients on similar positions in the codeword space. These codewords are the basis to generate a set of partitions $\{p_0, ..., p_i\} \in P \subset Y$. Our balancing goal is to minimize the differences on partition sizes: $|p_a| - |p_b|, \forall p_a, p_b \in P$.

After studying the properties of the space partitioning in the literature, we arrived at two families of methods that have the potential to meet the desired properties: sparse hashes and clustering. Sparse coding techniques are designed to generate overcomplete representations of the search space: our reasoning is that codebook atoms can act as the basis of the partitions. For clustering techniques, centroids and distance to centroids act as codebook and codewords respectively, using soft clustering for redundant partitioning. In the following sections, we will detail how we applied these families of methods.

3.1 Codebooks by Sparse Coding

Sparse codewords can be computed as sparse high-dimensional hashes. Sparse hashes offer a number of advantages over binary hashes for search space partitioning: sparse coding techniques are designed to be overcomplete, offer real-valued membership (e.g. representative hash values) and offer control over the sparsity of the solution and thus, redundancy. The steps for generating sparse hashes are:

- compute the dictionary/codebook D from training data;
- use D to create an hash/codeword with s non-zero coefficients and assigned them to the corresponding partitions;
- for search, inspect the s partitions with have non-zero coefficients.

The process for the generation of sparse hashes that follow Eq.1 goals, is to solve the following optimization problem:

$$\arg\min_x \|Dx - y\|_2 \quad \text{subject to} \quad \|x\|_0 \leq s, \tag{3}$$

where $D \in \mathbb{R}^{n \times k}$ is a dictionary, learned from the data, $y \in \mathbb{R}^n$ is the the original vector, $x \in \mathbb{R}^k$ is the sparse hash and s is the sparsity coefficient. Eq. 3 generates an hash with the desired properties, using a previously computed dictionary. Techniques for dictionary computation include K-SVD [1] and Stochastic Gradient Descent techniques. On this paper, we focus a K-SVD inspired method that takes into account the number of documents per bucket.

3.1.1 *KSVD and OMP.*

Dictionary computation requires solving the following optimization problem:

$$\begin{gathered} \arg\min_{D,X} \|DX - Y\|_2 \\ \text{subject to} \\ \|x\|_0 \leq s, \\ \text{for } x \in X \end{gathered} \tag{4}$$

where $D \in \mathbb{R}^{n \times k}$ is a dictionary, learned from the data, $Y \in \mathbb{R}^{m \times n}$ is the the original document vector space, $X \in \mathbb{R}^{m \times k}$ is the sparse hash and s is the sparsity coefficient. Solving for both D and X is computationally hard. KSVD alternatively optimizes the solution for D and X. KSVD updates each dictionary atom iteratively (represented by i), while fixing other atoms $j_{[0,k]} \neq i$.

$$\begin{gathered} \arg\min_{D_i,(x_i)_I} \|D_i(x_i)_I + (E_i)_I - Y\|_F^2 \\ E_i = \sum_{j_{[0,k]} \neq i} \|D_j x_j - Y\|_F^2 \end{gathered} \tag{5}$$

where $\|...\|_F$ is the Frobenius norm. Sparsity is enforced by using only the atoms with non-zero coefficients: I is the set of all index with non-zero coefficients that use atom i for reconstruction.

By fixing j atoms, the value for atom D_i can be computed by finding a rank-1 matrix approximation of E_i, $\hat{E_i}$, and factorizing the result into D_i and x_i.

$$\hat{E_i} = G \sum^{1} V^T \tag{6}$$

This decomposition will yield D_i as the first column of G and x_i as the first column of $V \times \sum^1$.

3.1.2 *Balanced KSVD with OMP.*

KSVD enforces the creation of sparse representations that group similar vectors in the original space on non-zero coefficients. When generating multiple codewords, KSVD will inherently create unbalanced representations, as the dictionary atoms are biased towards the principal directions of the data on the original space. As our goal is to minimize the differences between the number of elements per partition P_j and the mean number of documents per partition $\bar{P}$, we adapted KSVD to reduce the magnitude of dictionary atoms assigned with more documents. The KSVD alternate optimization process is similar to Eq.5; Our adaptation is applied to Eq.6 E decomposition; after the rank-1 approximation, we multiply the G matrix by the penalization factor B:

$$\begin{gathered} \text{balanced } \hat{E_i} = B \times G \sum^{1} V^T \\ B = \frac{1}{\left(\left|P_{j \in [0,k]}\right| + r\right)^e} \end{gathered} \tag{7}$$

where $\left|P_{j \in [0,k]}\right|$ contains the number of documents assigned to partitions j, computed using the previous iteration of the dictionary. e is the parameter to control the magnitude of the penalty and r is a smoothing factor to avoid division by zero for partitions with zero documents. This penalty distorts the generated dictionary atoms, creating non-orthogonal balanced representations. The regularization parameters r and s control the magnitude of this distortion.

3.1.3 *Random dictionary with OMP.*

We can also measure the impact of dictionary learning on the computation of sparse hashes, by testing OMP with a dictionary generated from the Gaussian distribution with zero mean and unit std. deviation.

$$D \in \mathbb{R}^{n \times k} \subset \mathcal{N}(0,1) \tag{8}$$

Random dictionaries show how OMP will cluster data without prior search space information from dictionary computation.

3.2 Codebooks by Soft Quantization

Our quantization process can be seen as a type of soft clustering, where the cluster membership is controlled by a fixed s sparsity factor. Our focus is to measure how well these clusters can represent neighbourhood data in a balanced way, and how using multiple clusters affects this process in an high dimensional feature space. Our clustering process is the following:

- find the centroids
- project the documents to s, redundant clusters
- search the matching cluster posting lists

Consider a set of cluster centroids $C \in \mathbb{R}^{n \times k}$. Our clustering process finds the set of closest centroids $c \in \mathbb{R}^{n \times s} \subset C$, and assigns the Euclidean distances to those centroids as the hash values:

$$\arg\min_c(\|c_i - y\|_2), \text{ for } c_{i \in [0,k]} \in C \text{ ,with } |c| = s$$

$$x_{i \in [0,k]} = \begin{cases} \|c_i - y\|_2, \text{ for } c_i \in c \\ 0, \text{ otherwise} \end{cases} \tag{9}$$

To find the set of centroids that best represent the feature space, we have selected three techniques, random sampling, k-means and fuzzy c-means. Alternative clustering techniques such as DBSCAN do not allow setting the number of clusters and thus, does not meet our desired properties.

Fuzzy c-means clustering [7] techniques extends the assignment of documents to clusters, by keeping membership information to multiple clusters (e.g. ratio of the distance to the centroids). It optimizes the intra-cluster objective function of k-means, combined with membership information, which allows documents to be in more than one clusters. In our preliminary experiments, fuzzy c-means produced very unbalanced clusters: all documents were assigned to only 20 clusters, regardless of the total number of generated centroids (512, 1024, 2048, 4096, 8192). Due to this extreme balance, we did not pursue further experiments using fuzzy c-means.

3.2.1 *k-means centroids.*

k-means is one the most widely applied clustering functions in nearest neighbour search. It tries to find the set of centroids $C \in \mathbb{R}^{n \times k}$ that minimizes the distances of the points to the centroids of their clusters. k-means tends to produce similarly sized clusters, which is a desirable property for our balanced partition goal (i.e.

higher focus on balancing cluster size for better partitioning). The k-means clustering process minimizes the following expression:

$$\arg\min_C \sum_{c_i \in C} \sum_{y_j \in P_i} \left\| c_i - y_j \right\|_2 \tag{10}$$

where $C \in \mathbb{R}^{n \times k}$ is the set of cluster centroids, $P_i, i \in [0, k]$ is the set of documents $y_j \in P$ that are assigned to centroid C_i. The k-means initialization requires the selection of a set of points as the initial centroids. We selected k-means++ [4] centroid initialization, as it selects points that give a good representation of the search space and lead to faster convergence, on a large set of experiments and datasets.

3.2.2 *Random centroids.*

We tested a random sampling technique that selects a random set of points C from the training data Y:

$$C \in \mathbb{R}^{n \times k} \subset Y \tag{11}$$

As with the random dictionary with OMP regression, this technique is a baseline to measure the impact of centroid selection for the creation of evenly balanced partitions.

4 EXPERIMENTS

We have described how we can create over-complete codebooks that generate sparse, high dimensional codewords. To measure how well the proposed methods meet our partitioning and retrieval goals, we will evaluate them from three perspectives:

- **Balanced partitioning**: measure how the tested methods manage to balance the size of the partitions;
- **Inter-partition retrieval**: measure the cumulative impact of searching on more than one partition;
- **Intra-partition retrieval**: measure whether the partitions capture the original space nearest neighbours;

Dataset: We tested the index partitioning methods on the Billion Vectors dataset [18, 19]. It contains 1 million descriptors from two feature types: GIST (960 dimensions) and SIFT features (128 dimensions). The datasets were split into a training, validation and test subsets [1]. We extracted 1000 queries per feature type from the test set. Having two types of features allows us to measure the partitioning impact of multiple dimensionalities and feature distributions.

Metrics: To assess load balancing quality, we measured the number of documents per partition p and the standard deviation σ of partition size versus the mean, median and maximum. We also used standard retrieval quality metrics, averaged over 1000 queries:

- 1-recall@r: average rate of queries for which the 1-nearest neighbor was returned. r changes with the number of candidates inspected.
- %kNN: average percentage of true k nearest neighbours retrieved.

Parameters: Based on preliminary experiments, we found that setting the exponent of the penalty to $c = 2$ and regularization factor to $r = 0.001$ offered the best balance between similarity and even balancing. We set the sparsity coefficient to $s = 10$ for all

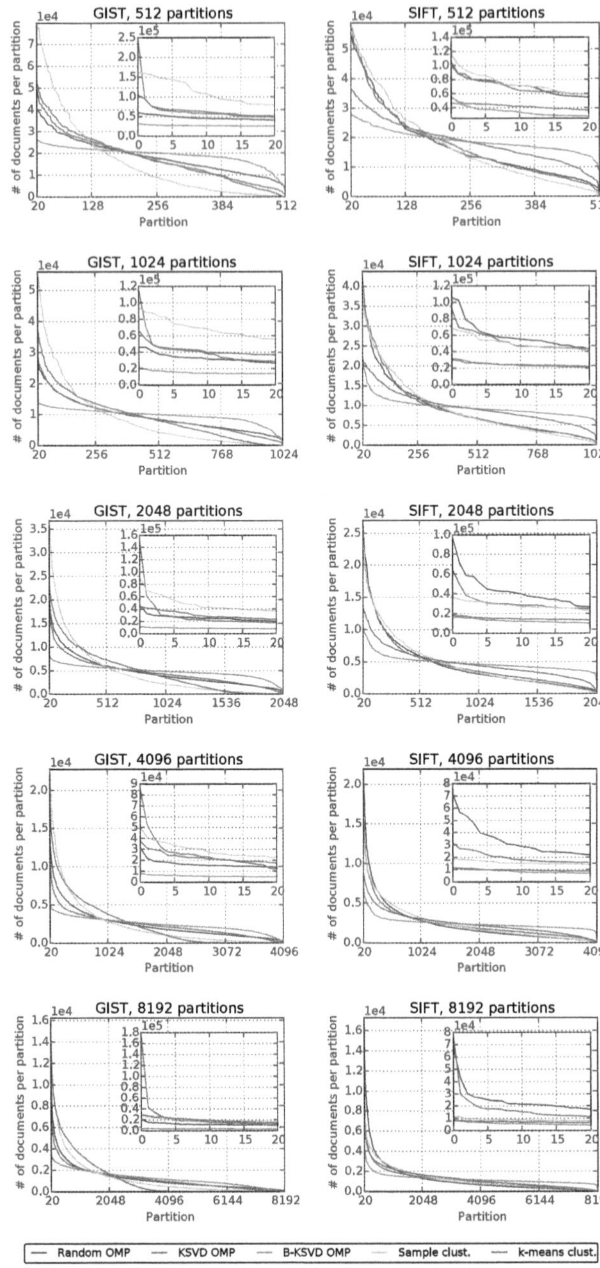

Figure 2: Sorted bucket distribution for multiple feature types and number of partitions. The smaller, inner chart shows the top 20 partition sizes, and the larger chart shows the remaining partition sizes.

algorithms, and varied the codeword size k and thus, number of partitions, (512, 1024, 2048, 4096, 8192).

4.1 Balanced partitioning

We defined balanced partition as the minimization of the differences in the number of documents per partition p (i.e. standard deviation

[1] http://corpus-texmex.irisa.fr/

Table 1: Partition balancing results: Max. is the size of the largest partition (bold values: lowest is best), Med is the size of the median partitions, partition size / 2 (bold values: closest to mean is best), and σ is the standard deviation of the partition sizes (bold values: lowest is best). The Mean value is the same for all methods for a set partition size, as all methods produce solutions with similar sparsity s. Max, Mean Med and σ values are on base 10^3.

	Partitions:	512			1024			2048			4096			8192		
	Mean:	19.5			9.8			4.9			2.4			1.2		
Algorithm	Features	Max	Med	σ	Max	Med	σ	Max	Med	σ	Max	Med	σ	Max	Med	σ
Random OMP	GIST	60.4	17.6	±9.7	46.2	8.2	±6.0	45.6	3.8	±3.9	31.4	1.8	±2.2	21.2	0.8	±1.3
KSVD OMP	GIST	245.9	16.7	±16.4	115.1	8.4	±7.6	148.0	4.3	±4.8	85.1	2.1	±2.6	176.2	0.9	±2.4
B-KSVD OMP	GIST	**33.0**	**20.1**	**±4.2**	**21.5**	**9.9**	**±2.4**	**11.5**	**4.9**	**±1.3**	**8.1**	**2.4**	**±0.9**	**4.5**	**1.1**	**±0.7**
Sample clust.	GIST	160.9	8.9	±27.0	94.3	4.3	±13.7	91.4	2.1	±7.6	50.2	1.0	±3.9	28.8	0.5	±2.1
k-means clust.	GIST	104.4	16.2	±14.9	66.2	8.0	±8.9	43.8	3.5	±5.3	37.6	1.0	±3.4	29.6	0.0	±2.3
Random OMP	SIFT	101.4	13.7	±15.9	106.0	6.7	±10.3	97.6	3.1	±6.0	71.5	1.4	±3.6	67.6	0.7	±2.1
KSVD OMP	SIFT	105.4	14.9	±16.0	91.9	6.5	±9.9	64.5	3.5	±4.8	31.6	1.8	±2.4	78.2	1.0	±1.5
B-KSVD OMP	SIFT	**46.4**	**18.5**	**±4.8**	**31.8**	**9.1**	**±3.0**	**16.5**	**4.6**	**±1.4**	11.8	**2.3**	**±0.8**	**8.3**	**1.1**	**±0.5**
Sample clust.	SIFT	116.6	13.0	±18.2	68.8	6.5	±9.7	36.6	3.3	±4.8	18.7	1.7	±2.4	11.6	0.8	±1.2
k-means clust.	SIFT	55.3	18.4	±8.4	30.0	9.0	±4.4	18.1	4.4	±2.4	**11.6**	2.2	±1.5	8.6	1.0	±1.0

Table 2: Intra-node, cumulative retrieval results for 1% and 10% global search limits (1×10^3 and 10×10^3 candidates per partition, respectively)

	Partitions:	512		1024		2048		4096		8192	
Algorithm	Features	%50NN	1-recall	%50NN	1-recall	%50NN	1-recall	%50NN	1-recall	%50NN	1-recall
					1% limit						
Random OMP	GIST	0.16	0.27	0.16	0.26	0.13	0.20	0.14	0.22	**0.16**	**0.28**
KSVD OMP	GIST	0.13	0.21	0.13	0.20	0.12	0.21	0.10	0.15	0.11	0.19
B-KSVD OMP	GIST	**0.19**	**0.30**	**0.20**	**0.29**	**0.18**	**0.27**	**0.16**	**0.26**	0.13	0.23
Sample clust.	GIST	0.09	0.15	0.16	0.25	0.05	0.09	0.02	0.03	0.03	0.05
k-means clust.	GIST	0.02	0.03	0.03	0.05	0.06	0.10	0.09	0.13	0.04	0.06
Random OMP	SIFT	0.14	0.20	0.21	0.30	0.16	0.23	0.21	0.36	0.19	0.27
KSVD OMP	SIFT	0.21	0.33	0.19	0.33	0.16	**0.24**	0.23	**0.37**	0.23	0.37
B-KSVD OMP	SIFT	0.25	0.40	0.23	**0.38**	**0.17**	**0.24**	0.19	0.27	0.22	0.34
Sample clust.	SIFT	**0.44**	**0.59**	**0.25**	0.37	0.13	0.19	0.07	0.11	0.03	0.05
k-means clust	SIFT	0.03	0.05	0.06	0.10	0.11	0.16	**0.25**	0.35	**0.46**	**0.59**
					10% limit						
Random OMP	GIST	0.34	0.44	0.42	0.56	0.49	0.60	0.53	0.62	0.28	0.41
KSVD OMP	GIST	0.26	0.35	0.29	0.39	0.33	0.47	0.38	0.51	0.41	0.50
B-KSVD OMP	GIST	0.22	0.33	0.28	0.39	0.36	0.50	0.47	0.60	0.57	0.69
Sample clust.	GIST	0.54	0.65	**0.68**	**0.78**	**0.72**	**0.82**	0.37	0.46	0.21	0.28
k-means clust.	GIST	**0.80**	**0.89**	0.44	0.53	0.21	0.27	**0.76**	**0.85**	**0.66**	**0.74**
Random OMP	SIFT	0.43	0.54	0.63	0.75	0.61	0.72	0.56	0.67	0.50	0.66
KSVD OMP	SIFT	0.56	0.69	0.62	0.75	0.65	0.77	0.41	0.52	0.50	0.62
B-KSVD OMP	SIFT	0.44	0.58	0.51	0.64	0.60	0.69	0.67	0.78	0.63	0.74
Sample clust.	SIFT	0.92	0.98	**0.95**	**0.98**	**0.89**	**0.95**	0.69	0.79	0.43	0.51
k-means clust.	SIFT	**0.93**	**0.99**	0.46	0.56	0.84	0.90	**0.96**	**0.99**	**0.95**	**0.99**

of the partition size distribution). For distributed retrieval, balanced partitions minimize the differences in the expected load on the nodes with the matching partitions (i.e. non-zero coefficients), at indexing and query time, as illustrated in Figure 1 (c). Thus, the goal of this experiment is to measure how the selected techniques distribute the documents across partitions, for multiple numbers of partitions and feature types. To create the partitions, documents were assigned to the partitions with corresponding non-zero codeword positions, for each partition method, feature type and number of partitions. This experiment shows the resulting partition sizes.

Figure 2 shows the behaviour of the partitioning algorithms for the GIST and SIFT features (different columns) and number of partitions (different rows). For readability, each chart is divided in two: the smaller chart shows the occupation of the top 20 partitions, where the variation in scale of number of documents is higher. The

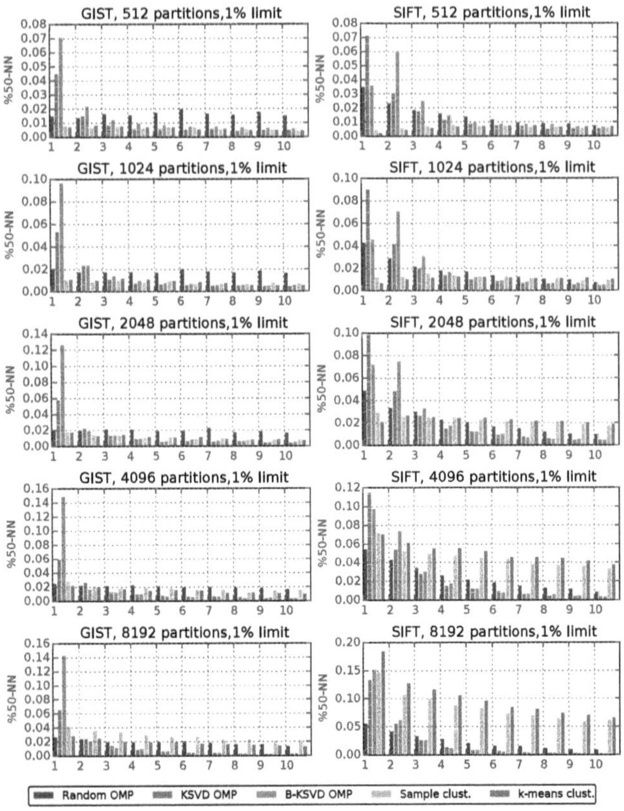

Figure 3: Inter-node partition %50-NN for individual partitions, for multiple feature types and number of partitions

larger chart shows the variation for the remaining partitions (20 to number of partitions k). The X-axis represents the partitions, sorted in descending order of number of indexed documents (i.e. partitions with more documents are to the left). The Y-axis represents the number of documents on that partition. Note that, as the goal is to show the relative differences between partitioning methods, the Y-axis scale is different across charts. Note that the sum of the sizes of the partitions is the same for all partitioning methods (index size $m \times s$). Table 1 shows the detailed std. deviation (σ), larger partition (Max), and median (Med) partition size ($k/2$).

KSVD learns a dictionary with the most prevalent directions of the data in the original space. Combined with OMP greedy atom selection, KSVD sparse representations are highly biased towards principal directions, which is clear on the top 20 charts. B-KSVD's bias managed to counteract KSVD's greediness and generated the most balanced solutions (σ columns on Table 1) The effect is more clear at the edge partitions (i.e. the ones with more documents and the ones with fewer documents): on the top 20 positions, B-KSVD is less affected than KSVD, by the most popular directions of the data; the occupation of the partition at median value is also consistently closer to the expected value (mean) that other methods, meaning the decrease in number of documents is much slower and gradual than the other retrieval methods tested. B-KSVD is also the most stable solution, offering the best balancing properties for all partition sizes and feature types.

k-means performance is greatly affected by feature type. For SIFT features, k-means partitioning balancing is in line with B-KSVD for the top 20 positions, with a faster decay in number of documents on the smaller partitions. For GIST features, the unbalanced distribution is more visible, and appears earlier (top 20).

On this experiment, we also measured the impact of the codebook computation, versus random and sampling techniques. Random dictionary OMP balancing varied greatly for the type of features used: for GIST, it is in line with k-means; for SIFT it has the most unbalanced distribution of all tested methods (e.g. partitions with over 1/8 of the total indexed documents). Sample clustering also shows large unbalances, where larger partitions clustered most of the documents. The large balancing variations for these methods shows that adjusting your dictionary to the data has a large impact on balancing partitions.

In addition to the type of features, the number of partitions impact is clearly visible. The tested partitioning methods are not designed to handle an higher number of partitions, and generates a large number of very small or empty partitions (visible on the left side of X-axis of Figure 2 charts). The exception is B-KSVD, that managed to keep even partitions, regardless of the number of partitions.

These experiment showed how different partitioning methods distribute documents across partitions. B-KSVD countered the greedy nature of regular KSVD and offered the most uniform partitions. On the following sections, we'll show how it affects the retrieval performance.

4.2 Searching redundant codewords

On this section, we will measure the retrieval impact of searching on over-complete partitions. An advantage of real-valued codewords over binary indexes is that codeword values represent document-partition membership likelihood. By having a measure of membership likelihood of documents and queries to partitions, one can prioritize candidate selection at two levels:

Inter-partition search: Table 2 shows the aggregated results for the search process. From each partition, we selected 0.1% and 1% of total index size, for a combined limit of 1% and 10%, respectively.

The advantages of KSVD based methods are clear on the limited search conditions (e.g. inspecting 1% of the index). When using smaller search limits, the reconstruction coefficient represents similarity in the original space better than distance to cluster centroids. For larger limits (10%) and more partitions, k-means and sample clustering methods are able to retrieve a larger set of candidates. Examining Table 2 and other experiments omitted due to space constraints, we concluded that 1-recall results follow the same pattern as %50NN. This means that both method families are able to index the first nearest neighbour at higher rates than the remaining 49 nearest neighbours.

Intra-partition search: On this experiment, we measure the retrieval performance of individual partitions, Figure 3. For each query, we selected 1000 candidates (i.e. 0.1% of total index size) for each corresponding partition, for a combined limit of 1%.

B-KSVD offers the best results on the first partition (i.e. higher membership) for GIST partitions (14% of 50 nearest neighbours, examining, 1000 documents, i.e. 0.1% of the index) The number of nearest neighbours decreases for lower membership partitions. The impact of the remaining partitioning methods is in the order of 2% of the 50 nearest neighbours, which is still an impressive value for 0.1% partition search limit.

For SIFT, the partition results show a different pattern. KSVD and B-KSVD also retrieve the most results on the top membership positions, for all but the 8192 partitions experiments. For larger numbers of partitions, clustering-based solutions offer better results. We reckon that the smaller partitions will mean that the remaining candidates will have an higher probability of being the nearest neighbours.

5 CONCLUSION

On this paper, we proposed balanced over-complete partitioning representations for distributed retrieval. We formalized the requirements to create overcomplete representations, to redundant document indexing, where partitions contain overlapping subsets of data. Parallel processing and redundancy are achieved searching the overcomplete partitions. We proposed representations based on sparse hashing and clustering models, and an adaptation to the KSVD algorithm, balanced KSVD (B-KSVD), that distributes hash values across positions, according to the global distribution.

We showed that computing codebooks that penalise larger partitions, creates more balanced partitions, and a corresponding positive retrieval impact. B-KSVD achieves 38% *1-recall* by inspecting only 1% of the full index, distributed over 10 partitions. We also observed that k-means partitioning performed better with more partitions with higher search limits. In addition, combining these techniques with effective single node retrieval techniques that can use the cluster membership value as an heuristic for search, can improve flexibility and performance of large scale distributed indexes.

ACKNOWLEDGEMENTS

This work has been partially funded by the CMU Portugal research project GoLocal Ref. CMUP-ERI/TIC/0033/2014, by the H2020 ICT project COGNITUS with the grant agreement No 687605 and by the project NOVA LINCS Ref. UID/CEC/04516/2013.

REFERENCES

[1] M. Aharon, M. Elad, and A. Bruckstein. 2006. K-SVD: An Algorithm for Designing Overcomplete Dictionaries for Sparse Representation. *IEEE Trans. on Signal Processing* 54, 11 (2006), 4311–4322.
[2] Mohamed Aly, Mario Munich, and Pietro Perona. 2011. Distributed Kd-Trees for Retrieval from Very Large Image Collections. In *Proc. of BMVC.*
[3] Alexandr Andoni and Piotr Indyk. 2008. Near-optimal Hashing Algorithms for Approximate Nearest Neighbor in High Dimensions. *ACM Commun.* 51, 1 (2008), 117–122.
[4] David Arthur and Sergei Vassilvitskii. 2007. k-means++: The advantages of careful seeding. In *Proc. of ACM-SIAM SODA.* 1027–1035.
[5] Artem Babenko and Victor Lempitsky. 2016. Efficient Indexing of Billion-Scale Datasets of Deep Descriptors. In *Proc. of IEEE CVPR.*
[6] Michal Batko, Fabrizio Falchi, Claudio Lucchese, David Novak, Raffaele Perego, Fausto Rabitti, Jan Sedmidubsky, and Pavel Zezula. 2010. Building a web-scale image similarity search system. *Multimed Tool Appl* 47, 3 (2010), 599–629.
[7] James C. Bezdek. 1981. *Pattern Recognition with Fuzzy Objective Function Algorithms.* Kluwer Academic Publishers, Norwell, MA, USA.
[8] Pedro Borges, André Mourão, and J. Magalhães. 2015. High-Dimensional Indexing by Sparse Approximation. In *ACM ICMR'15.* ACM.
[9] Stefan Büttcher, Charles LA Clarke, and Gordon V Cormack. 2010. *Information retrieval: Implementing and evaluating search engines.* Mit Press.
[10] A. Cherian, S. Sra, V. Morellas, and N. Papanikolopoulos. 2014. Efficient Nearest Neighbors via Robust Sparse Hashing. *IEEE TIP* 23, 8 (2014), 3646–3655.
[11] O. Chum, J. Philbin, and A. Zisserman. 2008. Near Duplicate Image Detection: min-Hash and tf-idf Weighting. In *Proc. of BMVC.*
[12] Mayur Datar, Nicole Immorlica, Piotr Indyk, and Vahab S. Mirrokni. 2004. Locality-sensitive hashing scheme based on p-stable distributions. In *Proc. of SCG.* ACM, 253–262.
[13] Jeffrey Dean and Sanjay Ghemawat. 2008. MapReduce: Simplified Data Processing on Large Clusters. *Commun. ACM* 51, 1 (2008), 107–113.
[14] Martin Ester, Hans-Peter Kriegel, Jrg Sander, and Xiaowei Xu. 1996. A Density-Based Algorithm for Discovering Clusters in Large Spatial Databases with Noise. In *Proc. of KDD.* 226–231.
[15] Kristen Grauman and Rob Fergus. 2013. *Machine Learning for Computer Vision.* Springer Berlin Heidelberg, Chapter Learning Binary Hash Codes for Large-Scale Image Search, 49–87. DOI: http://dx.doi.org/10.1007/978-3-642-28661-2_3
[16] G. E. Hinton and R. R. Salakhutdinov. 2006. Reducing the Dimensionality of Data with Neural Networks. *Science* 313, 5786 (2006), 504–507. DOI: http://dx.doi.org/10.1126/science.1127647
[17] A. E. Hoerl and R. W. Kennard. 2004. *Ridge Regression.* John Wiley and Sons, Inc. DOI: http://dx.doi.org/10.1002/0471667196.ess2280
[18] Hervé Jégou, M. Douze, and C. Schmid. 2011. Product Quantization for Nearest Neighbor Search. *IEEE Trans. on PAMI* 33, 1 (2011), 117–128. DOI: http://dx.doi.org/10.1109/TPAMI.2010.57
[19] H. Jégou, R. Tavenard, M. Douze, and L. Amsaleg. 2011. Searching in one billion vectors: re-rank with source coding. *ArXiv e-prints* (2011). arXiv:cs.IR/1102.3828
[20] Rongrong Ji, Ling-Yu Duan, Jie Chen, Lexing Xie, Hongxun Yao, and Wen Gao. 2013. Learning to Distribute Vocabulary Indexing for Scalable Visual Search. *IEEE Trans. on Multimedia* 15, 1 (2013), 153–166. DOI: http://dx.doi.org/10.1109/TMM.2012.2225035
[21] Y. Kalantidis and Y. Avrithis. 2014. Locally Optimized Product Quantization for Approximate Nearest Neighbor Search. In *Proc. of IEEE CVPR.* 2329–2336. DOI: http://dx.doi.org/10.1109/CVPR.2014.298
[22] Anagha Kulkarni and Jamie Callan. 2010. Document Allocation Policies for Selective Searching of Distributed Indexes. In *Proc. of ACM CIKM (CIKM '10).* 449–458. DOI: http://dx.doi.org/10.1145/1871437.1871497
[23] Michael S. Lewicki and Terrence J. Sejnowski. 2000. Learning Overcomplete Representations. *Neural Comput.* 12, 2 (Feb. 2000), 337–365. DOI: http://dx.doi.org/10.1162/089976600300015826
[24] Zhen Li, Huazhong Ning, Liangliang Cao, Tong Zhan, Yihong Gong, and Thomas S. Huang. 2011. Learning to Search Efficiently in High Dimensions. In *Neural Information Processing Systems.*
[25] Stuart Lloyd. 1982. Least squares quantization in PCM. *IEEE Trans. on Information Theory* 28, 2 (1982), 129–137.
[26] Joao Magalhaes and Stefan Rueger. 2007. High-dimensional Visual Vocabularies for Image Retrieval. In *ACM SIGIR'07.* ACM, New York, NY, USA, 815–816. DOI: http://dx.doi.org/10.1145/1277741.1277923
[27] Diana Moise, Denis Shestakov, Gylfi Gudmundsson, and Laurent Amsaleg. 2013. Indexing and Searching 100M Images with Map-reduce. In *ICMR'13.* 17–24. DOI: http://dx.doi.org/10.1145/2461466.2461470
[28] André Mourão and João Magalhães. 2015. Scalable Multimodal Search with Distributed Indexing by Sparse Hashing. In *ACM ICMR'15.* ACM, New York, NY, USA, 283–290. DOI: http://dx.doi.org/10.1145/2671188.2749310
[29] Marius Muja and David G. Lowe. 2014. Scalable Nearest Neighbor Algorithms for High Dimensional Data. *IEEE Trans. on PAMI* 36 (2014).
[30] Bruno A Olshausen and David J Field. 1996. Emergence of simple-cell receptive field properties by learning a sparse code for natural images. *Nature* 381, 6583 (1996), 607–609.
[31] Y. Pati, R. Rezaiifar, and P. Krishnaprasad. 1993. Orthogonal Matching Pursuit : recursive function approximation with application to wavelet decomposition. In *Asilomar Conf. on Signals, Systems and Computer.*
[32] Maxim Raginsky and Svetlana Lazebnik. 2009. Locality-sensitive binary codes from shift-invariant kernels. In *NIPS.* 1509–1517.
[33] Romain Tavenard, Hervé Jégou, and Laurent Amsaleg. 2011. Balancing clusters to reduce response time variability in large scale image search. In *International Workshop on Content-Based Multimedia Indexing (CBMI 2011).* Madrid, Spain. http://hal.inria.fr/inria-00576886 QUAERO.
[34] Robert Tibshirani. 1994. Regression Shrinkage and Selection Via the Lasso. *Journal of the Royal Statistical Society, Series B* 58 (1994), 267–288.
[35] A. Torralba, R. Fergus, and W.T. Freeman. 2008. 80 Million Tiny Images: A Large Data Set for Nonparametric Object and Scene Recognition. *IEEE Trans. on PAMI* 30, 11 (Nov 2008), 1958–1970. DOI: http://dx.doi.org/10.1109/TPAMI.2008.128
[36] Roger Weber, Hans-Jörg Schek, and Stephen Blott. 1998. A Quantitative Analysis and Performance Study for Similarity-Search Methods in High-Dimensional Spaces. In *Proc. of VLDB.* 194–205.
[37] Yair Weiss, Antonio Torralba, and Robert Fergus. 2008. Spectral Hashing. *NIPS* 9, 1 (2008), 6.
[38] Z. Yang, S. i. Kamata, and A. Ahrary. 2009. NIR: Content based image retrieval on cloud computing. In *Proc of ICIS,* Vol. 3. 556–559.
[39] Hui Zou and Trevor Hastie. 2005. Regularization and variable selection via the Elastic Net. *Journal of the Royal Statistical Society, Series B* 67 (2005), 301–320.

Deep Supervised Hashing for Multi-Label and Large-Scale Image Retrieval

Dayan Wu
Institute of Information Engineering, Chinese Academy of Sciences
School of Cyber Security, University of Chinese Academy of Sciences
Beijing, China
wudayan@iie.ac.cn

Zheng Lin
Institute of Information Engineering, Chinese Academy of Sciences
Beijing, China
linzheng@iie.ac.cn

Bo Li*
Institute of Information Engineering, Chinese Academy of Sciences
Beijing, China
libo@iie.ac.cn

Mingzhen Ye
Institute of Information Engineering, Chinese Academy of Sciences
Beijing, China
yemingzhen@iie.ac.cn

Weiping Wang
Institute of Information Engineering, Chinese Academy of Sciences
Beijing, China
wangweiping@iie.ac.cn

ABSTRACT

One of the most challenging tasks in large-scale multi-label image retrieval is to map images into binary codes while preserving multilevel semantic similarity. Recently, several deep supervised hashing methods have been proposed to learn hash functions that preserve multilevel semantic similarity with deep convolutional neural networks. However, these triplet label based methods try to preserve the ranking order of images according to their similarity degrees to the queries while not putting direct constraints on the distance between the codes of very similar images. Besides, the current evaluation criteria are not able to measure the performance of existing hashing methods on preserving fine-grained multilevel semantic similarity. To tackle these issues, we propose a novel Deep Multilevel Semantic Similarity Preserving Hashing (DMSSPH) method to learn compact similarity-preserving binary codes for the huge body of multi-label image data with deep convolutional neural networks. In our approach, we make the best of the supervised information in the form of pairwise labels to maximize the discriminability of output binary codes. Extensive evaluations conducted on several benchmark datasets demonstrate that the proposed method significantly outperforms the state-of-the-art supervised and unsupervised hashing methods at the accuracies of top returned images, especially for shorter binary codes. Meanwhile, the proposed method shows better performance on preserving fine-grained multilevel semantic similarity according to the results under the Jaccard coefficient based evaluation criteria we propose.

*Corresponding author

ICMR '17, June 6–9, 2017, Bucharest, Romania

DOI: http://dx.doi.org/10.1145/3078971.3078989

CCS CONCEPTS

•Information systems →Image search;

KEYWORDS

Multi-Label Image Retrieval; Deep Learning

ACM Reference format:
Dayan Wu, Zheng Lin, Bo Li, Mingzhen Ye, and Weiping Wang. 2017. Deep Supervised Hashing for Multi-Label and Large-Scale Image Retrieval. In *Proceedings of ICMR '17, June 6–9, 2017, Bucharest, Romania,* , 9 pages.
DOI: http://dx.doi.org/10.1145/3078971.3078989

1 INTRODUCTION

With the explosive growth of images on the web, much attention has been devoted to the nearest neighbor search via hashing methods. In this paper, we focus on deep supervised hashing for multi-label image data, an emerging stream of hashing methods that learn multilevel semantic similarity-preserving hash functions to encode input multi-label images into binary codes.

Deep supervised hashing methods try to perform simultaneous feature learning and hash-code learning with deep neural networks, which have shown better performance than traditional hashing methods with hand-crafted features. By leveraging supervised information, the output binary codes of deep supervised hashing methods can preserve semantic similarity between images.

However, most of these hashing methods aim at preserving simple binary semantic similarity (i.e. similar or dissimilar), which is not scalable in multi-label image retrieval [23]. Recently, several deep supervised hashing methods [10] [23] are proposed to learn hash functions that preserve multilevel semantic similarity (e.g. very similar, normally similar and dissimilar). More specifically, DSRH in [23] tries to preserve multilevel semantic similarity using a ranking list which decodes the multilevel similarity information, and IAH in [10] focuses on designing a deep architecture that learns instance-aware image representations for multi-label images. By using weighted triplet loss functions, extended from triplet loss functions designed for single-label images, DSRH and IAH achieve the goal of preserving multilevel semantic similarity between multi-label images. However, the weighted triplet loss functions focuses on preserving the correct order of images according to their similarity degrees to the queries, which puts no direct constraints on the distance between the codes of very similar images, indicating a room for improvement on the accuracies of top returned images. Besides, when the codes get shorter the overall retrieval performance slides down rapidly due to the quick decline of discriminability. Moreover, the traditional evaluation criteria can not measure the performance of the existing hashing methods on preserving fine-grained multilevel semantic similarity.

To address the above problems, we introduce a novel framework based on deep learning model for constructing hash functions that preserve multilevel similarity between multi-label images in the semantic space, named Deep Multilevel Semantic Similarity Preserving Hashing (DMSSPH). An overview of the proposed framework is illustrated in Figure 1. Here we use deep convolutional neural network (CNN) [8] to construct hash functions to learn directly from images, which provides much richer semantic information than the hand-crafted features. Meanwhile, a loss function is elaborately designed to maximize the discriminability of the output space by encoding the supervised information from the input image pairs, and simultaneously imposing regularization on the real-valued outputs to approximate the desired discrete values. To further compare the effectiveness of the existing methods on preserving fine-grained multilevel semantic similarity, we adopt the Jaccard coefficient based similarity measurement proposed in [22] and further propose the Jaccard coefficient based evaluation criteria. Compared with the existing methods, DMSSPH obtains much higher accuracies of top returned images, especially for shorter codes, which means the top returned images in our method are much more similar to the query images in the semantic space. Meanwhile, DMSSPH is better at preserving fine-grained multilevel semantic similarity according to the results under the Jaccard coefficient based evaluation criteria. In general, the contributions of this study can be summarized as follows:

(1) We propose a novel CNN model based framework, named DMSSPH, for learning hash functions that preserve multilevel semantic similarity between multi-label images. To the best of our knowledge, DMSSPH is the first pairwise label based deep supervised hashing method which can encode multi-label images to compact binary codes with their multilevel semantic similarity preserved.
(2) We adopt the semantic similarity measurement proposed in [22] and further propose the Jaccard coefficient based evaluation criteria. With the newly proposed evaluation criteria, we can give further comparisons of the proposed method with the existing methods on the effectiveness of preserving fine-grained multilevel semantic similarity.
(3) Experimental results under the traditional evaluation criteria demonstrate that the proposed method significantly improves the accuracies of top returned images, especially for shorter codes. Experimental results under the Jaccard coefficient based evaluation criteria prove that our method is better at preserving fine-grained multilevel semantic similarity.

The rest of the paper is organised as follows: Related work is briefly discussed in Section 2. Section 3 describes DMSSPH in detail. Section 4 extensively evaluates the proposed method on three multi-label image datasets. Finally, Section 5 concludes this paper.

2 RELATED WORK

Hashing methods can be roughly classified into two categories: data-independent methods and data-dependent methods. Here we mainly discuss data-dependent methods preserving the semantic structure which this paper focuses on. Here are some representative examples in this category. Iterative quantization with canonical correlation analysis (CCA-ITQ) [3] utilizes CCA with labels to reduce the dimensionality of input data and binarizes the outcome through minimizing the quantization error, where only the pointwise label information is exploited to guide hash function learning. Minimal loss hashing (MLH) [16] and its extension learn hash codes by minimizing the loss between the learned Hamming distance and the quantization error. Semi-supervised hashing (SSH) [18] minimizes an empirical error over the labeled pairs of points and makes hash codes balanced and uncorrelated to avoid overfitting. Supervised discrete hashing (SDH) [17] is proposed to directly optimize the binary codes to overcome the shortcomings of relaxation, and achieves improved retrieval performance.

While the hashing methods mentioned before have certainly achieved success to some extent, they all use hand-crafted visual features (e.g. SIFT), which cannot capture the semantic information beneath the drastic appearance variations in real-world data and thus limit the retrieval accuracy of the learned binary codes. To tackle this issue, most recently, several CNN-based hashing methods [14] [20] [13] [22] [9] [21] [11] [12] are proposed to learn image representations together with binary codes using the promising CNNs. [9] [22] enforce the network to learn binary-like outputs that preserve the semantic relations of image-triplets; [20] trains a CNN to fit the binary codes computed from the pairwise similarity matrix; [13] [21] train the model with a binary-like hidden layer for image classification tasks. [14] [11] try to incorporate CNN model into hash functions to learn binary codes with pairwise labels. However, the above methods can hardly deal with more complex multilevel semantic similarity between multi-label images. To tackle the issue, [10] and [23] are proposed. [23] tries to learn hash functions that preserve multilevel semantic similarity using a ranking list which decodes the multilevel similarity information. [10] focuses on designing a deep architecture that learns instance-aware image representations for multi-label images. By using weighted triplet loss functions, [10] and [23] achieve the goal of preserving multilevel semantic similarity between multi-label images. However, the weighted loss functions have no strong constraints on the distance between codes of very similar images, indicating a room for improvement on the accuracies of top returned images which are the focus of most users. Besides, they are not good at preserving fine-grained multilevel semantic similarity due to the coarse-grained definition of semantic similarity between multi-label images.

3 THE PROPOSED APPROACH

A hash function $h : R^M \rightarrow \{-1, 1\}$ is a mapping that projects a M-dimentional input into a binary code. Assume we are given a set

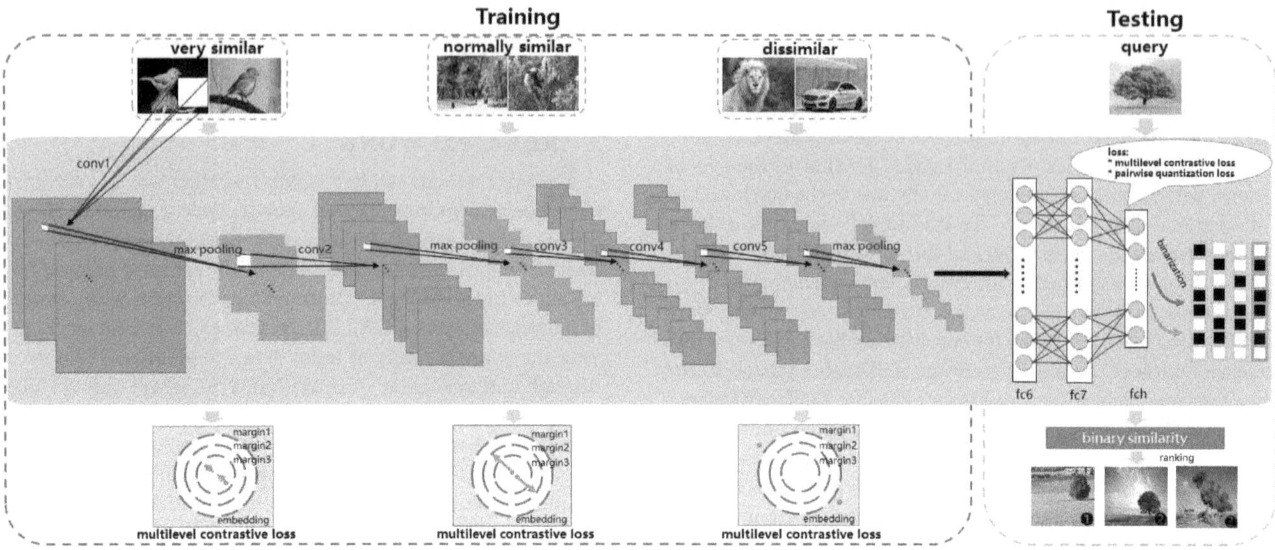

Figure 1: Overview of the proposed framework. The input to the proposed framework is in the form of two-tuples, i.e., very similar images, normally similar images and dissimilar images. Through the proposed architecture, the image tuples are first encoded into a pairwise of image feature vectors by five convolution layers (conv1-con5) and two fully-connected layers (fc6-fc7). Then each image vector in the two-tuple is converted to a hash code by a hash layer (fch). After that, these hash codes are used in a multilevel contrastive loss that aims to preserve multilevel similarities on images and a quantization loss that aim to obtain binary-like codes. Binary codes are obtained by quantizing the network outputs of images.

of class labels $L = \{L_1, L_2, ..., L_c\}$ and a data set $D = \{x_n\}_{n=1}^{N}$ where each data $x \in R^M$ is associated with a set of class labels $l \subseteq L$, we aim to learn a set of hash functions $h(x) = [h_1(x), h_2(x), ..., h_k(x)]$ which generate k-bits binary codes ($k \ll M$) while preserving sematic structure of data points with multiple labels.

3.1 Deep Hash Functions

We construct hash functions through incorporating the CNN model whose architecture is similar to the one proposed in [8], as shown in Figure 1. A deep feature representation is computed by forward propagating a mean-subtracted 227×227 image through five convolutional layers and two fully connected layers, and then fed into the last hash layer to generate a compact binary code. Accordingly, our deep hash function is defined as:

$$\begin{aligned} h(x; w) &= sign(f(x)) \\ f(x; w) &= w^T f'(x) \end{aligned} \tag{1}$$

where w denotes weights in the hash layer, $f'(.)$ denotes feature vectors from the outputs of the last full connected layers (fc7). Therefore, k-bits binary codes can be obtained through k such deep hash functions $h(x; w) = [h_1(x; w), h_2(x; w), ..., h_k(x; w)]$.

3.2 Loss Function

As mentioned above, our goal is to learn K deep hash functions which are used to generate K-bits binary codes while preserving multilevel sematic similarity between multi-label images. For this purpose, the codes of very similar images should be as close as possible, while the codes of normally similar images should be a certain distance away and that of dissimilar images being far away. Based on this objective, the loss function is naturally designed to differ the desired distance between the codes of two images according to their similarity degrees.

As shown in Figure 1, the proposed network is similar to the the Siamese structure [4], and an intuitive way to train the network is to adopt the loss function in a contrastive loss form. However, the conventional contrastive loss function doesn't apply to multi-label images because the similarity relationship between them is not binary. To this end, we extend the conventional contrastive loss function to multilevel contrastive loss function. Specifically, for a pair of images I_1, I_2 and their associated class label sets l_1, l_2, we define $n_1 = |l_1|$ which denotes the number of labels in l_1 and $n_2 = |l_1 \cap l_2|$ which denotes the number of shared labels in l_1 and l_2. Obviously $n_2 \leq n_1$. Further, we define $y = 0$ if $n_1 = n_2$, and $y = 1$ otherwise. The multilevel contrastive loss function is defined as:

$$\begin{aligned} L(I_1, I_2, n_1, n_2, y, m) &= \frac{1}{2}(1-y) D_H(h(I_1; w), h(I_2; w)) \\ &+ \frac{1}{2} y \max\left(m\left(\frac{n_1 - n_2}{n_1}\right) - D_H(h(I_1; w), h(I_2; w)), 0\right) \\ s.t. \quad & h(I_j; w) \in \{+1, -1\}^k, j \in \{1, 2\} \end{aligned} \tag{2}$$

where $D_H(\cdot, \cdot)$ denotes the Hamming distance between two binary vectors, and $m > 0$ is a margin threshold parameter. The first term punishes very similar ($l_1 \subseteq l_2$) images mapped to different binary codes, and the second term punishes normally similar or dissimialr images mapped to close binary codes when their Hamming distance falls below a certain margin threshold determined by their similarity degrees. Specifically, we claim I_1 and I_2 are dissimilar if they share no class labels (i.e. $n_2 = 0$), and we punish them as long as the margin between their binary codes is within the largest margin m.

Table 1: Configurations of the proposed network

Layer	Configurations
conv1	filter 96 × 11 × 11, stride 4 × 4, pad 0, LRN, pool 3 × 3
conv2	filter 256 × 5 × 5, stride 1 × 1, pad 2, LRN, pool 3 × 3
conv3	filter 384 × 3 × 3, stride 1 × 1, pad 1
conv4	filter 384 × 3 × 3, stride 1 × 1, pad 1
conv5	filter 256 × 3 × 3, stride 1 × 1, pad 1, pool 3 × 3
fc6	4096
fc7	4096
fch	k

For images that share at least one class label but not all labels (i.e. $0 < n_2 < n_1$), we treat them as normally similar images.

Suppose that there are N training pairs randomly selected from the training images $\{(I_{i,1}, I_{i,2}, n_{i,1}, n_{i,2}, y_i) \,|i = 1, 2, ..., N\}$, our goal is to minimize the overall loss function:

$$\mathcal{L} = \sum_{i=1}^{N} L\left(I_{i,1}, I_{i,2}, n_{i,1}, n_{i,2}, y_i, m_i\right) \tag{3}$$

3.3 Relaxation

The problem in Eqn.(2) is a discrete optimization, which is hard to solve. A commonly used relaxation method is to utilize *sigmoid* or *tanh* function to approximate the thresholding procedure. Nevertheless, such non-linear functions would inevitably slow down or even restrain the convergence of the network [8]. Unlike the normal relaxation methods, we impose the regularizer proposed in [14] on the real-valued network outputs to approach the desired discrete values (+1,-1). Besides, we replace the Hamming distance in Eqn.(2) by Euclidean distance, which is a normal relaxation trick for ease of optimization, then Eqn.(2) can be transformed to:

$$\begin{aligned} L_r(I_1, I_2, n_1, n_2, y, m) &= \frac{1}{2}(1-y)\,||f(I_1;w) - f(I_2;w)||_2^2 \\ &+ \frac{1}{2} y \max\left(m\left(\frac{n_1 - n_2}{n_1}\right) - ||f(I_1;w) - f(I_2;w)||_2^2, 0\right) \\ &+ \alpha\left(|||f(I_1;w)| - \mathbf{1}||_1 + |||f(I_2;w)| - \mathbf{1}||_1\right) \end{aligned} \tag{4}$$

where $\mathbf{1}$ is a vector of all ones, $||\cdot||_1$ is the L1-norm of vector, $|\cdot|$ is the element-wise absolute value operation, and α is a weight parameter that controls the strength of the regularizer.

Substituting Eqn.(4) into Eqn.(3), we rewrite the final relaxed loss function as follows:

$$\begin{aligned} \mathcal{L}_r = \sum_{i=1}^{N}\{ &\frac{1}{2}(1-y_i)\,||f(I_{i,1};w) - f(I_{i,2};w)\,||_2^2 \\ &+ \frac{1}{2} y_i \max\left(m_i\left(\frac{n_{i,1} - n_{i,2}}{n_{i,1}}\right) - ||f(I_{i,1};w) - f(I_{i,2};w)\,||_2^2, 0\right) \\ &+ \alpha\left(|||f(I_{i,1};w)\,| - \mathbf{1}||_1 + |||f(I_{i,2};w)\,| - \mathbf{1}||_1\right)\} \end{aligned} \tag{5}$$

3.4 Learning

We use back-propagation algorithm with mini-batch gradient descent method to train the network. Thus the gradients of Eqn.(5) w.r.t. $f(I_{i,j};w), \forall i, j$ need to be computed. Considering max operation and the absolute value operation in the objective function is non-differentiable at some certain points, we use subgradients instead, and define subgradients to be 1 at these points. For the sake of concision, we denote $f_{i,j}$ as $f\left(I_{i,j};w\right)$. The subgradients of the first two terms of Eqn.(5) and that of the regularizer are respectively written as:

$$\begin{aligned} \frac{\partial Term_1}{\partial f_{i,j}} &= (-1)^{j+1}(1-y_i)\left(f_{i,1} - f_{i,2}\right) \\ \frac{\partial Term_2}{\partial f_{i,j}} &= \begin{cases} (-1)^j\, y_i\left(f_{i,1} - f_{i,2}\right) & ||f_{i,1} - f_{i,2}||_2^2 < m_i\left(\frac{n_{i,1} - n_{i,2}}{n_{i,1}}\right) \\ 0 & \text{otherwise} \end{cases} \\ \frac{\partial Regularizer}{\partial f_{i,j}} &= \alpha\delta\left(f_{i,j}\right) \end{aligned} \tag{6}$$

where

$$\delta(x) = \begin{cases} 1 & -1 \le x \le 0 \; or \; x \ge 1 \\ 0 & \text{otherwise} \end{cases} \tag{7}$$

is applied on each element.

With the computed subgradients over mini-batches, the rest of the back-propagation algorithm can be done in standard manner.

3.5 Implementation Details

Our method is implemented with Caffe[1] [7]. The network structure is illustrated in Figure.1, and the detailed configurations of the network is shown in Table 1. All the convolution layers and the first two fully connected layers are equipped with the ReLU [15].

During training, the batch size is set to 32, the momentum to 0.9, and the weight decay to 0.004. Similar to [14], the initial margin threshold parameter margin $m*$ is heuristically set to $m* = 2k$ to encourage the codes of dissimilar images to differ in no less than $\frac{k}{2}$ bits. Then $m*$ is slightly adjusted to $m = (\lfloor \frac{m*}{4n_1} \rfloor + 1) \times 4n_1$ to encourage the codes of normally simialr images sharing $n_1 - t$ $(0 < t < n_1)$ class labels to differ in no less than $\frac{mt}{4n_1}$ bits.

We evaluate the retrieval peformances of DMSSPH when setting $\alpha = \{0.1, 0.01, 0.001\}$ respectively. Experimental results show that in most cases, the best retrieval performances are obtained when setting $\alpha = 0.01$, therefore we empirically set $\alpha = 0.01$ in the following experiments. Note that the value of α in [14] is set to 0.01 too.

To make better use of computational resources and storage space, we propose to generate image pairs online by exploiting all the unique pairs in each mini-batch. To cover those image pairs across batches, after each epoch we shuffle the whole training set.

4 EXPERIMENTS

4.1 Datasets

We test the proposed hashing method on three multi-label benchmark datasets, i.e., VOC2007 [1], VOC2012 [1] and MIRFLICKR-25K [5].

[1] http://caffe.berkeleyvision.org/

Table 2: Comparison of NDCG@100, ACG@100 and weighted mAP w.r.t. different number of bits on three datasets.

Methods	VOC 2007				VOC 2012				MIRFLICKR 25K			
	8 bits	16bits	24bits	32bits	8 bits	16bits	24bits	32bits	8 bits	16bits	24bits	32bits
NDCG@100												
DMSSPH	**0.5384**	**0.5965**	**0.6232**	**0.6353**	**0.5309**	**0.5939**	**0.6143**	**0.6309**	**0.4057**	**0.4648**	**0.4828**	**0.4952**
IAH	0.4015	0.5247	0.5708	0.5983	0.4025	0.5354	0.5873	0.6017	0.3123	0.4340	0.4735	0.4915
DSRH	0.3625	0.4586	0.4982	0.5320	0.3568	0.4557	0.5186	0.5482	0.3129	0.4073	0.4452	0.4690
ITQ+CNN	0.2995	0.4136	0.4245	0.4133	0.3526	0.3846	0.4278	0.4346	0.3062	0.3394	0.3804	0.3714
SH+CNN	0.3867	0.4205	0.4160	0.4104	0.4043	0.4032	0.4064	0.4028	0.2951	0.3568	0.3786	0.3817
LSH+CNN	0.2423	0.3305	0.3312	0.3584	0.2286	0.2811	0.2880	0.3283	0.2419	0.3217	0.3389	0.3526
ACG@100												
DMSSPH	**0.6791**	**0.7326**	**0.7595**	**0.7728**	**0.6406**	**0.6965**	**0.7161**	**0.7339**	**2.2349**	2.3973	2.4344	2.4716
IAH	0.5504	0.6723	0.7176	0.7448	0.5337	0.6600	0.6956	0.7163	2.1670	**2.4644**	**2.5764**	**2.6273**
DSRH	0.5101	0.6066	0.6441	0.6705	0.4829	0.5840	0.6388	0.6641	2.0122	2.3667	2.4725	2.5252
ITQ+CNN	0.4141	0.5242	0.5242	0.4960	0.4510	0.4631	0.4964	0.4994	1.9254	1.9828	2.0192	1.9276
SH+CNN	0.5101	0.5132	0.4921	0.4809	0.4987	0.4537	0.4513	0.4455	1.8106	1.8803	1.8889	1.8793
LSH+CNN	0.3335	0.4191	0.4017	0.4364	0.2931	0.3195	0.3297	0.3748	1.5112	1.7588	1.8052	1.9256
weighted mAP												
DMSSPH	**0.5881**	**0.6429**	**0.6744**	**0.6863**	**0.5532**	**0.6128**	**0.6334**	**0.6554**	1.7238	1.8474	1.8738	1.9040
IAH	0.5095	0.6094	0.6482	0.6732	0.4880	0.5972	0.6325	0.6518	1.7703	1.9115	1.9686	2.0004
DSRH	0.4723	0.5568	0.5902	0.6195	0.4415	0.5294	0.5831	0.6068	**1.7814**	**1.9511**	**2.0016**	**2.0302**
ITQ+CNN	0.3241	0.4108	0.4159	0.3926	0.3472	0.3646	0.4013	0.3934	1.4959	1.4731	1.5107	1.4762
SH+CNN	0.3900	0.4024	0.3903	0.3831	0.3840	0.3551	0.3501	0.3435	1.3606	1.4092	1.4071	1.3873
LSH+CNN	0.2972	0.3503	0.3368	0.3523	0.2566	0.2743	0.2776	0.3060	1.2969	1.4462	1.4468	1.5017

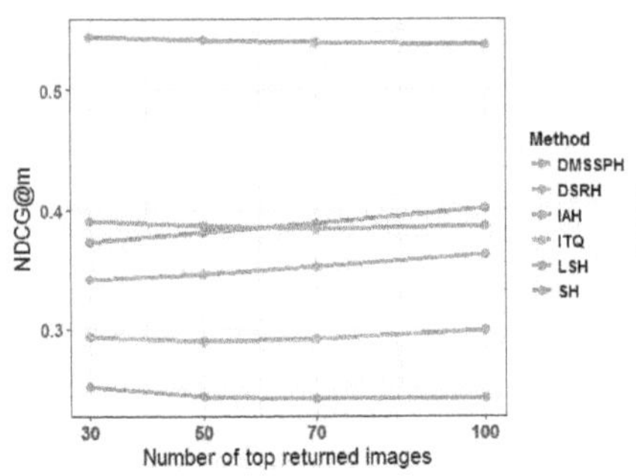

(a) VOC2007

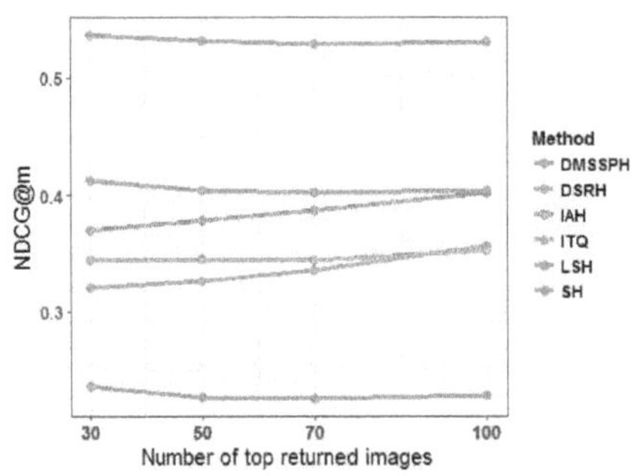

(b) VOC2012

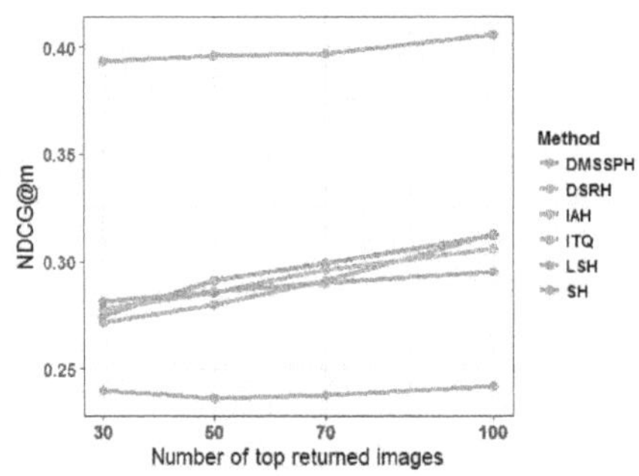

(c) MIRFLICKR

Figure 2: NDCG curves with 8 bits w.r.t. different numbers of top returned samples.

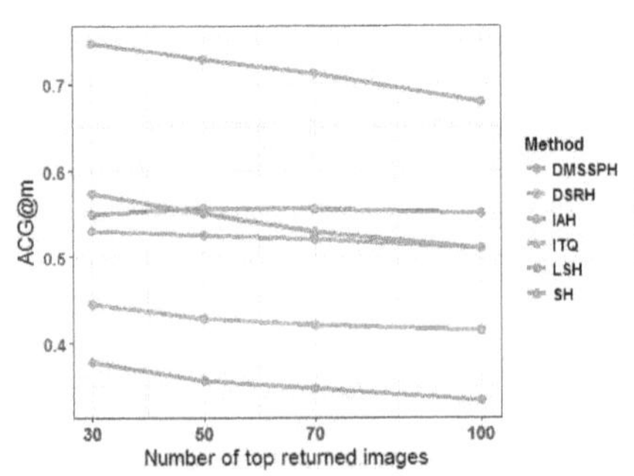

(a) VOC2007

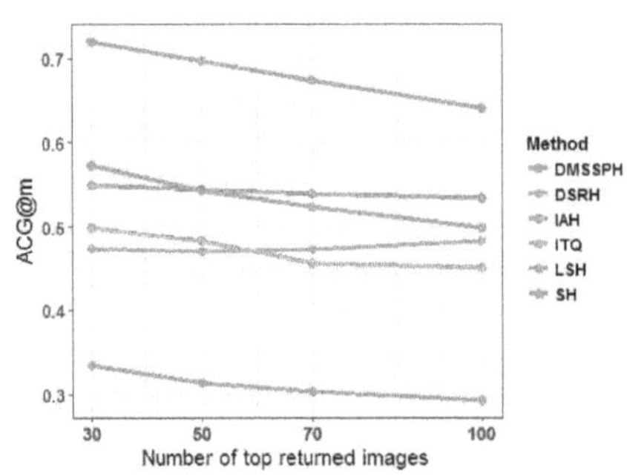

(b) VOC2012

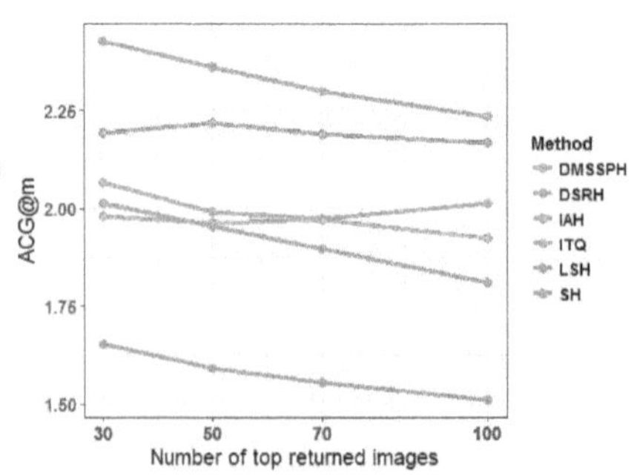

(c) MIRFLICKR

Figure 3: ACG curves with 8 bits w.r.t. different numbers of top returned samples.

VOC 2007 consists of 9,963 multi-label images which are collected from Flickr. There are 20 object classes in this dataset. On average, each image is annotated with 1.5 labels.

VOC 2012 consists of 22,531 multi-label images in 20 classes. Since the ground truth labels of the test images are not available, in our experiments, we only use 11,540 images from its training and validation set.

MIRFLICKR-25K consists of 25,000 multi-label images downloaded from Flickr. There are 38 classes in this dataset. Each image has 4.7 labels on average.

In each dataset, we randomly select 2,000 images as the test query set, and the rest images are used as training samples.

4.2 Evaluation Criteria

Following the previous work, the evaluation metrics used are: Normalized Discounted Cumulative Gain (NDCG) [6], Average Cumulative Gain (ACG) [6], and weighted mean Average Precision (weighted mAP) [23].

NDCG is a popular evaluation metric in information retrieval. Given a query image, the DCG score at the position m is defined as:

$$DCG@m = \sum_{j=1}^{m} \frac{2^{r(j)} - 1}{\log (j+1)} \tag{8}$$

where $r(j)$ denotes the similarity between the j-th position image and the query image, which is defined as:

$$r(j) = |l_q \cap l_j| \tag{9}$$

where l_q denotes the label set of the query image and l_j denotes the label set of the j-th position image. Then, the NDCG score at the position m can be calculated by $NDCG@m = \frac{DCG@m}{Z_m}$, where Z_m is the maximum value of $DCG@m$.

$ACG@m$ represents the sum of similarities between the query image and each of the top m retrieved images, which can be calculated by:

$$ACG@m = \sum_{j=1}^{m} \frac{r(j)}{m} \tag{10}$$

mAP is the mean of average precision for each query. Considering the multilevel semantic similarity relationship between multi-label images, we compute a weighted mAP using ACG:

$$mAP_w = \frac{1}{Q} \sum_{q=1}^{Q} AP_w(q) \tag{11}$$

$$AP_w(q) = \frac{\sum_{j=1}^{M} \prod (r(j) > 0) \, ACG@j}{M_{r>0}} \tag{12}$$

where Q is the number of test queries, M is the size of test query set, $\prod(.)$ is an indicator function and $M_{r>0}$ is the number of relevant data points.

We notice that r is defined as the number of shared labels between the query image and the retrieved images. However, r is not able to represent fine-grained multilevel semantic similarity between multi-label images. In Figure 4, all images on the right side share two labels with the query image, meaning that they are on the same similarity level due to the definition of r. In [22], the semantic similarity between multi-label images is measured by:

Figure 4: A sample of semantic similarity ranking according to the Jaccard coeffcient based evaluation criteria.

$$r(j) = \frac{|l_q \cap l_j|}{|l_q \cup l_j|} \tag{13}$$

In this way, images on the same similarity level according to the traditional similarity measurement can be further distinguished according to the Jaccard coeffcient based similarity measurement, as shown in Figure 4. In other words, the Jaccard coeffcient based similarity measurement can describe fine-grained multilevel semantic similarity. Accordingly, we redefine NDCG@m, ACG@m and weighted mAP, and denote them as J-NDCG@m, J-ACG@m and J-weighted mAP respectively.

4.3 Method Comparison

Comparative methods: We compare our method with LSH [2], SH [19], ITQ [3], DSRH [23] and IAH [10]. DSRH and IAH are two state-of-the-art supervised hashing methods aiming at preserving multilevel semantic similarity based on CNN models. SH and ITQ are two representative data-dependent hashing methods while LSH is the most famous data-independent hashing method. These methods were all implemented using source codes provided by the authors except for DSRH [2]. For fair comparison, all the CNN-based methods, including IAH, DSH, and DMSSPH, used the same network structure, as described in Section 3.5. For LSH, SH and ITQ, we used the features extracted from the activation of the full-connected layer fc7 of the same neural network pre-trained on the retrieval datasets, i.e., VOC2007, VOC2012 and MIRFLICKR-25K.

Parameter settings: The parameters of those comparative methods were all set based on the authors' suggestions in the original publications. It is important to note that the loss function defined in the source code of IAH is more elaborately designed than the one described in its original paper. Besides, we tried our best to maintain the original form of DSRH by carefully reading its source codes and configuration files.

Results on VOC2007: Our method dramatically outperforms other hashing methods on VOC2007, as listed in Table 2. More specifically, the NDCG@100 values of the proposed method indicate a $6.2\% \sim 34.1\%$ relative increase over the second best baseline. Besides, the values of ACG@100 indicate a relative increase of

[2]Since the released source code of DSRH is not implemented with Caffe, to be fair, we carefully reimplement DSRH based on Caffe

Table 3: Comparison of J-NDCG@100, J-ACG@100 and J-weighted mAP w.r.t. different number of bits on three datasets.

Methods	VOC 2007				VOC 2012				MIRFLICKR-25K			
	8 bits	16bits	24bits	32bits	8 bits	16bits	24bits	32bits	8 bits	16bits	24bits	32bits
J-NDCG@100												
DMSSPH	**0.4903**	**0.5540**	**0.5842**	**0.5906**	**0.4227**	**0.5504**	**0.5699**	**0.5909**	**0.4508**	**0.5056**	**0.5224**	**0.5325**
IAH	0.3453	0.4750	0.5243	0.5511	0.3496	0.4884	0.5321	0.5593	0.3780	0.4854	0.5118	0.5140
DSRH	0.3060	0.3990	0.4434	0.4847	0.3021	0.3981	0.4661	0.4966	0.3606	0.4569	0.4977	0.5138
ITQ+CNN	0.2630	0.3718	0.3749	0.3764	0.3153	0.3474	0.3906	0.4006	0.3456	0.3874	0.4226	0.4027
SH+CNN	0.3455	0.3813	0.3795	0.3760	0.3702	0.3756	0.3805	0.3772	0.3396	0.3954	0.4135	0.4176
LSH+CNN	0.2045	0.2916	0.2928	0.3204	0.2003	0.2524	0.2576	0.2953	0.2746	0.3486	0.3696	0.3836
J-ACG@100												
DMSSPH	**0.4188**	**0.4626**	**0.4861**	**0.4893**	**0.3426**	**0.4441**	**0.4566**	**0.4727**	**0.3328**	**0.3574**	**0.3677**	**0.3719**
IAH	0.3104	0.4056	0.4433	0.4602	0.3019	0.4059	0.4351	0.4525	0.2886	0.3465	0.3572	0.3547
DSRH	0.2750	0.3518	0.3807	0.4081	0.2651	0.3352	0.3850	0.4048	0.2853	0.3457	0.3660	0.3682
ITQ+CNN	0.2265	0.3054	0.2931	0.285	0.2594	0.2611	0.2885	0.2914	0.2576	0.2722	0.2837	0.2619
SH+CNN	0.2970	0.3035	0.2884	0.2812	0.3027	0.2724	0.2708	0.2664	0.2524	0.2671	0.2702	0.2714
LSH+CNN	0.1714	0.2232	0.2171	0.2434	0.1554	0.1737	0.1746	0.2065	0.2008	0.2301	0.2413	0.2524
J-weighted mAP												
DMSSPH	**0.3636**	**0.4091**	**0.4321**	**0.4408**	**0.2965**	**0.4000**	**0.4145**	**0.4321**	**0.2438**	0.2606	0.2650	0.2710
IAH	0.2863	0.3661	0.3986	0.4159	0.2825	0.3703	0.3969	0.4135	0.2331	0.2563	0.2607	0.2592
DSRH	0.2557	0.3224	0.3489	0.3748	0.2483	0.3121	0.3553	0.3739	0.2432	**0.2694**	**0.2775**	**0.2790**
ITQ+CNN	0.1765	0.2363	0.2319	0.2247	0.1999	0.2060	0.2333	0.2322	0.1939	0.1969	0.2050	0.1943
SH+CNN	0.2240	0.2369	0.2285	0.2226	0.2326	0.2139	0.2113	0.2060	0.1872	0.1936	0.1941	0.1930
LSH+CNN	0.1506	0.1847	0.1809	0.1934	0.1348	0.1484	0.1474	0.1692	0.1697	0.1870	0.1903	0.1948

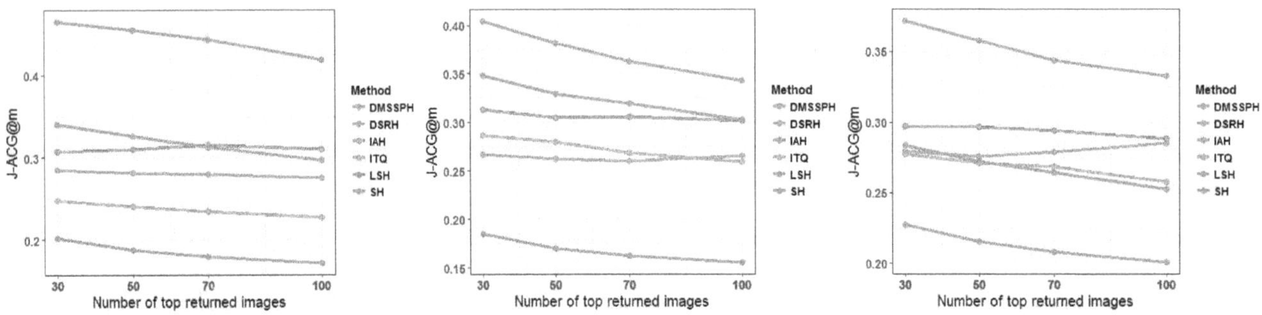

(a) VOC2007 (b) VOC2012 (c) MIRFLICKR

Figure 5: J-ACG curves with 8 bits w.r.t. different numbers of top returned samples.

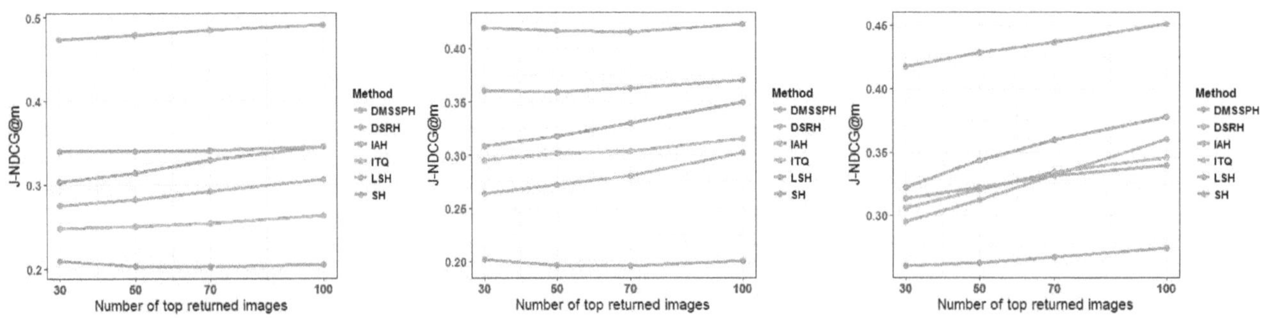

(a) VOC2007 (b) VOC2012 (c) MIRFLICKR

Figure 6: J-NDCG curves with 8 bits w.r.t. different numbers of top returned samples.

3.8% ~ 23.4% and the values of weighted mAP indicate a relative increase of 2.0% ~ 13.2%. In particular, our method achieves comparable or even better performance with shorter binary codes. For example, our method with 24-bits binary code outperforms all the other hashing methods with 32-bits binary codes in terms of NDCG@100, ACG@100 and weighted mAP. Besides, the CNN-based methods outperform the conventional hash learning methods by a large margin, validating the advantage of learning image representations over using hand-crafted features. Besides, with the decreasing of the number of top returned images, the advantages of the proposed method on NDCG and ACG present an increasing trends, as shown in Figure 2a and Figure 3a.

For the Jaccard coefficient based evaluation criteria, DMSSPH enlarges its advantages in all cases, as shown in Table 3. More specifically, the values of J-NDCG@100 indicate a 7.2% ~ 42.0% relative increase over the second best baseline, the values of J-ACG@100 indicate a relative increase of 6.3% ~ 34.9% and the values of J-weighted mAP indicate a relative increase of 6.0% ~ 27.0%. Figure 6a and Figure 5a plot the values of J-NDCG@m and J-ACG@m with varying m on VOC2007. As can be seen, our method maintains great advantages.

Results on VOC2012: Like VOC2007, the proposed method gains all-round advantages over all the other hashing methods on VOC2012, as can be seen in Table 2. To be more specific, the NDCG@100 values of the proposed method indicate a 4.9% ~ 32.0% relative increase over the second best baseline, the values of ACG@100 indicate a relative increase of 2.5% ~ 20.0% and the values of weighted mAP indicate a relative increase of 0.6% ~ 9.3%. Note that our method gains overwhelming advantages over other methods for shorter binary codes. DMSSPH further widens its advantages on NDCG@m and ACG@m over the other two CNN-based hashing methods when m decreases as Figure 2b and Figure 3b present.

As expected, our method outperforms all the other hashing methods on VOC2012 under the Jaccard coefficient based evaluation criteria, as can be seen in Table 3. More specifically, the values of J-NDCG@100 indicate a 5.6% ~ 20.9% relative increase over the second best hashing methods IAH, the values of J-ACG@100 indicate a relative increase of 4.5% ~ 13.5% and the values of J-weighted mAP indicate a relative increase of 4.5% ~ 5.0%. The values of J-NDCG@m and J-ACG@m with varying m on VOC2012 are ploted in Figure 6b and Figure 5b. Results indicate that the proposed method performs much better than other methods as m decreases.

Results on MIRFLICKR-25K: The proposed method maintain its advantages on NDCG@100, as illustrated in Table 2, meaning our method achieves better performance on the accuracies of top returned images. For ACG@100, the proposed method achieves the best performance with 8-bits binary code. However, for other cases, the proposed method is slightly inferior to the best one. For weighted mAP, our method achieves the third best performance among all methods and is also slightly inferior to the best method. With the decreasing of m, DMSSPH enlarges its advantages over other methods on NDCG@m and ACG@m, as clearly shown in Figure 2c and Figure 3c.

Table 3 shows that the proposed method substantially outperforms all the other methods under the Jaccard coefficient based evaluation criteria on MIRFLICKR-25K. More specifically, DMSSPH maintain its advantages on J-NDCG@100 while regaining the advantages on J-ACG@100. Besides, our method achieves the second best performance among all methods in term of J-weighted mAP and is slightly inferior to the best method DSRH. As expected, the results shown in Figure 6c and Figure 5c indicate that DMSSPH enlarges its advantages on J-NDCG@m and J-ACG@m as m decreases.

In general, we have the following observations: **First**, DMSSPH achieves promising performance on the accuracies of top returned images, especially for shorter binary codes, indicating the effectiveness of the strong constraints in our loss functions on the distance between the codes of very similar images, which can be observed from the comparisons of NDCG@m and J-NDCG@m; **Second**, DMSSPH substantially outperforms all the other methods under the Jaccard coefficient based evaluation criteria, proving that DMSSPH is better at perserving fine-grained multilevel semantic similarity.

5 CONCLUSION

In this paper, we have proposed a CNN-based hashing method for large-scale and multi-label image retrieval, called DMSSPH. We carefully design a loss function that makes the best of supervised information in the form of pairwise labels to maximize the discriminability of output binary codes, and simultaneously imposing regularization on the real-valued outputs to obtain the desired discrete values. We further introduce the Jaccard coefficient based evaluation criteria to further verify the effectiveness of our method on preserving fine-grained multilevel semantic similarity. Extensive experiments demonstrate that DMSSPH is better at preserving fine-grained multilevel semantic similarity and significantly improves the accuracies of top returned images, especially for shorter codes, which is essential for large-scale image retrieval.

ACKNOWLEDGMENTS

This work was supported by National Natural Science Foundation of China (No.61502478), National High-Tech Research and Development Program of China (2013AA013204) and National HeGaoJi Key Project (2013ZX01039- 002-001-001).

REFERENCES

[1] Mark Everingham, Luc Van Gool, Christopher KI Williams, John Winn, and Andrew Zisserman. 2010. The pascal visual object classes (voc) challenge. *International journal of computer vision* 88, 2 (2010), 303–338.
[2] Aristides Gionis, Piotr Indyk, Rajeev Motwani, and others. 1999. Similarity search in high dimensions via hashing. In *VLDB*, Vol. 99. 518–529.
[3] Yunchao Gong, Svetlana Lazebnik, Albert Gordo, and Florent Perronnin. 2013. Iterative quantization: A procrustean approach to learning binary codes for large-scale image retrieval. *IEEE Transactions on Pattern Analysis and Machine Intelligence* 35, 12 (2013), 2916–2929.
[4] Raia Hadsell, Sumit Chopra, and Yann LeCun. 2006. Dimensionality reduction by learning an invariant mapping. In *Computer vision and pattern recognition, 2006 IEEE computer society conference on*, Vol. 2. IEEE, 1735–1742.
[5] Mark J Huiskes and Michael S Lew. 2008. The MIR flickr retrieval evaluation. In *Proceedings of the 1st ACM international conference on Multimedia information retrieval*. ACM, 39–43.
[6] Kalervo Järvelin and Jaana Kekäläinen. 2000. IR evaluation methods for retrieving highly relevant documents. In *Proceedings of the 23rd annual international ACM SIGIR conference on Research and development in information retrieval*. ACM, 41–48.
[7] Yangqing Jia, Evan Shelhamer, Jeff Donahue, Sergey Karayev, Jonathan Long, Ross Girshick, Sergio Guadarrama, and Trevor Darrell. 2014. Caffe: Convolutional architecture for fast feature embedding. In *Proceedings of the 22nd ACM*

international conference on Multimedia. ACM, 675–678.

[8] Alex Krizhevsky, Ilya Sutskever, and Geoffrey E Hinton. 2012. Imagenet classification with deep convolutional neural networks. In *Advances in neural information processing systems*. 1097–1105.

[9] Hanjiang Lai, Yan Pan, Ye Liu, and Shuicheng Yan. 2015. Simultaneous feature learning and hash coding with deep neural networks. In *Proceedings of the IEEE Conference on Computer Vision and Pattern Recognition*. 3270–3278.

[10] Hanjiang Lai, Pan Yan, Xiangbo Shu, Yunchao Wei, and Shuicheng Yan. 2016. Instance-aware hashing for multi-label image retrieval. *IEEE Transactions on Image Processing* 25, 6 (2016), 2469–2479.

[11] Wu-Jun Li, Sheng Wang, and Wang-Cheng Kang. 2015. Feature learning based deep supervised hashing with pairwise labels. *arXiv preprint arXiv:1511.03855* (2015).

[12] Kevin Lin, Jiwen Lu, Chu-Song Chen, and Jie Zhou. 2016. Learning compact binary descriptors with unsupervised deep neural networks. In *Proceedings of the IEEE Conference on Computer Vision and Pattern Recognition*. 1183–1192.

[13] Kevin Lin, Huei-Fang Yang, Jen-Hao Hsiao, and Chu-Song Chen. 2015. Deep learning of binary hash codes for fast image retrieval. In *Proceedings of the IEEE conference on computer vision and pattern recognition workshops*. 27–35.

[14] Haomiao Liu, Ruiping Wang, Shiguang Shan, and Xilin Chen. 2016. Deep supervised hashing for fast image retrieval. In *Proceedings of the IEEE Conference on Computer Vision and Pattern Recognition*. 2064–2072.

[15] Vinod Nair and Geoffrey E Hinton. 2010. Rectified linear units improve restricted boltzmann machines. In *Proceedings of the 27th international conference on machine learning (ICML-10)*. 807–814.

[16] Mohammad Norouzi and David M Blei. 2011. Minimal loss hashing for compact binary codes. In *Proceedings of the 28th international conference on machine learning (ICML-11)*. 353–360.

[17] Fumin Shen, Chunhua Shen, Wei Liu, and Heng Tao Shen. 2015. Supervised discrete hashing. In *Proceedings of the IEEE Conference on Computer Vision and Pattern Recognition*. 37–45.

[18] Jun Wang, Sanjiv Kumar, and Shih-Fu Chang. 2010. Semi-supervised hashing for scalable image retrieval. In *Computer Vision and Pattern Recognition (CVPR), 2010 IEEE Conference on*. IEEE, 3424–3431.

[19] Yair Weiss, Antonio Torralba, and Rob Fergus. 2009. Spectral hashing. In *Advances in neural information processing systems*. 1753–1760.

[20] Rongkai Xia, Yan Pan, Hanjiang Lai, Cong Liu, and Shuicheng Yan. 2014. Supervised Hashing for Image Retrieval via Image Representation Learning.. In *AAAI*, Vol. 1. 2.

[21] Huei-Fang Yang, Kevin Lin, and Chu-Song Chen. 2015. Supervised learning of semantics-preserving hashing via deep neural networks for large-scale image search. *arXiv preprint arXiv:1507.00101* (2015).

[22] Ruimao Zhang, Liang Lin, Rui Zhang, Wangmeng Zuo, and Lei Zhang. 2015. Bit-scalable deep hashing with regularized similarity learning for image retrieval and person re-identification. *IEEE Transactions on Image Processing* 24, 12 (2015), 4766–4779.

[23] Fang Zhao, Yongzhen Huang, Liang Wang, and Tieniu Tan. 2015. Deep semantic ranking based hashing for multi-label image retrieval. In *Proceedings of the IEEE Conference on Computer Vision and Pattern Recognition*. 1556–1564.

Accelerated Nearest Neighbor Search with Quick ADC

Fabien André
Technicolor
fabien.andre@technicolor.com

Anne-Marie Kermarrec
Inria
anne-marie.kermarrec@inria.fr

Nicolas Le Scouarnec
Technicolor
nicolas.lescouarnec@technicolor.com

ABSTRACT

Efficient Nearest Neighbor (NN) search in high-dimensional spaces is a foundation of many multimedia retrieval systems. Because it offers low responses times, Product Quantization (PQ) is a popular solution. PQ compresses high-dimensional vectors into short codes using several sub-quantizers, which enables in-RAM storage of large databases. This allows fast answers to NN queries, without accessing the SSD or HDD. The key feature of PQ is that it can compute distances between short codes and high-dimensional vectors using cache-resident lookup tables. The efficiency of this technique, named Asymmetric Distance Computation (ADC), remains limited because it performs many cache accesses.

In this paper, we introduce Quick ADC, a novel technique that achieves a 3 to 6 times speedup over ADC by exploiting Single Instruction Multiple Data (SIMD) units available in current CPUs. Efficiently exploiting SIMD requires algorithmic changes to the ADC procedure. Namely, Quick ADC relies on two key modifications of ADC: (i) the use 4-bit sub-quantizers instead of the standard 8-bit sub-quantizers and (ii) the quantization of floating-point distances. This allows Quick ADC to exceed the performance of state-of-the-art systems, e.g., it achieves a Recall@100 of 0.94 in 3.4 ms on 1 billion SIFT descriptors (128-bit codes).

KEYWORDS

Large-Scale Multimedia Search; Multimedia Search Acceleration; Product Quantization; SIMD

ACM Reference format:
Fabien André, Anne-Marie Kermarrec, and Nicolas Le Scouarnec. 2017. Accelerated Nearest Neighbor Search with Quick ADC. In *Proceedings of ICMR '17, Bucharest, Romania, June 06-09, 2017,* 8 pages.
DOI: http://dx.doi.org/10.1145/3078971.3078992

1 INTRODUCTION

The Nearest Neighbor (NN) search problem consists in finding the closest vector x to a query vector y among a database of N d-dimensional vectors. Efficient NN search in high-dimensional spaces is a requirement in many multimedia retrieval applications, such as image similarity search, image classification, or object recognition. These problems typically involve extracting high-dimensional feature vectors, or descriptors, and finding the NN of the extracted descriptors among a database of descriptors. For images, SIFT [10] and GIST descriptors [12] are commonly used.

ICMR '17, June 6-9, 2017, Bucharest, Romania

978-1-4503-4701-3/17/06...$15.00
DOI: http://dx.doi.org/10.1145/3078971.3078992

Although efficient NN search solutions have been proposed for low-dimensional spaces, *exact* NN search remains challenging in high-dimensional spaces due to the notorious curse of dimensionality. As a consequence, much research work has been devoted to Approximate Nearest Neighbor (ANN) search. ANN search returns sufficiently close neighbors instead of the exact NN. Product Quantization (PQ) [7] is a widely used [9, 14] ANN search approach. PQ compresses high-dimensional vectors into short codes of a few bytes, enabling in-RAM storage of large databases. This allows fast answers to ANN queries, without SSD or HDD accesses.

The key feature of PQ is that it allows computing distances between uncompressed query vectors and compressed database vectors. This technique, known as Asymmetric Distance Computation (ADC), relies on cache-resident lookup tables. Although ADC is faster than distance computations in high-dimensional spaces, its efficiency remains low because it performs many cache accesses. To date, much of the research work has been devoted to the development of efficient inverted indexes [3, 13], which reduce the number of ADCs required to answer NN queries. Recently, there also has been an interest in increasing the performance of the ADC procedure itself with the introduction of PQ Fast Scan [1]. Unfortunately, PQ Fast Scan cannot be combined with efficient inverted indexes, limiting its usefulness in practical cases. In this paper, we introduce Quick ADC, a high-performance ADC procedure that can be combined with inverted indexes. More specifically, this paper makes two contributions, detailed in the next two paragraphs.

First, we detail the design of Quick ADC. Like PQ Fast Scan, Quick ADC replaces cache accesses by SIMD in-register shuffles to accelerate the ADC procedure. Exploiting SIMD in-register shuffles requires storing the lookup tables used by the ADC procedure in SIMD registers. However, these registers are much smaller than the lookup tables used by the conventional ADC procedure. Therefore, algorithmic changes are required to obtain small lookup tables that fit SIMD registers. PQ Fast Scan obtains such small lookup tables by grouping the codes of the database. This approach prevents PQ Fast Scan from being combined with inverted indexes. Quick ADC takes a different approach to obtain small lookup tables, which is compatible with inverted indexes. Namely, Quick ADC relies on two key ideas: (i) the use of 4-bit sub-quantizers, instead of the standard 8-bit sub-quantizers, and (ii) the quantization of floating-point distances to 8-bit integers.

Second, we implement Quick ADC and evaluate its performance in a wide range of scenarios. It is known that the use of 4-bit quantizers instead of the common 8-bit quantizer can cause a loss of recall [7]. However, we show that this loss is small or negligible, especially when combining Quick ADC with inverted indexes and Optimized Product Quantization (OPQ), a variant of PQ. On the SIFT1B dataset, Quick ADC achieves a better speed-accuracy trade-off than the state-of-art OMulti-D-OADC system [3, 5], e.g., Quick ADC achieves a Recall@100 of 0.94 in 3.4 ms (128-bit codes).

2 BACKGROUND

In this section, we describe how Product Quantizers (PQ) and Optimized Product Quantizers (OPQ) encode vectors into short codes. We then detail the ANN search process in databases of short codes. Lastly, we analyze the impact of PQ parameters on ANN search speed and recall.

2.1 Vector Encoding

Vector Quantizers. To encode vectors as short codes, PQ builds on vector quantizers. A vector quantizer, or quantizer, is a function q which maps a vector $x \in \mathbb{R}^d$, to a vector $c_i \in \mathbb{R}^d$ belonging to a predefined set of vectors C. Vectors c_i are called *centroids*, and the set of centroids C, of cardinality k, is the *codebook*. For a given codebook C, a quantizer which minimizes the quantization error must satisfy Lloyd's condition and map the vector x to its closest centroid c_i:

$$\mathrm{q}(x) = \underset{c_i \in C}{\arg\min} \, ||x - c_i||.$$

A vector quantizer can be used to encode a vector $x \in \mathbb{R}^d$ into a short code $i \in \{0 \ldots k-1\}$ using the encoder enc:

$$\mathrm{enc}(x) = i, \text{ such that } \mathrm{q}(x) = c_i$$

The short code i only occupies $b = \lceil \log_2(k) \rceil$ bits, which is typically much lower the $d \cdot 32$ bits occupied by a vector $x \in \mathbb{R}^d$ stored as an array of d single-precision floats (32 bit each). To maintain the quantization error low enough for ANN search, a very large codebook e.g., $k = 2^{64}$ or $k = 2^{128}$ is required. However, training such codebooks is not tractable both in terms of processing and memory requirements.

Product Quantizers. Product quantizers overcome this issue by dividing a vector $x \in \mathbb{R}^d$ into m sub-vectors, $x = (x^0, \ldots, x^{m-1})$, assuming that d is a multiple of m. Each sub-vector $x^j \in \mathbb{R}^{d/m}$, $j \in \{0, \ldots, m-1\}$ is quantized using a sub-quantizer q^j. Each sub-quantizer q^j has a distinct codebook $C^j = (c_i^j)_{i=0}^{k-1}$ of cardinality k. A product quantizer pq maps a vector $x \in \mathbb{R}^d$ as follows:

$$\begin{aligned}\mathrm{pq}(x) &= \left(\mathrm{q}^0(x^0), \ldots, \mathrm{q}^{m-1}(x^{m-1})\right) \\ &= (c_{i_0}^0, \ldots, c_{i_{m-1}}^{m-1})\end{aligned}$$

The codebook C of the product quantizer q is given by the cartesian product of the sub-quantizers codebooks:

$$C = C^0 \times \cdots \times C^{m-1}$$

The cardinality of the product quantizer codebook C is k^m. Thus, a product quantizer is able to produce a large number of centroids k^m while only requiring storing and training m codebooks of cardinality k. A product quantizer can be used to encode a vector x into a short code, by concatenating codes produced by sub-quantizers:

$$\mathrm{enc}(x) = (i_0, \ldots, i_{m-1}), \text{ such that } \mathrm{q}(x) = (c_{i_0}^0, \ldots, c_{i_{m-1}}^{m-1})$$

The short code $(i_0, \ldots, i_{m-1})$ requires $\lceil \log_2(k^m) \rceil = m \cdot b$ bits of storage, where $b = \lceil \log_2(k) \rceil$.

Optimized Product Quantizers. Cartesian k-means (CKM) [11] and Optimized Product Quantizers (OPQ) [5] and optimize the subspace decomposition by multiplying the vector x by an orthonormal matrix $R \in \mathbb{R}^{d \times d}$ before quantization. The matrix R allows for arbitrary rotation and permutation of vector components. An optimized product quantizer opq maps a vector x as follows:

$$\mathrm{opq}(x) = \mathrm{pq}(Rx), \text{ such that } R^T R = I,$$

where pq is a product quantizer. Optimized product quantizers can be used to encode vectors into short codes like product quantizers.

2.2 Inverted Indexes

The simplest search strategy, exhaustive search, involves encoding database vectors as short codes using PQ or OPQ and storing short codes in RAM. At query time, the whole database is scanned for nearest neighbors.

The more refined non-exhaustive search strategy relies on inverted indexes (or IVF) [7, 8] to avoid scanning the whole database. An inverted index uses a quantizer $\mathrm{q_i}$ to partition the input vector space into K Voronoi cells. Vectors lying in each cell are stored in an inverted list. At query time, the inverted index is used to find the closest cells to the query vector, which are then scanned. Inverted indexes therefore offer a lower query response time. When adding a vector x to an indexed database, its residual $\mathrm{r}(x)$ is first computed:

$$\mathrm{r}(x) = x - \mathrm{q_i}(x)$$

The residual $\mathrm{r}(x)$ is then encoded into a short code using a product quantizer. This code is then stored in the appropriate inverted list of the inverted index. Indexed databases therefore use two quantizers: a quantizer for the index ($\mathrm{q_i}$) and a product quantizer to encode residuals into short codes. The energy of residuals $\mathrm{r}(x)$ is smaller than the energy of input vectors x, thus there is a lower quantization error when encoding residuals into short codes. Non-exhaustive search therefore offers a higher recall than exhaustive search in addition to the lower response time. Inverted indexes however incur a memory overhead (usually 4 bytes per database vector). This memory overhead is negligible in the case of small databases (~ 4MB for 1 million vectors) and for large databases, exhaustive search is anyway hardly tractable. Non-exhaustive search is therefore preferred to exhaustive search in most cases.

2.3 ANN Search

ANN search in a database of short codes consists in three steps: *Index*, which involves retrieving inverted lists from the index, *Tables*, which involves computing lookup tables to speed up distance computations and *Scan* which involves computing distances between the query vector and short codes using the pre-computed lookup tables. Obviously, the step *Index* is only required for non-exhaustive search, and is skipped in the case of exhaustive search. We detail these three steps in the three following paragraphs.

Index. In this step, the Voronoi cell of the inverted index quantizer $\mathrm{q_i}$ in which the query vector y lies is determined. The residual $\mathrm{r}(y)$ of the query vector is also computed. In practice, to improve recall, the ma closest cells (typically, $ma = 8$ to 64) are selected. For the sake of simplicity, this section describes the ANN search process for $ma = 1$, but each operation is repeated ma times: ma cells are selected, ma sets of lookup tables are computed and ma cells are searched. In the case of exhaustive search no residual is computed and the query vector is used as-is. In the remainder of

Algorithm 1 ANN Search

1: **function** NNS($\{C^j\}_{j=0}^m$, *database*, y, R)
2: *list*, y' ← INDEX_GET_LIST(*database*, y)
3: $\{D^j\}_{j=0}^m$ ← COMPUTE_TABLES(y', $\{C^j\}_{j=0}^m$)
4: **return** SCAN(*list*, $\{D^j\}_{j=0}^m$)
5: **function** SCAN(*list*, $\{D^j\}_{j=0}^m$, R)
6: *neighbors* ← binheap(R) ▷ binary heap of size R
7: **for** $i \leftarrow 0$ to $|list| - 1$ **do**
8: $c \leftarrow list[i]$ ▷ ith pqcode
9: $d \leftarrow$ ADC(p, $\{D^j\}_{j=0}^m$)
10: *neighbors*. add((i, d))
11: **return** *neighbors*
12: **function** ADC(c, $\{D^j\}_{j=0}^{m-1}$)
13: $d \leftarrow 0$
14: **for** $j \leftarrow 0$ to m **do**
15: $d \leftarrow d + D^j[c[j]]$
return d

this section, $y' = r(y)$ for non-exhaustive search, and $y' = y$ for exhaustive search.

Tables. In this step, a set of m lookup tables are computed $\{D^j\}_{j=0}^m$, where m is the number of sub-quantizers of the product quantizer. The jth lookup table comprises the distance between the j sub-vector of y' and all centroids of the jth sub-quantizer:

$$D^j = \left(\left\| y'^j - C^j[0] \right\|^2, \ldots, \left\| y'^j - C^j[k-1] \right\|^2 \right) \tag{1}$$

Scan. In this step, the cells of the inverted index selected during the step *Index* are searched for nearest neighbors. This requires computing the distance between the query vectors and short codes using Asymmetric Distance Computation (ADC). ADC computes the distance between the query vector y and a short code c as follows:

$$\mathrm{adc}(y, c) = \sum_{j=0}^{m-1} D^j[c[j]] \tag{2}$$

Equation 2 is equivalent to:

$$\mathrm{adc}(y, c) = \sum_{j=0}^{m-1} \left\| y'^j - C^j[c[j]] \right\|^2 \tag{3}$$

Thus, ADC computes the distance between a query vector y' and a code c by summing the distances between the sub-vectors of y' and centroids associated with code c in the m sub-spaces of the product quantizer. When the number of codes in cells is large compared to k, the number of centroids of sub-quantizers, using lookup tables avoids computing $||y'^j - C^j[i]||^2$ for the same i multiple times. Thus, lookup tables therefore provide a significant speedup. While scanning inverted lists, neighbors and their associated distances are stored in a binary heap of size R (Algorithm 1, line 6).

2.4 Impact of PQ Parameters

The two parameters of a product quantizer, m, the number of sub-quantizers and k, the number of centroids of each sub-quantizer impact: (1) the memory usage of codes, (2) the recall of ANN search and (3) search speed. In practice, 64-bit codes (2^{64} centroids) or 128-bit codes (2^{128} centroids) are used in most cases.

The second tradeoff is between ANN accuracy and search speed. For a constant memory budget of $m \cdot b$ bits per code, the respective values of m and b impact accuracy and speed. Decreasing m, which implies increasing b, increases accuracy [7]. We discuss the effect of m and b on the time cost of the *Tables* and *Scan* steps of ANN search (Section 2.3). Each lookup table requires $k = 2^b$ l_2-norm computations in sub-spaces of dimensionality d/m. Thus, the complexity of computing all m lookup tables is $O(m \cdot 2^b \cdot d/m) = O(2^b \cdot d)$, and increases exponentially with b. In conclusion, decreasing m makes the *Tables* step more costly.

During the *Scan* step, each Asymmetric Distance Computation (ADC) (Algorithm 1, line 12) requires m accesses to lookup tables and m additions (Algorithm 1, line 15). Therefore, decreasing m decreases the number of operations required for each ADC, which is beneficial for search speed. However, decreasing m implies increasing b, and thus increasing the size of lookup tables. The size of all lookup tables $\{D^j\}_{j=0}^m$ is $m \cdot k \cdot \mathrm{sizeof(float)} = m \cdot 2^b \cdot 4$. It increases linearly with m and exponentially with b. Thus, decreasing m increases the size of lookup tables. As the size of lookup tables increases, they need to be stored in larger and slower cache levels which is detrimental to performance [1]. In conclusion, decreasing m, makes the *Tables* step less costly, except if it causes lookup tables to be stored in slower cache.

To illustrate this, we measure the recall (R@100) and the time cost of the *Tables* and *Scan* steps of ANN search for different $m \times b$ configurations producing 64-bit codes (Table 1). For 16×4 and 8×8, tables fit the L1 cache. The 8×8 configuration has a lower *Scan* time because it requires less additions and less accesses to lookup tables. The 4×16 configuration requires even less additions and table accesses but lookup tables are stored in the much slower L3 cache. Overall, the 4×16 configuration therefore has a higher *Scan* time. In all cases, the time cost of the *Tables* step increases with b.

Table 1: Speed-Accuracy tradeoff for 64-bit codes (SIFT1M, Exhaustive search)

$m \times b$	Size	Cache	R@100	Tables	Scan
16×4	1 KiB	L1	83.1%	0.001 ms	6.1 ms
8×8	8 KiB	L1	91.6%	0.005 ms	2.7 ms
4×16	1 MiB	L3	96.5%	0.77 ms	7.8 ms

3 QUICK ADC

3.1 Overview

The performance gains of Quick ADC are achieved by exploiting SIMD. Single Instruction Multiple Data (SIMD) instructions perform the same operation e.g., additions, on multiple data elements in one instruction. Consequently, SIMD enables large performance improvements. Thus, optimized linear algebra libraries rely on SIMD to offer high performance. Current CPUs include an SIMD unit in each core. SIMD therefore offers an additional level of parallelism over multi-core processing. ANN search parallelizes naturally over multiple cores by processing a distinct query on each core. With

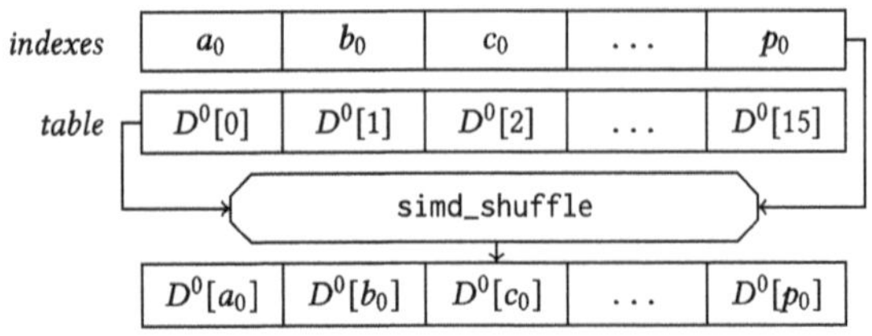

Figure 1: SIMD in-register shuffle

Quick ADC, we propose further increasing performance by speeding up ADC for each query, thanks to the use of SIMD. To process multiple data elements at once, SIMD instructions operate on wide registers. SSE instructions use 128-bit registers, while the newer AVX instructions use 256-bit registers.

The *Scan* step computes asymmetric distances between the query vector and all codes stored in selected cells. Each ADC requires (1) m accesses to cache-resident lookup tables and (2) m additions. If implementing additions using SIMD is straightforward, SIMD does not allow an efficient implementation of table lookup, even using `gather` instructions introduced in recent processors [1, 6]. SIMD can add 4 floating-point numbers (128 bits) or 8 floating-point numbers (256 bits) at once, there are only 2 cache read ports in each CPU core. Therefore, it is not possible to perform more than 2 cache accesses concurrently.

Therefore, efficiently implementing ADC using SIMD requires storing lookup tables in SIMD registers and performing lookups using SIMD in-register shuffles. The main challenge is that SIMD registers (128 bits) are much smaller than lookup tables, for common PQ configurations. In most cases, product quantizers use 8-bit sub-quantizers, which results in lookup tables of $k = 2^8 = 256$ floats (8192 bits). For this reason, Quick ADC relies on (i) the use of 4-bit quantizers instead of the common 8-bit quantizers, and (ii) the quantization of floats to 8-bit integers. We obtain lookup tables of $k = 2^4 = 16$ floats, which are then quantized to 8-bit integers. The resulting lookup tables comprise 16 8-bit integers (128 bits), and can be stored in SIMD registers. Once lookup tables are stored in SIMD registers, in-register shuffles can be used to perform 16 lookups in 1 cycle (Figure 1), enabling large performance gains.

In addition to the use of 4-bit quantizers and the quantization of floats to 8-bit integers, Quick ADC requires a minor change of memory layout. In the next sections, we detail this change of memory layout as well as our lookup tables quantization process and the SIMD implementation of distance computations.

3.2 Memory Layout

An SIMD in-register shuffle performs 16 lookups at once, but in a *single* lookup table e.g., D^0 (Figure 1). Therefore, to use shuffles efficiently, we need to operate on the first component of 16 codes $(a_0, \ldots, p_0)$ at once instead of the 16 components of a single code $(a_0, \ldots, a_{15})$. Its is crucial for efficiency that all values in an SIMD register can be loaded in a single memory read. This requires that $a_0, \ldots, p_0$ are *contiguous* in memory, which is not the case with the standard memory layout of inverted lists (Figure 2a). We therefore transpose inverted lists by blocks of 16 codes, so that analogous components of 16 codes are stored in adjacent bytes (Figure 2b).

a	$a_1\ a_0$	...	$a_{m-1}\ a_{m-2}$
b	$b_1\ b_0$	...	$b_{m-1}\ b_{m-2}$
	...	...	...
p	$p_1\ p_0$	...	$p_{m-1}\ p_{m-2}$

(a) Standard layout

a	b	c		p
$a_1\ a_0$	$b_1\ b_0$	$c_1\ c_0$	...	$p_1\ p_0$
...	...	...	...	...
$a_{m-1}\ a_{m-2}$	$b_{m-1}\ b_{m-2}$	$c_{m-1}\ c_{m-2}$	...	$a_{m-1}\ a_{m-2}$

(b) Transposed layout

Figure 2: Inverted list memory layouts. Each table cell represents a byte.

We divide each inverted list in blocks of 16 codes and transpose each block independently. Figure 2 shows the transposition of one block of 16 codes $(a, \ldots, p)$. This transposition is performed offline, and does not increase ANN query response time. The transposition is moreover very fast; the overhead on database creation time is less than 1%.

3.3 Quantization of Lookup Tables

In standard ADC, lookup tables store 32-bit floats. To be able to store tables of 16 elements in 128-bit registers, we quantize 32-bit floats to 8-bit integers using a scalar quantizer. Because there is no SIMD instruction to compare unsigned 8-bit integers, we quantize distances to signed 8-bit integers, only using their positive range. We quantize distances between a $qmin$ and $qmax$ bound into n = 127 bins (0-126) uniformly. The size of each bin is $\Delta = (qmax - qmin)/n$. Values larger than $qmax$ are quantized to 127.

We choose the minimum value accross all lookup tables $\{D^j\}_{j=0}^m$, which is the smallest distance we need to represent, as the $qmin$ value. Using the maximum possible distance i.e., the sum of the maximums of all lookup tables results in a too high quantization error. Therefore, to set $qmax$ we scan *init* vectors (typical *init*=200-1000) to find a temporary set of R nearest neighbor candidates, where R is the number of nearest neighbors requested by the user (Section 2.3). We use the distance of the query vector to the Rth nearest neighbor candidate i.e., the farthest nearest neighbor candidate, as the $qmax$ bound. All subsequent candidates will need to be closer to the query vector, thus $qmax$ is the maximum distance we need to represent.

3.4 SIMD Distance Computation

Although recent Intel CPUs offer 256-bit SIMD, we describe a version of Quick ADC which uses 128-bit SIMD for the sake of simplicity. Yet, we explain how to generalize it to 256-bit at the end of the section. Moreover, the 128-bit version of Quick ADC offers the best compatibility, notably with older Intel CPUs or ARM CPUs. In Algortihm 2, SIMD instructions are denoted by the prefix `simd_`. SIMD instructions use 128-bit variables, denoted by `r128`.

Algorithm 2 ANN Search with Quick ADC

1: **function** LOOKUP_ADD($comps, D^j, acc$) ▷ Fig. 3
2: r128 masked ← simd_and($comps$, 0x0f)
3: r128 partial ← simd_shuffle($comps, D^j$)
4: **return** simd_add_saturated($acc, partial$)
5: **function** QUICK_ADC_BLOCK($blk, \{D^j\}_{j=0}^{m-1}$)
6: r128 acc ← {0}
7: **for** $j \leftarrow 0$ to $m/2 - 1$ **do**
8: r128 $comps$ ← simd_load($blk + j \cdot 16$)
9: acc ← LOOKUP_ADD($comps, D^{2j}, acc$)
10: $comps$ ← simd_right_shift($comps$, 4) ▷ Fig. 4
11: acc ← LOOKUP_ADD($comps, D^{2j+1}, acc$)
return acc
12: **function** QUICK_ADC_SCAN($tlist, \{D^j\}_{j=0}^{m-1}, R$)
13: $neighbors$ ← binheap(R)
14: **for** blk in $tlist$ **do**
15: r128 acc ← QUICK_ADC_BLOCK($blk, \{D^j\}_{j=0}^{m-1}$)
16: EXTRACT_MATCHES($acc, neighbors$)
17: **return** $neighbors$

The QUICK_ADC_SCAN function (Algorithm 2, line 12) scans a block-transposed inverted list $tlist$ (Section 3.2) using m *quantized* lookup tables $\{D^j\}_{j=0}^{m-1}$, where m is the number of sub-quantizers of the product quantizer. Each lookup table is stored in a distinct SIMD register. The QUICK_ADC_SCAN function iterates over blocks blk of 16 codes (Algorithm 2, line 14). The QUICK_ADC_BLOCK function computes the distance between the query vector and the 16 codes $(a, \ldots, p)$ of the block blk.

Each block comprises $m/2$ rows of 16 bytes (128 bits). Each row stores the jth and $(j+1)$th components of 16 codes (Figure 2b). The QUICK_ADC_BLOCK function iterates over each row (Alorithm 2, line 7), and loads it in the *comps* register sequentially (Algorithm 2, line 8). Two lookup-add operations are performed on each row (Algorithm 2, line 9 and line 11): one for the $(2j)$th components, and one for $(2j+1)$th components of the codes. Figure 3 describes the succession of operations performed by the LOOKUP_ADD function for the first row ($j = 0$). As each byte of the first row stores two components, e.g., the first byte of the first row stores a_1 and a_0 (Figure 3), we start by masking the lower 4 bits of each byte (and with 0x0f), to obtain the first components $(a_0, \ldots, p_0)$ only. The remainder of the function looks up values in the D^0 table and accumulates distances in *acc* variable. Before the LOOKUP_ADD function can be used to process the second components $(a_1, \ldots, p_1)$, it is necessary that $(a_1, \ldots, p_1)$ are in the lowest 4 bits of each byte of the register. We therefore right shift the *comps* register by 4 bits (Figure 4) before calling LOOKUP_ADD (Algorithm 2, line 10). The EXTRACT_MATCHES function (Algorithm 2, line 16), the implementation of which is not shown, extracts distances from the *acc* register and inserts them in the binary heap *neighbors*.

Among 256-bit SIMD instructions (AVX and AVX2 instruction sets) supported on recent CPUs, some, like in-register shuffles, operate concurrently on two independent 128-bit lanes. This prevents use of 256-bit lookup tables (32 8-bit integers) but allows an easy

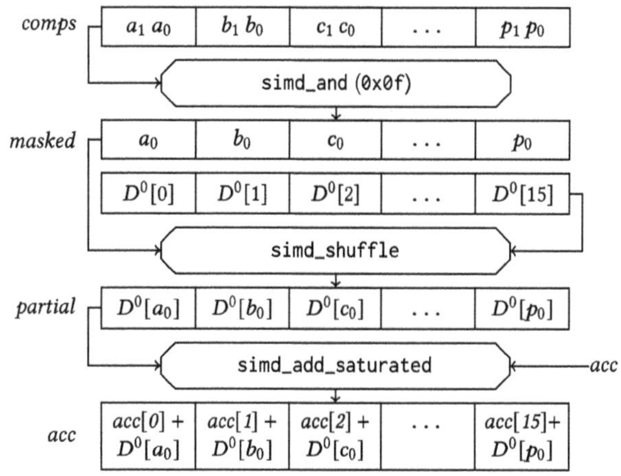

Figure 3: SIMD Lookup-add ($j = 0$)

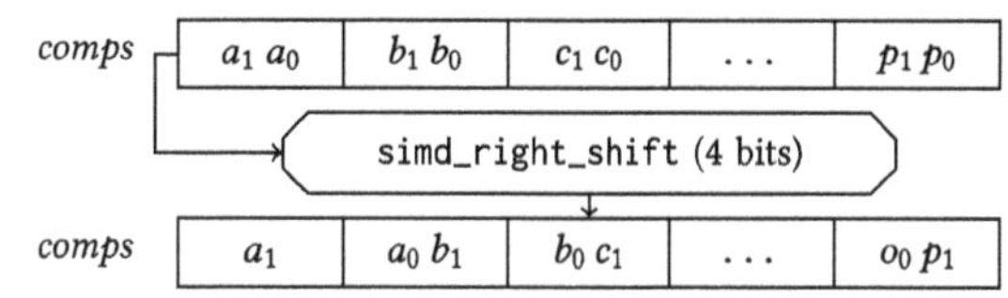

Figure 4: SIMD 4-bit Right Shift ($j = 0$)

generalization of the 128-bit version of Quick ADC. While the 128-bit version of Quick ADC iterates on block rows one by one (Algorithm 2, line 7), the 256-bit version processes two rows at once: one row in each 128-bit lane. The number of iterations is thus reduced from $m/2$ to $m/4$. Lastly, instead of storing each D^j table in a distinct 128-bit register, the tables D^j and D^{2j}, $j \in \{0, \ldots, m/2 - 1\}$, are stored in each of the two lanes of a 256-bit register.

4 EVALUATION

4.1 Experimental Setup

We implemented 256-bit Quick ADC in C++, using compiler intrinsics to access SIMD instructions. Our implementation is released under the Clear BSD license[1] and uses the AVX and AVX2 instruction sets. We used the g++ compiler version 5.3, with the options `-O3 -ffast-math -m64 -march=native`. Exhaustive search and non-exhaustive search (inverted indexes, IVF) were implemented as described in [7]. We use the yael library and the ATLAS library version 3.10.2. We compiled an optimized version of ATLAS on our system. To learn product quantizers and optimized product quantizers, we used the implementation [2] of the authors of [2, 4]. Unless otherwise noted, experiments were performed on our workstation (Table 2). To get accurate timings, we processed queries sequentially on a single core. We evaluate our approach on two publicly available[3] datasets of SIFT descriptors, one dataset of GIST descriptors, and one dataset of PCA-compressed deep features[4] (Table 3). For SIFT1B, the learning set is needlessly large to train product

[1] https://github.com/technicolor-research/quick-adc
[2] https://github.com/arbabenko/Quantizations
[3] http://corpus-texmex.irisa.fr/
[4] http://sites.skoltech.ru/compvision/projects/aqtq/

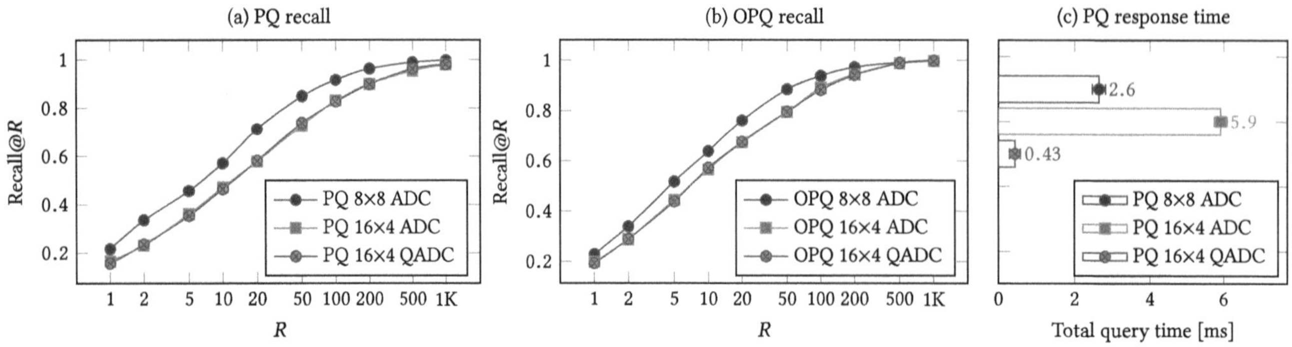

Figure 5: ADC and QADC response time and recall with PQ and OPQ (SIFT1M, Exhaustive search)

Table 2: Systems

	CPU	RAM
workstation	Xeon E5-1650v3	16GB DDR4 2133Mhz
server	Xeon E5-2630v3	128GB DDR4 1866Mhz

Table 3: Datasets

	Base set	Learning set	Query set	Dim.
SIFT1M	1M	100K	10K (1K)	128
SIFT1B	1000M	100M (2M)	10K (1K)	128
GIST1M	1M	500K	1K	960
Deep1M	1M	300K	1K	256

quantizers, so we used the first 2 million vectors. We used a query set of 1000 vectors for all experiments.

4.2 Exhaustive Search in SIFT1M

Using 16×4 Quick ADC (QADC) instead of 8×8 ADC offers a large performance gain, thanks to the use of SIMD in-register shuffles. It however also causes a decrease in recall which is cause by two factors: (1) use of 16×4 quantizers instead of 8×8 quantizers (Section 2.4) and (2) use of quantized lookup tables (Section 3.3). In this section, we evaluate the global decrease in recall caused by the use of 16×4 QADC instead of 8×8 ADC, but also the relative impact of factors (1) and (2). To do so, we use the SIFT1M dataset and follow an exhaustive search strategy. We do not use an inverted index and we encode the original vectors into short codes, not residuals. This maximizes quantization error and thus represents a worst-case scenario for QADC. We scan $init = 200$ vectors to set the $qmax$ bound for quantization of lookup tables (Section 3.3).

We observe that 16×4 ADC slightly decreases recall (Figure 5a). However, 16×4 QADC, which uses quantized lookup tables, does not further decrease recall in comparison with 16×4 ADC. OPQ yields better results than PQ in all cases (Figure 5b), which is consistent with [5, 11]. Moreover, the difference in recall between 8×8 ADC and 16×4 QADC is lower for OPQ than it is for PQ. OPQ optimizes the decomposition of the input vector space into m subspaces, which are used by the optimized product quantizer (Section 2.1). For $m = 16$, OPQ has more degrees of freedom than for $m = 8$ and is therefore able to bring a greater level of optimization.

For an exhaustive search in 1 million vectors, 16×4 QADC is ~14 times faster than 16×4 ADC and 6 times faster than 8×8 ADC (Figure 5c) (85% decrease in response time). Response times for PQ and OPQ are similar, so we report results for PQ. In practice, 8×8 ADC is much more common than 16×4 ADC [2–4, 11, 15], thus we only compare 16×4 QADC with 8×8 ADC in the remainder of this section. Overall, QADC therefore proposes trading a small decrease in recall, for a large improvement in response time.

Non-exhaustive search offers both a lower response time and a higher recall than exhaustive search (Section 2.2). For this reason, non-exhaustive search is preferred to exhaustive search in practical systems. Therefore, in the remainder of this section, we evaluate QADC in the context of non-exhaustive search, for a wide range of scenarios: SIFT, GIST descriptors, deep feature, PQ and OPQ, 64 and 128 bit codes. We show that in most cases, when combined with OPQ and inverted indexes, QADC offers a decrease in response time close to 70% for a small or negligible loss of accuracy.

4.3 Non-exhaustive Search in SIFT1M

Table 4 compares the Recall@100 (R@100) and total ANN search time (Total). The time spent in each of the search steps (Index, Tables, and Scan) detailed in Section 2.3 is also reported. All times are in milliseconds (ms). OPQ requires a rotation of the input vector before computing lookup tables (Section 2.1). We include the time to perform this rotation in the Tables column. When using inverted indexes, the parameters K, the total number of cells of the inverted index, and ma, the number of cells scanned to answer a query, impact response time and recall (Section 2.3). For datasets of 1 million vectors, we have found the parameters $ma = 24$ and $K = 256$ to offer the best tradeoff.

For this configuration, QADC offers a 75% decrease in scan time. In addition, QADC offers a 50-70% decrease in tables computation time, thanks to the use of 4-bit quantizers, which result in smaller and faster to compute small tables. Overall, this translates into a decrease of approximately 70% in total response time. The loss of recall is significantly lower with OPQ (-1.5%) than with PQ (-4.4%), as OPQ offers a lower quantization error than PQ.

Table 4: Non-exhaustive search, SIFT1M, 64 bit

PQ	ADC*	R@100	Index	Tables	Scan	Total
		SIFT1M, IVF, K=256, ma=24				
PQ	ADC	0.949	0.008	0.18	0.3	0.48
	QADC	0.907	0.008	0.055	0.072	0.14
		-4.4%		*-69%*	*-76%*	*-72%*
OPQ	ADC	0.963	0.008	0.21	0.29	0.52
	QADC	0.949	0.008	0.089	0.073	0.17
		-1.5%		*-59%*	*-75%*	***-67%***

* ADC: 8×8 ADC, QADC: 16×4 QADC

Table 5: Non-exhaustive search, GIST1M, 128 bit

PQ	ADC*	R@100	Index	Tables	Scan	Total
		GIST1M, IVF, K=256, ma=24				
PQ	ADC	0.675	0.038	0.77	0.71	1.5
	QADC	0.515	0.038	0.26	0.15	0.45
		-24%		*-67%*	*-79%*	*-71%*
OPQ	ADC	0.918	0.039	1.7	0.73	2.5
	QADC	0.872	0.038	1.2	0.16	1.4
		-5%		*-32%*	*-78%*	***-45%***

* ADC: 16×8 ADC, QADC: 32×4 QADC

4.4 Non-exhaustive Search in GIST1M

GIST descriptors have a much higher dimensionality (960 dimensions) than SIFT descriptors (128 dimensions). For this reason, GIST descriptors are often encoded into 128-bit codes instead of 64-bit codes [3, 11]. This corresponds to 16×8 codes for ADC and 32×4 codes for QADC. In this case, when combined with PQ, QADC offers a decrease of approximately 70% in total response time, as with 64-bit codes and SIFT descriptors (Table 5). However, the decrease in recall when using QADC with PQ is higher for GIST descriptors (-24%) than for SIFT descriptors (-4.4%). This loss of recall is limited to 5% when combining QADC with OPQ. The decrease in total response time is however less important for OPQ (-45%) than for PQ (-71%). This is because OPQ requires rotating the query vector when computing distance tables. Rotating 960-dimensional GIST descriptors is costly, increasing the time to compute distance tables, which in turn limits the gain in total response time.

4.5 Non-exhaustive Search in Deep1M

The Deep1M dataset comprises L_2-normalized deep features that are PCA-compressed to 256 dimensions. Due to their relatively low dimensionality, these vectors can be encoded into 64-bit codes. As for SIFT and GIST descriptors, QADC offers a 70% decrease in response time when combined with PQ. The decrease in recall (-13%) for Deep1M vectors is between the decrease in recall for SIFT descriptors (-4.4%) and the decrease in recall for GIST descriptors (-24%), which is consistent with the dimensionality of vectors. Once again, OPQ strongly limits the loss of recall (-2.2%). It also limits the gain in total response time (-62%), due to the time spent performing rotations.

Table 6: Non-exhaustive search, Deep1M, 64 bit

PQ	ADC*	R@100	Index	Tables	Scan	Total
		Deep1M, IVF, K=256, ma=24				
PQ	ADC	0.772	0.015	0.24	0.33	0.58
	QADC	0.669	0.013	0.082	0.076	0.17
		-13%		*-66%*	*-77%*	*-71%*
OPQ	ADC	0.922	0.013	0.34	0.32	0.67
	QADC	0.902	0.013	0.16	0.08	0.25
		-2.2%		*-53%*	*-75%*	*-62%*

* ADC: 8×8 ADC, QADC: 16×4 QADC

4.6 Non-exhaustive Search in SIFT1B

We conclude our experimental section by performing experiments on a large dataset of 1 billion SIFT descriptors. For this dataset, we use an inverted index with $K = 65536$ cells and scan $ma = 64$ cells to answer queries. This configuration has been shown to offer best performance [3]. We scan $init = 1000$ vectors before quantizing lookup tables (Section 3.3). For SIFT descriptors, we have shown that combining QADC with OPQ allows a higher recall, with no impact on total response time (Section 4.3). For this reason, we perform experiments with OPQ. As with the SIFT1M dataset, QADC offers a decrease of approximately 70% in response time (Table 7). However, for 64-bit codes the loss of recall is higher on SIFT1B (-7.3%) than on SIFT1M (-1.5%). Using 128-bit codes makes the loss of recall negligible (-1.1%) but increases memory use (Table 8). With 128-bit codes, the database uses 20GB of RAM, therefore we had to run this experiment on our server (Table 2).

4.7 Summary

Our experiments show that QADC offers large performance gains in all cases, at the expense of a small or negligible decrease in recall. For SIFT descriptors, this decrease is always negligible, even when using PQ (Section 4.3). For descriptors of higher dimensionality, the decrease in recall is greater (Section 4.4 and 4.5). Using OPQ brings this loss of recall down to low levels, but also slightly limits the gain in response time (-50% to -60% decrease in response time). Overall, QADC offers an interesting speed-accuracy tradeoff: a loss in recall of 1-5% for a decrease of response time of 50-70%. The case of large datasets is slightly less favorable for QADC: we observe a 7% decrease in accuracy on the SIFT1B dataset, even when using OPQ. However, even in this scenario, QADC exhibits similar or better performance than state-of-the-art systems. Thus, with 64-bit codes, QADC achieves a recall of 0.747 on the SIFT1B dataset in 1.7 ms, while the state-of-the-art OMulti-D-OADC system achieves the same recall in 2 ms [3]. With 128-bit codes, QADC achieves a recall of 0.94 in 3.4 ms while OMulti-D-OADC achieves a recall of 0.901 in 5 ms [3].

Table 7: Non-exhaustive search, SIFT1B, 64 bit

PQ	ADC *	R@100	Index	Tables	Scan	Total
		SIFT1B, IVF, K=65536, ma=64				
OPQ	ADC	0.806	0.52	0.51	4.2	5.2
	QADC	0.747	0.53	0.22	0.92	1.7
		-7.3%		*-57%*	*-78%*	***-68%***

* ADC: 8×8 ADC, QADC: 16×4 QADC

Table 8: Non-exhaustive search, SIFT1B, 128 bits

PQ	ADC *	R@100	Index	Tables	Scan	Total
		SIFT1B, IVF, K=65536, ma=64				
OPQ	ADC	0.95	0.73	1.1	10	12
	QADC	0.94	0.72	0.49	2.2	3.4
		-1.1%		*-57%*	*-78%*	***-72%***

* ADC: 16×8 ADC, QADC: 32×4 QADC

5 RELATED WORK

PQ Fast Scan. Both PQ Fast Scan [1] and Quick ADC speed up the scan of lists of short codes by taking advantage of SIMD. More specifically, PQ Fast Scan and Quick ADC store lookup tables in SIMD registers and use SIMD in-register shuffles in place of cache accesses. The main challenge is that lookup tables used for ANN search are much larger than SIMD registers. PQ Fast Scan tackles this issue by both altering (i) inverted lists (vector grouping) and (ii) lookup tables (minimum tables). PQ Fast Scan uses the standard 8-bit sub-quantizers, hence it incurs no loss of recall. However, because of the transformations it applies, PQ Fast Scan requires a minimum list size of 3 million codes [1]. This limits the applicability of PQ Fast Scan to exhaustive search or to very coarse (and thus inefficient [3, 7]) inverted indexes. On the contrary, Quick ADC imposes no constraints on list sizes, and may be combined with efficient inverted indexes (lists of 1000-10000 vectors) as shown in our experiments (Section 4).

Inverted Multi-index. Inverted multi-indexes [3] provide a finer partition (typical $K = 2^{28}$) of the vector space than inverted indexes (typical $K = 65536$). At query time, this finer partition allows scanning less vectors to achieve the same recall, therefore providing a significant speedup. Unlike PQ Fast Scan, Quick ADC does not require lists of a minimum size. Therefore, Quick ADC can also be combined with multi-indexes to further decrease response time.

Compositional Quantization Models. Recently, compositional vector quantization models inspired by PQ have been proposed. These models offer a lower quantization error than PQ or OPQ. Among these models are Additive Quantization (AQ) [2], Tree Quantization (TQ) [4] and Composite Quantization (CQ) [15]. These models also use cache-resident lookup tables to compute distances, therefore Quick ADC may be combined with them. However, this may require additional work as some of these models use more lookup tables than PQ or OPQ.

6 CONCLUSION

In this paper, we presented Quick ADC, a novel distance computation method for ANN search. Quick ADC achieves a 3 to 6 times speedup over the standard ADC method by efficiently exploiting SIMD. This efficient use of SIMD is enabled by two changes to the ADC procedure: (i) the use of 4-bit quantizers instead of the usual 8-bit quantizers, and (ii) the quantization of floating-point distances to 8-bit integers.

It is known that using 4-bit quantizers may cause a loss in recall [7]. However, through an extensive evaluation, we have shown that this loss is small or negligible when 4-bit quantizers are combined with OPQ and inverted indexes. In addition, we have shown that Quick ADC integrates well with other search acceleration methodes, in particular inverted indexes. Lastly, upcoming SIMD instruction sets (e.g., 512-bit AVX in Xeon Skylake CPUs), will allow Quick ADC to offer both greater speedups (twice more codes processed per cycle) and an even smaller loss of recall (6-bit quantizers instead of 4-bit quantizers).

ACKNOWLEDGEMENTS

Experiments presented in this paper were carried out using the Grid'5000 testbed, supported by a scientific interest group hosted by Inria and including CNRS, RENATER and several Universities as well as other organizations (see https://www.grid5000.fr).

REFERENCES

[1] Fabien André, Anne-Marie Kermarrec, and Nicolas Le Scouarnec. 2015. Cache locality is not enough: High-Performance Nearest Neighbor Search with Product Quantization Fast Scan. *PVLDB* 9, 4 (2015).
[2] Artem Babenko and Victor Lempitsky. 2014. Additive Quantization for Extreme Vector Compression. In *CVPR*.
[3] Artem Babenko and Victor Lempitsky. 2015. The Inverted Multi-Index. *TPAMI* 37, 6 (2015).
[4] Artem Babenko and Victor Lempitsky. 2015. Tree Quantization for Large-Scale Similarity Search and Classification. In *CVPR*.
[5] Tiezheng Ge, Kaiming He, Qifa Ke, and Jian Sun. 2014. Optimized Product Quantization. *TPAMI* 36, 4 (2014).
[6] Johannes Hofmann, Jan Treibig, Georg Hager, and Gerhard Wellein. 2014. Comparing the Performance of Different x86 SIMD Instruction Sets for a Medical Imaging Application on Modern Multi- and Manycore Chips. In *WPMVP*.
[7] Hervé Jégou, Matthijs Douze, and Cordelia Schmid. 2011. Product Quantization for Nearest Neighbor Search. *TPAMI* 33, 1 (2011).
[8] Hervé Jégou, Romain Tavenard, Matthijs Douze, and Laurent Amsaleg. 2011. Searching in one billion vectors: Re-rank with source coding. In *ICASSP*.
[9] Josip Krapac, Florent Perronnin, Teddy Furon, and Hervé Jégou. 2014. Instance Classification with Prototype Selection. In *ICMR*.
[10] David G. Lowe. 1999. Object Recognition from Local Scale-Invariant Features. In *ICCV*.
[11] Mohammad Norouzi and David J. Fleet. 2013. Cartesian K-Means. In *CVPR*.
[12] Aude Oliva and Antonio Torralba. 2001. Modeling the Shape of the Scene: A Holistic Representation of the Spatial Envelope. *IJCV* 42, 3 (2001).
[13] Yan Xia, Kaiming He, Fang Wen, and Jian Sun. 2013. Joint Inverted Indexing. In *ICCV*.
[14] Lingxi Xie, Richang Hong, Bo Zhang, and Qi Tian. 2015. Image Classification and Retrieval are ONE. In *ICMR*.
[15] Ting Zhang, Chao Du, and Jingdong Wang. 2014. Composite Quantization for Approximate Nearest Neighbor Search. In *ICML*.

Improving Small Object Proposals for Company Logo Detection

Christian Eggert
Dan Zecha
Stephan Brehm
Rainer Lienhart
christian.eggert@informatik.uni-augsburg.de
dan.zecha@informatik.uni-augsburg.de
stefan.brehm@informatik.uni-augsburg.de
rainer.lienhart@informatik.uni-augsburg.de
University of Augsburg
Universitätsstr. 6a
Augsburg 86199

ABSTRACT

Many modern approaches for object detection are two-staged pipelines. The first stage identifies regions of interest which are then classified in the second stage. Faster R-CNN is such an approach for object detection which combines both stages into a single pipeline. In this paper we apply Faster R-CNN to the task of company logo detection. Motivated by its weak performance on small object instances, we examine in detail both the proposal and the classification stage with respect to a wide range of object sizes. We investigate the influence of feature map resolution on the performance of those stages.

Based on theoretical considerations, we introduce an improved scheme for generating anchor proposals and propose a modification to Faster R-CNN which leverages higher-resolution feature maps for small objects. We evaluate our approach on the FlickrLogos dataset improving the RPN performance from 0.52 to 0.71 (MABO) and the detection performance from 0.52 to 0.67 (mAP).

CCS CONCEPTS

• **Computing methodologies → Interest point and salient region detections; Object detection; Object recognition;**

KEYWORDS

Object Proposals; Object Detection; Object Recognition; Region Proposal Network; RPN; Small objects; Faster R-CNN; Company Logos; Brand Detection

ACM Reference format:
Christian Eggert, Dan Zecha, Stephan Brehm, and Rainer Lienhart. 2017. Improving Small Object Proposals for Company Logo Detection. In *Proceedings of ICMR '17, Bucharest, Romania, June 06-09, 2017,* 8 pages.
https://doi.org/10.1145/3078971.3078990

ACM ISBN 978-1-4503-4701-3/17/06…$15.00
https://doi.org/10.1145/3078971.3078990

1 INTRODUCTION

Current object detection pipelines like Fast(er) R-CNN [7] [15] are built on deep neural networks whose convolutional layers extract increasingly abstract feature representations by applying previously learned convolutions followed by a non-linear activation function to the image. During this process, the intermediate feature maps are usually downsampled multiple times using max-pooling.

This downsampling has multiple advantages:

(1) It reduces the computational complexity of applying the model
(2) It helps to achieve a certain degree of translational invariance of the feature representation
(3) It also increases the receptive field of neurons in the deeper layers.

The flipside of these advantages is a feature map which has a significantly lower resolution than the original image. As a result of this reduced resolution it is difficult to associate features with a precise location in the original image.

Despite this potential drawback, this approach has been extremely successful in the areas of image classification and object detection. For most applications, pixel-accurate localization is not important.

In this paper we examine the suitability of feature representations from different levels of the feature hierarchy for the problem of company logo detection. Company logo detection is an application of object detection which attracts lots of commercial interest. On a superficial level, company logo detection is nothing but a special case of general object detection. However, company logos are rarely the objects which were intended to be captured when the picture was taken. Instead, they usually happen to get caught in the picture by accident. As a result, company logos tend to occupy a rather small image area.

Intersection over union (IoU) is the usual criterion by which the quality of the localization is assessed. By this measure, a detection which is off by a given amount of pixels has a greater influence on small object instances than large ones. Therefore, small object instances require a more precise localization than large instances in order to be classified as correct detections.

Another problem is, that small objects typically are detected with a lower confidence score than large objects. Experiments done by [5] show that this effect is not necessarily rooted in the low resolution of the objects and that detection performance can be improved by simply magnifying the test images.

Magnifying input images would also alleviate the former problem but this simple approach is not very appealing since the effort for applying the convolutions grows quadratically with the side length of the image. This is especially true for company logo detection in which the object is typically small compared to the image, resulting in much unnecessary computation.

Our contributions are as follows:

(1) We theoretically examine the problem of small objects at the proposal stage. We derive a relationship which describes the minimum object size which can reasonably be proposed and provide a heuristic for choosing appropriate anchor scales.
(2) We perform detailed experiments which capture the behavior of both the proposal and the classification stage as as a function of object size using features from different feature maps. Deeper layers are potentially able to deliver features of higher quality which means that individual activations are more specific to input stimuli than earlier layers. We show that in the case of small objects, features from earlier layers are able to deliver a performance which is on par with – and can even exceed – the performance of features from deeper layers.
(3) We evaluate our observations on the well-known FlickrLogos dataset [16] in the form of an extension to the Faster R-CNN pipeline

Since FlickrLogos has been originally been conceived as a benchmark for image retrieval we have re-annotated the dataset for the task of object detection[1].

2 RELATED WORK

Object proposals traditionally have played an important role in DCNN-based object detection due to the high computational cost of applying a DCNN in a sliding window fashion.

R-CNN [8] was one of the first approaches which applied DCNNs to object detection. External algorithms like Selective Search [19] or Edge Boxes [20] were used to generate regions of interest. The DCNN would extract a separate feature representation of each ROI which was subsequently used for classification through a support vector machine [3].

Fast R-CNN [7] is able to speed up object detection by not computing a separate feature representation for each ROI. It applies the convolutional layers of a DCNN across the complete image, generating a single feature map. For each ROI, an ROI-Pooling layer computes a fixed-dimensional representation from parts of the feature map, which is then used for classification. Faster R-CNN [15] finally incorporates the generation of object proposals into the network itself by introducing a region proposal network (RPN) which operates on the same single feature map of the image.

Some approaches to object detection can manage without explicitly generating object proposals. Two representatives of this class are YOLO [14] and SSD [12]. However, these algorithms are typically optimized for real-time object detection and usually do not perform as well on small object instances which limits their applicability for company logo detection.

Scale is a potentially bigger problem for Fast(er) R-CNN than for R-CNN since it does not rescale every ROI to a standard size. Therefore, some efforts have been made to mitigate this problem: [5] use a multi-scale approach while avoiding to build a complete image pyramid by using the initial feature representation of small objects to decide which ROIs should be examined in more detail. The corresponding image parts are packed into a new image which is magnified and a new feature map is being computed.

Other approaches build a multi-scale feature representation: [1] apply techniques like skip-pooling to create multi-scale feature representations. They also consider encoding the context of an object using features obtained by an recurrent network. Hypercolumns [9] attempt to construct a single multi-scale feature representation by concatenating feature maps generated on different levels of the DCNN while [17] combine predictions based on different feature maps to a single more accurate preduction. Most similar to the network architecture used in our work are Feature Pyramid Networks [11] (FPNs) which compute hierarchical feature maps on different scales but introduce another path to the network which aggregates the different feature map into a multi-scale representation.

All of these approaches focus on multi-scale feature representations to increase the performance of the classifier. However, in this work we focus on the limitations that are inherent in the choice of the anchor sets. By this, we mean the impact of anchors on the RPN performance, assuming a perfect classifier. Therefore the considerations in this paper are largely complementary to the previously mentioned approaches.

The specific problem of company logo detection with DCNNs has previously been studied by [5, 13] and [2]. All of these approaches use the above-mentioned R-CNN [8] or Fast R-CNN [7] pipelines using externally generated object proposals. In this paper we apply RPNs to this task and study the problems that arise for small objects.

3 SMALL OBJECTS IN FASTER R-CNN

Current object detection pipelines usually consist of two stages: First, they identify regions of interest (ROIs) from images. These ROIs serve as an attention model and propose potential object locations which are more closely examined in the second stage.

For our experiments we use a re-implementation of the Faster R-CNN [15] approach. Faster R-CNN extracts a feature representation of the image through a series of learned convolutions. This feature map forms the basis of both the object proposal stage and the classification stage. The first step is accomplished by a Region Proposal Network (RPN) which starts by generating a dense grid of anchor regions with specified size and aspect ratio over the input image.

For each anchor, the RPN – which is a fully convolutional network – predicts a score which is a measure of the probability of this anchor containing an object of interest. Furthermore, the RPN predicts two offsets and scale factors for each anchor which are part of a bounding box regression mechanism which refines the object's location. The refined anchors are sorted by score, subjected

[1] The updated annotations and evaluation script are made available here: http://www.multimedia-computing.de/flickrlogos

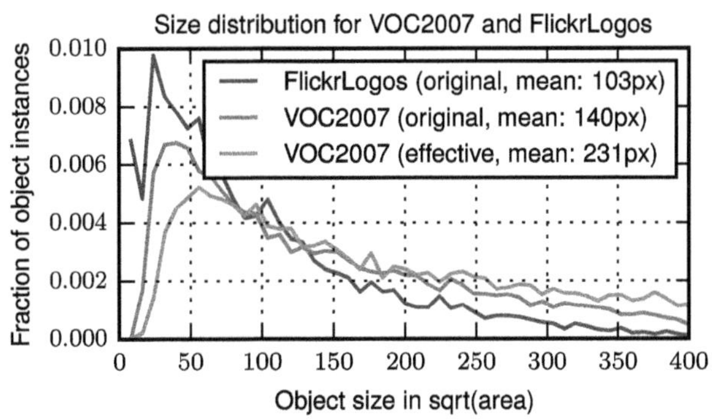

Figure 1: Distribution of object instance sizes in VOC2007 and FlickrLogos. The effective size distribution – induced by dynamic rescaling in Faster R-CNN – is shifted towards larger object instances.

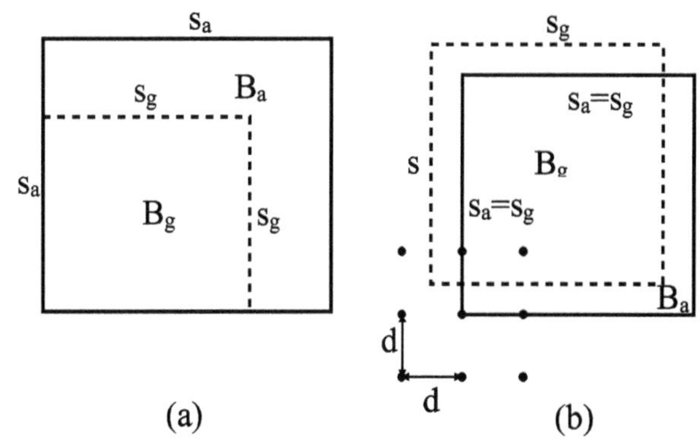

Figure 2: (a) IoU can be expressed as the ratio of bounding box areas in the case of aligned bounding boxes of equal aspect ratio. (b) Worst case displacement of two bounding boxes of equal size when anchors are sampled with stride *d*

to a non-maximum suppression and the best scoring anchors are kept as object proposals which are fed into the second stage of the network.

At training time, anchors are divided into positive and negative examples, depending on the overlap they have with a groundtruth instance. Typically, an anchor is considered to be a positive example if it has an IoU greater than 0.5 with a groundtruth object.

Ren et. al [15] use anchors whose side length are powers of two, starting with 128 pixels. This choice of anchors delivers good results on datasets such as VOC2007 [6] where the objects are typically relatively large and fill a sizeable proportion of the total image area. Furthermore, [15] also dynamically re-scale input images to enlarge the objects: Images are rescaled in a way so that their minimum side length is at least 600px but their maximum side length does not exceed 1000px. This rescaling results in a size distribution which is distinct from the one of the original VOC2007 dataset. Both the original and the resulting size distribution are illustrated in Figure 1.

Upscaling the input images typically improves the detection performance which is interesting, since upscaling cannot introduce new information. This has already been noted by [5] who attribute this property to the receptive field of the network.

Figure 1 also shows the size distribution of the FlickrLogos [16] dataset. The average object size is quite small compared with the average side length of the images (which is typically around 1000 pixels). Rescaling the images so that logo instances are on a comparable scale to the VOC2007 dataset would result in huge images. This means that upscaling of input images is typically not feasible for company logo detection.

Figure 1 also makes it clear, that an anchor of side length of 128*px* – which is the smallest anchor scale used in the default Faster R-CNN approach – is inadequate to cover the range of object sizes. In order to counter this problem one could simply add additional anchors using the same powers-of-two scheme used by [15]. However, we show that this scheme leads to difficulties – particularly for small objects – as it might fail to generate an anchor box with sufficient overlap.

To illustrate the problem we will imagine an object proposal system which has learned to perfectly predict the concept of a ROI as taught during the training phase. This means, we imagine a classifier which for every possible anchor is able to predict perfectly, whether the anchor has an IoU with a groundtruth instance of at least 0.5.

Assuming such a classifier, consider the situation in Figure 2a: We assume a quadratic groundtruth bounding box B_g of side length s_g and a quadratic anchor box B_a of side length s_a. Furthermore we will assume w.l.o.g. that $s_g \leq s_a$ and that both side lengths are related through a scaling factor $\alpha \geq 1$ by $s_a = \alpha s_g$. Under these conditions we can move B_g anywhere inside of B_a without changing the IoU.

In this case we can express the IoU as the ratio between the areas enclosed by these boxes:

$$t \leq IoU(B_g, B_a) = \frac{|B_g \cap B_a|}{|B_g \cup B_a|} = \frac{s_g^2}{s_a^2} = \frac{1}{\alpha^2} \quad (1)$$

In order for an anchor box to be classified as positive example we require the IoU to exceed a certain threshold t. It follows that for $\alpha > \sqrt{t}^{-1}$ an anchor is unable to cover a groundtruth box with sufficient overlap to be classified as a positive example. The same relationship holds for non-quadratic anchors – provided the aspect ratio of groundtruth boxes and anchor boxes match.

Therefore, the side length of anchor boxes of neighboring scales s_{a_1} and s_{a_2} should be related by $s_{a_2} = \sqrt{t}^{-1} s_{a_1}$.

For the previous considerations we assume that there exists an anchor position at which the corner of an anchor is completely aligned with the groundtruth instance. In practice this is not true since the feature map of the network upon which the RPN is based usually has a much smaller resolution than the original image. A downsampling factor d^{-1} between the original image and the feature map effectively results in a grid of anchors with stride d.

To examine the influence of feature map resolution on the RPNs potential to identify small object instances, we consider the situation in Figure 2b. We assume a quadratic groundtruth instance B_g and the existence of an anchor box B_a of identical scale and aspect ratio. In the worst case, both boxes are displaced against each other by a distance of $\frac{d}{2}$. The IoU between these boxes can be expressed by:

$$IoU(B_g, B_a) = \frac{(s_g - \frac{d}{2})^2}{(s_g - \frac{d}{2})^2 + 2(2\frac{d}{2}(s_g - \frac{d}{2}) + \frac{d^2}{4})} \quad (2)$$

Solving $t \leq IoU(B_g, B_a)$ for s_g while assuming $d > 0$ and $0 < t < 1$ and ignoring negative solutions for this quadratic expression, we obtain the following relationship for the minimum detectable object size:

$$\frac{d(t+1) + d\sqrt{2t(t+1)}}{2 - 2t} \leq s_g \quad (3)$$

For the VGG16 [18] architecture, which is commonly used as basis for Faster R-CNN, $d = 16$. Assuming $t = 0.5$, this translates into a minimum detectable object size of $s_g \approx 44px$. This suggests that for the small end of our size distribution a feature map of higher resolution is needed. For the *conv4* feature map ($d = 8$) the minimum detectable object size is given by $s_g \approx 22px$. Since we do not expect to reliably classify objects smaller than 30px we use the next power of two as smallest anchor size.

Making use of our previous result we choose as our anchor set $\mathcal{A} = \{32, 45, 64, 90, 128, 181, 256\}$ since we follow the recommendation of [15] and set $t = 0.5$.

3.1 Region Proposals of small objects

We want to evaluate the effectiveness of RPNs for different object sizes. The primary measure of an RPN's quality is the mean average best overlap (MABO). It measures the RPN's ability to generate at least one proposal region for each object with high overlap. If C represents the set of object classes, G_c the set of groundtruth objects of a particular class $c \in C$ and $\mathcal{L}$ the set of object proposals, we can evaluate the performance of the RPN for a particular class c via its average best overlap $ABO(c)$ given by:

$$ABO(c) = \frac{1}{|G_c|} \sum_{g \in G_c} \max_{l \in L} IoU(g, l) \quad (4)$$

where $IoU(g, l)$ is the intersection over union between the groundtruth item g and the proposal l. The MABO is the mean over all ABO values for each object class.

In order to examine the influence of object size on the performance of the RPN, we create differently scaled synthetic variants of the FlickrLogos [16] dataset by applying the following algorithm to each image:

We start by selecting the point which has the maximum distance between two non-overlapping groundtruth bounding boxes. This point defines two axes along which the image is to be partitioned into four parts. We ensure that the axes of the split do not intersect with any other groundtruth items. If no such split can be found, the image is discarded. For each of the resulting partitions which contain more than one groundtruth item, the process is applied recursively. After applying this algorithm, each image contains only a single object instance which is then rescaled to match the desired target size.

Using this algorithm we create 11 differently scaled versions of the test set which we call $F_{test,x}$ where $x \in \{10 * i + 20 | i = 0 \ldots 10\}$ represents the target object size, measured as square root of the object area. Additionally, we create a single training dataset F_{train}

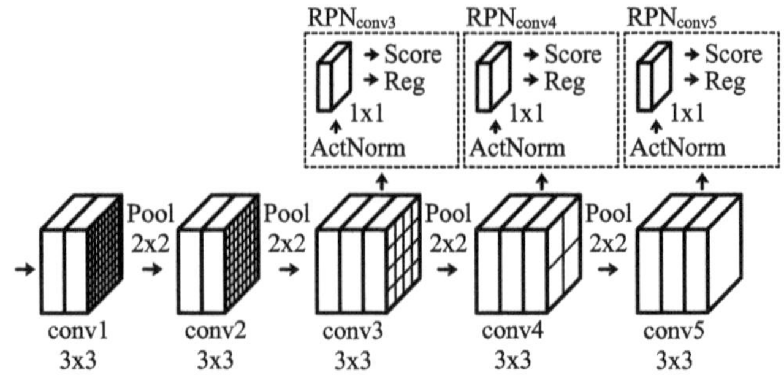

Figure 3: Template for the construction of our RPNs. The RPN uses the same number of channels as the preceeding feature map and outputs object proposals as a grid of predictions with the same resolution.

in which the objects are scaled in such a way that the square root of the object area is distributed evenly in the interval [20px, 120px].

In order to observe the performance of the RPN for different layers we create three RPNs: RPN_{conv3}, RPN_{conv4} and RPN_{conv5} based on the VGG16 [18] architecture used by [15] and attach RPN modules to the *conv3*[2], *conv4* and *conv5* layers, respectively. The template for this network is illustrated in Figure 3. Each network is trained separately with only one of the RPN modules active at a time.

The features are passed through a normalization layer which normalizes the activations to have zero-mean and unit-variance. This is similar to batch normalization [10]. However, we normalize the activations with respect to the training set and not with respect to the current batch as in [10]. We do this so that we can easily use an off-the-shelf Imagenet [4]-pretrained VGG16 network. Those pre-trained models usually have the property that the variance of activations decreases from layer to layer as the data progresses through the network. This property makes it hard to make certain changes to the network architecture. For example, adding additional branches of different depths will result in differently scaled activations in each branch which in turn leads to different effective learning rates in each branch. This normalization scheme circumvents this problem.

We place a standard RPN on top of this feature normalization which consists of a 3×3 convolution using the same number of channels than the preceeding layer. The output of this RPN is then used in two additional convolutional layers which predict anchor scores and regressors (see [15] for details). In the case of RPN_{conv3} we use the features from the *conv3* layer for predicting bounding boxes.

We fine-tune each of our RPNs on the F_{train} dataset for 40000 iterations with an initial learning rate of $\mu = 0.001$ on our set of anchors $\mathcal{A}$. The learning rate is decreased by a factor of $\gamma = 0.1$ after 30000 iterations. We then evaluate the trained RPNs on the different $F_{test,x}$ datasets while only considering the outputs for a single anchor at a time. As a result we are able to plot how effective the different feature maps are at predicting object proposals of

[2] *conv3* refers to the output of the last layer of the *conv3* block which is *conv3_3* when using the naming convention of [18]

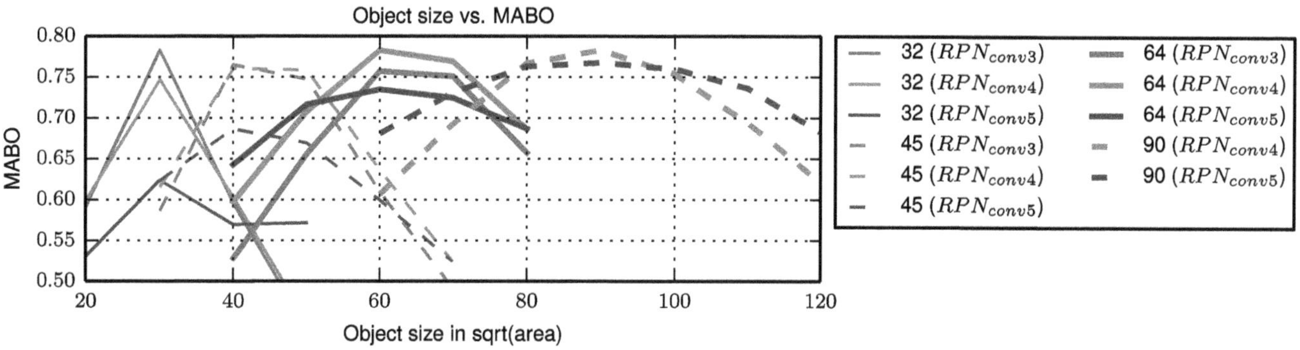

Figure 4: RPN performance (MABO) for different anchor sizes as a function of object size. (green) performance of *conv3*, (red) performance of *conv4*, (blue) performance of *conv5*. Proposals for small objects can be generated more effectively by earlier layers while the performance of the *conv5* layer drops noticeably.

a given size. Figure 4 shows the result of this experiment. Each point on the abscissa represents the result of an experiment with the corresponding $F_{test,x}$ dataset while the ordinate reports the performance for this experiment as MABO.

Figure 4 shows that for small objects the *conv5* feature map delivers results which are noticably inferior than the results generated by the *conv3* or *conv4* feature maps.

Another observation to be made is that earlier feature maps deliver a more localized response for every anchor than the *conv5* feature map. This manifests itself in a steeper performance drop as the object size moves away from the ideal anchor size. This is a consistent pattern over all examined object sizes: Even medium sized objects with a side length between 80px and 100px are better predicted by the *conv4* feature map. However, this in only true if the object size closely matches the anchor size. The *conv5* feature map is able to deliver a more stable performance over a larger range of object sizes.

3.2 ROI Classification of small objects

After identifying ROIs, Faster RCNN predicts a score and bounding box regressants for each ROI and for every class. In the original approach, this stage re-uses the previously computed *conv5* feature map which was used to generate the object proposals. An ROI-Pooling [7] layer projects the ROI coordinates identified by the RPN onto the feature map using the downsampling factor of the network. The corresponding area of the feature map is converted into a fixed-dimensional representation with a pre-determined spatial resolution (usually 7 × 7). Each of these feature representations is then fed into several fully connected layers for classification and class-specific bounding box regression.

We perform an analysis of the performance of the classification stage by object size which is similar to our analysis of the RPN. Unlike RPNs, where each anchor by virtue of its size and the overlap criterion self-selects appropriate training examples, the classification stage does not have this property. We therefore need to be careful about the size distribution in the training set.

For the scope of this paper we are interested in the maximum performance each feature map can deliver for a specific object

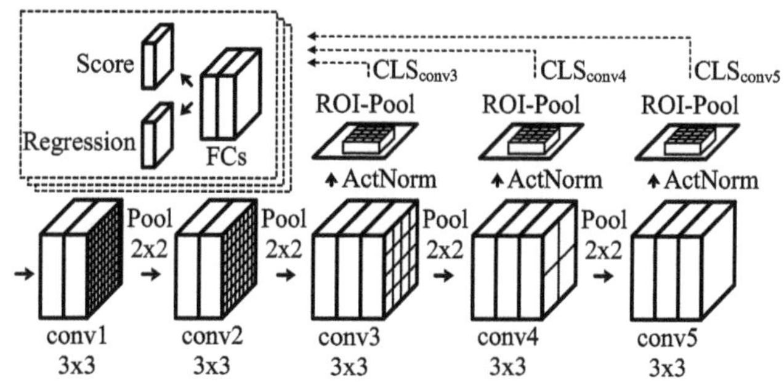

Figure 5: Template for the construction of our classification networks. The fully connected layers of the classification pipeline are attached to an ROI-Pooling layer operating on a specific feature map.

size. In order to avoid any effects from size distribution we ideally want a separate training set for each test set $F_{test,x}$. To reduce the training effort, we combine multiple sizes into a single training set. For this purpose we generate four training sets $F_{train,a,b}$ where a represents the minimum object size and b the maximum object size as the square root of the object area. We choose

$$(a, b) \in \{(20px, 60px), (40px, 80px), (60px, 100px), (80px, 120px)\}$$

to adequately cover the range of small objects in the FlickrLogos dataset (see Figure 1).

Similar to our evaluation of the RPN, we generate three versions of the classification pipeline: CLS_{conv3}, CLS_{conv4} and CLS_{conv5}. CLS_{conv5} is identical in architecture to the default pipeline described in [7]. The other two networks are similar: They only differ in the feature map that they are based on, and the normalization layer described in chapter 3. During training, we only train the fully-connected layers and compare these results to a network where all layers are optimized (CLS_{conv5}(all)).

We train each of these networks on all of the training sets $F_{train,a,b}$ for 40000 iterations, an initial learning rate of $\mu = 0.01$ with a reduction by a factor $\gamma = 0.1$ after 30000 iterations. Each

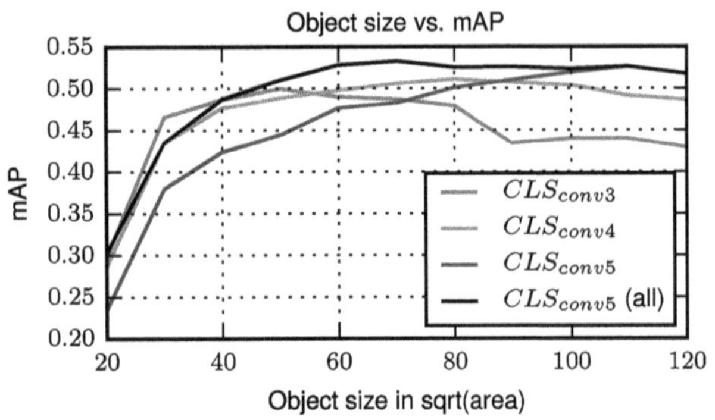

Figure 6: Performance of the classification pipeline by size. The performance for *conv5* features drops noticeably for small object sizes. However, a full optimization (*conv5* (all)) is able to adapt to a wide range of scales.

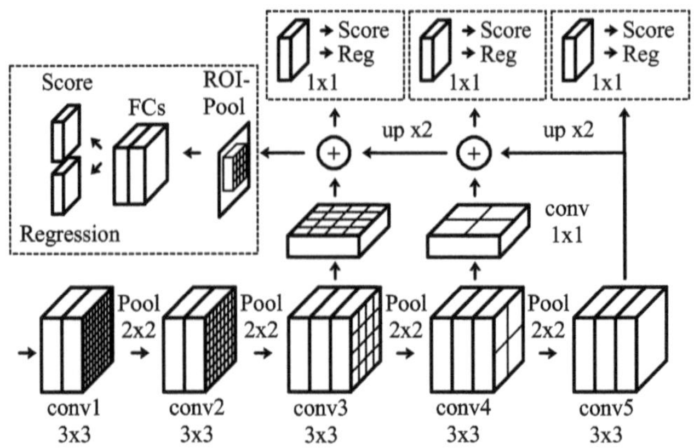

Figure 7: Our modified architecture (FPN16) which makes use of feature maps on multiple scales (batch normalization layers are not shown). In addition to the bottom-up feature extraction we add a top-down path which summarizes multi-scale feature representations into a single feature map.

of those models in evaluated according to their mean average precision (mAP) on all the test sets $F_{test,x}$ where $a \leq x \leq b$. Since the ranges of object sizes between the training sets overlap with each other, we obtain multiple mAP values for each object size x – represented by the test set $F_{test,x}$. We take the maximum mAP for each version of the classification pipeline. Since we are solely interested in the performance of the classification stage, we need to eliminate any potential influences between RPN and classification. We therefore assume a perfect RPN for this experiment and evaluate our networks using groundtruth bounding boxes as object proposals.

Figure 6 shows the results of this experiment. Unsurprisingly, the classification performance generally declines for small object instances across all feature maps. When only the fully connected layers are optimized we see a similar trend as in the region proposal network. For example, the CLS_{conv3} network delivers a better performance for small objects than the CLS_{conv5} network. When we allow all layers to adapt, this effect disappears. This behavior shows that DCNNs can potentially adapt to a wide range of input scales. However, it also suggests that once the network is trained, the filters in each feature map are optimized for a particular scale.

On the other hand, it is generally accepted that deeper layers are more specific in their activations to certain stimuli and are therefore better suited for computer vision tasks. Ideally, we want to have the best of both worlds: We want to select the feature map at which the filters are best suited for the scale of the object, but we also want high-quality deep features.

4 AN INTEGRATED DETECTION PIPELINE

While our anchor set has the potential to improve object proposals in most detection pipelines which utilize an RPN, we want to improve object proposals even further. In our previous experiments we have shown that the resolution of the feature map can have a strong influence on the performance of the RPN, particularly for small anchors. In the following, we want to explore, whether the performance can be improved further by incorporating information from deeper feature maps.

In the previous chapter we have also examined the scale behavior of the classification stage and have observed a similar behavior. But the behavior of both stages differs in a key point: The classification stage is able to accommodate a wide range of object sizes when all layers of the network are allowed to adapt. This is not the case for the RPN: Even when all layers are allowed to adapt, the scale of an object still determines which feature map is most effective in predicting the ROI. In other words, the performance of the RPN for small objects is mainly limited by the resolution of the anchor grid which is directly dependent on the resolution of the feature map.

However, the ability of the classification stage to adapt to a wide range of object sizes does not mean that it cannot benefit from information from earlier layers. In fact, our experiments described in chapter 3.2 suggest that once the network has been trained on objects of a certain size, the object size determines the feature map which is most effective for classification.

In order to take advantage of the information contained in earlier feature maps we modify our network architecture in the following way (inspired by Feature Pyramid Networks [11]): In addition to the bottom-up path which extracts the feature hierarchy, we introduce a second top-down path which allows the network to combine feature maps from multiple scales. This architecture is illustrated in Figure 7. High-level feature maps are upscaled by a factor of 2 to fit the resolution of the next lower-level feature map using bilinear interpolation. The lower-level features are allowed to adapt through a 1×1 convolution before being combined with the upscaled feature map by summation. This top-down path extends from the *conv5* feature map down to the *conv3* feature map.

We attach RPN modules at every intermediate feature map generated on the top-down path. Each module is responsible for generating object proposals suitable for its scale. In accordance with our observations from Figure 4 we use the following assignment of anchor sizes to feature maps:

Anchors with a side length $\leq$ 45*px* are assigned to the RPN attached to the *conv3* feature map. All anchors with a side length in the interval $[45px, 90px]$ are assigned to the RPN attached to the *conv4* feature map. Finally, all anchors scales $\geq 90px$ are assigned to the *conv5* feature map.

For generating object proposals we first take the individual proposals from each individual RPN on which we perform an individual non-maximum suppression – suppressing boxes with an IoU ≥ 0.7. The remaining proposals are merged and another non-maximum suppression is applied.

We attach the fully-connected layers of the classification stage at the feature map generated at the end of the top-down path. In principle, we could also extend the model to train multiple classifiers for separate scales. However, the vast majority ($> 1 * 10^8$) of learnable parameters of the VGG16 architecture are concentrated in the fully-connected layers of the network. A separate classifier for each feature map would inflate the already large model disproportionately. Since our previous experiments have shown the ability of the classifier to adapt to a wide range of objects, we do not consider this inflation justifiable.

As a sidenote on the implementation: Simply attaching additional arms to the existing VGG16 architecture proved unsuccessful. Since the original network operates on unnormalized input data, the magnitude of the activations varies strongly across the different layers. We have observed that fine-tuning such a network with added arms can destroy the pre-trained weights. In order to be able to make these extensions to the VGG16 network we also need to modify its base model. We introduce batch normalization [10] layers after every block of convolutions, that is after the *conv1*, *conv2*, etc. Additionally, we apply batch normalization directly on the network input, effectively standardizing the input data. We pretrain the network on the Imagenet [4] dataset before fine-tuning it on FlickrLogos.

5 EVALUATION

We evaluate the effectiveness of our approach separately for both stages of the pipeline along two dimensions: (1) The architecture of the underlying network and (2) the anchor set used to generate object proposals. We will refer to the unmodified original architecture as *VGG16* which uses only features from the *conv5* feature map. *FPN16* refers to our modified architecture which uses information from multiple scales using the top-down path. After extracting object proposals on the FlickrLogos dataset ($n = 2000$) we hold these proposals fixed and use them to train and evaluate the classification pipeline separately.

We first evaluate the impact of our extended anchor set on the unmodified original pipeline. For this purpose we evaluate three sets of anchors: As our baseline we evaluate the default anchor set $\mathcal{A}_{orig}$ which is used by the original Faster R-CNN implementation consisting of the scales $\mathcal{A}_{orig} = \{128, 256, 512\}$. $\mathcal{A}_{ext} = \{32, 64, 128, 256\}$ refers to the default anchor set which has been adapted for the size distribution of the FlickrLogos dataset (Figure 1) but is a straightforward extension using the default powers-of-two scheme. Finally, we evaluate an anchor set $\mathcal{A}_{prop}$ which implements our theoretical considerations from chapter 3.1 which aims to provide a more complete coverage of object scales. $\mathcal{A}_{prop} = \{32, 45, 64, 90, 128, 256\}$.

The results of this evaluation is shown in Table 1. Surprisingly, the original anchor set performs quite well, despite the fact that

Architecture	Anchor set	RPN	CLS	max. Recall
VGG16	$\mathcal{A}_{orig}$	0.52	0.51	0.56
VGG16	$\mathcal{A}_{ext}$	0.66	0.62	0.72
VGG16	$\mathcal{A}_{prop}$	0.68	0.66	**0.76**
FPN16	$\mathcal{A}_{ext}$	0.69	0.66	0.75
FPN16	$\mathcal{A}_{prop}$	**0.71**	**0.67**	**0.76**

Table 1: Evaluation of RPN and classification performance of both the original architecture and the proposed multiscale architecture for different anchor sets. RPN performance is measured in MABO and classification performance (CLS) is measured in mAP.

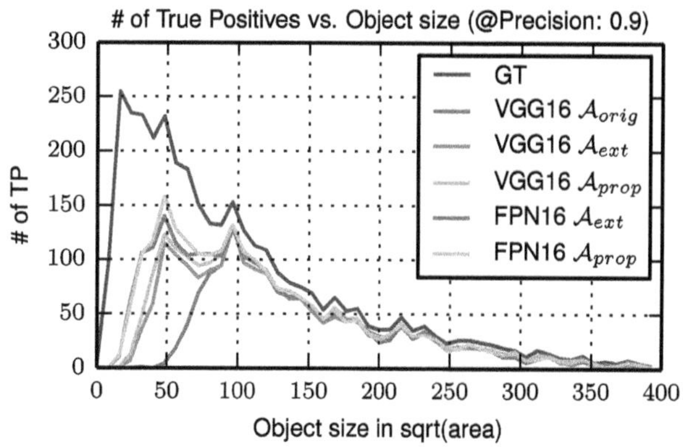

Figure 8: True positives as a function of groundtruth instance size on the FlickrLogos test set. An improved detection of small objects is the source of the overall performance increase as measured by the mAP.

it has not been tuned to the size distribution of the FlickrLogos dataset. However, the strong improvement of the extended anchor set makes it is quite clear that the orignal RPN is missing many small objects. Our proposed anchor set is able to achieve an even better performance which indicates that the powers-of-two scheme is indeed unable to find an anchor with sufficient overlap for some objects.

Table 1 also shows the benefit of of multi-resolution feature maps. We evaluate *FPN16* on the $\mathcal{A}_{ext}$ and the $\mathcal{A}_{prop}$ anchor sets. In both cases we are able to achieve a substantial improvement in the performance of the RPN. Unsurprisingly, the improved object proposals also have a positive impact on the overall detection performance. However, the relationship between MABO and mAP is not linear. This is probably due to the fact that small objects typically are detected with a lower confidence score than large objects.

Figure 9 shows two images with example detections while Figure 8 illustrated the distribution of true positives across all object sizes on the FlickrLogos test set for the approaches evaluated in Table 1. It is clear, that the overall performance increase as measured

Figure 9: (left) Example detections from the FlickrLogos dataset, comparing detections using the $\mathcal{A}_{orig}$ anchor set (VGG16). (right) Example detection using the $\mathcal{A}_{prop}$ anchor set (FPN16). The detection of small logo instances can be visibly improved using our proposed anchor set combined with classification using multiple feature maps.

by the mAP mostly originates in an improved detection of small objects.

6 CONCLUSION

We have performed a theoretical analysis of the region proposal stage and derived a relationship between feature map resolution and the minimum object size which can reasonably be detected, assuming a perfect classifier.

Our experiments of the scale behavior of the RPN on different feature maps have shown that feature map resolution plays an important role in reliably detecting small object instances. Small objects can often be detected more accurately on earlier feature maps despite the fact that these features might not be as expressive than features from deeper layers. This behavior persists, even when all layers of the network are being optimized.

We performed similar experiments on the classification stage and found it to exhibit the same behavior once the filters are fixed. However, we have also observed that the filters in the convolutional layers can adapt to a wide range of scales when given the chance.

Finally we have integrated our findings into the Faster R-CNN framework using an improved network architecture based on Feature Pyramid Networks. We were able to show that integrating features from multiple feature maps while at the same time selecting a suitable resolution for generating proposals can improve the performance of the RPN considerably.

7 ACKNOWLEDGEMENTS

This work was funded by GfK Verein. The authors would like to thank Carolin Kaiser, Holger Dietrich and Raimund Wildner for the great collaboration. Especially, we would like to express our gratitude for their help in re-annotating the FlickrLogos dataset.

REFERENCES

[1] S. Bell, C. L. Zitnick, K. Bala, and R. Girshick. 2016. Inside-Outside Net: Detecting Objects in Context with Skip Pooling and Recurrent Neural Networks. In *2016 IEEE Conference on Computer Vision and Pattern Recognition (CVPR)*. 2874–2883. https://doi.org/10.1109/CVPR.2016.314

[2] S. Bianco, M. Buzzelli, D. Mazzini, and R. Schettini. 2017. Deep Learning for Logo Recognition. *CoRR* abs/1701.02620 (2017). http://arxiv.org/abs/1701.02620

[3] Bernhard E. Boser, Isabelle M. Guyon, and Vladimir N. Vapnik. 1992. A Training Algorithm for Optimal Margin Classifiers. In *Proceedings of the Fifth Annual Workshop on Computational Learning Theory (COLT '92)*. ACM, New York, NY, USA, 144–152. https://doi.org/10.1145/130385.130401

[4] J. Deng, W. Dong, R. Socher, L. J. Li, Kai Li, and Li Fei-Fei. 2009. ImageNet: A large-scale hierarchical image database. In *2009 IEEE Conference on Computer Vision and Pattern Recognition*. 248–255. https://doi.org/10.1109/CVPR.2009.5206848

[5] C. Eggert, A. Winschel, D. Zecha, and R. Lienhart. 2016. Saliency-guided Selective Magnification for Company Logo Detection. In *2016 International Conference on Pattern Recognition (ICPR)*.

[6] M. Everingham, L. Van Gool, C. K. I. Williams, J. Winn, and A. Zisserman. 2010. The Pascal Visual Object Classes (VOC) Challenge. *International Journal of Computer Vision* 88, 2 (June 2010), 303–338.

[7] R. Girshick. 2015. Fast R-CNN. In *IEEE International Conference on Computer Vision*. 1440–1448. https://doi.org/10.1109/ICCV.2015.169

[8] R. Girshick, J. Donahue, T. Darrell, and J. Malik. 2014. Rich Feature Hierarchies for Accurate Object Detection and Semantic Segmentation. In *IEEE Conference on Computer Vision and Pattern Recognition*. 580–587. https://doi.org/10.1109/CVPR.2014.81

[9] B. Hariharan, P. Arbelaez, R. Girshick, and J. Malik. 2016. Object Instance Segmentation and Fine-Grained Localization using Hypercolumns. *IEEE Transactions on Pattern Analysis and Machine Intelligence* PP, 99 (2016). https://doi.org/10.1109/TPAMI.2016.2578328

[10] S. Ioffe and C. Szegedy. 2015. Batch Normalization: Accelerating Deep Network Training by Reducing Internal Covariate Shift. In *International Conference on Machine Learning*. 448–465.

[11] Tsung-Yi Lin, Piotr Dollár, Ross Girshick, Kaiming He, Bharath Hariharan, and Serge Belongie. 2016. Feature Pyramid Networks for Object Detection. *arXiv preprint arXiv:1612.03144* (2016).

[12] Wei Liu, Dragomir Anguelov, Dumitru Erhan, Christian Szegedy, Scott Reed, Cheng-Yang Fu, and Alexander C. Berg. 2016. SSD: Single Shot MultiBox Detector. (2016). http://arxiv.org/abs/1512.02325

[13] G. Oliveira, X. Frazao, A. Pimentel, and B. Ribeiro. 2016. Automatic graphic logo detection via Fast Region-based Convolutional Networks. In *2016 International Joint Conference on Neural Networks (IJCNN)*. 985–991. https://doi.org/10.1109/IJCNN.2016.7727305

[14] J. Redmon, S. Divvala, R. Girshick, and A. Farhadi. 2016. You Only Look Once: Unified, Real-Time Object Detection. In *2016 IEEE Conference on Computer Vision and Pattern Recognition (CVPR)*. 779–788. https://doi.org/10.1109/CVPR.2016.91

[15] S. Ren, K. He, R. Girshick, and J. Sun. 2016. Faster R-CNN: Towards Real-Time Object Detection with Region Proposal Networks. *IEEE Transactions on Pattern Analysis and Machine Intelligence* (2016). https://doi.org/10.1109/TPAMI.2016.2577031

[16] S. Romberg, L. G. Pueyo, Lienhart R., and R. van Zwol. 2011. Scalable logo recognition in real-world images. In *ACM International Conference on Multimedia Retrieval (ICMR '11)*. ACM, Article 25, 8 pages. https://doi.org/10.1145/1991996.1992021

[17] E. Shelhamer, J. Long, and T. Darrell. 2016. Fully Convolutional Networks for Semantic Segmentation. *IEEE Transactions on Pattern Analysis and Machine Intelligence* PP, 99 (2016). https://doi.org/10.1109/TPAMI.2016.2572683

[18] K. Simonyan and A. Zisserman. 2015. Very Deep Convolutional Networks for Large-Scale Image Recognition. In *International Conference on Learning Representations*.

[19] J. R. R. Uijlings, K. E. A. Sande, T. Gevers, and A. W. M. Smeulders. 2013. Selective Search for Object Recognition. *International Journal of Computer Vision* 104, 2 (2013), 154–171. https://doi.org/10.1007/s11263-013-0620-5

[20] L. Zitnick and P. Dollár. 2014. Edge Boxes: Locating Object Proposals from Edges. In *ECCV*. European Conference on Computer Vision.

Discrete Multi-view Hashing for Effective Image Retrieval

Rui Yang
School of Computer Science and Technology, Shandong University
1500 Shunhua Road
Jinan, Shandong, China 250101
yrui1023@163.com

Yuliang Shi*
School of Computer Science and Technology, Shandong University
1500, Shunhua Road
Jinan, Shandong, China 250101
shiyuliang@sdu.edu.cn

Xin-Shun Xu†
School of Computer Science and Technology, Shandong University
1500, Shunhua Road
Jinan, Shandong, China 250101
xuxinshun@sdu.edu.cn

ABSTRACT

Recently, hashing techniques have witnessed an increase in popularity due to their low storage cost and high query speed for large scale data retrieval task, e.g., image retrieval. Many methods have been proposed; however, most existing hashing techniques focus on single view data. In many scenarios, there are multiple views in data samples. Thus, those methods working on single view can not make full use of rich information contained in multi-view data. Although some methods have been proposed for multi-view data; they usually relax binary constraints or separate the process of learning hash functions and binary codes into two independent stages to bypass the obstacle of handling the discrete constraints on binary codes for optimization, which may generate large quantization error. To consider these problems, in this paper, we propose a novel hashing method, i.e., Discrete Multi-view Hashing (DMVH), which can work on multi-view data directly and make full use of rich information in multi-view data. Moreover, in DMVH, we optimize discrete codes directly instead of relaxing the binary constraints so that we could obtain high-quality hash codes. Simultaneously, we present a novel approach to construct similarity matrix, which can not only preserve local similarity structure, but also keep semantic similarity between data points. To solve the optimization problem in DMVH, we further propose an alternate algorithm. We test the proposed model on three large scale data sets. Experimental results show that it outperforms or is comparable to several state-of-the-arts.

CCS CONCEPTS

• **Computing methodologies → Learning paradigms;** • **Information systems → Multimedia and multimodal retrieval;**

*Corresponding author (shiyuliang@sdu.edu.cn).
†Corresponding author (xuxinshun@sdu.edu.cn).

ICMR '17, Bucharest, Romania
© 2017 ACM. 978-1-4503-4701-3/17/06...$15.00
DOI: http://dx.doi.org/10.1145/3078971.3078981

KEYWORDS

Multi-view; Hashing; Image Retrieval; Learning to Hash; Locally Linear Embedding

ACM Reference format:
Rui Yang, Yuliang Shi, and Xin-Shun Xu. 2017. Discrete Multi-view Hashing for Effective Image Retrieval. In *Proceedings of ICMR '17, Bucharest, Romania, June 06-09, 2017,* 9 pages.
DOI: http://dx.doi.org/10.1145/3078971.3078981

1 INTRODUCTION

Approximate nearest neighbor search (ANN), which involves retrieving relevant samples given a query, plays a fundamental role in many important applications, such as information retrieval, data mining and computer vision, etc. [30]. In the past several decades, many techniques have been developed for ANN search, e.g., KD tree [20], ball tree [13] and metric tree [24], etc. Recently, many hashing based methods have been proposed for ANN search task, which embed high-dimensional data into a low-dimensional Hamming space such that similar objects are indexed by binary codes with small Hamming distances. Due to their low cost for storage and high retrieval efficiency, in recent years, hashing techniques have attracted a lot of attention.

Generally, hashing approaches can be divided into two categories: data-independent and data-dependent methods [26, 27]. Data independent methods usually use random projections to get binary codes of data without considering specific data [22]. For example, locality-sensitive hashing (LSH) [3] is one of the most popular data-independent methods owing to its empirical success and elegant theoretic guarantee. Although LSH based algorithms have been successfully applied to many applications [8, 12], their performance is not satisfactory when short binary codes are used. Thus, they requires numerous tables with long codes for high accuracy. However, the numerous hashing tables will cost high storage and query time [3]. In addition, for some data, we can get some labeled information, e.g., tags/semantics, etc. However, data-independent methods cannot make use of such given information.

Due to the drawbacks of data-independent methods, many data-dependent methods have been proposed to learn more compact hash codes from specific data set. However, most existing data-dependent hashing methods [4, 8, 10, 17, 18, 28, 31, 35] only work on single-view data, which can be categorized as single-view hashing. For example, they only focus on using one type of visual descriptors to learn hash functions.

While in many real-world scenarios, multiple representations exist for a same object. For example, an image can be characterized by GIST, as well as a collection of scale-invariant feature transform (SIFT) descriptors. It has been proved in many applications that adaptively combining a set of diverse and complementary features gives better performance than using a single one. For instance, the content-based image retrieval systems gain significant performance improvements by fusing multiple features like color and texture [6, 32]. Note that some methods just simply concatenate different view features of a object as one vector to make use of multi-view features. However, many methods have shown that is not a good choice. Moreover, such methods may cause curse of dimensionality.

To make full use of information from multiple views, recently, some hashing methods have been proposed, which may fall into two classes: cross-view hashing and multi-view hashing. Specifically, cross-view hashing [2, 9, 25, 29, 36, 37] aims to use one view of a query and retrieve nearest neighbours in different views. While multi-view hashing aims at achieving better codes by leveraging auxiliary views than single-view hashing. Multi-view hashing assumes that all the views should be provided for a query when performing retrieval. A number of multi-view hashing methods have been proposed, such as Composite Hashing with Multiple Information Sources (CHMIS) [34], Multiple Feature Hashing (MFH) [21], Multiple Feature Kernel Hashing (MFKH) [11], and Multi-view Latent Hashing (MVLH)[19], etc.

As shown above, some multi-view hashing have been proposed. However, there are still some problems that need to be further considered. First, the discrete constraints imposed on the binary codes that the target hash functions generate will lead to mixed-integer optimization problem which is NP-hard. To tackle the optimization problem, these methods mentioned above usually relax binary constraints or separate the process of learning hash functions and binary codes into two independent stages during learning process, and then threshold the continuous outputs to be binary. This process greatly simplifies the optimization; however, it could generate large quantization error and get suboptimal solutions. Note that Shen et al. [17] proposed a discrete hashing method; however, it can only work on single view data. Second, many methods are unsupervised methods, e.g., CHMIS, MFH and MVLH. These methods can be easily applied to different data with a given distance metric; however, they cannot make use of supervised information, e.g., tags/semantics, which is very important to improve the performance and generate compact codes. Note that CHMIS considers that different features should play different roles in learning stage; however, it does not take the weight of similarity matrix in different views into account. Third, some supervised hashing approaches, e.g., MFKH, can make use of supervised information and keep semantic similarity between data points. But, in some cases, even if two samples share common labels, they may also have great difference in content. That means simply using label information to construct similarity matrix is not enough and may generate great errors.

Therefore, if a model could consider the above problems, it is expected to obtain better performance than state-of-the-art methods. Motivated by this, in this paper, we propose a novel supervised multi-view hashing framework for multi-view scenarios, i.e., Discrete Multi-view Hashing. Specifically, we reformulate the objective such that it can be solved without relaxing the binary constraints by introducing an auxiliary variable. In addition, to measure the similarity between data points, we construct similarity matrix by a new method based on Locally Linear Embedding (LLE) [14, 15], which cannot only preserve local similarity structure, but also keep the semantic similarity between data pairs. Experimental results on three data sets, i.e., CIFAR-10, Caltech256 and NUS-WIDE, demonstrate that DMVH outperforms or is comparable to several state-of-the-art hashing methods.

The rest of this paper is organized as follows. In Section 2, we give a brief introduction of Spectral Hashing (SH) and Locally Linear Embedding (LLE), which are highly related to our work. The details of our proposed method are given in Section 3. Section 4 describes the evaluation settings and experimental results of our proposed method and several compared state-of-the-arts on three real data sets. Finally, conclusions are given in Section 5.

2 RELATED WORK

2.1 Spectral Hashing

Spectral Hashing (SH) attempts to encode data into compact binary codes based on the assumption that two samples should have similar binary codes in Hamming space if they are similar in original space. At the same time, the basic SH formulation requires the codes to be balanced and uncorrelated. The balance condition means that each bit has around 50% chance of being 1 or −1. The uncorrelated requirement means that different bits are uncorrelated. Specifically, SH can be formulated as the following optimization problem.

$$\begin{aligned}&\sum_{i,j} S_{ij}\|y_i - y_j\|^2\\ &s.t.\ \ y_i \in \{-1,1\}^c, \sum_i y_i = 0, \frac{1}{N}\sum_i (y_i y_i^T) = I\end{aligned} \tag{1}$$

where S_{ij} is the similarity between the i-th and j-th samples, c is the length of binary codes, and N is the number of data samples, y_i is the hash code of the i-th sample. As mentioned previously, the constraint $\sum_i y_i = 0$ requires each bit to be balanced, and $\frac{1}{N}\sum_i (y_i y_i^T) = I$ requires the bits to be uncorrelated.

2.2 Locally Linear Embedding

Locally Linear Embedding (LLE) is a non-linear method for dimensionality reduction. It attempts to discover nonlinear structure in high dimensional data by exploiting the local symmetries of linear reconstructions. It is based on the assumption that, if there are enough data, each data point and its neighbours lie on or close to a locally linear patch. Therefore, a data point can be approximated as a weighted linear combination of its neighbours. LLE uses the following cost function to measure reconstruction error in original space.

$$\begin{aligned}&\min_{P}\sum_{i}\|x_i-\sum_{j}P_{ij}x_j\|^2\\&s.t.\ \sum_{j}P_{ij}=1\end{aligned}\tag{2}$$

where $P_{ij}=0$ if x_i and x_j are not neighbours.

Then, LLE assumes that such a linear combination should remain unchanged even after the manifold has been mapped to a low space, i.e.,

$$\begin{aligned}&\min_{Y}\sum_{i}\|y_i-\sum_{j}P_{ij}y_j\|^2\\&s.t.\ \sum_{i}y_i=0,\ \ \frac{1}{N}\sum_{i}y_i{y_i}^T=I_c\end{aligned}\tag{3}$$

where y_i is a low dimensional vector mapped from x_i.

3 DISCRETE MULTI-VIEW HASHING

In this section, we introduce our proposed Discrete Multi-View Hashing approach–DMVH. First, we show how to fuse multiple features of different views. Then, we introduce the similarity preservation method to map data into binary codes. Finally, we give the overall formulation of DMVH and an alternate solution to the optimization problem of DMVH.

3.1 Integration of Multiple Features

Suppose that the training data set contains N samples, i.e., $\{O_1,...,O_N\}$. For each sample, we have M different features of different views, i.e., $\{X^{(m)}=[x_1^{(m)},...,x_N^{(m)}]\in\mathbb{R}^{d_m\times N}\}_{m=1}^{M}$, where d_m is the dimension of the m-th view, M is the number of views. Usually, the features of different views have different dimensions. Thus, it is hard to fuse such features. To do this, in this paper, we use kernel function to prepare multiple features.

Specifically, we first construct L landmarks in each view space, i.e., $\{z_l^{(m)}\}_{l=1}^{L}$, which can be obtained by clustering or randomly chosen from the original N samples. Then, we construct kernel matrices $\{K^{(m)}\}_{m=1}^{M}\in\mathbb{R}^{L\times N}$ by the following kernel function.

$$K^{(m)}(z_p^{(m)},x_q^{(m)})=\frac{exp(-\|z_p^{(m)}-x_q^{(m)}\|/2\sigma_m^2)}{\sum_{p=1}^{L}exp(-\|z_p^{(m)}-x_q^{(m)}\|/2\sigma_m^2)},\forall p,q\tag{4}$$

where σ_m is the related scalable parameter.

Then, we define the fused kernel matrix $K=\sum_{m=1}^{M}\alpha_m K^{(m)}$, where $\alpha=[\alpha_1,...,\alpha_M]^T$ is a non-negative weight vector for different features satisfying $\sum_{m=1}^{M}\alpha=1$. We will show how to adaptively learn α in later subsection.

3.2 Similarity Preservation

One of the key problems in hashing algorithms is similarity preserving, which indicates that similar documents should be mapped to binary codes with short Hamming distance. To do this, we propose a new method to construct similarity matrix based on LLE, which can not only preserve local similarity structure, but also keep the semantic similarity between data pairs.

For each data point in the m-th view, e.g., $x_i^{(m)}$, we first find data set $Q_i^{(m)}$ in which all samples share common class labels with $x_i^{(m)}$. Then, we pick up G points $\{u_g^{(m)}\}_{g=1}^{G}$ from $Q_i^{(m)}$ to reconstruct $x_i^{(m)}$) if and only if $u_g^{(m)}$ is one of $x_i^{(m)}$'s G-nearest points in $Q_i^{(m)}$. Thus, seeking the sparse representation for $x_i^{(m)}$ leads to the following optimization problem:

$$\begin{aligned}&\min_{P^{(m)}}\sum_{i=1}^{N}\|x_i^{(m)}-\sum_{g=1}^{G}P_{ig}^{(m)}u_g^{(m)}\|_F^2\\&s.t.\ \sum_{g=1}^{G}P_{ig}^{(m)}=1\end{aligned}\tag{5}$$

By solving Eq. (5), we get

$$P_{ig}^{(m)}=\frac{\sum_{t=1}^{G}C_{gt}^{-1}}{\sum_{p=1}^{G}\sum_{q=1}^{G}C_{pq}^{-1}}\tag{6}$$

where, C is a local covariance matrix, $1\le g,t\le G$, which is computed as follows:

$$C_{gt}=(x_i^{(m)}-u_g^{(m)})^T(x_i^{(m)}-u_t^{(m)})\tag{7}$$

Usually, $P_{ig}^{(m)}$has a large value if its corresponding sample (i.e., $u_g^{(m)}$) has a great influence on $x_i^{(m)}$. This means that we can use it to construct the similarity matrix. For example, the element of similarity matrix $S^{(m)}$ can be defined as:

$$S_{ij}^{(m)}=\begin{cases}|P_{ig}^{(m)}| & if\ x_j^{(m)}\ is\ a\ neighbor\ of\ x_i^{(m)}\ in\ Q_i^{(m)}\\0 & otherwise\end{cases}\tag{8}$$

where $P_{ig}^{(m)}$ is the g-th element of $P_i^{(m)}$, which also means that $x_j^{(m)}$ is the g-th neighbor of $x_i^{(m)}$ in $Q_i^{(m)}$, i.e., $u_g^{(m)}$.

In addition, to ensure the symmetry of $S^{(m)}$, we further update it with $S^{(m)}\leftarrow((S^{(m)})^T+S^{(m)})/2$. Unlike previous methods, we do not directly sum similarity matrix in different views together. In order to measure the similarity on multiple features of different views, we calculate affinity matrix $S^{(m)}$ for the m-th view and sum them together by assigning different weight, i.e., $S=\sum_{m=1}^{M}\alpha_m S^{(m)}$, where α is a weight vector mentioned in Section 3.1.

Then the similarity preservation part can be formulated as follows:

$$\begin{aligned}&\min_{Y}\sum_{i,j}S_{ij}\|y_i-y_j\|^2\\&s.t.\ Y\in\{-1,1\}^{N\times c}\end{aligned}\tag{9}$$

where $y_i\in\{-1,1\}^{1\times c}$ is hashing codes corresponding to the i-th sample and c is the length of hash codes.

Generally, Eq.(9) can be rewritten as:

$$\begin{aligned}&\min_{Y,W,\alpha}tr(Y^T\widetilde{L}Y)\\&s.t.\ Y\in\{-1,1\}^{N\times c}\end{aligned}\tag{10}$$

where $tr(Y^T\widetilde{L}Y) = tr(Y^T(D-S)Y)$, D is a diagonal matrix whose entries are given by $D_{ii} = \sum_{j=1}^{N} S_{ij}$.

3.3 Objective Function

In order to obtain hash codes of new samples efficiently, we aim to learn a projection matrix W to map all samples into into binary codes, i.e., $Y = (\sum_{i=m}^{M} \alpha_m K^{(m)})^T W$, where $W \in \mathbb{R}^{L\times c}$. Thus, the objective function can be formulated as follows.

$$\begin{aligned}&\min_{Y,W,\alpha} tr(Y^T\widetilde{L}Y) + \gamma\|Y - (\sum_{m=1}^{M} \alpha_m K^{(m)})^T W\|_F^2 \\ &s.t.\ Y \in \{-1,1\}^{N\times c}, \sum_{m=1}^{M} \alpha = 1, \alpha_m \geq 0\end{aligned} \tag{11}$$

where the first item is used to keep similarity between samples, the second is introduced to map samples to Hamming space.

To solve the above optimization problem, we can relax the discrete constraints to bypass the difficulty of directly learning discrete binary codes, which has been taken in most existing approaches. However, this scheme may generate large quantization error, which makes the obtained binary codes sub-optimal. To tackle this problem, here we introduce an auxiliary matrix B into the objective function.

$$\begin{aligned}&\min_{Y,W,\alpha,B,R} tr(B^T\widetilde{L}B) + \beta\|Y - B\|_F^2 + \gamma\|B - K^T W\|_F^2 \\ &s.t.\ Y \in \{-1,1\}^{N\times c}, \sum_{m=1}^{M} \alpha = 1, \alpha_m \geq 0\end{aligned} \tag{12}$$

In addition, inspired by the success of Iterative Quantization [4], we further introduce an orthogonal matrix R to rotate the intermediate representation B into BR, which minimizes the quantization loss. Then, the final objective function becomes

$$\begin{aligned}&\min_{Y,W,\alpha,B,R} tr(B^T\widetilde{L}B) + \beta\|Y - BR\|_F^2 + \gamma\|B - K^T W\|_F^2 \\ &s.t.\ Y \in \{-1,1\}^{N\times c}, R^T R = I_c, \sum_{m=1}^{M} \alpha = 1, \alpha_m \geq 0\end{aligned} \tag{13}$$

In the following subsection, we show how to tackle the above optimization problem after we introduce B and R.

3.4 Optimization

Apparently, we cannot obtain a solution to the optimization problem of Eq. (13) with five matrix variables Y, W, B, R and α directly. Fortunately, it is easy to solve with respect to any one of the five variables while fixing the other four. Thus, in this paper, we propose an iterative procedure to find a solution to this problem. The detailed steps are listed as follows, which are repeated until convergency.

Step 1: Fixing W, Y, R and α, update B. We have the following sub-problem:

$$\min_{B} tr(B^T\widetilde{L}B) + \beta\|Y - BR\|_F^2 + \gamma\|B - K^T W\|_F^2 \tag{14}$$

Setting the derivative of Eq. (14) w.r.t. B to zero, we have

$$AB + BD + E = 0 \tag{15}$$

where $A = \widetilde{L} + \gamma I$, $D = \beta RR^T$, $E = -\beta YR^T - \gamma K^T W$. It ia a typical Sylvester equation; thus, we can obtain B easily.

Step 2: Fixing B, Y, R and α, update W. After dropping some irrelevant terms, the optimization problem is transformed into the following form.

$$\min_{W} \|B - K^T W\|_F^2 \tag{16}$$

It is a least squares problem of W, which has a closed-form solution, i.e.,

$$W = (KK^T)^{-1}KB \tag{17}$$

Step 3: Fixing B ,W, R and α, update Y. The problem is reduced to

$$\begin{aligned}&\min_{Y} \|Y - BR\|_F^2 \\ &s.t.\ Y \in \{-1,1\}^{N\times c}\end{aligned} \tag{18}$$

It is easy to find that Eq. (18) gets its minimum when

$$Y = sgn(BR) \tag{19}$$

Step 4: Fixing B, W, Y and α, update R. Then, the problem is transformed to

$$\begin{aligned}&\min_{R} \|Y - BR\|_F^2 \\ &s.t.\ R^T R = I_c\end{aligned} \tag{20}$$

This objective function is essentially the classic Orthogonal Procrustes problem [16], which can be solved efficiently by singular value decomposition. For example, let $U\Sigma V^T$ be the singular value decomposition of $B^T Y$. Then, we have

$$R = UV^T \tag{21}$$

which minimizes the objective function of Eq. (20).

Step 5: Fixing B, W, Y and R, update α. Once other variables are fixed, the optimization problem with respect to α can be formulated as a quadratic programming problem, i.e.,

$$\begin{aligned}&\min_{\alpha} \frac{1}{2}\alpha^T \widetilde{E}\alpha + h^T\alpha \\ &s.t.\ \sum_{m=1}^{M} \alpha = 1, \alpha_m \geq 0\end{aligned} \tag{22}$$

where

$$\widetilde{E}_{mn} = 2tr(K^{(m)})^T WW^T K^{(n)}), m, n = 1, ..., M$$

$$h_m = -2tr(W^T K^{(m)} B) + tr(B^T \widetilde{L}^{(m)} B), m = 1, ..., M$$

After the above optimization procedure, we directly get the binary codes of all training samples, i.e., Y. In addition, we also obtain W and R. Thus, we can also get the binary codes for new samples. For example, given a query x, it can be computed by first computing the hashing function $f(x) = K^T WR$, where K can be achieved by using Eq. (4). Then, the hashing code can be obtained through sign function $h(x) = sgn(f(x))$.

In addition, to have an overall look of the proposed method, we summarize it in **Algorithm 1**.

Table 1: mAP Comparisons on CIFAR-10 and Caltech256.

Method	CIFAR-10				Caltech256			
	24 bits	32 bits	48 bits	64 bits	24 bits	32 bits	48 bits	64 bits
ITQ	0.1483	0.1492	0.1513	0.1533	0.0249	0.0264	0.0308	0.0312
LFH	0.2585	0.2697	0.2775	0.2956	0.0640	0.0678	0.0708	0.0718
MFH	0.1275	0.1255	0.1239	0.1228	0.0220	0.0253	0.0266	0.0274
MFKH	0.1518	0.1636	0.1641	0.1848	0.0357	0.0382	0.0404	0.0408
MVLH	0.1790	0.1820	0.1842	0.1862	0.0541	0.0598	0.0635	0.0664
DMVH	**0.3093**	**0.3286**	**0.3370**	**0.3361**	**0.0719**	**0.0761**	**0.0846**	**0.0866**

Algorithm 1 Discrete Multi-view Hashing (DMVH)

Input:
Training set $\{X^{(m)}\}_{m=1}^{M}$; code length c; parameters β, γ; number of anchor points L.
Output:
Binary codes Y; auxiliary variable B; rotation matrix R; projection matrix W; non-negative weight vector α.

Initialize R, Y and W randomly, and $\{\alpha_m\}_{m=1}^{M} = \frac{1}{M}$;
Construct the landmark set $\{z_l^{(m)}\}_{l=1}^{L}$;
Define the kernel feature $\{K^{(m)}\}_{m=1}^{M}$ using Eq. (4);
Construct S get Laplacian matrix like Section 3.2 $\widetilde{L}$;
repeat;
  Update B by solving the Sylvester equation in Eq. (15);
  Update W using Eq. (17);
  Update Y according to Eq. (19);
  Update R using Eq. (21);
  Update α by solving problem Eq. (22);
until convergence

4 EXPERIMENTS

In this section, we show the experimental results on three data sets of the proposed method and compared methods. In addition, multi-modal problem can also be treated as multi-view problem. Thus, in the experiments, we evaluate the proposed method on both multi-feature and multi-modal problems. Specifically, we compare DMVH on two multi-feature data sets with three multi-view hashing methods: MFH [21], MFKH [11] and MVLH [19]. We also choose two classical single-view hashing methods as baseline models: ITQ [4] and LFH [35]. To make ITQ and LFH workable on multi-feature cases, we concatenate the features of different views into one vector as their input. In addition, in order to show that our method can handle multi-modal problems as well, we also test it on a multi-modal data set, and compare it with several multi-modal hashing methods, i.e., MFH, MFKH, MVLH, LSSH [36] and SCMH [33] . Note that LSSH and SCMH are cross-modal hashing methods. They construct correlation between multi-modal representations, then learn different binary codes for different modalities.

4.1 Datasets and Evaluation Metrics

We conduct our experiments on three benchmark data sets, i.e., **CIFAR-10** [7], **Caltech256** [5] and **NUS-WIDE**[1].

CIFAR-10 and Caltech256 are used as multi-feature data sets. CIFAR-10 is a labeled subset of the 80-million tiny images collection [23]. It consists of a total of 60,000 32×32 color images in 10 classes, each of which has 6,000 samples. Each sample is associated with a mutually exclusive class label. Caltech256 contains a total of 30,607 images of 256 object categories with more than 80 images per category. For both of two datasets, we use GIST (384-dimension for CIFAR, 512-dimension for Caltech256) and SIFT (300-dimension for CIFAR-10 and Caltech256) descriptors to produce two views of each image. For evaluation, we uniformly sample 1,000 images as queries, 3000 images as the training data, and the remaining images as the database. Since both of them are fully annotated, the ground truth neighbors can be easily retrieved based on the class labels.

NUS-WIDE is used as a multi-modal data set. It consists of 269,648 instances. Each instance manually annotated with at least one of 81 provided labels but some are scare. In our experiments, we select 10 most common concepts and delete all samples that do not contain one of these concepts at least; finally, we get 186,577 corresponding images. Each image is represented as a 500-D Bag-of-Visual-Words SIFT feature vector and each text is represented by a 1000-dimensional tag occurrence feature vector. For evaluation, we uniformly sample 1,000 images as queries, 5000 images as the training data, and the remaining images as the database. The ground truth neighbors are also defined by class labels.

To measure the performance of DMVH and compared methods, we use **Precision**, **Recall** and **mean Average Precision** (**mAP**) as evaluation metrics.

4.2 Parameters Setting.

There are several parameters that could affect the performance of DMVH, i.e., the number of landmarks L, the number of neighbors G, β and γ in Eq. (14). In all experiments, we empirically set $L = 300$ and $G = 7$. To determine the values of β and γ, we use a cross-validation process. Finally, we find that DMVH obtains the best performance when $\beta = 0.01$, $\gamma = 0.001$ on CIFAR-10 and $\beta = 0.005$, $\gamma = 0.001$ on Caltech256, respectively. On NUS-WIDE, we use the same cross-validation process to get the best values of β and γ, i.e., $\beta = 1$ and $\gamma = 0.005$.

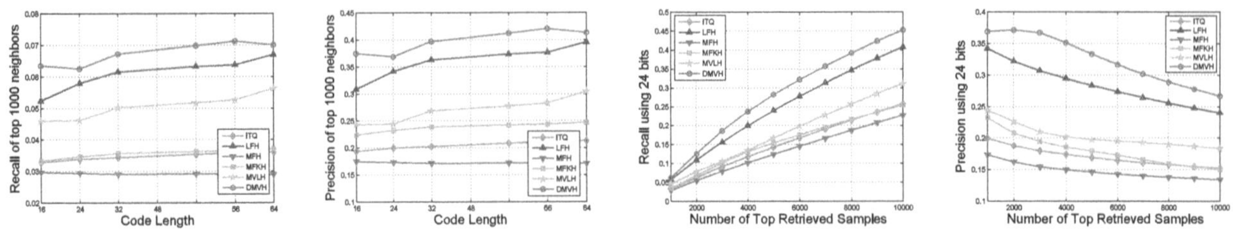

(a) (b) (c) (d)

Figure 1: Precision and recall results on CIFAR-10.

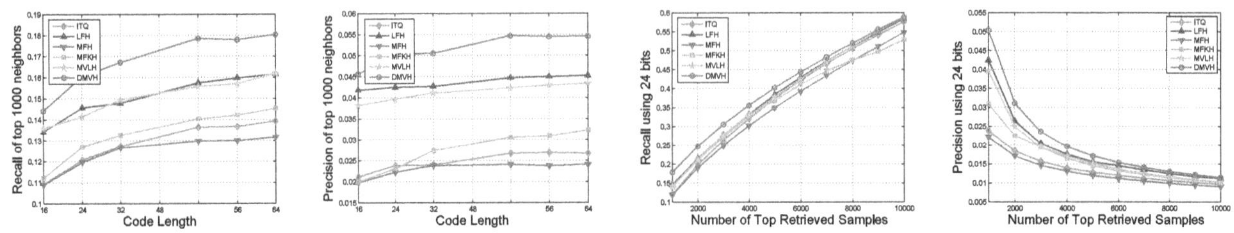

(a) (b) (c) (d)

Figure 2: Precision and recall results on Caltech256.

4.3 Results on Multi-Feature Datasets

The results on multi-feature data sets, i.e., CIFAR-10 and Caltech256, are shown in Table 1, Figure 1 and Figure 2. Specifically, the mAP values of different code lengths, i.e., from 24 to 64, on CIFAR-10 are summarized in Table 1. Figure 1 illustrates precision and recall curves of DMVH and all compared methods on CIFAR-10. Fig. 1 (c)-(d) show the precision and recall curves with 24-bit codes. Jointly analyzing Table 1 and Figure 1, we can observe

- DMVH obtains the best results on all cases.
- DMVH obtains much better results than compared methods.
- DMVH consistently achieves the best results on all cases with varying the number of retrieved samples.

Similar experiments are conducted on Caltech256. Results are shown in Table 1 and Figure 2. Table 1 contains the mAP values of the proposed method and other compared methods with different code lengths. The precision and recall curves are plotted in Figure 2. Specifically, Figure 2 (a) and (b) present the recall and precision curves with varying code lengths. Figure 2 (c)-(d) plot the recall and precision curves of all methods on 24 bits with varying the number of top retrieved samples. From these figures, we can find that DMVH get better results than other compared methods on all cases. From Table 1 and Figure 2, we can observe

- DMVH outperforms all other methods. Especially, with the code length increasing, its performance becomes much better than other methods.

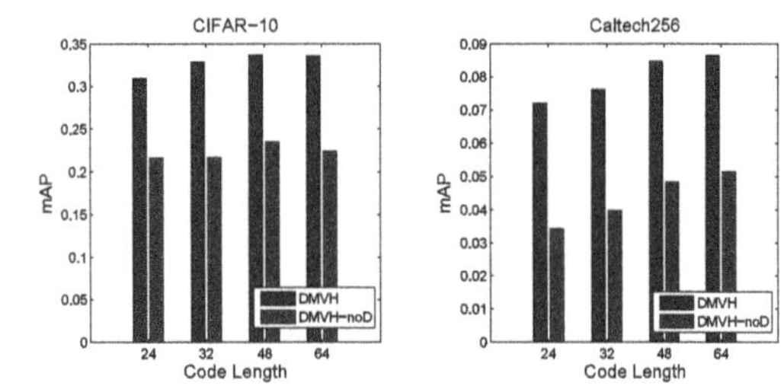

(a) (b)

Figure 3: Evaluation on effects of discrete constraints.

- DMVH obtains much better results than compared methods.
- DMVH consistently achieves the best results on all cases with varying the number of retrieved samples.

4.4 Effects of Discrete Constraints

In this section, we conduct experiments to confirm that keeping hashing codes discrete during training is helpful to learning high-quality hashing codes. In this experiment, we use $Y = BR$, instead of $Y = sgn(BR)$, during training stage, which is called DMVH-noD. The experimental results are shown in Figure 3. From this figure, we can find that DMVH obtains much better performance than DMVH-noD , which confirms that DMHV benefits much from keeping hashing codes discrete during training.

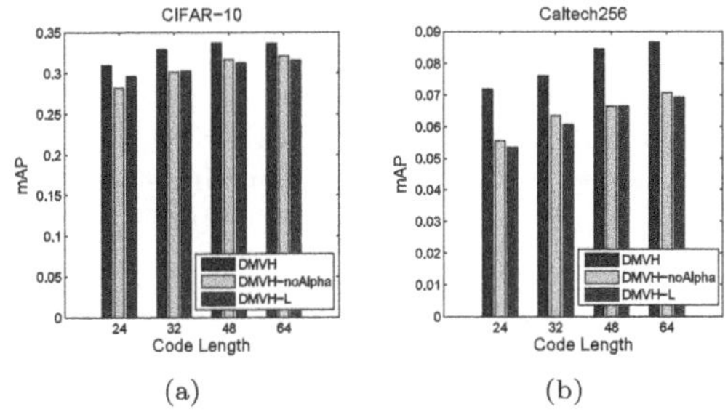

Figure 4: Evaluation on effect of similarity matirx.

4.5 Effects of Similarity Matrix

In addition, in DMVH, we make use of both semantic information and structure of samples to construct similarity matrix. To show this similarity matrix can better preserve the similarity between samples, we further conduct experiments on CIFAR-10 and Caltech256. Specifically, we first construct the other similarity matrix S which only uses label information, i.e., $S_{ij} = 1$ if samples i an j share at least one label, 0 otherwise. Then, we compare the performance of DMVH with different similarity matrices. The results are shown in Figure 4, which contains the values of mAP with different code lengths. DMVH-L means the proposed method working on the similarity matrix constructed only from label without structure information. DMVH-noAlpha means that when construct similarity matrix we sum similarity matrix together directly instead of assigning different weight. From this Figure, we can find that DMVH with our proposed similarity matrix obtains better results than that with the other two methods. This confirms that the similarity matrix containing structure information with different weight can improve the performance of DMVH.

4.6 Training Time Comparison

In Table 2, we report the comparison of training time on CIFAR-10 and Caltech256. The results are the time cost of different methods on the case with 64 bits. From this table, we can find that the training time of DMVH is a little longer than other methods. The main reason is that we need to solve Sylvester equation and quadratic programming problem during training stage, which will take more time. But, considering its better performance, the time cost is still acceptable.

4.7 Multi-View vs. Single-View

To further show that our multi-view scheme can indeed improve the retrieval performance by incorporating multiple views, we also compare performance of our method with multiple views and single view on CIFAR-10 and Caltech256. The single view scheme means that DMVH only work with one type of feature, i.e., SIFT or GIST. The mAP results are shown in Fig. 5. From Figure 5, our method with multiple views achieves the best results which demonstrates that integrating multiple views can achieve better performance than using single view. In addition, we also observe that the single view scheme with GIST obtains better results than that with SIFT. A reasonable explanation is that the GIST representation contains more information that the SIFT representation on these two data sets.

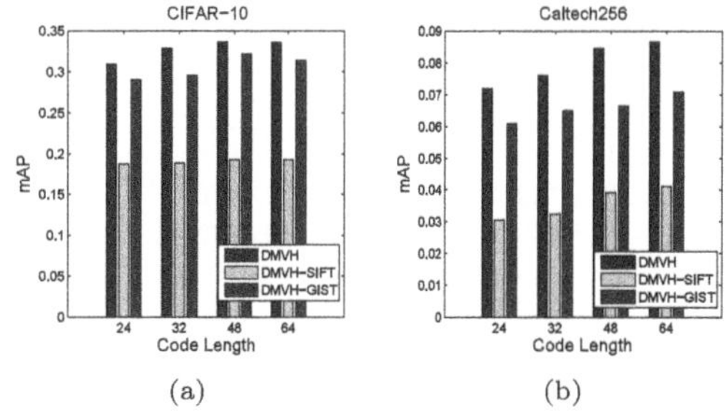

Figure 5: Comparisons of multiple views vs. single view on CIFAR-10 and Caltech256

Table 2: Training time comparison on case with 64 bits (in seconds).

Method	CIFAR-10	Caltech256
ITQ	1.14	1.27
LFH	41.6	30.9
MFH	38.7	72.9
MFKH	12.5	14.7
MVLH	19.7	20.0
DMVH	82.4	108.4

4.8 Evaluations on Multi-modal Data Set

In order to test that DMVH can also work on multi-modal data, we further conduct experiments on NUS-WIDE. Due to the fact that LSSH and SCMH are cross-modal hashing methods, we show their cross-modal retrieval performance, e.g., the performance of retrieving text with image (i.e., LSSH-I, and SCMH-I) and that of retrieving image with text (i.e., LSSH-T and SCMH-T). The mAP results of all methods with different code lengths are shown in Table 3. From this table, we can observe that DMVH obtains the best results on all cases. In addition, we can also find that those cross-modal methods generally obtain better results on cases that they use text to retrieve image than those they use image to retrieve text. The main reason may be that texts could better describe the content of images. To further observe the performance of DMVH and other compared methods, we also plot precision and recall curves of 64 bits in Figure 6 (a)-(b). From this figure, we can also observe that DMVH generally outperforms or is comparable to other methods.

The results on three data sets confirm that our method can obtain better results than other compared methods on most cases. This means that:

Table 3: mAP Comparison on NUS-WIDE.

Method	24 bits	32 bits	48 bits	64 bits
SCMH-I	0.5021	0.5046	0.5030	0.5016
SCMH-T	0.4836	0.4846	0.4875	0.4891
LSSH-I	0.3743	0.3730	0.3673	0.3719
LSSH-T	0.3612	0.3677	0.3736	0.3802
MFH	0.4085	0.4081	0.4059	0.4028
MFKH	0.3963	0.3961	0.4050	0.4073
MVLH	0.4337	0.4725	0.4780	0.4980
DMVH	**0.5126**	**0.5222**	**0.5295**	**0.5300**

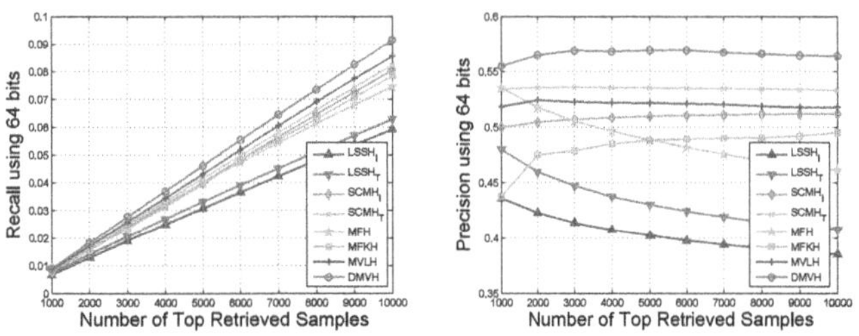

(a) (b)

Figure 6: Precision and recall results on NUS-WIDE

- The kernel function to map multiple features to kernel feature space can effectively exploit the structure information of multiple features of multiple views.
- The similarity matrix can effectively measure the similarity between samples.
- The scheme of learning binary codes directly can avoid large quantization error to some extent and obtain better binary codes than that of relaxation.

5 CONCLUSIONS

In this paper, we propose a novel hashing method which can make full use of multiple features from multiple views. To fuse features from different views, we adopt kernel function whose weights for different views are optimized during training stage. In addition, considering the significance of label information and the structure similarity of samples, we further propose a method to construct similarity matrix which can keep the semantic similarity and local similarity structure simultaneously. Furthermore, we introduce an auxiliary variable to learn high-quality discrete binary codes without relaxation. Finally, an alternating algorithm is proposed to tackle the optimization problems in the proposed method. The experimental results on three benchmark data sets demonstrate the proposed method outperforms or is comparable to other state-of-the-art hashing methods.

6 ACKNOWLEDGMENTS

This work was partially supported by National Natural Science Foundation of China (61573212, 61173068, 91546203), Program for New Century Excellent Talents in University of the Ministry of Education, the Taishan Industrial Experts Program of Shandong Province (TSCY20150305), the Key Science Technology Development Program of Shandong Province (2016GGX101044, 2016GGX101008, 2015GGE27033, 2016ZDJS01A09), and the Independent Innovation Foundation of Shandong Province (2014CGZH1106).

REFERENCES

[1] T.-S. Chua, J. Tang, R. Hong, H. Li, Z. Luo, and Y. Zheng. Nus-wide: a real-world web image database from national university of singapore. In *Proceedings of ACM International Conference on Image and Video Retrieval*, page 48, 2009.

[2] G. Ding, Y. Guo, and J. Zhou. Collective matrix factorization hashing for multimodal data. In *Proceedings of IEEE Conference on Computer Vision and Pattern Recognition*, pages 2075–2082, 2014.

[3] A. Gionis, P. Indyk, R. Motwani, et al. Similarity search in high dimensions via hashing. In *Proceedings of International Conference on Very Large Data Bases*, pages 518–529, 1999.

[4] Y. Gong and S. Lazebnik. Iterative quantization: A procrustean approach to learning binary codes. In *Proceedings of IEEE Conference on Computer Vision and Pattern Recognition*, pages 817–824, 2011.

[5] G. Griffin, A. Holub, and P. Perona. Caltech-256 object category dataset. Technical report, Technical report 7694, California Institute of Technology, 2007.

[6] J. He, J. Feng, X. Liu, T. Cheng, T.-H. Lin, H. Chung, and S.-F. Chang. Mobile product search with bag of hash bits and boundary reranking. In *Proceedings of IEEE Conference on Computer Vision and Pattern Recognition*, pages 3005–3012, 2012.

[7] A. Krizhevsky. Learning multiple layers of features from tiny images. Master's thesis, Department of Computer Science, 2009.

[8] B. Kulis and K. Grauman. Kernelized locality-sensitive hashing for scalable image search. In *Proceedings of IEEE International Conference on Computer Vision*, pages 2130–2137, 2009.

[9] Z. Lin, G. Ding, M. Hu, and J. Wang. Semantics-preserving hashing for cross-view retrieval. In *Proceedings of IEEE Conference on Computer Vision and Pattern Recognition*, pages 3864–3872, 2015.

[10] W. Liu, J. Wang, S. Kumar, and S.-F. Chang. Hashing with graphs. In *Proceedings of International Conference on Machine Learning*, pages 1–8, 2011.

[11] X. Liu, J. He, and B. Lang. Multiple feature kernel hashing for large-scale visual search. *Pattern Recognition*, 47(2):748–757, 2014.

[12] Y. Liu, J. Cui, Z. Huang, H. Li, and H. T. Shen. Sk-lsh: An efficient index structure for approximate nearest neighbor search. *Proceedings of International Conference on Very Large Data Bases*, 7(9):745–756, 2014.

[13] S. M. Omohundro. Efficient algorithms with neural network behavior. *Complex Systems*, 1(2):273–347, 1987.

[14] S. T. Roweis and L. K. Saul. Nonlinear dimensionality reduction by locally linear embedding. *Science*, 290(5500):2323–2326, 2000.

[15] L. K. Saul and S. T. Roweis. Think globally, fit locally: unsupervised learning of low dimensional manifolds. *The Journal of Machine Learning Research*, 4:119–155, 2003.

[16] P. H. Schönemann. A generalized solution of the orthogonal procrustes problem. *Psychometrika*, 31(1):1–10, 1966.

[17] F. Shen, C. Shen, W. Liu, and H. Tao Shen. Supervised discrete hashing. In *Proceedings of IEEE Conference on Computer Vision and Pattern Recognition*, pages 37–45, 2015.

[18] F. Shen, C. Shen, W. Liu, and H. Tao Shen. Supervised discrete hashing. In *Proceedings of IEEE Conference on Computer Vision and Pattern Recognition*, pages 37–45, 2015.

[19] X. Shen, F. Shen, Q.-S. Sun, and Y.-H. Yuan. Multi-view latent hashing for efficient multimedia search. In *Proceedings of ACM international Conference on Multimedia*, pages 831–834, 2015.

[20] C. Silpa-Anan and R. Hartley. Optimised kd-trees for fast image descriptor matching. In *Proceedings of IEEE Conference on Computer Vision and Pattern Recognition*, pages 1–8, 2008.

[21] J. Song, Y. Yang, Z. Huang, H. T. Shen, and R. Hong. Multiple feature hashing for real-time large scale near-duplicate video retrieval. In *Proceedings of ACM International Conference on Multimedia*, pages 423–432, 2011.

[22] J. Tang, Z. Li, M. Wang, and R. Zhao. Neighborhood discriminant hashing for large-scale image retrieval. *IEEE Transactions on Image Processing*, 24(9):2827–2840, 2015.

[23] A. Torralba, R. Fergus, and W. T. Freeman. 80 million tiny images: A large data set for nonparametric object and scene recognition. *IEEE Transactions on Pattern Analysis and Machine Intelligence*, 30(11):1958–1970, 2008.

[24] J. Uhlmann. Satisfying general proximity/similarity queries with metric trees. *Information Processing Letters*, 40(4):175–179, 1991.

[25] D. Wang, X. Gao, X. Wang, and L. He. Semantic topic multimodal hashing for cross-media retrieval. In *Proceedings of International Joint Conference on Artificial Intelligence*, pages 3890–3896, 2015.

[26] J. Wang, X.-S. Xu, S. Guo, L. Cui, and X. Wang. Linear unsupervised hashing for ann search in euclidean space. *Neurocomputing*, 171:283–292, 2016.

[27] S.-S. Wang, Z. Huang, and X.-S. Xu. A multi-label least-squares hashing for scalable image search. In *Proceedings of SIAM International Conference on Data Mining*, pages 954–962, 2015.

[28] Y. Weiss, A. Torralba, and R. Fergus. Spectral hashing. In *Advances in Neural Information Processing Systems*, pages 1753–1760, 2009.

[29] X.-S. Xu. Dictionary learning based hashing for cross-modal retrieval. In *Proceedings of ACM International Conference on Multimedia*, pages 177–181, 2016.

[30] T.-K. Yan, X.-S. Xu, S. Guo, and X.-L. Wang. Supervised robust discrete multimodal hashing for cross-media retrieval. In *Proceedings of ACM International Conference on Information and Knowledge Management*, pages 1271–1280, 2016.

[31] Y. Yang, F. Shen, H. T. Shen, H. Li, and X. Li. Robust discrete spectral hashing for large-scale image semantic indexing. *IEEE Transactions on Big Data*, 1(4):162–171, 2015.

[32] G. Ye, D. Liu, I.-H. Jhuo, S.-F. Chang, et al. Robust late fusion with rank minimization. In *Proceedings of IEEE Conference on Computer Vision and Pattern Recognition*, pages 3021–3028, 2012.

[33] D. Zhang and W.-J. Li. Large-scale supervised multimodal hashing with semantic correlation maximization. In *Proceedings of AAAI Conference on Artificial Intelligence*, pages 2177–2183, 2014.

[34] D. Zhang, F. Wang, and L. Si. Composite hashing with multiple information sources. In *Proceedings of ACM International Conference on Research & Development in Information Retrieval*, pages 225–234, 2011.

[35] P. Zhang, W. Zhang, W.-J. Li, and M. Guo. Supervised hashing with latent factor models. In *Proceedings of ACM International Conference on Research & Development in Information Retrieval*, pages 173–182, 2014.

[36] J. Zhou, G. Ding, and Y. Guo. Latent semantic sparse hashing for cross-modal similarity search. In *Proceedings of ACM International Conference on Research & Development in Information Retrieval*, pages 415–424, 2014.

[37] X. Zhu, Z. Huang, H. T. Shen, and X. Zhao. Linear cross-modal hashing for efficient multimedia search. In *Proceedings of ACM International Conference on Multimedia*, pages 143–152, 2013.

Quadruplet Networks for Sketch-Based Image Retrieval*

Omar Seddati
CS - TCTS Lab (UMONS)
Bd Dolez 31
Mons, Belgium
omar.seddati@umons.ac.be

Stéphane Dupont
TCTS Lab (UMONS)
Bd Dolez 31
Mons, Belgium
stephane.dupont@umons.ac.be

Saïd Mahmoudi
CS (UMONS)
Bd Dolez 31
Mons, Belgium
said.mahmoudi@umons.ac.be

ABSTRACT

Freehand sketches are a simple and powerful tool for communication. They are easily recognized across cultures and suitable for various applications. In this paper, we use deep convolutional neural networks (ConvNets) to address sketch-based image retrieval (SBIR). We first train our ConvNets on sketch and image object recognition in a large scale benchmark for SBIR (the sketchy database). We then conduct a comprehensive study of ConvNets features for SBIR, using a kNN similarity search paradigm in the ConvNet feature space. In contrast to recent SBIR works, we propose a new architecture the quadruplet networks which enhance ConvNet features for SBIR. This new architecture enables ConvNets to extract more robust global and local features. We evaluate our approach on three large scale datasets. Our quadruplet networks outperform previous state-of-the-art on two of them by a significant margin and gives competitive results on the third. Our system achieves a recall of 42.16% (at $k = 1$) for the sketchy database (more than 5% improvement), a Kendal score of $43.28\mathcal{T}_b$ on the TU-Berlin SBIR benchmark (close to $6\mathcal{T}_b$ improvement) and a mean average precision (MAP) of 32.16% on Flickr15k (a category level SBIR benchmark).

CCS CONCEPTS

• **Computing methodologies → Image representations; Neural networks;**

KEYWORDS

Sketch-based image retrieval; Quadruplet networks; Triplet networks; ConvNets; Metric learning; Sketch recognition

ACM Reference format:
Omar Seddati, Stéphane Dupont, and Saïd Mahmoudi. 2017. Quadruplet Networks for Sketch-Based Image Retrieval. In *Proceedings of ICMR '17, Bucharest, Romania, June 06-09, 2017,* 8 pages.
https://doi.org/http://dx.doi.org/10.1145/3078971.3078985

1 INTRODUCTION

Freehand sketches are attracting more and more interest in image processing research. Sketches are commonly used by humans and easily accessible with many of the devices that we now use on a daily basis.

In this work, we use ConvNets (state-of-the-art in the field of sketch classification) where they were able to significantly outperform previous state-of-the-art approaches [32, 33] that were using hand crafted features and more traditional computer vision schemes [12].

In the field of natural images, ConvNets activations have shown their ability to provide an effective descriptor for content-based image retrieval (CBIR) [1, 40]. In this paper, we present a comprehensive study of ConvNets features for sketch-based image retrieval. In the case of SBIR, we face the problem of cross-domain retrieval. As we can see in figure 1, the sketches represent queries while the results of the research are natural images. In order to offer a solution to this problem, we need a feature space where the sketch corresponding to an image has a representation close enough to the representation of this image. As for CBIR, a good retrieval system is able to give results that match the query semantics (global features) and details (local features). In this paper, we study in depth these two aspects of retrieval systems. We start with an evaluation of existing approaches and show how to improve retrieval performance. We introduce a new architecture called quadruplet to enhance both, local and global features. We use three different benchmarks to validate the results of our approach and show that the quadruplet based search outperforms previous state-of-the-art.

The paper is organized as follows. We start with a brief review of different approaches used in the field of sketch recognition and SBIR. Next we present the approach that we selected as a baseline and our quadruplet network. Then we proceed to the evaluation of our sketch retrieval system.

2 RELATED WORK

Works on sketch recognition goes back to the development of SketchPad more than 50 years ago [37]. Ever since, different computer vision approaches were used in order to achieve better results in multiple application domains. LaViola et al. [19] investigated recognition of mathematical sketches. Ouyang et al. [24] addressed chemical structure drawings recognition. Cao et al. [8] proposed a low dimensional symmetry aware flip invariant descriptor for sketches. Li et al. [21] exploited local feature representations (using star graph-based ensemble matching strategy) and global structures to address local and global variations. They trained an SVM classifier using bag-of-features (BOF) to select the top N sketch categories most similar to the query.

In addition to the sparse and abstract nature of hand drawings (compared to natural images), there is also a challenge related to the lack of available databases for model training and benchmarking.

*Produces the permission block, and copyright information

ICMR '17, June 06-09, 2017, Bucharest, Romania

ACM ISBN 978-1-4503-4701-3/17/06...$15.00
https://doi.org/http://dx.doi.org/10.1145/3078971.3078985

Figure 1: Samples from the sketchy database [27].

Eitz et al. [12] defined a taxonomy of 250 object categories. They gathered 20000 unique sketches to form the first large scale dataset of human sketches (TU-Berlin benchmark). For sketch category recognition, they used local feature vectors, bag-of-features representations [36], and multi-class support vector machines (SVMs). Yesilbek et al. [43] used IDM (Image Deformation Model) features and SVM classifiers. They demonstrated the importance of a good hyper-parameters optimization. Schneider et al. [30] modified the benchmark proposed by Eitz et al. [12] to make it more focused on the relevant aspect (what it looks like) rather than the original drawing intention. Later on, they used SIFT, GMM based Fisher vector encoding, and multi-class SVM to achieve sketch recognition.

In the related area of computer vision for natural images (photographs), supervised learning with ConvNets achieved state-of-the-art results [18, 39]. In general, ConvNets enable classification without requiring classic feature extraction approaches, as the model trains itself to extract relevant features from pixels. In the field of sketch recognition, Sarvadevabhatla et al. [28] used two popular ConvNets architectures (AlexNet ConvNet and a modified LeNet ConvNet) and fine-tuned their parameters on the sketch database. They used a subset of TU-Berlin sketch benchmark by retaining only 160 categories and 56 sketches from each category (as done in [30]). In contrast, Yang et al. [42] trained a ConvNet from scratch instead of fine tuning existing ones. They show that the receptive fields of the first layer ConvNet filters had to be increased (compared to typical settings for natural images) to improve generalization performance. In [32] Seddati et al. proposed a system for sketch recognition and similarity search (using ConvNets + kNN) and for the first time were able to outperform human performance in recognizing the sketch categories. In [44], the authors used a multi-scale multi-channel ConvNet for sketch recognition. Sarvadevabhatla et al. [29] propose a recurrent neural network architecture to exploit the sequential aspect of hand-drawn sketches. Zhang et al. [45] propose an approach to enhance sketch recognition through learning image-sketch shared latent structures.

In the last two decades, many sketch based image retrieval methods have also been proposed. One of the main challenge in this area is to find a common feature representation that enables to match sketches and images. Eitz et al. [13] introduced a benchmark for SBIR performance evaluation and proposed new descriptors based on bag-of-features. Szanto et al. [38] used edge histogram descriptors (EHD) and the histogram of oriented gradients (HOG). Wang et al. [41] used edge map descriptors and wavelet transform features to match sketches and images. Zhou et al. [46] used a saliency-based approach to select the main object in the image and extract features only for the salient region. Jin et al. [17] presented an approach based on a visual region descriptor where sketch-like representations are generated from images by using edge map generation and edge pixel screening. Then, the sketch-like representation is used for sketch-image matching. Bozas et al. [5] use a hashing algorithm for patch similarity within an overlapping spatial grid to rank sketch-image similarities. Bhattacharjee et al. [4] combine shape and appearance in a graph based re-ranking scheme. Bui et al. [7] explore triplets with several strategies for weight sharing. In [34] Seddati et al. proposed a system for real-time sketch recognition and SBIR using ConvNets features and edge detection. [11] use edge detection to generate sketch-like from images and histogram of line relationship to reduce noise. Li et al. [20] use local descriptors with product quantization and sparse coding.The similarity between the query and test data is achieved by comparing features histograms. Qi et al. [26] use a siamese ConvNet for SBIR. Niu et al. [23] generate visual words for images and sketches and use them to determine the relationship between two visual vocabularies. Sangkloy et al. [27] introduced a large scale benchmark for SBIR. They asked crowd workers to sketch particular photographic objects for 125 categories. The database contains 75,471 sketches of 12,500 objects. Thanks to this database, the authors were able to evaluate several approaches to SBIR taking into account the cross-domain challenge (being able to retrieve objects whose categories are different than the ones of the objects used during training). In their experiences they end up with a multi-task triplet network that gives their best results.

3 METHODOLOGY

In this section, we present the reasoning followed in this work in order to improve state-of-the-art SBIR techniques. We start with a brief description of our ConvNet training for sketch and image recognition. Then, we discuss the first approach that we selected for SBIR (a variant of the approaches proposed in [7, 27]). Finally, we introduce our quadruplet network and explain how this approach enhance ConvNet features for SBIR.

3.1 Sketch and image classification

In order to build our feature extractor, unlike the approach proposed in [27], we train **one ConvNet** for sketch and image object recognition. Our goal is to force the ConvNet to encode in a similar fashion the information coming from two inputs with the same category even if they belong to different domains (sketch vs natural image). This modification is meant to make easier the task of finding an embedding space for features corresponding to different domains.

During the training of our ConvNet (with a resnet-18 architecture [15]), we followed the standard approach:

- We resize the sketches and images to a resolution of 256 × 256.
- We present crops with a resolution of 224 × 224 as input to our ConvNet.
- We use mirroring for data augmentation.
- We use batch-normalization as a regularization technique.

The resulting ConvNet is used as an initialization for the following experiences. We experimented several finetuning approaches to enhance our ConvNet features for SBIR.

3.2 Triplet network for SBIR

In order to improve the features extracted with our ConvNet for SBIR we first train a triplet network [31]. In this kind of architecture, we generally have three copies of the same network with shared parameters. The input is in the form of Anchor, Positive and Negative. The goal is minimizing the distance between an anchor (a natural image) and a positive (a sketch corresponding to the anchor image) as shown in Figure 2, while maximizing the distance between this anchor and a negative (corresponding to a sketch from the same category but drawn for a different object). In our case we use the first eight layers of our object recognition ConvNet as a feature extractor. We add an embedding layer with 1024 neurons on the top of our feature extractor and we normalize the outputs of the embedding layer (l_2-norm). For each input (anchor, positive, negative) we compute the distances. Our goal is to have :

$$[D_{A,P} < D_{A,Nc}] \quad (1)$$

where :

- $D_{A,P}$: the distance between Anchor and positive.
- $D_{A,Nc}$: the distance between Anchor and Negative from the same category.

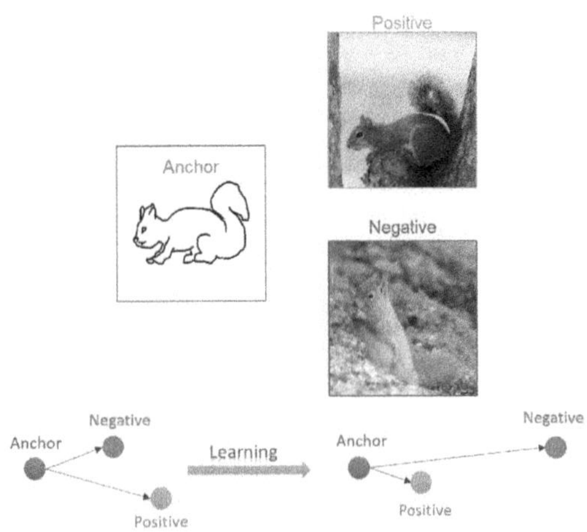

Figure 2: The triplet loss minimization [31].

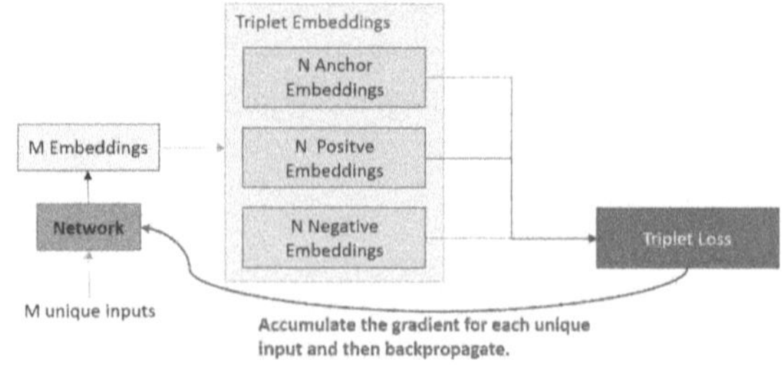

Figure 3: End-to-end training flow of [2].

In order to do that, we train our triplet network with the following loss function:

$$\sum_{i}^{N}[\left\|f(x_i^a) - f(x_i^p)\right\|_2^2 - \|f(x_i^a) - f(x_i^n)\|_2^2 + \alpha]_+ \quad (2)$$

where :
x_i^a: the feature vector of the anchor sketch.
x_i^p: the feature vector of the positive image.
x_i^n: the feature vector of the negative image.
α: by using this margin ($\alpha = 0.2$) we try to ensure a minimal distance between each pair of {anchor, positive} and {anchor, negative}.

During the training phase, we can expect that many of the triplets presented to the triplet network already respect the constraint of equation 1. These triplets will slow the training without intervening in the weight update. In order to avoid this limitation, we use the triplet Selection approach proposed in [2] (Figure 3). Instead of using three copies of the same network, we use one network that takes a mini-batch of samples and do the forward pass. Once we have the embedding outputs, we form triplets only with samples that violate the constraint of equation 1. For these triplets, we calculate the loss and back-propagate the error.

3.3 Multi-task triplet network for SBIR

In order to further improve triplet network features for SBIR, the authors of [7, 27] used multi-task learning. To do so, they add a classification branch to their triplet networks. The muti-task triplet network is able to achieve both, object classification and features embedding. Adding this secondary task improves the performance of the network embedding by preserving additional information that can be of great help especially for semantic retrieval. In our case, we add a **linear** layer for classification, in order to force as much as possible the previous layer (the embedding layer) to encode the input information in a fashion that preserves semantics and details. But the question that remains is whether the multi-task learning is the best way to build an embedding layer that encodes semantic information in a correct fashion for SBIR when using kNN? The experiments conducted in this work show that our quadruplet network is able to further enhance triplets representation.

3.4 Quadruplet network for SBIR

In this work, we introduce the quadruplet network (Figure 4). This architecture is similar to a triplet network, but we have an additional input. The input is in the form of Anchor (sketch), Positive (image),

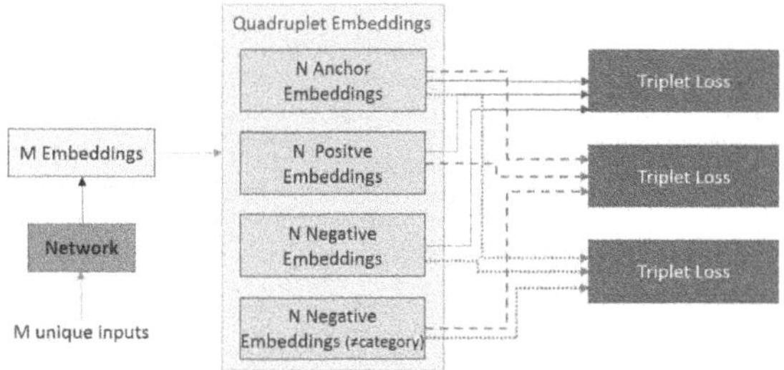

Figure 4: The quadruplet network.

Negative from the same category (image) and Negative from a different category (image). Our goal is to have :

$$[D_{A,P} < D_{A,Nc} < D_{A,N\neq c}] \tag{3}$$

where :

- $D_{A,P}$: the distance between Anchor and positive.
- $D_{A,Nc}$: the distance between Anchor and Negative from the same category.
- $D_{A,N\neq c}$: the distance between Anchor and Negative from a different category.

Instead of using multi-task learning to improve triplet categorical-level features, we add an input for examples that belong to a category different than the anchor. This additional input enables us to compute two more triplet loss functions:

$$\sum_i^N [\left\|f(x_i^a) - f(x_i^p)\right\|_2^2 - \|f(x_i^a) - f(x_i^{n2})\|_2^2 + \alpha]_+ \tag{4}$$

$$\sum_i^N [\|f(x_i^a) - f(x_i^n)\|_2^2 - \|f(x_i^a) - f(x_i^{n2})\|_2^2 + \alpha]_+ \tag{5}$$

where :
x_i^a: the feature vector of the anchor sketch.
x_i^p: the feature vector of the positive image.
x_i^n: the feature vector of the negative image.
x_i^{n2}: the feature vector of the negative image (category different than the anchor).

The quadruplet (Figure 5) encodes semantic information in a similar fashion to what triplet does for "local" information, which makes the embeddings obtained with quadruplet networks more suited for SBIR than those generated when using multi-task triplets.

3.5 Multi-task quadruplet network for SBIR

Once we validated the interest of using quadruplet networks, we start analyzing if there is a complementarity between the use of a multi-task approach and our quadruplet network. We start with checking the non-retrieved images during a retrieval test for both approaches. We use kNN with euclidean distance to retrieve the 10 closest neighbors (images) to the sketch query. We found that close to 87% of the non-retrieved images are shared for the two approaches, while the remaining examples are non-retrieved only by one of them. This observation leads us to believe that we can

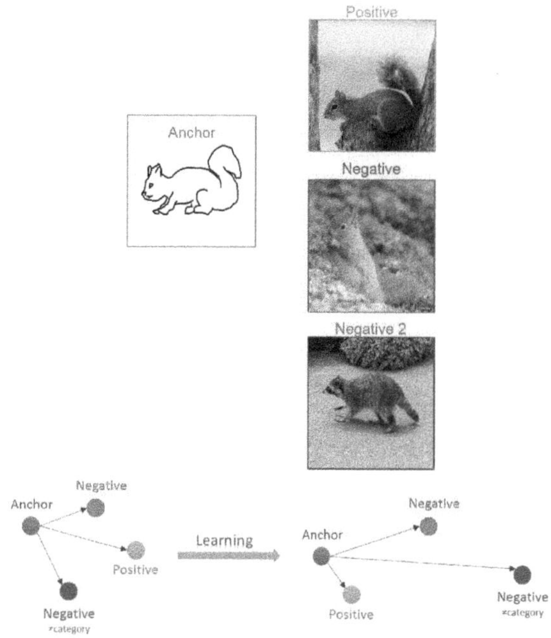

Figure 5: The quadruplet loss minimization.

combine both approaches to further improve the quadruplet features, which will be proved with the results of our experiments in the next section 4.

4 EXPERIMENTAL RESULTS

In this section we present the different results for the experiments conducted in this work. We start with a brief description for each of the benchmarks used to evaluate our approach. Then we report and discuss the outcomes of the various experiences carried out.

4.1 Benchmarks

In order to evaluate our approach we used various well-known benchmarks in the field of SBIR:

- The sketchy database [27]: a large scale collection for SBIR (Fig. 1). It contains 125 categories and 75,471 sketches of 12,500 objects. The crowd workers are asked to sketch particular photographic objects in order to give a fine-grained association between sketches and photos. For each category we have 100 images and at least 5 sketches per image. For the sketchy database we followed the guidelines of [27], 90% of the data are used for the training and the rest are used for test. All our experiments are based on ConvNets trained only on the sketchy database.
- TU-Berlin SBIR benchmark [14]: this benchmark is acquired in a controlled user study, where the authors gather more than 30,000 ratings for sketch/image pairs similarity. These ratings can be used to evaluate SBIR system results and compare them to human expectation. This benchmark contains 31 sketches and 40 ranked images

Table 1: Comparison of classification results on sketchy.

Method	mAP (%)
AlexNet [27]	77.29
GoogleNet [27]	80.85
Our resnet-18	**90.82**

Note: our resnet-18 was trained on images and sketches merged, the reported mAP is for sketch recognition.

for each sketch (1,240 benchmark images). This benchmark contains 100,000 more images collected from Flickr and used as distractor. During the evaluation, the 1,240 benchmark images are merged with the 100,000 distractor images. Then, each sketch query is used to rank the corresponding 40 benchmark images. Finally, the resulting 31 ordered lists are used to compute Kendal score.

- Flickr15k [16]: this is a category level SBIR benchmark, which means that if the retrieved image belongs to the same category as the query, we make the assumption that the result is correct. This benchmark has 33 sketch categories, for each category we have 10 sketches. It also contains 15,024 images with more than 60 categories and different number of images per category. The authors guidelines suggest to use the mean average precision (MAP) computed with a TRECVID tool for evaluation.

4.2 Evaluation and discussion

4.2.1 The sketchy database.
As explained in section 3.1, we start our experiments with training our ConvNet for object recognition using the images and sketches of the sketchy benchmark. All of our ConvNets are trained using the publicly available Torch toolbox [9]. The results are reported in Table 1.

Once our ConvNet training is done, we use the first eight layers of this ConvNet as initialization to train our triplets and quadruplets.

Note: in the rest of the paper we use the following annotation :

- classifL8: the output of layer 8 are used as features.
- quadruplet: quadruplet features.
- quadruplet_MT: multi-task quadruplet features.
- quadruplet_MT_v2: multi-task quadruplet features (_v2 indicates that during the training, the anchor is a **sketch** while the positive and negatives samples are **images**. The absence of _v2 at the end of an annotation states that during the training, the anchor is an **image** while the positive and negatives samples are **sketches**).
- triplet: triplet features.
- triplet-Cl-MT: classification multi-task triplet features. This triplet was trained differently than the others, we aim to reduce the distance between sketch/image pairs that belongs to the same category without taking into account the intra-categorical differences. We also use a multi-task learning scheme to strengthen the semantic capability of the generated features.
- triplet_MT: multi-task triplet features.

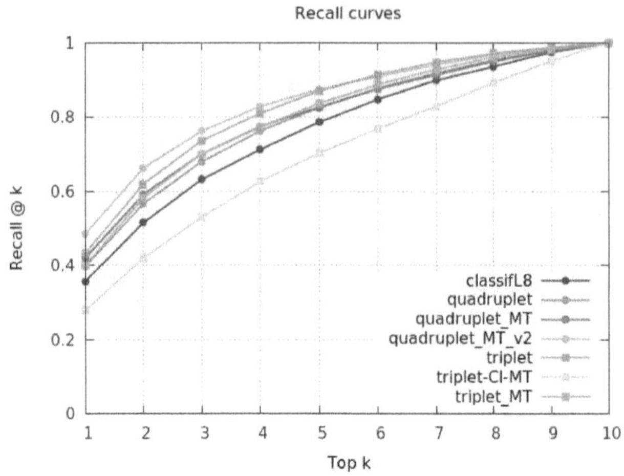

Figure 6: The recall curves for local features evaluation on the sketchy database.

A good retrieval system is able to give results that match the query semantics (global features) and details (local features). In order to evaluate the different approaches used in this work and demonstrate the interest of using quadruplet networks we use three different evaluation approaches on the sketchy database:

Local features evaluation: during this evaluation we make the assumption that the category is given and we evaluate how well the features do when it comes to sorting the results. In Figure 6 the recall curves are shown for local features evaluation on the sketchy database. We can see that our quadruplets features give the best results.

Global features evaluation: we use the sketch queries to retrieve images, if the result belongs to the same category as the query, the result is considered as correct. This category level evaluation enables us to evaluate if the shape information is correctly encoded. Figure 7 shows the mean average recall curves for global features evaluation. The triplet-Cl-MT gives the best result, which was not surprising since the training focus only on global information. But we can still see that quadruplets features are in second position, which means that quadruplet gives a better global representation than those obtained when using standard triplet approaches.

Standard evaluation: in this evaluation we follow the approach used in [27], each sketch query is used to retrieve 10 images, Figure 8 gives the mean average recall curves. This figure shows clearly that the multi-task quadruplet improves the SBIR performance. In Figure 9 we show the results reported in [27], these curves can be compared with those of Figure 8. We can easily conclude that our quadruplet outperforms previous state-of-the-art on the sketchy database (at $k = 1$ we achieved a recall of 42.16% compared to the 37.10% reported in [27]). Figure 10 shows some retrieval results of our proposed method (quadruplet_MT_v2) where the correct image is found at $k = 1$. In Figure 11 we have other examples where the image that matches the sketch query was not found at $k = 1$. We can notice that in several cases the retrieved images are close to the query, but it is still considered as wrong because of some limitations of the sketchy benchmark.

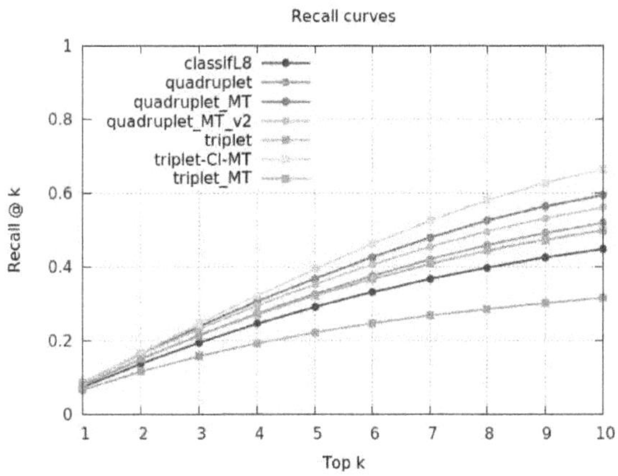

Figure 7: The recall curves for global features evaluation on the sketchy database.

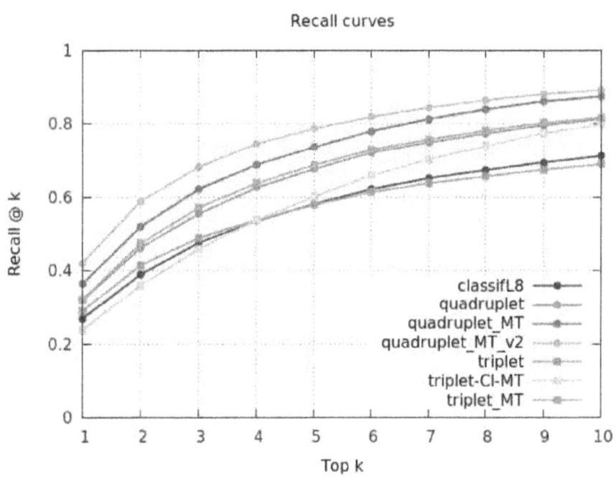

Figure 8: The recall curves for the sketchy database.

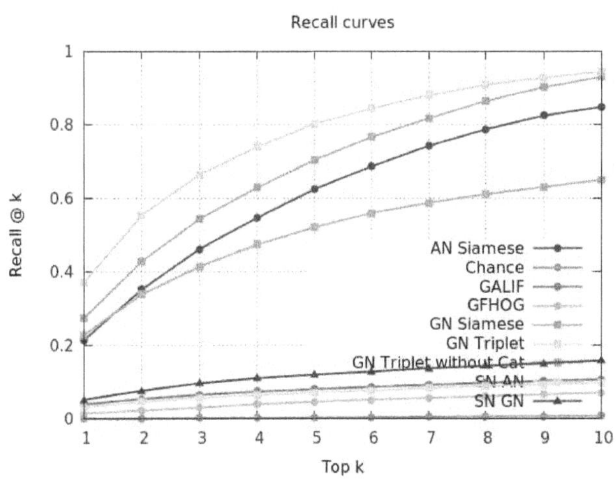

Figure 9: Recall curves for the different approaches used in [27].

Table 2: SBIR results comparison using Kendal's correlation on TU-Berlin SBIR benchmark.

Method	$\mathcal{T}_b$
quadruplet_MT	43.3
quadruplet_MT_v2	42
Triplet (fine-tuned final model) [7]	37.4
Triplet (sketch-photo) [7]	33.3
SHoG [14]	27.7
Triplet (sketch-edgemap) [7]	22.3
HoG (global) [14]	22.3
Structure Tensor [13]	22.3
Spark [14]	21.7
HoG (local) [10]	17.5
Shape Context [3]	16.1

Table 3: MAP comparison on Flickr15k.

Method	MAP (%)
Triplet (fine-tuned final model)* [7]	36.17
Triplet (sketch-photo, no-share)* [7]	32.87
quadruplet_MT	32.16
Triplet (sketch-photo, half-share)* [7]	31.38
quadruplet_MT_v2	28.10
Triplet (sketch-edgem, half-share)* [7]	24.45
Siamese CNN [26]	19.54
Perceptual Edge [25]	18.37
Extended GF-HoG [6]	18.20
GF-HoG [16]	12.22
SHoG [14]	10.93
SSIM [35]	9.57
SHoG [22]	9.11
Shape Context [3]	8.14
Structure Tensor [13]	7.98

4.2.2 *TU-Berlin SBIR benchmark.*

In addition to the sketchy database, we also used TU-Berlin SBIR benchmark to evaluate our system. We followed the guidelines of the authors and compute Kendal score. Our results and a comparison with others from previous state-of-the-art are reported in Table 2. The quadruplet networks show again their high performance and generalization capability.

4.2.3 *Flickr15k.*

We also evaluate our quadruplet networks on the Flickr15k benchmark. Table 3 presents a comparison of different MAP results. The authors of [7] found that using training data with more categories improves significantly the results on the Flickr15k benchmark. During training, they used in addition to the sketchy database pairs of images and sketches coming from other sources to form a new training dataset with 250 categories. In our case, we use half of the number of categories used in [7], but we still get competitive results and outperform all the other approaches.

Figure 10: Representative SBIR results on sketchy where the correct image (red box) is found at $k = 1$.

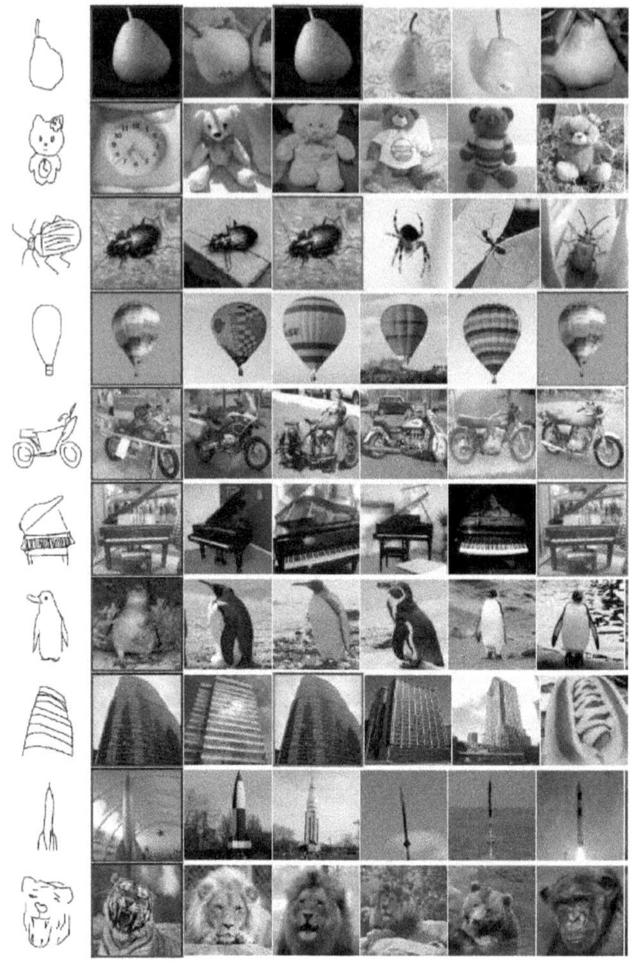

Figure 11: Representative SBIR results on sketchy where the ground-truth (blue box) is not found at $k = 1$.

5 CONCLUSIONS

In this paper, we introduce deep quadruplet networks architecture for SBIR. This new approach improves deep features for SBIR by projecting data in an embedding space suited for global and local information. The global information enables our system to retrieve images with objects that belongs to the same category as the query. While local information ease the identification of similarities that goes beyond object's shape similarity. We used three different benchmarks to evaluate our approach. The category level SBIR benchmark Flickr15k, where we achieved state-of-the-art result. We also outperform significantly previous state-of-the-art results on the sketchy database and the TU-Berlin SBIR benchmark. Beyond this we showed that quadruplet networks give better embedding than triplet networks, which means that this approach can be extended to improve performance in other domains where triplet networks are used.

REFERENCES

[1] Artem Babenko, Anton Slesarev, Alexandr Chigorin, and Victor Lempitsky. 2014. Neural codes for image retrieval. In *European conference on computer vision*. Springer, 584–599.

[2] Artem Babenko, Anton Slesarev, Alexandr Chigorin, and Victor Lempitsky. 2014. Neural codes for image retrieval. In *European conference on computer vision*. Springer, 584–599.

[3] Serge Belongie, Jitendra Malik, and Jan Puzicha. 2002. Shape matching and object recognition using shape contexts. *IEEE transactions on pattern analysis and machine intelligence* 24, 4 (2002), 509–522.

[4] Sreyasee Das Bhattacharjee, Junsong Yuan, Weixiang Hong, and Xiang Ruan. 2016. Query Adaptive Instance Search using Object Sketches. In *Proceedings of the 2016 ACM on Multimedia Conference*. ACM, 1306–1315.

[5] Konstantinos Bozas and Ebroul Izquierdo. 2012. Large scale sketch based image retrieval using patch hashing. In *International Symposium on Visual Computing*. Springer, 210–219.

[6] Tu Bui and John Collomosse. 2015. Scalable sketch-based image retrieval using color gradient features. In *Proceedings of the IEEE International Conference on Computer Vision Workshops*. 1–8.

[7] Tu Bui, Leonardo Ribeiro, Moacir Ponti, and John Collomosse. 2016. Generalisation and Sharing in Triplet Convnets for Sketch based Visual Search. *arXiv preprint arXiv:1611.05301* (2016).

[8] Xiaochun Cao, Hua Zhang, Si Liu, Xiaojie Guo, and Liang Lin. 2013. Sym-fish: A symmetry-aware flip invariant sketch histogram shape descriptor. In *Proceedings of the IEEE International Conference on Computer Vision*. 313–320.
[9] Ronan Collobert, Koray Kavukcuoglu, and Clément Farabet. 2011. Torch7: A matlab-like environment for machine learning. In *BigLearn, NIPS Workshop*.
[10] Navneet Dalal and Bill Triggs. 2005. Histograms of oriented gradients for human detection. In *Computer Vision and Pattern Recognition, 2005. CVPR 2005. IEEE Computer Society Conference on*, Vol. 1. IEEE, 886–893.
[11] Aishwarya Deore and BL Gunjal. 2016. Advanced Sketch Based Image Retrieval System Using Object Boundary Selection Algorithm. (2016).
[12] Mathias Eitz, James Hays, and Marc Alexa. 2012. How do humans sketch objects? *ACM Trans. Graph.* 31, 4 (2012), 44–1.
[13] Mathias Eitz, Kristian Hildebrand, Tamy Boubekeur, and Marc Alexa. 2010. An evaluation of descriptors for large-scale image retrieval from sketched feature lines. *Computers & Graphics* 34, 5 (2010), 482–498.
[14] Mathias Eitz, Kristian Hildebrand, Tamy Boubekeur, and Marc Alexa. 2011. Sketch-based image retrieval: Benchmark and bag-of-features descriptors. *IEEE transactions on visualization and computer graphics* 17, 11 (2011), 1624–1636.
[15] Kaiming He, Xiangyu Zhang, Shaoqing Ren, and Jian Sun. 2016. Deep residual learning for image recognition. In *Proceedings of the IEEE Conference on Computer Vision and Pattern Recognition*. 770–778.
[16] Rui Hu and John Collomosse. 2013. A performance evaluation of gradient field hog descriptor for sketch based image retrieval. *Computer Vision and Image Understanding* 117, 7 (2013), 790–806.
[17] Cheng Jin, Zheming Wang, Tianhao Zhang, Qinen Zhu, and Yuejie Zhang. 2015. A Novel Visual-Region-Descriptor-based Approach to Sketch-based Image Retrieval. In *Proceedings of the 5th ACM on International Conference on Multimedia Retrieval*. ACM, 267–274.
[18] Alex Krizhevsky, Ilya Sutskever, and Geoffrey E Hinton. 2012. Imagenet classification with deep convolutional neural networks. In *Advances in neural information processing systems*. 1097–1105.
[19] Joseph J LaViola Jr and Robert C Zeleznik. 2007. MathPad 2: a system for the creation and exploration of mathematical sketches. In *ACM SIGGRAPH 2007 courses*. ACM, 46.
[20] Qiang Li, Yahong Han, and Jianwu Dang. 2016. Sketch4Image: a novel framework for sketch-based image retrieval based on product quantization with coding residuals. *Multimedia Tools and Applications* 75, 5 (2016), 2419–2434.
[21] Yi Li, Yi-Zhe Song, and Shaogang Gong. 2013. Sketch Recognition by Ensemble Matching of Structured Features.. In *BMVC*, Vol. 1. 2.
[22] David G Lowe. 2004. Distinctive image features from scale-invariant keypoints. *International journal of computer vision* 60, 2 (2004), 91–110.
[23] Jianwei Niu, Jun Ma, Jie Lu, Xuefeng Liu, and Zeyu Zhu. 2017. M-SBIR: An Improved Sketch-Based Image Retrieval Method Using Visual Word Mapping. In *International Conference on Multimedia Modeling*. Springer, 257–268.
[24] Tom Y Ouyang and Randall Davis. 2011. ChemInk: a natural real-time recognition system for chemical drawings. In *Proceedings of the 16th international conference on Intelligent user interfaces*. ACM, 267–276.
[25] Yonggang Qi, Yi-Zhe Song, Tao Xiang, Honggang Zhang, Timothy Hospedales, Yi Li, and Jun Guo. 2015. Making better use of edges via perceptual grouping. In *Proceedings of the IEEE Conference on Computer Vision and Pattern Recognition*. 1856–1865.
[26] Yonggang Qi, Yi-Zhe Song, Honggang Zhang, and Jun Liu. 2016. Sketch-based image retrieval via Siamese convolutional neural network. In *Image Processing (ICIP), 2016 IEEE International Conference on*. IEEE, 2460–2464.
[27] Patsorn Sangkloy, Nathan Burnell, Cusuh Ham, and James Hays. 2016. The sketchy database: learning to retrieve badly drawn bunnies. *ACM Transactions on Graphics (TOG)* 35, 4 (2016), 119.
[28] Ravi Kiran Sarvadevabhatla and R Venkatesh Babu. 2015. Freehand sketch recognition using deep features. *arXiv preprint arXiv:1502.00254* (2015).
[29] Ravi Kiran Sarvadevabhatla, Jogendra Kundu, and others. 2016. Enabling My Robot To Play Pictionary: Recurrent Neural Networks For Sketch Recognition. In *Proceedings of the 2016 ACM on Multimedia Conference*. ACM, 247–251.
[30] Rosália G Schneider and Tinne Tuytelaars. 2014. Sketch classification and classification-driven analysis using fisher vectors. *ACM Transactions on Graphics (TOG)* 33, 6 (2014), 174.
[31] Florian Schroff, Dmitry Kalenichenko, and James Philbin. 2015. Facenet: A unified embedding for face recognition and clustering. In *Proceedings of the IEEE Conference on Computer Vision and Pattern Recognition*. 815–823.
[32] Omar Seddati, Stephane Dupont, and Saïd Mahmoudi. 2015. Deepsketch: deep convolutional neural networks for sketch recognition and similarity search. In *Content-Based Multimedia Indexing (CBMI), 2015 13th International Workshop on*. IEEE, 1–6.
[33] Omar Seddati, Stephane Dupont, and Saïd Mahmoudi. 2016. DeepSketch 2: Deep convolutional neural networks for partial sketch recognition. In *Content-Based Multimedia Indexing (CBMI), 2016 14th International Workshop on*. IEEE, 1–6.
[34] Omar Seddati, Stéphane Dupont, and Saïd Mahmoudi. 2016. DeepSketch2Image: Deep Convolutional Neural Networks for Partial Sketch Recognition and Image Retrieval. In *Proceedings of the 2016 ACM on Multimedia Conference*. ACM, 739–741.
[35] Eli Shechtman and Michal Irani. 2007. Matching local self-similarities across images and videos. In *Computer Vision and Pattern Recognition, 2007. CVPR'07. IEEE Conference on*. IEEE, 1–8.
[36] Josef Sivic, Andrew Zisserman, and others. 2003. Video google: A text retrieval approach to object matching in videos.. In *iccv*, Vol. 2. 1470–1477.
[37] Ivan E Sutherland. 1964. Sketchpad a man-machine graphical communication system. *Transactions of the Society for Computer Simulation* 2, 5 (1964), R–3.
[38] B Szántó, P Pozsegovics, Z Vámossy, and Sz Sergyan. 2011. Sketch4matchâĂŤContent-based image retrieval system using sketches. In *Applied Machine Intelligence and Informatics (SAMI), 2011 IEEE 9th International Symposium on*. IEEE, 183–188.
[39] Christian Szegedy, Wei Liu, Yangqing Jia, Pierre Sermanet, Scott Reed, Dragomir Anguelov, Dumitru Erhan, Vincent Vanhoucke, and Andrew Rabinovich. 2015. Going deeper with convolutions. In *Proceedings of the IEEE Conference on Computer Vision and Pattern Recognition*. 1–9.
[40] Ji Wan, Dayong Wang, Steven Chu Hong Hoi, Pengcheng Wu, Jianke Zhu, Yongdong Zhang, and Jintao Li. 2014. Deep learning for content-based image retrieval: A comprehensive study. In *Proceedings of the 22nd ACM international conference on Multimedia*. ACM, 157–166.
[41] Yuxin Wang, Miao Yu, Qi Jia, and He Guo. 2011. Query by sketch: An asymmetric sketch-vs-image retrieval system. In *Image and Signal Processing (CISP), 2011 4th International Congress on*, Vol. 3. IEEE, 1368–1372.
[42] Yongxin Yang and Timothy M Hospedales. 2015. Deep neural networks for sketch recognition. *arXiv preprint arXiv: 1501.07873* (2015).
[43] Kemal Tugrul Yesilbek, Cansu Sen, Serike Cakmak, and T Metin Sezgin. 2015. SVM-based sketch recognition: which hyperparameter interval to try?. In *Proceedings of the workshop on Sketch-Based Interfaces and Modeling*. Eurographics Association, 117–121.
[44] Qian Yu, Yongxin Yang, Yi-Zhe Song, Tao Xiang, and Timothy Hospedales. 2015. Sketch-a-net that beats humans. *arXiv preprint arXiv:1501.07873* (2015).
[45] Hua Zhang, Si Liu, Changqing Zhang, Wenqi Ren, Rui Wang, and Xiaochun Cao. 2016. Sketchnet: Sketch classification with web images. In *Proceedings of the IEEE Conference on Computer Vision and Pattern Recognition*. 1105–1113.
[46] Rong Zhou, Liuli Chen, and Liqing Zhang. 2012. Sketch-based image retrieval on a large scale database. In *Proceedings of the 20th ACM international conference on Multimedia*. ACM, 973–976.

On the Automatic Identification of Music for Common Activities

Karthik Yadati
Delft University of Technology
The Netherlands
n.k.yadati@tudelft.nl

Cynthia C. S. Liem
Delft University of Technology
The Netherlands
c.c.s.liem@tudelft.nl

Martha Larson
Radboud University & Delft University of Technology
The Netherlands
mlarson@science.ru.nl

Alan Hanjalic
Delft University of Technology
The Netherlands
a.hanjalic@tudelft.nl

ABSTRACT

In this paper, we address the challenge of identifying music suitable to accompany typical daily activities. We first derive a list of common activities by analyzing social media data. Then, an automatic approach is proposed to find music for these activities. Our approach is inspired by our experimentally acquired findings (a) that genre and instrument information, i.e., as appearing in the textual metadata, are not sufficient to distinguish music appropriate for different types of activities, and (b) that existing content-based approaches in the music information retrieval community do not overcome this insufficiency. The main contributions of our work are (a) our analysis of the properties of activity-related music that inspire our use of novel high-level features, e.g., drop-like events, and (b) our approach's novel method of extracting and combining low-level features, and, in particular, the joint optimization of the time window for feature aggregation and the number of features to be used. The effectiveness of the approach method is demonstrated in a comprehensive experimental study including failure analysis.

CCS CONCEPTS

•Information systems →Music retrieval; •Human-centered computing →*Social recommendation; Social media; Social tagging;*

KEYWORDS

Music recommendation; Activity; Workout music; Relax music; Study music

ACM Reference format:
Karthik Yadati, Cynthia C. S. Liem, Martha Larson, and Alan Hanjalic. 2017. On the Automatic Identification of Music for Common Activities. In *Proceedings of ICMR '17, Bucharest, Romania, June 06-09, 2017,* 9 pages.
DOI: http://dx.doi.org/10.1145/3078971.3078997

978-1-4503-4701-3/17/06...$15.00
DOI: http://dx.doi.org/10.1145/3078971.3078997

1 INTRODUCTION

In addition to "just" listening to music as a part of our leisure, we can also use music to facilitate our daily activities. For example, listening to appropriate music while studying can help us focus better [3]. While there exist online music services specialized in this direction (e.g., Focus at will and Brain FM), the mechanisms underlying their offerings are either automatic music generation or fully manual curation. Moreover, they only cover a limited scope of activities (e.g., focus only). A recent study on using "music as a technology" [5] to accomplish a goal highlights how little research has been done on developing music recommender systems for daily activities. Our paper delves into this area and investigates the main challenges in automating the process of identifying existing music for different daily activities.

The first challenge we face is deriving a list of daily activities for which music is sought. Instead of simply predefining this list, as is typically done in the existing work (e.g., [18]), we mine a social media sharing platform (YouTube) to derive a list of popular activities i.e., those activities that are found to have frequent mention when searching for activity-related music. Our mining approach is similar to that taken by recent work [9] on identifying common user-intent categories in online video search.

The second challenge we address in this paper is to find an appropriate approach to automatically recognize activity-related music categories. We start by looking at the available textual metadata that we typically find associated with the music tracks that are posted on YouTube and promoted as being suitable for a particular activity. Specifically, the fact that the titles of these music tracks in many cases contain genre/instrument information, leads us to investigate the usability of this specific information first.

Since our findings indicate that relying on music genre or presence of particular instruments is not a reliable approach to link a music track to a particular activity, we proceed by investigating how to develop an approach that works well for the posed problem. For this purpose, we look into the existing content-based approaches in the field of music information retrieval (MIR) and encounter several issues that need to be addressed. The first issue is the temporal variation of musical content in a given track. We hypothesize that the time resolution for feature extraction in standard MIR tasks is not appropriate to capture the variations for activity-based music classification. Traditional MIR tasks typically extract features at a resolution of 10-100 ms and then aggregate them over the entire music track (e.g., for emotion detection [8]) or a segment sampled from the track (e.g., for genre recognition [8]). In our paper, we propose to aggregate features over windows of different time resolution and identify the temporal resolution that can give optimal classification performance.

A related issue we address in this paper is how to represent a music track in the feature space in order to enable effective activity-based classification. We take as our starting point a standard set of low-level features that can be extracted from the music signal. Additionally, we also consider some other sources of information that we, either intuitively or through exploratory experiments, found relevant for the task. Specifically, we consider different dimensions of affect (arousal, valence and tension [12]) and the presence of events like onsets and drops [19]. We encode this information in an additional set of high-level features. Finally, we design a classifier with which we investigate the possibility of identifying different activity-related music categories, and the usefulness of different low- and high-level features for the task. Specifically, in parallel with optimizing the time window for feature aggregation as explained above, we also optimize the number of low-level features to be used.

In summary, the main contribution of this paper consists of the answers to the following research questions:

(1) *RQ1: Which activity categories are popular?* We mine music on YouTube to derive common categories of activities. By analyzing the textual metadata related to the activity-related music tracks, we identify the top-3 activity categories to focus on (Section 3).
(2) *RQ2: Is genre or instrument information helpful in predicting an activity-related music category?* This research question is addressed in Section 4 by using the textual metadata of the music tracks, and in particular the presence of genre/instrument related keywords.
(3) *RQ3: How to automatically identify music for a specific activity?* In Section 5, we investigate two aspects to dealing with this question, viz. the temporal resolution at which we should aggregate features and the types of features that would be helpful for the task.

The contributions listed above are presented after an analysis of the existing work on automatically associating music with daily activities, as well as different feature extraction strategies in Section 2. Experimental results assessing the performance of our proposed classification method and a failure analysis are presented and discussed in Section 6. Section 7 concludes the paper.

2 RELATED WORK

In this section, we look at two different aspects dealt in this paper: associating music with activities and different feature extraction strategies used in the MIR literature.

2.1 Associating music with activities

Wang et al. proposed a method that associates music with specific activities [18]. The authors use a predefined list of activities: running, walking, sleeping, working, studying and shopping, for which they recommend music. Sensors on the mobile phone are used to infer whether the user is in the middle of one of these activities, and then suitable music is recommended based on an analysis of low-level features extracted from the signal. To train the recommender system, playlists for specific activities are collected from an online music sharing platform. Next, a subset of 1200 songs is picked from these playlists and manually labeled with one or more activities as tags. A classification problem is then set up where a model is trained for each activity based on the mean and standard deviation of low-level features extracted from a 512 sample frame extracted every 30 seconds of the song. Wang et al. use the following features for classification: Zero crossing rate, Centroid, Rolloff, Flux, Mel-Frequency Cepstral Coefficients (MFCC), Chroma, Spectral Flatness Measure (SFM) and Tempo. The trained model then predicts activity-based tags for new songs. Similar work is reported by Dias et al. [6], where the system "Improvise" is designed to associate music with daily activities mentioned above.

In our approach, we focus on the categories of activities derived from social media data and base the classification process on a novel feature extraction approach that, as we will explain and demonstrate experimentally, is more suitable for the task.

2.2 Feature extraction

Typical MIR tasks, like genre recognition, mood classification or instrument recognition, have been addressed frequently in the past [8]. Characteristic for these tasks is the way of extracting audio features, namely at the frame (time interval) level and with typically rather small frames, e.g., 10-100 ms for timbre features. In order to extract temporal features, like rhythm, a larger time window with a couple of seconds in length is used. Recently, the research community working on extracting emotion from music argued for using longer time windows and tracking emotions over "emotionally stable" segments [1], [15]. We take this discussion a step further by investigating segments of differing lengths while aggregating features for music-to-activity mapping. Additionally, we enrich the set of common audio features by new high-level features that we find especially useful for the task.

3 WHICH ACTIVITIES ARE POPULAR?

In this section, we address RQ1, i.e., we identify types of activities during which users commonly listen to music. Many daily activities are potential occasions for listening to music. A priori, examples include commuting, taking a shower, cooking, cleaning the house, studying or working out. However, compiling an exhaustive list of music-accompanied activities would require difficult-to-acquire behavioral information. For this reason, we focus on activities that are publicly mentioned, and can be assumed to be important to a substantial portion of general population. We turn to social media platforms as an information sources. Specifically, we analyze textual metadata on YouTube for common mentions of activities, which we take as providing indication of their popularity and wide-spread importance to users seeking music online.

When listeners are searching music for specific activities, we assume that search queries could take on various common forms, e.g., "Music for *", where the wildcard * could refer to a specific activity (e.g., studying, workout or jogging). Our metadata analysis is based on the observation that this query consists of a conjunction or a preposition connecting the other two words. In order to construct queries that would allow us to identify common activities, we looked at all possible prepositions[1] and conjunctions[2] that can follow the word "music". In this way, we arrived at five different word pairs: "music for", "music to ", "music when ", "music while" and "music during". By enclosing the word pairs in quotations, we created a query that could be matched with track metadata (i.e., title and description).

YouTube is a rich source of music, and offers a wealth of music intended for different activities, e.g., Study[3] or Workout[4]. In general, such music takes form of long tracks with durations typically exceeding 30 minutes. We use the queries just discussed to identify these tracks on YouTube. For each of the 5 queries, we follow these steps to collect the tracks and the corresponding metadata:

(1) Using a web crawler, go through all the pages returned by YouTube for a given query and collect the unique identifiers of the videos as well as the titles.
(2) Download the mp3 audio of the videos and the corresponding metadata, e.g., title, description and likes.
(3) Remove duplicates in the search results and also remove the results that are not music tracks.

We accumulated a total of 2589 music tracks from YouTube and their textual metadata using our search queries. We used the titles of the collected music tracks to identify the most frequently occurring activities. We rely on the title of a track because it appeared to be the most informative about the music-type of the track. For example, the title "Workout Music - Best Workout Rock Music 2016 for GYM and Fitness" indicates that this track can be used while working out in the gym and it contains rock music released in the year 2016. We preprocess the titles by changing them into lower case, converting the -ing forms to their root words (e.g., studying is changed into study) and removing unicode characters, the standard English stop words, genre-related keywords, and numbers (e.g., years).

After this pre-processing, we counted the most frequently occurring terms in the titles, and arrived at the following top-3 activity-related keywords: "relax", "study" and "workout". Note that these keywords can be seen more as activity categories rather than single activities. Examples of single activities, e.g., for study music, include keywords like "work" and "office". Similarly, we find keywords like "run" and "exercise" in the titles of workout music. Our response to RQ1, is the top-3 activity categories, which we will focus on in the remainder of this paper. To provide an impression of these categories, we provide a list of associated keywords:

- *Relax*: relax, calm, soothe, peaceful, chill, meditation, stress relief, sleep
- *Study*: study, focus, concentration, office, work
- *Workout*: workout, training, exercise, gym, run

Our final dataset contains a total of 1272 (49%) *Relax* tracks, 567 (22%) *Study* tracks and 450 (17%) *Workout* tracks. The remaining 300 (12%) tracks were found not to belong to any of the above three categories of activity-related music, despite the presence of the relevant keywords. Although this set of tracks is not used as a classification target, we keep it as *Others* and use it for analysis later in this paper. In order to check for bias towards a particular Internet source, we also inspected the names of the channels from which the tracks were collected. We observed that the *Relax*, *Study* and *Workout* tracks were collected from 12, 10 and 9 different channels respectively, which gives a reasonable diversity of sources.

As a supplement to the keyword information above, Figures 1 - 3 show word clouds, which visualize the term clusters corresponding to our activity categories, which were generated using the titles of the tracks, as described above. Common stop words, numbers, urls have been removed and stemming has been applied. The word clouds allow us to observe the difference in terms that charaterize each of the three main activity categories we found. The word cloud for relaxation music contains keywords like "relax", "calm", "sleep", "heal", "meditate", "calm", "zen", "relief" and "lullaby". Similarly, "workout", "training", "gym", "fit" and "running" are the most frequently used keywords in the titles of workout music (Figure 3). Additionally, we observe the word cloud for the tracks not belonging to any of the above three categories labelled as "Others" in Figure 4. Observing Figure 4, we can say that there is a lot of music for babies, playing games, pets (Dogs) etc.

4 IS GENRE OR INSTRUMENT INFORMATION ENOUGH?

In this section, we address RQ2 and investigate whether genre or instrument information is helpful for predicting music for the top-3 activity categories identified in the previous section. For this investigation we do not develop nor implement any existing genre or instrument detection method. Rather we rely on the textual metadata carrying information about the music genre or instruments present in the titles and descriptions of the music tracks we crawled from YouTube. Our hypothesis is that if the link between the genre- or instrument-related textual metadata and a particular activity category is unambiguous, then it is meaningful to focus on the development, implementation and optimization of the corresponding content-based methods and algorithms as the means to solve the activity-related music classification problem.

The next question to answer is whether the specific genre- and instrument-related terms found in the term clusters are also distinctive per activity category. In order to answer this question, we pick the genre- and instrument-related keywords from the titles of tracks in each of the four term clusters and arrange them in Table 1. Please note that there is no particular order in which the genres or instruments are laid out in the table. Since the dataset contains both electronic and acoustic music, we list the instruments found only in acoustic music. Observing the table, we can say that investigating genre or instrument is not enough to associate music to activities. We can see that genres like classical music, electronic music and ambient music are present in three of the four clusters. In particular, house music is present in all the four clusters, thus also in the *Others* cluster consisting of the tracks for a wide range of activities other than the three targeted in this paper. Similarly, piano, guitar and violin are present in three of the four clusters.

We now take a look at example music tracks for genres and instruments that are common between different activity categories. First, we compare genres in *Relax* and *Study* categories and pick one of the common genres present in both the categories: *Trance*.

[1]https://www.englishclub.com/grammar/prepositions-list.htm
[2]http://www.english-grammar-revolution.com/list-of-conjunctions.html
[3]https://www.youtube.com/user/StudyMusicProject
[4]https://www.youtube.com/user/WorkoutMusicService

Figure 1: Cloud from *Relax* track titles

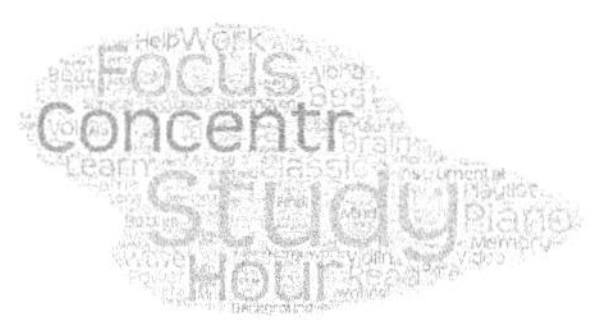

Figure 2: Cloud from *Study* track titles

Figure 3: Cloud from *Workout* track titles

Figure 4: Cloud from *Other* track titles

Listening to the examples of *Trance* music in *Relax* and *Study*, one can immediately identify a difference in texture where a *Study* music example has a slightly higher density than a *Relax* music example. Another difference is the presence of drop-like events [19] in a *Study* music example and a complete absence of such events in the *Relax* example. We refer to drop-like events as those that follow similar acoustic and rhythm patterns as drop events that are typically associated with electronic dance music (EDM). Drop events generally occur as combinations of two different events, viz. *drop* and *build*, defined as follows:

(1) Drop: A point in the EDM track, where the full bassline is re-introduced and generally follows a recognizable build section.
(2) Build: A section in the EDM track, where the intensity continuously increases and generally climaxes towards a drop.

These events are associated with the increasing intensity of the music and reaching a climax before the beat returns. We investigate these events because they represent the building up of intensity and changing of rhythm, which could be important for music for study (to not let the listener zone out) or workout (to push the listener to intensify the workout). Finally, the *Study* music examples were completely devoid of vocals, unlike the *Relax* music examples that have vocals at certain points in the track. This analysis revealed that even within one genre (*Trance*), some musical properties could make one track of that genre suitable for the *Relax* and the other track for the *Study* category.

Music for *Relax* is bound to be very different from the music for *Workout* as they are activities at the extremes of physical exertion with *Relax* requiring least physical activity and *Workout* requiring high level of physical activity. Even though we expect the two categories to be related to completely different music, they still have some genres in common, like *dubstep* and *hip hop*. Listening to an example for both the *Relax* and *Workout* category in the *dubstep* genre, one can clearly observe a difference in terms of tempo and texture. As expected, the tempo is higher and the music is more dense for the *Workout* example as compared to the *Relax* example. Listening to the *Workout* example, one can observe the prominence of the bassline, which is at times "naked" without melodic layers. In contrast, in the *Relax* example the bass is much less prominent. As indicated earlier, *Relax* music does not contain drops but there are many drops in the *Workout* example. Our conclusion here is therefore the same as above. Though the tracks belong to the same genre, there are significant variations that make it challenging to rely on genre information alone to distinguish between music for *Relax* and *Workout*.

Finally, we look at two examples from the same genre (*progressive house*), but from different activity categories: *Study* and *Workout*, and notice the presence of vocals in the *Workout* track. Another key difference is the presence of many drop-like events in the *Workout* track and limited number of such events in the *Study* track.

Based on the analysis reported above, we can conclude that genre- and instrument-related information alone is not sufficient to predict suitability of a music track for an activity. Observing the individual examples, we see the main reason for this is the local properties of a music track, i.e., localized variations in low-level features. In the subsequent section, we therefore propose a method which segments the tracks into windows of different time resolutions in order to investigate how to optimally capture these local variations for the posed classification task. Furthermore, the insights presented above motivate our decision to consider the presence/absence of drop-like events as one of the features in the design of activity-related music classification framework, as stated in Section 1.

5 HOW TO IDENTIFY MUSIC FOR ACTIVITY CATEGORIES

In this section, we describe our approach to developing an automatic classification method for activity-to-music mapping. Since the information on genre or instruments is not helpful in detecting music for a given activity, classification based on other and more relevant information needs to be developed.

We start off by noting that recent advances in deep learning, such as [13], may enable unsupervised extraction of relevant features. However, we would like the features that we identify as contributing towards identifying music for activities to be explainable, and we would also like to carry out an assessment of the temporal resolution that is appropriate for feature extraction. Explainability of deep learning pipelines for music currently still is in a pioneering phase [16]. For these reasons, we choose to investigate features and models that are already well understood and reflect different musical characteristics. More specifically, we take as input a basic set of low- and mid-level (rhythm and tonality related) features known from the MIR field. These features and their corresponding dimensionality (in parenthesis) are listed in Table 2.

In addition to the problem of understanding what features are suitable for the task in the first place, the main open issue related to how the features are extracted is the selection of the time window t to optimally aggregate the feature values in order to capture the above mentioned informative local signal variations in the best possible way. In order to discover the best value for t, we devise an algorithm that we run on our training data set and that uses repeated random sub-sampling validation [7] to test different values

Type of music	Genres	Instruments
Relax	classical, binaural, jazz, ambient, house, trance, dubstep, chillstep, hip hop, trap, rock, country, folk	piano, guitar, flute, saxophone, violin, drums
Study	classical, binaural, jazz, ambient, trance, Drum & bass, electronic, deep/electro/progressive house	piano, violin, guitar, viola
Workout	electro, dubstep, progressive house, rock, rap, EDM, hip hop, electronic, techno	piano, drum
Others	jazz, classical, binaural, house, ambient, rock, folk, dubstep, EDM, electronic, electro, trance	piano, saxophone, guitar, drums

Table 1: Genres and musical instruments present in each activity category.

Type of features	Features
Low-level features	Avg. loudness (1), dynamic complexity (1), pitch salience (2), spectral centroid (2), spectral complexity (2), spectral decrease (2), spectral energy (2), spectral entropy (2), spectral flux (2), spectral kurtosis (2), spectral rms (2), spectral rolloff (2), spectral skewness (2), spectral spread (2), zero crossing rate (2), MFCC (13), Image moments (162) [19]
Rhythm features	Number of beats (1), tempo (1), danceability (1), onset rate (1), statistical spectrum descriptor (168) [14], rhythm histogram (60) [14]
Tonal features	chromagram (12), key strength (1), pitch class profile (pcp) (36)
High-level features	Number of events (1) [19], Affect (3)

Table 2: Low-level/mid-level/high-level features we use for distinguishing between music for different activities.

of t. In the same algorithm, we also embed the search for the best value of another parameter d, which stands for the number of most discriminative features used for classification. We use a simple k-nearest neighbour (k-NN) classifier and repeat the algorithm to identify the combination of d and t that gives the best classification performance. The proposed algorithm is defined as follows:

(1) Consider the range of $t = 0.5, 1, 5, 10, 15, 20, 25, 30$ seconds
(2) For each value of t, follow these steps:
   (a) Extract features for each segment and combine them into a single feature vector.
   (b) Randomly divide the training data into X_{train} (90%) and X_{val} (10%).
   (c) Select a value of d from the set 10, 11, 12 ... to 50 features.
   (d) Use X_{train} for feature selection and pick the top-d most discriminating features. Before feature selection, we normalize each feature.
   (e) Use X_{train} with selected features to build a training model.
   (f) Use this model to predict labels in X_{val}.
   (g) Aggregate the segment-level labels using a majority vote to obtain a single label for a track and then compute the f-score.
   (h) Repeat steps 2 (d) – (g) for the whole range of d.
   (i) Repeat the whole process ten times for different X_{train} and X_{val} each time to obtain average validation performance.
(3) Choose the t with the best average validation performance.

In this paper, we aim to understand the phenomena underlying the activity-related music classification and *not* to optimize the classification itself. This is the reason for which we chose a simple and standard k-NN classifier, which has minimal number of parameters to be tuned. Regarding the range we considered for t, we also investigated the window sizes beyond 30 seconds (up to 60 sec) and found that the performance does not improve. For feature selection, we use a method that deploys mutual information and that is available in the feature selection toolbox [4]. Once we identify the best values of d and t, we evaluate the performance on the test set to predict the links between the music tracks and the activity categories.

The other features we introduce are based on intuition, informed by the analysis in Section 4. Here, we consider three affect dimensions, namely arousal, valence and tension, and assess their impact to activity-related music classification experimentally, using conventional scores [12]. We do the same with the feature encoding the number of drop-like events [19] found in a music track: while the consideration of this feature initially was also based on intuition, the potential of this feature has been strengthened by the analysis reported in the previous section. The affect scores are extracted over non-overlapping segments of duration t seconds (result of the algorithm described above) and for the events feature, we count the number of drop-like events in the entire music track.

6 EXPERIMENTAL EVALUATION

In this section, we evaluate our proposed method and also compare its performance to a number of existing methods and approaches that we found related to the problem addressed in this paper. Additionally, we report which features are the most discriminative for our classification task. Finally, we summarize the insights we gained from a failure analysis, based on which we propose topics for future research in this direction.

Window size(sec.)	F-score(relax)	F-score(study)	F-score(workout)	Overall F-score	No. of features
0.5	0.41	0.23	0.56	0.4	46
1	0.43	0.24	0.55	0.41	45
5	0.41	0.28	0.57	0.41	48
10	0.59	0.58	0.79	0.65	40
15	0.59	0.63	0.86	0.69	38
20	0.58	0.61	0.83	0.67	26
25	**0.60**	**0.69**	**0.89**	**0.73**	**25**
30	0.60	0.59	0.89	0.69	35

Table 3: F-scores for different classes and number of discriminative features across different window sizes.

Feature	F-score(relax)	F-score(study)	F-score(workout)	Overall F-score
Events (E)	0.79	0.64	0.72	0.72
Affect (A)	0.63	0.51	0.73	0.62
A + E	0.65	0.51	0.71	0.62

Table 4: F-scores using high-level features at a windows size of 25 sec.

6.1 Experimental design and results

For the experiment, we have a training set, containing 300 relax tracks, 250 study tracks and 250 workout tracks. For the test set, we use 50 each of relax, study and workout tracks. We focus on tracks that are specific for a single activity category, as reflected in our labels. Music suitable for multiple categories is an interesting topic for future work, but we do not look at it here.

For finding t and d according to the algorithm described in the previous section, we set $k = 10$ for the k-NN classifier after evaluating different values of k on a smaller development set (not included in the train and test set). For extracting low-level, tonal features and most of the rhythm related features, we use the Essentia framework [2]. For statistical spectrum descriptors and rhythm histogram, we use the source code provided by Lidy et al. [14]. For extracting the low-level features, we use a non-overlapping frame size of 100 ms. Regarding the high-level features, we use the method proposed in [19] to detect the drop-like events in a given music track. We rely on the dataset released by Yadati et al. [11] to train models and predict the presence of events in our dataset. Finally, for computing the affect scores, we use the MIRtoolbox [12] that gives us a 3-dimensional feature vector with one score per dimension.

Table 3 shows the f-scores per activity category obtained while executing the algorithm for optimizing the values of t and d, as introduced in the previous section. We note again that the classification here is performed using the low- and mid-level features only. It can be observed that the best classification performance was obtained at a window size of 25 seconds. Examining the f-scores obtained at this window size, we can say that the simple classifier performs reasonably well in distinguishing between music for the three different categories.

As indicated in the last column, for the window size of 25 seconds, the best number d of discriminative features to use is 25. Here, we list the features (and their dimensionality) that are found to be most discriminative in this case: tempo (1), dynamic complexity (1), danceability (1), onset rate (1), spectral centroid (1), spectral flux (1), image moments (6), PCP (4), rhythm pattern (4), rhythm histogram (3) and MFCC (2). This is a mix of rhythm features, low-level features and tonal features, with a majority of them being rhythm-related and with PCP being the only representative of the tonal features. A key observation here is that most of the selected features (tempo, danceability, rhythm pattern etc.) generally need longer time segments to be computed. We therefore believe that the flexibility we allowed in the selection of the time window t was critical for pushing these features forward as being most informative for classification and therefore also critical for getting the most out of the signal and achieving the best possible classification performance.

We also performed the classification based on the high-level features, first separately and then integrated with low- and mid-level features. We computed the affect features in the time interval corresponding to the optimal value of t, namely 25 seconds. Experiments using other window sizes showed, however, that this parameter is not critical, resulting in relatively constant classification performance. Computation of the event feature is not dependent on the time window as this is solely the number of drop-like events found in a music track. The classification results for different features and their combinations are presented in Table 4. We observe that the high-level features generally perform worse than low- and mid-level features. An interesting exception is the result obtained for the events feature and *Relax* category. The detector of the drop-like events that we adopted from [19] is namely known for its high precision and low recall. This is beneficial for the *Relax* music tracks having no drops and less beneficial for the tracks from other two categories where drop-like events are present, but because of the detector deployed, not well detectable. This result shows the potential of this feature to improve the overall classification performance upon the one obtained by using low- and mid-level features, however, under the condition that the detector of drop-like events performs well. We discuss this further in the next section.

So far, we looked at the performance of our method in isolation. We now compare our method with existing methods which classify music tracks into activities. Specifically, we compare it with the method proposed by Wang et al. [18] and also with two other methods that we devised as being representative of common approaches deployed in standard MIR classification tasks. The four methods entering a comparative analysis are:

(1) *Our method*: As a representative of our proposed approach we choose the method variant deploying low- and mid-level features with the best performance in Table 3, namely for the time window of 25 seconds and 25 features.
(2) *Full track*: We aggregate the low-level features, extracted from 50ms frames, over the entire track by computing the mean and variance. We then combine these features with other rhythm and tonal features extracted from the whole track. We perform feature selection and select the most discriminative features (51 in this case). Using a k-nearest neighbour classifier, we predict the labels of the music tracks in the test set and compute the f-scores for the three categories. Such a method is inspired from the field of static emotion recognition [8], which aggregates the features over the entire music track in order to give an affect score for a track.
(3) *One segment*: We select one 25-second segment from each track in the training data and extract the features as before. We then perform a feature selection and obtain the most discriminative features (49 in this case). We divide each music track in the test set into 25-second segments and select these 49 most discriminative features. Using a k-nearest neighbour classifier, we predict the labels of each 25-second segment in the test set and use a majority vote to get a single label for a track. We then compute the f-scores for the three categories. This method is inspired by existing MIR approaches, especially genre recognition [8], where a short segment taken from the track is used for feature extraction and classification.
(4) *Wang et al.*: Wang et al. extract features from a 512-sample frame every 30 seconds and compute the mean and variance of these features over the entire track. Then, they use an adaboost classifier to predict the labels of music tracks in the test set. We follow this procedure on our dataset and compute the f-scores for the individual categories.

Figure 5 summarizes the results of all four methods for the three target activity categories. We can clearly see that our method outperforms other methods. We further observe that the *Full track* method that aggregates features over the entire track performs better than the *One segment* method and the *Wang et al.* method at least in two categories: *Relax* and *Study*. From Table 3 and Figure 5, we can conclude that aggregating over a longer window size helps in classifying the music track into one of the three activity categories and, based on the experiments on our dataset, the best window size is 25 seconds.

6.2 Failure analysis and outlook

Through different experiments, we have shown that we can distinguish between music for different activities and that our method performs better than the related existing methods. However, even the best results are not perfect. In this section, we focus at these

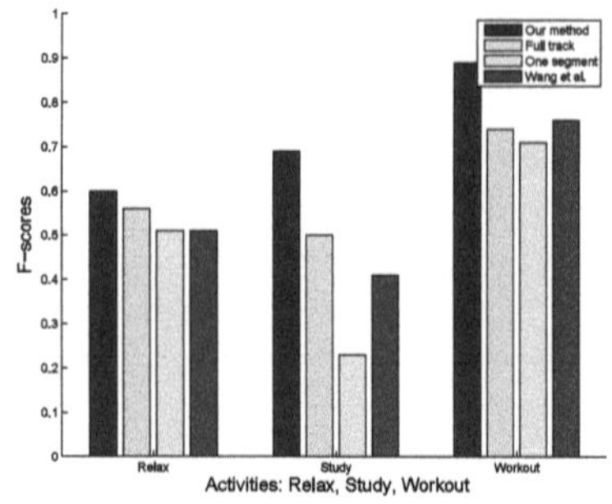

Figure 5: Comparison of performance for three activity categories across different methods.

imperfections by analyzing the failure cases where music tracks belonging to a certain activity category are assigned a wrong label.

Figure 6 illustrates the confusion matrix for the predicted labels on the test set and the numbers in the boxes indicate the number of correctly/wrongly classified samples. The first observation we make is that there is considerable confusion between the *Relax* and *Study* categories. Here, we take a look at individual examples and try to find patterns that lead to this confusion between *Relax* and *Study*. Using a majority vote to aggregate the labels seems to be the reason behind some of the misclassifications. One of the tracks in the relax category, which had 72 segments in total, is misclassified as a *Study* track because 33 segments are classified as *Relax*, 34 segments are classified as *Study* and the remaining segments are classified as *Workout*. A majority vote clearly finds that the track is *Study*, but the competition between *Relax* and *Study* categories was close. We also found many other examples where the difference between the number of segments classified as *Relax* and those classified as *Study* is low. There was even an example in the *Study* category that contained equal number of segments classified as *Relax* and *Study*, but the max operator chose the category of the track as *Relax*. In order to investigate this phenomenon further, we measured the mean and standard deviation of the difference between the number of segments in the top two categories for each example. For correctly classified examples, the mean is 48.6 while the standard deviation is 16.2. For incorrectly classified examples, the mean is 26 while the standard deviation is 6.1. We clearly see lower values for incorrectly classified examples, indicating that there is a closer competition between categories for incorrectly classified examples. Clearly, deploying majority vote has drawbacks as it does not reflect how strong the majority is. This calls for investigating different aggregation strategies that can combine the labels of individual segments into a single label for the track in a more robust fashion. Alternatively, we would also like to explore whether we could choose the segments in a smart way (analogous to feature selection) that are most discriminative for an activity category, which removes the need for an aggregation step. Another possible direction could be to consider the labels for the segments as a sequence instead of considering them as a bag of segments (current method). The temporal ordering could provide additional information that could reduce the misclassfication rate.

We initially hypothesized that drop-like events are completely absent in *Relax* music, while they are present in the other two categories. This is confirmed by the classification results reported in Table 4, in particular by a high f-score for *Relax* music when events feature is used. As explained in the previous section, this effect is additionally emphasized due to a strong bias of the event detector used towards high precision. However, there is more to it. Some of the *Study* music tracks also do not contain drop-like events and this resulted in a confusion between *Relax* and *Study* categories. Furthermore, there are similar numbers of drop-like events in some *Study* music and *Workout* music tracks, which results in lower f-scores for these two categories. Another reason for failure is that there are more subtle drop-like events in *Study* music while *Workout* music has more pronounced events and the drop detector missed detecting some of the subtle events.

Mapping between low-level features and affect is a difficult proposition and we have used an off-the-shelf toolbox to compute the affect scores for the music tracks. Observing the results reported in Table 4, the affect based classifier performs reasonably well, but there is a scope for improvement. We could look at different strategies to compute affect scores in the future and investigate its impact on the classification performance.

An aspect of activity-based music that needs further attention is the presence of distractors, which are musical characteristics that might distract the user from his/her activity. For instance, one of the observations in Section 4 was that *Study* music did not have any vocals while the other two types of music could contain vocals. In the future, one could investigate to which extent the presence/absence of vocals is informative as a feature for this classification task. In general, one could search for additional sources of information, e.g., user comments, that can help identify the distractors for different activities. Here are some examples of user comments that can be used to identify if the track is really useful for an activity:

- Comment on a relax music track: "There is a jarring piano sound in the middle!"
- Comment on a study music track: "This track contains vocals and distracting while working"

The biggest challenge we see when relying on user comments is to spot the comment with the relevant information among plenty of (largely noisy) comments posted by the users.

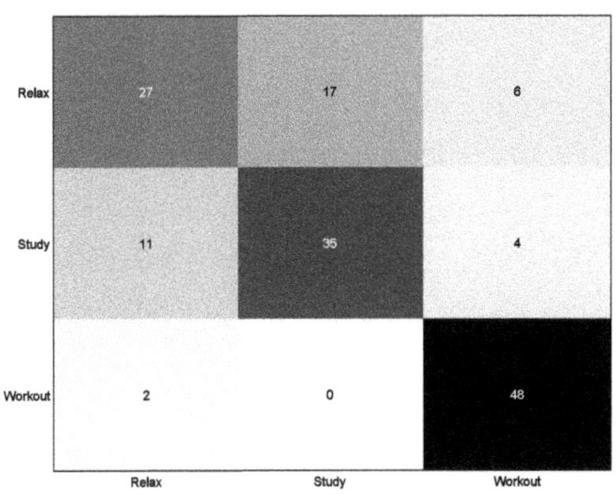

Figure 6: Confusion matrix for the best performing case of $t = 25$ seconds

7 CONCLUSION AND OUTLOOK

In this paper, we have addressed the challenge of identifying appropriate music for common daily activities. In this way, we made a critical step towards developing a music recommender system that takes into consideration both the aspects of what music is and what it can do for a listener. We have focused on the three activity categories that we found to be be common via a study of textual metadata on YouTube: *Relax*, *Study* and *Workout*.

One of our key findings is that standard music information retrieval (MIR) approaches, in particular, those focused on genre or instrument information, are not well-suited for addressing the problem of activity-based music classification. Another important finding is that this task requires more timeline information (25 seconds) for feature extraction from an audio track, i.e., the window size must be longer than what is currently conventional in the MIR literature.

Based on these findings we have developed a method that identifies the time resolution at which the low-level features should be aggregated and also the best number of discriminative features to be used. Using the features extracted at the identified temporal resolution, our classifier could successfully distinguish between music for the three different activity categories and also outperform existing methods.

This paper opens interesting perspectives for future work. From the musical content perspective, we plan to investigate additional information to improve the identification of music for activities. Here, we have taken a bag-of-segments approach. Moving forward, however, we anticipated that incorporation of the temporal order of the segments could, as mentioned above, provide further insight. Further, also as mentioned above, users post comments on YouTube for different music tracks. Some of these touch on the suitability of a music track is for a specific activity. These comments are a promising source of information. Additionally, high-level features, e.g., presence/absence of vocals, could also improve classification.

Our work here is based on the insight that there are general characteristics of music which have a similar reception across a broad population. In pursuit of these general characteristics, we focus on information about music tracks provided by uploaders. We adopt an assumption used recently in work on video uploader intent [10]: the fact that uploaders are publishing on a public platform, accessible to millions of users, makes it likely that they are taking the musical reception of the general population into account. The fact that we focus on here on broad consensus on which music is appropriate for which purposes, should not preclude future study of the role played by individual preferences in users' choices of music for different activities. Individual preferences should also be understood as preferences of groups of users who pattern together, such as introverts and extroverts, as studied by [17]. Moving forward, understanding where universal music preferences fall short of being useful will allow us to gain further insight into the performance of the classifier. Specifically, we would like to investigate the relatively large confusion between the music for the *Relax* and *Study* categories from a user's perspective. Such a user study would allow us to determine whether the classifier should be further improved, or whether the category labels must be refined to make it possible to cater for finer-grained preferences within the population.

REFERENCES

[1] Anna Aljanaki, Frans Wiering, and Remco C Veltkamp. 2015. Emotion based segmentation of musical audio. In *Proceedings of the 17th Conference of the International Society for Music Information Retrieval (ISMIR 2015)*.

[2] Dmitry Bogdanov, Nicolas Wack, Emilia Gómez, Sankalp Gulati, Perfecto Herrera, O. Mayor, Gerard Roma, Justin Salamon, J. R. Zapata, and Xavier Serra. 2013. ESSENTIA: an Audio Analysis Library for Music Information Retrieval. In *Proceedings of the 15th Conference of the International Society for Music Information Retrieval (ISMIR 2013)*.

[3] Sara Bottiroli, Alessia Rosi, Riccardo Russo, Tomaso Vecchi, and Elena Cavallini. 2014. The cognitive effects of listening to background music on older adults: processing speed improves with upbeat music, while memory seems to benefit from both upbeat and downbeat music. *Frontiers in Aging Neuroscience* 6 (2014), 284.

[4] Gavin Brown, Adam Pocock, Ming-Jie Zhao, and Mikel Luján. 2012. Conditional Likelihood Maximisation: A Unifying Framework for Information Theoretic Feature Selection. *J. Mach. Learn. Res.* 13 (Jan. 2012), 27–66.

[5] Andrew Demetriou, Martha Larson, and Cynthis C. S. Liem. 2016. Go With the Flow: When Listeners use Music as Technology. In *Proceedings of the 18th Conference of the International Society for Music Information Retrieval (ISMIR 2016)*.

[6] Ricardo Dias, Manuel J Fonseca, and Ricardo Cunha. 2014. A User-centered Music Recommendation Approach for Daily Activities.. In *Proceedings of the 1st Workshop on New Trends in Content-based Recommender Systems (CBRecSys)*.

[7] Werner Dubitzky. 2009. *Fundamentals of Data Mining in Genomics and Proteomics*. Springer-Verlag, Berlin, Heidelberg.

[8] Z. Fu, G. Lu, K. M. Ting, and D. Zhang. 2011. A Survey of Audio-Based Music Classification and Annotation. *IEEE Transactions on Multimedia* 13, 2 (April 2011), 303–319.

[9] Alan Hanjalic, Christoph Kofler, and Martha Larson. 2012. Intent and Its Discontents: The User at the Wheel of the Online Video Search Engine. In *Proceedings of the 20th ACM International Conference on Multimedia (MM '12)*.

[10] C. Kofler, S. Bhattacharya, M. Larson, T. Chen, A. Hanjalic, and S. F. Chang. 2015. Uploader Intent for Online Video: Typology, Inference, and Applications. *IEEE Transactions on Multimedia* 17, 8 (Aug 2015), 1200–1212.

[11] Martha Larson, Karthik Yadati, Mohammad Soleymani, and Pavala Shakthi Nathan Chandrasekaran Ayyanathan. 2014. MediaEval 2014 Crowdsourcing Task: Crowdsorting multimedia comments. (Oct 2014). http://osf.io/h92g8

[12] Olivier Lartillot and Petri Toiviainen. 2007. MIR in Matlab (II): A Toolbox for Musical Feature Extraction from Audio. In *Proceedings of the 9th International Society for Music Information Retrieval Conference (ISMIR 2007)*.

[13] Honglak Lee, Peter Pham, Yan Largman, and Andrew Y. Ng. 2009. Unsupervised feature learning for audio classification using convolutional deep belief networks. In *Advances in Neural Information Processing Systems (NIPS 2009)*.

[14] Thomas Lidy and Andreas Rauber. 2005. Evaluation of Feature Extractors and Psycho-acoustic Transformations for Music Genre Classification. In *Proceedings of the 6th International Conference on Music Information Retrieval (ISMIR 2005)*.

[15] Lie Lu, D. Liu, and Hong-Jiang Zhang. 2006. Automatic mood detection and tracking of music audio signals. *IEEE Transactions on Audio, Speech, and Language Processing* 14, 1 (Jan 2006), 5–18.

[16] J. Pons, T. Lidy, and X. Serra. 2016. Experimenting with musically motivated convolutional neural networks. In *Proceedings of the 14th International Workshop on Content-Based Multimedia Indexing (CBMI)*.

[17] Geen Russell. 1984. Preferred stimulation levels in introverts and extroverts: Effects on arousal and performance. *Journal of Personality and Social Psychology* 46, 6 (June 1984), 1303–1312.

[18] Xinxi Wang, David Rosenblum, and Ye Wang. 2012. Context-aware Mobile Music Recommendation for Daily Activities. In *Proceedings of the 20th ACM International Conference on Multimedia (MM 2012)*.

[19] Karthik Yadati, Martha Larson, Cynthia C. S. Liem, and Alan Hanjalic. 2014. Detecting Drops in Electronic Dance Music: Content based approaches to a socially significant music event. In *Proceedings of the 15th International Society for Music Information Retrieval Conference (ISMIR 2014)*.

Improving Context-Aware Music Recommender Systems: Beyond the Pre-filtering Approach

Martin Pichl, Eva Zangelere and Günther Specht
Databases and Information Systems
Department of Computer Science
University of Innsbruck
{firstname.lastname}@uibk.ac.at

ABSTRACT

Over the last years, music consumption has changed fundamentally: people switch from private, mostly limited music collections to huge public music collections provided by music streaming platforms. Thus, the amount of available music has increased dramatically and music streaming platforms heavily rely on recommender systems to assist users in discovering music they like. Incorporating the context of users has been shown to improve the quality of recommendations. Previous approaches based on pre-filtering suffered from a split dataset. In this work, we present a context-aware recommender system based on factorization machines that extracts information about the user's context from the names of the user's playlists. Based on a dataset comprising 15,000 users and 1.8 million tracks we show that our proposed approach outperforms the pre-filtering approach substantially in terms of accuracy of the computed recommendations.

CCS CONCEPTS

•**Information systems → Personalization;** *Clustering and classification;* **Recommender systems; Music retrieval; Collaborative filtering;**

KEYWORDS

Recommender Systems, Context, Personalization, User Modeling

ACM Reference format:
Martin Pichl, Eva Zangelere and Günther Specht. 2017. Improving Context-Aware Music Recommender Systems: Beyond the Pre-filtering Approach. In *Proceedings of ICMR '17, June 6–9, 2017, Bucharest, Romania, ,* 8 pages.
DOI: http://dx.doi.org/10.1145/3078971.3078982

1 INTRODUCTION

Recently, we are facing a fundamental change in the way people consume music: more and more people switch from private, mostly limited music collections to public music streaming collections containing several millions of tracks [23]. People increasingly do not store music locally on CDs and hard drives anymore. Instead, they access millions of tracks offered by cloud-based streaming services using various devices. To increase usability, streaming platforms heavily rely on recommender systems to help users in discovering music they like. Previous research has shown that the context of a user (i.e., occasion, event or emotional state) plays an important role for providing personalized music recommendations [20, 22]. Kamalzadeh et al. [16] showed that people listen to different music during different activities and found that people organize tracks in their music collections by the intended use (i.e., working or exercising). This finding is backed up by Cunningham et al. [10], who found that people create playlists that are intended for certain activities.

Over the last years, data for quantitatively validating these studies became available: music streaming platforms provide means for "social playlist generation"—playlists that are shared among friends or to the public. Particularly public playlists serve as an essential new data source for music recommender systems. For Spotify[1], a popular music streaming service, all user-created playlists are public by default[2] and thus can be crawled using the Spotify API[3]. Pichl et al. [27] propose an approach for clustering contextually similar playlists by exploiting the names of these playlists. The clusters are then leveraged in a collaborative filtering recommender system (CF) with pre-filtering [2], hence CF is applied to each cluster individually. Thus, the recommender system is applied to different parts of the dataset in isolation, a method that has drawbacks: the user profiles are split up among the different clusters and thus, there is no holistic view on the user. In addition, recommendation accuracy substantially varies among clusters, as these are different in size.

In this work, we follow up and complement the research of Pichl et al. [27] by utilizing their proposed playlist aggregation pipeline to implement a novel recommender system to overcome the drawbacks of contextual pre-filtering. Particularly, we are interested in how contextual clusters may be leveraged for music recommendations while ensuring that the drawbacks of the pre-filtering approach can be avoided. Therefore, we propose to make use of Factorization Machines (FM) [28] that are directly able to incorporate the contextual clusters extracted from the names of playlists for the computation of recommendations.

In several empirical experiments using k-fold cross-validation we show that our proposed factorization machine-based recommender system outperforms context-agnostic recommender systems, pre-filtering context-aware recommender systems as well

ICMR '17, June 6–9, 2017, Bucharest, Romania

ACM ISBN 978-1-4503-4701-3/17/06...$15.00
DOI: http://dx.doi.org/10.1145/3078971.3078980

[1] http://www.spotify.com
[2] https://developer.spotify.com/web-api/working-with-playlists/#public-private-and-collaborative-status
[3] http://developer.spotify.com/web-api/

as classification-based context-aware recommender systems substantially in terms of recall, precision and the F_1-measure. Our experiments show that factorization machines are particularly capable of tackling the major issue of the pre-filtering approach (i.e., splitting up the dataset). To foster reproducibility and repeatability, we make both our code and data used publicly available by publishing our recommender system and the evaluation framework utilized in this paper on GitHub[4].

The remainder of this paper is structured as follows. In the next section, we focus on related work before presenting our recommendation approach in Section 3. After that, we introduce the reader to our conducted experiments aiming to benchmark different recommendation systems including our proposed recommender system. In the subsequent sections, we present the results of the experiments and discuss them in Section 5. Finally, we wrap up our work in Section 6.

2 RELATED WORK

We classify related work into two main fields of research: context-aware music recommender systems and approaches concerned with leveraging new data sources for music recommendations.

It is widely agreed upon the fact that the user's context improves personalized recommendations [2]. This is why we can see a shift from purely content- or CF-based approaches towards more user-centric approaches incorporating the user's context [33]. In the field of music recommender systems, studies showed that users often seek for music that matches their current context (i.e., occasion, event or emotional state) [20, 22]. As for the different types of contexts, Kaminskas and Ricci [18] distinguish environment-related context (location, time, weather), user-related context (activity, demographic information, emotional state of the user) and multimedia context (text or pictures the user is currently reading or looking at). Examples for contextual information that is leveraged for music recommendations are emotion and mood [4, 7, 11, 31], the user's location [3, 9, 17, 19] or recommending music fitting to documents on the web a user reads at the moment [8]. As for the integration of contextual information into a recommender system, Adomavicius et al. [2] classify approaches modeling the user's context into contextual pre-filtering, contextual post-filtering and contextual modeling approaches. We consider the approach presented in this work as a contextual modeling approach as we do not filter the input or output data of the system.

As for music recommender systems based on novel publicly available data, Zangerle et al. [36] propose a music recommender system based on association rules computed based on user listening behavior extracted from #nowplaying tweets (tweets in which users state which musical track they are listening to at the moment). Moreover, context-aware approaches for music recommendations that are based on information extracted from public data sources have been proposed. Schedl and Schnitzer exploit #nowplaying tweets enhanced with acoustic features extracted from 7digital[5] and extract context information about these tracks by utilizing a web search on the track and artist [34]. In [35], Schedl et al. explore the use of geospatial information for a set of collaborative filtering approaches. Furthermore, also LastFM has been utilized for analyzing the listening behavior of users [12, 32]. Pichl et al. [27] extract contextual information from the names of playlists of Spotify users and incorporate these in the process of recommending tracks. The work presented in this paper builds upon this approach and aims to address the problems of the pre-filtering approach (as proposed by Pichl et al.) by using factorization machines. To the best of our knowledge, this is the first factorization machine-based recommendation approach for integrating contextual clusters derived from playlist names into a music recommender system.

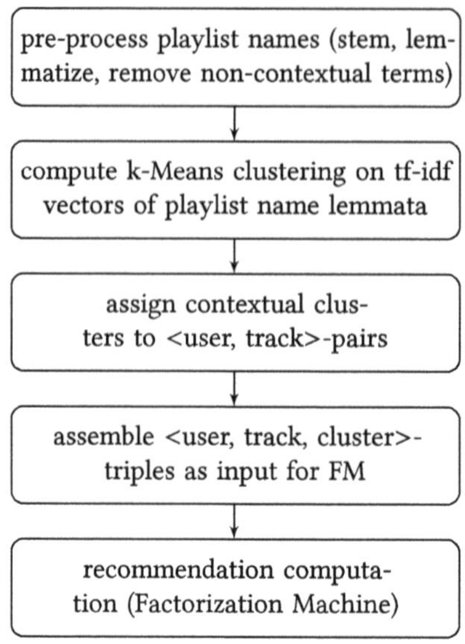

Figure 1: Pipeline for Computing Recommendations

3 METHODS

In this section, we present our proposed recommendation algorithm. First, we introduce the approach taken for computing clusters of contextually similar tracks. In a next step, we present the proposed recommendation framework, which leverages the information provided by these contextual clusters. Figure 1 depicts the overall workflow for the computation of music recommendations utilizing contextual clusters.

As the approach taken for computing contextual clusters relies on the work of Pichl et al. [27], we naturally utilize the same dataset for evaluating our approach (and comparing it to the original approach). This dataset contains 143,528 unique playlists created by 15,345 unique users who listened to 1,878,457 tracks in the form of $<user, track, artist, playlist>$-quadruples.

3.1 Playlist Aggregation and Cluster Generation

In a first step, we compute clusters of contextually similar playlists based on the context information extracted from the names of playlists. Therefore, we follow the method introduced by Pichl et al. [27], which we will shortly sketch in the following. As depicted in Figure 1, we firstly stem all playlist names and lemmatize the tokens in a first step. In a next step, we remove non-contextual terms

[4]https://github.com/dbis-uibk/MusicRecommenderEvaluator/
[5]http://www.7digital.com

such as genre, artist and track names as well as general stop words, as these do not contain any contextual information. We use the resulting bags of lemmata describing each playlist to compute the term frequency-inverse document frequency (tf-idf) [15] for each bag of lemmata representing a playlist name. Using tf-idf, we represent each playlist as a vector containing the tf-idf weights. This allows us to compute playlist similarities by computing the pairwise cosine similarity of the playlist vectors. Using the computed similarities, we span a distance matrix and finally find contextually similar playlists by applying k-Means to the playlists in the matrix. As we evaluate our approach using the same dataset as Pichl et al. [27], we set the number of clusters to $k = 23$, as proposed in the original approach. In the next step, we integrate the contextual clusters in the recommendation computation as presented in the following section.

3.2 Recommendation Computation

Our proposed recommendation approach aims to provide track recommendations for a given user in a given context. Particularly, we aim to model users by the tracks they listened to and enrich this information with the contexts in which each individual user has listened to those tracks. For the given input dataset, we assume that by adding a track to a playlist, the user expresses some preference for the track. For means of simplicity, we will describe a user-track interaction extracted from a playlist as "a given user listened to a given track". Furthermore, we infer from previous findings [10, 16], that user create playlists to listen to the contained tracks in the context specified by the playlist name.

The initial input dataset contains <*user*, *track*, *playlist*>-triples. We transform this dataset into a set of <*user*, *track*, *context_cluster*>-triples by applying the clustering method presented in Section 3.1 and assigning each user-track pair with one of the 23 contextual clusters in which the given user has listened to the given track. By adding a fourth factor *rating* to the dataset, we transform the recommendation computation task into a rating prediction task: for each unique <*user*, *track*, *context_cluster*>-triple, the *rating* r_{ijk} is 1 if the user u_i has listened to the track t_j in cluster c_k. Our dataset does not contain any implicit feedback by users (i.e., play counts, skipping behavior, session durations or dwell times during browsing the catalog). Therefore, we cannot estimate any preferences towards an item a user not listened to as proposed by [13]. Thus, for each <*user*, *track*, *context_cluster*> combination for which we cannot obtain a rating for, we assume the rating to be $r = -1$ (as proposed by [13]). The rating r_{ijk} for each user u_i, track t_j and cluster c_k can now defined as stated in Equation 1. Although there is a certain bias towards negative values as some missing values might be positive, Pan et al. [26] found that this method for rating estimation works well.

$$r_{ijk} = \begin{cases} 1 & if\ u_i\ listened\ to\ t_j\ in\ c_k \\ -1 & otherwise \end{cases} \quad (1)$$

To get a better understanding of the resulting dataset, we depict a sample of the dataset in Table 1. Based on this dataset, we train a classifier that decides whether a user has listened to a track in a contextual cluster or not. For this computation, we require a given user, track and cluster as input.

As for the actual computation of recommendations, we opt for factorization machines (FM) [28, 29], as these can be considered as state-of-the-art recommendation approach and have been shown to perform well for recommender systems [30]. FMs are a generalization of factorization models and allow to model interactions of input variables in a lower-dimensional space (i.e., interactions are mapped onto a latent features-space of lower dimension). As we aim to exploit the interaction effects of users, tracks and clusters with this recommender system, we chose to utilize a FM of the order $d = 2$ modeling all single and pairwise interactions between input variables as depicted in Equation 2.

$$\hat{r}_{FM} = w_0 + \sum_{i=1}^{n} w_i x_i + \sum_{i=1}^{m} \sum_{j=i+1}^{m} \langle \vec{v}_i, \vec{v}_j \rangle x_i x_j \quad (2)$$

Equation 2 shows that a FM computes rating predictions by modeling a global bias (w_0), the influence of the user, track as well as the clusters ($\sum_{i=1}^{m} w_i x_i$) along with the quadratic interaction effects of those ($\sum_{i=1}^{m} \sum_{j=i+1}^{m} \langle \vec{v}_i, \vec{v}_j \rangle$). However, instead of learning all weights $w_{i,j}$ for the interaction effects, a FM relies factorization to model the interaction as the inner product of low dimensional vectors ($\langle \vec{v}_i, \vec{v}_j \rangle$) [29].

To estimate the performance of the presented recommender systems we conduct a set of experiments as described in the following section.

4 EXPERIMENTS

In this section, we introduce the experiments conducted to evaluate the proposed approach and the baseline approaches aiming at answering our research questions. We start with a description of the dataset used for the evaluation before focusing on the experimental setup and the evaluation measures.

4.1 Dataset

For our experiments, we apply the proposed clustering method on the initial dataset and reshape the input dataset into a set containing <*user*, *track*, *context_cluster*, *rating*>-quadruples. We assign each track in a playlist with a rating value as described in Section 3.2. The rating indicates whether a certain user listened to a certain track in a certain cluster ($r = 1$) or not ($r = -1$). A fragment of the dataset is shown in Table 1. This excerpt shows that user 872 has listened to track 250246 in contextual cluster 0, whereas user 911 has listened to track 250246 in context 2. This dataset forms the foundation for our experiments, which are presented in the next section.

User	Track	Contextual Cluster	r
872	309275	0	1
872	309275	1	-1
911	250246	0	-1
911	250246	0	-1
911	250246	2	1

Table 1: Dataset Fragment

4.2 Baseline Recommender Systems

We compare our proposed FM approach to three baseline recommender systems: a CF-based system, a SVD-based system and a classification-based system. To incorporate context information in the CF- and SVD-based baseline approaches, we apply pre-filtering [2], where the computation of recommendations (CF or SVD) is performed on each contextual cluster individually. I.e., we compute the recommendations on a sub-dataset of the dataset restricted to a certain cluster. The classification-based system uses the computed contextual clusters as an input feature to the classifier. With those systems, we benchmark classical CF, approaches facilitating latent features (considered as state-of-the art in recent years) and a classification-based approach against our proposed factorization machine-based recommender system.

The first recommender system to benchmark is a collaborative filtering approach [1]. The idea behind CF is to recommend items the k-nearest neighbors of a user interacted with. For determining the nearest neighbors, we compute pairwise user similarities by computing the Jaccard Coefficient [14] of the set of tracks each of the two users listened to. Thus, we measure the number of commonly listened tracks in relation to the tracks both users listened to as depicted in Equation 3, where we denote S_i as the set of tracks a user i has listened to.

$$Jaccard_{i,j} = \frac{|S_i \cap S_j|}{|S_i \cup S_j|} \tag{3}$$

The second baseline recommender system is based on singular value decomposition (SVD) [21]. SVD predicts ratings by extracting a number of latent features from the user-item matrix R. In our setting, this is a sparse matrix containing all the binary ratings r_{ij} (cf. Equation 1) of all users u_i and the tracks t_j they listened to. These latent features, characterizing types of tracks, are computed by factoring the user-item matrix R into two matrices U and V, which represent the user and item factors. Hence, R is the cross product of U and V ($R = UV'$). We approximate U and V by minimizing the error to the known ratings r_{ij} using stochastic gradient descent optimization (SGD) [21].

Thirdly, we aim to compare our proposed approach with a classification-based recommendation approach as the performed recommendation computation can also be considered as a one-class classification problem [26]. Therefore, we implement a random forest classifier [24] as it has two main advantages: firstly, we only have to tune one parameter: the number of trees [25]. Secondly, all trees can be computed in parallel and the algorithm scales linearly with the number of trees.

Furthermore, we compare all recommender system to a random-choice baseline. The assumption behind this baseline is that the fundamental chances of guessing whether a track was listened by a user ($r = 1$) or not ($r = -1$) is 50%. Thus, the random baseline for the *precision* measure is 0.5. The same holds for RMSE and MAPE, where the random baseline is also 0.5. For the *recall* measure we cannot state a single baseline value, as recall is dependent on the number of recommendations n as explained in Section 4.4 and shown in Equation 8.

A detailed description of the evaluation is given in the next section.

4.3 Experimental Setup

To evaluate the performance of the different recommender systems, we conduct a 5-fold cross-validation. Therefore, we randomly split the dataset into five folds of equal size. Subsequently, we utilize four folds as training data and the remaining fold as test data. This process is repeated 5 times such that every fold serves as test data once. Due to the random selection of data for the folds, each fold contains an arbitrary number of relevant and irrelevant items. The relevant items are tracks a user has listened to within a certain cluster, whereas the latter are items a user did not listen to at all within a cluster.

For assessing the rating prediction performance of the different recommender systems, we compute the predicted rating $\hat{r}$ for each track in the current test set. Using the predicted ratings $\hat{r}$ as well as the actual ratings r in the test set, we compute the evaluation measures as described in Section 4.4. These evaluation measures are computed for each fold separately and before computing the measures, we perform a min-max scaling. For the results in Section 5, we compute the average across all folds.

For evaluating the top-n recommendations performance, we sort the result by the predicted rating $\hat{r}$ and subsequently use the top-n recommended tracks for the evaluation. We compare $\hat{r}$ to the actual rating r for the current user, track and cluster in the test set. For this comparison, we assume all track recommendations with $\hat{r} \geq 0.5$ as relevant for the user in the given context and hence, $\hat{r} = 1$.

As for the learning method utilized for the FM, we make use of Markov Chain Monte Carlo (MCMC) inference as proposed by Rendl et al. [28]. Generally, we tuned each of the recommender systems (except the random baseline), using k-fold cross-validation. For the random forest classifier, we train the random forest classifier with 1,000 trees. In preliminary experiments, we found that this is a sufficient number of trees to get stable results. Similarly, in our preliminary experiments we found that for CF, $n = 30$ and for SVD, $k = 50$ are suitable parameter options.

4.4 Evaluation Measures

In this section, we elaborate on the evaluation measures used for assessing the performance of the different recommendation algorithms.

For assessing the rating prediction task, we compute the different widely used error measures: root mean square error (RMSE) as well as the mean absolute percentage error (MAPE) as stated in Equations 4 and 5, where $\hat{r}$ is the predicted rating and r the actual rating as contained in the test set. For the results stated Table 2, we compute the average error among all ratings r_i in the test set. Please note that for computing the error measures, we scaled the predicted rating $\hat{r}$ between 0 and 1 using min-max scaling to be able to directly compare the evaluated approaches.

$$RMSE = \sqrt{\frac{\sum_{i=1}^{n}(r_i - \hat{r}_i)^2}{n}} \tag{4}$$

$$MAPE = \frac{1}{n}\sum_{i=1}^{n}\left|\frac{r_i - \hat{r}_i}{r_i}\right| \tag{5}$$

For measuring the performance of the top-n recommendations, we rely on *recall*, *precision* and the F_1-measure. For computing the *recall*-measure, we have to classify the tracks in the test set into relevant and non-relevant items. We consider an item as relevant, if the user has listened to this track in a certain cluster and thus $r = 1$. An item is considered as non-relevant for a given user if the user did not listen to it in a given cluster and thus, $r = -1$. For a certain user, a track can be relevant in certain clusters and simultaneously not relevant in other cluster. In case of the FM-based recommender, we have to transform the rating prediction task into a one-class classification task [26] on whether a given track relevant or not relevant for a given user in a given context to be able to compute the top-n measures. Therefore, we consider $\hat{r}$ as 1 if the computed probability that a user interacted with an item $P(r = 1)$ is higher than 50% as stated in Equation 6. As for the ranking, we rely on the predicted rating for ranking the recommendations to be able evaluate the top-n recommendations.

$$\hat{r} = \begin{cases} 1 & if\ P(r = 1) \geq 0.5 \\ -1 & otherwise \end{cases} \tag{6}$$

In Equations 7 and 8 we state how precision (P) and recall (R) are computed. Precision measures the number of true positives (TP) in relation to the number of recommendations n, which is the number of true positives plus the number of false positives (FP). We consider all items where $r = \hat{r} = 1$ as true positives. In contrast, Recall measures the ratio of true positives and the number of relevant items in the test set (RIT). These relevant items are the items a user has listened to in the given context and hence, have the rating $r = 1$. This recall computation implies that there is natural a cap of the recall determined by the number of recommendations n. The maximum recall is $\frac{n}{RIT}$. Hence, a low number of recommendations n naturally implies a low recall R.

$$P = \frac{TP}{TP + FP} \tag{7}$$

$$R = \frac{TP}{RIT} \tag{8}$$

For assessing the overall *precision*, *recall* and F_1-measure of the evaluated recommender systems, we compute the measures for each individual fold and compute the average among all users in a final step. We elaborate on the results of the presented evaluation in the following section.

5 RESULTS AND DISCUSSION

Based on the evaluation setup and measures described in the preceding section, we assess the performance of the following recommender systems: a pure CF-based recommender system (CF), context-aware CF with pre-filtering (PR-CF) as proposed by Pichl et al. [27], a SVD-based recommender system (SVD), a context-aware SVD-based recommender system with pre-filtering (PR-SVD), a context-aware random forest classifier-based recommender system (RF) as well as our proposed context-aware FM-based recommender system (FM). As outlined in Section 4.2, we consider the first five recommender systems as baseline approaches to our FM-based recommender. Additionally, we compare all recommender system against the random baseline (RB).

As described in Sections 4.3 and 4.4, we evaluate the rating prediction task and the top-n recommendations. Analogously to the previous section, we start with discussing the rating prediction before analyzing the top-n recommendations task.

Recommender	RMSE	MAPE
CF	0.921	0.424
Pre-filtering CF	0.914	0.418
SVD	0.913	0.417
Pre-filtering SVD	0.914	0.418
RF	0.520	0.209
FM	0.560	0.282

Table 2: Evaluation of the Rating Prediction Task (all Tracks)

The results of the rating prediction task applied to all items in the test set are stated in Table 2. We find that with respect to the rating prediction task, the presented classifier-based context-aware approaches (RF and FM) clearly outperform all other approaches. RF and FM reach a RMSE of 0.520 and 0.560 and a MAPE of 0.209 and 0.282, respectively. The proposed baseline approaches reach RMSE values of > 0.9 and MAPE values of > 0.4. However, we also observe that none of the algorithms outperforms the random baseline of 0.5 w.r.t. RMSE (in contrast to MAPE). We lead this back to the fact that as RMSE naturally is more sensitive to high deviations between r and $\hat{r}$. Furthermore, the high error rate can also be explained by the fact that there are far more tracks a user did not listen to in a given cluster than tracks a user did actually listen to in a given cluster (i.e., the underlying matrix is highly sparse). Therefore, computing the error measures incorporating all tracks in the data leads to results biased towards imprecise rating predictions of low ranked (and hence, irrelevant) items. As the majority of tracks within our dataset are not relevant for a given user in a given context, evaluating RMSE and MAPE of all tracks within the dataset naturally includes tracks are not relevant for a user. Our recommender systems considers all tracks with a predicted rating $\hat{r} < 0.5$ as irrelevant to the user and these tracks are naturally not shown in the list of recommendations. We argue that the error for tracks with ratings $\hat{r} < 0.5$ are irrelevant for ranking the tracks on the recommendation list. To illustrate this bias we repeat the experiment for all tracks the recommendation algorithms consider as relevant for the user (i.e., tracks with a predicted rating of $\hat{r} \geq 0.5$ after the min-max scaling). The results of this evaluation are depicted in Table 3.

Recommender	RMSE	MAPE
CF	0.389	0.151
Pre-filtering CF	0.143	0.021
SVD	0.366	0.177
Pre-filtering SVD	0.939	0.927
RF	0.415	0.172
FM	0.380	0.221

Table 3: Evaluation of the Rating Prediction Task (relevant Tracks)

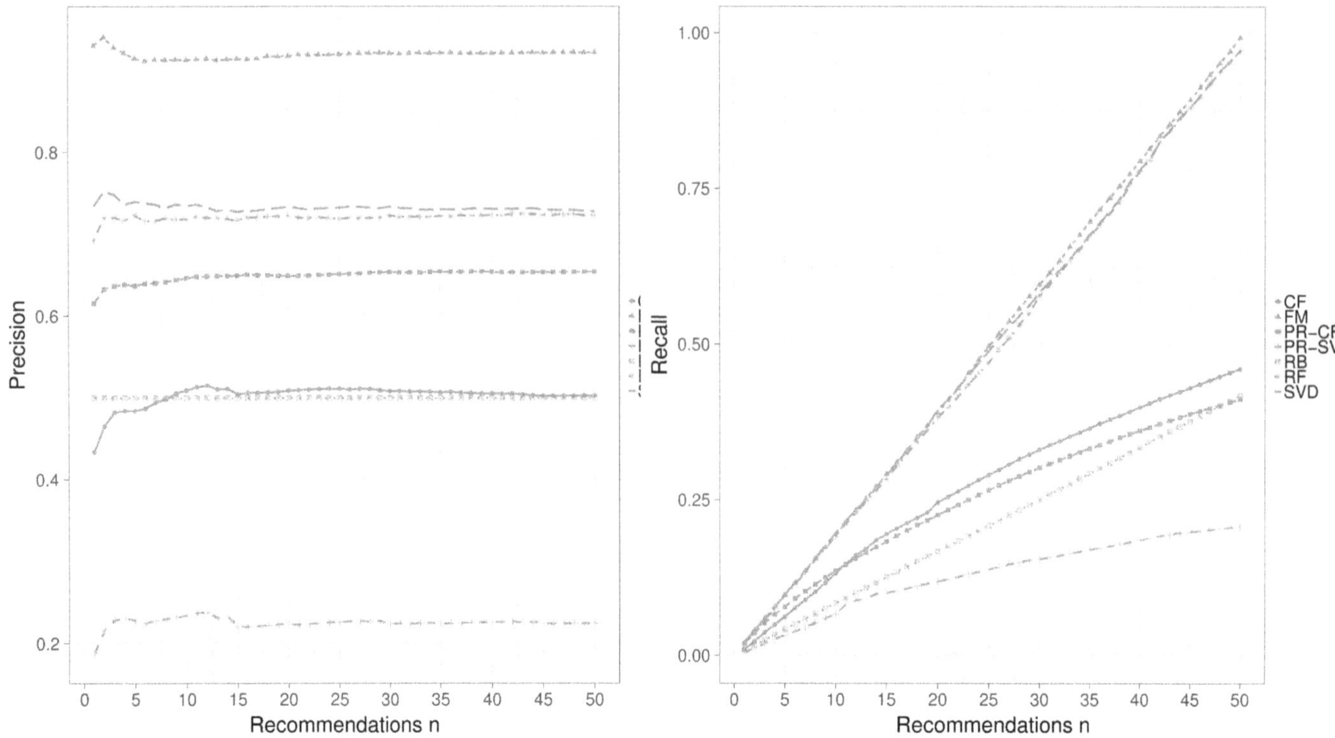

(a) Precision@n

(b) Recall@n

Figure 2: Evaluation: Recall and Precision for $n = \{1 \ldots 50\}$

When considering only tracks with a predicted rating of $\hat{r} \geq 0.5$, the results show that all algorithms except pre-filtering SVD outperform the baseline. The SVD-based recommender system even performs better than the RF-based one and slightly outperforms our proposed FM-based recommender. Furthermore, in this scenario, applying pre-filtering to CF improves results.

However, we argue that for the use cases we discuss later in this section, the top-n-recommendations evaluation is of higher importance as a user-centric evaluation that measures the utility of the top-n recommendations provided to the user is vital and of higher importance than actual error rates. Particularly, we argue that a top-n performance for low n is vital for users. Hence, we are particularly interested in the performance of the proposed recommendation approaches for lower n. Hence, not the precise rating prediction is crucial but ranking the track, such that the most relevant tracks for a user in a given context are listed within the top-n recommendations. This is, as the recommender system computes the list by sorting all potential track recommendations descending by the predicted rating $\hat{r}$ and returns the top-n tracks based in this list. Amongst others, in the remainder of the this section we empirically show the discrepancy between rating prediction accuracy and top-n prediction accuracy: although the RMSE and MAPE of CF is low, even lower than using RF, the performance evaluated measuring the accuracy of the top-n recommendations hardly outperforms the baseline.

For the presenting the results of the top-n performance evaluation of the proposed recommendations task, we depict the *precision-* and *recall*-curves in the Figures 2a and 2b for $n = \{1 \ldots 50\}$. Aiming at making the performance of the recommender systems easily comparable, we integrated both, the *precision-* and the *recall* into the F_1 measure and plot the F_1 measure in Figure 3. Figure 2b shows that the FM, RF and SVD-based approaches perform substantially better in terms of recall than the other baselines across all number of recommendations n. Notably, the pre-filtering SVD approach performs worse than the random baseline across all n. As for precision (shown in Figure 2a) we detect a similar behavior. Again, pre-filtering SVD reaches substantially lower precision values than the other approaches. Interestingly, the SVD approach performs better than the pre-filtering SVD approach and reaches values similar to the random baseline. The FM-based approach performs substantially better than SVD and RF, followed by pre-filtering CF.

When examining the F_1 results in Figure 3, we consequently observe that all approaches outperform the baseline approach for $n < 25$. For $n >= 25$, only pre-filtering SVD reaches F_1 values lower than the random baseline. Considering the *precision* and *recall* plots of the algorithms in Figures 2a and 2b respectively, we observe that pre-filtering SVD performs poorly independent of the evaluation measure. However, we also note that a recommender system based on latent features computed via SVD provides accurate results and reaches high *recall* values. From this, we derive that the implicitly computed latent features represent track-context associations.

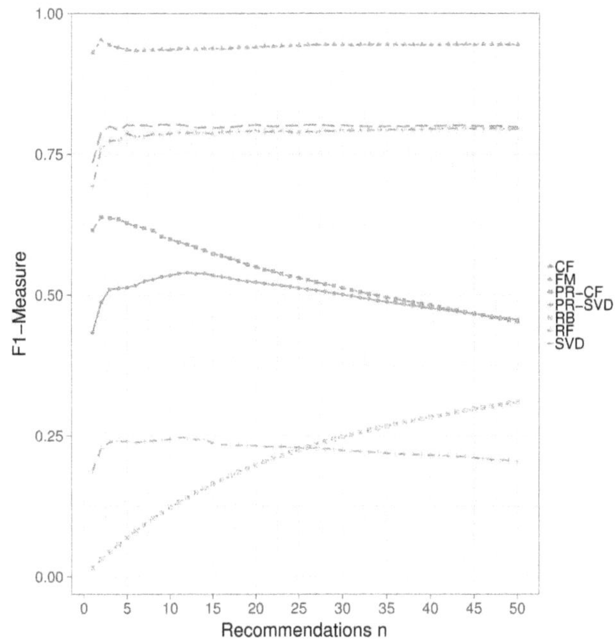

Figure 3: F1@n

Hence, pre-filtering limits the amount of input data available for computing latent features. Hence, we argue that pre-filtering SVD is not an effective approach for our recommendation task.

Moreover, we observe that all approaches besides pre-filtering SVD outperform classical CF. However, we have to note that CF hardly beats the random baseline, for which we assume that the chances to guess whether a track was listened by a user ($r = 1$) or not ($r = -1$) is 50%. We lead this back to a lack of non-boolean ratings as explicit ratings would allow a more precise computation of the user similarity and hence, more precise recommendations. We argue that this would improve the ordering of the tracks, which is especially crucial for the top-n recommendation task.

Additionally our experiments show that contextual pre-filtering is beneficial for CF. Pre-filtering CF beats the random baseline by a 46% higher F_1-score, which confirms the results of Pichl et al. [27]. However, as we observe in Figures 2a and 2b, pre-filtering is only highly beneficial for *precision*. The obtained *recall* value is slightly lower for the pre-filtering CF approach than for standard CF approach (-3,08%). We suspect two reasons for this: firstly, pre-filtering computes recommendations based on parts of the dataset. This is beneficial for the *precision*, as the number of recommendation candidates is limited. However, this configuration limits the *recall*. Secondly, as we compute user similarities on a restricted amount of data, not all similarities are captured which also possibly limits the set of possible recommendations.

Finally, we note that our proposed FM-based recommender system clearly outperforms all other approaches including SVD and RF in terms of *precision*, whereas the *recall* behaves similar for the three best approaches (FM, SVD and RF). We lead this behavior back to the way recall is computed. For each algorithm, the tracks are ordered by the predicted rating $\hat{r}$ and hence, by the likelihood of being relevant to a given user in a given context. Secondly, there is a natural upper bound of the recall dependent on the number of recommendations ($\frac{n}{RIT}$). As we sort recommendations by the predicted rating $\hat{r}$ evaluate the top-n tracks, the order of tracks is essential. The better an algorithm performs, the more relevant items with $\hat{r} = r = 1$ are contained in the top-n recommendations. This ultimately results in a higher number of RIT, as we compare the top-n recommendations to the actual rating value r. This is why the top-algorithms approach a recall of $n/50$.

Bollen et al. [6] addressed the problem of choice overload and state that user satisfaction is highest when presenting the user with top-5 to top-20 items—naturally assuming that the recommendation list contains a sufficient number of relevant items for the user. This is why we state the results for a small number of recommendations n in Table 4. Please note that we only list the top-3 algorithms here (FM, SVD and RF).

Recommender	F_1@1	F_1@5	F_1@10	F_1@20	F_1@50
FM	0.93	0.94	0.94	0.94	0.95
SVD	0.73	0.80	0.80	0.80	0.80
RF	0.69	0.79	0.79	0.79	0.80

Table 4: F_1-Measure for different n

The results in Table 4 show that for maximizing the user satisfaction according to Bollen et al. [6], our proposed FM-based approach clearly outperforms RF-based approaches (where we model the context explicitly) as well as SVD-based approaches (where we model the context-track associations implicitly via latent features). The FM model in Equation 2 depicts that the FM models the context explicitly as part of the variable's main effects: $\sum_{i=1}^{n} w_i x_i$ and additionally similar to the SVD approach implicitly in the pair-wise interactions: $\sum_{i=1}^{m} \sum_{j=i+1}^{m} \vec{v}_i, \vec{v}_j x_i x_j$. Underpinned by an empirical evaluation we argue that a hybrid approach combining regression with two-way interaction effects, where the weights of these effects are estimated via matrix factorization for classification (as provided by a factorization machine) is the best approach for context-aware music recommendation in a setting similar to the one presented in this work.

Summing up, in this work we show how contextual clusters can be leveraged for context-aware music recommendations. We find that contextual clusters can be leveraged for music recommendations without the drawbacks of the pre-filtering approach either by using a classifier approach or by incorporating latent features. Particularly, we find that by using Factorization Machines, the best results regarding the accuracy of recommendations can be obtained. Possible use cases for such recommender systems are (i) the generation of track suggestions during the playlist generation phase of a user and (ii) "contextual browsing" which helps users discovering music they like. For the first use case, the recommender system can recommend tracks that are likely to be interesting to the user that can be added to the currently curated playlist. Thus, the recommender system presents tracks to the user, which similar users added to contextually similar playlists. The second use case, the "contextual browsing", is based on the finding of Cunningham et al. [10] that people browse music collections to discover tracks they like to listen to during different activities or situations. After a user selects a certain context (or the context is automatically inferred), our recommender system can provide lists of interesting tracks for this specified context. This use case is similar to the classical top-n recommendation task we evaluated in Section 4.

6 CONCLUSION

In this work, we propose a novel approach for incorporating contextual clusters extracted from the names of user playlists for the computation of context-aware track recommendations. Particularly, we present a recommendation approach based on Factorization Machines. We evaluate the prediction accuracy of different recommendation approaches based on a dataset of 15,000 users. Our k-fold cross-validations show that contextual clusters can indeed contribute substantially to recommendation accuracy by relying on either a classifier-based approach or approaches facilitating latent features. Particularly, the obtained results show that our proposed factorization machined-based recommender system is able to outperform the baseline approaches substantially. We consider these findings highly promising. Hence, in future work, we aim to evaluate different FM-models and configurations. Particularly, we are also interested in the use of higher order factorization machines [5].

REFERENCES

[1] Gediminas Adomavicius and Alexander Tuzhilin. 2005. Toward the Next Generation of Recommender Systems: A Survey of the State-of-the-Art and Possible Extensions. *IEEE Trans. on Knowl. and Data Eng.* 17, 6 (June 2005), 734–749. DOI: http://dx.doi.org/10.1109/TKDE.2005.99

[2] Gediminas Adomavicius and Alexander Tuzhilin. 2010. Context-Aware Recommender Systems. In *Recommender Systems Handbook* (1st ed.), Francesco Ricci, Lior Rokach, Bracha Shapira, and Paul B. Kantor (Eds.). Springer-Verlag New York, Inc., New York, NY, USA, Chapter 7, 217–253.

[3] Anupriya Ankolekar and Thomas Sandholm. 2011. Foxtrot: a soundtrack for where you are. In *Proceedings of Interacting with Sound Workshop: Exploring Context-Aware, Local and Social Audio Applications.* ACM, 26–31.

[4] Linas Baltrunas, Marius Kaminskas, Bernd Ludwig, Omar Moling, Francesco Ricci, Aykan Aydin, Karl-Heinz Lke, and Roland Schwaiger. 2011. InCarMusic: Context-Aware Music Recommendations in a Car. In *E-Commerce and Web Technologies*, Christian Huemer and Thomas Setzer (Eds.). Lecture Notes in Business Information Processing, Vol. 85. Springer, 89–100.

[5] Mathieu Blondel, Akinori Fujino, Naonori Ueda, and Masakazu Ishihata. 2016. Higher-Order Factorization Machines. In *Advances in Neural Information Processing Systems.* 3351–3359.

[6] Dirk Bollen, Bart P. Knijnenburg, Martijn C. Willemsen, and Mark Graus. 2010. Understanding Choice Overload in Recommender Systems. In *Proceedings of the Fourth ACM Conference on Recommender Systems (RecSys '10).* ACM, New York, NY, USA, 63–70. DOI: http://dx.doi.org/10.1145/1864708.1864724

[7] Matthias Braunhofer, Marius Kaminskas, and Francesco Ricci. 2011. Recommending Music for Places of Interest in a Mobile Travel Guide. In *Proceedings of the Fifth ACM Conference on Recommender Systems (RecSys '11).* ACM, New York, NY, USA, 253–256. DOI: http://dx.doi.org/10.1145/2043932.2043977

[8] Rui Cai, Chao Zhang, Chong Wang 0002, Lei Zhang 0001, and Wei-Ying Ma. 2007. MusicSense: contextual music recommendation using emotional allocation modeling.. In *Proceedings of the 15th ACM International Conference on Multimedia (2007).*

[9] Zhiyong Cheng and Jialie Shen. 2014. Just-for-Me: An Adaptive Personalization System for Location-Aware Social Music Recommendation. In *Proceedings of the 2014 ACM International Conference on Multimedia Retrieval (ICMR).* Glasgow, UK.

[10] Sally Jo Cunningham, David Bainbridge, and A. Falconer. 2006. More of an Art than a Science': Supporting the Creation of Playlists and Mixes. In *Proceedings of the 7th International Symposium on Music Information Retrieval (ISMIR 2006).*

[11] Byeong-jun Han, Seungmin Rho, Sanghoon Jun, and Eenjun Hwang. 2010. Music emotion classification and context-based music recommendation. *Multimedia Tools and Applications* 47, 3 (2010), 433–460.

[12] David Hauger and Markus Schedl. 2012. Exploring Geospatial Music Listening Patterns in Microblog Data. In *Proceedings of the 10th International Workshop on Adaptive Multimedia Retrieval (AMR 2012).*

[13] Yifan Hu, Yehuda Koren, and Chris Volinsky. 2008. Collaborative Filtering for Implicit Feedback Datasets. In *Proceedings of the 2008 Eighth IEEE International Conference on Data Mining (ICDM 2008).* 263–272.

[14] Paul Jaccard. 1912. The Distribution of the Flora in the Alpine Zone. *New Phytologist* 11, 2 (1912), 37–50.

[15] Karen Sprck Jones. 1972. A statistical interpretation of term specificity and its application in retrieval. *Journal of Documentation* 28 (1972), 11–21.

[16] Mohsen Kamalzadeh, Dominikus Baur, and Torsten Mller. 2012. A Survey on Music Listening and Management Behaviours. In *Proceedings of the 13th International Symposium on Music Information Retrieval (ISMIR 2012).*

[17] Marius Kaminskas and Francesco Ricci. 2011. Location-Adapted Music Recommendation Using Tags. In *User Modeling, Adaption and Personalization.* Springer Berlin Heidelberg, 183–194.

[18] Marius Kaminskas and Francesco Ricci. 2012. Contextual music information retrieval and recommendation: State of the art and challenges. *Computer Science Review* 6, 2 (2012), 89–119.

[19] Marius Kaminskas, Francesco Ricci, and Markus Schedl. 2013. Location-aware Music Recommendation Using Auto-tagging and Hybrid Matching. In *Proceedings of the 7th ACM Conference on Recommender Systems (RecSys 2013).* 17–24.

[20] Ja-Young Kim and Nicholas J Belkin. 2002. Categories of Music Description and Search Terms and Phrases Used by Non-Music Experts.. In *ISMIR*, Vol. 2. 209–214.

[21] Yehuda Koren, Robert Bell, and Chris Volinsky. 2009. Matrix Factorization Techniques for Recommender Systems. *Computer* 42, 8 (Aug. 2009), 30–37. DOI: http://dx.doi.org/10.1109/MC.2009.263

[22] Jin Ha Lee and J Stephen Downie. 2004. Survey of music information needs, uses, and seeking behaviours: Preliminary findings.. In *ISMIR*, Vol. 2004. Citeseer, 5th.

[23] Jin Ha Lee, Yea-Seul Kim, and Chris Hubbles. 2016. A look at the cloud from both sides now: an analysis of cloud music service usage. In *Proceedings of the 17th International Society for Music Information Retrieval Conference (ISMIR 2016).*

[24] Andy Liaw and Matthew Wiener. 2002. Classification and regression by randomForest. *R news* 2, 3 (2002), 18–22.

[25] Thais Mayumi Oshiro, Pedro Santoro Perez, and José Augusto Baranauskas. 2012. How Many Trees in a Random Forest?. In *In Proceedings of the 8th International Conference Machine Learning and Data Mining in Pattern Recognition (MLDM 2012).* 154–168.

[26] Rong Pan, Yunhong Zhou, Bin Cao, Nathan N. Liu, Rajan Lukose, Martin Scholz, and Qiang Yang. 2008. One-Class Collaborative Filtering. In *Proceedings of the 2008 Eighth IEEE International Conference on Data Mining (ICDM '08).* IEEE Computer Society, Washington, DC, USA, 502–511. DOI: http://dx.doi.org/10.1109/ICDM.2008.16

[27] Martin Pichl, Eva Zangerle, and Günther Specht. 2015. Towards a Context-Aware Music Recommendation Approach: What is Hidden in the Playlist Name?. In *15th IEEE International Conference on Data Mining Workshops (ICDM 2015).* 1360–1365.

[28] Steffen Rendle. 2012. Factorization Machines with libFM. *ACM Trans. Intell. Syst. Technol.* 3, 3, Article 57 (May 2012), 22 pages.

[29] Steffen Rendle, Zeno Gantner, Christoph Freudenthaler, and Lars Schmidt-Thieme. 2011. Fast Context-aware Recommendations with Factorization Machines. In *Proceedings of the 34th International ACM SIGIR Conference on Research and Development in Information Retrieval.* 635–644.

[30] Steffen Rendle, Zeno Gantner, Christoph Freudenthaler, and Lars Schmidt-Thieme. 2011. Fast context-aware recommendations with factorization machines. In *Proceedings of the 34th international ACM SIGIR conference on Research and development in Information Retrieval.* ACM, 635–644.

[31] Seungmin Rho, Byeong-jun Han, and Eenjun Hwang. 2009. SVR-based Music Mood Classification and Context-based Music Recommendation. In *Proceedings of the 17th ACM International Conference on Multimedia (2009).* 713–716.

[32] Markus Schedl. 2016. The LFM-1b Dataset for Music Retrieval and Recommendation. In *Proceedings of the ACM International Conference on Multimedia Retrieval (ICMR).* New York, USA.

[33] Markus Schedl, Arthur Flexer, and Julin Urbano. 2013. The neglected user in music information retrieval research. *Journal of Intelligent Information Systems* 41, 3 (2013), 523–539.

[34] Markus Schedl and Dominik Schnitzer. 2013. Hybrid Retrieval Approaches to Geospatial Music Recommendation. In *Proceedings of the 35th Annual International ACM SIGIR Conference on Research and Development in Information Retrieval (SIGIR 2013).*

[35] Markus Schedl, Andreu Vall, and Katayoun Farrahi. 2014. User Geospatial Context for Music Recommendation in Microblogs. In *Proceedings of the 37th Annual International ACM SIGIR Conference on Research and Development in Information Retrieval (SIGIR 2014).*

[36] Eva Zangerle, Wolfgang Gassler, and Günther Specht. 2012. Exploiting Twitter's Collective Knowledge for Music Recommendations. In *Proceedings of the 2nd Workshop on Making Sense of Microposts (#MSM2012).*

Groups Re-identification with Temporal Context

Michal Koperski
INRIA
2004 Route Des Lucioles
Sophia Antipolis, France 06902
michal.koperski@inria.fr

Slawomir Bak
Disney Research
4720 Forbes Avenue
Pittsburgh, PA 15213
slawomir.bak@disneyresearch.com

Peter Carr
Disney Research
4720 Forbes Avenue
Pittsburgh, PA 15213
peter.carr@disneyresearch.com

ABSTRACT

Re-identification methods often require well aligned, unoccluded detections of an entire subject. Such assumptions are impractical in real world scenarios, where people tend to form groups. To circumvent poor detection performance caused by occlusions, we use fixed regions of interest and employ codebook-based visual representations. We account for illumination variations between cameras using a coupled clustering method that learns per-camera codebooks with entries that correspond across cameras. Because predictable movement patterns exist in many scenarios, we also incorporate temporal context to improve re-identification performance. This includes learning expected travel times directly from data and using mutual exclusion constraints to encourage solutions that maintain temporal ordering. Our experiments illustrate the merits of the proposed approach in challenging re-identification scenarios including crowded public spaces.

CCS CONCEPTS

• **Computing methodologies** → *Object recognition*; *Object identification*;

KEYWORDS

Computer Vision;People Re-Identification

ACM Reference format:
Michal Koperski, Slawomir Bak, and Peter Carr. 2017. Groups Re-identification with Temporal Context. In *Proceedings of ICMR '17, Bucharest, Romania, June 06-09, 2017,* 9 pages.
https://doi.org/http://dx.doi.org/10.1145/3078971.3078978

1 INTRODUCTION

Re-identification is the task of finding the same individual across a network of cameras. This problem is very challenging due to significant changes in appearance caused by variations in illumination, viewing angle and a person's pose. In this paper, we focus on re-identification in *crowded environments* with predictable movement patterns. For instance, people tend to maintain their ordering in queues, whether it be checking out at a grocery store or passing through airport security. Such scenarios are popular for re-identification (and extremely challenging), but have not been studied extensively.

Most re-identification approaches assume reliable detections [1, 7, 10, 19, 23, 32], which are not possible in crowd environments. Only a few methods have targeted more challenging scenarios where detections are less reliable and partially occluded [5, 14, 44]. To mitigate the impact of occlusions and poor detection alignment, we focus on re-identifying groups at *pinch points* like queues and doorways.

Instead of running an object detector, we define a fixed region of interest (ROI) on the image plane (see Fig. 1). We propose to represent the visual content within an ROI using a codebook. Codebooks [8, 34, 35] have shown high efficacy in scenarios where specialized object detectors fail. However, standard codebook learning approaches are inefficient in multi-camera environments when there are significant appearance changes between cameras. As a result, we propose a new coupled clustering method that generates per-camera codebooks with entries that correspond across cameras.

A codebook encoding of an ROI is usually not as distinctive as a full body-based descriptor (which can leverage the spatial locations of visual features). Therefore, we enhance our representation by incorporating temporal information. Predictable movement patterns exist in many scenarios, and these can be used to disambiguate people with otherwise similar appearances. In airports, for example, people tend to move from ticketing through security and then to their boarding gates (see Fig. 1). Our main contributions are:

- We propose a new coupled clustering method that learns codebooks for each camera pair with codewords corresponding across cameras. This copes with significant illumination changes of visual appearance between cameras.
- We integrate a temporal model into our matching strategy. The temporal model is jointly optimized using both visual appearance and temporal information. Initial parameters of the temporal model are first estimated using the visual appearance, and then they are used as a feedback to enhance the re-identification. Coherent re-identification matches in return provide better estimation of temporal parameters. By iterating, the method quickly converges to the optimal configuration.
- Because existing re-identification datasets have no temporal information, we collected a new **QUEUE** dataset that simulates a queue scenario in which people move from one location to another with significant variations in illumination. Recorded sequences come from non-overlapping cameras. We also modified existing re-identification datasets to simulate temporal information by adding synthetic timestamps.

ICMR '17, June 06-09, 2017, Bucharest, Romania

ACM ISBN 978-1-4503-4701-3/17/06...$15.00
https://doi.org/http://dx.doi.org/10.1145/3078971.3078978

Figure 1: Predictable movement patterns exist in many scenarios. We model the travel time between cameras to help disambiguate people with similar appearances. Because full body detectors are unreliable in crowded scenarios, we use a fixed region of interest (ROI) on the image plane and represent its visual appearance using a set of learned camera-specific codebooks that have corresponding entries (camera-specific codewords) across cameras. Learning corresponding entries facilitates matching under different imaging (illumination) conditions.

Our experiments illustrate the merits of joint optimization and achieve new state-of-the-art performance on multiple datasets outperforming existing approaches that only considered visual appearance models.

2 RELATED WORK

Re-identification remains an unsolved problem due to large intra-class and inter-class variations caused by changes in lighting, viewing angle and a person's pose. Most effective approaches learn robust metrics for matching [1, 6, 19, 23, 32, 33]. These methods learn a distance function among features from different cameras such that relevant dimensions are emphasized while irrelevant ones are discarded. Explicitly or implicitly, all of these approaches assume matching of full body appearance with negligible amounts of occlusion and cannot operate on images taken in crowded public spaces.

The recent work of [44] introduces *partial person re-identification* to address retrieval in more realistic scenarios where only a partial observation of a person is available for matching. It combines local patch level matching based on sparse coding with global, part-based matching that exploits spatial layout information.

Visual information from surrounding people has also been used to reduce ambiguity in person identification. In [5, 14, 43] we can find that group association between two or more people can give valuable information about the identity of an individual. [16, 21] employ dictionary learning to cope with detection misalignment. The bounding box images are divided into a set of stripes and per-stripe dictionaries are learned assuming well aligned person detections. [17, 18, 28] search for a set of linear transformations, which transform features from different viewpoints to the common embedding space. These methods implicitly assume spatial correspondence between features extracted from both viewpoints (otherwise it would not be clear which transformation should be applied). Thus the mentioned methods are more suitable for recognition of rigid objects. In contrast, our approach does not depend on spatial information. It is mostly invariant to camera viewpoint changes and easily incorporates multiple people into the appearance representation (see Fig. 1).

Although temporal cues are rarely used in recent re-identification methods[1], they were exploited in early person re-identification and multi-target tracking methods to infer camera topology which enabled tracking across multiple non-overlapping views [15, 26, 29]. These approaches usually exploit space-time cues to learn inter-camera relationships that are then used to constrain the re-identification search space. Camera topology together with temporal information can reduce the number of paths people might take, which constrains potential re-identification matches [31, 36]. Our approach is similar in spirit to these methods but introduces a new formulation that jointly learns models of both visual appearance and movement patterns.

Global motion patterns are learned in [26] for activity modeling. Activities were detected using the density of moving pixels and omitted visual appearance representations. Cross Canonical Correlation Analysis is introduced in [24, 25] to correlate activities across cameras with disjoint FOVs to infer the topology of a camera network. The FOVs of the cameras are segmented into regions within which the activity patterns were similar. Affinity matrices are employed to infer spatio-temporal camera topologies. [9] propose to use cameras topology to improve the global re-identification consistency. Unlike ours, it requires head, torso and leg detectors and it becomes effective in camera networks with at least 3 cameras.

A comprehensive review of camera topology estimation methods is presented in [40]. Similarly, temporal information has been used to constrain the re-identification search space [31, 36]. Re-identification that employs time-ordering constraints is widely applied in Intelligent Transportation Systems (ITS). [13] propose a method for car re-identification based on simple visual appearance model and the expected travel time between cameras. Simple appearance model makes it unsuitable for person re-identification and their temporal model must be initialized using the ground truth. The visual appearance of a car and an inductive loop (extracting speed and induction response amplitude) are used together with time information to predict when the vehicle would re-appear in the second camera [39]. Time ordering constraints are integrated using manually computed temporal windows which controlled feasibility.

[1]This phenomenon may be a result of the available re-identification datasets, which are often only a collection of bounding boxes extracted from disjoint camera views with no temporal information.

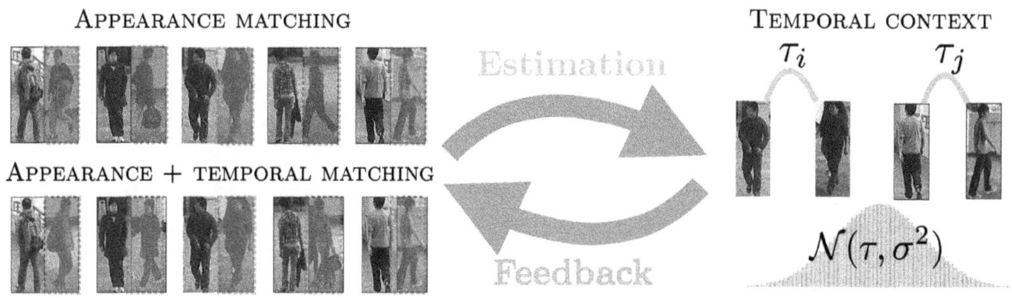

Figure 2: Learning and Leveraging Temporal Context. Actual travel times between cameras are estimated from reliable re-identification matches using only appearance information. Model parameters are then fit to these data samples. Re-identification with temporal context is then used to disambiguate detections with less distinctive visual appearances.

In these approaches, the visual appearance and temporal cues are often modeled independently. Our approach, on the other hand, jointly models visual appearance and temporal context using a feedback loop (see Fig. 2).

Re-identification usually treats every test case (query) as an independent retrieval task. In contrast, multi-target tracking algorithms [3, 41] typically conduct multiple queries simultaneously by posing a linear assignment problem [12, 41]. Prior work [37] extended this idea and proposed to compute m-suboptimal solutions to find consensus assignment. In this paper, we follow a similar idea and incorporate temporal context with multiple queries to simultaneously search for an optimal solution. This enforces mutual exclusion constraints, improving the re-identification accuracy.

3 METHOD

We define a region of interest (ROI) as rectangular bounding box containing sub-image for each camera. In contrast to the common re-identification problem where every ROI bounding box image contains a well detected individual, we consider crowded scenarios where ROI might contain multiple people, occluding each other. As object detectors might be infeasible in such scenario due to large and frequent occlusions, ROI is assumed to be fixed. However, as "pinch points" (doorways, gates, etc.) exist in many scenarios, these are our natural choices for ROIs.

Let A and B denote two cameras in a network. Each camera monitors a local region that people pass through, such as a gate or doorway (see Fig. 1). Suppose there are two ROI bounding boxes $\mathbf{b}_i$ and $\mathbf{b}_j$ captured from cameras A and B respectively at times t_i and t_j, and that appearance descriptors $\mathbf{x}_i$ and $\mathbf{x}_j$ are extracted from the visual content of each ROI bounding box.

We refer to triplets $\mathbf{o}_k = (\mathbf{b}_k, t_k, \mathbf{x}_k)$ as observations. From a Bayesian point of view, re-identification is the likelihood that observations $\mathbf{o}_i$ and $\mathbf{o}_j$ are different images of the same person. Most re-identification methods ignore the spatiotemporal information and only consider the similarity of the extracted appearance descriptors

$$\mathrm{P}_{\mathrm{ReID}}(\mathbf{o}_i, \mathbf{o}_j | i \equiv j) \propto \mathrm{P}_{\mathrm{App}}(\mathbf{x}_i, \mathbf{x}_j | i \equiv j). \quad (1)$$

In this work, we incorporate the expected movement patterns as well. Because we have restricted our camera views to each focus on a single localized region, the extracted bounding boxes locations are effectively constant (see Fig. 1). As a result, we formulate the likelihood as a product of appearance similarity and expected travel time between the two locations[2]

$$\mathrm{P}_{\mathrm{ReID}}(\mathbf{o}_i, \mathbf{o}_j) \propto \mathrm{P}_{\mathrm{App}}(\mathbf{x}_i, \mathbf{x}_j)\mathrm{P}_{\mathrm{Time}}(t_i, t_j), \quad (2)$$

where the conditional dependency $i \equiv j$ has been omitted for notational convenience. Re-identification is often used to match observations between cameras: given an observation $\mathbf{o}_j$ from camera B, the most likely observation of the same individual from camera A is

$$\begin{aligned} \mathbf{o}_i^* &= \arg\max_i \mathrm{P}_{ReID}(\mathbf{o}_i, \mathbf{o}_j) & (3)\\ &= \arg\min_i d^2_{ReID}(\mathbf{o}_i, \mathbf{o}_j) & (4)\\ &= \arg\min_i \left(\lambda d^2_{App}(\mathbf{x}_i, \mathbf{x}_j) + (1-\lambda) d^2_{Time}(t_i, t_j)\right), & (5) \end{aligned}$$

where $\lambda \in [0, 1]$ is a parameter that controls the relative influence of similar visual appearance and expected travel time. We will now describe the distance functions that reflect our appearance (d^2_{App}) and temporal models (d^2_{Time}).

3.1 Appearance Model

Crowded scenarios produce detections that are poorly aligned and/or partially occluded. To cope with these difficulties, we propose a visual appearance descriptor $\mathbf{x}_i$ based on a codebook approach.

Codebooks [8, 34, 35] have been used previously in re-identification [27, 42], but only in situations with well-aligned bounding boxes. Different codebooks were learned for different regions of the bounding box by dividing it into a fixed layout of rectangular patches (horizontal stripes or a dense grid). Although spatial structure is beneficial for recognition, it requires unoccluded, reliably aligned detections, which is impractical in crowded scenarios. Instead we learn a single codebook for the entire *ROI*. To achieve that we

[2] Our methodology easily extends to a model which does not require pre-defined fixed locations.

Figure 3: Sample images from the QUEUE dataset. The left column illustrates image pairs from QUEUE01 that were used for training codebooks; the right column illustrates image pairs from QUEUE02 simulating the queue scenario.

propose to densely sample random patches from *ROI*. And then compute codebook based on descriptors extracted from patches.

Two popular choices for converting visual features into codewords are *Bag-of-words* (BoW) [8] and *Fisher Vector* (FV) [34, 35]. Let $\mathcal{F} = \{\mathbf{f}_1, \ldots, \mathbf{f}_F\}$ be a set of image features extracted from training data. Image features are usually high-dimensional vectors (*e.g.* SIFT descriptors concatenated with color histograms) and are typically clustered into codewords. For example, $BoW = \{\mu_k : k = 1, \ldots, K\}$ uses k-means clustering to define codewords as the centers of the learned clusters. The number of the clusters K is the codebook size. BoW maps each image feature $\mathbf{f}_f$ to a codeword k using nearest neighbour lookup. The descriptor is a K-dimensional histogram of codeword frequencies.

FV is an extension of BoW. The distribution of features is modeled by a Gaussian Mixture Model (GMM). Let $FV = \{\mu_k, \Sigma_k, w_k : k = 1, \ldots, K\}$ be the parameters of a GMM fitting the distribution of image features, where w_k is the weight of the kth Gaussian with mean μ_k and covariance Σ_k. An image feature $\mathbf{f}_f$ is represented by the gradients of the likelihood of this feature being generated by a certain Gaussian. The gradients are computed over both μ and Σ variables. The resulting descriptor is a $2K$-dimensional vector (see [34, 35] for details).

Both BoW and FV can be learned using features from different cameras (*e.g.* from camera A and camera B) by combining them into a single set $\mathcal{F}^{A,B} = \{\mathbf{f}_1^A, \ldots, \mathbf{f}_{FA}^A, \mathbf{f}_1^B, \ldots, \mathbf{f}_{FB}^B\}$ and then performing clustering on $\mathcal{F}^{A,B}$ [27]. If there are strong appearance changes across the two cameras, a common mapping from image features to codewords might not be effective. Instead, we modify the underlying clustering method (k-means for BoW and GMM for FV) such that corresponding features will map to the same cluster even though they have different appearances due to illumination changes.

Coupled clustering. We propose to train codebooks on features extracted from corresponding images which are well aligned between cameras (see Train images from Fig. 3). Note that we only require correspondences when learning a codebook. At test time, our method does not require well-aligned detections.

Given corresponding features $\mathbf{f}^A$ and $\mathbf{f}^B$, we build $\mathcal{F}^{A|B} = \{(\mathbf{f}^A|\mathbf{f}^B)_1, \ldots, (\mathbf{f}^A|\mathbf{f}^B)_{FA|B}\}$, which is a set of concatenated corresponding image features from camera A and camera B. On such feature set we perform either k-means (in case of BoW) or GMM (in case of FV) clustering to obtain model parameters. For example, in case of k-means, we divide the coupled codebook $BoW^{A,B} = \{\mu_{A|B} : k = 1, \ldots, K\}$ into two codebooks $BoW^A = \{\mu_k^A : k = 1, \ldots, K\}$ and $BoW^B = \{\mu_k^B : k = 1, \ldots, K\}$ by extracting the first and second halves of the cluster center dimensions respectively. FV can be split analogously obtaining two GMM models: $FV^A = \{\mu_k^A, \Sigma_k^A, w_k : k = 1, \ldots, K\}$ and $FV^B = \{\mu_k^B, \Sigma_k^B, w_k : k = 1, \ldots, K\}$, where w_k are shared across the models. The appearance transfer function between cameras is learned implicitly due to the proposed coupled clustering method.

The concatenation step is crucial because it guides a clustering algorithm to find clusters that represent similar visual features from both cameras. In addition, it ensures codeword correspondence across cameras which is crucial for computing similarity between images (see Eq. (6)). Without the concatenation step, a clustering algorithm would find clusters based only on appearance features and would ignore which camera they were extracted from. Object appearance is usually more similar in multiple images from the same camera compared to images taken from two disjoint cameras. In standard clustering where the source of the image is ignored, the clusters may contain patches from only one camera.

In test stage, to compare two *ROIs* from different cameras, we densely sample random patches from *ROI* and based on them we compute codebook representation. We follow the same steps for a second *ROI*. Thanks to the proposed coupled clustering, the codebook representation of the same group of people across cameras, is much more consistent than representation based on standard codebook. Moreover, because we pick random patches from *ROI*, our method is much more robust in terms of misalignment and occlusions.

Appearance Dissimilarity Measure. Let $\mathbf{x}_i$ and $\mathbf{x}_j$ be extracted appearance representations (in our case, $\mathbf{x}_i$ and $\mathbf{x}_j$ are histograms (BoW) or *Fisher Vectors*). We compute the visual appearance dissimilarity using ℓ_2 norm:

$$d^2_{\text{App}}(\mathbf{x}_i, \mathbf{x}_j) = \|\mathbf{x}_i - \mathbf{x}_j\|_2^2. \tag{6}$$

3.2 Temporal Model and Joint Optimization

For simplicity, we assume that the amount of time a subject takes to travel between cameras A and B can be modeled as a normal distribution $\mathcal{N}(\tau, \sigma^2)$. Given the parameters (τ, σ^2) of the distribution and the times t_i and t_j of the two bounding boxes, the **Time Context Dissimilarity Measure** between the actual and expected elapsed time is

$$d^2_{\text{Time}}(t_i, t_j) = \frac{(t_j - t_i - \tau)^2}{2\sigma^2}. \tag{7}$$

Parameter Estimation. In practice, τ and σ are estimates of an unknown distribution $\mathcal{N}(\tau^*, \sigma^{*2})$. The parameters of the distribution could be estimated heuristically using the distribution of typical walking speeds if the path distance between cameras A and B is known. When that information is not available, we propose the following solution. Given an appearance dissimilarity function $d_{\text{App}}(\mathbf{x}_i, \mathbf{x}_j)$, we construct a binary threshold classifier $h(\mathbf{x}_i, \mathbf{x}_j) \mapsto \{0, 1\}$ to predict whether observations $\mathbf{o}_i$ and $\mathbf{o}_j$ contain indeed the same subject. We select the threshold ξ that achieves a 95% confidence level on the training data and use only these observation pairs $(\mathbf{o}_i, \mathbf{o}_j)$ — *e.g.* people with distinctive appearances that can be re-identified reliably — to estimate the parameters $(\tau\, \sigma^2)$ of the normal distribution (see Algorithm 1 steps 1 - 3).

Threshold ξ is learned on the training set, but parameters τ and σ are estimated at test time. Image pairs with distances below threshold ξ can be false positives. We exploit the fact that the variance of timestamp differences $t_{ij} = t_i - t_j$ of the true positives is low, while t_{ij} values of false matches form outliers. Based on this fact, we use Minimum Covariance Determinant [4, 38] (MCD) to estimate τ and σ parameters. The MCD method was designed to estimate unimodal Gaussian parameters from data containing outliers which is exactly our case.

Algorithm 1 Parameter Estimation algorithm

1: For each test query o_j compute:
   $o_i^* \leftarrow \arg\min_i d^2_{App}(x_i, x_j)$
2: Construct $\Delta T = \{t_{ij}\}$: $d_{App}(x_i, x_j) < \xi$
3: Compute initial estimates $\tau, \sigma \leftarrow MCD(\Delta T)$
4: **loop**
5:     For each test query o_j compute:
       $o_i^* \leftarrow \arg\min_i d^2(o_i, o_j)$ // see Eqs. 4-5
6:     Reconstruct ΔT using all (o_i^*, o_j)
7:     Update estimates $\tau, \sigma \leftarrow MCD(\Delta T)$
8: **end loop**

To improve the estimations of τ^* and σ^*, we propose to **jointly optimize** the parameters τ^* and σ^* based on information from re-identification stage and the current temporal model parameters (see Algorithm 1 steps 4 - 8). After the initial estimation of τ^* and σ^* based on the appearance-only model, we propose to re-estimate τ and σ. We do it based on current re-identification matches, which are obtained from our model using jointly appearance and temporal context (see Eq. (5)). Because the re-identification accuracy of the joint appearance and temporal context model is higher than the appearance only model, we can re-estimate (jointly optimize) τ and σ by taking into account timestamps of current matches. Better temporal context enables matching individuals with less discriminative visual appearance (e.g. common clothing colors such as black winter coats). These new matches are then used to refine the current temporal context model.

The Univariate Gaussian could be replaced with any density estimation technique. With sufficient data, we can fit more complex models (*e.g.* GMM). However as time information is not available in re-id benchmarks and our QUEUE dataset is relatively small, a single Gaussian distribution is effective.

3.3 Ordering Preference via Mutual Exclusion

In many re-identification experiments, each test query $\mathbf{o}_i$ is evaluated independently

$$\mathbf{o}_i^* = \arg\min_i d^2(\mathbf{o}_i, \mathbf{o}_j). \tag{4}$$

If multiple queries are conducted, it is entirely possible that different queries $\mathbf{o}_j$ and $\mathbf{o}_k$ from camera B will have the same best match $\mathbf{o}_i$ in camera A. By conducting multiple queries simultaneously, we can enforce mutual exclusion constraints and ensure that each query has a unique match. In scenarios where people are observed while passing through confined regions, such as a gates or doorways, and there is an expected path between cameras, the order of people observed in A should be similar to the order of people observed in B. By incorporating temporal context into the cost function and enforcing mutual exclusion constraints, we can implicitly encourage a preference for preserved ordering to improve the recognition of observations that do not have distinctive appearance descriptors. Given N observations from camera A and M observations from camera B, we formulate simultaneous re-identification queries as a linear assignment problem

$$\{\mathbf{o}_i^*\} = \arg\min_\pi \left(\sum_{j=1}^{M} d^2(\mathbf{o}_{\pi(j)}, \mathbf{o}_j) \right), \tag{8}$$

where π is M-vector mapping observations from camera B to observations in camera A. We encode the linear assignment problem into an $M \times N$ cost matrix $\mathrm{C} = \{c_{ij}\}_{M \times N}$ where $c_{ij} = d^2(\mathbf{o}_j, \mathbf{o}_i)$ and determine the optimal assignment using the Kuhn-Munkres (Hungarian) algorithm [20]. Our experiments evaluate the merits of conducting queries independently versus simultaneously with a preference for preserving ordering.

For clarity, we have described the simple case where every observation in B has a corresponding observation in A (another typical bias in most re-identification datasets). For more practical scenarios, our linear assignment formulation can be encoded in an augmented matrix to include 'no match' conditions as well [12].

4 EXPERIMENTS

We carried out experiments on four challenging datasets: **VIPeR** [11], **CUHK01** [22], **iLIDS-groups** [43], and our **QUEUE** dataset. The results are analyzed in terms of recognition rate using *rank-1 accuracy* as well as the *cumulative matching characteristic* (CMC) [11] curve. The CMC curve represents the expectation of finding the correct match in the top r matches. The curve can be characterized by a scalar value computed by normalizing the area under the curve referred to as *nAUC* value.

4.1 Datasets

VIPeR [11] is one of the most popular person re-identification datasets. It contains 632 image pairs of pedestrians captured by two outdoor cameras. **VIPeR** images contain large variations in lighting conditions, background, viewpoint, and image quality. Each bounding box is cropped and scaled to be 128×48 pixels.

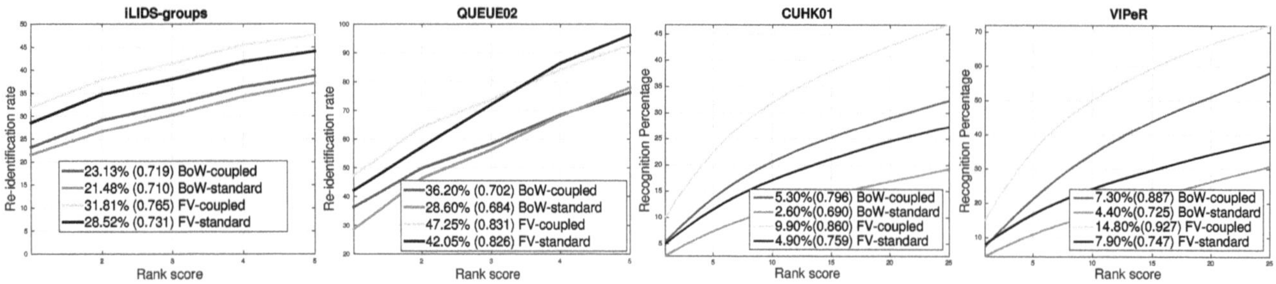

Figure 4: Performance comparison of different codebook models on iLIDS-groups, QUEUE02, CUHK01 and VIPeR. *Rank-1* identification rates as well as *nAUC* values (provided in brackets) are shown in the legend next to the method name. Coupled clustering significantly outperforms standard approaches for both BoW and FV model.

CUHK01 [22] contains 971 people captured with two cameras. For each person, 2 images from each camera are available. The first camera captures the side view of a pedestrian and the second captures a frontal or rear view. Each bounding box is scaled to be 160×60 pixels.

iLIDS-groups [43] contains 64 groups captured with two cameras in the airport. In most cases 4 images of each group are available. Thus the dataset contains 274 images of cropped groups. This dataset along with standard challenges like illumination changes across cameras, introduces some other challenges including occlusions because people in group tend to occlude each other. Additionally dataset was recorded at an airport where people are often occluded by luggage. Moreover people in groups very often change their relative positions across the cameras. We mentioned in Section 3.1 that we need patch correspondence between cameras to train the proposed coupled clustering codebook. Because iLIDS-groups is very noisy and contains multiple people, it is difficult to extract corresponding patches automatically. In the result we train a codebook using iLIDS-MA [2] dataset, which contains 3680 manually cropped images of 40 individuals, well aligned and acquired by the same camera pair.

QUEUE is our new dataset that contains two scenarios. The first **QUEUE01** consists of 23 individuals with 3379 images of people registered by two cameras in significantly different lighting conditions (see Fig. 3). This data was used for training the codebook. In the second scenario (**QUEUE02**), 23 individuals from **QUEUE01** were asked to move from the the one location to another, simulating a queue scenario (see Fig. 3). We manually annotated 15 groups; each group is described by unique group id and frame time-stamp from the video stream. As can be seen in Fig. 3 the queue is dense so some individual belongs to more than one group. To our best knowledge the **QUEUE02** is the only group re-identification dataset which provides timestamp information. **QUEUE02** is the only dataset which contains both: people groups and timestamps. We chose **iLIDS-groups**, because it contains groups of people. **VIPeR** and **CUHK01**, though they do not contain neither timestamp information nor groups of people were selected to show relative improvement of the proposed coupled clustering method compared with standard Bag of Words approaches.

Dataset	Codebook size				
	16	**20**	**64**	**128**	**256**
iLIDS-groups	29.3	31.8	29.2	29.0	-
QUEUE02	47.2	44.2	46.2	41.9	-
CUHK01	8.7	8.6	9.6	9.9	9.0
VIPeR	11.4	11.6	12.7	14.8	12.4

Table 1: Rank-1 accuracy w.r.t. codebook size for coupled clustering based on Fisher Vector.

4.2 Coupled Clustering

In this section we evaluate the proposed coupled clustering method from Section 3.1. We extract image features by densely sampling 24×12 pixel patches from ROI, ignoring their spatial locations. For each patch, we extract LAB and HSV histograms, each with 30 bins per channel. To keep only informative patches, we applied background subtraction. Please note that for **QUEUE02** we use fixed ROI, but for the other datasets (since we do not have access to original images containing whole scene) we use cropped images provided by the authors of datasets. Please note that in case **QUEUE02** our appearance model is based on Fisher Vector of randomly sampled patches within ROI and ignores patch locations, thus is invariant to small shifts of ROI. The resulting 180-dimensional feature vectors were used to generate codebooks using both BoW and FV. The appropriate size of each codebook was determined using cross validation: **CUHK01** FV(128) BoW (500), **VIPeR** FV(128) BoW (500), **iLIDS-groups** FV(20) BoW (300), **QUEUE02** FV(16) BoW(200).

In case of **CUHK01** and **VIPeR**, we followed the common evaluation protocol in re-identification. We split subjects from each dataset into training/testing: **VIPeR** - 316/316, **CUHK01** - 486/485.

In evaluation of the **iLIDS-groups** dataset we followed the same evaluation protocol as in [43], where the dataset was introduced. We randomly select one image from each group to build the gallery set and the rest of the images form the probe set. The selection procedure was repeated 10 times. To train the codebooks we use the iLIDS-MA dataset.

For **QUEUE02**, we split the data set into 11/12 groups, and similarly, we split QUEUE01 dataset to 10/13 individuals. In this way we assure that individuals from QUEUE01 who were used to train the codebook do not appear in the group from **QUEUE02** in the testing phase.

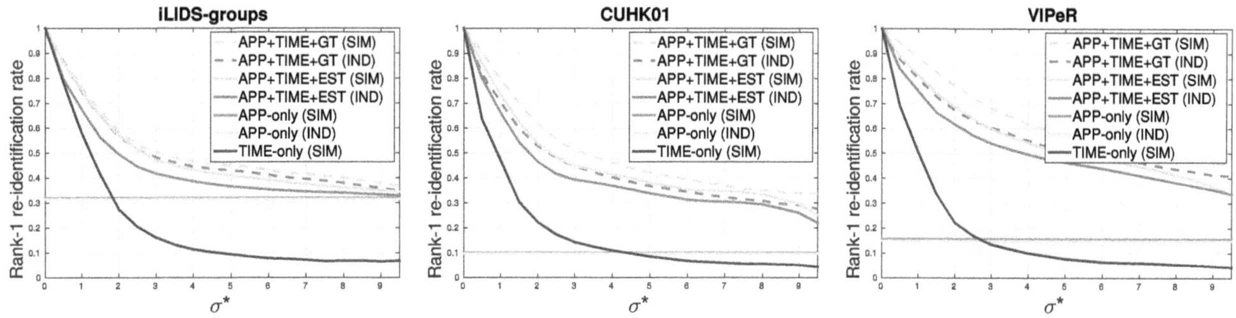

Figure 5: Rank-1 recognition rate based on the reliability of an expected travel time (simulated by synthesizing timestamps from different normal distributions with different standard deviations σ^*). Appearance-only models (magenta and cyan) are not affected by temporal context. Temporal context on its own (dark-blue) is powerful but degrades quickly as the variance in expected travel time increases (making temporal context less informative). Combining appearance and temporal context gives a significant boost in re-identification performance compared to using either model independently. Incorporating mutual exclusion constraints (green) generally leads to improved performance over independent queries (red).

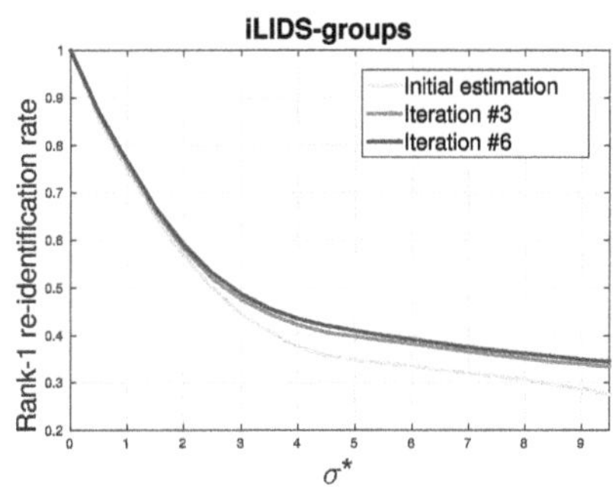

Figure 6: Rank-1 recognition rate with varying travel time consistency (using different standard deviations σ^* for synthetic timestamps). Iterative re-estimation of the unknown σ^* parameter improves overall Rank-1 accuracy.

When testing, we evaluate a single-shot scenario and repeat the codebook generation procedure 10 times for computing averaged CMC curves. Figure 4 illustrates CMC curves on the four datasets. It is apparent that our coupled clustering approach has a large margin of improvement over standard clustering on all datasets for both BoW and FV models. The significant performance gain is especially evident using FV codebooks. In table 1 we show Rank-1 accuracy w.r.t. FV codebook size. This experiment illustrates the merits of coupled clustering and confirms our claims that learning a generic codebook that maps features to codewords is not as effective as learning camera specific codebooks that map corresponding features across cameras to the same codewords. Note that the relatively small gain in performance on the **iLIDS-groups** dataset can be explained by the characteristics of the selected evaluation scheme. In the evaluation scheme proposed by the authors of the dataset, it is possible that both images from the same camera might be assigned to gallery and probe sets. Because re-identification on images from same camera is a much easier task, the advantages of the proposed coupled clustering are not evident on **iLIDS-groups** dataset.

4.3 Temporal Context

In this section, we evaluate the performance of the joint appearance and temporal context model (see Section 3.2 and Eq. (5)). We employ the previously learned coupled clustering FV codebooks (see Section 4.2) for an appearance model. We evaluate the benefit of temporal context by comparing the performance of the appearance-only model (see Eq. (1)) versus the appearance+temporal context model (see Eq. (2)). In both cases, the performance is measured when queries are conducted independently (IND) (see Eq. (5)) and by enforcing the proposed mutual exclusion constraints (Section 3.3) when performing all queries simultaneously (SIM) (see Eq. (8)).

VIPeR, **CUHK01** and **iLIDS-groups** do not contain timing information, so we simulate a queue scenario by assigning random timestamps to images from the first camera. Timestamps for images from the second camera are generated by sampling a normal distribution $\mathcal{N}(\tau^*, \sigma^{*2})$. In real-life τ^* and σ^{*2} parameters would be fixed and depend on crowd behavior. In practice, σ^{*2} controls how much the temporal order is preserved *w.r.t* the second camera. We set τ^* to 0 because it represents the expected time difference between images from two cameras and can be always normalized to 0. The above experimental setup gives us the opportunity to study the limits of the proposed method when temporal context is no longer informative.

Figure 5 illustrates the rank-1 recognition accuracy *w.r.t* σ^*. Performance of standard appearance-only re-identification (magenta and cyan) is invariant to σ^*. Temporal context on its own (dark blue) is quite powerful, but degrades quickly as flow from one camera to another is less ordered and the validity of the underlying assumption breaks down. Hybrid cost functions that consider both appearance and temporal context give significant improvement in performance.

The effect of estimating parameters τ and σ are evaluated by plotting the upper performance limit (dashed red & green) using

		CUHK01		VIPeR		iLIDS-groups		QUEUE02	
Method		*rank-1*	*rank-5*	*rank-1*	*rank-5*	*rank-1*	*rank-5*	*rank-1*	*rank-5*
KISSME [19]		16.41	38.02	19.60	49.53	9.57	31.64	32.14	79.46
XQDA [23]		63.21	83.00	40.00	68.13	26.15	46.76	25.89	92.86
Assoc. Groups of People [43]		-	-	-	-	22.50	45.0	-	-
Our (App - IND)		9.54	26.81	14.85	37.32	**31.38**	**47.37**	**47.25**	**96.20**
Our (App - SIM)		10.00	29.83	15.59	38.81	**31.88**	**48.65**	**55.46**	**100.00**
Our (App+Time+Est - IND)	s=0.5	79.98	92.00	83.77	98.52	71.55	100.00	100.00	100.00
	s=9.0	21.94	46.11	33.50	59.02	33.42	55.69		
Our (App+Time+Est - SIM)	s=0.5	**86.00**	**94.50**	**88.97**	**100.00**	**86.48**	**100.00**	**100.00**	**100.00**
	s=9.0	25.16	48.49	36.66	59.50	36.09	60.15		

Table 2: Performance comparison on CUHK01, VIPeR, iLIDS-groups and QUEUE02 datasets. We report *rank-1* and *rank-5* accuracy. Our appearance model outperforms standard metric learning approaches on group datasets. Integrating the temporal model together with our joint optimization consistently improves the re-identification performance in all datasets.

the true values of τ^* and σ^*. We then compare the performance of our temporal context model (solid red & green) estimated based on Algorithm 1. The results illustrate that there is a small performance drop using our estimation method. Incorporating mutual exclusion constraints (green) generally leads to improved performance over independent queries (red).

In Table 2 we report the performance on **QUEUE02**. This dataset contains real timestamps, so τ^* and σ^* are fixed. We use our proposed parameter estimation method to find τ and σ. Temporal context provides a significant boost in performance compared to appearance-only methods. Also, mutual exclusion leads to performance improvements.

Time Context Parameter Estimation In Section 3.2, we introduced an iterative algorithm to estimate the unknown parameters τ^* and σ^*. The experiments on **iLIDS-groups** shown in Fig. 6 confirm that iterative parameter re-estimation improves Rank-1 re-identification accuracy. After three iterations the algorithm converges and further parameter re-estimation does not translate into improvement in accuracy. Finally, the advantages of iterative parameter re-estimation is especially visible for cases with high $\sigma*$ (the ordering of people between cameras is rarely maintained). In such cases, the number of examples used for initial parameter estimation is small and insufficient to accurately estimate τ and σ.

4.4 State-of-the-art comparison

In this section we compare with two most common metric learning approaches: KISSME [19] and its extension - XQDA [23] that showed to be very effective while applied to re-identification problem [30]. We also report the results of [43] that proposed a dedicated descriptor for group re-identification. In Table 2 we report *rank-1* and *rank-5* accuracies on several re-identification datasets: **CUHK01**, **VIPeR** which contain well detected individuals, and group datasets: **iLIDS-groups** and **QUEUE02** which contain multiple people and a large amount of occlusion. The order of the datasets (from left column to right one) reflects the difficulty (*e.g.* VIPeR contains more variations in pose and image quality than CUHK01, and QUEUE02 contains significantly larger amount of occlusion than iLIDS-groups). Notice, that metric learning approaches perform relatively well on datasets that contain well detected individuals (CUHK01, VIPeR) but their performance degrades on group datasets (**iLIDS-groups**, **QUEUE02**). Our appearance model (App) ignores the spatial location of features, thus it is outperformed by metric learning approaches. However, with increasing difficulty of datasets, our codebook-based model outperforms metric learning approaches as the spatial information of features become less reliable. Notice that for iLIDS-groups and QUEUE02, our appearance-only model outperforms all other approaches, illustrating benefits of the proposed coupled clustering method. From Table 2 it is apparent that integrating the temporal model and using our joint optimization significantly increases the re-identification accuracy. In addition, we show that by applying mutual exclusion, we further improve the *Rank-1* and *Rank-5* accuracies (compare IND to SIM results). For datasets with simulated temporal information we also provide performance for two extreme values of σ^*. The results indicate that even if the ordering is rarely maintained ($\sigma^* = 9$) the proposed joint optimization still outperforms appearance-only model. The performance gain is even stronger when ordering is usually maintained between cameras ($\sigma^* = 0.5$).

5 SUMMARY

Many real-world scenarios have large amounts of occlusion and background clutter. Re-identification methods that require reliable detection will struggle in these circumstances. We propose a coupled clustering method that learns codebooks with entries that correspond across cameras and that is robust to both occlusion and alignment errors. We make use of common movement patterns by incorporating temporal context into the re-identification process. We show how the parameters of our model can be estimated from data, and illustrate the benefit of jointly optimizing appearance and temporal models. Our experiments demonstrate that methods based on coupled clustering and temporal context provided significant performance gains on challenging group re-identification datasets. Furthermore, we show how mutual exclusion constraints between multiple simultaneous queries (to preserve an ordering preference) also helps improve re-identification performance. Finally, our method has high practical impact in real-world scenarios, not only in terms of robustness, but also in usability (high Rank-1 accuracy).

REFERENCES

[1] Ejaz Ahmed, Michael Jones, and Tim K. Marks. 2015. An Improved Deep Learning Architecture for Person Re-Identification. In *CVPR*.

[2] Slawomir Bak, Etienne Corvee, Francois Bremond, and Monique Thonnat. 2012. Boosted human re-identification using Riemannian manifolds. *Image and Vision Computing* 30, 6-7 (2012), 443 – 452.

[3] Ben Benfold and Ian Reid. 2011. Stable Multi-Target Tracking in Real-Time Surveillance Video. In *CVPR*.

[4] R. W. Butler, P. L. Davies, and M. Jhun. 1993. Asymptotics for the Minimum Covariance Determinant Estimator. *The Annals of Statistics* 21, 3 (09 1993), 1385–1400.

[5] Y. Cai, V. Takala, and M. Pietikainen. 2010. Matching Groups of People by Covariance Descriptor. In *2010 20th International Conference on Pattern Recognition*. 2744–2747. https://doi.org/10.1109/ICPR.2010.672

[6] Dapeng Chen, Zejian Yuan, Gang Hua, Nanning Zheng, and Jingdong Wang. 2015. Similarity Learning on an Explicit Polynomial Kernel Feature Map for Person Re-Identification. In *CVPR*.

[7] Dong Seon Cheng, Marco Cristani, Michele Stoppa, Loris Bazzani, and Vittorio Murino. 2011. Custom Pictorial Structures for Re-identification. In *BMVC*.

[8] Gabriella Csurka, Christopher R. Dance, Lixin Fan, Jutta Willamowski, and Cedric Bray. 2004. Visual categorization with bags of keypoints. In *In Workshop on Statistical Learning in Computer Vision, ECCV*.

[9] Abir Das, Anirban Chakraborty, and Amit K. Roy-Chowdhury. 2014. Consistent Re-identification in a Camera Network. In *ECCV*.

[10] M. Farenzena, L. Bazzani, A. Perina, V. Murino, and M. Cristani. 2010. Person re-identification by symmetry-driven accumulation of local features. In *CVPR*.

[11] D. Gray, S. Brennan, and H. Tao. 2007. Evaluating Appearance Models for Recognition, Reacquisition, and Tracking. *PETS* (2007).

[12] Chang Huang, Bo Wu, and Ramakant Nevatia. 2008. Robust Object Tracking by Hierarchical Association of Detection Responses. In *ECCV*.

[13] Timothy Huang and Stuart Russell. 1997. Object Identification in a Bayesian Context. In *IJCAI*.

[14] Haruyuki Iwama, Yasushi Makihara, and Yasushi Yagi. 2012. Group Context-aware Person Identification in Video Sequences. *IPSJ Transactions on Computer Vision and Applications* 4 (2012), 87–99. https://doi.org/10.2197/ipsjtcva.4.87

[15] Omar Javed, Khurram Shafique, Zeeshan Rasheed, and Mubarak Shah. 2008. Modeling inter-camera space-time and appearance relationships for tracking across non-overlapping views. *Computer Vision and Image Understanding* 109, 2 (2008), 146 – 162.

[16] Xiao-Yuan Jing, Xiaoke Zhu, F. Wu, Xinge You, Qinglong Liu, Dong Yue, Ruimin Hu, and Baowen Xu. 2015. Super-resolution Person re-identification with semi-coupled low-rank discriminant dictionary learning. In *CVPR*.

[17] Meina Kan, Shiguang Shan, Haihong Zhang, Shihong Lao, and Xilin Chen. 2012. Multi-view Discriminant Analysis. In *Proc. of the 12th European Conf. on Computer Vision*. 808–821.

[18] Tae-Kyun Kim, Josef Kittler, and Roberto Cipolla. 2006. Learning Discriminative Canonical Correlations for Object Recognition with Image Sets. In *Proc. of the 9th European Conference on Computer Vision*. 251–262.

[19] Martin Koestinger, Martin Hirzer, Paul Wohlhart, Peter M. Roth, and Horst Bischof. 2012. Large Scale Metric Learning from Equivalence Constraints. In *CVPR*.

[20] H. W. Kuhn. 1955. The Hungarian method for the assignment problem. *Naval Research Logistics Quarterly* 2, 1-2 (1955).

[21] Sheng Li, Ming Shao, and Yun Fu. 2015. Cross-view Projective Dictionary Learning for Person Re-identification. In *IJCAI*.

[22] Wei Li, Rui Zhao, and Xiaogang Wang. 2012. Human Reidentification with Transferred Metric Learning. In *ACCV*.

[23] Shengcai Liao, Yang Hu, Xiangyu Zhu, and Stan Z. Li. 2015. Person Re-Identification by Local Maximal Occurrence Representation and Metric Learning. In *CVPR*.

[24] C.C. Loy, T. Xiang, and S. Gong. 2009. Multi-camera activity correlation analysis. In *CVPR*.

[25] Chen Change Loy, Tao Xiang, and Shaogang Gong. 2010. Time-Delayed Correlation Analysis for Multi-Camera Activity Understanding. *International Journal of Computer Vision* 90, 1 (2010), 106–129.

[26] C. C. Loy, T. Xiang, and S. Gong. 2012. Incremental Activity Modeling in Multiple Disjoint Cameras. *IEEE Transactions on Pattern Analysis and Machine Intelligence* 34, 9 (Sept 2012), 1799–1813.

[27] Bingpeng Ma, Yu Su, and Frederic Jurie. 2012. Local Descriptors Encoded by Fisher Vectors for Person Re-identification. In *ECCVW*.

[28] Y. Makihara, A. Mansur, D. Muramatsu, Z. Uddin, and Y. Yagi. 2015. Multi-view Discriminant Analysis with Tensor Representation and Its Application to Cross-view Gait Recognition. In *Proc. of the 11th IEEE Conf. on Automatic Face and Gesture Recognition (FG 2015)*. Ljubljana, Slovenia, 1–8.

[29] D. Makris, T. Ellis, and J. Black. 2004. Bridging the gaps between cameras. In *CVPR*.

[30] Tetsu Matsukawa, Takahiro Okabe, Einoshin Suzuki, and Yoichi Sato. 2016. Hierarchical Gaussian Descriptor for Person Re-Identification. In *The IEEE Conference on Computer Vision and Pattern Recognition (CVPR)*.

[31] Riccardo Mazzon, Syed Fahad Tahir, and Andrea Cavallaro. 2012. Person re-identification in crowd. *Pattern Recognition Letters* 33, 14 (2012), 1828 – 1837. Novel Pattern Recognition-Based Methods for Re-identification in Biometric Context.

[32] S. Paisitkriangkrai, C. Shen, and A. van den Hengel. 2015. Learning to rank in person re-identification with metric ensembles. In *CVPR*.

[33] Sateesh Pedagadi, James Orwell, Sergio A. Velastin, and Boghos A. Boghossian. 2013. Local Fisher Discriminant Analysis for Pedestrian Re-identification. In *CVPR*.

[34] Florent Perronnin, Yan Liu, Jorge Sanchez, and Herve Poirier. 2010. Large-Scale Image Retrieval with Compressed Fisher Vectors. In *CVPR*.

[35] Florent Perronnin, Jorge Sanchez, and Thomas Mensink. 2010. Improving the Fisher Kernel for Large-Scale Image Classification. In *ECCV*.

[36] A. Rahimi, B. Dunagan, and T. Darrell. 2004. Simultaneous calibration and tracking with a network of non-overlapping sensors. In *CVPR*.

[37] S. H. Rezatofighi, A. Milan, Z. Zhang, Q. Shi, A. Dick, and I. Reid. 2016. Joint Probabilistic Matching Using m-Best Solutions. In *CVPR*.

[38] Peter J. Rousseeuw and Katrien Van Driessen. 1999. A Fast Algorithm for the Minimum Covariance Determinant Estimator. *Technometrics* 41, 3 (Aug. 1999), 212–223.

[39] C. C. Sun, G. S. Arr, R. P. Ramachandran, and S. G. Ritchie. 2004. Vehicle Reidentification using multidetector fusion. *Transactions on Intelligent Transportation Systems* 5, 3 (2004).

[40] Xiaogang Wang. 2013. Intelligent multi-camera video surveillance: A review. *Pattern Recognition Letters* 34, 1 (2013), 3 – 19. Extracting Semantics from Multi-Spectrum Video.

[41] Li Zhang, Yuan Li, and R. Nevatia. 2008. Global data association for multi-object tracking using network flows. In *CVPR*.

[42] Rui Zhao, Wanli Ouyang, and Xiaogang Wang. 2014. Learning Mid-level Filters for Person Re-identification. In *CVPR*.

[43] Wei-Shi Zheng, Shaogang Gong, and Tao Xiang. 2009. Associating Groups of People. In *BMVC*.

[44] Wei-Shi Zheng, Xiang Li, Tao Xiang, Shengcai Liao, Jianhuang Lai, and Shaogang Gong. 2015. Partial Person Re-Identification. In *ICCV*.

Simple, Efficient and Effective Encodings of Local Deep Features for Video Action Recognition

Ionut C. Duta
University of Trento, Italy
ionutcosmin.duta@unitn.it

Bogdan Ionescu
University Politehnica of Bucharest, Romania
bionescu@imag.pub.ro

Kiyoharu Aizawa
University of Tokyo, Japan
aizawa@hal.t.u-tokyo.ac.jp

Nicu Sebe
University of Trento, Italy
niculae.sebe@unitn.it

ABSTRACT

For an action recognition system a decisive component is represented by the feature encoding part which builds the final representation that serves as input to a classifier. One of the shortcomings of the existing encoding approaches is the fact that they are built around hand-crafted features and they are not also highly competitive on encoding the current deep features, necessary in many practical scenarios. In this work we propose two solutions specifically designed for encoding local deep features, taking advantage of the nature of deep networks, focusing on capturing the highest feature response of the convolutional maps. The proposed approaches for deep feature encoding provide a solution to encapsulate the features extracted with a convolutional neural network over the entire video. In terms of accuracy our encodings outperform by a large margin the current most widely used and powerful encoding approaches, while being extremely efficient for the computational cost. Evaluated in the context of action recognition tasks, our pipeline obtains state-of-the-art results on three challenging datasets: HMDB51, UCF50 and UCF101.

KEYWORDS

Deep Feature Encoding; Video Classification; Action Recognition

1 INTRODUCTION

Human action recognition is one of the most challenging tasks in computer vision and multimedia, which receives a high attention from the research community due to a large number of potential applications. From the previous research works we can identify two main directions for this task. The first is based on hand-crafted features, represented by well-known descriptors, such as Histogram of Oriented Gradients (HOG) [6, 22], Histogram of Optical Flow (HOF) [22] and Motion Boundary Histograms (MBH) [7]. These descriptors are extracted from a video using different approaches to establish the region of extraction, such as at interest points [21], using a dense sampling [44, 49], along motion trajectories [40, 45, 47]. The second direction for this task relies on learning the features throughout a neural network, obtaining very competitive results [4, 19, 27, 35, 36, 41, 42, 51, 54]. Along the action recognition pipeline we can distinguish three main components: feature extraction, encoding and classification.

Feature encoding is used for building a final video representation which serves as input for a classifier and is one of the key components for the performance of the overall task pipeline. In this work we address the feature encoding step and propose solutions to improve it in the case of deep features. It is well-known that deep features are different from the hand-crafted ones. For instance, deep features contain high discriminative power while hand crafted features contain low level information. Therefore, a research question arises: *"Can we exploit the effectiveness of encoding with deep features?"* In general, for hand-crafted features adding more statistical information into the encoding step improves the results, this is one of the reasons for which improved Fisher Vectors (iFV) method [31] outperforms Vector of Locally Aggregated Descriptors (VLAD) [17]. However, for deep features this fact is not anymore checked. As a matter of fact, in our preliminary experiments and also in recent works such as [52], we can notice a completely different behavior of deep features compared to hand-crafted features, where a simpler encoding approach such as VLAD outperforms a method which relies on higher order information such as iFV. Thus, another question arises: *"Is it beneficial for the encoding step to rely on higher order information in case of deep features?"* Another important aspect is that with the current availability of a large number of already trained networks, many works are using these networks as a black box feature extraction tool, due to several reasons, such as the availability of not enough training data, of not enough resources, etc. Then, some techniques for hand crafted features are used to encode the extracted deep features. However, we argue that existing techniques (which are built around deep features) are not optimal also for deep features encoding. Therefore, investigating the encoding approaches for deep features is still an open area of research.

The main contributions of this work are the following: (1) we propose two encoding approaches specifically built for deep features. The first solution is extremely efficient for the computational cost, however less performant in terms of accuracy for more challenging datasets, while the other provided solution gives the best accuracy including for challenging datasets but being more demanding for the computational cost than the first solution. Our solutions take advantage of the convolutional networks, capturing the highest

ICMR '17, June 6–9, 2017, Bucharest, Romania
 ACM ISBN 978-1-4503-4701-3/17/06...$15.00
DOI: http://dx.doi.org/10.1145/3078971.3078988

feature response of the convolutional maps which actually results from the highest neuron activation from the network. Specifically, after we extract some local deep features from a video, we have two approaches to group the features: one is based on the channel information from the feature maps of the network and the other on the similarity information. In the end we perform a max-pooling over the resulted group of features. Our proposed solutions respect three essential characteristics for a highly competitive video representation: (i) simple and generic, our solutions are straightforward to implement and are highly discriminative, working even with a simple model such as a linear classifier; (ii) efficient, our proposed approaches are able to run faster than real-time; (iii) effective, our proposed methods outperform the other encoding approaches in terms of accuracy (such as, iFV and VLAD) by a large margin. (2) we propose a very competitive pipeline for action recognition to work with deep features. Our pipeline can be easily adopted to work with networks that are not specifically trained or fine-tuned for a particular dataset or even are trained on a different task. We cover all those cases in our work and we present a robust framework with state-of-the-art results on three challenging datasets for action recognition.

The rest of the paper is organized as following: Section 2 summarizes the related works. Section 3 introduces our encoding solutions. Section 4 presents the local deep feature extraction pipeline. The experimental evaluation is presented in Section 5. The conclusions are drawn in Section 6.

2 RELATED WORK

Due to the fact that feature encoding step is a key factor for the system performance, there are many works which are focused to build a powerful representation that serves as input for a classifier. Super vector-based encoding methods are among the most powerful representation generators. Improved Fisher Vectors (iFV) [31] is one of the state-of-the-art super vector-based encoding methods which performs a soft assignment of the features and incorporates first- and second-order information. Vector of Locally Aggregated Descriptors (VLAD) [17] is a simplification of iFV capturing only first-order information and performing a hard assignment of the features. Super Vector Coding (SVC) [57] method keeps the zero-order and first-order statistics, thus SVC can be seen as a combination between Vector Quantization (VQ) [37] and VLAD.

There are many works with the main goal to improve the aforementioned widely used approaches. The work in [28] proposes to improve VLAD by concatenating the second- and third-order statistics, and using supervised dictionary learning. The work in [24] uses Random Forests in a pruned version for the trees to build the vocabulary and then additionally concatenate second-order information similar as iFV. The works in [22, 23] consider a Spatial Pyramid approach to capture the information about features location, however, the scalability is an issue for this method, as it increases considerably the size of the final representation and it is not feasible for dividing the video in more than 4 segments. The work in [2] proposes to use intra-normalization to improve VLAD performance. The RootSIFT normalization is proposed in [1] to improve the performance of the framework for object retrieval

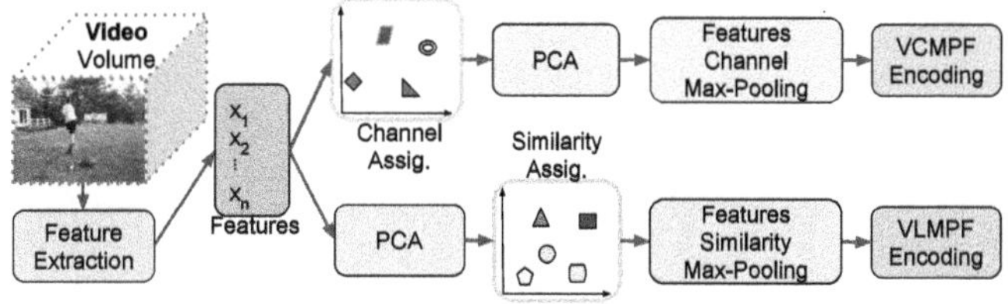

Figure 1: The pipelines for deep feature encoding.

by computing square root of the values to reduce the influence of large bin values. In [10] the VLAD approach is empowered with spatio-temporal information by considering the feature position within the video, while in [11] the performance of VLAD is boosted by using a double assignment approach. The work in [30] uses a multi-layer nested iFV encoding to boost the performance. Different from aforementioned methods which are initially built to encode hand-crafted features, our work proposes solutions specifically designed for local deep features encoding.

Recently, encouraged by deep learning breakthroughs, many works [4, 19, 27, 35, 36, 41, 42, 51, 54] encapsulate all three main steps: feature extraction, encoding and classification, in an end-to-end framework. The work in [35] uses two streams, to capture both appearance and motion information. The works in [14, 15] are based on rank pooling for encoding; the authors in [4] extend this idea to dynamic images to create a video representation. In [42] a 3D convolutional neural network is proposed which is able to learn both appearance and motion information from a video. Over the previous approaches, our proposed methods have the advantage of being able to use any available trained network without the need to train, re-train or fine tune it, obtaining impressive performance, even improving the original network results. Furthermore, our methods can easily combine different networks, with different source of information, to create an effective video representation.

3 DEEP FEATURE ENCODING

In this section we present our proposed encoding approaches for local deep features: VCMPF (Vector of Channel Max Pooled Features) and VLMPF (Vector of Locally Max Pooled Features). The overview of the main steps for each encoding method is illustrated in Figure 1.

3.1 VCMPF

The upper part of Figure 1 represents the path to obtain the VCMPF representation for a given video. We exploit the nature of deep features and obtain an automatic codebook represented by the channels of the network layer from where we extract the features (see Section 4 for details about feature extraction), thus we have 512 channels. Therefore, each local deep feature extracted from a video is a 512 dimensional vector, and each dimension represents the response for its corresponding channel. Formally, we can represent the codebook for the channels as $Ch=\{ch_1, ch_2, ..., ch_{512}\}$ and the extracted features for a given video are represented by $X=\{x_1, x_2, ..., x_n\} \in R^{n \times d}$, where d is the feature dimensionality and n is the total number of the local features of the video. In the assignment, for each local feature x_j ($j=1, ..., n$) we obtain the index

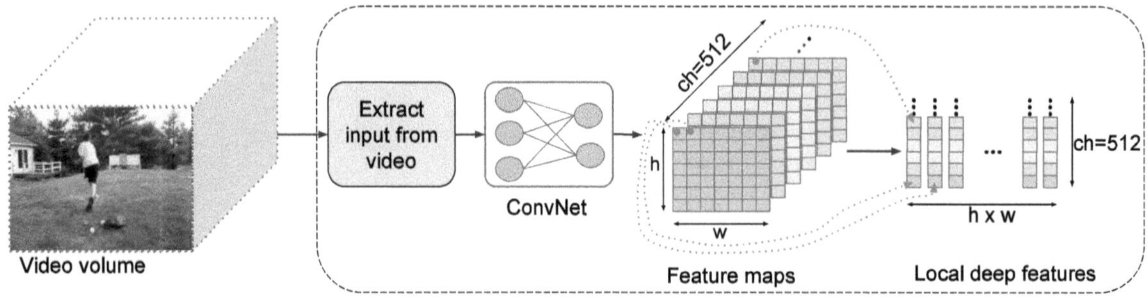

Figure 2: The pipeline for local deep feature extraction.

(within its vector) where the highest response (the maximum absolute value of the feature vector) is located and then we assign the feature to the corresponding channel with the obtained index. In this case the assignment step is extremely fast as it is not necessary to compute any distances, which in general is demanding for the computational cost.

The next step is to apply PCA over all features. This is an optional step, however, it can be useful in practice due to the high dimensionality of the local deep features. We apply PCA after the assignment step with the goal to conserve all 512 dimensions of the initial feature vector, and thus, keep all the initial channels as a codebook. The assignment step provides a division of the features in 512 groups. For each group i (i =1, ..., 512) we compute a vector representation $v^{ch_i}=[v_1^{ch_i}, v_2^{ch_i}, ..., v_{d^*}^{ch_i}]$, where d^* is the feature dimensionality after PCA. Each $v_s^{ch_i}$ (s iterates over the dimensions of the feature, s=1, ..., d^*) is formally computed as:

$$v_s^{ch_i} = \text{sign}(x_{j,s}) \max_{x_j \in ch_i} |x_{j,s}| \quad (1)$$

where sign() returns the sign of a number and |.| represents the absolute value. The equation above performs a max pooling over each group of features based on the channel assignment. With this approach we capture the highest feature responses over each channel. The concatenation of all $[v^{ch_1}, v^{ch_2}, ..., v^{ch_{512}}]$ gives the VCMPF encoding, which is a row vector with the size $512 \times d^*$.

3.2 VLMPF

For VLMPF, we initially learn a codebook with k-means, using a large set of randomly selected features extracted from a subset of videos. The resulted codebook $C=\{c_1, c_2, ..., c_k\}$ contains k visual words. In the bottom part of Figure 1 are presented the main steps to obtain the VLMPF representation. After we obtain the features for a video, we can optionally apply PCA to reduce their dimensionality. Then we perform a hard assignment of the features, where each local feature is assigned (based on the Euclidian distance) to its nearest visual word from the learned codebook C. Similar as above, for each resulted group of features we compute a vector representation $v^{c_i}=[v_1^{c_i}, v_2^{c_i}, ..., v_{d^*}^{c_i}]$, where $v_s^{c_i}$ is formally computed as:

$$v_s^{c_i} = \text{sign}(x_{j,s}) \max_{x_j : NN(x_j)=c_i} |x_{j,s}| \quad (2)$$

where $NN(x_j)$ denotes the nearest neighborhood visual word of the codebook C for the feature x_j.

This equation performs a max pooling over each group of features resulted from the similarity-based information. Basically, VLMPF retains the maximum response for each dimension and for each visual word separately. All concatenated vectors $[v^{c_1}, v^{c_2}, ..., v^{c_k}]$ provide the VLMPF encoding, which is represented by a row vector of $k \times d^*$ dimensions.

These two proposed approaches for deep feature encoding, represent a competitive and practical solution to encode the features extracted with convolutional neural network from the entire video.

4 DEEP FEATURE EXTRACTION

This section presents the framework to extract the local deep features for a video. The approaches based on convolutional networks (ConvNets) [4, 19, 27, 35, 36, 41, 42, 51, 54] have recently obtained very competitive results over traditional hand-crafted features.

Our framework for local feature extraction uses three streams: a spatial stream for capturing the appearance, a temporal stream for capturing the motion and a spatio-temporal stream for capturing at the same time both appearance and motion information. All these three networks are individually applied on a video to extract the local deep features. Figure 2 illustrates the framework for local deep feature extraction, where we initially obtain from a given video the requested input necessary for each network and then we extract the feature maps with spatial information.

In our framework the appearance information is obtained by using the VGG ConvNet in [36], which is a network with 19 layers. VGG19 is also characterized by a smaller size of the convolutional filters of 3×3 and the stride is only 1 pixel. These characteristics enable the network to explore finer-grained details from the feature maps. This network is trained on the ImageNet dataset [8], with state-of-the-art results for image classification. The VGG19 ConvNet requests as input an image with 224×224 pixels and three channels for the color information. We initially extract the individual frames from a video and then we accordingly resize them to the required input size of the network. For each individual frame we take the output of the last convolutional layer with spatial information, which for this network is represented by pool5. The motivation of choosing this layer is related to the fact that deeper layers provide high discriminative information. By taking a layer with spatial information we can extract local deep features for each frame of the video, instead of a global deep feature, increasing the robustness of the approach. The pool5 layer provides as output a feature map with a spatial size of 7×7 and 512 channels. From the obtained feature map we extract the local deep features by taking individually each spatial location and concatenate the values along all 512 channels, obtaining local deep features with 512 dimensions. Therefore, from each frame we extract 7×7=49 local deep features and each feature is a 512 dimensional vector. For each video we obtain in total $\#frames$×49 local deep features. In the experimental section we refer to the local deep features extracted from the Spatial Convolutional Network as SCN.

The motion information extraction is based on the re-trained network in [51]. This deep network, also VGG, is initially proposed in [36] and contains 16 layers. The authors in [51] re-trained the VGG ConvNet for action recognition task with new input data using several good practices for the network re-training, such as pre-training to initialize the network, smaller learning rate, more data augmentation techniques and high dropout ratio to prevent overfitting. The VGG ConvNet is re-trained for action recognition task using the UCF101 dataset [39]. For the temporal ConvNet the input consists in 10-stacked optical flow fields, each field provides an image for the vertical motion and another image for the horizontal motion information. Thus, the input for this network is represented by 20-stacked optical flow images. From a given video we extract the optical flow fields using the OpenCV implementation of the TVL1 algorithm [55]. Similar as in the previous ConvNet, for the temporal ConvNet we also take the output of the last convolutional layer with structure information represented by pool5 layer. The spatial size of this pool5 layer is also 7×7 and 512 channels. As illustrated in Figure 2, the final local deep features for an input are obtained by concatenating the values from each spatial location along all the channels, resulting in 49 local features for an input. The total number of local deep features extracted for a video when using temporal ConvNet is ($\#frames$−9)×49. We further refer to the local deep features extracted with Temporal Convolutional Network as TCN.

For the spatio-temporal stream we use the 3D ConvNet [42]. This network is trained on Sports-1M dataset [19] and contains 16 layers: 8 convolutional, 5 max-pooling, 2 fully connected layers, and the softmax output layer. The network is designed to capture both appearance and motion information by using 3D convolutional kernels. The input of the network is a 16 frame-long clip extracted from the video. Similar to the previous two networks used in our pipeline, we use a sampling step size of one frame to iterate over the frames of the video for creating the input clips. The last layer with spatial information has spatial size of the feature maps of 4×4. Due to this relatively small spatial size of the feature maps for this layer and also for having an equal size of the feature maps for all three networks, we extract for this spatio-temporal network the conv5b layer. The conv5b layer contains two feature maps, each of them 7×7×512. For obtaining a single feature map out of this two, we take maximum value for each position of the both feature maps from conv5b. After this step, we obtain the same size as previous two networks, therefore, we can apply the same framework to extract the local deep features. The total number of local deep features obtained with this network for a video is ($\#frames$−15)×7×7. We further refer to the features extracted with this Convolutional 3D network as C3D.

5 EXPERIMENTS

This section presents the experimental part where we evaluate the proposed approach for action recognition.

5.1 Datasets

We evaluate our framework on three of the most popular and challenging datasets for action recognition: HMDB51 [20], UCF50 [32], and UCF101 [39].

The HMDB51 dataset [20] contains 51 action categories, with a total of 6,766 video clips. It is one of the most challenging dataset with realistic settings. We use the original non-stabilized videos, and we follow the original protocol using three train-test splits [20]. We report average accuracy over the three splits as performance measure.

The UCF50 dataset [32] contains 6,618 realistic videos taken from YouTube. There are 50 human action categories mutually exclusive and the videos are split into 25 predefined groups. We follow the recommended standard procedure and perform leave-one-group-out cross validation and report average classification accuracy over all 25 folds.

The UCF101 dataset [39] is a widely adopted benchmark for action recognition, consisting in 13,320 realistic videos and 101 action classes. We follow for evaluation the recommended default three training/testing splits and report the average recognition accuracy over these three splits.

5.2 Experimental setup

For the motion stream of the local deep feature extraction pipeline, the work in [51] provides three trained models for each split of the UCF101 dataset. We accordingly use the models for each split of the UCF101 for feature extraction. For the other two datasets, HMDB51 and UCF50, we use only the model trained on the split1 of UCF101 to extract the local deep features. We compare our proposed encodings (VCMPF and VLMPF) with two state-of-the-art super vector-based encoding approaches represented by Vector of Locally Aggregated Descriptors (VLAD) [17] and Fisher Vectors (iFV) [31]. We set the size of the codebook to 256 visual words for our VLMPF, VLAD and iFV. This is a standard used size of the codebook in many works, and by keeping this setting we can easily and fairly compare different approaches. The codebook is learned from a randomly 500k sampled features from a subset of videos. Before classification, for VCMPF and VLMPF we individually normalize each representation resulted from each feature type by applying L2 normalization. Many works, such as [47, 44], show that iFV and VLAD perform better if after feature encoding the Power Normalization (PN) is applied followed by L2-normalization ($||sign(x)|x|^{\alpha}||$). Thus, we also adopted this normalization strategy for iFV and VLAD, setting α to the standard widely used value of 0.5. The reason for which iFV and VLAD work better when using PN is due to the fact that their resulted final representation contains large peaks within the vector and PN helps to reduce them and make the vector smoother. Instead, our proposed encodings do not provide a final vector containing large peaks, therefore, it is not necessary to apply also PN. For the classification part, in all the experiments we use a linear one-vs-all SVM with the parameter C=100.

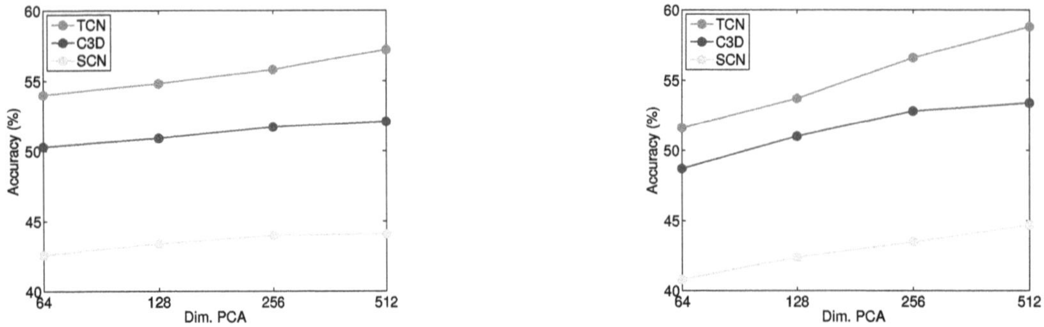

Figure 3: Evaluation of the dimensionality reduction with PCA for VCMPF (left) and VLMPF (right).

Table 1: Accuracy comparison on all three datasets. Best results are in bold.

	HMDB51 (%)						UCF50 (%)						UCF101 (%)					
	SCN		TCN		C3D		SCN		TCN		C3D		SCN		TCN		C3D	
	256	512	256	512	256	512	256	512	256	512	256	512	256	512	256	512	256	512
iFV	36.6	41.8	51.0	56.6	46.1	49.0	75.7	81.0	95.2	96.1	84.7	88.8	67.8	74.1	84.1	85.4	77.7	79.8
VLAD	37.2	40.3	51.1	53.9	46.8	49.1	78.4	80.2	95.5	95.4	86.4	89.0	69.9	73.4	83.7	85.2	78.6	81.4
VCMPF	**44.0**	44.1	55.8	57.2	51.7	52.1	**85.1**	85.1	**97.0**	**97.1**	93.4	**93.7**	78.3	**78.8**	**86.5**	**86.9**	83.5	84.1
VLMPF	43.5	**44.7**	**56.6**	**58.8**	**52.8**	**53.4**	84.7	**85.3**	96.8	96.8	**93.7**	**93.7**	**78.5**	78.6	85.9	**86.9**	**84.5**	**84.7**

5.3 Parameter tuning

We examine the influence on the accuracy of dimensionality reduction using PCA. The left graph from Figure 3 presents the evolution of the accuracy while the number of feature dimensions is changed for the VCMPF encoding approach. By reducing the feature dimensionality by a factor of two, a reasonable trade-off with the accuracy is achieved. In the right graph of Figure 3 we present the situation of decreasing the feature dimensionality in the case of VLMPF encoding approach where the best accuracy is obtained with all 512 dimensions, while the 256 dimensionality for the features represents the trade-off. Following this evaluation we use in the next experiments the feature with full dimensionality (512) and also reducing their dimensionality to 256 with PCA.

5.4 Comparison to other encodings

In this part we compare our proposed encoding approaches with other highly competitive encoding methods, such as improved Fisher Vectors (iFV) and Vector of Locally Aggregated Descriptors (VLAD). The comparison is conducted in both effectiveness and efficiency.

5.4.1 Effectiveness comparison. In Table 1 we present the accuracy comparison of our encoding with iFV and VLAD over all three datasets. For all three considered local deep features (SCN, TCN and C3D) we report the results for full feature dimensionality (512) and also after applying PCA to reduce their dimensionality by a factor of two. We can clearly see that both proposed encoding approaches, VCMPF and VLMPF, outperform by a large margin the state-of-the-art super vector-based encoding approaches iFV and VLAD over all three datasets and feature types. For instance, for C3D features with full dimensionality, VLMPF outperforms iFV by 4.4 percentage points and VLAD by 4.3 percentage points on the challenging HMDB51 dataset.

Very interestingly, in the case of deep features, iFV does not perform always better than VLAD, which is actually the case for hand-crafted features presented in many works, such as [44, 29]. It is well-known by the research community that for hand-crafted features iFV gives a better accuracy than VLAD, one of the reasons is due to the fact that iFV considers high order statistics to build the final representation. However, in the case of deep features, considering high statistical information for the encoding method does not guarantee an improvement for accuracy. However, our encoding methods, specially designed for encoding local deep features, give impressing results for all three datasets.

5.4.2 Efficiency comparison. For the efficiency comparison we randomly sampled 500 videos from HMDB51 dataset and we report the number of frames per second and the number of seconds per video that an encoding method is able to process. The timing measurements are performed on a single core Intel(R) Xeon(R) CPU E5-2690 2.60GHz.

Table 2 presents the efficiency comparison over all three deep features using both full dimensionality of the features (512) and reduced with PCA to 256. The table shows that our approaches are the most efficient. The most demanding for the computational cost is iFV and this is due to the computation of first- and second-order information and also to the use of a soft assignment approach. VLMPF is comparable with VLAD in computational cost, however VLAD is slightly slower due to the computation of the residuals. The fastest approach is our VCMPF, which outperforms including the other proposed encoding, and this is due to the assignment step which avoids the computation of the expensive distances. The last

Table 2: Computational efficiency comparison. We report the number of frames per second (fr/sec) and seconds per video (sec/vid). Last two columns show the dimensionality generated by each encoding method for 256 and 512 feature dimensionality. Best results are in bold.

	SCN 256		SCN 512		TCN 256		TCN 512		C3D 256		C3D 512		256	512
	fr/sec	sec/vid	fr/sec	sec/vid	fr/sec	sec/vid	fr/sec	sec/vid	fr/sec	sec/vid	fr/sec	sec/vid	dim	dim
iFV	253.2	0.357	168.7	0.536	301.4	0.300	197.6	0.457	308.7	0.293	202.3	0.447	131,072	262,144
VLAD	1967.5	0.046	1143.8	0.079	2213.8	0.041	1299.5	0.070	2372.5	0.038	1375.0	0.066	**65,536**	**131,072**
VCMPF	**4435.9**	**0.020**	**3485.1**	**0.026**	**4731.4**	**0.019**	**3612.5**	**0.025**	**5019.5**	**0.018**	**3682.2**	**0.025**	131,072	262,144
VLMPF	2049.4	0.044	1192.6	0.076	2329.2	0.039	1370.9	0.066	2455.0	0.037	1426.0	0.063	**65,536**	**131,072**

Table 3: Fusion strategies for VCMPF and VLMPF. DF (Deep Features) represent all three local deep features (SCN, TCN, C3D), except for UCF50 dataset where we excluded TCN features from the fusion; HMG (Histograms of Motion Gradients) [12]; and iDT (improved Dense Trajectories) [47] is represented with HOG, HOF, MBHx and MBHy. The best performance results are in bold for each fusion type over each feature representation combination. The best result over each dataset is also underlined.

(a) VCMPF

	HMDB51 (%)			UCF50 (%)			UCF101 (%)		
	DF	DF+HMG	DF+HMG+iDT	DF	DF+HMG	DF+HMG+iDT	DF	DF+HMG	DF+HMG+iDT
Early	64.2	66.6	69.9	94.4	95.3	96.6	**93.1**	**93.8**	**<u>94.1</u>**
sLate	61.5	63.2	66.5	93.0	94.1	95.6	91.3	91.9	92.3
wLate	63.2	63.9	68.2	93.9	94.9	96.5	91.7	92.2	92.9
sDouble	63.2	64.6	68.0	93.5	94.5	95.8	91.9	92.5	92.7
wDouble	**65.2**	**67.1**	**<u>70.5</u>**	**94.6**	**95.4**	**<u>96.9</u>**	**93.1**	**93.8**	**<u>94.1</u>**

(b) VLMPF

	HMDB51 (%)			UCF50 (%)			UCF101 (%)		
	DF	DF+HMG	DF+HMG+iDT	DF	DF+HMG	DF+HMG+iDT	DF	DF+HMG	DF+HMG+iDT
Early	65.3	66.7	70.2	94.5	95.3	96.7	**93.1**	**93.6**	**<u>94.1</u>**
sLate	63.6	64.7	68.0	93.5	94.4	95.6	91.5	92.0	92.3
wLate	65.1	65.7	69.3	93.9	94.9	96.5	91.7	92.2	93.0
sDouble	65.0	65.9	69.0	94.0	95.0	96.0	92.3	92.6	92.8
wDouble	**66.9**	**68.0**	**<u>71.6</u>**	**94.8**	**95.4**	**<u>96.9</u>**	**93.1**	**93.6**	**<u>94.1</u>**

two columns presents the dimensionality of a video representation generated by each encoding approach. VLAD and our proposed encoding approach, VLMPF, generate the lower dimensionality for a video representation.

5.5 Fusion strategies

In the previous experiments we show that our proposed approaches are superior to the other encoding methods. Also from the previous experiments we can notice that our VCMPF is not considerably affected by the dimensionality reduction to 256, while the accuracy for our VLMPF drops more. Considering this observation, for the next experiments we reduce the feature dimensionality to 256 for VCMPF, while for VLMPF we keep full dimensionality of 512. This setting provides also the same size of the video representation generated by VCMPF and VLMPF.

The UCF101 dataset is an extension of UCF50 and the TCN features are extracted using a network trained on UCF101. To avoid the risk of overfitting on UCF50 dataset we exclude the TCN features when performing any fusion. Therefore, for a fair comparison, in the next results, which are used as a comparison with the state-of-the-art, we use as deep features only SCN and C3D for UCF50 dataset.

As feature fusion, we use three combinations. (1) DF stands for deep features represented by fusing SCN, TCN and C3D (note that, as we said before, for UCF50 we excluded TCN features). (2) DF+HMG, we add to deep features a hand-crafted descriptor represented by Histogram of Motion Gradients [12], which is focused on capturing the motion information within the video in an efficient approach. (3) DF+HMG+iDT, in addition, we fuse the improved Dense Trajectories [47] descriptors represented by HOG, HOF, MBHx and MBHy. iDT represents a state-of-the-art approach for extracting hand-crafted descriptors. The hand-crafted descriptors are extracted using the code provided by the authors [12, 47], with the suggested default settings. All hand-crafted descriptors are individually encoded as suggested, using iFV, and then before classification, we individually apply on each resulted representation Power Normalization (with α=0.1) followed by L2 normalization as recommended in [12].

The fusion between features is performed using several strategies. "Early" represents an early fusion by concatenating each

Table 4: Comparison to the state-of-the-art.

HMDB51 (%)		UCF50 (%)		UCF101(%)	
Jain et al. [16] (2013)	52.1	Solmaz et al. [38] (2013)	73.7	Wang et al. [48] (2013)	85.9
Zhu et al. [58] (2013)	54.0	Reddy et al. [32] (2013)	76.9	Karpathy et al. [19] (2014)	65.4
Oneata et al. [26] (2013)	54.8	Shi et al. [34] (2013)	83.3	Simonyan et al. [35] (2014)	88.0
Wang et al. [47] (2013)	57.2	Wang et al. [45] (2013)	85.6	Wang et al. [46] (2015)	86.0
Kantorov et al. [18] (2014)	46.7	Wang et al. [47] (2013)	91.2	Sun et al. [41] (2015)	88.1
Simonyan et al. [35] (2014)	59.4	Ballas et al. [3] (2013)	92.8	Ng et al. [54] (2015)	88.6
Peng et al. [30] (2014)	66.8	Everts et al. [13] (2014)	72.9	Tran et al. [42] (2015)	90.4
Sun et al. [41] (2015)	59.1	Uijlings et al. [43] (2014)	80.9	Wang at al. [51] (2015)	91.4
Wang et al. [46] (2015)	60.1	Kantorov et al. [18] (2014)	82.2	Wang et al. [50] (2015)	91.5
Wang et al. [50] (2015)	65.9	Ciptadi et al. [5] (2014)	90.5	Zhang et al. [56] (2016)	86.4
Park et al. [27] (2016)	56.2	Narayan et al. [25] (2014)	92.5	Peng et al. [29] (2016)	87.9
Seo et al. [33] (2016)	58.9	Uijlings et al. [44] (2015)	81.8	Park et al [27] (2016)	89.1
Peng et al. [29] (2016)	61.1	Wang et al. [46] (2015)	91.7	Bilen et al. [4] (2016)	89.1
Yang et al. [53] (2016)	61.8	Peng et al. [29] (2016)	92.3	Diba et al. [9] (2016)	90.2
Bilen et al. [4] (2016)	65.2	Duta et al. [12] (2016)	93.0	Fernando et al. [14] (2016)	91.4
Fernando et al. [14] (2016)	66.9	Seo et al. [33] (2016)	93.7	Yang et al. [53] (2016)	91.6
Our VCMPF(DF)	65.2	Our VCMPF(DF)	**94.6**	Our VCMPF(DF)	**93.1**
Our VCMPF(DF) + iFV(HCF)	**70.5**	Our VCMPF(DF) + iFV(HCF)	**96.9**	Our VCMPF(DF) + iFV(HCF)	**94.1**
Our VLMPF(DF)	**66.9**	Our VLMPF(DF)	**94.8**	Our VLMPF(DF)	**93.1**
Our VLMPF(DF) + iFV(HCF)	**71.6**	Our VLMPF(DF) + iFV(HCF)	**96.9**	Our VLMPF(DF) + iFV(HCF)	**94.1**

resulted individual representation and then performing a final L2 normalization over the resulted final representation. "sLate" represents a late fusion by performing a sum over the classifiers output obtained from each individual feature type. "wLate" represents also a late fusion but using a weighted sum of the classifiers output. The weights combination is tuned taking values in the [0;1] interval with the step 0.1. In addition, we perform a double fusion, where besides the individual classifier output obtained for each feature type we use also the classifier obtained from the early fusion. We have also "sDouble" from sum over all classifiers output and "wDouble" for weighted sum over the classifiers output, with similar strategy as late fusion to establish the weights.

The results for each fusion strategy is presented in Table 3a for VCMPF and in Table 3b for VLMPF. We can notice that fusing hand-crafted descriptors with the deep features boosts the accuracy. In general, early fusion outperforms late fusion and the weighted sum over the classifiers output gives better results than just performing the sum. The double fusion combines the benefits of early and late fusion, achieving the best results overall that serves as comparison to the state-of-the-art.

5.6 Comparison to state-of-the-art

The comparison of our framework for action recognition to the state-of-the-art is presented in Table 4. We compare the state-of-the-art to both proposed solutions for feature encoding: VCMPF and VLMPF. For both solutions we present the results using only deep features (DF) represented by SCN, TCN and C3D (note that, as explained above, in all the cases we excluded TCN features for UCF50 dataset). In addition, we present the results where we combine our representation with the improved Fisher Vector (iFV) applied over hand-crafted features (HCF). The hand-crafted features are represented by Histogram of Motion Gradients (HMG) [12] and improved dense trajectories (iDT) approach (represented by the descriptors: HOG, HOF, MBHx andMBHy) [47]. It is important to mention that our results are obtained without re-training or fine-tuning the ConvNets for the datasets used in this work (except TCN features for UCF101). For instance, the competitive results on HMDB51 datasets are obtained using features extracted from three different ConvNets, none of which had access to any data from HMDB51 during the training. Our results outperform even recent works on action recognition, obtaining state-of-the-art results on all three datasets: HMDB51, UCF50 and UCF101.

6 CONCLUSION

In this work we present two competitive solutions specifically designed for encoding the local deep features. The provided solutions are useful in many practical scenarios for working with deep features to generate a robust final representation. In this work we show that our powerful encodings for deep features outperform by a large margin the existing state-of-the-art encoding approaches, which are built around hand-crafted features, such as VLAD and improved Fisher Vectors, this motivating the necessity of an encoding approach adapted for local deep features. Furthermore, our proposed solutions are highly efficient, being able to run faster than real time. Our encoding approaches provide a solution to encode the features extracted with a ConvNet over the entire video. Our proposed pipeline for action recognition is pushing the state-of-the-art further by 4.7, 3.2 and 2.5 percentage points on the HMDB51, UCF50 and UCF101 datasets respectively.

Acknowledgments. This work was partially supported by EIT Digital. Part of this work was funded under UEFISCDI research grant PN-III-P2-2.1-PED-2016-1065, agreement 30PED/2017, project SPOTTER.

REFERENCES

[1] R. Arandjelović and A. Zisserman. Three things everyone should know to improve object retrieval. In *CVPR*, 2012.
[2] R. Arandjelovic and A. Zisserman. All about VLAD. In *CVPR*, 2013.
[3] N. Ballas, Y. Yang, Z.-Z. Lan, B. Delezoide, F. Prêteux, and A. Hauptmann. Space-time robust representation for action recognition. In *ICCV*, 2013.
[4] H. Bilen, B. Fernando, E. Gavves, A. Vedaldi, and S. Gould. Dynamic image networks for action recognition. In *CVPR*, 2016.
[5] A. Ciptadi, M. S. Goodwin, and J. M. Rehg. Movement pattern histogram for action recognition and retrieval. In *ECCV*, 2014.
[6] N. Dalal and B. Triggs. Histograms of oriented gradients for human detection. In *CVPR*, 2005.
[7] N. Dalal, B. Triggs, and C. Schmid. Human detection using oriented histograms of flow and appearance. In *ECCV*. 2006.
[8] J. Deng, W. Dong, R. Socher, L.-J. Li, K. Li, and L. Fei-Fei. Imagenet: A large-scale hierarchical image database. In *CVPR*, 2009.
[9] A. Diba, A. M. Pazandeh, and L. Van Gool. Efficient two-stream motion and appearance 3d cnns for video classification. In *ECCV ws*, 2016.
[10] I. C. Duta, B. Ionescu, K. Aizawa, and N. Sebe. Spatio-temporal vlad encoding for human action recognition in videos. In *MMM*, 2017.
[11] I. C. Duta, T. A. Nguyen, K. Aizawa, B. Ionescu, and N. Sebe. Boosting VLAD with double assignment using deep features for action recognition in videos. In *ICPR*, 2016.
[12] I. C. Duta, J. R. R. Uijlings, T. A. Nguyen, K. Aizawa, A. G. Hauptmann, B. Ionescu, and N. Sebe. Histograms of motion gradients for real-time video classification. In *CBMI*, 2016.
[13] I. Everts, J. C. Van Gemert, and T. Gevers. Evaluation of color spatio-temporal interest points for human action recognition. *TIP*, 2014.
[14] B. Fernando, P. Anderson, M. Hutter, and S. Gould. Discriminative hierarchical rank pooling for activity recognition. In *CVPR*, 2016.
[15] B. Fernando, E. Gavves, J. Oramas, A. Ghodrati, and T. Tuytelaars. Rank pooling for action recognition. *TPAMI*, 2016.
[16] M. Jain, H. Jégou, and P. Bouthemy. Better exploiting motion for better action recognition. In *CVPR*, 2013.
[17] H. Jégou, F. Perronnin, M. Douze, J. Sanchez, P. Perez, and C. Schmid. Aggregating local image descriptors into compact codes. *TPAMI*, 34(9):1704–1716, 2012.
[18] V. Kantorov and I. Laptev. Efficient feature extraction, encoding and classification for action recognition. In *CVPR*, 2014.
[19] A. Karpathy, G. Toderici, S. Shetty, T. Leung, R. Sukthankar, and L. Fei-Fei. Large-scale video classification with convolutional neural networks. In *CVPR*, 2014.
[20] H. Kuehne, H. Jhuang, E. Garrote, T. Poggio, and T. Serre. Hmdb: a large video database for human motion recognition. In *ICCV*, 2011.
[21] I. Laptev. On space-time interest points. *IJCV*, 64(2-3):107–123, 2005.
[22] I. Laptev, M. Marsza lek, C. Schmid, and B. Rozenfeld. Learning realistic human actions from movies. In *CVPR*, 2008.
[23] S. Lazebnik, C. Schmid, and J. Ponce. Beyond bags of features: Spatial pyramid matching for recognizing natural scene categories. In *CVPR*, 2006.
[24] I. Mironică, I. C. Duţă, B. Ionescu, and N. Sebe. A modified vector of locally aggregated descriptors approach for fast video classification. *Multimedia Tools and Applications*, pages 1–28, 2016.
[25] S. Narayan and K. R. Ramakrishnan. A cause and effect analysis of motion trajectories for modeling actions. In *CVPR*, 2014.
[26] D. Oneata, J. Verbeek, and C. Schmid. Action and event recognition with fisher vectors on a compact feature set. In *ICCV*, 2013.
[27] E. Park, X. Han, T. L. Berg, and A. C. Berg. Combining multiple sources of knowledge in deep cnns for action recognition. In *WACV*, 2016.
[28] X. Peng, L. Wang, Y. Qiao, and Q. Peng. Boosting vlad with supervised dictionary learning and high-order statistics. In *ECCV*. 2014.
[29] X. Peng, L. Wang, X. Wang, and Y. Qiao. Bag of visual words and fusion methods for action recognition: Comprehensive study and good practice. *CVIU*, 150:109–125, 2016.
[30] X. Peng, C. Zou, Y. Qiao, and Q. Peng. Action recognition with stacked fisher vectors. In *ECCV*, 2014.
[31] F. Perronnin, J. Sánchez, and T. Mensink. Improving the fisher kernel for large-scale image classification. In *ECCV*. 2010.
[32] K. K. Reddy and M. Shah. Recognizing 50 human action categories of web videos. *Machine Vision and Applications*, 24(5):971–981, 2013.
[33] J.-J. Seo, H.-I. Kim, W. De Neve, and Y. M. Ro. Effective and efficient human action recognition using dynamic frame skipping and trajectory rejection. *IVC*, 2016.
[34] F. Shi, E. Petriu, and R. Laganiere. Sampling strategies for real-time action recognition. In *CVPR*, 2013.
[35] K. Simonyan and A. Zisserman. Two-stream convolutional networks for action recognition in videos. In *NIPS*, 2014.
[36] K. Simonyan and A. Zisserman. Very deep convolutional networks for large-scale image recognition. *arXiv preprint arXiv:1409.1556*, 2014.
[37] J. Sivic and A. Zisserman. Video google: A text retrieval approach to object matching in videos. In *Computer Vision, 2003. Proceedings. Ninth International Conference on*, pages 1470–1477, 2003.
[38] B. Solmaz, S. M. Assari, and M. Shah. Classifying web videos using a global video descriptor. *Machine vision and applications*, 2013.
[39] K. Soomro, A. R. Zamir, and M. Shah. Ucf101: A dataset of 101 human actions classes from videos in the wild. *arXiv preprint arXiv:1212.0402*, 2012.
[40] J. Sun, X. Wu, S. Yan, L.-F. Cheong, T.-S. Chua, and J. Li. Hierarchical spatio-temporal context modeling for action recognition. In *CVPR*, 2009.
[41] L. Sun, K. Jia, D.-Y. Yeung, and B. E. Shi. Human action recognition using factorized spatio-temporal convolutional networks. In *ICCV*, 2015.
[42] D. Tran, L. Bourdev, R. Fergus, L. Torresani, and M. Paluri. Learning spatiotemporal features with 3d convolutional networks. In *ICCV*, 2015.
[43] J. R. R. Uijlings, I. C. Duta, N. Rostamzadeh, and N. Sebe. Realtime video classification using dense hof/hog. In *ICMR*, 2014.
[44] J. R. R. Uijlings, I. C. Duta, E. Sangineto, and N. Sebe. Video classification with densely extracted hog/hof/mbh features: an evaluation of the accuracy/computational efficiency trade-off. *International Journal of Multimedia Information Retrieval*, 4(1):33–44, 2015.
[45] H. Wang, A. Kläser, C. Schmid, and C.-L. Liu. Dense trajectories and motion boundary descriptors for action recognition. *IJCV*, 103(1):60–79, 2013.
[46] H. Wang, D. Oneata, J. Verbeek, and C. Schmid. A robust and efficient video representation for action recognition. *IJCV*, 2015.
[47] H. Wang and C. Schmid. Action recognition with improved trajectories. In *ICCV*, 2013.
[48] H. Wang and C. Schmid. Lear-inria submission for the thumos workshop. In *ICCV Workshop*, 2013.
[49] H. Wang, M. M. Ullah, A. Klaser, I. Laptev, and C. Schmid. Evaluation of local spatio-temporal features for action recognition. In *BMVC*, 2009.
[50] L. Wang, Y. Qiao, and X. Tang. Action recognition with trajectory-pooled deep-convolutional descriptors. In *CVPR*, 2015.
[51] L. Wang, Y. Xiong, Z. Wang, and Y. Qiao. Towards good practices for very deep two-stream convnets. *arXiv preprint arXiv:1507.02159*, 2015.
[52] Z. Xu, Y. Yang, and A. G. Hauptmann. A discriminative cnn video representation for event detection. In *CVPR*, 2015.
[53] X. Yang, P. Molchanov, and J. Kautz. Multilayer and multimodal fusion of deep neural networks for video classification. In *ACMMM*, 2016.
[54] J. Yue-Hei Ng, M. Hausknecht, S. Vijayanarasimhan, O. Vinyals, R. Monga, and G. Toderici. Beyond short snippets: Deep networks for video classification. In *CVPR*, 2015.
[55] C. Zach, T. Pock, and H. Bischof. A duality based approach for realtime tv-l 1 optical flow. In *Pattern Recognition*. 2007.
[56] B. Zhang, L. Wang, Z. Wang, Y. Qiao, and H. Wang. Real-time action recognition with enhanced motion vector cnns. In *CVPR*, 2016.
[57] X. Zhou, K. Yu, T. Zhang, and T. S. Huang. Image classification using super-vector coding of local image descriptors. In *Computer Vision–ECCV 2010*, pages 141–154. 2010.
[58] J. Zhu, B. Wang, X. Yang, W. Zhang, and Z. Tu. Action recognition with actons. In *ICCV*, 2013.

Musical Instrument Recognition in User-generated Videos using a Multimodal Convolutional Neural Network Architecture

Olga Slizovskaia
Universitat Pompeu Fabra
Barcelona, Spain
olga.slizovskaia@upf.edu

Emilia Gómez
Universitat Pompeu Fabra
Barcelona, Spain
emilia.gomez@upf.edu

Gloria Haro
Universitat Pompeu Fabra
Barcelona, Spain
gloria.haro@upf.edu

ABSTRACT

This paper presents a method for recognizing musical instruments in user-generated videos. Musical instrument recognition from music signals is a well-known task in the music information retrieval (MIR) field, where current approaches rely on the analysis of the good-quality audio material. This work addresses a real-world scenario with several research challenges, i.e. the analysis of user-generated videos that are varied in terms of recording conditions and quality and may contain multiple instruments sounding simultaneously and background noise. Our approach does not only focus on the analysis of audio information, but we exploit the multimodal information embedded in the audio and visual domains. In order to do so, we develop a Convolutional Neural Network (CNN) architecture which combines learned representations from both modalities at a late fusion stage. Our approach is trained and evaluated on two large-scale video datasets: YouTube-8M and FCVID. The proposed architectures demonstrate state-of-the-art results in audio and video object recognition, provide additional robustness to missing modalities, and remains computationally cheap to train.

CCS CONCEPTS

•**Information systems → Multimedia and multimodal retrieval;** *Music retrieval;* •**Computing methodologies → Neural networks;** *Visual content-based indexing and retrieval;*

KEYWORDS

multimodal musical instrument classification; convolutional neural networks; multimodal video analysis; feature fusion; multimedia information retrieval

ACM Reference format:
Olga Slizovskaia, Emilia Gómez, and Gloria Haro. 2017. Musical Instrument Recognition in User-generated Videos using a Multimodal Convolutional Neural Network Architecture. In *Proceedings of ICMR '17, June 6–9, 2017, Bucharest, Romania,* , 7 pages.
DOI: http://dx.doi.org/10.1145/3078971.3079002

DOI: http://dx.doi.org/10.1145/3078971.3079002

1 INTRODUCTION

Humans recognize a musical instrument by combining multiple perception modalities. For example, we can distinguish a violin from a cello by its timbre, size, bow movements and relative position of the instrument with respect to the performer's body. Although the task is fairly easy for humans to perform, combining multimodal information is not trivial for machine learning algorithms.

Musical instrument recognition is a well-known problem in the music information retrieval (MIR) field. State-of-the-art methods are based on the combination of audio feature extraction (representative of the time-frequency distribution of the signal), automatic classification methods and context information on the music material under analysis. Nowadays, these algorithms provide good accuracy in recognizing musical instruments from monophonic audio recordings (i.e. single instrument playing), although the performance depends on the number of instruments and size of the audio collection used for training [17]. This performance significantly drops in polyphonic music scenarios (i.e. more than one instrument playing), where it is easier to recognize instruments if they are predominant in the audio signal [6].

Nevertheless, current approaches are based on the analysis of good-quality audio material and fail for real-world scenarios such as the one addressed here. Moreover, it's typical to find the presence of the sound of the instruments. In contrast, in this paper, our problem is to recognize the physical presence of the instruments by either sound or visual component. With this method, we hope to advance the field of indexing music videos in large-scale collections.

User-generated videos are widely found on social networks to share own musical performances, and they may contain multiple instruments, different types of noise, blur, compression artifacts, and they are varied in terms of recording conditions and quality [38]. Yet, despite these downsides, collections of user-generated videos are a rich source of knowledge. While the most important information comes from audio, visual content also plays an important role in detecting musical instruments in videos. Thus, different taxonomies for musical instruments rely on audio characteristics as well as on visual characteristics (such as a keyboard, wood, brass, bowed string). In this work, we explore the relationship between audio and visual cues and take advantage of complementary information provided by the nature of the task.

In particular, we benefit from the information embedded in the audio and visual domains by means of a Convolutional Neural Network (CNN) architecture. We train and evaluate it on two large-scale video datasets: YouTube-8M [2] and FCVID [46] which contain, respectively, more than 60000 and 5000 musical performance videos with musical instruments. The proposed architectures demonstrate state-of-the-art results in audio and video object recognition, provide additional robustness to missing modalities, and remains computationally cheap to train. In addition, our approach meets the standards of reproducible research.

Our contributions include: (1) a novel multimodal CNN architecture for audio-visual musical instruments recognition which outperforms unimodal state-of-the-art techniques with the largest musical performance videos datasets ever used in the literature; (2) evaluation on a few recent and popular audio-only and general-purpose CNN architectures in the context of user-generated musical performance videos; (3) both FCVID and YouTube-8M datasets have been constructed for visual concept recognition; this notwithstanding, we show in a set of experiments that audio information plays a crucial role in the categorization of musical videos and can significantly improve recognition performance over visual input.

2 RELATED WORK

The increasing popularity of deep neural networks in data analysis looks like a wildfire. The ideas of convolutional and recurrent neural networks smoldered for years until they were brought to the fore by enhanced computational abilities and the availability of massive labeled data collections. Nowadays, CNNs effectively deal with a huge number of unimodal tasks and become stronger for multimodal learning rapidly [22].

Video Recognition: The breakthrough in pattern recognition on static images was largely due to its impressive feature learning ability. The computer vision community has been struggled for decades to find a way to avoid handcrafted features for solving large-scale video analysis tasks in a unique non-specific way [23, 42].

Over the last years, most of the best solutions in action recognition [7, 15, 29, 37, 42], scene recognition [2, 23, 42] and general multi-label video classification [2, 23] tasks exploit either deep neural networks on raw spatio-temporal data [15, 23, 37, 42] or combine them with motion features such as improved Dense Trajectories (including HOG, HOF and MBH) [7, 42] and Optical Flow images [29]. The most straightforward way to incorporate temporal information in video CNNs is to switch from 2D convolutions to 3D convolutions [23, 42], although it leads to difficulties in the choice of parameters such as the optimal shape for the filters, the frame-rate for analysis or the clip size, to name a few.

Several alternative methods have been recently proposed, such as two-stream CNNs [15, 37], which use single-frame architecture for spatial modeling and precomputed multi-frame optical flow images for temporal modeling, while aggregating information at the prediction stage [37] or at several layers of the network [15]. The approach in [29] examines different feature-pooling methods on CNN architectures with up to 120 frames as well as the capability of Long Short-Term Memory networks to catch temporal information. Although this approach provides good results, its computational performance is far from satisfactory. A good compromise between accuracy and speed for large-scale video classification has been proposed by several teams of researchers [2, 23]. They build systems upon frame-level spatial features and exploit average pooling and Deep Bag of Frame (DBoF) pooling for clip-level and video-level predictions.

Audio Recognition: In recent years, there has been a strong interest in deep learning at the audio signal processing community. Apart from the tremendous attention received at speech recognition, important tasks in music information retrieval (MIR) have been addressed with deep learning methods. Among them, we find approaches for musical onset detection [35], musical instrument recognition [16, 26], automatic music transcription [36], acoustic event detection [14, 33], automatic tagging [9], audio source separation [8] and various classification tasks [18, 32].

Since research in this area is still very active, there is no generic architecture working well for all the mentioned problems. Although some end-to-end methods working with raw audio have been recently proposed [3, 43], they require huge data collections and a lot of time to train. The most common approaches first transform audio data into two-dimensional image-like representations (e.g. Short-Time Fourier Transform (STFT) spectrogram [8, 14], log mel-spectrogram [9, 16, 18, 35] or Constant-Q spectrogram [26, 36]) and then train various CNN architectures. Besides, most of the architectures are either shallow, consist of only straight layer connections, or exploit squared filter shapes, which came up directly from image processing. For our case, we explore few enhancements over traditional models, such as separable convolutions [11] and partially task-specific filter shapes [32].

Multimodal Learning: Different deep learning architectures have been proposed for audio-visual speech recognition [19, 20, 30], audio-visual emotion recognition [24, 31, 45, 47], cross-modal representation learning [3] or image classification and retrieval using images and text [39, 40].

Contrariwise, the majority of MIR-related multimodal research so far relies on handcrafted audio and visual descriptors and traditional machine learning algorithms. Among them, we would like to mention multimodal approaches on detecting the playing/non-playing activity [5], automatic music transcription [27], general-purpose audio/video classification [4, 28], and artist identification problem [34].

Depending on the task and method, there are a few approaches to aggregate information from different modalities. In multimodal deep learning [30], researchers distinguish three phases: feature learning, training, and testing. For multimodal fusion, both audio and visual information is available in all phases, while for cross-modality learning or shared representation learning [3], training and testing phases exploit either audio *or* video. Even for multimodal fusion, several aggregating strategies exist, namely, (1) early fusion [19, 30, 31], where the network learns hidden representation from concatenated multimodal input; (2) middle/slow fusion [15, 23], where the network may have multiple fusion layers and optimize several learning representation simultaneously; and (3) late fusion [30, 31, 45], where the networks for all data sources are optimized separately and the learned representations are then combined to model the joint distribution of multiple modalities. Although multimodal CNNs have been proposed before for video analysis tasks [3, 19, 20, 24, 30, 31, 45, 47], to the best of our knowledge, we present the first study in the context of multimodal musical instrument recognition in video recordings.

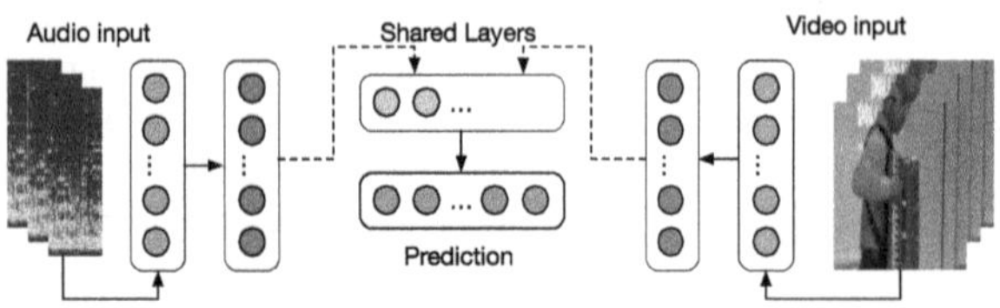

Figure 1: Schematic representation of our multimodal CNN architecture for musical instrument recognition.

3 PROPOSED METHOD

In this section, we describe our models for the task of multimodal musical instrument classification.

3.1 Visual-based recognition

Recent works [29, 44] report that spatio-temporal features can be better captured with long clips, while for short clips frame-level features have a greater impact on video object recognition performance [23]. Considering the fact that learning over long clips is a very time-consuming process, we follow the approach from [2] and extract frame-level features from videos.

For detecting instruments in static video frames, we experiment with Inception v3 architecture [41] since it's one of the most prominent and successful ones and it has been showed to provide a notable generalization ability in various tasks [18, 41]. We explore the influence of the total number of frames selected from the videos at the training phase. Moreover, we study the impact of fine-tuning the model over an independent set of images of musical instruments. The pretraining details are provided in Section 4.3.

3.2 Audio-based recognition

For audio feature representation learning, we have chosen the model from [16] (we refer to it later as *Han et al. 2016*) as a baseline. It's a classical deep CNN architecture with 8 convolutional layers stacked in a sequence, and followed by one fully connected layer. Max-pooling and dropout layers are placed after every second convolutional layer. All convolutional filters have shape of 3×3, which is similar to popular CNNs used in computer vision.

We also experiment with a modified model from [9] (we refer to it later as *Choi et al. 2016*) with a final classification softmax layer instead of gated recurrent unit layers. This architecture follows the idea of stacking convolutional layers as well, but has a larger receptive field and exploits more advanced activation function and batch normalization [21], the recent effective regularization technique.

In addition, we explore a recent Xception [11] architecture for audio-based instrument recognition. We modify the input layer so that the receptive field would be the same as in [9], and employ rectangular filters of size 48×3 at the first layer for better capturing the timbral characteristics of musical instruments. To reflect the changes of the input layer, we set the number of filters for separable convolutions equal to 768. The description of the network input is provided in Section 4.2.

3.3 Multimodal recognition

In this work, we investigate multimodal fusion strategy, so we use audio and video for both training and evaluation. Although the most direct approach for multimodal learning would be to train a model over concatenated audio-visual input (and thereby to fully integrate the modalities and learn a joint feature representation), earlier work in [30] demonstrates that there are almost no cross-modal connections in the resulting architecture. Moreover, such approach would limit us to a small number of hidden layers, which is not desirable. Thereby, following the literature [30, 45, 47], we individually train audio and video representation models and we then exploit learned features from the last layers of the networks to train and evaluate the joint model as shown in Figure 1. Since the specific parameters for the audio and visual networks change for each experiment, we comment on the architecture of the late fusion model. The input layer of the model takes a concatenated feature vector of size $(k + 1, n)$, where k is the number of video frames (plus one vector of the audio features), and n corresponds to the penultimate layer size in the audio and visual networks. The model consists of two fully-connected layers (each layer contains 1024 neurons and ReLU activation function) preceding the batch normalization, and a softmax prediction layer.

3.4 Implementation details

Our approach is implemented with Keras [10] and TensorFlow [1]. We found out that the best optimization strategy for video models consists of a Stochastic Gradient Descent (SGD) optimizer with an initial learning rate of 0.0001, and a momentum of 0.9. We halved the learning rate every 5 epochs. We set up the batch size to 64 and an early stopping criterion to 5 epochs for our visual-based experiments. For audio architectures, we use the Adam [25] optimizer with various batch sizes and 10 epochs for an early stopping criterion. All experiments are conducted on a single NVIDIA Titan X 12GB GPU. The code, extracted features, pre-trained models, and experimental results are available online[1].

4 EXPERIMENTS AND RESULTS

4.1 Datasets

FCVID: Fudan-Columbia Video Dataset (FCVID) [46] contains videos, labels, several pre-computed descriptors and a category hierarchy. For our task, we consider a subcategory of FCVID dataset namely *Musical Performance With Instruments* containing 12 different classes including popular instruments, chamber music, rock band and orchestral performances. The subset contains 5154 videos with a total length of almost 260 hours. All videos in the dataset have been manually annotated by a team of 20 people (at least 3 annotations per video). Unluckily, we could not find any information about human performance rate and agreement rate for this dataset.

YouTube-8M: YouTube-8M Dataset [2] is a recently released large-scale video benchmark that consists of about 8 million YouTube video corresponding with 4800 visual entities. The vocabulary for the dataset has been created by humans, while the labels for individual videos have been automatically obtained. To evaluate our task we check the dataset entities and select those of them that match

[1]http://github.com/Veleslavia/ICMR2017

Property	FCVID [46]	YouTube-8M [2]
Total number of categories	12	13 (46)
Total number of videos	5,154	60,862 (235,260)
Total video duration	259.84 hr	4,152.09 hr
Mean video duration	3.03 min	4.09 min
Videos per category (mean/std)	429 / 101	4,677 / 6,445
Videos used in experiments	5,154	60,802

Table 1: Statistics of the musical instruments sub-datasets extracted from FCVID [46] and YouTube-8M [2] datasets. Numbers in parenthesis correspond to sub-dataset statistics before undersampling.

musical instruments. We gather a dataset containing 235k videos of 46 classes. At the same time, we found out that the resulting dataset contains a number of fine-grained categories representing by only a few videos while the top-3 categories form 75% of the dataset. To be able to compare results to FCVID dataset and to avoid problems related to dataset granularity and high imbalance, we reduce the number of categories to 13 and adjust the classes distribution by undersampling the top-3 classes. The final dataset then contains more than 60k videos with a total length of about 4k hours, that is the largest musical instrument recognition dataset for today. It's also worth mentioning that the original vocabulary for the dataset contains only visual entities and it has been built with an emphasis on the ease of visual object recognition. The average human performance reported in [2] is 78.8% in precision and 14.5% in recall. For our experiments we sample videos from both datasets to train, validation, and test splits with ratio 70%, 15%, and 15% respectively. The details about the datasets can be found in Table 1.

4.2 Data Preprocessing

First, we separate audio and visual data and preprocess them individually. For audio, we convert the stereo input to mono by averaging the left and right channels and downsample it. We then compute two different one-channel log-mel-spectrogram representations following the models proposed in [9, 16]. The model [16] (*Han et al. 2016*) has an input size of 128×43 (128 mel-frequency bins and 43 time frames) that corresponds to approximately 3 seconds of audio converted by Short Time Fourier Transform (STFT) with a Hann window of size 1024 samples and a hop size of 512 samples. The model [9] (*Choi et al. 2016*) has an input size of 96×1366 (96 mel-frequency bins and 1366 time frames, respectively) that corresponds to approximately 30 seconds of audio converted by using a STFT with window size of 512 samples and hop size of 256 samples. For all the experiments we select 30 seconds from each video: for model *Han et al. 2016* we select 10 segments by 3 seconds, uniformly distributed in original audio (and average predictions over 10 segments); for the model *Choi et al. 2016* we investigate two segmentation strategies: central cropping (30 seconds from the middle of the audio, *CC*) and uniformly cropped segments (10 segments by 3 seconds, *UC*). To obtain a proper input for our visual model we take frames from videos with 1 fps frame rate, then resize every frame to size 256×256×3, make a central crop with size 224×224×3 and apply random horizontal flipping. In the experiments where different numbers of frames are evaluated, we randomly select k frames for every video.

For both datasets, we only have one label per video, so we assign a video-level label to every selected frame.

Dataset	FMs	PT	Steps	Time	Hit@1	Hit@3	F1
FCVID	20	No	32K	19h	42.30	64.53	43.16
FCVID	30	No	16K	11h	65.39	81.75	67.29
FCVID	30	Yes	16K	11h	68.77	84.26	70.33
FCVID	50	No	24K	22h	67.47	83.21	69.38
FCVID	50	Yes	21K	19h	**69.39**	**84.32**	**71.23**
FCVID	100	No	43K	98h	68.56	83.97	70.42
FCVID	100	Yes	36K	84h	67.76	83.50	69.16
YT-8M	10	No	58K	82h	61.15	78.45	52.19
YT-8M	20	Yes	57K	92h	**70.07**	**84.20**	**71.09**

Table 2: Comparison of clip-level performance for visual instrument classification model trained on different number of frames (FMs) with or without pre-training (PT) on ImageNet musical instruments. All rows use the same Inception v3 architecture.

4.3 Experimental setup

Metrics: For experimental evaluation we use three standard information retrieval metrics: accuracy (Hit@1, the success rate at top-1 prediction), top-3 accuracy (Hit@3, the success rate at top-3 predictions), and F1-measure (the harmonic mean of precision and recall).

Pre-training of Inception v3 model: Since it has been proved that pre-training helps to improve generalization ability and reduce training time [13], we initialize Inception v3 model with the model weights trained from ImageNet [12] and fine-tune the model on a subset of musical instrument images as described in [38].

4.4 Results

Visual-only classification results: Table 2 provides a summary of the visual-based musical recognition experiments. We observe that using pre-training and increasing the number of frames for training from 20 to 50 provides a significant improvement to the performance of the classifier ($F1$ = 71.23, FCVID) vs the baseline method ($F1$ = 43.16, FCVID). However, further increase of the number of frames to 100 does not yields higher performance. Our experiments also demonstrate noticeable success in using a pre-trained model compared with one with random initialization. The combination of two aspects also demonstrates noticeable performance improvement on YouTube-8M dataset (from $F1$ = 61.15 to $F1$ = 70.07). At the same time, increasing the number of frames causes longer training process (from 22 to 84 hours for FCVID dataset and from 82 to 92 hours for YouTube-8M dataset), while the use of the pre-trained model decreases training time (from 22 to 19 hours for the 50-frames model on FCVID dataset).

Audio-only classification results: Results for audio-based music instrument recognition are presented in Table 3. We observe that the highest accuracy is obtained by *(Choi et al. 2016)* for

Method	#Params	Dataset	Hit@1	Hit@3	F1
Han et al. [16]	1.5M	FCVID	64.13	76.82	53.64
Choi et al. [9] + CC	2.4M	FCVID	77.73	92.05	77.18
Choi et al. [9] + UC	2.4M	FCVID	**79.81**	**96.09**	78.71
Xception [11] + UC	9.6M	FCVID	78.69	94.44	**79.35**
Han et al. [16]	1.5M	YT-8M	59.37	70.87	56.50
Choi et al. [9] + UC	2.4M	YT-8M	**83.58**	94.23	**84.26**
Xception [11] + UC	9.6M	YT-8M	83.53	**94.69**	84.16

Table 3: Clip-level performance of different audio architectures and frame selection methods trained and evaluated on FCVID (top) and YouTube-8M datasets (bottom).

Method	Dataset	Hit@1	Hit@3	F1
Xception [11] / 50 frames	FCVID	**88.28**	**97.00**	**88.27**
Choi et al. [9] / 50 frames	FCVID	86.97	96.09	87.25
Xception [11] / 20 frames	YT-8M	82.64	91.37	78.95
Choi et al. [9] / 20 frames	YT-8M	**84.01**	**93.41**	**84.69**

Table 4: Overall performance of the proposed multimodal neural network for Choi and Xception feature representations.

both datasets (79.81 for FCVID and 83.58 for YouTube-8M), although results are very close to the ones obtained using the Xception architecture (78.69 for FCVID and 83.53 for YouTube-8M). For FCVID dataset we experimented with central cropped (CC) and uniformly cropped (UC) segments for *(Choi et al. 2016)* architecture. Since we obtained that the UC segments provide additional robustness, we use them throughout all the remaining experiments.

In addition, we observe that classification results are significantly higher than the ones obtained using *(Han et al. 2016)* and that audio-based classification significantly outperforms video-based classification ($F1 = 79.35$ for audio vs $F1 = 71.23$ for video, FCVID, and $F1 = 84.26$ for audio $F1 = 71.09$ for video, YouTube-8M).

Multimodal classification results: Results for the combination of audio and video models are shown in Table 4. We observe that the highest accuracy of the audio-visual approach for FCVID is obtained using the Xception architecture ($Hit@1 = 88.28$), and the results are slightly lower for Choi ($Hit@1 = 86.97$). These results are noticeably better than the ones obtained by audio-only architectures for FCVID dataset and significantly higher than the ones obtained using a video-only architectures. For YouTube-8M dataset we observe that the classification performance of our multimodal method is 13% higher than the visual-only method. With comparison to the audio-only approach our combined method demonstrates similar results.

Confusion matrices: Figure 2 shows the confusion matrices obtained for FCVID dataset using the three proposed approaches: audio-only, video-only, and multimodal. As it can be seen the confusion is significantly reduced in the proposed multimodal approach vs the alternative methods, specially in the cases of harmonica (where the percentage of correct predictions increases from 75-76% to 99%), and violin, accordion, guitar, chamberMusic (with respectively, 11%, 10%, 10%, 10% of increase with respect to the audio alone and 10%, 14%, 13%, 21% of increase with respect to the video alone).

Figure 3 shows the confusion matrices obtained for YouTube-8M dataset. We notice several significant differences with comparison to FCVID dataset. The first one is that the classification performance varies drastically between both categories and approaches. We believe that this is related to high imbalance of the categories and substantial diversity in videos. We notice that the video sequence in our data often doesn't contain the target instrument while being annotated to the certain category.

To test this assumption we carry out a simple experiment on human recognition performance. Given a video from YouTube-8M dataset we ask non-expert humans to label it with one of the considered categories. In case of presence of multiple instruments we ask to choose the predominant one. The total amount of evaluated videos is 547, evaluated by 20 different people without specific musical training. We obtain the human performance rate for our task to be equal to 86.00 in precision, 85.00 in recall, and 85.00 in F1-measure. Those results are comparable to our multimodal results ($F1 = 85.00$ vs $F1 = 84.69$). That allows us to conclude that the task (and dataset) is difficult to solve even by humans.

The feedback from our participants also contains claims that the instruments are often not present in videos from YouTube-8M dataset. Despite it's much easier and faster to recognize the instrument by its shape, they say that if the instrument is not present on the frame it's still possible to recognize it from the audio.

5 CONCLUSION

To summarize, this paper makes several contributions. First, we introduce a multimodal method for musical instrument recognition in user-generated videos. Second, we show the case when visual object recognition can be enhanced by adding audio information. Third, we evaluate several baseline convolutional neural network architectures for audio classification. Fourth, we investigate the influence of amount of frames used for image-based object recognition in video and the influence of using a pre-trained model. We evaluate our method on a heterogeneous large-scale dataset of user-generated videos so that it can be used with different datasets and scenarios.

Our results demonstrate that both modalities are important to obtain better performance. In addition, we show that the audio-only network and our multimodal approach perform very close to the human performance rate for the musical instrument subset of automatically annotated YouTube-8M dataset. This illustrates the fact that people may not only determine the video concept based on visual cues but also on the auditory ones. Moreover, the considered audio-only models clearly outperform the video-only models and the multimodal network performs better than those based on a single modality in one of the considered datasets, illustrating the advantage of multiple modalities.

In future work, we will investigate the prospects of joint multimodal hidden representation learning, cross-correlations between

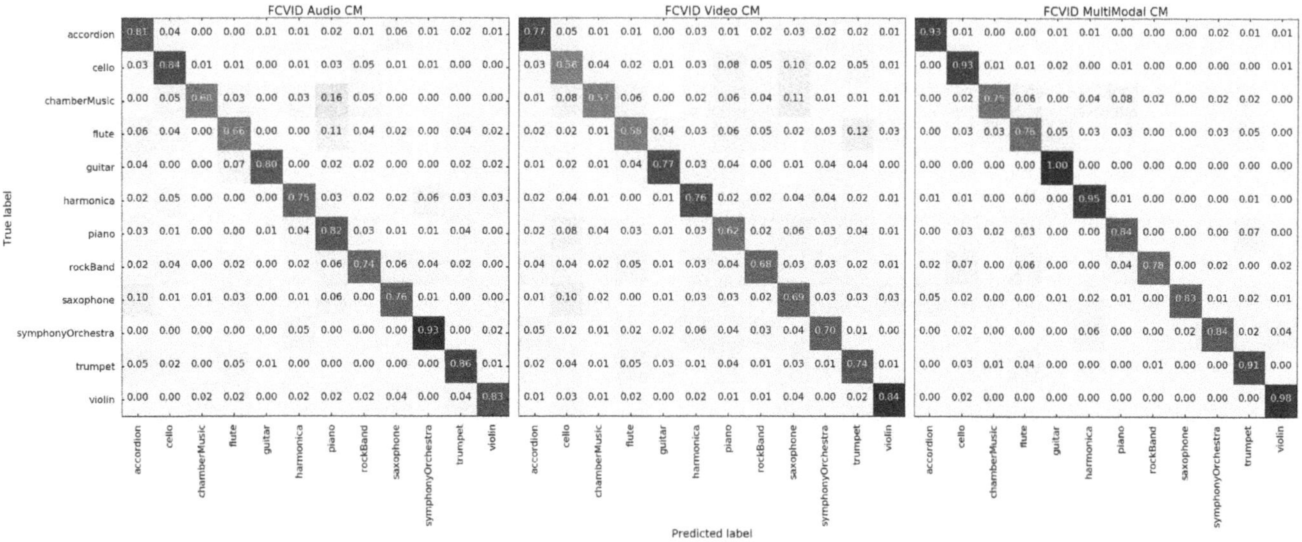

Figure 2: Comparison of confusion matrices for FCVID dataset. From left to right: audio-only recognition, video-only-recognition, multimodal recognition.

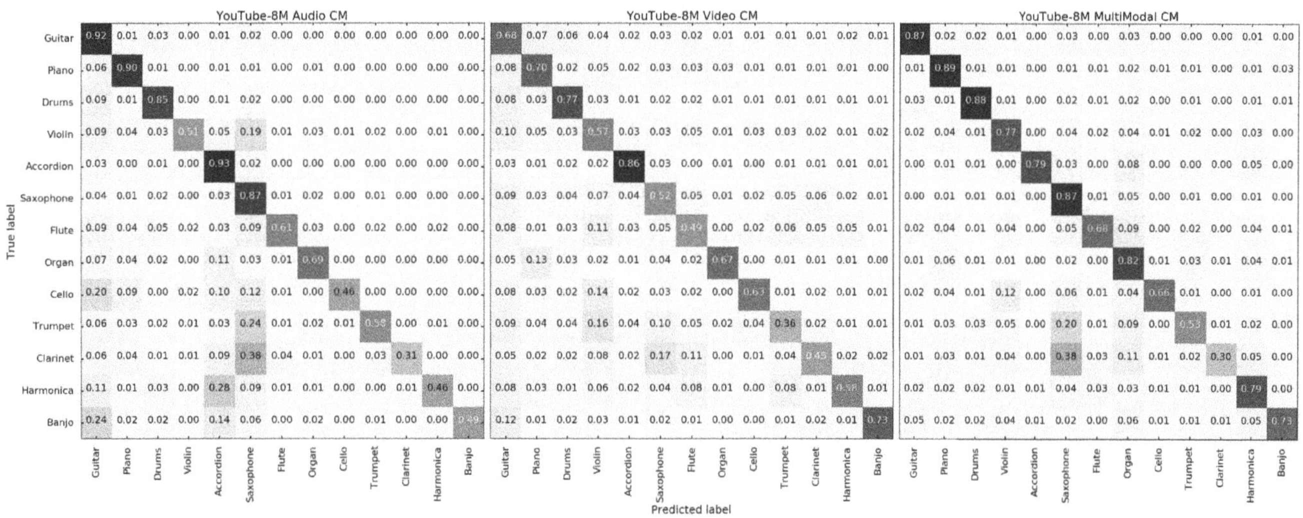

Figure 3: Comparison of confusion matrices for YouTube-8M dataset. From left to right: audio-only recognition, video-only-recognition, multimodal recognition.

audio and visual modalities, and the impact of dynamic video information.

ACKNOWLEDGMENTS

This work is partly supported by the Spanish Ministry of Economy and Competitiveness under the Maria de Maeztu Units of Excellence Programme (MDM-2015-0502), the CASAS Spanish research project (TIN2015-70816-R), and project TIN2015-70410-C2-1-R (MINECO/FEDER, UE). We gratefully acknowledge the support of NVIDIA Corporation with the donation of the Titan X GPU used for this research.

REFERENCES

[1] Martín Abadi, Ashish Agarwal, Paul Barham, Eugene Brevdo, Zhifeng Chen, Craig Citro, Greg S Corrado, Andy Davis, Jeffrey Dean, Matthieu Devin, and others. 2016. Tensorflow: Large-scale machine learning on heterogeneous distributed systems. *arXiv preprint arXiv:1603.04467* (2016).

[2] Sami Abu-El-Haija, Nisarg Kothari, Joonseok Lee, Paul Natsev, George Toderici, Balakrishnan Varadarajan, and Sudheendra Vijayanarasimhan. 2016. YouTube-8M: A Large-Scale Video Classification Benchmark. *CoRR* abs/1609.08675 (2016). http://arxiv.org/abs/1609.08675

[3] Yusuf Aytar, Carl Vondrick, and Antonio Torralba. 2016. Soundnet: Learning sound representations from unlabeled video. In *Advances in Neural Information Processing Systems*. 892–900.

[4] Ana M. Barbancho, Lorenzo J. Tardón, Javier López-Carrasco, Jana Eggink, and Isabel Barbancho. 2015. Automatic Classification of Personal Video Recordings Based on Audiovisual Features. *Know.-Based Syst.* 89, C (Nov. 2015), 218–227. DOI: http://dx.doi.org/10.1016/j.knosys.2015.07.005

[5] Alessio Bazzica, Cynthia CS Liem, and Alan Hanjalic. 2016. On detecting the playing/non-playing activity of musicians in symphonic music videos. *Computer Vision and Image Understanding* 144 (2016), 188–204.

[6] J. Bosch, J. Janer, Ferdinand Fuhrmann, and Perfecto Herrera. 2012. A Comparison of Sound Segregation Techniques for Predominant Instrument Recognition in Musical Audio Signals. In *13th International Society for Music Information Retrieval Conference (ISMIR 2012)*. Porto, Portugal, 559–564.

[7] Fabian Caba Heilbron, Victor Escorcia, Bernard Ghanem, and Juan Carlos Niebles. 2015. Activitynet: A large-scale video benchmark for human activity understanding. In *Proceedings of the IEEE Conference on Computer Vision and Pattern Recognition*. 961–970.

[8] Pritish Chandna, Marius Miron, Jordi Janer, and Emilia Gómez. 2017. Monoaural Audio Source Separation Using Deep Convolutional Neural Networks. In *13th International Conference on Latent Variable Analysis and Signal Separation (LVA ICA2017)*.

[9] Keunwoo Choi, George Fazekas, and Mark Sandler. 2016. Automatic Tagging Using Deep Convolutional Neural Networks. In *International Society of Music Information Retrieval Conference, New York, USA*. ISMIR.

[10] François Chollet. 2015. Keras. https://github.com/fchollet/keras. (2015).

[11] François Chollet. 2016. Xception: Deep Learning with Depthwise Separable Convolutions. *arXiv preprint arXiv:1610.02357* (2016).

[12] J. Deng, W. Dong, R. Socher, L.-J. Li, K. Li, and L. Fei-Fei. 2009. ImageNet: A Large-Scale Hierarchical Image Database. In *CVPR09*.

[13] Dumitru Erhan, Yoshua Bengio, Aaron Courville, Pierre-Antoine Manzagol, Pascal Vincent, and Samy Bengio. 2010. Why Does Unsupervised Pre-training Help Deep Learning? *J. Mach. Learn. Res.* 11 (March 2010), 625–660.

[14] Miquel Espi, Masakiyo Fujimoto, Keisuke Kinoshita, and Tomohiro Nakatani. 2015. Exploiting spectro-temporal locality in deep learning based acoustic event detection. *EURASIP Journal on Audio, Speech, and Music Processing* 1 (2015), 26.

[15] Christoph Feichtenhofer, Axel Pinz, and Andrew Zisserman. 2016. Convolutional two-stream network fusion for video action recognition. In *Proceedings of the IEEE Conference on Computer Vision and Pattern Recognition*. 1933–1941.

[16] Yoonchang Han, Jaehun Kim, and Kyogu Lee. 2016. Deep convolutional neural networks for predominant instrument recognition in polyphonic music. *arXiv preprint arXiv:1605.09507* (2016).

[17] Perfecto Herrera-Boyer, Geoffroy Peeters, and Shlomo Dubnov. 2003. Automatic Classification of Musical Instrument Sounds. *Journal of New Music Research* 32, 1 (2003), 3–21. DOI: http://dx.doi.org/10.1076/jnmr.32.1.3.16798

[18] Shawn Hershey, Sourish Chaudhuri, Daniel P. W. Ellis, Jort F. Gemmeke, Aren Jansen, Channing Moore, Manoj Plakal, Devin Platt, Rif A. Saurous, Bryan Seybold, Malcolm Slaney, Ron Weiss, and Kevin Wilson. 2016. CNN Architectures for Large-Scale Audio Classification. In *arXiv*. https://arxiv.org/abs/1609.09430

[19] Di Hu, Xuelong Li, and others. 2016. Temporal multimodal learning in audiovisual speech recognition. In *Proceedings of the IEEE Conference on Computer Vision and Pattern Recognition*. 3574–3582.

[20] Jing Huang and Brian Kingsbury. 2013. Audio-visual deep learning for noise robust speech recognition. In *2013 IEEE International Conference on Acoustics, Speech and Signal Processing*. IEEE, 7596–7599.

[21] Sergey Ioffe and Christian Szegedy. 2015. Batch Normalization: Accelerating Deep Network Training by Reducing Internal Covariate Shift. In *Proceedings of the 32nd International Conference on Machine Learning (ICML-15)*. 448–456.

[22] M. I. Jordan and T. M. Mitchell. 2015. Machine learning: Trends, perspectives, and prospects. *Science* 349, 6245 (2015), 255–260. DOI: http://dx.doi.org/10.1126/science.aaa8415

[23] Andrej Karpathy, George Toderici, Sanketh Shetty, Thomas Leung, Rahul Sukthankar, and Li Fei-Fei. 2014. Large-scale video classification with convolutional neural networks. In *Proceedings of the IEEE conference on Computer Vision and Pattern Recognition*. 1725–1732.

[24] Yelin Kim, Honglak Lee, and Emily Mower Provost. 2013. Deep learning for robust feature generation in audiovisual emotion recognition. In *2013 IEEE International Conference on Acoustics, Speech and Signal Processing*. IEEE, 3687–3691.

[25] Diederik Kingma and Jimmy Ba. 2014. Adam: A method for stochastic optimization. *arXiv preprint arXiv:1412.6980* (2014).

[26] Vincent Lostanlen and Carmine-Emanuele Cella. 2016. Deep convolutional networks on the pitch spiral for musical instrument recognition. In *Proceedings of the 17th International Society for Music Information Retrieval Conference (ISMIR)*. New York City, NY, USA.

[27] Bernardo Marenco, Magdalena Fuentes, Florencia Lanzaro, Martín Rocamora, and Alvaro Gómez. 2015. *A Multimodal Approach for Percussion Music Transcription from Audio and Video*. Springer International Publishing, Cham, 92–99. DOI: http://dx.doi.org/10.1007/978-3-319-25751-8_12

[28] L. Nanni, Y.M.G. Costa, D.R. Lucio, C.N. Silla Jr., and S. Brahnam. 2017. Combining visual and acoustic features for audio classification tasks. *Pattern Recognition Letters* 88 (2017), 49 – 56. DOI: http://dx.doi.org/10.1016/j.patrec.2017.01.013

[29] Joe Yue-Hei Ng, M. Hausknecht, S. Vijayanarasimhan, O. Vinyals, R. Monga, and G. Toderici. 2015. Beyond short snippets: Deep networks for video classification. In *2015 IEEE Conference on Computer Vision and Pattern Recognition (CVPR)*. 4694–4702. DOI: http://dx.doi.org/10.1109/CVPR.2015.7299101

[30] Jiquan Ngiam, Aditya Khosla, Mingyu Kim, Juhan Nam, Honglak Lee, and Andrew Y Ng. 2011. Multimodal deep learning. In *Proceedings of the 28th international conference on machine learning (ICML-11)*. 689–696.

[31] Lei Pang and Chong-Wah Ngo. 2015. Mutlimodal Learning with Deep Boltzmann Machine for Emotion Prediction in User Generated Videos. In *Proceedings of the 5th ACM on International Conference on Multimedia Retrieval (ICMR '15)*. ACM, New York, NY, USA, 619–622. DOI: http://dx.doi.org/10.1145/2671188.2749400

[32] Jordi Pons and Xavier Serra. 2017. Designing Efficient Architectures for Modeling Temporal Features with Convolutional Neural Networks. In *42th International Conference on Acoustics, Speech, and Signal Processing (ICASSP 2017)*. IEEE, New Orleans, USA.

[33] Justin Salamon and Juan Pablo Bello. 2016. Deep Convolutional Neural Networks and Data Augmentation for Environmental Sound Classification. *CoRR* abs/1608.04363 (2016). http://arxiv.org/abs/1608.04363

[34] Alexander Schindler and Andreas Rauber. 2015. *An Audio-Visual Approach to Music Genre Classification through Affective Color Features*. Springer International Publishing, Cham, 61–67. DOI: http://dx.doi.org/10.1007/978-3-319-16354-3_8

[35] Jan Schluter and Sebastian Bock. 2014. Improved musical onset detection with convolutional neural networks. In *2014 IEEE International Conference on Acoustics, speech and signal processing (ICASSP)*. IEEE, 6979–6983.

[36] S. Sigtia, E. Benetos, and S. Dixon. 2016. An End-to-End Neural Network for Polyphonic Piano Music Transcription. *IEEE/ACM Transactions on Audio, Speech, and Language Processing* 24, 5 (May 2016), 927–939. DOI: http://dx.doi.org/10.1109/TASLP.2016.2533858

[37] Karen Simonyan and Andrew Zisserman. 2014. Two-stream convolutional networks for action recognition in videos. In *Advances in Neural Information Processing Systems*. 568–576.

[38] Olga Slizovskaia, Emilia Gómez, and Gloria Haro. 2016. Automatic musical instrument recognition in audiovisual recordings by combining image and audio classification strategies. In *13th Sound and Music Computing Conference (SMC 2016)*. Hamburg, Germany.

[39] Kihyuk Sohn, Wenling Shang, and Honglak Lee. 2014. Improved multimodal deep learning with variation of information. In *Advances in Neural Information Processing Systems*. 2141–2149.

[40] Nitish Srivastava and Ruslan R Salakhutdinov. 2012. Multimodal learning with deep boltzmann machines. In *Advances in neural information processing systems*. 2222–2230.

[41] Christian Szegedy, Vincent Vanhoucke, Sergey Ioffe, Jon Shlens, and Zbigniew Wojna. 2016. Rethinking the inception architecture for computer vision. In *Proceedings of the IEEE Conference on Computer Vision and Pattern Recognition*. 2818–2826.

[42] Du Tran, Lubomir Bourdev, Rob Fergus, Lorenzo Torresani, and Manohar Paluri. 2015. Learning Spatiotemporal Features with 3D Convolutional Networks. In *Proceedings of the 2015 IEEE International Conference on Computer Vision (ICCV) (ICCV '15)*. IEEE Computer Society, Washington, DC, USA, 4489–4497. DOI: http://dx.doi.org/10.1109/ICCV.2015.510

[43] Aäron van den Oord, Sander Dieleman, Heiga Zen, Karen Simonyan, Oriol Vinyals, Alex Graves, Nal Kalchbrenner, Andrew W. Senior, and Koray Kavukcuoglu. 2016. WaveNet: A Generative Model for Raw Audio. *CoRR* abs/1609.03499 (2016). http://arxiv.org/abs/1609.03499

[44] Gül Varol, Ivan Laptev, and Cordelia Schmid. 2016. Long-term Temporal Convolutions for Action Recognition. *arXiv preprint arXiv:1604.04494* (2016).

[45] Baohan Xu, Yanwei Fu, Yu-Gang Jiang, Boyang Li, and Leonid Sigal. 2016. Video Emotion Recognition with Transferred Deep Feature Encodings. In *Proceedings of the 2016 ACM on International Conference on Multimedia Retrieval (ICMR '16)*. ACM, New York, NY, USA, 15–22.

[46] Jun Wang Xiangyang Xue Shih-Fu Chang Yu-Gang Jiang, Zuxuan Wu. 2015. Exploiting Feature and Class Relationships in Video Categorization with Regularized Deep Neural Networks. *arXiv preprint arXiv:1502.07209* (2015).

[47] Shiqing Zhang, Shiliang Zhang, Tiejun Huang, and Wen Gao. 2016. Multimodal Deep Convolutional Neural Network for Audio-Visual Emotion Recognition. In *Proceedings of the 2016 ACM on International Conference on Multimedia Retrieval*. ACM, 281–284.

A Spatio-Temporal Category Representation for Brand Popularity Prediction

Gijs Overgoor
Amsterdam Business School
University of Amsterdam
g.overgoor@uva.nl

Masoud Mazloom
Informatics Institute
University of Amsterdam
m.mazloom@uva.nl

Marcel Worring
Informatics Institute
University of Amsterdam
m.worring@uva.nl

Robert Rietveld
Amsterdam Business School
University of Amsterdam
r.l.rietveld@uva.nl

Willemijn van Dolen
Amsterdam Business School
University of Amsterdam
w.m.vandolen@uva.nl

ABSTRACT

Social media has become an important tool in marketing for companies to communicate with their consumers. Firms post content and consumers express their appreciation for the brand by following them on social media and/or by liking the firm generated content. Understanding the consumers' attitudes towards a particular brand on social media (i.e. liking) is important. In this paper, we focus on a method for brand popularity prediction and use it to analyze social media posts generated by various brands during a specific period of time. Existing instance-based popularity prediction methods focus on popularity of images, text, and individual posts. We propose a new category based popularity prediction method by incorporating the spatio-temporal dimension in the representation. In particular, we focus on brands as a specific category. We study the behavior of our method by performing four experiments on a collection of brand posts crawled from Instagram with 150,000 posts related to 430 active brands. Our experiments establish that 1) we are able to accurately predict the popularity of posts generated by brands, 2) we can use this post-level trained model to predict the popularity of a brand, 3) by constructing category representations we are

ACM Reference format:
Gijs Overgoor, Masoud Mazloom, Marcel Worring, Robert Rietveld, and Willemijn van Dolen. 2017. A Spatio-Temporal Category Representation for Brand Popularity Prediction. In *Proceedings of ICMR '17, June 6–9, 2017, Bucharest, Romania*, , 9 pages.
DOI: http://dx.doi.org/10.1145/3078971.3078998

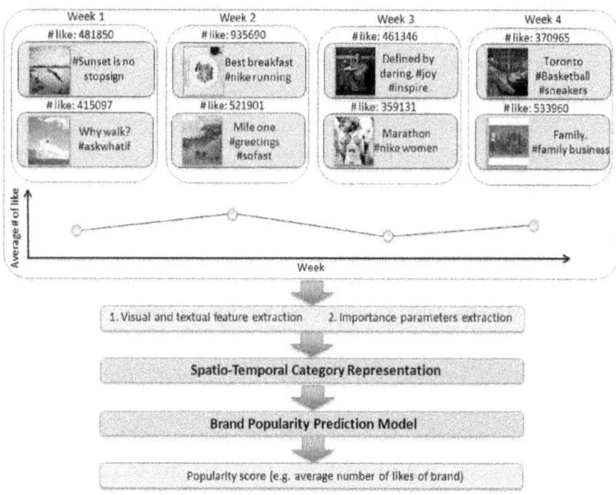

Figure 1: We propose a spatio-temporal category representation to model the temporal behavior of category specific content and use it for predicting the popularity of the category.

1 INTRODUCTION

Social media has become an integral part of people's lives and understanding the drivers behind popularity of content on social media brings us closer to understanding people's interests, opinions, and general behavior. Therefore, in recent years the prediction of the popularity of online content has been studied extensively [1, 3, 6, 7, 9, 12, 13]. However, modeling the user's interests is difficult as they are partly expressed implicitly via the visual and the textual content of the post the user generates. A further complicating factor is that the interests of the users change over time. Because of this [8], one would expect the popularity of content posted by brands to change over time as well. And indeed, some factors of popularity such as user activeness and image prevalence variability can be viewed as time-sensitive [20], which means that for a most accurate analysis of popularity one needs to address temporal dynamics. Various automated systems have been developed to extract important information from different types of user generated content using domain agnostic methods. These automated systems have given us the ability to gain insight in what is posted by users on a large scale. True insight, however, is only possible when it has a direct impact within the domain of study [15].

One particular domain in which insight in social media has an enormous impact is business and marketing. Social media enables businesses to reach thousands of users at the same time and opens a line of communication between them and consumers which is far more interactive and direct than what was available before. Analyzing and effectively using social media holds numerous opportunities

ICMR '17, June 6–9, 2017, Bucharest, Romania

ISBN 978-1-4503-4701-3/17/06...$15.00
DOI: http://dx.doi.org/10.1145/3078971.3078998

for enhancing customer engagement and brand development. Remarkable research efforts show that social media has dramatically altered the way companies market their businesses. In [10], Mangold *et al.* state that social media as a new channel and context, is crucial in today's marketing-mix. Zeng *et al.* in [22] describe how businesses profit from using social media as a source of information for business intelligence as well as an execution platform for product design and innovation, relationship management, and marketing. In [16, 17], the authors show the importance of analyzing social media from a business perspective. In [16], Risius *et al.* demonstrate the value of social media analytics for building brand loyalty. All these works [10, 16, 17, 22] use several statistics of user posts for analyzing different problems in business without analyzing their contents.

One of the interesting and challenging problems in the marketing and business community now is predicting the popularity of a brand based on the content of what they post. Brand popularity reflects a brand's recognition on social media, which comes from positive experiences of consumers. Understanding the drivers behind the popularity, therefore enables brands to enhance social media strategies for establishing a better relationship with consumers. Recent research on predicting the popularity of a user post has focused on visual and textual content [1, 3, 6, 7, 9, 12, 13], with methods depending on the type of platform and social context. Elaborating on the success of recent post popularity prediction in social media [1, 3, 6, 7, 9, 12, 13] we continue the study by predicting the popularity of brands. We follow [12] for analyzing the content generated by brands. In this paper, for the study of brand popularity prediction, we use the content of posts generated by the brands themselves instead of user posts for representing brands.

Up to now, focal priority has been cross-sectional modeling of popularity based on users and the content they generate, however as indicated before temporal dynamics are also of importance as users' interests change over time [8, 20]. Motivated by [8, 20], we propose a novel approach for incorporating the temporal dimension of content posted by brands to predict their popularity. In this paper we, therefore, incorporate the temporal dimension in the brand representation to account for changes over time in popularity that are not solely reflected by the content. We attempt to answer to the question: *How do the spatial and temporal properties of the content generated by a brand affect its popularity?.* Figure 1 visualizes our proposal for representing a brand and how we utilize it for the brand popularity prediction problem.

Of course popularity depends on how users express their opinions and this varies over the different social media platforms. Among those platforms, Instagram is used for self-expression by images with a description through captions and hashtags. Unlike some other social media platforms, the content that is generated by the brands will always be visible for users. As a consequence Instagram allows for visual marketing that is not controlled. Moreover, the hashtags allow brands to target individuals and engage with them directly. Consequently, top brands on Instagram are seeing a per-follower engagement[1] (i.e. likes per follower) rate of 4.21, which is 58 times higher than Facebook and 120 times higher than Twitter. These aspects make Instagram of particular interest in the research of brand popularity prediction. In this paper we, therefore, investigate brand popularity prediction on a dataset crawled from Instagram.

We make the following main contributions in this paper:

- We show the effectiveness of post popularity prediction on content generated exclusively by brands.
- We initiate the study of brand popularity prediction based on brand generated content on social media.
- We propose a spatio-temporal category representation for brand popularity prediction.
- We introduce a new dataset, for brand popularity prediction, obtained for free from Instagram by a simple crawling procedure.

We organize the remainder of this paper as follows. We start by considering related work in Section 2. Section 3 describes our problem formulation and we define our brand representation for predicting the popularity of brand. We introduce the experimental setup on our dataset in Section 4. Results are presented in Section 5. Finally, Section 6 concludes with a summary of our findings and a discussion of several possible directions for future work.

2 RELATED WORK

In the past few years, extensive research has been done in analyzing the content generated by users on social media. In this section, we first review existing studies in post popularity prediction, then we explain those works that focus on post popularity prediction using temporal information.

2.1 Post Popularity Prediction

Popularity prediction of user generated posts in social media has recently received a lot of attention from the research community [1, 3, 6, 7, 9, 12, 13]. While some of the work has focused on predicting the popularity of textual content, such as messages or tweets on Twitter [1, 7], recent research focuses on the image content [3, 6, 9, 12, 13].

Notable examples of text based popularity prediction are [7] and [1]. In [7], Hong *et al.* predict the number of retweets on twitter using textual features extracted from tweets. They report the effect of combining textual features with contextual features of the user as well as temporal dynamics of retweet chains and suggest the importance of including a temporal dimension into popularity prediction. Bae *et al.* in [1] report the relation between the sentiment and popularity of tweets. These works successfully predict popularity of posts using textual data. However, visual content, which is rich in information, is not addressed.

In [3, 6, 9, 12, 13], the authors focus primarily on extracting different visual features from posts for predicting the popularity of an image and measuring the impact of these features on popularity. In [9], Khosla *et al.* report the results of image popularity prediction using simple image features, such as color, gist, gradient, texture, and low-level and high-level deep learning features as indicators for objects in images. They consider the problem of popularity prediction as a learning to rank problem. In [13], McParlane *et al.* learn a binary classifier for investigating the popularity of a post. They report the effect of social factors of each post such as

[1]http://blogs.forrester.com/nate elliott/14 04 29 Instagram is the king of social engagement

how many followers a user has, the number of tags attached to the photo, and the length of the title. Moreover, they report the result of popularity prediction using content factors such as the number of faces in the images, analysis of the scene, and color features. Cappallo *et al.* in [3] learn a ranker by considering popular and unpopular latent factors. In [6, 12] the authors investigate the effect of sentiment analysis on the popularity of a post. Gelli *et al.* in [6] investigate the effect of visual sentiment analysis on images as well as contextual features used in [13]. They report the potential of predicting the popularity of images using visual sentiment scores as a feature, which was first introduced in [2] to detect sentiment in an image. Mazloom *et al.* in [12] initiate the problem of predicting popularity of brand-related user posts automatically in the business and marketing community. They further propose usage of an ensemble of cues, extracted from visual and textual channel of posts, which are important in analyzing brand popularity. All these works [6, 9, 12, 13] emphasize that visual and textual features are complementary in predicting the popularity of user generated posts. However, these works [3, 6, 9, 12, 13] don't address the use of temporal dynamics in popularity prediction. Different from these works, we propose to incorporate the temporal dimension of brand generated posts since multiple factors of popularity are time sensitive [20]. Moreover, [3, 6, 9, 12, 13] are limited to popularity prediction of individual posts. We aim for popularity of categories based on multiple posts.

2.2 Temporal Post Popularity Prediction

In [21], Yang *et al.* analyze the temporal dynamics in social media content. They propose the k-spectral centroid algorithm for clustering time series to find patterns in social media. McParlane *et al.* in [13] utilize time, day and season in their representation of posts for predicting popularity. The time at which content is posted can be classified into time of day (i.e. morning, afternoon, evening, night), whether it is a week or a weekend day and also the season in which the content is posted. Wu *et al.* in [20] argue how time plays a crucial role in social media popularity. To capture the temporal dynamics of image popularity, they factorize popularity in the user-item context and the time-sensitive context. Different from these works [13, 20, 21] which focus on considering temporal dynamics on user generated post popularity prediction, we aim to incorporate the temporal dimension of posts generated by a brand to construct a category representation for predicting the popularity of a brand.

3 OUR PROPOSAL

In this paper, we aim to predict popularity of a category by introducing a category representation that incorporates temporal dynamics. To that end we consider each individual brand as a category throughout this work. Our category popularity prediction framework consists of two main parts, schematically illustrated in Figure 2. In the training phase, at first, we construct a category representation from a dataset of content generated by categories. We use the average number of likes of categories as labels. Second, in the prediction phase, we construct a representation of new categories and compute a popularity score. Before introducing the proposed framework for popularity prediction, the notation and key concepts will be formally introduced.

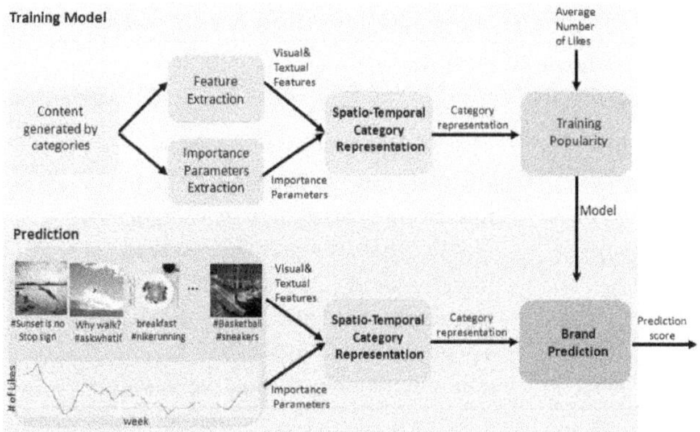

Figure 2: Dataflow for learning a category representation and using it for brand popularity prediction.

3.1 Problem Formalization

Given a specified category, popularity prediction of a category is the task of computing a score that shows how popular the category will be in comparison to other categories, based on the content that they generate. For consistency, we use B_x to indicate the given category x. We aim to construct a real-valued function $f(B_x)$ which produces a score for the popularity of B_x. By sorting all categories in a test set according to $f()$ in descending order, a list of most popular categories will be obtained.

Let $B = \{(B_1, y_1), (B_2, y_2), ..., (B_m, y_m)\}$ be a set of m categories, where y_i is the popularity score of category B_i. Suppose category B_i has been shared in total n_i posts during the specific period of time; $B_i = \{P_{i1}, P_{i2}, ..., P_{in_i}\}$, where P_{i1} and P_{in_i} are the first and last post shared by the category. Each post $P_{ij}, j = 1, ..., n_i$ has received a certain number of likes, α_{ij}, during a specific time which defines the popularity of post P_{ij}. Let $l_i = \{\alpha_{i1}, \alpha_{i2}, ..., \alpha_{in_i}\}$ be the set of popularity scores of B_i posts during the specific time period. We define $y_i = f(B_i) = \frac{1}{n_i} \sum_{j=1}^{n_i} \alpha_{ij}$, the average number of likes of the category's posts, as the popularity score of B_i.

The difficulty in constructing $f(B_x)$ largely depends on the representation of category B_x. We hypothesize that what makes a category become popular on the web, captured in the average number of likes a category will receive, depends on the content the category generates. The key idea of our proposal is to represent a category, based on the content shared on the web, as accurate as possible before predicting it's popularity.

Next, we show in section 3.2 how to construct a spatio-temporal category representation based on content generated and posted by a category. For the ease of reference, Table 1 lists the main notation used throughout this work.

3.2 Category Representation

Let us now explain how a specific category B_i can be represented using its generated content during a specific time. We propose to construct a category representation, $h(B_i)$,by a set of posts $P_{ij}, j = 1, ..., n_i$ generated and shared by B_i, α_{ij} the relative importance of P_{ij} based on the number of likes users gave to P_{ij}, and $\gamma_{it}, t =$

Table 1: Main notations used in this work

Notation	Definition
B	a set of categories
B_i	a set of posts of the ith category
P_{ij}	j^{th} post of category B_i
n_i	number of posts shared by category B_i
α_{ij}	number of likes which P_{ij} received
γ_{ij}	importance of category B_i in j^{th} week
y_i	popularity score of category B_i
$h(B_i)$	a representation of category B_i
$f()$	a function for computing the popularity

$1, ..., K$ the relative importance of B_i per week based on the moving average popularity time series, with $\sum_{t=1}^{K} \gamma_{it} = 1$ for all categories. Suppose $P_{ij} = (P_{ij}^v, P_{ij}^t)$ consists of two components namely visual and textual content respectively. To find different representations of post P_{ij}, we extract visual features, $z(P_{ij}^v)$, and textual features, $z(P_{ij}^t)$, of P_{ij} and use them for representing B_i.

Similar to [12], we use both visual and textual components in the representation of category B_i as they carry some information related to the popularity of a category. In addition, we make use of a third component, a temporal dimension, with which we aim to capture changing interests in time of users. Depending on how to use these components, we present three variants of category representation $h(B_i)$, namely

(1) Naive Category Representation (NCR): The construction of the naive brand category representation is simply an average pooling over all features of posts of B_i without considering importance parameters. The representation is defined as follows:

$$h_{NCR}^v(B_i) = \frac{1}{n_i} \sum_{j=1}^{n_i} z(P_{ij}^v) \tag{1}$$

where n_i is the total number of posts generated by category B_i.

(2) Weighted Category Representation (WCR): The construction of the weighted category representation is based on the weekly importance parameter γ_{it}. The weekly importance parameter is derived from the popularity time series of a category and it indicates the relative importance of a category per week compared to the other weeks. The representation is defined as follows:

$$h_{WCR}^v(B_i) = \sum_{t=1}^{K} \gamma_{it} \sum_{j \in I_{it}} \frac{z(P_{ij}^v)}{n_{it}} \tag{2}$$

where I_{it} is the set of posts of B_i within week t. K is the total number of weeks in the time series and n_{it} is the total number of posts generated by B_i in week t. The second sum in the formula shows the average pooling of visual features of posts per week.

(3) Spatio-Temporal Category Representation (STCR): This representation is based on both importance parameters, γ_{it}, and α_{ij}. The weighted aggregation based on the importance parameters is given by the following equation:

$$h_{STCR}^v(B_i) = \sum_{t=1}^{K} \gamma_{it} \sum_{j \in I_{it}} \frac{\alpha_{ij} * z(P_{ij}^v)}{A_{it}} \tag{3}$$

where A_{it} is the total number of likes B_i received in week t.

Replacing $z(P_{ij}^v)$ by $z(P_{ij}^t)$ in the above three equations, we produce $h_{NCR}^t(B_i)$, $h_{WCR}^t(B_i)$, and $h_{STCR}^t(B_i)$, three category representations using textual components of posts of B_i.

Next, we show in section 3.3 how to tackle brand popularity prediction using the different category representation methods.

3.3 Brand Popularity Prediction

After representing brands with the category representation, we use it for the problem of brand popularity prediction. Suppose $B = B_{TR} \cup B_{TE}$ is a set of m brands with $B_{TR} = \{(B_1, y_1), (B_2, y_2), ..., (B_e, y_e)\}$ is a training set consist of e brands and $B_{TE} = \{(B_{e+1}, y_{e+1}), ..., (B_m, y_m)\}$ is a test set consisting of the other brands in B. By dividing the brands in a train and test set using the formulas explained in section 3.2, we define B_{TR} and B_{TE} as two matrix representations of all brands:

$$\begin{aligned} B_{TR} &= [h(B_1), h(B_2), ..., h(B_e)] \\ B_{TE} &= [h(B_{e+1}), h(B_{e+2}), ..., h(B_m)] \end{aligned} \tag{4}$$

Each row of B_{TR} and B_{TE} represents a brand . We train a brand popularity model on B_{TR} and report the result of popularity prediction on B_{TE}.

Let $h(B_i)$ be the category representation of brand B_i and y_i show the popularity of B_i. The idea is to optimize w, parameter of function $f_w()$, on B_{TR} to minimize the error between y_i and $f_w(h(B_i)) = w^T h(B_i)$. We consider the problem of brand popularity prediction as a regression problem and try to optimize the following objective function:

$$\textstyle\sum_{i=1}^{e}(y_i - f_w(h(B_i))) - C \sum_{k=1}^{n} {w_k}^2 \tag{5}$$

which can be formulated as

$$\arg\max_w \textstyle\sum_{i=1}^{e} \log p(y_i | h(B_i), w) - C \sum_{k=1}^{n} {w_k}^2 \tag{6}$$

where $\log p(y_i | h(B_i), w) = \frac{1}{1+e^{-w^T h(B_i)}}$.

To solve the problem and find the optimal value of w we use L2 regularized L2 loss Support Vector Regression, as used in [9, 12], from the LIBLINEAR package [5]. After training the model and finding the optimum value of w on B_{TR}, we use it for prediction of brand popularity on B_{TE} and report the rank correlation between the predicted scores and grand truth.

4 EXPERIMENTAL SETUP

We investigate the effectiveness of our proposal for predicting popularity of a brand by performing a series of experiments on a dataset crawled from Instagram.

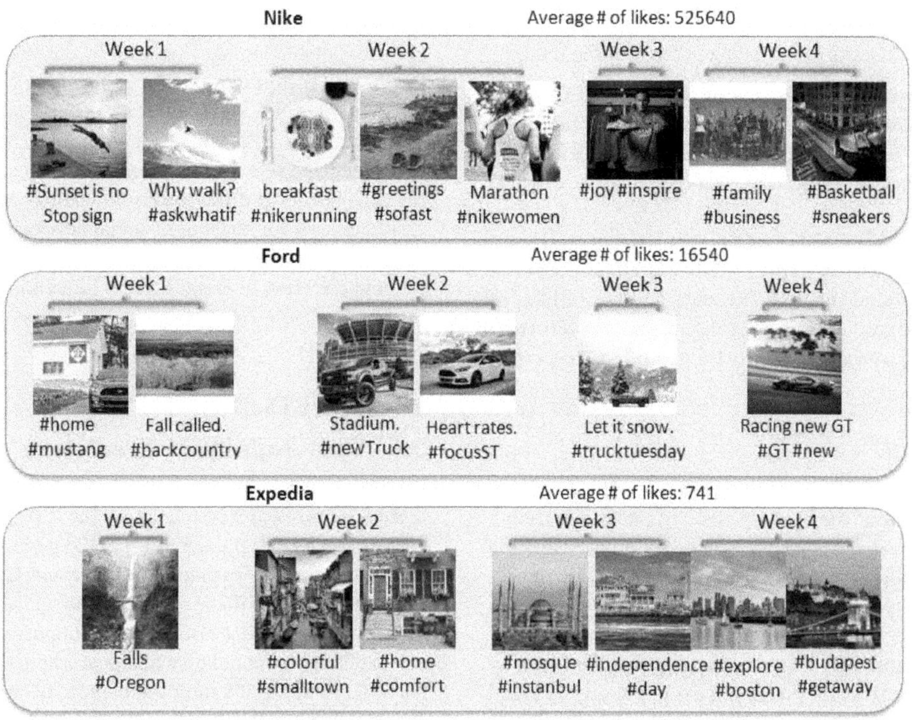

Figure 3: Example of three brands, *Nike, Ford, Expedia* and their generated content during four weeks from our dataset.

4.1 Dataset

Since there is no existing dataset for predicting the popularity of a brand, we created one by crawling the content brands post on Instagram. A grand variety of brands have adopted Instagram for the means of visual marketing. Unlike other social media platforms, the content that is generated by the brands will always be visible by users. Moreover, the hashtags allow brands to target certain individuals and engage with them directly. This makes our Instagram dataset especially relevant for the research on brand popularity prediction. Our dataset consists of 150,000 posts generated by 430 active brands, such as *Expedia, Ford, Nike* and *McDonald's*, across 27 different industries like *Travel, Automotive, Sports* and *Fast Food.* All the content is generated between 01/05/2015 and 30/04/2016 and the brands behind the content are considered active, which means that they at least generate content every week. Figure 3 shows examples of posts with the number of likes generated by three highly popular brands. [2]

The dataset is split into two parts, where two thirds are used for training the model and one third is used as a test set for evaluation of the model.

4.2 Implementation details

Feature extraction To represent a post in our dataset we use the following state of the art features:

Textual features We use the textual features used in [12]:

- *W2V* A trained deep neural network proposed in [14], which computes a 300 dimension vector by mapping each tag onto its Word2Vec representation. A post is then represented by average pooling of the W2V representation of all tags in the post.
- *Textual Sentiment* Represented by making use of SentiStrength [19]. First the stop words are removed and stemming is performed. The sentiment value of each tag is computed using SentiStrength to generate positive (ranging from 1 to 5) and negative (ranging from -1 to -5) sentiment scores.
- *Terms* a sparse representation with a length of 5250, where the length of the vector equals the number of unique tags that occur in at least 75 posts. Only the values of those elements corresponding to the tags of the post receive a weighting score.

Visual features We use the visual features as used in [12]:

- *CNN-Pool5* As low-level visual features, we used the 1024-dimensional features from pooling the last fully connected layer of the Deep Net in [18] which is trained on ImageNet [4]
- *Concepts* we extract the convolutional neural network features, initially proposed in [18] and trained to identify those 15,293 ImageNet [4] concept categories, for which at least 200 positive examples are available. We represent the image of each post by the 15,293-dimensional output of the softmax layer of the network as an effective representation has been shown in [11].
- *Visual Sentiment* A feature based on the Visual Sentiment Ontology which was first introduced in [2] to detect sentiment in an image. The sentiment ontology representation

[2] http://isis-data.science.uva.nl/Masoud/ICMR17Data

consist of a 1,200 dimensional vector with probabilities of Adjective Noun Pairs (ANP) being present in the image.

Popularity prediction As we mentioned in section 3.3, we use an L2 regularized L2 loss Support Vector Regression to predict the popularity of a brand. To find the optimal value of the regularization parameter C, we consider 5-fold cross-validation on C for $C \in \{0.001, 0.1, 1, 10, 100\}$.

Evaluation metric After predicting the popularity of each brand at test time we compute the Spearman's rank correlation between the prediction and ground truth, the average number of likes of the posts which the brand shared in Instagram, which returns a value between [-1, 1]. A value close to 1 corresponds to perfect correlation.

4.3 Experiments

Experiment 1: ***Post popularity prediction*** In this experiment we evaluate the popularity of the brand generated posts. We train a post level popularity model over all posts in the training set and use it for predicting the popularity of a post in the test set. We report the result of post popularity prediction using different visual and textual features, which we mentioned in section 4.2, on our test set. We also report the result of fusing visual and textual features, by an average pooling scenario, for predicting the popularity of brand generated post. The combination of features creates an overview of the current state of the art prediction methods on content generated exclusively by brands.

Experiment 2: ***Baseline: Brand popularity by post level training model*** We create and evaluate a baseline for brand popularity prediction using a post level training model. We use this model to predict the popularity score for each post of a brand in the test set. We obtain a popularity score for a brand in the test set by averaging the predicted score of each post of a brand. Then we report the rank correlation between the predicted scores and ground truth as a popularity of a brand. We also report the result of the brand popularity prediction using different visual and textual features and their fusion by average pooling.

Experiment 3: ***Brand popularity prediction using brand category representation*** In this experiment we evaluate the three category representation methods we explained in section 3.2 for predicting the popularity of a brand. We represent each brand in the train and test set using our proposal which is explained in section 3.3 and train a model on the train set and predict the popularity of a brand in the test set. We evaluate the effect of different visual and textual features for representing a brand category in brand popularity prediction. We also report the result of fusing all features by average pooling.

Experiment 4: ***Popularity prediction on an off-line collection*** In this experiment we evaluate the effect of our proposal for selecting those images from an off-line collection of images of a brand which are expected to get a high number of likes. For this purpose we randomly select 100 posts of each brand from the test set and use only the visual data. We extract the visual features per test image and apply the pre-trained models of experiment 1 to compute a popularity score. Then, we rank the images of the brand from the test set based on their popularity score and select the top p images as most promising for sharing in social networks. We evaluate the selection, by defining the popularity ratio as average number of matches between images selected by our method and images from the ground truth ranking. The value of the popularity ratio shows the quality of the approach for selecting images to be shared in social networks. Proximity of the popularity ratio to 1 indicates a better image selection. We report the accuracy of selecting popular images using different visual features by selecting 10, 20, 30, ..., 100 images for sharing in social networks. We also repeat this procedure by selection images of brands randomly. We repeat the random selection of images for 50 times and report the average of the results.

5 RESULTS

5.1 Post Popularity Prediction

We report the result of this experiment in Table 2. Starting with the textual features, the results show the 0.346, 0.481 and 0.145 rank correlation as a popularity of a brand generated post using *W2V*, *Terms*, and *Textual Sentiment* features respectively. Using an average pooling for fusing these textual features, the result reaches 0.494. The results in Table 1 also show the importance of visual features in predicting the popularity of a post where the results reach 0.341, 0.287, 0.293 and 0.366 rank correlation using *CNN-Pool5, Concepts, Visual Sentiment* and *fusion* of them respectively. The results depict that *Concepts* and *Sentiment* present in the image of a post holds information on the popularity of a post. People may respond to concepts in images positively or negatively and a post that contains those positive concepts generally attains more likes. At the end the result in Table 1 shows the significant improvement in predicting the popularity of a brand generated post by combining the textual and visual features. The result of rank correlation reaches 0.520.

The results of experiment 1 confirm that visual and textual features are complementary for predicting the popularity of a brand generated post. Moreover, in general, we are able to predict popularity of brand generated content.

5.2 Baseline: Brand popularity by post level training model

Table 3 shows the results of Experiment 2, where we use a post-level training model on predicting popularity of a brand. It shows the rank correlation reaches 0.474, 0.133, 0.143, and 0.479 using *W2V*, *Terms, Textual Sentiment,* and *fusing* these textual features respectively. The Table 3 also mention to the effect of visual feature on brand popularity, where the rank correlation reaches 0.408, 0.299, 0.399 and 0.411 using *CNN-Pool5, Concept, Visual Sentiment,* and *fusing* of visual features respectively. All visual features have a significant positive impact on brand popularity. Table 3 also confirms complementarity of the visual and textual features for brand popularity prediction by training a post-level popularity model, where the result reaches 0.500 rank correlation.

The results of experiment 2 show the ability of predicting the popularity of a brand using a trained model based on the content they generated. Again, the results confirm that visual and textual features are complementary for predicting the popularity of a brand.

Table 2: The result of predicting the popularity of brand generated posts.

	Textual Features				Visual Features				Multimodal
Features	W2V	Terms	Sentiment	Fusion	CNN-Pool5	Concept	Sentiment	Fusion	Fusion
Rank-correlation	0.346	0.481	0.145	0.494	0.341	0.287	0.293	0.366	**0.520**

Table 3: Brand popularity prediction by post level training model.

	Textual Features				Visual Features				Multimodal
Features	W2V	Terms	Sentiment	Fusion	CNN-Pool5	Concept	Sentiment	Fusion	Fusion
Rank-correlation	0.474	0.133	0.143	0.479	0.408	0.299	0.399	0.411	**0.500**

Table 4: Category representation for brand popularity prediction.

	Textual Features				Visual Features				Multimodal
Features	W2V	Terms	Sentiment	Fusion	CNN-Pool5	Concept	Sentiment	Fusion	Fusion
NCR	0.517	0.141	0.154	0.527	0.441	0.322	0.445	0.479	**0.554**
WCR	0.526	0.167	0.174	0.532	0.464	0.365*	0.461	0.497	**0.579**
STCR	0.532	0.197	0.204	0.540	0.487	0.394	0.471	0.511	**0.598**

5.3 Brand Popularity prediction by category representation

We show the result of experiment 3 in Table 4. Table 4 describes the result of brand popularity using our proposal for brand representation using visual, textual, and fusing of them.

Using *NCR* as a brand representation the result reaches 0.517, 0.141, 0.154 and 0.527 when we use *W2V, Terms, Textual Sentiment,* and *fusing* them respectively. On the other hand using visual features for the *NCR* representation of a brand, the result of brand popularity reaches 0.441, 0.322, 0.445 and 0.479 when we use *CNN-Pool5, Concepts, Visual Sentiment,* and *fusion* of all visual features respectively. Combining visual and textual features in the *NCR* representation of a brand, the rank correlation reaches 0.544.

The results in Table 4 also show the efficiency of using *WCR* as a method for brand representation in comparison with *NCR* method. We observe that the rank correlation using all textual and visual features reaches 0.526, 0.167, 0.174, 0.464, 0.365, 0.461 where features are *W2V, Terms, Textual Sentiment, CNN-Pool5, Concepts,* and *Visual Sentiment* respectively. By fusing textual features, visual features, and combining visual and textual features the rank correlation reaches to 0.532, 0.497, and 0.579 respectively. We observe 5% relative improvement in brand popularity prediction compared to *NCR*, showing the effect of considering the importance per week inside the brand representation.

The results in Table 4 emphasize the efficiency of considering the temporal behaviour of popularity of contents generated by a brand inside the brand representation. Using *STCR*, the rank correlation reaches 0.532, 0.197, 0.204, 0.540 using *W2V, Terms, Textual Sentiment,* and *fusing* them respectively. By visual feature to construct *STCR* the rank correlation reaches 0.487, 0.394, 0.471, 0.511 where the features are *CNN-Pool5, Concepts, Visual Sentiment,* and *fusion* respectively. The Table 4 show the best result of brand popularity reaches 0.598 where we fused the visual and textual features represented by *STCR*. By comparing the result of *STCR* by *NCR* and *WCR* we find that incorporating the importance of brand per week and importance of post inside the weak, we reach to more accurate brand representation.

The STCR addresses not only the weekly importance of certain images but also assigns weights to images within the week. It emphasises specifically the images of importance for the brand and combines it with the importance of a certain week in the brand popularity over time.

By comparing the result of our category representations with the baseline, experiment 2, we find 10%, 16%, and 20% relative improvement in brand popularity prediction when we use *NCR, WCR,* and *STCR* respectively.

The results of experiment 3 confirm that brand popularity prediction accuracy profits from constructing a representation of a brand. Moreover it depicts that a brand representation in which temporal behavior is incorporated is more representative for popularity prediction.

5.4 Popularity prediction on off-line collection

We show the results of experiment 4 in Figure 4. The results demonstrate the effectiveness of using different visual features for selecting those images from an offline collection which have the potential of getting more likes and becoming more popular. Figure 4 shows the result of image selection using our proposal always much better than random selection. When we request to select 30 images we reach 0.125 accuracy in popularity ratio using *Random* selection, whilst using *Concepts, Sentiments, CNN-Pool5* and *Fusion* of all visual features reach 0.280, 0.328, 0.371, and 0.410. The result shows that by considering fusion of all visual features, we come to an accurate set of selected images which depicts each type of visual features capture different aspects of popularity of a post.

We also observe from Figure 4 that the presence of *Visual Sentiment* for all brands has a positive effect on the predicted popularity. We further investigate which particular ANPs correlate most with the number of likes in different industries. In order to evaluate the correlation of visual sentiment with popularity, we compute the SVR weights separately for two industries, *Food* and *Fashion,* and

Figure 5: Experiment 4: ANPs that have a positive impact on popularity of (a) *Food industry* and (b) *Fashion industry*. Font size correlates with the importantnees of sentiments for both brands.

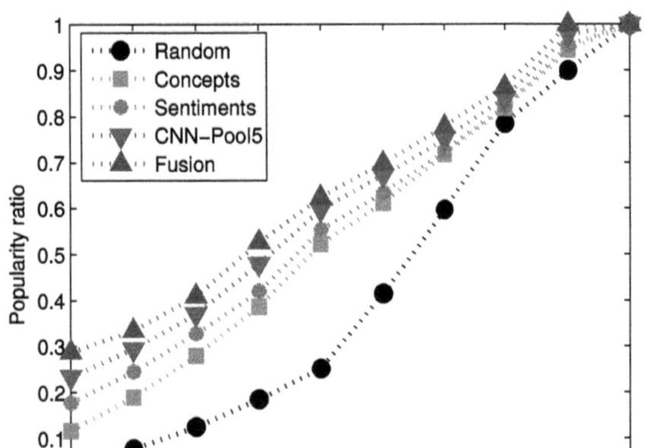

Figure 4: Experiment 4: Selection of images from an offline collection of brands predicted as more popular. Fusing all visual features help us to select more popular images.

then sort them for selection. The results in Figure 5, highlight the important sentiments with different impact on popularity for these brand industries.

The results of experiment 4 show that, in general, using a predicted model over the brand generated contents we have the ability of helping brands in selecting the content they should share on their page on social media.

6 CONCLUSION

In this paper we study the prediction of popularity of brands. We investigate how the visual and textual contents of brand generated posts impact their popularity. Different from existing works which focus more on predicting the popularity of user generated posts, we are the first to study brand popularity prediction. We incorporate the spatio-temporal behavior of the popularity of the posts generated by brand for representing brand. We study the behavior of our proposal for predicting the popularity of brands on a dataset crawled from Instagram.

The results of experiment 1 confirm complementarity of visual and textual features for predicting post popularity. In addition, it shows how we are able to accurately predict the popularity of content that is generated and posted exclusively by brands. The results of experiment 2 show that by using the post level training model we have the ability to predict the popularity of the brand. Experiment 3 displays that prediction of brand popularity is more accurate when a brand is represented as a category representation. Moreover, incorporation of the temporal dimension into the representation increases the predictability of brand popularity. Finally, experiment 4 reveals that using our proposal, where all channels are fused, we have the ability of selecting a set of off-line images of a brand likely to become more popular.

We conclude that for category popularity prediction it is beneficial to construct a category representation in which spatio-temporal dynamics are considered.

ACKNOWLEDGMENTS

This research is supported by the Amsterdam Academic Alliance Data Science (AAA-DS) Program Award to the UvA and VU Universities.

REFERENCES

[1] Y. Bae and H. Lee. Sentiment analysis of twitter audiences: Measuring the positive or negative influence of popular twitterers. *J. Am. Soc. Inf. Sci. Technol.*, 63(12):2521–2535, 2012.
[2] D. Borth, R. Ji, T. Chen, T. Breuel, and S.-F. Chang. Large-scale visual sentiment ontology and detectors using adjective noun pairs. In *MM*, 2013.
[3] S. Cappallo, T. Mensink, and C. G. Snoek. Latent factors of visual popularity prediction. In *ICMR*, 2015.
[4] J. Deng, W. Dong, R. Socher, L.-J. Li, K. Li, and L. Fei-Fei. ImageNet: A Large-Scale Hierarchical Image Database. In *CVPR*, 2009.
[5] R.-E. Fan, K.-W. Chang, C.-J. Hsieh, X.-R. Wang, and C.-J. Lin. LIBLINEAR: A library for large linear classification. *JMLR*, 9:1871–1874, 2008.
[6] F. Gelli, T. Uricchio, M. Bertini, A. Del Bimbo, and S.-F. Chang. Image popularity prediction in social media using sentiment and context features. In *MM*, 2015.
[7] L. Hong, O. Dan, and B. D. Davison. Predicting popular messages in twitter. In *WWW*, 2011.
[8] B. Jiang and Y. Sha. Modeling temporal dynamics of user interests in online social networks. *Procedia Computer Science*, 51:503–512, 2015.
[9] A. Khosla, A. Das Sarma, and R. Hamid. What makes an image popular? In *WWW*, 2014.
[10] W. G. Mangold and D. J. Faulds. Social media: The new hybrid element of the promotion mix. *Business horizons*, 52(4):357–365, 2009.
[11] M. Mazloom, A. Habibian, D. Liu, C. G. M. Snoek, and S.-F. Chang. Encoding concept prototypes for video event detection and summarization. In *ICMR*, 2015.
[12] M. Mazloom, R. Rietveld, S. Rudinac, M. Worring, and W. Van Dolen. Multimodal popularity prediction of brand-related social media posts. In *MM*, 2016.
[13] P. J. McParlane, Y. Moshfeghi, and J. M. Jose. Nobody comes here anymore, it's too crowded; predicting image popularity on flickr. In *ICMR*, 2014.

[14] T. Mikolov, I. Sutskever, K. Chen, G. S. Corrado, and J. Dean. Distributed representations of words and phrases and their compositionality. In *NIPS*, 2013.
[15] C. North. Toward measuring visualization insight. *IEEE Comput. Graph. Appl.*, 26(3), 2006.
[16] M. Risius and R. Beck. Effectiveness of corporate social media activities in increasing relational outcomes. *Information Management*, 52(7):824–839, 2015.
[17] B. Stieglitz, Dang-Xuan and Neuberger. Social media analytics - an interdisciplinary approach and its implications for information systems. *Business Horizons*, 6(2):89–96, 2014.
[18] C. Szegedy, W. Liu, Y. Jia, P. Sermanet, S. Reed, D. Anguelov, D. Erhan, V. Vanhoucke, and A. Rabinovich. Going deeper with convolutions. In *CVPR*, 2015.
[19] M. Thelwall, K. Buckley, G. Paltoglou, D. Cai, and A. Kappas. Sentiment strength detection in short informal text. *J. Am. Soc. Inf. Sci. Technol.*, 61(12):2544–2558, 2010.
[20] B. Wu, T. Mei, W.-H. Cheng, and Y. Zhang. Unfolding temporal dynamics: Predicting social media popularity using multi-scale temporal decomposition. In *AAAI*, 2016.
[21] J. Yang and J. Leskovec. Patterns of temporal variation in online media. In *WSDM*, 2011.
[22] D. Zeng, H. Chen, R. Lusch, and S.-H. Li. Social media analytics and intelligence. *Intelligent Systems*, 25(6):13–16, 2010.

Bridging the Aesthetic Gap: The Wild Beauty of Web Imagery

Miriam Redi
Bell labs
Cambridge,UK
miriam.redi@nokia.com

Frank Liu
Flickr
San Francisco,CA
fzliu@yahoo-inc.com

Neil O'Hare
Yahoo
Sunnyvale,CA
nohare@yahoo-inc.com

ABSTRACT

To provide good results, image search engines need to rank not just the most relevant images, but also the highest quality images. To surface beautiful pictures, existing computational aesthetic models are trained with datasets from photo contest websites, dominated by professional photos. Such models fail completely in real web scenarios, where images are extremely diverse in terms of quality and type (e.g. drawings, clip-art, etc). This work aims at bridging and understanding this "aesthetic gap". We collect a dataset of around 100K web images with 'quality' and 'type' (photo vs non-photo) annotations. We design a set of visual features to describe image pictorial characteristics, and deeply analyse the peculiar beauty of web images as opposed to appealing professional images. Finally, we build a set of computational aesthetic frameworks based on deep learning and hand-crafted features that take into account the diverse quality of web images, and show that they significantly outperform traditional computational aesthetics methods on our dataset.

ACM Reference format:
Miriam Redi, Frank Liu, and Neil O'Hare. 2017. Bridging the Aesthetic Gap: The Wild Beauty of Web Imagery. In *Proceedings of ICMR '17, Bucharest, Romania, June 6–9, 2017,* 9 pages.
https://doi.org/http://dx.doi.org/10.1145/3078971.3078972

Figure 1: Aesthetics in the wild web: photo VS graphics.

1 INTRODUCTION

To meet user expectations, web-scale image search engines need to surface not only the most relevant images for a query, but also the highest quality, most beautiful images [6]. Computational aesthetic models, which automatically assess the image aesthetic quality, can be very important in enabling this. [3, 14, 15]. Although effective, such methods generally use corpora automatically created from photography contest websites [12, 15, 20], where the average image quality tends to be very high, with few lower quality images, since photo contest participants are (semi) professional photographers.

Web image search, on the other hand, must deal with images from a wide variety of sources, including very bad quality images typically absent in photo contest websites. Additionally, according to our study, around 15% of the images in the web are *non-photographic*: clipart, drawings, etc. Because of these differences, aesthetic models trained solely on high-quality, photographic images will fail completely when confronted with such diverse content, thus making them not *generalizable* to real-case scenarios.

Given the importance of web image quality scoring, and the lack of methods to address this problem, in this work we take the first steps towards the complete understanding of image aesthetics in the wild. We collect a dataset of web images with aesthetic and image type annotations, and analyze this data to understand what makes web images different from professional images. We then build a set of computational aesthetics systems that, unlike previous work, are designed to take into account the diverse, and often poor, quality of web images, showing that it outperforms traditional computational aesthetic approaches when applied to images in the wild. Our contributions can be summarized as follows:

- We collect the first *large-scale aesthetic dataset for web images,* containing approximately 100K *web images* editorially annotated in terms of aesthetic quality and type (photo or non-photo), as shown in Sec. 3
- We design a set of hand-crafted *aesthetic visual features* and use them in Sec. 4 to analyse how image quality manifests itself differently in photographic web images, non-photographic web images, and professional images. We show that "visual beauty"

ICMR '17, June 6–9, 2017, Bucharest, Romania

ACM ISBN 978-1-4503-4701-3/17/06...$15.00.
https://doi.org/http://dx.doi.org/10.1145/3078971.3078972

means different things for different image types, and that certain features (e.g. sharpness) can be positively or negatively correlated with quality, depending on the image type. The findings also emphasize that it is misleading to think of image aesthetics prediction as a single, unified, task, but as a set of related problems, which differ significantly depending on the domain.
- We propose 3 distinct complete systems to rate the aesthetic value of images in the wild (Sec. 6). The first framework uses a type-aware approach, based on hand-crafted features and composed of a photo aesthetic model and a non-photographic aesthetic model. The other approaches use deep learning frameworks: one is trained from scratch using our collected dataset, while the second is trained on professional images and fine-tuned with web images.
- We evaluate our models against a set of diverse, real-world, web images (Sec. 6), for 3 different use-cases: image scoring, surfacing, and ranking. Our methods greatly outperform traditional state-of-the-art methods based on professional images. We find that, in some cases, methods based on hand-crafted features can be more effective than deep learning. Moreover, we find that transferring knowledge between aesthetic datasets through fine-tuning can massively improve performance for web image aesthetics ranking.

2 RELATED WORK

Our work relates to the computer vision research on the automatic assessment of non-semantic concepts such as memorability [10], emotions [17], interestingness [7], creativity [25], popularity [13], and aesthetics [3, 15]. Early work in image aesthetics designed aesthetic features for amateur vs professional photo classification [3, 12]. Since then, computational aesthetics researchers have proposed more discriminative visual features and attributes [4, 22], generic semantic features [19, 20], deep learning [14, 18], and effective ranking frameworks [28].

While we follow a similar research line, in this paper we explicitly explore the aesthetics of *web* images, as opposed to the *semi-professional* images analyzed in previous works. Our work is novel compared to the state-of-the-art in computational aesthetics in a number of ways:

Dataset. Computational aesthetics researchers have mainly worked with datasets derived from photo challenge websites such as DPChallenge.com [3, 12, 15, 20] or Photo.net [3]. The largest aesthetic database (AVA [20]) contains around 250,000 images with aesthetic, semantic and style labels. One major limitation of these ground truths is that their pictures come from professional/aspiring photographers: the quality of the photographs in such datasets is therefore extremely skewed towards 'beautiful' images, and so models based on this data will learn to discriminate between various levels of 'beautiful' images, but not learn to distinguish these from poor quality images. Luo et al. [15] attempted to partly solve this issue by creating a mixed dataset of professional and low quality images. However, subsequent studies [20] have pointed out that this dataset cannot be used in real scenarios due to its artificial nature. Unlike previous work, we build the first editorially annotated aesthetic groundtruth of images that truly represents the diversity of images on the web: while Geng *et al* [6]also evaluate against a corpus of web images, the diversity of their data is limited by the fact that they use only 100 seed queries, whereas our dataset is based on images sampled from over 8k queries.

Web images are extremely *diverse* along at least 2 dimensions. First, general web images come from a much more diverse set of sources and, unlike professional image websites, they contain many poor or average quality images. Second, not all images on the web are *photographic*: a significant percentage (around 15% in our study) is composed of *non-photographic* images, including clip-art, drawings, illustrations, digital artworks, etc. To replicate real a web image scenario we: (i) ensure wide diversity in image quality by sampling images from a large sample of queries issued to a commercial web search engine, *(ii)* ask editors to annotate image aesthetics on a 4-point scale that considers both objective quality and subjective beauty, spanning a range from 'bad' to 'exceptional', and *(iii)* annotate the presence of non-photographic images. The quality scale that we use encapsulates the highly related, but distinct notions of *aesthetic beauty* and *objective quality*. That is, unlike previoius work, not only do we aim to surface the most beautiful images, we also aim to detect (and demote in our ranking) the poorer quality images that are absent in other computational aesthetics datasets.

Schifanella et al. [27] built a corpus of Flickr images annotated with aesthetic degrees collected via crowdsourcing. While that work represents a first step towards the creation of non-professional image aesthetic datasets, 2 characteristics of their corpus make it unsuitable to explore the nature of images in the wild web: (1) their dataset is a single platform corpus, composed of Flickr images only, and so its images are much more uniform in nature and quality than the images available in the web, (2) in order to make the crowdsorucing task more reliable, they sampled images from 4 main topical categories only (people, urban, nature, animals), thus resulting in corpus that is lacking in diversity.

Analysis of Web image Aesthetics. This work is one of the first of its kind that performs a large comparative analysis of what visual features make different types of pictures beautiful. Previous work [10, 13, 25, 26] has highlighted the predictive power of single visual features for properties such as creativity, memorability, popularity, and portrait aesthetics. However, these works focus on the characteristics of a single dataset specifically tailored to explore such properties. In this paper, we perform a much broader analysis, and show that different image types, and those from different sources, manifest their 'quality' and 'beauty' in markedly different ways, emphasizing that a single notion of image beauty is not sufficient for all use cases.

Models. For the first time in computational aesthetics, in this paper we address the problem of scoring the aesthetics of non-photographic images, which comprise a non-trivial subset of web images. While researchers have previously built topic-specific models for a variety of photographic subjects [16, 23, 26], and classifiers to distinguish between photo and graphics [21], or between different image styles [11], the extent to which visual features can help understanding the beauty of non-photographic images has not been explored. In this paper, we build a a type-aware aesthetic model that scores photographic images differently from non-photographic images. Moreover, for the first time, we design a deep network to score *web* images in terms of beauty showing that it outperforms state-of-the art on both professional and web image datasets. Finally, we use the *finetuning* technique to re-learn the weights of a deep network originally designed to score professional images, thus taking advantage of a larger image quality range (from the high quality of professional images to the extreme low quality of web images).

Although aesthetics is an important dimension of visual perception, previous work in image search has rarely focused on aesthetic analysis [24]. In work that is closest to ours, Geng *et al* [6] investigate the role of 'attractiveness' in web image search. In addition to conducting a user study that validates the supreme importance of image attractiveness or beauty for users in web image search, the authors also evaluate models for scoring web images for aesthetic quality. Our work differs from that work in a number of important ways: (1) unlike that work, we investigate the differences between web image aesthetics and professional image aesthetics, both through qualitative analysis and comparative evaluation of aesthetic models, (2) we specifically investigate the importance of image type, in terms of photographic versus non-photographic images, for aesthetics, (3) we train a deep neural network for web image aesthetics, which shows improvements both over hand-crafted features trained on the same data, and a deep model trained on professional images.

3 WEB IMAGE AESTHETICS DATASET

In this section, we create a dataset of images that are commonly found on web image search platforms. To do so, we sample results of queries that are issued to a web image search engine. From the logs of a large commercial web image search engine, we randomly sample a set of 8,131 queries based on traffic (i.e. a query that has been issued 1,000 times is 100 times more likely to be sampled than a query that has been issued 10 times)[1]. This sampling methodology gives a mix of popular queries from the head of the distribution (e.g. 'miley cyrus') and rare queries at the tail of the distribution. We then run each query against a web-scale search engine, taking as our sample an average of 12 images per query from the top 500 results (this is to avoid bias caused by the ranking algorithm used). Each of the images was then annotated by professionally trained image editors, along 2 dimensions, *aesthetic quality* and *image type.*

Aesthetic Quality. Along with much of the related research [3], we adopt the definition of aesthetics as the perceived beauty and overall quality of photographs. We designed an annotation experiment specifically tailored for web images. We then asked professional annotators to judge images according to a 4-point scale. We define the point labels to cover the full range of quality degrees in the web, by first setting set the top (exceptional) and the bottom (bad) of this scale, and then inferring the middle grades, as follows:

(1) *Fair/Bad.* Low or extremely low quality images with technical flaws (blurred, over/underexposed, incorrectly framed), and without any artistic value.

[1] the query traffic volume is calculated against 6 months of log data.

	Photographic (%)	Non-photographic (%)	All (%)
Exceptional	2,055 (2.5)	360 (2.4)	2,415 (2.5)
Professional	42,247 (51.3)	4,241 (28.6)	46,488 (47.8)
Good	32,590 (39.6)	9,216 (62.2)	41,806 (43)
Fair/Bad	5,479 (6.7)	1,009 (6.8)	6,488 (6.7)
All	82,371	14,826	97,197

Table 1: Summary of annotations in image quality dataset. Percentages are column-wise (per image type).

(2) *Good.* Standard quality images without technical flaws (subject well framed, in focus, and easily recognizable), and without any artistic value.
(3) *Professional.* Professional-quality images (flawless framing, focus, and lightning).
(4) *Exceptional.* Very appealing images, showing both outstanding professional quality (photographic and/or editing techniques) and high artistic value.

Quality levels (1), (2), and (3) differ mainly in terms of *objective quality*: annotators need to look at how much the image is technically correct, rather than its aesthetic or artistic value. On the other hand, both *Professional* and *Exceptional* images must show high technical quality: when distinguishing between levels (3) and (4) images, annotators need instead to evaluate the artistic value, namely that aesthetic factor that makes pictures exceptionally beautiful.

Image Type. Since we are also interested in understanding aesthetic differences between photographic and non-photographic images, we also asked editors to annotate images as being *photographic,* namely images that represent scenes from the real world, or *non-photographic* images such as illustrations, computer-generated artworks, clipart, etc. 15% of the images in our corpus were annotated as non-photographic.

Table 1 summarises the annotated corpus, which will be used as a testbed for the experiments in this paper. In total, this effort yielded 97,197 annotations with 2,415 (2.5%) images annotated as *exceptional,* 46,488 annotated as *professional,* 41,806 annotated as *good,* and 6,488 images annotated as *fair/bad.* Overall, we can see that the majority of images are of either *Good* or *Professional* quality. For non-photographic images, however, a very large proportion are of *Good* quality, while a small but significant number of photos is labelled as *Professional,* and the number of fair/bad images is non-trivial (almost 7%).

We calculate the ratio of photographic images to non-photographic images for all of the queries in our data, and plot the sorted results in Figure 2 (the black area on the left represents queries for which all annotated images are photographic). 58% of queries have only photographic results, while 3.5% have exclusively non-photographic results, with the other 38.5% representing 'mixed' queries. This emphases the importance of properly understanding quality for different image types: many queries may return images of different types, and we need to be able to understand the quality of each in a reliable, and consistent way, especially, for example, if we need to rank them for the same query.

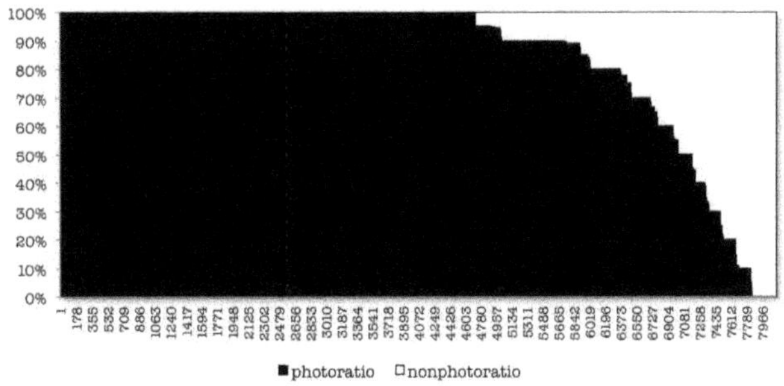

Figure 2: Photo / Non-photo ratio by query (sorted).

4 WHAT MAKES WEB IMAGE BEAUTY DIFFERENT?

To what extent does the way in which image quality manifests itself depend on image type? Does beauty have different meanings for different image types? To address these questions, in this section, we extract a set of interpretable visual features and perform an extensive analysis of the values such features take in relation to quality for different image types.

4.1 Visual Aesthetic Features

Similar to previous work [3, 15], we extract features describing image color, texture, quality and composition.

Color. Spatial/chromatic color distribution is one of the properties that is mostly related to the aesthetic [3] value of a picture. We compute a *Contrast* metric based on luminance values [25], perceptual metrics of *colorfulness* (the color vividness) and *naturalness* (the color perception accuracy) [9], average *Hue, Saturation,* and *Brightness (H,S,V)* across the whole image and for its *Central Quadrant, HSV Color Histograms* and the *HSV Contrasts* [17], i.e. the standard deviation of H, S and V Color Histograms.

Texture Similar to previous work [17], we describe the textural patterns using Haralick's features [8], namely the *Entropy, Energy, Homogeneity, Contrast* of the Gray-Level Co-occurrence Matrices.
Basic Quality Metrics. From previous work on aesthetics [26], we borrow a set of metrics describing the basic image quality, i.e. a set of rules that measure the signal integrity after registration, post-processing and compression. These metrics are crucial to estimate the level of degradation of web images, which are often poor in terms of visual quality. We compute the *Contrast Balance*, the *Exposure Balance*, the *JPEG Quality* (the amount of annoyance due to JPEG blocking artifacts) and the image *Sharpness.*

Composition. When evaluating pictorial aesthetics, a key criteria is the "mise en scene", i.e. the way in which objects are arranged in the space [5]. Similar to previous computational aesthetic work [26] we describe the spatial arrangement by evaluating the *Presence of Objects* in 9 image quadrants (3x3 image subdivision)a HOG-based [2] *Symmetry* feature, and a *Uniqueness* feature that records the originality of the image composition.

4.2 Analysis

In this Section, we are interested in understanding the differences in quality between (1) *non-photographic web images*, (2) *photographic web images*, and (3) *professsional photos.*

We compute, for each group, the Spearman Correlation coefficients between each of the visual features from Section 4.2 and the images' aesthetic scores[2]. The magnitude of the correlation coefficients allows us to understand how predictive each feature is. The sign of the coefficients indicates the impact of each feature for image aesthetics scoring: positive correlations show that high values of the feature correspond to high aesthetic degree, negative correlations mean that the feature is an indicator of lower quality, while near-zero coefficients show that the feature is not correlated with beauty or quality. In Figure 3 we show the correlation coefficients between the aesthetic scores of the 3 image types and the 27 most discriminative features, grouped by feature type. We can see that the aesthetic patterns of the three datasets are very distinct, with two mains sets of differences: the difference between all web images and professional photos, and between photographic and non-photographic content.

Web Images vs Professional Photos.

Basic Quality Metrics. We observe that, for *Jpeg quality, Contrast balance* and *Brightness Contrast,* the sign of the coefficient is positive for all image types: these features reflect basic quality requirements for any image. The correlation between quality/aesthetics and *Jpeg quality/Contrast balance* is much higher for web images than for AVA photos, because very poor quality images are not represented in the AVA dataset. Interetingly, *Sharpness* is a negative indicator of beauty for web images, while it is positively correlated with the AVA aesthetic scores. The sharpness feature captures the acutance of the shape surface and their edges (see Figure 1), which is a must in good professional photography. However, the wild web is full of non-standard pictures that show extremely sharp, textured patterns such as the one shown in Figure 1: even if the sharpness of their edges is extremely high, these images might not be considered as particularly attractive, thus making the sharpness feature negatively correlated with web image beauty.

Composition. We can also observe that the importance of the object position features varies between web and professional images. For beautiful AVA images, that typically should follow the professional rule of thirds, it is important that the object is not placed in the exact image center: it should cross one of the lines resulting from a 3x3 division of the image(among the object positions, *Presence of Objects (center)* is the most negatively correlated) . Unlike in professional pictures, among web images we can find huge volumes of badly cropped and incorrectly framed pictures: when objects are extremely non-centered, features such as *Presence of Objects (top/left)* or *(top/right)* take higher values: such features are highly negatively correlated with the quality of web images.

Photographic vs Non-photographic images.

One of the most notable patterns from the analysis in Figure 3 is that, in some cases, the aesthetics of non-photographic images are

[2]Since the purpose of this study is to understand what makes web images different from professional photographs, we choose to look at *interpretable* features only, namely the hand-crafted *Visual Aesthetic Attributes*

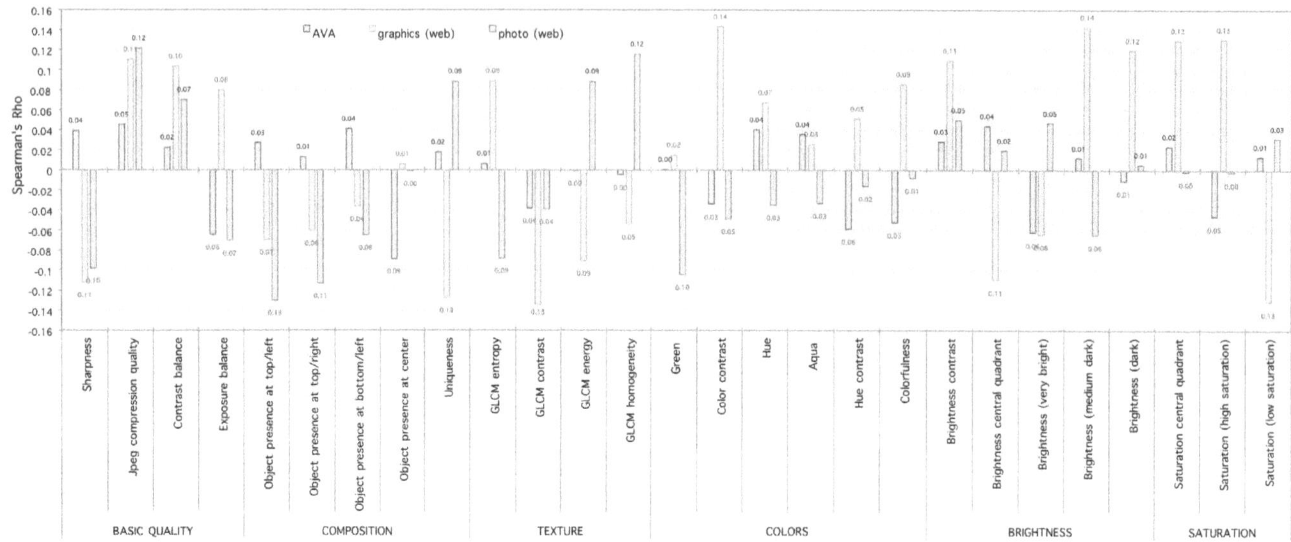

Figure 3: Analysis of the most relevant aesthetic features for professional, web photographic, and web non-photographics images

very different from both professional and web photographic images. This is because non-photographic images typically do not follow the same artistic criteria as photos. In Figure 1 we collected visual examples among the 5 top-ranked and 5 bottom-ranked photo and non-photo images according to 4 main discriminative features.

Basic Quality Metrics. While photographers like to experiment with the *Exposure Balance* to convey certain type of sentiments (negative correlation between exposure balance and photo aesthetic score), non-photographic image patterns need to be correctly exposed to be clearly distinguishable.

Composition. Unlike photos, the quality of non-photographic images is inversely correlated with its *Uniqueness*.

Texture. Overly simple graphics (i.e. with high *GLCM homogeneity, energy, and contrast*, and low *GLCM entropy*) appear to be considered less appealing, while photo homogeneity, on the other hand, seems to be highly correlated with photographic beauty.

Color. While over-contrasted photos tend to have lower aesthetic value, beautiful non-photographic images show higher levels of *Contrast*, due to the different pictorial style, and the synthetic generation of the colors. Good non-photographic images are also very *Colorful*, while too many colors in photos lead to an impoverishment of the aesthetic value. Non-photographic images labeled as 'Exceptional' show a darker background compared to average non-photographic images like clip-arts (typically drawn on white backgrounds), making the *Brightness* features inversely correlated with non-photographic beauty. Moreover, the colors of good non-photographic images tend to be more *Saturated* (non-photographic beauty is positively correlated with high values of saturation, and negatively with low saturation).

Discussion.
The differences discussed in this section serve to emphasise that not only does image quality vary with type, but that the correlation of many features with image aesthetic value changes from positive to negative depending on image type. This means that the lessons previously learnt on professional photographic images are not necessarily applicable to non-photographic and non-professional images, and that models trained on professional photographic images may be poor at predicting the quality of non-professional and/or non-photographic images. Since previous work has focused almost exclusively on professional photographic datasets, our findings here emphasize that web image aesthetics prediction is a sufficient sub-problem of computational aesthetics to warrant separate investigation. In the next Section, our experiments will show that models trained on such professional photographic data do, indeed, perform poorly when tasked with aesthetic scoring of web images.

5 MODELS FOR WEB IMAGE AESTHETICS

The findings from the previous section highlights the diverse quality and styles of web images, suggesting that we need to go beyond traditional computational aesthetic frameworks to understand the peculiarities of web images aesthetics and automatically assess their quality. We therefore design: (1) a type-aware framework to learn aesthetic models for both photographic and non-photographic images based on hand-crafted features, (2.1) a robust convolutional neural networks trained for web image aesthetics, and (2.2) a CNN trained for professional image aesthetic scoring and fine-tuned for web image aesthetics.

5.1 Hand-Crafted Type-Aware Model

Based on the features listed in Sec. 4.2, we now design an image aesthetic scorer able to first classify image type (photo/non-photo) and then score the image with a type-specific aesthetic classifier.

Photographic VS Non-photographic Image Classifier. We first build a model able to distinguish between photographic and non-photographic images, based on the *Visual Aesthetic Features*, the

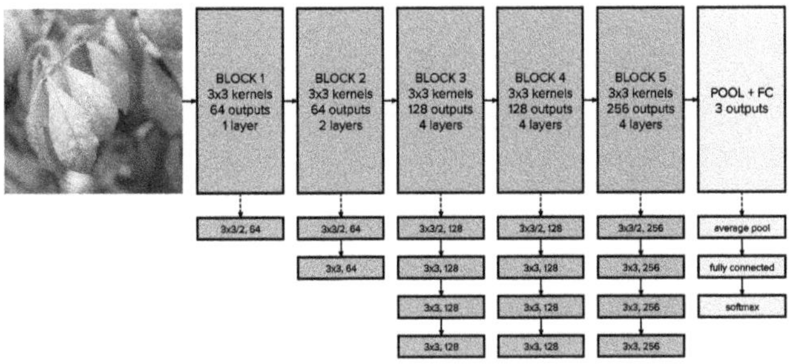

Figure 4: Convnet used to train the aesthetics network. Each layer is implicitly followed by Batch Normalization and ReLU.

type annotations collected, and a binary (photo/nonphoto) Random Forest classifier [1]. We evaluate the classifier using 5-fold cross-validation, and achieve an average accuracy of 82.14%, with 81% of graphics correctly classified and 83.28% of photos correctly classified. These results are in line with the state-of-the art performance of similar classifiers applied to web images [21].

Type-aware Aesthetic Classifier. To learn type-specific aesthetic models, we first partition our data according the original photo/non-photo annotations collected with our ground-truth. For each type-specific data partition, we then compute the *Visual Aesthetic Features* and use them as input for a Random Forest regression algorithm that will learn how to rank the images of a given type in terms of beauty. We therefore obtain 2 aesthetic models:

(1) A model estimating **non-photographic** aesthetics, trained on non-photographic images only.
(2) A model estimating **photographic** aesthetics, trained on photographic images only.

We then combine the Type-Aware classifier and our type-specific aesthetic models in an all-in-one **type-aware** classifier that scores the aesthetics of all images together. This model first classifies all images based on type (photographic or non-photographic), and then predicts the aesthetics score based on the appropriate model (i.e. model 1 or model 2).

5.2 Deep Web Aesthetics Models

5.2.1 Pure Web Aesthetics Model. Given the proven effectiveness of deep networks for aesthetic image scoring [14], we also design a CNN architecture for web image aesthetics. The architecture for this deep model is quite simple (see Figure 4), with body of the network consisting of only 3x3 convolutions, batch normalization, and ReLU activations. To minimize the number of total parameters, the tail end of the network utilizes global average pooling followed by a single densely connected (into softmax) layer with three outputs. These three outputs correspond to the probability that the photo falls into high (degrees 3/4), medium (degree 2), and low quality (degree 1) buckets.

We applied the following heuristic to calculate a score for the web images, given their three softmax outputs:

$$s = \frac{1}{2}(p_{HQ} - p_{LQ} + 1) \tag{1}$$

where p_{HQ} and p_{LQ} represent the high quality and low quality softmax probabilities, respectively.

Since we do not have enough non-photographic images to train a type-aware model, for the deep learning model we use as training all types of images, without distinguishing between photographic and non-photographic.

5.2.2 Finetuned Web Aesthetics Model. In addition to the model trained from scratch (discussed in the previous section), we also fine-tune a model first trained using AVA, an existing dataset for image aesthetics sourced from a photo challenge website. For training, we split the AVA dataset into three equal-sized classes by the aggregate score. By first training the network on a large dataset of professional or near-professional photographs, we hope to transfer some of the domain-agnostic high level knowledge to the final model. We further hypothesized that beginning the fine-tuning process using a lower learning rate would minimize any potential overfitting and lead to somewhat better generalizability. We use the same architecture as for the *pure web aesthetics model.* Unlike standard fine-tuning procedures, however, we initialize *the entire model* with weights learned from the AVA dataset, including the final parameterized output layer. In other words, none of the weights in the fine-tuned model are initialized from scratch.

6 WEB AESTHETICS PREDICTION EXPERIMENTS

Following the insights from Section 4, we present here aesthetics prediction experiments on web images and expose interesting findings about methods for web image aesthetics prediction.

6.1 Experimental Methodology

Baseline Models. We evaluate 2 baseline aesthetic prediction models, against which we compare our proposed models:

i) *Hand-crafted type-agnostic Model:* We train a simple predictor using the hand-crafted features described in Section 4.2, without using the type information to evaluate the role that the image type in web aesthetic assessment.

i) *AVA deep Model:* To evaluate our methods against state-of-the art computational aesthetics frameworks, we train a deep network purely on *AVA* images, using the same architecture as our web aesthetic classifier (see Sec. 5.2.1). We deviate from the binary classification used by [14] and instead split the entire AVA dataset into three evenly sized classes based on their average score. This was done to maintain a level of parity with the web aesthetics model.[3]

Proposed Models. We evaluate performances of our models:

1) The *Hand-crafted Type-aware Model* model described in Section 5.1 uses the hand-crafted features in Section 5 and random forests with 100 trees[4].

2) A *Pure Web Deep Model* trained from scratch on *web* images, as described in Section 5.2.1. We use standard stochastic gradient

[3]To verify the good accuracy of our AVA-based network, we compare it with state-of-the-art methods. To do so, we adapt our model to a binary classification task. We change the number of output classes, and use the same hyper-parameters and body. We show that it actually performs better than state-of-the-art, achieving an accuracy of 75.4% on a held out set of AVA images as opposed to the 75.1% of [14].
[4]We evaluate these parameters with cross-validation

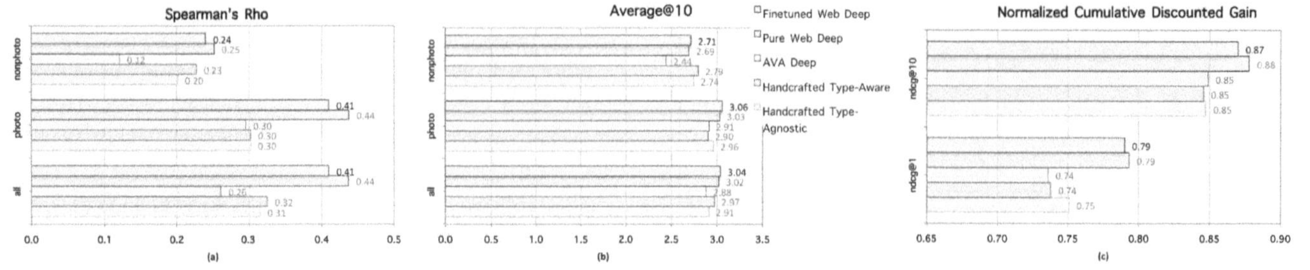

Figure 5: Aesthetic image ranking: comparison of models trained on our dataset vs traditional aesthetic models.

descent during training, with a batch size of 256, initial learning rate of 0.01, weight decay of 0.0001. The learning rate is decreased every 20 epochs for a total of 100 epochs over the training data. We hold out a small subset of the photos for validation purposes. This is done to ensure that we do not overfit to the data; during training, we ensured that the accuracy on the held out validation set did not exceed that of the training set by anything greater than a couple of percentage points. Once this was verified, we re-trained the entire model using all of the data and report results obtained by scoring each image with such model.

3) A *Finetuned Web Deep Model* classifier trained from scratch on *AVA* images, and then *fine-tuned* using *web* images as described in Section 5.2.2. We use here the same architecture as the *web* model. The learning rate starts off at 0.001, decreasing by a factor of ten every four epochs up to a total of 20 epochs. We also use the same train/test split.

Image Ranking. For the deep learning models, images are ranked based on Eq. 1. For the methods based on hand-crafted features, we rank based on the score output by the regression model. For evaluation, we split the web image dataset described Section 3 into 5 random partitions. For each of the methods tested, we perform 5-fold cross-validation experiments by training on 4 partitions and testing on the remaining one. We report the results obtained by ranking all images according to the scores produced for each partition.

Evaluation Metrics and Use cases. We evaluate the models using 3 metrics reflecting different use cases:

a) *Scoring images - Rho*: we want to understand how each method performs for overall *aesthetic scoring*, namely how well the scores produced by a method replicate the actual aesthetic ranking, not only giving high scores to beautiful images, but also low scores to bad images. To reflect this, we compute the correlation (Spearman) between the ranked list of predicted scores and the actual scores.

b) *Surfacing images - Average@10* : the average aesthetic score (from 1 to 4) in the top 10 images ranked by each method reflects how good each method is for the task of *surfacing* beautiful pictures: i.e. giving the top 10 to the highest quality pictures in the entire dataset. This metric evaluates how suitable the model would be for a recommendation task, to surface the best images in the entire collection.

c) *Per-query Ranking - NDCG@10, NDCG@1* : for an image search scenario, we are not so interested in the global ordering of images, but rather in how well the model can rank within the set of candidate images for a given query. For this we rank the images for each query separately, calculate the *Normalized Discounted Cumulative Gain (NDCG)* for each query, and then average this value over all queries. Note that this metric is different from *Average@10*, which simply looks at the global top 10 images based on each method.

6.2 Evaluation Results

We present the results of our aesthetics prediction for each evaluation metric in Figure 5.

Scoring Images. The classifier that best replicates the overall image aesthetic ranking (*rho*) for all type of images is our *Pure Web Deep*, thanks to the accuracy of the underlying deep learning framework combined with the wide quality range of the training data (web images). On the other hand, the *Handcrafted Type-Aware* model, although trained on the same data, is based on simple hand-crafted features, thus less able to capture non-linear associations between images and annotations, making it less predictive that the deep learning framework. The deep framework trained on *AVA* images, although still very predictive compared to a random classifier, is not able to rank images in terms of beauty as effectively as other frameworks: this is due to the fact that its training data does not include low quality images typical of web visual data, and so the model is not able to accurately score such images. In particular, we can see that the rank produced by the *AVA Deep* classifier has the lowest *rho* for non-photographic images, showing the importance of incorporating this type of image in the training data. For similar reasons, we can find also that the framework *fine-tuned* with web images has lower performances compared to *Pure Web Deep*.

Surfacing Most Beautiful Images. In terms of *Average@10*, we can observe similar patterns as before, but with a few differences. In particular, we can notice the superior performance of the *Handcrafted Type-Aware* model over the *Handcrafted Type-Agnostic* for the detection of the most beautiful non-photographic images: this is the only method that explicitly takes into account the image type when detecting beautiful images. Another interesting result regarding the *Finetuned Web Deep* model is that, unlike its low performances for complete image ranking, it appears to be the most accurate model in terms of *Average@10* for both *photographic* and *all* images. Such high performance is due to the mixed training information: by combining the knowledge on high-quality images from the *AVA* dataset with the knowledge on mid-low quality images from the *web* dataset, this framework is able to surface beautiful web images better than our *Pure Web Deep* trained from scratch with web images only.

Per Query Aesthetic Image Ranking. From Figure 5 (c), we can see that our *Pure Web Deep* method achieves very high performance for per-query aesthetic ranking, while, similarly to the scoring task, the models trained or fine-tuned over professional images show less accuracy. We also notice a significant difference between the hand crafted models and the the *Pure Web Deep* (+ 5% for NDCG@1).

Qualitative analysis. In Figure 6 we show photo and non-photo visual examples of beautiful and non-beautiful pictures according to the different models. By visually inspecting these results, we can observe some interesting patterns. Although the *Handcrafted Type-Aware* model does a good job in terms of image ranking, its lack of complexity results in a uniform "quality" modelling: the most beautiful images according to this algorithm tend to have an individual object on the foreground placed on the thirds lines, while bad images tend to be extremely dark or blurred. Thanks to its complex deep network, the *AVA Deep* model is able to discover a wide range of beautiful photographic images (and the few non-photo images that look like photographs), while, due to its lack of bad quality images, it is not able to correctly classify low-quality images: from the bottom ranked examples in Figure 6, it is very clear that the strawberry image should not be considered a very low quality image. Opposite to this, the *Pure Web Deep* model can correctly detect different types of bad images, while, due to the lack of extremely beautiful images in the training data, puts mid-high quality images at the top of the ranking. The *Finetuned Web Deep* model combines the best of both models: it can surface a diverse set of beautiful photographic and non-photographic images, while at the same time detecting low-quality images with different patterns.

Key Findings. To summarize, results suggest 4 main conclusions:

- Models trained purely on professional images do not perform well for images in the wild.
- Type-aware models are needed when the goal of the system is to surface beautiful non-photograhic images from the web.
- Deep frameworks work better than models based on hand-crafted features (excluding the above case) for scoring, ranking and surfacing beautiful images in the web. However, methods based on hand-crafted features are interpretable and they can be used when the main goal of the framework is to explain aesthetic phenomena.
- Fine-tuned CNNs transferring knowledge about professional image aesthetics to the task of surfacing (Average@10 metric) aesthetically pleasing images perform better than any other solution.

7 CONCLUSIONS AND FUTURE WORK

In this paper, we studied quality and aesthetics of web images. In particular, we emphasized the diversity of web images in the wild, which is in contrast to existing work on computational aesthetics, where features and models are designed to learn aesthetics from

Figure 6: Examples of beautiful and non-beautiful pictures according to our frameworks.

datasets of semi-professional images. We collected a dataset of approx. 100,000 images annotated with aesthetic scores and image type labels (photo/non-photo). We showed that this corpus contains many non-photographic images, and a non-trivial number of average or poor quality images. We designed a set of visual features to model image aesthetic value, and build 3 frameworks to automatically predict web image quality based on hand-crafted features and deep-learning. We evaluate our framework for different uses cases and expose interesting findings about how data, features, and learning algorithms impact aesthetic prediction.

The interpretability of the visual features we compute allows us to perform extensive analysis of the relations between features and aesthetics for professional photographs, web photographs and web graphics, and compare the three groups of pictures accordingly, showing that there are marked differences in the types of features that correlate with beauty and quality in each case. These differences explain the "aesthetic gap": web image aesthetic assessments is a very different problem to professional photo aesthetic assessments, since the nature of beautiful images is very different in each case.

This work represents a first study on the aesthetics of web images, opening many research questions regarding future work. We plan to improve our work by collecting more granular judgements regarding the non-photographic class of images: within the graphics pictures, we can find a wide variety of image sub-types (and therefore of aesthetic patterns), such as paintings, artworks, drawings, clipart, digital abstract art, etc. Such a detailed analysis would give us rich insights about the aesthetic value of different sub-groups of graphics, thus improving the global effectiveness of a real web image aesthetic classifier.

REFERENCES

[1] L. Breiman. Random forests. *Machine learning*, 45(1):5–32, 2001.

[2] N. Dalal and B. Triggs. Histograms of oriented gradients for human detection. In *Computer Vision and Pattern Recognition, 2005. CVPR 2005. IEEE Computer Society Conference on*, volume 1, pages 886–893. IEEE, 2005.

[3] R. Datta, D. Joshi, J. Li, and J. Z. Wang. Studying aesthetics in photographic images using a computational approach. In *European Conference on Computer Vision*, volume 3953 of *Lecture Notes in Computer Science*, pages 288–301. Springer

Berlin Heidelberg, 2006.
[4] S. Dhar, V. Ordonez, and T. L. Berg. High level describable attributes for predicting aesthetics and interestingness. In *Proceedings on IEEE Computer Society Conference on Computer Vision and Pattern Recognition*, CVPR, pages 1657–1664. IEEE Computer Society, 2011.
[5] M. Freeman. *The Photographer's Eye: Composition and Design for Better Digital Photos*, volume 1. Focal Press, 2007.
[6] B. Geng, L. Yang, C. Xu, X.-S. Hua, and S. Li. The role of attractiveness in web image search. In *Proceedings of the 19th ACM international conference on Multimedia*, pages 63–72. ACM, 2011.
[7] M. Gygli, H. Grabner, H. Riemenschneider, F. Nater, and L. V. Gool. The interestingness of images. In *Computer Vision (ICCV), 2013 IEEE International Conference on*, pages 1633–1640. IEEE, 2013.
[8] R. M. Haralick. Statistical and structural approaches to texture. *Proceedings of the IEEE*, 67(5):786–804, 1979.
[9] K.-Q. Huang, Q. Wang, and Z.-Y. Wu. Natural color image enhancement and evaluation algorithm based on human visual system. *Computer Vision and Image Understanding*, 103(1):52–63, 2006.
[10] P. Isola, J. Xiao, A. Torralba, and A. Oliva. What makes an image memorable? In *Computer Vision and Pattern Recognition (CVPR), 2011 IEEE Conference on*, pages 145–152. IEEE, 2011.
[11] S. Karayev, M. Trentacoste, H. Han, A. Agarwala, T. Darrell, A. Hertzmann, and H. Winnemoeller. Recognizing image style. *arXiv preprint arXiv:1311.3715*, 2013.
[12] Y. Ke, X. Tang, and F. Jing. The design of high-level features for photo quality assessment. In *Computer Vision and Pattern Recognition, 2006 IEEE Computer Society Conference on*, volume 1, pages 419–426. IEEE, 2006.
[13] A. Khosla, A. Das Sarma, and R. Hamid. What makes an image popular? In *Proceedings of the 23rd international conference on World wide web*, pages 867–876. International World Wide Web Conferences Steering Committee, 2014.
[14] X. Lu, Z. Lin, H. Jin, J. Yang, and J. Z. Wang. RAPID: Rating pictorial aesthetics using deep learning. In *Proceedings of the ACM International Conference on Multimedia*, pages 457–466. ACM, 2014.
[15] W. Luo, X. Wang, and X. Tang. Content-based photo quality assessment. In *ICCV), 2011*, pages 2206–2213. IEEE, 2011.
[16] Y. Luo and X. Tang. Photo and video quality evaluation: Focusing on the subject. In D. Forsyth, P. Torr, and A. Zisserman, editors, *Computer Vision âĂŞ ECCV 2008*, volume 5304 of *Lecture Notes in Computer Science*, pages 386–399. Springer Berlin Heidelberg, 2008.
[17] J. Machajdik and A. Hanbury. Affective image classification using features inspired by psychology and art theory. In *Proceedings of the international conference on Multimedia*, pages 83–92. ACM, 2010.
[18] L. Mai, H. Jin, and F. Liu. Composition-preserving deep photo aesthetics assessment. In *The IEEE Conference on Computer Vision and Pattern Recognition (CVPR)*, June 2016.
[19] L. Marchesotti, F. Perronnin, D. Larlus, and G. Csurka. Assessing the aesthetic quality of photographs using generic image descriptors. In *ICCV*, pages 1784–1791. IEEE, 2011.
[20] N. Murray, L. Marchesotti, and F. Perronnin. Ava: A large-scale database for aesthetic visual analysis. In *CVPR, 2012 IEEE Conference on*, pages 2408–2415. IEEE, 2012.
[21] T.-T. Ng, S.-F. Chang, and M.-P. Tsui. Lessons learned from online classification of photo-realistic computer graphics and photographs. In *Signal Processing Applications for Public Security and Forensics, 2007. SAFE'07. IEEE Workshop on*, pages 1–6. IET, 2007.
[22] M. Nishiyama, T. Okabe, I. Sato, and Y. Sato. Aesthetic quality classification of photographs based on color harmony. In *Proceedings on IEEE Computer Society Conference on Computer Vision and Pattern Recognition*, CVPR, pages 33–40, 2011.
[23] P. Obrador, X. Anguera, R. de Oliveira, and N. Oliver. The role of tags and image aesthetics in social image search. In *Proceedings of the First SIGMM Workshop on Social Media*, WSM '09, pages 65–72, New York, NY, USA, 2009. ACM.
[24] N. O'Hare, P. de Juan, R. Schifanella, Y. He, D. Yin, and Y. Chang. Leveraging user interaction signals for web image search. In *Proceedings of the 39th International ACM SIGIR conference on Research and Development in Information Retrieval*, pages 559–568. ACM, 2016.
[25] M. Redi, N. O?Hare, R. Schifanella, M. Trevisiol, and A. Jaimes. 6 seconds of sound and vision: Creativity in micro-videos. *Computer*, 2014.
[26] M. Redi, N. Rasiwasia, G. Aggarwal, and A. Jaimes. The beauty of capturing faces: Rating the quality of digital portraits. In *IEEE International Conference on Automatic Face and Gesture Recognition 2015*. IEEE, 2015.
[27] R. Schifanella, M. Redi, and L. M. Aiello. An image is worth more than a thousand favorites: Surfacing the hidden beauty of flickr pictures. In *Proceedings of THE 9TH INTERNATIONAL AAAI CONFERENCE ON WEB AND SOCIAL MEDIA (ICWSM-15)*, 2015.
[28] O. Wu, W. Hu, and J. Gao. Learning to predict the perceived visual quality of photos. In *ICCV*, pages 225–232. IEEE, 2011.

Multimodal Analysis of Image Search Intent

Intent Recognition in Image Search from User Behavior and Visual Content

Mohammad Soleymani
Swiss Center for Affective Sciences
University of Geneva
Geneva, Switzerland
mohammad.soleymani@unige.ch

Michael Riegler
Simula Research Laboratory and
University of Oslo
Oslo, Norway
michael@simula.no

Pål Halvorsen
Simula Research Laboratory and
University of Oslo
Oslo, Norway
paalh@simula.no

ABSTRACT

Users search for multimedia content with different underlying motivations or intentions. Study of user search intentions is an emerging topic in information retrieval since understanding *why* a user is searching for a content is crucial for satisfying the user's need. In this paper, we aimed at automatically recognizing a user's intent for image search in the early stage of a search session. We designed seven different search scenarios under the intent conditions of *finding* items, *re-finding* items and *entertainment.* We collected facial expressions, physiological responses, eye gaze and implicit user interactions from 51 participants who performed seven different search tasks on a custom-built image retrieval platform. We analyzed the users' spontaneous and explicit reactions under different intent conditions. Finally, we trained machine learning models to predict users' search intentions from the visual content of the visited images, the user interactions and the spontaneous responses. After fusing the visual and user interaction features, our system achieved the F-1 score of 0.722 for classifying three classes in a user-independent cross-validation. We found that eye gaze and implicit user interactions, including mouse movements and keystrokes are the most informative features. Given that the most promising results are obtained by modalities that can be captured unobtrusively and online, the results demonstrate the feasibility of deploying such methods for improving multimedia retrieval platforms.

CCS CONCEPTS

•Information systems → Image search; *Search interfaces;* **•Human-centered computing →** *Laboratory experiments;*

KEYWORDS

Search, multimedia, user interaction, intent, emotion, experiment, eye gaze, facial expression, computer vision

ACM Reference format:
Mohammad Soleymani, Michael Riegler, and Pål Halvorsen. 2017. Multimodal Analysis of Image Search Intent. In *Proceedings of ICMR '17, Bucharest, Romania, June 6–9, 2017,* 9 pages.
DOI: http://dx.doi.org/10.1145/3078971.3078995

978-1-4503-4701-3/17/06...$15.00.
DOI: http://dx.doi.org/10.1145/3078971.3078995

1 INTRODUCTION

A multimedia retrieval system that takes users' intent into account can optimize its ranking and visualization methods to better satisfy its users. In this context, users' search intention has a profound effect on the way they interact with an information retrieval system. It has been shown that search tasks are not solely performed with the goal of information search, but also to re-find specific content [36] and for entertainment [13]. The success of multimedia retrieval does not only rely on the relevance of the content to the query and the way the content is framed and depicted is equally important to users, given their search intention. This is more evident for the case of multimedia retrieval in which entertainment is a major motivator behind multimedia search [22]. Understanding *why* a user is embarking on a multimedia search process is not possible with information retrieval systems simply accepting query terms. Therefore, search motivation shall be determined from the implicit indicators and the context.

Due to its nature, intent in multimedia search is different from the classic web search intentions, i.e., *informational, navigational* and *transactional* intentions [7, 22]. Moshfeghi *et al.* [30] used the categories of *seeking information, re-finding an item* and two *entertainment* categories to adjust arousal and mood. They further attempted to automatically identify video search intentions from users implicit feedback, e.g., mouse movements. They could demonstrate the feasibility of intent recognition from users' implicit feedback. Users implicit feedback and behavioral responses have been also used to automatically determine topical relevance in information retrieval [1].

In this work, we aimed at automatically recognizing search intent early in an image search session. We targeted three scenarios, i.e., *finding* images, *re-finding* images and *entertainment.* Our *finding* category includes *seeking information* and *transactions* since we asked the participants to identify images to be downloaded and used for a certain purpose. The re-find category is similar to the category of *mental image* proposed in [26] in which a user has a specific image in mind that they want to find. Unlike the work in [30], we let the participants decide how they want to entertain themselves through image search, thus our mood and arousal adjustments are mixed. It is also worth noting that it is not as easy to adjust for arousal through images in contrast to videos that are used in [30].

We recruited 51 healthy participants to participate in an experiment performing image search tasks under different intent conditions. We built a custom image search interface using the Flickr[1] API. Given the role of emotions in the search intent process [30],

[1] http://www.flickr.com

we opted for recording and analyzing facial expressions and Galvanic Skin Response (GSR), in addition to the interactions analyzed in [30]. We also recorded eye gaze and pupil dilation which can capture interaction, attention and arousal [5, 20]. Additionally, we recorded implicit user interactions with the search interface, including key strokes, search logs and mouse movements. We analyzed these modalities and how they vary under different intent conditions. Moreover, we trained models to recognize intent early in the search session (first 30s) from the spontaneous reactions and implicit interactions. We also used the visual content from the visited images to recognize search intent sessions. In summary, our major contributions are as follows.

- We analyzed how facial expressions, eye gaze, queries and implicit user interaction vary by image search intent.
- We analyzed visual content features of the visited images and demonstrate how they can be utilized for search intent recognition.
- We built and evaluated a search intent recognition system through users spontaneous responses and interaction.

Thus, in contrast to the work presented in [30], which reported a user-dependent intent recognition in video search, we performed a user-independent intent recognition for image search. We also analyzed facial expressions, physiological responses, eye gaze, implicit user interactions and visual content of images and evaluated their effectiveness for intent recognition.

Using machine learning models to predict users' intentions from the collected information, our system achieved the average F-1 score of 0.722 for three classes in a user-independent cross-validation. Furthermore, experiments revealed that eye gaze and implicit user interactions are the most informative features. This is very promising because these modalities can be captured online, which demonstrates the potential of using such methods for improving multimedia retrieval platforms.

The remainder of this paper is organized as follows. The previous work is presented in Section 2. The experimental methodology and apparatus are explained in Section 3. Section 4 provides details about the image retrieval system in the experiments. Extracted features and statistical analysis on how they vary by intent conditions are reported in Section 5. Intent recognition and its results are given in Section 6, and the limitations of this work are discussed in Section 7. The work is finally concluded in Section 8.

2 BACKGROUND

There is a general belief in the multimedia community that intent in text search is different from the intent in multimedia search [22]. In addition to relevance, in multimedia search, the content and the presentation of multimedia items are also important to the user, i.e., *why* and for which purpose images and videos are taken, searched for and viewed. User intent in the area of multimedia can in general be divided in the domains of image and video search [22]. In each of the two domains, several models and categories of intent have been defined, which are conceptually similar, but named differently in different publications [14, 17, 24, 26].

In the image retrieval domain, the most important intent categories are *navigation* (find a specific image without knowing the content), *transaction* (find a specific image for further use), *knowledge orientation* (learn something by looking at an image) and *mental image* (know the content of the image beforehand) [26]. The following intent categories are identified in video search: *information* (obtain knowledge and gather new information), *experience learning* (acquire new skills or learn something), *experience exposure* (undergo a specific experience), *affect* (change mood or affective state) and *object* (the video itself as an object) [17]. Based on these intent categories, several researchers tried to perform intent classification from multimedia content. Hanjalic *et al.* [17] classified videos based on shot patterns, speech and metadata into three different categories (*information*, *experience* and *affect*) and reported a weighted F-1 score of 0.833 for the performance of the classification.

Lux et. al. [27] released and discussed an image dataset containing 1,309 images for five intent classes. The dataset and intent annotations for each image were collected in a user study, and for the intent classes, the categories presented in [26] were used. The intent dataset was used in [32] to explore if content-based visual features can be helpful to detect the photographers' intent (why the picture has been taken). This was done by performing unsupervised clustering of the images into five intent classes using global visual features. To evaluate the performance, the correlation between the human agreement with the clusters was compared, which revealed that content-based features can indeed be used to classify images based on the photographers' intent.

Moshfeghi *et al.* [30] studied the emotion and interaction in different video search intent scenarios. They recorded users' implicit feedback for four different intention classes, namely, *seeking information*, *re-finding* a particular information object, *entertainment* by adjusting arousal level, and *entertainment* by adjusting mood. They found significant differences between the emotional experiences of tasks in different intentions. They also found that the task difficulty and certainty perception varied by search intention. They could finally train a model to predict search intent, in a user-dependent cross-validation, with the accuracy of up to 57.29%.

Overall, the reviewed literature provides evidence for the usefulness of multimedia content and users' spontaneous reactions for recognizing intent in multimedia search. Nevertheless, predicting and using a user's intent during a multimedia search is still a rather unexplored field. Even though both content-based methods and user interactions features have been studied in such a context, to the best of our knowledge, this work is the first to combine both in a multimodal fusion and to explore the usefulness of additional modalities, i.e., eye gaze, physiological response and facial expression.

3 DATA COLLECTION

The experiment has received ethical approval from the ethical review board of the faculty of psychology and educational sciences, University of Geneva. 51 healthy participants with normal or corrected to normal vision were recruited through campus wide posters and Facebook. From these 51 participants, 18 were male and 33 were female, and the average age was 25.7 years (σ = 5.3). The participants were informed about their rights and the nature of

Figure 1: Our experimental setup including an eye gaze tracker, front-facing camera recording face videos and galvanic skin response.

the experiment. They then signed an informed consent form before the recordings. They received a monetary gratitude for their participation.

Our experiments were conducted in an acoustically isolated experimental booth with controlled lighting (shown in Figure 1). A video was recorded using an Allied Vision[2] Stingray camera at 60.03 frames/second with a 780 × 580 resolution. Stimuli were presented on a 23 inches screen (1920×1080), and the participants were seated approximately 60cm from the screen. Two Litepanels[3] daylight spot LED projectors were used to light up the participants' faces to reduce possible shadows. An infrared block filter was mounted on the lens to remove the reflection of the infrared light from the eye gaze tracker. Video was recorded using the Norpix Streampix software[4]. Eye gaze, pupil diameter and head distance were recorded using a Tobii[5] TX300 eye gaze tracker at 300Hz. The GSR was recorded using a Biopac[6] MP-36 at 125Hz through electrodes attached on distal phalanges of index and middle fingers. An experimental protocol was run by Tobii Studio, and the recordings were synchronized by a sound trigger that marked the frames before each stimulus for the camera. The same trigger was converted to a transistorfi?!transistor logic (TTL) trigger using a Brain Products StimTrak[7] and recorded alongside the GSR signals.

Our participants were first familiarized with the protocol and ratings in a test run, and then they performed search tasks under three different intent conditions. In this study, we were interested in assessing knowledge emotions in image search. Knowledge emotions are the emotions that arise as a result of the evaluation of one's knowledge, e.g., interest, confusion and surprise. Therefore, we asked the participants to self-report these emotions on a seven-point scale at the end of each session. In addition, we also asked the participants to report the level of control and boredom they felt using a similar seven-point scale rating.

The recorded database, except face videos are available for academic research[8]. For the face videos, we provide the landmarks, features and action units for the benefit of the community.

[2] https://www.alliedvision.com/
[3] http://www.litepanels.com
[4] https://www.norpix.com
[5] http://www.tobii.com/
[6] https://www.biopac.com/
[7] http://www.brainproducts.com/
[8] http://cvml.unige.ch/resources

Figure 2: An example of a search performed with our image retrieval system. With a double click on the enlarged image, the user chose the goal image.

4 IMAGE RETRIEVAL SYSTEM

To conduct the search experiments, we created our own custom image search tool. A snapshot of our image retrieval system is shown in Figure 2. The design of the tool was made in a way that it could easily be customized to the different search intents. The images are retrieved using the Flickr API. When the user performs a search by submitting a query, the tool returns a ranked list of images. The images are presented to the user in an image gallery depicting the first ten images as thumbnails with the first image enlarged at the bottom.

The experiments were conducted in seven sessions, under three intent conditions, namely, *entertainment, finding* and *re-finding* items. Each session lasted three minutes and sessions were presented in random order. We had three sessions for finding images for a specific purpose; three sessions for re-finding images that were displayed for 15 seconds before the search session and one free viewing *entertainment* session. For two search sessions, one in *finding* and one in *re-finding*, we slightly modified the search terms on the fly to observe the effect of goal obstruction on users behavior. The modification was performed by adding and removing random query terms before they were sent to Flickr. The search tasks were mostly about Geneva where the experiments were conducted. The image search task instructions are given in Table 1.

We discarded the data from the participants who misunderstood the instructions, and the sessions in which the majority of eye gaze samples were lost (due to extreme head pose and, in one case, device failure). Therefore, out of 357 possible search sessions, we could analyze 299 session that were consistently and correctly performed and recorded. In the analysis of behavioral responses, the data from the first seven participants were also discarded since we made a small change in the layout of the interface, after recording them, which made the eye gaze responses inconsistent.

5 EXTRACTED FEATURES AND MULTIMODAL ANALYSIS

5.1 User interactions and responses

The following modalities were recorded from the participants interacting with the search interface: visual, physiological, eye gaze and implicit user interactions. In this section, we describe the processing and feature extraction performed on these modalities. For

Table 1: The list of image search task instructions given to the users during the experiment.

Task	Instruction
Condition 1 (*entertainment*):	You can search/browse freely to look for your content of interest.
Condition 2-1 (*finding* items):	Please find 3 pictures to be used for advertising tourism in Geneva; they should all show jet d'eau.
Condition 2-2 (*finding* items):	Please find 3 pictures to be used for advertising tourism in Geneva; it should be from the city and with no picture from the lake.
Condition 2-3 (*finding* items):	Please find 3 pictures to be used for advertising tourism in Geneva; it should show Nations square.
Condition 3-1 (*re-finding* items):	Please try to re-find the example image shown below. The example image is a boy on a beach playing with a bucket.
Condition 3-2 (*re-finding* items):	Please try to re-find the example image shown below. The example image is a Swiss flag swung on the edge of a lake.
Condition 3-3 (*re-finding* items):	Please try to re-find the example image shown below. The image shows passengers boarding a Vietnam airlines plane on a cloudy day.

Table 2: The list of 17 features extracted from the logged implicit user interaction with the search tool. Each feature is extracted per user and per session.

Feature type	Description	#
Mouse clicks	Clicking rate per second (mean and standard deviation), type of clicked object (search button, next image, etc.)	8
Mouse movement	Distance moved in pixels per second, speed (pixels per second) of movement for each second (mean and standard deviation)	4
Key strokes	Keystroke rate per second (mean and standard deviation)	2
Search terms	Number of different query terms, complexity of query terms derived from the synsets tree length in the WordNet [2, 29]	2
Images	Number of displayed images	1

the analysis in this section, we analyzed user interactions features extracted from the full sessions. The visual content features and the user interactions features from the first 30 seconds were used for the intent recognition in Section 6.

5.1.1 Implicit user interaction. All implicit user interactions performed with the search tool were logged (see Table 2). This includes the clicks, mouse movements, displayed images and thumbnails, selected images, search queries and keystrokes. Additionally, we implemented the possibility to manipulate search queries in the background. All the information was collected using Java scripts and stored in a MySQL server using PHP for later analysis. From the collected data, we extracted different types of features for further analysis, including mouse movements, mouse clicks and keystrokes.

5.1.2 Eye gaze. Optical eye gaze trackers track the direction of gaze and provide the projected gaze. The eye gaze pattern and pupil diameter have been used for detecting boredom, mind-wandering and interest [3, 11, 20, 25]. Eye gaze trackers often record head distance and pupil diameter which are both shown to be useful for recognizing affective and cognitive states [20]. Head distance is a measure of body posture. Pupillary reflex is modulated by emotional arousal through increase in sympathetic activities [5]. Eye gaze features such as fixations and saccades were extracted by the eye gaze analysis software (Tobii Studio). Fixations are the points where eye gaze is maintained in the same location for a minimum amount of time (around 100ms). The number of eye fixations, the presence of eye gaze in the area of interest (AOI) and the saccadic movements vary in different cognitive and emotional states. Saccades are the eye movements between fixations. The absolute direction of saccades (measured by their absolute angle) and the relative direction with regard to the last saccade were calculated by Tobii studio. With a simplifying assumption of straight saccadic movements, we defined the scan path as the direct path between the consecutive fixations. In eye gaze analysis, an area of interest is often defined to study the gaze pattern locally. We defined the area of the enlarged image as the AOI. Inspired by the relevant literature [3, 11], 60 features were extracted from eye gaze, pupil diameter and head distance (see Table 3).

Table 3: The list of 60 eye gaze features. The functionals or statistical descriptives are mean, standard deviation, first and third quartiles, median, maximum and minimum.

Feature type	Description	#
AOI	Number of fixations in the AOI, the proportion of gaze duration in AOI	2
Fixation	Number of fixations, statistical descriptives on fixation duration	8
Saccade	Number of saccedes, statistical descriptives of saccade duration, absolute and relative saccadic directions	22
Scan path	Statistical descriptives of scan path distances and their speed	14

5.1.3 Facial expressions. Facial expressions were analyzed using the Affdex SDK [28]. The Facial Action Coding System (FACS) [12] is a taxonomy of facial movements that can describe facial expressions, e.g., lip puller, brow raise and dimpler. The intensity of 19 facial action units were detected at frame level by Affdex. Additionally, head pose direction was also extracted. The following seven functionals were applied to the features in each session for pooling: mean, standard deviation, median, maximum, minimum, first and third quartiles. This resulted in a feature vector with 154 elements for each session.

5.1.4 Galvanic skin response (GSR). GSR is a measurement of electrical conductance on skin through a pair of electrodes. The skin's electrical resistance measured by GSR fluctuates with the activity of sweat glands which are driven by the sympathetic nervous system. GSR responses consists of tonic (slow) and phasic (fast and often event-related) responses. GSR varies by emotional arousal and has been extensively used in emotion sensing [8, 23]. GSR provides a measure for detecting the presence and intensity of emotions. We used the open source TEAP toolbox[9] [34] to extract nine features from the GSR signals. In order to capture the phasic

[9]https://github.com/Gijom/TEAP

Table 4: The list of nine GSR features.

Feature type	Description
Number of peaks	Number of peaks in resistance exceeding 100Ω
Amplitude of peaks	GSR peak amplitude from the saddle point preceding the peak
Rise time	The time it takes GSR to reach its peak from the saddle point in seconds
Statistical moments	Mean, first and third quartile & standard deviation (electrical resistance in Ω)
Trend	Intercept and slope for the linear trend

responses, we extracted the peaks that appears in GSR signals and calculated their frequency of occurrence, amplitude and rise time. Statistical descriptives were also extracted that captures both tonic and phasic characteristics of electrodermal responses. The list of features are given in Table 4.

5.2 Visual content features

To explore how the content of the visited images are related to the intent categories, we extracted three sets of visual content features from the images. We decided to use one feature-set that extracts the overall visual similarities based on colors and textures in images visited for the same intent and another set that is able to emulate the visual perception of a human to explore if the visited images in intent classes are of differentiable nature according to their visual perception. Additionally, sentiment expressed by images, i.e., visual sentiment [4], may carry information about the intent categories that can be useful. For each of these three feature-sets, we created one feature vector containing the visual features of all images visited in the first 10, 20 and 30 seconds of the search session for each search task. The visual content features were only used for the intent recognition experiments in Section 6. We decided not to directly use features extracted from a deep convolutional neural network trained on Imagenet [10] since such features are related to the concepts present in images that can be associated with the specific tasks rather than intentions.

5.2.1 Joint composite descriptor (JCD). JCD is a set of global visual features that represent the texture and color of an image. The JDC features are joint descriptors, which combine two compact composite descriptors (fuzzy color and texture histogram and the color and edge directivity) in one. The combination of the two descriptors is possible because their color information originates from the same fuzzy color system. The result of the combination is a descriptor, which contains fuzzy color information, texture information and edge information [9]. By extracting this feature, we wanted to study the visual similarities in images visited in the same intent condition.

5.2.2 Tamura. The Tamura features are defined based on the assumption that textural features correspond to the perception of the human eyes [35]. Tamura compared coarseness, contrast, directionality, line-likeness, regularity and roughness, which are six different texture features, with psychological measures taken from experiment subjects. The three features that achieved the best results in his evaluation are coarseness, contrast and orientation. Coarseness measures the size texture primitives (also called texture elements or texels) [18]. Larger textures have larger primitives and fine textures have smaller ones. The contrast measures how distinctive the differences between the textures in the images are. The contrast can be considered as clear to identify if all areas can easily be distinguished from each other. The orientation describes the dominant orientation of the textures in the image. A single image can have only one dominant orientation or several of them. Moreover, an image can also have no orientation at all, which then is called isotropic. For the Tamura global image feature, coarseness, contrast and orientation are extracted from an image and stored in a histogram representation [19]. Using this feature, we want to explore if the intent classes are related to the visual perception and if this can help to classify the intent class.

5.2.3 Visual sentiment descriptors. A visual sentiment concept detector [21] was applied to the images that were visited during the search process. This sentiment detector was trained to detect a refined set of a large-scale visual sentiment concept ontology (VSO) that detects the presence of adjective-noun pairs in images. These adjective-noun pairs (ANP) were selected from social media data based on their relevance in expressing sentiment. The model that we used is an improved version of the original work [4] that uses a residual deep convolutional neural network (CNN) that is trained to detect adjectives, nouns and ANPs simultaneously [21]. This CNN generates probability estimates (softmax output) for 553 adjective-noun pairs that are then combined for the visited images to form feature vectors.

5.3 Statistical analysis

In this Section, we analyze how the features extracted from behavior, reported emotions and interactions differ under different intent scenarios. Participants self-reported a set of emotions, e.g., interest, boredom and confusion, at the end of each short search session. We calculated the Spearman rank correlation between all the self-reported emotions (see Table 5). As expected, interest and boredom are inversely correlated. The significant correlation between surprise and confusion ratings demonstrate that these emotions were co-occurring in search scenarios. We further looked into whether

Table 5: Spearman rank correlation coefficient between the ratings. * implies significance ($p < 0.01$).

Rating	Interest	Boredom	Confusion	Control	Surprise
Interest	-	-0.49*	-0.03	0.31*	0.22*
Boredom	-	-	-0.05	-0.29*	-0.19*
Confusion	-	-	-	-0.30*	0.46*
Control	-	-	-	-	-0.06

the reported emotions varied in different intent conditions. We performed a one-way ANOVA test on the ratings in three conditions and found significant differences for interest ($p = 0.00$, $F = 12.10$), boredom ($p = 0.01$, $F = 5.25$) and control ($p = 0.00$, $F = 16.93$). The distribution of the reported emotions in three different intent conditions are given in Figure 3. We performed a two-tailed t-test to check whether the perception of control was changed with manipulating the query terms, i.e., adding and removing random terms before sending the query to Flickr in two out of seven sessions. We did not find any significant difference between manipulated and

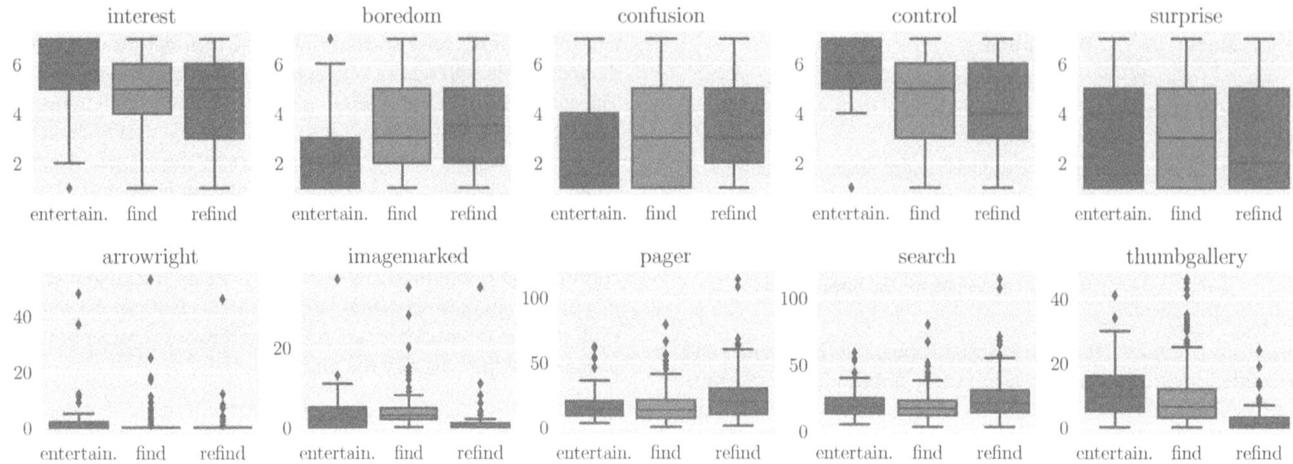

Figure 3: Self-reported emotions (top) and click frequency on different items (bottom) under different intent conditions.

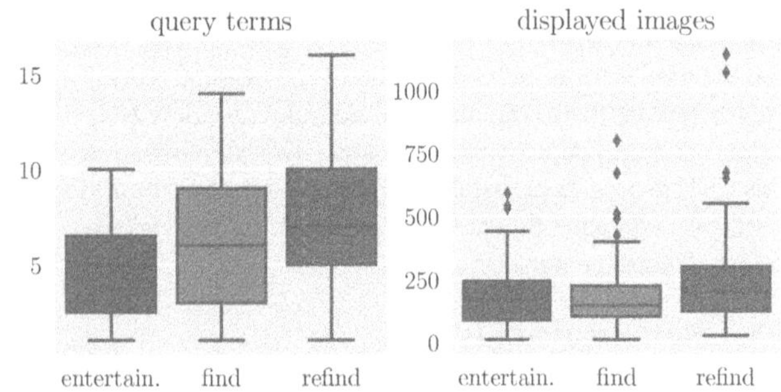

Figure 4: Box-plots showing the distributions of the number of images and the number query terms in each condition.

non-manipulated situations which demonstrated that our query manipulation was too weak and not effective in inducing the sense of goal obstruction.

Semantic complexity of a term is associated with its ambiguity, i.e., the number of different meanings that can be interpreted from the word. We calculated the query complexity using a synset tree; the deeper the vertex is in the tree the less ambiguous the term is [29]. The total complexity is calculated as follows. First, we get the synset tree for a given search term. In the tree, we iterate over all branches leading to the term. For all branches, we calculate the depth and sum it. The number and depth of branches is representative of the number of the meaning that can be derived and is a measure of complexity. For example, "cage" has three branches in the sysnet tree and each of them has a depth of one which makes its complexity score three. A one-way ANOVA test on the query term complexity showed a significant difference between different intent conditions. The *entertainment* condition queries had a much lower complexity compared to the *finding* and *re-finding* conditions. The *re-finding* condition had the highest complexity where the participants were trying to use generic terms describing the content they had in mind. Through fitting a linear model, we checked whether the complexity of the query terms varied over time. We found that, only in the *re-finding* condition, there was a significant increase in the complexity of the query terms ($slope = 0.05$, $p = 0.00$).

We also looked at the number of search terms used in each condition. A one-way ANOVA test showed significant differences between the number of query terms used in average ($p = 0.00$, $F = 17.75$). Similarly, the *entertainment* condition had the lowest average number of query terms followed by *finding* and *re-finding* conditions (see Figure 4).

To study the browsing pattern, we counted the number of browsed images per session. A one-way ANOVA test found a significant difference between the number of images displayed under three different conditions ($p = 0.00$, $F = 5.68$). Given the smaller number of query terms used in the *entertainment* condition, this demonstrates that the participants spent more time browsing rather than searching (see Figure 4).

We looked into two features from mouse movements under different intent conditions. The speed and the distance of mouse movement trajectories. A one-way ANOVA test showed significant differences for speech ($p = 0.00$, $F = 6.77$) and distance ($p = 0.01$, $F = 5.12$) under different intent conditions. Mouse movement was the fastest in the *entertainment* condition. However, the distance of the mouse trajectories was much shorter in average compared the *finding* and *re-finding* conditions. Therefore, participants spent less time exploring the interface with their mouse in the *entertainment* condition.

Mouse click features describe where on the interface the clicks occurred and at what time. We collected clicks based on the locations of the clicks, which are *arrowright* and *arrowleft*, *imagemarked* (enlarged image), *pager* (to change pages), *search* and *thumbgallery* (thumbnails). The distribution of the click frequencies is shown in Figure 3. A one-way ANOVA test showed significant differences between click frequencies for *imagemarked* ($p = 0.00$, $F = 22.66$), *pager* ($p = 0.00$, $F = 6.63$), *search* button ($p = 0.00$, $F = 7.00$) and *thumbgallery* ($p = 0.00$, $F = 43.78$). We also calculated the key stroke rates and found that the rate of key strokes were not different under the three intent conditions.

The aggregated heat maps of eye gaze on three different conditions are given in Figure 5. We can observe that users spent more time looking at the enlarged image in the *entertainment* conditions whereas they spent much less time in the *re-finding* condition. In

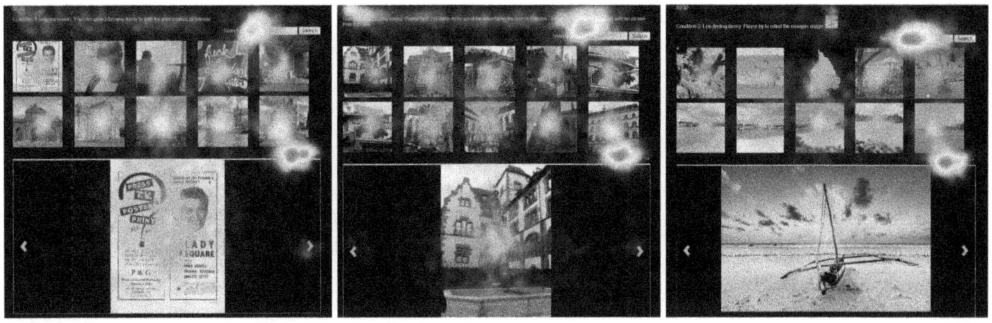

Figure 5: Eye gaze heat maps in different search intent conditions. From left to right: entertainment, finding and re-finding.

the re-find condition, the goal was to spot the image so they spent more time on queries and exploring the thumbnails.

Using the Affdex SDK [28], we also calculated the intensity of the following expressed emotions: sadness, joy, disgust, anger, contempt , surprise and engagement. The statistical analysis did not show any difference between the frequency of the expressed emotions under different conditions.

6 INTENT RECOGNITION

Predicting the search intent early on in a search session can help a retrieval system to adapt its results according to the user's need. Therefore, we attempted recognizing search intent from four different modalities, namely, facial expressions, physiological responses, eye gaze and implicit interactions, e.g., mouse movement. Inspired by the previous work that related visual content to the possible search intent [17, 26], we also extracted visual content features from the visited images and used them for intent recognition. We only extracted features from the first 10, 20 and 30 seconds of a search session to imitate a situation in which a retrieval system is predicting the search intent.

Using the extracted features from the first 10, 20 and 30 seconds, we trained Random Forest classifiers to tackle the classification. We opted for using an ensemble method due to its ability to perform well with lower number of samples and its robustness against over-fitting. The utilized features are described in Section 5. The performance of the classification was evaluated through a user-independent cross-validation, in which the samples from the same participants were never present in both train and test sets.

6.1 Experimental results and multimodal fusion

For all our classification experiments, we used the same Random Forest classifier with the respective features as input [6] with the following parameters: 300 trees, 100 iterations, unlimited maximal depth and a batch size of 100.

For the evaluation, we used user-independent cross-validation. Table 6 gives an overview of the classification results using the user interaction features, visual content features and fusions of them. We fused the modalities in two ways.

The first fusion method is *early fusion* which consists in concatenating different feature vectors into a single vector before being fed to a classifier. A problem with early fusion is that the combination of very diverse features, like user interaction features with visual features, can pose problems. For example, combining interaction features with a small number of dimensions with a visual feature-set with many thousand dimensions in an early fusion does not result to improved performance [16, 33].

The second utilized fusion method is *late fusion*. In late fusion or decision-level fusion, each modality has its own classifier. After these first classification steps, the output of all classifiers are combined to obtain a final result. This combination can be performed for example by simple majority vote, using another classifier or weighted sum of the scores. Because each feature is processed in a separate classifier, *late fusion* is more costly in terms of computational complexity. The choice of *late fusion* method depends on the dataset, the features and the metrics that are used to calculate the distances between the different features [15].

As shown in Table 6, the visual content features alone outperform the baseline, which we calculated using the ZeroR classifier. ZeroR assigns the label from the majority class to all the instances and provides a baseline. This is an indicator that the intent categories are somehow preserved in the visual features but single features are not very efficient to detect this. The same is true for all user interactions features. The performance of Tamura is particularly interesting since it should be able to give a similar perception to humans and indicates that different intent classes are perceived differently. The VSO features performed the best among the visual features. VSO features also performed better with more images, i.e., the longer the interaction window we analyzed. However, VSO features might have captured the concepts that are related to the tasks rather than intentions. Comparing visual content features and user interactions features, the user spontaneous and implicit interaction features perform better. Implicit interaction outperforms the visual content features. All sets of visual content features perform better than the face and GSR features.

Looking at the window length, the shorter segments yield better results for behavioral and interaction features whereas for content features longer segments mostly increased the performance. Overall, 30 seconds segments gives the best performance with late fusion reaching average F-1 score of 0.722 for three classes.

Early fusion does not lead to a large increase of the performance and for the user interactions features it even leads to a small decrease. Feature vectors from different modalities are of different size and simply concatenating them does not yield superior results (for example face compared to GSR). For the visual content features, the early fusion lead to a small increase, which was expected based on previous findings [16, 33]. Late fusion for all different combinations

Table 6: Classification performance based on the user interactions and visual content features in terms of weighted average of precision, recall and F-1 score. The results are reported for the first 10, 20 and 30 seconds. The best results are in boldface.

Features	Precision			Recall			F-1 score		
User interactions features	**10sec**	**20sec**	**30sec**	**10sec**	**20sec**	**30sec**	**10sec**	**20sec**	**30sec**
Face	**0.449**	0.444	0.392	**0.524**	0.520	0.458	**0.483**	0.479	0.421
Eye Gaze	**0.576**	0.542	0.562	**0.626**	0.587	0.572	**0.585**	0.548	0.536
GSR	**0.430**	0.363	0.421	**0.488**	0.413	0.438	**0.455**	0.386	0.422
Implicit user interaction	**0.693**	0.650	0.619	**0.724**	0.681	0.682	**0.698**	0.651	0.637
Visual content features	**10sec**	**20sec**	**30sec**	**10sec**	**20sec**	**30sec**	**10sec**	**20sec**	**30sec**
Tamura	0.392	0.396	**0.403**	0.478	0.482	**0.495**	0.43	0.433	**0.444**
JCD	**0.561**	0.532	0.46	0.512	**0.538**	0.468	0.475	**0.493**	0.463
VSO	0.502	0.617	**0.623**	0.583	0.627	**0.639**	0.539	0.601	**0.612**
Multimodal fusion	**10sec**	**20sec**	**30sec**	**10sec**	**20sec**	**30sec**	**10sec**	**20sec**	**30sec**
Early fusion user interactions and visual content	**0.581**	0.54	0.521	**0.677**	0.630	0.610	**0.625**	0.581	0.562
Late fusion user interactions and visual content	0.683	0.67	**0.743**	0.748	0.736	**0.748**	0.703	0.692	**0.722**
Baseline (ZeroR)	0.353	0.353	0.189	0.421	0.421	0.435	0.346	0.346	0.264

reaches the best results. In our experiments, we used the weighted sum of scores for late fusion. The scores were derived from the classifier by averaging the predicted class probability of the trees in a Random Forest (confidence score for each class). The overall best result is achieved fusing the user interactions features with the visual content features. We found that multimodal fusion achieves the best results for intent classification.

7 DISCUSSIONS

The intention categories in this work do not cover all possible search intent scenarios and are only three typical cases. To fully cover the whole spectrum of search intent, we need a finer granularity and additional intent categories specific to the image content. We did not witness significant emotional expressions, and this could be a result of the mental fatigue caused by the experiment or the artificial nature of the search tasks with less sense of ownership than genuine ones [31].

Another limitation of this work is the potential bias of the tasks cognitive load and behavioral responses elicited by instructions rather than intention. This might have resulted in different interaction and behavioral responses that are not necessarily related to intent. For example, the head pose or eye gaze position are more likely to be at the top to recall the task description in more difficult tasks compared to the easy one, i.e., entertainment.

The visual features used in this work show promising results. Nevertheless, further analysis is needed on content-based features. We hypothesize that emotional content of the query and retrieved results are related with search intent, e.g., positive sentiment might be associated with *entertainment* intent. However, what has been detected by visual sentiment features might not necessarily be related the intention, and the difference in the visual sentiment might be the result of the task at hand.

The intent recognition performance is similar to the one reported in [30], i.e., 51.4% in the early stage for four classes. However, our results are obtained using a user-independent cross-validation which is more generalizable and shows robustness to between-user variations. Nevertheless the performance of such a system shall be further evaluated in an operationalized system with a diverse set of scenarios in which intention can even change in the middle of a search session.

To the best of our knowledge, the relevance of the content to search intent has not been analyzed in text-content. Utilizing the language processing models to understand queries and retrieved content can be also useful for determining users search intent.

8 CONCLUSIONS

In this paper, we analyzed the spontaneous responses of users under different search intent conditions. We found that implicit user interaction including mouse movement to be the most informative channel of information for predicting the intent. Eye gaze behavior also showed promising power in differentiating between different intent conditions. However, despite the importance of emotions in the search process [30], facial expression and physiological responses underperformed in recognizing search intent compared to implicit user interactions. As we showed, the visual content of the browsed images can also provide hints on the underlying intention for image search. To summarize, we identified the best modalities for recognizing search intent and showed the feasibility of automatically identifying search intent early in a search session. If such automatic intent recognition method is deployed, the resulting intent-aware multimedia retrieval system can optimize its results by switching its ranking methods according to the user's underlying motivation.

9 ACKNOWLEDGMENTS

The work of Soleymani was supported by his Swiss National Science Foundation Ambizione grant. The work of Riegler and Halvorsen was supported by the Research Council of Norway as a part of the projects INTROMAT under grant agreement 259293 and EONS under grant agreement 231687. We thank David Sander for his kind assistance for the ethical review of the experiment. We also thank "Fondation Campus Biotech Genève" for providing access and support at their experimental facilities.

REFERENCES

[1] I. Arapakis, I. Konstas, and J. M. Jose. 2009. Using Facial Expressions and Peripheral Physiological Signals As Implicit Indicators of Topical Relevance. In *Proceedings of the 17th ACM International Conference on Multimedia (MM '09)*. ACM, New York, NY, USA, 461–470.

[2] S. Bird. 2006. NLTK: the natural language toolkit. In *Proceedings of the COLING/ACL on Interactive presentation sessions*. 69–72.

[3] N. Blanchard, R. Bixler, T. Joyce, and S. D'Mello. 2014. Automated Physiological-Based Detection of Mind Wandering during Learning. In *Proceedings of ITS*. Springer International Publishing, 55–60.

[4] D. Borth, T. Chen, R. Ji, and S.-F. Chang. 2013. SentiBank: Large-scale Ontology and Classifiers for Detecting Sentiment and Emotions in Visual Content. In *Proceedings of the 21st ACM International Conference on Multimedia (MM '13)*. ACM, New York, NY, USA, 459–460.

[5] Bradley, M. Margaret, Miccoli, Laura, Escrig, A. Miguel, Lang, and J. Peter. 2008. The pupil as a measure of emotional arousal and autonomic activation. *Psychophysiology* 45, 4 (July 2008), 602–607.

[6] L. Breiman. 2001. Random forests. *Machine learning* 45, 1 (2001), 5–32.

[7] A. Broder. 2002. A Taxonomy of Web Search. *SIGIR Forum* 36, 2 (Sept. 2002), 3–10.

[8] R. A. Calvo and S. D'Mello. 2010. Affect Detection: An Interdisciplinary Review of Models, Methods, and Their Applications. *IEEE Transactions on Affective Computing* 1, 1 (jan 2010), 18–37.

[9] S. Chatzichristofis, Y. Boutalis, and M. Lux. 2009. Selection of the proper compact composite descriptor for improving content based image retrieval. In *Procideeding of IASTED Int'l Conference on Signal Processing, Pattern Recognition and Applications*, Vol. 134643. 64.

[10] J. Deng, W. Dong, R. Socher, L.-J. Li, K. Li, and L. Fei-Fei. 2009. Imagenet: A large-scale hierarchical image database. In *Computer Vision and Pattern Recognition, 2009. CVPR 2009. IEEE Conference on*. IEEE, 248–255.

[11] S. D'Mello, A. Olney, C. Williams, and P. Hays. 2012. Gaze tutor: A gaze-reactive intelligent tutoring system. *International Journal of Human-Computer Studies* 70, 5 (2012), 377–398.

[12] P. Ekman and W. Friesen. 1978. *The Facial Action Coding System (FACS)*. Consulting Psychologists Press, Stanford University, Palo Alto.

[13] D. Elsweiler, S. Mandl, and B. Kirkegaard Lunn. 2010. Understanding Casual-leisure Information Needs: A Diary Study in the Context of Television Viewing. In *Symposium on Information Interaction in Context (IIiX '10)*. ACM, New York, NY, USA, 25–34.

[14] R. Fidel. 1997. The image retrieval task: implications for the design and evaluation of image databases. *New Review of Hypermedia and Multimedia* 3, 1 (1997), 181–199.

[15] I. Gialampoukidis, A. Moumtzidou, D. Liparas, S. Vrochidis, and I. Kompatsiaris. 2016. A hybrid graph-based and non-linear late fusion approach for multimedia retrieval. In *Proceedings of the 14th International Workshop on Content-Based Multimedia Indexing (CBMI)*. 1–6.

[16] A. H. Gunatilaka and B. A. Baertlein. 2001. Feature-level and decision-level fusion of noncoincidently sampled sensors for land mine detection. *IEEE Transactions on Pattern Analysis and Machine Intelligence* 23, 6 (2001), 577–589.

[17] A. Hanjalic, C. Kofler, and M. Larson. 2012. Intent and Its Discontents: The User at the Wheel of the Online Video Search Engine. In *Proceedings of the 20th ACM International Conference on Multimedia (MM '12)*. ACM, New York, NY, USA, 1239–1248.

[18] R. M. Haralick. 1979. Statistical and structural approaches to texture. *Proc. IEEE* 67, 5 (May 1979), 786–804.

[19] P. Howarth and S. Rüger. 2004. Evaluation of texture features for content-based image retrieval. In *Image and Video Retrieval*. Springer, 326–334.

[20] N. Jaques, C. Conati, J. M. Harley, and R. Azevedo. 2014. Predicting affect from gaze data during interaction with an intelligent tutoring system. In *Proc. of ITS*, Vol. 8474 LNCS. 29–38.

[21] B. Jou and S.-F. Chang. 2016. Deep Cross Residual Learning for Multitask Visual Recognition. In *Proceedings of the 2016 ACM on Multimedia Conference (MM '16)*. ACM, New York, NY, USA, 998–1007.

[22] C. Kofler, M. Larson, and A. Hanjalic. 2016. User Intent in Multimedia Search: A Survey of the State of the Art and Future Challenges. *Comput. Surveys* 49, 2, Article 36 (2016), 37 pages.

[23] S. D. Kreibig. 2010. Autonomic nervous system activity in emotion: A review. *Biological Psychology* 84, 3 (jul 2010), 394–421.

[24] C. Lagger, M. Lux, and O. Marques. 2012. What makes people watch online videos: An exploratory study. *Computer Entertainment* (2012).

[25] S. Lallé, C. Conati, and G. Carenini. 2016. Predicting Confusion in Information Visualization from Eye Tracking and Interaction Data. In *Proceedings of the Twenty-Fifth International Joint Conference on Artificial Intelligence (IJCAI'16)*. AAAI Press, 2529–2535.

[26] M. Lux, C. Kofler, and O. Marques. 2010. A classification scheme for user intentions in image search. In *CHI'10 Extended Abstracts on Human Factors in Computing Systems*. 3913–3918.

[27] M. Lux, M. Taschwer, and O. Marques. 2012. A Closer Look at Photographers' Intentions: A Test Dataset. In *Proceedings of the ACM Multimedia 2012 Workshop on Crowdsourcing for Multimedia (CrowdMM '12)*. ACM, New York, NY, USA, 17–18.

[28] D. McDuff, A. Mahmoud, M. Mavadati, M. Amr, J. Turcot, and R. e. Kaliouby. 2016. AFFDEX SDK: A Cross-Platform Real-Time Multi-Face Expression Recognition Toolkit. In *CHI Conference Extended Abstracts on Human Factors in Computing Systems*. 3723–3726.

[29] G. A. Miller. 1995. WordNet: a lexical database for English. *Commun. ACM* 38, 11 (1995), 39–41.

[30] Y. Moshfeghi and J. M. Jose. 2013. On cognition, emotion, and interaction aspects of search tasks with different search intentions. In *International conference on World Wide Web - WWW '13*. ACM Press, New York, New York, USA, 931–942.

[31] A. Poddar and I. Ruthven. 2010. The Emotional Impact of Search Tasks. In *Proc. of the 3rd Symposium on Information Interaction in Context (IIiX '10)*. 35–44.

[32] M. Riegler, M. Larson, M. Lux, and C. Kofler. 2014. How 'How' Reflects What's What: Content-based Exploitation of How Users Frame Social Images. In *Proceedings of the 22Nd ACM International Conference on Multimedia (MM '14)*. ACM, New York, NY, USA, 397–406.

[33] C. G. M. Snoek, M. Worring, and A. W. M. Smeulders. 2005. Early Versus Late Fusion in Semantic Video Analysis. In *Proceedings of the 13th Annual ACM International Conference on Multimedia (MULTIMEDIA '05)*. ACM, New York, NY, USA, 399–402.

[34] M. Soleymani, F. Villaro-Dixon, T. Pun, and G. Chanel. 2017. Toolbox for Emotional fEAture extraction from Physiological signals (TEAP). *Frontiers in ICT* 4 (2017), 1.

[35] H. Tamura, S. Mori, and T. Yamawaki. 1978. Textural features corresponding to visual perception. *IEEE Transactions on Systems, Man and Cybernetics* 8, 6 (1978), 460–473.

[36] J. Teevan, E. Adar, R. Jones, and M. A. S. Potts. 2007. Information Re-retrieval: Repeat Queries in Yahoo's Logs. In *Proc. of ACM SIGIR Conference on Research and Development in Information Retrieval (SIGIR '07)*. 151–158.

Nested Invariance Pooling and RBM Hashing for Image Instance Retrieval

Olivier Morère
Université Pierre et Marie Curie, Paris, France
olivier.morere@gmail.com

Jie Lin
Institute for Infocomm Research, Singapore
lin-j@i2r.a-star.edu.sg

Antoine Veillard
Université Pierre et Marie Curie, Paris, France
antoine.veillard@gmail.com

Ling-Yu Duan
School of EE&CS, Peking University, China
lingyu@pku.edu.cn

Vijay Chandrasekhar*
Institute for Infocomm Research / Nanyang Technological University, Singapore
vijay@i2r.a-star.edu.sg

Tomaso Poggio
Massachusetts Institute of Technology, USA
tp@ai.mit.edu

ABSTRACT

The goal of this work is the computation of very compact binary hashes for image instance retrieval. Our approach has two novel contributions. The first one is Nested Invariance Pooling (NIP), a method inspired from *i-theory*, a mathematical theory for computing group invariant transformations with feed-forward neural networks. NIP is able to produce compact and well-performing descriptors with visual representations extracted from convolutional neural networks. We specifically incorporate scale, translation and rotation invariances but the scheme can be extended to any arbitrary sets of transformations. We also show that using moments of increasing order throughout nesting is important. The NIP descriptors are then hashed to the target code size (32-256 bits) with a Restricted Boltzmann Machine with a novel batch-level regularization scheme specifically designed for the purpose of hashing (RBMH). A thorough empirical evaluation with state-of-the-art shows that the results obtained both with the NIP descriptors and the NIP+RBMH hashes are consistently outstanding across a wide range of datasets.

CCS CONCEPTS

•Information systems → Image search;

KEYWORDS

Image Instance Retrieval; CNN; Invariant Representation; Hashing; Unsupervised Learning; Regularization

1 INTRODUCTION

Small binary image representations such as 64-bit hashes are a definite must for fast image instance retrieval. Compact hashes provide more than enough capacity for any practical purposes, including internet-scale problems. In addition, a compact hash is directly addressable in RAM and enables fast matching using ultra-fast Hamming distances.

State-of-the-art global image descriptors such as Fisher Vectors (FV) [30], Vector of Locally Aggregated Descriptors (VLAD) [22] and Convolutional Neural Network (CNN) features [6, 24] allow for robust image matching. However, the dimensionality of such descriptors is typically very high: 4096 to 65536 floating point numbers for FVs [30] and 4096 for CNNs [24]. Bringing such high-dimensional representations down to compact hashes is a considerable challenge.

Deep learning has achieved remarkable success in many visual tasks such as image classification [24, 36], image retrieval [6], face recognition [37, 38] and pose estimation [41]. Here,we propose a deep learning framework for binary hashing that generates extremely compact, yet discriminative descriptors. A series of nested pooling layers introduced in the pipeline, provide higher invariance and robustness to common transformations like rotation and scale. A RBM layer for hashing is introduced at the end of the pipeline to map real-valued data to binary hashes. The proposed deep learning pipeline generates hashes that consistently and significantly outperform other state-of-the-art methods at code size from 256 down to very small sizes like 32 bits, on several popular benchmarks.

2 BACKGROUND AND RELATED WORK

Our image instance retrieval pipeline starts with the computation of high-dimensional vectors referred to as *global descriptors*, followed by a hashing step to obtain compact representations. Here, we review the state-of-the-art in *global descriptors* and hashing methods.

Global Descriptors. State-of-the-art *global descriptors* for image instance retrieval are based on either FV [30]/VLAD [22] or Convolutional Neural Networks (CNN) [6]. Several variants of FV/VLAD [8, 23, 26, 39] have been proposed, since it was first proposed for instance retrieval [30]. In recent work, CNN descriptors have begun being applied to the computation of global descriptors for image retrieval [5, 6, 34, 35, 40, 43].

Razavian et al. [34] evaluate the performance of CNN activations from fully connected layer on a wide range of tasks including instance retrieval, and show initial promising results. After that, Babenko et al. [6] show that a pre-trained CNN can be fine tuned

*O. Morère, J. Lin, A. Veillard and V. Chandrasekhar contributed equally to this work.

ICMR '17, June 6–9, 2017, Bucharest, Romania
© 2017 ACM. ACM ISBN 978-1-4503-4701-3/17/06...$15.00
DOI: http://dx.doi.org/10.1145/3078971.3078987

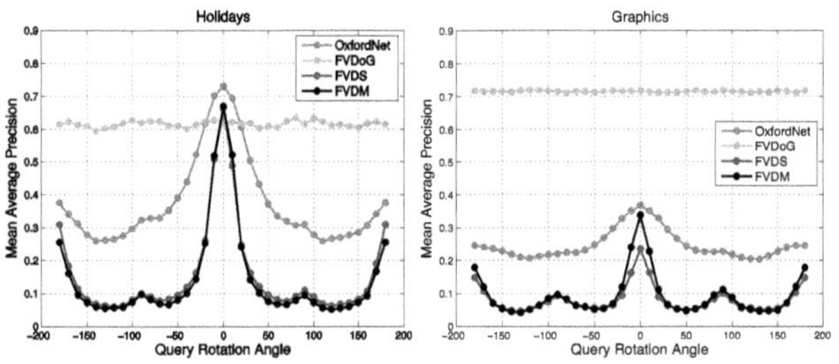

Figure 1: Comparison of CNN and FV descriptors retrieval performance with rotated queries on *Holidays* and *Graphics* datasets (see experimental section for details on datasets). FVDoG, FVDS, and FVDM are Fisher Vectors based on DoG interest points, Dense interest points at Single scale, and Dense interest points at Multiple scales respectively: all use the SIFT descriptor. FVDoG is robust to rotation, while CNN, FVDS and FVDM suffer a sharp drop in performance as query image is rotated.

with domain specific data (objects, scenes, etc.) to improve retrieval performance on relevant datasets. In [43], the authors propose extracting activations of fully connected layer from multiple regions sampled in an image, followed by aggregating VLAD descriptors on these local CNN activations. While this results in highly performant descriptors, the starting representations are orders of magnitude larger than descriptors proposed in this work. [4, 35] show that spatial max pooling of intermediate maps is an effective representation and higher performance can be achieved compared to using the fully connected layers. Babenko et al [5] in their very recent work, show that sum-pooling of intermediate feature maps performs better than max-pooling, when the image representation is whitened. Note that the approach in [5] provide limited invariance to translation, but not to scale or rotation. Another very recent work [40] proposes pooling across regional bounding boxes in the image, similar to the popular R-CNN approach [12] used for object detection.

Unlike FVs based on interest point detectors like the Difference-of-Gaussian (DoG) detector, CNN does not have a built-in mechanism to ensure resilience to geometric transformations like scale and rotation. In particular, the performance of CNN descriptors quickly degrade when the objects in the query and the database image are rotated or scaled differently. To illustrate this, in Figure 1, we show retrieval results when query images are rotated with respect to database images for descriptors: (a) Fisher Vectors based on Difference of Gaussian interest points and SIFT descriptors (FVDoG), (b) Fisher Vectors based on dense interest points and SIFT descriptors, at just one scale (FVDS), (c) Fisher Vectors based on dense interest points and SIFT descriptors, at multiple scales in the image (FVDM), and (d) CNN descriptors based on the first fully connected layer of *OxfordNet* [36]. Schemes apart from FVDoG suffer a sharp drop in performance as geometric transforms are applied. In this work, we focus on how to systematically incorporate groups of invariance into the CNN pipeline.

Hashing. In this work, we are focused on image instance retrieval with compact descriptors produced by unsupervised hashing on global descriptors. Semantic image retrieval with supervised hashing is outside the scope of this work. Examples of popular unsupervised hashing methods include Locality Sensitive Hashing (LSH) [9], Iterative Quantization (ITQ) [15], Spectral Hashing (SH) [42] and Restricted Boltzmann Machines (RBM) [18, 28]. Gong et al. propose the popular ITQ [15]. ITQ first performs Principal Component Analysis (PCA) to reduce dimensionality, then applies rotations to distribute variance across dimensions, and finally binarizes each dimension according to its sign. Besides hashing, quantization based methods such as Product Quantization (PQ) [22, 45, 46] divide the raw descriptor into smaller blocks and vector quantization is performed on each block. While this results in highly compact descriptors composed of sub-quantizer indices, the resulting representation is not binary and cannot be compared with Hamming distance.

3 CONTRIBUTIONS

The goal of this work is the computation of very compact binary hashes for image instance retrieval. To that end, we propose a multi-stage pipeline as shown on Figure 2 with the following contributions:

- First, we propose Nested Invariance Pooling (NIP), a method to produce compact global image descriptors from visual representations extracted from CNNs. Our method draws its inspiration from the *i-theory* [1–3], a mathematical theory for computing group invariant transformations with feed-forward neural networks. We specifically incorporate scale, translation and rotation invariance but the scheme can be extended to any arbitrary sets of transformations. We also show that using moments of increasing order throughout nesting is important. Resulting NIP descriptors are invariant to various types of image transformations and we show that the process significantly improves retrieval results while keeping dimensionality low (512 dimensions).
- Then, the NIP descriptors are hashed to the target code size (32-256 bits) with a Restricted Boltzmann Machine (RBM). We propose a novel batch-level regularization scheme specifically designed for the purpose of hashing, a scheme we refer to as RBMH from hereon.
- A thorough empirical evaluation with state-of-the-art shows that the results obtained both with the NIP descriptors and the NIP+RBMH hashes are consistently outstanding across a wide range of datasets. To the best of our knowledge, the results reported at 128 bits hashes are the highest reported results in state-of-the-art literature.

4 METHOD

4.1 Nested Invariance Pooling

Let an image $x \in E$ and a group G of transformations acting over E with group action $G \times E \rightarrow E$ denoted with a dot (.). The orbit of x by G is the subset of E defined as $O_x = \{g.x \in E | g \in G\}$. The orbit corresponds to the set of transformations of x under groups such as rotations, translations and scale changes. It can be easily shown that O_x is globally invariant to the action of any element of G and thus any descriptor computed directly from O_x would be globally invariant to G.

The *i-theory* builds invariant representations for a given object $x \in E$ in relation with a predefined template $t \in E$ from the

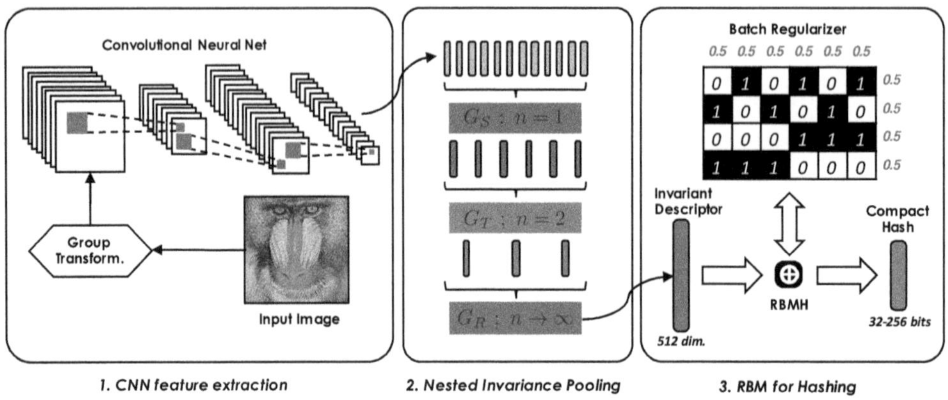

Figure 2: Our proposed pipeline for image instance retrieval applies Nested Invariance Pooling (NIP) to produce robust and compact descriptors from CNNs followed by an RBM specially regularized for Hashing (RBMH).

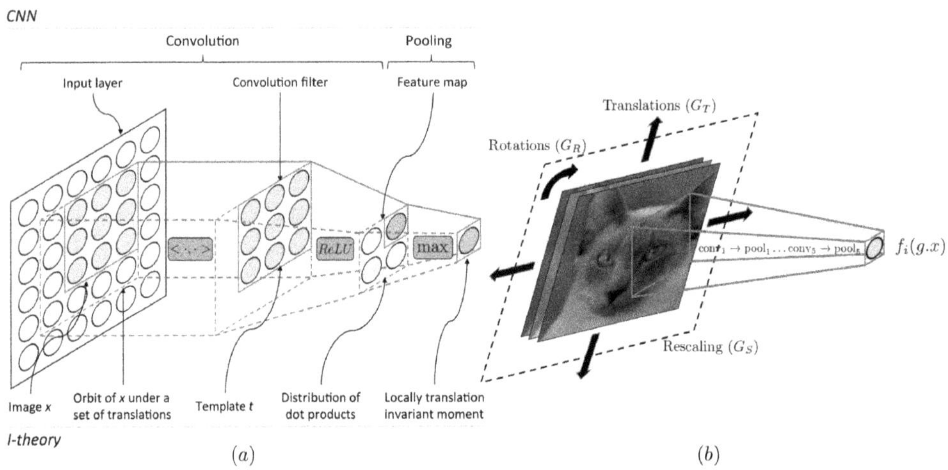

Figure 3: (a) A single convolution-pooling operation from a CNN schematized for a single input layer and single output unit. The parallel with *i-theory* shows that the universal building block of CNNs is compatible with the incorporation of invariance to local translations of the input according to the theory. (b) A specific succession of convolution and pooling operations learnt by the CNN (depicted in red) computes the *pool5* feature f_i for each feature map i from the RGB image data. A number of transformations g can be applied to the input x in order to vary the response $f_i(g.x)$.

distribution of the dot products $D_{x,t} = \{< g.x, t > \in \mathbb{R} | g \in G\} = \{< x, g.t > \in \mathbb{R} | g \in G\}$ over the orbit. The following representation (for any $n \in \mathbb{N}^*$) is proven to have proper invariance and selectivity properties provided that the group is compact or locally compact:

$$\mu_{G,t,n}(x) = \frac{1}{\int_G dg} \left(\int_G | < g.x, t > |^n dg \right)^{\frac{1}{n}} \quad (1)$$

Note that the sequence $(\mu_{G,t,n}(x))_{n \in \mathbb{N}^*}$ is analogous to a histogram. In practice, the theory extends well (with approximate invariance) to non-locally compact groups and even to continuous non-group transformations (e.g. out-of-plane rotations, elastic deformations) provided that proper class-specific templates can be chosen [2]. Recent work on face verification [25] and music classification [44] apply the theory to non-compact groups with good results.

Popular CNN architectures for classification such as *AlexNet* [24] and *OxfordNet* [36] share a common building block: a succession of convolution-pooling operations designed to model increasingly high-level visual representations of the data. As shown in Figure 3 (a), the succession of convolution and pooling operations in a typical CNN is in fact a way to incorporate local translation invariance strictly compliant with the framework proposed by the *i-theory*. The network architecture provides the robustness as predicted by the *i-theory*, while parameter tuning via back propagation ensures a proper choice of templates.

We build our NIP descriptors starting from the already locally robust *pool5* feature maps of *OxfordNet*. Global invariance to several transformation groups are then sequentially incorporated following the *i-theory* framework. The specific transformation groups considered in this study are translations G_T, rotations G_R and scale changes G_S. For every feature map i of the *pool5* layer ($0 \leq i < 512$), we denote $f_i(x)$ the corresponding unit's output. As shown on Figure 3 (b), transformations g are applied on the input image x varying the output of the *pool5* feature $f_i(g.x)$. Note that the transformation f_i is non-linear due to multiple convolution-pooling operations thus not strictly a mathematical dot product but can still be viewed as an inner product. Accordingly, the pooling scheme used by NIP with $G \in \{G_T, G_R, G_S\}$ is:

$$\mathcal{X}_{G,i,n}(x) = \frac{1}{\int_G dg}\left(\int_G f_i(g.x)^n dg\right)^{\frac{1}{n}} = \frac{1}{m}\left(\sum_{j=0}^{m-1} f_i(g_j.x)^n\right)^{\frac{1}{n}} \tag{2}$$

when O_x is discretized into m samples. The corresponding global image descriptors are obtained after each pooling step by concatenating the moments for the individual features:

$$\mathcal{X}_{G,n}(x) = (\mathcal{X}_{G,i,n}(x))_{0 \le i < 512} \tag{3}$$

As shown in Equation 2, the pooling operation has an order parameter n defining the "hardness" of the pooling. $n = 1$ is average pooling while $n \to +\infty$ on the other extreme is max-pooling. $n = 2$ is analogous to standard deviation. Subsequently, we refer to the moments for $n = 1, 2, +\infty$ as $\mathcal{A}_G$, $\mathcal{S}_G$ and $\mathcal{M}_G$.

Work on *i-theory* [44] has shown that it is possible to chain multiple types of group invariances one after the other [44]. We apply this principle on our NIP descriptors by making them invariant to several transformations. For instance, following scale invariance with average ($n = 1$) by translation invariance with hard max-pooling ($n \to +\infty$) is done by:

$$\begin{aligned} &\max_{g_t \in G_T}\left(\frac{1}{\int_{g_s \in G_S} dg_s}\int_{g_s \in G_S} f_i(g_t g_s.x)dg_s\right) \\ &= \max_{j \in [0, m_t - 1]}\left(\frac{1}{m_s}\sum_{i=0}^{m_s-1} f_i(g_{t,j} g_{s,i} t.x)\right) \end{aligned} \tag{4}$$

Operations are sometimes commutable (e.g. $\mathcal{A}_G$ and $\mathcal{A}_{G'}$) and sometimes not (e.g. $\mathcal{A}_G$ and $\mathcal{M}_{G'}$) depending on the specific combination of moments so the sequence of transformations does matter for NIP. The hardness parameter n must also be chosen carefully. Empirically, we found pooling progressively with increasing moments (e.g. $\mathcal{A}_G$, then $\mathcal{S}_G$, then $\mathcal{M}_G$) to work well as presented in the experiments section.

Figure 4 provides an insight on how adding different types of invariance with our NIP scheme will affect the matching distance on different image pairs of matching objects. With the incorporation of each new transformation group, we notice that the relative reduction in matching distance is the most significant with the image pair which is the most affected by the transformation group.

4.2 Restricted Boltzmann Machine for Hashing

The NIP descriptors are subsequently hashed to the target dimensionality with an RBM layer. The motivation is to obtain mutually independent dimensions while distributing variance evenly across them in a way similar to ITQ [15]. The main originality of our RBM is its batch-level regularization scheme which is specifically designed for hashing. We subsequently refer to this variant as RBMH.

An RBM is a bipartite Markov random field with the input layer $x \in R^I$ connected to a latent layer $z \in R^J$ via a set of undirected weights $W \in R^{IJ}$. The input and latent layers are also parameterised by their corresponding biases c and b, respectively. Since

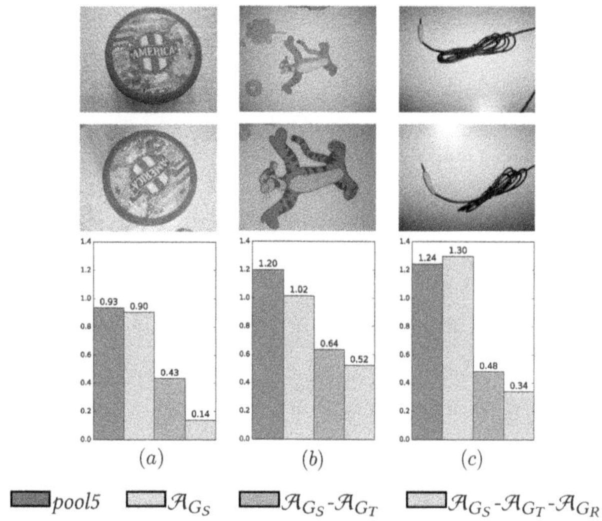

Figure 4: Distances for 3 matching pairs from the *UKB* dataset. For each pair, 4 pairwise distances (L_2-normalized) are computed corresponding to the following descriptors: *pool5*, $\mathcal{A}_{G_S}$, $\mathcal{A}_{G_S}$-$\mathcal{A}_{G_T}$ and $\mathcal{A}_{G_S}$-$\mathcal{A}_{G_T}$-$\mathcal{A}_{G_R}$. Adding scale invariance makes the most difference on (b), translation invariance on (c), and rotation on (a) which is consistent with the scenarios suggested by respective image pairs.

the units within a layer are conditionally independent pairwise, the activation probabilities of one layer can be sampled by fixing the states of the other layer, and using distributions given by logistic functions (a sigmoid activation function is chosen since binary hashes are desired):

$$P(z_j|x) = 1/(1 + \exp(-w_j x - b_j)), \tag{5}$$

$$P(x_i|z) = 1/(1 + \exp(-w_i^\top z - c_i)). \tag{6}$$

As a result, alternating Gibbs sampling can be performed between the two layers. The sampled states are used to update the parameters $\{W, b, c\}$ through batch gradient descent using the contrastive divergence algorithm [19] to approximate the maximum likelihood of the input distribution. The hashed descriptors are obtained by binarizing the latent units at 0.5.

Proper regularization is key during the training of RBM. The popular RBM proposed by Nair and Hinton [28] encourages latent representations to be sparse. This improves separability which is desirable for classification task. For hashing, it is desirable to encourage the representation to make efficient use of the limited latent subspace. RBMH achieves this goal by controlling sparsity in a way to maximize the entropy not only within every hash but also between the same bit of different hashes. This effectively encourages (a) half the bits to be active for a given hash, and (b) each hash bit to be equiprobable across images. We introduce a regularization term at the batch as in [13]. For a batch B, we define a regularization term:

$$h(B) = \sum_{x_\alpha \in B}\sum_{j\alpha} t_{j\alpha} \log z_{j\alpha} + (1 - t_{j\alpha})\log(1 - z_{j\alpha}), \tag{7}$$

where t_α are the target activations for each data sample α. We choose the $t^l_{j\alpha}$ such that each $\{t^l_{j\alpha}\}_j$ for fixed α and each $\{t^l_{j\alpha}\}_\alpha$ for fixed j is distributed according to the uniform distribution $U(0, 1)$

effectively maximizing entropy. The overall objective function becomes:

$$\underset{\{W,b,c\}}{\arg\min} - \sum_{\alpha} \log\left(\sum_{z_\alpha \in B} P(x_\alpha, z_\alpha) + \lambda h(B)\right), \quad (8)$$

with λ the regularization constant.

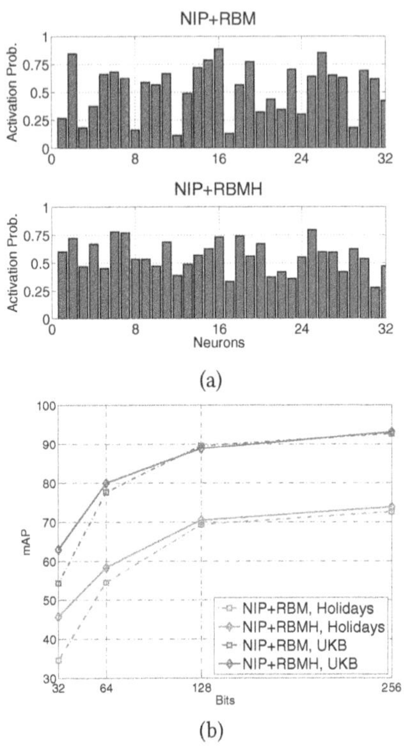

Figure 5: (a) Activation probabilities of hash bits between RBMH and the RBM proposed by Nair&Hinton [28]. We compute the statistics with 32 bits binary hashes on *Holidays* dataset (1491 images in total). (b) Comparison of our RBMH with RBM [28] in terms of mAP on *Holidays* and *UKB*. Both schemes are built upon the best NIP descriptors. RBMH outperforms RBM at very low code sizes.

Figure 5 shows the activation probabilities of the hash bits between RBMH and the RBM proposed by Nair and Hinton [28]. The comparison is for 32-bits hashes. In Figure 5 (a), the mean probability of activation is nearly 0.5 in both cases. Nevertheless, we can see that probabilities are much more evenly distributed across bits with BRMH. In Figure 5 (b), retrieval results on *UKB* and *Holidays* show that the RBMH is able to outperform the standard RBM specially at lower code sizes (32 or 64 bits).

5 EXPERIMENTS

5.1 Evaluation Framework

We evaluate the performances on 4 popular datasets for image instance retrieval: (1) **Holidays**. The INRIA Holidays dataset [21] consists of outdoor holiday pictures. There are 500 queries and 991 database images. (2) **UKB**. The University of Kentucky Benchmark dataset [29] consists of 2550 groups of common objects, 4 images per object. All 10200 images are used as queries. (3) **Oxford5K**. The Oxford buildings dataset [32] consists of 5063 images representing landmark buildings in Oxford. The query set contains 11 different landmarks, each represented by 5 queries. (4) **Graphics**. The Graphics dataset is part of the Stanford Mobile Visual Search dataset [7], which was used in the MPEG standard titled Compact Descriptors for Visual Search (CDVS) [20]. This dataset contains objects like CDs, DVDs, books, prints, business cards. There are 500 unique objects, 1500 queries, and 1000 database images. Note that *Graphics* is different from the other datasets as it contains images of rigid objects captured under widely varying scale and rotation changes.

For large-scale experiments, we present results on the 4 datasets combined with the 1 million MIR-FLICKR distractor images [27]. Most schemes, including our approach, require an unsupervised training step. We train on a randomly sampled set of 150K images from the 1.2 million *ImageNet* dataset [10]. No class labels are used in this work.

For the starting global descriptor representation, we use the *pool5* layer from the 16-layer *OxfordNet* [36], which is widely adopted in instance retrieval literature [5, 35, 40]. The input image size for *OxfordNet* is fixed at 224 × 224. The dimensionality of the *pool5* descriptor is 25088, organized as 512 feature maps of size 7 × 7.

For rotation invariance, rotated input images are padded with the mean pixel value computed from the ImageNet dataset. The step size for rotations is 10 degrees yielding 36 rotated images per orbit. For scale changes, 10 different center crops are considered varying from 50% to 100% of the total image. For translations, the entire feature map is used for every feature, resulting in an orbit size of 7 × 7 = 49.

For retrieval with floating point descriptors, L_2 normalization is first applied followed by L2 distance computation. For retrieval with binary descriptors, we use hamming distance computation. We evaluate retrieval results with mean Average Precision (mAP). To be consistent with the literature, 4× Recall @ $R = 4$ is provided for *UKB*.

Table 1: Retrieval results (mAP) for different sequences of transformation groups and moments. For *UKB*, 4× Recall @ $R = 4$ is shown between parentheses. G_T, G_R, G_S denote the groups of translations, rotations and scale changes respectively. Note that averages commute with other averages so the sequence order of the composition does not matter when only averages are involved. Best results are achieved by choosing specific moments. $\mathcal{A}_{G_S}$-$\mathcal{S}_{G_T}$-$\mathcal{M}_{G_R}$ corresponds to the best average performer. *fc6* and *pool5* are provided as a baseline.

Sequence	Dims	Dataset			
		Oxford5K	Holidays	UKB	Graphics
pool5	25088	0.427	0.707	0.823(3.11)	0.315
fc6	4096	0.461	0.782	0.910(3.50)	0.312
$\mathcal{A}_{G_T}$	512	0.477	0.800	0.924(3.56)	0.322
$\mathcal{A}_{G_R}$	25088	0.462	0.779	0.954(3.72)	0.500
$\mathcal{A}_{G_S}$	25088	0.430	0.716	0.828(3.12)	0.394
$\mathcal{A}_{G_T}$-$\mathcal{A}_{G_R}$	512	0.418	0.796	0.955(3.73)	0.417
$\mathcal{A}_{G_T}$-$\mathcal{A}_{G_S}$	512	0.537	0.811	0.931(3.61)	0.430
$\mathcal{A}_{G_R}$-$\mathcal{A}_{G_S}$	25088	0.494	0.815	0.959(3.75)	0.552
$\mathcal{A}_{G_T}$-$\mathcal{A}_{G_R}$-$\mathcal{A}_{G_S}$	512	0.484	0.833	0.971(3.82)	0.509
$\mathcal{A}_{G_S}$-$\mathcal{S}_{G_T}$-$\mathcal{M}_{G_R}$	512	**0.592**	**0.838**	**0.975(3.84)**	**0.589**

5.2 Results

Evaluation of NIP descriptors. As shown in Table 1, we first study the effects of incorporating various transformation groups and using different moments on NIP descriptors. We present results for all possible combinations of transformation groups for average pooling (order does not matter as averages commute) and for the single best performer which is $\mathcal{A}_{G_S}$-$\mathcal{S}_{G_T}$-$\mathcal{M}_{G_R}$ (order matters). First, we point out the effectiveness of the *pool5* layer. Although it performs notably worse than *fc6* as-is, a simple average pooling over the space of translations $\mathcal{A}_{G_T}$ makes it both better and 8 times more compact than *fc6*. Similar observations have also been reported by [4, 5]. Second, on average, accuracy significantly increases with the number of transformation groups involved. Third, choosing statistical moments different than averages further improve the retrieval results. In Table 1, we observe that $\mathcal{A}_{G_S}$-$\mathcal{S}_{G_T}$-$\mathcal{M}_{G_R}$ performs significantly better than $\mathcal{A}_{G_T}$-$\mathcal{A}_{G_R}$-$\mathcal{A}_{G_S}$. Notably, the best combination corresponds to an increase in the orders of the moments: $\mathcal{A}$ being a first-order moment, $\mathcal{S}$ second order and $\mathcal{M}$ of infinite order. A different way of stating this is that a more invariant representation requires higher and higher orders of pooling.

Table 2: Retrieval performance comparing NIP to other state-of-the-art methods. We include results in recent papers with comparable dimensionality of descriptors reported in those papers. L2 distance is used for all methods.

Method	Dims	Dataset		
		Oxford5K	Holidays	UKB
T-embedding [23]	1024	0.560	0.720	3.51
T-embedding [23]	512	0.528	0.700	3.49
FV+Proj [17]	512	-	0.789	3.36
FC+PCAWhitening [34]	500	0.322	0.642	-
FC+VLAD+PCA [43]	512	-	0.784	-
FC+Finetune+PCAWhitening [6]	512	0.557	0.789	3.30
Conv+MaxPooling [35]	256	0.533	0.716	-
FV+FC+PCAWhitening [31]	512	-	0.827	3.37
Conv+SPoC+PCAWhitening [5]	256	0.589	0.802	3.65
R-MAC+PCAWhitening [40]	512	**0.668**	-	-
R-MAC+PCAWhitening [40]	256	0.561	-	-
NIP (Ours)	512	0.592	**0.838**	**3.84**
NIP+PCAWhitening (Ours)	256	**0.609**	**0.836**	**3.83**

Overall, $\mathcal{A}_{G_S}$-$\mathcal{S}_{G_T}$-$\mathcal{M}_{G_R}$ improves results over starting representation *pool5* by 39% (*Oxford5K*) to 87% (*Graphics*) depending on the dataset. Better improvements with *Graphics* can be explained with the presence of many rotations in the dataset (smaller objects taken under different angles) while *Oxford5K* consisting mainly of upright buildings is less significantly helped by incorporating rotation invariance.

Comparing NIP with state-of-the-art including variants of VLAD/FV [17, 23], deep descriptors [5, 6, 35, 40] and descriptors combining deep CNN and VLAD/FV [31, 43]. As shown in Table 2, we observe that 512-D NIP descriptors largely outperform most state-of-the-art methods with 512 or higher dimensions, on all datasets. Following [5, 35, 40], we also perform PCA whitening (PCAW) to reduce the dimensionality of NIP to 256. One can see that the 256-D NIP descriptors yield superior performance to [5, 35, 40] on all datasets.

First, we compare NIP to the most related papers [5,35,40] which propose 256-D deep descriptors by aggregating convolutional features with various pooling operations [1]. [4, 5, 35] can be considered a special case of our work, with just one layer of pooling, which only provided limited levels of translation invariance. The very recently proposed Regional Maximum Activation of Convolutions (R-MAC) [40] reports outstanding results on building dataset *Oxford5K* with very small dimensionality (e.g. 0.668 mAP for 512-D R-MAC and 0.561 mAP for 256-D R-MAC). The authors propose a fast R-CNN type pooling [11], which is effective when the object of interest is in a small portion of the image. Such an approach will be less effective when the object of interest is affected by groups of distortions like rotation and perspective, and located at the centre of the image. Here, we observe that nested pooling over many types of distortions with progressively increasing moments is essential to achieving geometric invariance and high retrieval performance with low dimensional descriptors. Besides, we argue that the technique proposed in [40] can be incorporated with NIP to further improve performance.

Next, we note that [35] reports better results on *Holidays* (0.881 mAP) and *Oxford5K* (0.844 mAP), with very high-dimensional descriptors (from 10K to 100K). These very high dimensional descriptors are obtained by combining CNN descriptors with spatial max pooling [4]. In contrast, our results are generated using only 256 to 512 dimensional descriptors.

Table 3: Retrieval performance comparing NIP+RBMH to other state-of-the-art methods at small codesizes (from 32 to 512 bits). ADC denotes asymmetric distance computation [16, 22]. "FT" stands for fine-tuning.

Method	Dims (bits)	Dist.	Dataset		
			Oxford5K	Holidays	UKB
Binarized FV [30]	520(520)	Cosine	-	0.460	2.79
FV+SSH [16]	256(256)	ADC	-	0.544	3.08
FV+SSH [16]	128(128)	ADC	-	0.499	2.91
FV+SSH [16]	32(32)	ADC	-	0.334	2.18
FV+PQ [22]	128(128)	ADC	-	0.506	3.10
VLAD+PQ [45]	128(128)	L2	-	0.586	2.88
VLAD+CQ [45]	128(128)	L2	-	0.644	3.19
VLAD+SQ [46]	128(128)	L2	-	0.639	3.06
FC+FT+PCAW [6]	16(512)	L2	0.418	0.609	2.41
Conv+MaxPooling [35]	256(256)	Cosine	0.436	0.578	-
Binarized NIP (Ours)	512(512)	Hamming	**0.477**	**0.781**	**3.70**
NIP+RBMH (Ours)	256(256)	Hamming	**0.445**	**0.739**	**3.59**
NIP+RBMH (Ours)	128(128)	Hamming	**0.359**	**0.705**	**3.38**
NIP+RBMH (Ours)	32(32)	Hamming	**0.274**	**0.458**	**2.26**

Evaluation of NIP+RBMH binary hashes. NIP+RBMH binary hashes are produced by feeding invariant NIP descriptors into the proposed RBM hashing layer. Small scale retrieval results with NIP+RBMH are shown in Figure 6. We compare NIP+RBMH to other popular unsupervised hashing methods at code sizes

[1]Note that [5, 35, 40] extract deep descriptors from images with size larger than 576 × 576, while we use 224 × 224 in this work. As shown in [6], there is potential improvement if larger image size adopted in deep descriptors extraction.

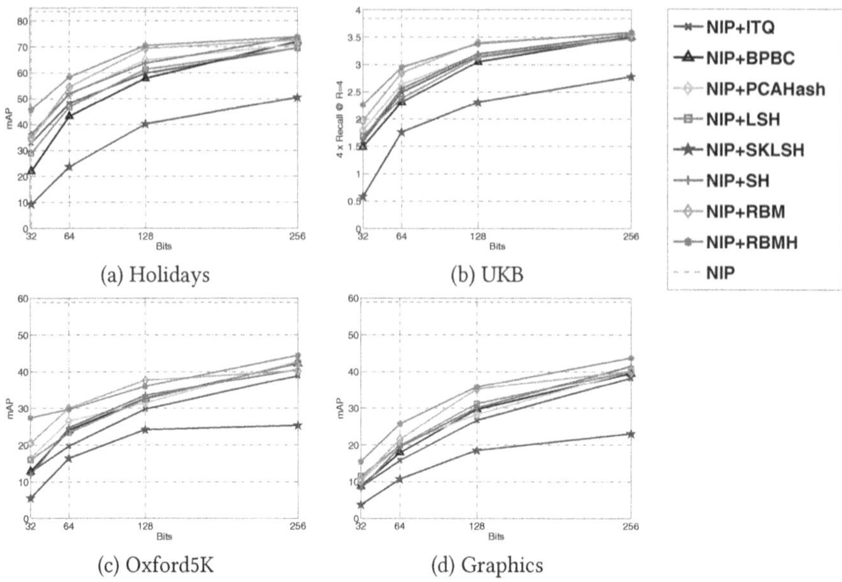

(a) Holidays (b) UKB (c) Oxford5K (d) Graphics

Figure 6: Comparison of RBMH with other hashing methods on 4 benchmark datasets. All methods are built upon the best NIP descriptors. To examine the effect of compression, we also present retrieval results using uncompressed NIP descriptors.

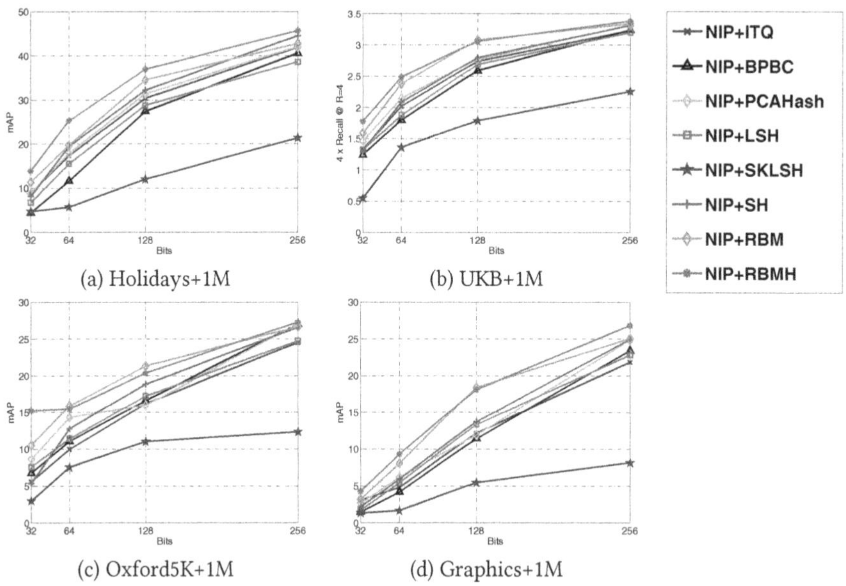

(a) Holidays+1M (b) UKB+1M (c) Oxford5K+1M (d) Graphics+1M

Figure 7: Comparison of RBMH with other hashing methods on large scale retrieval experiments. All methods are based on the best NIP descriptors.

from 32 to 256 bits, including *ITQ* [15], Bilinear Projection Binary Codes (*BPBC*) [14], *PCAHash* [15], *LSH* [9], *SKLSH* [33], *SH* [42] and *RBM* [18, 28]. We used the software provided by the authors in [15, 18] to generate results for the baseline hashing methods. In addition, we also include the results of 512-D NIP descriptors, as the baseline uncompressed scheme.

We observe that NIP+RBMH outperforms other methods at most code sizes on all data sets. First, there is a significant improvement at smaller code sizes like 32 bits, due to the proposed batch-level regularization: 0.457 vs. 0.369 in terms of mAP, compared to the second performing method RBM on *Holidays* at 32 bits. Second, the improvements of NIP+RBMH over other methods becomes smaller as code size increases (except SKLSH). For code size larger than 256 bits, the performances of all methods approach the upper bound, i.e., uncompressed NIP descriptors. Finally, compared to uncompressed NIP descriptors, there is a marginal drop for all methods on *UKB* at 256 bits, while performance gap is larger for other datasets.

Comparing NIP+RBMH with state-of-the-art including methods compressing VLAD/FV with direct binarization [30], hashing [16] and PQ [22, 46], methods based on compact deep descriptors [6, 35].

As shown in Table 3, first, a simple binarization strategy applied to our best performing NIP descriptor is sufficient to obtain significantly better accuracy than [6, 30] at comparable code size (512 bits), e.g., 3.7 vs. 2.79 in [30] for 4× Recall @ $R = 4$ on *UKB*. Second, NIP+RBMH outperforms state-of-the-art by a significant margin at comparable code sizes (from 32 to 256 bits). NIP+RBMH achieves the best performance on *Holidays* at small code size (128 bits), 0.705 vs. 0.644 mAP reported in [45] (to our knowledge, the state-of-the-art on this dataset with 128-bit descriptors). Note that Hamming distance is used for our binary descriptors, while other methods like PQ variants employ Euclidean distances (L2 or ADC), which typically result in higher accuracy than Hamming distance, at the expense of higher computational cost.

Large scale experiments. In Figure 7, we present large scale retrieval results, combining the 1 million MIR FLICKR distractor images with each data set respectively. Trends consistent with small scale retrieval results in Figure 6 are observed.

6 CONCLUSIONS

In this work, we proposed a method to produce global image descriptors from CNNs which are both compact and robust to typical geometric transformations. The method provides a practical and mathematically proven way for computing invariant object representations with feed-forward neural networks. To achieve global geometric invariance, we introduce a series of nested pooling layers at intermediate levels of the deep CNN network. We further introduce a RBM layer with a novel batch-level regularization scheme for generating compact binary descriptors. Through a thorough evaluation with state-of-the-art, we show that the proposed method outperforms state-of-the-art by a significant margin.

7 ACKNOWLEDGMENTS

This work was partially supported by grants from National Natural Science Foundation of China (U1611461, 61661146005) and National Hightech R&D Program of China (2015AA016302).

REFERENCES

[1] F. Anselmi, J. Z. Leibo, L. Rosasco, J. Mutch, A. Tacchetti, and T. Poggio. Magic materials: a theory of deep hierarchical architectures for learning sensory representations. *CBCL paper*, 2013.

[2] F. Anselmi, J. Z. Leibo, L. Rosasco, J. Mutch, A. Tacchetti, and T. Poggio. Unsupervised learning of invariant representations in hierarchical architectures. *arXiv:1311.4158*, 2013.

[3] F. Anselmi and T. Poggio. Representation learning in sensory cortex: a theory. *CBMM memo n 26*, 2010.

[4] Hossein Azizpour, Ali Sharif Razavian, Josephine Sullivan, Atsuto Maki, and Stefan Carlsson. From generic to specific deep representations for visual recognition. In *Computer Vision and Pattern Recognition Workshops*, 2015.

[5] A. Babenko and V. Lempitsky. Aggregating local deep features for image retrieval. In *International Conference on Computer Vision (ICCV)*, 2015.

[6] Artem Babenko, Anton Slesarev, Alexandr Chigorin, and Victor Lempitsky. Neural Codes for Image Retrieval. In *European Conference on Computer Vision (ECCV)*, 2014.

[7] V. Chandrasekhar, D.M.Chen, S.S.Tsai, N.M.Cheung, H.Chen, G.Takacs, Y.Reznik, R.Vedantham, R.Grzeszczuk, J.Back, and B.Girod. Stanford Mobile Visual Search Data Set. In *ACM Multimedia Systems Conference (MMSys)*, 2011.

[8] D. M. Chen, S. S. Tsai, V. Chandrasekhar, G. Takacs, R. Vedantham, R. Grzeszczuk, and B. Girod. Residual Enhanced Visual Vector as a Compact Signature for Mobile Visual Search. In *Signal Processing*, 2012.

[9] Mayur Datar, Nicole Immorlica, Piotr Indyk, and Vahab S. Mirrokni. Locality-Sensitive Hashing Scheme based on p-stable Distributions. In *Annual Symposium on Computational Geometry*, 2004.

[10] J. Deng, W. Dong, R. Socher, L.-J. Li, K. Li, and L. Fei-Fei. Imagenet: A large-scale hierarchical image database. In *Computer Vision and Pattern Recognition (CVPR)*, 2009.

[11] Ross Girshick. Fast R-CNN. In *International Conference on Computer Vision (ICCV)*, 2015.

[12] Ross Girshick, Jeff Donahue, Trevor Darrell, and Jitendra Malik. Rich feature hierarchies for accurate object detection and semantic segmentation. In *Computer Vision and Pattern Recognition (CVPR)*, 2014.

[13] Hanlin Goh, Nicolas Thome, Matthieu Cord, and Joo-Hwee Lim. Unsupervised and supervised visual codes with restricted Boltzmann machines. In *European Conference on Computer Vision (ECCV)*, 2012.

[14] Yunchao Gong, Sanjiv Kumar, Henry Rowley, and Svetlana Lazebnik. Learning Binary Codes for High-Dimensional Data Using Bilinear Projections. In *Computer Vision and Pattern Recognition (CVPR)*, 2013.

[15] Yunchao Gong, Svetlana Lazebnik, Albert Gordo, and Florent Perronnin. Iterative Quantization: A Procrustean Approach to Learning Binary Codes for Large-scale Image Retrieval. In *IEEE Transaction on Pattern Analysis and Machine Intelligence (PAMI)*, 2013.

[16] Albert Gordo, Florent Perronnin, Yunchao Gong, and Svetlana Lazebnik. Asymmetric distances for binary embeddings. *IEEE Transactions on Pattern Analysis and Machine Intelligence (PAMI)*, 36(1):33–47, 2014.

[17] A. Gordoa, J.A. Rodriguez-Serrano, F. Perronnin, and E. Valveny. Leveraging category-level labels for instance-level image retrieval. In *Computer Vision and Pattern Recognition (CVPR)*, 2012.

[18] G E Hinton and R R Salakhutdinov. Reducing the dimensionality of data with neural networks. *Science*, 313:504–507, 2006.

[19] Geoffrey E Hinton. Training products of experts by minimizing contrastive divergence. *Neural Computation*, 14(8):1771–1800, 2002.

[20] ISO/IEC-JTC1/SC29/WG11/N12202. *Evaluation Framework for Compact Descriptors for Visual Search*, 2011.

[21] H. Jégou, M. Douze, and C. Schmid. Hamming Embedding and Weak Geometric Consistency for Large Scale Image Search. In *European Conference on Computer Vision (ECCV)*, 2008.

[22] Hervé Jégou, Florent Perronnin, Matthijs Douze, Jorge Sánchez, Patrick Pérez, and Cordelia Schmid. Aggregating local image descriptors into compact codes. *IEEE Transactions on Pattern Analysis and Machine Intelligence (PAMI)*, 34(9):1704–1716, 2012.

[23] Hervé Jégou and Andrew Zisserman. Triangulation embedding and democratic aggregation for image search. In *Computer Vision and Pattern Recognition (CVPR)*, 2014.

[24] Alex Krizhevsky, Ilya Sutskever, and Geoffrey E Hinton. Imagenet classification with deep convolutional neural networks. In *Neural Information Processing Systems (NIPS)*, 2012.

[25] Q. L. Liao, J. Z. Leibo, and T. Poggio. Learning invariant representations and applications to face verification. In *Neural Information Processing Systems (NIPS)*, 2013.

[26] Jie Lin, Ling-Yu Duan, Tiejun Huang, and Wen Gao. Robust Fisher Codes for Large Scale Image Retrieval. In *International Conference on Acoustics and Signal Processing (ICASSP)*, 2013.

[27] B. Thomee Mark J. Huiskes and Michael S. Lew. New Trends and Ideas in Visual Concept Detection: The MIR Flickr Retrieval Evaluation Initiative. In *ACM International Conference on Multimedia Information Retrieval*, 2010.

[28] Vinod Nair and Geoffrey Hinton. 3D Object Recognition with Deep Belief Nets. In *Neural Information Processing Systems (NIPS)*, 2009.

[29] D. Nistér and H. Stewénius. Scalable Recognition with a Vocabulary Tree. In *Computer Vision and Pattern Recognition (CVPR)*, 2006.

[30] F. Perronnin, Y. Liu, J. Sanchez, and H. Poirier. Large-scale Image Retrieval with Compressed Fisher Vectors. In *Computer Vision and Pattern Recognition (CVPR)*, 2010.

[31] Florent Perronnin and Diane Larlus. Fisher vectors meet neural networks: A hybrid classification architecture. In *Computer Vision and Pattern Recognition (CVPR)*, 2015.

[32] J. Philbin, O. Chum, M. Isard, J. Sivic, and A. Zisserman. Object Retrieval with Large Vocabularies and Fast Spatial Matching. In *Computer Vision and Pattern Recognition (CVPR)*, 2007.

[33] M. Raginsky and S. Lazebnik. Locality-Sensitive Binary Codes from Shift-Invariant Kernels. In *Neural Information Processing Systems (NIPS)*, 2009.

[34] Ali Sharif Razavian, Hossein Azizpour, Josephine Sullivan, and Stefan Carlsson. CNN Features Off-the-Shelf: An Astounding Baseline for Recognition. In *Computer Vision and Pattern Recognition Workshops*, 2014.

[35] Ali Sharif Razavian, Josephine Sullivan, Atsuto Maki, and Stefan Carlsson. A baseline for visual instance retrieval with deep convolutional networks. In *International Conference on Learning Representations (ICLR)*, 2015.
[36] K Simonyan and A Zisserman. Very Deep Convolutional Networks for Large-Scale Image Recognition. In *International Conference on Learning Representations (ICLR)*, 2015.
[37] Yi Sun, Xiaogang Wang, and Xiaoou Tang. Deep learning face representation from predicting 10,000 classes. In *Computer Vision and Pattern Recognition (CVPR)*, 2014.
[38] Yaniv Taigman, Ming Yang, Marc'Aurelio Ranzato, and Lior Wolf. DeepFace: Closing the Gap to Human-Level Performance in Face Verification. In *Computer Vision and Pattern Recognition (CVPR)*, 2014.
[39] G. Tolias, Y. Avrithis, and H. Jegou. To aggregate or not to aggregate: Selective match kernels for image search. In *International Conference on Computer Vision (ICCV)*, 2013.
[40] Giorgos Tolias, Ronan Sicre, and Hervé Jégou. Particular object retrieval with integral max-pooling of CNN activations. In *arXiv:1511.05879*, 2015.
[41] Alexander Toshev and Christian Szegedy. Deeppose: Human pose estimation via deep neural networks. In *Computer Vision and Pattern Recognition (CVPR)*, 2014.
[42] Y. Weiss, A. Torralba, and R. Fergus. Spectral Hashing. In *Neural Information Processing Systems (NIPS)*, 2008.
[43] R. Guo Y. Gong, L. Wang and S. Lazebnik. Multi-scale orderless pooling of deep convolutional activation features. In *European Conference on Computer Vision (ECCV)*, 2014.
[44] C. Zhang, G. Evangelopoulos, S. Voinea, L. Rosasco, and T. Poggio. A deep representation for invariance and music classification. In *International Conference on Acoustics and Signal Processing (ICASSP)*, 2014.
[45] Ting Zhang, Chao Du, and Jingdong Wang. Composite quantization for approximate nearest neighbor search. In *International Conference on Machine Learning (ICML)*, 2014.
[46] Ting Zhang, Guo-Jun Qi, Jinhui Tang, and Jingdong Wang. Sparse composite quantization. In *Computer Vision and Pattern Recognition (CVPR)*, 2015.

Embedding Watermarks into Deep Neural Networks

Yusuke Uchida*
KDDI Research Inc.
Saitama, Japan

Yuki Nagai
KDDI Research Inc.
Saitama, Japan

Shigeyuki Sakazawa†
KDDI Research Inc.
Saitama, Japan

Shin'ichi Satoh
National Institute of Informatics
Tokyo, Japan

ABSTRACT

Significant progress has been made with deep neural networks recently. Sharing trained models of deep neural networks has been a very important in the rapid progress of research and development of these systems. At the same time, it is necessary to protect the rights to shared trained models. To this end, we propose to use digital watermarking technology to protect intellectual property and detect intellectual property infringement in the use of trained models. First, we formulate a new problem: embedding watermarks into deep neural networks. Second, we propose a general framework for embedding a watermark in model parameters, using a parameter regularizer. Our approach does not impair the performance of networks into which a watermark is placed because the watermark is embedded while training the host network. Finally, we perform comprehensive experiments to reveal the potential of watermarking deep neural networks as the basis of this new research effort. We show that our framework can embed a watermark during the training of a deep neural network from scratch, and during fine-tuning and distilling, without impairing its performance. The embedded watermark does not disappear even after fine-tuning or parameter pruning; the watermark remains complete even after 65% of parameters are pruned.

CCS CONCEPTS

•**Computing methodologies** →**Neural networks;**

KEYWORDS

deep neural networks; watermarking; regularizer

ACM Reference format:
Yusuke Uchida, Yuki Nagai, Shigeyuki Sakazawa, and Shin'ichi Satoh. 2017. Embedding Watermarks into Deep Neural Networks. In *Proceedings of ICMR '17, June 6–9, 2017, Bucharest, Romania*, , 9 pages.
DOI: http://dx.doi.org/10.1145/3078971.3078974

*The author is currently with DeNA Co., Ltd.
†The author is currently with Osaka Institute of Technology.

ICMR '17, June 6–9, 2017, Bucharest, Romania
 ACM ISBN 978-1-4503-4701-3/17/06...$15.00
DOI: http://dx.doi.org/10.1145/3078971.3078974

1 INTRODUCTION

Deep neural networks have recently been significantly improved. In particular, deep convolutional neural networks (DCNN) such as LeNet [25], AlexNet [23], VGGNet [28], GoogLeNet [29], and ResNet [16] have become *de facto* standards for object recognition, image classification, and retrieval. In addition, many deep learning frameworks have been released that help engineers and researchers to develop systems based on deep learning or do research with less effort. Examples of these great deep learning frameworks are Caffe [19], Theano [3], Torch [7], Chainer [30], TensorFlow [26], and Keras [5].

Although these frameworks have made it easy to utilize deep neural networks in real applications, the training of deep neural network models is still a difficult task because it requires a large amount of data and time; several weeks are needed to train a very deep ResNet with the latest GPUs on the ImageNet dataset for instance [16]. Therefore, trained models are sometimes provided on web sites to make it easy to try a certain model or reproduce the results in research articles without training. For example, Model Zoo[1] provides trained Caffe models for various tasks with useful utility tools. Fine-tuning or transfer learning [28] is a strategy to directly adapt such already trained models to another application with minimum re-training time. Thus, sharing trained models is very important in the rapid progress of both research and development of deep neural network systems. In the future, more systematic model-sharing platforms may appear, by analogy with video sharing sites. Furthermore, some digital distribution platforms for purchase and sale of the trained models or even artificial intelligence skills (e.g. Alexa Skills[2]) may appear, similar to Google Play or App Store. In these situations, it is necessary to protect the rights to shared trained models.

To this end, we propose to utilize digital watermarking technology, which is used to identify ownership of the copyright of digital content such as images, audio, and videos. In particular, we propose a general framework to embed a watermark in deep neural networks models to protect intellectual property and detect intellectual property infringement of trained models. To the best of our knowledge, this is first attempt to embed a watermark in a deep neural network. The contributions of this research are three-fold, as follows:

[1]https://github.com/BVLC/caffe/wiki/Model-Zoo
[2]https://www.alexaskillstore.com/

(1) We formulate a new problem: embedding watermarks in deep neural networks. We also define requirements, embedding situations, and attack types for watermarking deep neural networks.
(2) We propose a general framework to embed a watermark in model parameters, using a parameter regularizer. Our approach does not impair the performance of networks in which a watermark is embedded.
(3) We perform comprehensive experiments to reveal the potential of watermarking deep neural networks.

2 PROBLEM FORMULATION

Given a model network with or without trained parameters, we define the task of watermark embedding as to embed T-bit vector $b \in \{0, 1\}^T$ into the parameters of one or more layers of the neural network. We refer to a neural network in which a watermark is embedded as a *host network*, and refer to the task that the host network is originally trying to perform as the *original task*.

In the following, we formulate (1) requirements for an embedded watermark or an embedding method, (2) embedding situations, and (3) expected attack types against which embedded watermarks should be robust.

2.1 Requirements

Table 1 summarizes the requirements for an effective watermarking algorithm in an image domain [8, 15] and a neural network domain. While both domains share almost the same requirements, *fidelity* and *robustness* are different in image and neural network domains.

For fidelity in an image domain, it is essential to maintain the perceptual quality of the host image while embedding a watermark. However, in a neural network domain, the parameters themselves are not important. Instead, the performance of the original task is important. Therefore it is essential to maintain the performance of the trained host network, and not to hamper the training of a host network.

Regarding robustness, as images are subject to various signal processing operations, an embedded watermark should stay in the host image even after these operations. And the greatest possible modification to a neural network is fine-tuning or transfer learning [28]. An embedded watermark in a neural network should be detectable after fine-tuning or other possible modifications.

2.2 Embedding Situations

We classify the embedding situations into three types: train-to-embed, fine-tune-to-embed, and distill-to-embed, as summarized in Table 2.

Train-to-embed is the case in which the host network is trained from scratch while embedding a watermark where labels for training data are available.

Fine-tune-to-embed is the case in which a watermark is embedded while fine-tuning. In this case, model parameters are initialized with a pre-trained network. The network configuration near the output layer may be changed before fine-tuning in order to adapt the final layer's output to another task.

Distill-to-embed is the case in which a watermark is embedded into a trained network *without* labels using the distilling approach [17]. Embedding is performed in fine-tuning where the predictions of the trained model are used as labels. In the standard distill framework, a large network (or multiple networks) is first trained and then a smaller network is trained using the predicted labels of the large network in order to compress the large network. In this paper, we use the distill framework simply to train a network without labels.

The first two situations assume that the copyright holder of the host network is expected to embed a watermark to the host network in training or fine-tuning. Fine-tune-to-embed is also useful when a model owner wants to embed individual watermarks to identify those to whom the model had been distributed. By doing so, individual instances can be tracked. The last situation assumes that a non-copyright holder (e.g., a platformer) is entrusted to embed a watermark on behalf of a copyright holder.

2.3 Expected Attack Types

Related to the requirement for robustness in Section 2.1, we assume two types of attacks against which embedded watermarks should be robust: fine-tuning and model compression. These types of attack are very specific to deep neural networks, while one can easily imagine model compression by analogy with lossy image compression in the image domain.

Fine-tuning or transfer learning [28] seems to be the most feasible type of attack, because it reduces the burden of training deep neural networks. Many models have been constructed on top of existing state-of-the-art models. Fine-tuning alters the model parameters, and thus embedded watermarks should be robust against this alteration.

Model compression is very important in deploying deep neural networks to embedded systems or mobile devices as it can significantly reduce memory requirements and/or computational cost. Lossy compression distorts model parameters, so we should explore how it affects the detection rate.

3 PROPOSED FRAMEWORK

In this section, we propose a framework for embedding a watermark into a host network. Although we focus on a DCNN [25] as the host, our framework is essentially applicable to other networks such as standard multilayer perceptron (MLP), recurrent neural network (RNN), and long short-term memory (LSTM) [18].

3.1 Embedding Targets

In this paper, a watermark is assumed to be embedded into one of the convolutional layers in a host DCNN[3]. Let (S, S), D, and L respectively denote the size of the convolution filter, the depth of input to the convolutional layer, and the number of filters in the convolutional layer. The parameters of this convolutional layer are characterized by the tensor $W \in \mathbb{R}^{S \times S \times D \times L}$. The bias term is ignored here. Let us think of embedding a T-bit vector $b \in \{0, 1\}^T$ into W. The tensor W is a set of L convolutional filters and the order of the filters does not affect the output of the network if the

[3]Fully-connected layers can also be used but we focus on convolutional layers here, because fully-connected layers are often discarded in fine-tuning.

Table 1: Requirements for an effective watermarking algorithm in the image and neural network domains.

	Image domain	Neural networks domain
Fidelity	The quality of the host image should not be degraded by embedding a watermark.	The effectiveness of the host network should not be degraded by embedding a watermark.
Robustness	The embedded watermark should be robust against common signal processing operations such as lossy compression, cropping, resizing, and so on.	The embedded watermark should be robust against model modifications such as fine-tuning and model compression.
Capacity	The effective watermarking system must have the ability to embed a large amount of information.	
Security	A watermark should in general be secret and should not be accessed, read, or modified by unauthorized parties.	
Efficiency	The watermark embedding and extraction processes should be fast.	

Table 2: Three embedding situations. Fine-tune indicates whether parameters are initialized in embedding using already trained models, or not. Label availability indicates whether or not labels for training data are available in embedding.

	Fine-tune	Label availability
Train-to-embed		✓
Fine-tune-to-embed	✓	✓
Distill-to-embed	✓	

parameters of the subsequent layers are appropriately re-ordered. In order to remove this arbitrariness in the order of filters, we calculate the mean of W over L filters as $\overline{W}_{ijk} = \frac{1}{L}\sum_l W_{ijkl}$. Letting $w \in \mathbb{R}^M$ ($M = S \times S \times D$) denote a flattened version of $\overline{W}$, our objective is now to embed T-bit vector b into w.

3.2 Embedding Regularizer

It is possible to embed a watermark in a host network by directly modifying w of a trained network, as is usually done in the image domain. However, this approach degrades the performance of the host network in the original task as shown later in Section 4.2.6. Instead, we propose embedding a watermark while *training* a host network for the original task so that the existence of the watermark does not impair the performance of the host network in its original task. To this end, we utilize a *parameter regularizer*, which is an additional term in the original cost function for the original task. The cost function $E(w)$ with a regularizer is defined as:

$$E(w) = E_0(w) + \lambda E_R(w), \tag{1}$$

where $E_0(w)$ is the original cost function, $E_R(w)$ is a regularization term that imposes a certain restriction on parameters w, and λ is an adjustable parameter. A regularizer is usually used to prevent overfitting in neural networks. L_2 regularization (or weight decay [24]), L_1 regularization, and their combination are often used to reduce over-fitting of parameters for complex neural networks. For instance, $E_R(w) = ||w||_2^2$ in the L_2 regularization.

In contrast to these standard regularizers, our regularizer imposes parameter w to have a certain statistical bias, as a watermark in a training process. We refer to this regularizer as an *embedding regularizer*. Before defining the embedding regularizer, we explain how to extract a watermark from w. Given a (mean) parameter vector $w \in \mathbb{R}^M$ and an embedding parameter $X \in \mathbb{R}^{T\times M}$, the watermark extraction is simply done by projecting w using X, followed by thresholding at 0. More precisely, the j-th bit is extracted as:

$$b_j = s(\Sigma_i X_{ji} w_i), \tag{2}$$

where $s(x)$ is a step function:

$$s(x) = \begin{cases} 1 & x \geq 0 \\ 0 & \text{else.} \end{cases} \tag{3}$$

This process can be considered to be a binary classification problem with a single-layer perceptron (without bias)[4]. Therefore, it is straightforward to define the loss function $E_R(w)$ for the embedding regularizer by using (binary) cross entropy:

$$E_R(w) = -\sum_{j=1}^{T} \left(b_j \log(y_j) + (1-b_j)\log(1-y_j)\right), \tag{4}$$

where $y_j = \sigma(\Sigma_i X_{ji} w_i)$ and $\sigma(\cdot)$ is the sigmoid function:

$$\sigma(x) = \frac{1}{1+\exp(-x)}. \tag{5}$$

We call this loss function an *embedding loss* function. It may be confusing that an embedding loss function is used to update w, not X, in our framework. In a standard perceptron, w is an input and X is a parameter to be learned. In our case, w is an embedding target and X is a fixed parameter. The design of X is discussed in the following section.

This approach does not impair the performance of the host network in the original task as confirmed in experiments, because deep neural networks are typically over-parameterized. It is well-known that deep neural networks have many local minima, and that all local minima are likely to have an error very close to that of the global minimum [6, 9]. Therefore, the embedding regularizer only needs to *guide* model parameters to one of a number of *good* local minima so that the final model parameters have an arbitrary watermark.

3.3 Regularizer Parameters

In this section we discuss the design of the embedding parameter X, which can be considered as a secret key [15] in detecting and embedding watermarks. While $X \in \mathbb{R}^{T\times M}$ can be an arbitrary matrix, it will affect the performance of an embedded watermark because

[4]Although this single-layer perceptron can be *deepened* into multi-layer perceptron, we focus on the simplest one in this paper.

it is used in both embedding and extraction of watermarks. In this paper, we consider three types of X: X^{direct}, X^{diff}, and X^{random}.

X^{direct} is constructed so that one element in each row of X^{direct} is '1' and the others are '0'. In this case, the j-th bit b_j is *directly* embedded in a certain parameter $w_{\hat{i}}$ s.t. $X^{\text{direct}}_{j\hat{i}} = 1$.

X^{diff} is created so that each row has one '1' element and one '-1' element, and the others are '0'. Using X^{diff}, the j-th bit b_j is embedded into the *difference* between w_{i_+} and w_{i_-} where $X^{\text{diff}}_{ji_+} = 1$ and $X^{\text{diff}}_{ji_-} = -1$.

Each element of X^{random} is independently drawn from the standard normal distribution $\mathcal{N}(0, 1)$. Using X^{random}, each bit is embedded into all instances of the parameter w with *random* weights. These three types of embedding parameters are compared in experiments.

Our implementation of the embedding regularizer is publicly available from https://github.com/yu4u/dnn-watermark.

4 EXPERIMENTS

In this section, we demonstrate that our embedding regularizer can embed a watermark without impairing the performance of the host network, and the embedded watermark is robust against various types of attack.

4.1 Evaluation Settings

Datasets. For experiments, we used the well-known CIFAR-10 and Caltech-101 datasets. The CIFAR-10 dataset [22] consists of 60,000 32×32 color images in 10 classes, with 6,000 images per class. These images were separated into 50,000 training images and 10,000 test images. The Caltech-101 dataset [10] includes pictures of objects belonging to 101 categories; it contains about 40 to 800 images per category. The size of each image is roughly 300×200 pixels but we resized them in 32×32 for fine-tuning. For each category, we used 30 images for training and at most 40 of the remaining images for testing.

Host network and training settings. We used the wide residual network [33] as the host network. The wide residual network is an efficient variant of the residual network [16]. Table 3 shows the structure of the wide residual network with a depth parameter N and a width parameter k. In all our experiments, we set $N = 1$ and $k = 4$, and used SGD with Nesterov momentum and cross-entropy loss in training. The initial learning rate was set at 0.1, weight decay to 5.0×10^{-4}, momentum to 0.9 and minibatch size to 64. The learning rate was dropped by a factor of 0.2 at 60, 120 and 160 epochs, and we trained for a total of 200 epochs, following the settings used in [33].

We embedded a watermark into one of the following convolution layers: the second convolution layer in the conv 2, conv 3, and conv 4 groups. In the following, we mention the location of the host layer by simply describing the conv 2, conv 3, or conv 4 group. In Table 3, the number M of parameter w is also shown for these layers. The parameter λ in Eq. (1) is set to 0.01. As a watermark, we embedded $b = \mathbf{1} \in \{0, 1\}^T$ in the following experiments.

Table 3: Structure of the host network.

Group	Output size	Building block	M
conv 1	32×32	$[3 \times 3, 16]$	N/A
conv 2	32×32	$\begin{bmatrix} 3 \times 3, 16 \times k \\ 3 \times 3, 16 \times k \end{bmatrix} \times N$	$144 \times k$
conv 3	16×16	$\begin{bmatrix} 3 \times 3, 32 \times k \\ 3 \times 3, 32 \times k \end{bmatrix} \times N$	$288 \times k$
conv 4	8×8	$\begin{bmatrix} 3 \times 3, 64 \times k \\ 3 \times 3, 64 \times k \end{bmatrix} \times N$	$576 \times k$
	1×1	avg-pool, fc, soft-max	N/A

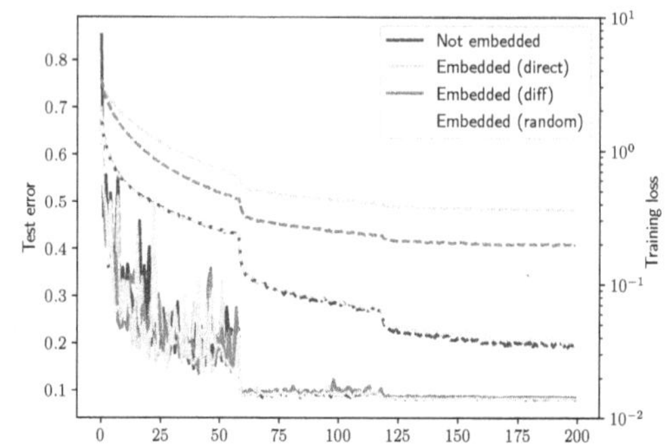

Figure 1: Training curves for the host network on CIFAR-10 as a function of epochs. Solid lines denote test error (y-axis on the left) and dashed lines denote training loss $E(w)$ (y-axis on the right).

Table 4: Test error (%) and embedding loss $E_R(w)$ with and without embedding.

	Test error	$E_R(w)$
Not embedded	8.04	N/A
direct	8.21	1.24×10^{-1}
diff	8.37	6.20×10^{-2}
random	7.97	4.76×10^{-4}

4.2 Embedding Results

First, we confirm that a watermark was successfully embedded in the host network by the proposed embedding regularizer. We trained the host network from scratch (train-to-embed) on the CIFAR-10 dataset with and without embedding a watermark. In the embedding case, a 256-bit watermark ($T = 256$) was embedded into the conv 2 group.

4.2.1 Test Error and Training Loss. Figure 1 shows the training curves for the host network in CIFAR-10 as a function of epochs. Not embedded is the case that the host network is trained without the embedding regularizer. Embedded (direct), Embedded (diff), and Embedded (random) respectively represent training curves with embedding regularizers whose parameters are X^{direct}, X^{diff}, and X^{random}. We can see that the training loss $E(w)$ with a watermark becomes larger than the not-embedded case if the parameters

X^{direct} and X^{diff} are used. This large training loss is dominated by the embedding loss $E_R(w)$, which indicates that it is difficult to embed a watermark directly into a parameter or even into the difference of two parameters. On the other hand, the training loss of Embedded (random) is very close to that of Not embedded.

Table 4 shows the best test errors and embedding losses $E_R(w)$ of the host networks with and without embedding. We can see that the test errors of Not embedded and random are almost the same while those of direct and diff are slightly larger. The embedding loss $E_R(w)$ of random is extremely low compared with those of direct and diff. These results indicate that the random approach can effectively embed a watermark without impairing the performance in the original task.

4.2.2 Detecting Watermarks. Figure 2 shows the histogram of the embedded watermark $\sigma(\Sigma_i X_{ji} w_i)$ (before thresholding) with and without watermarks where (a) direct, (b) diff, and (c) random parameters are used in embedding and detection. If we binarize $\sigma(\Sigma_i X_{ji} w_i)$ at a threshold of 0.5, all watermarks are correctly detected because $\forall j,\ \sigma(\Sigma_i X_{ji} w_i) \geq 0.5\ (\Leftrightarrow \Sigma_i X_{ji} w_i \geq 0)$ for all embedded cases. Please note that we embedded $b = \mathbf{1} \in \{0,1\}^T$ as a watermark as mentioned before. Although random watermarks will be detected for the non-embedded cases, it can be easily judged that the watermark is not embedded because the distribution of $\sigma(\Sigma_i X_{ji} w_i)$ is quite different from those for embedded cases.

4.2.3 Distribution of Model Parameters. We explore how trained model parameters are affected by the embedded watermarks. Figure 3 shows the distribution of model parameters W (not w) with and without watermarks. These parameters are taken only from the layer in which a watermark was embedded. Note that W is the parameter before taking the mean over filters, and thus the number of parameters is 3×3×64×64. We can see that direct and diff significantly alter the distribution of parameters while random does not. In direct, many parameters became large and a peak appears near 2 so that their mean over filters becomes a large positive value to reduce the embedding loss. In diff, most parameters were pushed in both positive and negative directions so that the differences between these parameters became large. In random, a watermark is diffused over all parameters with random weights and thus does not significantly alter the distribution. This is one of the desirable properties of watermarking related the security requirement; one may be aware of the existence of the embedded watermarks for the direct and diff cases.

The results so far indicated that the random approach seemed to be the best choice among the three, with low embedding loss, low test error in the original task, and not altering the parameter distribution. Therefore, in the following experiments, we used the random approach in embedding watermarks without explicitly indicating it.

4.2.4 Fine-tune-to-embed and Distill-to-embed. In the above experiments, a watermark was embedded by training the host network from scratch (train-to-embed). Here, we evaluated the other two situations introduced in Section 2.2: fine-tune-to-embed and distill-to-embed. For fine-tune-to-embed, two experiments were performed. In the first experiment, the host network was trained on the CIFAR-10 dataset without embedding, and then fine-tuned on the same CIFAR-10 dataset with embedding and without embedding (for comparison). In the second experiment, the host network is trained on the Caltech-101 dataset, and then fine-tuned on the CIFAR-10 dataset with and without embedding.

Table 5: Test error (%) and embedding loss $E_R(w)$ with and without embedding in fine-tuning and distilling.

(a) Fine-tune-to-embed (CIFAR-10 → CIFAR-10)		
	Test error	$E_R(w)$
Not embedded 1st	8.04	N/A
Not embedded 2nd	7.66	N/A
Embedded	7.70	4.93×10^{-4}
(b) Fine-tune-to-embed (Caltech-101 → CIFAR-10)		
	Test error	$E_R(w)$
Not embedded 2nd	7.93	N/A
Embedded	7.94	4.83×10^{-4}
(c) Distill-to-embed (CIFAR-10 → CIFAR-10)		
	Test error	$E_R(w)$
Not embedded 1st	8.04	N/A
Not embedded 2nd	7.86	N/A
Embedded	7.75	5.01×10^{-4}

Table 5 (a) shows the result of the first experiment. Not embedded 1st corresponds to the first training without embedding. Not embedded 2nd corresponds to the second training without embedding and Embedded corresponds to the second training with embedding. Figure 4 shows the training curves of these fine-tunings[5]. We can see that Embedded achieved almost the same test error as Not embedded 2nd and a very low $E_R(w)$.

Table 5 (b) shows the results of the second experiment. Not embedded 2nd corresponds to the second training without embedding and Embedded corresponds to the second training with embedding. The test error and training loss of the first training are not shown because they are not compatible between these two different training datasets. From these results, it was also confirmed that Embedded achieved almost the same test error as Not embedded 2nd and very low $E_R(w)$. Thus, we can say that the proposed method is effective even in the fine-tune-to-embed situation (in the same and different domains).

Finally, embedding a watermark in the distill-to-embed situation was evaluated. The host network is first trained on the CIFAR-10 dataset without embedding. Then, the trained network was further fine-tuned on the same CIFAR-10 dataset with and without embedding. In this second training, the training labels of the CIFAR-10 dataset were *not* used. Instead, the predicted values of the trained network were used as soft targets [17]. In other words, no label was used in the second training. Table 5 (c) shows the results for the distill-to-embed situation. Not embedded 1st corresponds to the first training and Embedded (Not embedded 2nd) corresponds to the second distilling training with embedding (without embedding). It was found that the proposed method also achieved low test error and $E_R(w)$ in the distill-to-embed situation.

[5] Note that the learning rate was also initialized to 0.1 at the beginning of the second training, while the learning rate was reduced to 8.0×10^{-4}) at the end of the first training.

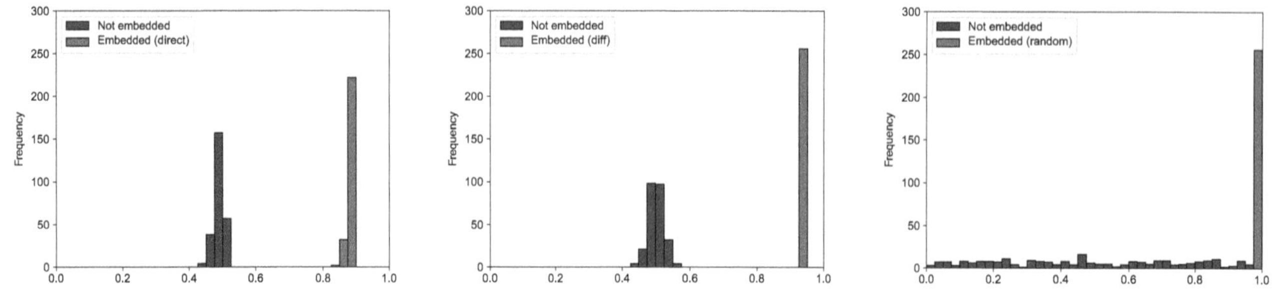

(a) direct (b) diff (c) random

Figure 2: Histogram of the embedded watermark $\sigma(\Sigma_i X_{ji} w_i)$ (before thresholding) with and without watermarks.

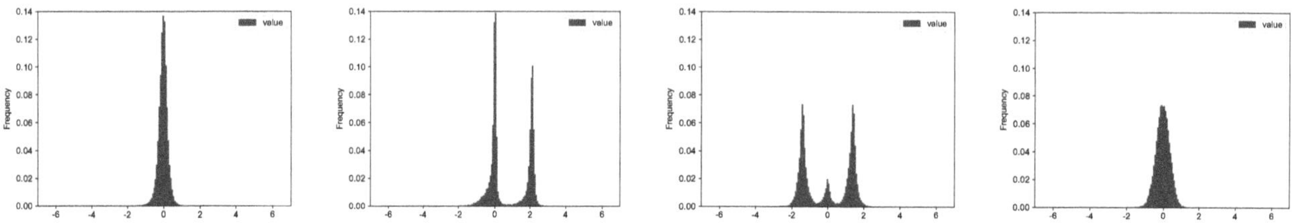

(a) Not embedded (b) direct (c) diff (d) random

Figure 3: Distribution of model parameters W with and without watermarks.

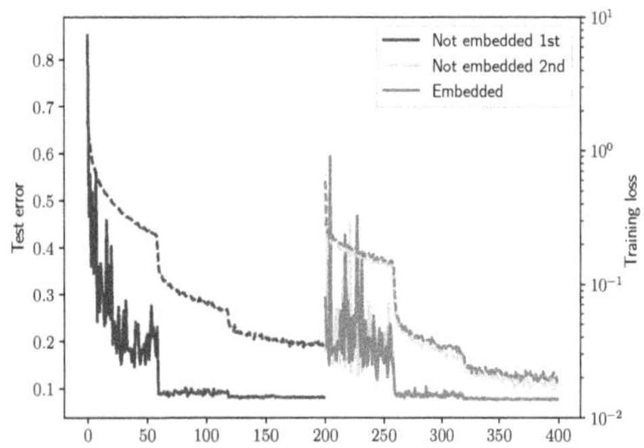

Figure 4: Training curves for fine-tuning the host network. The first and second halves of epochs correspond to the first and second training. Solid lines denote test error (y-axis on the left) and dashed lines denote training loss (y-axis on the right).

4.2.5 Capacity of Watermark. In this section, the capacity of the embedded watermark is explored by embedding different sizes of watermarks into different groups in the train-to-embed manner. Please note that the number of parameters w of conv 2, conv 3, and conv 4 groups were 576, 1152, and 2304, respectively. Table 6 shows test error (%) and embedding loss $E_R(w)$ for combinations of different embedded blocks and different number of embedded bits. We can see that embedded loss or test error becomes high if the number of embedded bits becomes larger than the number of parameters w (e.g. 2,048 bits in conv 3) because the embedding problem becomes overdetermined in such cases. Thus, the number of embedded bits should be smaller than the number of parameters w, which is a limitation of the embedding method using a single-layer perceptron. This limitation would be resolved by using a multi-layer perceptron in the embedding regularizer.

Table 6: Test error (%) and embedding loss $E_R(w)$ for the combinations of embedded groups and sizes of embedded bits.

(a) Test error (%)

Embedded bits	Embedded group		
	conv 2	conv 3	conv 4
256	7.97	7.98	7.92
512	8.47	8.22	7.84
1,024	8.43	8.12	7.84
2,048	8.17	8.93	7.75

(b) Embedding loss

Embedded bits	Embedded group		
	conv 2	conv 3	conv 4
256	4.76×10^{-4}	7.20×10^{-4}	1.10×10^{-2}
512	8.11×10^{-4}	8.18×10^{-4}	1.25×10^{-2}
1,024	6.74×10^{-2}	1.53×10^{-3}	1.53×10^{-2}
2,048	5.35×10^{-1}	3.70×10^{-2}	3.06×10^{-2}

Table 7: Losses, test error, and bit error rate (BER) after embedding a watermark with different λ.

λ	$\frac{1}{2}\|\|w - w_0\|\|_2^2$	$E_R(w)$	Test error	BER
0	0.000	1.066	8.04	0.531
1	0.184	0.609	8.52	0.324
10	1.652	0.171	10.57	0.000
100	7.989	0.029	13.00	0.000

4.2.6 Embedding without Training. As mentioned in Section 3.2, it is possible to embed a watermark to a host network by directly modifying the trained parameter w_0 as usually done in image domain. Here we try to do this by minimizing the following loss function instead of Eq. (1):

$$E(w) = \frac{1}{2}||w - w_0||_2^2 + \lambda E_R(w), \quad (6)$$

where the embedding loss $E_R(w)$ is minimized while minimizing the difference between the modified parameter w and the original parameter w_0. Table 7 summarizes the embedding results after minimizing Eq. (6) against the host network trained on the CIFAR-10 dataset. We can see that embedding fails for $\lambda \leq 1$ as bit error rate (BER) is larger than zero while the test error of the original task becomes too large for $\lambda > 1$. Thus, it is not effective to directly embed a watermark without considering the original task.

4.3 Robustness of Embedded Watermarks

In this section, the robustness of a proposed watermark is evaluated for the three attack types explained in Section 2.3: fine-tuning and model compression.

4.3.1 Robustness against Fine-tuning. Fine-tuning or transfer learning [28] seems to be the most likely type of (unintentional) attack because it is frequently performed on trained models to apply them to other but similar tasks with less effort than training a network from scratch or to avoid over-fitting when sufficient training data is not available.

In this experiment, two trainings we performed; in the first training, a 256-bit watermark was embedded in the conv 2 group in the train-to-embed manner, and then the host network was further fine-tuned in the second training without embedding, to determine whether the watermark embedded in the first training stayed in the host network or not, even after the second training (fine-tuning).

Table 8 shows the embedding loss before fine-tuning ($E_R(w)$) and after fine-tuning ($E'_R(w)$), and the best test error after fine-tuning. We evaluated fine-tuning in the same domain (CIFAR-10 → CIFAR-10) and in different domains (Caltech-101 → CIFAR-10). We can see that, in both cases, the embedding loss was slightly increased by fine-tuning but was still low. In addition, the bit error rate of the detected watermark was equal to zero in both cases. The reason why the embedding loss in fine-tuning in the different domains is higher than that in the same domain is that the Caltech-101 dataset is significantly more difficult than the CIFAR-10 dataset in our settings; all images in the Caltech-101 dataset were resized to 32×32[6] for compatibility with the CIFAR-10 dataset.

[6]This size is extremely small compared with their original sizes (roughly 300×200).

Table 8: Embedding loss before fine-tuning ($E_R(w)$) and after fine-tuning ($E'_R(w)$), and the best test error (%) after fine-tuning.

	$E_R(w)$	$E'_R(w)$	Test error
CIFAR-10 → CIFAR-10	4.76×10^{-4}	8.66×10^{-4}	7.69
Caltech-101 → CIFAR-10	5.96×10^{-3}	1.56×10^{-2}	7.88

4.3.2 Robustness against Model Compression. It is sometimes difficult to deploy deep neural networks to embedded systems or mobile devices because they are both computationally intensive and memory intensive. In order to solve this problem, the model parameters are often *compressed* [12–14]. The compression of model parameters can intentionally or unintentionally act as an attack against watermarks. In this section, we evaluate the robustness of our watermarks against model compression, in particular, against parameter pruning [14]. In parameter pruning, parameters whose absolute values are very small are cut-off to zero. In [13], quantization of weights and the Huffman coding of quantized values are further applied. Because quantization has less impact than parameter pruning and the Huffman coding is lossless compression, we focus on parameter pruning.

In order to evaluate the robustness against parameter pruning, we embedded a 256-bit watermark in the conv 2 group while training the host network on the CIFAR-10 dataset. We removed α% of the $3 \times 3 \times 64 \times 64$ parameters of the embedded layer and calculated embedding loss and bit error rate. Figure 5 (a) shows embedding loss $E_R(w)$ as a function of pruning rate α. Ascending (Descending) represents embedding loss when the top α% parameters are cut-off according to their absolute values in ascending (descending) order. Random represents embedding loss where α% of parameters are randomly removed. Ascending corresponds to parameter pruning and the others were evaluated for comparison. We can see that the embedding loss of Ascending increases more slowly than those of Descending and Random as α increases. It is reasonable that model parameters with small absolute values have less impact on a detected watermark because the watermark is extracted from the dot product of the model parameter w and the constant embedding parameter (weight) X.

Figure 5 (b) shows the bit error rate as a function of pruning rate α. Surprisingly, the bit error rate was still zero after removing 65% of the parameters and 2/256 even after 80% of the parameters were pruned (Ascending). We can say that the embedded watermark is sufficiently robust against parameter pruning because, in [13], the resulting pruning rate of convolutional layers ranged from to 16% to 65% for the AlexNet [23], and from 42% to 78% for VGGNet [28]. Furthermore, this degree of bit error can be easily corrected by an error correction code (e.g. the BCH code). Figure 6 shows the histogram of the detected watermark $\sigma(\Sigma_i X_{ji} w_i)$ after pruning for $\alpha = 0.8$ and 0.95. For $\alpha = 0.95$, the histogram of the detected watermark is also shown for the host network into which no watermark is embedded. We can see that many of $\sigma(\Sigma_i X_{ji} w_i)$ are still close to one for the embedded case, which might be used as a confidence score in judging the existence of a watermark (zero-bit watermarking).

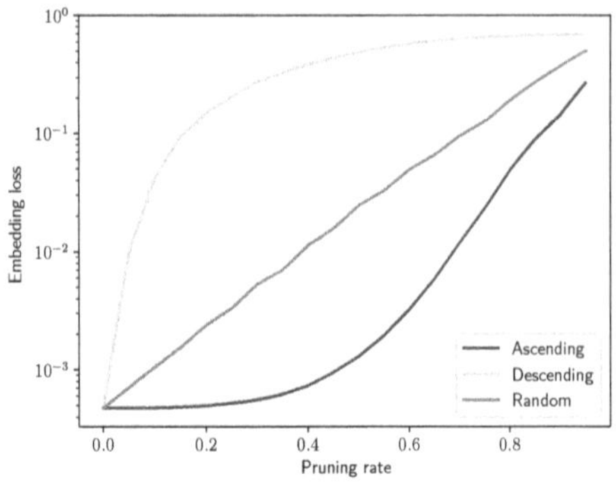

(a) Embedding loss.

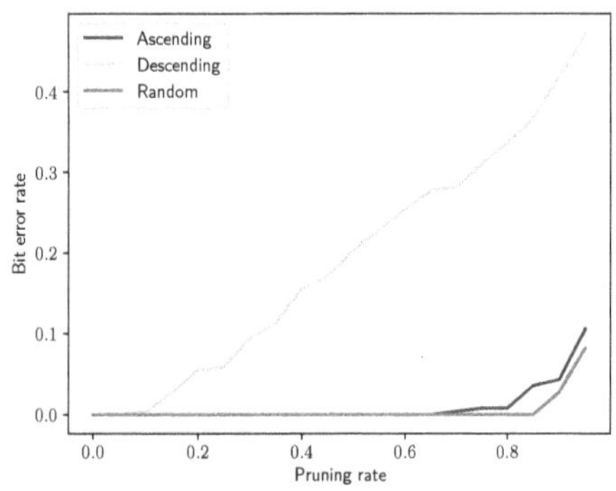

(b) Bit error rate.

Figure 5: Embedding loss and bit error rate after pruning as a function of pruning rate.

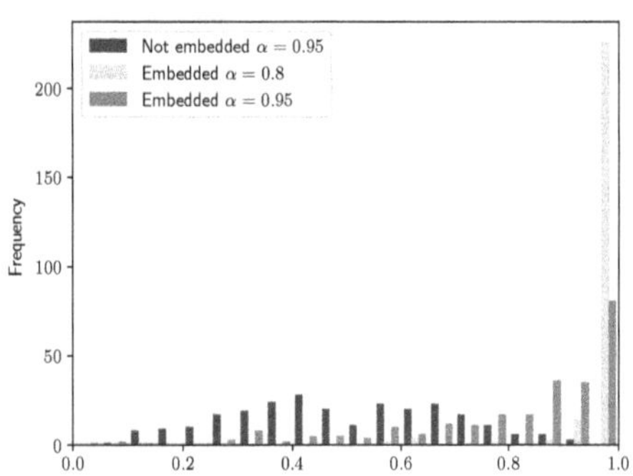

Figure 6: Histogram of the detected watermark $\sigma(\Sigma_i X_{ji} w_i)$ after pruning.

5 CONCLUSIONS AND FUTURE WORK

In this paper, we have proposed a general framework for embedding a watermark in deep neural network models to protect the rights to the trained models. First, we formulated a new problem: embedding watermarks into deep neural networks. We also defined requirements, embedding situations, and attack types for watermarking deep neural networks. Second, we proposed a general framework for embedding a watermark in model parameters using a parameter regularizer. Our approach does not impair the performance of networks into which a watermark is embedded. Finally, we performed comprehensive experiments to reveal the potential of watermarking deep neural networks as the basis of this new problem. We showed that our framework could embed a watermark without impairing the performance of a deep neural network. The embedded watermark did not disappear even after fine-tuning or parameter pruning; the entire watermark remained even after 65% of the parameters were pruned.

5.1 Future Work

Although we have obtained first insight into the new problem of embedding a watermark in deep neural networks, many things remain as future work.

Watermark overwriting. A third-party user may embed a different watermark in order to *overwrite* the original watermark. In our preliminary experiments, this watermark overwriting caused 30.9%, 8.6%, and 0.4% bit errors against watermarks in the conv 2, conv 3, and conv 4 groups when 256-bit watermarks were additionally embedded. More robust watermarking against overwriting should be explored (e.g. non-linear embedding).

Compression as embedding. Compressing deep neural networks is a very important and active research topic. While we confirmed that our watermark is very robust against parameter pruning in this paper, a watermark might be embedded in conjunction with compressing models. For example, in [13], after parameter pruning, the network is re-trained to learn the final weights for the remaining sparse parameters. Our embedding regularizer can be used in this re-training to embed a watermark.

Network morphism. In [4, 32], a systematic study has been done on how to morph a well-trained neural network into a new one so that its network function can be completely preserved for further training. This network morphism can constitute a severe attack against our watermark because it may be impossible to detect the embedded watermark if the topology of the host network is severely modified. We left the investigation how the embedded watermark is affected by this network morphism for future work.

Steganalysis. Steganalysis [21, 27] is a method for detecting the presence of secretly hidden data (e.g. steganography or watermarks) in digital media files such as images, video, audio, and, in our case, deep neural networks. Watermarks ideally are robust against steganalysis. While, in this paper, we confirmed that embedding watermarks does not significantly change the distribution of model parameters, more exploration is needed to evaluate robustness against steganalysis. Conversely, developing effective steganalysis against watermarks for deep neural networks can be an interesting research topic.

Fingerprinting. Digital fingerprinting is an alternative to the watermarking approach for persistent identification of images [2], video [20, 31], and audio clips [1, 11]. In this paper, we focused on one of these two important approaches. Robust fingerprinting of deep neural networks is another and complementary direction to protect deep neural network models.

REFERENCES

[1] X. Anguera, A. Garzon, and T. Adamek. 2012. MASK: Robust Local Features for Audio Fingerprinting. In *Proc. of ICME.*

[2] J. Barr, B. Bradley, and B. T. Hannigan. 2003. Using digital watermarks with image signatures to mitigate the threat of the copy attack. In *Proc. of ICASSP.* 69–72.

[3] J. Bergstra, O. Breuleux, F. Bastien, P. Lamblin, R. Pascanu, G. Desjardins, J. Turian, D. Warde-Farley, and Y. Bengio. 2010. Theano: a CPU and GPU Math Expression Compiler. In *Proc. of the Python for Scientific Computing Conference (SciPy).*

[4] Tianqi Chen, Ian Goodfellow, and Jonathon Shlens. 2016. Net2Net: Accelerating Learning via Knowledge Transfer. In *Proc. of ICLR.*

[5] F. Chollet. 2015. Keras. https://github.com/fchollet/keras. *GitHub repository* (2015).

[6] A. Choromanska, M. Henaff, M. Mathieu, G. Arous, and Y. LeCun. 2015. The Loss Surfaces of Multilayer Networks. In *Proc. of AISTATS.*

[7] R. Collobert, K. Kavukcuoglu, and C. Farabet. 2011. Torch7: A MATLAB-like environment for machine learning. In *Proc. of NIPS Workshop on BigLearn.*

[8] Ingemar Cox, Matthew Miller, Jeffrey Bloom, Jessica Fridrich, and Ton Kalker. 2008. *Digital Watermarking and Steganography* (2 ed.). Morgan Kaufmann Publishers Inc.

[9] Y. Dauphin, R. Pascanu, C. Gulcehre, K. Cho, S. Ganguli, and Y. Bengio. 2014. Identifying and attacking the saddle point problem in high-dimensional non-convex optimization. In *Proc. of NIPS.*

[10] L. Fei-Fei, R. Fergus, and P. Perona. 2004. Learning generative visual models from few training examples: an incremental Bayesian approach tested on 101 object categories. In *Proc. of CVPR Workshop on Generative-Model Based Vision.*

[11] J. Haitsma and T. Kalker. 2002. A Highly Robust Audio Fingerprinting System. In *Proc. of ISMIR.* 107–115.

[12] Song Han, Xingyu Liu, Huizi Mao, Jing Pu, Ardavan Pedram, Mark A. Horowitz, and William J. Dally. 2016. EIE: Efficient Inference Engine on Compressed Deep Neural Network. In *Proc. of ISCA.*

[13] Song Han, Huizi Mao, and William J. Dally. 2016. Deep Compression: Compressing Deep Neural Networks with Pruning, Trained Quantization and Huffman Coding. In *Proc. of ICLR.*

[14] Song Han, Jeff Pool, John Tran, and William J. Dally. 2015. Learning both Weights and Connections for Efficient Neural Networks. In *Proc. of NIPS.*

[15] F. Hartung and M. Kutter. 1999. Multimedia Watermarking Techniques. *Proc. IEEE* 87, 7 (1999), 1079–1107.

[16] K. He, X. Zhang, S. Ren, and J. Sun. 2016. Deep Residual Learning for Image Recognition. In *Proc. of CVPR.*

[17] Geoffrey Hinton, Oriol Vinyals, and Jeff Dean. 2014. Distilling the Knowledge in a Neural Network. In *Proc. of NIPS Workshop on Deep Learning and Representation Learning.*

[18] S. Hochreiter and J. Schmidhuber. 1997. Long Short-Term Memory. *Neural Computation* 9, 8 (1997), 1735–1780.

[19] Yangqing Jia, Evan Shelhamer, Jeff Donahue, Sergey Karayev, Jonathan Long, Ross Girshick, Sergio Guadarrama, and Trevor Darrell. 2014. Caffe: Convolutional Architecture for Fast Feature Embedding. In *Proc. of MM.*

[20] A. Joly, C. Frelicot, and O. Buisson. 2005. Content-based video copy detection in large databases: a local fingerprints statistical similarity search approach. In *Proc. of ICIP.* 505–508.

[21] J. Kodovsky, J. Fridrich, and V. Holub. 2012. Ensemble Classifiers for Steganalysis of Digital Media. *IEEE Trans. on Information Forensics and Security* 7, 2 (2012), 432–444.

[22] A. Krizhevsky. 2009. Learning multiple layers of features from tiny images. *Tech Report* (2009).

[23] Alex Krizhevsky, Ilya Sutskever, and Geoffrey E. Hinton. 2012. ImageNet Classification with Deep Convolutional Neural Networks. In *Proc. of NIPS.*

[24] Anders Krogh and John A. Hertz. 1992. A Simple Weight Decay Can Improve Generalization. In *Proc. of NIPS.*

[25] Y. Lecun, L. Bottou, Y. Bengio, and P. Haffner. 1998. Gradient-Based Learning Applied to Document Recognition. *Proc. IEEE* 86, 11 (1998), 2278–2324.

[26] M. Abadi, *et al.* 2016. TensorFlow: Large-Scale Machine Learning on Heterogeneous Distributed Systems. *arXiv:1603.04467* (2016).

[27] Liu Shaohui, Yao Hongxun, and Gao Wen. 2003. Neural network based steganalysis in still images. In *Proc. of ICME.*

[28] Karen Simonyan and Andrew Zisserman. 2015. Very deep convolutional networks for large-scale image recognition. In *Proc. of ICLR.*

[29] C. Szegedy, W. Liu, Y. Jia, P. Sermanet, S. Reed, D. Anguelov, D. Erhan, V. Vanhoucke, and A. Rabinovich. 2015. Going deeper with convolutions. In *Proc. of CVPR.*

[30] Seiya Tokui, Kenta Oono, Shohei Hido, and Justin Clayton. 2015. Chainer: a Next-Generation Open Source Framework for Deep Learning. In *Proc. of NIPS Workshop on Machine Learning Systems.*

[31] Y. Uchida, M. Agrawal, and S. Sakazawa. 2011. Accurate Content-Based Video Copy Detection with Efficient Feature Indexing. In *Proc. of ICMR.*

[32] Tao Wei, Changhu Wang, Yong Rui, and Chang Wen Chen. 2016. Network Morphism. In *Proc. of ICML.*

[33] S. Zagoruyko and N. Komodakis. 2016. Wide Residual Networks. In *Proc. of ECCV.*

Learning to Detect Misleading Content on Twitter

Christina Boididou, Symeon Papadopoulos, Lazaros Apostolidis, Yiannis Kompatsiaris
Information Technologies Institute, Centre for Research and Technology Hellas
Thessaloniki, Greece
{boididou,papadop,laaposto,ikom}@iti.gr

ABSTRACT

The publication and spread of misleading content is a problem of increasing magnitude, complexity and consequences in a world that is increasingly relying on user-generated content for news sourcing. To this end, multimedia analysis techniques could serve as an assisting tool to spot and debunk misleading content on the Web. In this paper, we tackle the problem of misleading multimedia content detection on Twitter in real time. We propose a number of new features and a new semi-supervised learning event adaptation approach that helps generalize the detection capabilities of trained models to unseen content, even when the event of interest is of different nature compared to that used for training. Combined with bagging, the proposed approach manages to outperform previous systems by a significant margin in terms of accuracy. Moreover, in order to communicate the verification process to end users, we develop a web-based application for visualizing the results.

CCS CONCEPTS

•Information systems → Information retrieval; Test collections; *Multimedia and multimodal retrieval;* **•Human-centered computing → Social networking sites;**

KEYWORDS

social media, verification, fake detection, news mining

ACM Reference format:
Christina Boididou, Symeon Papadopoulos, Lazaros Apostolidis, Yiannis Kompatsiaris. 2017. Learning to Detect Misleading Content on Twitter. In *Proceedings of ICMR '17, June 6–9, 2017, Bucharest, Romania, ,* 9 pages.
DOI: http://dx.doi.org/10.1145/3078971.3078979

1 INTRODUCTION

Recent years have seen tremendous increase in the use of social media platforms such as Twitter and Facebook as means of sharing news content and multimedia. The simplicity of the sharing process has led to large volumes of news content propagating over social networks and reaching huge numbers of readers in very short time. Especially multimedia content (images, videos) can rapidly reach massive audiences and become viral due to the fact that it is easily consumed and often carries a lot of entertainment value.

ACM ISBN 978-1-4503-4701-3/17/06...$15.00
DOI: http://dx.doi.org/10.1145/3078971.3078979

Figure 1: Examples of fake imagery that spread on Twitter during the Malaysian airlines incident on March 2014.

Given the speed of the news spreading process and the competition of news outlets and journalists to publish first, it is only natural that the verification of content is often carried out in a superficial manner or even neglected. This leads to the online appearance and spread of large amounts of misleading multimedia content. In particular, when a news event breaks (e.g., a natural disaster), and media coverage is of primary importance, news professionals often turn to social media to source newsworthy content. It is exactly this setting, when the risk of misleading content becoming viral is the highest. As misleading (or for the sake of brevity *fake*), we define any post that shares multimedia content that does not faithfully represent the event that it refers to. This could include: a) content from a past event that is reposted as referring to the current event, b) content that is deliberately manipulated, or c) content that is falsely used to represent an aspect of the current event. In a similar way, as *real*, we define posts that share content that faithfully represents the event in question. There are in-between cases: for instance, when a post acknowledges the misleading nature of the content it shares or refers to it with a sense of humour, it is hard to categorize as fake or real; these are out of the scope of this work.

The impact of fake content being widely disseminated can be quite severe. For example, after the Malaysia Airlines flight disappeared on March 2014 (Figure 1), numerous fake images that became soon viral on social media raised false alarms that the plane was detected. This deeply affected and caused emotional distress to people directly involved in the incident, such as the passengers' families. Examples such as this point to the need for means of identifying and debunking fake media content on social media. One of the first such attempts [8] used a supervised learning approach, in which a set of known fake and real tweets were used to train a model to distinguish between the two classes; experiments were conducted on a dataset around the Hurricane Sandy and a very high detection accuracy was reported. Yet, the fact that content from the same event was used both for training and testing was found to give an overly optimistic sense of accuracy, questioning its generalization ability to content from different events [3].

To address the limitations of state-of-the-art solutions on the problem, we present a robust approach for detecting in real time whether a media item shared by a tweet is fake or real. The proposed fake detection approach uses a variety of content-based and contextual features for the social media post in question, and leverages part of its own predictions for retraining, following a semi-supervised learning paradigm, to adapt the model to unseen content. Experiments on a public annotated corpus of multimedia tweets demonstrate the effectiveness of the proposed approach. Additionally, we propose a visualization method for communicating the result of automatic analysis to end users in an intuitive way.

2 RELATED WORK

Multimedia forensics. Although the field of multimedia forensics has led to a multitude of methods for detecting digital manipulation in digital content [18, 21], recent research has shown that tampered images found on the Web are very hard to detect [27, 28]. Moreover, in a lot of cases, forensics techniques are insufficient, e.g. when the multimedia item is just a reposting from a past event. Indeed, past studies have demonstrated that more than half of the videos around trending topics are repostings or remixes of past content [26]. Also, the verification methods employed by journalists [23], e.g. looking into the Exif metadata of content or getting in touch with the person that published it, are often not applicable due to the constraints of popular social media platforms. For instance, Twitter and Facebook remove the Exif metadata from posted content.

Assessing content credibility in social media. Castillo et al. focused on automatic methods for assessing the credibility of a given set of tweets. In particular, they analysed microblog posts related to trending topics and classified them as credible or not credible based on a number of features [5]. A similar approach was presented by Gupta et al. [8], demonstrating high classification accuracy on a dataset of tweets collected around Hurricane Sandy. A thorough experimental study of information credibility on Twitter was also based on information propagation processes in the context of news events [6]. Two models were developed, one that decides whether an information cascade corresponds to a newsworthy event and another one that evaluates the trustworthiness of the cascade. In contrast with the aforementioned approaches, Martinez-Romo et al. [13] conducted a study for detecting malicious tweets in trending topics focusing on statistical linguistic analysis, taking into account exclusively the tweets without considering any information from users. Finally, O'Donovan et al. [16] performed an analysis of the utility of various features when predicting content credibility.

Verification services and systems. Ratkiewicz et al. developed the Truthy system [17], a web service for tracking political memes and misinformation on Twitter, focusing on political astroturf. Truthy collects tweets, detects a number of memes in them, and offers a web interface that lets users annotate those memes they consider "truthy". In recent years, systems that are fully-automatic have been developed, such as TweetCred [7], a tool that computes credibility scores for a set of tweets, and Hoaxy [22], a platform for detecting and analysing online misinformation. Finally, semi-automatic systems have been also introduced, such as RumorLens [20], which combines human effort with computation to detect new rumours in Twitter, and TwitterTrails [14], which lets users investigate the propagation of a given rumour.

3 FAKE DETECTION FRAMEWORK

The proposed framework relies on two independent classification models built on the training data using two different sets of features, tweet-based (TB) and user-based features (UB). A bagging technique is used when building both models. At prediction time, an agreement-based retraining strategy is employed (`fusion`), which combines the outputs of the two models in a semi-supervised learning manner, to increase the generalization capabilities of the framework given tweets from a new unknown event. The outcome of the verification is then visualized to end users. A corpus of labelled posts is necessary (described in Section 4) in order to build the classification models and to generate the visualizations. Figure 2 depicts the main components of the proposed framework. The implementation of the framework is publicly available on GitHub[1].

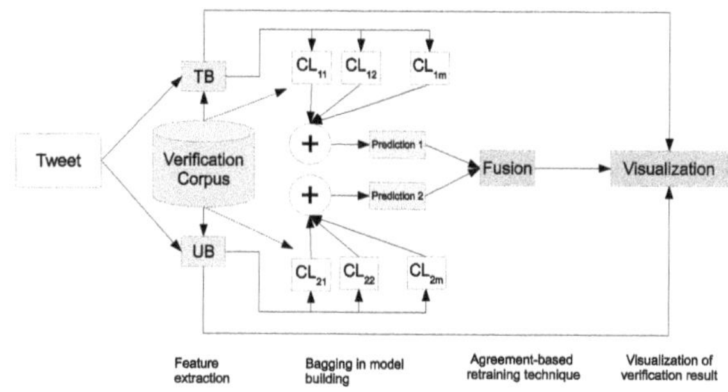

Figure 2: Overview of the proposed framework.

3.1 Feature Extraction

The selection of features used in our framework was carried out following a thorough study of the way in which news professionals, such as journalists, verify content on the Web. Based on relevant journalistic studies, such as [12], and the Verification Handbook [23], we have defined a set of features that are important for verification. These are not limited to the content itself, but also pertain to its source (Twitter account that posted the content) and to the location where it was posted. We decided to not use any image/video forensics features following the conclusion of our recent study [27] that Twitter media content is not amenable to image forensics. This was also confirmed by our recent MediaEval participations [2, 4], where the use of forensics features did not lead to consistent improvement. The feature extraction process produces a set of TB and UB features for each tweet (Table 1).

Tweet-based features (TB): We consider four types of feature related to tweets: a) text-based, b) language-specific, c) Twitter-specific, and d) link-based.
a) text-based: These are extracted from the text of the tweet, and capture characteristics such as the length of a tweet text and the number of words in it. They also include characteristics such as the number of question and exclamation marks, uppercase characters, as well as binary features indicating the existence or not of emoticons, special words ("please") and punctuation (colon).

[1] https://github.com/MKLab-ITI/computational-verification

Table 1: Overview of verification features. Link-based features are extracted in the TB case for external links that tweets may share, and in the UB case for the URL included in the account profile. Features with an asterisk were proposed in [3, 8] and will be denoted as Baseline Features (BF), while the full feature set (BF and newly proposed ones) as Total Features (TF).

Tweet-based Features (TB)		User-based Features (UB)	
text-based		**user-specific**	
#words*	has ''please''	#friends*	has location
length of text*	has colon	#followers*	has existing location
#question marks*	contains happy emoticon*	follower-friend ratio*	has bio description
#exclamation marks*	contains sad emoticon*	#media content	tweet ratio
contains question mark*	#uppercase chars*	has profile image	account age
contains exclamation mark*		has header image	is verified*
language-specific		has a URL*	#times listed*
#pos senti words*	contains 1st pers.pron.*		
#neg senti words*	contains 2nd pers.pron.*	**link-based (common for TB and UB)**	
#slangs	contains 3rd pers.pron.*	WOT score	alexa country rank
#nouns	readability	in-degree centrality	alexa delta rank
twitter-specific		harmonic centrality	alexa popularity
#retweets*	#mentions*		alexa reach rank
#hashtags*	#URLs*		
has external link			

b) language-specific: These are extracted for a predefined set of languages (English, Spanish, German), which are first detected using a language detection library[2]. They include the number of positive and negative sentiment words in the text. For English we use the list by Jeffrey Breen[3], for Spanish the adaptation of ANEW [19] and for German the Leipzig Affective Norms [10]. Additional binary features indicate whether the text contains personal pronouns (in the supported languages). An additional feature is the number of slang words in the tweet. This is extracted using slang words in English[4] and Spanish[5]. For German, no available slang list was found and hence no such feature is computed. Moreover, the number of nouns in the tweet text was also added as feature, and is computed based on the Stanford parser only for English [11]. Finally, to investigate whether the readability of the tweet text is related to its veracity, we use the *Flesch Reading Ease* method[6] to compute a readability score in the range [0, 100], with 0 representing the very hard-to-read text and 100 the very easy-to-read text. For the tweets written in a language, where the above features cannot be extracted, we consider the corresponding values missing.
c) twitter-specific: This set contains features related to the Twitter platform. These include the number of re-tweets, hashtags, mentions, URLs and a binary feature expressing whether any of the URLs points to external (non-Twitter) resources.
d) link-based: These include features that provide information about the links that are shared through the tweet. This set of features is common in both TB and UB sets, but in the latter it is defined in a different way (see link-based category in UB features). For TB, depending on the existence of an external URL in the tweet, its reliability is quantified based on a set of Web metrics: i) the WOT score[7], which is a way to assess the trust on a website using crowdsourced reputation ratings, ii) the in-degree and harmonic centralities[8], computed based on the links of the Web graph, and iii) four Alexa metrics (rank, popularity, delta rank and reach rank) based on the rankings API[9].

User-based features (UB): These are related to the Twitter account posting the tweet. We divide them in a) user-specific and b) link-based features.
a) user-specific: These include the user's number of friends and followers, the account age, the follower-friend ratio, tweet ratio (number of tweets/day divided by account age) and a number of binary features: whether the user is verified by Twitter, whether there is a biography in his/her profile, whether the user declares his/her location using a free text field, and whether the location text can be parsed into an actual location[10], whether the user has header or profile image, and whether a link is included in the profile.
b) link-based: In this case, depending on the existence of a URL in the Twitter profile description, we apply the same Web metrics as the ones used in the link-based TB features. If there is no link in the profile, the values of these features are considered to be missing.

After feature extraction, the next steps include pre-processing, cleaning and transformation. To handle the issue of missing values on some of the features, we use linear regression for estimating their values: we consider the attribute with the missing value as a dependent (class) variable and apply linear regression for numeric features. The method cannot support the prediction of boolean values and hence those are left missing. Only feature values from the training set are used in this process. Data normalization is also performed to scale the numeric feature values to the range [-1, 1].

3.2 Building the classification models

We use the TB and UB features to build two independent Random Forest classifiers (CL_1, CL_2), each of which is based on the respective set of features. To further increase classification accuracy, we make use of bagging: we create m different subsets of tweets from the training set, including equal number of samples for each class (some samples may appear in multiple subsets), leading to the creation of m instances of CL_1 and CL_2 (m = 9 in our experiments), as shown in Figure 2. The final prediction for each of the test samples is calculated using the majority vote among the m predictions.

[2]https://code.google.com/p/language-detection/
[3]https://github.com/jeffreybreen/twitter-sentiment-analysis-tutorial-201107
[4]http://onlineslangdictionary.com/word-list/0-a/
[5]http://www.languagerealm.com/spanish/spanishslang.php
[6]http://simple.wikipedia.org/wiki/Flesch_Reading_Ease
[7]https://www.mywot.com/
[8]http://wwwranking.webdatacommons.org/more.html
[9]http://data.alexa.com/data?cli=10&dat=snbamz&url=google.gr
[10]Based on https://github.com/socialsensor/geo-util project.

3.3 Agreement-based retraining

A key novelty in the proposed framework is an *agreement-based retraining* step (the fusion block in Figure 2) to improve the prediction accuracy for content associated with unseen events. This was motivated by an approach that was proposed for effectively tackling out-of-domain sentiment classification [25]. We combine the outputs of classifiers $\mathtt{CL}_1$, $\mathtt{CL}_2$ as follows: for each sample of the test set, we compare their predictions and depending on their agreement, we divide the test set in the *agreed* and *disagreed* subsets. The instances of the *agreed* set are assigned the agreed label (fake/real) assuming that it is correct with high likelihood, and are used to build a new classifier to handle the *disagreed* instances. To this end, we use two retraining techniques. First, we select the most effective of the independent classifiers $\mathtt{CL}_1$, $\mathtt{CL}_2$ based on their performance on the training set during cross-validation. Then, we either use just the agreed samples to train the CL classifier (denoted as CL(i)), or we use the entire set of initial training samples extending it with the set of agreed samples (denoted as CL(ii)). The goal is to adapt the initial model to the specific data characteristics of the new event. In that way, the model can predict more accurately the values of the samples for which $\mathtt{CL}_1$, $\mathtt{CL}_2$ did not initially agree. In the experimental section, we test both retraining variants.

3.4 Verification result visualization

The key idea for visualizing the results of the proposed verification process is to present the list of extracted features for the input tweet, and then for a selected feature to present its value in relation to the distribution that this feature has for real versus fake tweets, as computed with respect to the verification corpus (Section 4).

Figure 3 illustrates a screenshot of this application, which is publicly available[11]. In terms of usage, the end user first provides the URL or id of a tweet of interest, and then the application presents the extracted tweet- and user-based features and the verification result (fake/real) for the tweet in the form of a color-coded frame (red/green respectively). It also offers the possibility of inspecting the feature values. By selecting a feature, its value distribution appears (right column), separately for the fake and real tweets (side-by-side). Moreover, a textual description informs the user about the percentage of tweets of this class (fake or real) that have the same value for this feature. In that way, the investigator may better understand how the verification result is justified based on the individual values of the features in relation to the "typical" values that these features have for fake versus real tweets.

4 VERIFICATION CORPUS

Our fake detection models are based on a publicly available a verification corpus (VC) of fake and real tweets. More specifically, this consists of tweets related to the 17 events of Table 2, comprising in total 193 cases of real images, 218 cases of misused (fake) images and two cases of misused videos, associated with 6,225 real and 9,596 fake tweets posted by 5,895 and 9,216 unique users respectively.

The corpus comprises a set of tweets T that is collected with the help of a set of keywords K for each of the 17 events. The ground truth labels (fake/real) of these tweets are based on a set of online resources, which discussed and debunked images and videos widely

[11] http://reveal-mklab.iti.gr/reveal/fake/

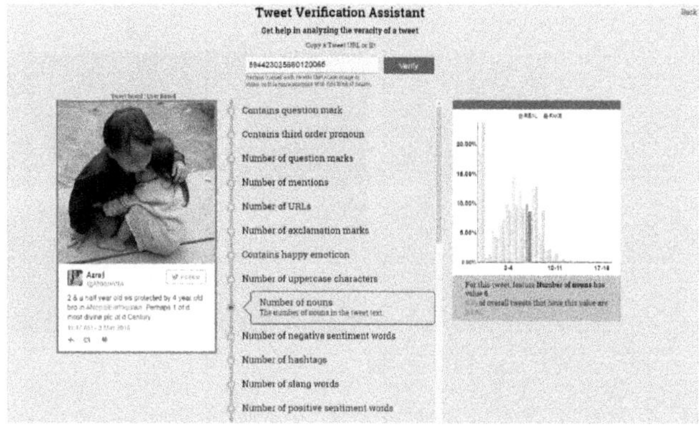

Figure 3: Snapshot of the Tweet Verification Assistant interface. Given a tweet, a user can explore the verification result, including the extracted feature values and their distribution on the Verification Corpus.

shared in the context of these events. Only resources were used that are reputable news providers and that adequately justified their decision about the veracity of each multimedia item. This led to a set of fake and real multimedia cases, denoted as I_F, I_R respectively, which were then used as seeds to create the reference verification corpus $T_C \subset T$. This includes exclusively tweets that contain at least one item from the two sets. In order not to restrict the tweets to only those that point to the exact seed URLs, a visual near-duplicate search technique was employed [24]. More specifically, the sets of fake and real images were used as visual queries and for each query it was checked whether each image tweet from T exists as an image item or a near-duplicate image item of the I_F or the I_R set. To ensure near-duplicity, a minimum threshold of similarity was empirically set, tuned for high precision. A small amount of the images exceeding the threshold were manually found to be irrelevant to the ones in the seed set and were then removed.

Several of the events, e.g., Columbian Chemicals, Passport Hoax and Rock Elephant, were actually hoaxes, hence all content associated with them is fake. Also, for several real events (e.g., MA flight 370) no real images (and hence no real tweets) were included in the dataset, since none came up as a result of the data collection.

As the aim of our work is to assess the generalization capability of the fake detection framework, we used every tweet in the corpus regardless of its language. The aim has been to use a comprehensive corpus, which contains the widest possible variety of fake tweets (even though this complicates the machine learning process due to missing feature values). Furthermore, we included content from different types of event. In terms of type of fake, we considered the following four categories: **a) reposting of real**: real photos from past events re-posted as being associated to a current event (Figure 4 (i)); **b) reposting of synthetic**: synthetic digital images, such as artworks or snapshots from movies, presented as real imagery about an event (Figure 4 (ii)); **c) speculations**: real photos from an ongoing event, expressing speculations regarding the association of persons or actions to the event (Figure 4 (iii)); **d) digital tampering**: digitally manipulated photos (Figure 4 (iv)).

(i) (ii) (iii) (iv)

Figure 4: Types of fake: (i) reposting of real photo depicting two Vietnamese siblings as being captured during the Nepal 2015 earthquakes; (ii) reposting of artwork as a photo from Solar Eclipse of March 2015; (iii) speculation of someone as being suspect of the Boston Marathon bombings in 2013; (iv) spliced sharks on a photo captured during Hurricane Sandy in 2012.

Table 2: List of events in VC: For each event, we report the number of unique real (if available) and fake images (I_R, I_F respectively), unique tweets that shared those images (T_R, T_F) and Twitter accounts that posted those tweets (U_R, U_F).

ID	Name	I_R	T_R	U_R	I_F	T_F	U_F
E1	Hurricane Sandy	148	4,664	4,446	62	5,559	5,432
E2	Boston Marathon bombing	28	344	310	35	189	187
E3	Sochi Olympics	-	-	-	26	274	252
E4	Bring Back Our Girls	-	-	-	7	131	126
E5	MA flight 370	-	-	-	29	501	493
E6	Columbian Chemicals	-	-	-	15	185	87
E7	Passport hoax	-	-	-	2	44	44
E8	Rock Elephant	-	-	-	1	13	13
E9	Underwater bedroom	-	-	-	3	113	112
E10	Livr mobile app	-	-	-	4	9	9
E11	Pig fish	-	-	-	1	14	14
E12	Nepal earthquake	11	1004	934	21	356	343
E13	Solar Eclipse	4	140	133	6	137	135
E14	Garissa Attack	2	73	72	2	6	6
E15	Samurai and Girl	-	-	-	4	218	212
E16	Syrian Boy	-	-	-	1	1786	1692
E17	Varoufakis and ZDF	-	-	-	1	61	59
	Total	193	6225	5895	220	9596	9216

From the corpus, we considered only unique posts by eliminating re-tweets. Finally, by manually checking the content of tweets, we ensured that no posts were included that featured funny/humorous content, nor posts that declared that their content is fake (both of which cases would be hard to classify as either real or fake).

5 EXPERIMENTAL STUDY

5.1 Overview

The aim of the conducted experiments was to evaluate the fake detection accuracy of different models on samples from new (unseen) events. We consider this an important aspect of a verification framework, as the nature of the untrustworthy (fake) tweets posted may vary across different events. Accuracy is computed as the ratio of correctly classified samples (N_c) over total number of test samples (N): $a = N_c/N$. The employed evaluation scheme can be thought of as a kind of *event-based cross-validation*: for each event E_i of the 17 events in the VC, we use the remaining 16 events for training. and E_i for testing. We denote each of these 17 splits as T_i. All models are built using Random Forests of 100 trees.

In addition, to compare the performance of our framework, with methods that participated in the recently organized Verifying Multimedia Use task in the context of *MediaEval* [1], we use the split proposed by the task organizers (denoted as $T18$): events $E1$-$E11$ are used for training, and events $E12$-$E17$ for testing.

5.2 New Features and Bagging

We first assess the contribution of the new features and bagging to the method's accuracy. To this end, we build the $\mathtt{CL}_1$, $\mathtt{CL}_2$ classifiers with and without the bagging technique. To create the models without bagging, we selected each time an equal number of random fake and real samples for training. We applied this procedure both for the Baseline (BF) and Total Features (TF) (cf. Table 1 caption). Table 3 presents the average accuracy for each setting.

We observe that the use of bagging led to considerably improved accuracy for both $\mathtt{CL}_1$ and $\mathtt{CL}_2$. In addition, further improvements are achieved when using the TF features over BF. We see that bagging led to an absolute improvement of approximately 10% and 15% in the accuracy of $\mathtt{CL}_1$ and $\mathtt{CL}_2$ respectively (when using the TF features), while the use of TF features over BF to an absolute improvement of approximately 18% on both classifiers (when bagging is used). Combined, the use of bagging and the newly proposed features led to an absolute improvement of more than 24% for both $\mathtt{CL}_1$ and $\mathtt{CL}_2$. Given the clear benefits of using bagging, in subsequent experiments, all reported results refer to classifiers with bagging.

Table 3: Comparison between CL_1, CL_2, and the effect of bagging and Total Features (TF) over Baseline Features (BF).

	$\mathtt{CL}_1$	$\mathtt{CL}_1$-bagging	$\mathtt{CL}_2$	$\mathtt{CL}_2$-bagging
TF	78.01	88.34	60.89	75.70
BF	64.14	70.57	51.15	57.40

Table 4: Accuracy for the entire set of features TF. Agreement levels between the CL_1 and CL_2 classifiers, agreed, disagreed and overall accuracy for each model (CL(i), CL(ii)) and each split.

Trial	Agreement percentage	Agreed accuracy	*CL(i)* disagreed accuracy	*CL(ii)* disagreed accuracy	*CL(i)* overall	*CL(ii)* overall	CL_1 bagging	CL_2 bagging
T1	71.54	95.11	57.89	62.75	84.54	86.05	74.10	90.56
T2	57.12	88.64	81.63	61.36	85.87	77.71	68.79	76.06
T3	67.73	93.73	83.40	85.20	90.36	91.09	90.58	68.83
T4	93.43	99.72	96.66	75.24	99.23	98.54	96.10	96.87
T5	78.82	96.81	76.76	82.58	92.33	93.77	90.07	83.79
T6	95.45	100	100	82.38	100	98.79	95.67	99.78
T7	57.95	90.19	66.59	96.87	89.54	93.18	92.95	54.09
T8	76.92	99	100	100	99.23	99.23	99.23	76.15
T9	89.38	99.29	100	94.81	99.38	99.02	96.01	92.12
T10	80	97.32	100	100	97.78	97.78	96.67	78.88
T11	82.85	100	100	60	100	93.57	91.42	91.42
T12	50.83	79.11	84.42	86.78	81.94	83.10	82.26	47.60
T13	54.90	91.89	69.16	45.07	81.59	71.11	67.47	78.77
T14	55.82	94.21	87.82	81.76	91.51	89.24	87.97	62.02
T15	61.46	95.29	88.03	95.36	93.66	95.64	83.90	62.15
T16	84.77	97.59	76.68	73.66	93.81	93.98	91.55	89.14
T17	42.29	80.43	68.93	89	86.89	85.73	85.57	40.98
T18	70.39	94.79	80.55	79.77	90.74	90.51	89.80	73.32
Average	**70.65**	**94.06**	**84.14**	**80.70**	**92.13**	**91.00**	**88.34**	**75.69**

5.3 Agreement-based retraining technique

We use the entire set of features (TF) for assessing the accuracy of the agreement-based retraining approach. Table 4 shows the scores obtained separately for each split. The first two columns present the agreement level and the accuracy of classifiers on the agreed set. We observe that on average the two classifiers' predictions (CL_1, CL_2) agree in the majority of tweets (Agreement (%) column); in particular, they agree on 70.65% of the tweets on average. On this set of tweets, the average accuracy (Agreed accuracy column) is extremely high (94.06%). One may also note that the higher the agreement level, the higher is the achieved accuracy on the agreed set. The next two columns present the accuracy on the disagreed samples, when using the two variations of the retraining process (CL(i) and CL(ii) in Section 3.3). The next two columns show the results while combining the accuracy of the agreed and disagreed samples. On average, the first retraining variation, i.e. using only the samples of the new event for training, slightly outperforms the second. For comparison purposes, the last two columns of the table present the scores of the CL_1 and CL_2 classifiers trained with the bagging technique and applied independently. Those correspond to the standard supervised learning paradigm [3, 8]. Comparing the average scores of the classifiers in the two last columns (88.34% and 75.69% respectively) with those of the agreement-based retraining technique (92.13% and 91%), one can see a clear improvement in terms of classification accuracy (approximately 4% when compared to the best CL_1 configuration).

5.4 Performance on different languages

We also assessed the classification accuracy of the framework for tweets written in different languages, i.e. the extent to which the framework is language-dependent.

We keep the five most used languages in the corpus (by number of tweets). Note that in many cases no language is detected, either because the text contains no text but just hashtags/URLs or the length of the text is too small to be detected by the language detector. For this reason, we also consider this category of tweets (denoted as NO-LANG), and thus compare between the following cases: English (EN), Spanish (ES), no language (NO-LANG), Dutch (NL) and French (FR). Table 5 shows the languages tested and the corresponding number of samples.

By using the total amount of features TF, we calculate the accuracy on each split ($T1$-$T18$) separately on the samples of each language. Figure 5 shows the results for each split when using the agreement-based retraining technique, according to the first and second variation of the method respectively. In most cases, it appears that fake detection accuracy remains relatively stable independent of language. The highest accuracy scores are achieved for NO-LANG followed by English and Spanish. Accuracy is somewhat lower for French and Dutch. This is an encouraging finding since it indicates that the framework is reliable even for languages, for which the language-specific features are not defined.

Table 5: Accuracy for most frequent languages on VC.

Language	EN	ES	NO LANG	NL	FR
Samples	12,301	1,107	729	279	271
Accuracy (%)	90.18	87.40	99.21	88.82	91.06

5.5 Comparison with state of the art

We also compare our method with the ones submitted to the MediaEval 2015 Verifying Multimedia Use task. These include the systems by UoS-ITI [15], MCG-ICT [9], and CERTH-UNITN [2]. For each of those, we only compare against their best *run*[12]. The comparison is done using the F1-score, which is the official metric of the task. According to the results (Table 6), the proposed method achieves the second best performance ($F = 0.934$), reaching almost

[12] In MediaEval, each system/team can submit up to five runs.

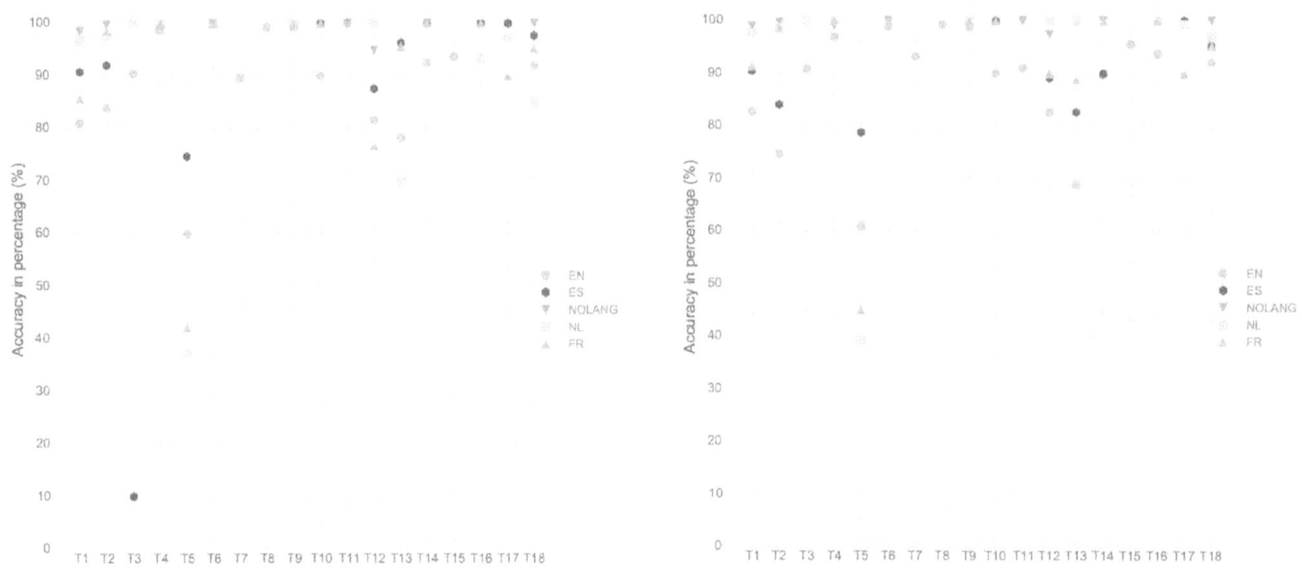

Figure 5: Language-based accuracy based on the `TF` features and the agreement-based retraining technique: left) using just the agreed samples for training (`CL(i)`), and right) using the agreed and the initial training samples for training (`CL(ii)`).

Table 6: Comparison among MediaEval 2015 submissions and the performance of our T18 run.

Method	F1-Score
`UoS-ITI` [15]	0.830
`MCG-ICT` [9]	0.942
`CERTH-UNITN` [2]	0.911
`Proposed`	0.934

equal performance to the best run by `MCG-ICT` [9] ($F = 0.942$). The latter, however, uses an approach that is tailored to the specifics of the dataset. In particular, `MGC-ICT` relies on a model that first clusters tweets into topics according to the multimedia resource that they contain. Then, it extracts topic-level features for building the fake detection classifier. It is important to note that the dataset of the task makes available a list of tweets, their associated multimedia item and label (fake/real). The way the dataset is structured makes the `MGC-ICT` possible to apply. However, in a realistic setting, unseen tweets do not appear in clusters (except in the case of highly popular media items that are shared concurrently by numerous different posts), which makes the application of such an approach much more complex and its results questionable. In contrast, our method leads to comparable performance without suffering from such limitations.

5.6 Verification visualization

To demonstrate the utility of the web-based verification application, we present an example case study where the proposed visualization approach is used on a tweet that shared fake multimedia content in the context of the March 2016 terrorist attacks in Brussels. The tweet (Figure 6) claimed that the shared video depicted one of the explosions in Zaventem airport, but the video is actually from another explosion in a different airport a few years ago. Indeed, the proposed classification framework flags the tweet as fake and presents the features' distributions in order to get useful insights about the reasons for this decision. Three sample tweet- and user-based feature distributions are illustrated in the upper and lower part of Figure 6 respectively. For example, in the first plot, the number of hashtags for this tweet is shown to be zero and at the same time the respective bar is highlighted. The plot informs that 63% of the overall training tweets that have this value are fake, a fact that partially justifies the classification result. In the two following plots that display the number of mentions and the text length, similar conclusions can be made about the veracity of the tweet. In the user-based feature value distributions, the date of creation, the number of friends and the followers/friends ratio seem to give some additional strong signals regarding the credibility of the account, and as a result the veracity of the posted tweet.

6 CONCLUSIONS AND FUTURE WORK

We presented a robust and effective framework for fake multimedia detection on Twitter. Using a specially collected verification corpus, we provided evidence of the high accuracy of the proposed framework over a number of events of different size and nature, as well as considerable improvements in accuracy as a result of the newly proposed features, the use of bagging, and the application of an agreement-based retraining method that outperforms standard supervised learning. We also demonstrated the utility of a novel visualization approach for explaining the verification result.

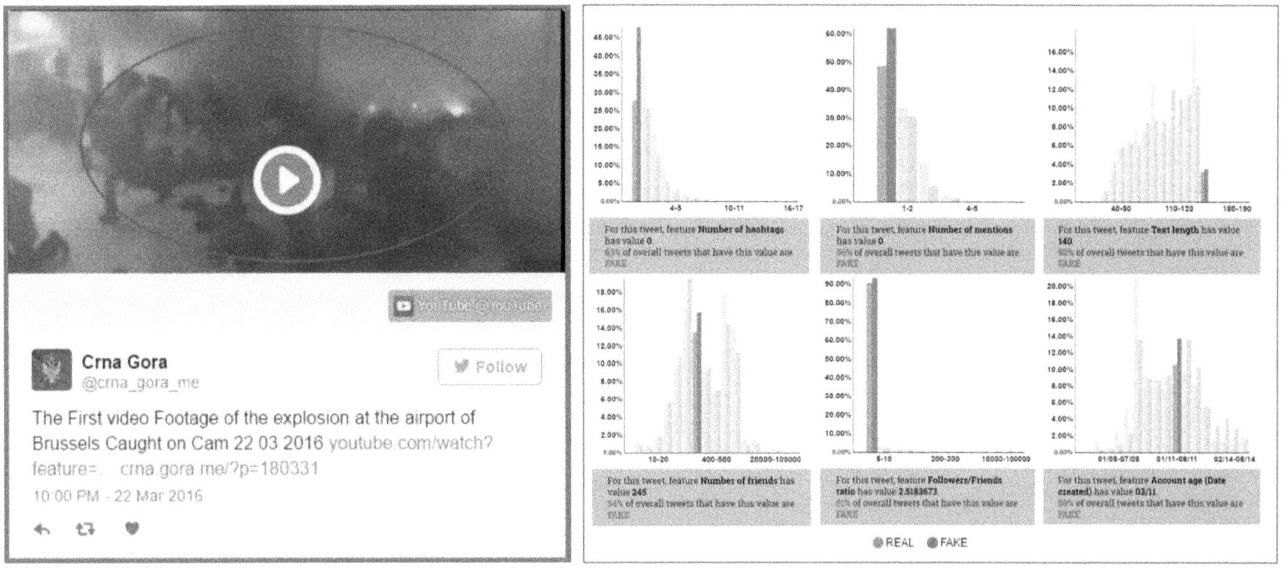

Figure 6: Tweet sharing fake video content and feature analysis produced by the Tweet Verification Assistant.

To use the proposed approach in real-time settings, one should be cautious of the following caveat. The agreement-based retraining method requires a number of samples from the new event in order to be applied. Hence, for the first set of arriving items, it is not possible to rely on this improved step. Yet, the rate at which new items arrive in the context of breaking news events could quickly provide the algorithm with a sizeable set of tweets.

In the future, we are interested in looking further into the real-time aspects of fake content detection, and conduct experiments that better simulate the fake content detection problem as an event evolves. We also plan to conduct user studies to test whether the proposed visualization is understandable and usable by news editors and journalists. Finally, we also plan to extend the framework to be applicable to content posted on platforms other than Twitter.

7 ACKNOWLEDGMENTS

This work has been supported by the REVEAL and InVID projects, under contract numbers 610928 and 687786 respectively, funded by the European Commission.

REFERENCES

[1] Christina Boididou, Katerina Andreadou, Symeon Papadopoulos, Duc-Tien Dang-Nguyen, Giulia Boato, Michael Riegler, and Yiannis Kompatsiaris. 2015. Verifying Multimedia Use at MediaEval 2015. In *MediaEval 2015 Workshop, Sept. 14-15, 2015, Wurzen, Germany.*

[2] Christina Boididou, Symeon Papadopoulos, Duc-Tien Dang-Nguyen, Giulia Boato, and Yiannis Kompatsiaris. 2015. The CERTH-UNITN Participation @ Verifying Multimedia Use 2015. (2015).

[3] Christina Boididou, Symeon Papadopoulos, Yiannis Kompatsiaris, Steve Schifferes, and Nic Newman. 2014. Challenges of Computational Verification in Social Multimedia. In *Proceedings of the Companion Publication of the 23rd International Conference on World Wide Web Companion.* 743–748.

[4] Christina Boididou, Symeon Papadopoulos, Stuart E. Middleton, Duc-Tien Dang-Nguyen, Michael Riegler, Andreas Petlund, and Yiannis Kompatsiaris. 2016. The VMU Participation @ Verifying Multimedia Use 2016. In *Working Notes Proceedings of the MediaEval 2016 Workshop, The Netherlands, Oct 20-21, 2016.*

[5] Carlos Castillo, Marcelo Mendoza, and Barbara Poblete. 2011. Information credibility on twitter. In *Proceedings of the 20th international conference on World wide web.* ACM, 675–684.

[6] Daniel Gayo-Avello, Panagiotis Metaxas, Eni Mustafaraj, Markus Strohmaier, Harald Schoen, Daniel Peter Gloor, Carlos Castillo, Marcelo Mendoza, and Barbara Poblete. 2013. Predicting information credibility in time-sensitive social media. *Internet Research* 23, 5 (2013), 560–588.

[7] Aditi Gupta, Ponnurangam Kumaraguru, Carlos Castillo, and Patrick Meier. 2014. Tweetcred: A real-time Web-based system for assessing credibility of content on Twitter. In *Proc. 6th International Conference on Social Informatics (SocInfo).*

[8] Aditi Gupta, Hemank Lamba, Ponnurangam Kumaraguru, and Anupam Joshi. 2013. Faking Sandy: characterizing and identifying fake images on Twitter during Hurricane Sandy. In *Proceedings of the 22nd international conference on World Wide Web companion.* 729–736.

[9] Zhiwei Jin, Juan Cao, Yazi Zhang, and Yongdong Zhang. 2015. MCG-ICT at MediaEval 2015: Verifying Multimedia Use with a Two-Level Classification Model.. In *MediaEval 2015 Workshop, Sept. 14-15, 2015, Wurzen, Germany.*

[10] Philipp Kanske and Sonja A Kotz. 2010. Leipzig affective norms for German: A reliability study. *Behavior research methods* 42, 4 (2010), 987–991.

[11] Dan Klein and Christopher D. Manning. 2003. Accurate Unlexicalized Parsing. In *Proceedings of the 41st Annual Meeting on Association for Computational Linguistics - Volume 1 (ACL '03).* Association for Computational Linguistics, Stroudsburg, PA, USA, 423–430.

[12] Nora Martin and BA Comm. 2014. Information Verification in the Age of Digital Journalism. In *Special Libraries Association Annual Conference, Vancouver.*

[13] Juan Martinez-Romo and Lourdes Araujo. 2013. Detecting malicious tweets in trending topics using a statistical analysis of language. *Expert Systems with Applications* 40, 8 (2013), 2992–3000.

[14] Panagiotis Metaxas, Samantha Finn, and Eni Mustafaraj. 2015. Using Twitter-Trails.com to Investigate Rumor Propagation. In *Proceedings of the 18th ACM Conference Companion on Computer Supported Cooperative Work & Social Computing.* ACM, 69–72.

[15] Stuart Middleton. 2015. Extracting attributed verification and debunking reports from social media: Mediaeval-2015 trust and credibility analysis of image and video. (2015).

[16] John O'Donovan, Byungkyu Kang, Greg Meyer, Tobias Hollerer, and Sibel Adalii. 2012. Credibility in context: An analysis of feature distributions in twitter. In *2012 International Conference on Privacy, Security, Risk and Trust (PASSAT) and 2012 International Conference on Social Computing (SocialCom).* IEEE, 293–301.

[17] Jacob Ratkiewicz, Michael Conover, Mark Meiss, Bruno Gonçalves, Snehal Patil, Alessandro Flammini, and Filippo Menczer. 2011. Truthy: mapping the spread of astroturf in microblog streams. In *Proceedings of the 20th international conference companion on World wide web.* ACM, 249–252.

[18] Judith A. Redi, Wiem Taktak, and Jean-Luc Dugelay. 2011. Digital Image Forensics: A Booklet for Beginners. *Multimedia Tools Appl.* 51, 1 (Jan. 2011), 133–162.

[19] Jaime Redondo, Isabel Fraga, Isabel Padrón, and Montserrat Comesaña. 2007. The Spanish adaptation of ANEW (affective norms for English words). *Behavior research methods* 39, 3 (2007), 600–605.

[20] Paul Resnick, Samuel Carton, Souneil Park, Yuncheng Shen, and Nicole Zeffer. 2014. Rumorlens: A system for analyzing the impact of rumors and corrections in social media. In *Proc. Computational Journalism Conference.*

[21] Anderson Rocha, Walter Scheirer, Terrance Boult, and Siome Goldenstein. 2011. Vision of the unseen: Current trends and challenges in digital image and video forensics. *ACM Computing Surveys (CSUR)* 43, 4 (2011), 26.

[22] Chengcheng Shao, Giovanni Luca Ciampaglia, Alessandro Flammini, and Filippo Menczer. 2016. Hoaxy: A Platform for Tracking Online Misinformation. In *Proceedings of the 25th Intern. Conf. Companion on World Wide Web.* 745–750.

[23] Craig Silverman. 2013. Verification handbook. (2013).

[24] Eleftherios Spyromitros-Xioufis, Symeon Papadopoulos, Ioannis Kompatsiaris, Grigorios Tsoumakas, and Ioannis Vlahavas. 2014. A Comprehensive Study Over VLAD and Product Quantization in Large-Scale Image Retrieval. *IEEE Transactions on Multimedia* 16, 6 (2014), 1713–1728.

[25] Adam Tsakalidis, Symeon Papadopoulos, and Ioannis Kompatsiaris. 2014. An Ensemble Model for Cross-Domain Polarity Classification on Twitter. In *Web Information Systems Engineering–WISE 2014.* Springer, 168–177.

[26] Lexing Xie, Apostol Natsev, Xuming He, John R Kender, Mark Hill, and John R Smith. 2013. Tracking large-scale video remix in real-world events. *Multimedia, IEEE Transactions on* 15, 6 (2013), 1244–1254.

[27] Markos Zampoglou, Symeon Papadopoulos, and Yiannis Kompatsiaris. 2015. Detecting image splicing in the wild (WEB). In *2015 IEEE International Conference on Multimedia & Expo Workshops (ICMEW).* IEEE, 1–6.

[28] Markos Zampoglou, Symeon Papadopoulos, and Yiannis Kompatsiaris. 2017. A Large-Scale Evaluation of Splicing Localization Algorithms for Web Images. *Multimedia Tools and Applications* 76, 4 (February 2017), 4801–4834.

On the Selection of Anchors and Targets for Video Hyperlinking

Zhi-Qi Cheng
City University of Hong Kong
Southwest Jiaotong University
zhiqicheng@gmail.com

Hao Zhang
City University of Hong Kong
hzhang57-c@my.cityu.edu.hk

Xiao Wu
Southwest Jiaotong University
wuxiaohk@home.swjtu.edu.cn

Chong-Wah Ngo
City University of Hong Kong
cscwngo@cityu.edu.hk

ABSTRACT

A problem not well understood in video hyperlinking is what qualifies a fragment as an anchor or target. Ideally, anchors provide good starting points for navigation, and targets supplement anchors with additional details while not distracting users with irrelevant, false and redundant information. The problem is not trivial for intertwining relationship between data characteristics and user expectation. Imagine that in a large dataset, there are clusters of fragments spreading over the feature space. The nature of each cluster can be described by its size (implying popularity) and structure (implying complexity). A principle way of hyperlinking can be carried out by picking centers of clusters as anchors and from there reach out to targets within or outside of clusters with consideration of neighborhood complexity. The question is which fragments should be selected either as anchors or targets, in one way to reflect the rich content of a dataset, and meanwhile to minimize the risk of frustrating user experience. This paper provides some insights to this question from the perspective of hubness and local intrinsic dimensionality, which are two statistical properties in assessing the popularity and complexity of data space. Based these properties, two novel algorithms are proposed for low-risk automatic selection of anchors and targets.

KEYWORDS

Video Hyperlinking; Hubness; Local Intrinsic Dimensions.

ACM Reference format:
Zhi-Qi Cheng, Hao Zhang, Xiao Wu, and Chong-Wah Ngo. 2017. On the Selection of Anchors and Targets for Video Hyperlinking. In *Proceedings of ICMR '17, Bucharest, Romania, June 6–9, 2017,* 7 pages.
DOI: http://dx.doi.org/10.1145/3078971.3079025

DOI: http://dx.doi.org/10.1145/3078971.3079025

1 INTRODUCTION

Link traversal is a usual practice for web page surfing. Extending such functionality for exploratory browsing of videos remains a new problem. Video hyperlinking, a new task initiated by [4, 12, 23], aims to enhance the accessibility of large video dataset by creating links across fragments of different videos. The usage scenario is that, rather than passively searching for video content of interest, users can comfortably jump between videos by traversing hyperlinks. Generally speaking, two fundamental problems of video hyperlinking are the selection of link anchors and targets, which refer to the sources and destination of hyperlinks. Ideally, anchors are "hubs" which lead users to different corners of the dataset, while targets are "authorities" which provide either detailed explanation of a concept or contextual information relevant to anchors.

The current research efforts on video hyperlinking include user-centric sampling of link anchors [1], contextual modeling of anchors [9, 21], the relationship between searching and hyperlinking [5, 13] and exploitation of rich multi-modal content in video [3, 8, 14]. One common theme among these studies is the query formulation of anchors for search of link targets. The employed techniques range from query expansion through linked data such as DBpedia and Freebase [14], term weighting for speech transcript [3] and selection of audio-visual concept classifiers for retrieval [3]. These efforts are mostly dedicated to the search of targets, either from the perspective of content relevancy to anchors [9] or link diversity [8]. To the best of our knowledge, except the ad-hoc heuristics presented in MediaEval benchmark evaluation [11], there is no formal study on the automatic identification of link anchors from large dataset.

This paper addresses the problem of both anchor and target selections from the viewpoint of data *popularity* and *uncertainty*, an issue not yet been considered in the literature. Popularity characterizes the frequency of signals, specifically hubs and outliers in this context, of a dataset. Naively, hubs could directly correspond to anchors and targets to encourage users to explore the major information sources in the close world of a dataset. Multimedia data, nevertheless, are unstructured and unordered in nature. Due to the lack of powerful techniques for semantic and context understanding, blindly bridging hubs can easily end up with the excessive number of false and redundant linking. As the purpose is essentially about recommendation, hyperlinking should be fundamentally different from video retrieval which provides a long list of search items for user selection. In principle, recommending false or redundant link will adversely impact user experience. It is easy to imagine the frustration of users when hyperlinks bring users to "middle of no way" with inconsistent or repeated information. Considering popularity without other factors such as data uncertainty and diversity could lead to meaningless hyperlinking in practice. This paper characterizes uncertainty as the complexity of *local* data distribution. Imagine that in a large dataset, the distribution of data changes when moving across different regions of the space. In regions of highly complex configuration, the probability of false linking will also proportionally increase. Creating hyperlinks with the potential risk in mind is thus important, for example, by introducing additional features for reducing data uncertainty.

To this end, this paper leverages two established studies, hubness [24] and local intrinsic dimension (LID) [2], to quantify anchors and targets based on statistical data properties. Hubness measures popularity by counting the number of times that a point in high-dimensional space appears among the k-nearest neighbors of other points. A popular point, or hub, can carry either blessing or warning signal. In retrieval for example, certain items share high similarity to disproportionally many other items, and thus are likely to be retrieved. Proper pre-processing of these items, such as by removing them from dataset, can improve search performance as studied in music retrieval community [17]. On the other hand, using hubs to initialize clustering algorithm, such as k-means, can boost performance [27]. LID, different from global dimensionality reduction techniques such as PCA, locally quantifies the intrinsic dimensionality of a point. In theory, a point embedded in a space with high number of LID will suffer from curse of dimensionality, due to the fact that distance or similarity measure becomes less meaningful in high dimensional space. LID of a point is calculated by the rate at which the number of neighboring points grows as the range of distances expands from that point [2].

By hubness and LID, this paper characterizes the statistical properties of anchors and targets in the Blip1000 dataset provided by Video Hyperlinking (LNK) of TRECVid 2016 [4] for case study. Particularly, the inter-play among hubness, LID and diversity are explored to provide an insightful look at the anchors, targets and multi-modal feature fusion. In addition, based on the result of analysis, we further propose two novel algorithms for automatic selection of link anchors and targets. The contribution of this paper is on quantifying the statistical properties of anchors and targets, and gives light in the way of selecting anchors and targets based on data popularity and risk.

2 DATA ANALYSIS

2.1 Hubness

Hubness characterizes the popularity of a fragment, defined as the number of times that a fragment is regarded as the k nearest neighbors of other fragments [24]. Let $\{x_1, ..., x_n\}$ be the n fragments drawn from a dataset, the hubness score of a fragment x is

$$N_k(x) = \sum_{i=1}^{n} p_{i,k}(x) \tag{1}$$

where

$$p_{i,k}(x) = \begin{cases} 1, & \text{if } x \text{ is among the } k \text{ nearest neighbor of } x_i, \\ 0, & \text{otherwise.} \end{cases} \tag{2}$$

Basically $N_k(x)$ counts the number of fragments that include x as their kth nearest neighbors under a predefined distance measure. Based on [24], the score can be utilized to categorize a fragment as hub if $N_k > k$, anti-hub if $N_k = 0$, and normal otherwise. In the context of hyperlinking, hubs are popular fragments that can potentially outreach to different "corners" of a dataset. A fragment with extremely high value of score, nevertheless, can be noise that might not worth linking. As studied in [18], removing these noises can improve the classification performance by 1%-5%.

By viewing $N_k(x)$ of all fragments as a probability distribution, the hubness of a dataset can be further characterized by the degree of skewness, defined as

$$S_{N_k} = \frac{E\left(N_k - \mu_{N_k}\right)^3}{\sigma_{N_k}^3} \tag{3}$$

which is the third moment of the distribution, with μ_{N_k} and σ_{N_k} as the mean and standard deviation respectively. According to [24], hubness exists in a dataset when $S_{N_k} > 1$. The bigger this value is, the less number of hubs in the dataset. In short, skewness gives a statistical sense of whether a dataset is appropriate for hyperlinking, and its degree indicates the proportion of fragments that could be regarded as hubs for hyperlinking.

2.2 Local intrinsic dimension (LID)

Intrinsic dimensionality refers to the minimal number of dimensions required to *globally* describe a dataset. Local intrinsic dimension (LID), instead, characterizes this property *locally* with respect to the neighbourhood structure of a fragment x. The higher the value of LID is for x, the more difficult or risky to describe the neighbourhood of x under a predefined distance function. In this paper, we employ Maximum Likelihood Estimation (MLE) [2] for calculation of LID. Consider n number of fragments in the vicinity of x with distance smaller than ω, and let $\{l_1, l_2, ..., l_n\}$ be their distances sorted in ascending order in the range of $[0, w)$. The LID of x is define as

$$\widehat{ID_L} = -\left(\frac{1}{n}\sum_{i=1}^{n} ln\frac{l_i}{\omega}\right)^{-1} \tag{4}$$

where l_i is a distance which is always larger than 0. Due to the problem of floating point representation, l_i may be treated as 0. In this case, l_i is set to the smallest value that can be recognized by the computer. LID in principle characterizes the risk of hyperlinking. Specifically, the chance of creating false links can be proportional to the number of LID. When the dimensionality is high, one may consider using a different distance measure or inclusion of multi-modal features to reduce the number of dimensions before link establishment.

2.3 Simulation

In this section, we use hubness and LID to analyze the statistical property of the Blip10000 dataset [25], which is the same dataset used by TRECVid 2016 benchmark for video hyperlinking [4]. The dataset consists of 340,342 fragments from around 3000 hours of videos.

2.3.1 Does hubness exist? As the dataset is huge, we employ sampling strategy to randomly select a subset of fragments for experiment. Three popularly employed features are considered in this simulation:

- CNN: Deep feature extracted from ResNet-50 [19]. The pool-5 feature, which is averagely pooled from the feature maps of last convolution layer, is employed. The dimension of feature is 2,048.
- Concept: High-level feature composed of the classifier responses of 1,000 ImageNet concepts [10]. The classifiers are learned with ResNet-50 and the feature is in 1,000 dimensions.
- Text: Bag-of-words feature extracted from automatic speech recognition (ASR) transcript and video metadata. The feature is weighted with TF-IDF and is in 32,797 dimensions.

Table 1 shows the simulation result. For all the three features, the skewness values are greater than 1.0, clearly indicating the existence of hubness in the dataset. Text feature, in particular, is much skew than CNN and Concept features. The high skewness can signal the less discriminative power of text than visual features for some fragments. We pick up the fragments with high value and notice that most of them correspond to lengthy speech with general content. Apparently these are not ideal candidates for link anchors.

When both visual features are early fused, the value of skewness increases. We speculate that fusion actually disambiguates some pairwise similarities due to the inclusion of new modality, resulting in less number of hubs and hence higher value of skewness. When all the three features are fused, the skewness value keeps increase. Nevertheless, the value is not as high as that of text feature alone. With the result, we conclude that multi-model fusion is likely to produce a better result in anchor or target selection than any of the three single modalities.

2.3.2 How popular and risky are the anchors? We use 122 anchors provided in the dataset for simulation. These anchors are manually identified as being the fragments of interest that users would likely to further explore more information from. We calculate the hub scores of the anchors using the combination of three features over the whole Blip10000 dataset. We set the number of nearest neighbors $k = 10$, and the result is shown in Figure 1. As a user is not likely to continue watching a video if no relevant content is found after few minutes, we consider only the first 3-minute of a fragment during the calculation. Among the 122 anchors,

Table 1: Skewness of hub scores in Blip10000 dataset. The experiment is run for multiple times. Each time the number of fragments being sample is in the range of 11,481 to 44,602. The last column corresponds to the skewness of distribution, by setting $k = 10$ nearest neighbors and using cosine similarity.

	dim	$S_{N_{10}}$
CNN	2,048	[0.94-1.83]
Concept	1,000	[1.42-2.03]
Text	32,797	[3.74-4.97]
CNN+Concept	3,048	[1.42-1.96]
CNN+Concept+Text	35,845	[2.68-3.97]

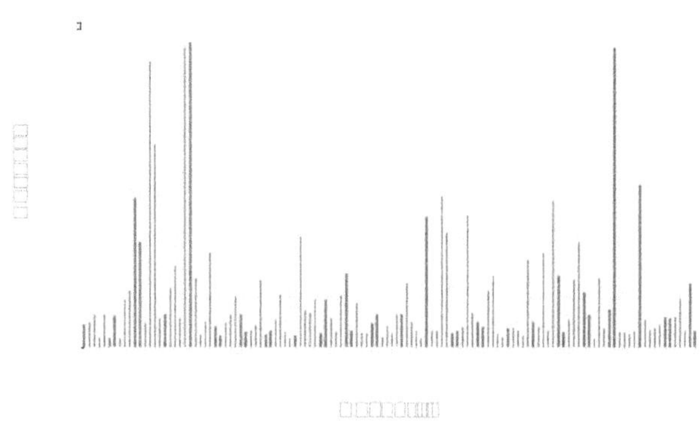

Figure 1: The hub score of 122 anchors in Blip10000.

114 of them are regarded as hubs for having values greater than 10, i.e., $N_k > k$. As shown in Figure 1, majority of anchors indeed have hub score much higher than $k = 10$.

We further investigate the interplay between hubness and LID. As shown in Figure 2, the average LID of anchors is 33, which is significantly less than the global intrinsic dimension (53) of the whole dataset calculated using [20]. As shown in Figure 2, majority of anchors are with values in the range of 20 to 40, basically showing low risk in hyperlinking in such a low dimensionality. Finally, we also take into consideration of the role of diversity in hyperlinking. We calculate diversity as the average pairwise distance between the 30 nearest neighbors of an anchor. The result is presented in Figure 2, where diversity is visualized by the radius of an anchor. It is not surprising to see that the value of diversity is somewhat inversely proportional to the hub score. Nevertheless, for anchors with higher LID value, the diversity value tends to be small. The result basically can give a clue that these are difficult anchors for hyperlinking.

Note that the 122 anchors actually belong to two sets. The first 28 are development anchors focusing on what people say [12], while the latter are 94 testing anchors conveying verbal visual information [15]. We also notice some fundamental difference between the two sets of anchors. Among the anchors with hubness > 122 as shown in Figure 1, 58% of them are from development anchors versus 42% from testing. Similarly in Figure 2, for LID > 50, there are 67% (33%) from development (testing) anchors. Based on this statistics,

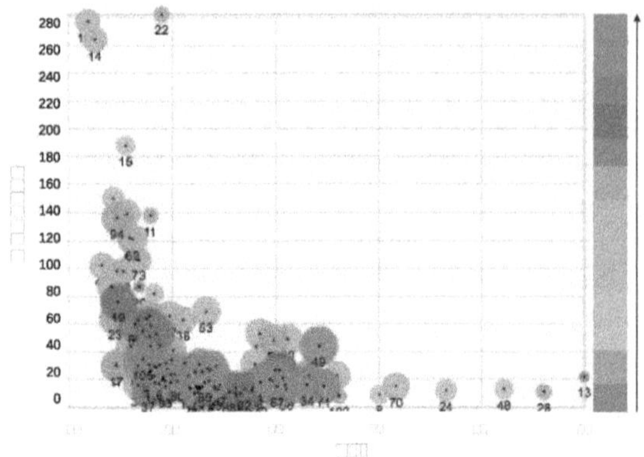

Figure 2: The relationship between hubness, LID, and diversity. The number indicates anchor ID. The color and size of radius show the diversity of an anchor.

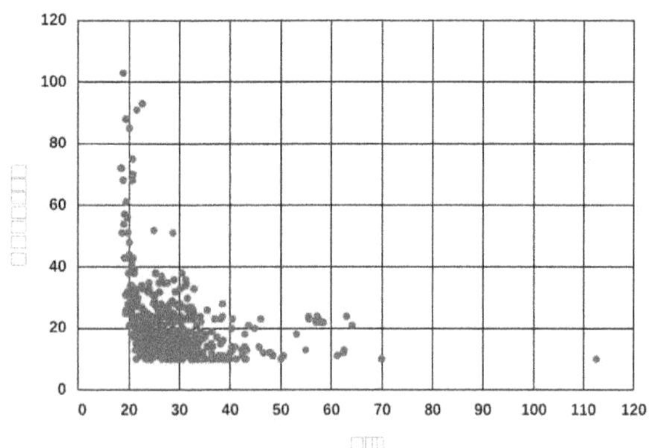

Figure 3: The distribution of 607 targets in the 2D space of LID and hubness.

we speculate that testing anchors shall generate overall better performance in hyperlinking.

2.3.3 How different are targets from anchors? We use 607 ground-truth link targets provided for 28 anchors in this simulation. Similar to anchors, these targets are manually judged as worth for hyperlinking. Figure 3 shows the distribution of target fragments in terms of hubness and LID. First, the hub scores are much lower than that of anchors. Second, a larger portion of fragments (94%) are cluttered in the LID interval of 20-40 than anchors. An interesting observation is that, different from anchors, a lower value of LID for a target may not correspond to a higher value of hub score. This can be explained by the fact that targets are more specific in content for detailing certain aspects of anchors, and thus are with lower hub scores than anchors. Similarly as in the previous subsection, we further investigate the degree of diversity for the targets. The average distance among the 30 nearest neighbors of targets is larger than that of anchors. The result shows that the neighborhood regions of targets are sparser or diverse.

3 ALGORITHM

We assume that the set of ground-truth anchors and targets are preferred examples for video hyperlinking. Based on the simulation results in Section 2.3, we speculate that both anchors and targets should have high value of hubness and diversity, while with lower value of LID. With this, we formulate the selection of anchors and targets as an optimization problem as following.

Let $X = [x_1, x_2, ..., x_n] \in R^{d \times n}$ as a dataset with n fragments, where x_i denotes the feature of ith fragment and d is feature dimension. The corresponding hub scores and LID values are denoted as $H = [h_1, h_2, ..., h_n] \in R^{n \times 1}$ and $D = [d_1, d_2, ..., d_n] \in R^{n \times 1}$ respectively. Furthermore, let A be an affinity matrix, where its element $A_{i,j}$ indicates the distance between fragments x_i and x_j. The optimization aims to select k out of n fragments as either anchors or targets with the objective function

$$\max_{Y} \left(\frac{Y^t H}{k} \quad \frac{Y^t D}{k} + \frac{Y^t A Y}{k\,(k \quad 1)} \right), \quad s.t. \sum_i y_i = k, y_i \in \{0, 1\} \tag{5}$$

where $Y = [y_1, y_2, ..., y_n] \in R^{n \times 1}$ is a binary indicator vector, with $y_i = 1$ means to select fragment x_i and otherwise. Basically the objective function is to sample a predefined number of fragments that are popular and diverse but with low risk in hyperlinking.

Optimizing Equation (5) is difficult, nevertheless, due to the 0-1 selection constraint imposed by the indicator vector. We relax the constraint to $y \in [0, 1]$, as following

$$\max_{Y} \left(\frac{Y^t H}{k} \quad \frac{Y^t D}{k} + \frac{Y^t A Y}{k\,(k \quad 1)} \right), \quad s.t. \sum_i y_i = k, y_i \in [0, 1] \tag{6}$$

making the formulation similar to the standard quadratic programming problem. The major difference lies in the constraint $y_i \in [0, 1]$ to prevent the solution from being dominated by a small number of fragments. In our solution, two Lagrangian multipliers, μ_i and β_i, are introduced for each variable $y_i \in Y$. Furthermore, an additional multiplier λ is used for the constraint $\sum_i y_i = k$. Equation (6) is turned into the form of

$$\max_{Y} \left(\frac{Y^t H}{k} \quad \frac{Y^t D}{k} + \frac{Y^t A Y}{k\,(k \quad 1)} \right) \quad \lambda(\sum_i yi \quad k) + \sum_i u_i y_i + \sum_i \beta_i (1 \quad y_i) \quad s.t. \sum_i y_i = k, y_i \in [0, 1] \tag{7}$$

Based on the Karush Kuhn Tucker (KKT) conditions [16], the solution that maximizes Equation (7) must satisfy the following first-order necessary conditions

$$\begin{cases} \left(\frac{H}{k} - \frac{D}{k} + \frac{2AY}{k(k-1)}\right)_i - \lambda + \mu_i - \beta_i = 0 \\ \sum_i u_i y_i = 0 \\ \sum_i \beta_i (1 - y_i) = 0 \end{cases} \quad (8)$$

where the subscript i can be viewed as index to a fragment. Since y_i, m_i and b_i are non-negative, the KKT conditions can be rewritten to

$$r_i(y) = \left(\frac{H}{k} - \frac{D}{k} + \frac{2AY}{k(k-1)}\right)_i \begin{cases} \leq \lambda & y_i = 0 \\ = \lambda & y_i \in (0,1) \\ > \lambda & y_i = 1 \end{cases} \quad (9)$$

which elegantly quantifies a fragment into three categories based on the value of λ. The value returned by the function r_i is treated as the "reward" of a fragment. To this end, we employ pairwise updating algorithm [22] for optimization. In each iteration, two variables y_i and $y_j, i \neq j$, will be updated as following

$$\hat{y_l} = \begin{cases} y_l, \ l \neq i, l \neq j; \\ y_l + \alpha, \ l = i; \\ y_l - \alpha, \ l = j; \end{cases} \quad (10)$$

By some mathematical manipulations, it can be shown that the value of α is

$$\alpha = \begin{cases} \min(y_j, i - y_i), & \sigma \geq 0 \ and \ \eta > 0; \\ \min\left(y_j, i - y_i, \frac{k(k-1)(r_j(y) - r_i(y))}{A_{ii} + A_{jj} - 2A_{ij}}\right), & \sigma < 0 \ and \ \eta > 0; \\ \min(y_j, i - y_i), & \sigma > 0 \ and \ \eta = 0; \end{cases} \quad (11)$$

where $\sigma = A_{ii} + A_{jj} - 2A_{ij}$ and $\eta = r_i(y) - r_j(y)$. To guarantee algorithm convergence, the pairs of fragments for updating should be carefully selected based on their rewards in Equation 9. Specifically, $r_i(y)$ should correspond to the fragment with the highest reward among the fragments whose rewards are smaller or equal to λ. While for $r_j(y)$, the fragment with the smallest reward among those whose rewards are larger or equal to λ should be selected.

3.1 Selection of anchors and targets

A critical step that governs the selection of fragments is the initialization of the binary indicator vector Y. In principle, the initialization tunes the optimization to favor selection of certain fragments. In the implementation, we leverage this trick for the selection of anchors and targets. We propose two algorithms: Hub-first and LID-first, where the former (latter) prioritizes fragments higher (smaller) in hubness (LID). The Hub-first algorithm initializes Y by setting $y_i = 1$ for variables that correspond to the fragments with the first k largest hub scores. Similarly for the LID-first algorithm which sets $y_i = 1$ for fragments corresponds to the first k smallest LID values. Based on the simulation results in 2.3, anchors are preferable to be high in hubness and low in LID. In such case, ideally either hub-first or LID-first is appropriate for identification of anchors. On the other hand, as targets are more specific in content, their hub scores are generally not as high as anchors. LID-first appears to be more appropriate for target selection.

4 EXPERIMENTS

The experiments are conducted on the full Blip10000 dataset [25]. The hubness, LID, and diversity of each fragment are offline precomputed over the whole dataset.

4.1 Anchor selection

The experiment assesses the ability to rank the 122 anchors provided by TRECVid LNK. As there is no ground-truth of whether one anchor is better than another for hyperlinking, we conduct the user study to evaluate the quality of anchors. Ideally, an anchor should deliver the message that users would like to further explore. A necessary though not sufficient condition is that such message should be unambiguous and explicit to most users. In this study, we recruit a total of 15 graduate students as evaluators, who are not native English speakers. They are instructed to watch 122 anchor fragments and then note down the messages of anchors in words. Note that the students are not familiar with video hyperlinking and Blip10000 dataset. Hence, the messages represent the understanding of key video content from their own perspectives. For each anchor, we manually check the 15 descriptions and then assign a score in the range between 0 and 15, indicating the number of descriptions that are consistent in meaning. Through this process, the quality of each anchor is reflected by a subjective score and used for the experiment.

We compare the performances of four algorithms: Hub, LID, Hub-first, and LID-first. The algorithm "Hub" ranks anchors based on their hub scores in descending order, and similarly for "LID" which performs ranking in ascending order of LID values. We assess the overall performance of top-K ranked anchors by averaging their subjective scores obtained in the user studies. The higher the average score is, the better an algorithm is. The result is presented in Table 2 using the combination of CNN, Concept and Text features. Overall, LID seems to be better coincident with human perception than hubness in evaluating the anchor qualities. Ranking anchors purely based on hub score runs into the risk of selecting noisy fragments, and the performance is consistently the worst across different values of top-K. Ranking anchors purely based on hub score runs into the risk of selecting noisy fragments. The performance is consistently the worst across different values of top-K, and sometimes is even worse than Random run. The proposed two algorithms, which takes into account the interplay among hubness, LID, and diversity, significantly outperforms the baselines Hub and LID. From the result, LID-first algorithm shows an edge

Table 2: Result of anchor selection. Oracle and Random are simulation runs, where the former shows the best possible performance and the latter selects anchor in random.

	K=10	K=20	K=40
Hub	3.53	4.67	5.60
LID	5.93	6.13	6.60
Hub-first	6.53	8.47	7.80
LID-first	7.40	8.26	8.33
Oracle	12.15	11.58	10.63
Random	4.40	5.13	5.33

Table 3: Comparison of target selection with mAP

	mAP@10	mAP@20	mAP@50
Hub	0.06	0.09	0.13
LID	0.08	0.11	0.15
Hub-first	0.09	0.13	0.17
LID-first	0.10	0.13	0.17

Table 4: Performance of LID-first algorithm on different features. The % in parenthesis indicates the relative improvement when LID-first is not in used.

	mAP@10	mAP@20	mAP@50
CNN	0.07 (1%)	0.11 (5%)	0.13 (5%)
Concept	0.04 (216%)	0.05 (163%)	0.07 (106%)
Text	0.04 (46%)	0.05 (71%)	0.08 (53%)
CNN+Concept	0.08 (32%)	0.11 (26%)	0.14 (24%)
LDA	0.02 (30%)	0.03 (42%)	0.05 (19%)
CM_LDA	0.04 (-8%)	0.08 (19%)	0.09 (18%)
CNN+ Concept+Text	0.10 (26%)	0.13 (23%)	0.17 (28%)

over Hub-first. We believe that this is due to the bias in the user study, where fragments with one single theme are likely to receive higher subjective score than fragments with multi-perspective themes. The result of LID-first is somewhat close to oracle, implying a certain degree of consistency between statistical analysis and human cognition of what should be an ideal anchor.

4.2 Target selection

In this experiment, we treat each anchor as a query and conduct search of top-K target candidates. The top-k candidates are then re-ranked respectively by four different algorithms. As in TRECVid LNK, the performance is measured by mean average precision (mAP) at a depth of K in a rank list. The mAP is calculated over 28 anchors which have ground-truth targets provided by TRECVid. The number of ground-truth targets for each anchor ranges from 9 to 38. Table 3 shows the performances of four different algorithms based on the fusion of three features. Similar performance trend is observed as anchor selection.

We further show the effect of different features and their combinations for target selection. In addition to CNN, Concept and Text, the feature being considered are the topic-level representation, which has been reported in [26] as reliable for video hyperlinking. Two kinds of topic modeling are considered: the classic Latent Dirichlet Allocation (LDA) [7] using text features, and cross-modal LDA (CM-LDA) using Concept and CNN features based on the implementation of [6]. Table 4 lists the result of the LID-first algorithm on different features. As can be seen, LID-first algorithm consistently introduce improvement for various features across different levels of depth. More importantly, such improvement is also noticed when different features are early fused, signifying the merit of manipulating hub, LID, and diversity for target selection.

5 DISCUSSION & CONCLUSION

We have presented the study of hubness and LID in quantifying the characteristics of anchors and targets. The study clearly shows the existence of hubness phenomenon in Blip10000 dataset. Particularly, the textual feature appears to be noisy resulting in fragments with extremely high hub scores. By fusion with deep and concept level features, the distribution of hubness is less skew implying a higher chance of achieving better performance with both text and visual features. Among the 122 anchors, 114 of them are regarded as hubs. Meanwhile, only 4 of them have local intrinsic dimensionality higher than the global intrinsic dimensionality of the entire dataset. When considering both hubness and LID, the majority of anchors are hubs with low to moderate risk in hyperlinking. By assuming that these are the required characteristics of anchors and targets, we take the bravery to propose the Hub-first and LID-first algorithms. Through the user study, surprisingly both algorithms somewhat align with human cognition of what could be think of as anchors. Furthermore, by applying the algorithms to re-rank targets, noticeable improvement is also attained across different modalities and their combinations. Basically, we can safely conclude that a fragment quantified as the hub with low local intrinsic dimensionality are likely to be a good anchor or target. Currently, it is still not clear of how the quality of anchors will correlate with the performance of target identification, which will be our future research direction.

ACKNOWLEDGMENTS

The work described in this paper was fully supported by a grant from the Research Grants Council of the Hong Kong Special Administrative Region, China (CityU 11250716), and National Natural Science Foundation of China (61373121).

REFERENCES

[1] Robin Aly, Roeland JF Ordelman, Maria Eskevich, Gareth JF Jones, and Shu Chen. 2013. Linking inside a video collection: what and how to measure?. In *WWW*. 457–460.

[2] Laurent Amsaleg, Oussama Chelly, Teddy Furon, Stéphane Girard, Michael E Houle, Ken-ichi Kawarabayashi, and Michael Nett. 2015. Estimating local intrinsic dimensionality. In *KDD*. 29–38.

[3] Evlampios Apostolidis, Vasileios Mezaris, Mathilde Sahuguet, Benoit Huet, Barbora Červenková, Daniel Stein, Stefan Eickeler, José Luis Redondo Garcia, Raphaël Troncy, and Lukás Pikora. 2014. Automatic fine-grained hyperlinking of videos within a closed collection using scene segmentation. In *ACM MM*. 1033–1036.

[4] George Awad, Jonathan Fiscus, Martial Michel, David Joy, Wessel Kraaij, Alan F Smeaton, Georges Quénot, Maria Eskevich, Robin Aly, and Roeland Ordelman. 2016. Trecvid 2016: Evaluating video search, video event detection, localization, and hyperlinking. In *Proc. TRECVid.*

[5] Werner Bailer, Michał Lokaj, and Harald Stiegler. 2014. Context in Video Search: Is Close-by Good Enough When Using Linking?. In *ICMR*. 209.

[6] Jingwen Bian, Yang Yang, Hanwang Zhang, and Tat-Seng Chua. 2015. Multimedia summarization for social events in microblog stream. *IEEE Trans. on Multimedia* 17, 2 (2015), 216–228.

[7] David M Blei, Andrew Y Ng, and Michael I Jordan. 2003. Latent dirichlet allocation. *JMLR* 3, Jan (2003), 993–1022.

[8] Rémi Bois, Vedran Vukotić, Anca-Roxana Simon, Ronan Sicre, Christian Raymond, Pascale Sébillot, and Guillaume Gravier. 2017. Exploiting Multimodality in Video Hyperlinking to Improve Target Diversity. In *MMM*. 185–197.

[9] Junwei Liang, Jia Chen, Poyao Huang, Xuanchong Li, Lu Jiang, Zhenzhong Lan, Pingbo Pan, Hehe Fan, Qin Jin, Jiande Sun, Yang Chen, Yi Yang, Alexandar Hauptmann. 2016. INF@TRECVID 2016 Video Hyperlinking. In *Proc. TRECVid.*

[10] Jia Deng, Wei Dong, Richard Socher, Li-Jia Li, Kai Li, and Li Fei-Fei. 2009. Imagenet: A large-scale hierarchical image database. In *CVPR*. 248–255.

[11] Maria Eskevich, Robin Aly, Roeland Ordelman, David N Racca, Shu Chen, and Gareth JF Jones. 2015. SAVA at MediaEval 2015: Search and anchoring in video archives. *MediaEval Workshop* (2015).

[12] Maria Eskevich, Robin Aly, David Racca, Roeland Ordelman, Shu Chen, and Gareth JF Jones. 2014. The search and hyperlinking task at MediaEval 2014. *MediaEval Workshop* (2014).

[13] Maria Eskevich, Gareth JF Jones, Robin Aly, Roeland JF Ordelman, Shu Chen, Danish Nadeem, Camille Guinaudeau, Guillaume Gravier, Pascale Sébillot, Tom De Nies, and others. 2013. Multimedia information seeking through search and hyperlinking. In *ICMR*. 287–294.

[14] Maria Eskevich, Gareth JF Jones, Robin Aly, Roeland JF Ordelman, Shu Chen, Danish Nadeem, Camille Guinaudeau, Guillaume Gravier, Pascale Sébillot, Tom De Nies, and others. 2013. Multimedia information seeking through search and hyperlinking. In *ICMR*. 287–294.

[15] Maria Eskevich, Martha Larson, Robin Aly, Serwah Sabetghadam, Gareth JF Jones, Roeland Ordelman, and Benoit Huet. 2017. Multimodal video-to-video linking: turning to the crowd for insight and evaluation. In *MMM*. 280–292.

[16] Anthony V Fiacco and Garth P McCormick. 1990. *Nonlinear programming: sequential unconstrained minimization techniques*. SIAM.

[17] Arthur Flexer, Dominik Schnitzer, and Jan Schlüter. 2012. A MIREX Meta-analysis of Hubness in Audio Music Similarity. In *ISMIR*. 175–180.

[18] Kazuo Hara, Ikumi Suzuki, Masashi Shimbo, Kei Kobayashi, Kenji Fukumizu, and Milos Radovanovic. 2015. Localized Centering: Reducing Hubness in Large-Sample Data.. In *AAAI*. 2645–2651.

[19] Kaiming He, Xiangyu Zhang, Shaoqing Ren, and Jian Sun. 2016. Deep residual learning for image recognition. In *CVPR*. 770–778.

[20] Elizaveta Levina and Peter J Bickel. 2004. Maximum likelihood estimation of intrinsic dimension. *Ann Arbor MI* 48109 (2004), 1092.

[21] Yuncheng Li, Xitong Yang, and Jiebo Luo. 2015. Semantic video entity linking based on visual content and metadata. In *ICCV*. 4615–4623.

[22] Hairong Liu, Xingwei Yang, Longin Jan Latecki, and Shuicheng Yan. 2012. Dense neighborhoods on affinity graph. *IJCV* 98, 1 (2012), 65–82.

[23] Paul Over, George Awad, Jon Fiscus, Martial Michel, David Joy, Alan Semeaton, Wessel Kraaij, Georges Quénot, Roeland Ordelman, and Robin Aly. 2015. TRECVid 2015–an overview of the goals, tasks, data, evaluation mechanisms, and metrics. In *Proc. TRECVid.*

[24] Miloš Radovanović, Alexandros Nanopoulos, and Mirjana Ivanović. 2010. Hubs in space: Popular nearest neighbors in high-dimensional data. *JMLR* 11, Sep (2010), 2487–2531.

[25] Sebastian Schmiedeke, Peng Xu, Isabelle Ferrané, Maria Eskevich, Christoph Kofler, Martha A Larson, Yannick Estève, Lori Lamel, Gareth JF Jones, and Thomas Sikora. 2013. Blip10000: A social video dataset containing spug content for tagging and retrieval. In *MMSys*. 96–101.

[26] Anca-Roxana Simon, Rémi Bois, Guillaume Gravier, Pascale Sébillot, Emmanuel Morin, and Sien Moens. 2015. Hierarchical topic models for language-based video hyperlinking. In *SLAM*. 31–34.

[27] Nenad Tomasev, Milos Radovanovic, Dunja Mladenic, and Mirjana Ivanovic. 2014. The role of hubness in clustering high-dimensional data. *IEEE Trans. on KDE* 26, 3 (2014), 739–751.

Visual Descriptors in Methods for Video Hyperlinking

Petra Galuščáková
Charles University
Faculty of Mathematics and Physics
Institute of Formal and Applied Linguistics
Prague, Czech Republic
galuscakova@ufal.mff.cuni.cz

Michal Batko
Masaryk University
Faculty of Informatics
Brno, Czech Republic
batko@fi.muni.cz

Jan Čech
Czech Technical University in Prague
Faculty of Electrical Engineering
Department of Cybernetics
Center for Machine Perception
Prague, Czech Republic
cechj@cmp.felk.cvut.cz

Jiří Matas
Czech Technical University in Prague
Faculty of Electrical Engineering
Department of Cybernetics
Center for Machine Perception
Prague, Czech Republic
matas@cmp.felk.cvut.cz

David Novák
Masaryk University
Faculty of Informatics
Brno, Czech Republic
david.novak@fi.muni.cz

Pavel Pecina
Charles University
Faculty of Mathematics and Physics
Institute of Formal and Applied Linguistics
Prague, Czech Republic
pecina@ufal.mff.cuni.cz

ABSTRACT

In this paper, we survey different state-of-the-art visual processing methods and utilize them in hyperlinking. Visual information, calculated using Features Signatures, SIMILE descriptors and convolutional neural networks (CNN), is utilized as similarity between video frames and used to find similar faces, objects and setting. Visual concepts in frames are also automatically recognized and textual output of the recognition is combined with search based on subtitles and transcripts. All presented experiments were performed in the Search and Hyperlinking 2014 MediaEval task and Video Hyperlinking 2015 TRECVid task.

KEYWORDS

Video retrieval, Hyperlinking, Information retrieval, Image processing

ACM Reference format:
Petra Galuščáková, Michal Batko, Jan Čech, Jiří Matas, David Novák, and Pavel Pecina. 2017. Visual Descriptors in Methods for Video Hyperlinking. In *Proceedings of ICMR '17, Bucharest, Romania, June 06-09, 2017,* 7 pages.
https://doi.org/10.1145/3078971.3079026

1 INTRODUCTION

The aim of this paper is to review methods for visual data processing and test them on hyperlinking problem. Some methods have already been utilized and described in our former work. Feature Signatures (Section 2.2) were described in the MediaEval 2014 report [17] and TRECVid results (Section 3) were described in the TRECVid report [19]. In addition to these results, we also closely analyze results achieved by Feature Signatures, show why they improve hyperlinking based on textual content (Section 2.3) and compare them to state-of-the-art CNN descriptors (Section 2.5). Moreover, we also present novel approaches to combination text-based retrieval with described visual descriptors (Section 2.4) and with detected visual concepts (Section 2.6). We also describe utilization of face descriptors (Section 2.7), which have not been used in hyperlinking before, according to our best knowledge.

Hyperlink is defined as "*an electronic link providing direct access from one distinctively marked place in a hypertext or hypermedia document to another in the same or a different document*" [31]. The source marked place of the link (e.g. relevant text, relevant part of an image or video) is called the *anchor*. Hyperlinking task focuses on automatic linking of the anchors to related targets. In this paper, we focus on hyperlinking in video collections. Both the anchors (or queries in our case) and targets are segments of video recording and they are defined by the video recording, beginning playback time and end playback time [36].

1.1 Evaluation Benchmarks

Hyperlinking of video data was also part of Search and Hyperlinking task at the 2014 MediaEval Multimedia Benchmark [15] and Video Hyperlinking task at 2015 TRECVid evaluation workshop [38]. Both tasks tested submitted systems using the same collection of TV broadcast programmes provided by BBC. The development set of the collection consisted of BBC TV programmes broadcast between 01.04.2008 and 11.05.2008, and the test set consisted of programmes broadcast between 12.05.2008 and 31.07.2008. Among other things, the collection contained news (e.g. *BBC Breakfast, BBC News at Ten*), documentaries (e.g. *The Life of Mammals, Wild China*), serials (e.g. *EastEnders, Two Pints of Lager and a Packet of Crisps*), entertainment programmes (e.g. *Top Gear, Hard Sell*), quiz shows (e.g. *Eggheads, The Weakest Link*), cookery shows (e.g. *Saturday Kitchen, Ready Steady Cook*), sport events (e.g. football matches, horse races), and children's programmes (e.g. *Big Barn Farm, Nina and the Neurons*). The collection also contained concerts (e.g. *Radio 1's Big Weekend, Glastonbury The Best Bits*) and music programmes (e.g. *Mad about Music, Later... with Jools Holland*). Thus the range of

ICMR '17, June 06-09, 2017, Bucharest, Romania

ACM ISBN 978-1-4503-4701-3/17/06.
https://doi.org/10.1145/3078971.3079026

topics of the videos was unrestricted and the collection contained many speakers, settings, accents, genres, and formality types. Apart from videos, the collection was also published with subtitles and three automatic transcripts provided by LIMSI [26], LIUM [43] and NST-Sheffield [27], manually entered metadata, automatically detected shots, a list of stable keyframes, prosodic features [16], and visual concepts [8, 46].

The set of query segments was in both tasks collected by hired participants of a user survey. In the 2014 MediaEval task, the focus was on a home user scenario. Participants searched the collection using a text-based search and watched some retrieved segments. Then, they marked anchors within these segments. Participants were also asked to state what kind of links would they like to find using marked segments. This information was further available in the evaluation but it was hidden to the task participants. 30 out of 36 collected queries were used for evaluation.

The 2015 Video Hyperlinking task was focused on media professionals and content creators. The anchors were created by journalist students and media professionals who were asked to locate segments which they would like to enrich by hyperlinks if they were content producers. Totally, 100 queries out of 135 collected were used for evaluation.

1.2 Hyperlinking Approaches

Ordelman et al. [36] state that the main difference between video hyperlinking task and other related problems such as video recommendation or near-duplicate detection is that video hyperlinking focuses on *"'give me more information about this anchor' instead of 'give me more based on this anchor or entity'"*. Thus the attention is focused on semantic similarity between the anchoring and target segments.

A full range of methods had been applied in the hyperlinking. In order to find the relevant segment, pre-segmentation of the videos is the dominant approach. Researchers use fixed length segments measured by time [10, 11, 33] or number of included words [29], sentence boundaries [9], shots [30, 41], visual similarity between frames [45] and boundaries defined by the TextTilling [3, 39] segmentation algorithm. However, some researches localize directly the jump-in points without any pre-segmentation. For example García et al. [20] put jump-in point to the place which maximizes their similarity function based on shared words and WordNet distances between words. Similarly, Preston et al. [42] represent each video by a probability density function and the points with the highest probabilities are the jump-in points.

Methods also differ in types of modalities which are used in the retrieval. Some of the authors only use textual information from transcripts and subtitles [20, 29]. Textual information can also be enriched by synonyms [41] or named entities [10, 34]. Textual query expanded by connected entities from Freebase, geographical entities from GeoNames, synonyms from Wordnet, and DBpedia words were used by Lokaj et al. [30]. Word vectors [32] can also be used as word representations [39]. Textual information is often combined with the visual information. The researches mostly employ visual concepts [28, 45, 49]. Şimon et al. [13] use bi-lingual LDA to create a probabilistic translation model between lexical transcripts and visual concepts. The results acquired by the text-based retrieval

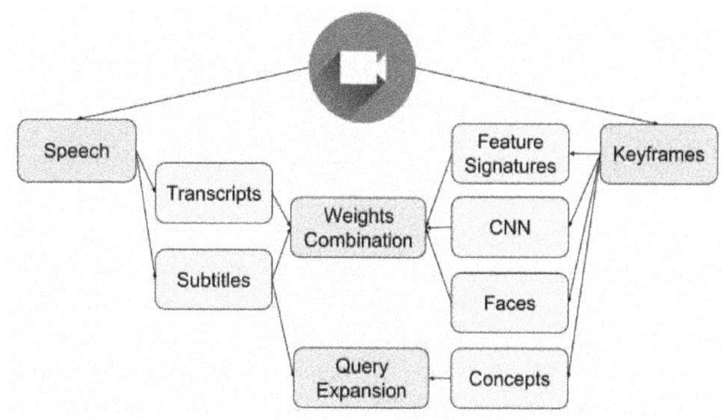

Figure 1: Visual methods overview.

using subtitles and transcripts can also be re-ranked using SIFT descriptors [30]. On the other hand, the approach by Werner and Ward [47] is purely based on the prosodic information. However, improvement achieved using multiple modalities is not definite. Even though, that some researches report an improvement using a combination of modalities, the best scoring approach at the 2015 TRECVid [11] only uses textual data.

The remainder of the paper is organized as follows. First, methods for calculating similarity between frames tested in MediaEval 2014 [17] will be described. Retrieval which utilizes Visual Similarity using Feature Signatures, which bring information about frame setting, will be compared with retrieval methods based purely on subtitles and transcripts. Results will be analyzed in respect to the TV broadcast data. In the following experiments, Feature Signatures will be compared with deep-learning based methods and face similarity algorithms will be utilized. Finally, the most promising approaches will be compared in the 2015 TRECVid evaluation benchmark.

2 VISUAL DESCRIPTORS IN MEDIAEVAL 2014

This section describes different visual descriptors (Feature Signatures, CNN and face descriptors) and different ways how to combine them with text-based retrieval (linear combination of weights and query expansion in which words from query are used together with detected concepts). Experiments with these descriptors were performed in MediaEval 2014 Benchmark and after the Benchmark on the same dataset. Overview of described methods is displayed in Figure 1.

2.1 Text-based Retrieval

In order to easily retrieve relevant video passages, recordings were divided into 50-second long segments. A new segment was created each 10 seconds – created segments can thus overlap. Text lying within the segment boundaries was then indexed. Similarly, we created a textual query from a query segment by utilizing all words in the subtitles lying within the query segment. Text-based retrieval can then be applied to the collection. In our experiments, we used the Terrier IR Framework [37] and its implementation of the Hiemstra Language Model [21] for retrieval, with its parameter set to 0.35. We used Porter stemmer and Terrier's stopwords list. In all experiments, we post-filtered retrieved segments and removed segments which partially overlapped with the query segment and also possibly with another higher ranked retrieved segment (further called removal of overlapping or *RO* filtering).

Manually created metadata available in the collection were utilized to further enrich the retrieval – title, episode title, description, short episode synopsis, service name, and program variant of the programmes were used specifically. Each segment was concatenated with the metadata of the corresponding full recording. Additionally, each query segment was concatenated with the metadata of the corresponding full recording. As the context of the query segment proved to be helpful in the former experiments, 200 seconds before the beginning of the query segment and 200 seconds after the end of the query segment were also utilized. The length of the context was tuned on the development data.

2.2 Feature Signatures

In order to represent video frames, *Feature Signatures* that approximate distribution of color and texture in the image can be used. Unlike modern CNN descriptors excellent in recognizing specific objects, this traditional descriptor can be used to identify keyframes with a similar background and setting. Feature Signatures have already been used in a known item search tasks [12]. The authors have created an efficient and effective sketch-based retrieval system [4, 5], where each keyframe is represented by a Feature Signature and users can query the database of Feature Signatures using simple signature-based sketches.

Visual Similarity was calculated between the query segment and each data segment. Distance was calculated between each keyframe in the query segment and each keyframe in data. Distance between segments was then calculated as a minimal similarity ($1 - distance$) between keyframes in the query and data segments. Finally, Visual Similarity of the segments was linearly combined with their Textual Similarity acquired from the text-based retrieval:

$$FinalScore(segment/query) = Score(segment/query) + Weight * VisualSimilarity(segment/query), \quad (1)$$

and the retrieved segments were scored according to the Final Score. The $Weight$ was tuned on the development data and it prefers textual information.

Position-color-texture Feature Signatures [23, 24, 44] were utilized to approximate a distribution of color and texture in each keyframe. This descriptor can be utilized in image retrieval tasks, where color and texture is meaningful for retrieval. Formally, given a feature space $\mathbb{F}$, the *Feature Signature* S^o of a multimedia object o is defined as a set of tuples $\{\langle r_i^o, w_i^o \rangle\}_{i=1}^n$ from $\mathbb{F} \times \mathbb{R}^+$, consisting of representatives $r_i^o \in \mathbb{F}$ and weights $w_i^o \in \mathbb{R}^+$. Image is then represented by a sequence of Feature Signatures which describe color of image regions. Example of image represented by Feature Signatures is displayed in Figure 2.

The distance between Features Signatures was calculated using the Signature Quadratic Form Distance [2]. Keyframe distances were calculated and provided by Department of Software Engineering at Charles University. Employing Feature Signatures enables visual similarity to work exceptionally well in detecting similar settings and backgrounds. This is particularly important in working with TV collections, in which a similar background occurs throughout the series. However Feature Signatures can fail to detect some details in keyframes, e.g. it is not possible recognize a particular person.

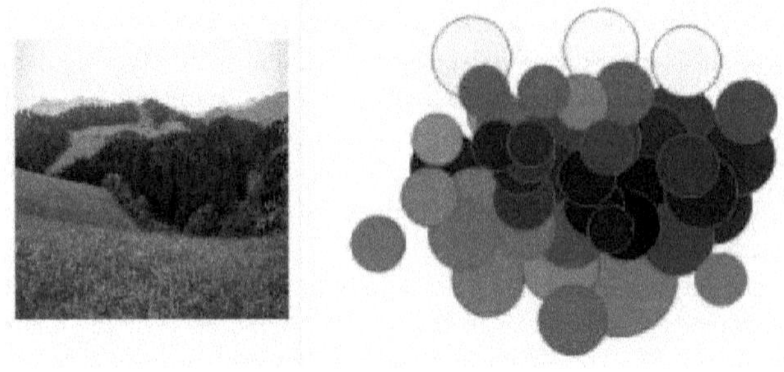

Figure 2: Representation of image using Feature Signatures.

2.3 MediaEval 2014 Results

The task was evaluated manually using crowd-sourcing methods and *MAP-bin* and *MAP-tol* evaluation measures [1]. Both these measures are adaptations of the *MAP* measure proposed for evaluation of video content retrieval to allow a segment retrieved near the relevant segment (but not necessarily overlapping it) to also be marked as relevant.

Comparison of results with utilization of Visual Similarity using Feature Signatures and using purely transcripts and subtitles is displayed in Table 1. The best results for both measures were achieved when the Visual Similarity was employed. The highest MAP-bin score was achieved on the subtitles when the overlapping segments were preserved. In general, differences between subtitles and automatic transcripts were minor, especially when additional visual information was used. The highest MAP-tol score was surprisingly achieved on the LIMSI transcripts when overlapping segments were filtered out. This may be caused by a precisely given timing of each word in the LIUM transcript. The timing of each word in the subtitles was approximated, based on the time of the beginning and the end of the utterance. In the case of the 15-second long tolerance windows, this approximation could decrease the score.

Transcript	Weights	RO	MAP-bin	MAP-tol
Subtitles	None	Yes	0.2689	0.2465
Subtitles	Visual	No	**0.3080**	0.0996
Subtitles	Visual	Yes	0.2724	**0.2580**
LIMSI	None	Yes	0.2659	0.2297
LIMSI	Visual	No	**0.3042**	0.0950
LIMSI	Visual	Yes	0.2692	**0.2414**
LIUM	None	Yes	0.2593	0.2547
LIUM	Visual	No	**0.2880**	0.0993
LIUM	Visual	Yes	0.2622	**0.2632**
NST-Sheffield	None	Yes	0.2611	0.2237
NST-Sheffield	Visual	No	**0.2949**	0.0914
NST-Sheffield	Visual	Yes	0.2655	**0.2440**

Table 1: Results with and without visual similarity utilization for different transcripts with and without RO filtering. Best results for each transcript are highlighted.

Visual Similarity calculated using Feature Signatures proved to be very helpful in the task. Even though the improvement in terms of MAP-bin score was minor, Feature Signatures improved the results consistently on all transcripts in both measures. Low MAP-tol scores achieved when overlapping segments were not filtered were caused by that MAP-tol measure takes into account each relevant segment only once. Overlapping retrieved segments thus lowered the score. Presented systems also achieved the overall highest results in the Benchmark [14].

Three examples in which Feature Signatures improved the retrieval quality are displayed in Figure 3. Color-position-based Feature Signatures work well for type of queries similar to Query 2. Even though that query and target keyframes are not necessarily from the same TV series or program, they are similar in terms of what color occurs in which part of the image. Similarly, the results in Query 11 are improved thanks to the retrieval of the same setting. In the Query 26, the only top relevant retrieved segment was the segment before the beginning of the query segment. This segment was retrieved thanks to its high Visual Similarity with the query segment. It did not occur among the top results retrieved using the text-based similarity only.

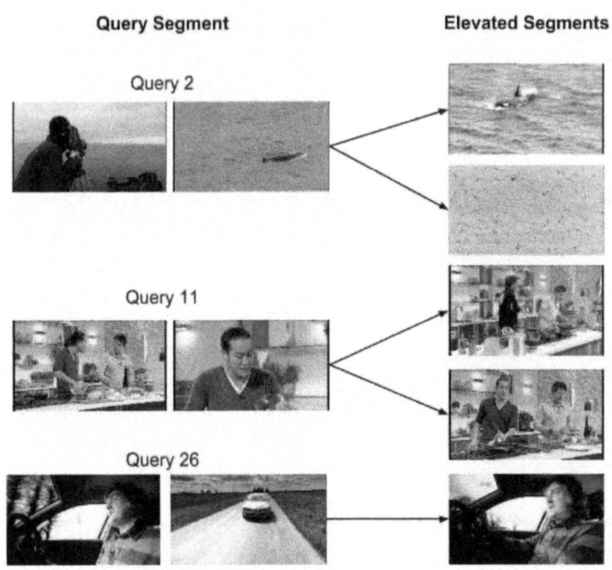

Figure 3: Examples in which employment of the Visual Similarity increased the retrieval quality.

Several keyframes of the query segments in which Visual Similarity decreased the results are in Figure 4. These keyframes display mainly persons and they do not contain any specific content or background. Therefore, even an optimal Visual Similarity calculation is hardly expected to improve the results in these cases.

2.4 Combination with Text-based Retrieval

In order to combine text-based retrieval with Visual Similarity between keyframes, maximum similarity between any keyframe from the query segment and any keyframe from the target segment was used in the presented experiments. However, this strategy is not

Figure 4: Examples in which employment of the Visual Similarity decreased the retrieval quality.

optimal as single keyframes can be similar to each other accidentally, e.g. both segments can contain black keyframes. Several other strategies were thus tested in follow-up experiments. Visual Similarity was also calculated as a sum over two or three most similar keyframes. Moreover, these two or three keyframes can be selected from segments with or without repetition – one keyframe thus can be taken into account either once or multiple times.

Additionally, in the case of calculating similarity using two keyframes, only keyframes which were similar enough to their adjacent keyframes were taken into account. This simulated that selected keyframes are specific representatives of the segments. Similarly, only keyframes which differed enough from the adjacent keyframes were taken into account, which simulated that selected keyframes are distinctive in comparison with their surrounding. In addition to maximum similarity, we also calculated average similarity between all pairs of keyframes in query and target segments.

Transcript	Keyframes	MAP-bin	MAP-tol
Subtitles	None	0.1463	0.1335
Subtitles	Max 1	0.1556	0.1389
Subtitles	Max 2	0.1622	**0.1445**
Subtitles	Max 3	**0.1623**	0.1423

Table 2: Results for Visual Similarity calculated using different number of keyframes. Best results are highlighted.

Each of these approaches increased both MAP-bin and MAP-tol scores. Highest achieved scores are tabulated in Table 2[1]. The approach which uses similarity between two keyframes (each one was selected from the segment without a repetition) achieved the most promising results. For three most similar keyframes, the MAP-bin score was even slightly higher but the improvement for the MAP-tol slightly dropped.

2.5 Object Recognition

In contrast to position-color-texture-based Feature Signatures, modern deep convolutional neural networks work particularly well for recognition and classification of object in the image [22]. Similarity between keyframes was thus also calculated using a CNN visual features calculated as the output from the last hidden layer fc7 of AlexNet [22]. These 4096-dimensional vectors were organized for efficient similarity search by a distance-based index [35] and this

[1] Even though, the experiments were performed on the same data as those in the previous section, the baseline system in these experiments uses 60-second long segments instead of 50 and no metadata and context are used.

system provided the similarity scores. Calculated object similarity was linearly combined with text-based similarity in the same way as similarity calculated using Feature Signatures. Similarly to Feature Signatures, CNN improved purely text-based retrieval but the improvement was smaller than in the case of the Feature Signatures and CNN were thus not applied on the 2015 TRECVid test data.

Both Visual Similarity calculation models were also combined. First, they were combined linearly with the output of text-based retrieval similarly as in the previous experiments. In order to acquire comparable scores, maxmin and mean normalization was applied to both visual similarity scores and both weights were jointly tuned. However, this approach did not outperform combination of text-based retrieval and Feature Signatures.

Scores were also combined using re-ranking. CNN were first applied and combined with text-based search in order to retrieve similar objects. Top retrieved results (10, 20, 50 and 100 items) then were re-ranked using Feature Signatures in order to sort target keyframes according to their "overall" similarity with the query keyframe. Although, this approach achieved a minor improvement, it again did not outperform results achieved by basic linear combination of text and Feature Signatures.

2.6 Concept Detection

Convolutional networks were also used to acquire textual descriptions of the concepts depicted in the keyframes. Concepts were created by image annotation system used in ImageCLEF 2014 Task [7]. This system first retrieves images similar to a given query image, or keyframe in our case, from annotated Profiset [6] using CNN. The word descriptions of the most similar images are then used for text analysis where the word semantic relationships are exploited to create a description of the query image. The description was created for each keyframe as a list of concepts (e.g. *people, indoors, young, two, canadian, plant, macro*) with a confidence score assigned to each concept.

Transcript	Concepts	Max Conc.	RO	MAP-bin	MAP-tol
Subtitles	No	–	No	0.2333	0.1375
Subtitles	Yes	–	No	**0.2414**	0.1603
Subtitles	Yes	5	No	0.2368	**0.1638**

Table 3: Query expansion by visual concepts with and without restriction of the maximum number of concept occurrences. Concepts are weighted by their confidence scores in both cases. Best results are highlighted.

Detected concepts were appended to the created text-based queries. When we used all detected concepts of all query keyframes, both the scores have decreased since the concepts then contained too much noise. Using only concepts with higher confidence scores and concepts with restricted number of occurrences (occurring up to two or three times in the query segment) allowed to increase these results but the scores were still lower than the baseline. However, assigning concept confidence scores as query term weights increased both the scores. Highest MAP-tol result was achieved using combination of concept term weighting and restriction of number of occurrences of each concept in query (up to six occurrences). The results achieved for query expansion using concepts are shown in Table 3.

2.7 Faces recognition

In addition to recognition of settings and particular objects, we also experimented with face recognition. Faces were detected by a commercial multi-view face detector[2]. Each face was geometrically aligned with a canonical pose by automatically extracted facial landmarks. Then a compact vectorial SIMILE descriptor [25] was calculated. A set of face descriptors representing person identities were thus available for each keyframe in which faces were detected. Faces were then compared by L2 distance on calculated descriptors.

In this way, it was possible to find occurrences of persons from query keyframes in the rest of the data. Detected similarity was first linearly combined with text-based similarity in the same way as Visual Similarity. This combination very slightly increased the MAP-bin score from 0.1463 to 0.1473 but MAP-tol score dropped from 0.1335 to 0.1322. Additionally, faces similarity was used for re-ranking top 1000 text-based retrieval results. In this case, both scores were improved. MAP-bin increased from 0.2051 to 0.2088 in the case when only faces with similarity score higher than a given threshold were used. MAP-tol score increased from 0.1162 to 0.1281 when all available faces were used. Due to unstable improvement achieved on the training data, this approach was not applied on the test data. We expect that employing recent deep net descriptors that are more powerful, e.g. [40], would further improve the performance.

3 TRECVID 2015 METHODS COMPARISON

The Search and Hyperlinking 2014 MediaEval task and Video Hyperlinking 2015 TRECVid task shared the same dataset but differed in the set of queries used for evaluation. Test set used for evaluation of the Search and Hyperlinking task was available for development purposes in the Video Hyperlinking task. Therefore, approaches which achieved the most promising results in the MediaEval 2014 experiments and in described follow-up experiments were submitted to the TRECVid 2015 Video Hyperlinking Task. In this section, we present the submitted systems.

3.1 *Baseline* run

Baseline is similar to the system described in Section 2.1 but there are some minor differences. Recordings were segmented into 60-second passages, only a title, a description and broadcast channel name were used as metadata information and context of 20 seconds was used. No automatic transcripts, only subtitles were used in the submitted runs. As the BBC collection contains numerous music programmes, the query segments were also expanded by audio information contained in each segment [18]. Sub-segments of each segment then were submitted to the Doreso service[3] for music identification which uses a fingerprinting technique. If the sub-segment contains any music, the song title and the artist are retrieved and this information is concatenated with the query segment. Music was detected in 10 out of 30 training queries but only in 7 out of 135 test queries. Each query was also further expanded

[2]Eyedea Recognition Ltd. http://www.eyedea.cz/
[3]http://developer.doreso.com

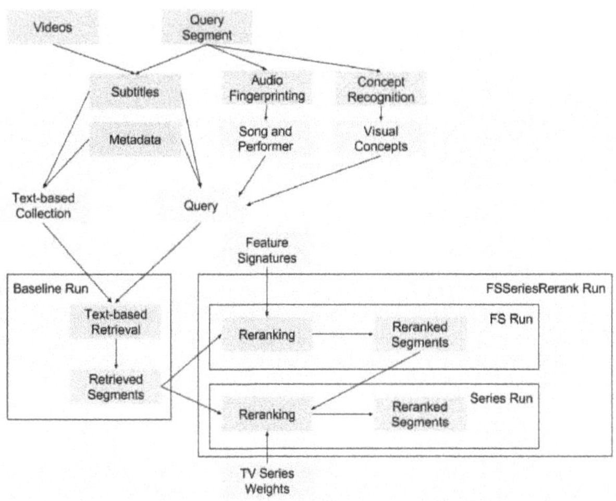

Figure 5: Retrieval processing system - strategy diagram.

by visual concepts contained in the source video segments which were weighted by confidence scores and only used if they occurred less than 7 times in segment as described in Section 2.6.

3.2 Tuning

The *Series* run achieved the highest improvement on the training data. It combines the *Baseline* run with information on whether the videos came from the same TV series. This information was used to pre-calculate a "series weight" for each video which was set to 0.13 if the query video and data video were from the same TV series; otherwise the weight was set to -0.15. These weights were tuned on the training data. Weights were linearly combined with the top 1000 retrieved results.

The *FS* run is similar to the highest ranked run submitted to the MediaEval 2014 Benchmark. In this run, the *Baseline* was expanded by the Visual Similarity between the query segment and data segments calculated using Feature Signatures as described in Section 2.2. Visual Similarity was calculated using two most similar keyframes as described in Section 2.4.

Finally, the *FSSeriesRerank* run is a combination of the *FS* and the *Series* runs. The top 1000 results returned by the *FS* system were linearly combined with the same weights as those used in the *Series* run and re-ranked accordingly.

3.3 Results

The strategy diagram of retrieval approaches is displayed in Figure 5. A performance comparison is reported in Table 4.

The best results are again achieved using Feature Signatures as the *FS* run outperforms the *Baseline* run. Even though that this improvement is not significant[4], it is in line with our previous experiments and it confirms that employment of Visual Similarity consistently improves text-based retrieval. Weighting using information about the same TV series did not outperform the *Baseline* run in any case; the *Baseline* run is significantly better than both

[4]Wilcoxon signed rank test [48]

Run Num.	Run Name	MAP-bin	MAP-tol
1	Series	0.1443	0.1131
2	FSSeriesRerank	0.1094	0.0838
3	FS	**0.1560**	**0.1234**
4	Baseline	0.1536	0.1214

Table 4: Performance comparison of results submitted to the Video Hyperlinking Task. Best results for each measure are highlighted.

Series and *FSSeriesRerank* runs, despite high improvement of reranking based on TV series achieved on the training data.

4 CONCLUSIONS

In the paper, we complexly reviewed image processing methods and tested them on the video hyperlinking task. We presented a range of image processing methods (Feature Signatures, CNN, concept detection and faces recognition) and experimented with their combination with text-based retrieval using transcripts and subtitles. All of these methods achieved improvement on the training data, comparing with text-based retrieval. Most promising methods which use Feature Signatures and detected concepts were also used in MediaEval and TRECVid benchmark experiments in which we confirmed that appropriate visual information improves results achieved using text-based retrieval. Even though that the improvement achieved by Feature Signatures was not significant, it was constantly better than text-based retrieval.

ACKNOWLEDGMENTS

The authors would like to thank to Jakub Lokoč and Martin Kruliš from the SIRET Group, Department of Software Engineering at Charles University for providing data. This research is supported by the Czech Science Foundation, grant number P103/12/G084.

REFERENCES

[1] Robin Aly, Maria Eskevich, Roeland Ordelman, and Gareth J. F. Jones. 2013. Adapting Binary Information Retrieval Evaluation Metrics for Segment-based Retrieval Tasks. *CoRR* abs/1312.1913 (2013).
[2] Christian Beecks, Merih Seran Uysal, and Thomas Seidl. 2010. Signature Quadratic Form Distance. In *Proc. of CIVR.* Xi'an, China, 438–445.
[3] Chidansh A. Bhatt, Nikolaos Pappas, Maryam Habibi, and Andrei Popescu-Belis. 2014. Multimodal Reranking of Content-based Recommendations for Hyperlinking Video Snippets. In *Proc. of ICMR.* Glasgow, UK, 225–232.
[4] Adam Blažek, Jakub Lokoč, Filip Matzner, and Tomáš Skopal. 2015. Enhanced Signature-Based Video Browser. In *Proc. of MMM (Lecture Notes in Computer Science)*, Vol. 8936. Sydney, Australia, 243–248.
[5] Adam Blažek, Jakub Lokoč, and Tomáš Skopal. 2014. Video Retrieval with Feature Signature Sketches. In *Proc of SISAP (Lecture Notes in Computer Science)*, Vol. 8821. Los Cabos, Mexico, 25–36.
[6] Petra Budikova, Michal Batko, and Pavel Zezula. 2011. Evaluation Platform for Content-based Image Retrieval Systems. In *International Conference on Theory and Practice of Digital Libraries (TPDL 2011).* 130–142.
[7] Petra Budíková, Jan Botorek, Michal Batko, and Pavel Zezula. 2014. DISA at ImageCLEF 2014: The Search-based Solution for Scalable Image Annotation. In *Proc. of CLEF.* Sheffield, UK, 360–371.
[8] Ken Chatfield, Relja Arandjelović, Omkar Parkhi, and Andrew Zisserman. 2015. On-the-fly Learning for Visual Search of Large-scale Image and Video Datasets. *International Journal of Multimedia Information Retrieval* (2015), 1–19.
[9] Shu Chen, Keith Curtis, David N. Racca, Liting Zhou, Gareth J.F. Jones, and Noel E. O'Connor. 2015. DCU ADAPT @ TRECVid 2015: Video Hyperlinking Task. In *Proc. of TRECVID.* Gaithersburg, MD, USA.
[10] Shu Chen, Gareth J. F. Jones, and Noel E. O'Connor. 2013. DCU Linking Runs at MediaEval 2013: Search and Hyperlinking Task. In *Proc. of MediaEval.* Barcelona, Spain.

[11] Zhiyong Cheng, Xuanchong Li, Jialie Shen, and Alexander G. Hauptmann. 2015. CMU-SMU@TRECVID 2015: Video Hyperlinking. In *Proc. of TRECVID*. Gaithersburg, MD, USA.

[12] Claudiu Cobârzan, Klaus Schoeffmann, Werner Bailer, Wolfgang Hürst, Adam Blažek, Jakub Lokoč, Stefanos Vrochidis, Kai Uwe Barthel, and Luca Rossetto. 2017. Interactive Video Search Tools: A Detailed Analysis of the Video Browser Showdown 2015. *Multimedia Tools and Applications* 76, 4 (2017), 5539–5571.

[13] Anca-Roxana Şimon, Ronan Sicre, Rémi Bois, Guillaume Gravier, Pascale Sébillot, and Emmanuel Morin. 2015. IRISA at TrecVid2015: Leveraging Multimodal LDA for Video Hyperlinking. In *Proc. of TRECVID*. Gaithersburg, MD, USA.

[14] Maria Eskevich, David N. Racca Aly, Robin and, Roeland Ordelman, Shu Chen, and Jones Gareth J.F. 2014. Search and Hyperlinking 2014 Overview. (2014). http://www.slideshare.net/mariaeskevich/search-and-hyperlinking-me14sh-task-overviewmero

[15] Maria Eskevich, Robin Aly, David N. Racca, Roeland Ordelman, Shu Chen, and Gareth J.F. Jones. 2014. The Search and Hyperlinking Task at MediaEval 2014. In *Proc. of MediaEval*. Barcelona, Spain.

[16] Florian Eyben, Felix Weninger, Florian Gross, and Björn Schuller. 2013. Recent Developments in openSMILE, the Munich Open-source Multimedia Feature Extractor. In *Proc. of ACMMM*. Barcelona, Spain, 835–838.

[17] Petra Galuščáková, Martin Kruliš, Jakub Lokoč, and Pavel Pecina. 2014. CUNI at MediaEval 2014 Search and Hyperlinking Task: Visual and Prosodic Features in Hyperlinking. In *Proc. of MediaEval*. Barcelona, Spain.

[18] Petra Galuščáková and Pavel Pecina. 2015. Audio Information for Hyperlinking of TV Content. In *Proc. of SLAM*. Brisbane, Australia, 27–30.

[19] Petra Galuščáková, Michal Batko, Martin Kruliš, Jakub Lokoč, David Novák, and Pavel Pecina. 2015. CUNI at TRECVID 2015 Video Hyperlinking Task. In *Proc. of TRECVID*. Gaithersburg, MD, USA.

[20] Fernando García, Emilio Sanchis, Marcos Calvo, Ferran Pla, and Lluís-F. Hurtado. 2013. ELiRF at MediaEval 2013: Similar Segments in Social Speech Task. In *Proc. of MediaEval*. Barcelona, Spain.

[21] Djoerd Hiemstra. 2001. *Using Language Models for Information Retrieval*. Ph.D. Dissertation. University of Twente, Enschede, Netherlands.

[22] Alex Krizhevsky, Ilya Sutskever, and Geoffrey E. Hinton. 2012. ImageNet Classification with Deep Convolutional Neural Networks. In *Advances in Neural Information Processing Systems 25*. 1097–1105.

[23] Martin Kruliš, Tomáš Skopal, Jakub Lokoč, and Christian Beecks. 2012. Combining CPU and GPU Architectures for Fast Similarity Search. *Distributed and Parallel Databases* 30, 3-4 (2012), 179–207.

[24] Martin Kruliš, Jakub Lokoč, and Tomáš Skopal. 2016. Efficient Extraction of Clustering-based Feature Signatures Using GPU Architectures. *Multimedia Tools and Applications* 75, 13 (July 2016), 8071–8103.

[25] Neeraj Kumar, Alexander C. Berg, Peter N. Belhumeur, and Shree K. Nayar. 2009. Attribute and Simile Classifiers for Face Verification. In *Proc. of ICCV*. Kyoto, Japan, 365–372.

[26] Lori Lamel and Jean-Luc Gauvain. 2008. Speech Processing for Audio Indexing. In *Proc. of GoTAL 2008, Advances in NLP*. Gothenburg, Sweden, 4–15.

[27] P. Lanchantin, P.-J. Bell, M.-J.-F. Gales, T. Hain, X. Liu, Y. Long, J. Quinnell, S. Renals, O. Saz, M.-S. Seigel, P Swietojanski, and P.-C. Woodland. 2013. Automatic Transcription of Multi-genre Media Archives. In *Proc. of SLAM Workshop*. Marseille, France, 26–31.

[28] H.A. Le, B. Huet Q.M. Bui and, B. Červenková, J. Bouchner, E. Apostolidis, F. Markatopoulou, A. Pournaras, V. Mezaris, D. Stein, S. Eickeler, and M. Stadtschnitzer. 2014. LinkedTV at MediaEval 2014 Search and Hyperlinking Task. In *Proc. of MediaEval*. Barcelona, Spain.

[29] Gina-Anne Levow. 2013. UWCL at MediaEval 2013: Similar Segments in Social Speech Task. In *Proc. of MediaEval*. Barcelona, Spain.

[30] Michał Lokaj, Harald Stiegler, and Werner Bailer. 2013. TOSCA-MP at Search and Hyperlinking of Television Content Task. In *Proc. of MediaEval*. Barcelona, Spain.

[31] Merriam-Webster Online. 2009. Merriam-Webster Online Dictionary. (2009). http://www.merriam-webster.com

[32] Tomas Mikolov, Scott Wen tau Yih, and Geoffrey Zweig. 2013. Linguistic Regularities in Continuous Space Word Representations. In *Proc. of HLT NAACL*. Atlanta, GA, USA.

[33] Usman Niaz, Bernard Merialdo, Claudiu Tanase, Maria Eskevich, and Benoit Huet. 2015. EURECOM at TrecVid 2015: Semantic Indexing and Video Hyperlinking Tasks. In *Proc. of TRECVID 2015*. Gaithersburg, MD, USA.

[34] Tom De Nies, Wesley De Neve, Erik Mannens, and Rik Van de Walle. 2013. Ghent University-iMinds at MediaEval 2013: An Unsupervised Named Entity-based Similarity Measure for Search and Hyperlinking. In *Proc. of MediaEval*. Barcelona, Spain.

[35] David Novák, Michal Batko, and Pavel Zezula. 2015. Large-scale Image Retrieval using Neural Net Descriptors. In *Proc. of SIGIR '15*. Santiago, Chile.

[36] Roeland Ordelman, Maria Eskevich, Robin Aly, Benoit Huet, and Gareth J. F. Jones. 2015. Defining and Evaluating Video Hyperlinking for Navigating Multimedia Archives. In *Proc. of WWW (Companion Volume)*. Florence, Italy, 727–732.

[37] I. Ounis, G. Amati, V. Plachouras, B. He, C. Macdonald, and C. Lioma. 2006. Terrier: A High Performance and Scalable Information Retrieval Platform. In *Proc. of SIGIR Workshop on Open Source Information Retrieval*. Seattle, WA, USA, 18–25.

[38] Paul Over, George Awad, Martial Michel, Jonathan Fiscus, Wessel Kraaij, Alan F. Smeaton, Georges Quéenot, and Roeland Ordelman. 2015. TRECVID 2015 – An Overview of the Goals, Tasks, Data, Evaluation Mechanisms and Metrics. In *Proc. of TRECVID*. Gaithersburg, MD, USA.

[39] Lei Pang and Chong-Wah Ngo. 2015. VIREO @ TRECVID 2015: Video Hyperlinking (LNK). In *Proc. of TRECVID 2015*. Gaithersburg, MD, USA.

[40] Omkar M. Parkhi, Andrea Vedaldi, and Andrew Zisserman. 2015. Deep Face Recognition. In *Proc. of BMVC*. Swansea, UK, 41.1–41.12.

[41] Zsombor Paróczi, Bálint Fodor, and Gábor Szücs. 2014. DCLab at MediaEval2014 Search and Hyperlinking Task. In *Proc. of MediaEval*. Barcelona, Spain.

[42] John Preston, Jonathon Hare, Sina Samangooei, Jamie Davies, Neha Jain, and David Dupplaw. 2013. A Unified, Modular and Multimodal Approach to Search and Hyperlinking Video. In *Proc. of MediaEval*. Barcelona, Spain.

[43] A. Rousseau, P. Deléglise, and Y. Estève. 2014. Enhancing the TED-LIUM Corpus with Selected Data for Language Modeling And More TED Talks. In *Proc. of LREC*. Reykjavik, Iceland, 3935–3939.

[44] Yossi Rubner and Carlo Tomasi. 2001. *Perceptual Metrics for Image Database Navigation*. Springer Science & Business Media, Norwell, MA, USA.

[45] Mathilde Sahuguet, Benoit Huet, Barbora Červenková, Evlampios Apostolidis, Vasileios Mezaris, Daniel Stein, Stefan Eickeler, José, Luis Redondo Garcia, Raphaël Troncy, and Lukáš Pikora. 2013. LinkedTV at MediaEval 2013 Search and Hyperlinking Task. In *Proc. of MediaEval*. Barcelona, Spain.

[46] T. Tommasi, R. Aly, K. McGuinness, K. Chatfield, R. Arandjelovic, O. Parkhi, R. J. F. Ordelman, A. Zisserman, and T. Tuytelaars. 2014. Beyond Metadata: Searching Your Archive Based on Its Audio-visual Content. In *Proc. of IBC*. Amsterdam, Netherlands.

[47] Steven D. Werner and Nigel G. Ward. 2013. Evaluating Prosody-Based Similarity Models for Information Retrieval. In *Proc. of MediaEval*. Barcelona, Spain.

[48] Frank Wilcoxon. 1945. Individual Comparisons by Ranking Methods. *Biometrics Bulletin* 1, 6 (1945), 80–83.

[49] Bin Xu, Weihang Liao, Zizheng Liu, Wentao Bao, Yiming Li, Daiqin Yang, Sihan Wang, Hongyi Liu, Yatong Xia, Yingbin Wang, and Zhenzheng Chen. 2015. IIPWHU@TRECVID 2015. In *Proc. of TRECVID*. Gaithersburg, MD, USA.

Linking Multimedia Content for Efficient News Browsing

Rémi Bois
CNRS, IRISA & INRIA Rennes
263 Avenue Général Leclerc
Rennes, France 35042
remi.bois@irisa.fr

Guillaume Gravier
CNRS, IRISA & INRIA Rennes
263 Avenue Général Leclerc
Rennes, France 35042
guillaume.gravier@irisa.fr

Éric Jamet
CRPCC, Université de Rennes 2
Place du recteur Henri Le Moal
Rennes, France 35043
eric.jamet@mshb.fr

Emmanuel Morin
LS2N, Université de Nantes
2 Chemin de la Houssinière
Nantes, France 44300
emmanuel.morin@univ-nantes.fr

Maxime Robert
CRPCC, Université de Rennes 2
Place du recteur Henri Le Moal
Rennes, France 35043
maxime.robert@univ-rennes2.fr

Pascale Sébillot
INSA, IRISA & INRIA Rennes
263 Avenue Général Leclerc
Rennes, France 35042
pascale.sebillot@irisa.fr

ABSTRACT

As the amount of news information available online grows, media professionals are in need of advanced tools to explore the information surrounding specific events before writing their own piece of news, e.g., adding context and insight. While many tools exist to extract information from large datasets, they do not offer an easy way to gain insight from a news collection by browsing, going from article to article and viewing unaltered original content. Such browsing tools require the creation of rich underlying structures such as graph representations. These representations can be further enhanced by typing links that connect nodes, in order to inform the user on the nature of their relation. In this article, we introduce an efficient way to generate links between news items in order to obtain an easily navigable graph, and enrich this graph by automatically typing created links. User evaluations are conducted on real world data in order to assess for the interest of both the graph representation and link typing in a press reviewing task, showing a significant improvement compared to classical search engines.

CCS CONCEPTS

• **Information systems → Nearest-neighbor search**; *Recommender systems*; • **Human-centered computing → *Hypertext / hypermedia***;

KEYWORDS

news graph; user evaluation; hyperlinking

ACM Reference format:
Rémi Bois, Guillaume Gravier, Éric Jamet, Emmanuel Morin, Maxime Robert, and Pascale Sébillot. 2017. Linking Multimedia Content for Efficient News Browsing. In *Proceedings of ICMR '17, Bucharest, Romania, June 06-09, 2017,* 7 pages.

ICMR '17, June 06-09, 2017, Bucharest, Romania

ACM ISBN 978-1-4503-4701-3/17/06...$15.00
https://doi.org/10.1145/3078971.3079023

1 INTRODUCTION

With content being massively made accessible grows the need to automatically extract information and organize multimedia collections so as to help users search and explore large amounts of content to gain knowledge and insight. Entity extraction and linking, along with topic and event detection, are now widely available to describe content and help search pieces of information. While these techniques are instrumental to content description and search, they are however not sufficient to user-friendly exploration and navigation of a collection to gain insight, e.g., to summarize or to synthesize information. In the absence of a precise search intent, exploration is much more adapted than search.

An efficient way to offer exploration capabilities is to make sense of the relation between pieces of content, with solutions ranging from topic detection, exhibiting relations existing between large sets of items, to hyperlinking, creating connections between individual items in the collection. A large spectrum exists between those two solutions, e.g., clustering, threads, ... But when collections grow, some of these approaches become unreliable. Clusters tend to multiply or become too large and threads lengthen to unmanageable sizes. Hyperlinking on the opposite can be controlled, offering only a small set of suggestions to continue the exploration of the collection. Nevertheless, when using hyperlinking, one can end up in closed loops, where only a small set of items are interconnected with no way to reach other parts of the collection.

In this article, we focus on language-based multimedia hyperlinking in the news domain, connecting elements from a multimedia collection with the goal of enabling easy exploration by analysts (journalists in our case). News data have been extensively studied, due to the relatively large accessibility and interest to both media professionals and general public, however mostly from the search angle. We rather focus on an exploration scenario without precise information need, where one typically has to get a comprehensive view on a topic or event in a limited amount of time. In this context, we consider hyperlinking and put forward the notion of *acceptable* graphs linking news pieces in such a way that users can easily find all relevant information on a topic by exploring the graph. The LIMAH project[1], in which this work finds its foundation, aims at creating such acceptable graphs.

[1] http://limah.irisa.fr/

Departing from standard approaches, e.g., $\mathcal{E}$-NN graphs, topic threading or event linking, we propose a novel nearest neighbor graph construction algorithm that creates hyperlinks in a reasonable number to avoid user overload and disorientation, yet ensuring relevance and serendipitous drift. Interestingly, the algorithm requires no threshold, making use of the intrinsic properties of the document representation space. We further propose a typology of links between pieces in the news domain along with rules for automatic link categorization. These two elements, graph construction and link categorization, result in an explorable organization of a large collection of news. The effectiveness of this organization, in particular that of link categorization, is assessed by means of user tests, where journalists were asked to write a synthesis on a particular topic in a limited amount of time.

2 NEWS BROWSING APPROACHES

In this section, we explore the approaches available to organize news collections and discuss how graph representations can help browsing news datasets.

2.1 Standard approaches

News collections structuring for search and exploration has been extensively studied and many solutions coexist, each with their pros and cons. One can distinguish between two main use-cases: the need to know "what has been happening in the last days/hours", and the need to know "how this relates to other news". The first one is typically targeting the general public who wants a quick tour of the main news, while the second one is usually more in line with professionals' needs.

Day to day news structuring answers the need of the general public to have an easy access to information. For this specific need, the clustering approach is most often used, in a Google News fashion. This approach consists in grouping together news articles that discuss the same specific event, and is manageable for small timeframes [16]. Most items in a cluster are very similar, and while some articles may bring more details or talk about a specific aspect of the topic at hand, it is assumed that users will most often read only one of the news pieces. Groups of clusters are sometimes arranged in topical categories to lower the information overload [12]. However, when considering more than a day worth of news, clustering leads to the creation of a large number of small sets of articles that are hard to comprehend.

Professionals such as journalists or press-attachés need a richer structuring of news data. To write their own piece of news or report, they try to gather as much information as possible, and need to go through most articles to unveil new details. The clustering approach described before can be reused for this task, and individual clusters can be organized as threads in order to ease intra-cluster navigation [10]. However, the same pitfalls appear when dealing with large timeframes, as the number of clusters to display becomes overwhelming [20]. Another approach consists in using timelines to represent the chronology of events [15, 21]. This allows to fuse clusters that deal with related events, e.g., the continuation of a story, thus reducing their number [1]. According to user studies, the temporal relation between news items is the most important to media professionals [8], allowing them to reveal the causes and consequences of some events. However, similarly to clustering, when considering large timeframes, it becomes hard to display the list of news stories that are available in the dataset.

Each one of these different ways of structuring news collections can be further enhanced by using multimedia analytics such as, e.g., automatically generated summaries, popularity measures, or links to external data [3].

2.2 Hyperlinking and graph representations

Hyperlinking of news pieces, i.e., creating links between two documents within a collection, allow users to directly go from one piece of news to another. By following links (that can be seen as user-independent recommendations), the user is able to navigate in an informed way, choosing his next step among a limited set of links that are related to the news item he is currently viewing [5]. When carefully crafted, those links can provide a highly navigable structure, as evidenced in a number of application domains [18], including news [13].

Structures created by the hyperlinking process can be seen as graphs, in which nodes correspond to documents, and edges are links between document pairs. More formally, a graph G is defined as a set of nodes V and a set of edges E such that $\forall e \in E, e = (v_i, v_j), v_i, v_j \in V^2$. The notion of navigability translates in this case into a set of characteristics for the graph, such as an easy access to most elements of the collection, combined with a limited set of suggestions for each item [18]. Navigable graphs allow for interesting applications, such as connecting the dots between two arbitrary pieces of information [19]. In the absence of pre-defined segments acting as the source of the links—the so-called anchors in [5]—, there are two main algorithms to create graphs that connect documents with hyperlinks: K nearest neighbors (K-NN) and $\mathcal{E}$ nearest neighbors ($\mathcal{E}$-NN) graphs. Both consist in creating links between related elements, called (nearest) neighbors, in a collection, relying on a content-based distance function that measures how similar two documents are. The neighbor selection criterion is either a fixed number of neighbors K for K-NN, or a distance threshold $\mathcal{E}$ for $\mathcal{E}$-NN.

In practice, finding the optimal threshold, K or $\mathcal{E}$, is difficult and requires some annotation to estimate the ratio of irrelevant links, a process that is often complex and subjective [7]. Moreover, graphs created with these methods exhibit some strong limitations in terms of navigability. K-NN graphs do not discriminate between news that are heavily discussed, and that could thus rightfully be linked to many other news pieces, and news that are reported by only a few medias, with few connections to other items. Using the same threshold K for the whole collection thus leads to links that are too few for some news items, or too numerous for others. The use of a distance threshold in $\mathcal{E}$-NN graphs skirts this issue by creating only relevant links. However, $\mathcal{E}$-NN graphs tend to create very large hubs [17], with a few nodes being connected to hundreds of others, causing navigation in such structures to be cumbersome. In experiments not reported in this paper, we also observed that combining a fixed number of neighbors and a distance threshold do not alleviate these issues.

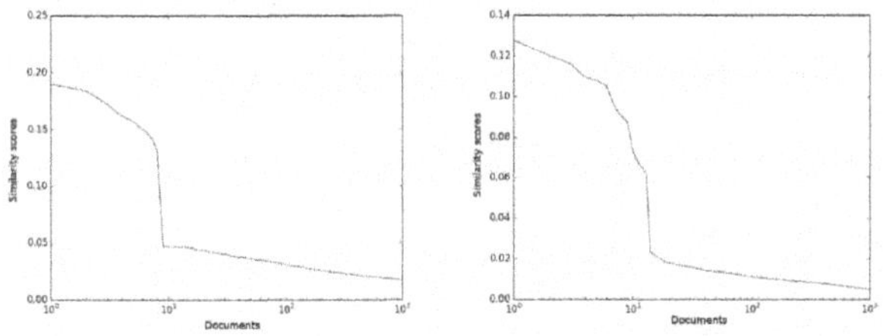

Figure 1: Illustration of similarity drops between close neighbors and far ones on two real-world examples.

Category	#nodes	nodes	degree	P (in %)	R (in %)
Science	16k	93 %	11	73.2	55.8
Business	15k	95.3 %	8	69.7	45.8
Health	14k	94.6 %	13	66.4	56.5
Entertain.	16k	96.5 %	17	74.3	59.2

Table 1: Number of nodes, amount of reachable nodes, median degree, precision and recall for adaptive nearest neighbors depending on the categories.

3 EXPLORABLE NEWS GRAPH

Nearest neighbors news graphs are attractive because of their practicality for navigation purposes but, as we just highlighted, current nearest neighbor graph construction algorithms fail at providing structures that are easily navigable by humans. In this section, we introduce an explorable news graph structure building on two key steps. First, the use of an adaptive nearest neighbors algorithm that creates news graphs with good explorability properties. Second, the automatic categorization of hyperlinks according to a typology adapted to the news domain.

3.1 Adaptive nearest neighbors

The main reason why $\mathcal{E}$-NN and K-NN graphs exhibit bad properties regarding navigability comes from the fact that they rely on a threshold that is the same for every item in the collection. This results in a difficult trade-off between the relevance of the hyperlinks and their number, with high fluctuations of the trade-off between items. We thus propose to adapt the threshold on a per node basis, automatically deciding on the appropriate number of near neighbors by detecting a large gap in the representation space between close neighbors and far ones. Such gaps are known to happen naturally in large collections such as social graphs [4] and are linked to the variations of the density of points in the representation space [11]. For an item i corresponding to node v_i, the gap corresponds to a drop in the similarity between item i and other items sorted in descending order of similarity. This is illustrated in Fig. 1 for two examples taken from a real-world dataset. Only items appearing before the gap are linked to item i.

Revealing those drops depends on two factors: a tailored representation space and an efficient drop detection algorithm. Preliminary experiments on embedded representations, e.g., averaged word2vec [14], revealed that such representations are good at ranking but tend to homogenize the representation space, situating most documents close one from another and thus flattening the similarity drop. We thus use a direct lexical similarity with tf-idf weighting for which large drops do exist and can be accurately detected based on a similarity ratio between consecutive documents after sorting documents in descending order of their similarity to a given node. For node v_i, drop detection is based on

$$\Delta_i(v_j, v_k) = 1 - \frac{\text{Sim}(v_i, v_k)}{\text{Sim}(v_i, v_j)}$$

where $\text{rank}_i(j) = \text{rank}_i(k) + 1$ in the list of documents sorted with respect to their similarities to item i of the collection. The adaptive nearest neighbors (ANN) approach can finally be written as

$$\text{ANN} = \left\{(v_i, v_j) \mid d(v_i, v_j) < d_i,\ \forall v_i, v_j \in V^2, v_i \neq v_j\right\}$$

with $d_i = d(v_i, argmax\,(\Delta_i(v_k, v_l))$, where the maximization is taken over all $v_k \in V$, $v_l \in V$ s.t. $\text{rank}_i(l) = \text{rank}_i(k) + 1$.

Table 1 reports the characteristics of ANN graphs computed over the News Aggregator dataset[2], which contains ~420k urls to news articles from a large number of publishers. This dataset comes from a five months monitoring of four Google News macro-categories—business, health, science and technology, and entertainment—within which articles on the same story form a cluster [6]. After retrieving all possible documents and filtering out clusters with less than 4 documents, we constructed ANN graphs over each category. For each category, we report the number of nodes, the ratio of nodes included in the largest component of the graph, the median number of links per node, as well as hyperlink recall and precision computed from the story cluster labels (a link is relevant if the two documents are within the same cluster). Note that the use of story-based cluster labels is only indicative of the overall objective of creating an easily navigable graph, where links between stories should appear to enable exploring the collection without searching for many entry points and to favor serendipitous drift. It is however encouraging to see that ANN graphs exhibit large precision values, indicating that few inter-cluster hyperlinks are created, however in sufficient number for most nodes to be part of a single connected component or, in other words, to enable a path between most pairs of nodes (>93 % overall). Results not reported within the scope of this paper show that ANN graphs offer much better trade-offs between precision and connectivity than K-NN and $\mathcal{E}$-NN graphs.

3.2 Link characterization

In spite of the limitation of the number of hyperlinks offered by the ANN approach, there still might be a significant number of hyperlinks per document. This calls for further organization of the collection to enhance navigation in the ANN graph and help users find their way by selecting appropriate hyperlinks to follow on. To this end, we propose to characterize links according to a typology arising from the needs in relation with large-scale news collection exploration.

News data depend a lot on chronology, which resulted in many approaches organizing collections as timelines so as to be able to follow the evolution of specific stories. The temporal relation is clearly the most important type of relations according to media professionals [8]. But it is insufficient alone, in particular when

[2] www.archive.ics.uci.edu/ml/datasets.html

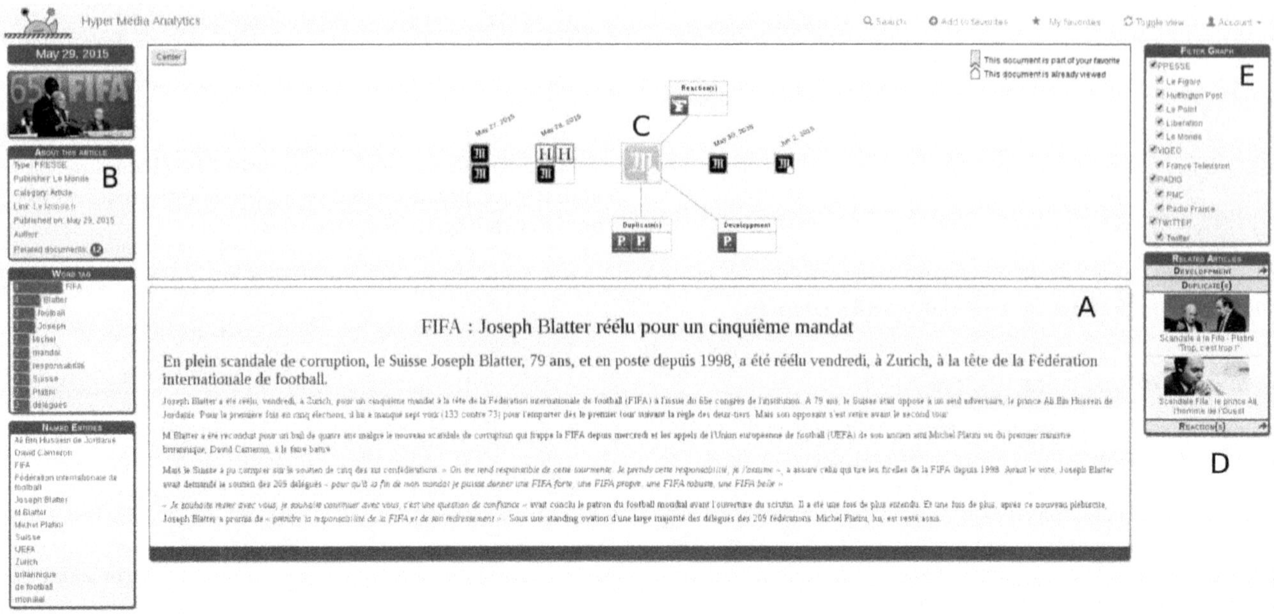

Figure 2: The LIMAH news exploration and analytics interface

exploring large news datasets that include articles with very similar content from different newswires that tends to clutter timelines. Extending temporal relations, we designed a typology consisting of 7 types of oriented links [2] defined as follows:

Near duplicate identifies a link between two nodes discussing the same event, where the target node provides little to no additional information compared to the source node.

Anterior/Posterior indicates a target node reporting on an event related to the source that occurred before (resp. after) the event of the source node.

Summary/Development corresponds to a link providing a subset (resp. superset) of information with respect to the source.

Reacts/In reaction to designates a reference (resp. followup) to another news piece in the collection.

These types of links are dual, e.g., a link with the *anterior* type between documents A and B necessarily coexists with an inverse link *posterior* between B and A. The anterior/posterior type, which is the most commonly found, allows to keep a sense of the chronology of news stories, and allows to decide whether one wants to know about past or future events. The near duplicate type allows a user to ignore some news pieces if he decides to, while still making them available. This is not only a way to discard articles, but also a way for professionals to decide which source of information they prefer when different newswires published similar information. A global filtering allowing only a few sources would not solve this issue as journalists reported that their preferred source changed according to the topic, e.g., changing source when going from the political aspects of a news story to its financial implications. The summary/development type serves a similar purpose and is a way to get the gist of an information, or on the opposite to further read about the very same event. Summaries often report short news from national press agencies and are only a few lines long. Developments are obviously longer and add context. They might correspond to editorials in which journalists comment the news in depth and often provide a variety of links to the various aspects of a story. Finally, the reaction links provide a specific type of followup, either by quoting a source, or by reporting the reaction of people of interest to a specific news piece, e.g., a politician answering an opponent's declaration. We chose to use this larger notion of reaction rather than to divide it into citation and response to avoid defining too many types whose semantics would be difficult to grasp.

Automatically categorizing links established within the ANN graph relies on a set of handcrafted rules. Near duplicates are detected first based on a cosine similarity over tf-idf weighted terms. Summaries and developments are then detected by comparing the length of document pairs. We finally assign the reaction type by detecting cue phrases such as "réagit" (reacted) or "répondu" (answered). Remaining links are considered as temporal relations and given the anterior/posterior type depending on publication dates.

4 EXPERIMENTS

Adaptive nearest neighbors news graphs with typed links offer significant explorability features whose benefit we evaluated by means of user studies, comparing search-only approaches and ANN graphs with and without link categorization on an information gathering task. We first describe the dataset and interface before discussing experiments and results.

4.1 Dataset and interface

Documents were extracted over a 3 week period (May 20–Jun 8, 2015) from a number of French newswire websites and include press articles (e.g. Le Monde, Libération, Le Figaro), videos (e.g. daily news from France 2, political news), and radio podcasts (e.g. news programs from France Inter, political interviews from RMC). Some of the topics discussed during the time the corpus was gathered had worldwide repercussions, such as the FIFA scandal or Lybian refugees crossing the Mediterranean sea. Others were dealing with French politics with the renaming of one of the main French political parties, or with local news. Podcasts and videos underwent speech transcription so as to enable indexing and segmentation. To deal with possibly long audio or video recordings, topic segmentation based on automatic transcripts [9] was used, each segment being treated as a document per se. In total, the resulting collection contains 4,966 news articles, 1,556 radio segments and 290 video segments.

We ran hyperlinking on the whole collection with adaptive nearest neighbor graphs and link categorization, creating 17,468 links in total: 10,980 temporal, 3,878 quasi-duplicates, 725 reactions, and 575 summaries/developments. Most links unsurprisingly depict temporal relations, leading us to primarily adopt a linear chronological view of the temporal relations related to a source document. Other types of relations appear either above or under the timeline, as illustrated in Fig. 2. Note that using a linear chronological view is only possible because adaptive nearest neighbors strongly limits the number of hyperlinks departing from the source. Furthermore, link categorization enables removing from the timeline links of a different nature, facilitating visualization and comprehension.

The starting point of the end-user interface, called LIMAH for Linking Media in Acceptable Hypergraphs, is a full-fledged search bar using keywords. Search classically returns a list of documents ranked by relevance, from which the user can choose an entry point for navigation. To facilitate the choice of a good entry point, in addition to a thumbnail of each relevant document, we display the number of links departing from each document, assuming that a document with a significant number of connections is deemed to be a better starting point for exploration than one with very few. Selecting an entry point brings the user to the content visualization and navigation part of the interface, illustrated in Fig. 2. In this view, the user can initially see the entry point document itself (A) and the links that departs from it. In addition to the original content, metadata and keywords are displayed (B), as both were judged crucial in the preliminary usefulness studies [8]. Links appear in one of two ways. The graph view (C) quickly shows how related documents appear on a navigable timeline, facilitating the comprehension of the development of a story. Users can navigate the timeline: a mouse-over on a node highlights the keywords in common with the entry point document; a click on a node enables viewing the content in zones A and C. Note that contrary to what is usually done in graph-based navigation interfaces, the entry point does not change while navigating and the graph displayed remains the graph depicting the documents related to the current entry point (indicated as a square on the graph). This avoids user disorientation, as it is difficult for users to apprehend the underlying graph structure if the subgraph displayed changes at every click. To enable further exploration, a double click on a node defines the node as the new entry point and changes the graph and recommendations displayed. For convenience, on the right side (D), hyperlinks are also provided as a list of recommendations organized by link types, omitting chronological links (i.e., anterior and posterior developments of the story) that only appear on the timeline. This recommendation view follows a standard web setting and is deemed as easier to apprehend than the graph view, though not as rich. At any time, filters listed in the top right section (E) allow selecting specific sources and a new entry point can be found from the search bar.

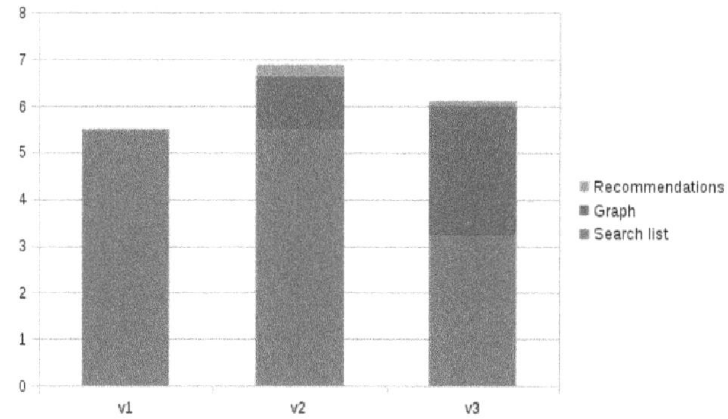

Figure 3: Number and origin of the articles viewed for the 3 versions of the LIMAH interface.

4.2 Experimental protocol

In order to evaluate the interest of the graph structure and link typing, we compare three versions of the LIMAH interface. Version 1 only provides the search engine, allowing for comparison with today's usage and with a technology that users are very familiar with. In this case, areas C, D, and E in Fig. 2 are hidden. Version 2 adds the recommendation and graph structure but converts all link types to either anterior or posterior, organizing data in a linear fashion. Recommendations in zone D are thus uncategorized and every link in zone C is shown on a timeline. Version 3 corresponds to the whole LIMAH interface, as presented before.

The study involved 25 journalism students in their 3rd, 4th, and 5th year of studies, split in three test pools: 8 users for versions 1 and 2 of the interface, and 9 of them for version 3. The user test involved a pre questionnaire, an information gathering task, a post questionnaire, and a final open discussion in which users could provide feedback on their use of the tool. Users were shown a short video explaining how to use the interface, and received no additional support during tests.

The information gathering task consisted in writing a synthesis about a particular subject in a limited amount of time, using the LIMAH interface to find as much relevant information on the topic as possible. The topic chosen was Solar Impulse 2, a solar-powered aircraft that circumnavigated the globe from March 2015 to July 2016. Bad weather conditions necessitating the plane to land and consequences of this unexpected halt are reported in 17 articles in the dataset, representing a total of 68 distinct information pieces over a long timespan. As the dataset comes from a large set of newswires, some pieces of information are repeated, while others are mentioned by only one or two sources. Users had to complete this task in 20 minutes, a time long enough to fully read a few articles, but short enough to forbid reading totally most of them.

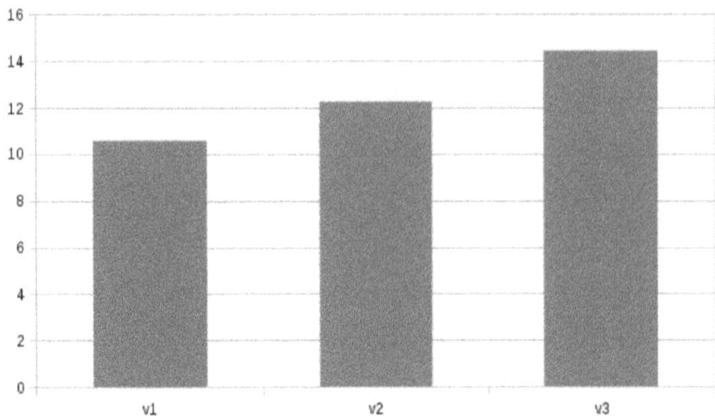

Figure 4: Knowledge extracted from the dataset depending on the version of the LIMAH interface.

4.3 Results

Fig. 3 first shows the average number of articles viewed by each user pool, as computed from the navigation logs, along with what feature of the interface was used to select an article (search, graph or recommendation). Clearly, the graph representation available in versions 2 and 3 allowed for more documents to be viewed when preparing the synthesis. Interestingly, comparing the number of articles viewed by users of versions 2 and 3 shows that typing links encouraged the use of the graph representation. For version 3, users clearly preferred navigating using the graph representation rather than the recommendation list, demonstrating the interest of this mean of visualization with a controlled-size neighborhood.

Apart from the number of articles considered for the synthesis, a measure of its exhaustiveness is also reported in Fig. 4. Exhaustiveness was measured by coding each synthesis according to the proportion of the 68 information pieces contained in the synthesis. Results clearly show that users of version 3 gathered significantly more information pieces than their counterparts, even though they viewed less documents than users of version 2. A detailed analysis of the information gathered by users revealed that versions 2 and 3 lead them to find a greater number of rare pieces of information that were available in less than 4 news items, as well as a greater number of important information, than with version 1, the difference being larger for version 3.

During the open discussion following the tests, users from version 3 were mostly positive about their experience with the tool, calling it "useful", with a "good accessibility", and an "interesting take on recommendation". A few users mentioned a difficulty to handle the back and forth between the graph representation and the search interface. They also had trouble drawing the line between articles relevant to the topic and articles that were not.

5 CONCLUSION

Appropriate graph representations of news articles can help professionals gather information more efficiently, as evidenced by the study presented in this paper. In particular, we experimentally demonstrated that categorizing automatically hyperlinks established between articles further improves the amount and quality of the information retrieved while exploring to gain insight on a particular topic. We also proposed an adaptive nearest neighbors algorithm that was shown to offer a better trade-off between relevance of the links and their number than standard nearest neighbors graph construction algorithms. The latter were found inadequate for navigation in preliminary studies not reported in the paper. The typology of links in the news domain is finally another contribution. While users did not comment the number of categories that were offered in the LIMAH interface, probably indicating that 7 link types was not an overwhelming amount, further studies on the ideal number of types would be of interest, in order to either increase this count, further refining the choices offered to users, or decrease this count, helping to alleviate the information overload. Automatic link categorization, currently based on handcrafted decision trees, was found accurate but could most likely be improved by either enriching the set of rules or using learning algorithms. Finally, the LIMAH interface could be improved by enriching the keywords and named entities currently extracted from each article. Users declared that linking those entities to external resources, such as the institutions' open data, would allow them to verify the relayed information. Interestingly, this can be seen as extending the graph to include links to data and knowledge sources rather than limiting hyperlinks to articles.

6 ACKNOWLEDGMENTS

This work was funded by the CominLabs excellence laboratory, and financed by the National Research Agency under reference ANR-10-LABX-07-01. We are immensely grateful to Arnaud Touboulic for his key contribution in the design and implementation of the LIMAH interface.

REFERENCES

[1] Amr Ahmed, Qirong Ho, Jacob Eisenstein, Eric Xing, Alexander J Smola, and Choon Hui Teo. 2011. Unified analysis of streaming news. In *20th International Conference on World Wide Web.* 267–276.

[2] Rémi Bois, Guillaume Gravier, Pascale Sébillot, and Emmanuel Morin. 2015. Vers une typologie de liens entre contenus journalistiques. In *22e Conférence Traitement Automatique des Langues Naturelles.* 515–521.

[3] Morgan Bréhinier, Sébastien Campion, and Guillaume Gravier. 2012. Texmix: An automatically generated news navigation portal. In *International Conference on Multimedia Retrieval.*

[4] Maximilien Danisch, Jean-Loup Guillaume, and Bénédicte Le Grand. 2013. Towards multi-ego-centred communities: A node similarity approach. *International Journal of Web Based Communities* 9, 3 (2013), 299–322.

[5] Maria Eskevich, Gareth J.F. Jones, Shu Chen, Robin Aly, Roeland Ordelman, Danish Nadeem, Camille Guinaudeau, Guillaume Gravier, Pascale Sébillot, Tom De Nies, Pedro Debevere, Rik Van de Walle, Petra GalušcĂąkovĂą, Pavel Pecina, and Martha Larson. 2013. Multimedia information seeking through search and hyperlinking. In *ACM International Conference on Multimedia Retrieval.* 287–294.

[6] Fabio Gasparetti. 2016. Modeling user interests from web browsing activities. *Data Mining and Knowledge Discovery* (2016), 1–46.

[7] Mouzhi Ge, Carla Delgado-Battenfeld, and Dietmar Jannach. 2010. Beyond accuracy: evaluating recommender systems by coverage and serendipity. In *4th Conference on Recommender Systems.* 257–260.

[8] Guillaume Gravier, Martin Ragot, Laurent Amsaleg, Rémi Bois, Grégoire Jadi, Éric Jamet, Laura Monceaux, and Pascale Sébillot. 2016. Shaping-up multimedia analytics: Needs and expectations of media professionals. In *22nd MMM Conference, Perspectives on Multimedia Analytics.* 303–314.

[9] Camille Guinaudeau, Guillaume Gravier, and Pascale Sébillot. 2012. Enhancing lexical cohesion measure with confidence measures, semantic relations and language model interpolation for multimedia spoken content topic segmentation. *Computer Speech and Language* 26, 2 (2012), 90–104.

[10] Ichiro Ide, Hiroshi Mo, Norio Katayama, and ShinâĂŹichi Satoh. 2004. Topic threading for structuring a large-scale news video archive. In *International Conference on Image and Video Retrieval.* 123–131.

[11] Hans-Peter Kriegel, Peer Kröger, Jörg Sander, and Arthur Zimek. 2011. Density-based clustering. *Wiley Interdisciplinary Reviews: Data Mining and Knowledge*

Discovery 1, 3 (2011), 231–240.

[12] G. Krishnalal, S. Babu Rengarajan, and K.G. Srinivasagan. 2010. A new text mining approach based on HMM-SVM for web news classification. *International Journal of Computer Applications* 1, 19 (2010), 98–104.

[13] Hyowon Lee, Alan F. Smeaton, Colin O'Toole, Noel Murphy, Seán Marlow, and Noel E. O'Connor. 2000. The Físchlár digital video recording, analysis, and browsing system. In *International Conference on Content-based Multimedia Information Access.* 1390–1399.

[14] Tomas Mikolov, Ilya Sutskever, Kai Chen, Greg S. Corrado, and Jeff Dean. 2013. Distributed representations of words and phrases and their compositionality. In *Advances in Neural Information Processing Systems.* 3111–3119.

[15] Philippe Muller and Xavier Tannier. 2004. Annotating and measuring temporal relations in texts. In *20th International Conference on Computational Linguistics.* 50–56.

[16] Dragomir R Radev, Sasha Blair-Goldensohn, Zhu Zhang, and Revathi Sundara Raghavan. 2001. Newsinessence: A system for domain-independent, real-time news clustering and multi-document summarization. In *1st International Conference on Human Language Technology Research.* 1–4.

[17] Miloš Radovanović, Alexandros Nanopoulos, and Mirjana Ivanović. 2010. Hubs in space: Popular nearest neighbors in high-dimensional data. *Journal of Machine Learning Research* 11, Sep (2010), 2487–2531.

[18] Klaus Seyerlehner, Peter Knees, Dominik Schnitzer, and Gerhard Widmer. 2009. Browsing music recommendation networks. In *10th International Society for Music Information Retrieval Conf.* 129–134.

[19] Dafna Shahaf and Carlos Guestrin. 2010. Connecting the dots between news articles. In *16th ACM SIGKDD International Conference on Knowledge Discovery and Data Mining.* 623–632.

[20] Amanda Sturgill, Ryan Pierce, and Yiliu Wang. 2010. Online news websites: How much content do young adults want. *Journal of Magazine & New Media Research* 11, 2 (2010), 1–18.

[21] Russell Swan and James Allan. 2000. Automatic generation of overview timelines. In *23rd Annual International ACM SIGIR Conference on Research and Development in Information Retrieval.* 49–56.

Multi-view Manifold Learning for Media Interestingness Prediction

Yang Liu
[1]Department of Computer Science
Hong Kong Baptist University
Hong Kong SAR, China
[2]IRACE, HKBU, Shenzhen, China
csygliu@comp.hkbu.edu.hk

Zhonglei Gu
Department of Computer Science
Hong Kong Baptist University
Hong Kong SAR, China
crossgate9@gmail.com

Yiu-ming Cheung
[1]Department of Computer Science
Hong Kong Baptist University
Hong Kong SAR, China
[2]IRACE, HKBU, Shenzhen, China
ymc@comp.hkbu.edu.hk

Kien A. Hua
Department of Computer Science
University of Central Florida
Orlando, Florida, USA
kienhua@cs.ucf.edu

ABSTRACT

Media interestingness prediction plays an important role in many real-world applications and attracts much research attention recently. In this paper, we aim to investigate this problem from the perspective of supervised feature extraction. Specifically, we design a novel algorithm dubbed Multi-view Manifold Learning (M^2L) to uncover the latent factors that are capable of distinguishing interesting media data from non-interesting ones. By modelling both geometry preserving criterion and discrimination maximization criterion in a unified framework, M^2L learns a common subspace for data from multiple views. The analytical solution of M^2L is obtained by solving a generalized eigen-decomposition problem. Experiments on the Predicting Media Interestingness Dataset validate the effectiveness of the proposed method.

KEYWORDS

Media interestingness analysis; multi-view manifold learning

ACM Reference format:
Yang Liu, Zhonglei Gu, Yiu-ming Cheung, and Kien A. Hua. 2017. Multi-view Manifold Learning for Media Interestingness Prediction. In *Proceedings of ICMR '17, June 6–9, 2017, Bucharest, Romania,* , 7 pages.
DOI: http://dx.doi.org/10.1145/3078971.3079021

ICMR '17, June 6–9, 2017, Bucharest, Romania
 ACM ISBN 978-1-4503-4701-3/17/06...$15.00
DOI: http://dx.doi.org/10.1145/3078971.3079021

1 INTRODUCTION

Media interestingness analysis, which aims to automatically analyze media data and identify the content which is considered to be interesting for the users, plays an important role in many real-world applications such as image/video retrieval, summarization, and recommendation [3, 11, 16, 19, 39, 46].

With the rapid development of computing resources, computational explorations on media interestingness analysis have received much attention recently. So far, the investigations have primarily focused on images and videos, for the vast amount of rich information these two types of media could provide. Dhar et al. utilized high-level image features, i.e., compositional attributes, content attributes, and sky-illumination attributes, to predict the interestingness of Flickr photos [9]. Gygli et al. presented a computational model that predicts the interestingness of images by measuring three important cues: unusualness, aesthetics, and general preferences [13]. Grabner et al. generated four different cues, i.e., emotion, complexity, novelty, and learning, from the low-level features, and constructed the interestingness predictor based on the combination of these cues [12]. Liu et al. introduced a method to measure the frame interestingness of a travel video by comparing the SIFT features of the frame with those of the web photos [23]. Jiang et al. conducted a pilot study to understand the human perception on video interestingness, and used a computational model to predict the interestingness of videos [16]. Soleymani validated that the intrinsic pleasantness, arousal, visual quality, and coping potential are important factors contributing to visual interest in digital photos and developed a system to detect these attributes from low-level features [39]. In a recently organized *Predicting Media Interestingness Task* [8], various computational models have been utilized to predict the interestingness of given images and videos [6, 22, 35, 37, 41, 44].

Although tremendous strides forward have already been made in analyzing and predicting media interestingness, most of the computational models still utilize manually selected or pre-defined features, which are somewhat subjective and might lose important structural and discriminant information. In order to automatically learn the useful and informative features for media interestingness prediction, we formulate the task as a supervised feature extraction problem and propose to utilize manifold learning to solve it, since the distributions of many kinds of media data, such as images and videos, match the manifold assumption very well [32, 34], which makes manifold learning being an appropriate tool for media data analysis. Moreover, the media data can often be characterized by features from multiple views [10, 18]. For instance, images or video frames could be taken from different angles or described by various kinds of visual features such as HoG, SIFT, GIST, etc. In order to explore multi-view media data under the manifold learning framework, we propose a novel algorithm dubbed Multi-view Manifold Learning (M^2L) to uncover the latent factors that distinguish interesting media data from non-interesting ones. The proposed method aims to preserve both the geometric structure and the interestingness information of the original dataset by mapping the multi-view data to a common subspace, in which the cross-view correlation is taken into consideration.

The rest of the paper is organized as follows. In Section 2, we briefly review some representative works on manifold learning for multimedia data analysis and multi-view dimensionality reduction. The details of the proposed method, M^2L, is presented in Section 3. In Section 4, we evaluate the performance of M^2L on the Predicting Media Interestingness Dataset [8]. The paper is concluded in Section 5.

2 RELATED WORKS

2.1 Manifold Learning for Multimedia Data Analysis

Manifold learning, which uncovers the intrinsic structure of data based on the assumption that the original observations lie on or close to the low-dimensional nonlinear manifold, has received much attention in the past two decades. The most representative manifold learning algorithms include isometric feature mapping (Isomap) [40], locally linear embedding (LLE) [36], and Laplacian eigenmaps (LE) [2]. Isomap is a global method, which aims to preserve the geometry at all scales by mapping the nearby data points on the manifold to nearby points in the low-dimensional space and the faraway points to faraway points. In contrast with Isomap, LLE and LE are local methods, which assume that the global structure can be uncovered by keeping all the local structures of the dataset, and thus only attempt to preserve the local geometry.

As the manifold assumption matches the distribution of multimedia data very well, manifold learning has played an important role in various applications of multimedia data analysis. Pless explored the video representation via Isomap [32]. Rahimi et al. investigated the appearance manifolds from video by exploiting the temporal coherence between frames and supervision from a user [34]. Yang et al. learned the hierarchical manifolds for multimedia document semantics understanding and cross-media retrieval [45]. Almeida et al. addressed the problem of video genre retrieval via reciprocal kNN graph based manifold learning [1, 31]. Shnitzer et al. applied a manifold learning technique, diffusion maps [5], to music analysis applications [38]. In our previous work, we proposed the hybrid manifold embedding for image classification [25]. Recently, we utilized supervised manifold regression to learn the compact representations of image/video data for media interestingness prediction [24].

2.2 Multi-view Dimensionality Reduction

Multi-view dimensionality reduction aims to find a common subspace for multiple views, where the cross-view correlation is preserved. The most classical method for multi-view dimensionality reduction is canonical correlation analysis (CCA), which aims to find the subspace where the correlations of data from two different views are maximized [15]. In [28], CCA was extended for multi-view scenarios. Luo et al. further proposed the tensor CCA for multi-view dimensionality reduction [27]. Zhang et al. presented a multi-view dimensionality co-reduction to explore the correlations within each view and maximize the dependence among different views [47].

Following the success of unsupervised multi-view dimensionality reduction, semi-supervised and supervised dimensionality reduction has been generalized for multi-view learning as well. Qian et al. introduced a semi-supervised multi-label multi-view dimensionality reduction framework based on reconstruction error minimization [33]. Wang et al. proposed a deep learning based multi-view dimensionality reduction scheme [42]. Kan et al. extended the classical linear discriminant analysis to the multi-view version [18].

Besides above general-purpose multi-view dimensionality reduction models, some methods have been presented for more specific applications in media data analysis. Li et al. studied the cross-view similarity search problem by mapping multiple views into a common Hamming space [21]. Farfade et al. modelled the problem of multi-view face detection using deep convolutional neural networks [10]. Jing et al. addressed the problem of web page classification using a semi-supervised intra-view and inter-view dimensionality reduction algorithm [17]. Zhu et al. proposed a block-row sparse multi-view multi-label learning method for image classification [48].

3 MULTI-VIEW MANIFOLD LEARNING

3.1 Problem Formulation

Let $\mathcal{X}$ be the set of data samples from V views: $\mathcal{X} = \{(\mathbf{x}_{11}, \mathbf{x}_{12}, ..., \mathbf{x}_{1V}), (\mathbf{x}_{21}, \mathbf{x}_{22}, ..., \mathbf{x}_{2V}), ..., (\mathbf{x}_{n1}, \mathbf{x}_{n2}, ..., \mathbf{x}_{nV})\}$, where $\mathbf{x}_{iv} \in \mathbb{R}^{D_v}$ $(i = 1, ..., n,\ v = 1, ..., V)$ denotes the i-th sample from the v-th view, n denotes the number of data samples in the set, V denotes the number of views, and D_v denotes the original dimension of the v-th view. To represent the data from different views, we define V data matrices: $\mathbf{X}_1 = [\mathbf{x}_{11}, \mathbf{x}_{21}, ..., \mathbf{x}_{n1}]$, $\mathbf{X}_2 = [\mathbf{x}_{12}, \mathbf{x}_{22}, ..., \mathbf{x}_{n2}]$, ..., and $\mathbf{X}_V = [\mathbf{x}_{1V}, \mathbf{x}_{2V}, ..., \mathbf{x}_{nV}]$. Meanwhile, we have the corresponding label of each of the n data samples:

$\mathbf{l} = [l_1, l_2, ..., l_n]$, where $l_i \in [0,1]$ is a real number denoting the corresponding label of the i-th data sample, 1 for extremely interesting and 0 for extremely non-interesting.

Given the above training set, Multi-view Manifold Learning (M^2L) aims to learn V transformation matrices $\mathbf{W}_v \in \mathbb{R}^{D_v \times d}$ ($d \ll D_v, v = 1, ..., V$), which are capable of projecting the original high-dimensional data from different views to a common subspace $\mathcal{Z} = \mathbb{R}^d$, where the manifold structure of the dataset could be well preserved, and the discriminant information could be maximized.

3.2 Geometry Preserving Criteria

In order to preserve the geometric structure of the dataset, we take both locality and globality into consideration. To describe the local structure for each view, we define a neighborhood graph matrix $\mathbf{N}^v$ for the v-th view ($v = 1, ..., V$). The element on the i-th row and the j-th column of $\mathbf{N}^v$ is given as follows:

$$N_{ij}^v = e^{-\frac{||\mathbf{x}_{iv} - \mathbf{x}_{jv}||^2}{2\sigma}}, \tag{1}$$

where the bandwidth σ is empirically set by $\sigma = \sum_{i=1}^{n} ||\mathbf{x}_{iv} - \mathbf{x}_{iv_K}||^2/n$ with $\mathbf{x}_{iv_K}$ being the K-th nearest neighbor of $\mathbf{x}_{iv}$. Accordingly, we construct the locality scatter matrix $\mathbf{S}_{lv}$ for the v-th view:

$$\mathbf{S}_{lv} = \sum_{i=1}^{n}\sum_{j=1}^{n} N_{ij}^v (\mathbf{x}_{iv} - \mathbf{x}_{jv})(\mathbf{x}_{iv} - \mathbf{x}_{jv})^T. \tag{2}$$

We then introduce the objective:

$$\{\mathbf{W}_1, ..., \mathbf{W}_V\} = \underset{\mathbf{W}_1,...,\mathbf{W}_V}{\arg\min}\ tr\Big(\sum_{v=1}^{V} \mathbf{W}_v^T \mathbf{S}_{lv} \mathbf{W}_v\Big), \tag{3}$$

where $tr(\cdot)$ denotes the trace operation. By minimizing the objective function in Eq. (3), the nearby data points in the original space of each view will also be close to each other in the common subspace, and thus the local structure is expected to be well captured.

To represent the global structure of each view, we construct the globality scatter matrix $\mathbf{S}_{gv}$:

$$\mathbf{S}_{gv} = \sum_{i=1}^{n}\sum_{j=1}^{n} (1 - N_{ij}^v)(\mathbf{x}_{iv} - \mathbf{x}_{jv})(\mathbf{x}_{iv} - \mathbf{x}_{jv})^T. \tag{4}$$

It is obvious that the larger the distance between $\mathbf{x}_{iv}$ and $\mathbf{x}_{jv}$, the smaller the N_{ij}^v, hence, the larger the $(1 - N_{ij}^v)$. This fact indicates that $\mathbf{S}_{gv}$ pays more attention to the relationship between faraway data points, which characterizes the structure of the v-th view from the global perspective. We then introduce the following objective:

$$\{\mathbf{W}_1, ..., \mathbf{W}_V\} = \underset{\mathbf{W}_1,...,\mathbf{W}_V}{\arg\max}\ tr\Big(\sum_{v=1}^{V} \mathbf{W}_v^T \mathbf{S}_{gv} \mathbf{W}_v\Big). \tag{5}$$

By maximizing the objective function in Eq. (5), the distant data points in the original space are still faraway from each other in the common subspace, and thus the global structure of the dataset is preserved.

3.3 Discrimination Maximizing Criteria

The idea behind the discriminant information maximization is straightforward: if two data points (no matter within the same view or from different views) possess similar interestingness levels, they should be close to each other in the learned subspace; otherwise, they should be faraway from each other. The more similar the interestingness levels, the closer the low-dimensional data points should be.

In order to describe the similarity between interestingness levels of different data samples, we define the label similarity matrix $\mathbf{A}$, where the element on the i-th row and the j-th column of $\mathbf{A}$ is given as follows:

$$A_{ij} = 1 - |l_i - l_j| \in [0, 1]. \tag{6}$$

Note that the representations of different views of the same data sample share the same label.

We then propose the following objective:

$$\{\mathbf{W}_1, ..., \mathbf{W}_V\} = \underset{\mathbf{W}_1,...,\mathbf{W}_V}{\arg\min}\ tr\Big(\sum_{u=1}^{V}\sum_{v=1}^{V}\sum_{i=1}^{n}\sum_{j=1}^{n} A_{ij}(\mathbf{W}_u^T\mathbf{x}_{iu} - \mathbf{W}_v^T\mathbf{x}_{jv})(\mathbf{W}_u^T\mathbf{x}_{iu} - \mathbf{W}_v^T\mathbf{x}_{jv})^T\Big). \tag{7}$$

By minimizing the objective function in Eq. (7), the data samples with similar or even the same interestingness levels will be close to each other in the learned common subspace, and thus the label similarity is well maintained.

To characterize the dissimilarity between data points, we define the discriminant matrix $\mathbf{B}$, where the element on the i-th row and the j-th column of $\mathbf{B}$ is given as follows:

$$B_{ij} = 1 - A_{ij} = |l_i - l_j| \in [0, 1]. \tag{8}$$

Then we present the following objective:

$$\{\mathbf{W}_1, ..., \mathbf{W}_V\} = \underset{\mathbf{W}_1,...,\mathbf{W}_V}{\arg\max}\ tr\Big(\sum_{u=1}^{V}\sum_{v=1}^{V}\sum_{i=1}^{n}\sum_{j=1}^{n} B_{ij}(\mathbf{W}_u^T\mathbf{x}_{iu} - \mathbf{W}_v^T\mathbf{x}_{jv})(\mathbf{W}_u^T\mathbf{x}_{iu} - \mathbf{W}_v^T\mathbf{x}_{jv})^T\Big). \tag{9}$$

By maximizing the objective function in Eq. (9), the data samples with different labels are expected to be faraway from each other in the learned common space, and thus the discriminant information can be well preserved.

3.4 Objective Function of M^2L

In order to preserve the geometric structure while maximizing the discriminant information, we integrate aforementioned four objectives (Eqs. (3), (5), (7), and (9)) into a unified formulation in Eq. (10), where $\alpha \in [0, 1]$ is a trade-off parameter to balance the weight of geometry information and that of discriminant information in the proposed learning framework.

$$\{\mathbf{W}_1,...,\mathbf{W}_V\} = \mathop{\arg\max}_{\substack{\mathbf{W}_1,...,\mathbf{W}_V \\ \mathbf{W}_v^T\mathbf{W}_v=\mathbf{I}_d \\ v=1,...,V}} tr\left(\frac{\alpha\sum_{v=1}^{V}\mathbf{W}_v^T\mathbf{S}_{gv}\mathbf{W}_v + (1-\alpha)\sum_{u=1}^{V}\sum_{v=1}^{V}\sum_{i=1}^{n}\sum_{j=1}^{n}B_{ij}(\mathbf{W}_u^T\mathbf{x}_{iu}-\mathbf{W}_v^T\mathbf{x}_{jv})(\mathbf{W}_u^T\mathbf{x}_{iu}-\mathbf{W}_v^T\mathbf{x}_{jv})^T}{\alpha\sum_{v=1}^{V}\mathbf{W}_v^T\mathbf{S}_{lv}\mathbf{W}_v + (1-\alpha)\sum_{u=1}^{V}\sum_{v=1}^{V}\sum_{i=1}^{n}\sum_{j=1}^{n}A_{ij}(\mathbf{W}_u^T\mathbf{x}_{iu}-\mathbf{W}_v^T\mathbf{x}_{jv})(\mathbf{W}_u^T\mathbf{x}_{iu}-\mathbf{W}_v^T\mathbf{x}_{jv})^T}\right) \tag{10}$$

3.5 Analytical Solution of M²L

Actually, Eq. (10) could be rewritten as follows:

$$\mathbf{W} = \mathop{\arg\max}_{\substack{\mathbf{W} \\ \mathbf{W}^T\mathbf{W}=\mathbf{I}_d}} tr\left(\frac{\mathbf{W}^T(\alpha\mathbf{S}_g + (1-\alpha)\mathbf{Q}_B)\mathbf{W}}{\mathbf{W}^T(\alpha\mathbf{S}_l + (1-\alpha)\mathbf{Q}_A)\mathbf{W}}\right), \tag{11}$$

where $\mathbf{W} = [\mathbf{W}_1^T, \mathbf{W}_2^T, \ldots, \mathbf{W}_V^T]^T$, $\mathbf{S}_g = diag(\mathbf{S}_{g1}, \mathbf{S}_{g2}, \ldots, \mathbf{S}_{gV})$, $\mathbf{S}_l = diag(\mathbf{S}_{l1}, \mathbf{S}_{l2}, \ldots, \mathbf{S}_{lV})$, $\mathbf{Q}_B = \begin{bmatrix} \mathbf{X}_1\mathbf{L}_{B11}\mathbf{X}_1^T & \cdots & \mathbf{X}_1\mathbf{L}_{B1V}\mathbf{X}_V^T \\ \vdots & \ddots & \vdots \\ \mathbf{X}_V\mathbf{L}_{BV1}\mathbf{X}_1^T & \cdots & \mathbf{X}_V\mathbf{L}_{BVV}\mathbf{X}_V^T \end{bmatrix}$, and $\mathbf{Q}_A = \begin{bmatrix} \mathbf{X}_1\mathbf{L}_{A11}\mathbf{X}_1^T & \cdots & \mathbf{X}_1\mathbf{L}_{A1V}\mathbf{X}_V^T \\ \vdots & \ddots & \vdots \\ \mathbf{X}_V\mathbf{L}_{AV1}\mathbf{X}_1^T & \cdots & \mathbf{X}_V\mathbf{L}_{AVV}\mathbf{X}_V^T \end{bmatrix}$. Here $\mathbf{L}_{Buv}$ and $\mathbf{L}_{Auv}$ $(u, v = 1, ..., V)$ are the (u, v)-th blocks of $\mathbf{L}_B$ and $\mathbf{L}_A$, respectively, i.e., $\mathbf{L}_B = \begin{bmatrix} \mathbf{L}_{B11} & \cdots & \mathbf{L}_{B1V} \\ \vdots & \ddots & \vdots \\ \mathbf{L}_{BV1} & \cdots & \mathbf{L}_{BVV} \end{bmatrix}$ and $\mathbf{L}_A = \begin{bmatrix} \mathbf{L}_{A11} & \cdots & \mathbf{L}_{A1V} \\ \vdots & \ddots & \vdots \\ \mathbf{L}_{AV1} & \cdots & \mathbf{L}_{AVV} \end{bmatrix}$, where $\mathbf{L}_B$ and $\mathbf{L}_A$ are two $nV \times nV$ Laplacian matrices [2] defined as $\mathbf{L}_B = \mathbf{Diag}_B - \mathbf{Adj}_B$ and $\mathbf{L}_A = \mathbf{Diag}_A - \mathbf{Adj}_A$, in which $\mathbf{Adj}_B = \mathbf{1}_{V\times V} \otimes \mathbf{B}$ and $\mathbf{Adj}_A = \mathbf{1}_{V\times V} \otimes \mathbf{A}$ are also $nV \times nV$ matrices, $\mathbf{1}_{V\times V}$ denotes the $V \times V$ matrix with all entries being 1, the symbol $\otimes$ denotes the Kronecker product operation on two matrices, and $\mathbf{Diag}_B$ and $\mathbf{Diag}_A$ are diagonal matrices defined as $(Diag_B)_{ii} = \sum_{j=1}^{nV}(Adj_B)_{ij}$ and $(Diag_A)_{ii} = \sum_{j=1}^{nV}(Adj_A)_{ij}$, respectively $(i = 1, ..., nV)$. Then the optimal $\mathbf{W}$ that maximizes the objective function in Eq. (11) is composed of the eigenvectors corresponding to the d largest eigenvalues of the following generalized eigen-decomposition problem:

$$(\alpha\mathbf{S}_g + (1-\alpha)\mathbf{Q}_B)\mathbf{w} = \lambda(\alpha\mathbf{S}_l + (1-\alpha)\mathbf{Q}_A)\mathbf{w}. \tag{12}$$

The detailed procedure of M²L is described in Algorithm 1.

Algorithm 1: Multi-view Manifold Learning (M²L)

Input: The training dataset $\mathcal{X} = \{(\mathbf{x}_{11}, ..., \mathbf{x}_{1V}), ..., (\mathbf{x}_{n1}, ..., \mathbf{x}_{nV})\}$ and the corresponding label set $\mathcal{L} = \{l_1, ..., l_n\}$; the subspace dimension d; and the balancing parameter α

Output: Transformation matrices $\mathbf{W}_1, \cdots, \mathbf{W}_V$

for $v = 1, ..., V$ **do**
  Construct $\mathbf{N}^v$ according to Eq. (1);
  Construct $\mathbf{S}_{lv}$ according to Eq. (2);
  Construct $\mathbf{S}_{gv}$ according to Eq. (4);
end
Construct $\mathbf{S}_l$: $\mathbf{S}_l \leftarrow diag(\mathbf{S}_{l1}, \mathbf{S}_{l2}, \ldots, \mathbf{S}_{lV})$;
Construct $\mathbf{S}_g$: $\mathbf{S}_g \leftarrow diag(\mathbf{S}_{g1}, \mathbf{S}_{g2}, \ldots, \mathbf{S}_{gV})$;
Construct $\mathbf{A}$ according to Eq. (6);
Construct $\mathbf{Adj}_A$: $\mathbf{Adj}_A \leftarrow \mathbf{1}_{V\times V} \otimes \mathbf{A}$;
Construct $\mathbf{Diag}_A$: $(Diag_A)_{ii} \leftarrow \sum_{j=1}^{nV}(Adj_A)_{ij}$;
Construct $\mathbf{L}_A$: $\mathbf{L}_A \leftarrow \mathbf{Diag}_A - \mathbf{Adj}_A$;
Construct $\mathbf{Q}_A$:
$$\mathbf{Q}_A = \begin{bmatrix} \mathbf{X}_1\mathbf{L}_{A11}\mathbf{X}_1^T & \cdots & \mathbf{X}_1\mathbf{L}_{A1V}\mathbf{X}_V^T \\ \vdots & \ddots & \vdots \\ \mathbf{X}_V\mathbf{L}_{AV1}\mathbf{X}_1^T & \cdots & \mathbf{X}_V\mathbf{L}_{AVV}\mathbf{X}_V^T \end{bmatrix};$$
Construct $\mathbf{B}$ according to Eq. (8);
Construct $\mathbf{Adj}_B$: $\mathbf{Adj}_B \leftarrow \mathbf{1}_{V\times V} \otimes \mathbf{B}$;
Construct $\mathbf{Diag}_B$: $(Diag_B)_{ii} = \sum_{j=1}^{nV}(Adj_B)_{ij}$;
Construct $\mathbf{L}_B$: $\mathbf{L}_B \leftarrow \mathbf{Diag}_B - \mathbf{Adj}_B$;
Construct $\mathbf{Q}_B$:
$$\mathbf{Q}_B = \begin{bmatrix} \mathbf{X}_1\mathbf{L}_{B11}\mathbf{X}_1^T & \cdots & \mathbf{X}_1\mathbf{L}_{B1V}\mathbf{X}_V^T \\ \vdots & \ddots & \vdots \\ \mathbf{X}_V\mathbf{L}_{BV1}\mathbf{X}_1^T & \cdots & \mathbf{X}_V\mathbf{L}_{BVV}\mathbf{X}_V^T \end{bmatrix};$$
Obtain $\mathbf{W}$ by solving the generalized eigen-decomposition problem:
$(\alpha\mathbf{S}_g + (1-\alpha)\mathbf{Q}_B)\mathbf{w} = \lambda(\alpha\mathbf{S}_l + (1-\alpha)\mathbf{Q}_A)\mathbf{w}$;
$[\mathbf{W}_1^T, \mathbf{W}_2^T, \ldots, \mathbf{W}_M^T] \leftarrow \mathbf{W}^T$;

4 EXPERIMENTAL RESULTS

4.1 Synthetic Example

First, we schematically illustrate the effect of M²L on a synthetic dataset. This synthetic dataset is composed of twelve two-dimensional data samples with two views, where $\mathbf{X}_1 = \begin{bmatrix} 1 & 1 & 1 & 1 & 2 & 2 & 2 & 2 & 3 & 3 & 3 & 3 \\ 1 & 2 & 3 & 4 & 3 & 4 & 5 & 6 & 5 & 6 & 7 & 8 \end{bmatrix}$ and $\mathbf{X}_2 = \begin{bmatrix} 0 & 1 \\ 1 & 0 \end{bmatrix}\mathbf{X}_1$, i.e., we interchange the two dimensions in view 1 to generate view 2. Moreover, we set the label vector $\mathbf{l} = [0, 0, 0, 0, 0.5, 0.5, 0.5, 0.5, 1, 1, 1, 1]$.

Figure 1 shows the projection directions learned by M²L and the corresponding one-dimensional mapping results for these two views (Figure 1(a) for view 1 and Figure 1(b) for view 2). For each view, we demonstrate three projection

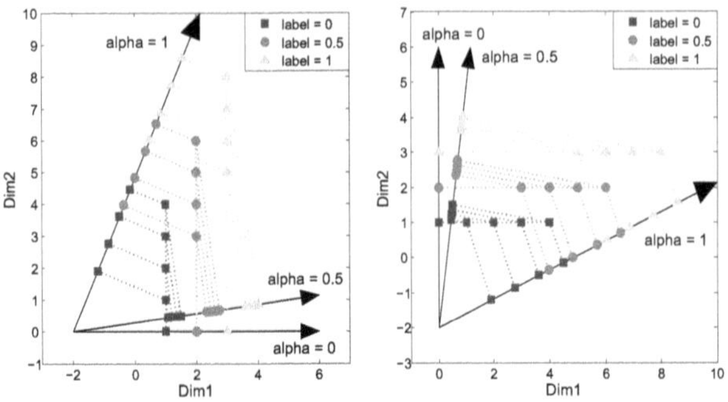

(a) (b)

Figure 1: Schematic illustration of M^{2}L on the synthetic example. (a) The original data in view 1 and the corresponding projections generated by M^{2}L. (b) The original data in view 2 and the corresponding projections generated by M^{2}L.

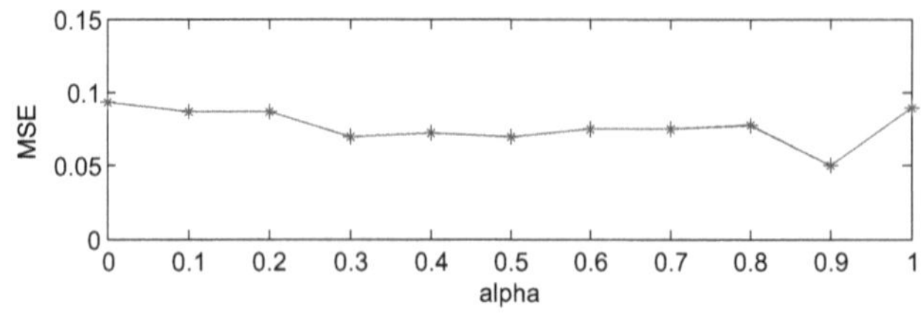

Figure 2: MSE of M^{2}L under various values of α.

Table 1: Performance (in terms of MSE) of PCA, MCCA, SMR, and M^{2}L with the corresponding reduced dimensions on Predicting Media Interestingness dataset

	PCA	MCCA	SMR	M^{2}L
MSE	0.1850	0.1197	0.0599	**0.0340**
Red. Dim.	37	$3 \times 5 = 15$	15	$\mathbf{2 \times 5 = 10}$

directions with $\alpha = 0$, 0.5, and 1 respectively. When $\alpha = 0$, the proposed M^{2}L considers only the discriminant information but ignores the geometric structure. Therefore, the data with different label values are well separated but the intra-class manifold information is lost in the one-dimensional subspace ($\mathbf{w}_1 = [1, 0]^T$ for view 1 and $\mathbf{w}_2 = [0, 1]^T$ for view 2). In contrast, when $\alpha = 1$, i.e., ignoring the discriminant information, the mapping results preserve the manifold structure well but the data with different labels are overlapped ($\mathbf{w}_1 = [0.4146, 1]^T$ and $\mathbf{w}_2 = [1, 0.4146]^T$). By setting $\alpha = 0.5$, both geometric structure and discriminant information are taken into consideration, and thus are well preserved ($\mathbf{w}_1 = [1, 0.1441]^T$ and $\mathbf{w}_2 = [0.144, 1]^T$). Interestingly, the relation between two views (i.e., the row exchange) is faithfully reflected by the corresponding projection vectors. Moreover, in the one-dimensional subspace, the mapping values of data from different views are similar if they possess the same label value; and are distinct from each other if the label values are different. This indicates that the learned common subspace preserves the label information consistently across different views.

4.2 Media Interestingness Prediction

In this subsection, we evaluate the performance of the proposed method on the Predicting Media Interestingness dataset [8]. The data is extracted from 78 Creative Commons licensed trailers of Hollywood-like movies. The trailers are further segmented into 7,396 shots, 5,054 of which are used for training and the remaining 2,342 shots are used for test. For each shot, the middle frame is extracted as its key frame and a set of low-level features of this key frame is computed as the original feature representation of the corresponding shot [8].

In our experiments, we utilize five types of features, i.e., 300-D dense Scale Invariant Feature Transform (dense SIFT) features [20, 26], 300-D HoG 2×2 features [7, 43], 59-D Local Binary Patterns (LBP) features [29], 512-D GIST features [30], and 128-D color histogram features. We thus have 5 views and the total dimension of these 5 views is 1,299. All data are manually annotated in terms of interestingness ranging from 0 to 1 by human assessors.

Firstly, we compare the proposed method M^{2}L with three dimensionality reduction methods, i.e., principal component analysis (PCA) [14], multi-view CCA (MCCA) [28], and supervised manifold regression (SMR) [24], where PCA is the most classical dimensionality reduction method, MCCA is a representative multi-view dimensionality reduction algorithm, and SMR is a recently proposed dimensionality reduction method for continuous labels. For MCCA and M^{2}L, we first map the original representations of 5 views to a low-dimensional common subspace, and then concatenate the reduced representations of these 5 views to a single feature vector. For PCA and SMR, we first concatenate the original representations of these 5 views to a 1,299-dimensional feature vector, and then map it to a low-dimensional subspace. After dimensionality reduction, we utilize ϵ-SVR on the low-dimensional data to predict the interestingness levels. We choose LIBSVM [4] and the RBF kernel, and the parameters in ϵ-SVR for the low-dimensional representations generated by PCA, MCCA, SMR, and M^{2}L are determined separately by a 5-fold cross validation technique on training data.

We also use the 5-fold cross validation technique on training data to determine the optimal value of α for M^{2}L. From Figure 2 we can see that the mean square error (MSE) value is relatively large when $\alpha = 0$ (preserving only the discriminant information) or $\alpha = 1$ (preserving only the geometric structure). The performance becomes better when both the geometric structure and the discriminant information are taken into consideration, and achieves the best when $\alpha = 0.9$. Therefore, we set $\alpha = 0.9$ for M^{2}L in the remaining experiments.

Table 1 reports the best performance (in terms of MSE, i.e., mean squared error) and the corresponding reduced dimension of aforementioned four algorithms. By learning

(a) Ground Truth = 0.5131 Predicted Value = 0.3897

(b) Ground Truth = 0.3618 Predicted Value = 0.3052

(c) Ground Truth = 0.0749 Predicted Value = 0.0735

(d) Ground Truth = 0.0559 Predicted Value = 0.0575

Figure 3: Examples of interesting and non-interesting video frames from the Predicting Media Interestingness dataset. (a) and (b) are examples of video frames with high interestingness values while (c) and (d) are examples of video frames with low interestingness values.

the intrinsic features from multiple views jointly, MCCA and M^2L outperform the classical PCA. By preserving the geometric structure and the discriminant information of the dataset, SMR and M^2L achieve better results than PCA and MCCA. By integrating the geometric structures of different views and the interestingness information of the original dataset under a multi-view manifold learning framework, M^2L performs the best in this experiment. Moreover, the reduced dimension of M^2L is the lowest among four methods, which indicates that the proposed method is capable of capturing the interestingness information of original dataset in a very low-dimensional subspace.

Figure 3 illustrates some examples of interesting and non-interesting video frames from the Predicting Media Interestingness dataset. Images in the top row of Figure 3 are two examples of video frames with high interestingness values and images in the bottom row are two examples of video frames with low interestingness values. We also list the ground truth and the predicted value on these video frames in the figure. We can observe that our predictions on these frames are consistent with the human judgment in terms of interestingness.

After having demonstrated the overall performance of M^2L on all five views, we further measure the MSE values of M^2L on individual views. Table 2 gives the results of M^2L on dense SIFT, HoG 2×2, LBP, GIST, and color histogram, respectively. We can observe that even using the low-dimensional representation from only one view can generate good result in predicting the media interestingness. Specifically, the performance of M^2L on LBP and GIST is better than that of PCA and MCCA with all five views; and the performance of

Table 2: Performance (in terms of MSE) of M^2L on individual views of Predicting Media Interestingness dataset

	SIFT	HoG	LBP	GIST	ColorHist
MSE	0.0462	0.0522	0.0813	0.0723	0.0360
Red. Dim.	2	2	2	2	2

M^2L on dense SIFT, HoG 2×2, and color histogram further outperforms SMR with all five views. The reason of achieving good performance on individual view might be that although only one view is used in prediction, the transformation matrix for that individual view is learned by considering the information from all the five views.

5 CONCLUSIONS

In this paper, we propose a novel Multi-view Manifold Learning (M^2L) algorithm to uncover the mapping between visual features and the corresponding interestingness levels. By modelling both geometric structures and interestingness information in a multi-view learning framework, the proposed algorithm shows good and explainable results in both synthetic example and real-world dataset.

For the future work, we are interested in mining the physical meaning of each dimension in the learned subspace, as well as its relations with the findings from psychology. Moreover, we aim to improve the proposed model by considering the high-order tensor structure and the dynamic nature of video data. Last but not least, we are going to investigate the possibility of extending the current method to the imbalanced version as most of the users only pay attention to the interesting media data rather than the non-interesting ones.

ACKNOWLEDGMENTS

The authors would like to thank the reviewers for their constructive comments and suggestions. This work was supported in part by the National Natural Science Foundation of China under Grants 61503317 and 61672444, in part by the Faculty Research Grant of Hong Kong Baptist University (HKBU) under Project FRG2/16-17/032, in part by the Hunan Provincial Key Laboratory of Intelligent Processing of Big Data on Transportation (No. JTKF2017001), Changsha University of Science & Technology, P.R. China, and in part by the Science and Technology Research and Development Fund of Shenzhen with Project Code JCYJ20160531194006833.

REFERENCES

[1] J. Almeida, D. C. G. Pedronette, and O. A. B. Penatti. 2014. Unsupervised manifold learning for video genre retrieval. In *Proc. CIARP*. 604–612.

[2] M. Belkin and P. Niyogi. 2003. Laplacian Eigenmaps for Dimensionality Reduction and Data Representation. *Neural Comput.* 15, 6 (2003), 1373–1396.

[3] P. R. Chakraborty, D. Tjondronegoro, L. Zhang, and V. Chandran. 2016. Automatic Identification of Sports Video Highlights Using Viewer Interest Features. In *Proc. ACM ICMR*. 55–62.

[4] C.-C. Chang and C.-J. Lin. 2011. LIBSVM: A Library for Support Vector Machines. *ACM Trans. Intell. Syst. Technol.* 2, 3 (2011), 27:1–27:27.
[5] R. R. Coifman and S. Lafon. 2006. Diffusion maps. *Applied and Computational Harmonic Analysis* 21, 1 (2006), 5 – 30.
[6] M. G. Constantin, B. Boteanu, and B. Ionescu. 2016. LAPI at MediaEval 2016 Predicting Media Interestingness Task. In *Proc. of the MediaEval 2016 Workshop.*
[7] N. Dalal and B. Triggs. 2005. Histograms of Oriented Gradients for Human Detection. In *Proc. CVPR.* 886–893.
[8] C.-H. Demarty, M. Sjöberg, B. Ionescu, T.-T. Do, H. Wang, N. Q. K. Duong, and F. Lefebvre. 2016. MediaEval 2016 Predicting Media Interestingness Task. In *Proc. of the MediaEval 2016 Workshop.*
[9] S. Dhar, V. Ordonez, and T. L. Berg. 2011. High level describable attributes for predicting aesthetics and interestingness. In *CVPR 2011.* 1657–1664.
[10] S. S. Farfade, M. J. Saberian, and L.-J. Li. 2015. Multi-view Face Detection Using Deep Convolutional Neural Networks. In *Proc. 5th ACM ICMR.* 643–650.
[11] L. Geng and H. J. Hamilton. 2006. Interestingness Measures for Data Mining: A Survey. *ACM Comput. Surv.* 38, 3 (2006).
[12] H. Grabner, F. Nater, M. Druey, and L. Van Gool. 2013. Visual Interestingness in Image Sequences. In *Proc. 21st ACM Multimedia.* 1017–1026.
[13] M. Gygli, H. Grabner, H. Riemenschneider, F. Nater, and L. V. Gool. 2013. The Interestingness of Images. In *Proc. ICCV.* 1633–1640.
[14] H. Hotelling. 1933. Analysis of a complex of statistical variables into principal components. *J. Educ. Psychol.* 24, 6 (1933), 417–441.
[15] H. Hotelling. 1936. Relations between two sets of variates. *Biometrika* 28 (1936), 321–377.
[16] Y.-G. Jiang, Y. Wang, R. Feng, X. Xue, Y. Zheng, and H. Yang. 2013. Understanding and Predicting Interestingness of Videos. In *Proc. 27th AAAI.*
[17] X.-Y. Jing, Q. Liu, F. Wu, B. Xu, Y. Zhu, and S. Chen. 2015. Web Page Classification Based on Uncorrelated Semi-supervised Intra-view and Inter-view Manifold Discriminant Feature Extraction. In *Proc. 24th IJCAI.* 2255–2261.
[18] M. Kan, S. Shan, H. Zhang, S. Lao, and X. Chen. 2016. Multi-View Discriminant Analysis. *IEEE Trans. Pattern Anal. Mach. Intell.* 38, 1 (2016), 188–194.
[19] H. Katti, K. Y. Bin, T.-S. Chua, and M. Kankanhalli. 2008. Pre-attentive discrimination of interestingness in images. In *Proc. ICME.* 1433–1436.
[20] S. Lazebnik, C. Schmid, and J. Ponce. 2006. Beyond Bags of Features: Spatial Pyramid Matching for Recognizing Natural Scene Categories. In *Proc. CVPR.* 2169–2178.
[21] K. Li, G. Qi, J. Ye, and K. Hua. 2016. Linear Subspace Ranking Hashing for Cross-modal Retrieval. *IEEE Trans. Pattern Anal. Mach. Intell.* PP, 99 (2016), 1–1.
[22] C. Liem. 2016. TUD-MMC at MediaEval 2016: Predicting Media Interestingness Task. In *Proc. of the MediaEval 2016 Workshop.*
[23] F. Liu, Y. Niu, and M. Gleicher. 2009. Using Web Images for Measuring Video Frame Interestingness. In *Proc. 21st IJCAI.*
[24] Y. Liu, Z. Gu, and Y.-M. Cheung. 2016. Supervised Manifold Learning for Media Interestingness Prediction. In *Proc. of the MediaEval 2016 Workshop.*
[25] Y. Liu, Y. Liu, K. C. C. Chan, and K. A. Hua. 2014. Hybrid Manifold Embedding. *IEEE Trans. Neural Netw. Learn. Syst.* 25, 12 (2014), 2295–2302.
[26] D. G. Lowe. 2004. Distinctive Image Features from Scale-Invariant Keypoints. *International Journal of Computer Vision* 60, 2 (2004), 91–110.
[27] Y. Luo, D. Tao, K. Ramamohanarao, C. Xu, and Y. Wen. 2015. Tensor Canonical Correlation Analysis for Multi-View Dimension Reduction. *IEEE Trans. Knowl. Data Eng.* 27, 11 (2015), 3111–3124.
[28] A.A. Nielsen. 2002. Multiset canonical correlations analysis and multispectral, truly multitemporal remote sensing data. *IEEE Trans. Image Process.* 11, 3 (2002), 293–305.
[29] T. Ojala, M. Pietikainen, and T. Maenpaa. 2002. Multiresolution gray-scale and rotation invariant texture classification with local binary patterns. *IEEE Trans. Pattern Anal. Mach. Intell.* 24, 7 (2002), 971–987.
[30] A. Oliva and A. Torralba. 2001. Modeling the Shape of the Scene: A Holistic Representation of the Spatial Envelope. *Int. J. Comput. Vision* 42, 3 (2001), 145–175.
[31] D. C. G. Pedronette, O. A.B. Penatti, and R. da S. Torres. 2014. Unsupervised manifold learning using Reciprocal kNN Graphs in image re-ranking and rank aggregation tasks. *Image and Vision Computing* 32, 2 (2014), 120–130.
[32] R. Pless. 2003. Image spaces and video trajectories: using Isomap to explore video sequences. In *Proc. ICCV.* 1433–1440.
[33] B. Qian, X. Wang, J. Ye, and I. Davidson. 2015. A Reconstruction Error Based Framework for Multi-Label and Multi-View Learning. *IEEE Trans. Knowl. Data Eng.* 27, 3 (2015), 594–607.
[34] A. Rahimi, B. Recht, and T. Darrell. 2005. Learning Appearance Manifolds from Video. In *Proc. CVPR.* 868–875.
[35] S. Rayatdoost and M. Soleymani. 2016. Ranking Images and Videos on Visual Interestingness by Visual Sentiment Features. In *Proc. of the MediaEval 2016 Workshop.*
[36] S. Roweis and L. K. Saul. 2000. Nonlinear Dimensionality Reduction by Locally Linear Embedding. *Science* 290, 5500 (2000), 2323–2326.
[37] Y. Shen, C.-H. Demarty, and N. Q. K. Duong. 2016. Technicolor at MediaEval 2016 Predicting Media Interestingness Task. In *Proc. of the MediaEval 2016 Workshop.*
[38] T. Shnitzer, R. Talmon, and J. J. Slotine. 2017. Manifold Learning With Contracting Observers for Data-Driven Time-Series Analysis. *IEEE Trans. Signal Process.* 65, 4 (2017), 904–918.
[39] M. Soleymani. 2015. The Quest for Visual Interest. In *Proc. 23rd ACM Multimedia.* 919–922.
[40] J. B. Tenenbaum, V. de Silva, and J. C. Langford. 2000. A Global Geometric Framework for Nonlinear Dimensionality Reduction. *Science* 290, 5500 (2000), 2319–2323.
[41] A. B. Vasudevan, M. Gygli, A. Volokitin, and L. V. Gool. 2016. ETH-CVL at MediaEval 2016: Textual-Visual Embeddings and Video2GIF for Video Interestingness. In *Proc. of the MediaEval 2016 Workshop.*
[42] W. Wang, R. Arora, K. Livescu, and J. Bilmes. 2015. On Deep Multi-View Representation Learning. In *Proc. 32nd ICML.* 1083–1092.
[43] J. Xiao, J. Hays, K. A. Ehinger, A. Oliva, and A. Torralba. 2010. SUN database: Large-scale scene recognition from abbey to zoo. In *Proc. CVPR.* 3485–3492.
[44] B. Xu, Y. Fu, and Y.-G. Jiang. 2016. BigVid at MediaEval 2016: Predicting Interestingness in Images and Videos. In *Proc. of the MediaEval 2016 Workshop.*
[45] Y. Yang, Y. T. Zhuang, F. Wu, and Y. H. Pan. 2008. Harmonizing Hierarchical Manifolds for Multimedia Document Semantics Understanding and Cross-Media Retrieval. *IEEE Trans. Multimedia* 10, 3 (2008), 437–446.
[46] G. Zen, P. de Juan, Y. Song, and A. Jaimes. 2016. Mouse Activity As an Indicator of Interestingness in Video. In *Proc. ACM ICMR.* 47–54.
[47] C. Zhang, H. Fu, Q. Hu, P. Zhu, and X. Cao. 2017. Flexible Multi-View Dimensionality Co-Reduction. *IEEE Trans. Image Process.* 26, 2 (2017), 648–659.
[48] X. Zhu, X. Li, and S. Zhang. 2016. Block-Row Sparse Multiview Multilabel Learning for Image Classification. *IEEE Trans. Cybern.* 46, 2 (2016), 450–461.

Utilising High-Level Features in Summarisation of Academic Presentations

Keith Curtis
ADAPT Centre
School of Computing
Dublin City University
Dublin, Ireland
Keith.Curtis@AdaptCentre.ie

Gareth J.F. Jones
ADAPT Centre
School of Computing
Dublin City University
Dublin, Ireland
Gareth.Jones@AdaptCentre.ie

Nick Campbell
ADAPT Centre
School of Computer
Science & Statistics
Trinity College Dublin
Dublin, Ireland
nick@tcd.ie

ABSTRACT

We present a novel method for the generation of automatic video summaries of academic presentations. We base our investigation on a corpus of multimodal academic conference presentations combining transcripts with paralinguistic multimodal features. We first generate summaries based on keywords by using transcripts created using automatic speech recognition (ASR). Start and end times for each spoken phrase are identified from the ASR transcript, then a value for each phrase created. Spoken phrases are then augmented by incorporating scores for human annotation of paralinguistic features. These features measure audience engagement, comprehension and speaker emphasis. We evaluate the effectiveness of summaries generated for individual presentations, created using speech transcripts and paralinguistic multimodal features, by performing eye-tracking evaluation of participants as they watch summaries and full presentations, and by questionnaire of participants upon completion of eye-tracking studies. Summaries were also evaluated for effectiveness by performing comparisons with an enhanced digital video browser.

CCS CONCEPTS

•**Computing methodologies** →**Video summarization;** Classification and regression trees; •**General and reference** →*Evaluation;*

KEYWORDS

Video summarisation; classification; evaluation; eye-tracking

ACM Reference format:
Keith Curtis, Gareth J.F. Jones, and Nick Campbell. 2017. Utilising High-Level Features in Summarisation
of Academic Presentations. In *Proceedings of ICMR '17, June 6–9, 2017, Bucharest, Romania*, , 7 pages.
DOI: http://dx.doi.org/10.1145/3078971.3079028

ICMR '17, June 6–9, 2017, Bucharest, Romania
 ACM ISBN 978-1-4503-4701-3/17/06...$15.00
DOI: http://dx.doi.org/10.1145/3078971.3079028

1 INTRODUCTION

Archives of multimedia content are currently growing very rapidly. Every minute in 2016, 300 hours of new video material was uploaded to YouTube, while 2.78 million videos were viewed, skype users made 104,300 calls, 38,050 hours of music were listened to on spotify and 38,194 new posts were made to Instagram. It is a growing challenge for users to be able to locate and browse content of interest in such multimedia archives - either in response to user queries or in more free or informal exploration of content. Browsing multimedia archives to find relevant information is extremely time consuming. While this is a challenging problem for multimedia including a video channel, this is particularly challenging for spoken content where a user must listen to the spoken audio track in a linear mode. This represents a growing challenge for accessing content considered relevant or of interest to users of multimedia archives where the significant information is in the audio of the multimedia file such as lectures, presentations etc. of which archives are growing rapidly.

The goal of this work is to provide an effective and efficient way to summarise audio-visual recordings where the significant information is in the audio stream. Existing multimedia information retrieval research has focused primarily on matching text queries against written meta-data or transcribed audio [2], in addition to seeking to match visual queries to low-level features such as colours and textures and shape and object recognition and person recognition, plus scene type classification - urban, countryside, and named individuals or places etc. [6]. In the case of multimedia content where the information is primarily visual, the content can be represented by multiple key-frames extracted using methods such as object recognition and facial detection. These are then matched against visual queries, and retrieved videos shown to the user using key-frame surrogates, with the user playing back in full videos which they believe to be relevant to the information need. Matching of the visual component of these queries is generally complemented by textual search against a transcript of any available spoken audio and any meta-data provided [9].

In this work we develop a novel video presentation summarisation algorithm to automatically generate summaries of academic presentations using classified areas of high audience engagement, audience comprehension, and areas of intentional or unintentional emphasis applied by the speaker. We address the following research question 'Can areas of special emphasis provided by the speaker, combined with detected areas of high audience engagement and high levels of audience comprehension, be used for effective summarisation of presentations?' We evaluate this summarisation approach using eye-tracking and by questionnaire. Our summarisation approach is also evaluated by comparisons to an enhanced digital video browser for quickly skimming presentations.

In section 2 of this paper we introduce relevant related work in video summarisation. Section 3 introduces the multimodal corpus used for these experiments while section 4 describes the classification of high level features used for creating these summaries. Section 5 describes the procedure for creating automatic summaries followed by section 6 which describes the evaluation tasks performed and results of these. Conclusions are offered in section 7 of the paper.

2 PREVIOUS WORK

This section looks at related work for the summarisation and skimming of academic presentations.

Ju et al. [8] present a system for analysing and annotating video sequences of technical talks. They use a robust motion estimation technique to detect key frames and segment the video into subsequences containing a single slide. Sub-sequences are stabilised to remove motion. Potential gestures are tracked using active contours. By successfully recognising all pointing gestures the authors are able to fully annotate presentations per slide. This first automatic video analysis system helps users to access presentation videos intelligently.

He et al. [5] use prosodic information from the audio stream to identify speaker emphasis during presentations, in addition to pause information to avoid selecting segments which start mid-phrase. They also garner information from slide transition points to indicate the introduction of a new topic or sub-topic. They develop three summarisation algorithms for slide transition based summary, pitch activity based summary and summary based on slide, pitch and user-access information. They use surveys for evaluation and find that computer generated summaries were rated poorly on coherence 5.3 to 3.5 in which participants complained that summaries jumped topics. In this work they also found that audio-visual presentations were less susceptible than the audio-only stream to pitch based emphasis analysis. This is the first work attempting to summarise presentation video by speaker emphasis. In this they found that speaker emphasis was not enough information to generate effective summaries.

Li et al. [10] develop and evaluate an enhanced digital video browser for browsing through different categories of digital video. The categories evaluated are Classroom, Conference, Sports, Shows, News and Travel. They evaluate the effectiveness of the following enhanced browser controls - Time Compression (TC), Pause Removal (PR), Table of Contents (TOC), Shot Boundary (SB), Timeline markers and jump controls. For browsing of conference presentations, TC and PR were found to be the most effective tools for improved video browsing with scores of 6.9 and 6.5 out of 7 respectively. This enhanced digital video browser gives us additional comparison method to evaluate the effectiveness of generated presentation summaries. From this work we gain the idea of an additional evaluation measure by comparison with the enhanced digital video browser.

Joho et al. [7] capture and analyse the user's facial expressions for the generation of perception-based summaries which exploit the viewer's affective state, perceived excitement and attention. Perception-based approaches are designed to overcome the semantic gap problem in summarisation by finding affective scenes in video. They find it unlikely that a single summary could be commonly seen as the highlight of videos by viewers. Results suggest that there were two or three at least distinguished parts of videos that can be seen as the highlight by various viewers.

Work by Pavel et al. [11] created a set of tools for creating video digests of informational video. Informal evaluation suggests these tools make it easier for authors of informational talks to create video digests. They also found that video digests afford browsing and skimming better than alternative video presentation techniques.

3 MULTIMODAL CORPUS

No standard publicly dataset exists for work of this nature, since we require recordings of the audience and of the speaker for academic presentations. For this work we used the International Speech Conference Multi-modal corpus (ISCM) from Curtis et al. [3]. This contains 31 academic presentations totalling 520 minutes of video, with high quality 1080p parallel video recordings of both the speaker and the audience to each presentation. We chose four videos from this dataset for our evaluation of our video summaries.

4 CLASSIFICATION OF HIGH-LEVEL FEATURES FOR SUMMARISATION

In this work, we develop a novel video summarisation algorithm to generate video summaries from the classification of high-level subjective concepts such as audience engagement, comprehension and speaker emphasis. In earlier work we developed effective technologies for automatic classification of these features. The following subsections briefly review this work and summarise our classification results on the ISCM corpus.

4.1 Classification of Audience Engagement

Prediction of audience engagement levels and applying ratings for 'good' speaking techniques [3] were performed by first employing human annotators to watch video segments of conference presentations and to provide a rating on an ordinal scale of how good that speaker was at presenting the material. Audience engagement levels were measured in a similar manner by having annotators watch video segments of the audience to academic presentations and to provide an estimate of just how engaged the audience appeared to be as a whole. Classifiers were trained on extracted audio-visual features using an Ordinal Class Classifier.

The qualities of a 'good' speaker can be predicted to an accuracy of 73% over a 4-class scale. Using speaker-based techniques alone, audience engagement levels can be predicted to an accuracy of 68% over the same scale. By combining with basic visual features from the audience as whole, this can be improved to 70% accuracy.

4.2 Identification of Emphasized Speech

Identification of intentional or unintentional emphasized speech [1] was performed by having human annotators label areas of emphasised speech. Human annotators were asked to watch through short video clips and to mark areas where they considered the speech to be emphasized, either intentionally or unintentionally. Analysis was performed on this data to attempt to identify existing conditions for areas in which annotators had marked emphasis. Basic audio-visual features of audio pitch and visual motion were then extracted from this data. From the analysis performed, it was clear that speaker emphasis occurred during areas of high pitch, but also during areas of high visual motion coinciding with areas of high pitch.

Candidate emphasised regions were marked from extracted areas of pitch within the top 1, 5, and top 20 percentile of pitch values, in addition to top 20 percentile of gesticulation down to the top 40 percentile of values respectively. All annotated areas of emphasis contained significant gesturing in addition to pitch with the top 20 percentile.

4.3 Predicting the Speakers Potential to be Comprehended

Prediction of audience comprehension [4] was performed. Human annotators were recruited through the use of crowdsourcing. Annotators were asked to watch each section of a presentation and to first provide a textual summary of the contents of that section of the presentation and following this to provide an estimate of how much they comprehended the material during that section. Audio-visual features were extracted from video of the presenter in addition to visual features extracted from video of the audience, and OCR over the slides for each presentation. Additional fluency features were also extracted from the speaker audio. Using the above described extracted features, a classifier was trained to predict the speakers potential to be comprehended.

We showed that it is possible to build a classifier to predict potential audience comprehension levels, obtaining accuracy over a 7-class range of 52.9%, and over a binary classification problem to 85.4%.

For the purpose of investigating the effect of these features on summarisation, in this study we rely on manual labels of these features within the investigated presentation recordings. This enables us to concentrate on the impact of the features without needing to consider the impact of errors in automatic feature detection.

5 CREATION OF PRESENTATION SUMMARIES

This section describes the steps involved in the generation of presentation summaries. Summaries are generated using transcripts created using automatic speech recognition (ASR), keywords, and annotated values for 'good' public speaking techniques, audience engagement, intentional or unintentional speaker emphasis and the speakers potential to be comprehended. Using the ASR outputs, we use pause information derived from the ASR output, which gives start and end times for each spoken phrase during the presentation. This provides a basis for the separation of presentations at the phrase-level. We first apply a ranking for each phrase based on the number of keywords, or words of significance, contained within it. For the first set of baseline summaries, we generate summaries by using the highest ranking phrases.

Additional ranking is applied to each sentence based on human annotations of 'good' speaking techniques. Combination of our baseline scores for each phrase with other features is carried out using a weighted linear summation of the available features. In the absence of a suitable training set to set optimal values of the summation weights, we select the weights based on our observed intuitions of their behaviour and significance Speaker Rating's are halved before applying this ranking to each phrase. We half the values for speaker ratings so as not to overvalue this feature, as these values are already encompassed for classification of audience engagement levels. Following this, audience engagement annotations are also applied directly. We take the true annotated engagement level and apply this ranking to each sentence contained within each segment throughout the presentation. As emphasis was not annotated for all videos, we use automatic classifications for intentional or unintentional speaker emphasis. For each classification of emphasis, we apply an additional ranking of 1 to the phrase containing that emphasised part of speech. Finally, we use the human annotated values for audience comprehension throughout the data-set. Once again the final comprehension value for each segment is also applied to each sentence within that segment. For weightings, we choose to half the Speaker Rating annotation, while choosing to keep the original for other annotations, this is to reduce the impact of Speaker Ratings on the final output. Points of emphasis receive a ranking of 1, while keywords receive a ranking of two, in order to prioritise the role of keywords in the summary generation process.

To generate the final set of video summaries, the highest ranking phrases in the set are selected. To achieve this, the final ranking for each phrase is normalised to between 0 and 1. By then assigned an initial threshold value of 0.9, and reducing this by 0.3 on each iteration, we select each sentence with a ranking above that threshold value. By calculating the length of each selected sentence, we can apply a minimum size to our generated video summaries. Final selected segments are then joined together to generate small, medium and large summaries for each presentation.

Algorithm 1 Generate Summaries

```
for all Sentence → S do
  if S_contains_Keyword then
    S ← S + 2
  end if
  Engagement → E
  SpeakerRating → SR
  Emphasis → Es
  Comprehension → C
  S ← S + E
  S ← S + SR/2
  S ← S + Es
  S ← S + C
end for
while Summary < length do
  if S ≥ Threshold then
    Summary ← S
  end if
end while
```

6 EVALUATION OF VIDEO SUMMARIES

In this study we hypothesise that the classification of areas of 'good' speaking techniques, audience engagement, intentional or unintentional speaker emphasis, and the speakers potential to be comprehended by the audience, can be used to improve summarisation methods for academic presentations. To evaluate this, we first crowdsource human evaluation tasks by asking workers to watch summaries generated using keywords alone and summaries generated using all available information. Additional evaluation of automatically generated presentation summaries is performed by eye-tracking of participants as they watch a full presentation video and an automatic video summary. The question being addressed by eye-tracking of participants, is whether or not participants spend a larger proportion of the time viewing slides during summaries than full presentations. A complimentary comparison is also performed against the use of an enhanced digital video browser, which removed pauses and allowed playback to be increased to 250% of the norm to support manual skimming, these were previously found to be very effective for gaining a quick overview of conference presentations.

6.1 Evaluation Between Summary Types

Table 1 lists results of the comparison between summaries built using keyword information only and summaries built using all available information - keywords in addition to classifier outputs of the concepts of engagement, 'good' speaking techniques, comprehension and emphasis. A total of 48 participants watched the summaries and answered the questionnaire on each summary. The questions addressed in this comparison are listed in the following section below, and answers are ranked on a Likert scale from 1 to 7.

Table 1: Total ranking per summary type for each video

Video	Q1	Q2	Q3	Q4	Q5
plen2_Key	3.5	5	4	5	4
	42	65	44	55	44
plen2_All	3.5	5	4	4	4
	42	61	43	52	43
prp1_Key	3.42	5	3	4	3
	41	58	38	46	38
prp1_All	3.42	5	3	4	3
	41	56	39	46	39
prp5_Key	5.08	6	5	5	5
	61	67	57	56	57
prp5_All	4.25	6	5	5	5
	51	66	58	55	58
spRT6_Key	3.5	5	3	3	3
	42	55	39	39	39
spRT6_All	3.42	5	3	4	3
	41	59	31	49	31

These results indicate that user's perceive little difference overall, between summaries generated using keyword information only, as summaries generated using all available information. The most notable results indicate that users perceive the keyword summary of prp_5 to be easier to understand than the summary created using all available information for this video. Interestingly, user's also perceive the summary generated using all available information from speechRT6 video to be much more coherent than the summary generated using only keyword information from this video. This may however be explained by the fact that speechRT6 was discovered by our classifiers to be less engaging and comprehensible than other videos in the collection, while prp_5 was found to be the most engaging video. This would indicate that the effectiveness of using engagement information depends on just how engaging the video was in the first place.

6.2 Gaze-Detection Evaluation

Eye-tracking was performed for evaluation of presentation summaries. Participants watched one full conference presentation whilst having their eye-movements tracked and answered a questionnaire on the same. Participants also watched a separate presentation summary, again whilst having their eye-movements tracked and answered a number of questions on same. The question being addressed here was whether or not participants spent a larger proportion of the time viewing the slides during summaries than full presentations, to support the hypothesis that summaries contain a higher concentration of new information than full videos.

Table 2: Eye-tracking video 1 slides scene by version

I	J	Variable	Measure	Diff	Error	Sig
summ	full	FD.M	Scheffe	-0.02	0.05	0.655
summ	**full**	**percent**	**Scheffe**	**11.07**	**4.97**	**0.043**
summ	**full**	**FCp100**	**Scheffe**	**37.32**	**14.32**	**0.021**

Table 2 shows a statistically significant difference between the summary and full versions, for the percentage of time fixated per scene and the number of fixations per 100 seconds. As also demonstrated in the core figures in table 5, this indicates a significant difference in the amount of time users spent fixating on the slides while watching the summary than the full video. This indicates that users found there to be a much higher concentration of new information during the summary than during the slides.

Table 3: Eye-tracking video 2 slides scene by version

I	J	Variable	Measure	Diff	Error	Sig
summ	full	FD.M	Scheffe	-0.08	0.08	0.337
summ	full	percent	Scheffe	-2.72	7.90	0.735
summ	full	FCp100	Scheffe	7.04	11.16	0.538

Again in Table 3, key differences are observed in the average fixation duration per scene, and to a lesser extent in the fixation count per 100 seconds, more clearly visible from the figures in Table 5, neither of these differences are statistically significant.

Table 4 shows that there is a significant difference in the mean fixation length over the slides during the summary than during the full presentation. As can be seen by looking at the core figures in Table 5, the averaged fixation duration is much shorter for fixations on slides. This indicates that users tend to read over slides in order to follow and absorb printed information.

Table 4: Eye-tracking video 3 slides scene by version

I	J	Variable	Measure	Diff	Error	Sig
summ	**full**	**FD.M**	**Scheffe**	**-0.15**	**0.05**	**0.009**
summ	full	percent	Scheffe	-2.67	6.54	0.689
summ	full	FCper100	Scheffe	16.91	13.54	0.232

Table 5: Eye-tracking video 4 slides scene by version

I	J	Variable	Measure	Diff	Error	Sig
summ	full	FD.M	Scheffe	-0.06	0.05	0.266
summ	**full**	**percent**	**Scheffe**	**15.68**	**6.42**	**0.028**
summ	**full**	**FCp100**	**Scheffe**	**54.96**	**16.98**	**0.006**

Table 5 shows a statistically significant difference between the summary and full versions, for the percentage of time fixated per scene and the number of fixations per 100 seconds. As demonstrated in the core figures in Table 5, this indicates a significant difference in the amount of time users spent fixating on the slides while watching the summary than the full video. This indicates that users found there to be a much higher concentration of new information during the summary than the full version.

Table 6: Totals per vid, version, scene (V.V.S = Vid,Version,Scene)

V.V.S.	FD.N	DF.M	FD.S	%	FC.S	FCp100
1.1.1	354.875	0.4213	143.874	66.608	354.875	164.294
1.1.2	62.5	0.9588	55.296	25.600	62.5	28.935
1.2.1	1223.5	0.4463	536.485	55.537	1223.5	126.978
1.2.2	299.5	1.2463	329.468	34.106	299.5	31.004
2.1.1	248.125	0.59	145.479	66.127	248.125	112.784
2.1.2	45.125	1.2438	6.518	25.69	45.125	20.511
2.2.1	923.125	0.6663	601.053	68.849	923.125	105.742
2.2.2	165.5	1.0775	160.774	18.416	165.5	18.958
3.1.1	140.125	0.4288	60.123	40.623	140.125	94.679
3.1.2	53.75	1.3375	69.969	47.276	53.75	36.318
3.2.1	596.5	0.58	332.088	43.297	596.5	77.771
3.2.2	294.875	1.3288	324.413	42.296	294.875	38.445
4.1.1	345.125	0.4475	149.583	79.144	345.125	182.606
4.1.2	40.375	0.6113	24.523	12.975	40.375	21.362
4.2.1	1194.75	0.505	594.019	63.464	1194.75	127.644
4.2.2	219.625	0.8137	181.351	19.375	219.625	23.464

Table 6 shows the averaged core values for eye-tracking measurements per video, version and scene, from which the above tables 2 - 5 are calculated. For this, version denotes either a summarisation video or the full video, whereas scene denotes either the area of the slides or the area around the speaker themselves. Measurements obtained include number of Fixations, Mean length of fixations, Total Sum of fixation lengths, percentage of time fixated per scene, average number of fixation counts and Number of fixation counts per 100 seconds.

6.3 Questionnaire for Eye-Tracking Participants

Following the participant's completion of eye-tracking experiment, they completed a questionnaire. This questionnaire asked participants how much they agreed with each of the 5 statements issued, depending on whether they watched a summary or the full video, on a 5-Likert scale.

The following is the five statements on each video for which participants indicated their level of agreement:

(1) The video / summary is easy to understand.
(2) The video / summary is enjoyable.
(3) The video / summary is informative.
(4) The video / summary is coherent.
(5) I would have preferred to see a summary of this video. / This would aid in deciding whether to watch the full video.

Participants indicated their level of agreement with each of the five statements on a 5-point Likert scale, from Strongly Disagree to Strongly Agree.

The following is the average rankings for each video based on answers given to the questionnaire listed above. Video summaries were rated as being slightly less easy to understand than full presentation videos, with the largest different being for video 2, prp1. All video summaries have also received high ratings for their ability to help users to decide whether they wished to watch the full presentation video. Summarisation videos all received good ranking for informativeness, with all videos receiving a ranking of over 2.5, the best of these is again video 2, prp 1, which received an overall informative ranking of 3.22. The video found to be the least informative was video 4, speechRT6. This video was chosen for summarisation evaluation as it had been found by our classifiers to be the least engaging and least comprehensible presentation from the collection. This video summary still received an overall informativeness ranking of 2.5 out of 5, indicating that this video summarisation strategy helps maintain coherence of presentation videos when generating summaries.

Most summaries evaluated were found to be slightly less enjoyable than their original. The exception to this is video 4, speechRT6. As explained previously this video was found by our classifiers to be the least engaging and least comprehensible video from the collection. That this video summary is found to be more enjoyable than in its original form indicates that watching summaries can be a good alternative to watching full presentations of which the user may not be very interested.

A word of warning with these results is that none of these results indicated below have shown to be statistically significant, limiting the conclusions which can be drawn from these results.

6.4 Evaluation by Comparison with Enhanced Digital Video Browser

For final evaluation of presentation summaries, we performed a comparison against the properties of an enhanced digital video browser as studied by [10]. In this work, they evaluated the effectiveness and most useful features of an enhanced digital video browser. Within the domain of conference presentations they found

Table 7: Averaged rankings per video

Video	Q1-avg	Q2-avg	Q3-avg	Q4-avg	Q5-avg
vid-1 (s)	1.75	1.75	2.625	2.625	3.75
vid-1 (f)	2.5	2.75	4	3.5	3.75
vid-2 (s)	2.8889	2.8889	3.2222	2.8889	4.3333
vid-2 (f)	4.5	4	3.7	4.1	4.1
vid-3 (s)	3	3.25	3.125	3.5	4.125
vid-3 (f)	4.125	3.625	4.5	4.5	3.125
vid-4 (s)	1.7	1.8	2.5	2.4	3.8
vid-4 (f)	2.3333	1.6667	3.3333	3.3333	4.2222

Table 8: Averaged rankings per summary or full video

Video	Q1-avg	Q2-avg	Q3-avg	Q4-avg	Q5-avg
Summ	2.3143	2.4	2.8571	2.8286	4
Full	3.4	3.0286	3.8571	3.8571	3.8286

that Time Compression and Pause Removal were rated by participants as the most useful features. For further evaluation of automatically generated presentation summaries, we compare against the use of an enhanced digital video browser providing the features of Pause Removal and Time Compression.

For these evaluations, participants were given 5 minutes to gain a clear and concise overview of a presentation which they had previously missed, in order to be able to take part in a meeting discussing what was presented. Participants were given an enhanced digital video browser which removed pauses and allowed participants to increase or decrease playback rate as required, up to a maximum of 250% normal speed. Using this, participants had 5 minutes to gain a clear and concise overview of one of the presentations, and then answered 3 questions on the use of this tool. Participants were also given an automatically generated summary of the presentation. This summary was under 5 minutes in length and participants were again given 3 questions to answer on the use of this tool.

The following is the three statements on each tool for which participants indicated their level of agreement:

(1) This tool is easy to use.
(2) This tool allowed me to gain a clear and concise overview of the presentation.
(3) This would be my tool of choice for tasks of this nature.

Table 9: Averaged rankings per video

Video	Q1-avg	Q2-avg	Q3-avg
video-1 summ	4.5625	4.375	3.625
video-1 enh	4.5	3.9375	3.9375
video-2 summ	4.75	4.6875	4.1875
video-2 enh	5.125	5.1875	4.75
video-3 summ	4.875	4.6875	4.75
video-3 enh	4.125	4.3125	4.375
video-4 summ	4.8125	4	4
video-4 enh	4.4375	4.0625	3.9375

Results in table 9 indicate that participants were found to be 4.5% more likely to find that generated summaries were easier to use than the enhanced digital video browser for gaining a quick, clear and concise overview of missed presentations. Participants were also 1.5% more likely to agree that automatically generated video summaries were better for gaining a clear and concise overview of missed presentations than was the use of enhanced digital video browser. However, they were still 2.6% more likely to choose the enhanced digital video browser as their tool of choice.

These results are not however statistically significant, meaning that effectively we ended up with very equal rankings between automatically generated video summaries and and the use of enhanced digital video browser for gaining a quick, clear and concise overview of missed presentations.

7 CONCLUSIONS

The results of eye-tracking experiments performed in this study indicate that generated summaries tend to contain a higher concentration of relevant information than full presentations, as indicated by the higher proportion of time participants spend carefully reading slides during summaries than during full presentations, and also by the lower proportion of time spent fixating on the speaker during summaries than during full presentations. We also find that watching generated presentation summaries is a good alternative to watching full presentations in which the viewer might not be fully interested. However the questionnaire did find that generated video summaries receive lower ratings than full video presentation for being easy to understand, enjoyable, informative and coherent.

More encouraging results are shown by our comparisons with an enhanced digital video browser, which show that our generated summaries compare quite favourably to the use of an enhanced digital video browser, though these results lack statistical significance. In this case generated video summaries receive slightly higher scores than an enhanced digital video browser for 'ease of use' and effectiveness for 'gaining a clear and concise overview of the presentation'. However, they receive slightly lower scores for 'tool of choice'. Given that the work of [10] showed that an enhanced digital video browser scores very favourably for skimming presentation videos, and our own comparisons which rate our generated summaries at least equal in terms of effectiveness, this is a very promising result for these summarisation tasks.

The results of this study indicate that while classification of areas of engagement, emphasis and comprehension can be useful for summarisation, this may depend on how engaging and comprehensible videos were in the first place.

While this work demonstrates potential to exploit non-verbal features effectively in summarisation of presentation videos, we need to conduct further work to more fully understand the potential contributions of each of these features in individual videos, and their potential utility in comparison to the use of transcripts and other potentially text annotations of the content.

ACKNOWLEDGMENTS

This research is supported by Science Foundation Ireland through the CNGL Programme (Grant 12/CE/I2267) in the ADAPT Centre (www.adaptcentre.ie) at Dublin City University.

REFERENCES

[1] J. Allwood, E. Ahlsén, S. Lanzini, A. Attaran, K. Curtis, G. J. Jones, N. Campbell, J. Frid, G. Ambrazaitis, M. S. Lundmark, et al. The 4th european and 7th nordic symposium on multimodal communication (mmsym 2016), copenhagen 29-30 september 2016: Extended abstracts. pages 6–7, 2016.

[2] G. Chechik, E. Ie, M. Rehn, S. Bengio, and D. Lyon. Large-scale content-based audio retrieval from text queries. In *Proceedings of the 1st ACM international conference on Multimedia information retrieval*, pages 105–112. ACM, 2008.

[3] K. Curtis, G. J. Jones, and N. Campbell. Effects of good speaking techniques on audience engagement. In *Proceedings of the 2015 ACM on International Conference on Multimodal Interaction*, pages 35–42. ACM, 2015.

[4] K. Curtis, G. J. Jones, and N. Campbell. Speaker impact on audience comprehension for academic presentations. In *Proceedings of the 18th ACM International Conference on Multimodal Interaction*, pages 129–136. ACM, 2016.

[5] L. He, E. Sanocki, A. Gupta, and J. Grudin. Auto-summarization of audio-video presentations. In *Proceedings of the seventh ACM international conference on Multimedia (Part 1)*, pages 489–498. ACM, 1999.

[6] M. J. Huiskes, B. Thomee, and M. S. Lew. New trends and ideas in visual concept detection: the mir flickr retrieval evaluation initiative. In *Proceedings of the international conference on Multimedia information retrieval*, pages 527–536. ACM, 2010.

[7] H. Joho, J. M. Jose, R. Valenti, and N. Sebe. Exploiting facial expressions for affective video summarisation. In *Proceedings of the ACM International Conference on Image and Video Retrieval*, page 31. ACM, 2009.

[8] S. X. Ju, M. J. Black, S. Minneman, and D. Kimber. Summarization of videotaped presentations: automatic analysis of motion and gesture. *IEEE Transactions on Circuits and Systems for Video Technology*, 8(5):686–696, 1998.

[9] M. S. Lew, N. Sebe, C. Djeraba, and R. Jain. Content-based multimedia information retrieval: State of the art and challenges. *ACM Transactions on Multimedia Computing, Communications, and Applications (TOMM)*, 2(1):1–19, 2006.

[10] F. C. Li, A. Gupta, E. Sanocki, L.-w. He, and Y. Rui. Browsing digital video. In *Proceedings of the SIGCHI conference on Human Factors in Computing Systems*, pages 169–176. ACM, 2000.

[11] A. Pavel, C. Reed, B. Hartmann, and M. Agrawala. Video digests: a browsable, skimmable format for informational lecture videos. In *UIST*, pages 573–582, 2014.

How to Make an Image More Memorable? A Deep Style Transfer Approach

Aliaksandr Siarohin
University of Trento
aliaksandr.siarohin@unitn.it

Gloria Zen
University of Trento
gloria.zen@unitn.it

Cveta Majtanovic
University of Novi Sad
and University of Trento
cveta.majtanovic@unitn.it

Xavier Alameda-Pineda
INRIA Grenoble
xavier.alameda-pineda@inria.fr

Elisa Ricci
Fondazione Bruno Kessler
and University of Perugia
eliricci@fbk.eu

Nicu Sebe
University of Trento
nicu.sebe@unitn.it

ABSTRACT

Recent works have shown that it is possible to automatically predict intrinsic image properties like memorability. In this paper, we take a step forward addressing the question: *"Can we make an image more memorable?"*. Methods for automatically increasing image memorability would have an impact in many application fields like education, gaming or advertising. Our work is inspired by the popular *editing-by-applying-filters* paradigm adopted in photo editing applications, like Instagram and Prisma. In this context, the problem of increasing image memorability maps to that of retrieving "memorabilizing" filters or style "seeds". Still, users generally have to go through most of the available filters before finding the desired solution, thus turning the editing process into a resource and time consuming task. In this work, we show that it is possible to automatically retrieve the *best* style seeds for a given image, thus remarkably reducing the number of human attempts needed to find a good match. Our approach leverages from recent advances in the field of image synthesis and adopts a deep architecture for generating a memorable picture from a given input image and a style seed. Importantly, to automatically select the best style a novel learning-based solution, also relying on deep models, is proposed. Our experimental evaluation, conducted on publicly available benchmarks, demonstrates the effectiveness of the proposed approach for generating memorable images through automatic style seed selection.

CCS CONCEPTS

•**Computing methodologies** →**Computer vision;** *Computational photography;*

KEYWORDS

Memorability; photo enhancement; deep style transfer; retrieval.

DOI: http://dx.doi.org/10.1145/3078971.3078986

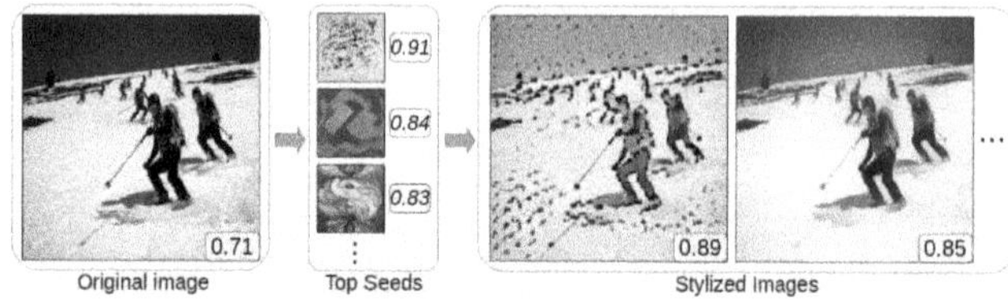

Figure 1: Sample results illustrating our idea (best viewed in colors). Given a generic image (left), automatically find the best style filters (center) that augment the memorability of the image (right). Memorability scores in the range [0,1] are reported in the small boxes.

ACM Reference format:
Aliaksandr Siarohin, Gloria Zen, Cveta Majtanovic, Xavier Alameda-Pineda, Elisa Ricci, and Nicu Sebe. 2017. How to Make an Image More Memorable? A Deep Style Transfer Approach. In *Proceedings of ICMR '17, June 6–9, 2017, Bucharest, Romania*, , 8 pages.
DOI: http://dx.doi.org/10.1145/3078971.3078986

1 INTRODUCTION

Today's expansion of infographics is certainly related to one of the everyday life idiom "A picture is worth a thousand words" (or more precisely 84.1 words [4]) and to the need of providing the fastest possible knowledge transfer in the current "information overload" age. A recent study [13] showed that everyone is bombarded by the equivalent of 174 newspapers of data every day. In this context, we ask ourselves: *Is it possible to transform a user-chosen image so that it has more chances to be remembered*?

For this question to be properly stated, it requires the existence of a measure of memorability, and recent studies proved that memorability is intrinsic to the visual content and is measurable [16, 17]. Indeed, these studies use *memory games* to provide an objective evaluation of image memorability, which has surprisingly low variance across trials. Recent studies have also provided tools to detect the visual features responsible for both memorable and easily forgettable images. For instance, images that tend to be forgotten lack distinctiveness, like natural landscapes, whereas pictures with people, specific actions and events or central objects are way more memorable [6]. Previous papers have also analyzed the relationship between emotions and memorability [8]. In a similar line of thought, researchers wondered how to accurately predict which images will be remembered and which will be not. Recent experiments showed near-human performance in estimating, measuring and predicting visual memorability [19], where MemNet, a model trained on the largest annotated image memorability dataset, LaMem, has been proposed.

While previous studies on automatic prediction of memorability from images paved the way towards the automatic recognition of image memorability, many questions are still open. For instance: *is it possible to increase the memorability of an image, while keeping its high-level content?* Imagine an advertising campaign concerning the design for a new product targeting a specific market sector. Once the very expensive designing phase is over, the client receives a set of images advertising the new product. Such images tell a story: in the attempt of increasing the image's memorability, the high-level content, that is *the meaning*, should remain intact. We therefore focus on how to automatically modify the style of the image, that is how to *filter* the image, so as to make it more memorable. Some popular commercial products are based on this image filtering philosophy, for other purposes than memorability though. For instance, Instagram[1], a photo and video sharing Internet platform launched in 2010, allows the users to filter the visual content with several pre-defined filters before sharing. Similarly, Prisma[2] turns user memories into art by using artificial intelligence. In parallel to the development of these commercial products, several recent research studies in computer vision and multimedia have focused on creating artistic images of high perceptual quality with artificial intelligence models. For instance, Gatys *et al.* [10] have proposed an approach where a deep network is used to manipulate the content of a natural image adapting it to the style of a given artwork. Subsequently, more efficient deep architectures for implementing a style transfer have been introduced [30]. Importantly, none of these commercial products and related research studies incorporate the notion of image memorability.

In this work, we propose a novel approach for increasing the memorability of images which is inspired by the *editing-by-filtering* framework (Fig. 1). Our method relies on three deep networks. A first deep architecture, the *Synthesizer* network, is used to synthesize a memorable image from the input picture and a style picture. A second network acts as a style *Selector* and it is used to retrieve the "best" style seed to provide to the Synthesizer, (*i.e.* the one that will produce the highest increase in terms of memorability) given the input picture. To train the Selector, pairs of images and vectors of memorability gap scores (indicating the increase/decrease in memorability when applying each seed to the image) are used. A third network, the *Scorer*, which predicts the memorability score from a given input image, is used to compute the memorability gaps necessary to train the Selector. Our approach is extensively evaluated on the publicly available LaMem dataset [19] and we show that it can be successfully used to automatically increase the memorability of natural images.

The main contributions of our work are the following:

- We tackle the challenging task of increasing image memorability while keeping the high-level content intact (thus modifying only the style of the image).
- We cast this into a style-based image synthesis problem using deep architectures and propose an automatic method to retrieve the style seeds that are expected to lead to the largest increase of memorability for the input image.
- We propose a lightweight solution for training the Selector network implementing the style seed selection process, allowing us to efficiently learn our model with a reduced number of training data while considering relatively large variations of style pictures.

2 RELATED WORKS

The concept of memorability and its relation with other aspects of the human mind has been long studied from a psychological perspective [3, 14, 25, 28]. Works in psychology and neuroscience mostly focused on visual memory, studying for instance the human capacity of remembering object details [6], the effect of emotions on memory [3, 28] or the brain's learning mechanisms, *e.g.* the role of the amygdala in memory [25, 28]. For a few years now, more automated studies on memorability have arisen: from the collection of image datasets specifically designed to study memorability, to user-friendly techniques to annotate these data with memorability scores. The community is now paying attention to understand the causes of visual memorability and its prominent links with, for instance, image content, low- and mid-level visual features and evoked emotions.

Isola *et al.* [16] showed that visual memorability is an intrinsic property of images, and that it can be explained by considering only image visual features. Besides the expected inter-subject variability, [16] reported a large consistency among viewers when measuring the memorability of several images. Typically, such measures are obtained by playing a memory game. Other studies proved that memorability can also be automatically predicted. Recently, Khosla *et al.* [19] used CNN-based features from MemNet to achieve a prediction accuracy very close to human performance, *i.e.* up to the limit of the inter-subject variability, thus outperforming previous works using hand-crafted features such as objects or visual attributes [17].

In parallel, large research efforts have been invested in understanding what makes an image memorable and, in a complementary manner, which is the relation between image memorability and other subjective properties of visual data, such as interestingness, aesthetics or evoked emotions. Gygli *et al.* [12] observed that memorability negatively correlates with visual interestingness. Curiously, they also showed that human beings perform quite bad at judging the memorability of an image, thus further justifying the use of memory games for annotation. In the same study, it was shown that aesthetic, visual interestingness and human judgements of memorability are highly correlated. Similar results were reported later on in [17], confirming these findings. A possible mundane interpretation of these findings is that people wish to remember what they like or find interesting, though this is not always the case.

Khosla *et al.* [19] showed that, with the exception of *amusement*, images that evoke negative emotions like *disgust*, *anger* and *fear*

[1] https://www.instagram.com
[2] http://prisma-ai.com

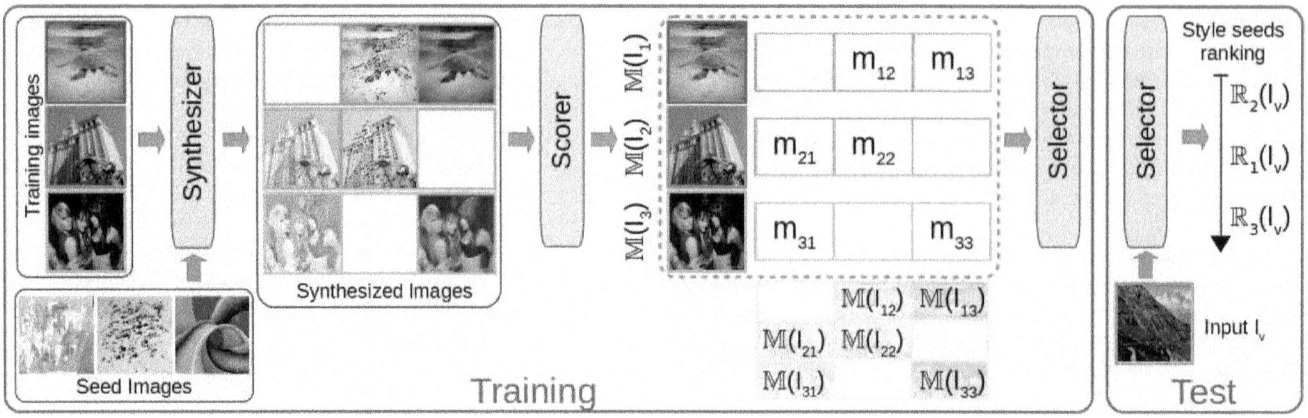

Figure 2: Overview of our method. At training time, the Synthesizer $\mathbb{S}$ and the Scorer $\mathbb{M}$ serve to generate the training data (highlighted with a red dotted frame) for the seed Selector $\mathbb{R}$. At test time, the seed Selector provides for each new image a sorted list of style seeds, based on the predicted memorability increase $\mathbb{R}_s(\mathbf{I}_v)$.

are more likely to be remembered. Conversely, images that evoke emotions like *awe* and *contentment* tend to be less memorable. Similarly, the authors of [15] showed that attributes like *peaceful* are negatively correlated with memorability. Other works showed that *arousal* has a strong effect on human memory [3, 8, 26] at two different stages: either during the encoding of visual information (*e.g.*, increased attention and/or processing) or post-encoding (*e.g.*, enhanced consolidation when recalling the stored visual information). Memorability was also investigated with respect to distinctiveness and low-level cues such as colors in [5] and with respect to eye fixation in [7, 19]. In more detail, [5] discussed how images that stand out of the context (*i.e.*, they are unexpected or unique) are more easily remembered and that memorability significantly depends upon the number of distinct colors in the image. These findings support our intuition that it is possible to manipulate an image to increase its memorability. Indeed, this can happen for example by indirectly modifying image distinctiveness or the evoked arousal. Along the same line of though, Peng *et al.* [27] attempted to modify the emotions evoked by an image adjusting its color tone and its texture-related features.

Recent works analyzed how images can be modified to increase or decrease their memorability [18, 19]. These are based on other contemporary studies that focused on generating memorability maps of images [20–22]. In particular, Khosla *et al.* [19] showed that by removing visual details from an image through a cartonization process the memorability score can be modified. However, they did not provide a methodology to systematically increase the memorability of pictures. The same group [18] also demonstrated that it is possible to increase the memorability of faces, while maintaining the identity of the person and properties like age, attractiveness and emotional magnitude. Up to our knowledge, this is the first attempt to automatically increase the memorability of generic images (not only faces).

3 METHOD

In this section we introduce the proposed framework to automatically increase the memorability of an input image. Our method is designed in a way such that the process of "memorabilizing" images is performed in an efficient manner while preserving most of the high-level image content.

3.1 Overview

The proposed approach co-articulates three main components, namely: the seed Selector, the Scorer and the Synthesizer, and so we refer to it as S^3 or *S-cube*. In order to give a general idea of the overall methodological framework, we illustrate the pipeline associated to S-cube in Figure 2. The Selector is the core of our approach: for a generic input image $\mathbf{I}$ and given a set of style image seeds $\mathcal{S}$, the Selector retrieves the subset of $\mathcal{S}$ that will be able to produce the largest increase of memorability. In details, the seed Selector predicts the expected increase/decrease of memorability that each seed $\mathbf{S} \in \mathcal{S}$ will produce in the input image $\mathbf{I}$, and consequently it ranks the seeds according to the expected increase of memorability. At training time, the Synthesizer and the Scorer are used to generate images from many input image-seed pairs and to score these pairs, respectively. Each input image is then associated to the relative increase/decrease of memorability obtained with each of the seeds. With this information, we can learn to predict the increase/decrease of memorability for a new image, and therefore rank the seeds according to the expected increase. Indeed, at query time, the Selector is able to retrieve the most memorabilizing seeds and give them to the Synthesizer. In the following, we first formalize the S-cube framework and then describe each of the three components in detail.

3.2 The S-cube approach

Let us denote the Scorer, the Synthesizer and the seed Selector models by $\mathbb{M}$, $\mathbb{S}$ and $\mathbb{R}$, respectively. During the **training phase** the three models are learned. The Scoring model $\mathbb{M}$ returns the memorability value $\mathbb{M}(\mathbf{I})$ of a generic image $\mathbf{I}$, and it is learned by means of a training set of images annotated with memorability: $\mathcal{M} = \{\mathbf{I}_i^M, m_i\}_{i=1}^I$. In addition to this training set, we also consider a generating set of natural images $\mathcal{G} = \{\mathbf{I}_g^G\}_{g=1}^G$ and a set of style seed images $\mathcal{S} = \{\mathbf{S}_s\}_{s=1}^S$. The Synthesizer produces an image from an image-seed pair,

$$\mathbf{I}_{gs} = \mathbb{S}\left(\mathbf{I}_g^G, \mathbf{S}_s\right). \quad (1)$$

The scoring model $\mathbb{M}$ and the Synthesizer $\mathbb{S}$ are the required steps to train the seed Selector $\mathbb{R}$. Indeed, for each image $\mathbf{I}_g^G \in G$ and for each style seed $\mathbf{S}_s \in S$, the synthesis procedure generates $\mathbf{I}_{gs}$. The Scoring model is used to compute the memorability score gap between the synthesized and the original images:

$$m_{gs}^{\mathbb{M}} = \mathbb{M}(\mathbf{I}_{gs}) - \mathbb{M}(\mathbf{I}_g^G). \quad (2)$$

The seed-wise concatenation of these scores, denoted by $\mathbf{m}_g^{\mathbb{M}} = (m_{gs}^{\mathbb{M}})_{s=1}^S$, is used to learn the seed Selector. Specifically, a training set of natural images labeled with the seed-wise concatenation of memorability gaps $R = \{\mathbf{I}_g^G, \mathbf{m}_g^{\mathbb{M}}\}_{g=1}^G$ is constructed. The process of seed selection is casted as a regression problem and the mapping $\mathbb{R}$ between an image and the associated vector of memorability gap scores is learned. This indirectly produces a ranking of the seeds in terms of their ability to memorabilize images (*i.e.* the best seed corresponds to the largest memorability increase).

During the **test phase** and given a novel image $\mathbf{I}_v$, the seed Selector is applied to predict the vector of memorability gap scores associated to all style seeds, *i.e.* $\mathbf{m}_v = \mathbb{R}(\mathbf{I}_v)$. A ranking of seeds is then derived from the vector $\mathbf{m}_v$. Based on this ranking the Synthesizer is applied to the test image $\mathbf{I}_v$ considering only the top Q style seeds $\mathbf{S}_s$ and produces a set of stylized images $\{\mathbf{I}_{qs}\}_{q=1}^Q$.

In the following we describe the three main building blocks of our approach, providing details of our implementation.

3.3 The Scorer

The scoring model $\mathbb{M}$ returns an estimate of the memorability associated to an input image $\mathbf{I}$. In our work, we use the memorability predictor based on LaMem in [19], which is the state of the art to automatically compute image memorability. In details, following [19] we consider a hybrid CNN model [31]. The network is pre-trained first for the object classification task (*i.e.* on ImageNet database) and then for the scene classification task (*i.e.* on Places dataset). Then, we randomly split the LaMem training setinto two disjoint subsets (of 22,500 images each), M and E. We use the pretrained model and the two subsets to learn two independent scoring models $\mathbb{M}$ and $\mathbb{E}$. While, as discussed above, $\mathbb{M}$ is used during the training phase of our approach, the model $\mathbb{E}$ is adopted for evaluation (see Section 4.1). For training, we run 70k iterations of stochastic gradient descent with momentum 0.9, learning rate 10^{-3} and batch size 256.

3.4 The Synthesizer

The Synthesizer takes as an input a generic image $\mathbf{I}_g$ and a style seed image $\mathbf{S}_s$ and produces a stylized image $\mathbf{I}_{gs} = \mathbb{S}(\mathbf{I}_g, \mathbb{S}_s)$. We use the strategy proposed in [30], which consists on training a different feed-forward network for every seed. As seeds, we use 100 abstract paintings from the DeviantArt database [29], and therefore we train $S = 100$ networks for 10k iterations with learning rate 10^{-2}. The most important hyper-parameter is the coefficient α, which regulates the trade-off between preserving the original image content and producing something closer to the style seed (see Figure

Figure 3: Sample results. (Left) Original images and applied style seeds. (Right) Synthesized images at varying parameter α, which regulates the trade-off between preserving the original content of the given image $\mathbf{I}_v$ and transferring the style $\mathbf{S}_s$.

3). In our experiments we evaluated the effect of α (see Section 4). It is worth noticing that the methodology proposed in this article is independent of the synthesis procedure. Indeed, we also tried other methods, namely Gatys *et al.* [9] and Li *et al.* [23], but we selected [30] since it showed very good performance while keeping low computational complexity. This is especially important in our framework since the Synthesizer is also used to generate the training set for learning $\mathbb{R}$.

3.5 The Seed Selector

The core part of our approach is the Selector. Given a training set of natural images labeled with the vector of memorability gaps: $R = \{\mathbf{I}_g^G, \mathbf{m}_g^{\mathbb{M}}\}_{g=1}^G$, the seed Selector $\mathbb{R}$ is trained minimizing the following objective:

$$L_{\mathbb{R}} = \sum_{g=1}^{G} \mathcal{L}\left(\mathbb{R}(\mathbf{I}_g^G), \mathbf{m}_g^{\mathbb{M}}\right). \quad (3)$$

where $\mathcal{L}$ is a loss function which measures the discrepancy between the learned vector $\mathbb{R}(\mathbf{I}_g^G)$ and the memorability gap scores $\mathbf{m}_g^{\mathbb{M}}$. By training the seed Selector with memorability gaps, we are learning *by how much each of the seeds increases or decreases the memorability of a given image.* This has several advantages. First, we can very easily rank the seeds by the expected increase in memorability they will produce if used together with the input image and the synthesis procedure. Second, if several seeds have similar expected memorability increase, they can be proposed to the user for further selection. Third, if all seeds are expected to decrease the memorability, the optimal choice of not modifying the image can easily be made. Fourth, once $\mathbb{R}$ is trained, all this information comes at the price of evaluating $\mathbb{R}$ for a new image, which is cheaper than running $\mathbb{S}$ and $\mathbb{M}$ S times.

Even if this strategy has many advantages at testing time, the most prominent drawback is that, to create the training set $\mathcal{R}$, one should ideally call the synthesis procedure for all possible image-seed pairs. This clearly reduces the scalability and the flexibility of the proposed approach. The scalability because training the model on a large image dataset means generating a much larger dataset (*i.e.*, S times larger). The flexibility because if one wishes to add a new seed to the set S, then all image-seed pairs for the new seed need to be synthesized and this takes time. Therefore, it would be desirable to find a way to overcome these limitations while keeping the advantages described in the previous paragraph.

The solution to these issues comes with a model able to learn from a partially synthesized set, in which not all image-seed pairs are generated and scored. This means that the memorability gap vector $\mathbf{m}_g^{\mathbb{M}}$ has missing entries. In this way we only require to generate *enough* image-seed pairs. To this aim, we propose to use a decomposable loss function $\mathcal{L}$. Formally, we define a binary variable ω_{gs} set to 1 if the gs-th image-seed pair is available and to 0 otherwise and rewrite the objective function in (3) as:

$$L_{\mathbb{R}} = \sum_{g=1}^{G}\sum_{s=1}^{S}\omega_{gs}\ell\left(\mathbb{R}_s(\mathbf{I}_g^G), m_{gs}^{\mathbb{M}}\right). \quad (4)$$

where $\mathbb{R}_s$ is the s-th component of $\mathbb{R}$ and ℓ is the square loss. We implemented this model using an AlexNet architecture, where the prediction errors for the missing entries of $\mathbf{m}_g^{\mathbb{M}}$ are not back-propagated. Specifically, we considered the pre-trained Hybrid-CNN and fine-tune only the layers fc6, fc7, conv5, conv4 using learning rate equal to 10^{-3}, momentum equal to 0.9 and batch size 64. The choice of Hybrid-CNN is considered more appropriate when dealing with generic images since the network is pre-trained both on images of places and objects.

4 EXPERIMENTAL VALIDATION

We assess the performance of our approach in successfully retrieving the most memorabilizing seeds to increase the memorability of arbitrary images (Sec. 4.2). The datasets and experimental protocol used in our study are described in Sec. 4.1.

4.1 Datasets and Experimental Protocol

In our experiments we consider two publicly available datasets, LaMem[3] and DeviantArt[4].

LaMem. The LaMem dataset [19] is the largest dataset used to study memorability. It is a collection of 58,741 images gathered from a number of previously existing datasets, including the affective images dataset [24], which consists of Art and Abstract paintings. The memorability scores were collected for all the dataset pictures using an optimized protocol of the memorability game. The corpus was released to overcome the limitations of previous works on memorability which considered small datasets and very specific image domains. The large appearance variations of the images makes LaMem particularly suitable for our purpose.

DeviantArt. This dataset [29] consists of a set of 500 abstract art paintings collected from deviantArt (dA), an online social network site devoted to user-generated art. Since the scope of our study requires avoiding substantial modifications of the high-level content of the image, we selected the style seeds from abstract paintings. Indeed, abstract art relies in textures and color combinations, thus an excellent candidate when attempting the automatic modification of the low-level image content.

Protocol. In our experiments using the LaMem dataset we consider the same training (45,000 images), test (10,000 images) and validation (3,741 images) data adopted in [19]. We split the LaMem training set into two subsets of 22,500 images each (see also Section 3.3), M and E, which are used to train two predictors $\mathbb{M}$ and $\mathbb{E}$, respectively. The model $\mathbb{M}$ is the Scorer employed in our framework, while $\mathbb{E}$ (which we will denote in the following as the external predictor) is used to evaluate the performance of our approach, as a proxy for human assessment. We highlight that $\mathbb{M}$ and $\mathbb{E}$ can be used as two independent memorability scoring functions, since M and E are disjoint. The validation set is used to implement the early stopping. To evaluate the performance of our scorer models M and E, following [19], we compute the rank correlation between predicted and actual memorability on LaMem test set. We obtain a rank correlation of 0.63 with both models, while [19] achieves a rank correlation of 0.64 training on the whole LaMem training set. As reported in [19], this is close to human performance (0.68).

The test set of LaMem (10k images) is then used (i) to learn the proposed seed Selector and (ii) to evaluate the overall framework (and the Selector in particular). In detail, we split LaMem test set into train, validation and test for our Selector with proportion 8:1:1, meaning 8,000 for training and 1,000 for validation and test. The training set for the Selector was already introduced as G. We denote the test set as V. The validation set is used to perform early stopping, if required.

Regarding the seeds, we estimated the memorability of all paintings of DeviantArt using $\mathbb{M}$ and selected the 50 most and the 50 least memorable images as seeds for our study (S). The memorability scores of the deviantArt images range from 0.556 to 0.938.

Baseline. To the best of our knowledge this is the first work showing that it is possible to automatically increase the memorability of a generic image. For this reason, a direct and quantitative comparison with previous studies is not possible. Indeed, the recent work [19] showed that it is possible to compute accurate memorability maps from images, which can be used as bases for further image manipulations. They also observed that using a memorability map for removing image details, such as through a cartoonization process, typically lead to a memorability decrease. Oppositely, we aim to effectively increase image memorability without modifying the high level content of the images. Therefore, the approach by [19] does not directly compare with ours. The only potential competitor to our approach would be [18], except that the method is specifically designed for face photographs. Indeed, the proposed approach aims to modify the memorability while keeping other attributes (age, gender, expression) as well as the identify untouched. Therefore, the principle of [18] cannot be straightforwardly transferred to generic images. Consequently, we define an *average* baseline B that consists on ranking the style seeds according to the average memorability increase for the training set, formulated as:

$$\bar{m}_s^{\mathbb{M}} = \frac{1}{G}\sum_{g=1}^{G} m_{gs}^{\mathbb{M}}. \quad (5)$$

4.2 Increasing image memorability

We first evaluate the performance of our method at predicting the memorability increase of an image-seed match, where the seed is taken from the set of style seeds S, and the generic image $\mathbf{I}_v^V$ is taken from a set of (yet) unseen images $V = \{\mathbf{I}_v^V\}_{v=1}^{V}$. We use two different performance measures: the mean squared error (MSE) and

[3] http://memorability.csail.mit.edu

[4] http://disi.unitn.it/~sartori/datasets/deviantart-dataset

		$A^{\mathbb{M}}$		$A^{\mathbb{E}}$		$\text{MSE}^{\mathbb{M}}$		$\text{MSE}^{\mathbb{E}}$	
α	$\bar{\omega}$	$\mathcal{B}$	S-cube	$\mathcal{B}$	S-cube	$\mathcal{B}$	S-cube	$\mathcal{B}$	S-cube
2	0.01	**63.21**	57.12	**60.96**	56.01	**0.0113**	0.0138	**0.0119**	0.0137
	0.1	64.49	**64.70**	61.07	**62.22**	**0.0112**	0.0114	**0.0117**	0.0119
	0.5	64.41	**67.18**	61.06	**64.38**	0.0112	**0.0102**	0.0117	**0.0106**
	1	64.41	**67.80**	61.06	**64.71**	0.0112	**0.0102**	0.0117	**0.0108**
10	0.01	**67.91**	64.74	**68.31**	64.74	**0.0126**	0.0151	**0.0134**	0.0163
	0.1	68.04	**72.25**	68.36	**70.96**	0.0125	**0.0116**	0.0132	**0.0121**
	0.5	67.99	**73.26**	68.31	**71.72**	0.0125	**0.0109**	0.0132	**0.0112**
	1	68.04	**73.26**	68.31	**71.75**	0.0125	**0.0108**	0.0132	**0.0111**

Table 1: Performance of our method S-cube compared to baseline $\mathcal{B}$ at varying percentage of training data $\bar{\omega}$ and style coefficient α, measured in terms of (left) accuracy A and (right) mean squared error (MSE). Performances have been evaluated using both the internal $\mathbb{M}$ and external $\mathbb{E}$ predictor.

the accuracy A, which are defined as follows:

$$\text{MSE}^{\mathbb{X}} = \frac{1}{SV} \sum_{s=1}^{S} \sum_{v=1}^{V} \left(m_{vs}^{\mathbb{X}} - \mathbb{R}_s(\mathbf{I}_v^V) \right)^2 \quad (6)$$

and

$$A^{\mathbb{X}} = \frac{1}{SV} \sum_{s=1}^{S} \sum_{v=1}^{V} (1 - |H(m_{vs}^{\mathbb{X}}) - H(\mathbb{R}_s(I_v^V))|) \quad (7)$$

where $\mathbb{X}$ indicates the internal or external predictor, respectively $\mathbb{X} = \{\mathbb{M}, \mathbb{E}\}$, and H is the Heaviside step function.

Table 1 reports the performance of both the proposed approach (S-cube) and the baseline (B) under different experimental setups. Indeed, we report the accuracy (left) and the MSE (right) evaluated using the scoring model $\mathbb{M}$ and the external scoring model $\mathbb{E}$ (left two and right two columns of each block), for different values of α and the average amount of image-seed matches $\bar{\omega}$. More precisely, $\bar{\omega} = 1$ means that all image-seed pairs are used, $\bar{\omega} = 0.1$ means that only 10% is used, and so on.

Generally speaking our method outperforms the baseline if enough image-seed pairs are available. We argue that, as it is well known, deep architectures require a *sufficient* amount of data to be effective. Indeed, when $\bar{\omega} = 0.01$, the network optimization procedure attemps to learn a regression from the raw image to a 100-dimensional space with, in average, only one of this dimensions propagating the error back to the network. Although this dimension is different for each image, we may be facing a situation in which not enough information is propagated back to the parameters so as to effectively learn a robust regressor. This situation is coherent when the scoring method changes from $\mathbb{M}$ to $\mathbb{E}$. We can clearly observe a decrease in the performance measures when using $\mathbb{E}$, as expected. Indeed, since the seed selector has been trained to learn the memorability gap of $\mathbb{M}$, the performance is higher when using $\mathbb{M}$ than $\mathbb{E}$.

Furthermore, we report the performance of our method using two different values of the style coefficient $\alpha = \{2, 10\}$. It can be noticed that our method performs better in terms of MSE when $\alpha = 2$, while accuracy is usually higher for $\alpha = 10$. What a priori could be seen as a divergent behavior, can be explained by the fact that imposing a higher weight to the style produces higher memorability gaps m_{gs}, thus it may generate a higher error in the estimation. We interpret these results as an indication that MSE and A can be good criteria for finding the best setup in terms of percentage of training data, but not necessarily to set other parameters.

	$A^{\mathbb{E}}$		$\text{MSE}^{\mathbb{E}}$	
$\bar{\omega}$	VGG16	AlexNet	VGG16	AlexNet
0.01	**61.56**	56.01	**0.0121**	0.0137
0.1	**64.76**	62.22	**0.0109**	0.0119
0.5	63.49	**64.38**	0.0111	**0.0106**
1	63.44	**64.71**	0.0111	**0.0108**

Table 2: Performances of our method S-cube based on AlexNet (fine-tuning Hybrid-CNN [31]) and VGG16 (pre-trained on ImageNet), measured in terms of $\text{MSE}^{\mathbb{E}}$ and $A^{\mathbb{E}}$, at varying percentage of training data $\bar{\omega}$.

	$A^{\mathbb{E}}$		$\text{MSE}^{\mathbb{E}}$	
S	B	S-cube	B	S-cube
20	60.66	**63.15**	0.0114	**0.0111**
50	61.09	**63.51**	0.0116	**0.0109**
100	61.06	**64.38**	0.0117	**0.0106**

Table 3: Performance of our method in terms of $\text{MSE}^{\mathbb{E}}$ and $A^{\mathbb{E}}$ ($\alpha = 2$ and $\bar{\omega} = 0.5$) at varying the cardinality S of the style seed set.

We also investigated the impact of the network depth and trained a seed Selector using VGG16 instead of AlexNet. We fine-tuned the layers fc6, fc7, and all conv5, using Nesterov momentum with momentum 0.9, learning rate 10^{-3} and batch size 64. Importantly, while AlexNet was trained as a hybrid-CNN [19], the pre-trained model for VGG16 was trained on ImageNet. We found very interesting results and report them in Table 2, for $\alpha = 2$. The behavior of AlexNet was already discussed in the previous paragraphs. Interestingly we observe similar trends in VGG. Indeed, when not enough training pairs are available the results are pretty unsatisfying. However, in relative terms, the results for small $\bar{\omega}$ are far better for VGG16 than for AlexNet. We attribute this to the fact that VGG16 is much larger, and therefore the amount of knowledge

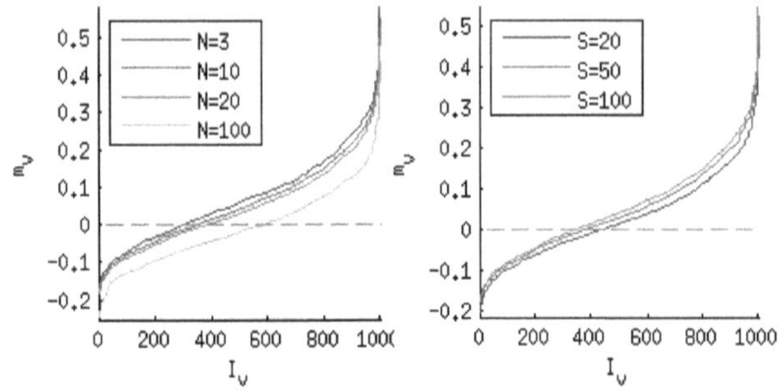

Figure 4: Sorted average memorability gaps $\bar{m}_v$ obtained with our method S-cube (left) averaging over varying number of top N seeds and (right) at varying the cardinality S of the seed set, with $N = 10$.

encoded in the pre-trained model has a stronger regularization effect in our problem than when using AlexNet. The main drawback is that, when enough data are available and since the amount of parameters in VGG16 is much larger than in AlexNet, the latest exhibits higher performance than the former. We recall that the seed Selector is trained with 8k images, and hypothesize that fine-tuning with larger datasets (something not possible if we want to use the splits provided in LaMem) will raise the performance of the VGG16-based seed Selector.

Furthermore, we studied the behavior of the framework when varying the size S of the seed set. Results are shown in Table 3. Specifically, we select two sets of 50 and 20 seeds out of the initial 100, randomly sampling these seeds half from the 50 most and half from the 50 least memorable ones. In terms of accuracy, the performance of both the proposed method and the baseline remain pretty stable when decreasing the number of seeds. This behavior was also observed in Table 1, especially for the baseline method. However, a different trend is observed for the MSE. Indeed, while the MSE of the proposed method increases when reducing the number of seeds (as expected), the opposite trend is found for the baseline method. We argue that, even if the baseline method is robust in terms of selecting the bests seeds to a decrease of the number of seeds, it does not do a good job at predicting the actual memorability increase. Instead, the proposed method is able to select the bests seeds and better measure their impact, especially when more seeds are available. This is important if the method wants to be deployed with larger seed sets. Application-wise this is quite a desirable feature since the seeds are automatically selected and hence the amount of seeds used is transparent to the user.

Finally, we assess the validity of our method as a tool for effectively increasing the memorability of a generic input image $\mathbf{I}_v$. In Figure 4 (left) we report the average memorability gaps $\bar{m}_v$ obtained over the test set V, when averaging over the top N seeds retrieved, with $N = 3, 10, 20$ and all the images. It can be noted that $\bar{m}_v$ achieve higher values when smaller sets of top N seeds are considered, as an indication that our method effectively retrieve the most memoralizable seeds. In Figure 4 (right) we report the average memorability gaps $\bar{m}_g$ obtained over the test set V with our mehtod S-cube, considering $N = 10$ and a varying number of style seeds S. It can be noted that a larger number of seeds allows to achieve higher increase. Figure 5 illustrates some "image memoralization" sample results obtained with our method.

Summarizing, we presented an exhaustive experimental evaluation showing several interesting results. First, the proposed S-cube approach effectively learns the seeds that are expected to produce the largest increase in memorability. This increase is consistently validated when measuring it with the external scorer $\mathbb{E}$. We also investigated the effect of the choice of architecture for the seed Selector and the effect of the amount of seeds in the overall performance. Finally, we have shown the per-image memorability increase when using the top few seeds, and varying the size of the seed set. In all, the manuscript provides experimental evidence that the proposed method is able to automatically increase the memorability of generic images.

5 CONCLUSIONS

This paper presented a novel approach to increase image memorability based on the *editing-by-filtering* philosophy. Methodologically speaking, we propose to use three deep architecures as the Scorer, the Synthesizer and the Selector. The novelty of our approach relies on the fact that the Selector is able to rank the seeds according to the expected increase of memorability and select the best ones so as to feed the Synthesizer. The effectiveness of our approach both in increasing memorability and in selecting the top memoralizable style seeds has been evaluated on a public benchmark.

We believe that the problem of increasing image memorability can have a direct impact in many fields like education, elderly care or user-generated data analysis. Indeed, memorabilizing images could help editing educational supports, designing more effective brain training games for elderly people, producing better summaries from lifelog camera image streams or leisure picture albums.

While in this work we focused on memorability, the architecture of our approach is highly versatile and can potentially be applied to other concepts such as aesthetic judgement, virality [1] or emotions [2]. A necessary condition to this is a sufficient precision of the Scorer, which should be as close to human performance as possible. When this condition does not occur, the automatic prediction can be replaced introducing a data annotation campaign. The philosophy followed in this study could be extended to take into account other image properties such as aesthetics or evoked emotions *simultaneously*. Indeed, image manipulations aimed to increase memorability may for example lead to aesthetically unpleasing images, which could be an undesired result for an advertising campaign or a life-log video summary. This is highly interesting and not straightforward, and we consider it as one of the main future work guidelines.

While literature on predicting image abstract concepts like memorability is quite huge, the literature in image synthesis with deep networks is still in its early infancy. A promising line of work is represented by Generative Adversarial Networks (GANs) [11]. However, it is not straightforward to apply GANs and still retaining the *editing-by-filters* philosophy. Indeed, one prominent feature of our methodology is that we keep the user in the loop of the image manipulation process, by allowing them to participate to the style selection, once the most promising seeds are automatically provided. Future research works will also investigate an alternative holistic approach based on GANs.

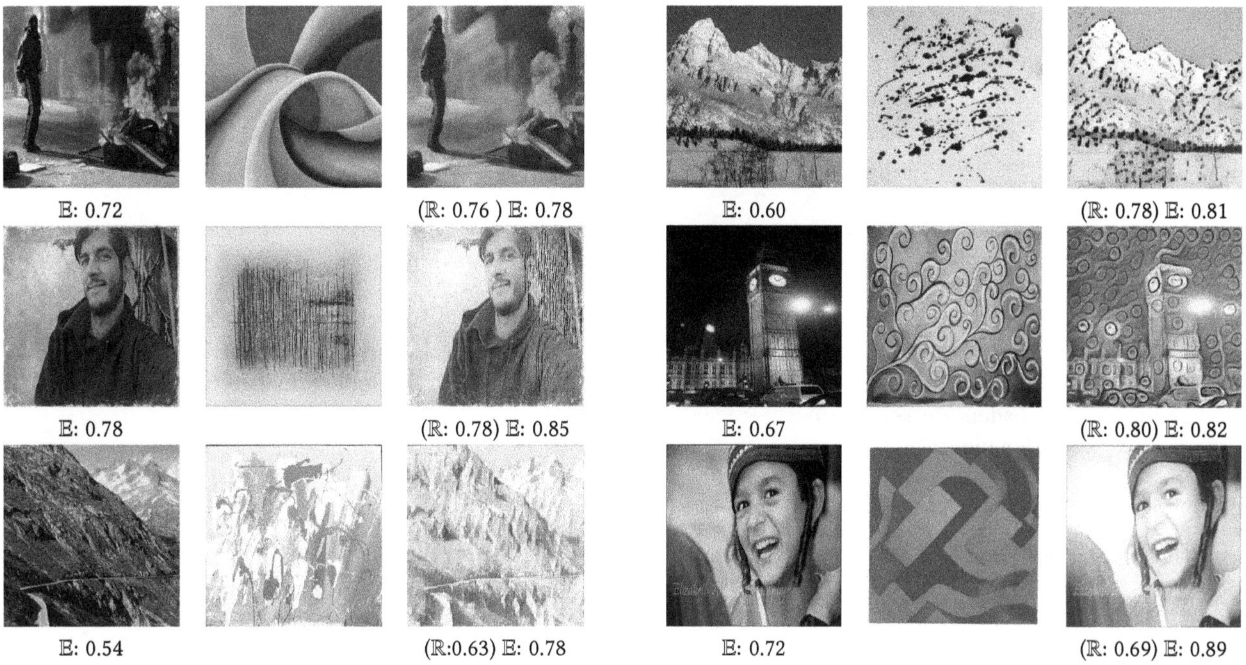

Figure 5: Sample results: (left) original input image, (center) retrieved style seed and (right) corresponding synthesized image. The memorability score measured with the external model $\mathbb{E}$ is reported below each image. The memorability score predicted by the Selector $\mathbb{R}$ based on the image-seed match is reported below the resulting synthesized image.

REFERENCES

[1] Xavier Alameda-Pineda, Andrea Pilzer, Dan Xu, Elisa Ricci, and Nicu Sebe. 2017. Viraliency: Pooling Local Virality. In *CVPR*.

[2] Xavier Alameda-Pineda, Elisa Ricci, Yan Yan, and Nicu Sebe. 2016. Recognizing emotions from abstract paintings using non-linear matrix completion. In *CVPR*.

[3] Adam K Anderson, Peter E Wais, and John De Gabrieli. 2006. Emotion enhances remembrance of neutral events past. *PNAS* 103, 5 (2006), 1599–1604.

[4] Alan F Blackwell. 1997. Correction: A picture is worth 84.1 words. In *ESP Student Workshop*.

[5] Michelle A Borkin, Azalea A Vo, Zoya Bylinskii, Phillip Isola, Shashank Sunkavalli, Aude Oliva, and Hanspeter Pfister. 2013. What makes a visualization memorable? *IEEE TVCG* 19, 12 (2013), 2306–2315.

[6] Timothy F Brady, Talia Konkle, George A Alvarez, and Aude Oliva. 2008. Visual long-term memory has a massive storage capacity for object details. *PNAS* 105, 38 (2008), 14325–14329.

[7] Zoya Bylinskii, Phillip Isola, Constance Bainbridge, Antonio Torralba, and Aude Oliva. 2015. Intrinsic and extrinsic effects on image memorability. *Vision research* 116 (2015), 165–178.

[8] Larry Cahill and James L McGaugh. 1995. A novel demonstration of enhanced memory associated with emotional arousal. *Consciousness and cognition* 4, 4 (1995), 410–421.

[9] Leon A Gatys, Alexander S Ecker, and Matthias Bethge. 2015. A neural algorithm of artistic style. *arXiv preprint arXiv:1508.06576* (2015).

[10] Leon A Gatys, Alexander S Ecker, and Matthias Bethge. 2016. Image style transfer using convolutional neural networks. In *CVPR*.

[11] Ian Goodfellow, Jean Pouget-Abadie, Mehdi Mirza, Bing Xu, David Warde-Farley, Sherjil Ozair, Aaron Courville, and Yoshua Bengio. 2014. Generative adversarial nets. In *NIPS*.

[12] Michael Gygli, Helmut Grabner, Hayko Riemenschneider, Fabian Nater, and Luc Gool. 2013. The interestingness of images. In *ICCV*.

[13] Martin Hilbert. 2012. How much information is there in the "information society"? *Significance* 9, 4 (2012), 8–12.

[14] R Reed Hunt and James B Worthen. 2006. *Distinctiveness and memory*. Oxford University Press.

[15] Phillip Isola, Devi Parikh, Antonio Torralba, and Aude Oliva. 2011. Understanding the intrinsic memorability of images. In *NIPS*.

[16] Phillip Isola, Jianxiong Xiao, Torralba Antonio, and Aude Oliva. 2011. What makes an image memorable?. In *CVPR*.

[17] Phillip Isola, Jianxiong Xiao, Devi Parikh, Antonio Torralba, and Aude Oliva. 2014. What makes a photograph memorable? *IEEE TPAMI* 36, 7 (2014), 1469–1482.

[18] Aditya Khosla, Wilma Bainbridge, Antonio Torralba, and Aude Oliva. 2013. Modifying the memorability of face photographs. In *ICCV*.

[19] Aditya Khosla, Akhil S Raju, Antonio Torralba, and Aude Oliva. 2015. Understanding and predicting image memorability at a large scale. In *ICCV*.

[20] Aditya Khosla, Atish Das Sarma, and Raffay Hamid. 2014. What makes an image popular?. In *WWW*.

[21] Aditya Khosla, Jianxiong Xiao, Phillip Isola, Antonio Torralba, and Aude Oliva. 2012. Image memorability and visual inception. In *SIGGRAPH Asia*.

[22] Aditya Khosla, Jianxiong Xiao, Antonio Torralba, and Aude Oliva. 2012. Memorability of image regions. In *NIPS*.

[23] Chuan Li and Michael Wand. 2016. Precomputed real-time texture synthesis with markovian generative adversarial networks. In *ECCV*.

[24] Jana Machajdik and Allan Hanbury. 2010. Affective image classification using features inspired by psychology and art theory. In *ACM Multimedia*.

[25] Stephen Maren. 1999. Long-term potentiation in the amygdala: a mechanism for emotional learning and memory. *Trends in neurosciences* 22, 12 (1999), 561–567.

[26] James L McGaugh. 2006. Make mild moments memorable: add a little arousal. *Trends in cognitive sciences* 10, 8 (2006), 345–347.

[27] Kuan-Chuan Peng, Tsuhan Chen, Amir Sadovnik, and Andrew C Gallagher. 2015. A mixed bag of emotions: Model, predict, and transfer emotion distributions. In *CVPR*.

[28] Elizabeth A. Phelps. 2004. Human emotion and memory: interactions of the amygdala and hippocampal complex. *Current opinion in neurobiology* 14, 2, 198–202.

[29] Andreza Sartori, Victoria Yanulevskaya, Almila Akdag Salah, Jasper Uijlings, Elia Bruni, and Nicu Sebe. 2015. Affective analysis of professional and amateur abstract paintings using statistical analysis and art theory. *ACM Transactions on Interactive Intelligent Systems* 5, 2 (2015), 8.

[30] Dmitry Ulyanov, Vadim Lebedev, Andrea Vedaldi, and Victor Lempitsky. 2016. Texture Networks: Feed-forward Synthesis of Textures and Stylized Images. *ICML*.

[31] Bolei Zhou, Agata Lapedriza, Jianxiong Xiao, Antonio Torralba, and Aude Oliva. 2014. Learning Deep Features for Scene Recognition using Places Database. In *NIPS*.

Cross-modal Image-Graphics Retrieval by Neural Transfer Learning

Fabian Junkert
RheinMain University of Applied Sciences
Unter den Eichen 5
Wiesbaden, Hessen 65197
fabian.junkter@student.hs-rm.de

Markus Eberts
RheinMain University of Applied Sciences
Unter den Eichen 5
Wiesbaden, Hessen 65197
markus.eberts@student.hs-rm.de

Adrian Ulges
RheinMain University of Applied Sciences
Unter den Eichen 5
Wiesbaden, Hessen 65197
adrian.ulges@hs-rm.de

Ulrich Schwanecke
RheinMain University of Applied Sciences
Unter den Eichen 5
Wiesbaden, Hessen 65197
ulrich.schwanecke@hs-rm.de

ACM Reference format:
Fabian Junkert, Markus Eberts, Adrian Ulges, and Ulrich Schwanecke. 2017. Cross-modal Image-Graphics Retrieval by Neural Transfer Learning. In *Proceedings of ICMR '17, June 6–9, 2017, Bucharest, Romania,* , 8 pages.
https://doi.org/http://dx.doi.org/10.1145/3078971.3078994

1 INTRODUCTION

Deep Convolutional Neural Networks (DCNNs) have recently led to remarkable break-throughs in image recognition. As demonstrated in the ImageNet Challenge (ILSVRC) [20], they recognize thousand object categories with near-human accuracy. One common use of DCNNs is *transfer learning*, where networks pre-trained on large-scale training data are applied to novel target problems. In this context, the DCNN – potentially refinded on data from the target domain – serves as an elaborate feature extractor for estimating the high-level semantics of an image. Such transfer learning offers the benefits of little training effort compared to learning from scratch, and often works even in case of limited training data in the target domain.

In this work, we explore transfer learning for *cross-modal image-graphics retrieval*: Given a set of 3D models and a photo of a real-world object depicting one of the models, our goal is to (1) retrieve the matching 3D model, (2) estimate the camera perspective from which the photo was taken, and (3) align a set of given 3D models from the same category so that camera perspective can be interpreted coherently. For all these subtasks, we apply view-based transfer learning by feeding signals from a pre-trained DCNN (we used the well-known Inception model [24]) to simple shallow classifiers (see Figure 1). Our experiments address the following questions:

- How well does an off-the-shelf DCNN generalize from low-quality rendered views to camera pictures?

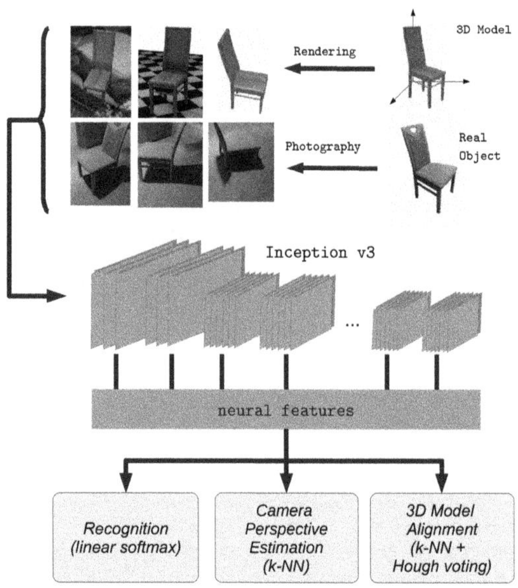

Figure 1: Image-graphics search includes recognition, the estimation of camera perspective, and the alignment of 3D models. We tackle all three subtasks by rendering training views and exploiting signals from the pre-trained DCNN Inception-v3 [24].

- The DCNN we use has been trained for the recognition of ImageNet categories. Which signals from the network are most useful for a precise recognition, alignment and camera perspective estimation?

We demonstrate in quantitative experiments on datasets of rendered graphics and real-world photos of chairs that Inception-v3 signals do offer impressive generalization capacities across forms of imagery and shapes, even yielding the capacity to precisely estimate camera perspective for novel objects. This capacity, however, strongly depends on the layer that neural features are drawn from and on the distance metric used to compare them.

ICMR '17, June 06-09, 2017, Bucharest, Romania

ACM ISBN 978-1-4503-4701-3/17/06...$15.00
http://dx.doi.org/10.1145/3078971.3078994

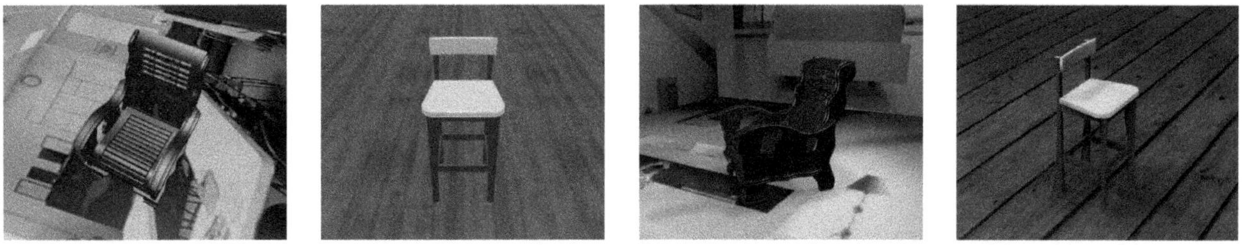

Figure 2: Sample training views of two objects with low-quality (left) vs. high-quality rendering (right). Views 1 and 3 use *Flickr skybox* background, Views 2 and 4 *Floor* textures.

2 RELATED WORK

Image-Graphics-Matching: The availability of large collections of images together with associated 3D models enables new and more reliable approaches for image retrieval. Eitz et al., for example, presented a system for 3D object retrieval based on a sketch of the searched object using bag-of-features and a feature transform based on a bank of Gabor filters [6]. A similar combination of interest points and visual vocabulary quantization was used in [21] for direct 2D-to-3D matching in large datasets. The problem of localizing and estimating the fine-pose of objects with given 3D models in an image was treated by Lim et al. [15]. In [1] a method was proposed to establish part-based correspondences between 3D CAD models and real photographs based on local histogram of oriented gradients (HoG) (see e.g. [5]) descriptors and linear discriminant analysis. This approach allowed aligning 3D models of chairs with corresponding 2D images in a wide variety of complex scenes.

DCNNs and Graphics: More recent approaches for image retrieval are based on DCNNs instead of analytically deduced feature detectors and descriptors and often combine the two data modalities (images and 3D models of an object) instead of processing them separatley. In [11] Hueting et al. presented a new analysis method using class-labeled image and noisy 3D model collections in an interweaved manner to consistently align the 3D models and resort the image collections based on pose and shape attributes. The authors showed that CNN based feature extraction outperforms classical feature desctiptors based on HOG and a Kernel Codebook encoding [7]. A similar approach was used in [4] to generate a proper three-dimensional headdress from a single photograph. Su et al. showed that 3D shapes can be recognized effectively from a collection of rendered 2D images using DCNNs [23]. Li et al. presented an embedding space joining 3D shapes and 2D images of objects [14]. The distances between embedded entities in this space reflect similarity between the underlying objects and therefore allow for cross-modality retrieval. Recently, Zamir et al. [28] presented a generic 3D representation based on DCNNs for object-centric camera pose estimation with an accuracy comparable to humans without the need of image rectification.

Peng et al. showed that DCNNs are invariant to various intra-class variations and proposed an optimal synthetic data generation strategy for training object detectors from CAD models [18]. The same authors in particular demonstrated that DCNNs learn better when low-level cues are simulated [19]. Aubry and Russell observed important differences across different DCNNs and their corresponding layers with respect to different scene factors and object categories [2]. Massa et al. [17] demonstrated that adapting the features of natural images to better align with those of CAD rendered views is crucial for DCNN based 2D-3D exemplar detection. They also showed that the adaptation can be learned by compositing rendered views of textured object models on natural images.

Transfer Learning with DCNNs: Pre-trained DCNNs have successfully been transferred to other application domains [24] such as object localization [30], image ranking [25] or image retrieval [26]. Here, one commonly used source is the large-scale ImageNet dataset, which has been shown to yield robust transfer even when subsampling training samples or classes [12] (the Inception-v3 network we use is also trained on ImageNet).

As DCNNs' feature maps – as opposed to hand-crafted features like HoG [5] – lack a straightforward interpretability, there have been efforts to inspect the properties of signals from different layers: Zeiler and Fergus visualize neurons by deconvolving their weight patterns [29]. Yosinski et al. [27] measure the performance drop when transfering CNN layers between subsets of the ImageNet dataset. They observed that neurons in higher layers tend to overspezialize, that transfer benefits decrease the more different the source and target domain, and that refining transferred layers can overcome co-adaption effects at the cut between transferred and target-learned neurons. Zhouh et al. [30] demonstrate that DCNNs trained for scene categorization evolve neurons strongly correlated with objects in the scene. Long and Wang [16] increase transferability by measuring and minimizing the domain discrepancy of inner layer's embeddings. Shafaei et. al. [22] showed that a DCNN trained on synthetic data performs similar to a network trained on real-world data for dense image classification.

Similar to this line of work, we also investigate the usefulness of features drawn from different layers of a DCNN. Our focus, however, is on the practical realization of cross-modal image-graphics search. Particularly, our experiments not only cover recognition but also the estimation of camera perspective or the pose of the depicted object respectively.

3 APPROACH

We take a view-based approach towards image-graphics search: 3D target models are represented by randomly sampled rendered views (Section 3.1). These views are passed to a DCNN, yielding feature maps from the network's different layers. These features (which we referred to "neural features" in the following) are pooled to a pre-defined size and employed by shallow learners, which –

given a query photo – infer *which* object/model is filmed from *what perspective* (Section 3.2). When indexing 3D models, we also align them to a coherent orientation, for which we conduct a voting over matches of neural features from different perspectives.

3.1 Rendering

We utilize the Blender Python API[1] to generate images of 3D models. All models are scaled to the same size and their center is shifted to the coordinate system's origin. The camera always points at the origin, with a roll angle of zero. Our system allows different sampling strategies for clutter, camera position, light colors and graphics levels (see Figure 2 for sample views):

- **Graphics level**: Sample views are rendered in two types of graphics settings: (1) *High-quality* (models are rendered with raytracing turned on and casted shadows). (2) *Low-quality* (standard phong illumination with no raytracing or casted shadows repectively).
- **Camera Position**: We use three different methods for sampling camera positions: (1) *Monte Carlo* (polar angle, azimuth angle and distance from the object are drawn from random distributions). (2) *Subdivision* (a uniform sampling of an object-centered sphere, calculated by multiple subdivison steps beginning with a cube[2]). (3) *Fixed height* (the model is orbited by the camera at a fixed height).
- **Background**: We test with three different types of backgrounds: (1) *Floor* (plane with one of 100 floor textures beneath the model). (2) *Skybox* (enclosing a skybox around the object with one of over 2000 random Flickr images applied to). (3) *Empty* (a plain white background).

3.2 Deep CNN and Transfer

Training views (as well as query photos) are fed to a DCNN acting as an elaborate feature extractor. We use the Inception-v3 network[3] by Szegedy et al. which was demonstrated to achieve state-of-the-art results on the ILSVRC dataset [24]. The network has been trained on the ILSVRC challenge training data (1,000 object classes, 1.2 mio. training images[4]). Its layout is illustrated in Figure 3. The intention of the model is to carefully balance computational overhead (i.e., limiting the number of network parameters and multiply-adds for feed-forward) while maintaining expressive power (see [24] for a more detailed discussion). The core is formed by 10 stacked so-called *Inception* modules. These are denoted with "mixed1–mixed10" in the Figure (as in the model itself). We will simply refer to them as "Layer 1–10" in the following. These Inception modules – each with similar (or identical) layout – comprise of different combinations of convolution and pooling operations, which were carefully designed to limit computational load: For example, the number of feature maps is reduced by 1x1 convolutions before applying higher-dimensional filters, and convolutions are separated (i.e., using subsequent 7x1 and 1x7 filters instead of one joint 7x7 filter).

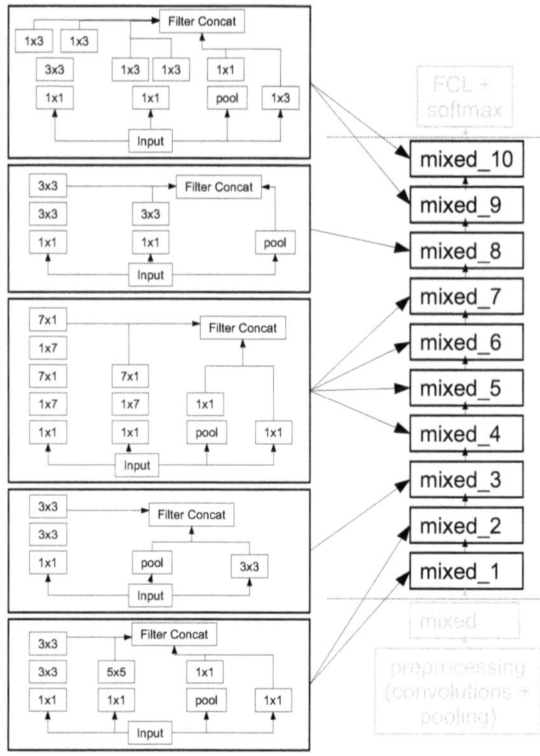

Layer	1-2	3-7	8	9-10
width × height	35×35	17×17	8×8	8×8
feature maps	288	768	1280	2048

Figure 3: Top: The Inception-v3 architecture contains 10 stacked Inception modules (data flow is bottom-up). Bottom: The dimensionality of features from the different Inception modules. Spatial resolution decreases over the layers, while the number of feature maps increases.

As illustrated in Table 3, the spatial resolution of feature maps decreases with the layers, while the number of feature maps increases (which is characteristic for DCNNs).

Transfer Our approach extracts the outputs of the 10 Inception modules and employs them off-the-shelf as feature vectors for transfer learning (i.e., we do not perform any adaptation of the DCNN to the target domain). We conduct an average pooling of the resulting feature maps, rescaling them to a size between 8×8 and 1×1 pixels. The resulting features are used either in a simple discriminative learner (to *recognize* the object in the picture) or in nearest neighbor matching (to estimate the most similar training *views* and thus infer camera perspective).

In the first setting – the **discriminative learner** – we define an output layer $\mathbf{y}$ containing one node for each 3D model in our index (which is supposed to be activated when the 3D model is visible in the scene). Given a (pooled and flattened) neural feature vector $\mathbf{x}^*$, the output layer is defined as:

$$\mathbf{y} = \text{softmax}\Big(W \cdot \mathbf{x}^* + \mathbf{b}\Big)$$

[1] https://www.blender.org/api
[2] http://www.gamedev.sk/triangulation-of-a-sphere
[3] https://github.com/tensorflow/models/tree/master/inception
[4] http://www.image-net.org/challenges/LSVRC/2012/

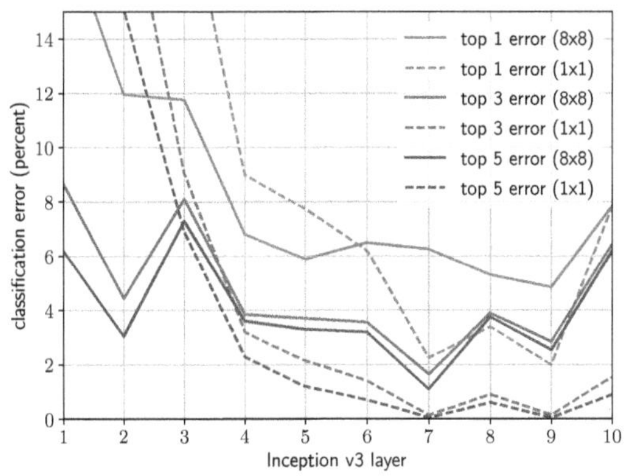

Figure 4: Recognition error plotted against the Inception-v3 Layer we pull neural features from (both pooled to 8×8 and 1×1).

(with weight matrix W and bias vector $\mathbf{b}$). The system is trained by minimizing cross-entropy with the Adam optimizer [13].

Our second setting – the **perspective estimator** – uses a nearest neighbor matching on the neural feature vectors using the *annoy* library[5]. We find the k views with Inception-v3 features closest to the query view (using either the Euclidean or angular distance), aggregate the corresponding camera positions (x_i, y_i, z_i), $i = 1, \ldots, k$ by a simple averaging, and assume the target view to be filmed from camera position $(\overline{x}, \overline{y}, \overline{z})$. Note that – since in our use case views are cropped to the target object – the distance between camera and object can be neglected. We further assume the camera to point towards the center of the object coordinate system, and the camera's roll angle to be zero (just like for our rendered training data in Section 3.1). Thus, we only determine polar and azimuth angle of the camera instead of its complete 6 DOF pose [3] or even a human pose [10].

4 EXPERIMENTS

We conducted experiments with respect to three tasks related to image-graphics search: *Recognition* (given a photo, which 3D model is visible in the scene), *3D Model Alignment* (given a set of 3D models, where is the coherent "front" direction), and *Camera Perspective* (given a photo, from which direction has the 3D model been filmed).

Our dataset is a subset of Aubry et al's [1] set of chairs collected from sketchup's 3D Warehouse[6]. We found lots of links to be unavailable and the majority of the retrieved models to be broken (i.e., parts were missing, normals flipped, scales incorrect or textures missing). We filtered those, and used the remaining dataset of 200 models of chairs[7]. As our experiments relate to a practical image-graphics search scenario (where the user takes a picture of the target object he is interested in), we assume the target object to be visually dominant in the scene. Otherwise its bounding box can be cropped via a simple user action. Correspondingly, we crop our training and test images to the object's bounding box.

[5]https://github.com/spotify/annoy
[6]3dwarehouse.sketchup.com
[7]Our reference models can be found here: http://www.cs.hs-rm.de/~ulges/pubs/chair_urls.txt

retrieval \ training		high-quality	low-quality
(high-quality) graphics	Top-1-Error	2.00	7.30
	Top-3-Error	0.15	1.45
	Top-5-Error	0.05	0.90
photos	Top-1-Error	39.02	45.12
	Top-3-Error	18.29	28.05
	Top-5-Error	7.32	19.51

Table 1: Recognition error (%) when generalizing between different levels of graphics and photos.

4.1 Recognition

It has been shown that the transferability of neural features varies over layers due to issues of abstraction and overspecialization [27]. Therefore, we investigate in a first experiment which Inception-v3 layers offer the most suitable features for the recognition of our graphics models. We train our softmax learner (Section 3.2) for 4000 training steps at a learning rate of 0.01 and batch size of 100. For each of our 200 target models, 200 training views and 10 test views were sampled (using Monte Carlo camera placement, floor background, and high-quality rendering). All views were cropped to the minimum quadratic region containing the target object. Results are illustrated in Figure 4, which shows that upper layers tend to offer better accuracy. The overadaptation to the ImageNet training problem [27] kicks in quite late (between Layers 9 and 10). Also, for recognition an aggressive pooling of feature maps to 1×1 yields better accuracy than 8×8 feature maps.

In a second experiment, we evaluate the generalization of DCNN features between different image sources (low-quality vs. high-quality graphics vs. photo stock). We tested only 1×1 features from Layer 9, and trained our softmax model both on low-quality graphics and high-quality views (with the same settings as above). Testing was done on the 2000 high-quality views from the first experiment ("(high-quality) graphics") and on 80 pictures we retrieved manually from the internet ("photos") showing chairs similar to some of our models, some cluttered, some with white background.

The results in Table 1 show that error rates are lower for high-quality training material, but in general inception features from low-quality views generalize both to high-quality graphics and to photos. Even though error rates on photos are higher in general, we found the system to yield reasonable matches in most cases – note that the photos we found online do not match the annotated reference model exactly, but we allowed a certain deviation in color and shape (which led to a considerable margin for subjectivity in our ground truth). Sample results can be found in Figure 5 (left). Due to copyright issues with the 80 web-crawled test photos, we display representative results for three self-captured test photos. For the first two, the highest-scored model (bottom) can be considered the closest match amongst our reference models, for the last one not.

Layer	# reference views			
	200	100	50	25
3	1.97	3.29 ± 1.08	3.90 ± 0.73	5.00 ± 1.05
4	2.06	3.27 ± 0.65	4.08 ± 1.04	4.65 ± 0.80
5	2.23	3.17 ± 0.56	3.29 ± 0.88	4.64 ± 0.55
6	2.41	3.06 ± 0.78	3.26 ± 1.01	4.87 ± 0.95
7	3.66	4.11 ± 0.91	4.78 ± 0.38	6.06 ± 0.55
8	2.62	3.78 ± 0.48	4.05 ± 0.95	5.61 ± 0.45

Table 2: Angle error of model alignment (in degrees) for Inception-v3 Layers 3 − 8 and when varying the number of reference views. For less than 200 reference views, results were averaged over 5 runs.

4.2 3D Model Alignment

Our second task is targeted at aligning 3D models with each other: Given a set of 3D models of a common category (all facing the same "front" direction), can we calculate the necessary rotation to align a new model with the existing ones? To begin with, we manually estimated the ground truth orientation for our 200 chair models and represented each model by a set of training views (using high-quality rendering, empty background, and fixed height camera position), i.e. the model was orbited in 2 degree steps, with the polar angle fixed at 90 degrees. This resulted in 180 views per model (36,000 views in total). We automatically cropped and rescaled the (potentially non-quadratic) object's bounding box. Each view was represented by neural features pooled to 8 × 8 (again, we tested all 10 Inception-v3 layers). We then created an index containing all views from $n \in \{25, 50, 100, 200\}$ random models.

To test model alignment, each of our 200 models were used once as a query q (q's views were removed from the index temporarily). We conducted a nearest neighbor search for every fourth of q's views (i.e., 45 query views in 8 degree steps). For each view v_i^q we estimated the nearest neighbor $n(v_i^q)$ and calculated the azimuth difference φ_i^q between v_i^q and $n(v_i^q)$. We estimate the rotation $\varphi^*(q)$ to align q with the models in the index by a simple voting (using the mode $Mo()$):

$$\varphi^*(q) := \mathrm{Mo}(\varphi_1^q, \ldots, \varphi_{45}^q)$$

Finally, we compute the mean angle error between our estimate φ^* and the ground truth rotation. Table 2 reports this error averaged over 5 runs with different random models in the index. We omit Layers 1 − 2 and 9 − 10, which gave slightly worse results than Layers 3 − 8, likely due to lack of abstraction or overspecialization. It can be seen that our average angle error is low, and that this behavior is quite stable over the inner Inception-v3 layers. Remarkably, alignment remains quite accurate even when reducing the number of models in our index: Even with only 25 reference models, the average angle error is only around 5 degrees. Overall, signals from intermediate layers of Inception-v3 allow us to reliably co-align 3d models (see Figure 5 for examples).

4.3 Camera Perspective Estimation

The last question we tackle is the estimation of camera perspective: Given a photo of an object and a set of 3D models of an object category (here, chairs), can we estimate from which perspective the target object is visible in the photo? Again, we exploit transfer learning with the Inception-v3 network. We conduct two types of experiments, one generalizing only between rendered views (referred to as "graphics–graphics" in the following), one generalizing from graphics to photos (referred to as "graphics-photo"). In some tests we included the query object in the training set ("same object"), in others we removed it ("cross-object"). Note that the latter case is particularly challenging, as we try to estimate the camera perspective for an *unknown* object from a known category.

In all experiments, we use training data of our 200 chair models generated by a uniform subdivision sampling of the upper hemisphere, obtaining 209 training views per object rendered with white background and low-quality, cropped to the object's bounding box as in the last experiment (see Figure 8, bottom for examples). Each such training view comes with a 3D camera position, whereas we limit the camera to point towards the object's center.

For test views, we estimate the camera position using k-NN matching with neural features (see Section 3.2). As an accuracy measure, we use the angle between the true camera position $\mathbf{x}$ and the estimated one $\mathbf{x}'$:

$$E(\mathbf{x}, \mathbf{x}') := \arccos\left(\frac{\mathbf{x}^\top \cdot \mathbf{x}'}{||\mathbf{x}|| \cdot ||\mathbf{x}'||}\right)$$

(with 0 degrees being optimal). We report this error averaged over all test views, and also the percentage of "inliers", i.e. test views for which $E(\mathbf{x}, \mathbf{x}')$ is less than 15 degrees.

graphics–graphics (same object): In our first experiment, test views were generated by the same subdivision sampling as the training views. By using different levels of subdivisions for training and testing, we obtain test views that deviate a bit in number (192) in perspective (by about 7 degrees) from the closest training views. We render test views with background using the "Flickr Skybox" approach (see Section 3). Out of the resulting 192 test views per object, we pick 20 random ones (resulting in 4000 test views in total). k-NN search runs with the angular distance metric using the annoy library[8] (setting the number of search trees to 100).

Figure 6 (left) illustrates the average angle error E when using features from different Inception-v3 layers, and when scaling the feature maps to different resolutions (using average pooling). We observe that a high spatial resolution is beneficial, with 8×8 feature maps providing the best overall results. More interestingly, the layer from which we pull CNN-features is crucial: While early layers do not provide a sufficient layer of abstraction, the last layers tend to overfit to the problem the object category recognition has been trained on. We made similar findings in Sections 4.1 and 4.2, and confirm them here for camera perspective estimation. Again, overspezialization kicks in quite late (in Layers 9 − 10), given that the network has been trained on very different data and for a very different task.

We also tested different values for the number of nearest neighbors k. It can be observed that by combining $k = 2$ matching views, accuracy can be improved even over the angle to the single best matching training view, which is about 7 degrees (control run, dashed line in Figure 6 left+center). This can be explained by symmetry effects: Imagine the two nearest neighbors found on opposite

[8]https://github.com/spotify/annoy

Figure 5: Left (Recognition): self-captured test photos (top) vs highest-scored 3D models (bottom), using 1 × 1 features from Layer 9. Right (3D Alignment): test views (top) vs matched training views of other chairs (bottom), using 8 × 8 features from Layer 6.

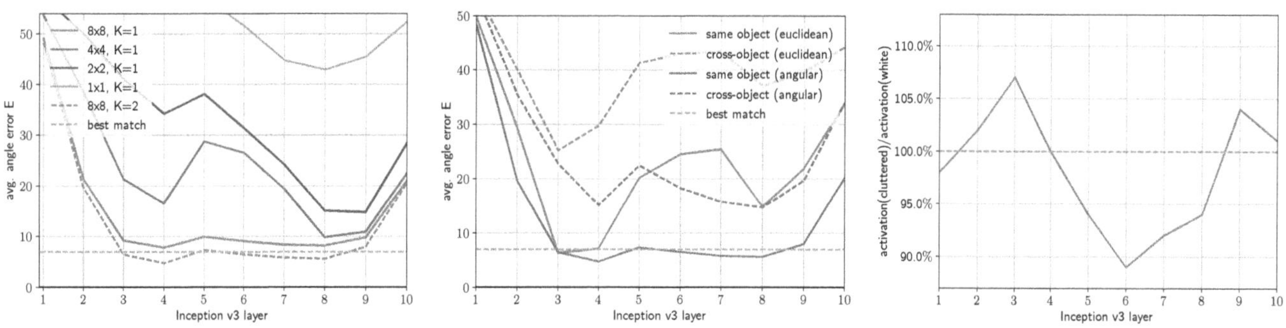

Figure 6: Left: The accuracy of camera perspective estimation (angular distance) is best when pulling features from intermediate Inception-v3 layers. Less aggressive pooling generally improves results. Center: Camera perspective estimation for known objects and when generalizing between objects. Right: Activations in the Inception layers differ between cluttered and white-background views.

sites of the ground truth perspective, which are combined (averaged) to a result closer to the query view than any single training view. We found results to be stable for $k = 2, \ldots, 5$ and decline when increasing k further.

graphics–graphics (cross-object): We repeat the same experiment as above (using $k = 2$). Only, when querying with a target view, we remove any views of the same object from the training data, enforcing generalization to new objects. Results are illustrated in Figure 6 (center), comparing the "same object" and "cross-object" settings both with Euclidean and angular distance. We observe that Inception-v3 features allow a remarkable robustness: In the cross-object experiment, there is generalization from plain white to textured background, from low-quality to high-quality graphics, and to novel objects. The best average angle error achieved is around 16° (green dashed line). In this case, for 86% of queries, the angle error was below 15°. Note, however, that the combination of Inception layer and distance measure is crucial for this robustness. For the Euclidean distance, upper layers give low accuracy and generalization to new objects remains poor.

To investigate the difference between the angular and Euclidean metric, we fed the network 1165 pairs of images, one with white background, the other with random floor background (camera perspective and target object were identical) and plotted how the Euclidean norm of neural activations in the Inception-v3 layers differs between both cases (Figure 6). The horizontal line (100%) stands for equal activation with/without clutter. We see that for Layers 5 – 8, there is indeed a strong discrepancy between cluttered and white-background scenes, with the white-background scenes yielding up to 10% *stronger* activations. Correspondingly, the discrepancy between the Euclidean distance and the angular distance (which normalizes out this activation gap) is strongest in Layers 5 – 8. Here, the Euclidean distance fails, while the angular distance benefits from the stronger abstraction capacities of upper layers and even manages to generalize to novel objects.

graphics–photo: Finally, we also tested camera perspective estimation on camera-captured photos. Therefor, we acquired pictures of chairs with ground truth camera perspectives in collaboration with a furniture store, where we collected 263 views of 41 chairs.

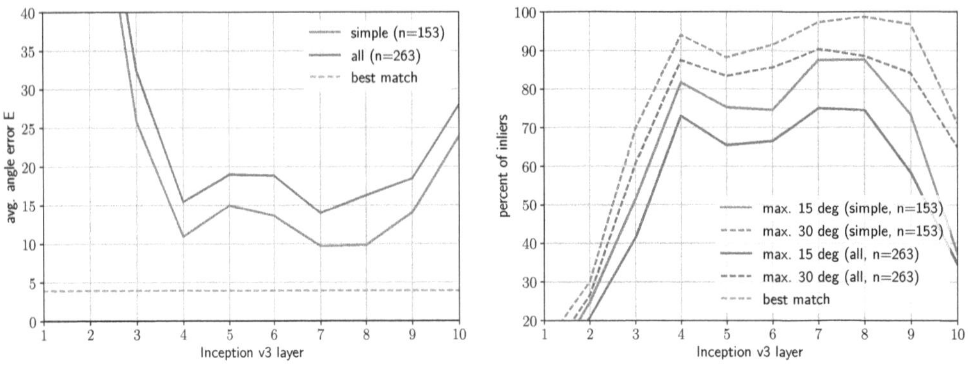

Figure 7: Quantitative results on photos of chairs (average angle error left, percentage of inliers right).

Figure 8: Sample results on photos of chairs (query photos at the top, best-matching training view at the bottom), using 8×8-pooled tensors from Inception-v3 Layer 8. The results illustrate the strong invariance properties of the CNN's inner signals, generalizing from graphics to cluttered views, and between different object colors and designs. The second-to-last result shows a typical inaccuracy due to different object shapes, the last result a failure (due to occlusion and object color). Queries 1 and 2 were in the "simple" subset.

None of these chairs was identical to any of our 200 reference 3D models. However, we labeled 61 views as *similar* to at least one of our reference chairs. We also did a more general annotation of photos into 110 'challenging' ones (where the object differed significantly in both shape and color from any known training model, or was partially occluded) and 153 'simple' ones (unoccluded object, and at least some similarity in shape and/or color to a reference model). Examples can be found in Figure 8, where the two leftmost pictures are "simple" cases and the other four "challenging".

To obtain ground truth camera perspectives, each photo was taken twice, once with a checkerboard marker placed on the seat (see the rightmost example in Figure 8). We assume the center of the checkerboard to be a sufficiently accurate estimate of the chair's bounding boxes' center (which is also the center of the 3D models' coordinate system). In a second picture the marker was removed and the actual test picture was taken from the same perspective. Note that most test pictures were taken from the target chair's front side so the marker was fully visible. The intrinsic parameters of the camera where determined using the GML C++ Camera Calibration Toolkit[9]. The position and orientation of the calibrated camera with respect to the checkerboard, i.e relative to the seat's center, were determined by solving the perspective-n-point problem [8, 9] using OpenCV functionality. Finally all test pictures were cropped manually.

Quantitative results (k-NN matching with the angular distance, $k = 2$ and 100 search trees) are illustrated in Figure 7. Results are in line with the "cross-object" experiment shown in Figure 6 (center+right): The best results are achieved for upper layers of the Inception-v3 network, with Layers 7 and 8 providing the best accuracy. Over the simple (all) cases, an average angle error of $< 10°$ ($< 14°$) is achieved, with inlier rates ($< 15°$) of 88% (75%). We see that generalization from graphics to photographs and to novel objects is possible. This is confirmed by some representative sample

[9]http://graphics.cs.msu.ru/en/node/909

results illustrated in Figure 8: There is a strong generalization to novel shapes (Examples 3 and 4) and color (Example 2). Except slight inaccuracies, pose estimates are widely correct. In the last example, camera perspective estimation fails (there is partial occlusion by the marker and the object differs in color and shape). Note, however, that even in the last example, the lower part of the chair is matched correctly.

5 CONCLUSIONS

In this work, we have shown that off-the-shelf signals pulled from a state-of-the-art Deep Convolutional Neural Network can be used for various tasks related to view-based image-graphics retrieval, including not only recognition but also model alignment and camera perspective estimation. Using simple linear and nearest neighbor models, strong robustness was achieved with respect to clutter and variations of shape/design on a dataset of 200 chair models. We observed that intermediate layers offer the best transfer, that pooling matters (strong pooling for recognition, weak pooling for perspective estimation), and that an angular distance is recommended to achieve robustness to clutter. Our results suggest Inception-v3 signals as a powerful baseline for benchmarking camera perspective estimation.

As future work, we plan to investigate a fine-tuning of Inception-v3 itself on rendered views from our target domain. We also want to replace our nearest neighbor view matching – which suffers from discretization effects due to the limited number of reference views – with a layered regression model on top of Inception-v3 features.

ACKNOWLEDGEMENT

This work was funded by the program "Forschung für die Praxis" of the Hessen State Ministry for Higher Education, Research and the Arts / Germany. We thank the Müllerland GmbH in Görgeshausen / Germany for data acquisition support.

REFERENCES

[1] Mathieu Aubry, Daniel Maturana, Alexei Efros, Bryan Russell, and Josef Sivic. 2014. Seeing 3D chairs: Exemplar Part-based 2D-3D Alignment using a Large Dataset of CAD models. In *Proc. CVPR*. 3762–3769.

[2] Mathieu Aubry and Bryan C. Russell. 2015. Understanding Deep Features With Computer-Generated Imagery. In *Proc. ICCV*. 2875–2883.

[3] Eric Brachmann, Frank Michel, Alexander Krull, Michael Ying Yang, Stefan Gumhold, and carsten Rother. 2016. Uncertainty-Driven 6D Pose Estimation of Objects and Scenes From a Single RGB Image. In *Proc. CVPR*.

[4] Menglei Chai, Tianjia Shao, Hongzhi Wu, Yanlin Weng, and Kun Zhou. 2016. AutoHair: Fully Automatic Hair Modeling from a Single Image. *ACM Trans. Graph.* 35, 4, Article 116 (2016), 12 pages.

[5] Navneet Dalal and Bill Triggs. 2005. Histograms of Oriented Gradients for Human Detection. In *Proc. CVPR*. 886–893.

[6] Mathias Eitz, Ronald Richter, Tamy Boubekeur, Kristian Hildebrand, and Marc Alexa. 2012. Sketch-Based Shape Retrieval. *ACM Trans. Graph. (Proc. SIGGRAPH)* 31, 4 (2012), 31:1–31:10.

[7] Jan C. Gemert, Jan-Mark Geusebroek, Cor J. Veenman, and Arnold W. Smeulders. 2008. Kernel Codebooks for Scene Categorization. In *Proc. ECCV*. 696–709.

[8] Johann August Grunert. 1841. Das Pothenot'sche Problem, in erweiterter Gestalt; nebst Bemerkungen über seine Anwendungen in der Geodäsie. *Grunerts Archiv für Mathematik und Physik* 1 (1841), 238–248.

[9] Joel A. Hesch and Stergios I. Roumeliotis. 2011. A Direct Least-Squares (DLS) method for PnP.. In *Proc. ICCV*, D. N. Metaxas and et al. (Eds.). 383–390.

[10] Chaoqun Hong, Jun Yu, Jian Wan, Dacheng Tao, and Meng Wang. 2015. Multimodal Deep Autoencoder for Human Pose Recovery. *IEEE Trans. Image Processing* 24, 12 (2015).

[11] Moos Hueting, Maks Ovsjanikov, and Niloy J. Mitra. 2015. CrossLink: Joint Understanding of Image and 3D Model Collections Through Shape and Camera Pose Variations. *ACM TOG* 34, 6 (2015), 233:1–233:13.

[12] Mi-Young Huh, Pulkit Agrawal, and Alexei A. Efros. 2016. What makes ImageNet good for transfer learning? *CoRR* abs/1608.08614 (2016). http://arxiv.org/abs/1608.08614

[13] Diederik P. Kingma and Jimmy Ba. 2014. Adam: A Method for Stochastic Optimization. *CoRR* abs/1412.6980 (2014). http://arxiv.org/abs/1412.6980

[14] Yangyan Li, Hao Su, Charles Ruizhongtai Qi, Noa Fish, Daniel Cohen-Or, and Leonidas J. Guibas. 2015. Joint Embeddings of Shapes and Images via CNN Image Purification. *ACM TOG*, Article 234 (2015), 12 pages. https://doi.org/10.1145/2816795.2818071

[15] J. J. Lim, H. Pirsiavash, and A. Torralba. 2013. Parsing IKEA Objects: Fine Pose Estimation. In *Proc. ICCV*. 2992–2999. https://doi.org/10.1109/ICCV.2013.372

[16] Mingsheng Long and Jianmin Wang. 2015. Learning Transferable Features with Deep Adaptation Networks. *CoRR* abs/1502.02791 (2015). http://arxiv.org/abs/1502.02791

[17] Francisco Massa, Bryan C. Russell, and Mathieu Aubry. 2016. Deep Exemplar 2D-3D Detection by Adapting From Real to Rendered Views. In *Proc. CVPR*.

[18] Xingchao Peng, Baochen Sun, Karim Ali, and Kate Saenko. 2014. Exploring Invariances in Deep Convolutional Neural Networks Using Synthetic Images. *CoRR* abs/1412.7122 (2014).

[19] Xingchao Peng, Baochen Sun, Karim Ali, and Kate Saenko. 2015. Learning Deep Object Detectors From 3D Models. In *Proc. ICCV*. 1278–1286.

[20] Olga Russakovsky, Jia Deng, Hao Su, Jonathan Krause, Sanjeev Satheesh, Sean Ma, Zhiheng Huang, Andrej Karpathy, Aditya Khosla, Michael Bernstein, Alexander C. Berg, and Li Fei-Fei. 2015. ImageNet Large Scale Visual Recognition Challenge. *Proc. IJCV* 115, 3 (2015), 211–252.

[21] Torsten Sattler, Bastian Leibe, and Leif Kobbelt. 2011. Fast Image-Based Localization using Direct 2D-to-3D Matching. In *Proc. ICCV*. 667–674.

[22] Alireza Shafaei, James J. Little, and Mark Schmidt. 2016. Play and Learn: Using Video Games to Train Computer Vision Models. *CoRR* abs/1608.01745 (2016). http://arxiv.org/abs/1608.01745

[23] Hang Su, Subhransu Maji, Evangelos Kalogerakis, and Erik G. Learned-Miller. 2015. Multi-view convolutional neural networks for 3d shape recognition. *CoRR* abs/1505.00880 (2015).

[24] Christian Szegedy, Vincent Vanhoucke, Sergey Ioffe, Jonathon Shlens, and Zbigniew Wojna. 2015. Rethinking the Inception Architecture for Computer Vision. *CoRR* abs/1512.00567 (2015). http://arxiv.org/abs/1512.00567

[25] Jiang Wang, Yang Song, Thomas Leung, Chuck Rosenberg, Jingbin Wang, James Philbin, Bo Chen, and Ying Wu. 2014. Learning Fine-Grained Image Similarity with Deep Ranking. In *Proc. CVPR*. 1386–1393.

[26] Artem Babenko Yandex and Victor Lempitsky. 2015. Aggregating Local Deep Features for Image Retrieval. In *Proc. ICCV*. 1269–1277.

[27] Jason Yosinski, Jeff Clune, Yoshua Bengio, and Hod Lipson. 2014. How transferable are features in deep neural networks? *CoRR* abs/1411.1792 (2014). http://arxiv.org/abs/1411.1792

[28] Amir Roshan Zamir, Tilman Wekel, Pulkit Agrawal, Colin Wei, Jitendra Malik, and Silvio Savarese. 2016. Generic 3D Representation via Pose Estimation and Matching. In *Proc. ECCV*. 535–553.

[29] Matthew D. Zeiler and Rob Fergus. 2013. Visualizing and Understanding Convolutional Networks. *CoRR* abs/1311.2901 (2013). http://arxiv.org/abs/1311.2901

[30] Bolei Zhou, Aditya Khosla, Àgata Lapedriza, Aude Oliva, and Antonio Torralba. 2014. Object Detectors Emerge in Deep Scene CNNs. *CoRR* abs/1412.6856 (2014). http://arxiv.org/abs/1412.6856

DRAW: Deep Networks for Recognizing Styles of Artists Who Illustrate Children's Books

Samet Hicsonmez
Hacettepe University
samethicsonmez@hacettepe.edu.tr

Nermin Samet
Middle East Technical University
nermin.samet@metu.edu.tr

Fadime Sener
University of Bonn
sener@informatik.uni-bonn.de

Pinar Duygulu
Hacettepe University
pinar@cs.hacettepe.edu.tr

Figure 1: First and second columns show pages from [1] and the other columns show more examples from the same illustrators. Top: Korky Paul, middle: Debi Gliori, bottom: Axel Scheffler. As seen the styles are distinctive for illustrators.

ABSTRACT

This paper is motivated from a young boy's capability to recognize an illustrator's style in a totally different context. In the book "We are All Born Free" [1], composed of selected rights from the Universal Declaration of Human Rights interpreted by different illustrators, the boy was surprised to see a picture similar to the ones in the "Winnie the Witch" series drawn by Korky Paul (Figure 1). The style was noticeable in other characters of the same illustrator in different books as well. The capability of a child to easily spot the style was shown to be valid for other illustrators such as Axel Scheffler and Debi Gliori. The boy's enthusiasm let us to start the journey to explore the capabilities of machines to recognize the style of illustrators.

We collected pages from children's books to construct a new illustrations dataset consisting of about 6500 pages from 24 artists. We exploited deep networks for categorizing illustrators and with around 94% classification performance our method over-performed the traditional methods by more than 10%. Going beyond categorization we explored transferring style. The classification performance on the transferred images has shown the ability of our system to capture the style. Furthermore, we discovered representative illustrations and discriminative stylistic elements.

KEYWORDS

Deep Learning for Art Analysis; Illustrator Classification; Convolu-tional Neural Networks

ACM Reference format:
Samet Hicsonmez, Nermin Samet, Fadime Sener, and Pinar Duygulu. 2017. DRAW:
Deep networks for Recognizing styles of Artists Who illustrate children's books. In *Proceedings of ICMR '17, June 6–9, 2017, Bucharest, Romania, ,* 9 pages.
DOI: http://dx.doi.org/10.1145/3078971.3078982

1 INTRODUCTION

Illustrations help us to understand the message clearly and have been widely used in printed and visual media. Yet, the role of illustrations in children's books is more than being a simple picture accompanying the text. For the children who don't know how to read, those are the illustrations that make the children to understand the story. Those images help them to identify the characters, scenes and events in the books and let them to be prepared for the fascinating world of words when they start to read by themselves[1].

This fact inspires many artists to draw illustrations for children's books. On the other hand, understanding, predicting, and analyzing people's taste of reading is a challenging problem, since the taste can depend on individuals' philosophical, psychological, political backgrounds. When it comes to children's books, especially from a child's perspective the choice mostly depends on the visual illustrations. Discovering the taste requires the understanding of the style characteristics of the illustrators. Motivated by this observation, in this study we aim to understand the style of artists who draw children's books.

Automatic understanding of artistic images could assist in organizing large collections and could be useful for art recommendation systems. However, it is a difficult task mostly due to varying stylistic behavior of different artists. Particularly with the increase of deep structures there has been an interest towards this relatively less explored area.

There have been recent efforts to understand aesthetic perception of art works such as investigating the potential of a computer to make aesthetic judgements [43], quantifying creativity [16], aesthetic analysis of images by feature discovery [6], and analyzing the artistic influence by comparing them to others [38]. Even though classifying art is qualitative [13], classification of art works has also emerged as another line of work. Bar et. al. [4] worked on classification of artistic styles by presenting a perceptiveness of deep neural network features in identifying artistic styles in paintings. Li et. al. [31] worked on automatically classifying paintings as aesthetic or not. Lyu et. al. [34] focused on painter authentication. Identification of painters is also studied based on wavelet analysis of brush strokes in paintings [25, 32]. In [39, 45] they aimed to classify fine-art paintings using CNNs on "Wikiart paintings" [27] data set. In [45] they conducted experiments on their proposed CNN which is very similar to AlexNet [29]. Best result is achieved when network is first trained on ImageNet dataset [37], then transfer learning applied to the network.

Inspired by capabilities of humans who are able to recognize objects regardless being in art or photography, Cai et. al. worked on automatically identifying objects in cross domains [5]. In [10, 11], the authors focus on recognizing objects in paintings learned from natural images.

Collecting and labelling a dataset for artistic images is also a challenging task. Mensink et. al. [36] introduced a diverse dataset of over 1 million artworks, 700,000 of which are prints to support and evaluate art classification. Carneiro et. al. [7] presented a database of monochromatic artistic images. Crowley et al. [10, 11] annotate a subset of publicly available 'Your Paintings' [2] data set images with ten category labels from the PASCAL VOC data set [17]. In [28] presented a dataset which contains 4266 paintings from 91 different painters. Karayev et. al. [27] presented two novel data sets, one of them contains 80K Flickr photographs annotated with 20 style labels such as vintage, romantic, HDR etc., and the second one consist of 85K art paintings from 25 art styles like Baroque, Roccoco, Cubism etc.

Some works concentrated on transferring artistic styles from style images such as paintings to content images such as selfie pictures [15, 22, 26]. In [21], the artistic style transfer pipeline tries to minimize feature reconstruction loss and style reconstruction loss at the same time by using features from pre-trained CNN model with forward and backward passes. Since backward computations increases computation time, to overcome this, [26] proposed a similar approach with using forward passes to minimize both feature and style reconstruction losses. Kyprianidis et. al. [30] presented a survey on state of the art techniques for transforming images and videos into artistically stylized renderings.

The studies that try to identify the style or genre for art images could be considered similar to ours [9, 27, 35, 39]. However, they define style as a more generic term shared by several artists. The work in [46] that identifies the authorship of photographs, that is the photographer, is the most similar one to ours. Deep networks are also utilized in that study for qualitative evaluations.

In the illustrator identification domain, based on our knowledge the only work is [40] where they tried to identify only four illustrators on a very small data set. They utilized several low-level descriptors such as HOG, GIST and SIFT and used a bag of words model to classify illustrations. In this work, we collected a larger data set and used their results as our baselines.

In some recent studies, illustrations are considered in the form of clip arts. In [19], a style similarity metric is designed by combining color, shading, texture and stroke features with relative comparisons collected via AMT, and this work was leveraged in [20] to obtain aesthetically coherent clusters for visualizations of clip art datasets. In [18], an unsupervised approach is proposed for stylistic comparison of illustrations again in the form of clip-arts. The illustrations that we consider are specific to the artistic drawings in children books, and they are more challenging than the illustrations in clip-arts.

Our contributions: We have several important contributions that will be described in detail in the following sections: **(1)** We attack to the problem of classifying styles of illustrators which is a more challenging task than classifying the content. **(2)** We have constructed a new dataset of illustrations. Based on our knowledge this is the first comprehensive dataset specific to artistic illustrations from books. **(3)** We focus on illustrations in children's books which have distinct characteristics in the sense that the imagination could lead to extreme characters and settings to happen that are difficult to be found in most of the photographs and paintings. **(4)** We explored different deep networks and compared them with low level features. **(5)** We tested three different strategies for categorisation: novel instance recognition from seen books as well as unseen books, and book recognition. **(6)** We exploited the style transfer method and showed the qualitative results for transferring styles from illustrators to cartoon images and natural photographs as well as to the illustrations of other illustrators. **(7)** Further, we provided quantitative results for illustrator to illustrator transfer utilizing the style categorization. **(8)** We compared different methods and features in choosing representative illustrators and discriminative patches.

[1] http://www.maaillustrations.com/blog/article/the-role-of-illustration-in-childrens-book/

Table 1: **Summary statistics of our Illustration dataset.**

Id - Illustrator	Dataset Book Cnt	Dataset Image Cnt	Id - Illustrator	Dataset Book Cnt	Dataset Image Cnt
01- Axel Scheffler	13	532	13- Korky Paul	15	427
02- Ayse Inal	4	120	14- Leo Lionni	10	314
03- Beatrix Potter	9	269	15- Marc Brown	17	360
04- Behic Ak	12	385	16- Maurice Sendak	7	263
05- Bill Peet	11	513	17- Mo Willems	6	268
06- David Mckee	12	199	18- Mustafa Delioglu	9	160
07- Debi Gliori	12	275	19- Patricia Polacco	9	284
08- Dr. Seuss	15	455	20- Ralf Butschkow	6	152
09- Eric Carle	14	304	21- Rosa Curto	8	288
10- Eric Hill	9	148	22- Serap Deliorman	5	158
11- Feridun Oral	5	140	23- Stephen Cartwright	5	179
12- Kevin Henkes	3	86	24- Tony Ross	7	189
	Total Number of	Illustrators: 24	Books: 223	Illustrations: 6468	

Figure 2: Example illustrations from our data set. Three consecutive illustrations in a column correspond to a single illustrator. The order of illustrators is the same as in Table 1. Note that, the styles are distinctive for illustrators. However, due to the variety in individual's styles some instances are difficult to categorise correctly.

2 DATASET

We constructed a new data set consisting of 6468 distinct illustrations from 24 different illustrators. Focusing on the popular children's books, we mostly selected the illustrators who created more than a single basic character. The pages are collected either directly scanning from printed books or from publicly available e-books and read aloud videos over YouTube. Table 1 shows summary of our dataset and Figure 2 represents some example illustrations.

In building the dataset, we are inspired from [40] in which a dataset consisting of 248 illustrations of Axel Scheffler, 243 illustrations of Debi Gliori, 249 illustrations of Korky Paul and 234 illustrations of Dr. Seuss was generated. We almost doubled the examples for three of the illustrators, and included 20 other illustrators. Within its current form the dataset is unique: although large scale datasets exist for paintings [11, 27, 28], based on our knowledge this is the first comprehensive dataset for illustrations.

Note that, in the painting datasets there are a variety of artists following the same artistic style, and thus the dataset is deep in the sense that the number of examples per style is large. However, each illustrator has only a limited set of books and therefore the number of examples per category is not possible to reach to the numbers in painting datasets. Similarly, the number of categories can only be extended within some limits when we force each illustrator to have more than a single specific character or book series. We continue to extend the dataset and will make it publicly available within the copyright limitations.

3 DISCOVERING STYLE OF ILLUSTRATORS

In the following, we will first describe the details of our method in categorizing the style of illustrators using deep networks. Then, we will discuss about approaches to transfer style and to discover representative elements.

3.1 Deep Learning For Style Recognition

Instead of creating a model from scratch, we used three well-known CNN models in training: AlexNet [29], VGG-19 [41] and GoogLeNet [44]. We used Caffe [24] framework to train deep networks on a Tesla K40 12GB GPU. We employed both end-to-end training and transfer learning. To train an end-to-end model, we enlarged our data set which is comparably small, by applying data augmentation.

For small data sets like ours, it is not practical and meaningful to fully train very deep networks. Thus, we fully trained only the AlexNet as being relatively shallow. We first subtracted the mean of RGB values over our illustrations dataset for each pixel and obtained the centered raw RGB values. We augmented our training and validation data using only horizontal reflections to reduce overfitting. The batch sizes are chosen as 128 and 40 for train and validation respectively. Base learning rate is set to 0.01 with a momentum of 0.9 and the learning rate is decreased by a factor of 10 after each 40K iterations.

Considering the fact that our dataset is comparably small, alternatively we applied transfer learning. For this purpose, we used VGG-19, AlexNet and GoogLeNet models pre-trained on a large scale ImageNet dataset. Our hyper parameters are nearly the same for fine tuning on AlexNet and VGG-19 except learning rate and batch sizes. Due to the memory issues, we were able to train VGG-19 with train batch sizes of 32. We selected learning rate accordingly and set it to 0.0004. Base learning rate for AlexNet is 0.0001 and all other parameters for SGD are same as end-to-end training. To train GoogLeNet we used quick solver [3] properties with initial learning rate of 0.01.

3.2 Style transfer

Inspired by the recent work on transferring artistic style of paintings [22], we transfer the style from one illustration to another. Besides showing the ability of style generation, this task is also important to understand the capability of deep models to capture the style separated from the content.

Style transfer model [22] combines the appearance of a style image, e.g. an artwork, with the content of another image, e.g. an arbitrary photograph, by minimizing the loss of content and style. In our case, style is learned from an illustration of a particular illustrator, and transferred to another image. The target image could be a cartoon, a natural photograph, or another illustration from another artist. We expect the resulting image to contain the content of the target image drawn with the style of source illustration.

However, it is difficult and subjective to judge the quality of the resulting images. In this study, focusing on the style transfers from one illustration to another, we propose to compare the style of the resulting illustration with the original style from the categorisation perspective. Our intuition here is that if we use the resulting image as a test instance on our deep networks, and classify them correctly then we could infer that deep models can capture styles.

3.3 Discovering representatives

Here we try to understand style of illustrators in terms of discriminative and representative examples. We utilised two methods for this purpose. The first method [14] was initially proposed for discovering architectural elements of different cities. It takes a positive set of images from which we want to extract discriminative patches, and a global negative set. It uses HOG features [12] to represent the images. We have used this method both to find representative illustrations for different artists and also for discovering the discriminative parts in the illustrations. However, since this algorithm takes days to complete on a powerful laptop, we were able to run it only for a few of illustrators.

The second method that we utilised [23] focuses on eliminating the outliers from a candidate set of positive examples to capture the representative elements in an iterative fashion. The method was proposed to recognise faces from noisy weakly labeled images collected from web. Being flexible, we exploited this method with HOG [12], color dense SIFT [33], and VGG [41] features.

4 EXPERIMENTS

In this section, we first present detailed experimental evaluations to recognize style of illustrators using deep networks. We also provide experimental results of conventional classification methods as a baseline to compare with deep architectures. Then, we present our results on style transfer and representative element discovery.

4.1 Style recognition with deep networks

We used two different settings for categorisation. In the first setting, we treated each page as an independent instance and constructed training, validation and test sets by randomly selecting instances from the entire collection. In the second setting, we tested a more challenging case, and removed some of the books entirely from the training set. Results of both settings will be discussed in the following.

To analyze and understand the results further, we exploited the method of [47]. Figure 4 shows per-unit visualizations from different layers of VGG-19 network. In every image, first column corresponds to synthetic images which cause high activation using regularized optimization, and second column shows crops from our training dataset that cause highest activation for that unit. As it is shown, our network is able to find parts and objects such as eyes, fish, car/wheel, house, plant, people and clothes, and even discriminate poses such as side views of humans and animals, as well as hair, fur or ears.

Instance categorisation: In this setting, our goal is classify illustrations on a randomly carved data. Here, we don't care about the books and thus we put all the illustrations from all the books of

Table 2: Illustration Classification Experiments. Fine Tuning is applied for VGG19 and GoogLeNet networks, while full training is performed for Alexnet.

Method	Augmentation	Accuracy(%)
Alexnet	Yes	68.75
VGG 19	No	93.47
VGG 19	Yes	93.24
GoogLeNet	No	94.07
Dense SIFT	-	82.71
Color Dense SIFT	-	84.35

Table 3: Classification results using GoogLeNet finetuning.

	Metrics			Metrics	
Id	F1 Score	Accuracy	Id	F1 Score	Accuracy
01	0.96	0.94	13	0.95	1.0
02	0.96	0.91	14	0.99	0.98
03	0.93	0.91	15	0.97	0.96
04	0.94	0.93	16	0.99	0.98
05	0.98	0.98	17	0.98	1.0
06	0.94	0.92	18	0.88	0.78
07	0.74	0.69	19	0.87	0.91
08	0.98	0.99	20	0.93	0.90
09	0.92	0.96	21	0.92	0.91
10	0.95	0.90	22	0.90	0.94
11	0.84	0.85	23	0.95	0.97
12	1.0	1.0	24	0.97	1.0

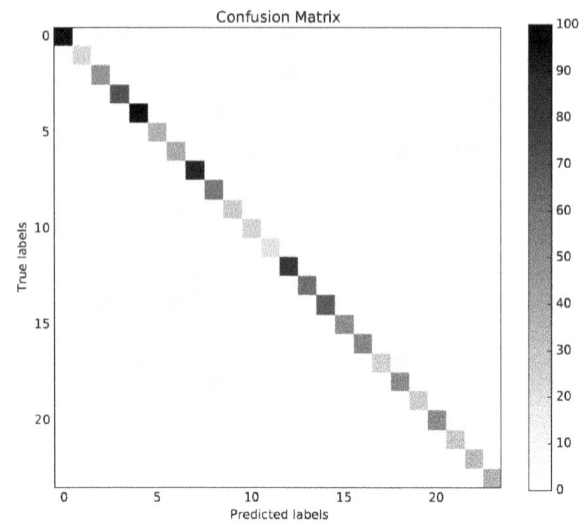

Figure 3: Confusion Matrix for GoogleNet Finetune Test.

Table 4: Experiments on unseen books.

Network	book based instance categorisation	book categorisation
VGG 19	78.96	90.00
GoogLeNet	79.27	88.33
Dense SIFT	69.34	-
Color Dense SIFT	70.00	-

an illustrator all together and then we construct training, validation and test sets by selecting fixed percentage of the instances randomly.

For this group of experiments we utilized several deep networks including end-to-end training of a network and fine tuning. Table 2 summarizes the results in terms of the network architecture used, test type such as fully training or fine tuning the network, and whether data augmentation is used or not. For all experiments on deep networks, we used 70% of the data as training set and, 10% of the data as validation set. The rest which is 20% is used for testing.

As expected fully training a deep network gives less accuracy than fine tuning. Thus, in the next group of experiments we focused only on the fine tuning. Also note that, using augmented data for fine tuning a model doesn't improve the accuracy much. Thus, we preferred not to use augmented data while fine tuning a model. GoogLeNet has much less parameters and less error rate than VGG-19 on ImageNet data set. Our results are in line with the same observation and GoogLeNet beats VGG-19 with a very small difference. Since GoogLeNet has the best performance, in the following experiments we report only the GoogLeNet results. Figure 3 and Table 3 depicts confusion matrix and class-based F1 and accuracy results respectively.

Book based instance categorisation: Since illustrators are likely to have varying styles in different books, in this setup we attack a more challenging problem of recognizing the style on novel books. Instead of carving illustrations from one illustrator, we split our data in terms of books into training/validation and test sets. Thus, training and test sets do not share illustrations from the same book. Some illustrators have fewer books than others, but to measure the accuracy we make sure that every illustrator have at least one book in the test set. Note that, this setting is similar to recognizing unseen categories, and especially in the case of domain transfer problem. Leaving out some books mean having unseen characters and contents. Therefore, our recognition performance on this setting proves the capability of our method in recognizing the style but not the specific characters. Notice that the results are lower than the results of instance recognition as expected (see Table 4) .

Book categorisation: We further used this network to predict the illustrator of each illustration book. Note that, in the previous settings our goal was to predict the illustrator of a single page. To predict the illustrator of a book, we used majority voting and selected the illustrator as the one having the largest number of pages assigned. We evaluated the performance of book categorisation with 60 different illustration books using results of VGG-19 model, and obtained 90% accuracy on predicting illustrator of a given book. Table 4 presents the performance on book recognition.

4.2 Style recognition with conventional methods

As a baseline method, we utilized conventional feature extraction methods that are shown to have the highest accuracies in [40]. We extracted Dense SIFT [33] and Color Dense SIFT [33] features

Figure 4: Visualizations from different layers. The network is able to capture parts and objects shared in drawings of different illustrators: eyes, wheels, buildings, pointy tree like structures, hairy or furry heads, big ears, human upper body, etc.

from every illustration and then generated a code book for Bag-of-words [42] representation using k-means clustering. We use Support Vector Machines to train our model. In particular LIBSVM library [8] is used for SVM classification. We use one versus all approach for training where to prepare the training set for a class, we provide the negative samples from all other classes. A test example is fed into multiple classifiers and it is assigned to the class with the highest confidence value. Half of the data set is used to train SVMs, and the rest is used for testing the models. We observe Hellinger's kernel boosts the performance by almost 20% over other kernels. As seen in Table 2 and Table 4 the results are much lower compared to the results of deep network architectures.

4.3 Style Transfer on Illustration Dataset

In style transfer experiments, we first selected a simple content image (cartoon image or a natural photograph) gathered from web and has no relation with our data set. Then, we randomly chose a group of illustrations from different illustrators as style images. In our second experiment, we challenged the problem and selected an illustration from our data set as the content image. In this setting, style image is an illustration from our data set, and content image is again an illustration but belongs to a different illustrator. We performed style transfer using each style and content image, and looked for the recognizing performance of our deep model on the resulting images. We use fine tuned GoogLeNet in all style transfer experiments.

Figure 5 illustrates the style transfer results for the given style and content images. As it could be seen, our model mostly succeed to capture the styles, except for 'Debi Gliori' on both content images, who has the worst classification performance in the previous experiments as well due to large variations in her style.

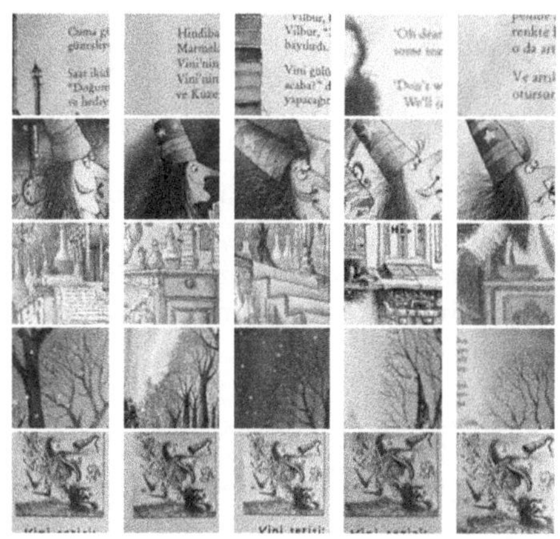

Figure 8: Discriminative patches from Korky Paul obtained by [14]. The first four rows correspond to discriminative stylistic parts seen in his illustrations. Note that the writing style is also captured as discriminative. However, as in the last row repeating images at the back pages of all books were also selected as discriminative as a failure case.

4.4 Representative and discriminative elements

First, we aimed to find representative illustrations of each illustrator. As depicted in Figure 6, we compared the method in [14], with the method in [23] first using HOG features in both methods. Then, we utilised color dense SIFT and VGG19 fined tuned features with [23] as well. Note that, since [14] produces patches while [23] gives images, only way to compare results of both algorithms was to find images which contain most of the extracted patches. While [14] is likely to choose the pages with text as considering the font style being discriminative, [23] is more likely to capture the style forced

Figure 5: Example results for style transfer. First column shows selected style images. 2nd, 4th and 6th columns present content images: a simple cartoon, an illustration from a different illustrator and a natural image respectively. 3rd, 5th and 7th columns belong to resulting images. The style images are from Marc Brown, Maurice Sendak, Korky Paul, Dr. Seuss, Debi Gliori and content images are from Ayse Inal, Ralf Butschkow, Rosa Curto, Leo Lionni, Behic Ak in the given order. Red boxes show the failure cases.

Figure 6: First 20 representative instances obtained by [14] (top-left), and by the method of [23] using HOG (top-right), color dense SIFT (bottom-left), and VGG19 finetuned (bottom-right) features.

by the chosen feature. VGG19 was able to capture the dark colors and the strokes better than the others. Since the visual examples are subjective, in order to quantitatively compare the performance of different methods for selection of representatives we used the categorisation performance. For the first 50 images [14] resulted in 1 incorrect classification and the others reported 100% accuracy. For a better analysis though we should look at the full list and find better comparative measures. Figure 7 shows the representatives for some other illustrators using VGG19 features with [23]. As a final experiment, we explored the patches extracted by [14] in Figure 8 for the Korky Paul images. As seen, we are able to select stylistic elements like the head of the witch, leafless trees, or furniture, and even the typeface of fonts as discriminative elements.

5 CONCLUSION

We attacked the problem of recognizing style of illustrators as a pioneering work in this area. On the new dataset constructed we reported qualitative and quantitative results for three different

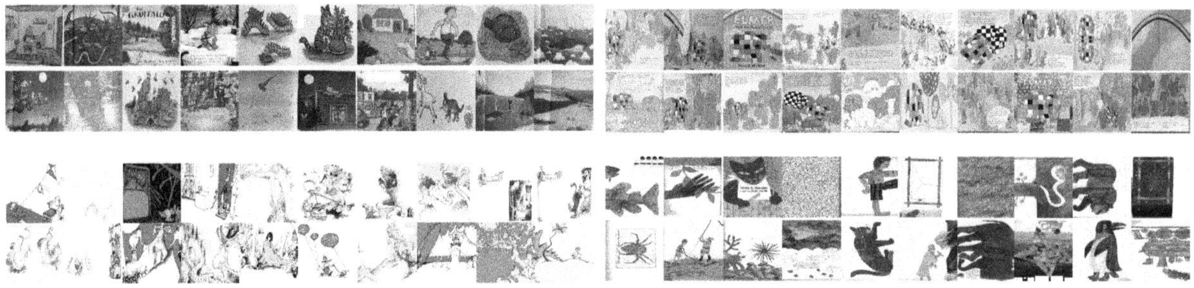

Figure 7: Representative instances for some other illustrators using the method in [23] by VGG19 fine tuned features.

applications: illustrator recognition, style transfer and representative instance selection. In our future work, we plan to expand the dataset with more illustrators. Moreover, better metrics are required to evaluate the quality of style transfer and selection of representatives.

REFERENCES

[1] 2008. We Are All Born Free: The Universal Declaration of Human Rights in Pictures. Frances Lincoln. (2008). http://www.goodreads.com/book/show/3082451-we-are-all-born-free

[2] 2012. BBC Your Paintings. (2012). Dataset available at http://www.bbc.co.uk/arts/.

[3] 2014. Caffe Model Zoo: GoogLeNet Model. (2014). Model available at https://github.com/BVLC/caffe/tree/master/models/bvlc_googlenet.

[4] Yaniv Bar, Noga Levy, and Lior Wolf. 2014. Classification of artistic styles using binarized features derived from a deep neural network. In *Workshop at the European Conference on Computer Vision*. Springer, 71–84.

[5] Hongping Cai, Qi Wu, Tadeo Corradi, and Peter Hall. 2015. The Cross-Depiction Problem: Computer Vision Algorithms for Recognising Objects in Artwork and in Photographs. *CoRR* abs/1505.00110 (2015). http://arxiv.org/abs/1505.00110

[6] Allan Campbell, Vic Ciesielksi, and AK Qin. 2015. Feature discovery by deep learning for aesthetic analysis of evolved abstract images. In *International Conference on Evolutionary and Biologically Inspired Music and Art*. Springer International Publishing, 27–38.

[7] Gustavo Carneiro, Nuno Pinho da Silva, Alessio Del Bue, and João Paulo Costeira. 2012. Artistic image classification: An analysis on the printart database. In *European Conference on Computer Vision*. Springer, 143–157.

[8] Chih-Chung Chang and Chih-Jen Lin. 2011. LIBSVM: A library for support vector machines. *ACM Transactions on Intelligent Systems and Technology* 2 (2011), 27:1–27:27. Issue 3. Software available at http://www.csie.ntu.edu.tw/~cjlin/libsvm.

[9] Wei-Ta Chu and Yi-Ling Wu. 2016. Deep Correlation Features for Image Style Classification. In *Proceedings of the 2016 ACM on Multimedia Conference (MM '16)*. 402–406.

[10] E. J. Crowley and A. Zisserman. 2014. In Search of Art. In *Workshop on Computer Vision for Art Analysis, ECCV*.

[11] E. J. Crowley and A. Zisserman. 2014. The State of the Art: Object Retrieval in Paintings using Discriminative Regions. In *British Machine Vision Conference*.

[12] Navneet Dalal and Bill Triggs. 2005. Histograms of oriented gradients for human detection. In *2005 IEEE Computer Society Conference on Computer Vision and Pattern Recognition (CVPR'05)*, Vol. 1. IEEE, 886–893.

[13] Paul DiMaggio. 1987. Classification in art. *American sociological review* (1987), 440–455.

[14] Carl Doersch, Saurabh Singh, Abhinav Gupta, Josef Sivic, and Alexei A. Efros. 2012. What Makes Paris Look like Paris? *ACM Transactions on Graphics (SIGGRAPH)* 31, 4 (2012), 101:1–101:9.

[15] Vincent Dumoulin, Jonathon Shlens, and Manjunath Kudlur. 2017. A Learned Representation For Artistic Style. *ICLR* (2017). https://arxiv.org/abs/1610.07629

[16] Ahmed Elgammal and Babak Saleh. 2015. Quantifying Creativity in Art Networks. *arXiv preprint arXiv:1506.00711* (2015).

[17] M. Everingham, L. Van Gool, C. K. I. Williams, J. Winn, and A. Zisserman. 2011. The PASCAL Visual Object Classes Challenge 2011 (VOC2011) Results. (2011). http://www.pascal-network.org/challenges/VOC/voc2011/workshop/index.html

[18] T. Furuya, S. Kuriyama, and R. Ohbuchi. 2015. An unsupervised approach for comparing styles of illustrations. In *2015 13th International Workshop on Content-Based Multimedia Indexing (CBMI)*. 1–6. DOI: http://dx.doi.org/10.1109/CBMI.2015.7153615

[19] Elena Garces, Aseem Agarwala, Diego Gutierrez, and Aaron Hertzmann. 2014. A Similarity Measure for Illustration Style. *ACM Trans. Graph.* 33, 4, Article 93 (July 2014), 9 pages. DOI: http://dx.doi.org/10.1145/2601097.2601131

[20] Elena Garces, Aseem Agarwala, Aaron Hertzmann, and Diego Gutierrez. 2016. Style-based exploration of illustration datasets. *Multimedia Tools and Applications* (2016), 1–20. DOI: http://dx.doi.org/10.1007/s11042-016-3702-x

[21] Leon A. Gatys, Alexander S. Ecker, and Matthias Bethge. 2015. A Neural Algorithm of Artistic Style. *CoRR* abs/1508.06576 (2015). http://arxiv.org/abs/1508.06576

[22] Leon A Gatys, Alexander S Ecker, and Matthias Bethge. 2016. Image style transfer using convolutional neural networks. In *Proceedings of the IEEE Conference on Computer Vision and Pattern Recognition*. 2414–2423.

[23] Eren Golge and Pinar Duygulu-Sahin. 2015. FAME: face association through model evolution. In *Proceedings of the IEEE Conference on Computer Vision and Pattern Recognition Workshops*. 43–49.

[24] Yangqing Jia, Evan Shelhamer, Jeff Donahue, Sergey Karayev, Jonathan Long, Ross Girshick, Sergio Guadarrama, and Trevor Darrell. 2014. Caffe: Convolutional Architecture for Fast Feature Embedding. *arXiv preprint arXiv:1408.5093* (2014).

[25] C Richard Johnson, Ella Hendriks, Igor Berezhnoy, Eugene Brevdo, Shannon Hughes, Ingrid Daubechies, Jia Li, Eric Postma, and James Z Wang. 2008. Image Processing for Artist Identification - Computerized Analysis of Vincent van Gogh's Painting Brushstrokes. *IEEE Signal Processing Magazine* (July 2008).

[26] Justin Johnson, Alexandre Alahi, and Li Fei-Fei. 2016. Perceptual losses for real-time style transfer and super-resolution. *arXiv preprint arXiv:1603.08155* (2016).

[27] Sergey Karayev, Matthew Trentacoste, Helen Han, Aseem Agarwala, Trevor Darrell, Aaron Hertzmann, and Holger Winnemoeller. 2013. Recognizing image style. *arXiv preprint arXiv:1311.3715* (2013).

[28] Fahad Shahbaz Khan, Shida Beigpour, Joost Van de Weijer, and Michael Felsberg. 2014. Painting-91: a large scale database for computational painting categorization. *Machine vision and applications* 25, 6 (2014), 1385–1397.

[29] Alex Krizhevsky, Ilya Sutskever, and Geoffrey E Hinton. 2012. Imagenet classification with deep convolutional neural networks. In *Advances in neural information processing systems*. 1097–1105.

[30] Jan Eric Kyprianidis, John Collomosse, Tinghuai Wang, and Tobias Isenberg. 2013. State of the" Art&# x201D;: A Taxonomy of Artistic Stylization Techniques for Images and Video. *IEEE Transactions on Visualization and Computer Graphics* 19, 5 (2013), 866–885.

[31] C. Li and T. Chen. 2009. Aesthetic Visual Quality Assessment of Paintings. *IEEE Journal of Selected Topics in Signal Processing* 3, 2 (April 2009), 236–252.

[32] Jia Li and J. Z. Wang. 2004. Studying Digital Imagery of Ancient Paintings by Mixtures of Stochastic Models. *Trans. Img. Proc.* 13, 3 (March 2004), 340–353. DOI: http://dx.doi.org/10.1109/TIP.2003.821349

[33] David G Lowe. 2004. Distinctive image features from scale-invariant keypoints. *International journal of computer vision* 60, 2 (2004), 91–110.

[34] Siwei Lyu, Daniel Rockmore, and Hany Farid. 2004. A digital technique for art authentication. *Proceedings of the National Academy of Sciences of the United States of America* 101, 49 (2004), 17006–17010.

[35] Shin Matsuo and Keiji Yanai. 2016. CNN-based style vector for style image retrieval. In *Proceedings of the 2016 ACM on International Conference on Multimedia Retrieval*. ACM, 309–312.

[36] Thomas Mensink and Jan Van Gemert. 2014. The rijksmuseum challenge: Museum-centered visual recognition. In *Proceedings of International Conference on Multimedia Retrieval*. ACM, 451.

[37] Olga Russakovsky, Jia Deng, Hao Su, Jonathan Krause, Sanjeev Satheesh, Sean Ma, Zhiheng Huang, Andrej Karpathy, Aditya Khosla, Michael Bernstein, Alexander C. Berg, and Li Fei-Fei. 2015. ImageNet Large Scale Visual Recognition Challenge. *International Journal of Computer Vision (IJCV)* 115, 3 (2015), 211–252.

DOI: http://dx.doi.org/10.1007/s11263-015-0816-y
[38] Babak Saleh, Kanako Abe, Ravneet Singh Arora, and Ahmed Elgammal. 2014. Toward automated discovery of artistic influence. *Multimedia Tools and Applications* (2014), 1–27.
[39] Babak Saleh and Ahmed Elgammal. 2015. Large-scale Classification of Fine-Art Paintings: Learning The Right Metric on The Right Feature. *arXiv preprint arXiv:1505.00855* (2015).
[40] Fadime Sener, Nermin Samet, and Pinar Duygulu Sahin. 2012. Identification of illustrators. In *European Conference on Computer Vision*. Springer Berlin Heidelberg, 589–597.
[41] K. Simonyan and A. Zisserman. 2014. Very Deep Convolutional Networks for Large-Scale Image Recognition. *CoRR* abs/1409.1556 (2014).
[42] Josef Sivic, Bryan C Russell, Alexei A Efros, Andrew Zisserman, and William T Freeman. 2005. Discovering object categories in image collections. (2005).
[43] Emily L. Spratt and Ahmed M. Elgammal. 2014. Computational Beauty: Aesthetic Judgment at the Intersection of Art and Science. In *Computer Vision - ECCV 2014 Workshops - Zurich, Switzerland, September 6-7 and 12, 2014, Proceedings, Part I.* 35–53. DOI: http://dx.doi.org/10.1007/978-3-319-16178-5_3
[44] Christian Szegedy, Wei Liu, Yangqing Jia, Pierre Sermanet, Scott Reed, Dragomir Anguelov, Dumitru Erhan, Vincent Vanhoucke, and Andrew Rabinovich. 2015. Going deeper with convolutions. In *Proceedings of the IEEE Conference on Computer Vision and Pattern Recognition*. 1–9.
[45] W. R. Tan, C. S. Chan, H. E. Aguirre, and K. Tanaka. 2016. Ceci n'est pas une pipe: A deep convolutional network for fine-art paintings classification. In *2016 IEEE International Conference on Image Processing (ICIP)*. 3703–3707. DOI: http://dx.doi.org/10.1109/ICIP.2016.7533051
[46] Christopher Thomas and Adriana Kovashka. 2015. Who's Behind the Camera? Identifying the Authorship of a Photograph. *arXiv preprint arXiv:1508.05038* (2015).
[47] Jason Yosinski, Jeff Clune, Anh Nguyen, Thomas Fuchs, and Hod Lipson. 2015. Understanding Neural Networks Through Deep Visualization. In *Deep Learning Workshop, International Conference on Machine Learning (ICML)*.

AMECON: Abstract Meta-Concept Features for Text-Illustration

Ines Chami[1]* Youssef Tamaazousti[2]* Hervé Le Borgne[2]
[1]Stanford University, Institute for Computational and Mathematical Engineering, California, USA
[2]CEA, LIST, Laboratory of Vision and Content Engineering, F-91191 Gif-sur-Yvette, France
*Both authors contributed equally to this work.

ABSTRACT

Cross-media retrieval is a problem of high interest that is at the frontier between computer vision and natural language processing. The state-of-the-art in the domain consists of learning a common space with regard to some constraints of correlation or similarity from two textual and visual modalities that are processed in parallel and possibly jointly. This paper proposes a different approach that considers the cross-modal problem as a supervised mapping of visual modalities to textual ones. Each modality is thus seen as a particular projection of an abstract meta-concept, each of its dimension subsuming several semantic concepts ("meta" aspect) but may not correspond to an actual one ("abstract" aspect). In practice, the textual modality is used to generate a multi-label representation, further used to map the visual modality through a simple shallow neural network. While being quite easy to implement, the experiments show that our approach significantly outperforms the state-of-the-art on Flickr-8K and Flickr-30K datasets for the text-illustration task. The source code is available at http://perso.ecp.fr/~tamaazouy/.

CCS CONCEPTS

•**Computing methodologies → Computer vision representations; Learning latent representations;** Image representations;

KEYWORDS

Multi-Modal Common Space; Text-Illustration; Neural Networks; Abstract Meta Concepts

ACM Reference format:
Ines Chami[1]* Youssef Tamaazousti[2]* Hervé Le Borgne[2] . 2017. AMECON: Abstract Meta-Concept Features for Text-Illustration. In *Proceedings of ICMR '17, June 06-09, 2017, Bucharest, Romania*, , 9 pages.
DOI: http://dx.doi.org/10.1145/3078971.3078993

1 INTRODUCTION

Many works deal with multi-modal tasks, either to retrieve an image given a text query (text illustration) or to linguistically describe an image (image captioning) or to classify bi-modal documents. Most of these approaches aim at learning a joint embedding for both modalities into a common latent space, in which vectors from the two different modalities are directly comparable [7, 11, 16, 17, 32].

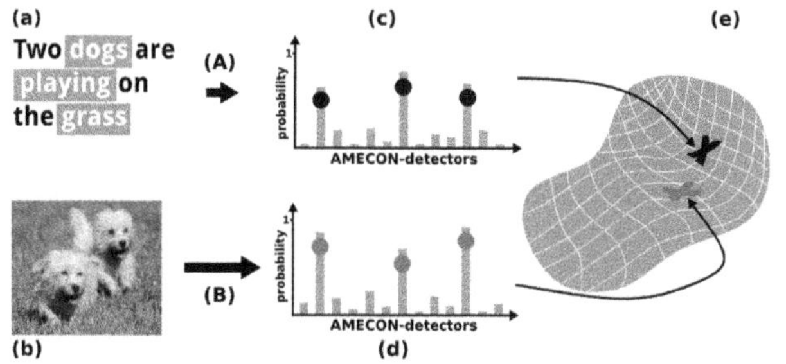

Figure 1: Given an input text (a) and an input image (b), our method computes the AMECON-features for each modality (textual (c) and visual (d)) and matches them in the AMECON Space (e). The key novelty of our approach is that, each dimension of our AMECON representation (each *bar* in (c) and (d)) corresponds to the output probability of an *abstract meta-concept* detector applied on the input data. For instance, here the two input data are close together in the AMECON space (e) since they both have the *same* three abstract meta-concepts (identified by circles on features) that are highly activated. The size of the arrows (A) and (B) highlights the *asymmetry* of our approach. In fact, it shows that more computations are needed to project (on the AMECON space) the visual features than the textual ones. Best view in color.

Two families of approaches emerge when reviewing the literature about the design of such a common latent space. The first, specifically focuses on learning the latent space from *existing* textual and visual features. These last, typically result from an embedding representation, such as the word2vec [22] features for textual content and one layer from a pre-trained Convolutional Neural Network (CNN) [3, 25] for the visual modality. Then, the latent space is learned according to a certain principle from aligned textual and visual data described with these features. By "aligned data", one must understand that an image is for example aligned with its caption, in the sense that their respective contents are supposed to match. Regarding the principle used to learn the latent space, the seminal work of Hardoon [11] consisted in maximizing the correlation of the aligned data once projected in the common space. More recently, Frome *et al.* [7] proposed a visual visual-semantic embedding that maps the visual representation to the language model by learning a similarity metric that produces a higher score for aligned data than non-aligned ones. The second family of approaches relies on deep networks to model a full multi-modal embedding. This is the case of [16] who proposed to infer the correspondences between images and their sentence description. First, they use a Region Convolutional Neural Network (RCNN) [8] as image representation and a

Bidirectional Recurrent Neural Network (BRNN) [24] to textual one. Second, they define a loss that encourages aligned image-sentences pairs to have a higher score than misaligned pairs. A RNN is then learned to generate a description for new images. Another interesting recent work is that of [35] who learn a text-image embedding using a two-view neural network. Two layers of non-linearities are used on top of a CNN-based visual representation and sentences represented by Fisher vectors [19]. They define a loss that tends to force aligned images and sentences to be reciprocal first neighbours within the latent space. Other related works are detailed in Sec. 2.

Our initial motivation is the same as the work of [7], that aimed at matching the visual and textual representations. However, our model differs from the previous work by proposing very different pipelines to process both modalities. Indeed, most of previous works use two similar pipelines in parallel, one for each modality that only differ by the features considered, then determine a method to design a common space. We adopt a different point of view, considering that the visual and the textual modalities should not (yet) be processed *symmetrically*. It refers to the well-known semantic gap [26] that reflects the fact that textual features are closer to human understanding (and language) than the pixel-based features. Despite the progresses due to deep learning in visual recognition, we argue that gap is still relevant to consider. We thus propose to consider the Abstract MEta-CONcept (AMECON) principle for a multi-modal (texts and images) alignment. As explained in the following, the AMECON models a higher-level representation of the human knowledge, that is "meta" since each of its dimension subsumes several semantic concepts and "abstract" because each of them may not correspond to a unique existing semantic concept.

A *semantic concept* can be named by a word from the vocabulary of a given language. In line with [1, 10, 27], a *meta-concept* is defined by a concept subsuming several semantic concepts. Moreover, a concept can be qualified as *abstract* when it does not reflect a notion that is explicit in a given language. For example, it is sometimes handy to use some words from a foreign language when it does not really exist in ours. However, in the case of AMECONs, they can be even more abstract, in the sense they can represent some notion where seemingly unrelated concepts can be mapped together because of some invisible intrinsic quality that they share but which is not obvious to humans. We consider that each modality, namely visual and textual, described in its original feature space is an (imperfect) observation of the AMECON space from a particular point of view. A key particularity of our approach is that the mapping from one modality to this space is specific to said modality. For reasons given above, the proposed AMECON space is much closer to the textual embedding space than to the visual one. In practice, on the one hand, the *textual modality* is mapped through vector quantization of the textual features, because we consider they are close enough from the human conceptual space. On the other hand, we learn a mapping from the *visual modality* to the AMECON space with a multi-layer perceptron. It takes the visual features as input and the target (labels) are derived from the textual features by local hard coding. An overview of our approach is illustrated in Figure 1.

Our proposal is thus a new method to build a multi-modal common latent space. It particularly, matches visual content to sentences and thus aims to perform cross-modal or bi-modal tasks. In this paper, we focus on the Text-Illustration task (*i.e.*, retrieve best images from a textual query). While being quite easy to implement, our method exhibits performance above the current state-of-the-art on Text-Illustration. Indeed, we conducted extensive experiments (in Sec. 4) on two publicly available benchmarks, namely Flickr-8k and Flickr-30k, on which our method significantly outperforms the previous works. We also conducted (in Sec. 5) an in-depth analysis of the proposed model to highlight its insights, including an ablation study that shows the relative importance of each component.

2 RELATED WORK

In its seminal work on the design of common space to visual and textual data, Hardoon proposed to maximize the correlation between the projections of both modalities using the Canonical Correlation Analysis (CCA) and its kernelized version (KCCA) [11]. This work has then be extended by [9] who added a third view that reflects the "semantic classes" derived from the ground-truth or the keywords used to download the images. This work also proposed to derive this third view from unsupervised clustering of the tags to avoid the use of ground truth. While being very different from our approach since it relies on a symmetric projection of both modalities through KCCA, such a clustering of tags relates to the process we use to define the projection of the textual features on the AMECON space. However, while [9] uses the clusters to define a third view that is further projected on the KCCA space, our approach uses it as a codebook to directly encode the textual projection.

In the vein of reflecting semantics, [4] proposed to build semantic features into the common space, that is to say to create a signature where each dimension is a given semantic concept that is estimated by a learned binary classifier [31]. Contrary to ours, these concepts are neither meta nor abstract. However, one could image to apply the approach of [1] to get meta-concepts in the common space. Still, a major difference with our work is that each concept is obtained by supervised classification, while in our case, the *abstract* concepts deeply result from an unsupervised approach.

A major drawback of KCCA-based approaches is their tendency to group the projections with respect to each modality rather than the actual semantic of the content. To compensate this effect, [32] proposed to quantify the common space then code each modality according to the resulting codebook. Their method also include a "completion" of each projected modality. Such a completion compensates the modality separation identified in the common space and can be effective for retrieval even without quantization [33].

Rather than relying on an a priori principle such as maximizing the correlation, other works consider deep neural networks with other type of constraint. Ngiam *et al.* [23] used a deep autoencoder to learn a common space for videos and speech audio data. It allows them to manage the absence of a modality and thus perform cross-modal retrieval. As already cited in the introduction, Frome *et al.* proposed DeViSE [7] that learns a similarity metric between the top layer of a visual network and a skip-gram text model (*word2vec*), optimizing an objective function that forces the similarity of a given image to the relevant label to be higher than that to other randomly chosen text terms. This is probably the work that is closer to ours, in the sense that it tries to directly match the visual representation to the textual one. However, our work differs from them on several points. Indeed, our approach transforms explicitly the textual information into labels to use a supervised classification scheme to map the visual representation. Thereby, the advantage of our approach is to design a non-linear mapping between both modalities while DeViSE only proposes a linear transformation between the original features. In [17] and [16], visual data is also aligned with sentences, thanks to a structured loss that forces aligned sentences and images to be close reciprocal neighbours. In the same vein but with a lighter architecture [35] tends to preserve the local neighbourhood of corresponding text and images by forcing the distances of correct matches in the latent space to be smaller than the wrong ones. The main difference between our approach and these deep learning-based approaches is that they rely on a quite *symmetric* scheme where both modalities are processed similarly. While our *asymmetric* approach seems more straightforward, it remains conceptually simpler and has much better performances.

Let note that, a recently released pre-print [6] also proposes an *asymmetric* method that matches text features to CNN-based image representations. The key differences with our work is the mapping as well as the common space. In fact, our common latent space is based on the proposed AMECON principle while they directly use the original visual features as the common space. Also interesting, the asymmetry of both approaches limits the performances on the inverse cross-modal task. Indeed, our method works very well on Text-Illustration but does not work so well on the inverse task (*i.e.*, image-captioning). The same phenomenon seems to appear in [6], since they only evaluate their method on image-captioning. Hence, for these *asymmetrical* approaches, getting good performances on one direction of cross-modal task when building the common latent space on the inverse direction, remains an open problem.

3 PROPOSED APPROACH

Our approach to build a multi-modal common space is named "Abstract Meta-Concept" (**AMECON**). It consists to match texts and images in an AMECON common latent space (described in Sec. 3.1) where the cues (visual, textual or both) contribute to activate the different *abstract meta-concept* detectors. In Sec. 3.2, we describe how to learn the abstract meta-concepts and how to generate AMECON features for the text modality. Sec. 3.3 details the learning of AMECON features for the visual modality. In this paper, we focus on the application of AMECON to the Text-Illustration task.

3.1 AMECON Space

Let first recall that a *semantic-concept* is *any* word (associated to a particular *notion*) from the real-world vocabulary used by humans (*e.g*, bicycle plant, bird, etc.).

Definition 1. An *abstract meta-concept* is both, an *abstract* concept and a *meta*-concept. An abstract concept describes a concept that is not associated to a semantic connotation (that does not exist in the real-world vocabulary used by humans) and a meta-concept is a concept that subsumes others (at least one). Note that, the subsumed concepts can be either semantic or even abstract.

Definition 2. An *abstract meta-concept detector* ($\chi_i(\mathbf{x})$) is a visual $\chi_i^V(\mathbf{x})$ or textual $\chi_i^T(\mathbf{x})$ classifier that takes as input a mid-level representation (visual $\mathbf{x}^V$ or textual $\mathbf{x}^T$) of an input data and an AMECON-model (that has been learned with positive and negative samples of that abstract meta-concept) and returns the probability of presence of that abstract meta-concept given the input data.

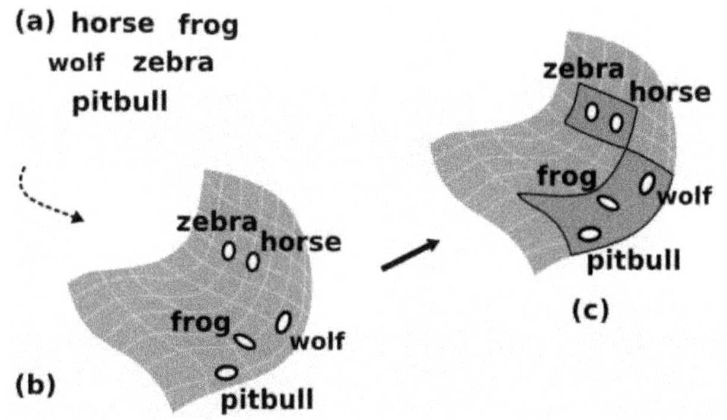

Figure 2: Illustration of the proposed AMECON principle. Given a set of words from a training corpus (a) and their projection in a word embedding space (b), our method clusters the space (c) such that each cluster is an *abstract meta-concept* that corresponds to an *abstract* concept (do not exist in the real-world) and a *general* concept (group of concepts). For instance, the blue cluster in (c) is *general* since it subsumes the vectors of many words and is *abstract* since no semantic connotation can be attributed to it. Indeed, the abstraction comes from the fact that inside the group, the words are not semantically related which makes the group *noisy* and thus prevents a human to attribute it a *correct* semantic concept. Best view in color.

Let us consider a visual representation of an image I noted χ^V and a linguistic representation of a text $\mathcal{T}$ noted χ^T, such that each dimension χ_i^V or χ_i^T reflects the *same* abstract meta-concept. Their integration into a unique multi-modal description χ results from a scheme where each representation (visual or textual) is an imperfect representation of the corresponding abstract meta-concept. Therefore, we name "AMECON Space" the space containing these abstract meta-concept and illustrate the principle in Figure 1.

Formally, the proposed multi-modal representation corresponds to a C-dimensional vector $\chi(\mathbf{x}) = [\chi_1(\mathbf{x}), \ldots, \chi_C(\mathbf{x})]$, where each dimension $\chi_i(\mathbf{x})$ is the output of an abstract meta-concept classifier that can be obtained by one or both modalities. More specifically, $\chi_i(\mathbf{x}) = max(\chi_i^T(\mathbf{x}), \chi_i^V(\mathbf{x}))$ with $\chi_i^T(\mathbf{x})$ and $\chi_i^V(\mathbf{x})$ are respectively the *textual* and *visual* abstract meta-concept detectors. Note that, we have as many visual classifiers as textual ones, thus the visual (χ^V) and textual representation (χ^T) are both of size C.

This scheme has the advantage to consider both modalities for *bi-modal* tasks (bi-modal retrieval and classification) or only one modality for *mono-modal* tasks (cross-modal retrieval and classification). More precisely, in the former case, it is straightforward to compute $\chi_i(\mathbf{x})$ since both modalities are available while in the latter case, where only one modality is available, we set the output values (of the detectors) of the missing modality to zero, resulting to consider only the available modality. Moreover, for cross-modal retrieval where we need to retrieve the nearest documents from another modality, we simply use the k-Nearest Neighbours algorithm since both modalities are represented in the *same* AMECON space.

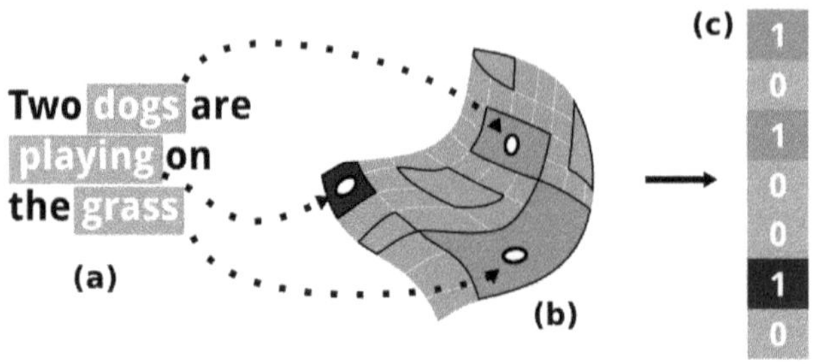

Figure 3: Illustration of the proposed textual AMECON-features. Given an input caption (a), our method first selects the non stop-words (coloured in gray), computes their mid-level features and projects them in the clustered word embedding (b) that corresponds to our AMECON space. After the projection, when a word embedding representation falls in an abstract meta-concept (*e.g*, blue cluster), its associated dimension is activated (*e.g*, 3rd dimension). All other dimensions are filled with a zero-value. Applying this process on all the selected words and pooling their *binary* textual AMECON features together, results in a *binary* multi-label representation (c). Best view in color.

3.2 Textual AMECON-Features

3.2.1 Learning the AMECONs. We propose to learn the abstract meta-concepts (AMECONs) using unsupervised clustering. Hence, the AMECONs verifies its two definitional characteristics: (i) it groups similar data into a generic cluster that thus corresponds to a *meta*-concept and (ii) because of the unsupervised aspect, the resulting clusters do not have any explicit semantic connotation (*i.e* do not exist in the real-world vocabulary of humans) making them *abstract*-concepts. More generally, AMECONs are obtained through unsupervised clustering of textual mid-level features (*e.g.*, word2vec [22]). In that sense, our method adopts a "bottom-up" approach, generating high-level knowledge from low-level data in the same vein as [1] for the *meta* aspect. Note that, in [27] and [10], the *meta* concepts are obtained through *manual* annotations. An illustration of our AMECON principle is given in Figure 2.

To learn the AMECONs in practice, we collect all the words of a training corpus and represent them in an embedding space (*e.g.*, word2vec) of dimension d. Then, we group the word vectors representations using a clustering algorithm (*e.g* K-means) that results into C clusters (C being chosen arbitrarily or obtained through cross-validation). Each cluster is an AMECON that is represented by the corresponding cluster-center $(\mathbf{c}_i)_{i=1,\ldots,C} \in \mathbb{R}^d$. Hence, within an AMECON cluster, words have *similar* semantic connotations (*i.e.*, similar in the sense of the word representation used). Here, we used the K-means algorithm for clustering but obviously, other unsupervised algorithms (*e.g.*, spectral-clustering, MeanShift, etc.) could be used. Note that, the number of AMECONs (C) directly corresponds to the dimensionality of the AMECON Space presented in the previous section.

3.2.2 Learning the Textual AMECON-Features. The set of C abstract meta-concepts is now seen as a codebook that we use to encode any piece of information. In the case of textual information, we adopt a coding scheme similar to local soft coding [20], originally introduced as locality-constrained linear coding [34], that is nevertheless binarized. Given a caption $\mathcal{T}$ composed of n words, we compute the mid-level representation $\mathbf{x}_j^T \in \mathbb{R}^d$ of each word, resulting into a set of n vectors $\{\mathbf{x}_j^T\}_{j=1,\ldots,n}$ in the word embedding space.

The jth word is then encoded according to the codebook in the C-dimensional vector, its kth dimension being:

$$\chi_{bin,j}^T(k) = \begin{cases} 1 & \text{if } k \in NN^m(\mathbf{x}_j^T) \\ 0 & \text{otherwise} \end{cases} \tag{1}$$

where $NN^m(\mathbf{x}_j^T)$ is the set of indexes of the m nearest AMECON clusters of $\mathbf{x}_j^T$ in the word embedding space. It is thus a "local hard coding" of $\mathbf{x}_j^T$ according to the codebook. We add the index notation $\cdot_{bin}$ to highlight it is a binary vector. The parameter m can be set arbitrarily or determined by cross-validation. The representation, in this C-dimensional space, of the ith caption result from the pooling of its word's representation:

$$\chi_{bin,i}^T = \underset{j=1\ldots n}{\mathcal{P}}(\chi_{bin,j}^T), \tag{2}$$

where $\mathcal{P}$ is the pooling operator that can be *max* or *sum* pooling. In the following we use the same notation for the representation of a word j and that of caption i since both of them lie in the same space. Our proposal to compute the textual AMECON-features for an input caption is illustrated in Figure 3.

3.3 Visual AMECON-Features

In this section, we describe the proposed method to learn and compute the AMECON-features for the image modality. More precisely, we first represent images through mid-level features extracted from a pre-trained CNN. Our goal is to project these mid-level features into the learned AMECON Space. To do this, we propose (in Sec. 3.3.1) to approach the projection problem as a *classification problem* with CNN features as inputs and the corresponding textual AMECON-features as ground-truth labels. We then, propose (in Sec. 3.3.2) to solve this classification problem using a shallow neural network.

3.3.1 Textual AMECON-Features as Image Labels. At the core of our approach, we associate visual mid-level features to *binary* textual AMECON features. It is posed as a classification problem with CNN features as input data and AMECON features as ground-truth labels. Indeed, the textual AMECON features being binary, they can be used as ground-truth labels for a multi-label supervised classification problem (reduced to a single label if the textual document is a unique word). Figure 4 illustrates the pipeline.

Formally, let consider a training database $\mathcal{D}$ containing N pairs of text-image $(\mathcal{T}^i, I^i)$. From each image I^i and caption $\mathcal{T}^i$, we respectively extract their mid-level features $\mathbf{x}_i^V$ and $\mathbf{x}_i^T$. For each *textual* mid-level features we compute the corresponding AMECON-features as depicted in Sec. 3.2. We then use these binary features as ground-truth labels (during training) for the visual mid-level features $\mathbf{x}_i^V$. In the next section, we describe the classification algorithm used to solve this multi-label classification problem.

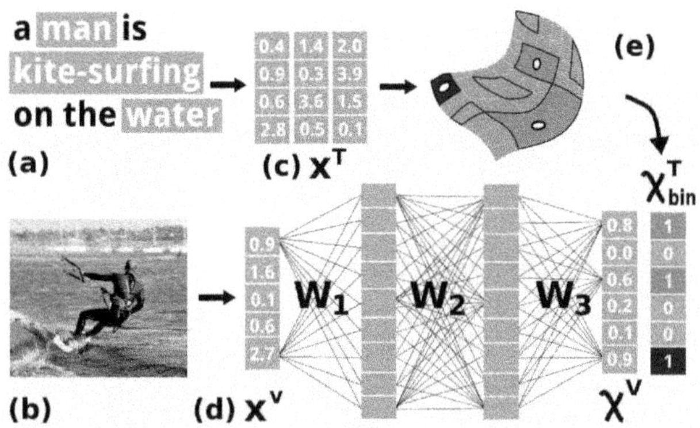

Figure 4: Illustration of the learning of the visual AMECON features. Given an input image (b) and its associated caption (a), we first represent the three selected words and the image through mid-level features (one layer of a CNN (d) for the image and word2vec features (c) for the words). Then, we project the word2vec features in the AMECON space (e) and compute the *binary* textual AMECON-features χ^T_{bin} of the caption. This latter, is then used as output layer (ground-truth label for the input image vector). A shallow neural-network is finally learned to map from the CNN features to the *binary* textual AMECON-features. Best view in color.

3.3.2 Learning the Visual AMECON-Features. To learn the mapping of visual mid-level features to the AMECON Space, we use a shallow neural-network classification algorithm. Formally, let re-consider the *training* database $\mathcal{D}$ of N text-image pairs $(\mathcal{T}^i, I^i)$. Each image I^i is represented as mid-level features $\mathbf{x}_i^V$ – *e.g* one layer of a pre-trained CNN – and its corresponding caption is represented using textual mid-level features $\mathbf{x}_i^T$ which are mapped to *binary* textual AMECON features $\chi^T_{bin,i}$ that result from the aggregation via Eq. (2). As depicted in the previous section, the mid-level visual features $\mathbf{x}_i^V$ are used as inputs and the textual features $\chi^T_{bin,i}$ are used as ground-truth labels.

To solve the above classification problem, we use an L-layer perceptron. The input layer is the visual mid-level features $\mathbf{x}^V$, the output layer is the *predicted visual* AMECON representation χ^V, and the neural network contain $L-1$ hidden layers. More concretely, by applying an affine transformation on $s(\mathbf{x}^V)$, followed by an element-wise ReLU activation $f(z) = max(0, z)$ we obtain the first hidden layer $h_1(\mathbf{x}^V)$ of the L-layer neural-network through:

$$h_1(\mathbf{x}^V) = f(W_1\mathbf{x}^V + b_1). \tag{3}$$

The following hidden layers are expressed by:

$$h_l(h_{l-1}) = f(W_l h_{l-1} + b_l), \forall l \in [2, \ldots, L-2], \tag{4}$$

where W_l parametrizes the affine transformation of the lth hidden layer and b_l are the bias terms. In the same vein, we compute the output layer χ^V by:

$$\chi^V(h_{L-1}) = \sigma(W_L h_{L-1} + b_L), \tag{5}$$

where $\sigma(z) = \frac{1}{1+e^{-z}}$ is the sigmoid function that maps the raw scores to the predicted probabilities. We then implement the sigmoid cross-entropy loss function $\mathcal{L}$ that is computed for N samples through:

$$\mathcal{L} = \frac{1}{N}\sum_{i=1}^{N} \chi^T_{bin,i}\log(\chi_i^V) + (1 - \chi^T_{bin,i})\log(1 - \chi_i^V), \tag{6}$$

where $\chi^T_{bin,i}$ and χ_i^V are the C-dimensional AMECON features for the ith example. The use of a *sigmoid cross-entropy* loss is better adapted to the *multi-label* problem than the commonly used *softmax* loss, since it leads to model the marginal probabilities while *softmax* leads to model the joint probability of the prediction. The cost function $\mathcal{L}$ is then minimized through asynchronized stochastic gradient descent.

Note that the training dataset $\mathcal{D}$ is composed of real-world images and texts that may contain very rich information. For instance, sentences may contain many entities and relations between them while images may contain very localized entities. Thus, it is important to consider this complex information in our model. For the text modality, our textual AMECON feature directly models this rich information by considering each word (that corresponds to *local* information) separately before pooling them together. Regarding the image modality, we follow the local schemes of [3, 29] which models the rich information through the pooling of features extracted from local regions. Practically, we extract a set of R regions $\{\mathcal{R}_i, i \in [1, R]\}$ that have been identified into an image I. From each region, we extract a visual mid-level feature $\mathbf{x}^{V,\mathcal{R}_i}$. Then, all these local features are pooled into a global representation of the image through:

$$\mathbf{x}^V = \mathop{\mathcal{P}}_{i=1\ldots R}(\mathbf{x}^{V,\mathcal{R}_i}), \tag{7}$$

where $\mathcal{P}$ is the pooling operator (max or sum). The resulting mid-level visual features $\mathbf{x}^V$ that models the local information of images are thus used as inputs of the neural-network.

During the test phase, given an input image, we extract its mid-level features according to Eq. (7), then compute its projection into the AMECON space through a forward pass on the learned network, which results in the *predicted* visual AMECON feature χ^V. In this space, features that are projection from visual and textual data are directly comparable which allows us to perform multi-modal tasks.

4 EXPERIMENTS

In this section, we evaluate the performance of our approach in a cross-modal retrieval task namely "Text-Illustration" (*i.e* retrieving the best representative images given a text query) through two datasets. Before comparing the results of our method to the state-of-the-art in Sec. 4.3, we describe (in Sec. 4.1) the different datasets that we use and the implementation details (in Sec. 4.2).

4.1 Datasets

We evaluate our system on two commonly used datasets for the task of Text-Illustration, namely Flickr-8K [13] and Flickr-30K [37]. Both of them contain images from Flickr groups, but they differ by their size. In fact, the former (Flickr-8k) contains 8,000 images while the latter consists of 31,783 images. Moreover, each image is associated to five captions (sentences) thus, they also differ by their number of texts, *i.e.*, 40,000 captions for Flickr-8k and 158,915 for Flickr-30k. We use the official training, validation and testing splits that consists of 6,000 images in Flickr-8k and 29,783 in Flickr-8k for training, and 1,000 images for validation and test sets in both datasets. In each subset, the images are associated to their five captions. Since, even the test images are associated to *five* captions and not *one*, different evaluation protocols have been used in the literature. Thus, we used the most common protocol [16, 17, 36] where each caption is treated individually – *i.e.* each of the 5,000 captions has to be illustrated by one image from the whole test set of 1,000 images. For both datasets, we adopt recall at top K retrieved results (denoted R@K in the following) as an evaluation metric. We follow the literature and set $K \in \{1, 5, 10\}$.

4.2 Implementation Details

Representations: For all experiments, the mid-level features used to represent words and images are respectively the word2vec [22] representation (300-dimensional vector) and the penultimate fully-connected layer (4096-dimensional vector) extracted from a pre-trained CNN. Once the mid-level features are computed for each modality, they are projected in the AMECON Space (Sec. 3.1). More precisely, each textual caption is represented through the binary textual AMECON feature, as depicted in Sec. 3.2.2 (with max-pooling for $\mathcal{P}$) and each image is represented through the visual AMECON features with respect to the method described in Sec. 3.3.2. Note that, for the captions, we apply pre-processing that aims to remove *stop-words* following the pipeline provided by [2]. It is also worth noting that during training, each image I^i is associated to five captions $(\mathcal{T}_1^i, \ldots, \mathcal{T}_5^i)$. Thus, we use them as five *different* training examples that result in the following set of text-image pairs $\{(I^i, \mathcal{T}_1^i), \ldots, (I^i, \mathcal{T}_5^i)\}$. Regarding, the CNN features used to represent images, we used the pre-trained VGG network of [30] that has been trained on a diversified set of ImageNet [5], which gives slightly better results than the standard VGG [25]. Note that, our method could also benefit from other best representations such as [12, 14, 28]. As depicted in Sec. 3.3.2, each image is represented by the pooling of a global representation (from the whole image) and local features (from local regions). Regarding the exact regions extracted from each image, we follow [29] and extract the full image as region $\mathcal{R}_0$ and choose the following $\mathcal{R}_{i>0}$ according to a regular grid at a smaller scale (2/3 of the image size). We use the *max*-pooling operator in Eq. (7) and the euclidean distance to compute the similarity in the AMECON space.

Neural Networks: We used the Caffe framework [15] to train the networks using standard parameters (*e.g.*, learning rate: 10^{-4}, momentum: 0.9, weight decay: $5 \cdot 10^{-4}$, batch size: 512). The networks were trained with full back propagation *from scratch, i.e.*, using a random initialization (with respect to a Gaussian law) of the weights. Regarding the architecture of the neural network in Sec. 3.3.2, we used a standard multi-layer perceptron and tested different architectures through cross-validation on each dataset. More precisely, we tested with one to three hidden layers (the L parameter of Eq. 4 is set to 3, 4 or 5) and for each layer, we set a number of hidden units to one of the following values: {2048, 3072, 4096}. Note that, the number of hidden-units is set according to each hidden layer, *i.e*, one layer can be of size 4096 and the other of size 1024. We conducted an in-depth analysis about the network architecture in Sec. 5.4. Regarding the input and output layers, they respectively corresponds to the visual CNN features (4096 units) and to the *binary* textual AMECON feature (C units since the AMECON space has C dimensions). The C parameter has also been set by cross-validation and we conducted an analysis on its impact in Sec. 5.2. Also important, each layer of the multi-layer perceptron is followed by a ReLU and a dropout function.

4.3 Text-Illustration Results

In this section, we evaluate our method for the text-illustration task on the two datasets presented above. We compare our method to the methods of the literature that reports the best results for text-illustration. All scores of the comparison methods are those released in the original papers, except those of Tran *et al.* [32]. Indeed, this very recent paper achieves great results on multi-modal tasks but uses another evaluation protocol different from ours. Thus, we re-implemented their method and evaluated it with our protocol for a fair comparison. Regarding the parameters (network architecture, C and m) of our method, they have been set by cross-validation on the validation set of each dataset. For instance, on Flickr-8k, the best performances on the validation set are obtained with $C = 1,000$, $m = 3$ and an architecture of 2 layers with 4096 units each. The results on the two datasets are presented in Table 1.

The best results of the literature on the two datasets were achieved by the method of [16] (BRNN). However, it is important to consider that above their interesting vision-language integration method, they use a costly representation on the visual side. More precisely, from each image they extract 2,000 salient regions through a RCNN then pool the local features of the top 19 detections, which is *unfair* with respect to other methods. On our side, we only extract 5 regions per image, and attain much better results (*e.g.*, an absolute improvement of 4.1 points of R@1 on FlickR-8k and 3.1 points of R@1 on Flickr-30k). Moreover, our proposal outperforms all other methods on the two datasets. Specifically, it outperforms the best method (except BRNN) with an improvement of, 4.1 to 5.8 absolute points of R@K on FlickR-8k and, 3.0 to 5.7 absolute points of R@K on Flickr-30k.

As said in Sec. 2, here we evaluate our method on one direction of cross-modal retrieval, namely *text-illustration*. By construction, our method could also technically deal with the inverse cross-modal retrieval task that consist to retrieve texts from image queries, which is also well known as *image-captioning*. The performances of our proposal on that task are still below those of the state-of-the-art, certainly due to the *asymmetrical* property of our approach. As said above, getting good performances on one direction of cross-modal task when building the common latent space on the inverse direction, remains an open problem.

5 ANALYSIS

5.1 Impact of Each Component

The goal of this section is to compare our proposal to baseline methods in order to demonstrate the utility of each component. Roughly, on the textual side, our method represents each word of an input caption with a word embedding vector (word2vec) and projects them in the AMECON space. We then use a *hard-coding* process to compute the textual AMECON features. Thus, in this section, we denote our method by $\mathbf{T_{loc}}$+$\mathbf{C_{hard}}$+$\mathbf{V_{loc}}$, with $\mathbf{T_{loc}}$

Method	**Denotation**	**Flickr-8k**			**Flickr-30k**		
		R@1	**R@5**	**R@10**	**R@1**	**R@5**	**R@10**
Karpathy *et al.* [17]	DeFrag	9.7	29.6	42.5	10.3	31.4	44.5
Kiros *et al.* [18]	MNLM	10.4	31.0	43.7	11.8	34.0	46.3
Mao *et al.* [21]	m-RNN	11.5	31.0	42.4	12.6	31.2	41.5
Karpathy *et al.* [16]	BRNN*	11.8	32.1	44.7	15.2	37.7	50.5
Yan *et al.* [36]	DCCA	12.7	31.2	44.1	12.6	31.0	43.0
Tran *et al.* [32]	MACC†	10.2	29.3	41.4	12.4	33.5	46.1
Our Approach	AMECON	**15.9**	**37.9**	**49.5**	**18.3**	**41.3**	**53.5**

Table 1: Comparison of our approach with state-of-the-art methods on the Text-Illustration task through the FlickR-8k and FlickR-30k datasets. The second columns states the denotation of the different methods. Each method is evaluated on its R@1, R@5 and R@10. All scores are those released in the original papers, except those marked with † that were re-implemented by ourselves for fair comparisons. The Method marked with * was achieved using a costly visual representation that consists to pool the top-19 features after an extraction of 2,000 regions per images.

meaning a *local* textual representation (extracted from *each word* w.r.t Eq. (1)) in the sentence, $\mathbf{C}_{\mathbf{hard}}$, a *hard*-coding process, and $\mathbf{V}_{\mathbf{loc}}$ a *local* visual representation (extracted from each *local region* w.r.t Eq.(7)). We thus compare our method to three baseline methods that differ from ours by one or two component which are replaced by baseline components. The following items describe the baseline methods:

- $\mathbf{T}_{\mathbf{loc}}$+$\mathbf{C}_{\mathbf{hard}}$+$\mathbf{V}_{\mathbf{glob}}$: In this baseline method, we use a *global* visual representation instead of a *local* one. More specifically, the visual CNN features are extracted only from the *global* image;
- $\mathbf{T}_{\mathbf{loc}}$+$\mathbf{C}_{\mathbf{soft}}$+$\mathbf{V}_{\mathbf{loc}}$: Here, we use a *soft*-coding process instead of a *hard*-coding one. Indeed, for each dimension of the textual AMECON features, we compute the euclidean distance between the word embedding vector and the vector representing the corresponding AMECON cluster;
- $\mathbf{T}_{\mathbf{glob}}$+$\mathbf{C}_{\mathbf{soft}}$+$\mathbf{V}_{\mathbf{loc}}$: In this baseline approach, we use a *global* textual representation instead of a *local* one. Practically, for an input caption, we compute the word features for all words and then average them in a vector that corresponds to a *global* representation of that caption. This latter is then projected to the AMECON space through Eq (1) and coded with *soft*-coding.

The results are presented in Table 2. Our method clearly outperforms the three baselines. More precisely, $\mathbf{T}_{\mathbf{loc}}$+$\mathbf{C}_{\mathbf{hard}}$+$\mathbf{V}_{\mathbf{loc}}$ is better than $\mathbf{T}_{\mathbf{loc}}$+$\mathbf{C}_{\mathbf{soft}}$+$\mathbf{V}_{\mathbf{loc}}$ which proves the utility of the *hard*-coding process. Our method also outperforms $\mathbf{T}_{\mathbf{loc}}$+$\mathbf{C}_{\mathbf{hard}}$+ $\mathbf{V}_{\mathbf{glob}}$ and $\mathbf{T}_{\mathbf{glob}}$+$\mathbf{C}_{\mathbf{soft}}$+$\mathbf{V}_{\mathbf{loc}}$ which demonstrates the utility of the modelization of the local visual and textual information in our scheme. Moreover, the results of the baseline $\mathbf{T}_{\mathbf{glob}}$+$\mathbf{C}_{\mathbf{soft}}$+$\mathbf{V}_{\mathbf{loc}}$ are very low, which confirms the clear need of *binary* outputs in the textual AMECON features and a computation of *locality* (projection *each* word in the AMECON space), at least on the textual modality.

Method	**R@1**	**R@5**	**R@10**
$\mathbf{T}_{\mathbf{loc}}$+$\mathbf{C}_{\mathbf{hard}}$+$\mathbf{V}_{\mathbf{glob}}$	12.8	32.5	43.0
$\mathbf{T}_{\mathbf{glob}}$+$\mathbf{C}_{\mathbf{soft}}$+$\mathbf{V}_{\mathbf{loc}}$	1.5	3.5	5.1
$\mathbf{T}_{\mathbf{loc}}$+$\mathbf{C}_{\mathbf{soft}}$+$\mathbf{V}_{\mathbf{loc}}$	13.1	30.6	41.5
$\mathbf{T}_{\mathbf{loc}}$+$\mathbf{C}_{\mathbf{hard}}$+$\mathbf{V}_{\mathbf{loc}}$	**15.9**	**35.9**	**48.0**

Table 2: Comparison of our method (denoted $\mathbf{T}_{\mathbf{loc}}$+$\mathbf{C}_{\mathbf{hard}}$+$\mathbf{V}_{\mathbf{loc}}$) to three baseline methods, that are described in Sec. 5.1. The evaluation is carried in a Text-Illustration task through the FlickR-8K dataset, with C = 700 and m = 3.

5.2 Impact of the Number of AMECONs

In this section, we study the impact of the parameter C in Equations (1) and (2), that corresponds to the number of abstract meta-concepts (clusters) and thus to the dimensionality of the AMECON Space. To evaluate its impact on our method, we set it to the seven values of the following set: {100, 300, 500, 700, 1000, 1100, 1300}. For instance, $C = 700$ means that the clustering algorithm (Sec. 3.2.1) was set to output 700 clusters that directly correspond to the AMECONs. Therefore, the dimensionality of our textual AMECON features (Sec. 3.3.1) is 700 and the mapping for the visual side is from a 4096-dimensional CNN features to a 700-dimensional textual AMECON features.

The results of our method for the different values of the C parameter evaluated on the FlickR-8k dataset are presented in Figure 5. We clearly observe that increasing the C parameter significantly improves the retrieval results. It is also important to note that, from 700 to 1, 300 the results are quite similar, meaning that our method is quite robust to the number of selected clusters (AMECONs).

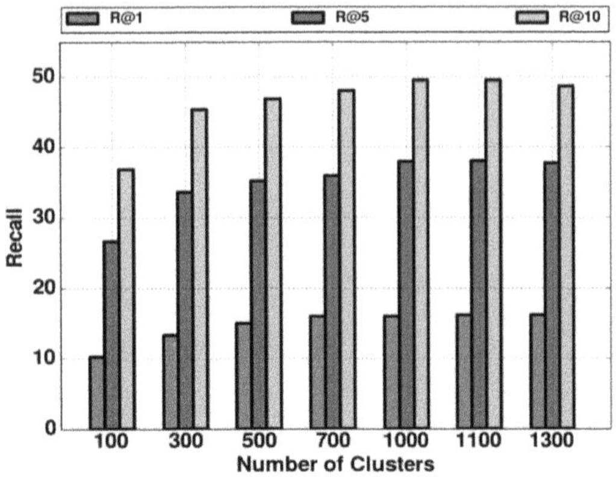

Figure 5: Evaluation of the impact of the number of selected clusters on our method in Text-Illustration through the FlickR-8k dataset. The graph presents the recall (R@1, R@5 and R@10) according to the number of clusters. Best view in color.

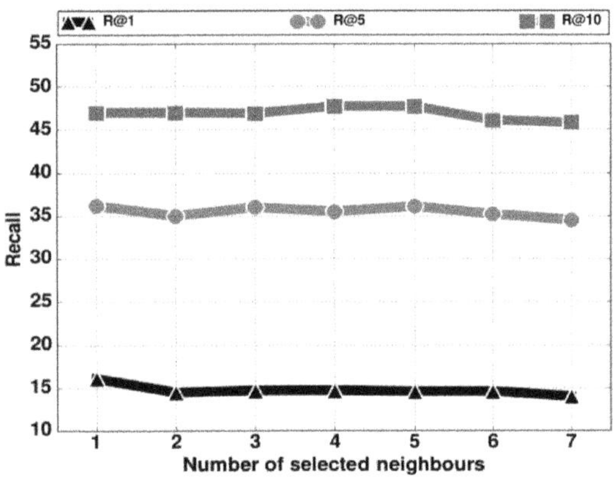

Figure 6: Evaluation of the impact of the number of selected neighbours (m parameter of Eq. (1)) on our method in Text-Illustration through the FlickR-8k dataset. The graph presents the R@1, R@5 and R@10 according to the number of selected neighbours. Here we report the scores with C = 700 and a 2-layer architecture with 4096 units each. Best view in color.

5.3 Impact of the Number of Neighbours

In this section, we evaluate the impact of the m parameter of Equation (1) that corresponds to the number of selected neighbours when performing the hard-coding process for each word. To evaluate its impact on our method, we set it in the seven values of the following set: $\{1, 2, 3, 4, 5, 6, 7\}$. For instance, $m = 3$ means that three dimensions are activated in the textual AMECON features computed by Equation (2).

The results of our method for the different values of the m parameter evaluated on the FlickR-8k dataset are presented in Figure 6. We clearly observe that the three curves (R@1, R@5 and R@10) are quite *flat*. This latter, means that our method is desirably highly robust to the m parameter.

L	Architecture	R@1	R@5	R@10
2	2048-2048	14.6	35.4	46.8
2	3072-2048	15.2	**36.6**	47.8
2	3072-3072	15.0	36.3	47.8
2	4096-3072	**16.2**	**36.6**	**48.0**
2	4096-4096	15.9	35.9	**48.0**
3	2048-2048-2048	13.0	33.6	45.0
3	3072-3072-3072	14.5	35.5	47.0
3	4096-4096-4096	15.8	36.4	47.7

Table 3: Text-illustration results on the FlickR-8K dataset with different network architectures. The first column indicates the number of hidden-layers in the architecture and the second indicates the number of units per hidden-layer. Here we report the scores with C = 700 meaning that we have 700 units in the output layer and m = 3.

5.4 Neural-Network Architecture

In this section, we evaluate the results of our method for different neural-network architectures. We conducted the experiment on the Flickr-8k dataset with the C and m parameters respectively fixed to 700 and 3. Since the C parameter is fixed to 700, the dimensionality of the textual AMECON features and thus the number of units in the output layer of the neural-network are 700. Regarding the hidden-layers of the neural-network, we set the L parameter of Equation (4) to two values (2 and 3). The size of each hidden-layer was set to one of the following values $\{2048, 3072, 4096\}$.

The results are given in Table 3. We observe that the best results are given with only 2 hidden-layers, which is desirable since no high computational complexity is needed to achieve great performance. Regarding the number of units in each hidden-layer, we can roughly say that increasing the number of units leads to better performance.

6 CONCLUSION

We introduced the Abstract Meta-Concept principle to build a multimodal common space and we demonstrated its ability on a Text-Illustration task. Contrary to most of recent work on this topic, we consider an *asymmetric* scheme to process both modalities and the unifying common space contains concepts that are *abstract* and that *subsumes* several semantic-concepts.

We evaluated our method on a Text-Illustration task and obtained significantly better results than recent methods on publicly available benchmarks, namely Flickr-8k and Flickr-30k. We also conducted an in-depth analysis of the parameters of our method, including an ablation study that shows the relative importance of each component of the proposed pipeline.

Above the formal definition of the AMECON and the experiments that demonstrate its efficiency on a particular application task, the proposed principle would be confirmed if one could demonstrate its success on the inverse retrieval task, namely image captioning (*i.e.*, retrieving the best captions given an image query).

REFERENCES

[1] Alessandro Bergamo and Lorenzo Torresani. 2012. Meta-class features for large-scale object categorization on a budget. In *CVPR*.
[2] Steven Bird, Ewan Klein, and Edward Loper. 2009. *Natural language processing with Python.* " O'Reilly Media, Inc.".
[3] Ken Chatfield, Karen Simonyan, Andrea Vedaldi, and Andrew Zisserman. 2015. Return of the devil in the details: Delving deep into convolutional nets. In *BMVC*.
[4] Jose Costa Pereira, Emanuele Coviello, Gabriel Doyle, Nikhil Rasiwasia, Gert Lanckriet, Roger Levy, and Nuno Vasconcelos. 2014. On the role of Correlation and Abstraction in Cross-Modal Multimedia Retrieval. *PAMI* (2014).
[5] J. Deng, W. Dong, R. Socher, L.-J. Li, K. Li, and L. Fei-Fei. 2009. ImageNet: A Large-Scale Hierarchical Image Database. In *CVPR*.
[6] Jianfeng Dong, Xirong Li, and Cees G. M. Snoek. 2016. Word2VisualVec: Image and Video to Sentence Matching by Visual Feature Prediction. In *ArXiv 1604.06838*.
[7] Andrea Frome, Greg S Corrado, Jon Shlens, Samy Bengio, Jeff Dean, Tomas Mikolov, and others. 2013. Devise: A deep visual-semantic embedding model. In *NIPS*.
[8] Ross Girshick, Jeff Donahue, Trevor Darrell, and Jitendra Malik. 2014. Rich Feature Hierarchies for Accurate Object Detection and Semantic Segmentation. In *CVPR*.
[9] Yunchao Gong, Qifa Ke, Michael Isard, and Svetlana Lazebnik. 2014. A Multi-View Embedding Space for Modeling Internet Images, Tags, and Their Semantics. *IJCV* (2014).
[10] Amirhossein Habibian, Thomas Mensink, and Cees G.M. Snoek. 2015. Discovering Semantic Vocabularies for Cross-Media Retrieval. In *ICMR*.
[11] David R. Hardoon, Sandor R. Szedmak, and John R. Shawe-Taylor. 2004. Canonical correlation analysis: An overview with application to learning methods. *Neural Computation* (2004).
[12] Kaiming He, Xiangyu Zhang, Shaoqing Ren, and Jian Sun. 2016. Deep residual learning for image recognition. In *CVPR*.
[13] Micah Hodosh, Peter Young, and Julia Hockenmaier. 2013. Framing image description as a ranking task: Data, models and evaluation metrics. *Journal of Artificial Intelligence Research* (2013).
[14] Gao Huang, Zhuang Liu, Kilian Q Weinberger, and Laurens van der Maaten. 2016. Densely connected convolutional networks. In *ArXiv 1608.06993*.
[15] Yangqing Jia, Evan Shelhamer, Jeff Donahue, Sergey Karayev, Jonathan Long, Ross Girshick, Sergio Guadarrama, and Trevor Darrell. 2014. Caffe: Convolutional architecture for fast feature embedding. In *ACM Multimedia*.
[16] Andrej Karpathy and Li Fei-Fei. 2015. Deep visual-semantic alignments for generating image descriptions. In *CVPR*.
[17] Andrej Karpathy, Armand Joulin, and Li Fei Fei. 2014. Deep fragment embeddings for bidirectional image sentence mapping. In *NIPS*.
[18] Ryan Kiros, Ruslan Salakhutdinov, and Richard S. Zemel. 2014. Unifying Visual-Semantic Embeddings with Multimodal Neural Language Models. In *ArXiv 1411.2539*.
[19] B. Klein, G. Lev, G. Sadeh, and L. Wolf. 2015. Fisher vectors derived from hybrid gaussian-laplacian mixture models for image annotation. In *CVPR*.
[20] Lingqiao Liu, Lei Wang, and Xinwang Liu. 2011. In Defense of Soft-assignment Coding. In *ICCV*.
[21] Junhua Mao, Wei Xu, Yi Yang, Jiang Wang, and Alan L. Yuille. 2014. Explain Images with Multimodal Recurrent Neural Networks. In *ArXiv 1410.1090*.
[22] Tomas Mikolov, Ilya Sutskever, Kai Chen, Greg S Corrado, and Jeff Dean. 2013. Distributed representations of words and phrases and their compositionality. In *NIPS*.
[23] Jiquan Ngiam, Aditya Khosla, Mingyu Kim, Juhan Nam, Honglak Lee, and Andrew Y Ng. 2011. Multimodal deep learning. In *ICML*.
[24] M. Schuster and K. K. Paliwal. 1997. Bidirectional recurrent neural networks. *Signal Processing* (1997).
[25] Karen Simonyan and Andrew Zisserman. 2015. Very deep convolutional networks for large-scale image recognition. In *ICLR*.
[26] Arnold W. M. Smeulders, Marcel Worring, Simone Santini, Amarnath Gupta, and Ramesh Jain. 2000. Content-Based Image Retrieval at the End of the Early Years. *PAMI* (2000).
[27] Youssef Tamaazousti, Hervé Le Borgne, and Céline Hudelot. 2016. Diverse Concept-Level Features for Multi-Object Classification. In *ICMR*.
[28] Youssef Tamaazousti, Hervé Le Borgne, and Céline Hudelot. 2017. MuCaLe-Net: Multi Categorical-Level Networks to Generate More Discriminating Features. In *CVPR*.
[29] Youssef Tamaazousti, Hervé Le Borgne, and Adrian Popescu. 2016. Constrained Local Enhancement of Semantic Features by Content-Based Sparsity. In *ICMR*.
[30] Youssef Tamaazousti, Hervé Le Borgne, Adrian Popescu, Etienne Gadeski, Alexandru Ginsca, and Céline Hudelot. 2017. Vision-Language Integration using Constrained Local Semantic Features. *CVIU* (2017).
[31] Lorenzo Torresani, Martin Szummer, and Andrew Fitzgibbon. 2010. Efficient Object Category Recognition Using Classemes. In *ECCV*.
[32] Thi Quynh Nhi Tran, Hervé Le Borgne, and Michel Crucianu. 2016. Aggregating Image and Text Quantized Correlated Components. In *CVPR*.
[33] Thi Quynh Nhi Tran, Hervé Le Borgne, and Michel Crucianu. 2016. Cross-modal Classification by Completing Unimodal Representations. In *ACM Multimedia Workshop*.
[34] Jinjun Wang, Jianchao Yang, Kai Yu, Fengjun Lv, Thomas Huang, and Yihong Gong. 2010. Locality-constrained linear coding for image classification. In *CVPR*.
[35] Liwei Wang, Yin Li, and Svetlana Lazebnik. 2016. Learning Deep Structure-Preserving Image-Text Embeddings. In *CVPR*.
[36] Fei Yan and Krystian Mikolajczyk. 2015. Deep correlation for matching images and text. In *CVPR*.
[37] Peter Young, Alice Lai, Micah Hodosh, and Julia Hockenmaier. 2014. From image descriptions to visual denotations: New similarity metrics for semantic inference over event descriptions. *ACL* (2014).

Leveraging Semantic Facets for Adaptive Ranking of Social Comments

Elaheh Momeni
University of Vienna
Vienna, Austria
elaheh.momeni-ortner@univie.ac.at

Reza Rawassizadeh
Dartmouth College
Hanover, NH
rrawassizadeh@acm.org

Eytan Adar
University of Michigan
Ann Arbor, MI
eadar@umich.edu

ABSTRACT

An essential part of the social media ecosystem is user-generated comments. However, not all comments are useful to all people as both authors of comments and readers have different intentions and perspectives. Consequently, the development of automated approaches for the ranking of comments and the optimization of viewers' interaction experiences are becoming increasingly important. This work proposes an adaptive faceted ranking framework which enriches comments along multiple semantic facets (e.g., subjectivity, informativeness, and topics), thus enabling users to explore different facets and select combinations of facets in order to extract and rank comments that match their interests. A prototype implementation of the framework has been developed which allows us to evaluate different ranking strategies of the proposed framework. We find that adaptive faceted ranking shows significant improvements over prevalent ranking methods which are utilized by many platforms such as YouTube or The Economist. We observe substantial improvements in user experience when enriching each element of a comment along multiple explicit semantic facets rather than in a single topic or subjective facets.

CCS CONCEPTS

•**Information systems** →**Information retrieval;**

KEYWORDS

Adaptive Ranking; Social Comment; Semantic Facets

ACM Reference format:
Elaheh Momeni, Reza Rawassizadeh, and Eytan Adar. 2017. Leveraging Semantic Facets for Adaptive Ranking of Social Comments. In *Proceedings of ICMR '17, June 6–9, 2017, Bucharest, Romania,* , 9 pages.
DOI: DOI:http://dx.doi.org/10.1145/3078971.3079004

1 INTRODUCTION

Online social media systems provide commenting features to support augmentation of social objects – ranging from YouTube videos, Flickr images, SoundCloud audio fragments to more classic news articles. Many platforms also (such as Facebook) allow commenting on any type of media object by embedding some javascript. Good comments contribute multiple perspectives and observations, answer questions, form hypotheses, and generally contribute to the development of the "social media object". Unfortunately, most comment presentation systems only provide simple temporal streams. These contain a diversity of focus, usefulness, and quality (with many comments being abusive or off-topic). Due to the substantial number of comments, without a mechanism for end-users to unravel comment streams and identify those likely to be of interest, most end-users tend to become inundated by the number of comments and disillusioned by their experience. End-users may even stop their participation and contributions.

The usual method to provide comment recommendation support is simply to ask end-users to evaluate contributions by others. This wisdom-of-the-crowd approach (crowd-based ranking) allows all users to vote on or rate comments. However, Liu et al. [10] show that voting is influenced by a number of factors (including the "rich get richer" phenomenon) that may distort accuracy. An alternative method has relied on classification to determine the usefulness of comments, with the training data being a set of majority-agreed labeled comments [15]. This approach avoids some of the biases that arise from crowd voting, but removes control from the end-user and thus does not permit individual users to adapt the ranking according to their preferences.

In this work, we propose and evaluate an adaptive faceted ranking framework for social media comments that addresses this problem and allows end users to identify comments of interest to them. We investigate how to design appropriate faceted ranking strategies for commenting systems and analyse the impact of different types of facets on the ranking performance.

This enables comments to be accessed and ordered in multiple ways rather than in a single topic order [1, 2], which was demonstrated in the past to be more in line with users' desires and in addition it overcomes the cold-start problem. This framework enables users to explore different semantic facets and select combinations of facets in order to rank and extract comments that match their interests or are relevant to selected facets.

For example, a YouTube video, *"Steve Jobs' 2005 Stanford Commencement Address"*[1] contains more than 20,000 comments. Authors of the comments have discussed different aspects of Steve Jobs's life subjectively and objectively. The commenting system of YouTube currently provides 20 comments per page using reverse-chronological ranking or top recommended comments using votes of the other users (crowd-based ranking). So, if a user is interested to read informative comments, available ranking features do not satisfy the information need of the user as many subjective and personal opinions comments are positioned at the top of these

 ACM ISBN 978-1-4503-4701-3/17/06...$15.00
DOI: DOI:http://dx.doi.org/10.1145/3078971.3079004

[1] https://www.youtube.com/watch?v=UF8uR6Z6KLc

ranking lists. Instead, our ranking framework proposes a set of semantic facets such as topics, informativeness, subjective opinions, enabling users to select combinations of facets to suit users' needs and rank comments with regard to their interests or relevance to selected facets. Furthermore, users by exploring various facets can have a better overview of the content discussed among authors and discover interesting discussions. For example, our framework also recommends as a type of facet a list of topics discussed among comments such as "Japan" or "Bill Gates" for the example video. So, users discover that there are some discussions about Steve Job's life in Japan and they can select two facets, "Japan" and "Informative" to read informative comments related to this topic.

To investigate the utility of our framework, we implemented a Web-based prototype [11], which enables end-users to interactively rank comment feeds using adaptive faceted ranking, thus allowing us to evaluate their experiences. The framework also enables users to vote whether comments match their interests or are relevant to their selections of facets to assess the ranking method's effectiveness. To investigate our framework, we experimented with two different classes of media objects – videos and news articles – using comments harvested from the popular online media platforms, YouTube (youtube.com) and The Economist (economist.com). We investigated two platforms, which are dynamic, deal with large content, and handle millions of comments, to demonstrate the scalability of our approach. Then, we present two studies: (1) a study on the effectiveness of adaptive faceted ranking and facet selection strategies and (2) a study on semantic enrichment and facet extraction from comments.

Accordingly, this work makes the following contributions:

- It demonstrates operationalisation of usefulness through strategies based on semantic enrichment and novel facet extraction and selection from comments.
- It reveals a framework and its building blocks that allow various faceted ranking strategies for content exploration of commenting systems, thus leveraging extracted facets to directly enable end-users to rank social media comments based on their preferences and interests.
- It presents an evaluation environment to compare the proposed framework with prevalent default methods utilized by many platforms. It also investigates the effectiveness of strategies for the selection of different types of facets.

In this work, we present a number of promising findings. We find that our proposed system shows significant improvements over prevalent default methods utilized by many platforms, such as reverse-chronological ranking or crowd-based ranking for enabling end-users to identify comments of interest to them. More precisely, for Economist comments, considering the interestingness dimension, adaptive faceted ranking reaches an effectiveness level of 0.85 in MAP (Mean Average Precision), while the standard reverse-chronological ranking and crowd-based ranking only reach 0.40 and 0.50 MAP respectively. For YouTube comments, adaptive faceted ranking reaches an effectiveness level of 0.71 in MAP, while the standard reverse-chronological ranking and crowd-based ranking only reach 0.46 and 0.26 MAP respectively. Next, we find that not all types of facets are equally useful, but instead that effectiveness varies according to three types of facets selected for this study: Topic-related facets, Subjective facets, and Objective facets.

We believe that this is the first study that investigates the effectiveness of different ranking methods on social media comments, explores appropriate faceted ranking strategies on commenting systems, and proposes different methods to extract various semantic facets.

2 RELATED WORK

Existing approaches for ranking of user-generated content as typically found in social media systems generally adopt one of three approaches:

Machine-based ranking approaches Some available approaches employ machine-learning methods to assess and rank content with regard to the defined "value". Siersdorfer et al. [15] and Momeni et al. [13] propose a classifier for the curation of useful comments on social media objects such as YouTube videos. A method for assessing the quality and credibility of a given set of tweets was proposed by Castillo et al. [4]. However, machine-based approaches which are trained as classifiers to rank comments are based on a set of majority-agreed labeled comments. This avoids some of the biases that emerge due to crowd-based voting, but removes control from end-users and thus does not permit individual requester to adapt ranking of comments based on their preferences [12]. This work proposes an adaptive faceted ranking framework that tackles this problem and allows end-users to identify comments of interest to them.

Personalized approaches For postings in micro-blogging platforms (such as Twitter), ranking and filtering methods based on collaborative filtering techniques are proposed by Hong et al., Das Sarma et al, and Paek et al. [5, 6, 14]. Furthermore, for posting in online forums, Lampe et al. [9] recommended that for ranking comments, patterns recognized by setting filters of users can be used to minimize the cost of settings for other users. These approaches provide personalized ranking of content, however they do not enable end-users to interact with the system and adapt the ranking with regard to their preferences.

Topic-based browsing approaches Other adaptive ranking solutions have focused on topic-based browsing which groups the comments into coherent topics and creates interfaces that enable users to browse their feeds more efficiently. Abel et al. [1] propose strategies for inferring facets and facet values on Twitter by enriching the semantics of individual Twitter messages. Topic modeling based methods (both on users and content) feature prominently in this space. Bernstein et al. [2] propose a browsable tag cloud of all the topics in a user's feed, allowing users to more easily find tweets related to their interests.

However, comments are often very brief and topics discussed alongside comments are very noisy. Furthermore, as comments have multiple explicit dimensions (such as language tone, physiological aspects, etc), grouping them exclusively based on topic results in a single imperfect faceted ranking does not enable users to rank comments with regard to other potentially useful facets. We propose instead that a system that combines higher level features alongside topic classification is desirable.

3 ADAPTIVE FACETED RANKING

This work proposes a framework for enabling adaptive faceted ranking on comments attached to social media objects (such as

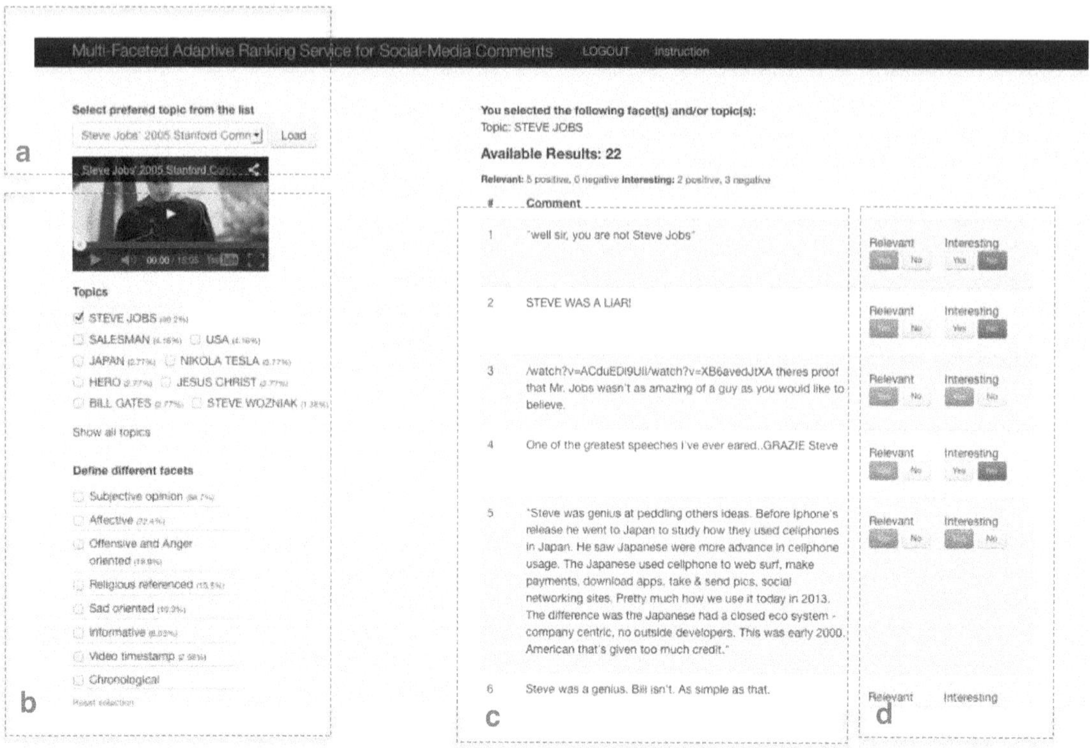

Figure 1: User interface of our developed prototype

comments on an online video or a news article). Our goal is to help users explore the comment stream by offering facilities to adapt the ranking of comments on the fly according to users' preferences.

User-Experience of Adaptive Faceted Ranking: To investigate the utility of our framework, we built a prototype Web-based interface [11][2] for our proposed ranking framework (Figure 1). With this prototype, end-users can experience the faceted adaptive ranking of social media comments and we can evaluate and track the end-users' interactions. For example, Alice as a user of the system wants to explore *informative* comments about Steve Jobs. She pulls up the interface, sees at the top of the interface (Figure 1-a) a drill-down list and selects a media object (an online video or news article). This triggers the system to crawl all comments related to the media object, enrich each comment along different semantic facets (such as *Subjective Opinion*, *Informative*, and *Topics*), dynamically extracts a set of facets for a set of comments, and recommends a list of facets on the left side of the interface (Figure 1-b). Additionally, in order to enable users to quickly acquire information about recommended facets, the system also shows percentages of related comments to the facet on the media object beside each facet. Alice now sees a list of facets (topic-based facets at the top and feature-based facets in the lower part). She explores facets and in addition to *"Informative"* facet, she can also see *"Nikola Tesla"* and other topics as facets. So, she selects a combination of facets based on her preferences. This triggers the system to present a ranked list of comments with high informative scores related to Steve Jobs on the right side of the interface (Figure 1 part-c). Also, the framework provides the conversation thread of each comment to Alice, helping her to understand the context of a comment. Finally, Alice can browse ranked comments and vote whether the comments match her interests and are relevant to her selection of facets (Figure 1 part-d).

For this prototype, three types of facets were implemented: **Topic-related facets**, topics discussed within comments on a media object. **Subjective facets**, such as comments with subjective tone, highly affective language, offensive and anger oriented, and sad oriented. **Objective facets**, such as informative, video timestamp, and religion referenced. Table 2 shows an overview of a set of semantic facets developed for this prototype and Table 4 shows some examples of comments for different facets. Related works on available approaches for analyzing free-text user-generated content in social media encourage the usage of these facets. Table 2 shows related work for each facet.

It should be noted that the set of facets explored in this work comprises a minimum set which demonstrates the effectiveness of using adaptive faceted ranking. However, it is not necessarily a complete set of useful facets. Some facets we developed include emotional facets such as "Subjective opinion" and "Affective" or ideological beliefs such as "Religious referenced", but other emotional facets such as anxiety or other ideological beliefs such as political orientation would be worth considering. Furthermore, we designed the presentation of facets as simple check boxes, our goal

[2]The development of the backend of the interface uses the REST style, permitting the interface to be easily integrated in any social media platform.

Feature	Description
Text Statistics	#Words, #Verbs, #Adjective, #Adverb, average length of sentences
Punctuation Marks	#Punctuation marks
#Named Entities	#Named Entities
NE Types Variety	#Distinct types of named entities
Readability	How difficult it is to parse the comment using Gunning's Fog Index
Psychological Characteristics	psychological dimensions of content of comment relies on the LIWC Scores[16]: Swear, Sadness, Anger, Anxiety, Religion, Positive Sentiment, and Negative Sentiment scores
Term Conformity	Distance between terms, t, of a comment, c, compared to other comments on the same media object, calculated using: $\Sigma_{t \in c} tfidf(t, c)$
Linkage Variety	#Hyperlinks in a comment
Subjectivity Tone	Measures the subjectivity degree of a comment. The Subjectivity Lexicon [18] is used to calculate subjectivity.

Table 1: Overview of basic features

Facet	Description
	Subjective Facets (SF)
Subjective opinion	Represents direct score of the "Subjectivity Tone" feature (Encouraged Wagner et al. [17]).
Offensive and angry	Calculated using average values of "Anger" and "Swear" features (Encouraged by Momeni et al. [13]).
Sad	Calculated using average values of "Sadness" and "Negative emotion" features (Encouraged by Wagner et al.et al. [17]).
Affective	Calculated using $\frac{\#Positive\ emotion + \#Negative\ emotion}{\#Words}$ (Encouraged by Castillo et al. [4]
	Objective Facets (OF)
Informativeness	The extent to which an author provides useful information. Exploits a trained classification model using "Readability", "#Named Entities", "Linkage Variety", "Subjectivity Tone", and "'Term Conformity" features (Encouraged dby Momeni et al. [13])).
Religious referenced	The extent to which an author employs religion-oriented words such as "mosque" or "church". Represents direct score of the "Religion" feature (Encouraged by Momeni et al. [13]).
Video timestamp	Particular facet for video. The extent to which a comment points to a part of a video. Extracting entities related to time using extracted named entities and NE-related features (Encouraged by Momeni et al. [13]).
	Topic Facets (TF)
Topic	A multi facet which shows various topics discussed among comments using extracted named entities and NE-related features (Encouraged by Bernstein et al. [2])

Table 2: Overview of our samples proposed facets.

being to analyse the effectiveness of faceted ranking rather than design of the facets. Nevertheless, we believe that different designs and orderings of facets may have a significant impact on the user interaction and experience, although this investigation is beyond the scope of this work.

System Architecture: The proposed framework consists of four main components:

1. ***Semantic Enrichment Component:*** As comments do not explicitly feature facets, this component enriches each comment along a set of semantic facets. It first extracts a set of basic features considering the text of the comment (such as text statistics, subjectivity tone, etc) and using some lexicons. Table 1 shows an overview of a set of basic features. Second, it enriches each comment along various semantic facets. As shown in Table 2, proposed facets by framework are categorized into three broad types of facets. We developed facets using three methods: (1) Representing direct value of basic features, extracted from texts of comments (such as "Subjective opinion" or "Religious referenced"). (2) Calculating a synthesis value of some basic features' values (such as "Offensive and Anger oriented", which is calculated using average values of "Anger" and "Swear" features) (3) Assessing a value, exploiting trained classification models and basic features based on standard classification approaches (for example, "Informative" facet uses the logistic regression classifier and a subset of basic features). As the classification model for the trained facet is developed using binary classes (whether a comment is informative or not), we used prediction confidence scores for ranking comments. Considering topic-related facet - by experimenting with a number of topic labelling approaches (see Study 2), we found that named entities are useful proxies for the topics of the comments.

2. ***Facet Extraction and Selection Component:*** It is important to recommend the user most important and relevant set of facets, therefore this component operates on semantically enriched comments, extracts a set of facets, selects a list of proposed facets dynamically, and recommends the list of selected facets to the user. For example if a set of comments contains 100 topics as facets and some topics are relevant to only a very small set of comments (only relevant to 2 comments), then this component does not recommend these topics as facets. For a dynamic selection of facets, we chose Greedy Count a core algorithm. The algorithm ranks the facets for selection according to the number of top-n comments in the ranked result list and is similar to the Most Frequent heuristic selection used by [8].

3. ***Ranking Component:*** This component enables an individual user to explore proposed facets and select a combination of facets and then it ranks comments accordingly. For every ranking, the system returns a count of how many matching comments were tagged with each value within each combination of facet. Multiple selections of facets are treated as an 'and' rather than an 'or'. This means that the values of facets are combined conjunctively for the ranking of comments.

4. ***Feedback Collector:*** The goal of this component is to enable end-users to provide implicit and explicit feedback. This feedback facilitates the evaluation of different strategies related to various facet types. Implicit activities of users in the system such as exploration and selection of facets can be used as implicit feedback, and, furthermore, the system provides users with the chance to vote (explicit feedback) if a comment is "relevant" and/or "interesting". We have used these two scores to capture both the specific relevance of the comments to the facets and users' interests. This framing, we believe, is more interpretable from end-users' perspectives (as compared to "usefulness") and is also more nuanced than an up- or down- vote or simple score. Notably, a relevant comment is not necessarily interesting (and vice versa).

4 EXPERIMENTS

We now turn to evaluation of the framework. Specifically, our first study investigates answers to the following two questions: How well does adaptive faceted ranking compare to the prevalent ranking methods, such as reverse-chronological or crowd-based ranking? Which type of facets perform best in the ranking process and what are effective strategies for selecting and building facets? The second study evaluates particular aspects of the proposed framework such as: How accurate is semantic enrichment and facet extraction? Considering the topics discussed within comments as one type of facet, which topic-identification algorithm is most appropriate for comments?

Datasets: We investigate our experiments on two datasets from real-world comments harvested from the popular online media platforms, YouTube and The Economist. These provide free-text comments on different types of media objects (videos and news articles) from a variety of people with different backgrounds and intentions.

Dataset 1-YouTube Dataset: The YouTube dataset was provided by Momeni et al. [13] and extended by this work for the evaluation of the proposed ranking framework with two prevalent ranking methods: reverse-chronological and crowd-based ranking. The history timeline provided by About.com was used to identify popular topics of different time periods. Examples of topics are the "Irish civil war" and "1936 Olympics" as events,"old New York" and "old Edinburgh" as places, and "Neil Armstrong" and "Princess Diana" as people. Next, via the YouTube API a search was conducted with each of these topics. Those videos with the highest number of comments or a high number of views (and at least 100 comments) were selected. In total, 308 videos were included in this data set. From those, 91, 778 comments were crawled. For each video, the latest 1, 000 comments were crawled by using the reverse-chronological option offered by the YouTube API, permitting an evaluation of the effectiveness of reverse-chronological ranking. Furthermore, in this work, the top 50 crowd-based comments were crawled for each video by using the "Top Comments" option offered by the YouTube user-interface.

Dataset 2-Economist Dataset: For the second dataset, a set of comments occurring on the GD ("Daily Chart") of the The Economist platform between November 2011 to October 2013 were collected [7], resulting in a dataset of 15,870 comments across 546 posts containing one or more comments. GD is a publicly accessible blog that is part of The Economist online. Each workday the blog publishes "charts, maps and infographics", which are mostly static but sometimes include interactive visualisations. Posts also include a one or two paragraph text article contextualising the graphic. Collected comments are pseudoanonymous and appear below the visualisation in paged blocks of twenty. Comments are sorted in reverse chronological order by default, but we also collected the order of comments using recommendation scores, provided by the platform itself.

4.1 Study 1: Effectiveness of Adaptive Faceted Ranking Strategies

In this study, we conducted a laboratory study in order to, firstly, evaluate the effectiveness of the faceted framework and, secondly, investigate the effectiveness of strategies for the selection of different types of facets. We gave users a short period of time to explore a comment feed using three different ranking interfaces, and then asked them to provide us feedback. In this study, beside our approach (**Adaptive Faceted, AF**) we consider two popular default ranking methods: (1) **Reverse-Chronological (RC):** This method orders comments according to the time of posting (e.g., called *"Newest first"* by YouTube), and (2) **Crowd-Based (CB):** This method ranks comments by enabling each user to vote and judge the contributions of others, such as thumbs-up/thumbs-down or voting style. Accordingly, the platforms rank comments using these votes (e.g., called *"Top Comments"* by YouTube).

Participants: We recruited study participants from two large universities (names omitted for anonymity) by distributing calls for participation through internal science mailing lists. From the respondents, we randomly selected 45 subjects. Participant ages ranged from 20 to 57 with a median of 29. 26 subjects are students and 19 are other professionals such as administrative staff, lecturers, etc. Participants received a gift voucher as renumeration for evaluating the system.

Method: The study utilized a within-subjects design to directly compare adaptive faceted ranking to the prevalent ranking methods. To ensure that any observed differences were due to the propose interface and not to nuances of layout or colouring, users in same interface saw ranked list of comment using reverse-chronological and crowd-based methods. Participants received an online instruction page. They were asked to perform the following steps: (1) Use a prototype developed for this study (see Figure1) to select a title from a list of 30 YouTube videos or 30 Economist GDs. We restricted the media to 30 to ensure that each media was approximately the same length and quality. The participants then chose and watched a video or read a GD article. (2) Use the prototype to retrieve a ranked list of the top 30 comments for a video or a GD based on reverse-chronological order and vote on each comment. (3) Use the prototype to retrieve a ranked list of the top 30 comments for a video or a news article based on crowd-based order (these were the top ranked comments highlighted by YouTube or recommended by The Economist) and vote on each comment. (4) Use the prototype to retrieve a ranked list of the top 30 comments for the same video in accordance with their preferences by selecting combinations of facets and topics and vote on each comment. Participants were given 5 minutes in each step. In the facet-based ranking, each comment is voted along two dimensions: (1) **Interestingness:** If it contains interesting content for user personally and not necessarily for other users. (2) **Relevance:** If it contains relevant content to user's selected facets and topics. It is important to note that in our setting *relevance* is a meaningless concept without selecting a particular facet. Therefore, in the chronological and crowd-based ranking modes, only the *interestingness* is rated. This is due to the fact that a comment is only considered relevant when it is relevant to the selected facets of the user. For example, when a user selects the subjectivity facet, in our experiment, the relevant comments are comments with higher subjectivity tone, but they are not necessarily relevant to the topic of the video. Additionally, we also explained that the comment does not necessarily have to be directly relevant to the video content.

We restricted the size of the ranked list of comments to 30 in order to minimize judgment fatigue. Additionally, due to the fact that different combinations of facets result in various numbers of comments, we excluded all rankings which resulted in less than three comments (76 rankings out of 462 rankings). For example, if particular combinations for a video result in only one comment which is relevant, then MAP and P@10 are given the value of 1. This result would have skewed our evaluation and for this reason we omitted those instances. Finally, in order to determine the type or types of facets that are most effective, we asked our study participants to explore different combinations of facets:

- **TF**: selecting combinations of only topic facets.
- **SF**: selecting combinations of only subjective facets.
- **OF**: selecting combinations of only objective facets.
- **Any**: any combination of facets.

To measure the effectiveness of the different facets, we rely on standard information retrieval effectiveness measures: *Mean Average Precision* (MAP) as well as *Precision* at 10 and 20 documents respectively (P@{10,20}). With these measures, we consider the use case that a user is interested in finding many relevant and interesting comments for each facet selection. While P@k is a set-based measure, MAP takes the ranking of relevant/interesting items into account as well.

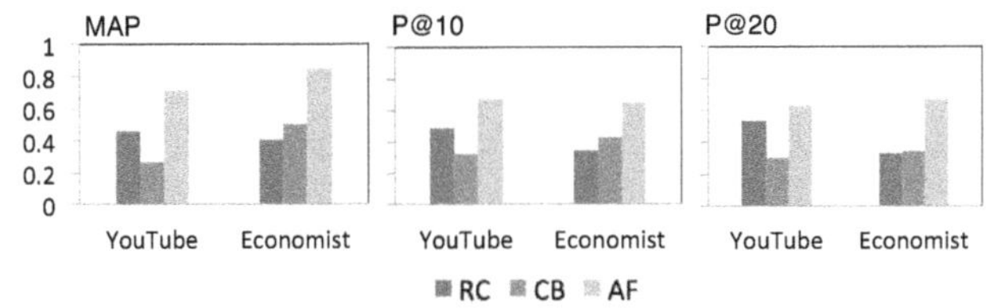

Figure 2: Comparison of the effectiveness of the adaptive faceted (AF) ranking to two prevalent ranking methods: Reverse-Chronological (RC) and Crowd-based (CB)

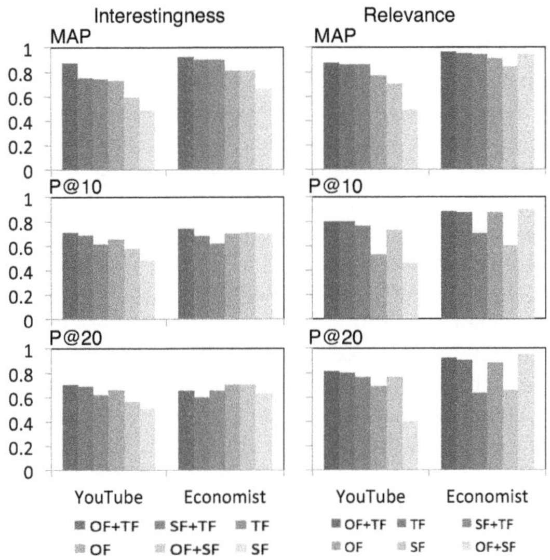

Figure 3: Comparison of effectiveness of different strategies for the selection of different types of facets. Values sorted by MAP values in decreasing order, therefore legends are different.

Results: Figure 2 shows the effectiveness of the faceted ranking compared to the prevalent ranking methods. In total, participants votes on 462 ranking lists (375 for YouTube dataset and 87 for Economist dataset). When considering the first default ranking method, the reverse-chronological ranking, the measures indicate that this ranking is at least partially effective for both platforms (MAP of .46 and .41 for YouTube and Economist respectively). Approximately half of the comments retrieved are *interesting* to the users. Furthermore, in consideration of the second ranking method, crowd-based ranking, the effectiveness measures indicate that the effectiveness of this ranking type is associated with the culture of the platform. It is less effective compared to the reverse-chronological ranking for the YouTube dataset, while it is more effective than reverse-chronological ranking for the Economist dataset (MAP of .26 and .51 for YouTube and Economist respectively). Approximately one third of the comments retrieved for YouTube set and half of the comments retrieved for Economist set are determined to be *interesting* to the users. In contrast, in the ranking of comments retrieved with our adaptive faceted ranking strategy, approximately every two out of three results are deemed to be interesting for both platforms (MAP of .71 and .85 for YouTube and Economist respectively).

Thus, overall we have shown that the adaptive faceted ranking method yields considerable improvements in terms of effectiveness compared to prevalent ranking methods.

Figure 3 shows the effectiveness of combinations of different types of facets. We observe that the combinations which exploit topic and objective facets (OF+TF) considerably outperform other combinations with respect to *interestingness* (MAP of .87 and .92 for YouTube and Economist respectively). However, the other strategy which exploits topic and subjective facets (SF+TF) performs only slightly worse (MAP of .75 and .90 for YouTube and Economist respectively). In particular, we observe that combinations which exploit topic facets (TF, OF+TF, and SF+TF) perform better than combinations without topic facets (SF+OF, SF, and OF), while two combinations which take into consideration subjective facets (SF, OF+SF) perform considerably lower than other combinations. The worst performing strategy is using only subjective facets. This is due to the fact that among faceted rankings based on subjective facets, most of rankings were based on "Offensive and angry" facet. Therefore, most of ranked comments were off-topic and vague and consequently users have less personal interest about these comments. Nevertheless, such a facet can assist the moderators of platforms to filter and extract off-topics and vague comments. The results are similar when considering *relevance* instead of *interestingness.* Also for the *relevance* dimension, we observe that the combination which exploits topic and objective facets (OF+TF) considerably outperform other combinations (MAP of .87 and .96 for YouTube and Economist respectively) and combinations which exploit topic facets perform better than combinations without topic facets.

While these results are useful for an initial analysis, a statistical analysis is required to draw more confident conclusions about how the effectiveness of strategies differs.

For each dataset we considered 3 sets: (1) all positive and negative interesting votes collected for the faceted ranking results, (2) all positive and negative interesting votes collected for the reverse-chronological ranking results, and (3) all positive and negative interesting votes collected for the crowd-based ranking results. Then we applied 2 Pearson's Chi-squared tests (1) between the first and second sets, and (2) between the first and third sets. The results of this study (shown in the top part of Table 3 indicate that adaptive faceted ranking is statistically significantly different from reverse-chronological ranking (RC) and crowd-based (CB) ranking. These results confirm our hypothesis which proposed that faceted ranking would outperform the two other ranking methods. Furthermore, we also present the mean and standard deviation values of positive votes on comments for different facets to help understand the magnitude and direction of the differences.

Additionally, we applied Pearson's Chi-squared tests between sets related to different adaptive faceted rankings with varying combinations of types of facets. More precisely, we applied a test for each set related to each combination of facets and the set related to all types of facets (without taking into consideration the type of facets). The results of this study (shown in the lower part of Table 3) indicate that the adaptive faceted rankings which use a combination of topic-related facets and objective facets are statistically significantly different from the faceted ranking with other combinations of facets. These results confirm that the combination

Ranking	YouTube			Economist		
	X2	Mean	STD	X2	Mean	STD
RC	25.26**	12.2	5.7	105.4**	10.15	7.65
CB	90.58**	8	2.2	103.8**	10.38	7.55
AF (OF+TF)	68.07*	21.8	7.8	5.575*	25.9	8.6
AF (SF+TF)	4.591	16.7	8.4	0.046	18.5	7.3
AF (OF+SF)	2.358	12	3.6	0.002	14	5.7
AF (TF)	0.056	14.9	7.8	1.401	19.6	8.5
AF (SF)	49.25*	11	6.6	42.27*	12	4.6
AF (OF)	5.787	15	7.8	0.021	20	7.3
AF	–	14.6	8.0	–	21.33	8.7

Table 3: The results of statistical significance tests. Adaptive faceted ranking strategy (AF) is compared to the reverse-chronological (RC) and crowd-based (CB) ranking (upper part), and to different strategies for selecting facets (lower part). All rows for which there is sufficient evidence ($p < 0.0001$) that the two predicted samples come from different distributions are marked with "" and ($p < 0.01$) are marked with "*". The mean and standard deviation of different ranking strategies are shown on the right.**

Facet	Full agreement	Moderate agreement
Subjective	*"One of the greatest speeches i've ever eared..GRAZIE Steve"*	*'Diana died, Barry manakee died, Kanga tryon died in the same year as Diana, the driver of the white fiat died,......everyone had a connection with the tampax. I wonder what will happen if Kate crosses him"*
Informative	*"Austria and Hungry was a major ally of Germany. They helped the Germans annihilate the russian army."*	*"No, the allies started this mess, it was their incompetence that led to ww2, if they were not so damn hard on Germany there wouldn't be a mad man like Hitler coming to power"*
Affective	*"Such an awful thing to happen to such a peaceful and talented man :(R.I.P John Lennon."*	*"If there was one thing everyone involved in the war could agree on, it's that they did not like Versailles."*

Table 4: Examples of comments that achieved full vs. moderate annotator agreement. The three facets shown are those with the lowest inter-annotator agreement.

of objective and topic facets is more effective when compared with combinations of other types of facets. Furthermore, it is indicated that the adaptive faceted rankings, which use a combination of only subjective facets, are statistically significantly different from the faceted ranking with all types of different combinations of facets. This result confirms that a combination of only subjective facets is less effective when compared with combinations of other types of facets.

Our results demonstrate that combinations of different facets perform better than faceted rankings which use only one type of facet, such as subjective facets or topics alone. We can also conclude that topic-related facets are very important to a successful ranking strategy, in terms of both relevance and degree of interest. Nevertheless, different combinations of objective or subjective facets with topic facets perform slightly better and are more effective when comments do not explicitly represent a specific topic. In addition, objective facets are more desirable than subjective facets or topics alone. Therefore, users should be made aware of objective and topic facets in higher positions of a facet order. Finally, we believe that chronological ranking is still useful for users with particular tasks in mind. Therefore, we suggest that chronological ordering may be designed and developed as one of the facets to be suggested to users. Considering crowd-based ranking, the effectiveness of this method is influenced by the culture of the platform.

4.2 Study 2: Semantic Enrichment Performance

As the results of the first study are influenced by the performance of facets, this study investigates a particular aspect of the framework, that is the evaluation of the performance of the semantic enrichment component.

First part of this study evaluates the performance of the subjective and objective facets and, in addition, describes the process of developing the Informativeness classification model. Second part investigates effectiveness of different topic-labelling approaches for topic facets.

4.2.1 Evaluation of Subjective and Objective Facets: ***Crowd-sourced annotated comment*** In order to create a training set and evaluate the accuracy of our semantic enrichment approach, we created a ground truth dataset by annotating a subset of the comments. Specifically, for ten randomly selected media objects, 100 comments were randomly chosen (thus in total 1,000 comments). The comments were annotated with respect to *Informative, Subjectivity, Affect, Offensiveness, Video Timestamp, Sadness, Offensive and Anger,* and *Religious referenced.* For the annotation process, we relied on crowdsourcing and employed workers via Amazon's Mechanical Turk[3] platform. To ensure worker quality and attention, workers had to answer two objective questions per task ("1-What is the first word of the comment?" and "2-Select 1-4 keywords that represent the most important terms in the comment"). The answers to these questions can be computed automatically. Those who did not answer the quality questions satisfactorily were excluded from further participation. Additionally, workers had to provide binary judgments for each of the seven facets listed above. Thus, overall nine questions (including two honey pot questions) had to be answered by each worker for each comment.

Having collected three judgments per comment, we first determine the inter-rater agreement for each facet based on Fleiss' Kappa. The results are shown on the left side of the Table 5. The agreement is close to perfect for the *Video Timestamp* facet. This is not surprising, considering the unique syntax of a timestamp. The agreement is also high for *Offensive and Angry* comments while workers had most difficulty to agree on *Subjective, Informative* and *Affective* comments. Examples of comments labelled with these facets (with high and low agreement) are shown in Table 4. Overall, we consider a Kappa above .65 for all facets. Comments were labeled along different facets based on majority agreement (when two out of three coders agreed).

Training setup of informative classification model: *"Informative"* facet exploits a trained classification model. This part reports how we trained this classifier. For training the informative classifier, we selected a balanced set of 400 informative comments and 400 NOT informative comments from our crowdsourcing-based annotated comments. Only comments for which at least two out of three coders agreed were selected. We investigated the performance of two classifier models, logistic regression and Naive Bayes. Classifiers were trained using combinations of basic features described above (see Table1). Best performance is achieved by using a subset of features ("Readability", "#Named Entities", "Linkage Variety", "Subjectivity Tone", and "Term Conformity") and the logistic regression classifier (.86 precision , .61 recall, and .71 F1). To determine influential features, in addition to interpreting the

[3] https://www.mturk.com/mturk/

Facet	Agreement	Precision	Recall	F1
Video Timestamp	0.97	0.91	0.91	0.91
Subjectivity	0.67	0.95	0.98	0.97
Sad	0.78	0.78	0.65	0.71
Religious referenced	0.76	0.58	0.88	0.70
Offensive and Angry	0.79	0.66	0.90	0.76
Affective	0.75	0.92	0.91	0.92
Informative	0.70	0.86	0.61	0.71

Table 5: Overview of enrichment performance across all facets ordered by their accuracy. Second column shows coders' inter-agreement for each proposed facet based on Fleiss' Kappa.

statistically significant coefficients of the best performing logistic regression model (using all sets of features), we also ranked the best performing features according to their Information Gain Ratio.

Results: semantic enrichment performance The performance of our semantic enrichment approach is shown in Table 5. We measure the performance of our semantic enrichment approach by Precision, Recall, and F1 for each facet. It is evident that our approach is highly effective for a number of facets. We are able to achieve a high F1 score, coupled with high precision and recall for enrichment related to the facets *Subjectivity*, *Affective*, and *Video timestamp*. However, the enrichment of facets *Informativeness*, *Religious referenced*, *Sad*, *Offensive and angry* proves to be more difficult. This difference in enrichment performance is a reflection of the difficulties that the human annotators experienced with the task.

4.2.2 Evaluation of Topic-based Facets. Topic labels of comments can be used to provide coherent topical facets. However, topics discussed alongside comments are very noisy due to their short nature. Therefore, exploring performance of different topic labeling approaches for selecting the most appropriate approach is useful. In this study, we empirically evaluate three topic labeling approaches:

1. TF-IDF based on Unigrams: The unigrams with the highest TF-IDF score were utilized. This approach does not require external resources and it is not computationally expensive.

2. Entity-Based: The Named Entities (NEs) appearing in a comment are considered to be indicators of the topics the comment discusses. They are ranked in order of their frequency of occurrence. For the extraction of NEs, we employed the semantic enrichment service AlchemyAPI [4].

3. Topic Modeling (LDA): Finally, we experimented with statistical topic modeling, in particular Latent Dirichlet Allocation (LDA) [3]. An LDA model was trained by aggregating all comments on a media object and inferring the topic distribution from this aggregate (the following standard hyper-parameters were used: $\alpha = 50/T$, $\beta = 0.01$ and T = 1000). From the proposed topics produced, the comment was labeled with the term carrying the highest weight.

Crowdsourcing-based evaluation In order to evaluate the three approaches, we randomly picked 1,000 of our available comments and presented the comments along with their extracted topic labels to Amazon Mechanical Turk workers. For example for a comment: *"For my money Mullen is the Tony Hawk of technical street skating. he pretty much invented it. First on a freestyle board, and then went on to make normal sized boards his bitch."*, three label topics *"Board"*, *"TONY HAWK"*, and *"Matter"* were extracted using TF-IDF based, Named entity based, and LDA based respectively. Or for a comment *"i lie. sometime i speak of the truth. Every lie and truth has a plan and meaning. "*, two label topics *"Lie"*, *"War"* were extracted using TF-IDF based and LDA based, as comment does not contain any named entity. Each worker was shown a comment and a proposed topic label (selected from one of our three approaches). The workers had to answer three questions about the comment – two questions regarding quality (the same quality questions used in our crowdsourcing-based annotating phase in feature-based evaluation to put off MTurk spammers.) and one question regarding the relevance of the topic label to the comment. In this setup, we make use of binary relevance assessments. Thus, for each of the 1,000 comments we generated three topic recommendations and collected three worker judgments for each pair of topic label and comment.

Results: topic labeling For the purposes of this study, the outcomes are binary. When considering comments with one or more Named Entities (among 1,000 comments only 420 comments contain Named Entities), the error rate is 3.85% for Entity based, 26.93% for TF-IDF based, and 69.67% LDA based topic labeling. For comments without Named Entities (67% of the comments), the TF-IDF based topic labeling outperforms the LDA based (the error rate is 28.78% for TF-IDF based and is 71.63% for LDA based). We find that the LDA Analysis generally does not provide meaningful topic terms. Also, providing interpretable descriptions for topic models is a difficult problem. These results show that for the problem of extracting a relevant topic label from a comment, the Entity-Based approach performs better than the investigated alternatives for those comments when Named Entities occur. Nevertheless, it should be noted that NER tools are not perfect - extracted Named Entities can be ambiguous and their disambiguation sometimes goes wrong, especially in short texts. This is a limitation for the topic extraction approach based on NEs. Consequently, additional fine tuning is required when relying on Named Entities such as topic proxies.

5 CONCLUSIONS

In this work, using semantic enrichment in a novel adaptive faceted ranking framework results in a set of semantic facets, enabling adaptive ranking of social comments for end-users. Our experimental results demonstrate that adaptive faceted ranking outperforms other prevalent ranking methods and users can easily find interesting comments based on their preferences. Adaptive faceted ranking combining various types of facets outperforms faceted ranking based on a single type of facet. Also, the type of the facet influences the effectiveness of ranking results, that is objective facets are more effective than subjective or topic facets. In the future, we will explore the use of personalized ordering of facets and ranking strategies to further improve the interestingness and relevancy to individual users. This exploration will require further work in user modelling, model similarity, and facet selection optimisation. Finally, different designs and orderings of facets may also have a significant impact on users' interactions with the system and the results achieved, and these are aspects which we will also explore further.

[4]http://www.ibm.com/watson/alchemy-api.html

REFERENCES

[1] Fabian Abel, Ilknur Celik, Geert-Jan Houben, and Patrick Siehndel. 2011. Leveraging the Semantics of Tweets for Adaptive Faceted Search on Twitter. In *Proceedings of the 10th International Conference on The Semantic Web (ISWC'11)*.

[2] Michael S. Bernstein, Bongwon Suh, Lichan Hong, Jilin Chen, Sanjay Kairam, and Ed H. Chi. 2010. Eddi: interactive topic-based browsing of social status streams. In *Proceedings of the 23nd annual ACM symposium on User interface software and technology (UIST '10)*.

[3] D.M. Blei, A.Y. Ng, and M.I. Jordan. 2003. Latent dirichlet allocation. *the Journal of machine Learning res* (2003).

[4] Carlos Castillo, Marcelo Mendoza, and Barbara Poblete. 2011. Information credibility on twitter. In *Proceedings of the 20th international conference on World wide web (WWW '11)*. https://doi.org/10.1145/1963405.1963500

[5] Anish Das Sarma, Atish Das Sarma, Sreenivas Gollapudi, and Rina Panigrahy. 2010. Ranking mechanisms in twitter-like forums. In *Proceedings of the third ACM international conference on Web search and data mining (WSDM '10)*.

[6] Liangjie Hong, Ron Bekkerman, Joseph Adler, and Brian D. Davison. 2012. Learning to rank social update streams. In *Proceedings of the 35th international ACM SIGIR conference on Research and development in information retrieval (SIGIR '12)*.

[7] Jessica Hullman, Nicholas Diakopoulos, Elaheh Momeni, and Eytan Adar. 2015. Content, Context, and Critique: Commenting on a Data Visualization Blog. In *Proceedings of the 18th ACM Conference on Computer Supported Cooperative Work & Social Computing (CSCW '15)*. 1170–1175.

[8] Jonathan Koren, Yi Zhang, and Xue Liu. 2008. Personalized Interactive Faceted Search. In *Proceedings of the 17th International Conference on World Wide Web (WWW '08)*.

[9] Cliff A.C. Lampe, Erik Johnston, and Paul Resnick. 2007. Follow the reader: filtering comments on slashdot. In *Proceedings of the SIGCHI Conference on Human Factors in Computing Systems (CHI '07)*.

[10] Jingjing Liu, Yunbo Cao, Chin Y. Lin, Yalou Huang, and Ming Zhou. 2007. Low-Quality Product Review Detection in Opinion Summarization. In *Proceedings of the 2007 Joint Conference on Empirical Methods in Natural Language Processing and Computational Natural Language Learning (EMNLP-CoNLL)*.

[11] Elaheh Momeni, Simon Braendle, and Eytan Adar. 2015. *Adaptive Faceted Ranking for Social Media Comments*. Springer International Publishing, Cham, 789–792.

[12] Elaheh Momeni, Claire Cardie, and Nicholas Diakopoulos. 2015. A Survey on Assessment and Ranking Methodologies for User-Generated Content on the Web. *ACM Comput. Surv.* 48, 3, Article 41 (Dec. 2015), 49 pages.

[13] Elaheh Momeni, Claire Cardie, and Myle Ott. 2013. Properties, Prediction, and Prevalence of Useful User-generated Comments for Descriptive Annotation of Social Media Objects. In *The 7th International AAAI Conference on Weblog and Social Media (ICWSM2013)*. AAAI, Boston, USA.

[14] Tim Paek, Michael Gamon, Scott Counts, David Maxwell Chickering, and Aman Dhesi. 2010. Predicting the Importance of Newsfeed Posts and Social Network Friends.. In *AAAI*. AAAI Press.

[15] Stefan Siersdorfer, Sergiu Chelaru, Wolfgang Nejdl, and Jose San Pedro. 2010. How useful are your comments?: analyzing and predicting youtube comments and comment ratings. In *Proceedings of the 19th international conference on World wide web (WWW '10)*. ACM, 10. https://doi.org/10.1145/1772690.1772781

[16] Yla R. Tausczik and James W. Pennebaker. 2010. The Psychological Meaning of Words: LIWC and Computerized Text Analysis Methods. (2010). http://homepage.psy.utexas.edu/homepage/students/Tausczik/Yla/index.html

[17] Claudia Wagner, Matthew Rowe, Markus Strohmaier, and Harith Alani. 2012. What Catches Your Attention? An Empirical Study of Attention Patterns in Community Forums. In *ICWSM'12*.

[18] Theresa Wilson, Janyce Wiebe, and Paul Hoffmann. 2005. Recognizing contextual polarity in phrase-level sentiment analysis. In *Proceedings of the conference on Human Language Technology and Empirical Methods in Natural Language Processing (HLT '05)*. Association for Computational Linguistics, Stroudsburg, PA, USA, 347–354.

Multi-task Deep Neural Network for Joint Face Recognition and Facial Attribute Prediction

Zhanxiong Wang[1†], Keke He[1†],Yanwei Fu[2*]
Rui Feng[1], Yu-Gang Jiang[1], and Xiangyang Xue[12]
[1]School of Computer Science, Shanghai Key Laboratory of Intelligent Information Processing, Fudan University, China
[2]School of Data Science, Fudan University, China
{15210240046,kkhe15,yanweifu,fengrui,ygj,xyxue}@fudan.edu.cn

ABSTRACT

Deep neural networks have significantly improved the performance of face recognition and facial attribute prediction, which however are still very challenging on the million scale dataset, i.e. MegaFace. In this paper, we for the first time, advocate a multi-task deep neural network for jointly learning face recognition and facial attribute prediction tasks. Extensive experimental evaluation clearly demonstrates the effectiveness of our architecture. Remarkably, on the largest face recognition benchmark – MegaFace dataset, our networks can achieve the Rank-1 identication accuracy of 77.74% and face verication accuracy 79.24% TAR at 10^{-6} FAR, which are the best performance on the small protocol among all the publicly released methods.

KEYWORDS

face identification, face verification, deep learning, multi-task learning and facial attribute prediction

ACM Reference format:
Zhanxiong Wang[1†], Keke He[1†],Yanwei Fu[2] and Rui Feng[1], Yu-Gang Jiang[1], and Xiangyang Xue[12] . 2017. Multi-task Deep Neural Network for Joint Face Recognition and Facial Attribute Prediction. In *Proceedings of ICMR '17, June 6–9, 2017, Bucharest, Romania,* , 10 pages.
DOI: http://dx.doi.org/10.1145/3078971.3078973

1 INTRODUCTION

Face recognition as a typical biometric-based technique, has received a great deal of research attention over the last few decades. Instead of authenticating people by passwords, PINs, tokens and so on, face recognition enables the identification or verification by biological facial traits. This thus facilitates a wide range of applications such as financial monitoring, building access control, station ticket check system and so forth.

Recently, with the renaissance of convolution neural networks, encouraging breakthroughs have been achieved on the leading Labeled Faces in the Wild (LFW) benchmark [15]. Particularly, some methods [32, 36] have surpassed human performance and achieved near perfect results. To further study face recognition in a dataset of billions of faces, MegaFace dataset [18] has been collected to simulate a more realistic application scenario and evaluate the face recognition algorithms in a million scale of distractors. Critically, recognizing faces is still very challenging "in the wild", since the human face image often changes dramatically caused by the variances of head pose, camera viewpoints, occlusion and illumination conditions.

The standard practices looked at solving this problem by increasing either the depth of neural network, or the number of training images, or both. This nevertheless requires prohibitive cost of computational resources. In contrast, humans recognize one's identity mostly by identifying the facial traits or facial attributes [31]. For example, the police are interested in identifying a suspect, in most scenarios, by collecting the facial traits of the suspect from the eyewitnesses. Interestingly, previous work [24, 35] revealed that identity-related attributes such as gender are implicitly encoded in the nodes of deep neural network for identity discrimination. Thus orthogonal to the standard practices and inspired by humans' ability, we advocate utilizing facial attributes to help face recognition and vice versa.

In this paper, we propose a novel multi-task deep learning architecture to enable the jointly learning facial attribute prediction and face recognition tasks. Specifically, since the existing face recognition dataset do not have pre-labelled facial attributes, the attribute labels are generated by majority-voting manner of prediction of attribute classifiers pre-trained on the auxiliary dataset. With the labelled attributes, we propose our multi-task face recognition network of both Full-Model and Fast-Model. Our architecture learns for both face recognition and facial attribute prediction tasks. The experiments on the challenging MegaFace dataset clearly show that the state-of-the-art performance is obtained. To further reveal the insights of our network, further ablation study on both MegaFace and LFW dataset is conducted and validates the efficacy of our framework.

*Yanwei Fu is the corresponding authour.
†The first two authors contribute equally to this paper.

ICMR '17, June 6–9, 2017, Bucharest, Romania
© 2017 ACM. ACM ISBN 978-1-4503-4701-3/17/06...$15.00
DOI: http://dx.doi.org/10.1145/3078971.3078973

To sum up, the contributions of our work are three points. (1) To the best of our knowledge, we for the first time, propose a multi-task deep neural network structure of jointly learning the two highly corrected tasks – facial attribute prediction and face recognition. These two tasks can greatly help each other and thus improve the performance over the state-of-the-art algorithms. Our experimental results achieve the best performance on the MegaFace challenge with the comparable evaluation protocol.(2) Due to the highly cost of our Full-Model, we propose a Fast-Model for learning the multiple tasks. The Fast-Model is a reasonable good and fast version of the Full-Model in term of running cost and performance. (3) We also systematically explore the alternative choices of different structures and configures in our network in both our intuitive explanations and experimental validation. The validation reveals the insights of the details how we design the network.

2 RELATED WORK

2.1 Face Recognition Analysis

Face detection and face alignment. Viola and Jones [40, 41] made the first work to enable face detection applicable in real-world scenarios by building cascaded classifiers upon Harr-like features. On top of HOG features, the generic object detector – deformable part model (DPM) [9] can be used for face detection. The detected faces will be aligned by face alignment algorithms [4, 14, 30, 39, 46, 47, 50, 51, 55]. Recently, with the CNNs based face detection algorithms [6, 29, 56] and face alignment algorithms [4, 50, 51], extremely remarkably high and reliable performance on face detection and face alignment can be obtained on the LFW benchmark.

Face verification and face identification. They are two primary tasks of face recognition. Face verification is a one-to-one matching by given a pair of query images and judge whether this pair is the same person. Starting from [7], the idea of selecting a pair of face images to a distance begins. Given positive pairs, siamese networks [20, 27, 36] restrict the similarity metric to be small, and vice versa. Face identification is a one-to-many matching which identifies the face image from many existing facial images. It has been widely studied recently [3, 11, 32–35, 37]. Wen *et al.* [43] proposed a novel discriminative feature learning approach for deep face recognition by joint supervision of the center loss and soft-max loss.

Different from all previous works, we for the first consider jointly learning the facial attributes and face identity in a single framework with the shared deep architecture. We argue that facial attribute can help face recognition significantly and vice versa. For example, in criminal investigation when police identify the face images of a suspect from their own face dataset, they can identify the suspect by personal facial traits such as facial hair type, eye types, nose and so on. Our experiments validate that the remarkable high results have been achieved on the benchmark dataset.

2.2 Facial Attribute Analysis

Facial attribute analysis has also been studied recently and achieved a series of breakthroughs in recent years. In general, the works of facial attribute analysis can be categorized as three classes according to the different visual features and varying network structures.

Firstly, traditional manually designed features such as SIFT [25] and LBP [28] are employed to either holistically describe the entire face, or selected key facial regions such as check and mouth. The attribute classifiers [19, 21] are thus built upon extracted features.

Secondly, deep features based facial attribute analysis has been studied recently [24, 42, 53]. Zhong et al. [53] adopted the off-the-shelf CNN face recognition features for Support Vector Machine (SVM) classifiers to predict facial attributes.

Thirdly, facial attribute prediction is one sub-task of multi-task framework in [1, 31]. Rudd *et al.* [31] introduced a mixed objective optimization network which took account of different distribution of attribute labels. Facial attributes have been directly used to build the face identification classifier in [19]. Comparing with [1, 19, 31], we for the first time, equally and jointly model the facial attribute and face identity.

2.3 Multi-Task Learning

Multi-task Learning (MTL) is one type of transfer learning and addresses the problem of learning to share information and exploiting the similarity among different tasks on the same dataset. It has been applied to many computer vision tasks such as pose estimation and action recognition [54] and semantic classification and information retrieval [23]. Recently MTL has also been employed in face-related tasks, for example, facial landmark detection [29, 52] and [1, 8, 31]. Comparing with these works and to the best of our knowledge, this is the first published work of jointly learning facial attributes and face recognition in the same single deep architectures.

3 THE ATTRIBUTE-CONSTRAINED DEEP FACE RECOGNITION ARCHITECTURE

We advocate the face attribute-constrained deep architecture for face recognition. In contrast, the methods on face recognition [43, 45] did not directly use the information of face attributes. Actually, the face attributes are very useful cues for face related tasks.

3.1 Architecture Overview

Figure 1 illustrates our full model for attribute-constrained face recognition architecture. The whole architecture has two steps: facial attribute prediction step (Sec. 3.2) and face recognition network step (Sec. 3.3).

As most existing face recognition datasets do not have facial attribute labelled, the first step is to generate attribute labels by an off-the-shelf facial attribute prediction algorithm in Sec.3.2. In the second step, we take as input of our network,

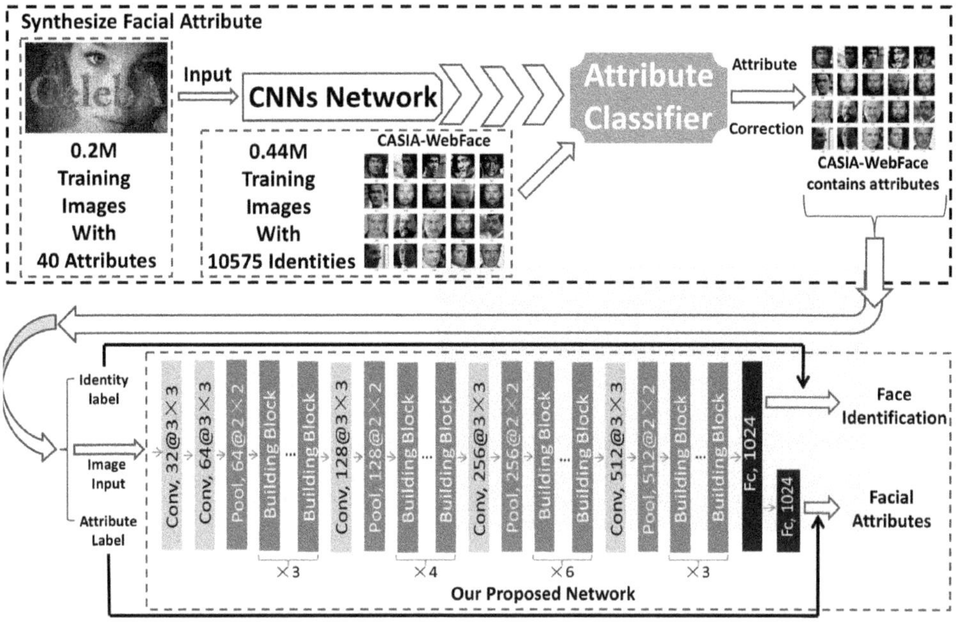

Figure 1: The overview of deep face recognition architecture. Note that: (1) the ×3,×4,×6 and ×3 indicates the corresponding number of building blocks. (2) number@size indicates the number and the size of convolutional filters.

Table 1: Selected attributes of the CelebA Dataset.

Group	Attributes
eye	Narrow Eyes
nose	Big Nose, Pointy Nose
global	Chubby, Double Chin, High Cheekbones, Male

the generated attribute labels, together with cropped training images and the corresponding face identity labels in Sec. 3.3. We also introduce a fast version of our network in Sec. 3.4.

3.2 Facial Attribute Prediction

In this work, we propose employing the facial attributes as the constraints for face recognition. Such facial attributes thus should be invariant to the visual appearance of one person in difference situation. In other word, the attributes related to biometrics (e.g. Big Nose) are more desirable than the other appearing facial attributes (e.g. wearing glasses). The full list of attributes used in our framework are shown in Tab. 1.

We predict these facial attributes of each identity in a transferrable manner. Specifically, we use CelebA dataset [24] (totally 0.2 M facial images) to train the facial attribute classifier (MOON model [31]). The trained model can thus be utilized to predict the facial attributes on the CAISIA-WebFace [49] dataset, which is the training data of our proposed network. For each identity, we assume that the selected facial (in Tab. 1) should be consistent. Thus majority voting can be further employed to adjust the results of facial attribute prediction. For example, the dataset includes 15 face images of Bruce Lee: if 14 of images are predicted to male and only one is predicted to female, then the majority voting will constrain all images of Bruce Lee with male attribute. Such a majority voting manner intrinsically helps prune noise and outlying prediction of classifiers for biometrics-related attributes in Tab. 1.

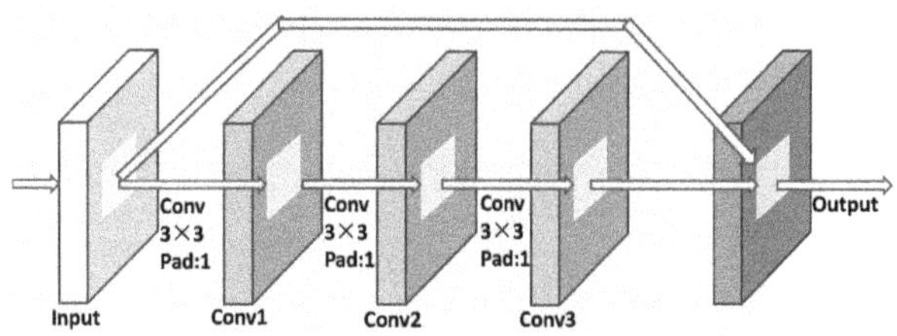

Figure 2: Building Block Structure(Full-Model). Each convolutional layer has padding 1 and stride 1.

3.3 Face Recognition Network Architecture

As illustrated in Fig. 1, this face recognition step intrinsically is organized as the network directly for face identification task, *i.e.*, a classification task for each identity. As for face verification task, we extract the features of each image by using the output of network as the representation; and given a pair of images, we compute their cosine distance and set the threshold to judge whether this pair is the same person or not. The network thus has four types of layers, namely,

Convolutional layers, aims at analyzing the input data stream with the size of 3×3 of receptive field, the stride 1 and padding 0. The four convolutional layers (yellow blocks in Fig. 1) have 32, 64, 64, 64, and 64 filters respectively. From the first convolutional layer to the second convolutional layer, the number of filters is doubled to preserve enough feature information for the following layers.

Max-pooling layers, have the filters of size 2×2 and stride 2. All four layers maintain the same number filters of previous layers and halves the size of feature map to save the computational cost.

Building blocks layers, have four groups with the number of building blocks of 3, 4, 6 and 3 respectively. For each group, we use the same structure as shown in Fig. 2, i.e., it has 3 convolutional filters as main road and one bypass [12] which is element-wise summed as the output. The number of convolutional filters of each group is 64, 128, 256 and 512 individually.

Fully connected layers, extract the 1024−dimensional vector for face recognition tasks. To better model the correlations among the facial attributes, we use one additional fully connected layer with 1024−dimensional output for facial attribute prediction only. The output vectors will model the visual features of face images. The batch normalization [16] is used after each convolutional layer and fully connected layer, then we use PReLU activation [13] after the batch normalization.

To better facilitate face recognition task, we employ facial attributes generated in Sec. 3.2 to help face recognition tasks. We argue that if our network wants to successfully recognize one identity from face image, it should also be able to trustably predict its corresponding biometric traits on faces, i.e. the facial attributes in Tab. 1; and vice versa. Thus, we build a deep network to jointly learn the facial attribute prediction and face identification tasks.

The network in Fig. 1 is denoted as $f(\mathbf{I};\Theta)$, where Θ is the parameter set of the deep architecture and we use $\mathbf{I}$ to denote the training images. Suppose we have M facial attributes and P face identities. We model the minimization of the expected loss as follows,

$$\{\Theta, W_a, W_p\} = \operatorname{argmin} \mathcal{L}(\mathbf{I};\Theta, W_a, W_p) \qquad (1)$$

where $\mathcal{L}(\mathbf{I};\Theta, W_a, W_p)$ is the loss function of the task and defined as

$$\mathcal{L}(\mathbf{I};\Theta, W_a, W_p) = \lambda_1 \mathcal{L}_a(W_a \cdot g(f(\mathbf{I};\Theta))) + \lambda_2 \mathcal{L}_p(W_p \cdot f(\mathbf{I};\Theta)) \qquad (2)$$

where $W_a \subseteq \mathbb{R}^{1024\times M}$ and $W_p \subseteq \mathbb{R}^{1024\times P}$ are the learned weights for facial attribute and face identification tasks; we use mean square error loss for facial attribute $\mathcal{L}_a(\cdot)$; and we use soft-max loss for face identification task $\mathcal{L}_p(\cdot)$. The shared parameters Θ are jointly optimized by these two tasks. $g(\cdot)$ indicates the second fully connected layer for facial attribute only in Fig. 1.

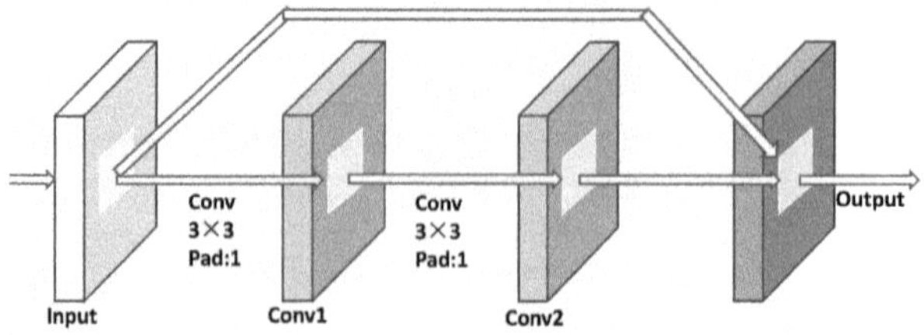

Figure 3: Building Block Structure(Fast-Model).

3.4 The building blocks of Fast-Model

Our network requires significant amount of computational cost on the building blocks in Fig. 2. Thus, in order to be able to balance the computational efficiency and accuracy, we simplify the building block structure in Fig. 3 and propose a Fast-Model. Particularly, the building block in our Fast-Model contains only 2 convolutional layers (Fig.3) comparing with the 3 convolutional layers in Full-Model. This will greatly reduce the computing cost and thus improve training speed, while our experiments show that the performance of Fast-Model is still very good.

4 EXPERIMENTS

4.1 Datasets and settings

Our models are trained on CASIA-WebFace [49] and CelebA [24], and we test our results on the widely used face datasets, MegaFace [18]. We further employ the LFW [15] dataset to evaluate the key components of our networks. Specifically,

CASIA-WebFace is currently the largest publicly released dataset for face verification and identification tasks. It contains 10,575 celebrities and 494,414 face images which are crawled from the web. Each person has 46.8 images on average.

CelebA is a facial attribute dataset which contains approximately $200k$ images. Each image is annotated with 5 landmarks (two eyes, the nose tips, the mouth corners) and binary labels of 40 attributes.

MegaFace is a very challenging dataset to evaluate the performance of face recognition algorithms. It includes gallery set and probe set. The gallery set consists of $690K$ different individuals with more than 1 million images. This images are collected from a subset of Flickr photos [38]. The sample images are shown in Fig. 5. The probe set used in the challenge are two existing databases: *Facescrub* [26] and *FGNet* [10]. *Facescrub* dataset is publicly available dataset, containing over 100K face images of 530 identities. *FGNet* dataset is a face aging dataset, consists of 1002 images of 82 individuals. Each identity has average 12 images ranging from 0 to 69. The gallery set are used as the distractors[1] to evaluates the performance of algorithms with the increasing size of "distractors" (going from 10 to $1M$). It has been showed that training image size have a significant impact on the performance of the algorithm. To evaluate to algorithm

[1] it means who are not in the testing set, i.e. faces of unknown persons.

Figure 4: Some face images in LFW dataset. The face image pairs in red bounding box are the same person pairs and the yellow images are the negative pairs.

Figure 5: Some face images in MegaFace dataset.

more fairly, MegaFace challenge has two protocols (large or small training set). The training set is defined as large if it contains more than $0.5M$ images and $20K$ subjects. Otherwise, it is defined as small. Our training set has 0.44M images and 10k subjects which belong to the small training set protocol, in contrast to the previous work of 200M images [32] and 1.3M images [22]. We conduct our experiments on Facescrub.

LFW contains 13, 233 web-collected images of 5749 different identities. These images has large variations in illuminations, pose and expression. LFW includes 6000 face pairs in 10 splits; each split with half positive pairs (the same persons) and half negative pairs (different persons). The sample images can be viewed in Fig 4.

4.2 Competitors

Our model is compared against the exiting methods on face recognition tasks reported from the official websites of MegaFace[2]. We mainly compare those publicly released methods including Google FaceNet [32], Center Loss [43], Lightened CNN [44], and LBP [2], and Joint Bayes model [5].

As an open challenge, there are lots of methods from the commercial companies such as FaceAll, NTechLAB, SIAT_MMLAB, BareBonesFR, 3DiVi Company. Since the details of these methods are not still kept unknown to the community, it is hard to judge whether these methods are comparable with us. However, we still list these methods as a general reference.

[2] http://megaface.cs.washington.edu/results/facescrubresults.html

For facial attribute prediction, we compare with the state-of-the-art method – MOON [31].

4.3 Evaluation metrics

For MegaFace dataset [18], there are two recognition tasks, i.e., *identification* and *verification*. We evaluate our models on both settings with the provided toolkit. The face attribute prediction is also evaluated here.

Face Identification. Given a probe photo (Facescrub) and a gallery containing at least one photo of the same identity, we need to compute the similarity between each of the gallery images and the probe face image given, as well as the rank orders of all the gallery images. Results are presented with Cumulative Match Characteristics (CMC) curves. It indicates the probability that a correct gallery image can be found in the first thousan images.

Face Verification. Given a pair of photos, we need to determine the person in the two images is the same or not. MegaFace challenges provides 4 billion negative pairs between probe and gallery datasets. The verification result is report with Receiver Operating Characteristic (ROC) curves. It explores the trade off between True Accept Rate (TAR) and False Accept Rate (FAR).

Facial attribute prediction. Given one attribute, we will compute the accuracy of facial attribute prediction. Note that the MegaFace dataset did not provide the ground-truth labels for the facial attributes. Since exhaustively annotating all the images used in MegaFace is expensive, we randomly sample 1000 images from faceScrub dataset and invite three annotators who are unknown to our projects to label the selected facial attributes. The ground-truth facial attributes are majority-voted among these three annotators. This sampled dataset is utilized to evaluate our algorithms.

In the real-world scenario, face recognition should achieve high accuracy with millions of distractors. In the MegaFace challenging setting, we compare Rank-1 identification accuracy with at least 1M distractors on the face identification task. For the face verification, verification accuracy at low false accept rate FAR $= 10^{-6}$ is adopted. These two evaluation settings show the incredible difficulty of MegaFace challenging.

4.4 Parameter settings

To train the CNN model, we randomly select one face image from each identity as the validation set and the remaining images as the training set. We train our model for 70k iterations with $\lambda_1 = 0, \lambda_2 = 1$ in Eq 2. The training images are horizontally flipped for data augmentation. The base learning rate is set as 0.01, and gradually decreased by 1/10 at $40k$, $58k$. The size of input image is $112 \times 96 \times 3$. We use the stochastic gradient descent algorithm with mini-batch size of 40 in Full-Model and mini-batch size of 48 in Fast-Model. Dropout is used for fully connected layers and the ratio is set to 0.5. For fair comparison, all the CNN models share the same base architecture and the details are given in Fig 1.

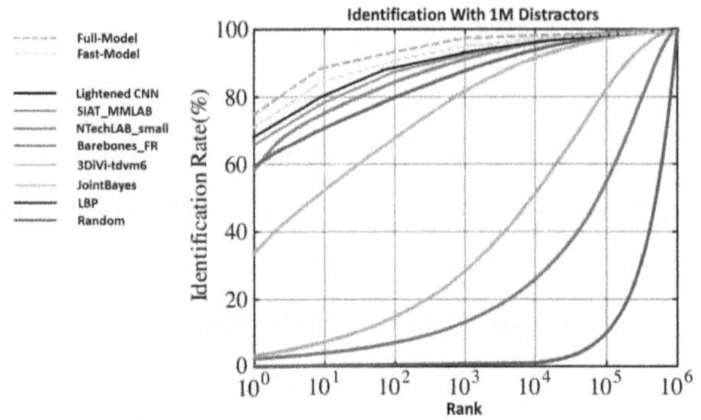

Figure 6: CMC curves of different methods (under the protocol of small training set) with 1M distractors. Note that the results of other other methods are reproduced from the official website of MegaFace dataset.

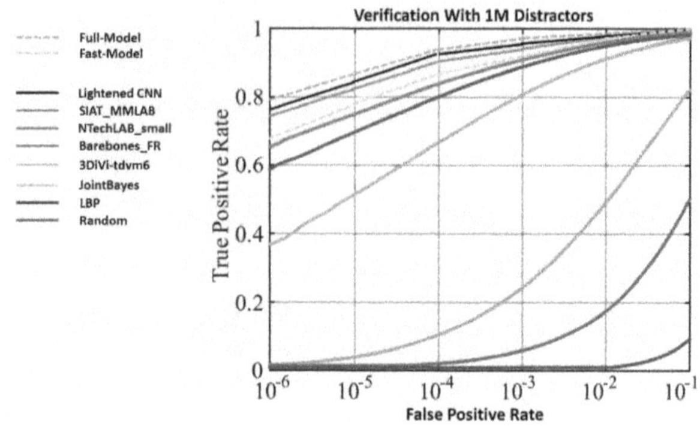

Figure 7: ROC curves of different methods (under the protocol of small training set) with 1M distractors. Note that the results of other other methods are reproduced from the official website of MegaFace dataset.

We also fine-tune our model for 30k iterations with $\lambda_1 = 0.1, \lambda_2 = 1$ in Eq 2. The base learning rate is set as 0.001, and gradually decreased by 1/10 at $10k$, $20k$. The remaining parameter settings are consistent with the above. We implement our method using the open source deep learning framework Caffe [17]. For all the experiments, we train the deep model from the scratch and we only use a single end-to-end model for all the testing.

4.5 Preprocessing

We use the annotations [3] from[48] to improve the quality of training set. Then we preprocess the CASIA-WebFace dataset with the following 3 steps, i.e. *face detection, face landmark detection* and *face alignment.* (1) For face detection and face landmark detection, we use the the public tools [51]. If the detection step is failed, we discard the image; otherwise, we crop the face image with the provided bounding box. (2) We employ the method of [44] to detect the five facial landmarks (two eyes, nose and mouth corners). (3) We use the codes in [44] for face alignment. The obtained faces are normalized and resized to 112 × 96 RGB images. Finally, we obtain roughly 0.44M remaining images of 10,575 unique identities from CASIA-WebFace dataset.

4.6 Running cost

Our Full-Model get converged with 100,000 iteration and it takes 17 hours on CASIA-WebFace with one NVIDIA TITANX GPUs. The batch size is 40, and it takes around 11 GB GPU memory. The Fast-Model gets converged with 100,000 iteration and it costs 14 hours on one NVIDIA TITANX GPUs. The batch-size is fixed as 48 which uses round 10 GB GPU memory.

4.7 Experiment on MegaFace

We evaluate face identification and face verification tasks on the standard settings of the challenging MegaFace benchmark.

[3] http://zyb.im/research/mm16.html

Table 2: Face identification Rank-1 results on MegaFace with 1M distractors. 'Rels' indicates whether the details of this method are publicly released.

Method	Rels	Protocol	Acc. (%)
Google - FaceNet v8 [32]	✓	Large	70.50
NTechLAB - Large	×	Large	73.30
Faceall Co. - Norm_1600	×	Large	64.80
Faceall Co. - FaceAll_1600	×	Large	63.98
Lightened CNN [44]	✓	Small	67.11
Center Loss [43]	✓	Small	65.23
LBP [2]	✓	Small	3.02
Joint Bayes [5]	✓	Small	2.33
NTechLAB -Small	×	Small	58.22
3DiVi Company	×	Small	33.71
SIAT_MMLAB	×	Small	65.23
Barebones FR	×	Small	59.36
Fast-Model (without Attribute)	✓	Small	70.28
Fast-Model	✓	Small	73.07
Full-Model (without Attribute)	✓	Small	74.25
Full-Model	✓	Small	**77.74**

For face identification, we plot the CMC curve of different methods with 1M distractors as shown in Fig 6 and list the Rank-1 identification accuracy at Tab. 2. In face verification, we plot the ROC curve of different methods also with 1M distractors listed in Fig. 7 and we compare the verification TAR at 10^{-6} FAR accuracy at Tab. 3. Comparing with all competitors, we want to highlight that *our method achieves the best performance on the small protocol among all the publicly released methods on MegaFace dataset*; specifically, we have

(1) our Full-Model beats the other methods on the protocol of small training set on the identification task. For face identification, our methods (both Full-Model and Fast-Model) has larger area under CMC curve than the

Table 3: Face verification on MegaFace with 1M distractors (TAR at 10^{-6} FAR). 'Rels' indicates whether the details of this method are publicly released.

Method	Rels	Protocol	Acc. (%)
Lightened CNN [44]	✓	Small	77.46
Center Loss [43]	✓	Small	76.52
LBP [2]	✓	Small	2.17
Joint Bayes [5]	✓	Small	1.46
Barebones FR	×	Small	59.04
NTechLAB - Small	×	Small	66.37
3DiVi Company	×	Small	36.93
SIAT_MMLAB	×	Small	76.72
Fast-Model (without Attribute)	✓	Small	58.20
Fast-Model	✓	Small	68.56
Full-Model (without Attribute)	✓	Small	76.22
Full-Model	✓	Small	**79.24**

other competitor methods as shown in Fig 6. This proves the efficacy of our model. Table 2 further shows the results on Rank-1 accuracy. As can be seen from the table, our Full-Model achieves 77.74% Rank-1 accuracy, outperforming all the other methods of the small protocol by clear margins (> 10%). Furthermore, it is also worth noticing that our model even outperform some models trained with very large training set (i.e., large protocol), e.g., Beijing Facecall Co. and Google's FaceNet. For example, Google - FaceNet v8 is trained on 200M face images; in contrast, our training set has only $0.44M$ face images.

(2) our Full-Model beats the other methods on the protocol of small training set on the verification task. The results are compared in Fig. 7 and Tab. 3. As we can see from the figure, our Full-Model can obtain the verification accuracy 79.24%; it shows 1.78% improvement over the second best method – Lightened CNN [44]. Note that, we argue that the verification task is more sensible to the scale of training data, and thus on the large protocol, the other competitors such as Google FaceNet v8 [32] achieving 86.47% enable better performance than ours (79.24%). However, our Full-Model on identification task can still beat Google FaceNet v8 [32] even in large protocol.

(3) our Fast-Model is very efficient and it can beat most of competitors on the small protocol. On face identification task, our Fast-Model achieve 73.07% and outperforms all the other methods on the small protocol. On face verification task, the result of Fast-Model is 68.56% which is higher than almost all the other methods with the only two exceptions – Lightened CNN [44] and Center Loss [43]. It shows that our Fast-Model is a reasonable good and fast version of our Full-Model in terms of running cost and performance.

(4) our Full-Model/Fast-Model with attribute constraints beats the models without learning attribute tasks. We compare another variants of our model, i.e., directly using our network for face recognition without learning

Table 4: Results of facial attribute prediction. Our model is compared agains MOON. Each row is corresponding to one task of attribute prediction.

	MOON(%)	Ours (%)
Narrow Eyes	83.40	**85.60**
Big_nose	71.00	**75.30**
Pointy_nose	70.50	**73.90**
Chubby	93.30	**93.50**
Double_Chin	94.80	**96.70**
High_cheekbones	74.10	**76.80**
Male	96.90	**97.30**

facial attribute tasks. The experiments show that the results without attribute constraints are inferior to those of their corresponding models with attribute constraints on both identification and verification tasks. This validates that the jointly learning two tasks can help improve the performance of face recognition.

(5) our facial attribute prediction beat the results of MOON [31]. We also compare the results of jointly learned framework against the model of only learning the facial attribute task, i.e., MOON. Note that without learning the face recognition task, our model can be degraded into MOON. The results are compared in Tab. 4. On all the attributes, our methods achieve higher prediction accuracy than MOON. This validates that our multi-task framework can help with facial attribute prediction.

4.8 The ablation study on MegaFace and LFW dataset

To better reveal the insights and evaluate the key components of our model, we compare the variants of our model on the LFW and MegaFace dataset. For LFW dataset, we evaluate algorithms with the standard protocol of unrestricted labeled data [15]. We test our algorithm on 6000 face pairs and mean accuracy is reported.

Our building block structure is important to guarantee the good performance on the benchmark. We further investigate different variants of building block structures listed in Fig. 8. Particularly, there are 3 variant structure compared here, i.e. the building blocks of Fast-Model, Full-Model and the variants-block. The variants-Block takes two convolutional layer on the main road, and one convolutional layer on the bypass. We compare the results of Rank-1 identification accuracy on MegaFace and LFW datasets in Tab. 5. For all the three methods, the only difference is the structure of building blocks. We highlight that (1) the building blocks of our Full-Model structure outperforms the other structures on both two datasets. This reveals that arranging the convolutional layers in a deeper structure (*i.e.* 3 layers in the main road of our Full-Model) can indeed extract more discriminative features, and thus improve the recognition accuracy. (2) Comparing the building block of Full-Model block with that of variants-block model, we conjecture that

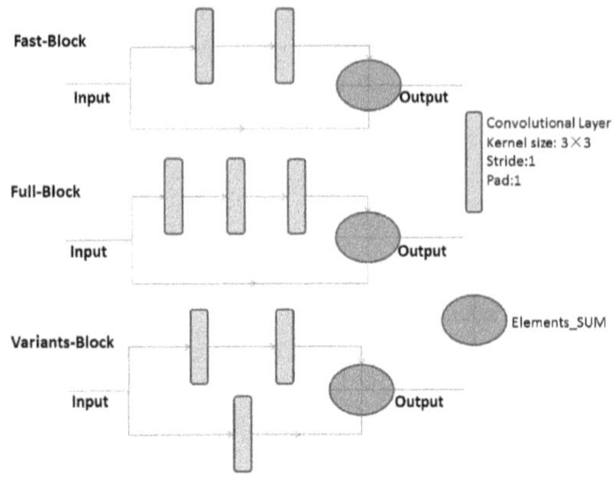

Figure 8: Different building blocks.

Table 5: Comparison of building block structure.

Method Names	MegFace (%)	LFW (%)
Fast-Block	73.07	97.62
Full-Block	**77.74**	**98.15**
Variants-Block	69.63	97.50

Table 6: Comparison of different configurations.

Method Names	MegFace (%)	LFW (%)
Configuration-1	**73.07**	**97.62**
Configuration-2	72.05	97.50
Configuration-3	69.40	97.60

convolutional layer at different lines (*i.e.* both main pass and by-pass in variants-block model) may confuse the residual learning of features, and thus it will harm the performance of corresponding architectures.

The different configurations of the last layer of our network in Fig. 1. We compare different configurations of the final layer of our network. Specifically, we use the Fast-Model to retrain the network with 3 different structures listed in Fig. 9. For a faire comparison, all the other settings and structures are the same except the last layer. (1) Configuration-1 is the structure is used in our Full-Model and Fast-Model. (2) Configuration-2 is a shared structure of both tasks. (3) Configuration-3 enforces another independent fully connected layer for each individual task. The result on both MegaFace and LFW datasets are shown in Tab. 6. The results of our configuration is better than those of the others. We argue that these attributes have relatively high correlation and such correlation should be modeled separately beyond the face recognition task. Thus another fully connected layer is introduced in our configuration to help model the correlation among attribute. As results, it enables the better performance than the other two configurations.

The benefits of different kinds of facial attributes. It is another interesting question of which type/group of facial attributes in Tab 1 can mostly help the face identification

Figure 9: Different configurations of the last layers.

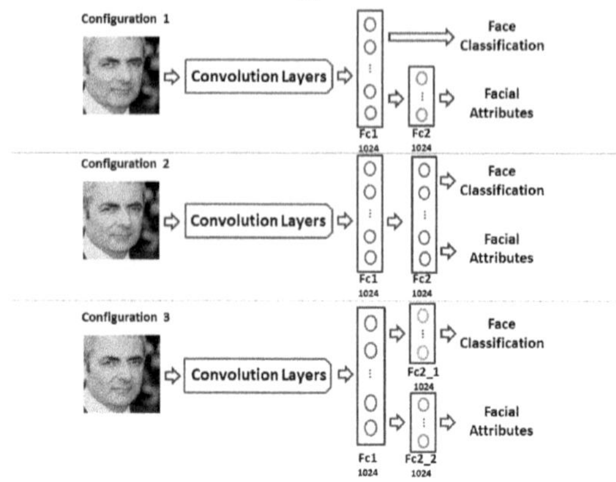

Table 7: Comparison of different groups of face attributes on face identification.

Method Names	MegFace (%)	LFW (%)
No attribute	70.28	97.20
Eye attribute	72.23	97.49
Nose attributes	71.72	97.63
Global attributes	71.92	97.45
All attributes	**73.07**	**97.62**

tasks. To answer this question, we design another set of experiments. Particularly, still with the same Fast-Model structure, we compare the methods (1) without attribute, (2) with only eye attribute, (3) with nose attribute, (4) with global attribute and (5) with all attributes. The results are listed in Tab 7. Comparing the model without attribute, it is obviously that using all facial attributes can improve face recognition performance. Further, we find that the eye attribute is more important than Global attributes in term of the identification accuracy on both dataset.

5 CONCLUSIONS

In this paper, we for the first time propose a novel joint deep architecture for face recognition and facial attribute prediction. In contrast to previous work of only considering one task only, our experimental results clearly show the benefit of the jointly learning structures and learning in such a way can help to capture both global feature and local attribute information simultaneously.

6 ACKNOWLEDGEMENT

This work is supported by the National Key Research and Development Plan (#2016YFC0801003), Shanghai Municipal Science and Technology Commission (#16JC1420401), Shanghai Sailing Program (#17YF1427500), the Shanghai Municipal R&D Foundation (#16511105402), Application of big data computing platform in Smart Lingang New City based BIM and GIS (#ZN2016020103).

REFERENCES

[1] Abrar H Abdulnabi, Gang Wang, Jiwen Lu, and Kui Jia. 2015. Multi-task cnn model for attribute prediction. *IEEE TMM* (2015).

[2] Timo Ahonen, Abdenour Hadid, and Matti Pietikainen. 2006. Face description with local binary patterns: Application to face recognition. *IEEE TPAMI* (2006).

[3] Lacey Best-Rowden, Hu Han, Charles Otto, Brendan F Klare, and Anil K Jain. 2014. Unconstrained face recognition: Identifying a person of interest from a media collection. *IEEE Transactions on Information Forensics and Security* (2014).

[4] Xudong Cao, Yichen Wei, Fang Wen, and Jian Sun. 2014. Face alignment by explicit shape regression. *IJCV* 107, 2 (2014), 177–190.

[5] Dong Chen, Xudong Cao, Liwei Wang, Fang Wen, and Jian Sun. 2012. Bayesian face revisited: A joint formulation. In *ECCV*.

[6] Dong Chen, Shaoqing Ren, Yichen Wei, Xudong Cao, and Jian Sun. 2014. Joint cascade face detection and alignment. In *ECCV*.

[7] Sumit Chopra, Raia Hadsell, and Yann LeCun. 2005. Learning a similarity metric discriminatively, with application to face verification. In *CVPR*.

[8] Max Ehrlich, Timothy J Shields, Timur Almaev, and Mohamed R Amer. 2016. Facial attributes classification using multi-task representation learning. In *CVPR Workshops*.

[9] Pedro F. Felzenszwalb, Ross B. Girshick, David McAllester, and Deva Ramanan. 2010. Object Detection with Discriminatively Trained Part-Based Models. *IEEE TPAMI* (2010).

[10] Yanwei Fu, Timothy M. Hospedales, Tao Xiang, Yuan Yao, and Shaogang Gong. 2014. Interestingness Prediction by Robust Learning to Rank. In *ECCV*.

[11] M. Guillaumin, J. Verbeek, and C. Schmid. 2009. Is that you? Metric Learning Approaches for Face Identification. In *CVPR*.

[12] Kaiming He, Xiangyu Zhang, Shaoqing Ren, and Jian Sun. 2015. Deep residual learning for image recognition. *arXiv preprint arXiv:1512.03385* (2015).

[13] Kaiming He, Xiangyu Zhang, Shaoqing Ren, and Jian Sun. 2015. Delving Deep into Rectifiers: Surpassing Human-Level Performance on ImageNet Classification. In *CoRR, vol. abs/1502.01852*.

[14] G. B. Huang, V. Jain, and E. Learned-Miller. 2007. Unsupervised Joint Alignment of Complex Images. In *IEEE International Conference on Computer Vision*. 1–8. DOI:http://dx.doi.org/10.1109/ICCV.2007.4408858

[15] Gary B Huang, Manu Ramesh, Tamara Berg, and Erik Learned-Miller. *Labeled faces in the wild: A database for studying face recognition in unconstrained environments*. Technical Report.

[16] Sergey Ioffe and Christian Szegedy. 2015. Batch Normalization: Accelerating Deep Network Training by Reducing Internal Covariate Shift. In *ICML*.

[17] Y. Jia, E. Shelhamer, J. Donahue, S. Karayev, J. Long, R. Girshick, S. Guadarrama, and T. Darrell. 2014. Caffe: Convolutional architecture for fast feature embedding. *arXiv* (2014).

[18] Ira Kemelmacher-Shlizerman, Steven M Seitz, Daniel Miller, and Evan Brossard. 2016. The MegaFace Benchmark: 1 Million Faces for Recognition at Scale. In *CVPR*.

[19] Neeraj Kumar, Alexander Berg, Peter N Belhumeur, and Shree Nayar. 2011. Describable visual attributes for face verification and image search. *IEEE TPMAI* (2011).

[20] Neeraj Kumar, Alexander C. Berg, Peter N. Belhumeur, and Shree K. Nayar. 2009. Attribute and Simile Classifiers for Face Verification. In *ICCV*.

[21] Neeraj Kumar, Alexander C Berg, Peter N Belhumeur, and Shree K Nayar. 2009. Attribute and simile classifiers for face verification. In *ICCV*. IEEE, 365–372.

[22] Jinguo Liu, Yafeng Deng, and Chang Huang. 2015. Targeting ultimate accuracy: Face recognition via deep embedding. *arXiv preprint arXiv:1506.07310* (2015).

[23] Xiaodong Liu, Jianfeng Gao, Xiaodong He, Li Deng, Kevin Duh, and Ye-Yi Wang. Representation learning using multi-task deep neural networks for semantic classification and information retrieval.

[24] Ziwei Liu, Ping Luo, Xiaogang Wang, and Xiaoou Tang. 2015. Deep learning face attributes in the wild. In *ICCV*.

[25] David G. Lowe. 2004. Distinctive Image Features from Scale-Invariant Keypoints. *International Journal of Computer Vision* 60 (2004).

[26] Hong-Wei Ng and Stefan Winkler. 2014. A data-driven approach to cleaning large face datasets. In *ICIP*.

[27] Hieu V. Nguyen and Li Bai. 2010. Cosine Similarity Metric Learning for Face Verification. In *ACCV*.

[28] Timo Ojala, Matti Pietikäinen, and Topi Mäenpää. 2002. Gray Scale and Rotation Invariant Texture Classification with Local Binary Patterns. *IEEE TPAMI* (2002).

[29] Rajeev Ranjan, Vishal M Patel, and Rama Chellappa. 2016. Hyperface: A deep multi-task learning framework for face detection, landmark localization, pose estimation, and gender recognition. *arXiv preprint arXiv:1603.01249* (2016).

[30] Shaoqing Ren, Xudong Cao, Yichen Wei, and Jian Sun. 2014. Face alignment at 3000 fps via regressing local binary features. In *CVPR*. IEEE.

[31] Ethan M. Rudd, Manuel Gunther, and Terrance E. Boult. 2016. MOON:A Mixed Objective Optimization Network for the Recognition of Facial Attributes. In *ECCV*.

[32] Florian Schroff, Dmitry Kalenichenko, and James Philbin. 2015. Facenet: A unified embedding for face recognition and clustering. In *CVPR*.

[33] William Robson Schwartz, Huimin Guo, and Larry S Davis. 2010. A robust and scalable approach to face identification. In *ECCV*.

[34] Yi Sun, Ding Liang, Xiaogang Wang, and Xiaoou Tang. 2015. Deepid3: Face recognition with very deep neural networks. *arXiv preprint arXiv:1502.00873* (2015).

[35] Yi Sun, Xiaogang Wang, and Xiaoou Tang. 2015. Deeply learned face representations are sparse, selective, and robust. In *CVPR*.

[36] Yaniv Taigman, Ming Yang, Marc'Aurelio Ranzato, and Lior Wolf. 2014. Deepface: Closing the gap to human-level performance in face verification. In *CVPR*. 1701–1708.

[37] Yaniv Taigman, Ming Yang, MarcAurelio Ranzato, and Lior Wolf. 2015. Web-scale training for face identification. In *CVPR*.

[38] Bart Thomee, David A Shamma, Gerald Friedland, Benjamin Elizalde, Karl Ni, Douglas Poland, Damian Borth, and Li-Jia Li. 2015. The new data and new challenges in multimedia research. *arXiv preprint arXiv:1503.01817* (2015).

[39] Georgios Tzimiropoulos and Maja Pantic. 2014. Gauss-newton deformable part models for face alignment in-the-wild. In *CVPR*. IEEE, 1851–1858.

[40] Paul Viola and Michael Jones. 2001. Rapid Object Detection using a Boosted Cascade of Simple Features. In *CVPR*.

[41] P. Viola, J. Platt, and C. Zhang. 2005. Multiple instance boosting for object detection. In *NIPS*.

[42] Jing Wang, Yu Cheng, and Rogerio Schmidt Feris. 2016. Walk and Learn: Facial Attribute Representation Learning from Egocentric Video and Contextual Data. *arXiv preprint arXiv:1604.06433* (2016).

[43] Yandong Wen, Kaipeng Zhang, Zhifeng Li, and Yu Qiao. 2016. A discriminative feature learning approach for deep face recognition. In *ECCV*.

[44] Xiang Wu, Ran He, and Zhenan Sun. 2015. A Lightened CNN for Deep Face Representation. *arXiv preprint arXiv:1511.02683* (2015).

[45] Xiang Wu, Ran He, Zhenan Sun, and Tieniu Tan. 2016. A Light CNN for Deep Face Representation with Noisy Labels. *arxiv* (2016).

[46] Xuehan Xiong and Fernando De la Torre. 2013. Supervised descent method and its applications to face alignment. In *CVPR*.

[47] Heng Yang, Wenxuan Mou, Yichi Zhang, Ioannis Patras, Hatice Gunes, and Peter Robinson. 2015. Face Alignment Assisted by Head Pose Estimation. *arXiv preprint arXiv:1507.03148* (2015).

[48] Hao Ye, Weiyuan Shao, Hong Wang, Jianqi Ma, Li Wang, Yingbin Zheng, and Xiangyang Xue. 2016. Face Recognition via Active Annotation and Learning. In *Proceedings of the 2016 ACM on Multimedia Conference*. 1058–1062.

[49] Dong Yi, Zhen Lei, Shengcai Liao, and Stan Z Li. 2014. Learning face representation from scratch. *arXiv preprint arXiv:1411.7923* (2014).

[50] Jie Zhang, Shiguang Shan, Meina Kan, and Xilin Chen. 2014. Coarse-to-fine auto-encoder networks (cfan) for real-time face alignment. In *ECCV*. Springer.

[51] K. Zhang, Z. Zhang, Z. Li, and Y. Qiao. 2016. Joint Face Detection and Alignment Using Multitask Cascaded Convolutional Networks. *IEEE SP Letters* (2016).

[52] Zhanpeng Zhang, Ping Luo, Chen Change Loy, and Xiaoou Tang. 2014. Facial landmark detection by deep multi-task learning. In *ECCV*.

[53] Yang Zhong, Josephine Sullivan, and Haibo Li. 2016. Face Attribute Prediction Using Off-the-Shelf CNN Features. In *arxiv*.
[54] Qiang Zhou, Gang Wang, Kui Jia, and Qi Zhao. 2013. Learning to share latent tasks for action recognition. In *ICCV*.
[55] Shizhan Zhu, Cheng Li, Chen Change Loy, and Xiaoou Tang. 2015. Face Alignment by Coarse-to-Fine Shape Searching. In *CVPR*.
[56] Xiangxin Zhu and Deva Ramanan. 2012. Face detection, pose estimation, and landmark localization in the wild. In *CVPR*.

Finger Vein Image Retrieval via Coding Scale-varied Superpixel Feature

Kuikui Wang
Shandong University
Jinan, Shandong,China
sarahkuikui@163.com

Lu Yang
Shandong University of Finance and Economics
Jinan, Shandong,China
yangluhi@163.com

Gongping Yang*
Shandong University
Jinan, Shandong,China
gpyang@sdu.edu.cn

Xin Luo
Shandong University
Jinan, Shandong,China
luoxin.lxin@gmail.com

Kun Su
Shandong University
Jinan, Shandong,China
nukus@sdu.edu.cn

Yilong Yin
Shandong University
Jinan, Shandong,China
ylyin@sdu.edu.cn

ABSTRACT

Finger vein image retrieval is one significant technique for performing fast identification especially in large-scale applications. However, most existing retrieval methods were based on fixed-scale feature of non-overlapped rectangular image block, in which the representation ability of feature and the local consistency of vein pattern were both overlooked. And the weak encoding (*e.g.*, predefined threshold based binarization) was also limited the retrieval performance. Focusing on these problems, this paper proposes a novel finger vein image retrieval framework based on similarity-preserving encoding of scale-varied superpixel feature. In the framework, locally consistent pixels in one superpixel are used as a unit of feature representation, and the feature length is varied with the category of the superpixel classified by the variance of lowest dimensional feature. Additionally, the feature compaction and feature rotation based encoding can minimize the quantization loss and preserve the similarity between the scale-varied feature and the encoded binary codes. Experimental results on six public finger vein databases demonstrate that the superiority of the proposed coding scale-varied superpixel feature based retrieval approach over the state-of-the-arts.

CCS CONCEPTS

• **Security and privacy** → **Biometrics**;

KEYWORDS

Finger vein recognition; Image retrieval; Scale-varied feature; Superpixel; Similarity-preserved encoding

*This author is the corresponding author.

ICMR '17, June 6–9, 2017, Bucharest, Romania
© 2017 ACM. ACM ISBN 978-1-4503-4701-3/17/06...$15.00.
DOI: http://dx.doi.org/10.1145/3078971.3078975

ACM Reference format:
Kuikui Wang, Lu Yang, Gongping Yang, Xin Luo, Kun Su, and Yilong Yin. 2017. Finger Vein Image Retrieval via Coding Scale-varied Superpixel Feature. In *Proceedings of ICMR '17, June 6–9, 2017, Bucharest, Romania,* , 8 pages.
DOI: http://dx.doi.org/10.1145/3078971.3078975

1 INTRODUCTION

Recent years, lots of promising results about the recognition accuracy of finger vein have been reported [9, 10, 14, 15, 26]. But the recognition efficiency is still an intractable problem. Obviously, exhaustively one-to-one matching cannot satisfy the real-time requirement of personal identification, especially in large-scale applications. In biometrics, quickly searching the database by fast comparison between the probe image and all enrolled images, and returning a set of limited candidates to be matched with the probe image is an effective and prevalent solution. And, in finger vein recognition, there are also some related methods, in which image classification and image retrieval are two popular ways of the fast candidate search.

In classification based candidate search, the enrolled images are grouped into several classes by the domain knowledge based predefined rules, the unsupervised clustering algorithm, and so on. The existing finger vein image classification methods are all based on unsupervised k-means clustering. In clustering, image quality features (*i.e.*, gradient, image contrast and information entropy) and image content features (*i.e.*, moment invariant, wavelet coefficient and Gabor filters) [19], the extracted vein pattern and its subset [18], and the number of vein points in image block [16] were separately used to represent finger vein image. The main difference is that the clustering algorithm was only performed once in the latter two methods, but the former method built a two-level classification framework by executing the clustering algorithm twice respectively based on quality features and content features. On the basis of enrolled image classification, the probe image can be matched with the only part of enrolled images, which are in the same class with it, instead of all enrolled images in traditionally exhaustive matching.

In another candidate search method, *i.e.*, image retrieval, simple feature (*e.g.*, compact binary codes) based fast exhaustive matching between the probe image and all enrolled images or hashing method is performed firstly, and then only the top t candidate identities in matching scores based ordered rank or in collision times based ordered rank will be matched with the probe image. So, the number of candidates in image retrieval is t, but it in image classification is tth (Supposing there are t predefined image classes). If the number of enrolled images is very large, there will be much fewer candidates in image retrieval than in image classification. With this point of view, image retrieval may be a preferable solution to do fast personal identification rather than image classification.

In finger vein recognition, there are two typical image retrieval methods, *i.e.*, locality sensitive hashing (LSH) based method [20] and vocabulary tree (VT) based method [21]. In the former method, the extracted vein pattern was firstly partitioned into non-overlapped rectangular grids, and then the number of vein points in each grid was binarized by a predefined threshold to finish the encoding. Lastly, LSH method was employed to select the candidates for the probe image. Like this method, the image was also partitioned into non-overlapped rectangular grids in the latter method. Each image block, represented by a 16-dimensional local binary pattern (LBP) histogram, was encoded in searching its nearest leaf node of a vocabulary tree. More specifically, the nearest node, to the probe image block, in each layer of the tree was labeled by 1, and others were labeled by 0. And, the Hamming distance based exhaustive matching was used for candidate selection.

We give a more visualized description of two mentioned finger vein image retrieval methods in Table 1. From the table, it can be easily summarized that, 1)The rectangular grid based finger vein image partitioned may separate local vein pattern into two or more different blocks. In other words, local consistency of finger vein image was broken in grid partition. 2) The used feature may be weak in representation of image block, which causes that the discrimination of image block is not exploited completely. More important, the difference of image blocks was totally neglected. But, in finger vein image, the block filled with vein pattern is believed to be more discriminative than it without vein pattern. Accordingly, it is better to deal with different image blocks individually. 3) To achieve better retrieval accuracy, the discriminative information of the extracted feature must be preserved as much as possible in encoding. But the discrimination of the feature was likely discounted in above two encoding methods. Obviously, the predefined threshold based binarization is not a strong encoding method. And in search path based encoding, the quantization loss may be accumulated layer by layer, owing to the difference between the probe block and its nearest tree node in each layer, used to label the block, may be large. Therefore, exploring a new feature with more describing ability to finger vein image and encoding method with less quantization loss may have potential to further improve the retrieval performance.

In this paper, we present a novel finger vein image retrieval framework to achieve similarity-preserving binary codes from scale-varied superpixel feature. Firstly, a superpixel segmentation method, named simple linear iterative clustering (S-LIC) [1], is employed to partition finger vein image into multiple superpixels. Next, these superpixels are classified into three groups according to the amount of vein pattern in superpixel, measured by the variance of the low-dimensional feature, and the features with different scales (*i.e.*, dimensions), called scale-varied feature, are used to represent superpixels in different groups. Thirdly, the concatenated features of all superpixels are compacted by principal component analysis (PCA) and further encoded into the similarity-preserving binary patterns by iterative quantization (ITQ) [6, 7]. Finally, the Hamming distance based exhaustive matching is utilized for candidate selection. As shown in the experiments, the proposed retrieval method achieves better performance than the state-of-the-arts on four public finger vein databases, one fused large database and one deformation database.

The rest of the paper is organized as follows. The proposed scale-varied superpixel feature and similarity-preserving coding based retrieval framework is presented in Section 2. And the experimental results on multiple finger vein databases are reported and analyzed in Section 3. Lastly, we draw the conclusion of the paper in Section 4.

2 CODING SCALE-VARIED SUPERPIXEL FEATURE BASED RETRIEVAL FRAMEWORK

In this section, the proposed scale-varied superpixel feature and similarity-preserving encoding based retrieval framework is described. The proposed framework mainly contains four key steps: superpixel segmentation, scale-varied feature extraction, similarity-preserving encoding and exhaustive matching based candidate selection in Hamming space. The outline of our finger vein image retrieval framework is illustrated in Fig. 1. In this framework, we focus on exploring new feature with more describing ability to finger vein image and encoding method with less quantization loss. To achieve the powerful finger vein feature, local consistent pixels are clustered into one superpixel, and local features with different scales are extracted from different superpixel according to the discrimination of the superpixel. Additionally, inspired by iterative quantization (ITQ), the scale-varied features are compacted and further encoded by minimizing the quantization loss, which is helpful to the retrieval efficiency and the retrieval accuracy both.

In the following, three main steps, *i.e.*, superpixel segmentation, scale-varied feature extraction, similarity-preserving encoding, are presented in detail.

2.1 Superpixel Segmentation

Here, the reason of using superpixel segmentation, not rectangular grid based image partition, and the used segmentation

Table 1: Visualized description of two finger vein image retrieval methods

Method	Image partition	Base feature	Encoding	Candidate selection
LSH based method [20]	Non-overlapped image blocks	Number of vein points	Predefined threshold based binarization	Locality sensitive hashing
VT based method [21]	Non-overlapped image blocks	16-dimensional LBP histogram	Search path of nearest leaf node	Exhaustive matching in Hamming space

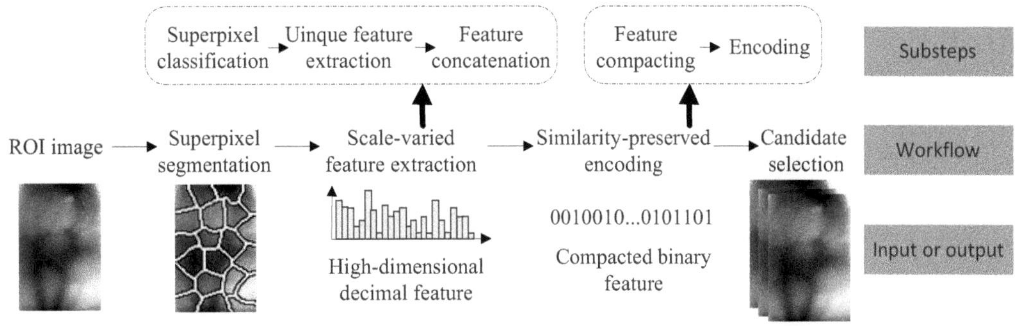

Figure 1: Outline of proposed finger vein image retrieval framework.

method are given. In finger vein recognition, some feature extraction methods [4, 5, 23], and even two existing image retrieval methods [20, 21], analyzed in Introduction, are based on rectangular image block. However, recently superpixel based finger vein features [11, 26] have achieved more promising recognition performance than rectangular block based ones. To intuitively show the difference between rectangular image block and superpixel, a comparison is given in Fig. 2. We can see from the figure that, superpixel segmentation tries to group vein pattern and non-vein pattern into different clusters and most superpixels only contain vein pattern or non-vein pattern. (It is should be noted that, superpixel segmentation is inevitably limited by the pixel location and the number of superpixels.) But, there may be some rectangular image blocks with half vein pattern and half non-vein pattern. A typical example is labeled by the red rectangular in the figure. Therefore, superpixel is better than rectangular image block to describe the local consistency characteristic of finger vein image. It is mainly attributed to that the location and gray value of pixel are both considered in superpixel segmentation, but only pixel location is considered in rectangular grid based image partition. In other words, superpixels are segmented in accordance with the distribution of vein pattern, and explore more intrinsic characteristics of finger vein image, which may be the underlying reason for its superior recognition performance in feature extraction.

Based on the above analysis, finger vein image is partitioned by a superpixel segmentation method, named simple linear iterative clustering (SLIC). The used SLIC method is adapted from k-means clustering approach. At beginning of segmentation, k superpixel centers are initialized. In each of following iteration, each superpixel is associated with its nearest superpixel center in assignment step, and the superpixel center is updated in update step. And the iteration is terminated until the the residual error, between the current

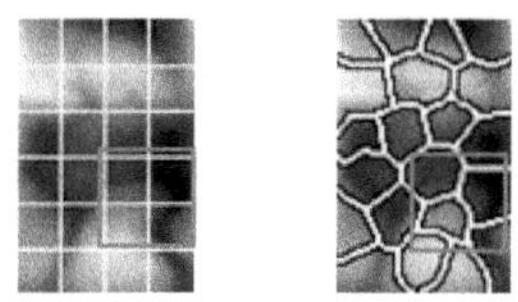

Figure 2: Comparison between (a) Rectangular image blocks and (b) Superpixels [1].

superpixel center locations and the previous ones, converges. It should be noted that, in each assignment, only pixels located in a region centered the superpixel center with fixed size are considered, and the differences of space and gray value between the considered pixel and superpixel center are both measured. Assuming the coordinate and the gray value of one pixel (or one superpixel center) are separately denoted by g and $[x, y]$. The distance between pixel i and superpixel center j can be formally written as:

$$d_g = \sqrt{(g_j - g_i)^2} \tag{1}$$

$$d_c = \sqrt{(x_j - x_i)^2 + (y_j - y_i)^2} \tag{2}$$

$$D = \sqrt{(d_g')^2 + (d_c')^2} \tag{3}$$

in which d_g' and d_c' are the normalized value of d_g and d_c. And, the number of superpixel in one image is set as 126 in our work.

2.2 Scale-varied Feature Extraction

The proposed scale-varied feature is presented in this section. As we introduced in Fig. 1, the scale-varied feature extraction mainly consists of three substeps, *i.e.*, superpixel classification, unique feature extraction and feature concatenation. A more definite explanation of scale-varied feature is illustrated in Fig. 3. The superpixels in one image are firstly classified into

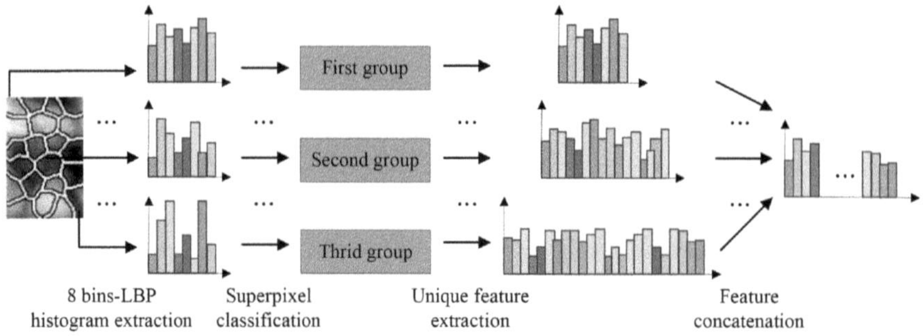

Figure 3: Illustration of scale-varied feature extraction.

three different groups according to the amount of vein pattern in each superpixel. And then, the superpixels classified into different groups will be represented by the features with varied scale. The features of all superpixels are concatenated finally.

Superpixel classification. In finger vein image, the image patch filled with vein pattern is believed to be more informative than the patch without vein pattern. And, we can see from the superpixel image in Fig. 2(b) that, the amount of vein pattern is varied from one superpixel to another. Therefore, it is better to deal with the superpixel individually. Here, the amount of vein pattern in each superpixel is roughly measured by the variance of the frequency numbers in a low-dimensional feature histogram. In other words, the superpixel with larger variance may have more vein pattern than others, and need high-dimensional histogram to represent. Another reason of using feature variance based superpixel classification is that, the more discriminative feature, evenly distributed at each bin of the histogram, is hoped.

Specifically, the LBP histogram feature is taken as an example to explain the classification of superpixel. For each pixel in one superpixel, the decimal LBP code is extracted, and further mapped into the corresponding bin of a histogram. And in the histogram, a small bin number is set. Next, all superpixels in one image are sorted in increasing sequences of the variance of frequency numbers on all bins in the built histogram, and evenly divided into three groups. More specifically, the first one-third superpixels and the last one-third ones separately belong to the first group and the third group, and the others in the middle constitute the second group. Assuming the histogram is denoted by $h = \{h_i, i = 1, 2, ..., n\}$ (n=8 in our experiments), the variance of the histogram can be represented by:

$$V_h = \frac{\sum_{i=1}^{n} (h_i - h_m)^2}{n} \tag{4}$$

in which h_m is the mean value of n frequency numbers. Three typical superpixels from different groups and their histograms with 8 bins are shown in Fig. 4. There is no vein pattern in the superpixel labeled in the first group, and the gray value is limited in a small range. But, the superpixel labeled in the second group, especially the one labeled in the third group, is filled with vein pattern, and the gray value varied largely. Additionally, the variance of frequency numbers (*i.e.*, the heights of bins) in the first two histograms, which is from the superpixels labeled in the third and second groups, is clearly larger than it in the last histogram, which is from the superpixel labeled in the first group. And the variance in the first histogram is largest. So, large difference can be found in the histograms of different superpixels, and the histogram with 8 bins is weak to represent superpixel filled with lots of vein pattern in the second and third groups.

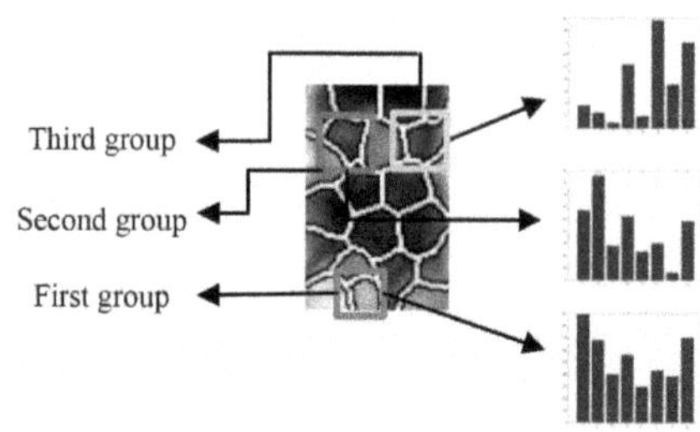

Figure 4: Typical superpixels in different groups and their histograms.

Unique feature extraction and concatenation. In fact, the feature with larger scale has bigger describing ability, and can exploit more discriminative information from image. Consequently, the superpixel, filled with a lot of vein pattern, in the last two groups, should be represented by the histogram with more bins. In our work, the superpixels in second group and these in third group are respectively represented by the histogram with 16 bins and it with 24 bins. Therefore, given the group label for each superpixel in one image, the unique LBP histogram is built for the superpixel. The histograms of all superpixels in one image are concatenated in order of superpixel number, which is assigned according to the superpixel position in the image. So, the decimal frequency number in the concatenated histogram is used as the image feature.

As we introduced, there are 126 superpixels in each image and the feature dimension (*i.e.*, the number of histogram bins) of one superpixel in the first, second and third group is separately 8, 16 and 24. Therefore, for one image, it will be a 2016-dimensional (*i.e.*, 42×8+42×16+42×24) decimal feature vector. Accordingly, to improve the retrieval speed, it is very essential to compact the feature vector, and further convert it into binary pattern.

2.3 Similarity-preserving Encoding

Here, the extracted high-dimensional and decimal scale-varied feature is compacted and encoded into a low-dimensional binary code vector. **Firstly**, principal component analysis (PCA) [22] is employed to conduct the feature compacting. Assuming there are N training images and their scale-varied features are demoted by $A_n, n = 1, 2, ..., N$. The covariant matrix of these training features can be calculated by Eq. 5:

$$C = \frac{1}{N}\sum_{n=1}^{N}(A_n - \overline{A})^T(A_n - \overline{A}) \quad (5)$$

where $\overline{A}$ is the mean vector of all training feature vectors. Next, the eigenvectors of the covariant matrix C is computed, and the top k eigenvectors are used as PCA basis, denoted by $W = [\lambda_1, \lambda_2, ...\lambda_k]$. Based on the computed PCA basis W, the high-dimensional scale-varied feature can be compacted as follows:

$$D_n = A_n * W, n = 1, 2, ..., N \quad (6)$$

In this paper, we set k=64, which means the compacted scale-varied feature of each image is 64-dimensinal.

Secondly, the similarity-preserving encoding method (*i.e.*, ITQ [6, 7]) is performed on the compacted decimal feature to obtain the binary codes, which will further improve the retrieval speed on the basis of feature compacting. Although the search speed is one important benchmark in image retrieval, the high retrieval accuracy is another principal target, which requires the quantization loss in encoding to be as less as possible to preserve the discrimination of the compacted scale-varied feature.

In considering of both retrieval efficiency and retrieval accuracy, a similarity-preserving encoding method is employed, which minimizes the quantization loss and preserves the similarity between the compacted feature and the encoded binary pattern by rotating the images. More specifically, the rotation of an image matrix is achieved by the multiplication of the matric and an orthogonal matrix. If the encoded binary codes and the orthogonal rotation matrix are denoted by B and R, the similarity-preserving binary codes can be obtained by minimizing the following objective function:

$$Q(B, R) = ||B - D * R||_F^2 \quad (7)$$

in which $D = [D_1, D_2, ..., D_n]$ is the compacted scale-varied feature of all training images, and $|| \bullet ||_F$ is the Frobenius norm. And the objective function is solved by alternating minimization algorithm, in which R is randomly initialized firstly, and then in each iteration, two alternating steps are performed, *i.e.*, 1) fix R and update B; 2) fix B and update R. Based on the learned orthogonal rotation matrix, each image can be encoded with the minimized quantization loss, resulting in a 64-dimensional binary retrieval codes.

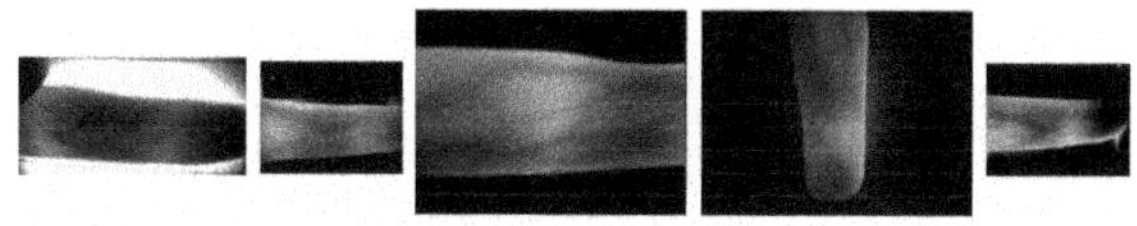

Figure 5: Typical finger vein images. Images in (a)-(d) are separately from four public databases and the one in (e) is from SDUD database.

3 EXPERIMENTS

In this section, we compare the proposed method and the state-of-the-art methods in terms of retrieval accuracy and retrieval efficiency, and also evaluate the robustness of our method on one deformation database and the adaption of our method to other descriptor.

3.1 Database and Experiment Settings

In order to comprehensively evaluate the performance of the proposed retrieval method, the experiments are conducted on six finger vein databases. There are four public databases, including POLYU [9], SDUMLA [25], MMCBNU [12] and FVUSM [2]. And the other two databases are the fusion database [21], built by integrating the above four public databases, and ourselves-built deformation database, named SDUD. In SDUD, there are largely relative variations (*e.g.*, image translation, image rotation and so on) between genuine images. The details of these six databases are given in Table 2, and the typical images are shown in Fig. 5.

As the state-of-the-art biometrics related image retrieval literatures [8, 17], the retrieval performance is evaluated by the most popular retrieval accuracy and penetration rate. The retrieval accuracy is defined as the ratio of the probe images, whose enrolled genuine images are correctly retrieved, to all probe images. And it can be formally represented by Formula 8.

$$\text{Retrieval accuracy} = \frac{\mathrm{N_a}}{\mathrm{N}} \quad (8)$$

where N is the total number of probe images and N_a is the number of probe images for which the correct identities are given in the retrieval candidate list. In addition, the penetration rate denotes the average ratio of retrieved enrolled images to all enrolled images in the database for all probe images,

$$\textit{Penetration}\ \text{rate} = \frac{1}{N}\sum_{i=1}^{N}\frac{L_i}{M} \quad (9)$$

where M is the total number of enrolled images in database and L_i represents the number of enrolled images retrieved in the candidate list for the ith probe image. In all, an effective retrieval scheme will achieve high retrieval accuracy and low penetration rate.

Additionally, in the experiments, we take each finger as one identity and the average retrieval performance in six-fold cross validation on public and fusion databases and eight-fold cross validation on deformation database is reported. All experiments are conducted in MATLAB on a PC with Intel

Table 2: Six finger vein databases used in experiments

Database	Finger number	Image number per finger	Image size(pixels)
POLYU [9]	312	6/12	513*256
SDUMLA [25]	636	6	320*240
MMCBNU [12]	492	12	640*480
FVUSM [2]	600	12	640*480
FUSIOND	2040	6	96*64
SDUD	57	8	320*240

Table 3: Retrieval accuracy (%) of proposed methods with different scale features

LBP histogram	POLYU	SDUMLA	FVUSM	MMCBNU	FUSIOND
8 bins	71.15	71.17	80.72	48.64	56.64
16 bins	77.94	80.32	83.16	52.81	64.55
24 bins	80.93	81.29	83.74	56.33	65.18
Scale-varied	100	99.94	100	100	99.88

i7-4790 3.60GHz CPU and 8.00G memory. Moreover, the region of interest (ROI) used in the experiments are cropped from finger vein images by the methods in Refs. [9, 13, 24] and normalized into 96×64 pixels. And local binary pattern (LBP) [11] (in Section 3.2-3.5) and Weber Local Descriptor (WLD) [3] (in Section 3.6) are separately used as local feature to represent each superpixel.

3.2 Comparison with Single Scale Feature

To prove the advantage of the proposed scale-varied feature, its comparison with single scale feature is performed on four public databases and the fusion database. Three single scale features are considered, *i.e.*, 8 bins-LBP histogram, 16 bins-LBP histogram and 24 bins-LBP histogram. And the proposed similarity-preserving encoding is performed for each kind of feature to generate the 64 bits-binary retrieval codes. The retrieval accuracies, based on top 5 candidates, of different features are reported in Table 3.

The table shows that, compared with the single scale features, the proposed scale-varied feature improves the retrieval accuracy significantly on these five considered databases. There may be two potential reasons. Firstly, relatively large histogram in scale-varied feature is more effective in representation of the superpixels with vein pattern. Secondly, the category of superpixel is hidden in the scale-varied features, which is also helpful for the improvement of the retrieval performance. And it also can be observed that the retrieval accuracy is gradually improved with the increment of the feature dimension (*i.e.*, the bin number of LBP histogram). The main reason is that the high dimensional histogram has more powerful describing ability, and can explore more discriminative information.

3.3 Comparison with State-of-the-arts

Here, the retrieval performance of the proposed method and the state-of-the-arts [20, 21] are evaluated on the fusion database. The used image feature and encoding method are both different in three involved retrieval methods. The penetration rate-retrieval accuracy curves of these methods are illustrated

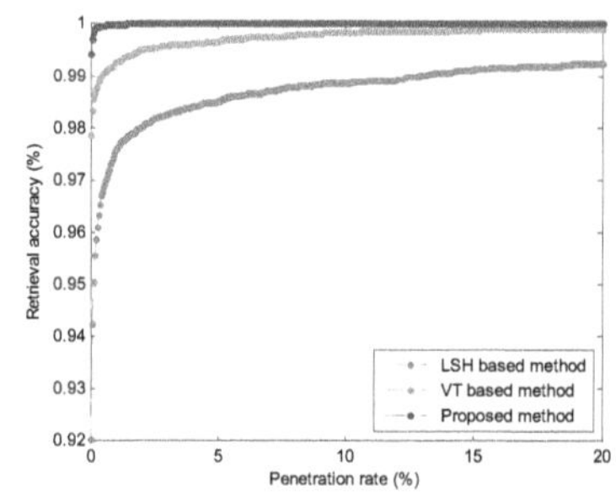

Figure 6: Comparison between proposed method and two state-of-the-arts on fusion database

in Fig. 6. It can be easily seen from the figure that, the proposed scale-varied feature and similarity-preserving encoding combined retrieval method achieves the best performance on the large fusion database. The best performance is mainly attributed to the powerful and discriminative superpixel feature and quantization loss-minimalized encoding method. More specifically, neighboring pixels with similar gray values are grouped into one superpixel, and this kind of local consistent image patch is more powerful than image block in the representation of finger vein image. What's more, in scale-varied feature, the superpixels with vein pattern are represented by large scale histogram than others, which can explore more discriminative information. And the category of superpixel, hidden in scale-varied feature, also increases the discrimination of retrieval feature. In other words, the number of vein points in LSH based method and the 16-bins LBP histogram in VT based method is both inferior to the proposed scale-varied feature in exploring discriminative information. Last, the similarity-preserving encoding minimalizes the quantization loss and keeps the discrimination of retrieval feature, but the encoding in two existing methods (*i.e.*, binarization and nearest leaf node searching), cause the larger quantization loss, and suppress the discrimination of the retrieval feature.

Table 4: Retrieval time (s) of different methods on fusion database

Method	Feature extraction	Encoding	Candidate selection	Total time
LSH based method [20]	0.9616	3.77e-04	0.0328	0.9944
VT based method [21]	0.0158	0.0175	0.1016	0.1349
Proposed method	0.0212	0.0193	0.0038	0.0443

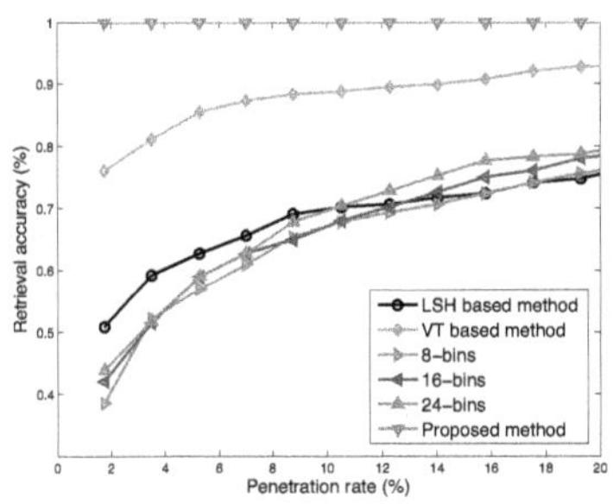

Figure 7: Comparison of proposed methods with different scale features and two old methods on deformation database

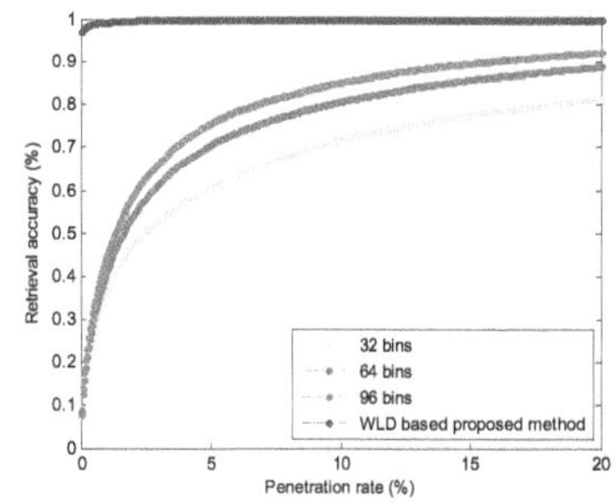

Figure 8: Retrieval performance of WLD based retrieval methods on fusion database

3.4 Computational Time Measurement

We discuss the retrieval efficiency of three involved methods. For one image, the computational time in three steps, *i.e.*, feature extraction, encoding and candidate selection, is measured. And the average time cost of every image in the fusion database is shown in Table 4. The table indicates that the proposed method outperforms two state-of-the-arts on the retrieval efficiency. The LSH based method spends much more time than our method and VT based one, and the time is mainly cost in repeated line tracking based vein pattern extraction. Generally, in order to extract plentiful vein pattern, the predefined tracking times is very large, which causes big time cost. Additionally, in comparison of VT based method and the proposed method, the former method pays more time cost in candidate selection. The extremely long retrieval codes in VT based method are the main reason, As the same exhaustive matching in Hamming space is used to list candidate in two methods. In detail, the dimension of the codes in the three layer and three branches based vocabulary tree is 39×96 for one image, but it is only 64 in the proposed method. Besides, the proposed method spends more time in feature extraction than other two methods, and it mainly caused by the additional superpixel classification.

3.5 Robustness to Image Deformation

To verify the robustness of our method to relative variations in genuine images, the retrieval performance of different methods is evaluated on ourselves-built deformation finger vein database (*i.e.*, SDUD database). The experimental results of different methods are shown by the penetration rate-retrieval accuracy curves in Figure 7. And the experiment results show that the proposed retrieval method not only outperforms two state-of-the-art methods but also achieves better performance than single scale feature based methods, which is same as the performance on the public and fusion databases. More importantly, the performance improvement on deformation database is larger than it on public and fusion databases, and it indicates that expect from more discriminative feature and less quantization loss, the proposed method has more robustness than other methods to the image deformation. On one side, superpixel is robust than the rectangular image block. In other words, the pixels in two images, which are with similar gray values but relative position variation, can be grouped into two corresponding superpixels, but may be divided into multiple rectangular blocks without correspondence. One other side, the better retrieval performance of scale-varied feature is also attributed to the hidden superpixels category and the contribution of superpixels in each category. In detail, the contribution of one kind of superpixels is likely to be similar in genuine images, but it in imposter images may be totally different.

3.6 Adaption Ability to Other Descriptor

Other descriptor (*e.g.*, weber local descriptor (WLD) [3]), instead of LBP descriptor, is used in this experiment to demonstrate the universality of the proposed method. Here, the superpixels in one image is also classified into three groups according to the variance of the frequency numbers in 32 bins-WLD histogram, and superpixels in each group are separately represented by 32 bins-histogram, 64 bins-histogram and 96 bins-histogram. The scale-varied WLD histogram based retrieval method is compared with three single scale histogram based methods, and the experimental results are illustrated in Fig. 8. It can be noted that with the increase of the number of bins in histogram, the retrieval accuracy is improved. More importantly, the scale-varied WLD retrieval feature achieves better performance than other single scale WLD features, which is similar to the performance of LBP feature. So, this experiment proves the adaption of the proposed retrieval method to other descriptor in some degree.

4 CONCLUSIONS

This paper proposes a novel finger vein image retrieval method for large scale identity authentication applications, which is based on scale-varied feature and similarity-preserving encoding. The main contributions of this paper consist of four points. First, considering the difference in the discrimination of image patches (*i.e.*, superpixel), scale-varied feature is proposed to powerfully represent all kinds of superpixels. The discrimination information of each superpixel is deeply explored by this feature, and the hidden category and distribution of superpixels further enhance its representation ability. Second, the quantization loss minimized encoding method used in this paper can greatly preserve the similarity of the scale-varied feature and the encoded binary patterns. In other words, the combination of scale-varied feature and similarity-preserving encoding can generate very discriminative retrieval codes. Third, ahead of encoding, the scale-varied feature is compacted, which is helpful for improving the retrieval efficiency. Last, the experimental results show that, the proposed method outperforms the state-of-the-arts, and has large robustness to image deformation and desirable adaption ability to other image descriptors.

However, it is a pity that the superpixel category is given according to the variance of frequency number in its feature histogram. In other words, the superpixel classification is feature-dependent. How to classify the superpixels independently is one worthy future work.

ACKNOWLEDGMENTS

The authors would also like to thank the anonymous reviewers for their valuable comments and helpful suggestions. The work is supported by the National Science Foundation of China under Grant No.: 61472226,61573219 and National Science Foundation of China Joint Fund with Guangdong under Key Project under Grant No.: U1201258.

REFERENCES

[1] Radhakrishna Achanta, Appu Shaji, Kevin Smith, Aurelien Lucchi, Pascal Fua, and Sabine Süsstrunk. 2012. SLIC superpixels compared to state-of-the-art superpixel methods. *IEEE transactions on pattern analysis and machine intelligence* 34, 11 (2012), 2274–2282.

[2] Mohd Shahrimie Mohd Asaari, Shahrel A Suandi, and Bakhtiar Affendi Rosdi. 2014. Fusion of band limited phase only correlation and width centroid contour distance for finger based biometrics. *Expert Systems with Applications* 41, 7 (2014), 3367–3382.

[3] Jie Chen, Shiguang Shan, Chu He, Guoying Zhao, Matti Pietikainen, Xilin Chen, and Wen Gao. 2010. WLD: A robust local image descriptor. *IEEE transactions on pattern analysis and machine intelligence* 32, 9 (2010), 1705–1720.

[4] Lumei Dong, Gongping Yang, Yilong Yin, Fei Liu, and Xiaoming Xi. 2014. Finger vein verification based on a personalized best patches map. In *Biometrics (IJCB), 2014 IEEE International Joint Conference on*. IEEE, 1–8.

[5] Lumei Dong, Gongping Yang, Yilong Yin, Xiaoming Xi, Lu Yang, and Fei Liu. 2015. Finger vein verification with vein textons. *International Journal of Pattern Recognition and Artificial Intelligence* 29, 04 (2015), 1556003.

[6] Yunchao Gong and Svetlana Lazebnik. 2011. Iterative quantization: A procrustean approach to learning binary codes. In *Computer Vision and Pattern Recognition (CVPR), 2011 IEEE Conference on*. IEEE, 817–824.

[7] Yunchao Gong, Svetlana Lazebnik, Albert Gordo, and Florent Perronnin. 2013. Iterative quantization: A procrustean approach to learning binary codes for large-scale image retrieval. *IEEE Transactions on Pattern Analysis and Machine Intelligence* 35, 12 (2013), 2916–2929.

[8] Aglika Gyaourova and Arun Ross. 2012. Index codes for multibiometric pattern retrieval. *IEEE transactions on information forensics and security* 7, 2 (2012), 518–529.

[9] Ajay Kumar and Yingbo Zhou. 2012. Human identification using finger images. *IEEE Transactions on Image Processing* 21, 4 (2012), 2228–2244.

[10] Fei Liu, Gongping Yang, Yilong Yin, and Shuaiqiang Wang. 2014. Singular value decomposition based minutiae matching method for finger vein recognition. *Neurocomputing* 145 (2014), 75–89.

[11] Fei Liu, Yilong Yin, Gongping Yang, Lumei Dong, and Xiaoming Xi. 2014. Finger vein recognition with superpixel-based features. In *Biometrics (IJCB), 2014 IEEE International Joint Conference on*. IEEE, 1–8.

[12] Yu Lu, Shan Juan Xie, Sook Yoon, Zhihui Wang, and Dong Sun Park. 2013. An available database for the research of finger vein recognition. In *Image and Signal Processing (CISP), 2013 6th International Congress on*, Vol. 1. IEEE, 410–415.

[13] Yu Lu, Shan Juan Xie, Sook Yoon, Jucheng Yang, and Dong Sun Park. 2013. Robust finger vein ROI localization based on flexible segmentation. *Sensors* 13, 11 (2013), 14339–14366.

[14] Naoto Miura, Akio Nagasaka, and Takafumi Miyatake. 2004. Feature extraction of finger-vein patterns based on repeated line tracking and its application to personal identification. *Machine Vision and Applications* 15, 4 (2004), 194–203.

[15] Naoto Miura, Akio Nagasaka, and Takafumi Miyatake. 2007. Extraction of finger-vein patterns using maximum curvature points in image profiles. *IEICE TRANSACTIONS on Information and Systems* 90, 8 (2007), 1185–1194.

[16] R Raghavendra, Jayachander Surbiryala, and Christoph Busch. 2015. An efficient finger vein indexing scheme based on unsupervised clustering. In *Identity, Security and Behavior Analysis (ISBA), 2015 IEEE International Conference on*. IEEE, 1–8.

[17] Yijing Su, Jianjiang Feng, and Jie Zhou. 2016. Fingerprint indexing with pose constraint. *Pattern Recognition* 54 (2016), 1–13.

[18] Jayachander Surbiryala, R Raghavendra, and Christoph Busch. 2015. Finger vein indexing based on binary features. In *Colour and Visual Computing Symposium (CVCS), 2015*. IEEE, 1–6.

[19] Dun Tan, Jinfeng Yang, Yihua Shi, and Chenghua Xu. 2013. A Hierarchal Framework for Finger-Vein Image Classification. In *2013 2nd IAPR Asian Conference on Pattern Recognition*. IEEE, 833–837.

[20] Darun Tang, Beining Huang, Rongfeng Li, and Wenxin Li. 2010. A person retrieval solution using finger vein patterns. In *Pattern Recognition (ICPR), 2010 20th International Conference on*. IEEE, 1306–1309.

[21] Kuikui Wang, Lu Yang, Kun Su, Gongping Yang, and Yilong Yin. 2016. Binary search path of vocabulary tree based finger vein image retrieval. In *Biometrics (ICB), 2016 International Conference on*. IEEE, 1–8.

[22] Jian-Da Wu and Chiung-Tsiung Liu. 2011. Finger-vein pattern identification using principal component analysis and the neural network technique. *Expert Systems with Applications* 38, 5 (2011), 5423–5427.

[23] Xiaoming Xi, Gongping Yang, Yilong Yin, and Lu Yang. 2014. Finger vein recognition based on the hyperinformation feature. *Optical Engineering* 53, 1 (2014), 013108–013108.

[24] Lu Yang, Gongping Yang, Yilong Yin, and Rongyang Xiao. 2013. Sliding window-based region of interest extraction for finger vein images. *Sensors* 13, 3 (2013), 3799–3815.

[25] Yilong Yin, Lili Liu, and Xiwei Sun. 2011. SDUMLA-HMT: a multimodal biometric database. In *Chinese Conference on Biometric Recognition*. Springer, 260–268.

[26] Lizhen Zhou, Gongping Yang, Yilong Yin, Lu Yang, and Kuikui Wang. 2016. Finger Vein Recognition Based on Stable and Discriminative Superpixels. *International Journal of Pattern Recognition and Artificial Intelligence* 30, 06 (2016), 1650015.

Joint Saliency Estimation and Matching using Image Regions for Geo-Localization of Online Video

Haoyue Shi
School of Electronics Engineering and Computer Science, Peking University
No.5 Yiheyuan Road
Beijing, P. R. China 100871
hyshi@pku.edu.cn

Jia Chen*
Language Technologies Institute, Carnegie Mellon University
5000 Forbes Avenue
Pittsburgh, PA, USA 15213
jiac@cs.cmu.edu

Alexander G. Hauptmann
Language Technologies Institute, Carnegie Mellon University
5000 Forbes Avenue
Pittsburgh, PA, USA 15213
alex@cs.cmu.edu

Abstract

In this paper, we study automatic geo-localization of online event videos. Different from general image localization task through matching, the appearance of an environment during significant events varies greatly from its daily appearance, since there are usually crowds, decorations or even destruction when a major event happens. This introduces a major challenge: matching the event environment to the daily environment, e.g. as recorded by Google Street View. We observe that some regions in the image, as part of the environment, still preserve the daily appearance even though the whole image (environment) looks quite different. Based on this observation, we formulate the problem as joint saliency estimation and matching at the image region level, as opposed to the key point or whole-image level. As image-level labels of daily environment are easily generated with GPS information, we treat region based saliency estimation and matching as a weakly labeled learning problem over the training data. Our solution is to iteratively optimize saliency and the region-matching model. For saliency optimization, we derive a closed form solution, which has an intuitive explanation. For region matching model optimization, we use self-paced learning to learn from the pseudo labels generated by (sub-optimal) saliency values. We conduct extensive experiments on two challenging public datasets: Boston Marathon 2013 and Tokyo Time Machine. Experimental results show that our solution significantly improves over matching on whole images and the automatically learned saliency is a strong predictor of distinctive building areas.

CCS Concepts

• **Information systems** → **Multimedia and multimodal retrieval**; *Image search*; *Video search*; • **Computer systems organization** → Neural networks;

Keywords

Video Geo-Localization, Region Saliency, Region Matching

*Jia Chen is the corresponding author

ICMR '17, June 06-09, 2017, Bucharest, Romania

ACM ISBN 978-1-4503-4701-3/17/06...$15.00
https://doi.org/http://dx.doi.org/10.1145/3078971.3078996

ACM Reference format:
Haoyue Shi, Jia Chen, and Alexander G. Hauptmann. 2017. Joint Saliency Estimation and Matching using Image Regions for Geo-Localization of Online Video. In *Proceedings of ICMR '17, Bucharest, Romania, June 06-09, 2017,* 9 pages.
https://doi.org/http://dx.doi.org/10.1145/3078971.3078996

1 Introduction

The popular smartphones with high quality cameras have enabled people to capture events all over the world by videos and share them via social media conveniently. When an event happens, different cameras may record it at different positions from different perspectives of view. For example, videos from surveillance cameras usually record the event from a fixed location from an aerial (usually 45-degree from top to down) view; videos from television reporters usually cover the event in a rather professional perspective (helicopter view or first person view) at major locations; the videos from passers-by usually capture event from a personal perspective at side locations that are often not covered by the news reporters. On the one hand, finding the location of the video content is the basic and essential element behind various event analysis tasks such as cross camera person tracking and scene reconstruction. On the other hand, unlike EXIF meta-data in images, most of the videos shared online do not come with GPS information together.

In this paper, we study the problem of automatic event video localization. The input of event video localization is the query, event video, and the database, environment images with GPS information, which could be street view images if the event video is taken on the ground or satellite images if the event video involves a 45-degree view. The task is to geo-localize the event video by matching its content to the database. To be specific, event video and environment images belong to two different domains and this is actually a cross-domain matching problem.

Abundant research works have been conducted in a related problem: general image localization through matching[1, 2, 7, 9] on public image datasets such as Paris dataset[18] and Oxford building[17]. Most of the query images in these datasets are photos of the landmarks in regular days. However, the appearance of the location could change a lot when an event happens. Here we give an example of location appearance change: Boston Marathon 2013 finish line explosion event. As shown in Figure 1, the appearance of the finish line (near the Boston Public Library) was quite different from the regular day appearance: additional audience stands were added to the sidewalk and blue end banner was raised. When an event happens, e.g. parade, protest or attack, the appearance of the district is usually changed to some extent by either manual decoration or manual destruction. Thus, such dramatic appearance change is very common and unneglectable in event video localization task. To the best of our knowledge, the only public dataset that is built to take into account large appearance change is the Tokyo Time Machine (Tokyo TM) dataset[1]. However, it only contains daily street view images while the variety in event videos is much larger, including both 45 degree view and street view on event days.

Figure 1: Comparison between the satellite image (regular appearance) and the video appearance of the place near Boston Public Library (the finish line of Boston Marathon 2013). The regions in red frames are salient, while those in blue frames are non-salient.

The major challenge of event video localization lies in cross-domain large appearance change. We observe that despite the large appearance change of the whole environment during the event, certain parts of the environment preserves their daily environment appearance. That is, though the whole appearance of each frame is quite different from daily environment image, some regions in a frame are similar to the regions in the daily environment images. Based on this key observation, we formulate the task as a joint saliency estimation and matching problem, which simultaneously outputs the matching score and the matched region as supporting evidence. Such problem formulation benefits us in three aspects.

First, by explicitly introducing saliency estimation in the model, we are able to distinguish between meaningful matching and meaningless matching. For example, the matching between building areas across two images is meaningful since building areas are usually discernible for localization. The matching between road and tree areas across two images is meaningless since such matching could occur everywhere and is not helpful to localization. Saliency estimation helps to distinguish between these two types of matching and its result will be used to down-weight the meaningless matching and emphasize on meaningful matching in our joint model.

Second, joint modeling preserves the interdependency between saliency estimation and matching. Region saliency is actually domain dependent and depends to matching. For example, if a video frame region matches many irrelevant environment images district A , it is not reliable to localize the video in district A based on this frame region. That is, this video frame region is not salient in district A. Now consider the same video frame region but the environment images of a different district B. The same video frame region may only match a few relevant environment images in district B, which means that it is reliable to localize the video based on this frame region in district B. That is, the same video frame region turns to be salient in district B. In our solution, we capture such interdependency between saliency estimation and matching.

Third, addition output of matched region makes the system output more explainable. For example, when the system fails, the "matched" region will be shown to users that there is not enough discernible environment clues in the video content so that it fails reasonably. Given such supporting evidence, the users will be more likely to trust the system as they learn to know the capability limit of the system in their usage.

Our solution is composed of three components:

- *Automatic weak label generation:* we first generate the labels, which indicate whether two images are matched, by their GPS coordinate. If their distance in the GPS coordinate system is less than a threshold, we label them as matched, otherwise unmatched.
- *Saliency estimation with region matching fixed:* we derive a closed form solution for saliency value, which has an intuitive explanation.
- *Self-paced learning for region matching model:* we leverage self-paced learning to learn region matching model from pseudo labels generated by saliency estimation.

The contributions of this paper are threefold.

(1) We formulate the event video localization task as a region based joint saliency estimation and matching problem.
(2) We derive an iterative solution to the non-convex optimization problem, which is composed of two steps: closed form solution for saliency estimation and self-paced learning for region matching model.
(3) Our solution output is not only accurate but also interpretable by human beings.

The rest of the paper is organized as follows. Section 2 introduces related work. Section 3 formalizes the problem for the video event localization task. Section 4 gives the solution to the problem. Section 5 presents the experiment results. Section 6 draws some conclusions and the work in the future.

2 Related Work

As we have mentioned in Section 1, early work by Hays and Efros [9] revealed the feasibility of the image localization task. Zamir and Roshan [23] used SIFT descriptors for image localization by voting, and constructed a dataset based on Google Street-View to test the efficiency of the algorithm. Lin et al. [14] proposed the first ground-to-overhead geo-localization method, of which the key idea is to learn the relationship between the ground-level images and their over-head appearances. After that, Lin et al. [15] then published an approach by convolutional neural network(CNN) to learn deep representations for ground-to-overhead geo-localization. Vo and Hays [22] then explored several deep CNN architectures for the cross-domain matching and improved the accuracy of image geo-localization. What's more, Bansal et al. [3] proposed a method to capture the structure of self-similarity of patterns on facades for image geo-localization.

Leung et al. [13] designed a monocular vision based particle filter localization system for urban settings that uses aerial reference map. However, because of the great similarity between the task of image localization and video localization, researchers often treat them as the same task.

Visual place recognition is a similar task of image geo-localization. Arandjelovic et al. [1] developed NetVLAD, a CNN architecture of which the main component is the VLAD ("Vectors of Locally Aggregated Descriptors") layer and got the state-of-the-art performance on two challenging place recognition datasets.

While attention-based models are widely used in recognition tasks, many recent works show that attention-based model can improve the performance of machine learning models [16, 24]. The key idea of attention-based model is to add attention information to build a representation. This idea is intuitive. For example, when looking at an image, we human beings often recognize the objects on it and then receive the information from the background, rather than receiving information simultaneously from the foreground objects and background scenes. In our approach, we compute the attention to each region by its saliency.

In machine learning, a sequence of gradually added training samples [4] is called a curriculum. Inspired by the cognitive process of humans and animals, a straightforward way to generate such a sequence is to add samples based on their "easiness" to learn. However, such "easiness" is based on specific problem and hard to generalize. In order to solve this problem, Self-Paced Learning (SPL) was introduced by Kumar et al. [12], which embeds curriculum designing into model learning. In SPL, the curriculum is gradually generated by the model itself based on what it has learned, and it's also a general implementation for curriculum learning. Following that, several works have improved self-paced learning [10, 11, 20]. In this paper, we propose self-paced learning method to automatically estimate the saliency score for each region of a frame.

3 Problem Formulation

The event video localization task is to retrieve environment images from database given the query event video. The database images are automatically downloaded from online map service given a circle or rectangle shaped district where the event happened. If the video is taken on the ground, the database images will be Google street view images; if the video is taken from a 45 degree up to down perspective of view, the database images will be Google satellite images. The details of database image generation will be elaborated in section 4.

A query video is composed of frames $\{q\}$. As we process one frame per time in matching the database, we abbreviate one frame from the query video as query for the ease of representation. The environment image from the database is denoted as d and the database is denoted as $D = \{d\}$. We divide images into a three-level spatial pyramid of regions: 1×1, 2×2, 3×3 as shown in Figure 2. We assign each region a saliency score s to indicate how import the region is in matching. Please refer to Section 5 for region division details. We use subscript to represent region index. That is, we have saliency score $s(q_i)$ for region i in query q and $s(d_j)$ for region j in the database image d. We define the non-negative matching score between two regions as $m(q_i, d_j; \Theta)$, where Θ is the parameters to be learn. The similarity of two regions is proportional to their matching score. For the ease of notation, we will use $m(q_i, d_j; \Theta)$ and $m(q_i, d_j)$ interchangeably in the following.

Figure 2: The regions of an image

Now we have defined regions in the image, saliency score on regions and matching score between regions. Putting all these together, we define the matching score between query and database image as weighted sum of region matching scores:

$$M(q, d) = \sum_{i,j} w_{ij}\, m(q_i, d_j) \quad (1)$$

$$w_{ij} = s(q_i) + s(d_j) \quad (2)$$

where the weight w_{ij} is defined as the sum of saliency score of both regions. On the one hand, if both regions are salient and their matching score is high, such region pair contribute much to the final matching score $M(q, d)$. On the other hand, even if the matching score between two regions is high, but if both regions are not salient (e.g. road or tree), such region pair doesn't contribute much to the final matching score $M(q, d)$.

In the training stage, we automatically generate the labels of image pairs from database D by leveraging the GPS information assigned to each environment image. The label $y_{(q,d)}$ of image q and d is 1 if two images are matched and 0 vice versa. The training data is denoted as:

$$\begin{gathered} D_{train} = \{(q, d, y_{(q,d)})\} \\ q \in D, d \in D \end{gathered} \quad (3)$$

The details of automatically generating D_{train} from D are given in section 4. Note that the labels are given on image pairs rather than region pairs. As the matching model $m(q_i, d_j; \Theta)$ is defined on region pair, the labels are actually weak labels. We use contrastive noise loss function as $L(q, d, y)$:

$$\begin{aligned} L(q, d, y) &= L_P(q, d, y) + L_N(q, d, y) \\ L_P(q, d, y) &= -y \sum_{y_{(q,d)}=1} M(q, d) \\ L_N(q, d, y) &= -(1-y) \sum_{y_{(q,d)}=0} \max(0, \Delta - M(q, d)) \end{aligned} \quad (4)$$

where Δ is a hyper-parameter to keep unmatched pairs having small matching scores, L_P is the loss function for matched pairs, L_N is the loss function for unmatched pairs. We use eq (1) to expand image matching $M(q,d)$ term in the loss function:

$$\begin{aligned} L(q,d,y) &= -y \sum_{y_{(q,d)}=1} M(q,d) - (1-y) \sum_{y_{(q,d)}=0} \max(0, \Delta - M(q,d)) \\ &= -y \sum_{i,j} \sum_{y_{(q,d)}=1} w_{ij}\, m(q_i,d_j) \\ &\quad - (1-y) \sum_{i,j} \sum_{y_{(q,d)}=0} w_{ij} \max(0, \Delta' - m(q_i,d_j)) \\ &= \underbrace{\sum_{i,j} w_{ij} L_P(q_i,d_j)}_{L_P(q,d)} + \underbrace{\sum_{i,j} w_{ij} L_N(q_i,d_j)}_{L_N(q,d)} \end{aligned} \tag{5}$$

In the last step substitution, we denote

$$\begin{aligned} L_P(q_i,d_j,y) &= -y \sum_{i,j} \sum_{y_{(q,d)}=1} m(q_i,d_j) \\ L_N(q_i,d_j,y) &= -(1-y) \sum_{i,j} \sum_{y_{(q,d)}=0} \max(0, \Delta' - m(q_i,d_j)) \end{aligned} \tag{6}$$

The last step in eq (6) shows that the two components in image level loss, $L_P(q,d,y)$ and $L_N(q,d,y)$, are weighted sum of the two components in region level loss, $L_P(q_i,d_j,y)$ and $L_N(q_i,d_j,y)$, respectively. Furthermore, if we consider the region level label to be the same as its corresponding image level label, i.e. $y_{(q_i,d_j)} = y_{(q,d)}$, we could see that region level loss $L_P(q_i,d_j,y)$, $L_N(q_i,d_j,y)$ in eq (5) has exactly the same form of image level loss $L_P(q,d,y)$, $L_N(q,d,y)$ in eq (4). However, recall that the major challenge in event video localization, large appearance change, leads to the fact that $y_{(q,d)} = 1$ doesn't imply that $y_{(q_i,d_j)} = 1, \forall q_i \in q, \forall d_j \in d$. In our problem formulation, we solve this issue by multiplying a region pair dependent weight w_{ij} to each region level loss $L_P(q_i,d_j)$. Note that w_{ij} is defined by saliency $s(q_i)$ and $s(d_j)$. That is, we could suppress the influence of "wrong" region level label to the final loss function through saliency.

We recap all the above deduction into one main problem.

main problem:

$$\begin{aligned} min_{S,\Theta} L(q,d,y;S,\Theta) &= -y \sum_{i,j} \sum_{y_{(q,d)}=1} w_{ij}\, m(q_i,d_j;\Theta) \\ &\quad - (1-y) \sum_{i,j} \sum_{y_{(q,d)}=0} w_{ij} \max(\Delta' - m(q_i,d_j;\Theta)) \\ w_{ij} &= s(q_i) + s(d_j) \\ s.t. &\ ||s(q)||_2 = 1 \quad \forall q \\ &\ ||s(d)||_2 = 1 \quad \forall d \\ &\ s(q_i), s(d_j) \in [0,1] \\ &\ y \in \{+1, 0\} \end{aligned}$$

The notations introduced in this section are summarized in table 1.

q_i	region i in the query image q
d_j	region j in the database image d
$s(q_i), s(d_j)$	the saliency of the region q_i, d_j
$m(q_i,d_j)$	non-negative matching score between region q_i and d_j

Table 1: Notations introduced in this section.

Figure 3: An example for collecting training data with Google Map.

4 Solution

The main problem is non-convex and very difficult to optimize. One typical solution is to use cyclic coordinate method (CCM)[8]. To be specific, we iteratively optimize the objective function by fixing S with respect to Θ and vice versa. The major problem in such approach is that the quality of the solution depends highly on the initialization as it converges to a local minimum. To be specific, if we get a good estimation of S, it is relatively easy to get a good solution for Θ as the final loss function puts more emphasis on the correct region pair matching and vice versa. Thus, we propose a region based joint model on saliency estimation and region matching for training.

4.1 Cyclic Coordinate Training

Our pipeline is composed of five main steps:

1. *Image level (weak) label generation.* In this step, we generate the weak labels based on GPS information automatically. Google Map provides satellite images, as well as street view images, together with their GPS information to users, so that we can download them conveniently as database. Figure 3 (color masked) shows the region that our database for Boston dataset (introduced in Section 5) covers. The colored masks are drawn by Google Map automatically, indicating the buildings. After the generation of our database, we sample images in the range that the database covers randomly. Google Map provides four different perspectives of view from each point. If we just move the sampling point a little, the image with the same perspective would not change a lot. Thus, we can get two different images containing almost the same scene, and that is the rationality of our method to generate weak labels automatically. More specifically, we use Euclidean distance to judge whether two sampling points are near to each other. We set the matching label of two images q, d using

$$y_{(q,d)} = \begin{cases} 1 & dist(q,d) \le \theta \\ 0 & dist(q,d) > \theta \end{cases} \tag{7}$$

where q is the sampled image, d is the image from our database, $dist(q,d)$ is the Euclidean distance between the locations of q and d in the real world, θ is a hyper-parameter that denotes the distance threshold of matching. In addition, by zooming, rotating and shifting, we can augment our database to let it contain images with larger diversity. Thus, we have completed the generation of training data D_{train}. For database generation, we set $\theta = 25m$.

2. *Initialization of matching model.* In this step, we choose a good initialization of matching model. The maching model is a weighted Siamese network for region matching as shown in Figure 4. We will elaborate more details in step 4. The initialization is done by starting from the degenerate case where the entire image is treated as one region. In this case, the region pairs are exactly image pairs

(q, d); region pair labels are the exactly image pair labels $y_{(q,d)}$; w_{ij} is set to 1.

3. *Saliency Estimation.* Apply the matching model $m(q_i, d_j; \Theta)$ on regions and optimize the main problem with respect to saliency S. This problem can be decomposed to $|Q| + |D|$ separate linear objective quadratic constraint convex optimization problems:

$$\begin{aligned} \max_{s(q)} & \sum_{q_i \in q} (m_{i\cdot}^+ - m_{i\cdot}^-) s(q_i) \\ s.t. & ||\mathbf{s}(q)||_2 = 1 \\ & s(q_i) \in [0, 1] \end{aligned} \tag{8}$$

where

$$m_{i\cdot}^+ = \sum_{\{d_j | y(q_i, d_j) = 1\}} m(q_i, d_j)$$
$$m_{i\cdot}^- = \sum_{\{d_j | y(q_i, d_j) = 0\}} \min(0, m(q_i, d_j) - \Delta')$$

We can add the other $|D|$ formulas with respect to d analogously. This problem has closed form solution:

$$\begin{aligned} \mathbf{m}_q &= [\dots, m_{i\cdot}^+ - m_{i\cdot}^-, \dots] \geq \mathbf{0} \\ \hat{\mathbf{s}}(q) &= \frac{\mathbf{m}_q}{||\mathbf{m_q}||_2} \end{aligned} \tag{9}$$

Here, $m_{i\cdot}^+, m_{i\cdot}^-$ correspond to the matching status of q_i to regions in positive labels and those in negative labels. Note that $m(q_i, d_j)$ is always non-negative due to our constraint in the section of problem formulation, $m_{i\cdot}^+$ is always non-negative and $m_{i\cdot}^-$ is always non-positive. Hence, we have the solution vector $\mathbf{m}_q = [\dots, m_{i\cdot}^+ - m_{i\cdot}^-, \dots] \geq \mathbf{0}$. Analogously, we can compute the solution for $\hat{\mathbf{s}}(d)$.

The solution saliency $\hat{\mathbf{S}} = \{\hat{\mathbf{s}}(q)\} \cup \{\hat{\mathbf{s}}(d)\}$ can be used to generate pseudo labels on region level. The label is called "pseudo" because we fix the parameter Θ from an imperfect matching model $m(q_i, d_j; \Theta)$ to get the solution.

With the hypothesis that different parts of a building would not look very different, if an image pair (q, d) is labelled as matched, then the pair of salient regions (q_i, d_j) with high $s(q_i)$ and $s(d_j)$ should be matched with high level confidence. Oppositely, if an image pair (q, d) is labelled as unmatched, the pair of salient regions (q_i, d_j) with high $s(q_i)$ and $s(d_j)$ should be unmatched with high level confidence, too. Thus, we use Eq (2) (i.e. the sum of $s(q_i)$ and $s(d_j)$) to measure the confidence of the pseudo label $y_{(q,d)}$ for region pair (q_i, d_j). For simplification, here we threshold on the confidence w_{ij} of pseudo label $y_{(q,d)}$ to get positive region pair label. We will give a formal treatment of the mathematical rationale behind thresholding in section 4.2. All the region pairs from negative image pair is considered as negative region pairs.

4. *Region based matching optimization.* Given the region pair labels generated in step 3, we could rewrite the loss function in eq (6) as:

$$L(q_i, d_j, y) = \sum_{y_{(q_i, d_j)} = 1} w_{ij} \cdot y_{(q_i, d_j)} \cdot m(q_i, d_j) + \tag{10}$$

$$\sum_{y_{(q_i, d_j)} = 0} w_{ij} (1 - y_{(q_i, d_j)}) \cdot \max(0, \Delta' - m(q_i, d_j)) \tag{11}$$

, which is actually a pairwise weighted version of the vanilla siamese region matching model.

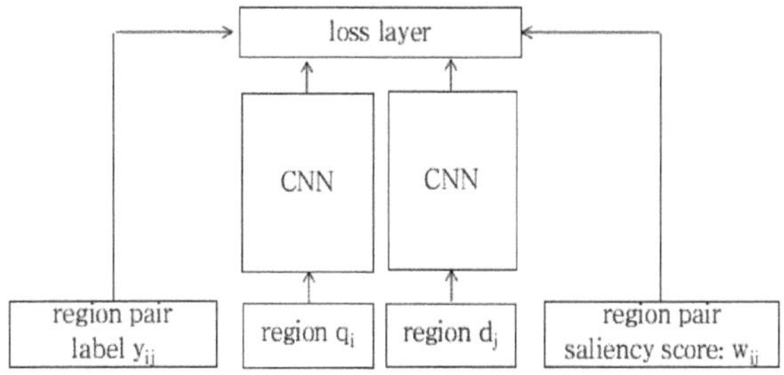

Figure 4: Region matching model in step 4

5. We repeat step 3 and step 4 and gradually lower the confidence level for the pseudo label as the model becomes more and more accurate and we could rely on more region pair labels generated.

4.2 Self-paced Training

In fact, the confidence lowering procedure in step 5 could be controlled by a pace function[11] on w_{ij} and we could justify the mathematical rationale behind our pipeline by self-paced learning. In self-paced learning, a pace function $f(\mathbf{w}; k)$ determines a learning scheme, where k increases with the learning step number to control the learning pace.

In the pace function, it is required that $||\mathbf{w}||_1$ increases with respect to pace step k, which means that we'll select more region pairs for training as the learning step number increases. Adding the pace function to the loss function in eq (6), we get:

$$L(q, d, y, k) = \sum_{y_{(q_i, d_j)} = 1} w_{ij} L_P(q_i, d_j) + \sum_{y(q_i, d_j) = 0} w_{ij} L_N(q_i, d_j) + f(\mathbf{w}; k) \tag{12}$$

This is the self-paced version loss of the *main problem.* Here we use the typical linear scheme pace function:

$$f(\mathbf{w}; k) = -\frac{1}{k} ||\mathbf{w}||_1 \tag{13}$$

The solution to the self-paced version doesn't change for steps 1 and 2 as they don't touch the loss function. Step 3 has only one minor change in the loss function of its subproblem (8):

$$\max_{s(q)} \sum_{q_i \in q} (m_{i\cdot}^+ - m_{i\cdot}^- - \underbrace{1/k}_{\text{change}}) s(q_i) \tag{14}$$

Its closed form solution also changes correspondingly:

$$\begin{aligned} m_q^i &= \begin{cases} m_i^+ - m_i^- - \frac{1}{k} & \text{if } m_i^+ - m_i^- > \frac{1}{k} \\ 0 & \text{if } m_i^+ - m_i^- <= \frac{1}{k} \end{cases} \\ \hat{s}(q) &= \frac{m_q}{||m_q||_2} \end{aligned} \tag{15}$$

We see that the solution is actually soft thresholding on the $s(q_i)$. We have solution in the same form for $\mathbf{s}(d)$. As $w_{ij} = s(q_i) + s(d_j)$, thresholding on $s(q_i)$ and $s(d_j)$ equals to thresholding on w_{ij}. Step 4 remains unchanged as it fixes variable w.

In summary, our method can be described as Algorithm 1.

4.3 Inference

After refining the matching model, we propose a corresponding region-based metric to measure the similarity between two images q and d, which is

$$sim_R(q, d) = -\sum_{q_i \in q} \min_{d_j \in d} \frac{|q_i|}{|q|} w_{ij} ||f(q_i) - f(d_j)||_2 \tag{16}$$

Algorithm 1 Joint Saliency Estimation and Matching Optimization

input: training dataset D_{train}, pre-trained matching model parameters Θ, self-paced function f and stepsize μ
output: saliency score S and region matching model Θ^*

```
Initialize S, k and the matching model Θ* = Θ
while not converged do
    Estimate saliency score with Eq (9)
    Select "easy" region level positive labels by thresholding on
    s(q_i) and s(d_j) using Eq (15)
    Refine Θ* with the loss function Eq (11)
    increase k by μ
end while
return S, Θ*
```

where $|q_i|$ and $|q|$ is the size of region q_i and image q, $f(q_i)$ and $f(d_j)$ are the last fully connected layer outputs of CNN in the region matching model.

Our method of video geo-localization is based on such fact: if a video has not been edited, the geo-location of it should not vary a lot in a short time. To find the geo-location of a video, we first retrieve K most similar images in the database for each frame, and collect $K \times F$ images (may overlap) in the database. Then, we cluster the images in the database into C clusters, based on their representative vectors in the feature space. The video will be localized to the average GPS coordinate of the largest cluster.

5 Experiments

In this section, we first give introduction to the two datasets we used to test our model; next, we briefly introduce the evaluation metrics and baseline we applied. We report the experimental results on joint model based geo-localization and saliency estimation in the last two sub-sections, and give some analysis.

5.1 Datasets

We use two challenging datasets, Boston Marathon 2013[6] and Tokyo Time Machine [1, 21]. Table 2 shows the summary of the two datasets we used.

5.1.1 Boston Dataset Chen et al. [6] collected video clips which are related to the event of Boston Marathon bombing from the internet. This is a dataset which focus on a real event. In the videos, the streets look very different from daily appearance due to the event. Figure 5 shows some example videos. In this dataset, they also provide 10,000 satellite environment images in the surrounding region of the event location. The region contains 562 buildings in total. We uniformly sampled 2,500 GPS locations in this region. For each GPS coordinate, we collected 4 images from 4 different perspectives of view (10,000 images in total). We also collected the same number of images as queries for training at randomly sampled GPS locations in the same way to collect database. For testing, we labeled the ground truth of geo-location for 100 sampled frames from 37 45-degree-view video clips. Some example frames are shown in Figure 5. Each frame may have multiple relevant images in the database.

5.1.2 Tokyo Time Machine Dataset Tokyo Time Machine (TokyoTM) dataset was released by Arandjelovic et al. [1], generated from

Figure 5: Sample video clips collected from the internet.

downloaded Time Machine panoramas. In this dataset, the appearances of buildings also change a lot, since the pictures were taken at different time in different days.

Dataset	Database	Query set
Tokyo Time Machine-train	49,104	7,277
Tokyo Time Machine-val	49,056	7,186
Tokyo 24/7 (-test)	75,984	1,125
Boston-train	8,000	8,000
Boston-val	2,000	2,000
Boston-test	10,000	37 video clips

Table 2: The size of the dataset we used in the experiments. The train/val(idation)/test dataset is mutually disjoint geographically.

5.2 Evaluation Metrics and Baselines

We test the performance of our model with adopting two common metrics: mean average precision (MAP) and recall on top$N$:
1. *MAP* For a query image, the average precision $AveP$ of each query is computed. Then $MAP = \frac{\sum_{i=1}^{|Q|} AveP(i)}{|Q|}$, where $|Q|$ is the number of queries. This metric shows the general performance for a model.
2. *Recall on Top N*. We retrieve N most similar images for each query. This metric is helpful to reveal the application value for a method, since we often retrieve top N images for image retrieval tasks, like geo-localization.

We applied our method introduced in Section 4 with VGG-CNN-M model as a base CNN model and we introduce the following baselines:
VGG-CNN-M-*sim*: it calculates similarity

$$sim(q, d) = -||f(q) - f(d)||_2 \tag{17}$$

using the $fc7$ layer output of the model released by Chatfield et al. [5].
VGG-CNN-M-sim_R: it estimates the saliency score using the VGG-CNN-M model, and then compute the similarity between image q and d by Eq (16).
IBFT-*sim*: it applies image-level based fine-tuning to the matching model, and use Eq (17) as the metric of similarity.
JSEM-sim_R: it is the full joint saliency estimation and matching model with the similarity measurement Eq (16) proposed in this paper.
Manually-labeled-sim_R: For Boston dataset, we also manually label the building contour in the image using LabelMe [19].
We treat building areas as foreground and other areas as background. We manually set the saliency value of a region based on its

intersection percentage with the foreground, and use this saliency value from additional building contour labeling in similarity measurement sim_R. It could be treated as a kind of upper bound.

5.3 Evaluation of Geo-Localization

Model	Boston	Tokyo TM
VGG-CNN-M-*sim*	28.85	26.83
VGG-CNN-M-sim_R	35.67	24.34
IBFT-*sim*	37.50	23.91
JSEM-sim_R	**58.33**	**37.01**
Manually-labeled-sim_R	63.40	-

Table 3: MAP (×100) on the two datasets.

Query Frame

Ground Truth

Ground Truth Ranking in All Database Images				
VGG-CNN-M-*sim*	6	3	10	108
JSEM-sim_R	1	1	1	12

Table 4: Case study on Boston Dataset.

Boston: The result reported in Table 3 shows that our model has significantly improved the mean average precision (MAP) on the geo-localization task. For the convenience of view, Table 4 shows some case study on this task, from which we can easily see that the rankings of ground truth images raise a lot. In CNN, we resize the frames into a 224 × 224 square shape. Thus, we show the frames and database in such square shapes rather than rectangular ones in Figure 5. Besides, the "recall on top K" result on Boston dataset is reported in Table 5.

TokyoTM: We also run experiments on the Tokyo TM dataset and show results in Table 3 and Table 6.

The experimental result proves the effectiveness of our model, showing that our model obtains the best recall for every N, and beats the baselines on the metric MAP. That is, our model not only performs well generally, but also has application value for real image retrieval tasks. However, it's interesting that the model IBFT-*sim* performs similar to VGG-CNN-M-*sim* on Tokyo TM dataset. It suggests that fine-tuning based only on the limited training dataset could easily cause over-fitting. This also shows that saliency score is an important part to improve the performance of the model, and make the model more robust.

5.4 Analysis of Learned Saliency

To give further supporting evidences for the effectiveness of our method, we analyze the learned saliency qualitatively and quantitatively. We first conduct case study on some salient and non-salient regions, and then report the Pearson correlation with manually labeled saliency score on some randomly selected samples.

We applied the method introduced in Section 4 to estimate the saliency score for each region of a given image. Figure 6 shows the 8 most salient and 8 most non-salient regions together with their saliency scores from the Tokyo TM database. The salient regions are all buildings with distinctive structure($a - h$) while the non-salient regions are images from road($i - k$), trees(m and n), sky(o) and indistinctive building regions(l and p).

We also analyze the correlation between learned saliency with saliency calculate from manually labeled building contour in manually-labeled-sim_R, which could be treated as ground truth saliency score. The Pearson correlation is 0.7625, showing that our estimated saliency score has strong relation with the ground truth saliency score. Figure 7 shows the case study of our region based saliency estimation on two specific images.

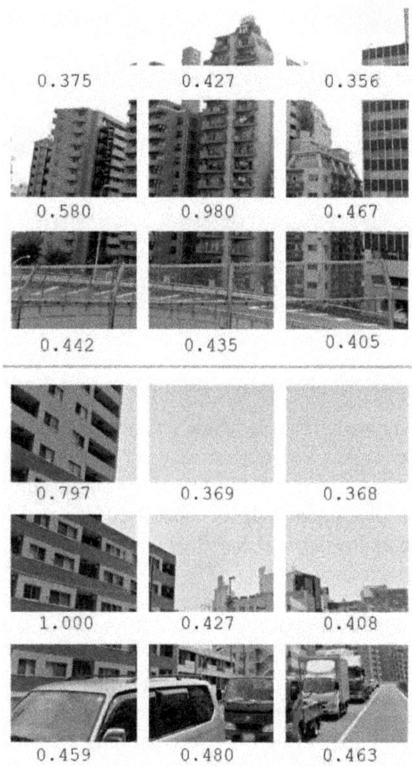

Figure 7: Case study of region-based saliency estimation.

6 Conclusions and Future Work

We study automatic geo-localization of online event videos, which is the key component supporting various event analysis tasks such as cross camera tracking and 3d reconstruction. The major challenge lies in large appearance change of the environment due to human activity during the event. To solve this problem, we formulate the problem as region based joint saliency estimation and matching, and propose a solution, which iteratively estimates saliency and optimizes region based matching model. For the step of saliency optimization, we derived a closed form solution, which has an intuitive explanation. For region based matching model optimization, we apply self-paced learning algorithm to learn from the pseudo labels generated by saliency value estimated by matching. We conduct experiments on Boston Marathon 2013 dataset and Tokyo Time Machine datas et to test the performance of our model. The experiments have shown that our solution significantly

Model	N = 1	N = 2	N = 3	N = 4	N = 5	N = 10	N = 15	N = 20	N = 25
VGG-CNN-M-*sim*	7.05	13.85	21.41	25.44	30.23	44.33	51.89	62.97	69.77
VGG-CNN-M-sim_R	8.31	15.87	23.43	30.23	35.52	53.40	73.05	80.35	84.13
IBFT-*sim*	7.56	15.62	23.93	37.03	42.82	56.93	67.25	78.84	85.89
JSEM-sim_R	16.12	27.96	39.80	51.39	58.44	78.84	84.63	89.67	95.21

Table 5: Recall on top N on Boston dataset.

Model	N = 1	N = 2	N = 3	N = 4	N = 5	N = 10	N = 15	N = 20	N = 25
VGG-CNN-M-*sim*	5.67	10.17	14.42	17.97	20.33	32.86	46.57	58.16	68.32
VGG-CNN-M-sim_R	5.91	10.87	15.84	18.68	21.04	36.17	47.28	61.47	70.92
IBFT-*sim*	7.57	11.58	15.60	18.91	23.17	34.04	46.57	55.79	68.09
JSEM-sim_R	9.22	15.60	21.28	25.77	28.84	48.70	63.83	74.23	84.87

Table 6: Recall on Top N on Tokyo TM dataset.

Figure 6: 8 most salient regions(top) and 8 most non-salient regions in Tokyo TM database, with their saliency score.

improves over matching on whole image and the automatically learned saliency has a strong correlation with manual labels on region saliency, proving that our model has significant application value. In the future, we will try more sophisticated CNN based models such as Resnet and NetVLAD in our matching model to improve performance.

7 Acknowledgement

This material is based in part upon work supported by the National Science Foundation under Grant Number IIS- 1638429. Any opinions, findings, and conclusions or recommendations expressed in this material are those of the author(s) and do not necessarily reflect the views of the National Science Foundation.

References

[1] R. Arandjelović, P. Gronat, A. Torii, T. Pajdla, and J. Sivic. 2016. NetVLAD: CNN architecture for weakly supervised place recognition. In *IEEE Conference on Computer Vision and Pattern Recognition*.

[2] Relja Arandjelović and Andrew Zisserman. 2013. All about VLAD. In *Computer Vision and Pattern Recognition, 2013. CVPR 2013. IEEE Conference on*. IEEE.

[3] Mayank Bansal, Kostas Daniilidis, and Harpreet Sawhney. 2012. Ultra-wide baseline facade matching for geo-localization. In *European Conference on Computer Vision*. Springer, 175–186.

[4] Yoshua Bengio, Jérôme Louradour, Ronan Collobert, and Jason Weston. 2009. Curriculum learning. In *Proceedings of the 26th annual international conference on machine learning*. ACM, 41–48.

[5] Ken Chatfield, Karen Simonyan, Andrea Vedaldi, and Andrew Zisserman. 2014. Return of the devil in the details: Delving deep into convolutional nets. *arXiv preprint arXiv:1405.3531* (2014).

[6] Jia Chen, Junwei Liang, Han Lu, Shoou-I Yu, and Alexander G. Hauptmann. 2016. Videos from the 2013 Boston Marathon: An Event Reconstruction Dataset for Synchronization and Localization.

[7] Christopher B Choy, JunYoung Gwak, Silvio Savarese, and Manmohan Chandraker. 2016. Universal Correspondence Network. In *Advances in Neural Information Processing Systems 29*.

[8] Jochen Gorski, Frank Pfeuffer, and Kathrin Klamroth. 2007. Biconvex sets and optimization with biconvex functions: a survey and extensions. *Math. Meth. of OR* 66, 3 (2007), 373–407. https://doi.org/10.1007/s00186-007-0161-1

[9] James Hays and Alexei A Efros. 2008. IM2GPS: estimating geographic information from a single image. In *Computer Vision and Pattern Recognition, 2008. CVPR 2008. IEEE Conference on*. IEEE, 1–8.

[10] Lu Jiang, Deyu Meng, Teruko Mitamura, and Alexander G Hauptmann. 2014. Easy samples first: Self-paced reranking for zero-example multimedia search. In *Proceedings of the 22nd ACM international conference on Multimedia*. ACM, 547–556.

[11] Lu Jiang, Deyu Meng, Qian Zhao, Shiguang Shan, and Alexander G Hauptmann. 2015. Self-Paced Curriculum Learning.. In *AAAI*, Vol. 2. 6.

[12] M Pawan Kumar, Benjamin Packer, and Daphne Koller. 2010. Self-paced learning for latent variable models. In *Advances in Neural Information Processing Systems*. 1189–1197.

[13] Keith Yu Kit Leung, Christopher M Clark, and Jan P Huissoon. 2008. Localization in urban environments by matching ground level video images with an aerial image. In *Robotics and Automation, 2008. ICRA 2008. IEEE International Conference on*. IEEE, 551–556.

[14] Tsung-Yi Lin, Serge Belongie, and James Hays. 2013. Cross-view image geolocalization. In *Proceedings of the IEEE Conference on Computer Vision and Pattern Recognition*. 891–898.

[15] Tsung-Yi Lin, Yin Cui, Serge Belongie, and James Hays. 2015. Learning deep representations for ground-to-aerial geolocalization. In *2015 IEEE Conference on Computer Vision and Pattern Recognition (CVPR)*. IEEE, 5007–5015.

[16] Volodymyr Mnih, Nicolas Heess, Alex Graves, and others. 2014. Recurrent models of visual attention. In *Advances in Neural Information Processing Systems*. 2204–2212.

[17] James Philbin, Ondrej Chum, Michael Isard, Josef Sivic, and Andrew Zisserman. 2007. Object retrieval with large vocabularies and fast spatial matching. In *2007 IEEE Computer Society Conference on Computer Vision and Pattern Recognition (CVPR 2007), 18-23 June 2007, Minneapolis, Minnesota, USA*.

[18] James Philbin, Ondrej Chum, Michael Isard, Josef Sivic, and Andrew Zisserman. 2008. Lost in quantization: Improving particular object retrieval in large scale image databases. In *2008 IEEE Computer Society Conference on Computer Vision and Pattern Recognition (CVPR 2008), 24-26 June 2008, Anchorage, Alaska, USA*.

[19] Bryan C. Russell, Antonio Torralba, Kevin P. Murphy, and William T. Freeman. 2008. LabelMe: A Database and Web-Based Tool for Image Annotation. *International Journal of Computer Vision* 77, 1 (2008), 157–173.

[20] Kevin Tang, Vignesh Ramanathan, Li Fei-Fei, and Daphne Koller. 2012. Shifting weights: Adapting object detectors from image to video. In *Advances in Neural Information Processing Systems*. 638–646.

[21] A. Torii, R. Arandjelović, J. Sivic, M. Okutomi, and T. Pajdla. 2015. 24/7 place recognition by view synthesis. In *CVPR*.

[22] Nam N Vo and James Hays. 2016. Localizing and Orienting Street Views Using Overhead Imagery. In *European Conference on Computer Vision*. Springer, 494–509.
[23] Amir Roshan Zamir and Mubarak Shah. 2010. Accurate image localization based on google maps street view. In *European Conference on Computer Vision*. Springer, 255–268.
[24] Yin Zheng, Richard S Zemel, Yu-Jin Zhang, and Hugo Larochelle. 2015. A neural autoregressive approach to attention-based recognition. *International Journal of Computer Vision* 113, 1 (2015), 67–79.

Panorama to Panorama Matching for Location Recognition

Ahmet Iscen[1] Giorgos Tolias[2] Yannis Avrithis[1] Teddy Furon[1] Ondřej Chum[2]
[1] Inria, Rennes, France
[2] Visual Recognition Group, Faculty of Electrical Engineering, CTU in Prague, Czech Republic

ABSTRACT

Location recognition is commonly treated as visual instance retrieval on "street view" imagery. The dataset items and queries are panoramic views, *i.e.* groups of images taken at a single location. This work introduces a novel panorama-to-panorama matching process, either by aggregating features of individual images in a group or by explicitly constructing a larger panorama. In either case, multiple views are used as queries. We reach near perfect location recognition on a standard benchmark with only four query views.

CCS CONCEPTS

•Information systems → Image search; •Computing methodologies → Visual content-based indexing and retrieval;

KEYWORDS

image retrieval; location recognition

ACM Reference format:
A. Iscen, G. Tolias, Y. Avrithis, T. Furon and O. Chum. 2017. Panorama to Panorama Matching for Location Recognition. In *Proceedings of ICMR '17, Bucharest, Romania, June 6–9, 2017,* 5 pages.
DOI: http://dx.doi.org/10.1145/3078971.3079033

1 INTRODUCTION

Location recognition has been treated as a visual instance retrieval task for many years [1, 3, 11, 23, 25, 33]. Additional, task-specific approaches include ground truth locations to find informative features [25], regression for a more precise localization [18, 31], or representation of the dataset as a graph [7]. A dense collection of multiple views allows 3D representations are possible, *e.g.* structured from motion [12], searching 2D features in 3D models [19, 24], or simultaneous visual localization and mapping [8]. However, this does not apply to sparse "street-view" imagery [30, 32], where dataset items and queries are groups of images taken at a single location, in a panorama-like layout.

Several approaches on visual instance retrieval propose to jointly represent a set of images. These sets of images can appear at the query or at the database side. In the former case, these images are different views of the same object or scene [2, 27] and finally performance is improved. This joint representation, which commonly is an average query vector constructed via aggregation, is presumably more robust than each individual query vector. On the other hand, when aggregating images on the database side it is better to group them together by similarity [14]; images are assigned to sets, and a joint representation is created per set.

This work revisits location recognition by aggregating images both on query and database sides. Our method resembles implicit construction of a panorama, *i.e.* images are combined in the feature space and not in the image space, but we also experiment with an explicit construction. Contrary to the general case of visual instance retrieval, it is easy to obtain multiple query images, e.g. capturing them with a smartphone or with multiple cameras in the case of autonomous driving. On the database side, location provides a natural way of grouping images together. Thus, contrary to generic retrieval, the images to be aggregated on the query and database sides, may not be similar to each other; they rather depict whatever is visible around a particular location.

We significantly outperform the state of the art without any form of supervision other than the natural, location-based grouping of images, and without any costly offline process like 3D reconstruction. Indeed we are reaching near perfect location recognition on the Pittsburgh dataset [32] even when we use as few as four views on the query side.

2 BACKGROUND

This section describes the related work on Convolutional Neural Network (CNN) based descriptors for image retrieval and on image set joint representations. Our approach applies these methods on the dataset and query images.

2.1 CNN Descriptors for Retrieval

CNN-based global descriptors are becoming popular in image retrieval, especially for instance-level search. Existing works [4, 17, 22, 29] employ "off-the-shelf" networks, originally trained on ImageNet, to extract descriptors via various pooling strategies. This offers invariance to geometric transformation and robustness to background clutter. Other approaches [5, 9, 20] fine-tune such networks to obtain descriptor representations specifically adapted for instance search.

NetVLAD [1] is a recent work that trains a VLAD layer on top of convolutional layers in an end-to-end manner. It is tuned for the location recognition task. The training images are obtained from panoramas, fed to a triplet loss to make it more compatible with image retrieval. As a result, their representation outperforms existing works in standard location recognition benchmarks.

2.2 Representing Sets of Vectors

Two common scenarios aggregate a set of vectors into a single vector representation for image retrieval. The first case involves aggregation of a large number of local descriptors, either to reduce

978-1-4503-4701-3/17/06.
DOI: http://dx.doi.org/10.1145/3078971.3079033

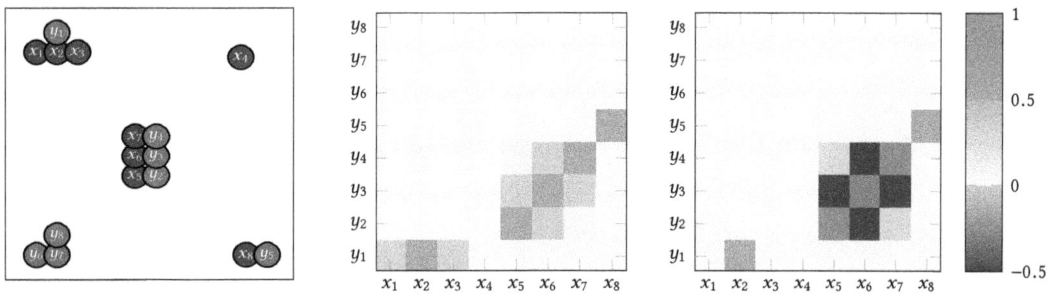

Figure 1: Left: Toy example of two vector sets X, Y on the 2D plane are shown on the left. Middle: Pairwise similarity between all vectors, cross-matching with sum-vectors, *i.e.* $X^\top Y$ (3). Only for visualization purposes, and since we are dealing with unnormalized 2D vectors, the similarity between vectors x, y is defined as $e^{\|x-y\|^2}$. Right: weighted pairwise-similarity between all vectors, cross-matching with pinv-vectors, *i.e.* $G_X^{-1}X^\top YG_Y^{-1}$ (4).

the number of descriptors [26, 28], or to create a global descriptor [10, 16]. In the other case, which is exploited in this work, a set of global image descriptors is aggregated into a single vector representation to construct a joint representation for a set of images [14].

In particular, we follow the two *memory vector* construction strategies proposed by Iscen et al. [14]. The first method simply computes the sum of all vectors in a set. Given a set of vectors represented as the columns of a $d \times n$ matrix $\mathbf{X} = [\mathbf{x}_1, \ldots, \mathbf{x}_n]$ with $\mathbf{x}_i \in R^d$, the *sum* memory vector is defined as

$$m(\mathbf{X}) = \mathbf{X}\mathbf{1}_n. \tag{1}$$

Assuming linearly independent columns ($n < d$), the second method is based on the Moore-Penrose pseudo-inverse $\mathbf{X}^+$ [21], given by

$$m^+(\mathbf{X}) = (\mathbf{X}^+)^\top \mathbf{1}_n = \mathbf{X}(\mathbf{X}^\top\mathbf{X})^{-1}\mathbf{1}_n. \tag{2}$$

It is theoretically optimized for high dimensional spaces and performs better in practice. This paper refers to the sum memory vector (1) as *sum-vector*, and to the pseudo-inverse memory vector (2) as *pinv-vector*.

Aggregating Dataset Images. The main purpose of aggregating dataset images is to reduce the computation cost of similarity search at query time [14]. Dataset vectors are assigned to sets in an offline process, and each set is represented by a single (memory) vector. At query time, the similarity between the query vector and each memory vector is computed, and memory vectors are ranked accordingly. Then the query is only compared to the database vectors belonging to the top ranked sets. This strategy eliminates the exhaustive computation of the similarities query vs. dataset vectors. Existing works use random assignments to create the sets, or weakly-supervised assignment based on k-means or kd-tree [13, 14].

Aggregating Query Images. Aggregation of query images has been also studied for instance-level object retrieval. Multiple images depicting the query object allow to better handle the problems of occlusion, view-point change, scale change and other variations. Arandjelovic et al. [2] investigate various scenarios, such as average or max pooling on query vectors and creating SVM models. Recently, Sicre and Jégou [27] have shown that aggregating query vectors with pinv-vector improves the search quality.

Aggregation of dataset images offers speed and memory improvements at the cost of performance loss. On the other hand, aggregation of query images is only applicable in the particular case of multiple available query images and offers performance improvements at no extra cost. Our approach adopts aggregation on both sides for the first time while enjoying speed, memory and performance improvements.

3 PANORAMA TO PANORAMA MATCHING

This section describes our contribution for location recognition. We assume that for each possible location we are given a set of images covering a full 360 degree view while consecutive images have an overlap (see Figure 2). We propose two ways to construct a *panoramic representation* of each location: an implicit way by vector aggregation and an explicit way by image stitching into a panorama and extraction of a single descriptor.

3.1 Implicit Panorama Construction

We form a panoramic representation by aggregating the descriptors of images from the same location. In this way, we implicitly construct a panorama in the descriptor space. In order to achieve this, we employ two approaches for creating memory vectors, *i.e.* sum-vector (1) and pinv-vector (2).

In contrast to previous works that aggregate the image vectors only on the dataset side [14] or only on the query side [27], we rather do it for both. This requires that the query is also defined by a set of images which offer a 360 degree view. A realistic scenario of this context is autonomous driving and auto-localization where the query is defined by such a set of images.

Assume that n images in a dataset location are represented by $d \times n$ matrix $\mathbf{X}$ and that k images in the query location by $d \times k$ matrix $\mathbf{Y}$. Analyzing the similarity between the two sum-vectors is straightforward. Panorama similarity is given by the inner product

$$s(\mathbf{X}, \mathbf{Y}) = m(\mathbf{X})^\top m(\mathbf{Y}) = \mathbf{1}_n^\top \mathbf{X}^\top \mathbf{Y}\mathbf{1}_k. \tag{3}$$

Similarly, panorama similarity for pinv-vectors is given by

$$s^+(\mathbf{X}, \mathbf{Y}) = m^+(\mathbf{X})^\top m^+(\mathbf{Y}) = \mathbf{1}_n^\top G_\mathbf{X}^{-1}\mathbf{X}^\top \mathbf{Y} G_\mathbf{Y}^{-1}\mathbf{1}_k, \tag{4}$$

where $G_\mathbf{X} = \mathbf{X}^\top\mathbf{X}$ is the Gram matrix for $\mathbf{X}$. Compared to (3), the sum after cross-matching is weighted now, and the weights are given by $G_\mathbf{X}^{-1}$ and $G_\mathbf{Y}^{-1}$. This is interpreted as "democratizing" the result of cross-matching; the contribution of vectors that are similar within the same set are down-weighted, just as in handling the burstiness phenomenon for local descriptors [16]. We visualize this with a toy example in Figure 1. Unweighted cross-matching is

Figure 2: Example of all images assigned to a single location (first two rows) and the corresponding panorama (last row) covering a full 360 degree view, constructed by automatic stitching.

Query:
Rank-1:
Query:
Rank-1:

Figure 3: Two examples of failures with *pan2pan/net*. We show the query and the top ranked image from the dataset.

dominated by "bursty" vectors in the same cluster. Democratization down-weights these contributions.

3.2 Explicit Panorama Construction

Our second approach explicitly creates a panoramic image. The descriptors are then extracted from the panorama. Given that images of a location are overlapping, we construct a panoramic image using an existing stitching method. In particular, we use the work of Brown and Lowe [6], which aligns, stitches, and blends images automatically based on their local SIFT descriptors and inlier correspondences. Figure 2 shows a stitched panoramic image. Once stitching is complete, we extract a single global descriptor from the panorama image, capturing the entire scene.

4 EXPERIMENTS

In this section, we describe our experimental setup, and compare our method to a number of baselines using the state-of-the-art NetVLAD network in a popular location recognition benchmark.

4.1 Experimental Setup

The methods are evaluated on the Pittsburgh dataset [32] referred to as Pitt250k. It contains 250k database and 24k query images from Google Street View. It is split into training, validation, and test sets [1]. We evaluate our approach on the test set, which consists of 83,952 dataset images and 8,280 query images. Each image is associated with a GPS location and 24 images are associated with the same GPS location. Therefore, each panoramic representation aggregates 24 images. There is a total of 345 query locations and 3,498 dataset locations. We use NetVLAD for our descriptor representation in all experiments. While the original representation is $d = 4{,}096$ dimensional, we also experiment with reducing dimensionality to $d = 256$ by PCA.

The standard evaluation metric is Recall@N. It is defined to equal 1 if at least one of the top N retrieved dataset images is within 25 meters from the spatial location of the query. Average is reported over all queries. We follow this protocol for the baseline and other cases where the query images are used individually.

Aggregating on the query side implies that there is a single query per location: the number of queries decreases from 8,280 to 345. We report the average recall@N from these 345 panorama queries. Section 4.3 also experiments with a larger number of random queries, each capturing only a fraction of the panoramic view. In this case, recall@N is averaged over those random queries. Aggregating on the dataset side does not affect the standard evaluation.

4.2 Panorama Matching

We refer to our proposed method as panorama to panorama or *pan2pan* matching, in particular *pan2pan/sum* and *pan2pan/pinv* when aggregating descriptors with sum-vector and pinv-vector respectively; and as *pan2pan/net* when using a NetVLAD descriptor from an explicit panorama. We compare against the following baselines: image to image matching (*im2im*) as in the work by Arandjelovic et al. [1], image to panorama matching (*im2pan*) corresponding to dataset-side aggregation as in the work by Iscen et al. [14], and panorama to image matching (*pan2im*) corresponding to query-side aggregation as in the work by Sicre and Jégou [27].

Figure 4 compares all methods for different descriptor dimensions. Clearly, panorama to panorama matching outperforms all other methods. The improvement is consistent for all N and significant for low N: pan2pan/net obtains 98% recall@1! There are only 7 failure queries. Two of them are shown in Figure 3. One is a challenging query depicting an indoor parking lot and the other

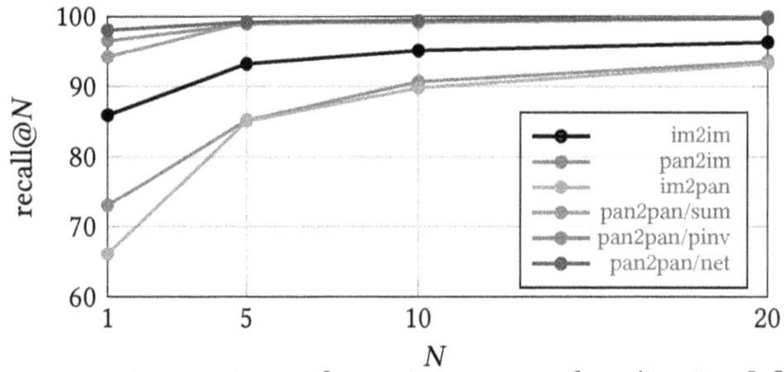

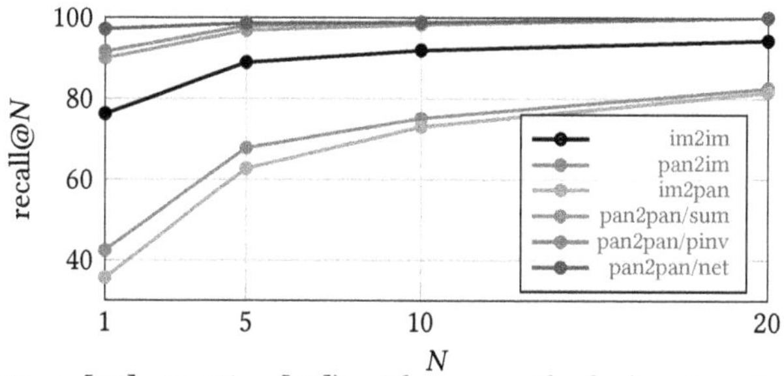

Figure 4: Comparison of existing approaches (im2im [1], im2pan [14], pan2im [27]) with our methods (pan2pan/sum, pan2pan/pinv and pan2pan/net) for the full 4096D (left) and for reduced dimensionality to 256D (right).

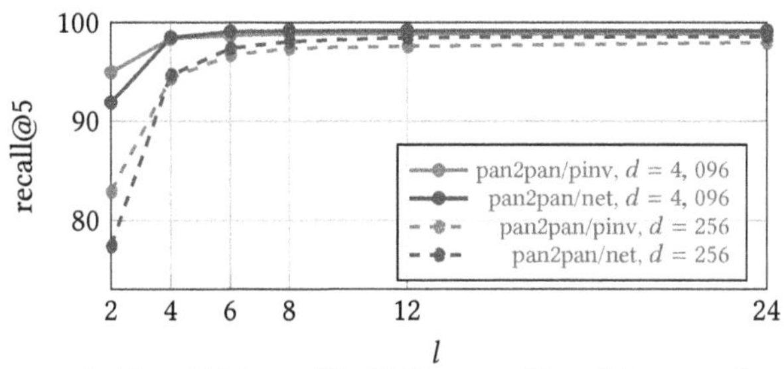

Figure 5: Recall@5 on Pitt250k, sampling l images from each query panorama and using NetVLAD descriptors of two different dimensionalities d. We report average measurements over 10 random experiments and compare our methods pan2pan/pinv and pan2pan/net.

actually retrieves the same building, which is incorrectly marked in the dataset's ground truth.

The recall is not only improved, but the search is also more efficient both speed-wise ($24^2\times$ faster) and memory-wise (24× less memory). Instead of comparing a given query image against 83k vectors, we only make 3.5k comparisons. Additional operations are introduced when aggregating the set of query images, but this cost is fixed and small compared to the savings from the dataset side.

Comparing to results in prior work, im2pan behaves as in the work of Iscen et al. [14] when compared to the baseline im2im. That is, memory compression and speed up at the cost of reduced performance. However, pan2im does not appear to be effective in our case, in contrast to the work of Sicre and Jégou [27]. On the contrary, pan2pan significantly improves the performance while enjoying both memory compression and search efficiency.

4.3 Sparse Panorama Matching

Aggregating on the dataset side is performed off-line. However, the user is required to capture images and to construct a full panorama (24 images in our case) at query time. Even though this is not a daunting task given the advances of smartphones and tablets, we additionally investigate a scenario where the user only captures a partial panoramic view.

In particular, we randomly sample a subset of l images from the query location and consider them as the query image set. Explicit panorama construction is no longer possible because the sampled images may not overlap and so we cannot stitch them. In this case, we feed sampled images through the convolutional layers only, and stack together all activations before pooling them through the NetVLAD layer (pan2pan/net for sparse panoramas).

Figure 5 shows the results. Our methods have near-perfect performance even for a small number of sampled images. When the user only takes four random photos, we are able to locate them up to 99% recall@5. Another interesting observation is that pan2pan/pinv outperforms pan2pan/net for $l = 2$, which is expected due to the nature of pinv-vec construction. It is theoretically shown to perform well even if all the vectors in the set are random, as shown in the original paper [14].

4.4 Comparison to Diffusion-based Retrieval

This work casts location recognition as a retrieval task. Query expansion techniques significantly improve retrieval performance. We compare to the state-of-the-art retrieval method by Iscen et al. [15], a kind of query expansion based on graph diffusion. In this method, an image is represented by individual region descriptors and at query time all query regions are processed. We compare to this method by considering that regions and images in [15] correspond to images and panoramas respectively in our scenario.

Our pan2pan/pinv and pan2pan/net approaches achieve 96.5% and 98% recall@1 respectively, while the approach [15] gives 91.9%. Even though query expansion improves the baseline, it does not help as much as our methods. This can be expected because [15] is based on many instances of the same object, which is not the case for location recognition on street view imagery.

5 CONCLUSIONS

Our method is unsupervised and conceptually very simple, yet very effective. Besides the performance gain, we make significant savings in space by aggregating descriptors of individual images over each group. The need for multiple query views is not very demanding because only four views are enough—an entire query panorama is definitely not needed.

Although our aggregation methods have been used for instance retrieval in the past, we are the first to successfully aggregate on both dataset and query-side for location recognition (which in fact has failed for instance retrieval [26]). An interesting finding is that although the NetVLAD descriptor has been explicitly optimized to aggregate CNN activations on the location recognition task, in some cases it is preferable to aggregate individual views into a pinv-vector rather than extracting a single NetVLAD descriptor from an explicit panorama.

Acknowledgments. The authors were supported by the MSMT LL1303 ERC-CZ grant. The Tesla K40 used for this research was donated by the NVIDIA Corporation.

REFERENCES

[1] R. Arandjelović, P. Gronat, A. Torii, T. Pajdla, and J. Sivic. NetVLAD: CNN architecture for weakly supervised place recognition. In *CVPR*, 2016.

[2] R. Arandjelovic and A. Zisserman. Multiple queries for large scale specific object retrieval. In *BMVC*, 2012.

[3] R. Arandjelovic and A. Zisserman. Dislocation: Scalable descriptor distinctiveness for location recognition. In *ACCV*, 2014.

[4] A. Babenko and V. Lempitsky. Aggregating deep convolutional features for image retrieval. In *ICCV*, 2015.

[5] A. Babenko, A. Slesarev, A. Chigorin, and V. Lempitsky. Neural codes for image retrieval. In *ECCV*, 2014.

[6] M. Brown and D. G. Lowe. Automatic panoramic image stitching using invariant features. *IJCV*, 74:59–73, 2007.

[7] S. Cao and N. Snavely. Graph-based discriminative learning for location recognition. In *CVPR*, 2013.

[8] M. Cummins and P. Newman. Fab-map: Appearance-based place recognition and mapping using a learned visual vocabulary model. In *ICML*, 2010.

[9] A. Gordo, J. Almazan, J. Revaud, and D. Larlus. Deep image retrieval: Learning global representations for image search. *ECCV*, 2016.

[10] P.-H. Gosselin, N. Murray, H. Jégou, and F. Perronnin. Revisiting the fisher vector for fine-grained classification. *Pattern recognition letters*, 49, 2014.

[11] J. Hays and A. A. Efros. Im2gps: estimating geographic information from a single image. In *CVPR*, 2008.

[12] A. Irschara, C. Zach, J.-M. Frahm, and H. Bischof. From structure-from-motion point clouds to fast location recognition. In *CVPR*, 2009.

[13] A. Iscen, L. Amsaleg, and T. Furon. Scaling group testing similarity search. In *ICMR*, 2016.

[14] A. Iscen, T. Furon, V. Gripon, M. Rabbat, and H. Jégou. Memory vectors for similarity search in high-dimensional spaces. *IEEE Trans. Big Data*, 2017.

[15] A. Iscen, G. Tolias, Y. Avrithis, T. Furon, and O. Chum. Efficient diffusion on region manifolds: Recovering small objects with compact cnn representations. In *CVPR*, 2017.

[16] H. Jégou and A. Zisserman. Triangulation embedding and democratic kernels for image search. In *CVPR*, June 2014.

[17] Y. Kalantidis, C. Mellina, and S. Osindero. Cross-dimensional weighting for aggregated deep convolutional features. In *ECCVW*, 2016.

[18] A. Kendall, M. Grimes, and R. Cipolla. Posenet: A convolutional network for real-time 6-dof camera relocalization. In *ICCV*, 2015.

[19] Y. Li, N. Snavely, D. Huttenlocher, and P. Fua. Worldwide pose estimation using 3d point clouds. In *ECCV*, 2012.

[20] F. Radenović, G. Tolias, and O. Chum. CNN image retrieval learns from BoW: Unsupervised fine-tuning with hard examples. *ECCV*, 2016.

[21] C. R. Rao and S. K. Mitra. Generalized inverse of a matrix and its applications. In *Sixth Berkeley Symposium on Mathematical Statistics and Probability*, 1972.

[22] A. S. Razavian, J. Sullivan, S. Carlsson, and A. Maki. Visual instance retrieval with deep convolutional networks. *ITE Transactions on Media Technology and Applications*, 4, 2016.

[23] T. Sattler, M. Havlena, K. Schindler, and M. Pollefeys. Large-scale location recognition and the geometric burstiness problem. In *CVPR*, 2016.

[24] T. Sattler, B. Leibe, and L. Kobbelt. Improving image-based localization by active correspondence search. In *ECCV*, 2012.

[25] G. Schindler, M. Brown, and R. Szeliski. City-scale location recognition. In *CVPR*, 2007.

[26] M. Shi, Y. Avrithis, and H. Jégou. Early burst detection for memory-efficient image retrieval. In *CVPR*, 2015.

[27] R. Sicre and H. Jégou. Memory vectors for particular object retrieval with multiple queries. In *ICMR*, 2015.

[28] G. Tolias, Y. Avrithis, and H. Jégou. To aggregate or not to aggregate: Selective match kernels for image search. In *ICCV*, December 2013.

[29] G. Tolias, R. Sicre, and H. Jégou. Particular object retrieval with integral max-pooling of cnn activations. *ICLR*, 2016.

[30] A. Torii, R. Arandjelovic, J. Sivic, M. Okutomi, and T. Pajdla. 24/7 place recognition by view synthesis. In *CVPR*, 2015.

[31] A. Torii, J. Sivic, and T. Pajdla. Visual localization by linear combination of image descriptors. In *ICCVW*, 2011.

[32] A. Torii, J. Sivic, T. Pajdla, and M. Okutomi. Visual place recognition with repetitive structures. In *CVPR*, 2013.

[33] W. Zhang and J. Kosecka. Image based localization in urban environments. In *3DPVT*, 2006.

Concept Language Models and Event-based Concept Number Selection for Zero-example Event Detection

Damianos Galanopoulos
Information Technologies Institute (ITI), CERTH
Thermi, Greece, 57001
dgalanop@iti.gr

Foteini Markatopoulou
Information Technologies Institute (ITI), CERTH
Thermi, Greece, 57001
Queen Mary University of London
markatopoulou@iti.gr

Vasileios Mezaris
Information Technologies Institute (ITI), CERTH
Thermi, Greece, 57001
bmezaris@iti.gr

Ioannis Patras
Queen Mary University of London
Mile end Campus, UK, E14NS
i.patras@qmul.ac.uk

ABSTRACT

Zero-example event detection is a problem where, given an event query as input but no example videos for training a detector, the system retrieves the most closely related videos. In this paper we present a fully-automatic zero-example event detection method that is based on translating the event description to a predefined set of concepts for which previously trained visual concept detectors are available. We adopt the use of Concept Language Models (CLMs), which is a method of augmenting semantic concept definition, and we propose a new concept-selection method for deciding on the appropriate number of the concepts needed to describe an event query. The proposed system achieves state-of-the-art performance in automatic zero-example event detection.

CCS CONCEPTS

• **Information systems → Query representation; Video search;**

KEYWORDS

Zero-example multimedia event detection; Video search; Query representation

ACM Reference format:

Damianos Galanopoulos, Foteini Markatopoulou, Vasileios Mezaris, and Ioannis Patras. 2017. Concept Language Models and Event-based Concept Number Selection for Zero-example Event Detection. In *Proceedings of ICMR '17, Bucharest, Romania, June 06-09, 2017,* 5 pages.
https://doi.org/10.1145/3078971.3079043

1 INTRODUCTION

Multimedia-event detection is a very important task that deals with automatically detecting the main event presented in a video. As a video event we consider a complex activity involving people interacting with other people and/or objects, e.g.,"Renovating a home". Typically, multi-class classification is used to train event detectors on ground-truth annotated video samples. However, collecting ground-truth annotated data is difficult and time consuming. As a result, the more practically applicable but also more challenging zero-example event detection task has gained significant attention. The objective of this task is to retrieve the most closely related videos from a large video collection, given any abstract event description for which training samples are not available.

Recent studies typically start by analysing the textual event description so as to transform it to a meaningful set of keywords. At the same time, a predefined set of concepts is used, in the one hand to find which of these concepts are related to the extracted keywords and consequently to the event description, and on the other hand, to train visual concept detectors that will be used to annotate the videos with these semantic concepts. The distance between the event's concept vector and each videos concept vector is calculated and the videos with the smallest distance are selected as being the most closely related to the given event. In this work we improve such a typical system in the following ways: i) We adopt an efficient way for augmenting the definition of each semantic concept in the concept pool, ii) We present a new strategy for deciding on the appropriate number of concepts for representing the event query, iii) We combine these in a zero-example event detection method that outperforms the state-of-the-art techniques.

2 RELATED WORK

Zero-example event detection is an active topic with many literature works proposing ways to build event detectors without any training samples using solely the event's textual description. Research towards this problem was mainly triggered a few years ago when the TRECVID benchmark activity introduced the 0Ex task as a subtask of the Media Event Detection (MED) task [9]. A similar to zero-example event detection problem, known as zero-shot learning (ZSL), also appears in the image recognition task. A new unseen category, for which training data is not available, is asked to be detected in images [3, 7, 12]. It should be noted that although the two problems have many common properties, zero-example event detection is a more challenging problem as it focuses in more

ACM ISBN 978-1-4503-4701-3/17/06...$15.00
https://doi.org/10.1145/3078971.3079043

complex queries, where multiple actions, objects and persons interact with each other compared to the simple object or animal classes that appear in ZSL [19].

The problem of zero-example event detection is typically addressed by transforming both the event textual description and the available videos into concept-based representations. Specifically, a large pool of concept detectors is used to annotate the videos with semantic concepts, the resulted vectors, a.k.a. model vectors, contain the scores indicating the degree that each of the concepts is related to the video. The query description is analysed and the most related concepts from the pool are selected. Finally, the distance between the model vectors and the event concept vectors is calculated and the most related videos are retrieved [1, 4, 18, 21].

Concept detectors are typically trained on external ground-truth annotated datasets using for example deep nets (DCNNs) or low-lever features from different modalities [10]. The simpler way of translating an event query into keywords is space separating the event's textual description, removing the stop-words and using simple NLP rules [16]. Then, each of the keywords is compared with each of the concepts and the top-related concepts are selected to represent the event. Typically, a fixed number is used to decide how many concepts will be selected for each event query [2, 18]. However, adjusting the number of concepts based on the textual description has not been investigated. A semi-automatic approach is proposed by [2]; initially, the system automatically detects the concepts that are related to an event query. Subsequently, a human manually removes the noisy ones. The authors argue on the importance of such human intervention due to the big influence that the selection of the wrong concepts for an input query has on the system's accuracy. Furthermore, comparing each keyword with a single concept may be suboptimal. In some works the augmentation of concepts with synonyms is proposed, while the authors in [18] proposed a method where Concept Language Models are built using online sources, such as Google and Wikipedia, for augmenting the concept definitions with more information. In [20], logical operators are used to discover different types of composite concepts, which leads to better event detection performance. More clever ways of augmenting the concept pool should be found. In [4] instead of calculating concept-related event and video vectors both the videos and the event queries are embedded into a distributional semantic space, then the similarity between these representations is measured. Xiaojun et al. [11] proposed a zero-example event detection method, which initially learns a skip-gram model in order to find the semantic correlation between the event description and the vocabulary of concepts. Then, external video resources are retrieved and dynamic composition is used in order to calculate the optimal concept weights that will be aligned with each testing video based on the target event. Although this approach presents very promising results, the retrieval of external videos and the concept weight calculation are computational expensive. Finally, works in [14] and [13] focus on the improvement of the system's retrieval accuracy by using pseudo-relevance feedback.

3 PROPOSED APPROACH

In this section we present a fully automatic zero-example event detection system as presented in Fig. 1. The proposed system takes as input the event kit, i.e., a textual description of the event query, and retrieves the most related videos from the available event collection. An example of an event kit is presented in Fig. 2. As it can be seen it is a textual description of the requested event that includes the event's title, a short definition of the event and visual and audio cues that are expected to appear in those videos that contain this event. The complete procedure is split into two major components. The first component (upper part of Fig. 1) builds the event detector i.e., a vector of the mostly related concepts based on the event kit. The second component (lower part of Fig. 1) calculates the video model vectors, i.e., annotates the videos with semantic concepts. Finally, the output of the two components is compared, using a similarity measure, and the video model vectors that are closer to the concept event detector are retrieved.

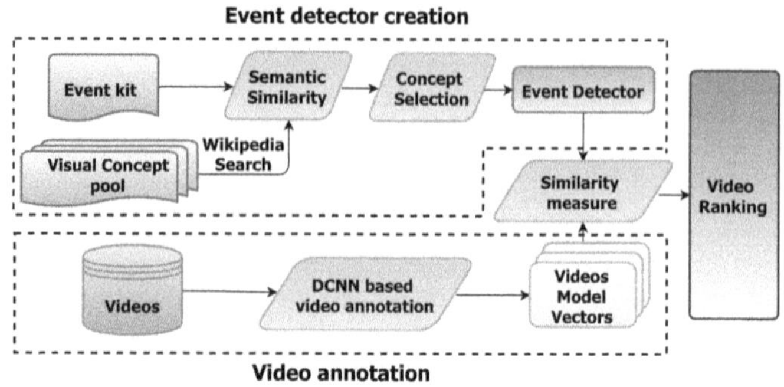

Figure 1: The proposed pipeline for zero-example event detection.

3.1 Building an Event Detector

An event detector is a k-element vector $\mathbf{d}$ of the most related concepts to the event query. Each element indicates the degree that each of the k concepts is related to the target event query. To calculate the event detector we propose a method as follows (algorithm 1): Firstly, we check if the entire event title is semantically close to any of the available concepts from the concept pool, i.e., we check if the semantic relatedness between the event title and each of the concepts is above a (rather high) threshold. If so, we consider that the event is well-described entirely by this (or those) concepts and the relatedness value of these is used to form the event detector $\mathbf{d}$. The Explicit Semantic Analysis (ESA) measure [17] is used to calculate the semantic relatedness of two words or phrases. The ESA measure calculates the similarity distance between two terms by computing the cosine similarity between their corresponding weighted vectors of Wikipedia articles. We choose this measure because it is capable of handling more complex phrases and not only simple words. If the above process does not detect any related concepts, then an Event Language Model (ELM) and Concept Language Models (CLM) are built as follows.

(a) Event Language Model (ELM) and Concept Language Model (CLM). An ELM is a set of N word and phrases that are extracted from the event kit. We build an ELM using the event title, and the visual and audio cues, by simply space separating them. A CLM is a set of M words or phrases that are extracted w.r.t. to a specific concept definition. A CLM is built for each concept using

Event Title: Attempting a bike trick.

Definition: One or more people attempt to do a trick on a bicycle, motorcycle, or other type of motorized bike. To count as a bike for purposes of this event, the vehicle must have two wheels (excludes unicycles, ATVs, etc).

Visual cues:
- **Scene:** outdoors, often in skate park, parking lot or street.
- **Objects/People:** person riding a bike, bike, ramps, helmet, concrete floor, audience.
- **Activities:** riding bike on one wheel, standing on top of bike, jumping with the bike (especially over or onto objects), spinning or flipping bike.

Audio cues:
- **Audio:** sounds of bike hitting surface during the trick, audience cheering.

Figure 2: The event kit text for the event class "Attempting a bike trick"

Algorithm 1: Building an event detector

```
Input  :Event_Title; List_of_visual_concepts
Output:Event detector d
i ← 0;
forall list_of_visual_concepts do
    score ← ESA(visual_concept_Title, Event_Title)
    if score > Threshold then
        d(i) ← score;
        i + +;
if size ofD > 0 then
    return d ;
else
    build ELM;
    forall list_of_visual_concepts do
        build CLM;
        W ← ESA(ELM,CLM);
        vector_of_concepts_scores(j) ← D_H(W) ;
    S ← sort(vector_of_concepts_scores);
    area ← calculate the area below S;
    for i ← 2 to sizeof(S) do
        tmp ← calculate the area below the curve between S_1, S_i;
        if tmp > area*X% then
            break;
    d = S_1, ..., S_i;
    return d ;
```

the top articles in Wikipedia. The retrieved articles are transformed in a Bag-of-Words (BoW) representation from which the top-M words, which are the most characteristic words of this particular visual concept, are kept. For example, the top retrieved words for the concept "*palace*" are "*palace*","*crystal*", "*theatre*", "*season*", "*west*", "*east*", "*spanish*", "*gates*", "*hotel*". After building the ELM and CLMs, we calculate a single value per concept that denotes the semantic relation of this concept with the ELM. To do that, for each CLM we calculate a $N \times M$ distance matrix W. Each element of the matrix contains the semantic relatedness (in terms of the ESA measure) between pairs of words appearing in the ELM and CLM. Given the matrix W a single score is calculated by applying to W the Hausdorff distance, defined as $D_{\mathcal{H}}(\text{EML}, \text{CLM}) = \text{median}\left(\max_{1 \leq j \leq N}(\mathbf{d_j})\right)$ where $\mathbf{d_j} = [W_{1,j}, W_{2,j}, \ldots, W_{M,j}]$. The single values calculated per concept, by repeating the above process for every CLM, are concatenated into a single k'-element vector $\mathbf{d}'$ and a process is followed for deciding the appropriate number of concepts that will be finally kept for representing the event query.

(b) Event-based concept number selection. In contrast to [18] and [2], where the number of selected concepts is fixed across the different events and motivated by statistical methods such as PCA [15], where a fraction of components are enough to efficiently or even better describe the data, we propose a statistical strategy that decides on the appropriate number of concepts k, where $k \leq k'$, that should be kept for an event query. Specifically, our strategy orders the vector of concepts scores $\mathbf{d}'$ in descending order, constructs an exponential curve, and then selects the first k concepts so that the corresponding area under the curve is at the $X\%$ of the total area under the curve. This procedure, consequently returns different number of selected concepts for different target events. For example for the event "*Attempting ordering the a bike trick*" the selected concepts are the following four: "*ride a dirt bike*", "*mountain biking*", "*put on a bicycle chain*", "*ride a bicycle*", while for the event "*Cleaning an appliance*" only the concept "*clean appliance*" is selected. The final event detector is a k-element vector that contains the relatedness scores of the selected concepts.

3.2 Video Annotation and Retrieval

Initially, each video is decoded into as set of keyframes at fixed temporal intervals. Then, a set of pre-trained concept-based DCNNs are applied to every keyframe and each keyframe is represented by the direct output of those networks. Finally, a video model vector is computed by averaging (in terms of arithmetic mean) the corresponding keyframe-level representations. Each element of a model vector indicates the degree that each of the predefined concepts appears in the video.

The distance between an event detector and each of the video-level model vectors is calculated, and the h videos with the smallest distance are retrieved. As distance measure we choose the histogram intersection, which calculates the similarity of two discretized probability distributions and is defined as follows:
$K_{\cap}(a, b) = \sum_{i=1}^{k} min(a_i, b_i)$.

4 EXPERIMENTAL RESULTS

We use the TRECVID MED14TEST dataset [9] that contains approximately 25.000 videos. We evaluate all the methods on the 20 MED2016 [5] Pre-Specified events (E021-E040) for which event kits are provided. We use a concept pool that consist of 13.488 semantic concepts collected from two different sets: i) 12.988 concepts from the *ImageNet* "fall" 2011 dataset [8] and ii) 500 high level concepts from the *EventNet* [6] dataset. Each video was decoded into 2 keyframes per second and each keyframe was annotated with all the above concepts. In order to obtain scores regarding the 12.988 ImageNet concepts we use the pre-trained GoogLeNet provided by [22], while we use the EventNet [6] network for gathering scores w.r.t. the 500 event-based concepts. The final video model vector is calculated by averaging the scores of the keyframe representations in terms of arithmetic mean. We evaluate all the methods in terms of the Mean Average Precision (MAP).

In our first set of experiments we investigate how different parameters of our method affect the final performance. Firstly, in Table 1, we compare 3 different types of ELMs (CLM was kept the same for all of the three ELMs). The first ELM is built solely from the event title, the second ELM uses both the event title and visual cues

ELM type	Event Title	Visual	Audio-Visual
MAP	0.091	0.122	**0.133**

Table 1: Comparison between different types of ELM

CLM type	Concept Title	Wikipedia
MAP	0.092	**0.133**

Table 2: Comparison between different types of CLM

and the third one uses the event title, visual and audio-visual cues. According to Table 1 the more information is given for building an ELM the better the overall accuracy, i.e., the third ELM that uses the complete event kit description (except for the event definition) outperforms the other two that use sub-parts of the event kit.

Similarly, in Table 2 and Figure 3 we compare 2 different types of CLMs. The first CLM uses solely the concept name, along with any available description of it. The second CLM augments the concept name with terms in Wikipedia as described in Section 3.1; the top-10 words of the BoWs representation from the top-10 retrieved documents are used. Similar to the ELMs, the more information provided for building a CLM the better the overall accuracy, i.e., augmenting a concept with information captured from Wikipedia improves the video detection performance. We noticed that 7 out of 20 events had the same performance irrespective of the used CLM types. This happened because existing concepts in our initial pool can describe adequately these specific events.

Figures 4 and 5 present how the different quota of the area under the curve (AUC) (which implies different number of the

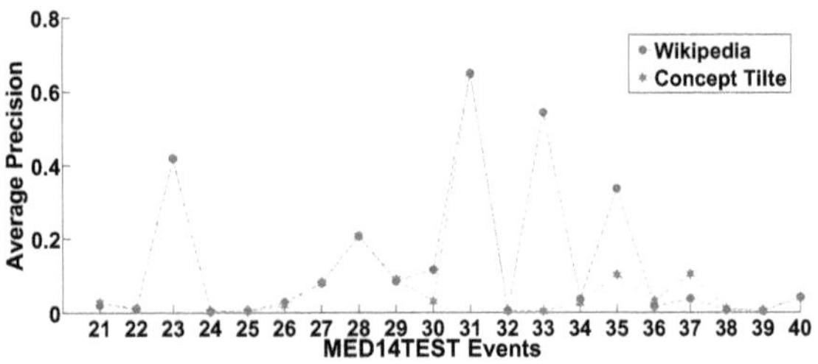

Figure 3: The performance for different types of CLM for the 20 MED14TEST events

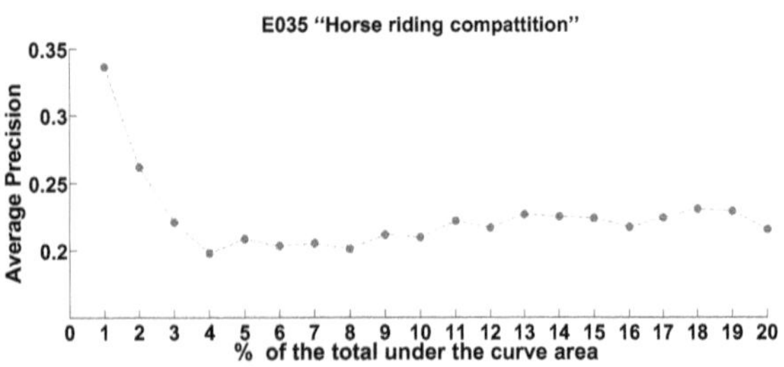

Figure 4: The performance of different quota of under the curve area for the E035 event

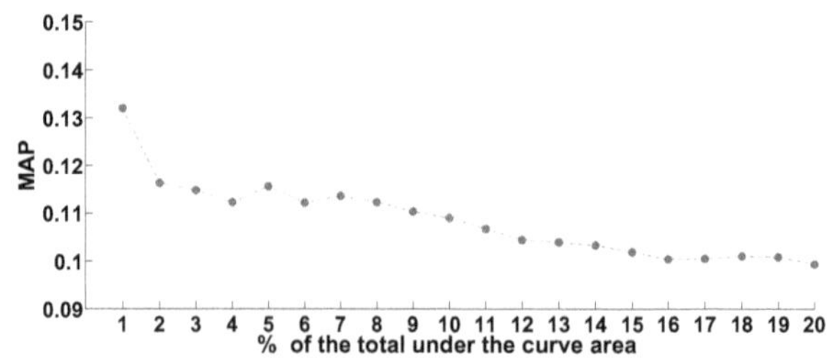

Figure 5: The overall performance of different quota of under the curve area for MED14TEST dataset

Method	MAP
AutoSQGSys [13]	0.115
Concept Bank [1]	0.129
Tzelepis et al. [18]	0.119
Proposed System	**0.133**

Table 3: Comparison between different zero-example event detection systems

top-k selected concepts in every event), affects the performance of our method. In Fig. 4 we observe that the better AP w.r.t the event "Horse riding competition" are achieved for small values of the AUC. This indicates that selecting more concepts that are not highly related with the event query adds noise to the retrieval process that consequently reduces the overall accuracy. Similar conclusions for the overall performance can be reached w.r.t. Fig. 5. The best performance is achieved when the 1% of the AUC is chosen. In this case the average number of selected concepts is 20.1, but each event has different number of concepts. For example the event "*Attempting a bike trick*" needs only 4 concepts while event "*Winning a race without a vehicle*" needs 38 concepts.

In our second set of experiments, we compare the proposed method with the following three state-of-the-art ones: i) AutoSQGSys System [13], ii) Concept Bank system [1] and iii) Tzelepis et al. zero-example method [18], where a fixed number of selected concepts was used. The results of [13] and [1] are picked up from the corresponding papers while the [18] method was re-implemented in order to be suitable for our experiment set-up. According to Table 3 the proposed method outperforms all of the other approaches reaching a MAP of 0.133.

5 CONCLUSION

In this paper we present a fully-automatic method for zero-example video event detection. The augmentation of the concept descriptions with extra information in combination with the proposed strategy for deciding on the appropriate number of concepts for representing the event query outperforms all the state-of-the-art approaches presented in this paper.

ACKNOWLEDGMENTS

This work was supported by the EU's Horizon 2020 research and innovation programme under grant agreements H2020-693092 MOVING and H2020-687786 InVID.

REFERENCES

[1] Y.J Lu, H. Zhang, M. de Boer, C.W. Ngo. 2016. Event Detection with Zero Example: Select the Right and Suppress the Wrong Concepts. In *Proceedings of the 2016 ACM on International Conference on Multimedia Retrieval (ICMR '16)*. ACM, New York, NY, USA, 127–134.

[2] Y.J. Lu, H. Zhang, M. de Boer, C.W. Ngo. 2016. Event detection with zero example: select the right and suppress the wrong concepts. In *Proceedings of the 2016 ACM on International Conference on Multimedia Retrieval*. ACM, 127–134.

[3] M. Elhoseiny, B. Saleh, A. Elgammal. 2013. Write a classifier: Zero-shot learning using purely textual descriptions. In *Computer Vision (ICCV), IEEE Int. Conf. on.* IEEE, 2584–2591.

[4] M. Elhoseiny, J. Liu, H. Cheng, H. Sawhney, A. Elgammal. 2015. Zero-shot Event Detection by multimodal distributional semantic embedding of videos. *arXiv preprint arXiv:1512.00818* (2015).

[5] G. Awad, J. Fiscus, M. Michel et al. 2016. Trecvid 2016: Evaluating video search, video event detection, localization, and hyperlinking. In *Proceedings of TRECVID*, Vol. 2016.

[6] G. Ye, Y. Li, H. Xu, et al. 2015. Eventnet: A large scale structured concept library for complex event detection in video. In *Proceedings of the 23rd ACM international conference on Multimedia*. ACM, 471–480.

[7] M. Norouzi, T. Mikolov, S. Bengio et al. 2013. Zero-shot learning by convex combination of semantic embeddings. *arXiv preprint arXiv:1312.5650* (2013).

[8] O. Russakovsky, J. Deng, H. Su et al. 2015. Imagenet large scale visual recognition challenge. *International Journal of Computer Vision* 115, 3 (2015), 211–252.

[9] P. Over, G. Awad, M. Michel et al. 2015. TRECVID 2015 – An Overview of the Goals, Tasks, Data, Evaluation Mechanisms and Metrics. In *Proceedings of TRECVID 2015*. NIST, USA.

[10] S. Wu, S. Bondugula, F. Luisier et al. 2014. Zero-shot Event Detection using Multi-modal Fusion of Weakly Supervised Concepts. In *Computer Vision and Pattern Recognition (CVPR), IEEE Conf. on.* IEEE, 2665–2672.

[11] C. Xiaojun, Y. Yi, L. Guodong, Z. Chengqi, H. Alexander G. 2016. Dynamic concept composition for zero-example event detection. (2016), 20–26.

[12] Z. Fu, T. Xiang, E. Kodirov, S. Gong. 2015. Zero-shot object recognition by semantic manifold distance. In *Proceedings of the IEEE Conference on Computer Vision and Pattern Recognition*. 2635–2644.

[13] L. Jiang, S.I. Yu, D. Meng, T. Mitamura, A.G. Hauptmann. 2015. Bridging the ultimate semantic gap: A semantic search engine for internet videos. In *Proceedings of the 5th ACM on International Conference on Multimedia Retrieval*. ACM, 27–34.

[14] L. Jiang, T. Mitamura, S.I. Yu, A.G. Hauptmann. 2014. Zero-example event search using multimodal pseudo relevance feedback. In *Proceedings of International Conference on Multimedia Retrieval*. ACM, 297.

[15] Ian Jolliffe. 2002. *Principal component analysis*. Wiley Online Library.

[16] Y.J. Lu. 2016. Zero-Example Multimedia Event Detection and Recounting with Unsupervised Evidence Localization. In *Proceedings of the 2016 ACM on Multimedia Conference*. ACM, 1464–1468.

[17] E. Gabrilovich, S. Markovitch. 2007. Computing Semantic Relatedness Using Wikipedia-based Explicit Semantic Analysis.. In *IJCAI*, Vol. 7. 1606–1611.

[18] C. Tzelepis, D. Galanopoulos, V. Mezaris, I. Patras. 2016. Learning to detect video events from zero or very few video examples. *Image and vision Computing* 53 (2016), 35–44.

[19] Y.-G. Jiang, S. Bhattacharya, S.-F. Chang, M. Shah. 2012. High-level event recognition in unconstrained videos. *International Journal of Multimedia Information Retrieval* (2012), 1–29.

[20] A. Habibian, T. Mensink, C. Snoek. 2014. Composite concept discovery for zero-shot video event detection. In *Proc. of Int. Conf. on Multimedia Retrieval*. ACM, 17.

[21] A. Habibian, T. Mensink, C. Snoek. 2014. VideoStory: A New Multimedia Embedding for Few-Example Recognition and Translation of Events. In *Proc. of the ACM Int. Conf. on Multimedia*. ACM, 17–26.

[22] P. Mettes, D. Koelma, C. Snoek. 2016. The ImageNet Shuffle: Reorganized Pre-training for Video Event Detection. *arXiv preprint arXiv:1602.07119* (2016).

Tiny Transform Net for Mobile Image Stylization

Shilun Lin
Tencent
cirolin@tencent.com

Pengfei Xiong
Tencent
pumbaaxiong@tencent.com

Hailong Liu
Tencent
hailongliu@tencent.com

ABSTRACT

Artistic stylization is an image transformation problem that renders an image in the style of another one. Existing methods either regard image style transfer as an optimization of perceptual loss function based on a pre-trained network, or train a feed forward network that achieves style transfer through one forward propagation. However, time-consuming optimization processes or relatively large feed forward networks are unacceptable for mobile application. In this work we propose a tiny transform net to accomplish image stylization on mobile devices. The advantages of our proposed architecture come from that: (i) The size of the carefully designed network is less than 40KB, which is more than 166 times smaller than the current popular network; (ii) Progressive training is put forward to keep the training stable, which is implemental to achieve semantics aware stylization; (iii) Deep convolutional network inference algorithm is reconstructed on mobile platform to reduce the overhead of storage and time. In addition, well-trained tiny transform nets and demo application will be made available.

KEYWORDS

Mobile Image Stylization; Convolutional Neural Network; Deep Learning; Tiny Transform Net

ACM Reference format:
Shilun Lin, Pengfei Xiong, and Hailong Liu. 2017. Tiny Transform Net for Mobile Image Stylization. In *Proceedings of ICMR '17, Bucharest, Romania, June 06-09, 2017,* 5 pages.
https://doi.org/http://dx.doi.org/10.1145/3078971.3079034

1 INTRODUCTION

Image stylization can be regarded as a kind of texture transfer which synthesise textures from source image to target image. At the same time, content structure of the latter is preserve by constraining the texture synthesis. Most previous works have achieved noteworthy results. For instance, Efros and Freeman achieve texture synthesis by patch based texture "growing" and introduce a correspondence map to constrain the texture synthesis procedure [2]. However, it is difficult to extract the semantic information (such as objects) in the content image only by using low-level image features. So semantics aware stylization can not be implemented without high-level representation.

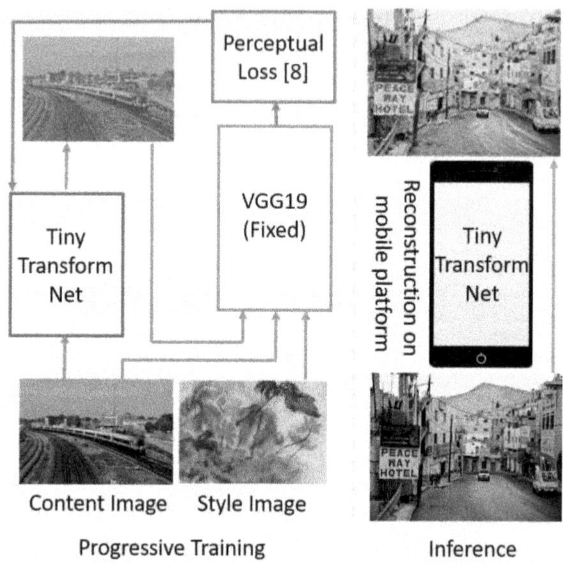

Figure 1: The flowchart of tiny transform network training and mobile image stylization inference.

Recently, researchers gradually shift their attention to image stylization based on deep features. The optimization-based method [3] obtained excellent visual results. It takes a long time to convert a noisy image into a stylized image by optimization algorithms such as L-BFGS. Feed-forward based method [8] significantly improves the efficiency of stylization. However, the relatively large model limits its application in the mobile terminal. In this paper, we try to use some hints given by experiments on convolutional network design to guide the construction of our network. The tiny transform net with Squeeze-Res module is proposed and trained step by step, which obtains visually appealing results with about 166 times fewer parameters and less than 40KB model size. The reconstruction of forward propagation algorithm allows our system to run smoothly on mobile devices. Fig. 1 shows the flowchart of our image stylization system.

2 RELATED WORK

2.1 Style Transfer

More recently, it has been shown that a well trained deep convolutional classifier can serve as a feature extractor to drive style transfer. Gatys *et al.* [3] formulate style transfer

ACM ISBN 978-1-4503-4701-3/17/06...$15.00
https://doi.org/http://dx.doi.org/10.1145/3078971.3079034

as an optimization problem that combines image stylization with content constraint. They use the off-the-shelf VGG-19 network [13] to extract style and content representations form a style image, a content image and a stylized image(using noise image as initialization). Two sets of representations are compared to generate loss and gradients are computed by back propagation. Gradient-based optimization is carried out to refine the stylized image. This method is time consuming, especially on mobile devices with limited computing resources, due to the need for hundreds of iterations to obtain visually acceptable stylized images. Johnson *et al.* address this issue by introducing a feed-forward style transform network trained to minimize the perceptual loss [8]. When the transform network is trained, it only requires one forward propagation from content image to stylized image. This yields a much faster method, but each relatively large transform network (6.5MB) only corresponds to one style. In mobile applications, such a large model is not acceptable, especially when the application contains a variety of styles. In addition, tiny networks require less computing resources. Therefore, it is essential to design a tiny and efficient transform network for mobile image stylization.

2.2 Design of Convolutional Neural Network

As one of the most widely used techniques in artificial neural network (ANN), convolution has made great success in the field of computer vision. In the aspect of convolution filter design, the early work by LeCun *et al.* [10] apply 5×5×Channels filters to digit recognition applications. And the current VGG architectures [13] extensively use 3×3 filters. Models such as Network-in-Network [11] and the GoogLeNet [14] utilize 1×1 filters in some layers. For the design of convolutional modules, Simoyan and Zisserman [13] propose the VGG block stacked by a plurality of 3×3 convolution layers. Szegedy *et al.* [14] come out with Inception modules , which are comprised of a number of different dimensionalities of filters, usually including 1×1 and 3×3, plus sometimes 5×5 and sometimes 1×3 and 3×1. He *et al.* [4] propose residual block with bypass connections and build up a deeper convolutional network, named ResNet, with up to 152 layers that deliver outstanding ImageNet [1] accuracy. Iandola *et al.* put forward the SqueezeNet which achieves AlexNet-level accuracy with 50 times fewer parameters [6]. These efforts are instructive to the design of tiny network for mobile image stylization.

3 METHODOLOGY

3.1 Tiny Transform Net

Mobile image stylization requires a fast and tiny transform network. Because tiny model makes the size of the application acceptable when it needs to support a variety of styles. Besides that, tiny model with fewer parameters is generally faster. In this section, design strategies for our proposed tiny transform net will be described. Primarily, reduce the number of large feature maps. On the one hand, the convolution operation of large feature map is more time-consuming. On the other hand, the total quantity of parameters in a convolutional layer equal to (number of input channels)×(number of filters)×(filter_weight×filter_height). Reducing the number of large feature maps can be considered as decreasing the number of input channels to the following convolutional layer which can effectively make the model tiny. Secondly, for transform network, the stylized image should share structure with the content image. He *et al.* [4] argue that bypass connections make it smooth for the network to learn the identify mapping which is an appealing property for stylization. With the purpose of designing a tiny model, the ordinary residual module is squeezed. Each Squeeze-Res module contains two convolutional layers. The number of parameters in the module is effectively controlled by using 1×1 kernel and small number of features map (half of the second layer) in the first layer. The second layer plays a role in maintaining the learning capability of transform network. Experiments by Ulyanov *et al.* [15] show that instance normalization can significantly improve the quality of style transfer. Therefore, instance normalization is eventually added to all convolution layers (including fractional convolution layers) except the last one to eliminate instance-specific contrast information from the content image. The architecture of tiny transform net is shown in Fig. 2.

3.2 Progressive Training

The tiny transform net proposed in the previous section has about 166 times fewer parameters than the network presented in [8]. Fewer parameters make the learning capacity of the model weaker, which leads to the difficulty of direct training in practice. Through experiments we found that stylized image generated by direct training network is visually rough. It is like adding a stylized mask to the input image rather than the semantics aware stylization. To achieve semantics aware style transfer, network sensitivity to general objects is one of the key elements. Furthermore, we also need to take the fact that different objects require varying degrees of stylization into account. The former is eased by using VGG-19 as loss network. In this section, progressive training strategy is put forward to tackle the latter problem. Instead of learning the mapping from content image to final stylized image directly, we divide the learning process into several stages and train the network step by step. At the beginning, the network is trained to generate an image that is close to the input content image. At this step, the network can be viewed as an encoder plus a decoder like the "unrolling" structure mentioned in literature [5]. From the perspective of function, the learning of this stage provides a stable foundation for the further stylization training. Then, gradually increase the intensity of style transfer by adjusting the proportion of style in perceptual loss. This helps the network to learn the mapping from the original image to light stylized image, and then to heavy stylized image gradually. In this phase, different object try to find the appropriate style transfer degree in a relatively small space of exploration. For instance, stylization of background objects have been completed in the

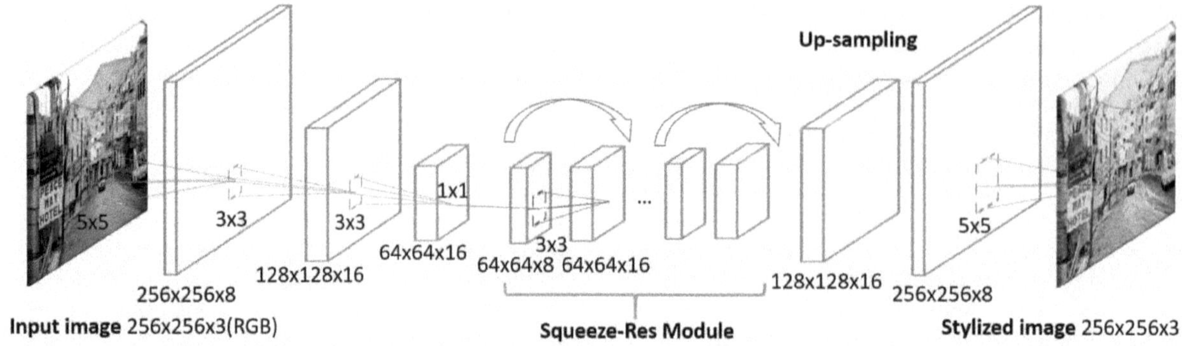

Figure 2: Architecture of the tiny transform net.

light stylized stage. Main objects are further processed in the stage of heavy stylization, which makes the final output sophisticated.

3.3 Optimization on Mobile Platform

Both time overhead and memory capacity need to be considered while algorithm is transplanted onto embedded systems. Existing methods apply dependent libraries corresponding to mobile version to accelerate traditional matrix operations. However, these dependent libraries can not play the maximum role due to the multi-thread mechanism. Furthermore, the size of application will be increased along with library size. Take Android platform as an example. The tiny transform net takes 2 seconds to process a 256×256 image without any acceleration. The time consumption can be decreased to 350 milliseconds with BLAS (Basic Linear Algebra Subprograms) library, but the application size will increase 40KB. To address this issue, we reconstructed deep convolutional network inference algorithm in three respects. Firstly, most of the time consumed in matrix multiplication on convolutional layers. Thus, we applied neon and assemble acceleration to classical convolutional layers with various kernel sizes and strides, which speed up around 12 times (170 milliseconds per image) compared to direct matrix operations in arithmetic. Secondly, parallel computing is carried out compatible with assemble, which further accelerated 2 times. Memory capacity has a great influence on time consumption in Android platform due to its multi-thread mechanism. Finally, a global parameter space is created for all layers. Weights and temporary variables used in each layer can share this space while algorithm execution layer by layer. Also a locking mechanism is designed to avoid memory conflicts. This operation accompanied by some code level optimization allows a real-time procession in about 50 milliseconds. Further, based on our algorithm, other existing methods like model sparse compression and fixed point quantization can also be applied for further acceleration.

4 EVALUATION

Microsoft COCO dataset [12] is used to train the tiny transform net and all images are resized to 256×256. VGG-19 provides feature space which contains content and style information. Feature maps extracted from layer conv4_2 serve as content representation. Style representation consist of activations at layers conv1-5_1. Adam [9] is applied to jointly minimise the distance between the style representations of style image and stylized image, and the content loss calculated by content representations of content image and stylized image. For progressive training, the initial ratio style/content is set to 100 and increased by 100 every 10,000 iterations. Our experiments are based on Caffe [7], a popular deep learning framework.

After about 80,000 iterations, the loss function reaches convergence and learning of tiny transform net is completed. As illustrated in Fig. 3, tiny transform nets achieve visually appealing results. In these results it is clear that the trained network does not blindly add some characteristic patches extracted from the style image to the content image. It is aware of the semantic content in images and implements fine-grained style transfer on them. For example in the image (h), starlight is added to the branches so that the whole tree looks very lively. In image (e), waves are integrated into the mountains, like rivers flowing through the mountains. We consider two potential factors contributing to this result. One is that the outstanding VGG-19 network is trained on the large scale ImageNet dataset. Using VGG-19 network to generate loss introduces the priori knowledge for general object recognition which makes the tiny transform net more sensitive to general objects. Furthermore, different objects require varying degrees of style. Progressive training divides the whole learning process into several stages (from light to heavy stylization as shown in Fig. 4). Thorough learning of each stage helps to carry out corresponding degree of style transfer to different objects.

The size of tiny transform net is less than 40KB which is more than 166 times smaller than the popular network presented in [8]. Table 1 presents the speed of various stylization approaches on a desktop computer. The tiny transform net is more than 1,700 times and 1.6 times faster than the optimization-based method proposed by Gatys *et al.* [3] and the remarkable feed-forward method [8] on GPU respectively. Reconstruction of CNN forward propagation algorithm is implemented so that processing time reduced from 2 seconds

Figure 3: Example results of style transfer using tiny transform net. Picture (a) is the content image. Pictures (b)-(h) are produced by tiny transform nets using The Muse of Pablo Picasso, Mosaic, The Scream of Edvard Munch, The Great Wave off Kanagawa of Hokusai, The Chinese Ink Painting, Sketch and The Starry Night of Vincent van Gogh as style images respectively during training.

Figure 4: Results of progressive training.

per image to about 50 milliseconds per image, which allows our system to run on mobile devices in real time.

Table 1: Speed comparison on various methods.

method	Gatys [3]	Johnson [8]	**Ours**(GPU/CPU)
256×256	15.86s	0.015s	0.009s/0.072s
512×512	54.85s	0.05s	0.028s/0.296s

5 CONCLUSION

This paper proposes a well-structured tiny transform net. Thanks to the progressive training strategy, it achieves visually engaging stylization with model size less than 40KB. An optimized inference algorithm ensures that the system can run on mobile devices efficiently. Additionally, finely trained model and online demo will be released.

REFERENCES

[1] Jia Deng, Wei Dong, Richard Socher, Li-Jia Li, Kai Li, and Li Fei-Fei. 2009. Imagenet: A large-scale hierarchical image database. In *Computer Vision and Pattern Recognition, 2009. CVPR 2009. IEEE Conference on*. IEEE, 248–255.

[2] Alexei A Efros and William T Freeman. 2001. Image quilting for texture synthesis and transfer. In *Proceedings of the 28th annual conference on Computer graphics and interactive techniques*. ACM, 341–346.

[3] Leon A Gatys, Alexander S Ecker, and Matthias Bethge. 2016. Image style transfer using convolutional neural networks. In *Proceedings of the IEEE Conference on Computer Vision and Pattern Recognition*. 2414–2423.

[4] Kaiming He, Xiangyu Zhang, Shaoqing Ren, and Jian Sun. 2016. Deep residual learning for image recognition. In *Proceedings of the IEEE Conference on Computer Vision and Pattern Recognition*. 770–778.

[5] Geoffrey E Hinton and Ruslan R Salakhutdinov. 2006. Reducing the dimensionality of data with neural networks. *science* 313, 5786 (2006), 504–507.

[6] Forrest N Iandola, Song Han, Matthew W Moskewicz, Khalid Ashraf, William J Dally, and Kurt Keutzer. 2016. SqueezeNet: AlexNet-level accuracy with 50x fewer parameters and¡ 0.5 MB model size. *arXiv preprint arXiv:1602.07360* (2016).

[7] Yangqing Jia, Evan Shelhamer, Jeff Donahue, Sergey Karayev, Jonathan Long, Ross Girshick, Sergio Guadarrama, and Trevor Darrell. 2014. Caffe: Convolutional architecture for fast feature

embedding. In *Proceedings of the 22nd ACM international conference on Multimedia*. ACM, 675–678.
[8] Justin Johnson, Alexandre Alahi, and Li Fei-Fei. 2016. Perceptual losses for real-time style transfer and super-resolution. In *European Conference on Computer Vision*. Springer, 694–711.
[9] Diederik Kingma and Jimmy Ba. 2014. Adam: A method for stochastic optimization. *arXiv preprint arXiv:1412.6980* (2014).
[10] Yann LeCun, Bernhard Boser, John S Denker, Donnie Henderson, Richard E Howard, Wayne Hubbard, and Lawrence D Jackel. 1989. Backpropagation applied to handwritten zip code recognition. *Neural computation* 1, 4 (1989), 541–551.
[11] Min Lin, Qiang Chen, and Shuicheng Yan. 2013. Network in network. *arXiv preprint arXiv:1312.4400* (2013).
[12] Tsung-Yi Lin, Michael Maire, Serge Belongie, James Hays, Pietro Perona, Deva Ramanan, Piotr Dollár, and C Lawrence Zitnick. 2014. Microsoft coco: Common objects in context. In *European Conference on Computer Vision*. Springer, 740–755.
[13] Karen Simonyan and Andrew Zisserman. 2014. Very deep convolutional networks for large-scale image recognition. *arXiv preprint arXiv:1409.1556* (2014).
[14] Christian Szegedy, Wei Liu, Yangqing Jia, Pierre Sermanet, Scott Reed, Dragomir Anguelov, Dumitru Erhan, Vincent Vanhoucke, and Andrew Rabinovich. 2015. Going deeper with convolutions. In *Proceedings of the IEEE Conference on Computer Vision and Pattern Recognition*. 1–9.
[15] Dmitry Ulyanov, Andrea Vedaldi, and Victor Lempitsky. 2016. Instance Normalization: The Missing Ingredient for Fast Stylization. *arXiv preprint arXiv:1607.08022* (2016).

Query and Keyframe Representations for Ad-hoc Video Search

Foteini Markatopoulou
Information Technologies Institute (ITI), CERTH
Thermi, Greece, 57001
Queen Mary University of London
markatopoulou@iti.gr

Damianos Galanopoulos
Information Technologies Institute (ITI), CERTH
Thermi, Greece, 57001
dgalanop@iti.gr

Vasileios Mezaris
Information Technologies Institute (ITI), CERTH
Thermi, Greece, 57001
bmezaris@iti.gr

Ioannis Patras
Queen Mary University of London
Mile end Campus, UK, E14NS
i.patras@qmul.ac.uk

ABSTRACT

This paper presents a fully-automatic method that combines video concept detection and textual query analysis in order to solve the problem of ad-hoc video search. We present a set of NLP steps that cleverly analyse different parts of the query in order to convert it to related semantic concepts, we propose a new method for transforming concept-based keyframe and query representations into a common semantic embedding space, and we show that our proposed combination of concept-based representations with their corresponding semantic embeddings results to improved video search accuracy. Our experiments in the TRECVID AVS 2016 and the Video Search 2008 datasets show the effectiveness of the proposed method compared to other similar approaches.

CCS CONCEPTS

• **Information systems → Query representation**; **Video search**;

KEYWORDS

Video search; zero-shot learning; visual analysis

ACM Reference format:
Foteini Markatopoulou, Damianos Galanopoulos, Vasileios Mezaris, and Ioannis Patras. 2017. Query and Keyframe Representations for Ad-hoc Video Search. In *Proceedings of ICMR '17, Bucharest, Romania, June 06-09, 2017,* 5 pages.
https://doi.org/10.1145/3078971.3079041

1 INTRODUCTION

Ad-hoc video search (AVS) [1] is the problem of retrieving, from a large video collection, video fragments (e.g., video shots) that are related to a given query. A query refers to an ad-hoc textual description, e.g. "Find shots of a woman wearing glasses". This problem is closely related to the simpler problem of concept-based video search, where a set of video shots is retrieved given a specific keyword (a.k.a. concept). In the latter case supervised learning (e.g., deep convolutional neural networks (DCNNs)) can be used to annotate the video shots with concepts. However, AVS is more complicated because an input query could be any complex or also abstract textual description for which annotated data does not exist; as a result, unsupervised learning and natural language processing (NLP) need to be employed for generating a common representation of queries and videos.

In this work we present a fully-automatic AVS method that uses solely a natural-language textual query to retrieve related video shots from a video collection. The novelty of our method is: a) An efficient algorithm that performs a number of NLP and semantic analysis steps to translate a query into a set of predefined concepts. b) A new approach that projects the concept-based video shot and query representations into a common semantic embedding space. And c) the combination of two different measures for the distance between the video shots and the target query, calculated on the concept-based and the semantic embedding representations respectively. Our AVS method was evaluated on the TRECVID AVS 2016 [1] and Video Search 2008 [5] datasets. The results show that it outperforms other state-of-the-art approaches.

2 RELATED WORK

Fully-automatic AVS is a very challenging problem, where the complete video search is performed without any user intervention. Typically, the query is broken down to a set of concepts using NLP. Each video shot from the test video collection is annotated with the same set of concepts, e.g., using DCNNs, and a distance measure is applied in order to retrieve those video shots that are closer to the concept-based query representation [3, 4, 12, 13, 15, 17, 20, 23]. Building the concept-based query representation starts by using simple NLP rules, e.g., removing stop-words, extracting nouns, verbs etc. or simply space-separating the whole query, which results to a set of terms for the query. Then, the semantic relation between each of the terms and the concepts is calculated, and the most semantically similar concepts to these terms are selected. The novelty of [20] is that they also enrich each concept with additional information captured by Google or Wikipedia, while in [4] an inverted index structure is used in order to associate the query with the concepts. A semi-automatic system is presented in [21], where the user is asked to choose keywords given a test query. All the above methods

ICMR '17, June 06-09, 2017, Bucharest, Romania

ACM ISBN 978-1-4503-4701-3/17/06...$15.00
https://doi.org/10.1145/3078971.3079041

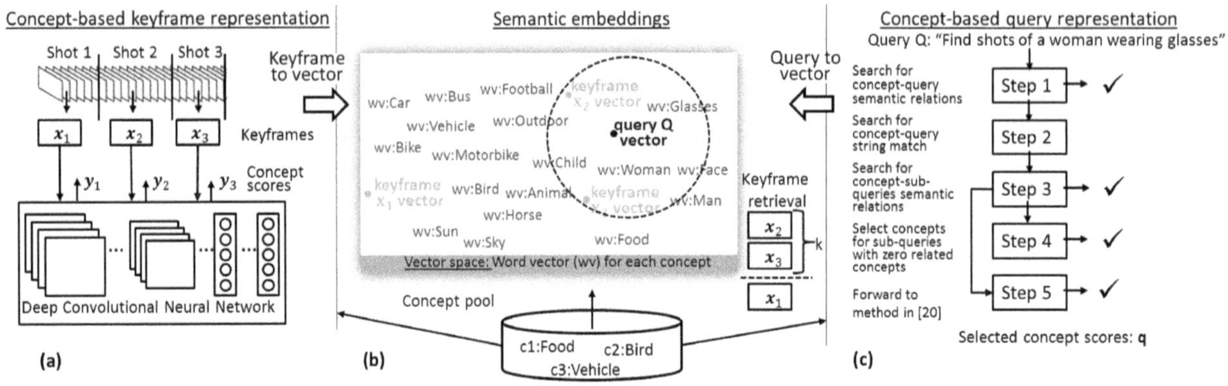

Figure 1: Overview of the proposed ad-hoc video search method.

treat the query as a set of simple terms. However, detecting the most useful parts of it, e.g., subsequences that contain the main content that the user asks for retrieval, could further improve the video search accuracy. Such a method is proposed in this paper. In contrast to the above methods, in [6], query models are trained with videos retrieved from websites, which is significantly slower compared to all the other methods discussed here.

Some recent methods for concept-based search, for example word2vec [10, 11, 14], train semantic embedding spaces of words or sentences from a large corpus using simple architectures of neural networks. After the embedding space is established, both video shots and concepts can be projected to it in order to directly measure their distance [15], [7], [19]. For example, in [15] images are mapped into a semantic embedding space by combining the class label embeddings with the concept detection results. All the methods in this paragraph aim to retrieve images for a single unknown concept label, which is a simpler problem compared to the one that we investigate, i.e., retrieving video shots given a complex textual query. In addition, combining the distances of the video shots from the target query calculated with respect to both concept-based and semantic embedding representations has not been investigated before.

3 THE PROPOSED METHOD

3.1 Overview

Assume that a text query Q and a set of keyframes $\mathbf{X} = \{\mathbf{x}_i\}_{i=1}^N$ are given, where one keyframe $\mathbf{x}_i \in \mathbb{R}^d$ has been extracted from each shot of the videos in a collection. Our goal is to retrieve for query Q the k keyframes from $\mathbf{X}$ that are most closely related to it. The overview of our method is presented in Fig. 1. Given a pre-defined concept pool $C = \{c_j\}_{j=1}^T$, our method represents both the keyframes (Fig. 1 (a)) and the query (Fig. 1 (c)) as vectors of related concepts. Then, these concept-based representations are projected into a common semantic embedding space (Fig. 1 (b)). Finally, the k-nearest keyframe representations to the query representation are retrieved using a distance measure.

3.2 Concept-based Keyframe Representation

Our method initially applies a DCNN $D : \mathbb{R}^d \Rightarrow [0,1]^T$, that has been trained on the T concepts, in every keyframe $\mathbf{x}_i$ in order to calculate concept-based representations $\mathbf{Y} = \{\mathbf{y}_i\}_{i=1}^N$. The DCNN's output for an input keyframe $\mathbf{x}$, $D(\mathbf{x}) = \mathbf{y}$, is a vector $\mathbf{y} \in [0,1]^T$ that indicates the model's belief that each of the concepts in C appears in the input keyframe.

3.3 Concept-based Query Representation

A set of NLP steps is applied in order to translate the query in a set of related concepts chosen from the concept set C. Let $C^Q = \{c_1^Q, c_2^Q, ..., c_{T'}^Q\} \subseteq C$ be the set of concepts selected for the query Q, where $T' \leq T$, and $\mathbf{q} = [q_1, q_2, ..., q_{T'}] \in [0,1]^{T'}$ a vector that indicates the degree to which each of the selected concepts in C^Q is related to Q. The following steps focus on analysing different parts of the query, instead of treating it as a set of single terms (words), which results to more distinctive retrieved concepts. Starting from the empty set $C^Q = \emptyset$ we calculate C^Q and $\mathbf{q}$ as follows:

Step one: The complete textual description of Q is compared with each concept in C for "semantic relatedness" in terms of the Explicit Semantic Analysis (ESA) measure (which returns a real number in the [0,1] interval) [8]. Those concepts that are semantically close to the query, i.e., the concepts that have ESA value higher than a threshold θ, are added in the set C^Q. If at least one concept is selected in this way, we assume that the entire query is very well described by these concepts and the query processing stops; otherwise, we continue with step two.

Step two: This step searches if any of the concepts in our concept pool appears in any part of the test query by string matching. Some (complex) concepts may describe part of the query quite well, but appear in a way that is difficult to detect them due to the subsequent linguistic analysis, e.g., breaking down the query to sub-queries. Any concept that appears in the query is added in the set C^Q and the query processing continues in step three.

Step three: Queries are complex sentences, but this step automatically transforms them into elementary *sub-queries*; i.e., meaningful smaller phrases or terms that are included in the original query. For example, the query "Find shots of one or more people at train station platform" is split into the following four sub-queries:

"people", "train station platform", "persons" and "train station". Then, each of the *sub-queries* is translated to a concept vector. To identify the sub-queries, part-of-speech tagging and stop-word removal are used together with a task-specific set of NLP rules. For example, extracting "Noun - Verb - Noun" sequences and considering them as sub-queries. The motivation is that such a triad is much more characteristic of the original query than any of the single terms alone. Then, the ESA measure is calculated between each sub-query and each of the concepts in the pool. Concepts that exceed the threshold θ are added in the set C^Q. In the case that for all of the sub-queries at least one concept has been selected, the query processing stops. If for a subset of the sub-queries no concepts have been selected then these sub-queries are propagated to step four. Finally, if for all the sub-queries no concepts have been selected then the test query and all of the sub-queries are propagated to step five.

Step four: For a subset of the sub-queries no concepts were selected. For each of these sub-queries, the concept with the highest value of ESA measure is selected in this step (i.e., threshold θ is ignored), and then the query processing stops.

Step five: For some queries, the processing step up to step three did not select any concepts. In this case, the query and the sub-queries are served as input to the zero-example event detection system of [20], which returns a ranked list of the most relevant concepts in accordance with relatedness scores, based on the ESA measure. In [20] the concepts are enriched with additional information captured by Google or Wikipedia, which virtually augments the concept pool. Then, the query processing has been completed.

Finally, the query's concept vector $\mathbf{q} \in [0, 1]^{T'}$ is formed by the corresponding scores of the selected concepts. If a concept has been selected in steps 1, 3, 4 or 5 then the corresponding vector's element is assigned with the relatedness score (calculated using the ESA measure); if it has been selected in step 2, it is set equal to 1. A complete example of applying the above steps in a query is presented in Table 1.

3.4 Semantic Embeddings for Concept-based Query and Keyframe Representations

Given a semantic embedding space $S \subseteq \mathbb{R}^m$, we project both the concept-based keyframe (Section 3.2) and the query (Section 3.3) representations into S, in order to directly measure their distance. Initially, we calculate the set $S^C = \{s(c_1), s(c_2), ..., s(c_T)\}$ of the semantic embedding vectors $s(c_j) \in S$ associated with each concept in C, by applying a pre-trained word2vec model [14].

Then, similarly to [15], our method calculates a keyframe semantic embedding vector $f(\mathbf{x}) \in \mathbb{R}^m$, as the combination of the semantic embeddings of the R-top retrieved concepts for $\mathbf{x}$, according to the concept-based keyframe representation $\mathbf{y} \in \mathbf{Y}$, weighted by their corresponding concept detection scores:

$$f(\mathbf{x}; \mathbf{y}, S^C) = \frac{1}{Z} \sum_{r=1}^{R} y_{g(\mathbf{x},r)} \cdot s(c_{g(\mathbf{x},r)}), \tag{1}$$

where $g(\mathbf{x}, r)$ denotes the r-th most likely concept label for the input keyframe $\mathbf{x}$ according to $\mathbf{y}$, $Z = \sum_{r=1}^{R} y_{g(\mathbf{x},r)}$ the normalization term and R a parameter that considers the maximum number of embeddings that will be combined.

Table 1: Concept-based query representation example.

	Query: ***Find shots of three people or more walking or bicycling on a bridge during daytime***		
	Sub-queries	C^Q ($\theta = 0.8$)	q
Step 1	*Find shots of...daytime*	$\emptyset$	-
Step 2	***three people or more*** *walking or bicycling on a bridge during daytime*	three or more people	1.0
Step 3	people walking	walking	1.0
	bicycling	bicycle-built-for-two	1.0
		bicycles	0.85
		bicycling	0.84
	bridge	suspension bridge	1.0
		bridges	0.84
	Sub-query *daytime* also found but without corresponding concepts with ESA distance > θ		
Step 4	daytime	daytime outdoor	0.74

Subsequently, we calculate the semantic embedding vector associated with the concept-based query representation by extending the above process as follows. Given the set of concepts C^Q assigned to this query and the corresponding ESA scores $\mathbf{q}$, described in Section 3.3, our method calculates the semantic embedding vector h(Q) for query Q, as the combination of the semantic embeddings of the concepts assigned to this query weighted by their corresponding ESA score:

$$h(Q; \mathbf{q}, S^C) = \frac{1}{Z'} \sum_{l=1}^{T'} q_l \cdot s(c_l^Q), \tag{2}$$

where $Z' = \sum_{l=1}^{T'} q_l$ the normalization term.

After the concept-based keyframe representations have been calculated (Section 3.2), our system measures their distance from the concept-based query representation (Section 3.3), e.g. by calculating the euclidean distance. Similarly, the distance between the semantic embedding keyframe representations and the semantic embedding query representation is calculated and the two distance vectors are combined in terms of arithmetic mean. The k keyframes with the smallest distance are then retrieved.

4 EXPERIMENTAL STUDY

4.1 Dataset and Experimental Setup

Our experiments were performed on the TRECVID AVS 2016 (AVS16) [1] and Video Search 2008 (VS08) [5] datasets that consist of approx. 600 and 100 hours of internet archive videos and are evaluated on 30 and 48 queries, respectively. Ground-truth annotated training data does not exist for these queries. The AVS problem as defined in TRECVID [1] was examined, i.e., given a query, the goal was to retrieve the 1000 video shots that are mostly related with it. We analyze our results in terms of mean extended inferred average precision (MXinfAP), which is an approximation of the mean average precision suitable for the partial ground-truth that accompanies the TRECVID dataset [22].

In order to create the concept-based keyframe representations, each keyframe was automatically annotated with 1000 ImageNet [18] and 346 TRECVID SIN [2] concepts. Regarding the 1000 ImageNet concepts, we applied five pre-trained ImageNet DCNNs on the keyframes and fused their outputs in terms of arithmetic mean to obtain a single score for each of the 1000 concepts. Regarding the 346 SIN concepts, we fine-tuned (FT) two pre-trained ImageNet DCNNs on the 346 concepts using the TRECVID AVS development dataset [1] and the extension strategy proposed in [16], where one extension layer with 4096 neurons was used. We used the last layer of each of these networks to train support vector machine classifiers (SVMs) for each concept. The keyframe score per concept was the average of the probabilities that the two SVM models returned. Each keyframe was finally represented by a 1345-element vector by simply concatenating the score vectors for the ImageNet and the TRECVID SIN concepts. The threshold θ for deciding whether to select a concept or not in our method (Section 3.3) was set to 0.8. The pre-trained Google News Corpus word2vec model [1] was used for calculating the semantic embeddings of the concept-based representations (Section 3.4). In our preliminary experiments, small fluctuations of the overall accuracy were observed for different values of parameter R (Eq. 1), consequently and based on these experiments we set it to 70. The euclidean distance was used for measuring the distance between the keyframe and query representations.

4.2 Experimental Results

Table 2: Experiments (MXInfAP (%)) on the AVS16 dataset to investigate the parameters of the proposed method.

Steps	All	Excluding one step: step 1	step 2	step 3	step 4	step 5
(a) Concept-based representation (Sections 3.2 + 3.3)	5.94	5.92	5.74	3.96	5.95	4.53
(b) Semantic embeddings (Section 3.4)	3.77	3.86	2.98	3.22	3.75	2.80
(c) Combination	6.35	**6.51**	5.77	4.37	6.27	4.99

Table 3: MXInfAP (%) for different compared AVS methods.

Methods	AVS16		VS08	
(a) Literature methods				
Tzelepis et al. [20]	4.16		8.27	
Ueki et al. [21]	5.65		7.24	
Norouzi et al. [15]	3.14		7.30	
(b) Top-4 TRECVID finalists				
Top-1	Le et al. [4]	5.4	Tang et al.	6.7
Top-2	Markat. et al. [13]	5.1	Snoek al.	5.4
Top-3	Liang et al. [6]	4.0	Ngo et al.	4.2
Top-4	Zhangy et al. [23]	3.8	Mei et al.	4.1
Proposed	**6.35**		**9.11**	

Table 2 presents the results of some intermediate experiments that we performed in order to investigate the performance when: i) the transformation to the semantic embedding space is ignored (Table 2 (a)), ii) the final distance from the query is calculated solely in the semantic embedding space (Table 2 (b)), iii) the complete process is used, i.e., the final distance is the combination of the distances calculated in i) and ii) (Table 2 (c)). For each of the above cases, we also examine the usefulness of each of the steps presented in Section 3.3, i.e., each column shows the corresponding results when one of the steps is excluded. According to Table 2 we conclude as follows: Concept-based representations perform very well on the AVS problem, outperforming the semantic embedding representations. However, combining the two types of representations further improves our method, reaching a MXInfAP of 6.35 %. Almost all of the steps one to five of Section 3.3 contribute to the improved translation of the query into related concepts; excluding one step reduces the performance in most cases. One exception is observed w.r.t. step 1. However, excluding step 1 and evaluating w.r.t. the VS08 dataset slightly reduced the accuracy, which lead us to propose the use of all five steps. Furthermore, step 4 only marginally affects the performance; thus, sub-queries that do not present high semantic relatedness with any of the concepts could be ignored when for at least one sub-query one or more concepts have been selected. Similar conclusions were reached on the VS08 dataset.

Table 3 compares the proposed method with 11 different literature ones. The top part of the table refers to those methods that were re-implemented in order to be adapted for this problem and datasets, whereas in the lower part we introduce the results of the top-four finalists in the AVS16 and the VS08 tasks. Especially for comparing with [21] we used a modified version that does not require the user's involvement. In this modified version, we automatically split the query into several keywords after removing the stop-words, and for each keyword the concept with the highest ESA value is selected. Overall, as we can see in Table 3, for both datasets our proposed method performs very well compared to the other methods. Specifically, it outperforms all the compared methods, achieving an MXinfAP of 6.35% and 9.11% for AVS16 and VS08, respectively.

5 CONCLUSIONS AND FUTURE WORK

In this work we presented a fully-automatic method that combines video concept detection and query analysis for ad-hoc video search. Extensive experiments reveal the usefulness of the proposed NLP steps for translating a textual query to related predefined concepts and the usefulness of combining different types of keyframe-query representations (e.g., concept-based representations, semantic embeddings). Our proposed method was compared with many state-of-the-art AVS systems and was shown to outperform all fully-automatic entries to the TRECVID AVS 2016 benchmarking activity. In our future work we will investigate the use of different types of semantic embeddings, e.g., [9], and also the influence of the different keyframe-query representations on different types of queries, i.e., in which cases concept-based representations outperform semantic embeddings or the combination of both.

ACKNOWLEDGMENTS

This work was supported by the EU's Horizon 2020 research and innovation programme under grant agreements H2020-693092 MOVING and H2020-687786 InVID.

[1]https://s3.amazonaws.com/dl4j-distribution/GoogleNews-vectors-negative300.bin.gz

REFERENCES

[1] G. Awad, J. Fiscus, and M. Michel et al. 2016. TRECVID 2016: Evaluating Video Search, Video Event Detection, Localization, and Hyperlinking. In *TRECVID 2016 Workshop.* NIST, USA.

[2] G. Awad, C. G. M. Snoek, and A. F. Smeaton et al. 2016. TRECVid Semantic Indexing of Video: A 6-Year Retrospective. *ITE Transactions on Media Technology and Applications* 4, 3 (2016), 187–208.

[3] M. Elhoseiny, B. Saleh, and A. Elgammal. 2013. Write a Classifier: Zero Shot Learning Using Purely Textual Descriptions. In *Int. Conf. on Computer Vision.*

[4] D.-D. Le et al. 2016. NII-HITACHI-UIT at TRECVID 2016. In *TRECVID 2016 Workshop.* Gaithersburg, MD, USA.

[5] G. Awad et al. 2008. TRECVID 2008–Goals, Tasks, Data, Evaluation Mechanisms and Metrics. In *TRECVID 2008 Workshop.* NIST, USA.

[6] J. Liang et al. 2016. Informedia @ Trecvid 2016. In *TRECVID 2016 Workshop.* Gaithersburg, MD, USA.

[7] Z. Fu, T. Xiang, and E. Kodirov et al. 2015. Zero-Shot Object Recognition by Semantic Manifold Distance. In *IEEE Conf. on Computer Vision and Pattern Recognition (CVPR).*

[8] E. Gabrilovich and S. Markovitch. 2007. Computing Semantic Relatedness Using Wikipedia-based Explicit Semantic Analysis.. In *IJCAI*, Vol. 7. 1606–1611.

[9] A. Habibian, T. Mensink, and C. G.M. Snoek. 2014. VideoStory: A New Multimedia Embedding for Few-Example Recognition and Translation of Events. In *Proceedings of the 22nd ACM International Conference on Multimedia (MM '14).* ACM, NY, USA, 17–26.

[10] T. Kenter, A. Borisov, and M. de Rijke. 2016. Siamese CBOW: Optimizing Word Embeddings for Sentence Representations. *CoRR* abs/1606.04640 (2016).

[11] R. Kiros, Y. Zhu, and R. Salakhutdinov et al. 2015. Skip-Thought Vectors. In *Advances in Neural Information Processing Systems.* Curran Associates, 3294–3302.

[12] Y.-J. Lu, H. Zhang, and M. de Boer et al. 2016. Event Detection with Zero Example: Select the Right and Suppress the Wrong Concepts. In *ACM Int. Conf. on Multimedia Retrieval (ICMR) (ICMR '16).* ACM, NY, USA, 127–134.

[13] F. Markatopoulou and A. Moumtzidou et al. 2016. ITI-CERTH participation to TRECVID 2016. In *TRECVID 2016 Workshop.* Gaithersburg, MD, USA.

[14] T. Mikolov, I. Sutskever, and K. Chen et al. 2013. Distributed Representations of Words and Phrases and Their Compositionality. In *26th Int. Conf. on Neural Information Processing Systems (NIPS'13).* Curran Associates, USA, 3111–3119.

[15] M. Norouzi, T. Mikolov, and S. Bengio et al. 2013. Zero-Shot Learning by Convex Combination of Semantic Embeddings. *CoRR* abs/1312.5650 (2013).

[16] N. Pittaras, F. Markatopoulou, and V. Mezaris et al. 2017. *Comparison of Fine-Tuning and Extension Strategies for Deep Convolutional Neural Networks.* Springer, Cham, 102–114.

[17] B. Romera-Paredes and P. H.S. Torr. 2015. An embarrassingly simple approach to zero-shot learning. *32nd Int. Conf. on Machine Learning (ICML)* (2015).

[18] O. Russakovsky, J. Deng, and H. Su et al. 2015. ImageNet Large Scale Visual Recognition Challenge. *Int. Journal of Computer Vision (IJCV)* 115, 3 (2015), 211–252.

[19] R. Socher, M. Ganjoo, and C. D Manning et al. 2013. Zero-Shot Learning Through Cross-Modal Transfer. In *Advances in Neural Information Processing Systems.* Curran Associates, 935–943.

[20] C. Tzelepis, D. Galanopoulos, and V. Mezaris et al. 2016. Learning to Detect Video Events from Zero or Very Few Video Examples. *Image Vision Computing* 53 (Sept. 2016), 35–44.

[21] K. Ueki, K. Kikuchi, and T. Kobayashi. 2016. Waseda at TRECVID 2016: Ad-hoc Video Search. In *TRECVID 2016 Workshop.* Gaithersburg, MD, USA.

[22] E. Yilmaz, E. Kanoulas, and J. A. Aslam. 2008. A Simple and Efficient Sampling Method for Estimating AP and NDCG. In *31st ACM SIGIR Int. Conf. on Research and Development in Information Retrieval.* ACM, USA, 603–610.

[23] H. Zhang, L. Pang, Y. Lu, and C. Ngo. 2016. VIREO@TRECVID 2016: Multimedia Event Detection, Ad-hoc Video Search, Video to Text Description. In *TRECVID 2016 Workshop.* Gaithersburg, MD, USA.

Manga FaceNet: Face Detection in Manga based on Deep Neural Network

Wei-Ta Chu
National Chung Cheng University
Chiayi, Taiwan
wtchu@ccu.edu.tw

Wei-Wei Li
National Chung Cheng University
Chiayi, Taiwan
welcometoway@gmail.com

ABSTRACT

Among various elements of manga, character's face plays one of the most important role in access and retrieval. We propose a DNN-based method to do manga face detection, which is a challenging but relatively unexplored topic. Given a manga page, we first find candidate regions based on the selective search scheme. A deep neural network is then proposed to detect manga faces of various appearance. We evaluate the proposed method based on a large-scale benchmark, and show performance comparison and convincing evaluation results that have rarely done before.

CCS CONCEPTS

•Computing methodologies → Object detection;

KEYWORDS

Manga; face detection; convolutional neural network

ACM Reference format:
Wei-Ta Chu and Wei-Wei Li. 2017. Manga FaceNet: Face Detection in Manga based
on Deep Neural Network. In *Proceedings of ICMR '17, June 6–9, 2017, Bucharest, Romania, ,* 5 pages.
DOI: http://dx.doi.org/10.1145/3078971.3079031

(a) (b) (c) (d) (e) (f)

Figure 1: Sample manga faces.

1 INTRODUCTION

Face detection is a fundamental step to many computer vision and multimedia applications. This topic has been widely studied for natural images. However, much fewer studies have been proposed for manga (Japanese comics). Manga is one of the biggest book sales in the world. Although the book market slumped, in Japan the market of compiled manga books keep creating record-high sales and reach around 2.4 billion US dollars in year 2014 [1]. As more and more manga books are digitized, efficient access and retrieval of manga is urgently demanded [6].

There are at least three differences between faces in natural images and in manga. First, we focus on the largest comics market, i.e., Japanese comics (manga). In most manga, only black-and-white and sometimes gray information is available, which is different from color information in natural images. Second, there are extreme variations in faces in different manga. Figure 1(a) and Figure 1(b) show two normal frontal faces, while Figure 1(c) and Figure 1(d) show drastically different visual appearance especially on eyes. Third, manga faces do not entirely possess properties of human faces. The spatial layout, visual appearance, and expression of manga faces may not physically reasonable (Figure 1(e) and Figure 1(f)). The methods proposed for human face detection are thus not able to be directly employed in manga face detection.

Some works were proposed to detect manga faces. Sun and Kise [8] extracted Haar-like features, and concatenated a sequence of weak classifiers to construct a face detector. For a limited dataset, frontal manga faces can be detected. Focusing on colorful comics images, Takayama et al. [9] detected skin color and the jaw contour to find character's face. The symmetric property of face was then adopted to filter out noises. This method may not be generic to faces in different poses. In [12], the deformable part model (DPM) was used to consider pose and spatial variations. This approach achieved performance better than the conventional HOG-based (histogram of oriented gradient) approach. Chu and Chao [3] attempted to avoid visual variations by first detecting character's eyes, and then expanded the eye regions to find the face.

The aforementioned methods are mostly ad-hoc approaches and are hard to be generalized. In addition, most of them were not evaluated on a large-scale dataset, making the conclusion not convincing enough. Thanks to the recently proposed Manga109 dataset [6], now we have more resource to train the face detector, and can evaluate the proposed method at a larger scale. We propose a deep-based manga face detection framework. The selective search [10] scheme is adopted to first detect regions with objects. Each region is then examined by a deep neural network that extracts features and classifies the input region as a face or not.

Contributions of this paper are twofold. First, we construct a deep manga face detection framework to resist visual variations. Second, we evaluate performance of the proposed framework based on large-scale benchmark to facilitate fair comparison in the future.

The rest of this paper is organized as follows. Section 2 provides details of the deep framework. Section 3 shows performance of the

ICMR '17, June 6–9, 2017, Bucharest, Romania
 ACM ISBN 978-1-4503-4701-3/17/06…$15.00
DOI: http://dx.doi.org/10.1145/3078971.3079031

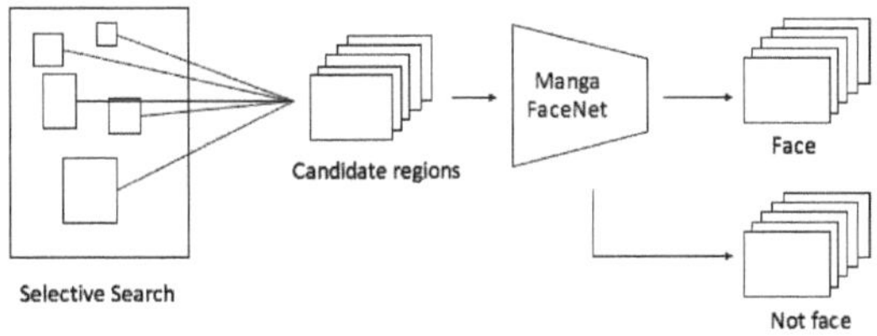

Figure 2: Overview of the manga face detection framework.

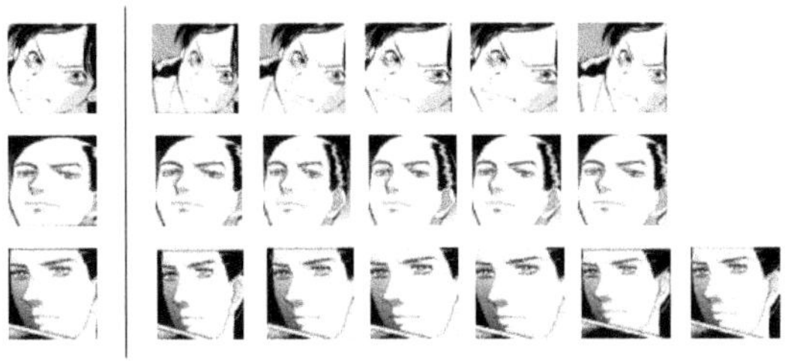

Figure 3: Left: ground truth; right: the regions found by selective search with large overlap with the ground truth. All regions are resized to 40×40.

proposed method as well as comparison with existing methods, and conclusion is given in Section 4.

2 MANGA FACE DETECTION

2.1 System Overview

Figure 2 shows overview of the proposed method. Given a manga page, we first employ the selective search scheme [10] to detect regions probably containing objects. Each region is then examined by the proposed deep neural network, named Manga FaceNet, to see whether this region is a manga face or not.

Recently the power of deep learning has been demonstrated in many domains. Not only for image classification [5] or object detection [7] for natural images, now the effectiveness of deep learning on sketch or line drawings have also been demonstrated [11] [13]. We therefore propose to construct a deep neural network called Manga FaceNet to do this task.

Before training, we randomly select 66 manga titles from the Manga109 dataset, and from each title we select 50 manga pages as the evaluation dataset. From each page, we manually define the bounding box of each manga face.

To train the proposed network, we extract positive samples and negative samples in the following way. Given each manga page, we employ the selective search scheme [10] to find regions of objects. The regions that have more than 70% overlap with any truth bounding box and contain frontal faces are considered as positive samples. On the other hand, the regions that have less than 30% overlap with any truth bounding box are considered as negative samples. Figure 3 illustrates results of sampling by showing just a few positive samples because of space limitation. We can see that the selective search may detect several regions corresponding to the same ground truth.

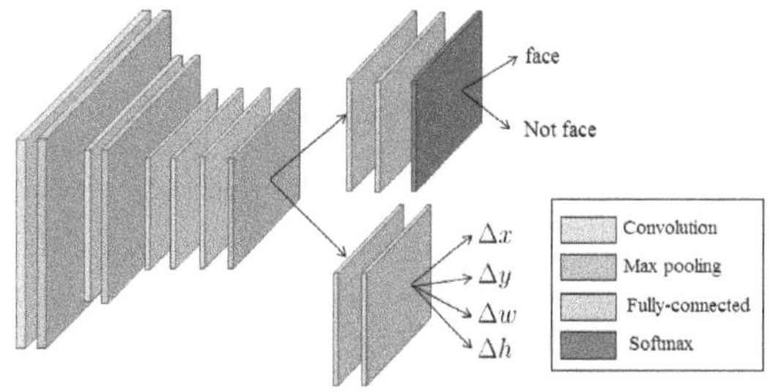

Figure 4: Structure of the Manga FaceNet.

2.2 Manga FaceNet

Based on the training data, we construct a face detector based on convolutional neural networks (CNN). Figure 4 shows structure of the proposed Manga FaceNet. Given a candidate region found by selective search, we resize it into 40×40 pixels and input it to a CNN consisting of five convolutional layers to do feature extraction. The output of the fifth convolutional layer is flattened to be a vector, which is then input to two branches. The top branch is a classification network consisting of two fully-connected layers. The activation function of the last fully-connected layer is softmax, and thus it outputs the probability of a given region being a manga face or not. To train the top branch of Manga FaceNet, the loss function is set as:

$$L_1 = \frac{-1}{N} \sum (y_g \log y_p + (1 - y_g) \log(1 - y_p)), \quad (1)$$

where y_p is the predicted probability of the given data being a manga face, and y_g is the ground truth where $y_g = 1$ if the given region is really a face, and $y_g = 0$ otherwise.

For the bottom branch of Manga FaceNet, we attempt to further consider the spatial displacement of a given training region to its corresponding ground truth, in order to more finely evaluate the goodness of a region being a manga face. Associated with each region, the spatial displacement and aspect ratio to the corresponding ground truth are further considered. More particularly, taking the original manga page as a coordinate system, assume that the left-top corner of a given region is at (x', y'), and its width and height are w' and h', respectively. For its corresponding ground truth, assume its left-top corner is at (x, y), and its width and height are w and h, respectively. Motivated by the settings in [7], the horizontal and vertical spatial displacements are calculated and normalized as $\Delta x = \frac{x'-x}{w}$, and $\Delta y = \frac{y'-y}{h}$, respectively. The width difference Δw and the height difference Δh are calculated as $\Delta w = \log \frac{w'}{w}$, and $\Delta h = \log \frac{h'}{h}$, respectively. Similar to the top branch of Manga FaceNet, we design two fully-connected layers to estimate the spatial displacement and aspect ratio change. Given a candidate region, if the predicted value of spatial displacement and aspect ratio difference are $\Delta\hat{x}$, $\Delta\hat{y}$, $\Delta\hat{w}$, and $\Delta\hat{h}$, respectively. The loss function to train the bottom branch of Manga FaceNet is the mean square error:

$$L_2 = \frac{1}{N} \sum (\Delta x - \Delta\hat{x})^2 + (\Delta y - \Delta\hat{y})^2 + (\Delta w - \Delta\hat{w})^2 + (\Delta h - \Delta\hat{h})^2, \quad (2)$$

where N is the number of training regions.

Table 1: Detailed Manga FaceNet configuration.

input (40 × 40 gray images)				
conv3-32 maxpooling dropout(0.25)	conv3-64 maxpooling dropout(0.25)	conv3-128	conv3-128	conv3-128 maxpooling dropout(0.25)
fully-connected (256 nodes) (both branches) dropout(0.5)(both branches)				
fully-connected (4 nodes) (bottom branch) fully-connected (2 nodes) – softmax (top branch)				

Overall, the top branch and the bottom branch of the Manga FaceNet are jointly trained by considering the integrated loss

$$L = \lambda_1 L_1 + \lambda_2 L_2, \quad (3)$$

where both weighting parameters λ_1 and λ_2 are currently set as 1.

Table 1 shows detailed configurations of Manga FaceNet. The input region is processed through five convolutional layers, as shown in the second row of Table 1, from left to right. The convolutional parameters are denoted as "conv⟨receptive field size⟩ - ⟨number of channels⟩". The ReLU activation function is used in all convolutional layers. The first, the second, and the fifth convolutional layers are followed by max pooling and dropout with ratio 0.25. Results of convolution are input to two fully-connected layers, where the first one consists of 256 nodes, and the second one consists of 4 nodes and 2 nodes for the bottom branch and the top branch, respectively. The activation function of the final fully-connected layer of the top branch is softmax.

We adopt mini-batch of size 100, and the learning process updates network parameters for 60 epochs. The learning algorithm is RMSprop, with the learning rate 0.001. We employ a strategy similar to the "image-centric" sampling strategy [4] to the train the network. A mini-batch contains positive samples and negative samples both sampled from the same manga title, i.e., more like "manga-title-centric" sampling.

3 EVALUATION

3.1 Dataset and Evaluation Settings

As we mentioned before, we evaluate the proposed system based on a large-scale manga benchmark, i.e., the Manga109 dataset [6]. We randomly select 66 titles from the 109 titles, and from each title we select 50 manga pages and manually define ground truths of manga faces. There are 14,405 faces in total.

According to the framework shown in Figure 2, we first detect object regions by the selective search scheme, and then estimate the probability of each region being a face. If the probability is larger than a threshold τ, we say the test region is a manga face.

One may wonder that if the selective search scheme is able to detect regions covering manga faces. To verify this, we calculate the ratio of manga faces that can be included in the regions found by selective search. According to our experiment, this ratio is around 92%. In the following experiments, we will use precision and recall values to measure performance of manga face detection. Because of the designed procedure shown in Figure 2, the value 0.92 is therefore the upper bound of the recall value we can obtain.

Table 2: Performance comparison between methods.

Methods	Precision	Recall	F-measure
OpenCV (pre-trained)	0.48	0.04	0.07
OpenCV (trained with manga) [8]	0.15	0.95	0.26
Eye-based method [3]	0.42	0.55	0.48
Manga FaceNet (top branch only)	0.57	0.70	**0.63**
Manga FaceNet (both branches)	0.79	0.56	**0.66**
Manga FaceNet (both) + VGG	0.97	0.46	**0.62**

3.2 Performance of Manga Face Detection

Table 2 shows performance comparison between different manga face detection methods. As we expect, the Adaboost method originally designed for detecting real human faces and is embedded in the OpenCV library does not work well (the first row). To decrease the mismatch problem between real human faces and manga faces, we retrain the OpenCV model based on our manga data. This is more like the method proposed in [8], though the training data are not the same. From the second row of Table 2, we see that the recall rate can be largely improved, while the precision rate largely decreases. Overall, only 0.26 F-measure can be obtained by the Adaboost method. The eye-based method [3] works better, but is still not promising. Intuitively the shapes of eyes is similar to round or elliptical. However, eyes are the most important features to show different artists' drawing styles or to show different characters. Accurately detecting eyes is thus not a trivial problem.

The fourth row shows performance of the proposed Manga FaceNet (top branch only), with threshold τ mentioned above set as 0.8. We see significant improvement can be obtained by the proposed deep-based method. When both branches are considered in training, the best performance as F-measure equal to 0.66 can be obtained (the fifth row). When a large number of manga pages (and thus a large number of manga faces) are available, precision of face detection is more important than recall in some applications, e.g., style analysis proposed in [3]. Therefore, for the regions determined as faces by Manga FaceNet, we further extract CNN features based on the VGG-f framework [2], and then construct a support vector machine to further verify them as face or non-face. As shown in the last row of Table 2, this process largely improves precision, with the cost of recall decrease.

Figure 6 further shows performance variations of Manga FaceNet (MF) and Manga FaceNet with VGG (MF+VGG), in terms of PR curves obtained based on different thresholds τ's. The MF+VGG approach hardly achieves high recall, but its precision is significantly higher than the MF approach. In addition, we see the MF+VGG approach relatively achieves more stable performance (precision ranges from 0.94 to 0.98, while recall ranges from 0.41 to 0.54).

Figure 5 shows sample manga face detection results for a manga page. It can be easily seen that the proposed method can much more accurately detect manga faces than the method originally designed for human face detection.

3.3 Discussion

Although the proposed Manga FaceNet largely improves detection performance, it is still far from perfect. The top row of Figure 7

(a) (b) (c) (d)

Figure 5: Sample detection results. (a) Ground truth; (b) OpenCV trained with manga; (c) the method in [3]; (d) our results.

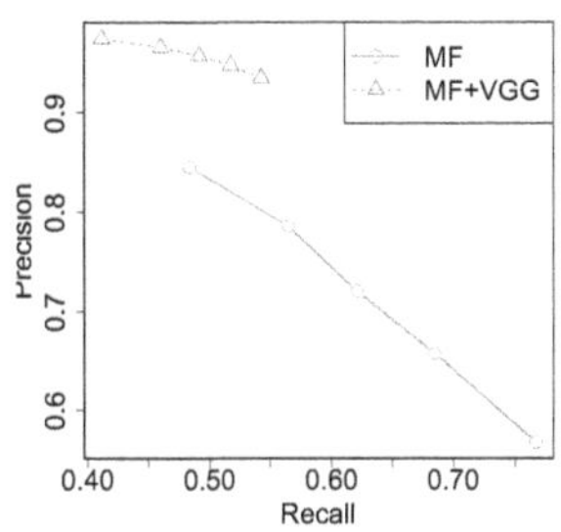

Figure 6: PR curves of two variants of the proposed method.

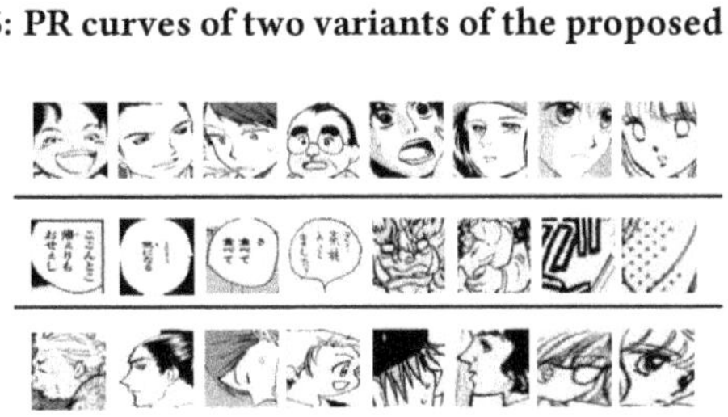

Figure 7: Sample face detection results. Top row: detected faces; middle row: false alarms; bottom row: miss.

shows correctly detected faces. The middle row shows false alarms. We observe that speech balloons or regions with large white area and symmetry may be falsely detected as faces. The bottom row shows miss cases. Apparently side faces are often missed in the current work. This is also a challenging issue in real human face detection. In the future, we will jointly consider side faces in the deep framework and try to improve recall rates.

4 CONCLUSION

We have presented a deep-based face detection method specially for Manga. Given a manga page, we first find candidate regions by the selective search scheme, and then determine each region as a manga face or not by the proposed Manga FaceNet. In addition to classification label, we also jointly consider spatial displacement and aspect ratio in the proposed network. Being able to model high variations on visual appearance and expression, the proposed method significantly outperforms the methods designed for real human faces and the conventional manga face detection methods. In the future, we would like to design a more elegant framework to enhance the ability of detecting side faces, in order to improve recall values.

ACKNOWLEDGMENTS

The work was partially supported by the Ministry of Science and Technology of Taiwan under the grant MOST105-2628-E-194-001-MY2, MOST104-2221-E-194-014, and MOST103-2221-E-194-027-MY3.

REFERENCES

[1] Anime News Network 2015. *Japanese Manga Book Market Rises to Record 282 Billion Yen.* Anime News Network. http://www.animenewsnetwork.com/news/2015-01-23/japanese-manga-book-market-rises-to-record-282-billion-yen/.83614.

[2] K. Chatfield, K. Simonyan, A. Vedaldi, and A. Zisserman. 2014. Return of the Devil in the Details: Delving Deep into Convolutional Nets. In *Proceedings of British Machine Vision Conference.*

[3] W.-T. Chu and Y.-C. Chao. 2014. Line-based Drawing Style Description for Manga Classification. In *Proceedings of ACM International Conference on Multimedia.* 781–784.

[4] R. Girshick. 2015. Fast R-CNN. In *Proceedings of International Conference on Computer Vision.* 1440–1448.

[5] A. Krizhevsky, I. Sutskever, and G.E. Hinton. 2012. ImageNet Classification with Deep Convolutional Neural Networks. In *Proceedings of Neural Information Processing Systems.*

[6] Y. Matsui, K. Ito, Y. Aramaki, A. Fujimoto, T. Ogawa, T. Yamasaki, and K. Aizawa. 2016. Sketch-based Manga Retrieval Using Manga109 Dataset. *Multimedia Tools and Applications* (2016).

[7] S. Ren, K. He, R. Girshick, and J. Sun. 2015. Faster R-CNN: Towards Real-Time Object Detection with Region Proposal Networks. In *Proceedings of Neural Information Processing Systems.*

[8] W. Sun and K. Kise. 2010. Similar Partial Copy Detection of Line Drawings Using a Cascade Classifier and Feature Matching. In *Proceedings of International Workshop on Computational Forensics.* 121–132.

[9] K. Takayama, H. Johan, and T. Nishita. 2012. Face Detection and Face Recognition of Cartoon Characters Using Feature Extraction. In *Proceedings of IIEEJ Image Electronics and Visual Computing Workshop.*

[10] J.R.R. Uijlings, K.E.A. van de Sande, T. Gevers, and A.W.M. Smeulders. 2013. Selective Search for Object Recognition. *International Journal of Computer Vision* 104, 2 (2013), 154–171.

[11] F. Wang, L. Kang, and Y. Li. 2015. Sketch-based 3D Shape Retrieval Using Convolutional Neural Networks. In *Proceedings of IEEE International Conference on Computer Vision and Pattern Recognition.* 1875–1883.

[12] H. Yanagisawa, D. Ishii, and H. Watanabe. 2014. Face Detection for Comic Images with Deformable Part Model. In *Proceedings of IIEEJ Image Electronics and Visual Computing Workshop.*

[13] F. Zhu, J. Xie, and Y. Fang. 2016. Learning Cross-Domain Neural Networks for Sketch-Based 3D Shape Retrieval. In *Proceedings of AAAI Conference on Artificial Intelligence.* 3683–3689.

Generative Adversarial Networks for Multimodal Representation Learning in Video Hyperlinking

Vedran Vukotić
INSA Rennes, INRIA/IRISA
Rennes, France
vedran.vukotic@irisa.fr

Christian Raymond
INSA Rennes, INRIA/IRISA
Rennes, France
christian.raymond@irisa.fr

Guillaume Gravier
CNRS, INRIA/IRISA
Rennes, France
guillaume.gravier@irisa.fr

ABSTRACT

Continuous multimodal representations suitable for multimodal information retrieval are usually obtained with methods that heavily rely on multimodal autoencoders. In video hyperlinking, a task that aims at retrieving video segments, the state of the art is a variation of two interlocked networks working in opposing directions. These systems provide good multimodal embeddings and are also capable of translating from one representation space to the other. Operating on representation spaces, these networks lack the ability to operate in the original spaces (text or image), which makes it difficult to visualize the crossmodal function, and do not generalize well to unseen data. Recently, generative adversarial networks have gained popularity and have been used for generating realistic synthetic data and for obtaining high-level, single-modal latent representation spaces. In this work, we evaluate the feasibility of using GANs to obtain multimodal representations. We show that GANs can be used for multimodal representation learning and that they provide multimodal representations that are superior to representations obtained with multimodal autoencoders. Additionally, we illustrate the ability of visualizing crossmodal translations that can provide human-interpretable insights on learned GAN-based video hyperlinking models.

CCS CONCEPTS

•Information systems →Multimedia information systems; *Document representation;* **•Computing methodologies →***Neural networks;*

KEYWORDS

video hyperlinking; multimedia retrieval; multimodal embedding; multimodal autoencoders; representation learning; unsupervised learning; generative adversarial networks; neural networks

ACM Reference format:
Vedran Vukotić, Christian Raymond, and Guillaume Gravier. 2017. Generative Adversarial Networks for Multimodal Representation Learning in Video Hyperlinking. In *Proceedings of ICMR '17, June 6–9, 2017, Bucharest, Romania,* , 4 pages.
DOI: DOI:http://dx.doi.org/10.1145/3078971.3079038

ACM ISBN 978-1-4503-4701-3/17/06...$15.00
DOI: DOI:http://dx.doi.org/10.1145/3078971.3079038

1 INTRODUCTION

Automatic generation of hyperlinks in video collections presents a problem of growing interest, where video segments are interlinked by their high level semantic similarity, based on one or more of their modalities. Video hyperlinking consists of establishing links between relevant video segments within a collection. Links are defined between source video segments, called anchors (video segments that the users are viewing and query for additional relevant video segments), and target video segments (video segments relevant for to each queried anchor). For every anchor, a multimodal retrieval task is performed and a set containing the most relevant related targets is returned. Automatic generation of hyperlinks within large video collections has been a subject studied and evaluated yearly as part of the MediaEval and TRECVID initiatives, within their Search and Hyperlinking benchmark [1]. There are different approaches to handling multiple modalities in multimodal retrieval and thus in video hyperlinking. Straightforward approaches using multiple modalities consist either in comparing each modality separately, combining the scores or rankings, or in combining descriptors from each modality. These methods however do not fully exploit the multimodality of the datasets. Regardless of classical methods such as canonical correlation analysis (CCA), the state of the art methods yielding a joint multimodal representation space from the initially disjoint representations heavily rely on multimodal autoencoders [3, 5].

Multimodal AEs operate with representations of each modality (in our case, speech and visual representations). It is possible to translate from one initial representation space to the other, but not completely to the original space. Being able to visualize the crossmodal mappings (e.g., what images are expected given a certain speech transcript) in video hyperlinking can offer important human-interpretable insight about the learned model and explain its performance. Recently, generative adversarial networks [6] have become popular as means of generating realistic artificial data in the original, initial space (as opposed to the original representation space). Even more recently, generative adversarial autoencoder models have been conditioned on the input with one modality (CGAN), while allowing them to generate realistic artificial data of the other modality [13] thus allowing for crossmodal translation from one initial space (e.g., text) to the other initial space (e.g., image), as opposed to crossmodal translation between representation spaces. We explore the possibility of using CGANs in video hyperlinking and creating models that not only provide good multimodal embeddings but also provide human-interpretable visualizations of what the model has learned.

Multimodal AEs are trained in an unsupervised manner on a dataset of finite, often limited size. It is possible to enlarge the dataset by applying random transformations and noise to the existing samples but the amount of samples will sill remain limited. In this work, we explore the possibility of using CGANs to tackle this problem. A generator network can generate an unlimited number of synthetic samples to train with and can constantly be improved by competing with the discriminator network. The discriminator network can also benefit from the additional synthetic samples and provide even better multimodal embeddings.

2 RELATED WORK

Multimodal AEs are commonly deployed in tasks where multiple modalities are used. Such tasks include but are not limited to classification [3, 10] and retrieval [5, 7]. More specifically, in video hyperlinking, the current state of the art is a variation on multimodal AEs, consisting of two interlocked crossmodal DNNs, translating in opposing directions [14, 15] that achieved the best performance at the latest TRECVID evaluation [2].

Generative adversarial networks have been first introduced by [6] as a two-network generative-discriminative model for generating high-quality, single-modal, realistic samples that could be mistaken for real samples from the dataset the model is trained on. GANs quickly became popular and are now used in a multitude of tasks, such as generating super-resolution images, inpainting, de-occlusion and many others. Conditional GANs [9] have been shown to generate realistic samples of one modality, given a conditioning input of another modality. A typical example of a crossmodal CGAN model is text to image synthesis [13, 16] but the conditioned input is not necessarily bound to multiple modalities and can be conditioned also on the same modality.

For the purpose of multimodal retrieval, we focus on crossmodal / multimodal CGANs and ways to obtain meaningful multimodal representations from them. While multimodal setups are currently less explored, there is a lot of evidence that GANs learn meaningful representations in single-modal setups [4, 8, 11], most notably in the generator network. These representations are obtained in a completely unsupervised manner and can be used to model changes in style, pose, color or even style and structure in RGBD data. Evidence suggests that both the generator network and the discriminator network can produce meaningful single-modal representations [12]. Our work falls into the category of text to image CGANs [13, 16], where we explore the possibility of obtaining good multimodal representations from the discriminator, while using the generator to visualize crossmodal mappings for the purposes of multimodal retrieval in video hyperlinking and to improve the embeddings from the discriminator network.

3 METHODOLOGY

We split the work in two separate parts. In the first part, we evaluate the current state of the art multimodal AEs. In the second part, we evaluate the feasibility of using CGANs to perform multimodal embedding and we compare the resulting representations against the current state of the art in the setup of multimodal retrieval within the video hyperlinking domain.

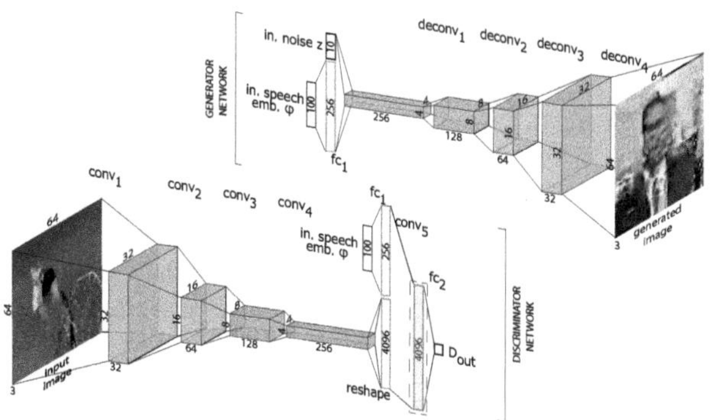

Figure 1: Used CGAN architecture, consisting of a generator and a discriminator network. Multimodal embeddings are obtained in the discriminator, after the last, 1D convolution operation, as denoted with a dashed rectangle.

3.1 Multimodal Autoencoders

Multimodal AEs with two separate input and output branches [10], one for each modality have been shown to perform better than simple AEs where the two modalities are concatenated. Recently, BiDNN, a variation with two disjoint but tied networks, working in opposing directions has been shown to define the new state of the art in video hyperlinking [2]. We compare our proposed model against both classical multimodal AEs and the recent BiDNN variation. However, multimodal AEs need existing continuous representations as inputs. We opt for averaged Word2Vec for representing speech and VGG-19 features for representing video keyframes.

3.2 Unsupervised Multimodal Representation Learning with CGANs

The CGAN architecture we evaluate is based on the GAN-CLS text to image model [13]. The model consists of a generator network G and a discriminator network D. The generator network takes a noise vector z, sampled from a $\mathcal{U}(-1, 1)$ distribution and a text embedding φ, and generates a synthetic image $\hat{x} = G(z, \varphi)$. The generator consists of a separate fully-connected layer with a leaky-ReLU activation function (that allows for a small non-zero gradient on the negative side) for modeling the text embeddings. This is then concatenated with the noise input. A standard deconvolutional network follows. The discriminator network takes an image x and a text embedding φ and determines whether the pair is real or artificial $D(x, \varphi)$. Contrary to the basic CGAN model that only differentiates between real and synthetic images, CGAN-CLS is trained on three pairs. In our case {real image, real text}, {incorrect image, real text} and {synthetic image, real text}. As we are doing unsupervised learning, pairs with a non-matching image and text are chosen at random from different video segments and the dataset is not split. Pairs of real maching and non-matching text-image pairs are necessary to train the discriminator. The discriminator consists of a series of convolutional layers with batch normalization, followed by a leaky-ReLU for modelling the input image and a full-connected leaky-ReLU layer to model the text embeddings. The two branches are then concatenated and a 1×1 convolution is performed, followed by batch normalization and a leaky-ReLU activation before obtaining the discriminator score. For multimodal

Table 1: **Visualization of generated synthetic images given automatic transcripts (in lowercase, with some stop words removed) as input. In the last column, a real image from the video segment corresponding to the input automatic transcript is shown. CGANs provide good visualizations of the video hyperlinking model: in the last row, given speech transcripts related to war thematic, the model is expecting a news presenter, while the actual video segment contains footage from the war zone.**

Input - Automatic Speech Transcript	Generated Images	Real Image
"...insects emerged to take advantage of the abundance . the warm weather sees the arrival of migrant birds stone chests have spent the winter in the south ..."	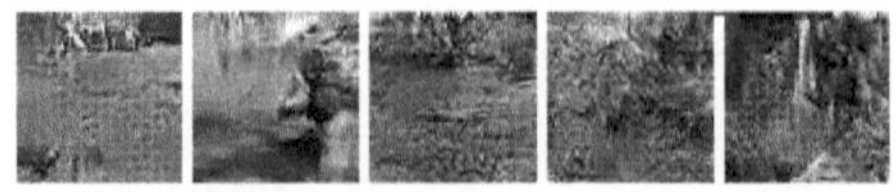	
"...second navigation of the united kingdom . the north sea , it was at the north yorkshire moors between the 2 , starting point for the next leg of our journey along the coast ..."		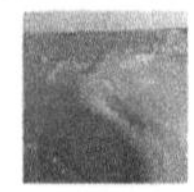
"...the role of my squadron afghanistan is to provide the the reconnaissance capability to use its or so forgave so using light armor of maneuvering around the area of ..."		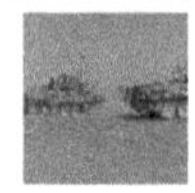

embedding, we use the vector obtained after the final 1×1 convolution of the discriminator. To maintain the losses of both the generator and the discriminator at similar levels (having a discriminator that is performing too well would prevent the generator from converging), the generator is updated four times more often than the discriminator. A cosine distance between the obtained multimodal embeddings is used to measure the similarity of the desired video segments both in the case of multimodal AEs and CGANs.

4 EXPERIMENTS

In this section we first define the dataset and the specific hyper-parameters of each architecture and then analyze and discuss the results of each experiment.

4.1 Dataset and Single-Modal Representations

We test all the methods in a video hyperlinking setup on a BBC video hyperlinkig dataset with segments and the groundtruth obtained post-evaluation during MediaEval 2014. The task considered is that of ranking target segments given a source segment acting as a query. We use only the video segments that contain both speech transcripts and video keyframes (10,321 in total). Speech is represented with averaged embeddings of size 100 from a skip-gram *Word2Vec* model with hierarchical sampling and a window size of 5 [2]. Regarding the visual stream, a representative keyframe is chosen for each video segment by computing a histogram for each pixel over all the keyframes and choosing the keyframe closest to the medianas a representative of each short video segment. Such an image is then downsampled and cropped to a size of 64×64 pixels. To obtain a sensible comparison, the same data and image sizes are used for all the methods. The CGAN model works directly with the text embeddings and images. Multimodal AEs also need visual embeddings as inputs. We obtained them from the same images, with a VGG-19 network (pretrained on ImageNet) and they are of size 4096. Table 2 show the initial single-modal results, which are 56.55% for speech transcripts and 52.41% for video keyframes, in terms of precision at 10 [1].

Table 2: **Comparison of initial modal single-modal representations and multimodal embeddings obtained with different methods. For each method, precision at 10 and its respective standard deviation are reported.**

Representation	P_{10} (%)	σ (%)
Speech Transcripts Only	56.55	-
Visual Only (VGG-19)	52.41	-
Multimodal AE	57.94	0.82
BiDNN	59.66	0.84
CGAN	**62.84**	**1.36**

4.2 Multimodal Autoencoders

We evaluate both classical multimodal AEs and BiDNNs, their state-of-the-art variation in video hyperlinking. We chose an AE architecture with separate input and output branches of size 1000 for each modality (first and last layers of consisting of two separate hidden layers of size 1000 each) and a common hidden layer or size 1000. For BiDNNs, we use the implementation provided by [2]. We use only the video segments that contain multimodal information (both speech transcripts and visual information) and we use averaged *Word2Vec* embeddings for speech and VGG-19 embeddings for the keyframes, as defined in section 4.1. BiDNNs expectedly outperform classical multimodal autoencoders and obtain a precision at 10 of 59.66%.

4.3 Multimodal Embedding with CGANs

To evaluate the feasibility of obtaining multimodal embeddings with CGANs, we used the architecture described in Sec. 3.2 with a speech embedding of dimension 100, a noise input of size 10, a fully connected layer for modeling text of size 256 and 4 *"deconvolutional"* layers of increasing size, each with 256, 128, 64 and 32 feature maps respectively in the generator network. The output of the generator is an image of size 64×64. The discriminator network consists of an image input of size 64×64 followed by 4 convolutional layers with batch normalization, each with 32, 64, 128 and 256 feature maps respectively and decreasing sizes and a speech embedding input of size 100, followed by a fully connected layer of size 256. The two branches are then concatenated and followed by another, final convolution. We trained the network for 1000 epochs by using the Adam optimizer with a learning rate r of 0.0001, a momentum β of 0.5 and a batch size of 64. As specified in Section 3.2, we use the one-dimensional convolutional layer in the discriminator that follows the merging of the two branches, before batch normalization and activation as a multimodal embedding layer, as illustrated in Figure 1. Other layers did not perform well and provided a lower or equal quality than the initial single-modal inputs. The generator network does not only provide a mean to visualize crossmodal mappings but is also crucial for obtaining high-quality embeddings in the discriminator by competing with it and providing additional synthetic samples.

Compared to multimodal AEs, CGANs are computationally expensive to train (20h on a GPU, compared to a few hours on a CPU for BiDNN), even for small images, and require both modalities to be present. However, the discriminator of a CGAN provides multimodal embeddings that are greatly improved over the initial representation spaces or each modality. The results are shown in Table 2. Representations learned with a CGAN not only outperformed multimodal AEs but they also significantly ($p = 99.9\,\%$ with a single-sided t-test) outperformed the state of the art BiDNN model and obtained 62.84%.

4.4 Crossmodal Visualizations

The existence of a generator network is crucial to train a discriminator that provides well-performing multimodal embeddings. Interestingly, the generator network can also be used to visualize crossmodal mappings in video hyperlinking. The generator can straightforwardly create synthetic images given an embedding of the speech transcripts as input. Examples of images generated for real transcripts on a few video segments, as well as their real visual counterparts are displayed in Table 1. The generator can also be reversed by simply applying the transposed learned kernels in an inversed architecture and slicing the obtained vector. In this case, given an image, embeddings in the textual domain can be obtained. A few examples of that translation are shown in Table 3.

5 CONCLUSIONS AND FUTURE WORK

In this work we experimentally demonstrated the interest of CGANs as an alternative method to design multimodal embeddings. While CGANs are more computationally intensive to train than multimodal autoencoders, and are thus limited to smaller image sizes, they can provide better multimodal embeddings in the last layer of their discriminator network that outperform embeddings of multimodal autoencoders. The generator network, that provides unlimited synthetic samples and is crucial for training the discriminator, can additionally be used to visualize one modality from another and provide human-interpretable insights of the crossmodal translations learned with this type of video hyperlinking models. To use CGANs for multimodal embedding more efficiently, it is necessary to investigate different architectures that are able to converge with bigger image sizes within a feasible training timeframe and evaluate possible methods of decreasing the training time for uses where online learning is required.

6 ACKNOWLEDGMENTS

We gratefully acknowledge the support of NVIDIA Corporation with the donation of the Titan X GPU used for this research.

Table 3: Visualization of the top words in the representation space of automatic transcripts, given an input image.

Input Image	Top Words in the Speech Modality
	britain, protecting, shipyard, carriers, jobs, vessels, current, royal, aircraft, securing, critics, flagships, foreclosures, economic, national
	north, central, rain, northern, eastern, across, scotland, southwest, west, north-east, northeast, south, affecting, england, midlands
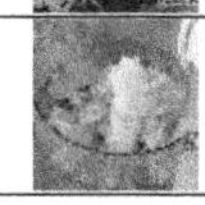	pepper, garlic, sauce, cumin, chopped, ginger, tomatoes, peppers, onion, crispy, parsley, grated, coconuts, salt, crust

REFERENCES

[1] George Awad, Jonathan Fiscus, Martial Michel, David Joy, Wessel Kraaij, Alan F Smeaton, Georges Quénot, Maria Eskevich, Robin Aly, and Roeland Ordelman. 2016. Trecvid 2016: Evaluating video search, video event detection, localization, and hyperlinking. In *Proceedings of TRECVID*, Vol. 2016.

[2] Rémi Bois, Vedran Vukotić, Ronan Sicre, Christian Raymond, Guillaume Gravier, and Pascale Sébillot. 2016. IRISA at TRECVid2016: Crossmodality, Multimodality and Monomodality for Video Hyperlinking. In *Working Notes of the TRECVid 2016 Workshop*.

[3] Miriam Cha, Youngjune Gwon, and H. T. Kung. 2015. Multimodal sparse representation learning and applications. *CoRR* abs/1511.06238 (2015).

[4] Xi Chen, Yan Duan, Rein Houthooft, John Schulman, Ilya Sutskever, and Pieter Abbeel. 2016. Infogan: Interpretable representation learning by information maximizing generative adversarial nets. In *Advances in Neural Information Processing Systems*. 2172–2180.

[5] Fangxiang Feng, Xiaojie Wang, and Ruifan Li. 2014. Cross-modal retrieval with correspondence autoencoder. In *ACM Intl. Conf. on Multimedia*. 7–16.

[6] Ian Goodfellow, Jean Pouget-Abadie, Mehdi Mirza, Bing Xu, David Warde-Farley, Sherjil Ozair, Aaron Courville, and Yoshua Bengio. 2014. Generative adversarial nets. In *Advances in neural information processing systems*. 2672–2680.

[7] Hungtsung Lu, Yuanming Liou, Hungyi Lee, and Linshan Lee. 2015. Semantic Retrieval of Personal Photos Using a Deep Autoencoder Fusing Visual Features with Speech Annotations Represented as Word/Paragraph Vectors. In *Annual Conf. of the Intl. Speech Communication Association*.

[8] Alireza Makhzani, Jonathon Shlens, Navdeep Jaitly, Ian Goodfellow, and Brendan Frey. 2015. Adversarial autoencoders. *arXiv preprint arXiv:1511.05644* (2015).

[9] Mehdi Mirza and Simon Osindero. 2014. Conditional generative adversarial nets. *arXiv preprint arXiv:1411.1784* (2014).

[10] Jiquan Ngiam, Aditya Khosla, Mingyu Kim, Juhan Nam, Honglak Lee, and Andrew Y Ng. 2011. Multimodal deep learning. In *Intl. Conf. on Machine Learning*.

[11] Guim Perarnau, Joost van de Weijer, Bogdan Raducanu, and Jose M Álvarez. 2016. Invertible Conditional GANs for image editing. (2016).

[12] Alec Radford, Luke Metz, and Soumith Chintala. 2015. Unsupervised representation learning with deep convolutional generative adversarial networks. In *ICLR 2016*.

[13] Scott Reed, Zeynep Akata, Xinchen Yan, Lajanugen Logeswaran, Bernt Schiele, and Honglak Lee. 2016. Generative adversarial text to image synthesis. In *Proceedings of The 33rd International Conference on Machine Learning*, Vol. 3.

[14] Vedran Vukotić, Christian Raymond, and Guillaume Gravier. 2016. Bidirectional Joint Representation Learning with Symmetrical Deep Neural Networks for Multimodal and Crossmodal Applications. In *Proc. of the ACM International Conference on Multimedia Retrieval*.

[15] Vedran Vukotić, Christian Raymond, and Guillaume Gravier. 2016. Multimodal and Crossmodal Representation Learning from Textual and Visual Features with Bidirectional Deep Neural Networks for Video Hyperlinking. In *ACM Multimedia 2016 Workshop: Vision and Language Integration Meets Multimedia Fusion (iV&L-MM'16)*. ACM, Amsterdam, Netherlands.

[16] Han Zhang, Tao Xu, Hongsheng Li, Shaoting Zhang, Xiaolei Huang, Xiaogang Wang, and Dimitris Metaxas. 2016. StackGAN: Text to Photo-realistic Image Synthesis with Stacked Generative Adversarial Networks. *arXiv preprint arXiv:1612.03242* (2016).

Efficient Indexing of Regional Maximum Activations of Convolutions using Full-Text Search Engines

Giuseppe Amato, Fabio Carrara, Fabrizio Falchi, Claudio Gennaro
ISTI-CNR, via G. Moruzzi 1, 56124, Pisa, Italy
{name.surname}@isti.cnr.it

ABSTRACT

In this paper, we adapt a surrogate text representation technique to develop efficient instance-level image retrieval using Regional Maximum Activations of Convolutions (R-MAC). R-MAC features have recently showed outstanding performance in visual instance retrieval. However, contrary to the activations of hidden layers adopting ReLU (Rectified Linear Unit), these features are dense. This constitutes an obstacle to the direct use of inverted indexes, which rely on sparsity of data. We propose the use of deep permutations, a recent approach for efficient evaluation of permutations, to generate surrogate text representation of R-MAC features, enabling indexing of visual features as text into a standard search-engine. The experiments, conducted on Lucene, show the effectiveness and efficiency of the proposed approach.

KEYWORDS

Similarity Search, Permutation-Based Indexing, Deep Convolutional Neural Network

ACM Reference format:
Giuseppe Amato, Fabio Carrara, Fabrizio Falchi, Claudio Gennaro. 2017. Efficient Indexing of Regional Maximum Activations of Convolutions using Full-Text Search Engines. In *Proceedings of ICMR '17, June 6–9, 2017, Bucharest, Romania, ,* 4 pages.
DOI: http://dx.doi.org/10.1145/3078971.3079035

1 INTRODUCTION

Deep learning has rapidly become the state-of-the-art approach for many computer vision tasks such as classification [21], content-based image retrieval [3, 12], cross-media retrieval [10], smart cameras [1]. A practical and convenient way of using Deep Convolutional Neural Networks (DCNNs) to support fast content-based image retrieval is to treat the neuron activations of the hidden layers as global features [12, 22, 27]. Recently, Tolias et al. [31] have gone further, proposing to use Regional Maximum Activation of Convolutions (R-MAC) as a compact and effective image representation for instance-level retrieval. This feature is the result of the spatial aggregation of the activations of a convolution layer of a DCNN, therefore is robust to scale and translation. Gordo et al. [17] extended the R-MAC representation by improving the region pooling mechanism and including it in a differentiable pipeline trained end-to-end for retrieval tasks.

However, these features are typically of high dimensionality, which prevents the use of space-partitioning data structure, such as kd-tree [9]. For instance, in the well-known AlexNet architecture [21] the output of the sixth layer (fc6) has 4,096 dimensions, while the R-MAC extracted by Gordo et al. [17] produces a 2048-dimensional image descriptor.

To overcome this problem, various partitioning methods have been proposed. In particular, the inverted multi-index uses product quantization both to define the coarse level and for coding residual vectors [6, 25]. This approach combined with binary compressed techniques outperforms the state of the art by a large margin [13]. Our approach, as we will see, is implemented on top of an existing text retrieval engine and requires minimal pre-processing.

Mohedano et al. [23] propose a sparse visual descriptor based on a Bag of Local Convolutional Features (BLCF), which allows fast image retrieval by means of an inverted index. This method, however, relies on a priori learning of a codebook (which involves the use k-means) and the VGG16 [30] pre-trained network, which makes it difficult to retrain the whole pipeline on new set of images.

Our approach to tackle the dimensionality curse problem is still based on the application of approximate access methods, but relies on the permutation approach similar to [5, 11, 14, 24]. The key idea is to represent metric objects (i.e., features) as sequences (permutations) of reference objects, chosen from a predefined set of objects. Similarity queries are executed by searching for data objects whose permutation representations are similar to the query permutation representation. Each permutation is generated by sorting the entire set of reference objects according to their distances from the object to be represented. The total number of reference objects to be used for building permutations depends on the size of the dataset to be indexed and can amount to tens of thousands [5]. In these cases, both indexing time and searching time is affected by the cost of generating permutations for objects being inserted or for the queries.

In this paper, we propose an adaptation of surrogate text representation [15] suitable to regional maximum activations of convolutions features, which exploits the so-called deep permutation approach introduced in [4]. An advantage of this approach lies in its low-computational cost since does not require the distance calculation between the reference objects and the objects to be represented.

The rest of the paper is organized as follows. Section 2 provides background for the reader. In Section 3, we introduce our approach to generate permutations for R-MAC features. Section 4 presents some experimental results using real-life datasets. Section5 concludes the paper.

ACM ISBN 978-1-4503-4701-3/17/06...$15.00
DOI: http://dx.doi.org/10.1145/3078971.3079035

2 BACKGROUND

2.1 Permutation-Based Approach

Given a domain $\mathcal{D}$, a *distance function* $d : \mathcal{D} \times \mathcal{D} \to \mathbb{R}$, and a fixed set of reference objects $P = \{p_1 \dots p_n\} \subset \mathcal{D}$ that we call *pivots* or *reference objects*, we define a permutation-based representation Π_o (briefly *permutation*) of an object $o \in \mathcal{D}$ as the sequence of pivots identifiers sorted in ascending order by their distance from o [5, 11, 14, 24].

Formally, the permutation-based representation $\Pi_o = (\Pi_o(1), \dots, \Pi_o(n))$ lists the pivot identifiers in an order such that $\forall j \in \{1, \dots, n-1\}$, $d(o, p_{\Pi_o(j)}) \leq d(o, p_{\Pi_o(j+1)})$, where $p_{\Pi_o(j)}$ indicates the pivot at position j in the permutation associated with object o. If we denote as $\Pi_o^{-1}(i)$ the position of a pivot p_i, in the permutation of an object $o \in \mathcal{D}$, so that $\Pi_o(\Pi_o^{-1}(i)) = i$, we obtain the equivalent *inverted* representation of permutations $\Pi_o^{-1} = (\Pi_o^{-1}(1), \dots, \Pi_o^{-1}(n))$. In Π_o the value in each position of the sequence is the identifier of the pivot in that position. In the inverted representation Π_o^{-1}, each position corresponds to a pivot and the value in each position corresponds to the rank of the corresponding pivot. The inverted representation of permutations Π_o^{-1}, is a vector that we refer to as *vector of permutations*, and which allows us to easily define most of the distance functions between permutations.

Permutations are generally compared using Spearman rho, Kendall Tau, or Spearman Footrule distances. In our implementation, we apply a simple algebraic transformation to permutations in order to compute the same ranking scores that we would obtain with the Spearman Rho distance using dot products. Due to the lack of space, we do not present the proof of this result, however, further details can be found in [15].

2.2 Deep Features

Recently, a new class of image descriptor, built upon Deep Convolutional Neural Networks, have been used as effective alternative to descriptors built using local features such as SIFT, SURF, ORB, BRIEF, etc. DCNNs have attracted enormous interest within the Computer Vision community because of the state-of-the-art results [21] achieved in challenging image classification challenges such as ImageNet Large Scale Visual Recognition Challenge (ILSVRC). In computer vision, DCNN have been used to perform several tasks, including image classification, as well as image retrieval [8, 12] and object detection [16], to cite some. In particular, it has been proved that the multiple levels of representation, which are learned by DCNN on specific task (typically supervised) can be used to transfer learning across tasks [12, 27]. The activation of neurons of a specific layers, in particular the last ones, can be used as features for describing the visual content.

2.3 R-MAC Features

Recently, image descriptors built upon activations of convolutional layers have shown brilliant results in image instance retrieval [7, 28, 31]. Tolias et al. [31] proposed the R-MAC feature representation, which encodes and aggregates several regions of the image in a dense and compact global image representation. To compute a R-MAC feature, an input image is fed to a fully convolutional network pre-trained on ImageNet [29]. The output of the last convolutional layer is max-pooled over different spatial regions at different position and scales, obtaining a feature vector for each region. These vectors are then $l2$-normalized, PCA-whitened, $l2$-normalized again, and finally aggregated by summing them together and $l2$-normalizing the final result. The obtained representation is an effective aggregation of local convolutional features at multiple position and scales that can be compared with the cosine similarity function.

Gordo et al. [17] built on the work of Tolias et al. [31] and inserted the R-MAC feature extractor in a end-to-end differentiable pipeline in order to learn a representation optimized for visual instance retrieval through back-propagation. The whole pipeline is composed by a fully convolutional neural network, a region proposal network, the R-MAC extractor and PCA-like dimensionality reduction layers, and it is trained using a ranking loss based on image triplets. The obtained pipeline can extract an optimized R-MAC feature representation that outperforms methods based on costly local features and spatial geometry verification.

An additional performance boost is obtained using state-of-the-art deep convolutional architectures, such as very deep residual networks [18], and aggregating descriptors extracted at multiple resolutions. A multi-resolution R-MAC descriptor is obtained feeding the network with images at different resolutions and then aggregating the obtained representations by summing them together and then performing a final $l2$-normalization.

In our work, we used the ResNet-101 trained model provided by [17] as a R-MAC feature extractor, which has been shown to achieve the best performance on standard benchmarmks. We extracted the R-MAC features using fixed regions at two different scales as proposed in [31] instead of using the region proposal network. Defined S as the size in pixel of the minimum side of an image, we extracted both single-resolution descriptors (with $S = 800$) and multi-resolution ones (aggregating descriptors with $S = 550$, 800 and 1050).

3 SURROGATE TEXT REPRESENTATION FOR DEEP FEATURES

As introduced above, the basic idea of permutation-based indexing techniques is to represent feature objects as permutations built using a set of reference object identifiers as permutants.

Using the permutation-based representation, the similarity between two objects is estimated computing the similarity between the two corresponding permutations, rather than using the original distance function. The rationale behind this is that, when permutations are built using this strategy, objects that are very close one to the other, have similar permutation representations as well. In other words, if two objects are very close one to the other, they will sort the set of reference objects in a very similar way.

Notice however that the relevant aspect when building permutations is the capability of generating sequences of identifiers (permutations) in such a way that similar objects have similar permutations as well. Sorting a set of reference objects, according to their distance with the object to be represented is just one, yet effective, approach.

When objects to be indexed are vectors as in our case of deep features, we can use the approach presented in [4], which allows us to generate sequence of identifiers not associated with reference objects. The basic idea is as follows. Permutants are the indexes of elements of the deep feature vectors. Given a deep feature vector, the corresponding permutation is obtained by sorting the indexes of the elements of the vector, in descending order with respect to the values of the corresponding elements. Suppose for instance the feature vector is $fv = [0.1, 0.3, 0.4, 0, 0.2]$[1]. The permutation-based representation of fv is $\Pi_{fv} = (3, 2, 5, 1, 4)$, that is permutant (index) 3 is in position 1, permutant 2 is in position 2, permutant 5 is in position 3, etc. The permutation vectors, introduced in Section 2 is $\Pi^{-1}_{fv} = (4, 2, 1, 5, 3)$, that is permutant (index) 1 is in position 4, permutant 2 is in position 2, permutant 3 is in position 1, etc.

The intuition behind this is that features in the high levels of the neural network carry out some sort of high-level visual information. We can imagine that individual dimensions of the deep feature vectors represent some sort of visual concept, and that the value of each dimension specifies the importance of that visual concept in the image. Similar deep feature vectors sort the visual concepts (the dimensions) in the same way, according to the activation values.

Without entering the technical details of this approach (for that, we refer the reader to [4]), let us just stress the fact that although the vector of permutations are of the same dimension of DCNN vectors, the advantage consists in that they be easily encoded into an inverted index. Moreover, following the intuition that the most relevant information of the permutation is in the very first, we can truncate the vector of permutations to the top-K (i.e., truncated permutations at K). The element of the vectors beyond K can be ignored, this approach allows us to modulate the size of vectors and reduce the size of the index by introducing more sparsity.

In order to index the permutation vectors with a text-retrieval engine as Lucene, we use the surrogate text representation introduced in [15], which simply consists in assigning a codeword to each item of the permutation vector Π^{-1} and repeating the codewords a number of times equal to the complement of the rank of each item within the permutation. For instance, let τ_i be the codeword corresponding to the i-th component of the permutation vector, for the vector $\Pi^{-1}_{fv} = (4, 2, 1, 5, 3)$, we generate the following surrogate text: "$\tau_1\ \tau_1\ \tau_2\ \tau_2\ \tau_2\ \tau_2\ \tau_3\ \tau_3\ \tau_3\ \tau_3\ \tau_3\ \tau_4\ \tau_5\ \tau_5\ \tau_5$".

4 EXPERIMENTAL EVALUATION

The assessment of the proposed algorithm in a multimedia information retrieval task was performed using the R-MAC features extracted as explained above from *INRIA Holidays* [19] and *Oxford Buildings* [26] datasets.

INRIA Holidays [19] is a collection of 1,491 images, which mainly contains personal holidays photos. The images are of high resolution and represent a large variety of scene type (natural, man-made, water, fire effects,etc). The authors selected 500 queries and manually identified a list of qualified results for each of them. As in [20], we merged the Holidays dataset with the distraction dataset MIRFlickr including 1M images [2].

Oxford Buildings [26] is composed by 5062 images of 11 Oxford landmarks downloaded from Flickr. A manually labelled groundtruth is available for 5 queries for each landmark, for a total of 55 queries. As for *INRIA Holidays*, we merged the dataset with the distraction dataset Flickr100k including 100k images [3].

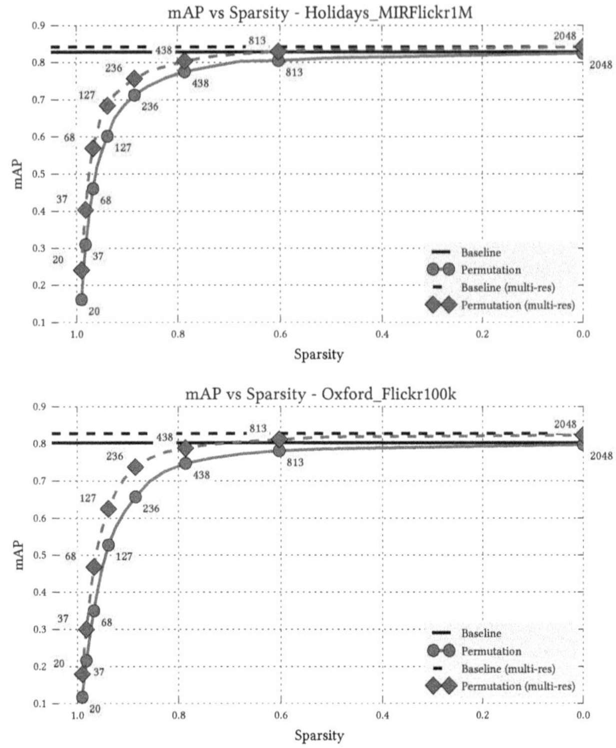

Figure 1: mAP vs sparsity for increasing values of K (reported near each point). Note that, the sparsity of the dataset is given by $\frac{K}{2048}$. The horizontal lines represent the levels of *mAPs* for the baselines, i.e., using the original R-MAC vectors.

We generated different sets of permutations from the original features with different values of K (i.e., we consider truncated at K of the permutations), and for each K, we measured the *mAP* obtained and the query execution times. Results on both datasets are reported in Figure 1. The experiments show the *mAP* of our Lucene implementation as function of the sparsity of the database introduced by the truncation at K. The greater is K (indicated near the point in the graphs) the lower is the sparsity, and hence the greater is the *mAP*. The levels of *mAPs* for the baselines, i.e., using the original R-MAC vectors, are also reported in the figure. These levels can be considered as the upper-bounds for our approach since we are dealing with an approximate approach. However, as it is possible to see, for a sparsity level of about 80%, we reach satisfactory levels of effectiveness.

In order to see the impact of the sparsity of the database, in Figure 2 we report the average query time versus the parameter K. Clearly, by increasing K the query time increases. However, for larger database sizes, a strategy of query reduction similar to the one presented in [2] can be used.

[1] In reality, the number of dimensions is 2,048 or more.

[2] http://press.liacs.nl/mirflickr/

[3] http://www.robots.ox.ac.uk/~vgg/data/oxbuildings/

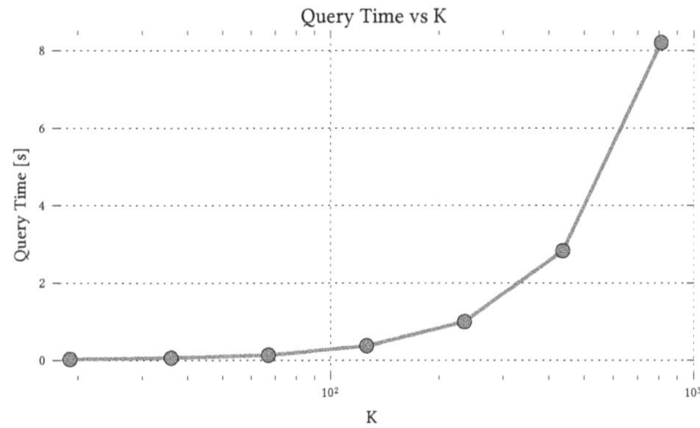

Figure 2: Average query times in seconds on INRIA Holidays dataset + MIRFlickr1M distractor set for different values of K on Lucene.

5 CONCLUSION

In this paper, we present an approach for indexing R-MAC features as permutations built upon the full-text retrieval engine Lucene that exploits surrogate text representation. The advantage is that comparing to the classical approach based on permutation, this technique does not need to compute distances between pivots and data objects but uses the same activation values of the neural network as a source for associating Deep Feature vectors with permutations.

In this preliminary study, we obtained encouraging results on two important benchmarks of image retrieval. In future, we plan test our approach on the more challenging Yahoo Flickr Creative Commons 100 Million (YFCC100M) dataset available at http://bit.ly/yfcc100md.

REFERENCES

[1] Giuseppe Amato, Fabio Carrara, Fabrizio Falchi, Claudio Gennaro, Carlo Meghini, and Claudio Vairo. 2017. Deep learning for decentralized parking lot occupancy detection. *Expert Systems with Applications* 72 (2017), 327–334.

[2] Giuseppe Amato, Franca Debole, Fabrizio Falchi, Claudio Gennaro, and Fausto Rabitti. 2016. Large Scale Indexing and Searching Deep Convolutional Neural Network Features. In *Proceeding of the 18th International Conference on Big Data Analytics and Knowledge Discovery (DaWaK 2016)*. Springer. to appear.

[3] Giuseppe Amato, Fabrizio Falchi, Claudio Gennaro, and Fausto Rabitti. 2016. YFCC100M HybridNet fc6 Deep Features for Content-Based Image Retrieval. In *Proceedings of the 2016 ACM Workshop on Multimedia COMMONS*. ACM, 11–18.

[4] Giuseppe Amato, Fabrizio Falchi, Claudio Gennaro, and Lucia Vadicamo. 2016. Deep Permutations: Deep Convolutional Neural Networks and Permutation-Based Indexing. In *International Conference on Similarity Search and Applications*. Springer, 93–106.

[5] Giuseppe Amato, Claudio Gennaro, and Pasquale Savino. 2014. MI-File: using inverted files for scalable approximate similarity search. *Multimedia Tools and Applications* 71, 3 (2014), 1333–1362. DOI: http://dx.doi.org/10.1007/s11042-012-1271-1

[6] Artem Babenko and Victor Lempitsky. 2012. The inverted multi-index. In *Computer Vision and Pattern Recognition (CVPR), 2012 IEEE Conference on*. IEEE, 3069–3076.

[7] Artem Babenko and Victor Lempitsky. 2015. Aggregating local deep features for image retrieval. In *Proceedings of the IEEE international conference on computer vision*. 1269–1277.

[8] Artem Babenko, Anton Slesarev, Alexandr Chigorin, and Victor Lempitsky. 2014. Neural codes for image retrieval. In *Computer Vision–ECCV 2014*. Springer, 584–599.

[9] Jon Louis Bentley. 1975. Multidimensional binary search trees used for associative searching. *Commun. ACM* 18, 9 (1975), 509–517.

[10] Fabio Carrara, Andrea Esuli, Tiziano Fagni, Fabrizio Falchi, and Alejandro Moreo Fernández. 2016. Picture it in your mind: Generating high level visual representations from textual descriptions. *arXiv preprint arXiv:1606.07287* (2016).

[11] Edgar Chávez, Karina Figueroa, and Gonzalo Navarro. 2008. Effective Proximity Retrieval by Ordering Permutations. *Pattern Analysis and Machine Intelligence, IEEE Transactions on* 30, 9 (2008), 1647–1658.

[12] Jeff Donahue, Yangqing Jia, Oriol Vinyals, Judy Hoffman, Ning Zhang, Eric Tzeng, and Trevor Darrell. 2013. Decaf: A deep convolutional activation feature for generic visual recognition. *arXiv preprint arXiv:1310.1531* (2013).

[13] Matthijs Douze, Hervé Jégou, and Florent Perronnin. 2016. *Polysemous Codes*. Springer International Publishing, Cham, 785–801.

[14] Andrea Esuli. 2012. Use of permutation prefixes for efficient and scalable approximate similarity search. *Information Processing & Management* 48, 5 (2012), 889–902.

[15] Claudio Gennaro, Giuseppe Amato, Paolo Bolettieri, and Pasquale Savino. 2010. An Approach to Content-Based Image Retrieval Based on the Lucene Search Engine Library. In *Research and Advanced Technology for Digital Libraries*, Mounia Lalmas, Joemon Jose, Andreas Rauber, Fabrizio Sebastiani, and Ingo Frommholz (Eds.). Lecture Notes in Computer Science, Vol. 6273. Springer Berlin Heidelberg, 55–66. http://dx.doi.org/10.1007/978-3-642-15464-5_8

[16] Ross Girshick, Jeff Donahue, Trevor Darrell, and Jitendra Malik. 2014. Rich feature hierarchies for accurate object detection and semantic segmentation. In *Proceedings of the IEEE conference on computer vision and pattern recognition*. 580–587.

[17] Albert Gordo, Jon Almazan, Jerome Revaud, and Diane Larlus. 2016. End-to-end learning of deep visual representations for image retrieval. *arXiv preprint arXiv:1610.07940* (2016).

[18] Kaiming He, Xiangyu Zhang, Shaoqing Ren, and Jian Sun. 2015. Deep Residual Learning for Image Recognition. *arXiv preprint arXiv:1512.03385* (2015).

[19] Hervé Jégou, Matthijs Douze, and Cordelia Schmid. 2008. Hamming Embedding and Weak Geometric Consistency for Large Scale Image Search. In *Computer Vision – ECCV 2008*, David Forsyth, Philip Torr, and Andrew Zisserman (Eds.). Lecture Notes in Computer Science, Vol. 5302. Springer Berlin Heidelberg, 304–317. http://dx.doi.org/10.1007/978-3-540-88682-2_24

[20] H. Jégou, M. Douze, and C. Schmid. 2009. Packing bag-of-features. In *Computer Vision, 2009 IEEE 12th International Conference on*. 2357 –2364. DOI: http://dx.doi.org/10.1109/ICCV.2009.5459419

[21] Alex Krizhevsky, Ilya Sutskever, and Geoffrey E Hinton. 2012. Imagenet classification with deep convolutional neural networks. In *Advances in neural information processing systems*. 1097–1105.

[22] Yann LeCun, Yoshua Bengio, and Geoffrey Hinton. 2015. Deep learning. *Nature* 521, 7553 (2015), 436–444.

[23] Eva Mohedano, Kevin McGuinness, Noel E. O'Connor, Amaia Salvador, Ferran Marques, and Xavier Giro-i Nieto. 2016. Bags of Local Convolutional Features for Scalable Instance Search. In *Proceedings of the 2016 ACM on International Conference on Multimedia Retrieval (ICMR '16)*. ACM, New York, NY, USA, 327–331.

[24] David Novak, Martin Kyselak, and Pavel Zezula. 2010. On locality-sensitive indexing in generic metric spaces. In *Proceedings of the Third International Conference on Similarity Search and Applications (SISAP '10)*. ACM, 59–66.

[25] Loïc Paulevé, Hervé Jégou, and Laurent Amsaleg. 2010. Locality sensitive hashing: A comparison of hash function types and querying mechanisms. *Pattern Recognition Letters* 31, 11 (2010), 1348–1358.

[26] J. Philbin, O. Chum, M. Isard, J. Sivic, and A. Zisserman. 2007. Object Retrieval with Large Vocabularies and Fast Spatial Matching. In *Computer Vision and Pattern Recognition, 2007. CVPR 2007. IEEE Conference on*. 1–8.

[27] Ali S Razavian, Hossein Azizpour, Josephine Sullivan, and Stefan Carlsson. 2014. CNN features off-the-shelf: an astounding baseline for recognition. In *Computer Vision and Pattern Recognition Workshops (CVPRW), 2014 IEEE Conference on*. IEEE, 512–519.

[28] Ali Sharif Razavian, Josephine Sullivan, Stefan Carlsson, and Atsuto Maki. 2014. Visual instance retrieval with deep convolutional networks. *arXiv preprint arXiv:1412.6574* (2014).

[29] Olga Russakovsky, Jia Deng, Hao Su, Jonathan Krause, Sanjeev Satheesh, Sean Ma, Zhiheng Huang, Andrej Karpathy, Aditya Khosla, Michael Bernstein, Alexander C. Berg, and Li Fei-Fei. 2015. ImageNet Large Scale Visual Recognition Challenge. *International Journal of Computer Vision (IJCV)* 115, 3 (2015), 211–252. DOI: http://dx.doi.org/10.1007/s11263-015-0816-y

[30] Karen Simonyan and Andrew Zisserman. 2014. Very deep convolutional networks for large-scale image recognition. *arXiv preprint arXiv:1409.1556* (2014).

[31] Giorgos Tolias, Ronan Sicre, and Hervé Jégou. 2015. Particular object retrieval with integral max-pooling of CNN activations. *arXiv preprint arXiv:1511.05879* (2015).

Family Photo Recognition via Multiple Instance Learning

Junkang Zhang
Southeast University
School of Automation
Nanjing, China 210096
jkzhang@seu.edu.cn

Siyu Xia
Southeast University
School of Automation
Nanjing, China 210096
xsy@seu.edu.cn

Ming Shao
University of Massachusetts Dartmouth
Department of Computer and Information Science
Dartmouth, MA 02747-2300, USA
mshao@umassd.edu

Yun Fu
Northeastern University
Department of ECE, College of Engineering
Boston, MA 02115, USA
yunfu@ece.neu.edu

ABSTRACT

Family photo recognition is an important task in social media analytics. Previous methods use singleton global features and conventional binary classifiers to distinguish family group photos from non-family ones. Different from them, we propose a novel family recognition approach with three dedicated local representations under Multiple Instance Learning framework, where geometry, kinship and semantic features are integrated to overcome issues in the previous work. Experimental results show that our method achieves the state-of-the-art result among global-feature models.

KEYWORDS

Family photo recognition, Group photo analysis, Multiple Instance Learning, Social Media

1 INTRODUCTION

On social media websites like Facebook and Flickr, people tend to share group photos taken with different people. Typically, people's relations in these photos vary from kinships among family members to social relations such as friends and colleagues. As we usually employ different approaches to identify kinship relations or non-kinship ones, it is vital to detect the kinships within the photo before further processing it. In this paper, we will focus on the family photo recognition task. Specifically, we try to distinguish family group photos (i.e. almost everyone in the photo can be linked via kinships) from non-family ones (i.e. no kinship exists in the photos).

To solve this binary classification problem, various feature descriptors have been designed based on multiple types of discriminative cues in group photos, including geometry cues (i.e. spatial layout of faces is different between two categories), appearance cues (i.e. facial familial features between family members), and semantic cues (i.e. a photo's contexts vary with its category). Chen et al [4] connected faces of different attributes and positions into a graph, and used subgraphs patterns [17] to describe people's relations in a photo. Wang et al [16] obtained a geometry feature by fitting faces' layout with a polygon and extracting its frequency patterns. Besides, they proposed an appearance feature which took the average of all pairwise kinship features in a photo as its descriptor. In their more recent work [15], they designed an improved appearance model using deep facial features, and a new semantic descriptor by mining a photo's contexts, e.g. objects, scenes and events. Overall, all these methods focused on the photo's global representations, and used one singleton feature vector to describe each image. Nevertheless, they ignored the discriminative cues lying in the image's local parts, which hinders them from achieving better recognition performance.

According to our observation, the most discriminative cues lie in local parts of a photo instead of the whole picture. Take appearance cues as an example. In the photo of the British Royal Family (Fig. 2), Charles (in red box) having kinship relations with more than half people (in blue boxes) can be utilized to distinguish this photo from non-family ones. While Kate, his daughter-in-law (in green box), without kinship relation to anyone may not contribute to the recognition. Hence, in [15, 16], the proposed global kinship feature for a photo by computing the average of all pairwise facial similarity vectors would be less discriminative, as the useful local cues (e.g. similarity vectors linked to Charles) were diluted by many non-discriminative information (e.g. vectors linked to Kate). And it is the same along with geometry and semantic cues. Therefore, an effective model that employs local cues of photos to discriminate family group photos from non-family ones is intended.

In this paper, we propose to solve this problem via Multiple Instance Learning (MIL) which takes multiple local representations of a photo as input and predicts its category. Since the previously proposed descriptors are not suited to MIL's settings, we also design three local feature descriptors corresponding to the geometry, appearance and semantic cues

ICMR '17, June 06-09, 2017, Bucharest, Romania
© 2017 ACM. 978-1-4503-4701-3/17/06...$15.00
DOI: http://dx.doi.org/10.1145/3078971.3079036

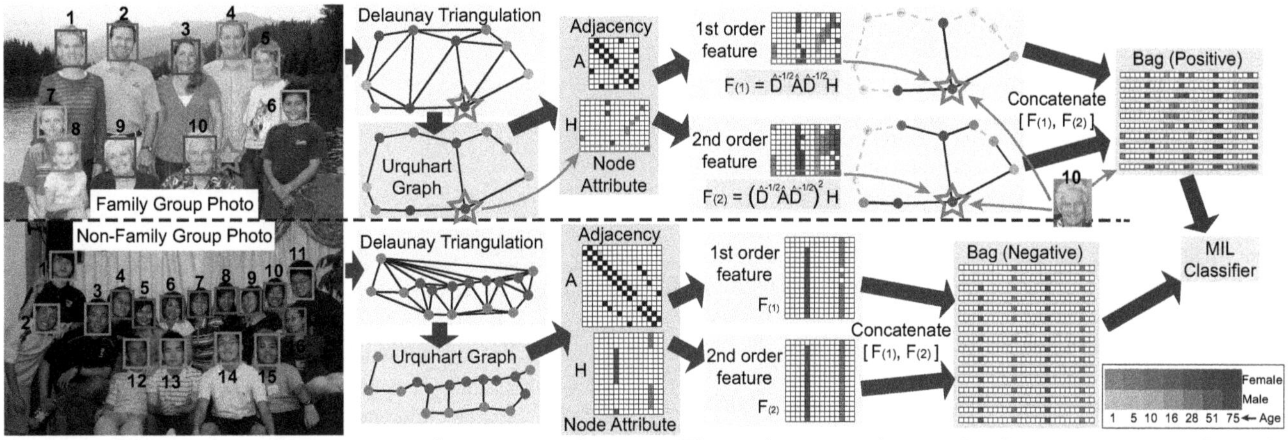

Figure 1: Illustration of our proposed geometry feature. The red stars point to the features extracted on the No. 10 face in the family photo. Non-white colors in matrices and vectors indicate non-zero values. Best viewed in color.

respectively. In the geometry feature, we connect all faces in a photo into a Urquhart Graph, and find the attribute relations in each node's neighborhood as the node's local descriptor. In the appearance feature, we take the average kinship similarity between a face and all other people as the face's local representation. While for the semantic feature, we extract multi-scale features at various positions of the photo as its local descriptor. In the rest of the paper, we will discuss our method in detail in Section 2, provide the experimental results in Section 3, and conclude our method in Section 4.

2 PROPOSED METHOD

2.1 Multiple Instance Learning (MIL)

Different from traditional binary classifiers which use one feature vector for each image, MIL describes data using labeled *bags* which contains multiple unlabeled *instances*. A bag with N instances is defined as $X_i = \{\mathbf{x}_{i1}, \mathbf{x}_{i2}, ..., \mathbf{x}_{iN}\}$, and the bag is labeled by $y_i \in \{1, -1\}$, while the instances' labels $y_{i1}, y_{i2}, ..., y_{iN} \in \{1, -1\}$ are unknown. The bag is positive ($y_i = 1$) if at least one of its instance is positive ($\exists j, y_{ij} = 1$), otherwise it is negative ($y_i = -1$), which can be described as

$$y_i = \max_j(y_{ij}) \tag{1}$$

In this paper, we use the Multiple Instance Boosting (MI-Boosting) framework [18] for bag classification. In detail, first, the boosting classifier h outputs its prediction on an instance $\mathbf{x}_{ij}$ as $h_{ij} = h(\mathbf{x}_{ij}) \in \Re$. Then, a sigmoid function is applied to transform the classifier's output into the *instance's probability of being positive*

$$p_{ij} = p(y_{ij} = 1|\mathbf{x}_{ij}) = 1/\big(1 + \exp(-h_{ij})\big) \tag{2}$$

Since Eq. (1) is not differentiable, we approximate the *bag's probability of being positive* via Generalized Mean function

$$p_i = p(y_i = 1|X_i) = \Big(\frac{1}{N}\sum_{j=1}^{N} {p_{ij}}^r\Big)^{1/r} \tag{3}$$

Finally, the negative log likelihood loss function is adopted

$$L(h) = -\sum_{X_i} \big(\mathbf{1}_{(y_i=1)} \log p_i + \mathbf{1}_{(y_i=-1)} \log(1 - p_i)\big) \tag{4}$$

where $\mathbf{1}_{(statement)} = 1$ if the statement is true, otherwise $\mathbf{1}_{(statement)} = 0$. Readers can refer to [1] for a detailed derivation process of MI-Boosting. When doing prediction, we regard a bag to be positive if $p_i \geq 0.5$, otherwise negative.

We select Gradient Boosting Decision Tree (GBDT) [3, 6] as our boosting classifier. In GBDT's training process, we only need to provide first-order gradient of the loss function over the classifier's output

$$\frac{\partial L}{\partial h_{ij}} = \begin{cases} -\frac{{p_{ij}}^r(1-p_{ij})}{\sum_j {p_{ij}}^r} & , y_i = 1 \\ \frac{p_i}{1-p_i}\frac{{p_{ij}}^r(1-p_{ij})}{\sum_j {p_{ij}}^r} & , y_i = 0 \end{cases} \tag{5}$$

Readers can refer to [3, 6] for more details on GBDT.

In our case, family photos are regarded as positive bags, and non-family photos are negative bags. In each bag, multiple local feature vectors are taken as instances. Therefore, we aim to find discriminative local information (i.e. positive instances) in family photos which can distinguish them from non-family ones.

2.2 Geometry Feature

Our proposed geometry representation aims at modeling the local relationship pattern between a centering person and his/her spatially neighboring people. We observe that this representation has different patterns in family and non-family photos. In family photos, the surrounding faces usually have obvious deviations from the centering person in their ages and genders due to the nature of family structures. While in non-family photos, such deviations, especially the age differences, are less common. For example, in the family photo in Fig. 1, faces surrounding the No. 10 face have different ages and/or genders from him. However, in the non-family photo in Fig. 1, no age variation is observed among neighboring faces. As a result, this discriminative local pattern which lies in the neighborhood of a person can be utilized for family photo recognition.

Note that Chen et al's model [4] also extracted the local structural information (i.e. subgraphs) in a face graph. However, it only computed the occurrence of a certain subgraph instead of the detailed relationship patterns in it. Besides, the total number of possible subgraphs was so huge that they would overload MIL with an enormous number of instances. Therefore, we need to design a new approach to extract the local spatial relationships among faces.

An illustration of our geometry feature extraction process is depicted in Fig. 1. First of all, all N faces in a photo are connected into an unweighted Urquhart Graph (UG) based on the pixel distances between each other. In detail, faces are first connected via Delaunay Triangulation, and then a UG is created by removing the longest edges in each triangles.

Afterwards, the UG is described by an adjacency matrix $\mathbf{A}_{N\times N}$, where $\mathbf{A}_{ij}=1$ indicates the edge between the ith and the jth nodes (faces). In addition, we describe each node by its age and gender attributes. Since we have 7 age categories (i.e. 1, 5, 10, 16, 28, 51, 75) and 2 gender categories (i.e. female and male), each node can be represented by a D-Dimension vector $\mathbf{h}_{D\times 1}$ ($D=14$) with only one element being 1 and the rest being 0. And the attributes of all nodes in the photo are summarized into a matrix $\mathbf{H}_{N\times D}=[\mathbf{h}_1,\mathbf{h}_2,...,\mathbf{h}_N]^T$. With $\mathbf{A}$ and $\mathbf{H}$, a simple way to describe the neighbors' attributes around every nodes is

$$\mathbf{F}=\mathbf{AH} \tag{6}$$

where the ith row in $\mathbf{F}_{N\times D}$ counts the attributes' occurrence in all neighboring nodes which connect the ith centering node via only one edge. This row vector can be directly used as the instance representation of the ith node in MIL. Yet in this formulation, each row of $\mathbf{A}$ is unnormalized which would change the scale of $\mathbf{F}$. Hence, we adopt a normalized form of Eq. (6) [10]

$$\mathbf{F}=\hat{\mathbf{D}}^{-\frac{1}{2}}\hat{\mathbf{A}}\hat{\mathbf{D}}^{-\frac{1}{2}}\mathbf{H} \tag{7}$$

where $\hat{\mathbf{A}}=\mathbf{A}+\mathbf{I}$ in which the centering node is also counted, and $\hat{\mathbf{D}}=\text{diag}(\sum_j \hat{\mathbf{A}}_{ij})$ is the diagonal node degree matrix of $\hat{\mathbf{A}}$.

Furthermore, we want to find a node's neighboring attribute patterns at any distances. Thus we define the nth order pattern as

$$\mathbf{F}^{(n)}=\big(\hat{\mathbf{D}}^{-\frac{1}{2}}\hat{\mathbf{A}}\hat{\mathbf{D}}^{-\frac{1}{2}}\big)^n\mathbf{H} \tag{8}$$

through which all neighboring nodes linked to the centering node within n edges will be included in the pattern. In the family photo in Fig. 1, an example of extracting 1st and 2nd order features from the No. 10 face (with a red star) is shown. As can been seen in the figure, local feature instances in the family photo (positive bag) are obviously different from those in the non-family photo (negative bag).

2.3 Kinship (Appearance) Feature

Since previous appearance features [15, 16] are unsuited for the MIL framework, and various kinship verification models (e.g. [12, 14]) are also unsuitable for this task due to lack of kinship labels, we redesign a local representation based on [15] to extract local kinship similarities between one face and all other faces in the photo.

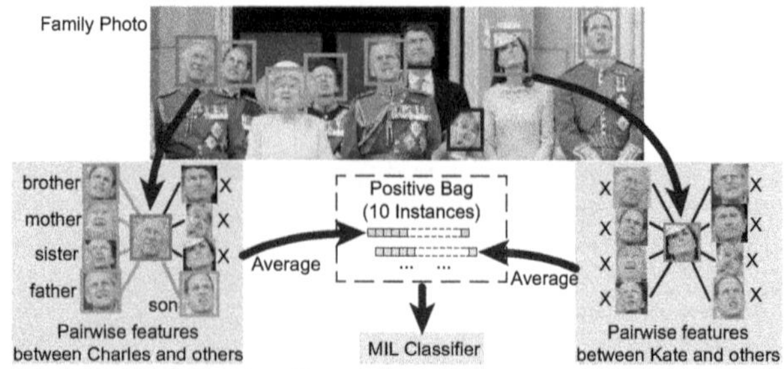

Figure 2: Illustration of our appearance feature.

As mentioned in Section 1, we find that in a family photo, certain people (e.g. Charles in red box in Fig. 2) have more kinship relations with the rest people, while others have less. On the contrary, kinship relations should rarely be observed in non-family photos. Meanwhile, we know that kinship relations between two faces are often expressed through the similarities in facial traits. Inspired by these knowledge, we can extract the facial feature similarities between a person and the resting people as a local kinship descriptor in a group photo.

In the beginning, we adopt a similar process with that in [15]. In brief, we first extract facial features $\mathbf{f}_i$ over all faces in a photo. Then, we compute the pairwise features between all possible face pairs in the photo as $\mathbf{f}_{ij}^{pair}=|\mathbf{f}_i-\mathbf{f}_j|$. Based on the pairwise age differences, all pairwise features are divided into 4 categories $\{[0,10],(10,20],(20,40],(40,\infty)\}$. In each category, two codebooks will be trained via K-means algorithm. One codebook is trained on the pairwise features in family photos, while another one is trained on features in non-family photos. Afterwards, each pairwise feature is encoded [5] by both codebooks of its category as $\mathbf{f}_{ij}^{map}$.

After we obtain the mapped pairwise features, we extract the local appearance similarity feature over each face in a group photo which is different from [15]. For face i in a photo, its local feature is computed as the average of all pairwise features between i and others

$$\mathbf{f}_i^{local}=\text{mean}\big(\{\mathbf{f}_{ij}^{map}|\forall j, j\neq i\}\big) \tag{9}$$

and it is regarded as an instance in the bag. In a positive bag (i.e. family photo), some instances are more likely to be positive (e.g. Charles's feature in Fig. 2), and some are negative (e.g. Kate's feature in Fig. 2). While in a negative bag (i.e. non-family photo), all instances should be negative.

2.4 Semantic Feature

We also propose a local semantic representation for family photo recognition. We find that the category of a photo is closely correlated with its contexts like locations, events, etc. Furthermore, the photo's contexts are closely related with the contained objects which often occupy a small portion of the image. For example, a dog's or a cat's occurrence often indicates a family residence, and further implies that the photo is probably a family one. On the contrary, beer bottles and glasses seldom contribute to the evidence of a family photo, since they often indicate a gathering or a party with friends. Therefore, the local objects in an image can be extracted to aid family photo recognition.

We design a simple method for local semantic feature extraction for MIL. First, a group photo is resized into various scales based on the average eye distances of its faces. Then, fixed-sized image patches are extracted from the multi-scale images by a sliding window which moves at a fixed step size. Afterwards, features of all patches are computed via the Deep Residual Network [9] which is trained on the ImageNet dataset [13] including 1000 object classes. Finally, all patches' feature vectors in a bag (photo) are regarded as its instances.

3 EXPERIMENTS

3.1 Settings

We evaluate our method on the dataset used in [4] which is a subset of the Images of Groups Dataset [7]. All photos are collected from Flickr. Each photo's label along with each face's eyes positions, age and gender are provided. There are totally 1177 family photos and 1267 non-family photos.

In our geometry feature, we extract 1st, 2nd and 3rd order features and concatenate them into a 42-D instance vector. In our kinship feature, we adopt [2] to align all faces, and extract deep facial features by [11]. In our semantic feature, the sliding window's size is 224×224, and its moving step is 112. The largest scale of a image is set so that the window width is $8\sqrt{2}$ times of a photo's average eye distance. And the following scales are reduced by $\sqrt{2}$ times from the previous scales until a window cannot be fitted into the image.

In Eq. (3) of MIL, we set $r = 5$. In GBDT, we set $\gamma = 0$, $\lambda = 10$ and $tree\,depth = 5$ [3] for all features. For kinship and semantic features, GBDT is trained under $learning\,rate = 0.1$ and $tree\,number = 500$. For geometry feature, we set $learning\,rate = 0.01$ and $tree\,number = 5000$ to get the best result. All codes are implemented in Matlab.

3.2 Results

For each feature, a 5-fold cross validation is performed, and the average classification accuracy from all folds is reported in Table 1. We compare our results with previous methods which use global features. As mentioned before, those methods describe each photo by one global feature vector and do classification via conventional binary classifiers.

As can be seen in Table 1, our geometry feature achieves the accuracy of 92.2% which is the state-of-the-art accuracy among all feature descriptors. This result verifies the effectiveness of the MIL framework in family photo recognition. Meanwhile, in each feature categories, our proposed semantic and geometry features outperform previous best results by 6.4% and 1.9% respectively. This proves that local semantic and geometry cues in a photo can be utilized for family photo recognition. And such local descriptors combined with MIL can perform better than global descriptors.

It is also shown that our kinship feature cannot rival the previous best kinship model. We think this is due to the noises (i.e. non-kinship relations) which appears in family photos. For example, in Fig. 2, Charles has no kinship relations with three people (linked via black lines), while these relations are also included in his local kinship features.

Table 1: Family photo recognition results using different features. Bold digits indicate the best results in each feature category. Red digits indicate the best result among all features.

Feature Type	Method	Accuracy(%)
Semantic	Wang et al.'s [15]	75.0
	Our Method	**81.4**
Kinship	Wang et al.'s [16]	89.4
	Wang et al.'s [15]	**91.0**
	Our Method	90.3
Geometry	Chen et al.'s [4]	90.3
	Wang et al.'s [15, 16] *	86.3
	Our Method	92.2

*No age or gender information required.

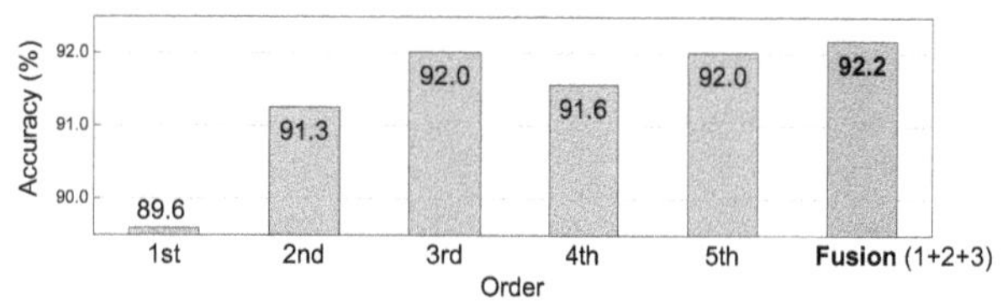

Figure 3: Recognition performance of geometry feature under different orders.

3.3 Geometry Feature Analysis

We also analyze the performance of our geometry feature under different orders. In Fig. 3, accuracies using features from the 1st to the 5th order and the concatenation of 1st, 2nd and 3rd order features are compared. As can be seen, the increase in order leads to better performance prior to 3rd order features, but no improvement is observed after 3rd order. Also, the concatenation of 1st, 2nd and 3rd order features works better than single-order features.

4 CONCLUSION

In this paper, we handled the family group photo recognition task by the proposed local features and the MIL technique. The experimental results showed that the local representations can be more discriminative than global descriptors in this task. Besides, our proposed semantic and geometry features are proved more effective than previous methods when combined with MIL. In our following works, we hope to find a fusion algorithm for different local features to achieve better recognition performance. Also, we wish to apply the current framework into the kinship recognition task in family group photos similar with [8].

ACKNOWLEDGMENTS

This work is supported by the Fundamental Research Funds for the Central Universities award under Grant 2242017K40120, the National Natural Science Foundation of China under Grant 61671151, and Priority Academic Program Development of Jiangsu Higher Education Institutions award.

REFERENCES

[1] Boris Babenko, Piotr Dollár, Zhuowen Tu, and Serge Belongie. 2008. Simultaneous Learning and Alignment: Multi-Instance and Multi-Pose Learning. In *Workshop on Faces in 'Real-Life' Images: Detection, Alignment, and Recognition.*

[2] T. Baltruaitis, P. Robinson, and L. P. Morency. 2016. OpenFace: An open source facial behavior analysis toolkit. In *2016 IEEE Winter Conference on Applications of Computer Vision (WACV).* 1–10.

[3] Tianqi Chen and Carlos Guestrin. 2016. XGBoost: A Scalable Tree Boosting System. In *Proceedings of the 22nd ACM SIGKDD International Conference on Knowledge Discovery and Data Mining.* 785–794.

[4] Yan-Ying Chen, Winston H. Hsu, and Hong-Yuan Mark Liao. 2012. Discovering Informative Social Subgraphs and Predicting Pairwise Relationships from Group Photos. In *Proceedings of the 20th ACM International Conference on Multimedia.* 669–678.

[5] Adam Coates, Andrew Y Ng, and Honglak Lee. 2011. An analysis of single-layer networks in unsupervised feature learning. In *International conference on artificial intelligence and statistics.* 215–223.

[6] Jerome H. Friedman. 2001. Greedy Function Approximation: A Gradient Boosting Machine. *The Annals of Statistics* 29, 5 (2001), 1189–1232.

[7] A. C. Gallagher and T. Chen. 2009. Understanding images of groups of people. In *2009 IEEE Conference on Computer Vision and Pattern Recognition.* 256–263.

[8] Y. Guo, H. Dibeklioglu, and L. v. d. Maaten. 2014. Graph-Based Kinship Recognition. In *2014 22nd International Conference on Pattern Recognition.* 4287–4292.

[9] K. He, X. Zhang, S. Ren, and J. Sun. 2016. Deep Residual Learning for Image Recognition. In *2016 IEEE Conference on Computer Vision and Pattern Recognition (CVPR).* 770–778.

[10] Thomas N Kipf and Max Welling. 2016. Semi-Supervised Classification with Graph Convolutional Networks. *arXiv preprint arXiv:1609.02907* (2016).

[11] Omkar M. Parkhi, Andrea Vedaldi, and Andrew Zisserman. 2015. Deep Face Recognition. In *Proceedings of the British Machine Vision Conference (BMVC).* Article 41, 41.1-41.12 pages.

[12] Joseph P Robinson, Ming Shao, Yue Wu, and Yun Fu. 2016. Families in the Wild (FIW): Large-Scale Kinship Image Database and Benchmarks. In *Proceedings of the 2016 ACM on Multimedia Conference.* ACM, 242–246.

[13] Olga Russakovsky, Jia Deng, Hao Su, Jonathan Krause, Sanjeev Satheesh, Sean Ma, Zhiheng Huang, Andrej Karpathy, Aditya Khosla, Michael Bernstein, Alexander C. Berg, and Li Fei-Fei. 2015. ImageNet Large Scale Visual Recognition Challenge. *International Journal of Computer Vision* 115, 3 (2015), 211–252.

[14] Joseph Robinson Shuyang Wang and Yun Fu. 2017. Kinship Verification on Families in the Wild with Marginalized Denoising Metric Learning. In *12th IEEE Conference on Automatic Face and Gesture Recognition.*

[15] Xiaolong Wang, Guodong Guo, Michele Merler, Noel C. F. Codella, Rohith MV, John R. Smith, and Chandra Kambhamettu. 2017. Leveraging multiple cues for recognizing family photos. *Image and Vision Computing* 58 (2017), 61 – 75. DOI: http://dx.doi.org/10.1016/j.imavis.2016.07.006

[16] X. Wang, G. Guo, M. V. Rohith, and C. Kambhamettu. 2015. Leveraging geometry and appearance cues for recognizing family photos. In *2015 11th IEEE International Conference and Workshops on Automatic Face and Gesture Recognition (FG),* Vol. 1. 1–8.

[17] Xifeng Yan and Jiawei Han. 2002. gSpan: graph-based substructure pattern mining. In *2002 IEEE International Conference on Data Mining, 2002. Proceedings.* 721–724.

[18] Cha Zhang, John C. Platt, and Paul A. Viola. 2006. Multiple Instance Boosting for Object Detection. In *Advances in Neural Information Processing Systems 18.* 1417–1424.

TaiChi: A Fine-Grained Action Recognition Dataset

Shan Sun, Feng Wang*, Qi Liang, Liang He
Shanghai Key Laboratory of Multidimensional Information Processing
Dept. of Computer Science and Technology, East China Normal University
52141201004@stu.ecnu.edu.cn,fwang@cs.ecnu.edu.cn,51151201039@stu.ecnu.edu.cn,lhe@cs.ecnu.edu.cn

ABSTRACT

In this paper, we introduce TaiChi which is a fine-grained action dataset. It consists of unconstrained user-uploaded web videos containing camera motion and partial occlusions which pose new challenges to fine-grained action recognition compared to the existing datasets. In this dataset, 2,772 samples of 58 fine-grained action classes are manually annotated. Additionally, we provide the baseline action recognition results using the state-of-the-art Improved Dense Trajectory feature and Fisher Vector representation with an MAP (Mean Average Precision) of 51.39%.

KEYWORDS

Fine-grained action recognition dataset; Tai Chi; benchmark dataset

ACM Reference format:
Shan Sun, Feng Wang*, Qi Liang, Liang He. 2017. TaiChi: A Fine-Grained Action Recognition Dataset. In *Proceedings of ICMR '17, June 6–9, 2017, Bucharest, Romania,* , 5 pages.
DOI: http://dx.doi.org/10.1145/3078971.3079039

1 INTRODUCTION

With the explosive growth of videos on the Internet, numerous works have been devoted to automatic understanding of the video content. Among them, human action recognition attracts a lot of research attention since it is widely used in various applications such as video surveillance, indexing, and event recounting. Human action recognition is faced with a number of challenges such as complex human actions, large intra-class variability, background motion, and occlusions. A lot of approaches have been proposed to tackle these issues. Most existing works focus on classifying coarsely-grained actions with relatively large inter-class variations, for instance, to distinguish *football* from *basketball* sports. Meanwhile, fine-grained human action recognition is rarely studied. Fine-grained human action recognition aims to distinguish between different actions with low inter-class variability. Compared to the traditional action recognition, fine-grained actions are usually with small spatial and temporal scales. In many cases, a fine-grained action is a part of a higher-level action, and shares the same context with other fine-grained actions. For instance, *throwing* and *slam dunk* are two fine-grained actions in action *basketball*, and they share the same background, actors, and objects. The traditional coarsely-grained action recognition distinguishes *basketball* from other actions, but rarely distinguishes *throwing* from *slam dunk*. However, the distinction of highly similar actions is necessary for many applications. For instance, for one who wants to learn basketball from online videos, s/he would like to search the clips containing action *throwing* or *slam dunk* in order to practice the specific skills rather than the clips simply labelled as *basketball*.

Fine-grained action recognition presents more detailed understanding of the video content. However, it has not been extensively studied. One reason for the lack of research on fine-grained action recognition is the absence of benchmark datasets. Most existing datasets such as the KTH [1], the Weizmann [2], the Hollywood [4, 5], the UCF databases [3, 6, 7, 9] and the CCV [10] are without fine-grained labels. With these datasets, we can distinguish *basketball* from *football*, but cannot learn how to distinguish *throwing* from *slam drunk*. The MPII database [13] released in 2013 is finely labelled. However, all the videos are captured in a fixed kitchen with a stationary camera and mainly focus on the hand actions, which cannot meet the requirements of the realistic applications. The FGA-240 [14] dataset is another fine-grained action dataset with a very large scale. However, only the videos containing actions are released, while the start and the end frames of each action are not annotated.

In this paper, we introduce and release a new fine-grained action dataset called TaiChi, which is composed by videos about Tai Chi sports. Tai Chi is a traditional Chinese art. It expresses as a kind of sport composed of slow, soft, and continuously flowing movements. There are currently lots of Tai Chi genres in different styles, and [16] provides a glance of Tai Chi styles. The Tai Chi sport is composed of a number of moves, and each move consists of a few basic actions of different body parts. Different Tai Chi genres develop different Tai Chi moves, but they share the same basic Tai Chi actions. The basic Tai Chi actions compose numerous Tai Chi moves by different permutations. We take the basic Tai Chi actions as the fine-grained actions in our dataset which are very similar to each other. Specifically, the TaiChi dataset contains 58 fine-grained Tai Chi actions of different body parts such as hand, arm, leg, and foot. The

*Corresponding author.

ICMR '17, June 6–9, 2017, Bucharest, Romania

DOI: http://dx.doi.org/10.1145/3078971.3079039

Figure 1: Samples for 6 action classes of the TaiChi dataset.

videos are all downloaded from the Internet†. Figure 1 shows some examples of the TaiChi dataset.

The main contribution of our work includes: (1) A novel dataset for fine-grained action recognition is released which presents different challenges including low intra-class variability, varying backgrounds, and partial occlusions. (2) A baseline is provided as the benchmark which employs the state-of-the-art Improved Dense Trajectory feature and Fisher Vector representation. The remaining of this paper is organized as follows. Section 2 discusses the related action datasets. Section 3 introduces the TaiChi dataset in detail. The baseline approach and the results on the TaiChi dataset are presented in Section 4. Finally, Section 5 concludes this paper.

2 RELATED WORK

2.1 Action datasets

Action recognition has been studied for decades and quite a number of action datasets are released to tackle various challenges [1–10]. The KTH [1] database released in 2004 is a relatively early database, and still widely used.The videos in the KTH database are recorded by the authors, and the actors in the videos perform six types of simple actions (walking, jogging, running, boxing, hand waving, and hand clapping). Similar to the KTH database, the Weizmann [2] released in 2005 includes nine simple human actions. The videos in these two databases are recorded in constrained environments and the humans can be easily segmented from the backgrounds. Thus, the researchers can focus on discriminating different human actions without considering the backgrounds.

With the advances achieved in action recognition, the varying environments and backgrounds are taken into consideration. A number of databases are released to include various backgrounds. The UCF Sports database [3] is composed of nine kinds of sports taking place in unconstrained environments. The videos are collected from broadcast television channels such as BBC and ESPN. Similarly, the HOHA [4] and the Hollywood2 [5] are composed of movie clips captured by professional filming crew. Hollywood2 [5] includes twelve kinds of human actions such as "answering phone" and "kissing". As the early attempts to build action databases, these databases are usually small scale in terms of the numbers of action categories and video clips.

The recently released databases [6–10] are more challenging and larger scale and more action categories. For instance, the UCF101 [9] consists of 101 kinds of sport actions and 13,320 video clips. Furthermore, they are composed of unconstrained user-uploaded web videos, which pose various challenges to researchers such as partial occlusions, camera motion, and diverse subjects. As shown in Table 1, all these five databases are composed with video clips collected from web. Compared with the early datasets, the numbers of actions are much larger. Furthermore, the diversity of actions is increasing, e.g., from sports to daily actions and from one-person actions to multi-person actions. With these datasets, researchers develop a great number of approaches to address different challenges in action recognition. However, there is usually large variability among different actions in these datasets which cannot be used for fine-grained action recognition.

2.2 Fine-grained action datasets

Fine-grained action recognition poses a number of new challenges to researchers. However, only few datasets focus on this issue. The SALADS [11] and the JIGSAWS [12] are two datasets on fine-grained action which contain video data as well as the accelerometer data. They are in small scales and rarely used. The MPII database [13] is built specifically for fine-grained action recognition, which is composed of 65 actions in a kitchen. All videos in the MPII databse are recorded in the same kitchen, and the background is static. This ignores the challenges for action recognition in the realistic environments. Furthermore, the MPII databse only contains actions of hand. FGA-240 [14] database is another large-scale database for fine-grained action recognition. It is composed of sports videos from web. However, the start and end frames of each action are not annotated, which limits its use in algorithm developing.

In this paper, we build a benchmark dataset for fine-grained action recognition by considering various challenges. In our TaiChi dataset, the videos are downloaded from YouTube and other Tai Chi sports video websites, which introduce different challenges including camera motion, various backgrounds, varying lighting conditions, partial occlusions, and low video qualities. to fine-grained action recognition. Table 1 compares the TaiChi and the related datasets in detail.

3 TAICHI DATASET ANNOTATIONS

We download 100 videos of Tai Chi sports from YouTube and Tai Chi websites [17], which are captured by non-professional cameramen. The videos contain camera motion, partial occlusions, and various backgrounds. Furthermore, the players in these videos are usually not professional and thus their moves

†Note that we don't own the copyright of the videos and only provide them for non-commercial research purposes.

Table 1: Summary of the related datasets and TaiChi.

Dataset	# Classes	# Clips	Background	Camera Motion	Frame Labels	Release Year	Resource
KTH [1]	6	2,391	Static	Yes	-	2004	Author recorded
Weizmann [2]	9	81	Static	No	-	2005	Author recorded
UCF Sports [3]	9	182	Dynamic	Yes	-	2008	TV shows
Hollywood2 [5]	12	1,707	Dynamic	Yes	-	2009	Movies
UCF11 [6]	11	1168	Dynamic	Yes	-	2009	YouTube
UCF50 [7]	50	6,681	Dynamic	Yes	-	2012	YouTube
HMDB51 [8]	51	6,766	Dynamic	Yes	-	2011	Movies, YouTube, Web
CCV [10]	20	9,317	Dynamic	Yes	-	2011	YouTube
UCF101 [9]	101	13,320	Dynamic	Yes	-	2012	YouTube
MPII [13]	65	5,609	Static	No	Yes	2013	Author recorded
FGA-240 [14]	240	>130,000	Dynamic	Yes	No	2015	YouTube
TaiChi	**58**	**2,772**	**Dynamic**	**Yes**	**Yes**	**2017**	**YouTube, Web**

are not strictly standard, which brings intra-class variations to action recognition.

As described in Section 1, each video contains a number of TaiChi moves, and each move consists of several basic actions of different body parts. In our dataset, we annotate the basic Tai Chi action for fine-grained action recognition. The start and the end frames of each action as well as its category are manually annotated. In total, the TaiChi dataset includes 2,772 annotations of 58 fine-grained Tai Chi action categories as listed in Table 2. These actions are divided into nine groups according to the moving body parts including hand, palm, arm, fist, foot, leg, step, knee, and whole body groups as shown in Table 2 from the top to the bottom. Some actions of the same body part are put into different groups. For instance, hand may act as a fist or palm in different actions, and we divide them into different groups. The statistics of these actions are also provided in Table 2.

In the TaiChi dataset, all the actions are annotated and double-checked by Tai Chi players. The annotators are provided with the sets of frames of web videos and asked to annotate the start and the end frames of the defined actions. As shown in Table 2, there are 25 to 257 positive samples for each category. Since fine-grained actions have relatively lower intra-class variability, these samples are enough for action recognition.

4 BASELINE

4.1 Experiment setup

Recently the improved dense trajectories [15] have shown its effectiveness for capturing motion information of videos and achieve the state-of-the-art results for action classification when combined with the Fisher Vector representation. Following [15], we extract the improved dense trajectories of videos and compute the histograms of oriented gradients (HOG), the histograms of flow (HOF), and motion boundary histograms (MBH) around the trajectories to represent the local information. For trajectory shape, HOG, HOF, MBHx, and MBHy features, PCA (Principle Component Analysis) is used to reduce the dimensionalities by a factor of 2. Following the implementation in [15], the square-root trick is applied on HOG, HOF, MBHx and MBHy descriptors. When encoding Fisher vectors, 256,000 samples are randomly chosen to train Gaussian Mixture Model with 256 Gaussians. Power ($\alpha = 0.5$) and L_2 normalization are used before concatenating different types of descriptors into the final representation. For classification, we train one-vs-all support vector machines (SVMs) using linear kernel function by fixing $C = 100$ as suggested in [15].

Following the settings of the UCF101 dataset [9], we apply a three-split setup by dividing all samples in the TaiChi dataset into 3 splits. Samples from the same video (with the same Tai Chi player) are put into the same split. For experiments, 3-fold cross validation is employed by using 2 splits for training and another one for testing. Thus, the players in the training and the testing sets are different. Since most action categories are defined around a single part of the body, a couple of actions of different categories may take place at the same time. Therefore, we filter the negative samples which overlap with the positive samples when training SVMs. Only those clips which do not overlap with the positive samples are chosen as negative samples. The details of train/test split of our experiments and the final positive/negative samples for each action are released together with the annotations on http://ac.ica.stc.sh.cn/papers/TaiChiDataset.rar.

4.2 Experiment results

We report the average precision (AP) of 58 classes in the TaiChi dataset in Table 2 by employing the baseline approach described in Section 4.1. The MAP (Mean Average Precision) for the nine predefined groups are: hand (47.37%), palm (36.51%), arm (53.19%), fist (50.20%), foot (54.83%), leg (63.65%), step (48.20%), knee (63.37%), and whole body (57.58%).

For the per-class AP, large variation is observed among different action categories even in the same group. For example, in group "hand", the action "Sweeping hand downwards" achieves an AP of 85.32%, while the action "Hooking hand" only achieves 6.12%. Figure 2 illustrates some samples of action categories which get the best and the worst performances. In Figure 2, we manually label the body part (with the yellow circle) which is key to detect the action in each

Table 2: The statistics of the TaiChi dataset and the baseline results.

ID	Action Category	Sample Number	AP (%)	Confused Actions
1	Setting hands apart	91	15.49	7,34,35
2	Down pushing both hands	32	51.59	54,56,19
3	Loosing hand	30	3.01	55,56,26
4	Stretch hand back	34	46.89	56,14,32
5	Crossing hands	25	49.13	14,56,28
6	Hooking hand	29	6.12	39,42,21
7	Hand lifting	37	58.06	20,53,1
8	Putting a hand on another	30	65.69	48,30,56
9	Pulling hand back	31	54.42	53,1,58
10	Sweeping hand downwards	32	85.32	3,51,54
11	Erecting hand	36	63.60	56,1,9
12	Pushing one hand	30	69.09	56,35,36
13	Setting palms down	37	40.75	54,48,1
14	Pushing palms forward	55	18.76	56,1,5
15	Turning palms over	30	8.61	56,21,53
16	Drawing palm back	50	45.23	56,40,1
17	Putting a palm above another	33	33.30	58,15,56
18	Pushing palms up and forward	61	72.43	13,48,24
19	Rotating the arms	52	71.48	32,41,42
20	Raising both arms	38	96.89	-
21	Setting arm upwards	57	34.19	44,52,53
22	Setting arms liking playing lute	34	19.62	51,1,10
23	Lifting arm	32	39.74	48,1,18
24	Stretching arm	44	54.56	58,7,35
25	Pushing arms apart	33	71.43	8,15,24
26	Rotating arm	30	29.59	56,11,27
27	Setting ball-arms	47	24.88	39,43,11
28	Bending arm	44	56.34	50,5,8
29	Pushing arm forward	30	55.46	48,1,56
30	Moving arms liking grounder	32	61.62	42,21,31
31	Circling arms forward to beast	29	63.57	27,39,7
32	Circling arms backwards	33	65.31	19,56,2
33	Making a fist	23	4.15	56,41,1
34	Moving fist	40	72.83	1,2,41
35	Punching	41	70.73	12,13,9
36	Pushing fists upward	34	73.11	35,8,13
37	Raising foot	25	65.15	55,16,3
38	Rotating foot outwards	32	66.13	28,48,56
39	Drawing foot back	124	51.01	11,43,3
40	Rotating foot outwards	41	48.06	56,3,19
41	Landing the foot	42	44.64	2,42,54
42	Stretching foot forwards	95	40.59	52,41,6
43	Taking foot back	32	46.76	39,49,19
44	Kicking with the heel	27	76.19	25,1,7
45	Setting legs apart	38	89.61	38,39
46	Lifting leg	26	34.54	21,53,39
47	Kicking down	31	66.82	34,42,22
48	Setting bow-step	163	32.02	35,36,29
49	Setting empty-step	67	25.28	39,35,56
50	Stepping backwards	34	71.87	28,34,18
51	Crouch step	55	89.69	6
52	Stepping forwards	29	22.09	42,2,11
53	Lifting knee	62	56.35	9,1,6
54	Bending knees	46	70.39	2,42,51
55	Move upper body backward	84	60.62	3,15,16
56	Turning left/right	257	39.99	3,18,24
57	Squatting down	28	40.91	51,10
58	Standing up	59	88.79	17,48,56
Mean Average Precision(%)		**51.39**		

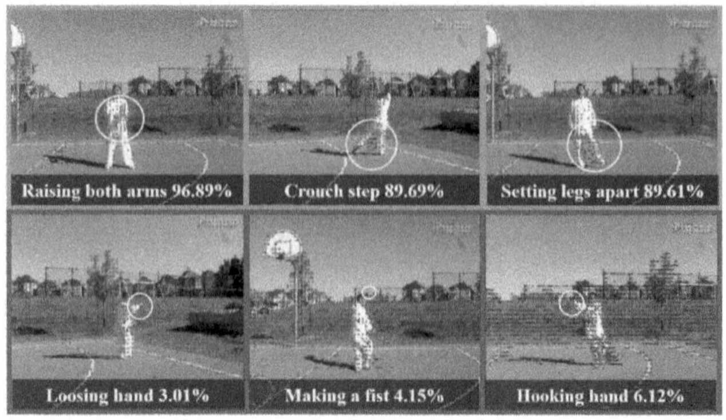

Figure 2: Trajectory visualization of actions with the best (the first row) and the worst (the second row) performances. We manually labelled the key part for the specific action in yellow circle.

sample. According to the manual labels, trajectories are concentrated in the key parts in the best performed actions. For the actions with the worst performance, the key body parts of the actions only present motion of small scales in spatial or temporal dimensions, and the resulting trajectories can hardly represent the target action. Therefore, the performances are quite poor.

The rightmost column of Table 2 lists the three action categories which are the most confusing for each action during classification. From Table 2, we can see that the well-performed actions are rarely confused with other actions, while the actions with poor performances are actually confused with multiple other actions. The whole-body actions are confusing with various actions, while the actions in a specific part are less confusing. Thus, locating the key moving body part is important for action recognition. In fine-grained actions, there are a great number of actions that move in a limited extent or move too fast to generate trajectories. This is a distinct peculiarity of fine-grained actions different from coarsely-grained actions.

5 CONCLUSION

In this paper, we construct a new fine-grained action dataset composed by Tai Chi sports videos collected from webs which contain background motion and partial occlusions. Based on this dataset, we evaluate the state-of-the-art action recognition approach and discuss the differences in detecting coarsely-grained actions and fine-grained actions. The dataset as well as the improved dense trajectory features are provided as a benchmark for further research on fine-grained action recognition.

ACKNOWLEDGMENTS

The work described in this paper was supported by the National High-tech 863 Program of China (No. 2015AA015801), the National Natural Science Foundation of China (No. 61375016) and the Science and Technology Commission of Shanghai Municipality (No. 16511102702).

REFERENCES

[1] C. Schuldt, I. Laptev, and B. Caputo. Recognizing human actions: a local SVM approach. In ICPR, 2004.
[2] M. Blank, L. Gorelick, E. Shechtman, M. Irani, and R. Basri. Actions as space-time shapes. In ICCV, 2005.
[3] M. D. Rodriguez, J. Ahmed, and M. Shah. Action MACH: a spatio-temporal Maximum Average Correlation Height filter for action recognition. In CVPR, 2008.
[4] I. Laptev, M. Marszalek, C. Schmid, and B. Rozenfeld. Learning Realistic Human Actions from Movies. In CVPR, 2008.
[5] M. Marszalek, I. Laptev, and C. Schmid. Actions in context. In CVPR, 2009.
[6] J. Liu, J. Luo, and M. Shah. Recognizing realistic actions from videos in the wild. In CVPR, 2009.
[7] K. Reddy, and M. Shah. Recognizing 50 human action categories of web videos. In MVAP, 2012.
[8] H. Kuehne, H. Jhuang, E. Garrote, T. Poggio, and T. Serre. Hmdb: A large video database for human motion recognition. In ICCV, 2011.
[9] K. Soomro, A. R. Zamir, and M. Shah. UCF101: A Dataset of 101 Human Actions Classes From Videos in The Wild. arXiv preprint arXiv:1212.0402, 2012.
[10] Y.-G. Jiang, G. Ye, S.-F. Chang, D. Ellis, and A. C. Loui. Consumer Video Understanding: A Benchmark Database and An Evaluation of Human and Machine Performance. In ICMR, 2011.
[11] S. Stein, and S. J. Mckenna. Combining Embedded Accelerometers with Computer Vision for Recognizing Food Preparation Activities. In UbiComp, 2013.
[12] Y. Gao, S. S. Vedula, C. E. Reiley, N. Ahmidi, B. Varadarajan, H. C. Lin, L. Tao, L. Zappella, B. Bejar, D. D. Yuh, et al. JHU-ISI Gesture and Skill Assessment Working Set (JIGSAWS): A Surgical Activity Dataset for Human Motion Modeling. In MICCAI Workshop: M2CAI, 2014.
[13] B. Schiele, M. Andriluka, S. Amin, and M. Rohrbach. A Database for Fine Grained Activity Detection of Cooking Activities. In CVPR, 2013.
[14] C. Sun, S. Shetty, R. Sukthankar, and R. Nevatia. Temporal Localization of Fine-Grained Actions in Videos by Domain Transfer from Web Images. In ACM MM, 2015.
[15] H. Wang, and C. schmid. Action Recognition with Improved Trajectories. In ICCV, 2013.
[16] "BeginnersTaiChi," http://www.beginnerstaichi.com/tai-chi-styles-for-beginners.html
[17] "ChinaTaiChi," http://www.cntaijiquan.com/

Conditional Fast Style Transfer Network

Keiji Yanai and Ryosuke Tanno
The University of Electro-Communications, Tokyo
1-5-1 Chofugaoka
Chofu-shi, Tokyo 182-8585
yanai@cs.uec.ac.jp,tanno-r@mm.inf.uec.ac.jp

ABSTRACT

In this paper, we propose a conditional fast neural style transfer network. We extend the network proposed as a fast neural style transfer network by Johnson et al. [8] so that the network can learn multiple styles at the same time. To do that, we add a conditional input which selects a style to be transferred out of the trained styles. In addition, we show that the proposed network can mix multiple styles, although the network is trained with each of the training styles independently. The proposed network can also transfer different styles to the different parts of a given image at the same time, which we call "spatial style transfer". In the experiments, we confirmed that no quality degradation occurred in the multi-style network compared to the single network, and linear-weighted multi-style fusion enabled us to generate various kinds of new styles which are different from the trained single styles. In addition, we also introduce a mobile implementation of the proposed network which runs in about 5 fps on an iPhone 7 Plus.

Figure 1: The world's first real-time multi-style-mixing transfer app, *"DeepStyleCam"*, running in about 5 fps on an iPhone 7 Plus. See the demo video in the supplementary material. This app is available on the iOS App Store. Please search for *"DeepStyleCam"*.

KEYWORDS

neural style transfer, CNN, conv-deconv network

ACM Reference format:
Keiji Yanai and Ryosuke Tanno. 2017. Conditional Fast Style Transfer Network. In *Proceedings ofICMR '17, Bucharest, Romania, June 6–9, 2017,* 4 pages.
https://doi.org/10.1145/3078971.3079037

1 INTRODUCTION

The neural style transfer method was proposed by Gatys et al. [4, 5] in 2015. This method synthesizes an image which has the style of a given style image and the contents of a given content image using Convolutional Neural Network (CNN). For example, by integrating the style of Gogh's starry night and the content of a lion photo, we obtain a lion painting in the style of Gogh. This method enables us to modify the style of an image keeping the content of the image easily. It replaces the information which are degraded while the signal of the content image goes forward through the CNN layers with style information extracted from the style image, and reconstructs a new image which has the same content as a given content images and the same style as a given style image.

However, since the method proposed by Gatys et al. required forward and backward computation iteratively to synthesize a composite image (in general several hundreds times), the processing time tends to become longer (several tens of seconds) even using GPU. Then, several methods using only feed-forward computation of CNN to realize style transfer have been proposed so far [8, 11]. One of them is the method proposed by Johnson et al. [8]. They proposed perceptual loss functions to train a ConvDeconv-style network as a feed-forward style transfer network. Their network consists of down-sampling layers, convolutional layers and up-sampling layers, which accepts an content image and outputs an synthesized image integrated with a fixed pre-trained style. ConvDeconv-style networks are commonly used for image transformation tasks such as super-resolution [1] and coloring of gray-scale images [6]. In their method, they train a ConvDeconv-style network so that the style matrix of its output image becomes closer to the style matrix of the given fixed style image and the CNN features of the input image leaves unchanged by using the proposed perceptual losses. By using the perceptual loss functions, we do not need to prepare transferred target images as ground-truth images.

However, their feed-forward style transfer network can treat only one fixed style. If transferring ten kinds of styles, we have to train different ConvDeconv networks independently and have to hold all the network parameters. This is inconvenient for mobile implementation in terms of required memory size. Then, in this paper, we modified Johnson et al.'s method so that a single ConvDeconv network can train multiple styles at the same time by adding an conditional input. We call our network as "a conditional fast style transfer network".

By adding an conditional input which selects a style to be transferred to a given input image among the trained styles, we have enabled a ConvDeconv style fast style transfer network to train multiple styles with one network. This network cannot only select

ICMR '17, June 6–9, 2017, Bucharest, Romania

ACM ISBN 978-1-4503-4701-3/17/06...$15.00.
https://doi.org/10.1145/3078971.3079037

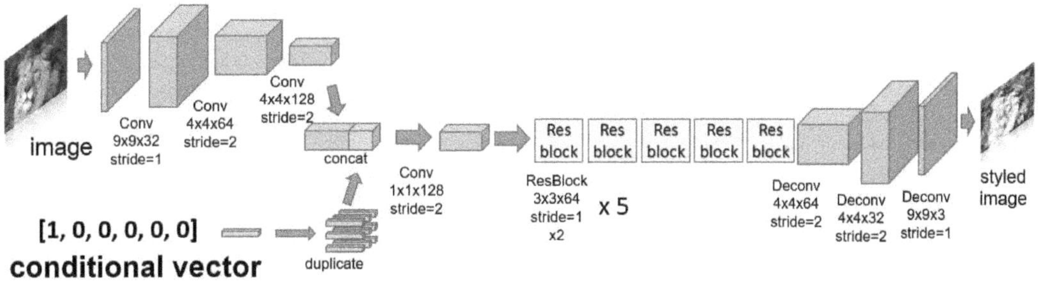

Figure 2: A conditional fast style transfer network.

one of the style out of the pre-trained styles but also mix multiple styles with arbitrary mixing weights. In addition, this network has ability to perform spatial style transfer which means that it can transfer different styles to the different parts of a given image through one-time feed-forward computation of the network according to the conditional signal.

In this paper, we introduce our conditional fast style transfer network and show its effectiveness regarding multiple style transfer, linear weighting style mixing, and spatial style transfer.

Note that recently Dumoulin et al. [2] proposed a method to learn multiple styles with the ConvDeconv style fast style transfer network proposed by Johnson et al. They used Instance Normalization [12] instead of Batch Normalization [7] for normalization of activation signals, and they proposed to replace scale and bias parameters of instance normalization layers depending on the styles. They call this as "conditional instance normalization". The idea on introducing conditions for style selection is similar to ours. However, they introduced a new special layer, "conditional instance normalization" layer, which is needed to be newly implemented for the existing deep learning frameworks such as Caffe, Tensorflow and Chainer, while in our method we added an additional input signal which is concatenated with an internal activation signal and we introduced one additional 1×1 convolution layer to integrate an internal signal and a style signal. We use only common layers in the proposed networks. In addition, in their method, to mix multiple styles, they have to calculate linear-weighted scale and bias parameters in advance, while we just assign weight values to the multiple elements of the conditional input vector such as $(0.2, 0.3, 0.1, 0.4)$.

2 CONDITIONAL FAST STYLE NETWORK

We modified the ConvDeconvNetwork used in [8] by adding a style condition input and an additional 1×1 convolutional layer for fusion of feature map activations and a conditional signal as shown in Figure 2. This network is inspired by Iizuka et al's CNN-based coloring work [6]. They proposed adding a scene contextual stream to the ConvDeconv-style colorization network. They transform a scene vector, which is an output vector of scene recognition network, to a scene feature map by making the same size of copies as the activation feature map, and concatenate it with the intermediate feature map of the activations of the ConvDeconv colorization network. With this improvement, they achieved coloring depending on the scene content of a target image.

When training, we prepare s style images, and make a mini-batch with the combinations of one content training image and all

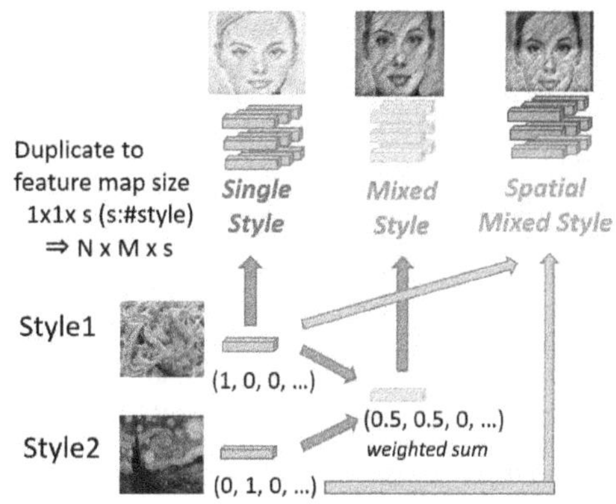

Figure 3: Three different ways to create the conditional input: (1) single style (2) mixed style by linear-weighting (3) spatially mixed style.

the style training images. That is, one mini-batch contains s combinations. To train the network, we provide a content image and one-hot conditional vectors which are s-dimensional binary vectors where the corresponding element to each of the styles is one and the rest elements are all zero. As shown in Figure 2, the conditional vector is $(1, 0, 0, \ldots)$ for the style no.1, while it is $(0, 1, 0, \ldots)$ for the style no.2. As a loss function, we use the perceptual loss proposed by Johnson et al. [8]. In the same way, we use VGG-16 [10] as the loss network, and optimize the weights of the network so that the content feature of the output image extracted from the CONV3_3 layer of VGG-16 gets closer to the one of the input content image and the style features of the output image extracted from the CONV1_2, CONV2_2, CONV3_3 and CONV4_3 layers from VGG-16 get closer to the ones of the correpending style image. Note that content features are feature map activations, while style features are the elements of Gram matrix of feature map activations. The loss functions can be written as follows:

$$
\begin{aligned}
L(w) &= \lambda_s L_s(w) + \lambda_c L_c(w) \\
&= \frac{1}{4} \sum_{l \in \{1\_2, 2\_2, 3\_3, 4\_3\}} ||G(\phi_l(I_{out}(w))) - G(\phi_l(I_s))||^2 \\
&+ \sum_{l \in \{3\_3\}} ||\phi_l(I_{out}(w))) - \phi_l(I_c)||^2
\end{aligned}
$$

where w represents the network parameter set, and $I_{out}(w)$, I_c, and I_s represents the image generated by the network with the parameter set w, a content training image and a style training image, respectively. Please refer the detail on training to [8].

When generating images, we provide a content input image and and a style conditional vector which indicates the styles a user like to transfer to the input image. Although at the time of training we use only one-hot vectors as a style vector, at the time of image generation, we can use the vector each of the elements of which is between 0 and 1 as a style-mixing weight vector. By using the vector which have two or more non-zero elements, we can mix multiple weights as shown in Figure 3(2). This is an interesting characteristic. We guess this comes from the linearity of neural networks. As a matter of course, by providing an one-hot vector as a conditional vector, we can select one single style among the pre-trained styles as shown in Figure 3(1).

In addition, this network has ability to perform spatial style transfer. As shown in Figure 3(3), if we combine multiple style vectors spatially, we can achieve spatial style transfer easily. In this case, we can use mixed style weight vectors as base style vectors.

3 EXPERIMENTAL RESULTS

In the experiment, we trained the network with 13 style images shown in the top row of Figure 4. From the second column to the fifth in the figure, we show the output images generated by single style transfer with the proposed multiple style transfer network using one-hot vectors as conditional vectors. Compared to the same transformation results shown in Figure 5 by single style transfer networks, the quality of the generated images are comparable, which shows the effectiveness of the proposed network. Regarding the processing speed, both are almost the same, since only one convolution layer is added to the original one.

In Figure 4 from the sixth column to the most left, we show the mixed-style transferred images. By adding the style no.10 to the style no.4, the result image became brighter. By mixing multiple styles, we can create new styles as we like. Random weight mixing is also interesting as shown in the left of the figure. Figure 6 shows results when changing the weights gradually between the style no.7 to no.8.

Figure 7 shows the results of spatial style transfer with the proposed network. The images in the left and the right were transformed with three different random weights regarding three vertically-divided regions. The images in the middle were transformed with three different random weights regarding three horizontally-divided regions. For future work, it is an interesting application to combine it with semantic segmentation.

4 IMPLEMENTATION AS IOS APP

We have implemented the proposed method. We modified the CNN network so that the amount of computation is reduced one tenth compared to the original multi-style network. Regarding mobile implementation, we followed the work on Efficient Mobile CNN Implementation [13]. In the method, CNN networks are directly converted to a C source code which utilized multi-threading and iOS Accelerate Framework for CNN computation. We have realized a real-time multi-style-mixing transfer app running in about 5 fps on an iPhone 7 Plus as show in Figure 1. The demo video of this app is attached as the supplementary material.

We shrunk the ConvDeconvNetwork compared to [8] to save computation costs. We added one down-sampling layer and up-sampling layer, replaced 9x9 kernels with smaller 5x5 kernels in the first and last convolutional layers, and reduced five Residual Elements into three. The detail of the network architecture is shown in Figure 8. We confirmed that these network shrinking did not harm the quality of outputs significantly. To accelerate computation of deconvolution layers, we use the sub-pixel convolutional layer proposed by Shi et al. [9], which realizes a deconvolution layer with n kernels and stride 2 using a convolution layer with $4n$ kernels and stride 1.

In addition, we implemented color preserving mode [3] which transfers selected styles only into gray-scale elements of an input image. It can keep the color of the content image while changing only the intensity of pixels, which is especially suitable for food images.

5 CONCLUSIONS

We proposed a conditional fast style network which we added a conditional vector input to the standard ConvDeconv network. Although at the time of training we use only one-hot vectors as a style vector, at the time of image generation, we can use the vector each of the elements of which is between 0 and 1 as a style-mixing weight vector. By only changing a style input vector, we can mix multiple styles out of the pre-trained styles with arbitrary weights. In addition, we implemented the world's first real-time multi-style-mixing transfer app running in about 5 fps on an iPhone 7 Plus. The app for iOS can be downloaded from http://bit.ly/deepstylecam.

For future work, we will extend the proposed method for unseen style transfer and an end-to-end network combining the proposed network with semantic segmentation.

Acknowledgment This work was supported by JSPS KAKENHI Grant Numbers 15H05915, 17H05972 and 17H06026.

REFERENCES

[1] C. Dong, C. C. Loy, K. He, and X. Tang. 2014. Learning a deep convolutional network for image super-resolution. In *Proc. of European Conference on Computer Vision*. 184–199.

[2] V. Dumoulin, J. Shlens, and M. Kudlur. 2016. A Learned Representation For Artistic Style. In *arXiv:1610.07629*.

[3] L. A. Gatys, M. Bethge, A. Hertzmann, and E. Shechtman. 2016. Preserving Color in Neural Artistic Style Transfer. In *ArXiv:1606.05897*.

[4] L. A. Gatys, A. S. Ecker, and M. Bethge. 2015. A Neural Algorithm of Artistic Style. In *arXiv:1508.06576*.

[5] L. A. Gatys, A. S. Ecker, and M. Bethge. 2016. Image Style Transfer Using Convolutional Neural Networks. In *Proc. of IEEE Computer Vision and Pattern Recognition*.

[6] S. Iizuka, E. Simo-Serra, and H. Ishikawa. 2016. Let there be Color!: Joint End-to-end Learning of Global and Local Image Priors for Automatic Image Colorization with Simultaneous Classification. *ACM Transactions on Graphics (Proc. of SIGGRAPH 2016)* 35, 4 (2016).

[7] S. Ioffe and C. Szegedy. 2015. Batch normalization: Accelerating deep network training by reducing internal covariate shift. In *Proc. of International Conference on Machine Learning*. 448–456.

[8] J. Johnson, A. Alahi, and L. F. Fei. 2016. Perceptual Losses for Real-Time Style Transfer and Super-Resolution. In *Proc. of European Conference on Computer Vision*.

[9] W. Shi, J. Caballero, F. Huszar, J. Totz, A. P. Aitken, R. Bishop, D. Rueckert, and Z. Wang. 2016. Real-Time Single Image and Video Super-Resolution Using an Efficient Sub-Pixel Convolutional Neural Network. In *Proc. of IEEE Computer Vision and Pattern Recognition*.

[10] K. Simonyan, A. Vedaldi, and A. Zisserman. 2015. Very Deep Convolutional Networks for Large-Scale Image Recognition. In *International Conference on Learning Representations*.

[11] D. Ulyanov, V. Lebedev, A. Vedaldi, and V. Lempitsky. 2016. Texture networks: Feed-forward synthesis of textures and stylized images. In *Internation Conference on Machine Learning*.

[12] D. Ulyanov, A. Vedaldi, and V. Lempitsky. 2016. Instance Normalization: The Missing Ingredient for Fast Stylization. In *arXiv:1607.08022*.

[13] K. Yanai, R. Tanno, and K. Okamoto. 2016. Efficient Mobile Implementation of A CNN-based Object Recognition System. In *Proc. of ACM International Conference Multimedia*.

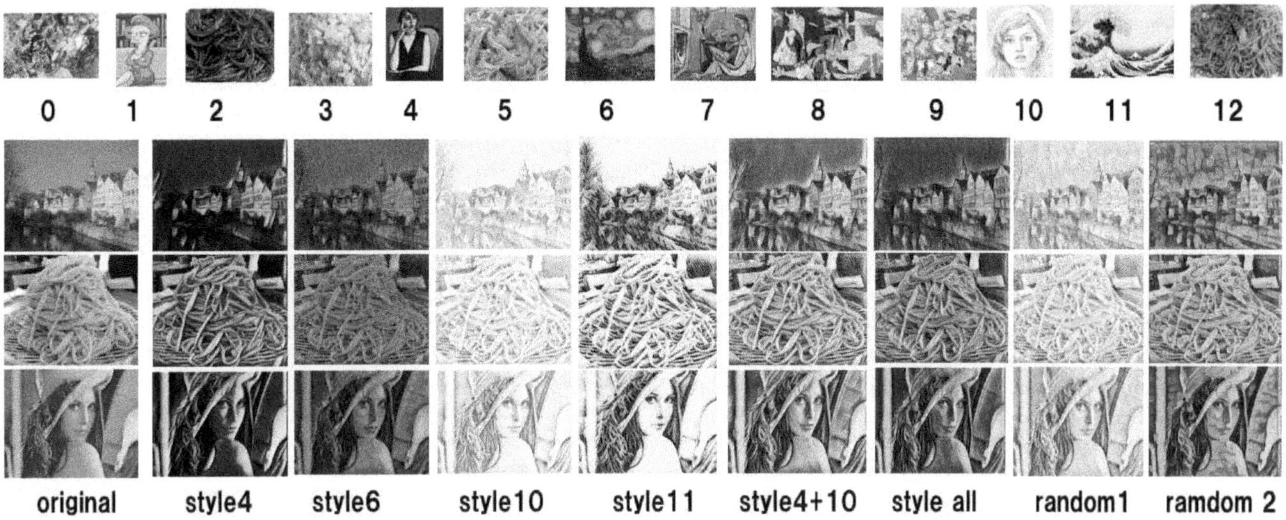

Figure 4: Results by the network trained with 13 styles shown in the top row. From Column 2 to 5, the results with a single style, and from column 6 to 9, the results with mixed styles.

Figure 5: Results by the single network which is equivalent to the one proposed by Johnson et al. [8].

Figure 6: Gradual change of the weights between style no.7 and no.8.

Figure 7: Results of the spatial style transfer.

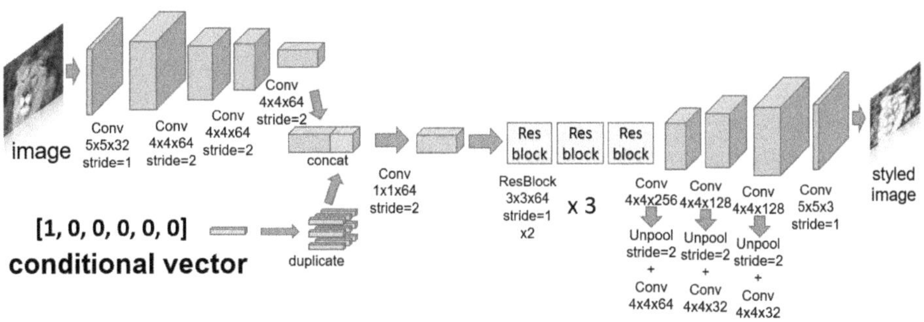

Figure 8: A modified conditional fast style transfer network for mobile implementation.

Improving Image Classification using Coarse and Fine Labels

Anuvabh Dutt
Univ. Grenoble Alpes, CNRS,
Grenoble-INP, LIG
France 38000
anuvabh.dutt@univ-grenoble-alpes.fr

Denis Pellerin
Univ. Grenoble Alpes, CNRS,
Grenoble-INP, GIPSA-Lab
France 38000
denis.pellerin@gipsa-lab.grenoble-inp.fr

Georges Quénot
Univ. Grenoble Alpes, CNRS,
Grenoble-INP, LIG
France 38000
georges.quenot@imag.fr

ABSTRACT

The performance of classifiers is in general improved by designing models with a large number of parameters or by ensembles. We tackle the problem of classification of coarse and fine grained categories, which share a semantic relationship. On being given the predictions that a classifier has for a given test sample, we adjust the probabilities according to the semantics of the categories, on which the classifier was trained. We present an algorithm for doing such an adjustment and we demonstrate improvement for both coarse and fine grained classification. We evaluate our method using convolutional neural networks. However, the algorithm can be applied to any classifier which outputs category wise probabilities.

KEYWORDS

Hierarchical classification, Ensemble learning, Image classification

ACM Reference format:
Anuvabh Dutt, Denis Pellerin, and Georges Quénot. 2017. Improving Image Classification using Coarse and Fine Labels. In *Proceedings of ICMR '17, June 6–9, 2017, Bucharest, Romania*, , 5 pages.
DOI: http://dx.doi.org/10.1145/3078971.3079042

1 INTRODUCTION

In this work, we present a simple method for increasing image classification accuracy by utilizing hierarchical relationships between classes. We enforce a consistency relationship between the classifier output probabilities for coarse and fine classes. We perform our experiments on the CIFAR-100 data set, using deep convolutional network (DCNN) architectures. We improve the classification accuracy for three different architectures, including the current state-of-the-art. The proposed method relies only on probabilistic outputs from a classifier. Hence, in principle it can be used with other machine learning models, such as SVM with Platt normalization.

2 RELATED WORK

Most current work involves fine tuning a trained classifier to achieve good performance on a new data set that is different from the one on which the training was done. There is little work that addresses the issue of adapting a classifier to situations where the data distribution remains the same but the label distribution changes.

[8] proposes a probabilistic framework to adapt the predictions of a classifier, based on the sequence of images that are presented to the classifier at test time. Their work is concentrated on a flat distribution of categories. In our case, we are concerned with adjusting and correcting our classifier by taking into account hierarchical relationships among object categories. This adjustment is by taking into consideration just one given test sample and not the previously seen test samples. The correction they do also takes into account the feedback from the prediction, that is whether the classifier was correct or not.

More closely related is the work of [5]. Given query images, they aim to identify the semantic subspace out of all categories, to which the test images belong. However, they work in a setting involving a single classifier with high capacity, trained on large amounts of data. Their aim is to select a relevant 'portion' of this trained classifier in order to discriminate over a subset of categories. In our setting, we aim to 'transfer knowledge' between two distinct classifiers which were trained separately. The only information we use during inference is the given hierarchy of categories and a single test sample.

Other work which involves use of label hierarchy are [7] and [2]. [7] use label relationships to train for *different* tasks: classification and detection. [2] use semantic relationships for similarity search and to speed up their proposed method.

3 METHOD

3.1 Problem Setting

We work in a standard multi-class classification setting. For each data point, $x \in \mathcal{X}$, the goal is to assign a class label $y \in \mathcal{Y} = \{l_1, ..., l_N\}$. The assignment of labels for each input depends on the output of a classifier, $f : \mathcal{X} \rightarrow \mathcal{Y}$, as $f(x) = argmax_y f_y(x)$. We consider a probabilistic classifier, which predicts a probability distribution over $\mathcal{Y}$. This is often obtained by applying a `softmax` transformation to the final model output.

We consider a setting with two sets of class (or category) labels corresponding to a two-level hierarchy with N_c *coarse* labels $\mathcal{Y}_c = \{c_1, ..., c_{N_c}\}$ and N_f *fine* labels $\mathcal{Y}_f = \{f_1, ..., f_{N_f}\}$. The hierarchical relation is defined by a function s from $\{1, ..., N_f\}$ to $\{1, ..., N_c\}$ specifying that the category with label $c_{s(j)}$ is the super-category of the category with label f_j. The goal is to aid the classifier in improving its predictions by augmenting the information contained in its parameters with the additional information from the hierarchy of labels.

ICMR '17, June 6–9, 2017, Bucharest, Romania

978-1-4503-4701-3/17/06...$15.00
DOI: http://dx.doi.org/10.1145/3078971.3079042

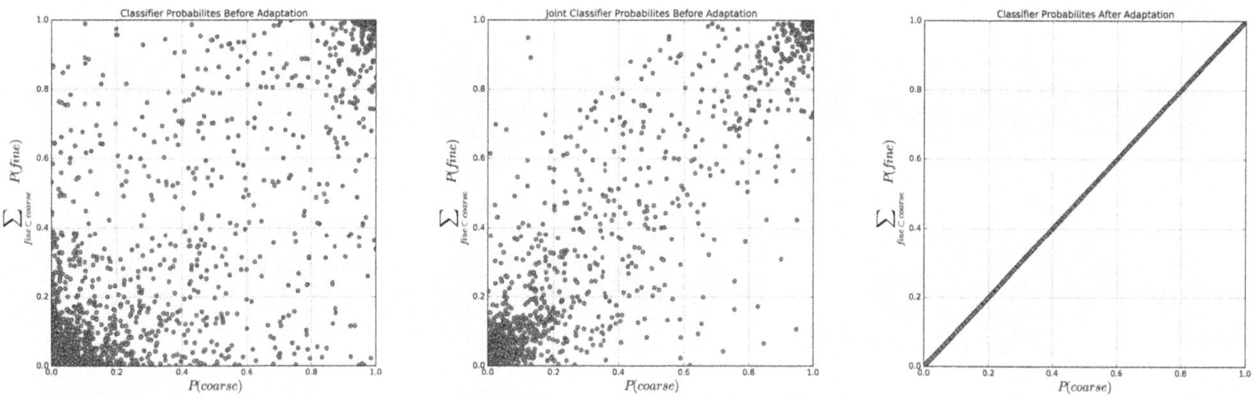

Figure 1: Distribution of probabilities for a coarse class obtained from coarse grain classification (horizontal axis) and from total fine grain classifications (vertical axis). Left and middle: Softmax values from classifiers, respectively for separate coarse and fine classifications, and for joint classification. Right: Probabilities adjusted to enforce that $P(coarse) = \sum P(fine)$.

Given different such models, each of which are trained on different levels of the hierarchy of classes, we would like to get an improvement in the model performance at minimum additional cost. Obtaining pre-trained models is quite straightforward and there is a vast collection available [1, 10].

Suppose we are given one classifier trained on N_c classes and another classifier which is trained on N_f classes. Each of the N_f classes are *fine* classes of the N_c *coarse* classes. Any given test sample will be assigned a probability of being correct by both classifiers. From this setting we make two observations:

(1) It is intuitive to reason that the probability of being correct at the *coarse* level should be greater than the probability of being correct at the *fine* level. This is due to the fact that the classifier has to discriminate among fewer classes at the coarse class level than at the fine class level.
(2) The probability assigned at the coarse class level is distributed among the fine classes which belong to this particular coarse class.

Figure 1 left shows the probability obtained from two classifiers trained at the coarse and fine levels. The horizontal axis shows the probability assigned to test samples for being in a particular coarse class (in this case, class 1 from CIFAR-20. See section 4). The vertical axis shows the total probability assigned to the corresponding fine classes, on being given the same test sample. Green dots denote data points which actually belong to the coarse class. We see that there are points for which the assigned coarse class probability is not the same as the total probability that is assigned to its corresponding fine classes.

3.2 Classifier Adaptation

From figure 1 left, we see that the previous observations do not hold for all data points. We want to enforce the condition that the confidence that a classifier has for a coarse class should be equal to the total confidence that a classifier has, for all fine classes of the coarse class in consideration. Formally, this is denoted as:

$$\forall i \in \{1, ..., N_c\} \; P(c_i|x) = \sum_{s(j)=i} P(f_j|x) \tag{1}$$

This state is depicted in figure 1, right. For all data samples, equation 1 will be satisfied if we map them to the diagonal. This procedure is outlined in algorithm 1.

In order to control the degree to which we enforce equation 1, we introduce an interpolation factor, α. In algorithm 1, the term α, is present inside the `for` loop. This term allows us to linearly interpolate between the original probabilities and the *degree* of adjustment that we want to carry out. In other words, it controls the extent of transformation from figure 1 left to right. A value of $\alpha = 1$ is the situation shown in figure 1 right and a value of $\alpha = 0$ is the situation in figure 1 left. It is to be noted that $\alpha = 0$ means that we are not performing any adjustment. The value of this hyper-parameter can be adjusted during inference and allows flexibility during inference.

Since, we modify the output probabilities based on the test sample, we term this procedure the *classifier adaptation* step.

3.3 Inference with Classifier Adaptation

Given the trained models, inference is done by using algorithm 1. For each test sample, first we obtain the probabilities from the coarse and fine classifiers. These probabilities are input to algorithm 1. The output of the algorithm are adjusted probabilities. The final prediction corresponds to the class having the maximum probability after the adjustment. The cost involved in doing this step is linear in the number of the super-classes. The interpolation factor, α, can be tuned using a validation set to obtain the best results.

Note that the adjustment of probabilities is done according to the hierarchy of all the labels. It is not the case that only the true label of the sample is being used.

4 EXPERIMENTS

Data Set. Experiments were conducted using the CIFAR-100 data set [6]. This data set contains 50,000 training images and 10,000 test

ALGORITHM 1: Classifier Adjustment

Input: Probabilities from coarse and fine classifiers
Output: Adapted classification probabilities, adjusted_coarse[i], adjusted_fine[i]

```
coarse[i], fine[i] //Lists of coarse and fine classes;
fine_coarse[j] // Coarse class of fine classes j;
P_coarse[i], P_fine[j] // Probability of coarse and fine classes;
Q_coarse[i] = Σ_{fine_coarse[j]=i} P_fine[j] // sum of probability of coarse
  classes of class i;
for i = 1, #coarse do
    target_prob = (P_coarse[i] + Q_coarse[i]) / 2;
    adjusted_coarse[i] =
    (1 − α)× P_coarse[i] + α× target_prob ;
    if Q_coarse[i] != 0 then
        for fine_coarse[j] = i do
            fine_target_prob =
            (P_fine[j] × target_prob[i]) / Q_coarse[i] ;
            adjusted_fine[j] =
            (1 − α)× P_fine[j] + α× fine_target_prob;
        end
    else
        adjusted_fine[j] =
        adjusted_coarse[i] / (Σ_{fine_coarse[j]=i} 1)
    end
end
```

images. These images are split into 100 mutually exclusive classes that we shall consider as the fine classes and refer to as CIFAR-100. These 100 classes are grouped into 20 coarse classes that we shall refer to as CIFAR-20. Each coarse class has exactly 5 fine classes.

Classifiers. Three deep convolutional neural network(DCNN) architectures were used: ALL-CNN-C [9], ResNet-164 [3], DenseNet-100 [4]. We retrained all these models on CIFAR-100 and CIFAR-20 ourselves. We additionally trained them on the fused set of concepts "CIFAR-120" that directly compute both the coarse and fine class probabilities at once. In this latter case, the softmax output layer is split in two parts, corresponding to the 100 fine and 20 coarse classes. The results obtained for CIFAR-100 are slightly different from those reported in the corresponding papers. Standard data augmentation was used during training, which is horizontal flips with 0.5 probability and random crops of 32×32 after padding each training image with 4 pixels on each side. The hyper-parameters and learning rate schedules were set according to the reported values for each model in their corresponding papers.

Experiments on separate models. The three different network architectures were trained on both CIFAR-100 and CIFAR-20 separately. After training, we applied our method as outlined in algorithm 1. In all cases we obtain a lower error rate. The error rates obtained with no ($\alpha = 0$) and full ($\alpha = 1$) adjustment are shown in tables 1 and 2 ("Separate" columns). It is important to point out that we obtain this gain in performance without any re-training and the adjustment time is negligible compared to the network training times. Figure 2 (blue dots) shows the change in error with respect to the degree of our adaptation scheme. We observe that on increasing the value of α, we obtain a decrease of the error. Hence,

Model	Separate	Joint	Ensemble
All-CNN-C initial	30.65%	29.63%	29.43%
All-CNN-C adjusted	29.64%	29.94%	28.48%
ResNet-164 initial	23.32%	23.35%	21.09%
ResNet-164 adjusted	22.21%	23.45%	20.48%
DenseNet-100 initial	21.07%	21.33%	18.89%
DenseNet-100 adjusted	19.98%	21.47%	18.25%

Table 1: CIFAR-100 error rates before and after adjustment of probabilities.

Model	Separate	Joint	Ensemble
All-CNN-C initial	20.72%	19.74%	19.78%
All-CNN-C adjusted	18.42%	18.48%	17.58%
ResNet-164 initial	15.25%	14.62%	13.76%
ResNet-164 adjusted	12.77%	13.94%	11.72%
DenseNet-100 initial	13.74%	13.16%	12.11%
DenseNet-100 adjusted	11.32%	12.31%	10.22%

Table 2: CIFAR-20 error rates before and after adjustment of probabilities.

steadily going from the situation depicted in figure 1 left to the one depicted in figure 1 right is better in the case of predictions from separate models.

Experiments on joint training. The three different network architectures were trained on CIFAR-120 (joint training). After training, we applied our method as outlined in algorithm 1. We obtain a lower error rate for coarse classification but a higher one for fine classification. The error rates obtained with no ($\alpha = 0$) and full ($\alpha = 1$) adjustment are shown in tables 1 and 2 ("Joint" columns). Figure 2 (green squares) shows the change in error with respect to the degree of our adaptation scheme. We observe that on increasing the value of α, we obtain a decrease (resp. increase) of the error.

Experiments on model ensembles. Exploiting the hierarchical relationship among the labels has some similarity with ensemble learning in the case of separate models, since we fuse the output of two trained models. The main difference is that we train with coarse and fine classes instead of two trainings with either twice the coarse classes or twice the fine classes. We did a contrast experiment by doing such a double training and simply averaging the predicted probabilities. The "ensemble" predictions are better than the adjusted ones either from separate or from joint trainings in all cases except for the All-CNN-C network on the coarse categories. It is also possible to do adjustment from ensemble prediction and it once again always leads to improved performance as shown in Figure 2 (orange diamonds).

5 DISCUSSION AND CONCLUSION

We presented a simple method, the classifier adaptation step, to improve fine grained classification using semantic hierarchical relations among different object categories. The information contained in the label hierarchy is complementary to the information that a

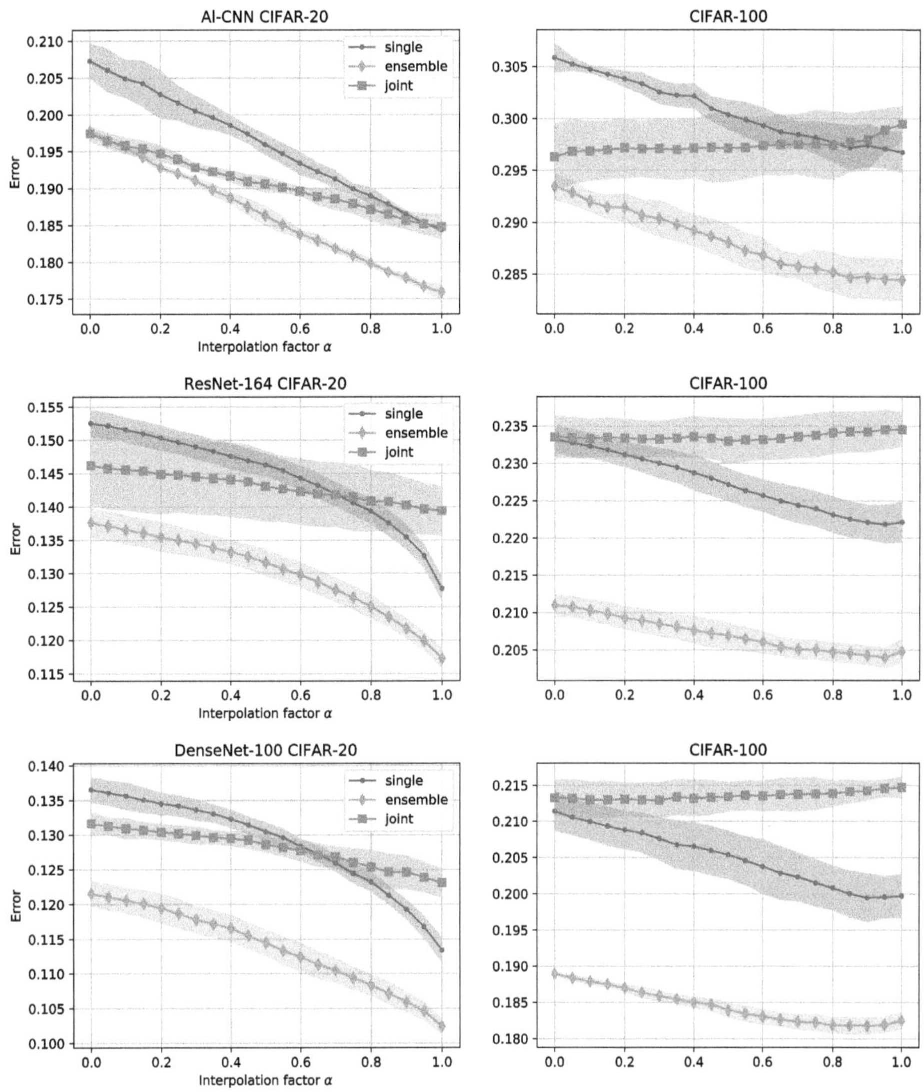

Figure 2: Classification error with respect to interpolation. Left: Coarse categories, Right: Fine categories(CIFAR-100). For each series, we report mean ± 1 standard deviation.

classifier learns from just the labels of training data. Our experimental results show that using the information from the relationship among labels, our method is able to reduce the error rate of a classifier. The classifier adaptation step is also able to improve on the predictions of an ensemble of models. This implies that hierarchical relationship is not exploited implicitly by classifiers and need to be enforced. As a future line of work, we would like to have a joint training of classifiers with multiple hierarchy levels for the labels.

We show that this holds for relatively simple CNN architectures, like the All-CNN-C, and also for very competitive models like ResNet-164 and DenseNet-100. The results obtained are promising because our proposed method is able to correct the predictions of different CNN architectures, even those with a large number of learnable parameters.

The classifier adaptation step, that we present, can in principle be applied to any classifier whose outputs are probabilities corresponding to categories. In the interest of time, we have performed experiments only on CNN models.

We evaluated our hypothesis successfully on the CIFAR-100 dataset, which has two levels of hierarchy. As future work, we will evaluate our approach on the much larger ILSVRC-2012 data set. This data set is organized according to the WordNet hierarchy and it should be possible to organize the training set in a hierarchical order.

ACKNOWLEDGMENTS

This work has been partially supported by the LabEx PERSYVAL-Lab (ANR-11-LABX-0025-01)

REFERENCES

[1] BVLC. *Caffe Model Zoo.* https://github.com/BVLC/caffe/wiki/Model-Zoo.

[2] Jia Deng, Alexander C Berg, and Li Fei-Fei. 2011. Hierarchical semantic indexing for large scale image retrieval. In *Computer Vision and Pattern Recognition (CVPR), 2011 IEEE Conference on.* IEEE, 785–792.

[3] Kaiming He, Xiangyu Zhang, Shaoqing Ren, and Jian Sun. 2016. Identity mappings in deep residual networks. In *European Conference on Computer Vision.* Springer, 630–645.

[4] Gao Huang, Zhuang Liu, Kilian Q Weinberger, and Laurens van der Maaten. 2016. Densely connected convolutional networks. *arXiv preprint arXiv:1608.06993* (2016).

[5] Yangqing Jia and Trevor Darrell. 2013. Latent task adaptation with large-scale hierarchies. In *Proceedings of the IEEE International Conference on Computer Vision.* 2080–2087.

[6] Alex Krizhevsky and Geoffrey Hinton. 2009. Learning multiple layers of features from tiny images. (2009).

[7] Joseph Redmon and Ali Farhadi. 2016. YOLO9000: Better, Faster, Stronger. *CoRR* abs/1612.08242 (2016). http://arxiv.org/abs/1612.08242

[8] Amelie Royer and Christoph H Lampert. 2015. Classifier adaptation at prediction time. In *Proceedings of the IEEE Conference on Computer Vision and Pattern Recognition.* 1401–1409.

[9] Jost Tobias Springenberg, Alexey Dosovitskiy, Thomas Brox, and Martin Riedmiller. 2014. Striving for simplicity: The all convolutional net. *arXiv preprint arXiv:1412.6806* (2014).

[10] TensorFlow. *Model Zoo.* https://github.com/tensorflow/models.

Fast Multi-Modal Unified Sparse Representation Learning

Mridula Verma*
Department of Computer Science and Engineering
Indian Institute of Technology (BHU)
Varanasi, Uttar Pradesh 221005
mridula.rs.cse13@iitbhu.ac.in

Kaushal Kumar Shukla
Department of Computer Science and Engineering
Indian Institute of Technology (BHU)
Varanasi, Uttar Pradesh 221005
kkshukla.cse@iitbhu.ac.in

ABSTRACT

Exploiting feature sets belonging to different modalities helps in improving a significant amount of accuracy for the task of recognition. Given representations of an object in different modalities (e.g. image, text, audio etc.), to learn a unified representation of the object, has been a popular problem in the literature of multimedia retrieval. In this paper, we introduce a new iterative algorithm that learns the sparse unified representation with better accuracy in a lesser number of iterations than the previously reported results. Our algorithm employs a new fixed-point iterative scheme along with an inertial step. In order to obtain more discriminative representation, we also imposed a regularization term that utilizes the label information from the datasets. Experimental results on two real benchmark datasets demonstrate the efficacy of our method in terms of the number of iterations and accuracy.

CCS CONCEPTS

•Computing methodologies →Computer vision; Machine learning approaches;

KEYWORDS

Cross-modal retrieval, unified representation learning, Accelerated Gradient Methods, Fixed-point Theory

ACM Reference format:
Mridula Verma and Kaushal Kumar Shukla. 2017. Fast Multi-Modal Unified Sparse Representation Learning. In *Proceedings of ICMR '17, June 6–9, 2017, Bucharest, Romania*, , 5 pages.
DOI: http://dx.doi.org/10.1145/3078971.3079040

1 INTRODUCTION

Enormous advancement in information systems and Internet technology has boosted the performances of the recognition and retrieval systems. Availability of a large amount of cross-modal information of an object extends the requirement of advanced knowledge extraction algorithms. A simple instance of such information is a web page having contents on a topic in form of different representations (e.g. Wikipedia; where domains are text and images). In order to use these representations for efficient retrieval, there is a direct need for an approach that efficiently handles this heterogeneous gap [19].

One class of approaches to handle such cross-domain information is the subspace learning methods such as Canonical Correlation Analysis (CCA) and Partial Least Squares (PLS), where the main objective is to learn the projections from individual domains to a common latent subspace. A few significant contributions in this direction include [8, 12, 14] and references therein. A significant contribution is by [16] that proposed a supervised CCA, named Generalized Multiview Analysis (GMA). In this paper authors proposed an efficient algorithm that exploits the label information of the objects for the purpose of cross-view classification and retrieval. Another method in this direction includes latent subspace learning via matrix factorization [4, 7]. Our work concerns the iterative methods for the multi-view learning, on which few popular contributions include [20, 21]. Following the similar trend recently in [19] authors proposed a joint dictionary learning method for cross-modal retrieval task, namely Multi-modal Unified Representation Learning (MURL). They have used the ℓ_1-norm to impose the sparsity in the learned model, as well as utilized the discriminant information of objects using *can-not-link* (i.e. the pair of objects belonging to different classes) and *must-link* (i.e. pair of objects belonging to the same class) pairs among data objects representations in different domains. They have utilized accelerated gradient method [3] to find out optimal multimodal unified sparse representations. Similar to their work, in authors utilized iterative schemes to solve the problem of multi-view learning.

The mathematical theory of accelerated gradient methods is rooted from the field of the Operator Theory and Functional Analysis. In a generalized infinite dimensional Hilbert space, such methods are called the inertial-based forward-backward splitting methods, which are linked from the area of fixed-point theory [9]. The fixed-point theory is a field of pure mathematics, where the new iterative schemes are designed and mathematically analyzed. For example, the iteration of classic accelerated gradient method was defined by the Picard fixed-point iterative scheme [11], which is considered to be the oldest fixed-point iterative scheme. Several other schemes are introduced henceforth such as Mann [10], s-iteration [1], normal s-iteration [15] and others [17] etc.

In this paper, we consider a non-smooth non-convex minimization framework to solve the multi-modal unified sparse representation learning problem, which optimizes the unified representation and the corresponding dictionaries. In order to solve this problem, we alternatively optimize the unified representation and the dictionaries respectively, keeping the other term fixed at a time. Our main contribution is a new optimization algorithm to learn the unified representation which takes lesser number of iterations with

*Corresponding author

ICMR '17, June 6–9, 2017, Bucharest, Romania
© 2017 ACM. ACM ISBN 978-1-4503-4701-3/17/06...$$15.00
DOI: http://dx.doi.org/10.1145/3078971.3079040

better results. An initial experimental analysis of the algorithm has been done in [18] for the high-dimensional regression problem. The algorithm provides a new formulation of inertial-based proximal gradient method, which exploits the extra gradient method of the fixed point theory. In this paper we will analyze the performance of the algorithm for learning the unified representation from different cross-modal domains. We performed extensive experiments on two benchmark cross-modal datasets, namely, *Wikipedia* and *NUS-WIDE*, that have textual and visual information about different objects. To the best of our knowledge, this is the first time when the extra gradient based approach has been applied and analyzed for the task of cross-modal retrieval.

2 PROBLEM FORMULATION AND PROPOSED APPROACH

For the problem of cross-modal retrieval, we adapt the formulation given in [19]. Let there are N objects with K representations. An object belonging to k^{th} modality is denoted as $X^k = [x_1^k, \cdots, x_N^k] \in \mathbb{R}^{d_k \times N}$, where $k = 1, \cdots, K$ and d_k is the dimensionality of kth modal. Thus, an individual object $x_i = \{x_i^1, \cdots, x_i^K\}$ has K representations. The problem of cross-domain retrieval is to retrieve p top-matched objects belonging to any modality. The objective is to learn a unified representation using information from all the modalities i.e. joint dictionary learning. Let $Z = [z_1, \cdots, z_N] \in \mathbb{R}^{P \times N}$ be the unified representation and $D^k = [d_1^k, \cdots, d_P^k] \in \mathbb{R}^{d_k \times P}$ is the dictionary corresponding to k-th modality. Following [19], the main objective function is to solve,

$$\min_{D^k, Z} \sum_{k=1}^{K} \|X^k - D^k Z\|_F^2 + \lambda_1 \|Z\|_1 + \lambda_2 tr(ZLZ^T)$$
$$\|d_p^k\|_2^2 \leq 1, \forall k = 1, \cdots K, p = 1, \cdots, P, \tag{1}$$

where, $L = D - W$, D is a diagonal matrix with $D_{ii} = \sum_j w_{ij}$, and

$$w_{ij} = \begin{cases} 1, & (x_i, x_j) \in \mathcal{S} \\ -\alpha, & (x_i, x_j) \in \mathcal{D} \\ 0, & \text{otherwise.} \end{cases} \tag{2}$$

Here $\mathcal{S}$ is the set of pairs of similar objects (objects belonging to same class), and $\mathcal{D}$ is the set of pairs where the class of objects are dissimilar. Since the problem in equation (1) is non-convex with both the variables, but convex with one of the variable keeping the other fixed, we solve the problem first for Z, keeping D^k fixed and vice-versa. First we keep the dictionary fixed and optimize the following problem:

$$\min_{Z} \sum_{k=1}^{K} \|X^k - D^k Z\|_F^2 + \lambda_1 \|Z\|_1 + \lambda_2 \, tr(ZLZ^T). \tag{3}$$

Due to the ℓ_1-norm term, the above equation is non-smooth. In order to effectively learn the unified representation Z, we present New Accelerated Gradient Algorithm NAGA as described in algorithm 1. This algorithm is applicable to solve the problem of minimizing the sum of a smooth convex loss function $f(\cdot)$ with gradient having Lipschitz constant L, and a non-smooth convex regularization function $g(\cdot)$. We rewrite (3) in terms of a loss function and regularization function as follows:

$$f(Z) = \sum_{k=1}^{K} \|X^k - D^k Z\|_F^2 + \lambda_2 \, tr(ZLZ^T), \quad g(Z) = \|Z\|_1. \tag{4}$$

The mathematical framework of the proximal gradient algorithms, includes a nonexpansive operator corresponding to both the functions f and g in Hilbert space $\mathcal{H}$ which forms a fixed-point problem and then iteratively solve to get the fixed-point solution. Here the nonexpansive operator can be designed as $\mathcal{T} = J_{c_n}^{\nabla f, prox_{\lambda g}} = prox_{c_n \lambda g}(I - c_n \nabla f)$ for $c_n \in (0, 2/L)$. Thus, the iterative scheme for the classical proximal gradient method becomes,

$$Z_{n+1} = J_{c_n}^{\nabla f, prox_{\lambda g}}(Z_n), \tag{5}$$

which is a Picard iterative scheme. Note that the Picard Iterative scheme is defined as follows,

$$x_{n+1} = \mathcal{T}(x_n), \tag{6}$$

where T is a nonexpansive operator, and the sequence $\{x_n\} \in \mathcal{H}$, for $n = 1, 2, \cdots, \mathbb{N}$. In order to accelerate the convergence, an additional inertial term is introduced to the traditional proximal gradient method (5), as follows,

$$Y_n = Z_n + \alpha_n (Z_n - Z_{n-1}) \tag{7}$$
$$Z_{n+1} = J_{c_n}^{\nabla f, prox_{\lambda g}}(Y_n). \tag{8}$$

It should be noted that the term $\alpha_n \in (0, 1)$ is a generalized term, that was defined by different expressions, such as in [3, 5]. In our experiments, the sequence α_n is generated in a way similar to [5]. More detail on the theoretical relation between the proximal gradient algorithm and the fixed-point theory is given in [11]. The main idea behind NAGA is the acceleration of a proximal gradient algorithm which employs the normal s-iteration fixed point iterative scheme [15]. The normal s-iteration scheme (also called the hybrid Picard-Mann iteration) is defined as follows,

$$x_{n+1} = \mathcal{T}((1 - \beta_n) x_n + \beta_n \mathcal{T}(x_n)), \tag{9}$$

where we set sequence $\{\beta_n\} \in (0, 1)$ for $n = 1, 2, \cdots, \mathbb{N}$.

Algorithm 1 NAGA for multimodal unified representation learning

1: **procedure** NAGA-MURL(c_0, β_0)
2: Initialize: $Z_0, Z_1 \in \mathcal{H}, \alpha_0 = 1$
3: **repeat**
4: Find c_n using backtracking stepsize rule
5: Compute α_n and β_n such that $\alpha_n, \beta_n \in (0, 1)$
6: $W_n \leftarrow Z_n + \alpha_n (Z_n - Z_{n-1})$
7: $V_n \leftarrow (1 - \beta_n) W_n + \beta_n J_{c_n}^{\nabla f, prox_{\lambda g}}(W_n)$
8: $Z_{n+1} \leftarrow J_{c_n}^{\nabla f, prox_{\lambda g}}(V_n)$
9: **until** converge
10: **return** Z_n
11: **end procedure**

It should be noted that the proximity operator with respect to the ℓ_1 norm function is the shrinkage operator defined as $prox_t(x_i) = (|x_i| - t)_+ sgn(x_i)$, where sgn is the signum function. We have considered that the value of L is not known in advance and thus we adapt the backtracking line search in each iteration, as considered in [3].

After getting the optimal value of Z, we will solve for corresponding dictionary D^k keeping Z fixed. For this, we used the approach of Lagrange dual as used in [19]. We adapted the conjugate gradient method to solve for the dictionaries D^k. The initial dictionaries are obtained using k-SVD [2]. These two steps of learning the unified representation and dictionaries are repeated until we get the convergence. After learning the dictionaries, in order to get the new representation of a test object x_t^k belonging to the kth modality, we solve the following problem:

$$\min_{z_t} \|x_t^k - D^k z_t\|_F^2 + \lambda_1 \|z_t\|_1 \tag{10}$$

It is easy to observe that the above problem follows the framework of popular Lasso problem. To solve the above problem we again adapt the NAGA algorithm. The value of λ_1 is computed using the backtracking line search approach same as before.

3 EXPERIMENTS AND RESULT ANALYSIS

We consider two modalities (i.e. text and image) in our cross-modal retrieval experiments. We performed our experiments on two benchmark datasets, namely Wiki [13] and NUS-WIDE [6]. Wiki dataset consists of 2866 image-text pairs with 128-dimensional visual features and 10-dimensional textual features. Here image-text pairs belong to ten categories. We have taken 2173 training sample pairs and 693 testing sample pairs in our experiments. The second dataset is NUS-WIDE, that consists of the tagged images from Flickr. We choose 15 categories with 600 images in each category. There are 500 visual features and 1000 textual features. For this dataset, we choose 60%-40% training-testing sample partition.

The value of sparsity controlling parameter λ_1 is set as $\{\theta \times \lambda_{max}\}$, where λ_{max} is set as $\|X^{k^T} D^k\|_\infty$ and the value of θ is chosen in the range of {1-0.0001}. We performed 5-fold cross-validation for tuning the parameter θ. For the stopping criteria, the tolerance value (the difference between two consecutive function values) is set to 10e-5, which also notifies the convergence. The maximum number of iterations is set to 10e4. All the vectors are initialized with a zero-valued component. Values of c_n and L are initialized with 1, and β_n is set to $\frac{1}{(n+1)}$. All the tests are performed on Intel Core i7 processor with 10GB RAM, under MATLAB computing environment. We have used MALSAR package [22] in our experiments.

It should be noted that it is the first time that a new proximal gradient method with extra-gradient and inertial step is applied to the task of multi-modal unified sparse representation learning. Our first result shows the main contribution of this work, which is the faster convergence of the algorithm for finding the multi-modal unified sparse representation learning. Figure 1 shows the results for both the datasets. In figure 1(a) and 1(c), we have shown the log-log plot between the value $F(Z_n) - F(Z^*)$ for both MURL and NAGA-MURL algorithms. Here Z_n is the value of Z at n^{th} iteration of algorithm 1 and Z^* is the optimal value. It can be easily observed that the convergence rate of NAGA-MURL is faster than that of the MURL approach. In addition, we have shown the function values $F(Z^n)$ at each iteration for both the algorithms, which directly implies that the function values decrease significantly faster with NAGA-MURL than the MURL approach.

Table 1: Mean Avg. Precision on the Wiki Dataset

Methods	Image Sample	Text Sample	Average
PCA	0.1423	0.1103	0.1263
PLS	0.1481	0.1349	0.1415
CCA	0.1590	0.1362	0.1476
MURL	0.1894	0.1565	0.1729
NAGA-MURL	**0.1902**	**0.1596**	**0.1816**

Table 2: Mean Avg. Precision on the NUS-WIDE Dataset

Methods	Image Sample	Text Sample	Average
PCA	0.0912	0.0794	0.853
PLS	0.1352	0.1181	0.1267
CCA	0.1126	0.1065	0.1096
MURL	0.1653	0.1394	0.1524
NAGA-MURL	**0.1697**	**0.1402**	**0.1549**

Table 3: Number of Iterations and computational time to converge for both Datasets

	WIKI	
Methods	# of Iterations	computational time
MURL	99	2.7522
NAGA-MURL	**31**	**1.612**
	NUS-WIDE	
Methods	# of Iterations	computational time
MURL	1957	127.7921
NAGA-MURL	**465**	**62.7285**

We compared the accuracy results of our algorithm with PCA, PLS, CCA and MURL. The standard metric to measure the performance of a cross-modal retrieval model is mean average precision (MAP), which are compared in tables 1 and 2. It can be concluded that for both the datasets the values of MAP is consistently better for the NAGA-MURL algorithm.

The comparison between the two proximal gradient methods are shown in table 3. The first proximal gradient method is accelerated gradient method used by MURL, and the second is the proposed NAGA used by the NAGA-MURL approach. It is clear from the table that the MAP values achieved by NAGA-MURL in a lesser number of iterations than that of MURL. For both the datasets, NAGA-MURL takes less than half number of iterations of MURL. The computational time is also shown in the table which shows that the NAGA-MURL approach gives better results in lesser number of iterations and less time. In the end, we demonstrate the precision-recall curves for the algorithms on both the datasets in figure 2. We can imply from the figure that the precision-recall curve for both the MURL and NAGA-MURL algorithms are comparable and better than that of the PCA, PLS and CCA approaches.

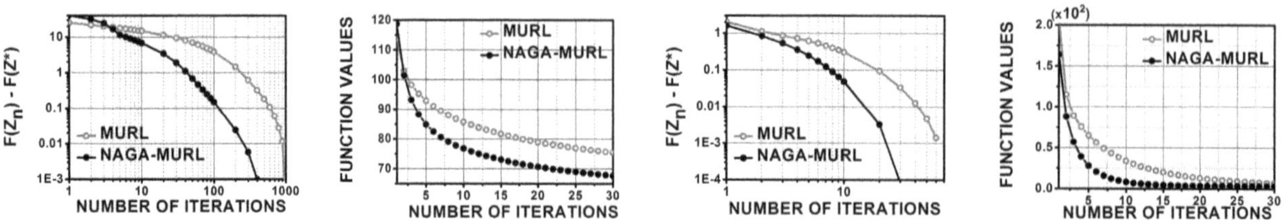

(a) Conv Rate on NUS (b) Func Values on NUS (c) Conv Rate on WIKI (d) Func Values on WIKI

Figure 1: Performance of NAGA-MURL in comparison to MURL on both the datasets.

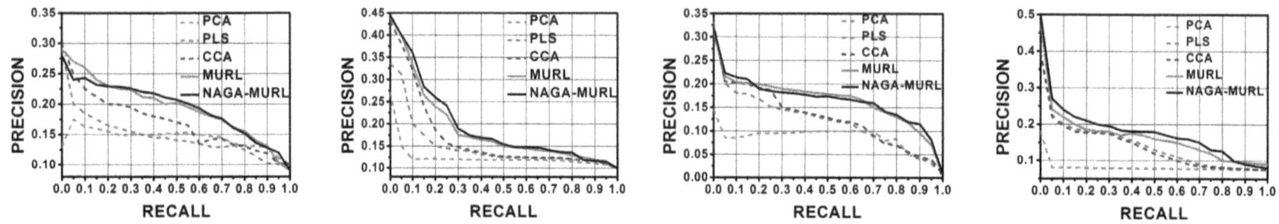

(a) Wiki Image query (b) Wiki Text query (c) NUS Image query (d) NUS Text query

Figure 2: Precision-recall curves on both the datasets for the two cross-modal retrieval tasks.

We conclude this section with some examples of the retrieved images for an image query and a text query for both the Wiki and NUS-WIDE datasets. In table 4, the left-most column is the query image/text, and the next 5 columns are the corresponding retrieved images.

4 CONCLUSION

In this paper, we present an experimental analysis of a new optimization technique for learning multi-modal unified sparse representations. The presented technique is based on a new fixed point iterative scheme, which is accelerated using an inertial step. Results with two benchmark cross-modal datasets are shown. We conclude that presented algorithm gives better performance than the previous algorithm, in terms of the number of iterations required to converge and accuracy. In future, we aim to perform mathematical analysis of the algorithm. We also intend to apply this technique as the deep learning optimization approach.

REFERENCES

[1] R. P. Agarwal, Donal O'Regan, and D. R. Sahu. 2007. Iterative construction of fixed points of nearly asymptotically nonexpansive mappings. *Journal of nonlinear and convex analysis* 8, 1 (April 2007), 61–79.

[2] M. Aharon, M. Elad, and A. Bruckstein. 2006. K-SVD: An Algorithm for Designing Overcomplete Dictionaries for Sparse Representation. *IEEE Transactions on Signal Processing* 54, 11 (Nov 2006), 4311–4322. DOI: http://dx.doi.org/10.1109/TSP.2006.881199

[3] Amir Beck and Marc Teboulle. 2009. A Fast Iterative Shrinkage-Thresholding Algorithm for Linear Inverse Problems. *SIAM Journal on Imaging Sciences* 2, 1 (2009), 183–202. DOI: http://dx.doi.org/10.1137/080716542 arXiv:http://dx.doi.org/10.1137/080716542

[4] Juan C. Caicedo and Fabio A. González. 2012. Multimodal Fusion for Image Retrieval Using Matrix Factorization. In *Proceedings of the 2Nd ACM International Conference on Multimedia Retrieval (ICMR '12)*. ACM, New York, NY, USA, Article 56, 8 pages. DOI: http://dx.doi.org/10.1145/2324796.2324860

[5] A. Chambolle and Ch. Dossal. 2015. On the Convergence of the Iterates of the "Fast Iterative Shrinkage/Thresholding Algorithm". *Journal of Optimization Theory and Applications* 166, 3 (2015), 968–982. DOI: http://dx.doi.org/10.1007/s10957-015-0746-4

[6] Tat-Seng Chua, Jinhui Tang, Richang Hong, Haojie Li, Zhiping Luo, and Yantao Zheng. 2009. NUS-WIDE: A Real-world Web Image Database from National University of Singapore. In *Proceedings of the ACM International Conference on Image and Video Retrieval (CIVR '09)*. ACM, New York, NY, USA, Article 48, 9 pages. DOI: http://dx.doi.org/10.1145/1646396.1646452

[7] R. Gaurav, M. Verma, and K. K. Shukla. 2016. Informed Multimodal Latent Subspace Learning via Supervised Matrix Factorization. In *Proceedings of the Tenth Indian Conference on Computer Vision, Graphics and Image Processing (ICVGIP '16)*. ACM, New York, NY, USA, Article 36, 8 pages. DOI: http://dx.doi.org/10.1145/3009977.3010012

[8] David R. Hardoon, Sandor R. Szedmak, and John R. Shawe-taylor. 2004. Canonical Correlation Analysis: An Overview with Application to Learning Methods. *Neural Comput.* 16, 12 (Dec. 2004), 2639–2664. DOI: http://dx.doi.org/10.1162/0899766042321814

[9] Dirk A. Lorenz and Thomas Pock. 2015. An Inertial Forward-Backward Algorithm for Monotone Inclusions. *Journal of Mathematical Imaging and Vision* 51, 2 (2015), 311–325. DOI: http://dx.doi.org/10.1007/s10851-014-0523-2

[10] W. Robert Mann. 1953. Mean Value Methods in Iteration. *Proc. Amer. Math. Soc.* 4, 3 (1953), 506–510. http://www.jstor.org/stable/2032162

[11] Neal Parikh and Stephen Boyd. 2014. Proximal Algorithms. *Found. Trends Optim.* 1, 3 (Jan. 2014), 127–239. DOI: http://dx.doi.org/10.1561/2400000003

[12] J. Costa Pereira, E. Coviello, G. Doyle, N. Rasiwasia, G. R. G. Lanckriet, R. Levy, and N. Vasconcelos. 2014. On the Role of Correlation and Abstraction in Cross-Modal Multimedia Retrieval. *IEEE Transactions on Pattern Analysis and Machine Intelligence* 36, 3 (March 2014), 521–535. DOI: http://dx.doi.org/10.1109/TPAMI.2013.142

[13] Nikhil Rasiwasia, Jose Costa Pereira, Emanuele Coviello, Gabriel Doyle, Gert R.G. Lanckriet, Roger Levy, and Nuno Vasconcelos. 2010. A New Approach to Cross-modal Multimedia Retrieval. In *Proceedings of the 18th ACM International Conference on Multimedia (MM '10)*. ACM, New York, NY, USA, 251–260. DOI: http://dx.doi.org/10.1145/1873951.1873987

[14] Roman Rosipal and Nicole Krämer. 2006. Overview and Recent Advances in Partial Least Squares. In *Proceedings of the 2005 International Conference on Subspace, Latent Structure and Feature Selection (SLSFS'05)*. Springer-Verlag, Berlin, Heidelberg, 34–51. DOI: http://dx.doi.org/10.1007/11752790_2

[15] D. R. Sahu. 2011. Applications of the S-iteration Process to Constrained Minimization Problems and Split Feasibility Problems. *Fixed Point Theory* 12, 1 (2011), 187–204.

[16] A. Sharma, A. Kumar, H. Daume, and D. W. Jacobs. 2012. Generalized Multiview Analysis: A discriminative latent space. In *2012 IEEE Conference on Computer Vision and Pattern Recognition*. IEEE Computer Society, Washington, DC, USA,

Table 4: Example of cross-modal retrieval on both datasets

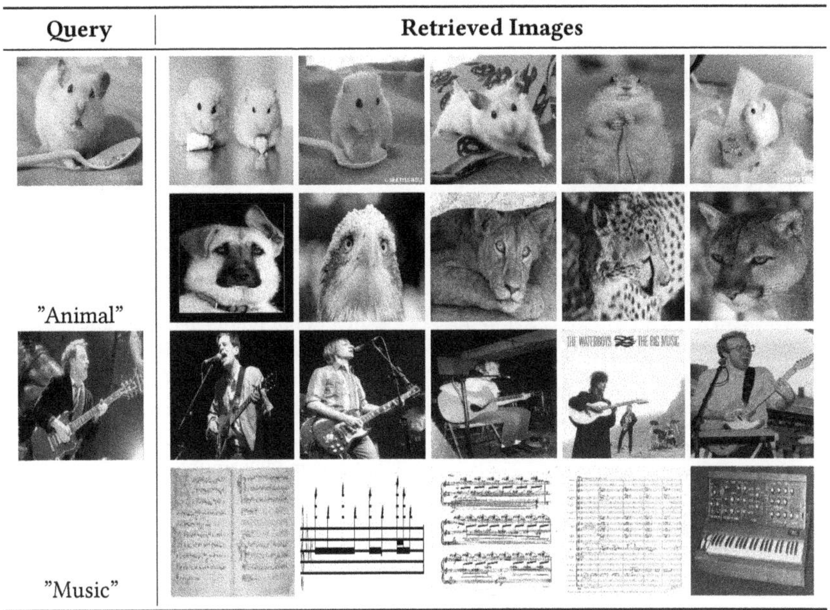

2160–2167. DOI: http://dx.doi.org/10.1109/CVPR.2012.6247923

[17] M. Verma, P. Jain, and K. K. Shukla. 2016. A New Faster First Order Iterative Scheme for Sparsity-based Multitask Learning. In *Proceedings of 2016 IEEE International Conference on Systems, Man, and Cybernetics.* IEEE SMC, Budapest, Hungary, 6.

[18] Mridula Verma and K. K. Shukla. 2017. A new accelerated proximal technique for regression with high-dimensional datasets. *Knowledge and Information Systems* (2017), 1–16. DOI: http://dx.doi.org/10.1007/s10115-017-1047-z

[19] K. Wang, W. Wang, and L. Wang. 2015. Learning unified sparse representations for multi-modal data. In *2015 IEEE International Conference on Image Processing (ICIP).* IEEE, Canada, 3545–3549. DOI: http://dx.doi.org/10.1109/ICIP.2015.7351464

[20] F. Wu, Z. Yu, Y. Yang, S. Tang, Y. Zhang, and Y. Zhuang. 2014. Sparse Multi-Modal Hashing. *IEEE Transactions on Multimedia* 16, 2 (Feb 2014), 427–439. DOI: http://dx.doi.org/10.1109/TMM.2013.2291214

[21] J. Yu, Y. Rui, and B. Chen. 2014. Exploiting Click Constraints and Multi-view Features for Image Re-ranking. *IEEE Transactions on Multimedia* 16, 1 (Jan 2014), 159–168. DOI: http://dx.doi.org/10.1109/TMM.2013.2284755

[22] J. Zhou, J. Chen, and J. Ye. 2011. *MALSAR: Multi-tAsk Learning via StructurAl Regularization.* Arizona State University. http://www.public.asu.edu/~jye02/Software/MALSAR

Badminton Video Analysis based on Spatiotemporal and Stroke Features

Wei-Ta Chu
National Chung Cheng University
Chiayi, Taiwan
wtchu@ccu.edu.tw

Samuel Situmeang
National Chung Cheng University
Chiayi, Taiwan
samuel.situmeang@ymail.com

ABSTRACT

Most of the broadcasted sports events nowadays present game statistics to the viewers which can be used to design the gameplay strategy, improve player's performance, or improve accessing the point of interest of a sport game. However, few studies have been proposed for broadcasted badminton videos. In this paper, we integrate several visual analysis techniques to detect the court, detect players, classify strokes, and classify the player's strategy. Based on visual analysis, we can get some insights about the common strategy of a certain player. We evaluate performance of stroke classification, strategy classification, and show game statistics based on classification results.

CCS CONCEPTS

•Computing methodologies → Activity recognition and understanding; •Human-centered computing → *Visual analytics;*

KEYWORDS

Badminton video, stroke classification, strategy classification, game statistics

ACM Reference format:
Wei-Ta Chu and Samuel Situmeang. 2017. Badminton Video Analysis based on Spatiotemporal
and Stroke Features. In *Proceedings of ICMR '17, June 6–9, 2017, Bucharest, Romania*, , 4 pages.
DOI: http://dx.doi.org/10.1145/3078971.3079032

1 INTRODUCTION

Game statistics are important to show details of sports events. In tennis, games statistics consist of each player's number of winners, unforced errors, aces, and so on. They help coaches to design the strategy to improve their player's performance. For viewers, game statistics would improve accessing the point of interest of a game. However, research on badminton videos specifically has been rare, and most past researches either concentrates on tennis videos or generalize it to racket sports [17][1][14]. Badminton is the fastest racket game [13], and this makes playing pattern and speed different from other racket games.

ICMR '17, June 6–9, 2017, Bucharest, Romania
 ACM ISBN 978-1-4503-4701-3/17/06...$15.00
DOI: http://dx.doi.org/10.1145/3078971.3079032

Focusing on tennis videos, Reno et al. [17] proposed a background subtraction algorithm, which facilitates accurate player and ball segmentation. Barnett and Clarke [2] proposed to predict outcomes of tennis matches. They showed how the standard statistics published by the The Association of Tennis Professionals can be combined to predict the serving statistics. Polk et al. [14] presented a tennis visualization system to show detailed information of a match in an organized way. Rea et al. [16] built event hidden Markov models with binary classification according to the player's positions in the court.

Relatively fewer badminton-related studies have been proposed. Chen and Wang [5] proposed a method based on 2-D seriate images to discover statistics of a badminton match. Careelmont [3] conducted badminton shot classification in compressed videos. The shuttlecock was detected and the stroke type was recognized based on the shuttlecock trajectory. Dierickx [7] continued Careelmont's work and improved performance of the trajectory extractor significantly. Overall, these works focus on shuttlecock trajectory extraction in order to facilitate classification.

We see most badminton-related works were limited to stroke classification. In this paper, we try to integrate visual analysis techniques to detect the court, detect players, classify strokes, and classify the player's strategy. Based on visual analysis, we attempt to get insights about the common strategy of a certain player.

The rest of this paper is organized as follows. Section 2 describes details of court detection. Section 3 introduces main visual analysis techniques. Section 4 provides evaluation results, followed by the conclusion and future works in Section 5.

2 COURT DETECTION

We follow the framework proposed in [9] to detect the court. This method was originally designed to find tennis court, and we slightly modify some components to detect the court in badminton videos.

Figure 1 shows the court detection framework. Because in most cases the court lines are white, the first step of this framework is white pixel extraction. Intuitively, pixels with intensity values higher than a predefined threshold are detected as white pixels. However, many other objects such as advertisement logos, net, spectators, and the player's clothes can also be white. We therefore devise a texture filtering process as the second step to remove noise.

The idea to remove noise is to exclude white pixels that are not at lines or corners. Motivated by the corner and edge principal values proposed in [10], we consider gradient information of a local patch W centered by each white pixel located at (x, y), and construct a structure matrix $\boldsymbol{A}$:

$$\boldsymbol{A} = \sum_{u \in W} \sum_{v \in W} w(u, v) \begin{bmatrix} I_x^2 & I_x I_y \\ I_x I_y & I_y^2 \end{bmatrix} \tag{1}$$

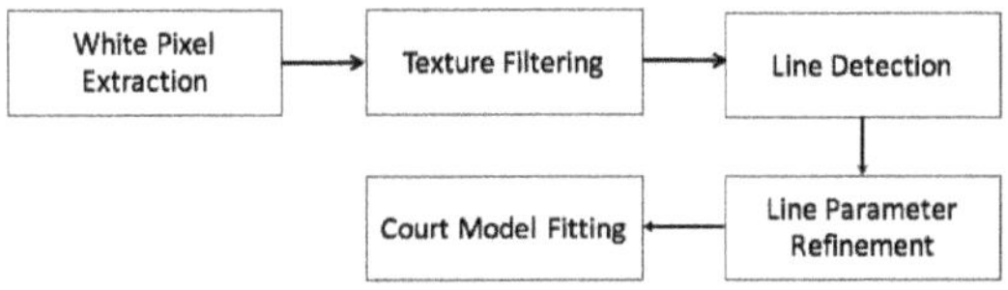

Figure 1: Overview of the court detection framework.

where $w(u, v)$ is the weighting function, and I_x and I_y are the partial derivatives in the horizontal and vertical aspects, respectively.

We then calculate the eigenvalues λ_1 and λ_2 of the structure matrix $\boldsymbol{A}$. Assuming that $\lambda_1 \leq \lambda_2$, based on the numerical values of the eigenvalues, the following observations can be made:

- If $\lambda_1 \approx 0$ and $\lambda_2 \approx 0$, then the white pixel at (x, y) has no feature of interest and should be excluded in the following process.
- If $\lambda_1 \approx 0$ and λ_2 is large, then the white pixel at (x, y) is probably on an edge and is retained.
- If both λ_1 and λ_2 are large, then the white pixel at (x, y) should be right on a corner and is retained.

Based on filtered white pixels, the Hough transform was used to detect court lines. In our work, we adopt a more recent probabilistic Hough transform [12] (PHT) to obtain more reliable results. In contrast to the standard Hough transform that takes all candidate pixels into account, PHT takes only a random subset of them to avoid noise but remain the ability to detect lines.

Results of the Hough transform or PHT may be a bundle of detected lines, which all lie close together. We thus adopt the line parameter refinement process in [9] to remove duplicate lines.

Finally, the final step shown in Figure 1 is court model fitting. At this step we need to find the mapping between the detected lines on video frames and the predefined court model. To do this, four different intersection points between court lines are extracted, and the the planar homography matrix is estimated to do projective mapping from the court in video frames to the predefined court. Details of homographic mapping please refer to [9].

With the homography matrix, we can calibrate different video frames and represent player's positions in a standardized coordinate system, which is important when we try to develop a computational model to do strategy analysis.

3 BADMINTON VIDEO ANALYSIS

We develop three important components to facilitate getting insights from game statistics. First, because how players move conveys rich cues to understand the game, we detect player's position and map it on the court model. Second, how a player hits the shuttlecock directly show the player's performance and influence game results. We therefore do stroke classification based on player's posture. Finally, we jointly consider player's movement and stroke sequences to do strategy classification.

3.1 Player Detection and Tracking

Because players may wear clothes in various color, it is not plausible to construct a generic model to describe players in various games. Instead, we construct a background model describing the color distribution of the court. With this model, the probability of each pixel belonging to the background is estimated. The pixels with low probability being the background are viewed to present players or court lines. Obviously we can easily eliminate court line pixels thereafter because we have already detected court lines (Sec. 2).

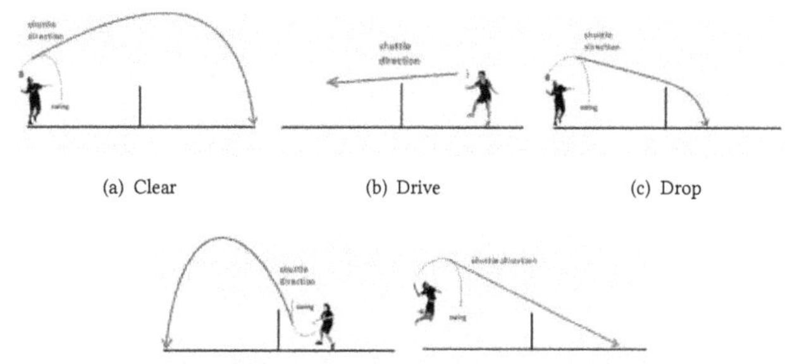

(a) Clear (b) Drive (c) Drop

(d) Lob (e) Smash

Figure 2: Illustration of five different strokes [11].

Although the color of a badminton court looks smooth and regular, the lighting condition, object movement, and many other factors dynamically change the color distribution. The key issue is thus how to create a background model and update the model parameters dynamically to adapt to background changes, including the change of scene illumination and scene composition. Inspired by [18], we construct a Gaussian mixture model (GMM) to describe the background. Given a video sequence $f_1, f_2, ..., f_N$, where f_i denotes the ith video frame, we first describe the color distribution of the region inside the court by a GMM $\mathcal{M}$, based on the observations of the first M frames, i.e., $f_1, ..., f_M$. Every time when a new frame is coming, say f_{M+1}, we update the parameters of the GMM $\mathcal{M}$ to adapt to the latest color distribution [19]. In this work, the number of frames to be considered in background model construction is 500, i.e., $M = 500$. We use three Gaussian mixtures to construct the model, and the standard expectation-maximum algorithm is used to find parameters.

For each pixel j of a video frame f_i, we estimate the probability of this pixel being the background as $p(j|\mathcal{M})$. If the probability $p(j|\mathcal{M})$ is less than a predefined threshold δ, we view the pixel j as a candidate foreground pixel. Based on detected candidate foreground pixels, we conduct morphological operations, i.e., dilation and erosion, to further remove noise. Connected components are then determined based on the remaining foreground pixels, and finally we detect the largest connected component (CC) as the player. Note that we respectively detect the largest CC in the top half and the bottom half of a video frame, which correspond to the player far from the camera and close to the camera.

To determine the player's position, we find the bounding box of the largest connected component. The middle point of the bottom border of this box is then defined as the player's position. With the homography matrix determined in Sec. 2, we can map the player's position from video to the court model.

3.2 Stroke Classification

There are several types of strokes in badminton games, and a high level of skill is required by a player to perform all of them effectively.

In this work, we generalize the strokes to six types, namely *clear*, *drive*, *drop*, *lob*, *smash*, and all other strokes are viewed as *others*. Figure 2 illustrates the first five strokes.

- Clear: Shuttle travels high and deep.
- Drive: Shuttle travels fast and flat skimming the net.
- Drop: Shuttle travels downwards.
- Lob: The aim is to lift or lob the shuttle over the opponent and to make the shuttle land closely to the baseline.
- Smash: Shuttle travels at speed in downward direction.
- Others: Other types of strokes or player standing without hitting the shuttle.

The idea to classify the stroke a player invokes is based on pose recognition. Based on the bounding box of a player, we extract histogram of oriented gradient (HOG) [6] as the representation. Based on HOG, we construct a classifier based on support vector machine (SVM) [4] to do stroke classification.

3.3 Strategy Classification

Strategy refers to the general plan that a player decides on to defeat the opponent, on the basis of some specific tactics [8]. Currently, we roughly classify strategies in badminton into either offensive or defensive strategies. Given a play, we detect player's position and classify strokes for each frame. A sequence of frames is then represented by a sequence of observations showing the evolution of player's position and strokes. More particularly, the observations are stroke type s and the bottom player's position in the court model (x, y). Note that we divide the court (bottom half) into nine equally-sized regions, and the player's position is spatially quantized into one of the nine regions. The representation of player's position is then $r = Q(x, y)$, where Q is the quantization function. A play consisting of T frames is then represented as $\boldsymbol{O} = (\boldsymbol{o}_1, ..., \boldsymbol{o}_T)$, where $\boldsymbol{o}_i = (s_i, r_i)$ is a tuple showing the stroke type and position.

Given a set of observation sequences $\{\boldsymbol{O}_1, ..., \boldsymbol{O}_K\}$, where K is the total number of training sequences, we construct hidden Markov models (HMMs) to do strategy classification. This model is trained based on the standard Baum-Welch algorithm [15]. We respectively collect training data of the offensive strategy and the defensive strategy, and separately train a model for each strategy. Given a play, we respectively input the observation sequence $\boldsymbol{O}$ to these two models λ_1 and λ_2. The probability of this play being an offensive strategy is estimated as $p(\boldsymbol{O}|\lambda_1)$, and the probability of being a defensive strategy is estimated as $p(\boldsymbol{O}|\lambda_2)$. The strategy of this play is finally determined as $i^* = \arg\max_i p(\boldsymbol{O}|\lambda_i)$.

4 EVALUATION

4.1 Dataset and Evaluation Setup

We collect the evaluation dataset from BadmintonWorld.TV channel in YouTube. In this work, we mainly focus on the match from top-down camera view, and eliminate highlight replay. Each video is divided into two or four parts according to the number of sets in the match. The third set is divided into two parts because the players must switch their position when a player's score reaches 11 points. Length of each set differs from two to eleven minutes, and the average length of a play is around 10 seconds. Resolution of each video is 854 × 480. There are 6 videos covering 558 plays in total. Table 1 shows detailed information of the dataset.

Table 1: Detailed information the evaluation dataset.

Match	Sets		
	1	2	3
TOTAL BWF World Championships 2015 Badminton Day 7 F M3-MS Chen vs Lee	32 plays	36 plays	
Victor Korea Open 2016 Badminton F M4-MS Son Wan Ho vs Qiao Bin	32 plays	44 plays	27 plays
Victor Korea Open 2016 Badminton SF M3-MS Wong Wing Ki Vincent vs Qiao Bin	38 plays	37 plays	
Yonex Denmark Open 2016 Badminton F M5-WS Akane Yamaguchi vs Tai Tzu Ying	36 plays	34 plays	30 plays
Yonex Denmark Open 2016 Badminton SF M4-WS Carolina Marin vs Akane Yamaguchi	32 plays	38 plays	38 plays
BCA Indonesia Open 2016 Badminton F M3-MS Jan O Jorgensen vs Lee Chong Wei	32 plays	37 plays	35 plays

(a) Clear (b) Drive (c) Smash (d) Smash → Clear (e) Lob → Drive

Figure 3: Sample images of correct stroke classification (left three) and false classification (right two).

To evaluate stroke classification, 600 images are manually extracted and cropped from badminton videos. In this work, we only do stroke classification for the bottom player. For each stroke type we collect 100 images. The resolution of these images is 120 × 150.

4.2 Performance of Player Detection

Denote the region of the detected player as D and the region of the ground truth G, we say the player is correctly detected if $\frac{D \cap G}{D \cup G} > 0.5$. Overall, we obtain 85.45% accuracy in player detection. One problem of the proposed player detection module is that shadow of the player may be misclassified as a part of the player, and disturbs player's positions.

4.3 Performance of Stroke Classification

We adopt the five-fold cross validation scheme to evaluate stroke classification. At each fold, we use 480 stroke images for training and 120 stroke images for testing. The number of correctly classified strokes divided by 120 is calculated as the classification accuracy. Overall, we obtain 83.33% average accuracy.

Figure 3 shows sample images of correct classification and false classification. The left three strokes are correctly classified into clear, drive, and smash, respectively. Figure 3(d) is actually a smash stroke, but is misclassified into clear. By comparing Figure 3(d) with Figure 3(a), we see the similarity between these two poses. Figure 3(e) is actually a lob, but is misclassified into drive. We again observe the similarity between Figure 3(e) and Figure 3(b). To achieve more accurate classification, we will further consider motion information in the future.

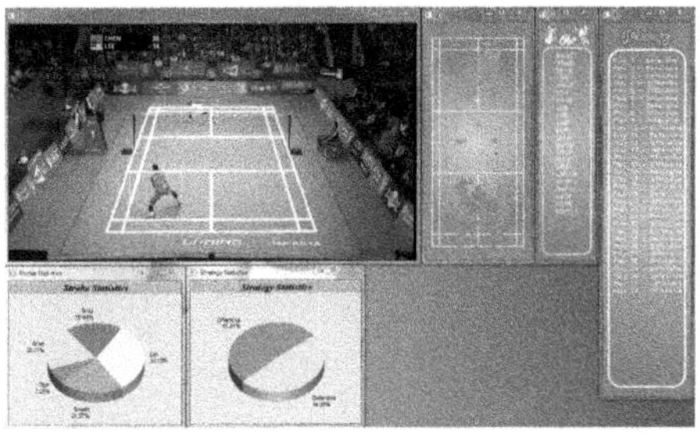

Figure 4: The interface to show game statistics. The windows from left to right, top to bottom, show the original video, player's position evolution, stroke classification results, strategy classification results, distribution of strokes, and distribution of strategies.

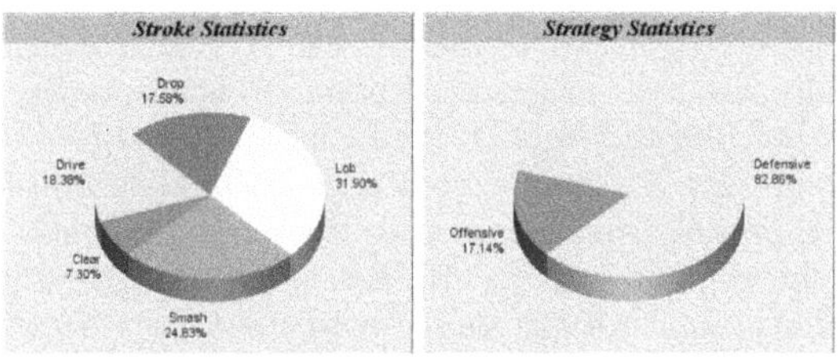

Figure 5: Sample distributions of strokes (left) and strategies (right).

4.4 Performance of Strategy Classification

We also use the five-fold cross validation scheme to evaluate strategy classification. At each fold, we use 18 plays for training and 6 plays for testing. Based on automatically extracted spatiotemporal features, the average strategy classification accuracy is 70%. Currently we don't work perfectly in stroke classification and player position detection. If the strategy classification model is constructed based on manually-corrected spatiotemporal features and stroke classification results, this system can achieve 83.33% average accuracy in strategy classification.

4.5 Badminton Video Statistics

Based on classification results of stroke classification, player detection, and strategy classification, we can see details of a badminton match, and provide more cues and insights by visualization. Figure 4 shows the interface showing various classification and detection results. From left to right, top to bottom, the sub-windows in Figure 4 are the original video, continuous player's positions illustrated in the court model, stroke classification results, strategy classification results, stroke distribution, and strategy distribution.

To get more insights, we can go into the details of each set. Figure 5 shows the stroke distribution and the strategy distribution of the game "TOTAL BWF World Championships 2015 Chen vs Lee". In this set, we observe Lee's stroke and strategy statistics. Lee used more lob strokes than other strokes. Statistics of the strategy shows that Lee focuses on defensive strategies. In fact, he was forced to do this, because his opponent attacked quite a lot in this set. Lee lost this set in the end.

5 CONCLUSION

In this paper, we integrate several visual analysis techniques to detect the court, detect the players, classify strokes, and classify player's strategy. We propose an adaptive background modeling to facilitate player detection. Based on player's pose, we classify the stroke a player invokes. By modeling the evolution of player's position and stroke information, we recognize a player's strategy. With these results, we visualize information of a badminton match, which can be used to analyze the player's performance and understand the characteristics of this match.

In the future, more elegant strategy modeling and more spatiotemporal features are to be pursued. In addition, motion information will be considered in stroke classification and strategy classification.

ACKNOWLEDGMENTS

The work was partially supported by the Ministry of Science and Technology of Taiwan under the grant MOST105-2628-E-194-001-MY2, MOST104-2221-E-194-014, and MOST103-2221-E-194-027-MY3.

REFERENCES

[1] T. Asano, Y. Serikawa, and S. Itoh. 2015. Quantitative Analysis of Tennis Ball Rotation and Trajectory. In *Proceedings of IEEE International Symposium on Industrial Electronics*. 906–911.

[2] T. Barnett and S.R. Clarke. 2005. Combining Player Statistics to Predict Outcomes of Tennis Matches. *IMA Journal of Management Mathematics* 16, 2 (2005), 113–120.

[3] S. Careelmont. 2013. *Badminton Shot Classification in Compressed Video with Baseline Angled Camera.* Master Thesis, University of Ghent.

[4] C.-C. Chang and C.-J. Lin. 2011. LIBSVM: A Library for Support Vector Machines. *ACM Transactions on Intelligent Systems and Technology* 2, 3 (2011), 1–27.

[5] B. Chen and Z. Wang. 2007. A Statistical Method for Analysis of Technical Data of a Badminton Match based on 2-d Seriate Images. *Tsinghua Science and Technology* 12, 5 (2007), 594–601.

[6] N. Dalal and B. Triggs. 2005. Histograms of Oriented Gradients for Human Detection. In *Proceedings of IEEE International Conference on Computer Vision and Pattern Recognition*. 886–893.

[7] T. Dierickx. 2014. *Badminton Game Analysis from Video Sequences.* Master Thesis, University of Ghent.

[8] J. Downey. 2007. *Tactics in Badminton Singles.* http://www.badminton-information.com/jake-downey-biography-badminton-books.html.

[9] D. Farin, S. Krabbe, W. Effelsberg, and P.H.N. de With. 2004. Robust Camera Calibration for Sport Videos using Court Models. In *Proceedings of SPIE Storage and Retrieval Methods and Applications for Multimedia*, Vol. 5307. 80–91.

[10] C. Harris and M. Stephens. 1988. A Combined Corner and Edge Detector. In *Proceedings of Fourth Alvey Vision Conference*. 147–151.

[11] Master Badminton 2017. *Badminton Techniques, Shots and Skills.* Master Badminton. http://www.masterbadminton.com/badminton-techniques.html.

[12] J. Matas, C. Galambos, and J. Kittler. 2000. Robust Detection of Lines Using the Progressive Probabilistic Hough Transform. *Computer Vision and Image Understanding* 78, 1 (2000), 119–137.

[13] Oceania Badminton Confederation 2011. *World's Fastest Racquet Sport.* Oceania Badminton Confederation. http://websites.sportstg.com/assoc_page.cgi?c=1-1065-0-0-0&sID=13337&&news_task=DETAIL&articleID=5850561.

[14] T. Polk, J. Yang, Y. Hu, and Y. Zhao. 2014. TenniVis: Visualization for Tennis Match Analysis. *IEEE Transactions on Visualization and Computer Graphics* 20, 12 (2014), 2339–2348.

[15] L. Rabiner. 1989. A Tutorial on Hidden Markov Models and Selected Applications in Speech Recognition. *Proc. IEEE* 77, 2 (1989), 257–286.

[16] N. Rea, R. Dahyot, and A. Kokaram. 2005. Classification and Representation of Semantic Content in Broadcast Tennis Videos. In *Proceedings of IEEE International Conference on Image Processing*. 1204–1207.

[17] V. Reno, N. Mosca, M. Nitti, T. Dorazio, D. Campagnoli, A. Prati, and E. Stella. 2015. Tennis Player Segmentation for Semantic Behavior Analysis. In *Proceedings of IEEE International Conference on Computer Vision Workshop*. 718–725.

[18] Z. Zivkovic. 2004. Improved Adaptive Gaussian Mixture Model for Background Subtraction. In *Proceedings of International Conference on Pattern Recognition*. 28–31.

[19] Z. Zivkovic and F. van der Heijden. 2006. Efficient Adaptive Density Estimation per Image Pixel for The Task of Background Subtraction. *Pattern Recognition Letters* 27, 7 (2006), 773–780.

Expo: An Expectation–oriented System for Selecting Important Photos from Personal Collections

Andrea Ceroni
L3S Research Center
ceroni@L3S.de

Vassilios Solachidis
ITI / CERTH
vsol@iti.gr

Claudia Niederée
L3S Research Center
niederee@L3S.de

Olga Papadopoulou
ITI / CERTH
olgapapa@iti.gr

Vasileios Mezaris
ITI / CERTH
bmezaris@iti.gr

ABSTRACT

The diffusion of digital photography lets people take hundreds of photos during personal events, such as trips and ceremonies. Many methods have been developed for summarizing such large personal photo collections. However, they usually emphasize the coverage of the original collection, without considering which photos users would select, i.e. their expectations. In this paper we present *Expo*, a system that aims at selecting which photos users perceive as most important and would have selected, thus meeting their expectations. It does not rely on any manually provided annotation, thus keeping the effort of users low. Photos are processed by applying a wide set of image processing techniques and a subset of a required size is selected. Users can review and modify the automatic selection. The system can also be used to gather training data by letting users select their preferred photos from the imported collections.

CCS CONCEPTS

- **Information systems → Multimedia information systems**;

KEYWORDS

Photo Selection; User Expectations; Image Importance; Coverage

1 INTRODUCTION

With digital photography, taking pictures is effortless and makes people easily ending up with hundreds of photos of personal events like holidays, trips, ceremonies. Different methods and applications have been developed to summarize such large collections and make their revisiting less onerous. They are usually centered around the concept of coverage, generating summaries that resemble the original collection. This is achieved either by clustering and picking representatives from each cluster [5, 8, 12] or by explicitly modeling and optimizing coverage [13, 14]. However, these strategies ignore user expectations, i.e. which photos users would select as most important for revisiting or preservation purposes. We argue that selecting photos that are important to users from personal collections is different than generating comprehensive summaries, as the set of important images might not fully cover the original collection [4]. For instance, users might not like photos of boring moments of a trip.

We present *Expo*, an expectation–oriented system for selecting photos from personal collections. Differently from previous systems (e.g. [2, 11]), it aims at emulating human selections by identifying those photos that users perceive as most important for revisiting or preservation, meeting their expectations. A demonstrative video is available[1]. To make selections, *Expo* relies on the method proposed by Ceroni et al. [4], which has been proved to be more effective in emulating user selections than methods based on coverage (e.g. [12–14]). It considers information at both image- and collection-level (by applying image quality assessment, concept detection, face detection, near-duplicate detection, event-based clustering) and estimates the selection probability of images via supervised Machine Learning.

Photos are first processed to extract the information required by the back-end selection method, which identifies the requested number of most important images. Users can browse the images, seeing also the information extracted from them and used in the selection process, as well as revise the automatic selection according to their preferences. The photos are organized in clusters (sub-events), to make browsing and reviewing easier for the users. *Expo* keeps the level of user investment low by not requiring any manual annotation. The system can also be used to acquire training data by letting users import new collections and manually select their preferred photos from them. Each imported collection and the associated selection data are sent to a common repository and used to re-train the model.

2 RELATED WORK

Different photo selection and summarization works are driven by the aspect of coverage, identifying clusters of images based on time and visual content and then picking a number of representative from each cluster [5, 8, 12]. Our selection method [3, 4] differs from them as it does not impose such a strict

[1] www.l3s.de/~ceroni/IPV/ICMR_2017_demo.mp4

ICMR '17, June 6–9, 2017, Bucharest, Romania

ACM ISBN 978-1-4503-4701-3/17/06...$15.00
DOI: http://dx.doi.org/10.1145/3078971.3079011

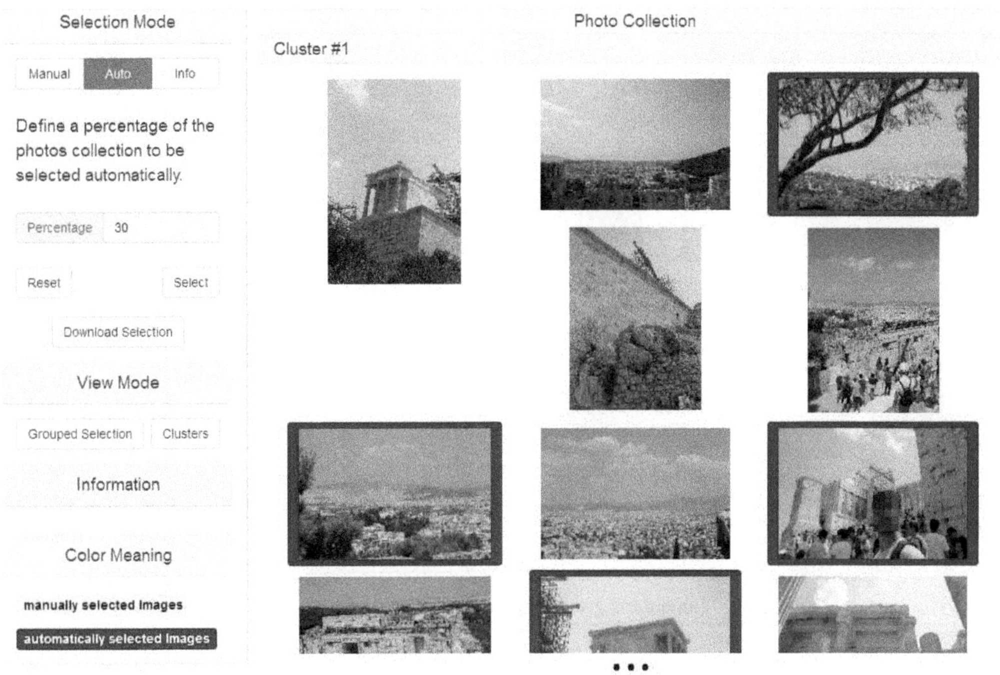

Figure 1: Performing automatic selections with *Expo*.

notion of coverage, but rather considers clusters and other global information together with image-level information, learning their different impact in a single model. The works in [13, 14] are closer to ours, as they consider coverage in a relaxed way as one dimension of a multi-goal optimization, but coverage still has the highest importance in the optimization and the summaries are not evaluated based on user assessments. Moreover, they make partial use of manually created text to associate semantic descriptors to images, while our system does not require any manual input, once the selection model has been learned.

Also available systems for photo selection and summarization [2, 11] are strongly based on coverage and diversity aspects and rely on a consistent amount of human supervision. These are the main differences from our system, which rather aims at identifying those photos that users perceive as most important for revisiting or preservation without any online input, after having learned the importance of coverage, diversity, and other aspects from human selections. Batko et al. [2] create textual and visual summaries of personal photo collections by combining clustering methods and image annotation tools. This requires a considerable effort to manually annotate pictures in the clusters. In [11], collections are first organized in clusters and images in the clusters are ranked based on visual quality, aesthetics, and the presence of faces. However, the weights of the different aspects are defined in presets and not learned from user selections, like our method does.

3 EXPECTATION-ORIENTED SELECTION

In this Section, we provide an overview of the main steps of the expectation-oriented selection method presented in [4], which is used in our system. Please refer to the original paper for further details.

Different image processing techniques are applied on input photo collections to extract features from them. These are: concept detection [9], to capture the semantic content of images beyond aesthetic and quality indicators; face detection [4], reflecting the importance of the presence of people in photos; near-duplicate detection [1], to take the redundancy of many pictures of the same scene as a signal of importance, and to eliminate very similar images; quality assessment [10], as good quality photos might be preferred in case of comparable photos; event clustering [6] and collection-level information for sake of browsing and to reflect the role of coverage in photo selection. This information is made visible to the user when browsing collections within the system.

Each photo is represented as a feature vector $\boldsymbol{f}_p$ by using the information listed above and a SVM trained on the data considered in [4] is used to predict the probability $I = SVM\left(\boldsymbol{f}_p\right)$ of each photo p to be selected, i.e. its importance. Finally, after predicting the importance of all the photos in the collection, the photos are ranked based on their importance and the top-n are selected. The parameter n, specified by the user, represents the desired size of the selection.

(a) Images grouped by clusters (sub-events).

(b) Images grouped by selection decisions.

Figure 2: Different ways of showing photos: grouping either by clusters (2a) or by selection decisions (2b).

4 SYSTEM DEMONSTRATION

In this Section we provide information regarding the implementation of the system (4.1) as well as the use cases that it supports (4.2).

4.1 Implementation and Functionalities

The system has been implemented as a Web application using the Java Play Framework[2], which simplifies the development of web applications with Java and Scala. The image processing techniques listed in Section 3 are exposed as RESTful Web Services, which are called once for each input collection. The classifier used for importance prediction has been built using the Support Vector Machine implementation of LibSVM[3] (with Gaussian Kernels) and has been trained on the dataset of [4].

The user interface is shown in Figure 1. Images are organized in clusters (sub-events) to simplify the browsing. The panel on the left-hand side contains all the functionalities available in the system. In the *Auto* mode, the one shown in the picture, users specify the number of images to select (as a percentage of the whole collection) and run the automatic selection. The selected images get a blue border and users

[2]https://www.playframework.com/

[3]http://www.csie.ntu.edu.tw/~cjlin/libsvm/

Figure 3: Looking at the features extracted from images.

can revise the selection according to their preferences. Besides organizing photos in clusters (Figure 2a), the "Grouped Selection" view (Figure 2b) shows all the selected images together to give an overall view of the selection.

Clicking on *Info*, the user can look at the information extracted from images. For instance, Figure 3 shows the information extracted from the image with blue border. Finally, clicking on *Manual*, users can produce their own selections manually and submit them (along with the whole collection) as training data for future re-training of the selection model.

4.2 Use Cases

The *Expo* system supports two use cases, one for the automatic identification of important images and one for providing new training data by performing manual selections.

Making Automatic Selections. The main functionality offered by the system to end users is automatically identifying those photos that are likely to be perceived as important by the owner of the collection, thanks to the underlying selection method aiming at meeting user selections and expectations. Starting from such automatic selection, the user can revise it according to his/her preferences. The availability of a fairly good initial selection alleviates the manual revision, which would become cumbersome when starting from scratch. At the end of the process, the selected photos can be downloaded and used in place of the whole collection, for instance, when looking back at the associated event in the future or sharing photos with relatives and friends. Such tasks would be more demanding and, to some extent, frustrating, if no selection was available and the original, potentially large collection had to be used.

Gathering Training Data. The system can be used to acquire new training data for the selection model. Users upload new photo collections, select their preferred photos from scratch, and submit the selection information and the whole collection to a central repository. Such collections annotated with user selections are used to re-train the model and to better match user expectations and selection patterns. This can be the starting point for user personalization, as previously investigated in [7].

5 CONCLUSION

In this paper we presented *Expo*, an expectation–oriented system for selecting pictures from personal collections. It offers a solution for the management of large personal photo collections by generating sets of highly important photos, which are more enjoyable for revising and sharing purposes. Differently from previous summarization systems based on the concept of coverage, it aims at emulating human selections by exploiting a selection method [4] that selects those pictures that users perceive as most important for revisiting or preservation, thus meeting their expectations. The notion of image importance has been learned from user selection patterns. *Expo* keeps the level of user investment low by not requiring any manual annotation. Users can review and modify the automatic selection according to their preferences. The system can also be used to gather training data by letting users select preferred photos from the imported collections.

Acknowledgments This work was funded by the German Research Foundation (DFG) in the context of the SPP 1921 on *Intentional Forgetting in Organisationen*, project *Managed Forgetting*.

REFERENCES

[1] K. Apostolidis, C. Papagiannopoulou, and Vasileios Mezaris. 2014. CERTH at MediaEval 2014 Synchronization of Multi-User Event Media Task. In *Proc. of MediaEval 2014 Workshop*.

[2] Michal Batko, Petra Budikova, Petr Elias, and Pavel Zezula. 2014. CLAN Photo Presenter: Multi-modal Summarization Tool for Image Collections. In *Proc. of ICMR '14*.

[3] Andrea Ceroni, Vassilios Solachidis, Mingxin Fu, Nattiya Kanhabua, Olga Papadopoulou, Claudia Niederée, and Vasileios Mezaris. 2015. Investigating human behaviors in selecting personal photos to preserve memories. In *International Conference on Multimedia & Expo Workshops (ICMEW '15)*.

[4] Andrea Ceroni, Vassilis Solachidis, Claudia Niederée, Olga Papadopoulou, Nattiya Kanhabua, and Vasileios Mezaris. 2015. To Keep or not to Keep: An Expectation-oriented Photo Selection Method for Personal Photo Collections. In *Proc. of ICMR '15*.

[5] Wei-Ta Chu and Chia-Hung Lin. 2008. Automatic Selection of Representative Photo and Smart Thumbnailing Using Near-duplicate Detection. In *Proc. of MM '08*.

[6] Matthew Cooper, Jonathan Foote, Andreas Girgensohn, and Lynn Wilcox. 2005. Temporal event clustering for digital photo collections. *In ACM TOMCCAP* (2005).

[7] Mingxin Fu, Andrea Ceroni, Vassilios Solachidis, Claudia Niederée, Olga Papadopoulou, Nattiya Kanhabua, and Vasileios Mezaris. 2015. Learning personalized expectation-oriented photo selection models for personal photo collections. In *International Conference on Multimedia & Expo Workshops (ICMEW '15)*.

[8] Jun Li, Joo Hwee Lim, and Qi Tian. 2003. Automatic summarization for personal digital photos. In *Proc. of ICICS-PCM '03*. DOI:https://doi.org/10.1109/ICICS.2003.1292724

[9] Foteini Markatopoulou, Nikiforos Pittaras, Olga Papadopoulou, Vasileios Mezaris, and Ioannis Patras. 2015. A Study on the Use of a Binary Local Descriptor and Color Extensions of Local Descriptors for Video Concept Detection. In *MultiMedia Modeling*.

[10] E. Mavridaki and Vasileios Mezaris. 2014. No-Reference blur assessment in natural images using Fourier transform and spatial pyramids. In *Proc. of ICIP '14*.

[11] Stefanie Nowak, Ronny Paduschek, and Uwe Kühhirt. 2011. Photo Summary: Automated Selection of Representative Photos from a Digital Collection. In *Proc. of ICMR '11*.

[12] Mohamad Rabbath, Philipp Sandhaus, and Susanne Boll. 2011. Automatic Creation of Photo Books from Stories in Social Media. *ACM TOMM* (2011).

[13] Boon-Siew Seah, Sourav S. Bhowmick, and Aixin Sun. 2014. PRISM: Concept-preserving Social Image Search Results Summarization. In *Proc. of SIGIR '14*.

[14] Pinaki Sinha, Sharad Mehrotra, and Ramesh Jain. 2011. Summarization of Personal Photologs Using Multidimensional Content and Context. In *Proc. of ICMR '11*.

Multimodal Video Retrieval with the 2017 IMOTION System

Luca Rossetto Ivan Giangreco Claudiu Tănase Heiko Schuldt
Department of Mathematics and Computer Science, University of Basel, Switzerland
(luca.rossetto|ivan.giangreco|c.tanase|heiko.schuldt)@unibas.ch

ABSTRACT

The IMOTION system is a multimodal content-based video search and browsing application offering a rich set of query modes on the basis of a broad range of different features. It is able to scale with the size of the collection due to its underlying flexible polystore called $ADAM_{pro}$ and its very effective retrieval engine Cineast, optimized for multi-feature fusion. IMOTION is simultaneously geared towards precision-focused searches, i.e., known-item search with image or text queries, and recall-focused, exploratory searches. In this demo, we will present the 2017 IMOTION system deployed on the IACC.3 collection consisting of 600 hours of Internet Archive video, which was also used in the TRECVID 2016 Ad-Hoc Video Search and in the 2017 Video Browser Showdown (VBS) challenge in which IMOTION ranked first. Conference attendees will have the chance to interact with the 2017 IMOTION system and quickly solve various retrieval tasks.

KEYWORDS

Content-based retrieval; Video retrieval; Multi-modal retrieval; Indexing; Video browsing

ACM Reference format:
Luca Rossetto Ivan Giangreco Claudiu Tănase Heiko Schuldt. 2017. Multimodal Video Retrieval with the 2017 IMOTION System. In *Proceedings of ICMR '17, Bucharest, Romania, June 6–9, 2017,* 4 pages.
DOI: http://dx.doi.org/10.1145/3078971.3079012

1 INTRODUCTION

Information retrieval technologies are key enablers of a range of applications in an environment where finding the right information and data becomes critical in many sectors, for efficient decision-making, research, or creative thinking. Multimedia content deserves a particular treatment given its unstructured (non-symbolic) and hidden (semantic gap) meaning to the computer. This calls for research on the way it can be indexed, queried, and stored efficiently.

The IMOTION system [14] is a content-based video search engine that provides fast and intuitive *known item search* in large video collections. In this paper, we pay special attention to the extensions and improvements we brought to the system after the publication of [16]. In this demo, we showcase the IMOTION system with all the available features and query modalities using a collection of 600 hours of video (IACC.3). We present the 2017 IMOTION system [16] which won the 2017 iteration of the Video Browser Showdown (VBS) [4]. Conference attendees will be able to interactively use the system and explore the collection using all available modes.

This paper is structured as follows: Section 2 introduces the system architecture; Section 3 presents the capabilities of the system from the features, the query modalities and the user interaction point of view. The demo plan is discussed in Section 4. Section 5 presents related work and Section 6 concludes.

ACM ISBN 978-1-4503-4701-3/17/06...$15.00.
DOI: http://dx.doi.org/10.1145/3078971.3079012

Table 1: Overview of feature data sources and query modes

Feature		Query Modality
Low-level	Image	Query-by-Sketch, Query-by-Example, Relevance Feedback
	Motion	Query-by-Motion
Mid-level	On-screen Text	Text-based Retrieval
	Spoken Audio	
High-level	Automated Image Captioning	
	User-provided Information	
	Semantic Concepts	Weighted Boolean retrieval

2 SYSTEM ARCHITECTURE

The IMOTION system is an extension of the vitrivr open source retrieval stack [15] and hence follows its architecture. It shares the polystore ($ADAM_{pro}$) [6] and the retrieval engine (Cineast) [13] with vitrivr while extending both, mainly by making use of text-based retrieval capabilities which are based on Apache Solr[1], and by using a custom user interface (see Figure 1) optimized for the challenges of the VBS 2017 competition.

3 IMOTION SYSTEM CAPABILITIES

In this section, we present in detail the system capabilities and the broad range of retrieval modes of the system. We give an overview of the features and query modalities summarized in Table 1.

3.1 Features

Low-level Image Features The color category contains low-level image features such as global and localized color histograms and regional color aggregations such as the color

[1] https://lucene.apache.org/solr/

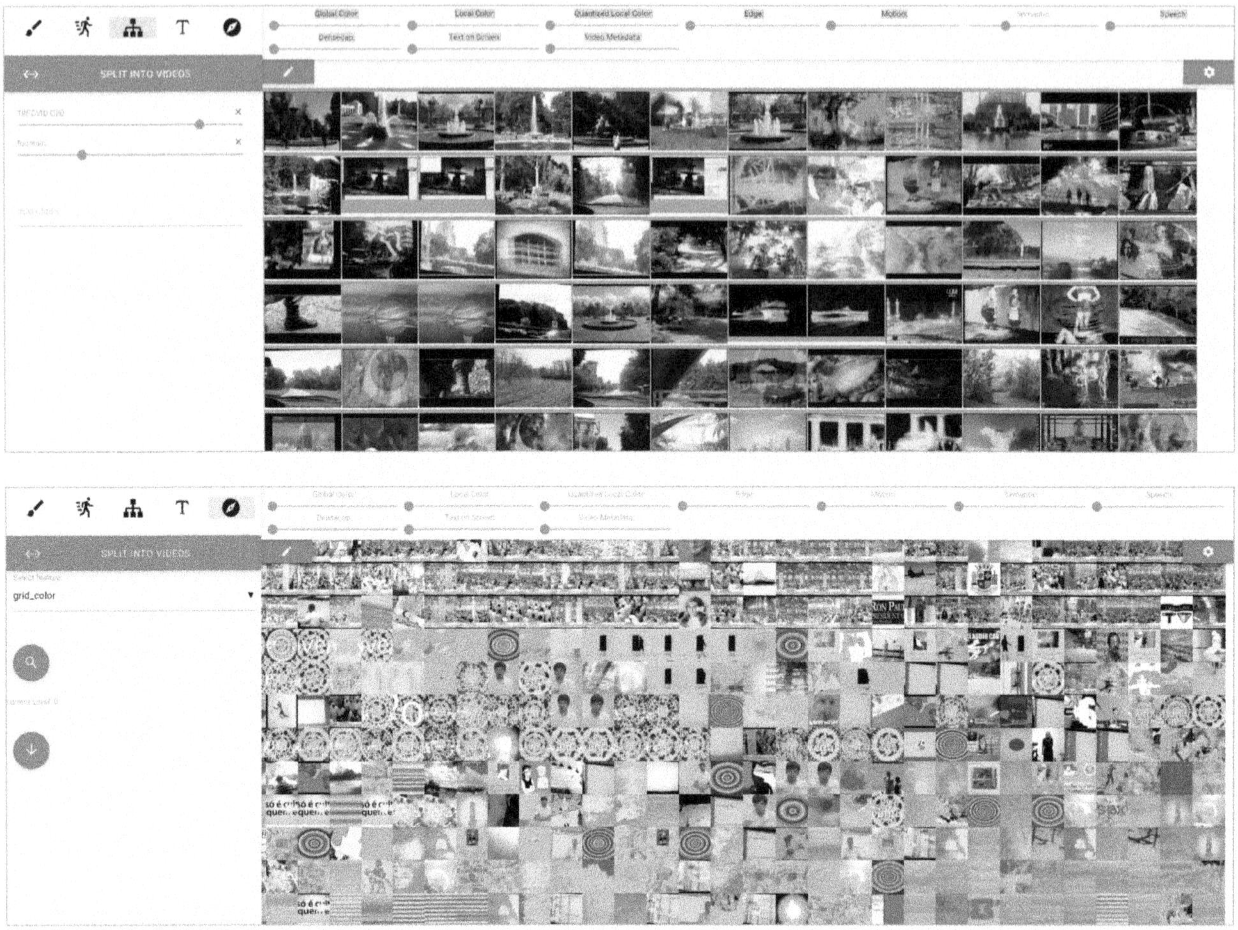

Figure 1: Screenshots of the GUI of the 2017 IMOTION system. Top: known-item search GUI. Bottom: exploratory search GUI.

layout descriptor. Similarly, the edge feature category contains features concerned with localized directional and non-directional edge histograms.

Low-level Motion Features To describe motion, localized directional histograms of sparse trajectories are used. During extraction, background–foreground separation is done by stabilizing the frame with a homographical model and the foreground region is estimated by thresholding the result of a spatio-temporal Gaussian blurring convolution.

OCR Since many videos contain sequences prominently featuring text on screen, we apply the Tesseract [18] optical character recognition system to every keyframe. For videos segmented into five or fewer shots, we sample the videos additionally at a 10 second interval. Because the output of the OCR is non-predictable for images which do not contain any text, it is filtered using the ratio of special characters to regular characters in order to reduce the amount of noise produced.

Speech-to-Text The metadata provided with the video collection contains among other things the output of an automatic speaker recognition (ASR) process [5, 9] which tries to detect all speakers within a video and timestamp every spoken word. We use this ASR data and transform it into artificial close captions by thresholding the detected words by confidence value and by mapping them to the boundaries of the shots. These captions are then aggregated into one document per shot such that each document contains all words spoken during the shot as well as the ones from the previous and the subsequent shot. This windowing is done in order to increase the chances of retrieving sequences in over-segmented video regions.

Automated Image Captioning We apply the DenseCap [7] image captioning neural network to all keyframes of the collection to produce one or several simple textual descriptions of the depicted scene. These captions are then grouped into one document per keyframe and subsequently loaded into Solr. The captioning is able to label a wider range of objects since the network is not trained to recognize objects directly but rather to pair textual descriptions to images and is hence not limited to a fixed set of classes.

User-provided Information For each video, the collection also contains a file with metadata. Even though these files are encoded in XML, the structure is of little benefit which is why we flatten these documents by removing all XML tags. The remaining text documents are also added to Solr. Since this is the only instance where we have one document per video rather than one per shot, we return one in ten shots of all videos which match a query on this modality.

Semantic Concept Instances The system can filter results by various semantic categories, which are obtained by binarizing prediction outputs of a total of 655 external classifiers. We apply various object and concept detectors on keyframes of the video collection and store the top 600 instances per detector. A custom network [12] is used to detect 325 common objects, defined by entry-level nouns (e.g., 'dog'). In addition, we added 365 labels corresponding to classes in the Places2 [22] dataset representing environments (e.g., 'amusement park') and 80 object category labels learned from human annotation in the MSCOCO [10] detection dataset (e.g., 'snowboard'). Scores for the 30 topics we extracted for TRECVID AVS 2016 [20] are also present as categories. Since all these lists are precomputed, we store them directly in the browser-based user interface to reduce runtime system load on the back-end.

3.2 Query Modalities

The following query modalities of IMOTION can be used either sequentially (for incremental query refinement) or concurrently (combined search).

Query-by-Sketch To be able to specify queries visually, the system offers a sketch canvas. The user has the possibility to input a rough visual representation of the desired content which is then processed by the same visual features which were used to process the videos.

Query-by-Example In contrast to the *Query-by-Sketch* modality, Query-by-Example does not use a user created object for querying but rather the internal description of an already known object. This way a user has the possibility to extend upon previously retrieved results.

Relevance Feedback In extension to *Query-by-Example*, relevance feedback enables a user to construct a query based on multiple previously retrieved results by labeling them either as relevant or irrelevant. The system then also uses the internal representations of these positive and negative examples to construct a new result.

Query-by-Motion Similar to *Query-by-Sketch*, the user has the possibility to specify flow-fields which roughly describe the motion within the video sequence. The interface allows switching between foreground and background motion sketching. Foreground flow fields model prominent moving objects and background flow fields model camera movement or movements of small objects. It should be noted that an empty motion canvas essentially means querying for still sequences.

Text-based Retrieval The text retrieval modality allows for querying using keywords. It makes use of the text-based retrieval capabilities provided by Apache Solr, i.e., computing the relevance using term frequency/inverse document frequency (TF-IDF).

Weighted Boolean Retrieval For the *Semantic Concept Instances*, we use pre-computed lists of relevant shots per topic. All list elements have a score which was determined by the rank of the detector output, the score ramps in the interval [0.0, 1.0] over the length of the list. By selecting a concept as relevant and thereby adding all elements of its corresponding list to the result set, the UI also adds a weight slider for the concept as shown in Figure 1 on the left. Using these sliders, the user can specify the relevance of a topic with respect to the others which provides more overall flexibility than basic Boolean retrieval.

3.3 User Interaction

3.3.1 Precision-focused searches (Known-item Search). For precision-focused searches, i.e., known-item searches, the IMOTION system provides a search interface as shown in Figure 1: query results are displayed with a thumbnail of the shot and a border which indicates its relevance to the query. The sliders on top control the weights of the various similarity measures. Changing the value of one of these sliders updates the scores of the individual results and re-orders them correspondingly in real time. In cases where the correct result is difficult to identify based on this grid representation, the user has the option to re-group the results by video. The results are then grouped chronologically within a video (horizontally) while the videos are ordered by maximum shot score (vertically). For every shot, the user also has the option to load the previews of the surrounding shots or of all shots from the same video in order to be able to gain a better overview of the entire video. It is also possible to start the video playback from every shot at the relevant position.

3.3.2 Recall-focused searches (Exploratory search). In order to complement the Query-by-Sketch/Example approach with exploratory navigation, the system offers multiple 2D-embeddings of the collection, based on different similarity metrics. These embeddings manifest in the UI as a separate view whereupon keyframes are placed in a large complete 572×572 grid. The embedding method assigns the keyframes to grid positions such that distance relations in a given feature space are best preserved.

An important feature is the seamless two-way transfer between search and embedding mode. Any thumbnail from the results pane can be instantly centered in the 2D map in order to allow exploration of its neighbors. Conversely, every object of the 2D map can be used as query, with optional refinement.

The 2D embeddings are obtained by in three steps: a sampling is first reprojected to 2D space using t-distributed Stochastic Neighbor Embedding [11], then mapped to coarse grid coordinates using optimal linear assignment (we use an implementation of the Jonker-Volgenant algorithm [8]), 2D positions of the full set are then estimated using Gaussian RBF interpolation and finally mapped to fine grid coordinates by greedy assignment.

4 DEMONSTRATION

For this demonstration conference attendees will have the chance to perform known-item searches with one of the pre-selected visual or textual queries, try AVS-style topics or simply explore the video collection with the 2017 IMOTION system. The presented system will be in the setup used for the 2017 Video Browser Showdown, using the IACC.3 video collection of over 600 hours from the Internet Archive.

5 RELATED WORK

Content-based interactive video retrieval has attracted a relatively small but dedicated research community. The Video Browser Showdown [4] is an annual competitive live benchamrking event where particpating teams are asked to submit in a limited time (no more than 5 minutes) results matching an ad-hoc video query. These queries have been only of the Known Item Search variety (one unique correct result in the entire collection) until the 2017 edition of VBS, where more exploratory AVS queries have been introduced. The AVS queries (e.g., "Find all shots of women wearing glasses"), as well as the pre-defined video collection are based on the TRECVID [1] 2016 Ad-Hoc Video Search task. This demo uses some results from the IMOTION team's participation in this task [20].

The field of content-based video retrieval without the interactivity constraint is more prominent in the literature. Two essential benchmarks for such search systems are the TRECVID and MediaEval challenges. Without the response time restrictions, content analysis systems in this field are able to make use of computationally heavier methods such as Deep Neural Networks for various classification tasks [21]. An important recent development in real-time search borrowed from this body of work consists of tagging the collection with semantic classifiers or using hidden layer activations as features in the pre-processing phase [20].

Recent high-performing approaches in video browsing revolve around retrieval of simplified sketches (e.g., by using simple color signatures [3]) and displaying the collection in a more informative way (e.g., using a graph-based keyframe arrangement for browsing [2]). A more in-depth sketch analysis where deep semantic classifiers are employed for sketch auto-completion has been demonstrated in earlier work [19]. For a comprehensive review of video search or browsing methods and systems, readers can refer to [17].

6 CONCLUSION

In this paper, we have presented the 2017 edition of the IMOTION system and we have shown how it can be used in an interactive demonstration for retrieving video sequences using a large variety of features and query modalities.

ACKNOWLEDGEMENTS

This work was partly supported by the Chist-Era project IMOTION with contributions from the Swiss National Science Foundation (SNSF, contract no. 20CH21_151571).

REFERENCES

[1] George Awad, Jonathan Fiscus, Martial Michel, David Joy, Wessel Kraaij, Alan F. Smeaton, Georges Qunot, Maria Eskevich, Robin Aly, Gareth J. F. Jones, Roeland Ordelman, Benoit Huet, and Martha Larson. 2016. TRECVID 2016: Evaluating Video Search, Video Event Detection, Localization, and Hyperlinking. In *Proceedings of TRECVID 2016*. NIST.

[2] Kai Uwe Barthel, Nico Hezel, and Radek Mackowiak. 2016. Navigating a graph of scenes for exploring large video collections. In *Proceedings of the 22nd International Conference on Multimedia Modeling (MMM 2016)*. Springer, Miami, FL, USA, 418–423.

[3] Adam Blažek, Jakub Lokoč, Filip Matzner, and Tomáš Skopal. 2015. Enhanced signature-based video browser. In *Proceedings of the 21st International Conference on Multimedia Modeling (MMM 2015)*. Springer, Sydney, NSW, Australia, 243–248.

[4] Claudiu Cobârzan, Klaus Schoeffmann, Werner Bailer, Wolfgang Hürst, Adam Blažek, Jakub Lokoč, Stefanos Vrochidis, Kai Uwe Barthel, and Luca Rossetto. 2016. Interactive video search tools: A detailed analysis of the video browser showdown 2015. *Multimedia Tools and Applications* (2016), 1–33.

[5] Jean-Luc Gauvain. 2010. The Quaero Program: Multilingual and Multimedia Technologies. In *Proceedings of the International Workshop on Spoken Language Translation (IWSLT 2010)*.

[6] Ivan Giangreco and Heiko Schuldt. 2016. ADAM_{pro}: Database Support for Big Multimedia Retrieval. *Datenbank-Spektrum* 16, 1 (2016), 17–26.

[7] Justin Johnson, Andrej Karpathy, and Li Fei-Fei. 2016. DenseCap: Fully Convolutional Localization Networks for Dense Captioning. In *Proc. of the International Conference on Computer Vision and Pattern Recognition (CVPR 2016)*. IEEE.

[8] R. Jonker and A. Volgenant. 1987. A shortest augmenting path algorithm for dense and sparse linear assignment problems. *Computing* 38, 4 (1987), 325–340.

[9] Lori Lamel. 2012. Multilingual Speech Processing Activities in Quaero: Application to Multimedia Search in Unstructured Data. In *Proc. of the International Conference on Human Language Technologies -fi The Baltic Perspective*. 1–8.

[10] Tsung-Yi Lin, Michael Maire, Serge Belongie, James Hays, Pietro Perona, Deva Ramanan, Piotr Dollár, and C Lawrence Zitnick. 2014. Microsoft coco: Common objects in context. In *Proc. of the European Conference on Computer Vision (ECCV 2014)*. Springer, 740–755.

[11] Laurens van der Maaten and Geoffrey Hinton. 2008. Visualizing Data using t-SNE. *Journal of Machine Learning Research* 9, Nov (2008), 2579–2605.

[12] Luca Rossetto, Ivan Giangreco, Silvan Heller, Claudiu Tănase, Heiko Schuldt, Stéphane Dupont, Omar Seddati, Metin Sezgin, Ozan Can Altıok, and Yusuf Sahillioğlu. 2016. IMOTION–Searching for Video Sequences Using Multi-Shot Sketch Queries. In *Proceedings of the 22nd International Conference on Multimedia Modeling (MMM 2016)*. Springer, Miami, FL, USA, 377–382.

[13] Luca Rossetto, Ivan Giangreco, and Heiko Schuldt. 2014. Cineast: a multi-feature sketch-based video retrieval engine. In *Proceedings of the International Symposium on Multimedia (ISM 2014)*. IEEE, Taichung, Taiwan, 18–23.

[14] Luca Rossetto, Ivan Giangreco, Heiko Schuldt, Stéphane Dupont, Omar Seddati, T. Metin Sezgin, and Yusuf Sahillioglu. 2015. IMOTION - A Content-Based Video Retrieval Engine. In *Proceedings of the 21st International Conference on MultiMedia Modeling (MMM 2015) (Lecture Notes in Computer Science)*, Vol. 8936. Springer, Sydney, NSW, Australia, 255–260.

[15] Luca Rossetto, Ivan Giangreco, Claudiu Tanase, and Heiko Schuldt. 2016. vitrivr: A Flexible Retrieval Stack Supporting Multiple Query Modes for Searching in Multimedia Collections. In *Proceeding of the International Conference on Multimedia (ACM MM 2016))*. ACM, Amsterdam, The Netherlands, 1183–1186.

[16] Luca Rossetto, Ivan Giangreco, Claudiu Tănase, Heiko Schuldt, Stéphane Dupont, and Omar Seddati. 2017. Enhanced Retrieval and Browsing in the IMOTION System. In *Proceedings of the 23rd International Conference on Multimedia Modeling (MMM 2017)*. Springer, Reykjavik, Iceland, 469–474.

[17] Klaus Schoeffmann, Frank Hopfgartner, Oge Marques, Laszlo Boeszoermenyi, and Joemon M. Jose. 2010. Video Browsing Interfaces and Applications: a Review. *SPIE Reviews (Online)* 1 (March 2010), 1–35.

[18] Ray Smith. 2007. An Overview of the Tesseract OCR Engine. In *Proceedings of the International Conference on Document Analysis and Recognition (ICDAR 2007)*. IEEE, 629–633.

[19] Claudiu Tanase, Ivan Giangreco, Luca Rossetto, Heiko Schuldt, Omar Seddati, Stephane Dupont, Ozan Can Altiok, and Metin Sezgin. 2016. Semantic Sketch-Based Video Retrieval with Autocompletion. In *Proc. of the International Conference on Intelligent User Interfaces (IUI 2016)*. ACM, Sonoma, CA, USA, 97–101.

[20] Claudiu Tanase, Luca Rossetto, Ivan Giangreco, Heiko Schuldt, Stéphane Dupont, and Omar Seddati. 2016. The IMOTION System at TRECVID 2016: The Ad-Hoc Video Search Task. (2016).

[21] Kazuya Ueki, Kotaro Kikuchi, Susumu Saito, and Tetsunori Kobayashi. 2016. Waseda at TRECVID 2016: Ad-hoc Video Search. (2016).

[22] Bolei Zhou, Aditya Khosla, Agata Lapedriza, Antonio Torralba, and Aude Oliva. 2016. Places: An image database for deep scene understanding. *arXiv preprint arXiv:1610.02055* (2016).

The JORD System - Linking Sky and Social Multimedia Data to Natural Disasters

Kashif Ahmad
University of Trento, Trento, Italy
kashif.ahmad@unitn.it

Micheal Riegler
Simula Research Laboratory, Oslo, Norway
michael@simula.no

Ans Riaz
University of Trento, Trento, Italy
ans.riaz@unitn.it

Nicola Conci
University of Trento, Trento, Italy
nicola.conci@unitn.it

Duc-Tien Dang-Nguyen
Dublin City University, Dublin, Ireland
duc-tien.dang-nguyen@dcu.ie

Pål Halvorsen
Simula Research Laboratory, Oslo, Norway
paalh@simula.no

ABSTRACT

Being able to automatically link social media information and data to remote-sensed data holds large possibilities for society and research. In this paper, we present a system called JORD that is able to autonomously collect social media data about technological and environmental disasters, and link it automatically to remote-sensed data. In addition, we demonstrate that queries in local languages that are relevant to the exact position of natural disasters retrieve more accurate information about a disaster event. To show the capabilities of the system, we present some examples of disaster events detected by the system. To evaluate the quality of the provided information and usefulness of JORD from the potential users point of view we include a crowdsourced user study.

CCS CONCEPTS

•**Information systems** →**Information extraction;**

KEYWORDS

Information Retrieval; Natural Disaster; Social Media; event detection

ACM Reference format:
Kashif Ahmad, Micheal Riegler, Ans Riaz, Nicola Conci, Duc-Tien Dang-Nguyen, and Pål Halvorsen. 2017. The JORD System - Linking sky and social multimedia data to Natural Disasters. In *Proceedings of ICMR '17, June 6–9, 2017, Bucharest, Romania,* , 5 pages.
DOI: http://dx.doi.org/10.1145/3078971.3079013

1 INTRODUCTION

During the last few decades, satellite data has been widely used to explore the surface of the Earth and its environment. Being able to cover a large spatio-temporal area, remote sensed data has been proved very effective and inherently useful in different applications like disaster management [9]. Recently, NASA released a dataset from the longest running satellite program called Landsat[1]. Landsat has been heavily used by researchers in the last decades where useful techniques have been developed, e.g., automatic detection of forest fires, sandstorms or floods [6, 8]. The latest Landsat dataset contains images shot by the Landsat 8 satellite, and it is available via Amazon Webservices[2]. Such a dataset provides many opportunities for society, and researchers can benefit from remote sensed data to develop new applications integrating satellite images in detection, retrieval and monitoring services.

Nevertheless, remote-sensed data also brings some challenges. For example, satellite images have a low temporal frequency, and more importantly, they only give a birds'-eye view of an actual event. For instance, nowadays, floods can be detected in satellite images (St-George seen from NASA MODIS satellite[3]) as shown in Figure 1, but it becomes difficult to understand the impact of the event on the people living in the area, both from practical and societal view point.

Figure 1: Based on a satellite image (flood in St George), it is almost impossible to give a clear statement about the impact on the environment and society (image: NASA MODIS Satellite)

On the other hand, over the last few years social media has emerged as an important source of information and rapid communication in emergency situations [14]. Particularly, Twitter has proved to be very effective in dissemination of news about natural disasters [1]. Moreover, as demonstrated in [12], there are many situations in which news agencies could not provide information at all or in time, about emergency situations, simply due to the

ICMR '17, June 6–9, 2017, Bucharest, Romania
© 2017 ACM. ACM ISBN 978-1-4503-4701-3/17/06...$15.00
DOI :http://dx.doi.org/10.1145/3078971.3079013

[1] http://landsat.usgs.gov/
[2] https://aws.amazon.com/public-data-sets/landsat/
[3] http://www.aerometrex.com.au/blog/?p=289

unavailability of reporters in the area. In such cases, social media plays an important role [3].

A rather recent trend is to combine content from social media with remote sensed data, e.g., in the MediaEval benchmark initiative with the "placing" task[4] where researchers try to predict geo-coordinates for images and videos from Flickr. Additionally, a task to build a system that links social multimedia to events, which can be detected in satellite images, has been introduced as a challenge at ACM MM 2016[5]. This clearly shows that the multimedia research community is interested in this new direction.

To this aim, we propose a system called *JORD*, which is to the best of our knowledge the first one, that is able to combine satellite images with information from social media (e.g., Twitter, Flickr and Youtube) and news items collected in real-time (as fast as possible after the event occurs). It also provides query refinement by automatically generating queries in all local languages that are relevant to the position of a disaster. With a system combining multimedia mining [10], retrieval [2] and linking [5] methods, we are able to tell a much clearer and more useful story to the users. JORD is able to link social multimedia data to events that are detected in satellite images. For instance, JORD is able to link an automatically detected sandstorm to social media reports found in Flickr, Youtube, Twitter and web pages. The linked information then can be used by the users of the system to get a clearer picture of the event and its possible impacts on the environment and the society. Moreover, the proposed system can also be helpful to follow up and monitor the process of rebuilding of infrastructure and other rehabilitation activities.

The main advantages of JORD are that it (i) collects data about events autonomously, continuously, and automatically in real-time from a disaster database (ii) automatically filters irrelevant information (iii) is able to link this information automatically with satellite and social media data using information retrieval and (iv) allows query refinement for the retrieval of information using automatic language detection and translation.

For the demonstration purposes, we will give a live demo of the system where it will be demonstrated how our system is able to collect and explore different multimedia data along with satellite images for natural and technological disasters. We will also show how JORD can facilitate users to find information about disasters from different sources in one go.

2 METHODOLOGY

Figure 2 provides a block diagram of JORD. It is composed of three main parts (highlighted with different colors in Figure 2): (i) multimedia data retrieval from social media, (ii) filtering and (iii) linking social media data with remote-sensed data and events. We provide a detailed description of all parts of the system which includes the natural disasters we target, query refinement through translation, multimedia data retrieval from social media, filtering and linking multimedia data from social media with remote sensed data.

[4]http://multimediaeval.org/mediaeval2016/placing/

[5]http://www.acmmm.org/2016/wp-content/uploads/2016/03/ACMMM16_GC_Sky_and_the_Social_Eye_latest.pdf

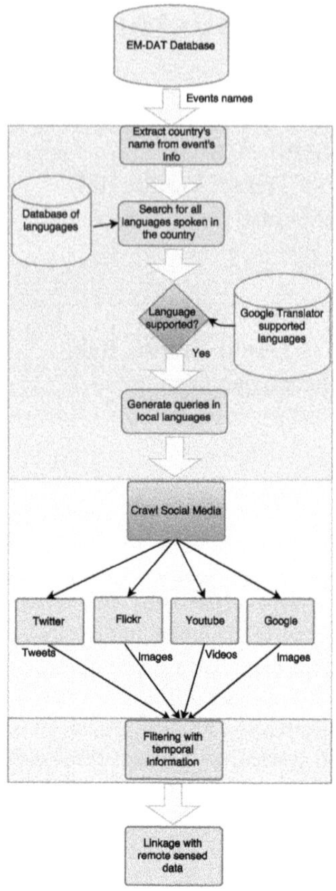

Figure 2: Block diagram of the proposed JORD system.

2.1 Target Events

As one can see in Figure 2, JORD first extracts a list of natural and technological disasters from the EM-DAT database [7] in real-time. This means that as soon as a new event occurs in the database, JORD starts collecting and linking information about it. EM-DAT is an international disaster database (supported by the World Health Organisation WHO) that provides information of natural and technological disasters that have occurred all over the world as fast as possible. We test our system with 82 recent natural and technological disasters. However, it is important to point out that JORD is able to collect, retrieve and link an unlimited number of events, and can operate in both a live mode as an quasi autonomous system and an on demand mode controlled by a user. Moreover, the events are not limited to a certain continent or region.

2.2 Query Refinement and Translation

The EM-DAT database provides the time period and location information for each disaster. Our system utilizes this information for the retrieval of related social multimedia data, such as videos, images and text. Furthermore, JORD supports query refinement by collecting additional tags for the underlying events by determining and translating them to the local languages of the area where the disaster occurred. By looking at news or social media posts, one can easily observe that during natural and technological disasters the local community usually initiates the process of spreading news about an event. This normally happens by commenting, posting and sharing information using different channels and media types right after an event occurs. Furthermore, people living in the proximity of the event usually tend to post and share information in their local languages. Based on these observations, our system automatically generates queries in all local languages that are relevant to the position of a disaster.

The translated queries are used in the next part of JORD, which is responsible for collecting multimedia data. During data analysis, we observed that the combination of translated and the original queries results in a larger amount of retrieved data per query (for some events, a search based on only English queries results in very little or no result). Moreover, user feedback revealed that the information retrieved with translated queries are more relevant to underlying events.

2.3 Social Media Platforms

In recent years, social networks, such as Twitter and Flickr, have emerged as important sources of information that report events in real-time, and provide a much broader story [4, 13]. With respect to Twitter, for example, the majority of the users use Twitter for breaking news, and thereby become a part of the process by commenting, posting and sharing information at the moment when an event occurs [1]. Similarly, Flickr and YouTube facilitate users to share audio-visual contents about an event whenever it happens. Therefore, it is important to include social media information in our system, and to get an overview of social media content for an event, we crawl four different social media platforms, i.e., Twitter, YouTube, Flickr, and also Google image search. It is important to mention that queries in local languages, generated by our system during query refinement phase, are supported by three platforms including Twitter, YouTube and Google. Flickr supports queries in English only.

2.4 Filtering and Linkage with satellite Data

Another challenge that we tackle is how to ensure that the retrieved information is relevant to the event. To solve this problem, we filtered the downloaded data using time information provided by EM-DAT database for each event. The final step of our system is the use of geo-location information to link the retrieved social media data and the remote-sensed images (before and after a disaster). To this aim, we rely on Google Earth and the geo-location information.

3 SYSTEM ARCHITECTURE

Figure 3 shows the block diagram of the architecture of our proposed system, which is composed of three main components: (i) Front View with a user friendly interface allowing users of the proposed system to interact with the tool according to their need (2) Controller, which is basically composed of the crawler with query refinement capabilities; (3) Database Model, which represents the structure of the database to store retrieved data. A reliable database, and a user friendly interface is always very crucial in such applications. To this aim, in order to host huge amounts of data, we carefully design the structure of the database for the proposed tool. Moreover, we tried our best to keep the database as simple as possible by avoiding the complexity of foreign keys and associations. Every kind of information required in the platform is stored in a proper way by allocating a separate table for it.

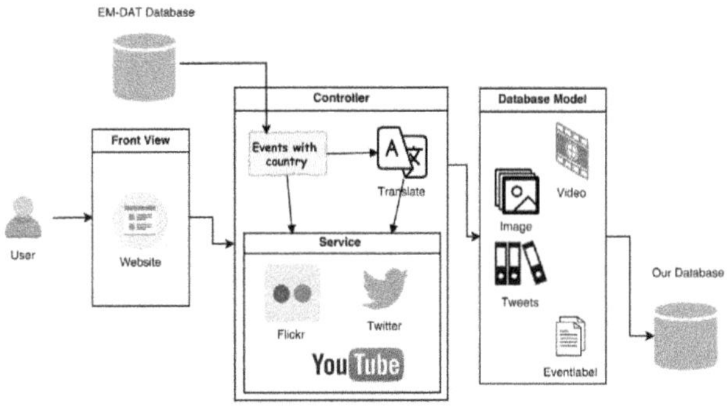

Figure 3: System architecture of JORD.

All in all, we have 4 tables in our database, one containing information of events for which our crawler use to search data in social media platforms. Similarly, for each type of data, retrieved from social media platforms, we have a separate table, which facilitates information retrieval and report generation. Our database also keeps meta data along with the images, videos and tweets downloaded from social media. Similarly, the front view is designed in a way to fully facilitate users with less efforts on the user's side. A number of functionalities have been provided, to facilitate users, in the tool. For instance, users can search for a particular disaster as well as for a particular type of data. As far as the controller unit is concerned, it is composed of the crawler, which searches for images, videos and tweets in social media, with query refinement capabilities, and is implemented in PHP. To this aim, respective Apis have been integrated in the crawler to download multimedia data along with meta data, and store it in the database.

The crawler can be configured in two different ways (automatically in a certain interval or manually) regarding how often the social media should be crawled). For query refinement and translation, the Google Translator Api[6] is used in combination with a database of spoken local languages per country in our pipeline. The list of local languages along with the country names are retrieved from InfoPlease[7]. Infoplease is a free encyclopedia almanac, atlas, dictionary, and thesaurus. Thus, JORD automatically extracts country information, where the disaster has been occurred, from the EM-DAT database and checks for the local languages spoken in that country, and subsequently generates new queries in local languages via Google Translator.

4 SYSTEM EVALUATION

Figure 4 shows a sample output for a flood query in Kenya. As can be seen in Figure 4, JORD combines the information from different sources, and presents a more detailed story about the disaster. To evaluate the system, in terms of if the retrieved multimedia contents about the disaster events are correct and useful for the users, we conducted a crowdsourcing study on Microworkers. We

[6] https://cloud.google.com/translate/docs/
[7] http://www.infoplease.com/ipa/A0855611.html

asked workers to give their opinion about the retrieved multimedia contents related to underlying events. We paid each worker 1.50 USD and tried to be as fair as possible regarding the discarding of workers. As shown in [11], controlling and discarding workers too much can lead to an undesired outcome of the study, which we tried to avoid by accepting almost every worker if they did the task in a reasonable way (which means did not try to cheat).

For the evaluation, we asked the crowd-workers five different questions: The first question, (i) "Do you think the system provided information was useful?", aims to get feedback from workers about the usefulness of the collected multimedia data using a scale from one to five from not useful to very useful. (ii) "From these three possible events, which one do you think has been the one presented to you?" (a list of three possible event names, which also contains similar types of events but in different location and time period, is presented to the user, two are wrong, one is the event retrieved by the system). This question was used to evaluate if JORD can help the user to understand the retrieved event and if the presented information is useful. The third question (iii) asked the workers to state how useful they find the three different type of multimedia content (images, tweets and videos) from a scale from one to five from not useful to very useful. The fourth question (iv) was a simple yes or no question where we asked the workers if they would use such a system or not. The final question (v) was an open question where the crowdworkers had to reason their yes or no from the previous question. This question we used to filter out workers that did the task not correctly. We checked each answer manually for each worker. If the answer made sense and showed that the worker answered it carefully we accepted it. If not we did not include it in the final evaluation. In total, we had 385 workers working on the task. We discarded 36, because they did not answer the open question in a way that it appeared that they conduced the task properly. This resulted in answers from at least five distinct users per event[8]

The first question (i) where the workers had to state if they find the system useful or not, had an average of 4.47 for all workers. This is a clear indication that workers find the system and the provided information useful.

For the second question (ii) where the workers had to chose the correct event out of three possible ones, only 19 workers out of 349 failed to correctly recognize the event presented to them. A closer investigation showed that all of them had just the country wrong but gave a correct answer about the disaster. This shows two important things. Firstly, that the retrieved information of JORD is accurate and can help users to get more information about events and secondly, that connecting it to satellite images is important to improve understanding of the event in terms of location.

For the third question (iii) where the workers had to report how useful they find different types of multimedia content we got an average of 4.23 for images, 4.08 for tweets and 4.44 for videos. Based on this, we can see a tendency that users find videos most useful and tweets least. We think that this might be due to the fact that a video usually contains more information than a text or image and

[8]The created dataset including the crowdsourcing study, the events and the results from the crowdsourcing study can be requested by mailing one of the authors. We cannot make it public available due to copyright restrictions.

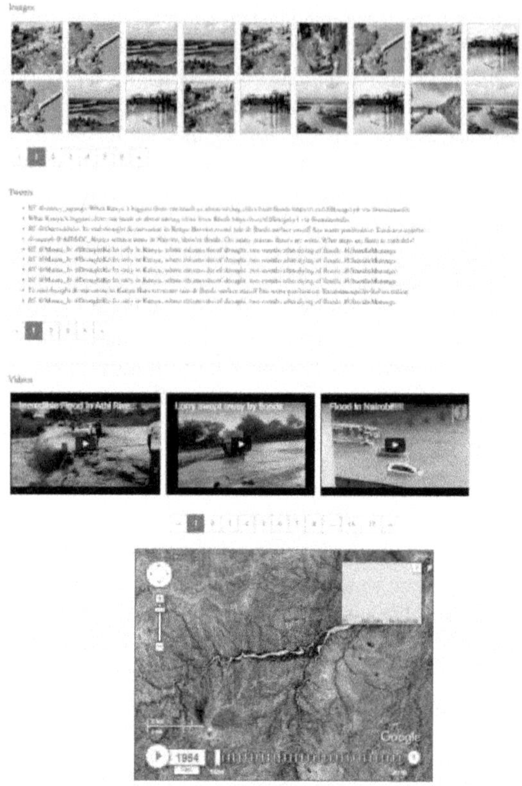

Figure 4: A sample output of JORD in terms of retrieved images (at the top), Tweets, Videos and the satellite data.

that it helps people more to understand and experience the current situation.

The last two questions (iv) and (v) are evaluated together. For the first question (iv), 336 from 349 workers (around 96%) stated that they find the system useful. This is a promising indicator that such a system would be useful and used by users.

5 CONCLUSION

In this demo paper, we presented a demo of JORD, which is able to autonomously and automatically retrieve social media data from various social platforms and links it to remote-sensed data. We demonstrated that queries in local languages that are relevant to the position of natural disasters retrieve more accurate information about a disaster event. We also showed that JORD automatically finds interesting events and used these events to query social media. The evaluation of the JORD system was carried out through crowdsourcing study where workers were asked to evaluate the usefulness of the system and to identify an event presented to them with collected images, tweets and videos. The evaluation indicates that JORD works very accurate without human input, and it can be used to collect and merge a large number of event based data for technological and environmental disasters from different sources. In future, we plan to include more different social media platforms and also to improve the representation of the retrieved and linked information to the users.

REFERENCES

[1] Farzindar Atefeh and Wael Khreich. 2015. A survey of techniques for event detection in twitter. *Computational Intelligence* 31, 1 (2015), 132–164.

[2] Shih-Fu Chang. 2016. New Frontiers of Large Scale Multimedia Information Retrieval. In *Proceedings of the ACM International Conference on Multimedia Retrieval (ICMR)*. 5–5.

[3] Marc Cheong and Vincent Lee. 2010. Twittering for Earth: A study on the impact of microblogging activism on Earth Hour 2009 in Australia. In *Proceedings of the Asian Conference on Intelligent Information and Database Systems*. Springer, 114–123.

[4] Xiaowen Dong, Dimitrios Mavroeidis, Francesco Calabrese, and Pascal Frossard. 2015. Multiscale event detection in social media. *Data Mining and Knowledge Discovery* 29, 5 (2015), 1374–1405.

[5] Berna Erol, Jonathan J Hull, and Dar-Shyang Lee. 2003. Linking multimedia presentations with their symbolic source documents: algorithm and applications. In *Proceedings of the eleventh ACM International Conference on Multimedia (MM)*. ACM, 498–507.

[6] Adrian Fisher, Neil Flood, and Tim Danaher. 2016. Comparing Landsat water index methods for automated water classification in eastern Australia. *Remote Sensing of Environment* 175 (2016), 167–182.

[7] Debarati Guha-Sapir, Regina Below, and Philippe Hoyois. 2015. EM-DAT: International disaster database. *Catholic University of Louvain: Brussels, Belgium* (2015).

[8] John Kansas, Javier Vargas, Hans G Skatter, and others. 2016. Using Landsat imagery to backcast fire and post-fire residuals in the Boreal Shield of Saskatchewan: implications for woodland caribou management. *International Journal of Wildland Fire* 25, 5 (2016), 597–607.

[9] Sian Lewis. 2009. Remote sensing for natural disasters: Facts and figures. *Science and Development Network* (2009).

[10] TN Manjunath, Ravindra S Hegadi, and GK Ravikumar. 2010. A survey on multimedia data mining and its relevance today. *IJCSNS* 10, 11 (2010), 165–170.

[11] M. Riegler, V. R. Gaddam, M. Larson, R. Eg, P. Halvorsen, and C. Griwodz. 2016. Crowdsourcing as self-fulfilling prophecy: Influence of discarding workers in subjective assessment tasks. In *14th Workshop CBMI*. 1–6. DOI: http://dx.doi.org/10.1109/CBMI.2016.7500256

[12] Brian Stelter and Noam Cohen. 2008. Citizen journalists provided glimpses of Mumbai attacks. *The New York Times* 30 (2008).

[13] C. Tzelepis, Z. Ma, V. Mezaris, B. Ionescu, and others. 2016. Event-based Media Processing and Analysis: A Survey of the Literature. *Image and Vision Computing* (2016).

[14] Jie Yin, Andrew Lampert, Mark Cameron, Bella Robinson, and Robert Power. 2012. Using social media to enhance emergency situation awareness. *IEEE Intelligent Systems* 27, 6 (2012), 52–59.

LireSolr – A Visual Information Retrieval Server

Mathias Lux
Klagenfurt University
Univeristätsstrasse 65-67
Klagenfurt, Austria
mlux@itec.aau.at

Michael Riegler
Simula Research Laboratory
Martin Linges v 17/25
Oslo, Norway
michael@simula.no

Pål Halvorsen
Simula Research Laboratory
Martin Linges v 17/25
Oslo, Norway
paalh@simula.no

Glenn MacStravic
World Intellectual Property Organization
34, chemin des Colombettes
Geneva, Switzerland
glenn.macstravic@wipo.int

ABSTRACT

In this paper, we present LireSolr, an open source image retrieval server, build on top of the LIRE library and the Apache Solr search server. With LireSolr, visual information retrieval can be run on a server, which allows better distribution of workloads and simplifies applications in several areas including mobile and web. Furthermore, we showcase several example scenarios how LireSolr can be used to point out the broad range of possibilities and applications. The system is easy to install and setup, and the large number of retrieval tools either provided by LIRE or by other Apache Solr is made easily available on the search server. Moreover, our tool demonstrates how predictions from CNNs can easily be used to extend the visual information retrieval functionality.

CCS CONCEPTS

•**Information systems** → **Search engine architectures and scalability;**

KEYWORDS

Visual information retrieval

ACM Reference format:
Mathias Lux, Michael Riegler, Pål Halvorsen, and Glenn MacStravic. 2017. LireSolr – A Visual Information Retrieval Server. In *Proceedings of ICMR '17, Bucharest, Romania, June 06-09, 2017,* 4 pages.
DOI: http://dx.doi.org/10.1145/3078971.3079014

1 INTRODUCTION

Large scale image retrieval is typically a problem of indexing large amounts of visual data and searching in indexes that cannot be held in the main memory of a server or desktop computer. Especially for projects, where retrieval is not the main goal, but merely a requirement among others, practitioners and researchers typically employ tools to fulfill their needs. In this demo, we present and demonstrate such a tool called LireSolr. It provides functionality for large scale visual retrieval by extending the popular Apache Solr[1] server by adding functionality for indexing and searching images. All benefits of the Solr server can be employed, i.e., handling text associated to images and distribution of search over multiple nodes. Moreover, the tool presented is fully open source and can be extended to fit the needs of new requirements. While being robust and scalable, it is available without any cost and the underlying technology, Apache Solr, is backed by a lively community of developers as well as large companies. While there are commercial products and services available, our tool allows for full control which data is indexed and how and where the data is stored, which is often a requirements for projects dealing with sensible data, i.e. medical image retrieval.

Our tool, LireSolr, supports visual features that are encoded in a numerical vector. This includes – besides the obvious global features – local feature histograms as well as features created by deep learning, e.g., using convolutional neural networks (CNN). In addition to these basic functionalities, bag of visual word approaches for image retrieval are also included since they come natural for a text based search engine. Main contributions of LireSolr are a binary data format for handling image features efficiently within Solr, means for search and sorting as well as implementations of hashing and permutation based approximate indexing. Moreover, common indexing tasks are covered by a modular and parallel approach to indexing.

This paper presents LireSolr in form of a demo. It first outlines features, benefits, and intended use of LireSolr. Then setup and deployment in a typical scenarios as well as a detailed web based demo application is discussed. Finally we provide pointers to the demo and summarize our findings. It's important to point out that the demo can be easily installed on computers supporting Docker[2] and Java and can therefore immediately be used for research projects, evaluations and even commercial applications.

2 LIRESOLR

LireSolr can be described as a set of classes adding additional functions to the Apache Solr server utilizing the LIRE library [7]. It

978-1-4503-4701-3/17/06...$15.00
DOI: http://dx.doi.org/10.1145/3078971.3079014

[1] http://lucene.apache.org/solr/, last visited 2017-02-02
[2] https://www.docker.com/, last visited 2017-02-02

includes tools for indexing, searching and result sorting, and it provides multiple ways to add visual features to indexes. The main architectural idea was to integrate visual features in a memory preserving way, which allows immediate access and approximate search. Within the Apache Solr server byte array data is typically handled in the so called *DocValues* structure, which is intended for use with non-text data. From Apache Solr major version 4 to version 6, the support for DocValues has been extended extensively, and LireSolr uses DocValues cached in main memory. Indexing is typically done in a two-step approach. First, visual features are extracted from images and stored within an XML file in the format required by Apache Solr for indexing new documents. Feature vectors are stored in the XML file using Base64 encoding of the byte arrays. Second, these XML file are sent to Apache Solr. LireSolr then decodes the Base64 encoded feature vectors on the server side and hands them to Apache Solr to store the vectors again as compressed byte arrays.

For approximate indexing, LireSolr supports two different ways. The first approach is BitSampling, which is a LSH based hashing approach [9]. In this approach, randomly generated hash functions are used to create terms for text based candidate search. As these hashes are roughly power law distributed, LireSolr implements a term dictionary and the inverse document frequency (IDF) of the hashes to find and select hashes, which do not match the majority of the data set, but are relatively more discriminating. Therefore, the candidate set and the query get smaller, and as a direct result, the search gets considerably faster. The second approach is based on Metric Spaces [4]. A set of reference points is selected from the data set, and these are used to generate a sorted list of nearest neighbors. The ordering of this list reflects the relevance of the reference points to describe a data point and is encoded within Apache Solr using the term frequency. The length of the query can be adapted at search time, i.e., a fast search would be to use a very small number, say the five nearest reference points, for search. A more accurate, but slower, search would use more reference points.

For searching, LireSolr provides a two-step approximate approach, where feature as well as hashing approach can be selected. First hashes (or reference points) are used to identify a candidate result set, which is then ranked using the actual image features. Moreover, the query length and the number of candidate results from the hash based (or metric space based) search can be configured at run time to control speed versus accuracy of retrieval. While this is implemented within a specific request handler class for Apache Solr, one can use the common text search for identifying a candidate set. There are multiple ways to perform such feat including searches based on text queries, like searches using boosted terms or searches that do not sort, but only filter based on terms. For this approach, LireSolr implements a sorting function, which can be used to sort candidate sets retrieved by the Apache Solr text search.

For handling images, LireSolr provides multiple ways to read images from storage (hard drives, SANs, etc.) and to read pre-processed image features vectors from text files. For both sources, LireSolr generates the required hashes utilizing a configurable number of CPU cores and stores the results in XML files for easy upload to Solr.

3 TYPICAL SETUP AND USAGE

The intended use of LireSolr is for end users, namely developers and researchers who do not intend to extend on the features, but want to use them within their own projects. LireSolr is managed by a Gradle build file and can be easily compiled and packaged for deployment. Installation, however, requires multiple steps including (i) the setup of Apache Solr; (ii) installing a dedicated Solr core for LireSolr; (iii) adding the Lire indexing format, the request handler class and the sorting function to the Solr core configuration; and (iv) configuring the schema of the core to be able to handle the required index fields correctly. In addition, a sample web application can be installed. There is a detailed guide available for setting up Apache Solr and configuring it for LireSolr on Github [6].

A more convenient and faster way to use LireSolr is to pull the Docker image. Docker is an open source container management tool and run-time environment, which allows to package software in a container. The container can then be pulled (meaning downloaded from a central repository) and run on client having the Docker run-time installed. The LireSolr Docker image[3] provides a pre-configured Apache Solr server with a LireSolr core and a sample web application. Data can be indexed using the Apache Solr web interface, and the index can be searched using the web application. A tool for indexing recent photos on Flickr for LireSolr is provided. A detailed guide is given on the LireSolr Github page [6].

Having LireSolr up and running, one can use the Apache Solr API to index and search for images. The LireSolr request handler supports multiple operations including retrieving random images, searching based on a query image defined by either an URL or a database id (if it is already in the index), extraction of visual features, and extraction of hashes (or lists of reference points). The sorting function can be used to sort results of a text search, either for hashes or actual textual documents attached to the images. The following three examples show how these methods can be used to construct actual search use cases.

3.1 Scenario A – Usage of the request handler

A common way is to query for similar images by specifying the query image by URL. See below for an example URL request to the Apache Solr server defining the visual features in the field argument (in this example one feature, the pyramid histogram of oriented gradients, PHOG [1], is used) and using *accuracy* and *candidates* parameters to configure the approximate search. The default method is the metric spaces indexing. To be able to use BitSampling, the parameter *ms* has to be set to false.

```
<solrserver>lireq?field=ph&url=<imgurl>&ms=true& \\
   rows=20&accuracy=0.35&candidates=1000
```

The example presented above retrieves data sets for 20 similar images from the Apache Solr server. For the actual search process in a first step, the query image is downloaded from the URL, decoded and the PHOG feature is extracted. Then, the reference point list is generated. From this list, the index is queried (employing the nearest 35% of the reference point list as defined in the *accuracy*

[3] https://hub.docker.com/r/dermotte/liresolr/, last visited 2017-02-02.

parameter) using the text search capabilities to retrieve 1000 candidate results. Finally the candidate set is re-ranked and the top 20 results are returned.

The result is returned as JSON document, but can be requested as a CSV file or an XML document as well. The listing below gives a shortened version of the response. In the header, the time for finding the candidate set (*RawDocsSearchTime*) and the time for re-ranking (*ReRankSearchTime*) are given in milliseconds in addition to the number of documents matching the approximate query (*RawDocsCount*). Each result has a property *d*, which gives the distance from the query to the matching result according to the employed visual feature and distance function.


```
{
  "responseHeader":{
  ...,
  "QueryField":"ph_ha",
  "QueryFeature":"PHOG",
  "DocValuesOpenTime":"0",
  "RawDocsCount":"19104",
  "RawDocsSearchTime":"6",
  "ReRankSearchTime":"3",
  "docs":[{
      "imgurl":"http://farm1....jpg",
      "id":"http://www.flickr.com/..2081/",
      "d":0.0,
      "title":"70210083149099",
      "authorid_s":"http://www.flic...",
      "authorname_ws":"Amsterdam DNA"},
    ...
    ]
}
```


Using LireSolr like this comes in handy if the client uses JavaScript or supports JSON encoded data out of the box, as most mobile or web platforms do.

3.2 Scenario B – Sorting the result of text searches

In this example, we show how one can combine text searches and image feature based re-ranking by employing the distance function *lirefunc* provided by LireSolr. In a first step, the request handler has to be used to extract the visual feature from a given image as shown in the example below. The result includes a property *histogram*, which can then be used as second parameter for the sorting function.

```
<solrserver>lireq?extract=<imgurl>&field=ph
```

One has to make sure that the extracted feature is the same as the one given in the first parameter of *lirefunc*, otherwise, the Base64 encoded parameter cannot be parsed. Note that the following query does not use the LireSolr request handler, but the standard Apache Solr one (*select* instead of *lireq*). The sort order can be configured by appending asc (ascending) or desc (descending). If the actual distance value that is used for sorting is needed, one has to add it to the results fields using the *fl* parameter, i.e., with `fl=*,lirefunc(ph,<base64>)`.

```
<solrserver>select?q=title:flower& \\
   sort=lirefunc(ph,<base64>)%20asc
```

3.3 Scenario C – Using text based search for two step search

Using LireSolr, one may also use a text-based search for a two-step search. This example, using the text search handler for approximate image search, is also based on two steps. First, we need to extract the histogram as well as the hashes needed for search like in above example:

```
<solrserver>lireq?extract=<imgurl>&field=ph
```

Following the extraction, we can build a text query using the *bs_query* property of the JSON response, which returns the Bit-Sampling hashes and the *histogram* property. If Metric Spaces is used, the *ms_query* property should be set. Compared to the above Scenario A, the user has tighter control over the query, i.e., using a filter query, shortening or boosting it, but looses control over the re-rank process as all candidate results need to be ranked. The final query to the Apache Solr server would then be:

```
<solrserver>select?wt=json&q=ph_ha:(<hashes>)*& \\
   sort=lirefunc(ph,<base64>)%20asc
```

4 DEMO

The demo of LireSolr combines the Solr with LireSolr and provides (i) an indexing routine for recent additions to Flickr, (ii) an integration of predictions from the ResNet50 model [5] for text based search and (iii) a web application providing a front end for search. Moreover, the demo can be installed easily and filled with own photos.

The demo is based on the LireSolr Docker image and – under the assumption that Docker is installed – can be started with:

```
$> docker run -p 8983:8983 dermotte/liresolr:latest
```

With the Docker container running, the admin console can be accessed by connecting to http://localhost:8983 with a browser. At this point, no photos are indexed. To add recent Flickr photos to the index, there is a small utility prepared within LireSolr. If Java is installed, the utility can be created by downloading the LireSolr source and running the following command.

```
$> gradlew.bat createCommandlineDownloader
```

The resulting file *flickrdownloader.jar* will download a number of recent photos from Flickr using the Atom feed for new photos and create an XML file. In the XML file for each image title, image URL, page URL, author name and ID and the extracted features as well as BitSampling hashes are stored. The number of photos as well as the output XML file can be configured by using the switches -n for defining a number of photos and -o for giving either the term auto for automatic file naming or the output file name. The tool can be run – also multiple times to index more photos – with:

```
$> java -jar flickrdownloader.jar -o auto
```

The resulting XML file can either be uploaded to Solr using the admin interface, or it can be further enriched with predictions from the ResNet CNN model [5] before uploading. For this purpose, we employed *Keras*[4], a wrapper for TensorFlow and Theano. For reflecting the accuracy of the predictions in the index, we use an

[4]https://keras.io/, last visited 2017-02-02

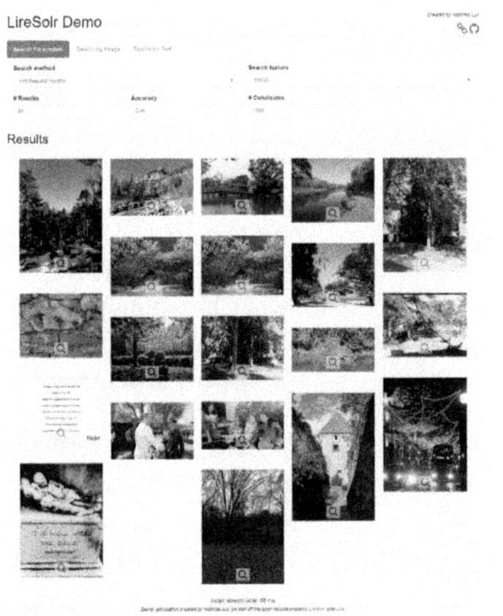

Figure 1: Sample application built with LireSolr showing results for a query image using the PHOG visual feature. Images are loaded from the Flickr servers. If a user deletes an image it is not available any more for the demo, like the image in the first column, third row.

approach similar to the one employed for approximate search with reference points. Predicted categories are added as terms, and the term frequency reflects the class score (probability $p \in [0, 1]$ for each of the 1,000 inception classes) of the predicted class using $tf = \lceil p * 10 \rceil$. If for instance car is predicted with a probability of $p = 0.31$ the term car is added to the index three times. A Python script provided in the LireSolr Github repository can be used to create a new XML file with the additional fields for upload taking the original XML file from the flickrdownloader.jar tool as input.

As soon as there are images in the index, http://localhost:8983/solr/lire.html can be accessed and random images will be shown on first start. There are three different types of searches available in the demo front end: (i) Any image in the index an be used to search for similar ones, (ii) image queries can be specified by URL, and (iii) one can use text based search as provided by Apache Solr, i.e., for searching through the predicted classes. The image search can be configured by selecting the visual feature to search for, the search approach as outlined in the scenarios above and the accuracy and number of candidates for approximate search. Moreover, the predicted classes can be used for a similarity search using the MoreLikeThis handler in Apache Solr. In the demo, six different global features are supported out of the box: The pyramid histogram or oriented gradient, PHOG [1], the compact composite descriptors CEDD and JCD [2, 3], and the MPEG-7 features ColorLayout and ScalableColor [8]. Fig. 1 is a screen shot of the demo web application showing the results of a image query using the PHOG visual feature and BitSampling hashing for approximate search.

5 CONCLUSIONS

We have presented our demo of LireSolr, which adds the functionality of LIRE and more to the Apache Solr search server. We discussed

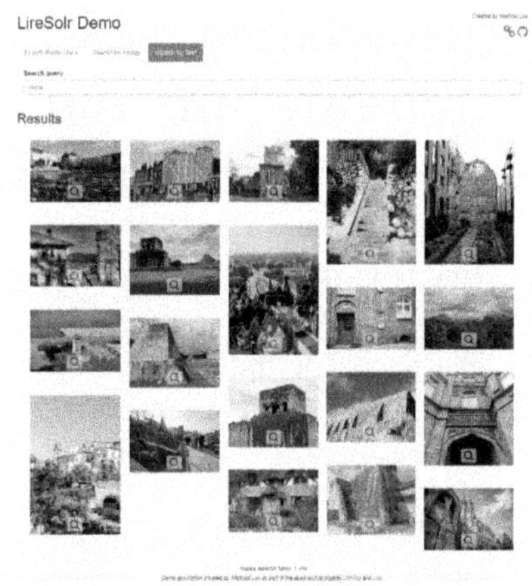

Figure 2: Example for text search in the category predictions created by the CNN ResNet50 model

the extension in detail and showed how to set up the system for a local installation to be used in any project requiring content-based image retrieval capabilities. Moreover, we provided and explained three typical use scenarios that should help the reader to get started using the system. Finally, we described our particular demo indexing and search application which is using LireSolr for indexing and searching Flickr images and has an integration of the ResNet50 model for text-based search. LireSolr is ongoing work, and in the future, we would like to include features extracted from neural network models for search and indexing. Furthermore, we are going to explore possibilities how global, local and CNN features and predictions can be fused at runtime to cover a broad range of requirements.

REFERENCES

[1] A. Bosch, A. Zisserman, and X. Munoz. Representing shape with a spatial pyramid kernel. In *Proceedings of the 6th ACM international conference on Image and video retrieval*, pages 401–408. ACM, 2007.

[2] S. A. Chatzichristofis and Y. S. Boutalis. CEDD: color and edge directivity descriptor: a compact descriptor for image indexing and retrieval. In *International Conference on Computer Vision Systems*, pages 312–322. Springer, 2008.

[3] S. A. Chatzichristofis, Y. S. Boutalis, and M. Lux. Selection of the proper compact composite descriptor for improving content based image retrieval. In *Proc. of the 6th IASTED International Conference*, volume 134643, page 064, 2009.

[4] C. Gennaro, G. Amato, P. Bolettieri, and P. Savino. An approach to content-based image retrieval based on the lucene search engine library. In *International Conference on Theory and Practice of Digital Libraries*, pages 55–66. Springer, 2010.

[5] K. He, X. Zhang, S. Ren, and J. Sun. Deep residual learning for image recognition. *CoRR*, abs/1512.03385, 2015.

[6] M. Lux. LireSolr Github repository: https://github.com/dermotte/liresolr, 2017.

[7] M. Lux and S. A. Chatzichristofis. LIRE: Lucene image retrieval: An extensible Java CBIR library. In *Proc. of ACM MM*, pages 1085–1088, 2008.

[8] B. S. Manjunath, P. Salembier, and T. Sikora. *Introduction to MPEG-7: multimedia content description interface*, volume 1. John Wiley & Sons, 2002.

[9] S. Rüger. Multimedia information retrieval. *Synthesis Lectures on Information Concepts, Retrieval, and Services*, 1(1):1–171, 2009.

VideoAnalysis4ALL: An On-line Tool for the Automatic Fragmentation and Concept-based Annotation, and the Interactive Exploration of Videos

Chrysa Collyda
CERTH-ITI
6th Km Charilaou-Thermi Road
Thessaloniki, Greece
ckol@iti.gr

Evlampios Apostolidis
CERTH-ITI
6th Km Charilaou-Thermi Road
Thessaloniki, Greece
apostolid@iti.gr

Alexandros Pournaras
CERTH-ITI
6th Km Charilaou-Thermi Road
Thessaloniki, Greece
apournaras@iti.gr

Foteini Markatopoulou
CERTH-ITI
Thermi, Greece, 57001
Queen Mary University of London
markatopoulou@iti.gr

Vasileios Mezaris
CERTH-ITI
6th Km Charilaou-Thermi Road
Thessaloniki, Greece
bmezaris@iti.gr

Ioannis Patras
Queen Mary University of London
Mile end Campus, E14NS
London, United Kingdom
i.patras@qmul.ac.uk

ABSTRACT

This paper presents the VideoAnalysis4ALL tool that supports the automatic fragmentation and concept-based annotation of videos, and the exploration of the annotated video fragments through an interactive user interface. The developed web application decomposes the video into two different granularities, namely shots and scenes, and annotates each fragment by evaluating the existence of a number (several hundreds) of high-level visual concepts in the keyframes extracted from these fragments. Through the analysis the tool enables the identification and labeling of semantically coherent video fragments, while its user interfaces allow the discovery of these fragments with the help of human-interpretable concepts. The integrated state-of-the-art video analysis technologies perform very well and, by exploiting the processing capabilities of multi-thread / multi-core architectures, reduce the time required for analysis to approximately one third of the video's duration, thus making the analysis three times faster than real-time processing.

CCS CONCEPTS

• **Computing methodologies → Visual content-based indexing and retrieval; Video segmentation;** • **Human-centered computing → Web-based interaction;**

KEYWORDS

Web-based on-line video analysis; video segmentation; video anno-tation; video content exploration

ICMR '17, June 06-09, 2017, Bucharest, Romania

ACM ISBN 978-1-4503-4701-3/17/06...$15.00
https://doi.org/http://dx.doi.org/10.1145/3078971.3079015

ACM Reference format:
Chrysa Collyda, Evlampios Apostolidis, Alexandros Pournaras, Foteini Markatopoulou, Vasileios Mezaris, and Ioannis Patras. 2017. VideoAnalysis4ALL: An On-line Tool for the Automatic Fragmentation and Concept-based Annotation, and the Interactive Exploration of Videos. In *Proceedings of ICMR '17, Bucharest, Romania, June 06-09, 2017,* 5 pages.
https://doi.org/http://dx.doi.org/10.1145/3078971.3079015

1 INTRODUCTION

Driven by the recent advances in video capturing and sharing technologies, in the last years there is a rapidly growing volume of video content distributed on the web through several channels, such as video-sharing platforms (e.g., YouTube and Vimeo), social networks (e.g., Facebook and Twitter) and on-line archives of content providers (e.g., broadcasters and news organizations). This trend, combined with the users' needs for finding and consuming the most appropriate and desirable content from vast amounts of information, highlights the necessity for making video content searchable and easily accessible, e.g., via some form of links in fragments of it, similar in principle to the hyperlinks between pieces of textual information. To this direction, semantically coherent fragments of a video must be identified and enriched with suitable human-interpretable annotations, that would make these pieces of video content searchable and linkable with related content.

The last years several technologies were introduced for the annotation of videos. Some of them, such as the ELAN [10], ANVIL [14] and EMXARaLDA [18] tools, offer an interactive environment for multi-layered, time-aligned video annotation with transcripts and annotations from various (pre-defined or customizable) categories. Other tools, such as the MobilVox [1], the Sloth [2] and the one in [17] support manual tagging of spatial and temporal fragments of a video with a set of multi-modal annotations (i.e., text, image, audio) in a way similar to the one applied by the YouTube [3] video

[1] https://www.youtube.com/watch?v=WB7M757Pw3I
[2] https://cvhci.anthropomatik.kit.edu/~baeuml/projects/a-universal-labeling-tool-for-computer-vision-sloth/
[3] https://support.google.com/youtube/answer/92710?topic=14354&hl=en

annotation framework. This spatiotemporal video tagging functionality is extended in other approaches, such as the BeaverDam [24] and the VideoJot [6], which enable a region-based, frame-by-frame annotation of videos through the demarcation and labeling of objects that appear within them with the help of bounding boxes or more arbitrary shapes. Furthermore, technologies for commenting and annotating (also streaming) videos through an interactive manual process were developed by the Universities of Harvard [4] and Minnesota [5]. The aforementioned manual solutions for video annotation are labour-intensive and time-demanding, so a set of semi-automatic approaches for reducing the video labeling workload were also introduced. Some of them, such as the Semantic Video Annotation Suite [22], automatically define the shots and the keyframes of the video and assist the manual shot-level annotation of the video by providing a customizable set of MPEG-7 annotations, while others, such as the Vatic [26] framework and the web-based tool of [3], enable the semi-automatic annotation of videos through an interactive user interface that enables the selection, labeling and tracking of specific areas of video frames.

In a slightly different direction, a number of technologies that support the exploration of video collections based on the semantic content of their videos have also been introduced. However, these frameworks require a prior analysis of the entire video collection in order to extract conceptual information about the videos, and they use this information for concept-based video retrieval through a video search engine. For example, the MediaMil system [25] used a lexicon of 100 automatically detected semantic concepts in the videos of the collection and offered a "query-by-concept" mechanism to facilitate users to access news video archives at a semantic level. Another interactive video search engine, VERGE, that extracts and exploits different types of visual information and is capable of retrieving and browsing video collections by integrating multimodal indexing and retrieval modules was presented in [19]. Alternatively, multi-modal approaches that combine different streams of the media content have been also proposed, such as the AXES-LITE video search engine [11], which integrates algorithms for text-based, visual-concept-based and visual-similarity-based retrieval of videos; and, the interactive system of [12], which represents the visual content of a video collection with the help of over 2500 high-quality pre-trained semantic concept detectors and applies text analysis on ASR and OCR data, allowing users to do multi-modal text-to-video and video-to-video search in large video collections. Many more interactive video search engines have been presented, e.g., [23], [13], [15] and [20].

The above overview indicates that most stand-alone existing video labeling tools require the involvement of the user in a labour-intensive and time-demanding video annotation process, while techniques for the automatic analysis and annotation of video have been integrated in prototype video search engines, but these usually do not give to the everyday user the possibility to analyze and annotate his/her own video content. Motivated by the lack of tools that an average user of the Web can employ for performing fine-grained video segmentation and labeling in a fully automatic way, we built an on-line, freely accessible web application that enables users to upload or submit videos of various genres and automatically perform: i) fragmentation of these videos into shots and scenes, ii) semantic annotation of the defined video fragments and iii) interactive exploration of their videos at a fine-grained level with the help of human-understandable visual concepts.

[4]http://annotation.chs.harvard.edu/video.php
[5]https://ant.umn.edu/

2 THE ON-LINE VIDEO ANALYSIS TOOL

The developed on-line tool integrates a set of video analysis technologies (reported in Section 3), and performs temporal fragmentation of a video and semantic annotation of the defined video fragments with the help of a vocabulary of visual concepts. The application allows the user to submit a video for analysis through the user interface depicted in Fig. 1. The submission can be done either via specifying the URL of an on-line available video, or by uploading a local copy of it from the user's machine. A variety of different video formats is supported, including mp4, webm, avi, mov, wmv, ogv, mpg, flv, and mkv. After fetching the video file, the tool decomposes the video into two different granularities, namely shots (i.e., the elementary structural parts of the video) and scenes (i.e., the story-telling parts of the video). Following, a few hundred visual concept detectors are evaluated for each keyframe extracted from the detected shots, and through this process the developed tool defines a shot-level concept-based annotation of the given video file. After submitting a video for analysis, the user can close the user interface and be notified by e-mail when the analysis results are ready; alternatively, he/she can keep the user interface open and monitor the progress of the analysis.

When the analysis is completed the results are presented to the user through the user interface presented in Fig. 2. With the help of this interactive environment the user is able to: i) explore the shot- and scene-level structure of the video, and select video fragments of these two different granularities (Fig. 2(b) shows the window that pops-up after clicking the "See all shots and scenes of the video" link); ii) see the concept-based annotation of each shot of the video (Fig. 2(a) depicts the top-10 concepts for the 49th shot of the video); iii) perform a concept-based search within the collection of detected shots by selecting a concept from the given list of concepts (Fig. 2(c) illustrates the retrieved video shots and the concept-based annotation of a selected one, after searching for the concept "Car"). As shown by the capabilities explained above and presented in Fig. 2, the developed tool automatically defines semantically annotated video fragments that are easily searchable and linkable with related content, with the help of a set of high-level visual concepts. Last but not least, the video files submitted for analysis and the corresponding analysis results are available for inspection via the user interface for approximately 48 to 72 hours after their analysis is completed; after this time period they are automatically deleted from our server.

3 VIDEO ANALYSIS TECHNOLOGIES AND USER INTERFACE

This section gives insights about the video analysis methods integrated in the tool, namely the algorithms for shot segmentation (Section 3.1), scene segmentation (Section 3.2) and concept detection (Section 3.3), and reports on the technologies utilized for building its interactive user interfaces (Section 3.4).

Figure 1: The user interface that allows to submit a video for analysis and to monitor the progress of the process.

3.1 Video shot segmentation

The video is temporally segmented into shots, i.e., sequences of frames captured uninterruptedly by a single camera, based on a variation of the algorithm in [1]. The employed method defines the boundaries of each shot by detecting the abrupt and gradual shot transitions. The latter is performed by evaluating the visual resemblance between consecutive and neighboring frames of the video with the help of local (ORB [5]) and global (HSV histograms) descriptors. Following, the boundaries of each shot of the video are determined through the comparison of the computed similarity scores and patterns against experimentally pre-specified thresholds and models that indicate the existence of abrupt and gradual shot transition. The resulting set of transitions is re-assessed with the help of a flash detector that eliminates falsely identified abrupt transitions due to short-term camera flashes, and a pair of dissolve and wipe detectors (based on [4] and [2] respectively) that remove erroneously detected gradual transitions due to swift camera and/or object movement. The union of the resulting sets of detected abrupt and gradual transitions forms the output of the applied technique. Finally, three representative keyframes are extracted from each shot of the video through a simple frame-sampling strategy that selects three uniformly distributed frames of the shot, and provided for further processing by the scene segmentation and concept detection algorithms of the tool.

3.2 Video scene segmentation

Building upon the outcomes of the shot segmentation analysis, the integrated scene segmentation algorithm from [9] specifies the story-telling parts of the video by grouping shots into sets that correspond to individual scenes of the video, i.e., semantically and temporally coherent segments that cover either a single event or several related events that take place in parallel. This grouping is performed by evaluating the content similarity and the temporal consistency among the shots of the video. Content similarity in the utilized method is expressed by assessing the visual similarity among the keyframes of different shots of the video through the extraction and matching of HSV histograms. Visual similarity and temporal consistency then are taken into account during the shot grouping into scenes that is performed with the help of two extensions of the Scene Transition Graph (STG) algorithm [27]. The first one decreases the computational load of STG-based shot grouping by taking into account shot linking transitivity and by exploiting the fact that scenes are by definition convex sets of shots, while the second extension builds on the former and constructs a probabilistic framework that eliminates the need for manual selection of the STG parameters. Based on these extensions the applied technique can identify the scene-level structure of videos belonging to different genres, and provide results that match well the human expectations.

3.3 Video concept detection

The integrated concept detection algorithm annotates each shot of the video by evaluating the existence of a set (several hundreds) of visual concepts in the middle keyframe of the shot. Video concept detection is performed using a modification of the deep multi-task learning algorithm (DMTL_LC) presented in [16]. DMTL_LC combines multi-task learning with deep learning and also constraints the network's concept-related parameters by considering the concept correlations between pairs of concepts. For the developed tool, a pre-trained ImageNet [8] deep network was fine-tuned using the DMTL_LC method on 345 TRECVID SIN concepts [7]. During the analysis, each video keyframe is forward propagated by the fine-tuned network. Then, the output of the network is refined by employing the re-ranking method proposed in [21] and finally, the refined scores are used to annotate the given keyframe and the corresponding shot of the video. Based on these computed shot-level annotations, a scene-level labeling is also automatically defined for each detected scene of the video, by max pooling the scores of the detected concepts in the shots that compose each individual scene.

3.4 UI implementation

The interactive user interface of the tool follows the HTML5 standard and integrates technologies of the JQuery JavaScript library [6] (version 1.9.1). For the presentation of the analysis results the web interface utilizes the JqPlot [7] plotting and charting plugin of the JQuery JavaScript framework, while the selection of the video fragment that is shown in the player is based on the use of media fragment URI references with the new HTML5 video tag. The user interface is fully compatible with Mozilla Firefox (version 41.0 or

[6] https://jquery.com/
[7] http://www.jqplot.com/

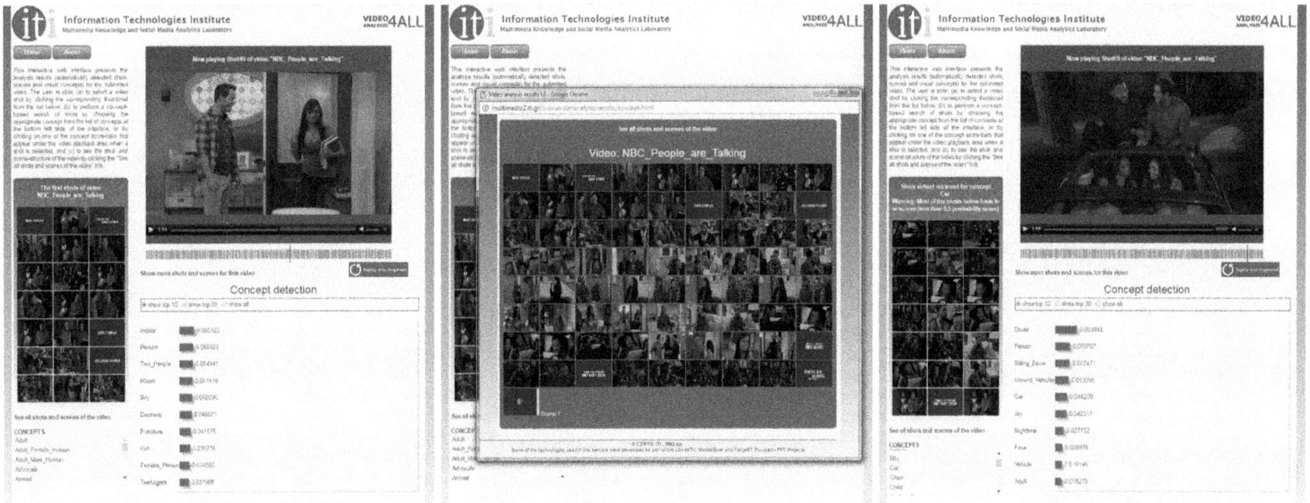

(a) The concept-based annotation of a selected shot. (b) The shot- and scene-level structure of the video. (c) The search results for the concept "Car".

Figure 2: The user interface for the presentation and management of the analysis results.

newer), Chrome (version 45.0 or newer) and Opera (version 32.0 or newer), while it is partially compatible with Internet Explorer (version 11.0 or newer) and Safari (version 5.1 or newer). Please note that the developed user interface for the presentation of the analysis results is also fully operable with the latter two browsers, however the playback functionality of the video player might not be optimal in some cases due to slight differences between the way that each browser handles these fragments (i.e., a few frames can be added in the beginning or at the end of a shot in some cases).

4 PERFORMANCE AND TESTING

The back-end services of the demo run on a PC with an Intel i7-4770K at 3.50 GHz, 16GB of RAM and a 384-core NVIDIA GeForce GTX 650 graphics card. By exploiting the multi-thread and multi-core processing capabilities of the available CPU and GPU, the analysis is faster than real-time video processing (where real-time processing would have a processing time equal to the video's duration); though, delays may be noticed if multiple analysis requests are sent to service, since the latter applies a queuing strategy on the incoming analysis requests and the analysis is performed in a one-by-one basis (and not in parallel). In particular the shot and scene segmentation is performed 4 to 6 times faster than real-time processing, depending on the resolution of the given video. The time required for concept detection is related to the number of detected shots (since this type of analysis is performed on a per shot/keyframe basis, as described above). Based on the fact that the service needs approximately 0.15 sec. per keyframe and according to a set of evaluations that included several different types of videos (e.g., news videos, documentaries, sitcoms, talk shows), we can state that the entire video fragmentation and annotation analysis is about three times faster than real-time processing (depending again on the number of the detected shots). We should mention that a bit of extra time is needed for fetching the video file in the service (i.e., for video transfer) and for transcoding it after the analysis, so that it can be displayable by the video player in different browser-player configurations. Our on-line tool for video fragmentation and annotation can be accessed and tested at http://multimedia2.iti.gr/onlinevideoanalysis/service/start.html.

5 CONCLUSIONS

This paper demonstrated the developed on-line tool for automatic video fragmentation and concept-based annotation. Details about the use and functionalities of the tool were given with the help of indicative snapshots of the implemented user interfaces. The integrated methods for video analysis and the employed technologies for building the tool were presented, and information about the performance of the developed technologies was given. The demo will show that our on-line tool is a fully automatic tool for video fragmentation and annotation, and for the creation of semantically annotated video fragments that are searchable using a set of human-interpretable concept labels.

ACKNOWLEDGMENTS

This work was supported by the EU's Horizon 2020 research and innovation programme under grant agreements H2020-687786 InVID, H2020-693092 MOVING and H2020-732665 EMMA.

REFERENCES

[1] E. Apostolidis and V. Mezaris. 2014. Fast shot segmentation combining global and local visual descriptors. In *Proceedings of the 2014 IEEE International Conference on Acoustics, Speech and Signal Processing*. 6583–6587.

[2] K. d. Seo, S. J. Park, and S. h. Jung. 2009. Wipe scene-change detector based on visual rhythm spectrum. *IEEE Transactions on Consumer Electronics* 55, 2 (May 2009), 831–838.

[3] A. Ioannidou, E. Apostolidis, C. Collyda, et al. 2017. A web-based tool for fast instance-level labeling of videos and the creation of spatiotemporal media fragments. *Multimedia Tools and Applications* 76, 2 (2017), 1735–1774.

[4] C.-W. Su, H.-R. Tyan, H.-Y. Mark Liao, et al. 2002. A motion-tolerant dissolve detection algorithm. In *Proceedings of the IEEE International Conference on Multimedia and Expo*, Vol. 2. 225–228 vol.2.

[5] E. Rublee, V. Rabaud, K. Konolige, et al. 2011. ORB: An efficient alternative to SIFT or SURF. In *2011 International Conference on Computer Vision*. 2564–2571.

[6] M. Riegler, M. Lux, V. Charvillat, et al. 2014. VideoJot: A Multifunctional Video Annotation Tool. In *Proceedings of the International Conference on Multimedia Retrieval (ICMR '14)*. ACM, New York, NY, USA, Article 534, 534:534–534:537 pages.

[7] O. Paul, A. George, M. Martial, et al. 2015. TRECVID 2015 – An Overview of the Goals, Tasks, Data, Evaluation Mechanisms and Metrics. In *TRECVID 2015 Workshop*. NIST, USA.

[8] O. Russakovsky, J. Deng, H. Su, et al. 2015. ImageNet Large Scale Visual Recognition Challenge. *International Journal of Computer Vision (IJCV)* 115, 3 (2015), 211–252.

[9] P. Sidiropoulos, V. Mezaris, I. Kompatsiaris, et al. 2011. Temporal Video Segmentation to Scenes Using High-Level Audiovisual Features. *IEEE Transactions on Circuits and Systems for Video Technology* 21, 8 (Aug 2011), 1163–1177.

[10] P. Wittenburg, H. Brugman, A. Russel, et al. 2006. ELAN: a Professional Framework for Multimodality Research. In *Proceedings of the 5th International Conference on Language Resources and Evaluation (LREC 2006)*. 1556–1559.

[11] S. Chen, K. McGuinness, R. Aly, et al. 2012. The AXES-lite video search engine. In *2012 13th International Workshop on Image Analysis for Multimedia Interactive Services*. 1–4. https://doi.org/10.1109/WIAMIS.2012.6226778

[12] S. Xu, H. Li, X. Chang, et al. 2015. Incremental Multimodal Query Construction for Video Search. In *Proceedings of the 5th ACM on International Conference on Multimedia Retrieval (ICMR '15)*. ACM, New York, NY, USA, 675–678. https://doi.org/10.1145/2671188.2749413

[13] W. Hürst, A. Ip Vai Ching, M. A. Hudelist, et al. 2016. A New Tool for Collaborative Video Search via Content-based Retrieval and Visual Inspection. In *Proceedings of the 2016 ACM on Multimedia Conference (MM '16)*. ACM, New York, NY, USA, 731–732. https://doi.org/10.1145/2964284.2973824

[14] M. Kipp. 2012. ANVIL: A Universal Video Research Tool. In *Handbook of Corpus Phonology*, J. Durand, U. Gut, and G. Kristofferson (Eds.). Oxford Univ. Press.

[15] Y.-J. Lu, P. A. Nguyen, H. Zhang, and et al. 2017. *Concept-Based Interactive Search System*. Springer International Publishing, Cham, 463–468. https://doi.org/10.1007/978-3-319-51814-5_42

[16] F. Markatopoulou, V. Mezaris, and I. Patras. 2016. Deep Multi-task Learning with Label Correlation Constraint for Video Concept Detection. In *Proceedings of the 2016 ACM on Multimedia Conference (MM '16)*. ACM, NY, 501–505.

[17] M. Martin, J. Charlton, and A. M. Connor. 2016. Mainstreaming video annotation software for critical video analysis. *CoRR* abs/1604.05799 (2016).

[18] C. Meissner and A. Slavcheva. 2013. Review of EXMARaLDA. *Language Documentation and Conservation* 7 (2013), 31–40.

[19] A. Moumtzidou, T. Mironidis, F. Markatopoulou, and et al. 2017. *VERGE in VBS 2017*. Springer International Publishing, Cham, 486–492. https://doi.org/10.1007/978-3-319-51814-5_46

[20] T. D. Ngo, V.-T. Nguyen, V. H. Nguyen, and et al. 2015. *NII-UIT Browser: A Multimodal Video Search System*. Springer International Publishing, Cham, 278–281. https://doi.org/10.1007/978-3-319-14442-9_28

[21] B. Safadi and G. Quénot. 2011. Re-ranking by Local Re-scoring for Video Indexing and Retrieval. In *Proceedings of the 20th ACM International Conference on Information and Knowledge Management*. ACM, New York, NY, USA, 2081–2084.

[22] P. Schallauer, O. Sandra, and H. Neuschmied. 2008. Efficient semantic video annotation by object and shot re-detection. In *3rd International Conference on Semantic and Digital Media Technologies*.

[23] K. Schoeffmann, M. J. Primus, B. Muenzer, and et al. 2017. *Collaborative Feature Maps for Interactive Video Search*. Springer International Publishing, Cham, 457–462. https://doi.org/10.1007/978-3-319-51814-5_41

[24] A. Shen. 2016. *BeaverDam: Video Annotation Tool for Computer Vision Training Labels*. Master's thesis. EECS Department, University of California, Berkeley.

[25] C. G. M. Snoek, M. Worring, J. van Gemert, et al. 2005. MediaMill: Exploring News Video Archives Based on Learned Semantics. In *Proceedings of the 13th Annual ACM International Conference on Multimedia (MULTIMEDIA '05)*. ACM, New York, NY, USA, 225–226. https://doi.org/10.1145/1101149.1101188

[26] C. Vondrick, D. Patterson, and D. Ramanan. 2013. Efficiently Scaling up Crowdsourced Video Annotation. *International Journal of Computer Vision* (2013), 184–204.

[27] M. Yeung, B.-L. Yeo, and B. Liu. 1998. Segmentation of Video by Clustering and Graph Analysis. *Comp. Vision and Image Underst.* 71, 1 (1998), 94 – 109.

Visually Browsing Millions of Images Using Image Graphs

Kai Uwe Barthel
Visual Computing Group
HTW Berlin
12459 Berlin, Germany
barthel@htw-berlin.de

Nico Hezel
Visual Computing Group
HTW Berlin
12459 Berlin, Germany
hezel@htw-berlin.de

Klaus Jung
Visual Computing Group
HTW Berlin
12459 Berlin, Germany
klaus.jung@htw-berlin.de

ABSTRACT

We present a new approach to visually browse very large sets of untagged images. High quality image features are generated using transformed activations of a convolutional neural network. These features are used to model image similarities, from which a hierarchical image graph is build. We show how such a graph can be constructed efficiently. In our experiments we found best user experience for navigating the graph is achieved by projecting subgraphs onto a regular 2D image map. This allows users to explore the image collection like an interactive map.

CCS CONCEPTS

• **Human-centered computing** → **Visualization techniques; Visualization systems and tools;** • **Mathematics of computing** → *Graph theory;*

KEYWORDS

Image Graph, Exploration, Browsing, Visualization, Navigation, Convolutional Neural Networks, CBIR.

ACM Reference format:
Kai Uwe Barthel, Nico Hezel, and Klaus Jung. 2017. Visually Browsing Millions of Images Using Image Graphs. In *Proceedings of ICMR '17, Bucharest, Romania, June 06-09, 2017,* 5 pages.
DOI: http://dx.doi.org/10.1145/3078971.3079016

Figure 1: www.picsbuffet.com allows users to visually explore one million images from the Pixabay stock agency.

1 INTRODUCTION

Searching particular images in untagged image collections with several millions of entries is very time consuming. As human perception is limited, overview is quickly lost if too many images are shown. Due to this, most applications display about 20 images per screen. Since most users only look at the first few pages, just a tiny fraction of the collection is viewed. Up to now image search systems do not allow visual browsing or exploration of the entire collection. While there has been a lot of effort to improve CBIR, there is very little support for exploratory image search.

For the Video Browser Showdown 2016 [15] we have proposed a new video browsing system [2]. No keywords were available, only automatically generated image features and visual exploration techniques were allowed. Our graph-based video browser obtained the best results in the competition. We show how this idea can be extended for exploring very large archives of (untagged) images.

ICMR '17, June 6-9, 2017, *Bucharest, Romania*

978-1-4503-4701-3/17/06...$15.00
DOI: http://dx.doi.org/10.1145/3078971.3079016

2 RELATED WORK

An overview of various visual browsing models for image exploration was given in [6]. If the total number of images is too high, pre-calculated image distance tables cannot be stored and a real time computation is impossible. Therefore image browsing techniques for huge collections require an off-line preparation step. Some authors use visual attributes to split images into subsets [10]. Others [16, 18] use techniques such as ISOMAP or self-organizing maps (SOMs) to generate visually sorted arrangements of search results. These approaches help to get a better overview, but they suffer from unequally positioned and overlapping images. In all cases, only few images of the entire image set are shown and there is no way to experience the relationships with other images.

Chen et. al [3] proposed an image pyramid to explore image collections. An improved version was presented in [12], however the complexity of the used kernelized sorting was too high for very large image sets. In [1] we have described how an image pyramid which allows combined image search and visual navigation can be constructed efficiently even for very large amounts of images. A demonstrator of this approach using 830000 stock photos from Pixabay can be found at www.picsbuffet.com (Figure 1). The images were sorted using a hierarchical, torus-shaped SOM, where every place on a regular rectangular image map could be occupied only by one image. Our system achieved superior visual sorting quality compared to the other systems described above.

Using a 2D projection, the complex relationships between all images cannot be preserved. Another important disadvantage of regular 2D sortings is their inability to handle changes of the image collection. Removed images will result in holes in the image map. If images are added, a new sorting process becomes necessary, which will change the previous order of the images.

Graph-based approaches [11] are able to better preserve the image relationships and can handle changes of the image archive easier. However, it is not clear how to visualize the "high-dimensional" graph in such a way that it can easily be perceived and navigated by the user. The meanwhile abandoned *Google Image Swirl* [8] was an example of a graph-based image browsing tool. Image navigation was rather difficult and only a fraction of the available screen space was used. In this paper we propose a graph-based image browsing approach not suffering from these problems. Subsets of images are successively extracted from the graph and regularly arranged onto a 2D surface while preserving the order of the previously displayed images. This creates "an endless map" and reduces the amount of dimensions of the graph the user has to deal with, but still allows to maintain the complex inter-image relationships.

3 PROPOSED SYSTEM

Visual exploration or visual browsing of a graph-based image collection requires three associated problems to be solved:

(1) *Semantic image features*: High quality image features are crucial to model inter image similarities. The calculated similarities from these features need to be close to the similarities the user perceives. In addition the size of the features should be very compact.
(2) A *hierarchical image graph* needs to be constructed. Similar images should be connected and other images should be accessible by traversing the graph. Lower layers of the graph should connect very similar images, while higher layers should connect less related images.
(3) Graph *visualization and navigation*: The images should be displayed such that they can easily be recognized. Navigation to other images should be easy and understandable.

3.1 Generating Semantic Features

Convolutional neural networks (CNNs) are not only able to achieve high accuracy rates for image classification tasks, the activations of a hidden layer can also serve as good feature vectors for image retrieval [9]. The outputs of a neural network trained for a particular set of categories do not perform well in general image retrieval tasks. Early layers describe primitive visual features such as colors or patterns, while later layers represent semantic information [13]. Intermediate layers can be seen as abstract representations of the visual content, and are therefore less dependent on the categories of the trained network. Existing trained networks can be reused for feature extraction. In order to determine how to generate good feature vectors, we tested different state-of-the-art CNNs [4, 5, 7, 17] regarding their image retrieval quality. The models were chosen by their classification accuracy and their diversity. The networks were trained using the ILSVRC2012 data set [14] or the entire ImageNet set. To evaluate the retrieval quality, we used a test set with 1000 images and 100 categories. Neither the images nor the categories were part of the trainging image sets. Best results in regard to the mean average precision (MAP) were obtained using the Deep Residual Learning Networks from [5]. The 2048 activations before the fully connected layer of ResNet-200 were taken as initial feature vectors. By applying a L1-normalization followed by a PCA we could improve the retrieval quality and compress the feature vectors to only 64 dimensions stored as byte values. The best metric for comparing these feature vectors was the L1 distance.

3.2 Building the Image Graph

The image graph has to be constructed such that similar images are connected and other related images can be reached by navigating the edges of the graph. For a non-hierarchical image graph the following requirements are to be met for each image:

(a) Connected images should be very similar.
(b) The number of connections should not be too high or low.
(c) The path to any other images should be as short as possible. This implies that the graph needs to be connected.

The definition of a general optimization rule for building the graph is rather difficult and it is not clear how these requirements should be weighted. In [2] we have presented an algorithm to construct a hierarchical image graph. To fulfill requirement (a) we used an edge swapping scheme. For requirement (b) we decided to keep the number of connections constant and to connect each image with four other images. Requirement (c) was simplified to only check the connectivity of the entire graph.

The image graph is built in three steps. First all images are sorted using a torus shaped 2D-SOM. The positions of the sorted images serve as initial non-hierarchical graph: Every image is connected with its four adjacent neighbors (Figure 2, top). In the next step this graph is improved by swapping edges. Two non-touching edges are swapped if this decreases the sum of the edge distances (1). Each swap improves the overall quality of the image graph. Swapping is stopped when the improvement gets too small.

$$\text{dist}_{AX} + \text{dist}_{EY} < \text{dist}_{AE} + \text{dist}_{XY} \quad (1)$$

The final step consists of generating hierarchical versions of the previously constructed non-hierarchical graph. The graph of the next hierarchy level is initialized as a copy of the actual graph. By successively removing images that are very similar to their connected neighbors a reduced graph is obtained. If image A is removed (Figure 2, bottom), the images B, C, D and E are reconnected with two new edges depending on the minimum of $\text{dist}_{BC} + \text{dist}_{DE}$, $\text{dist}_{BD} + \text{dist}_{CE}$, and $\text{dist}_{BE} + \text{dist}_{CD}$. For each hierarchy level three quarters of the images are removed, as this corresponds to a resolution reduction by a factor of two on a 2D map.

Building the image graph requires to calculate distances between image pairs. If the number of images is too high, only a sparse distance lookup table containing a set of the most similar images can be used. A dense lookup table would be to large due to the quadratic storage requirements. However, as our image features are rather small, the L1-distances between image features can also be computed on the fly. The memory requirements for storing the graph are linear with respect to the number of images.

Compared to the graph-building process described above we have improved the algorithm in several aspects. Random edge swapping is a way to generate good image graphs, however, the process is rather slow and the quality of the graphs varies, depending on the initial sorting of the SOM and the order in which edge swaps were tested. This signifies that the optimization process easily gets stuck in local minima. One way to improve the final graph quality is to allow temporal degradations by modifying Equation (1) to

$$\text{dist}_{AX} + \text{dist}_{EY} - \text{dist}_{AE} - \text{dist}_{XY} < -\theta_t \qquad (2)$$
$$\text{with} \quad \theta_{t+1} = \beta\theta_t \quad \text{and} \quad \beta < 1$$

The initial value of the swapping threshold θ_0 is set to the average distance value. With each iteration the value of θ_t is gradually decreased towards zero by a factor β less than one. This results in a process like simulated annealing, and leads to image graphs with better quality, but the choice of the optimal factor β is not obvious.

However, the main remaining problem is the slow convergence of this approach. The main reason for this is the low probability of finding two edges that improve the graph quality if they are swapped. Despite the quadratic time complexity for building the graph, we have developed an algorithm that speeds up the process significantly. Instead of trying to find pairs of edges to be swapped, we use Algorithm 1 to improve the graph. The probability of finding a sequence of edge reconnections that in sum improve the graph quality is much higher compared to previous approach, in addition this approach is parameter free. Figure 3 shows a comparison of the previous and the improved edge swapping algorithm. It also turned out that presorting using a SOM is not necessary. Building the graph can be started with a random assignment where every image is connected to four other images. A further speedup can be achieved by tracking the distances of the linked images. Edges with high distances are chosen with higher probability. Applying these improvements allows to build a graph of one million images in one hour on a single core using an Intel Xeon E3-1230 v3 CPU.

Algorithm 1: Improved Edge Swapping Algorithm

Remove a random $edge_{kl}$ (connecting $image_k$ and $image_l$)
$gain = dist_{kl}$
for $i \leftarrow 1$ *to* $maxTries$ **do**
  Connect $image_l$ with $image_m$, which is a random image from the list of the most similar images of $image_l$
  $gain = gain - dist_{lm}$
  From $image_m$ remove the edge with highest distance (let this be $edge_{mn}$ and $image_n$)
  $gain = gain + dist_{mn}$
  if $gain - dist_{kn} > 0$ **then**
    Connect $image_n$ with $image_k$, **return** // improvement
  else
    $image_l \leftarrow image_n$
  end
end
Undo all changes, **return** // no improvement was found

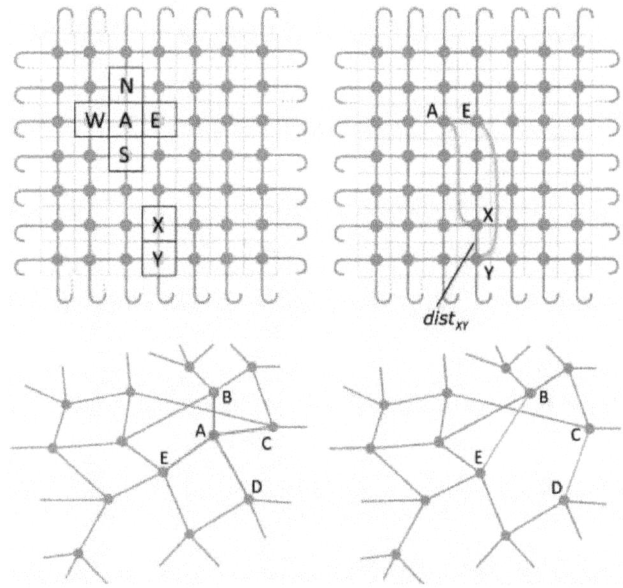

Figure 2: Top left: initial image graph based on 2D-sorting, top right: edges are swapped if this decreases the total distance. Bottom: The next hierarchy level is generated by successively removing images with low edge distances.

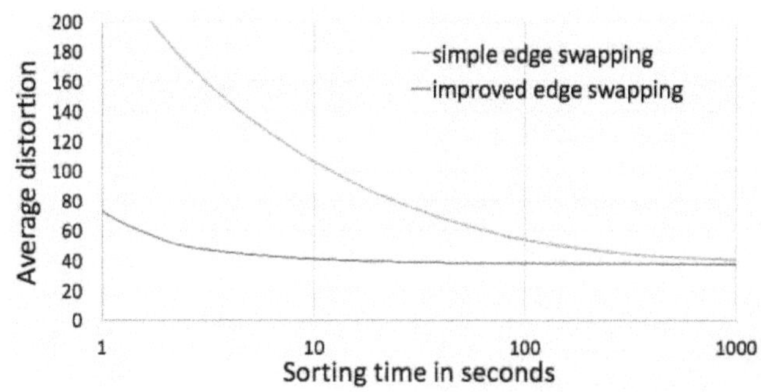

Figure 3: Quality over time for building a graph with 10000 RGB colors, improved edge swapping is significantly faster.

3.3 Visualizing and Navigating the Graph

As described before, a 2D projection of the entire graph cannot preserve the complex image relationships and will result in similarity discontinuities. Our approach is to combine the graph navigation with a 2D projection. By dynamically querying the image graph, projecting and showing only a sub-graph, it is possible to preserve the complex inter-image relationships for display and navigation. Starting from an image in focus, the connected edges are recursively followed until the desired amount of neighboring images has been retrieved. In a next step these images are sorted with a SOM, which maps the images according to their similarities onto a regular 2D image map (Figure 4). If the user does not find the desired image a user action may be necessary to navigate to other parts of the graph. This is achieved by dragging the 2D-map such

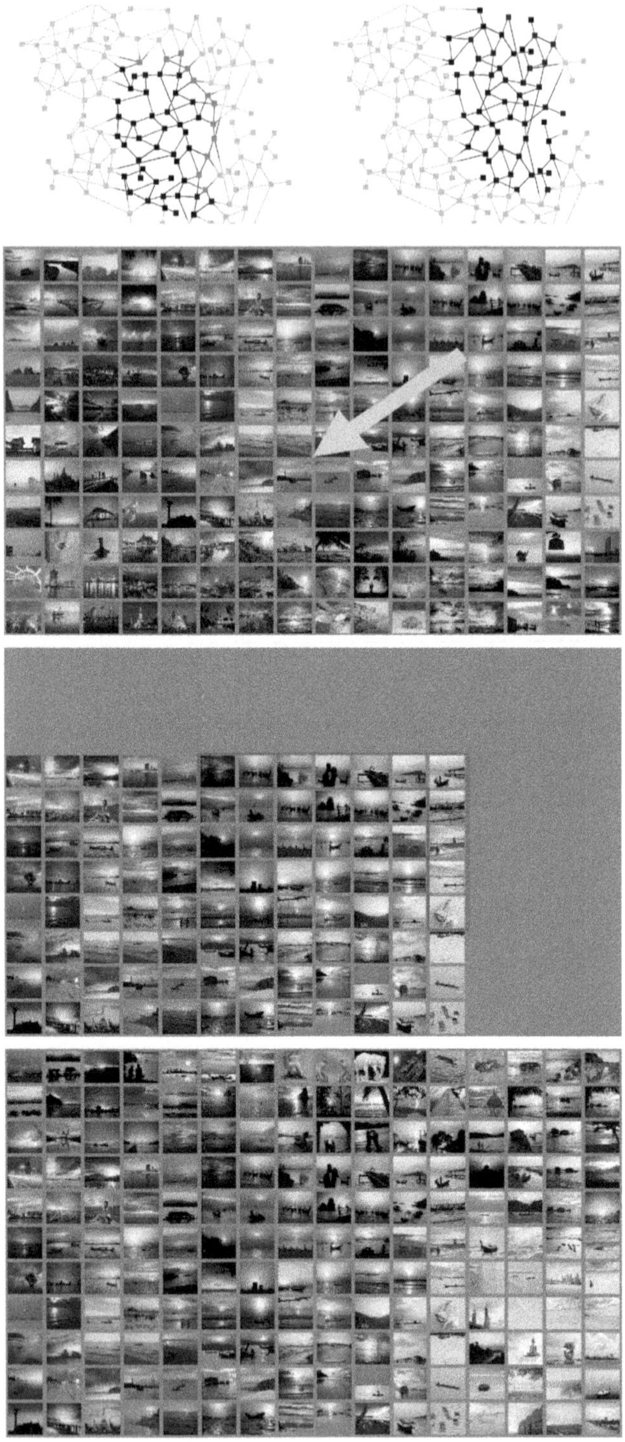

Figure 4: Navigating the graph. Dragging the map (indicated by the arrow) will change the sub-graph to be displayed. The images which are used to retrieve further images from the graph are indicated in red. Previously displayed images that remain in the view port keep their positions. Newly retrieved images are visually sorted and added to the map.

that the region where the searched images are anticipated becomes visible. Dragging the map moves some images out of the viewport and leaves some empty space on the opposite side. The inverse direction of the mouse drag indicates the images of interest (shown in red in Figure 4) and instructs the system to retrieve their neighboring vertices from the graph. Images that are already displayed or just have been moved out of the viewport are ignored. The newly retrieved images are mapped to the most suitable empty places, being defined by the highest surrounding image similarities. This sorting again is performed using a SOM, however the positions of the previously displayed images remain unchanged.

If the total number of retrieved images is chosen to be larger than the number of images that are shown in the viewport, then the "newly" revealed images can be pre-sorted. This will give the impression as if a large continuous map was available. To emphasize a realistic navigation experience previous arrangements are cached.

The user may change the zoom factor to get an overview or to see more similar images. In this case the closest sub-graph of the next hierarchy level needs to be selected and displayed. In order for the user not to get lost a smooth transition from the old map to the new map is performed.

4 DEMO SYSTEM

We have implemented a prototype of the new image browsing system. The user interface and experience is very similar to our picsbuffet image browser (Figure 1). However, there are much less abrupt changes of image concepts.

As the entire image graph is stored, the adaptation to a user interaction can be performed very quickly. The only needed operations are the retrieval of the connected images and their sorting. Both steps can be done very efficiently in a fraction of a second.

If a new image is added to the graph, the four most similar images will be connected with the new image. This will change the number of edges, but the visualization process can cope with varying numbers of connections per image. The same is true for removed images. For an image to be removed, all its connections have to be removed as well. If the image collection has undergone substantial changes, it might be useful to reorganize the entire image graph in order to keep the number of connections per image constant. An implementation of this demo can be found at www.visual-computing.com

5 CONCLUSION & FUTURE WORK

We have presented a new approach to visually explore large collections of untagged images. Organizing all images with a graph helps to preserve inter-image relations much better than static 2D sortings. As subgraphs are projected on a 2D map the user can navigate the image collection similar to interactive maps and will not be aware of the underlying graph structure.

Future work will focus on further speeding up the graph building process by either using fast presorting techniques or by better determining possible edge swap candidates. In addition we will enable visual image exploration using keywords. If keywords are available for the images then it is very easy to use a keyword search to directly access the most interesting sub-graph. For collections with untagged images we determine feature vectors of typical keywords, which can be used as search query.

REFERENCES

[1] Kai Uwe Barthel, Nico Hezel, and Radek Mackowiak. 2015. ImageMap - Visually Browsing Millions of Images.. In *MMM (2) (Lecture Notes in Computer Science)*, Xiangjian He, Suhuai Luo, Dacheng Tao, Changsheng Xu, Jie Yang, and Muhammad Abul Hasan (Eds.), Vol. 8936. Springer, 287–290.

[2] Kai Uwe Barthel, Nico Hezel, and Radek Mackowiak. 2016. *Navigating a Graph of Scenes for Exploring Large Video Collections.* Springer International Publishing, Cham. 418–423 pages. DOI: https://doi.org/10.1007/978-3-319-27674-8_43

[3] Jau-Yuen Chen, Charles A. Bouman, and John C. Dalton. 1998. Similarity pyramids for browsing and organization of large image databases.. In *Human Vision and Electronic Imaging (SPIE Proceedings)*, Bernice E. Rogowitz and Thrasyvoulos N. Pappas (Eds.), Vol. 3299. SPIE, 563–575.

[4] Kaiming He, Xiangyu Zhang, Shaoqing Ren, and Jian Sun. 2016. Deep Residual Learning for Image Recognition.. In *CVPR.* IEEE Computer Society, 770–778.

[5] Kaiming He, Xiangyu Zhang, Shaoqing Ren, and Jian Sun. 2016. Identity Mappings in Deep Residual Networks.. In *ECCV (4) (Lecture Notes in Computer Science)*, Bastian Leibe, Jiri Matas, Nicu Sebe, and Max Welling (Eds.), Vol. 9908. Springer, 630–645.

[6] Daniel Heesch. 2008. A Survey of Browsing Models for Content Based Image Retrieval. *Multimedia Tools Appl.* 40, 2 (Nov. 2008), 261–284. DOI: https://doi.org/10.1007/s11042-008-0207-2

[7] Sergey Ioffe and Christian Szegedy. 2015. Batch Normalization: Accelerating Deep Network Training by Reducing Internal Covariate Shift.. In *ICML (JMLR Workshop and Conference Proceedings)*, Francis R. Bach and David M. Blei (Eds.), Vol. 37. JMLR.org, 448–456.

[8] Yushi Jing, Henry A. Rowley, Charles R. Rosenberg, Jingbin Wang, Ming Zhao, and Michele Covell. 2010. Google image swirl, a large-scale content-based image browsing system.. In *ICME.* IEEE Computer Society, 267.

[9] Alex Krizhevsky, Ilya Sutskever, and Geoffrey E. Hinton. 2012. ImageNet Classification with Deep Convolutional Neural Networks.. In *NIPS*, Peter L. Bartlett, Fernando C. N. Pereira, Christopher J. C. Burges, Léon Bottou, and Kilian Q. Weinberger (Eds.). 1106–1114.

[10] Guoping Qiu, Jeremy Morris, and Xunli Fan. 2007. Visual guided navigation for image retrieval. *Pattern Recognition* 40, 6 (2007), 1711–1721.

[11] Shi Qiu, Xiaogang Wang, and Xiaoou Tang. 2013. Visual Semantic Complex Network for Web Images.. In *ICCV.* IEEE Computer Society, 3623–3630.

[12] Novi Quadrianto, Kristian Kersting, Tinne Tuytelaars, and Wray L. Buntine. 2010. Beyond 2D-grids: a dependence maximization view on image browsing.. In *Multimedia Information Retrieval* (2010-04-12), James Ze Wang, Nozha Boujemaa, Nuria Oliver Ramirez, and Apostol Natsev (Eds.). ACM, 339–348.

[13] Ali Sharif Razavian, Hossein Azizpour, Josephine Sullivan, and Stefan Carlsson. 2014. CNN Features off-the-shelf: an Astounding Baseline for Recognition. *CoRR* abs/1403.6382 (2014).

[14] Olga Russakovsky, Jia Deng, Hao Su, Jonathan Krause, Sanjeev Satheesh, Sean Ma, Zhiheng Huang, Andrej Karpathy, Aditya Khosla, Michael S. Bernstein, Alexander C. Berg, and Fei-Fei Li. 2015. ImageNet Large Scale Visual Recognition Challenge. *International Journal of Computer Vision* 115, 3 (2015), 211–252.

[15] K. Schoeffmann, D. Ahlstroem, W. Bailer, and C. Cobarzan. 2013. The Video Browser Showdown: a live evaluation of interactive video search tools. *International Journal of Multimedia Information Retrieval, Springer Verlag London* (2013), pp. 1–15.

[16] Grant Strong, Enamul Hoque, Minglun Gong, and Orland Hoeber. 2010. *Organizing and Browsing Image Search Results Based on Conceptual and Visual Similarities.* Springer Berlin Heidelberg, Berlin, Heidelberg, 481–490. DOI: https://doi.org/10.1007/978-3-642-17274-8_47

[17] Christian Szegedy, Wei Liu, Yangqing Jia, Pierre Sermanet, Scott E. Reed, Dragomir Anguelov, Dumitru Erhan, Vincent Vanhoucke, and Andrew Rabinovich. 2015. Going deeper with convolutions.. In *CVPR.* IEEE Computer Society, 1–9.

[18] Jingdong Wang, Liyan Jia, and Xian-Sheng Hua. 2011. Interactive browsing via diversified visual summarization for image search results. *Multimedia Syst.* 17, 5 (2011), 379–391.

A Generic Framework for Social Event Analysis

Shengsheng Qian, Tianzhu Zhang, and Changsheng Xu
National Lab of Pattern Recognition, Institute of Automation, CAS, Beijing, China
University of Chinese Academy of Sciences, Beijing, China
{shengsheng.qian,tzzhang,csxu}@nlpr.ia.ac.cn

ABSTRACT

Social event is something that occurs at specific place and time associated with some specific actions, and it consists of many stories over time. With the explosion of Web 2.0 platforms, a popular social event that is happening around us and around the world can spread very fast. As a result, social event analysis becomes more and more important for users to understand the whole evolutionary trend of social event over time. However, it is very challenging to do social event analysis because social event data from different social media sites have multi-modal, multi-domain, and large-scale properties. The goal of our research is to design advanced multimedia techniques to deal with the above issues and establish an effective and robust social event analysis framework for social event representation, detection, tracking and evolution analysis. (1) For social event representation, we propose a novel cross-domain collaborative learning algorithm based on non-parametric Bayesian dictionary learning model. It can make use of the shared domain priors and modality priors to collaboratively learn the data's representations by considering the domain discrepancy and the multi-modal property. (2) For social event detection, we propose a boosted multi-modal supervised Latent Dirichlet Allocation model. It can effectively exploit multi-modality information and utilize boosting weighted sampling strategy for large-scale data processing. (3) For social event tracking, we propose a novel multi-modal event topic model, which can effectively model the correlations between textual and visual modalities, and obtain their topics over time. (4) For social event evolution analysis, we propose a novel multi-modal multi-view topic-opinion mining model to conduct fined-grained topic and opinion analysis for social events from multiple social media sites collaboratively. It can discover multi-modal topics and the corresponding opinions over time to understand the evolutionary processes of social event. Extensive experimental results show that the proposed algorithms perform favorably against state-of-the-art methods for social event analysis.

KEYWORDS

social event; multi-modal; multi-domain; large-scale

ICMR '17, June 6–9, 2017, Bucharest, Romania

ACM ISBN 978-1-4503-4701-3/17/06...$15.00
DOI: http://dx.doi.org/10.1145/3078971.3079007

ACM Reference format:
Shengsheng Qian, Tianzhu Zhang, and Changsheng Xu. 2017. A Generic Framework for Social Event Analysis. In *Proceedings of ICMR '17, June 6–9, 2017, Bucharest, Romania*, , 4 pages.
DOI: http://dx.doi.org/10.1145/3078971.3079007

1 INTRODUCTION

With the rapid development of Internet, more and more social networking sites (e.g., Flickr, YouTube, Facebook, and Google News) appear and allow users to conveniently share their ideas, pictures, posts, activities, and events. Therefore, when a popular event is happening around us, it can spread very fast in different social media sites with substantial amounts of multimedia data including images, videos, and texts. Most of these multimedia contents associated with social events uploaded by users are related to some specific topics, and it is very time-consuming for people to manually identify or cluster them to obtain the whole topic evolution of an event in real-world scenarios. For example, users may want to know the whole evolutionary process of the event "The Arab Spring" from start to end. Given the well-defined query, users can search it on Google and obtain a lot of related information. However, all returned results only tend to show what has happened recently and the related information associated with the event is too scattered. As a result, users have to repeatedly switch back and forth from one to another in order to completely understand the theme of the event. Usually, it is time-consuming for users to browse such huge documents and almost impossible to capture the whole evolutionary process of the event. Therefore, it is important and necessary to propose a generic framework for social event analysis to know the evolutionary trend of social event over time automatically. Based on the framework, for the event "The Arab Spring", we can visualize its whole evolutionary process in the map over time, and it is much easier for users to understand what has happened to the Arab Spring.

To achieve this goal, we propose a generic framework as shown in Figure 1 for social event analysis including social event representation, detection, tracking, and evolution analysis. In the proposed framework, we have designed specific model for each task to overcome the challenges, such as multi-modal, multi-domain, and large-scale properties in social event data. The details are as follows. (1) Social event representation aims to learn the semantic-based multi-modal event description by exploiting the multi-modal data from multi-domain social media resources, including the textual information and visual information. To achieve this goal, we propose a generic cross-domain collaborative learning algorithm based on the non-parametric Bayesian dictionary learning model. As a result, our model can effectively make use of the virtues of different information sources to complement and enhance each

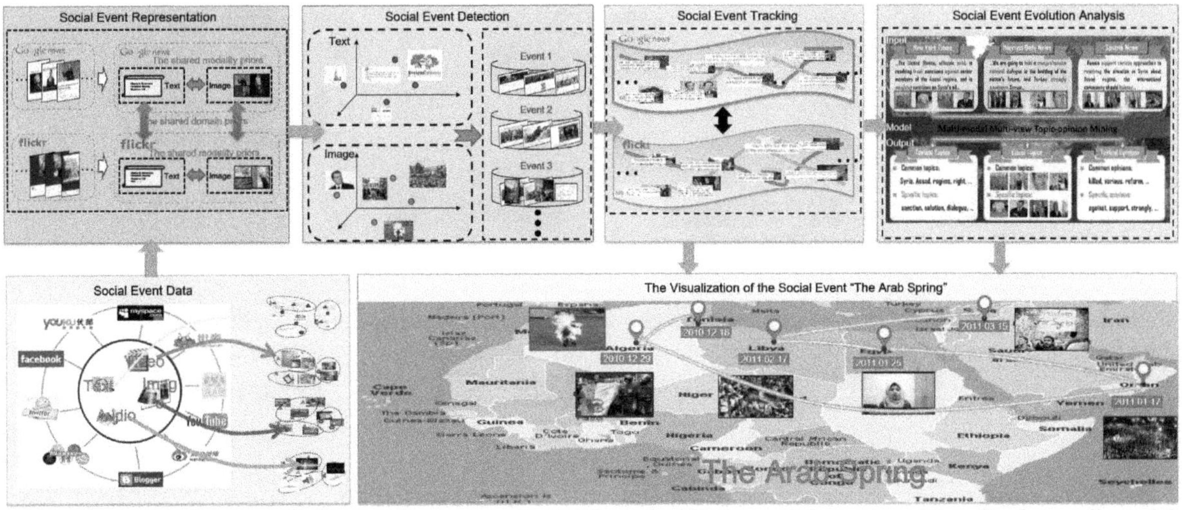

Figure 1: A generic framework for social event analysis. The input is the social event multimedia data collected from multiple social media sites. The proposed framework includes four major parts: social event representation, social event detection, social event tracking, and social event evolution analysis. After doing social event analysis, we can visualize the whole evolutionary process of social event in the map over time.

other for feature representation. (2) Social event detection is to automatically mine and identify social events from large-scale social media data. To exploit the supervised category information of the large-scale data, we propose a novel boosted multi-modal supervised Latent Dirichlet Allocation by integrating a supervised topic model in the boosting framework, which can effectively process large-scale data iteratively. (3) The goal of social event tracking is to obtain the evolutionary processes of social events over time. To track multiple social events from multiple platforms with multiple modalities, we propose a novel incremental topic model learning algorithm to obtain the evolutionary trends of social events and generate effective event summary details over time. (4) To do social event evolution analysis, we propose a novel multi-modal multi-view topic-opinion mining model by considering multi-view and multi-modal properties for topic and opinion learning in multiple collection sources. As a result, the proposed model can discover multi-modal topics and the corresponding opinions in multiple views, and visualize the evolutionary process of social event over time. The above four models are closely related with each other, and extensive experimental results have demonstrated the effectiveness of the proposed models for social event analysis.

2 SOCIAL EVENT ANALYSIS

In this Section, we introduce the proposed generic framework for social event analysis including social event representation, detection, tracking, and evolution analysis.

Social Event Representation: The goal of social event representation is to utilize the multi-modal data from multi-domain social media resources to learn semantic multi-modal event description. In the real-world scenario, different social media platforms (different domains), such as Google News and Flickr, have large amounts of multimedia data, including texts, images, and videos, related with the same social event. If we can aggregate the relevant data across different domains for social event analysis, they can complement and enhance each other, especially when the strengths of one domain complement the weaknesses of the other. Our goal is to design an effective algorithm to exploit the multi-domain multi-modal data for social event representation.

Recently, most existing cross domain learning methods have been proposed, and could be categorized into two categories including (1) cross-domain feature learning in multimedia by adopting a cross-domain constraint to make different domains share a common feature space [13]. (2) personalization recommendation in social links by modeling cross-network user behaviors [1].The existing methods are not suitable for social event representation learning, because social event data have multi-domain, multi-modal, and supervised properties.

To address the above issues, we propose a generic cross-domain collaborative learning algorithm via a discriminative non-parametric Bayesian dictionary learning model for cross-domain data analysis [8]. Compared with existing cross-domain learning methods, our proposed algorithm mainly has the following advantages: (1) To deal with the domain discrepancy, we adopt the shared domain priors across multiple domains to make them share a common feature space. (2) To make use of the multi-modal property, we learn the sparse representation of multi-modal data by introducing the shared modality priors to infer the sparse structure shared among different modalities of media data. (3) To make use of class label information of cross-domain data, we learn the discriminative dictionary which is shared by all the classes and utilize the latent probability vector to control the probability of selection of the dictionary atoms for a single class data. As a result, the proposed algorithm can effectively explore the virtues of different information sources to complement and enhance each other for the feature representation learning of multi-modal cross domain data.

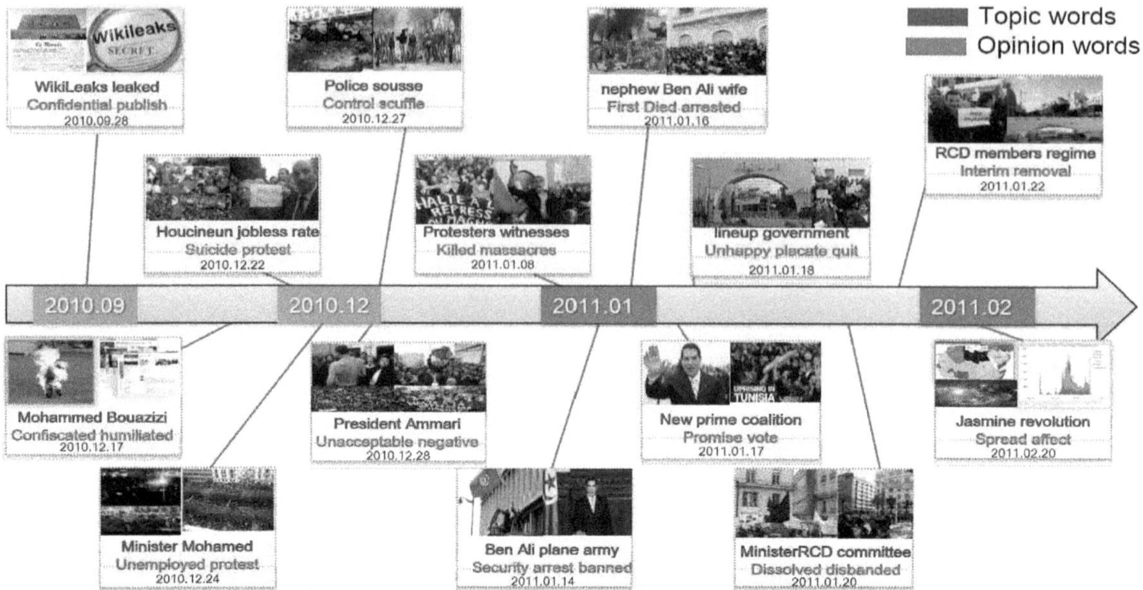

Figure 2: The learned topics and opinions for social event "Syria civil war" based on the proposed generic framework. We can visualize the learned topic and opinion words over time. Based on the visualization, it is quite clear to know the whole evolutionary process of social event.

Social Event Detection: The social event detection is to automatically discover and identify relevant social events from the large-scale social media data. In the real-world scenario, there are a large amounts of event data uploaded by users from different social media sites, and it is very difficult and time-consuming to manually identify or cluster them. Therefore, automatically mining and identifying social events from massive social media data is important and helpful to better browse, search and monitor social events by users or governments. Recently, how to address these challenges for automatically mining and monitoring social events has drawn much attention in the multimedia research community, such as social event classification [4], and investigating event detection [2]. Most of these methods mainly focus on feature designing for social event modeling, such as textual features, visual feature or their combination. However, most of these methods ignore the semantic relationship among multiple modalities and the multi-class property of social events. In the multi-modal topic model methods, such as mmLDA [12] and Corr-LDA [3], they can consider the multi-modal information to obtain the semantic feature representation among multiple modalities. However, they have two limitations: (1) they do not utilize the supervised category information to boost the classification accuracy. (2) all the above topic models ignore the document weight distribution and it is time-consuming to train the models on a large-scale dataset.

To deal with these issues, we propose a novel boosted multi-modal supervised Latent Dirichlet Allocation for social event classification by integrating a supervised topic model, denoted as multi-modal supervised Latent Dirichlet Allocation, in the boosting framework [10]. Compared with existing methods, our model mainly has the following advantages: (1) Our BMM-SLDA can effectively exploit the multi-modality and the multi-class property of social events jointly, and make use of the supervised category label information to classify multi-class social event directly. (2) It is suitable for large-scale data analysis by utilizing boosting weighted sampling strategy to iteratively select a small subset of data to efficiently train the corresponding topic models. (3) It effectively exploits social event structure by the document weight distribution with classification error and can iteratively learn new topic model to correct the previously misclassified event documents.

Social Event Tracking: The goal of social event tracking is to associate all stories of social event over time. It can provide informative summary details on what has happened in the real world and could yield important knowledge on the evolutionary trends of social event over time. Moreover, social event tracking is helpful to browse, search, and monitor social events and understand their evolution by users. Users may be interested in multiple events and their evolution. For instance, they might want to know the evolutionary trend of social event such as "the war in Afghanistan" or "the 2011 England Riot". Thus, for the better understanding, it is important to obtain the whole processes of multiple events by social event tracking. Many methods have been proposed, such as social event tracking[2] and social event evolution[14]. While the existing methods mainly focus on feature designing to calculate the similarity of social event documents, which can improve experimental performance, the semantic relationship and importance of those features have not been studied in details. To deal with the above issues, many topic models [3, 7] have been proposed to explore multi-modal topics for social event analysis. However, these methods need the strong relativity between the textual and visual information, and do not consider richer information in multi-modal event documents including long textual information and the corresponding visual information from Flickr or Google News, which cannot be suitable for social event modeling.

To overcome these issues, we propose a novel multi-modal event topic model to effectively fuse multi-modality information and consider visual-representative topics and non-visual-representative topics together [11]. Based on this model, we propose a novel multi-modal social event tracking and evolution algorithm to obtain the evolutionary trends of social events and generate effective event summary details over time. Compared with existing methods, our model mainly has the following advantages: (1) The model is suitable for multimedia documents from various social media platforms, which is able to not only effectively capture their multi-modal topics, but also obtain the evolutionary trends of social events over time. (2) The model can exploit the multi-modal property of social event, which can effectively model social media documents including long text with related images and learn the correlations between textual and visual modalities to separate the visual-representative topics and non-visual-representative topics. (3) We propose a novel incremental topic model for social event tracking, which can obtain the whole evolutionary processes of events with textual and visual topics over time and help understand the events.

Social Event Evolution Analysis: The social evolution analysis is achieved via topic-opinion Mining, which is to exploit multiple social media resources to conduct the fined-grained topic-opinion analysis. For example, for the political controversial events such as "The crises in Libya", every news media over a controversial topic not only has many different aspects, but also has its own opinion tendencies, and there is no absolute true opinion for this topic. Therefore, social event fined-grained topic-opinion mining is important to automatically understand the topics of the hot political controversial social events and the corresponding opinions in different news medias. How to conduct topic-opinion mining in multiple views across different collections has attracted much research interest. Basically, there are two major research topics: (1) A fine-grained topic analysis by adopting an extended cross-collections LDA to discover common topics across all collections as well as model their similarities and differences across multiple collections [6]. (2) The combination of topic and opinion mining by adopting the extended topic model methods or other latent variable models to learn the topic and the corresponding opinion simultaneously [5]. These two research topics focus on topic and opinion mining in textual content analysis by utilizing a latent model for cross-collection data modeling. However, both the topics and opinions in multiple collections have the multi-view property, and the media data have the multi-modal property. The existing methods do not still consider these properties well.

To deal with these issues, we propose a novel multi-modal multi-view topic-opinion mining model for social event analysis in multiple collection sources [9]. Compared with existing topic-opinion mining methods, our model mainly has the following advantages: (1) The model can effectively take into account multi-modal and multi-view properties jointly in a unified and principled way for the fine-grained social event modeling. (2) The model is able to not only discover multi-modal common topics from all collections as well as summarize the similarities and differences of these collections along each specific topic, but also automatically mine multi-view opinions on the learned topics across different collections. (3) The model is general and can also be applied for many other applications in multimedia, such as opinion mining and sentiment analysis, multi-view association visualization, and topic-opinion mining for movie review.

3 RESULTS

We have conducted both qualitative and quantitative evaluations for social event representation, detection, tracking, and evolution analysis. All results have demonstrated the effectiveness of the proposed models for social event analysis. In Figure 2, we show an example of the learned topics and opinions over time for the social event "Syria civil war".

4 CONCLUSION

In this research, we propose a generic framework for social event analysis including social event representation, detection, tracking and evolution analysis. The extensive results have demonstrated the effectiveness of the proposed models. In the future, we will do some research on social event prediction and develop a real system for social event analysis.

5 ACKNOWLEDGMENT

This work was supported in part by National Natural Science Foundation of China (No. 61225009, 61303173, 61432019, 61572498)

REFERENCES

[1] Fabian Abel, Samur Araújo, Qi Gao, and Geert-Jan Houben. 2011. Analyzing Cross-System User Modeling on the Social Web. In *Web Engineering - 11th International Conference, ICWE 2011, Paphos, Cyprus, June 20-24, 2011*. 28–43.

[2] James Allan, Ron Papka, and Victor Lavrenko. 1998. On-line New Event Detection and Tracking. In *SIGIR*. 37–45.

[3] David M. Blei and Michael I. Jordan. 2003. Modeling Annotated Data. In *SIGIR*. 127–134.

[4] Xueliang Liu and Benoit Huet. 2013. Heterogeneous Features and Model Selection for Event-based Media Classification. In *ICMR*. 151–158.

[5] Samaneh Moghaddam and Martin Ester. 2011. ILDA: Interdependent LDA Model for Learning Latent Aspects and Their Ratings from Online Product Reviews. In *SIGIR '11*. 665–674.

[6] Michael Paul and Roxana Girju. 2009. Cross-cultural Analysis of Blogs and Forums with Mixed-collection Topic Models. In *EMNLP '09*. 1408–1417.

[7] Duangmanee Putthividhya, Hagai Thomas Attias, and Srikantan S. Nagarajan. 2010. Topic regression multi-modal Latent Dirichlet Allocation for image annotation.. In *CVPR*. 3408–3415.

[8] Shengsheng Qian, Tianzhu Zhang, Richang Hong, and Changsheng Xu. 2015. Cross-Domain Collaborative Learning in Social Multimedia. In *Proceedings of the 23rd Annual ACM Conference on Multimedia Conference, MM '15, Brisbane, Australia, October 26 - 30, 2015*. 99–108.

[9] Shengsheng Qian, Tianzhu Zhang, and Changsheng Xu. 2016. Multi-modal Multi-view Topic-opinion Mining for Social Event Analysis. In *Proceedings of the 2016 ACM Conference on Multimedia Conference, MM 2016, Amsterdam, The Netherlands, October 15-19, 2016*. 2–11.

[10] Shengsheng Qian, Tianzhu Zhang, Changsheng Xu, and M. Shamim Hossain. 2014. Social Event Classification via Boosted Multimodal Supervised Latent Dirichlet Allocation. *TOMCCAP* 11, 2 (2014), 27:1–27:22.

[11] Shengsheng Qian, Tianzhu Zhang, Changsheng Xu, and Jie Shao. 2016. Multi-Modal Event Topic Model for Social Event Analysis. *IEEE Trans. Multimedia* 18, 2 (2016), 233–246.

[12] Daniel Ramage, Paul Heymann, Christopher D. Manning, and Hector Garcia-Molina. 2009. Clustering the Tagged Web. In *WSDM*. ACM.

[13] Xiaoshan Yang, Tianzhu Zhang, and Changsheng Xu. 2015. Cross-Domain Feature Learning in Multimedia. *IEEE Transactions on Multimedia* 17, 1 (2015), 64–78.

[14] Jianwen Zhang, Yangqiu Song, Changshui Zhang, and Shixia Liu. 2010. Evolutionary Hierarchical Dirichlet Processes for Multiple Correlated Time-varying Corpora. In *KDD '10*.

Semi-Automatic Retrieval of Relevant Segments from Laparoscopic Surgery Videos

Stefan Petscharnig
Alpen-Adria-Universität Klagenfurt
Universitätsstraße 65-67
Klagenfurt, Austria 9020
stefan.petscharnig@itec.aau.at

ABSTRACT

Over the last decades, progress in medical technology and imaging technology enabled the technique of minimally invasive surgery. In addition, multimedia technologies allow for retrospective analyses of surgeries. The accumulated videos and images allow for a speed-up in documentation, easier medical case assessment across surgeons, training young surgeons, as well as they find the usage in medical research. Considering a surgery lasting for hours of routine work, surgeons only need to see short video segments of interest to assess a case. Surgeons do not have the time to manually extract video sequences of their surgeries from their big multimedia databases as they do not have the resources for this time-consuming task. The thesis deals with the questions of how to semantically classify video frames using Convolutional Neural Networks into different semantic concepts of surgical actions and anatomical structures. In order to achieve this goal, the capabilities of predefined CNN architectures and transfer learning in the laparoscopic video domain are investigated. The results are expected to improve by domain-specific adaptation of the CNN input layers, i.e. by fusion of the image with motion and relevance information. Finally, the thesis investigates to what extent surgeons' needs are covered with the proposed extraction of relevant scenes.

CCS CONCEPTS

• **Information systems → Video search**; • **Computing methodologies →** *Supervised learning by classification*;

KEYWORDS

Endoscopic Video Retrieval, Endoscopic Image Classification

ACM Reference format:
Stefan Petscharnig. 2017. Semi-Automatic Retrieval of Relevant Segments from Laparoscopic Surgery Videos. In *Proceedings of ICMR '17, June 6–9, 2017, Bucharest, Romania*, , 5 pages.
DOI: http://dx.doi.org/10.1145/3078971.30790082

ICMR '17, June 6–9, 2017, Bucharest, Romania
 ACM ISBN 978-1-4503-4701-3/17/06...$15.00
DOI: http://dx.doi.org/10.1145/3078971.30790082

1 INTRODUCTION

Minimally invasive surgery methods aim at reducing wound healing time as well as associated pain and risk of infections. These methods were enabled by the advance of several medical and technical technologies, such as operating methods, electro surgery, precision instruments, and imaging technology. Therefore, a camera is introduced into the human body via a small incision enabling surgeons to perform the surgery. During a surgery, the surgeon is able to record video as well as image data. The recorded data can later be used for documentation purpose, medical research, education of young surgeons, as well as for the improvement of surgery techniques. Thus, huge amounts of multimedia data are produced in such surgery contexts. Considering the fact that full surgeries last for hours of routine work and only minutes of medically relevant events, surgeons do not have the resources for a manual analysis of these huge amounts of data. In current practice, the additionally recorded images play a central role for quick assessment of a case. These images capture the important moments or situations of the corresponding surgery. Yet, the images on their own are not sufficient for a full, systematic documentation of a medical case in laparoscopic surgery (which is for example a necessity in medical research). In order to be able to share, discuss, and learn from medical cases, doctors need to be able to quickly extract relevant video scenes from surgeries showing important temporal dynamic information. The main problem is that manual browsing in such video collections is a tedious and time-consuming task.

The use case of relevant scene extraction is depicted in Figure 1. A surgeon is interested in retrieving a relevant scene of a specific operation from a multimedia database. Therefore, the surgeon selects an image captured during surgery. Using this query image, a bookmark (linking to the appropriate video and the corresponding playback time stamp) is created. Please note that in practice there is no way for a trivial interlinking of captured images and recorded videos and the multimedia databases can grow to thousands of hours of surgery videos. The boundaries of the relevant segment including the retrieved playback position are automatically identified. Current literature does not provide solutions for such use cases.

We aim at approaching the aforementioned problem based on two main building blocks. The first building block is a semantic classification of surgery frames, either belonging to a surgical action or anatomical structure category. On

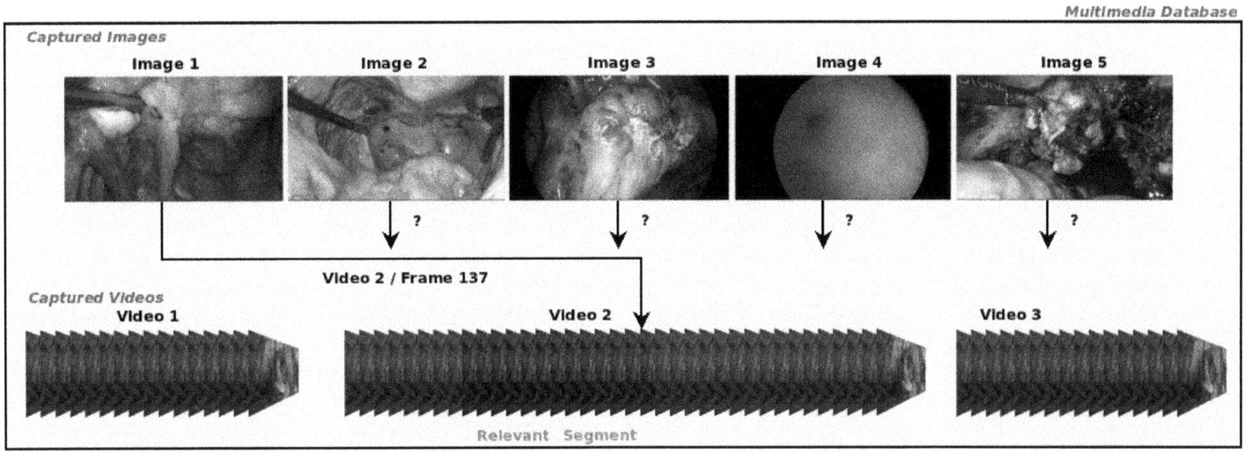

Figure 1: Use case overview: A surgeon browses the captured images which is interlinked to a video and playback time stamp. We aim at the extraction of the relevant scene containing the query image.

the short term, this will enable medical experts to browse surgeries by their chosen semantic content classes of interest and thereby speed-up the process of manual scene-extraction. In order to reach this objective, the thesis considers existing CNN architectures, transfer learning and domain-relevant input fusion. The second building block, is the automatic interlinking of a video segment and the corresponding manually captured images. As in the aforementioned use case, we aim at extracting the video and playback time stamp using state of the art methods of content base image retrieval. For the calculation of begin and end time of segments of interest, a domain-specific algorithm exploiting semantic similarity using the developed CNN models is developed.

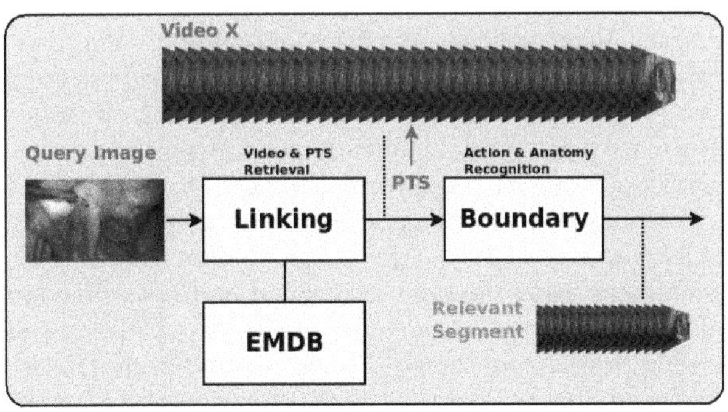

Figure 2: System overview: linking and boundary components extract a relevant scene from an endoscopic multimedia database (EMDB) given an image of interest.

A system approaching this problem consists of a linking and boundary component (c.f. Figure 2). Its input is a query image and a given endoscopic multimedia database (EMDB). Within the linking component, the system links the given query image to a video and a respective playback time stamp using a retrieval method, e.g. off-the-shelf CNN features (neural codes). The video and playback time stamp are input to the boundary component, which uses CNN-based action and anatomy recognition to determine the action at the current playback time stamp. The action recognition can be multi-modal, e.g. motion vectors or relevance masks from the video shall be considered as well. Using action and antomy recognition, we the boundary component determines an upper and lower time-bound for the relevant scene resulting in the output of the relevant scene.

2 RELATED WORK

This section describes work related to the thesis. For the use case of interstitial lung diseases, Li et al. [5] provide a simple CNN model containing a single convolutional layer. They yield per–class precision and recall between 0.8 and 0.9 for classification into five classes (normal, emphysema, ground glass, fibrosis, and micro-nodules) outperforming the SIFT feature as well as Restricted Boltzmann Machines. The authors of [2] propose a deep CNN model containing five convolutional layers for the classification of CT images into seven classes of interstitial lung diseases (healthy, ground glass opacity, micronodules, consolidation, reticulation, and honeycombing). Their results imply that, for this use case, their CNN approach outperforms other CNNs as well as state-of-the-art methods using handcrafted features. In the work of Yan et al. [23], a multi–stage deep learning framework is presented. Using the proposed framework, the authors try to solve the problem of body-part recognition in MRI images. In total, they achieve best performance regarding recall, precision and f–score compared against logistic regression, SVMs, and CNNs. The importance of CNNs in medical applications is also apparent from their use within other applications such as nucleus segmentation [22], polyp detection in colonoscopy videos [11], microcalcification detection in digital breast tomosynthesis [17], mitosis detection in breast cancer histology [1], and short–term breast cancer risk prediction [14]. Our work is delimited to the aforementioned research as in contrast to the classification of a state (e.g., healthy or consolidation, type of tissue), we aim at classifying both, anatomical structures and surgical actions. Furthermore, there haven't been any efforts made regarding the classification of images extracted from laparoscopic surgery videos. Fine tuning and transfer learning effects of CNNs were covered in recent literature [19, 20]. These pieces of work are based on the use cases of lymph node detection, interstitial lung disease classification, polyp detection and image quality assessment in colonoscopy, pulmonary embolism detection in computed tomography images, and intima-media boundary segmentation in ultrasonographic images. Their results imply that CNNs are suitable for computer aided diagnosis problems, and transfer learning from large–scale annotated natural image datasets is beneficial for performance. Due to the classical use cases of computer aided diagnosis, medical imaging research focuses on image classification. For colonic polyp classification, Riberio et al. proposed transfer learning using off-the-shelf CNN features [16]. For a comprehensive survey on deep learning in medical image analysis please refer to [6] In the domain of cataract surgery videos, Quellec et al. propose a temporal segmentation and recognition of tasks. The temporal segmentation is based on the detection of idle phases which is achieved by nearest neighbor search in a reference dataset [15]. Primus et al. provide a video segmentation for endoscopic surgeries based spatial and temporal motion changes [9]. For the use case of cholecystectomy, a special form of laparoscopic surgeries, Primus et al. provide a rule-based method to temporally segment a surgery into different phases [13]. The recognition of number and kind of used instrument (which was topic of their previous work [12]) act as main indication for a surgery phase. The work of Twinanda et al. [21] also focuses on the use case cholecystectomy. They successfully apply CNNs, SVMs and HHMMs for detection of surgical phases. Shot boundary detection in cholecystectomy surgery videos using Gaussian Mixture Models and a Variational Bayesian Algorithm was investigated by Loukas et al. [7]. The envisioned classification is different from the use cases mentioned above, as in cholecystectomy there are predefined surgical phases, whereas in other fields of laparoscopic surgery (such as as gynaecology) there is no general consensus for such surgical phases. Muenzer et al. [10] propose three irrelevance classes for endoscopic video frames: dark, blurry, and out of patient. Furthermore their work provides visual feature extraction methods to obtain irrelevance indicators for each class on a per-image basis as well as a framework for detecting irrelevant video segments of the three aforementioned categories. The problem of image to video linking for endoscopic surgeries (strictly speaking: retrieving a video from an endoscopic video database based on a query image) was already studied by Roldan-Carlos et al. [4], Beecks et al. [3], and Schoeffmann et al. [18]. In [4], retrieval based on global features (Color and Edge Directivity Descriptor CEDD, auto color correlogram, and pyramid histogram of oriented gradients PHOG) fusion methods by rank and score, as well as a localized version of CEDD using the SIMPLE approach on every fifth video frame is evaluated. They report that they were able to correctly map 78.3%, 78.5%, and 79.8% of the queries to the correct video sequence using the approaches Sum of Ranks, Sum of Scores, and SIMPLE-CEDD respectively. The work done in [3] was performed on the same dataset and also utilized a description for every fifth frame. The authors approached this problem by using feature signatures and also compared various signature matching distances to the baseline of [4]. Their results imply that feature signatures using a unidirectional approach based on L1 distance improved the state-of-the-art by approximately 10%. This work was improved by Schoeffmann et al. [18] by investigating further distance measures including signature matching distance (SMD), signature quadratic form distance (SQFD), and the earth movers distance (EMD) over various signature sizes. Their results imply that on the used dataset, the correct video segment can be retrieved for more than 88% of the query images. For more information on content-based methods in endoscopic images and videos, please refer to [8].

3 CONTRIBUTIONS

This section introduces the research questions and the methodology for approaching them. The main research questions are formulated in an abstract way and the contributions are summarized in concrete sub-questions following the description of the approach.

RQ 1: Transfer Learning and Multi-modal Classification of Laparoscopic Video Frames with Convolutional Neural Networks: How good can surgical actions and anatomy be recognized? This research question aims at the classification of semantic content classes in laparoscopic surgery videos based on a single-frame CNN classification model. Together with medical experts from LKH Villach, we define a set of surgical actions and anatomic structures relevant to laparoscopic surgeries in the special use case of gynecology. We plan to create a dataset with at least 2000 cross-validated images per class. We conduct a baseline evaluation by using off-the-shelf features extracted from an already pre-trained Convolutional Neural Network. We use these extracted features as input for an SVM classifier and measure its predictive performance, i.e. precision and recall. Furthermore, we evaluate training a CNN from scratch using the same predefined network architecture and compare the results. We also investigate whether transfer learning (initializing the CNN with weights from a network trained on another dataset) is beneficial in the domain of laparoscopic surgery in gynecology. Therefore, we consider different levels of transfer learning (by partially re-using the trained weights) and compare the results to the aforementioned approaches in terms of predictive performance and training time. Eventually, we plan to investigate early fusion of the still-image with additional inputs, i.e. motion vectors extracted from the videos, optical flow, or already existing domain-specific approaches such as fusing the image with a per-pixel relevance estimation. The results of these investigations address the following concrete research questions:

RQ 1.1 Exploring a baseline of the predictive performance for the recognition of semantic concepts in laparoscopic surgery: To what extent are CNNs capable of recognizing surgical actions and anatomy from a still image?

RQ 1.2 Does transfer learning allow for the improvement of the predictive performance, or the reduction of training time compared to training from scratch?

RQ 1.3 Is it better to partially train the network from scratch rather than fully deploy transfer learning considering training time and predictive performance?

RQ 1.4 By how much can the provided baseline be improved when considering additional CNN inputs such as motion vectors from a surgery video, optical flow, and already existing domain-specific approaches such as fusing the image with a per-pixel relevance estimation?

RQ 2: Automatic extraction of surgery scenes using a query image: How good can we cover the surgeons' needs? We aim at the automatic extraction of scenes from the full surgery video based on frames manually captured by the surgeon through an expert system. Therefore, we investigate the problem of finding a video and playback position to a query image using state-of-the-art local image descriptors CEDD and Feature Signatures, image similarity metrics PSNR and SSIM, as well as deep learning based methods using histograms of class confidences and neural codes. For evaluation of this approach, we build a dataset containing video sequences and corresponding images which were created by a surgeon in a real-world scenario. We evaluate the approaches in terms of recall (i.e. the correct video was found) and temporal deviation of the correct playback time stamp, as well as their computational efficiency (computation time and storage requirements). Furthermore, we plan to incorporate the knowledge from RQ1 by using the CNN models in order to develop a similarity-based shot boundary detection algorithm. This algorithm enables us to define the start and end time stamp of the shot in which the query image was taken. We aim at conducting a qualitative evaluation of the results with five surgeons against a naive baseline. The qualitative evaluation shall focus on the question whether the extracted scenes are relevant and appropriate in terms of duration.

RQ 2.1 How good perform state-of-the-art methods for interlinking images to video and their respective playback positions in terms of recall, temporal deviation and computational efficiency within a successfully found video?

RQ 2.2 To what extent do automatically extracted scenes overlap with semantic boundaries determined by medical experts, when using a naive baseline as well as a similarity-based method for shot boundary detection?

4 WORK IN PROGRESS

For the use case of image to video interlinking, we already have evaluated global features, visual quality metrics, and off-the-shelf CNN features over different sampling strategies. Our results show that off-the-shelf CNN features work best even for sparse sampling, i.e. 82.6% videos correctly linked at a sampling interval of four seconds. The average temporal deviation from the true playback time stamp is 4.83s. Off-the-shelf CNN features have the drawback of big descriptor sizes. We aim at approaching this problem by quantization for off-the-shelf features, which has shown promising results in first experiments, i.e. 81.2% correctly linked videos at an average temporal deviation of 4.96s for the same feature and configuration as mentioned above. For comparison, a simple (yet computationally very expensive) PSNR baseline achieves a performance of 78.3% video recall and an average temporal deviation of 7.61s for this configuration. We also have dealt with classification of laparoscopic surgery frames into semantic content classes for gynecology. We aim at lassifying surgical actions (blunt dissection, coagulation, cold cutting, hf-cutting, hysterectomy using sling, injection, suction and irrigation, and suturing) as well as anatomical structures (colon, liver, ovaries, oviduct, uterus). We base our work on an action video dataset comprising 486,771 unique frames and an anatomy dataset comprising 33,732 unique frames summing up to 1,105 unique shots that have been extracted from 111 raw gynecological surgery videos.

5 ACKNOWLEDGEMENTS

This work was supported by Universität Klagenfurt and Lakeside Labs GmbH, Klagenfurt, Austria and funding from the European Regional Development Fund and the Carinthian Economic Promotion Fund (KWF) under grant KWF 20214 u. 3520/ 26336/38165.

REFERENCES

[1] S. Albarqouni, C. Baur, F. Achilles, V. Belagiannis, S. Demirci, and N. Navab. 2016. AggNet: Deep Learning From Crowds for Mitosis Detection in Breast Cancer Histology Images. *IEEE Transactions on Medical Imaging* 35, 5 (2016), 1313–1321.

[2] M. Anthimopoulos, S. Christodoulidis, L. Ebner, A. Christe, and S. Mougiakakou. 2016. Lung Pattern Classification for Interstitial Lung Diseases Using a Deep Convolutional Neural Network. *IEEE Transactions on Medical Imaging* 35, 5 (2016), 1207–1216.

[3] Christian Beecks, Klaus Schoeffmann, Mathias Lux, Merih Seran Uysal, and Thomas Seidl. 2015. Endoscopic Video Retrieval: A Signature-based Approach for Linking Endoscopic Images with Video Segments. In *Proceedings of the IEEE International Symposium on Multimedia 2015 (ISM 2015)*, Alberto Del Bimbo, Shu-Ching Chen, Haohong Wang, Heather Yu, and Roger Zimmermann (Eds.). IEEE, Los Alamitos, CA, 1–6.

[4] Jennifer Roldan Carlos, Mathias Lux, Xavier Giro-i Nieto, Pia Munoz, and Nektarios Anagnostopoulos. 2015. Visual information retrieval in endoscopic video archives. In *Content-Based Multimedia Indexing (CBMI), 2015 13th International Workshop on.* IEEE, 1–6.

[5] Qing Li, Weidong Cai, Xiaogang Wang, Yun Zhou, David Dagan Feng, and Mei Chen. 2014. Medical image classification with convolutional neural network. In *Control Automation Robotics & Vision (ICARCV), 2014 13th International Conference on.* IEEE, 844–848.

[6] Geert Litjens, Thijs Kooi, Babak Ehteshami Bejnordi, Arnaud Arindra Adiyoso Setio, Francesco Ciompi, Mohsen Ghafoorian, Jeroen AWM van der Laak, Bram van Ginneken, and Clara I Sánchez. 2017. A Survey on Deep Learning in Medical Image Analysis. *arXiv preprint arXiv:1702.05747* (2017).

[7] Constantinos Loukas, Nikolaos Nikiteas, Dimitrios Schizas, and Evangelos Georgiou. 2016. Shot boundary detection in endoscopic surgery videos using a variational Bayesian framework. *International Journal of Computer Assisted Radiology and Surgery* 11, 11 (2016), 1937–1949.

[8] Bernd Münzer, Klaus Schoeffmann, and Laszlo Böszörmenyi. 2017. Content-based processing and analysis of endoscopic images and videos: A survey. *Multimedia Tools and Applications* (2017), 1–40.

[9] B. Münzer, K. Schoeffmann, and L. Böszörmenyi. 2013. Relevance Segmentation of Laparoscopic Videos. In *2013 IEEE International Symposium on Multimedia*. 84–91.

[10] B. Münzer, K. Schoeffmann, and L. Böszörmenyi. 2013. Relevance Segmentation of Laparoscopic Videos. In *2013 IEEE International Symposium on Multimedia*. 84–91.

[11] Sun Young Park and Dusty Sargent. 2016. Colonoscopic polyp detection using convolutional neural networks. In *SPIE Medical Imaging*. International Society for Optics and Photonics, 978528–978528.

[12] M. J. Primus, K. Schoeffmann, and L. Böszörmenyi. 2015. Instrument classification in laparoscopic videos. In *2015 13th International Workshop on Content-Based Multimedia Indexing (CBMI)*. 1–6.

[13] M. J. Primus, K. Schoeffmann, and L. Böszörmenyi. 2016. Temporal segmentation of laparoscopic videos into surgical phases. In *2016 14th International Workshop on Content-Based Multimedia Indexing (CBMI)*. 1–6.

[14] Yuchen Qiu, Yunzhi Wang, Shiju Yan, Maxine Tan, Samuel Cheng, Hong Liu, and Bin Zheng. 2016. An initial investigation on developing a new method to predict short-term breast cancer risk based on deep learning technology. In *SPIE Medical Imaging*. International Society for Optics and Photonics, 978521–978521.

[15] G. Quellec, M. Lamard, B. Cochener, and G. Cazuguel. 2014. Real-Time Segmentation and Recognition of Surgical Tasks in Cataract Surgery Videos. *IEEE Transactions on Medical Imaging* 33, 12 (2014), 2352–2360.

[16] Eduardo Ribeiro, Andreas Uhl, Georg Wimmer, and Michael Häfner. 2016. Transfer Learning for Colonic Polyp Classification Using Off-the-Shelf CNN Features. In *International Workshop on Computer-Assisted and Robotic Endoscopy*. Springer, 1–13.

[17] Ravi K Samala, Heang-Ping Chan, Lubomir M Hadjiiski, Kenny Cha, and Mark A Helvie. 2016. Deep-learning convolution neural network for computer-aided detection of microcalcifications in digital breast tomosynthesis. In *SPIE Medical Imaging*. International Society for Optics and Photonics, 97850Y–97850Y.

[18] Klaus Schoeffmann, Christian Beecks, Mathias Lux, Merih Seran Uysal, and Thomas Seidl. 2016. Content-based retrieval in videos from laparoscopic surgery. *Proc. SPIE* 9786, 97861V–97861V–10.

[19] H. C. Shin, H. R. Roth, M. Gao, L. Lu, Z. Xu, I. Nogues, J. Yao, D. Mollura, and R. M. Summers. 2016. Deep Convolutional Neural Networks for Computer-Aided Detection: CNN Architectures, Dataset Characteristics and Transfer Learning. *IEEE Transactions on Medical Imaging* 35, 5 (2016), 1285–1298.

[20] N. Tajbakhsh, J. Y. Shin, S. R. Gurudu, R. T. Hurst, C. B. Kendall, M. B. Gotway, and J. Liang. 2016. Convolutional Neural Networks for Medical Image Analysis: Full Training or Fine Tuning? *IEEE Transactions on Medical Imaging* 35, 5 (2016), 1299–1312.

[21] A. P. Twinanda, S. Shehata, D. Mutter, J. Marescaux, M. de Mathelin, and N. Padoy. 2017. EndoNet: A Deep Architecture for Recognition Tasks on Laparoscopic Videos. *IEEE Transactions on Medical Imaging* 36, 1 (2017), 86–97.

[22] F. Xing, Y. Xie, and L. Yang. 2016. An Automatic Learning-Based Framework for Robust Nucleus Segmentation. *IEEE Transactions on Medical Imaging* 35, 2 (2016), 550–566.

[23] Z. Yan, Y. Zhan, Z. Peng, S. Liao, Y. Shinagawa, S. Zhang, D. N. Metaxas, and X. S. Zhou. 2016. Multi-Instance Deep Learning: Discover Discriminative Local Anatomies for Bodypart Recognition. *IEEE Transactions on Medical Imaging* 35, 5 (2016), 1332–1343.

On the Effectiveness of Distance Measures for Similarity Search in Multi-Variate Sensory Data*

Yash Garg
CIDSE, Arizona State University
Tempe, USA 85281
ygarg@asu.edu

Silvestro Roberto Poccia
University of Turin
Corso Svizzera 185
Turin, Italy 10149
poccia@di.unito.it

ABSTRACT

Integration of rich sensor technologies with everyday applications, such as gesture recognition and health monitoring, has raised the importance of the ability to effectively search and analyze multi-variate time series data. Consequently, various time series distance measures (such as Euclidean distance, edit distance, and dynamic time warping) have been extended from uni-variate to multi-variate time series. In this paper, we note that the naive extensions of these measures may not necessarily be effective when analyzing multi-variate time series data. We present several algorithms, some of which leverage external metadata describing the potential relationships, either learned from the data or captured from the metadata, among the variates. We then experimentally study the effectiveness of multi-variate time series distance measures against human motion data sets.

CCS CONCEPTS

•Information systems →Similarity measures; Multimedia and multimodal retrieval;

KEYWORDS

Action recognition, similarity measures, DTW, SAX

ACM Reference format:
Yash Garg and Silvestro Roberto Poccia. 2017. On the Effectiveness of Distance Measures for Similarity Search in Multi-Variate Sensory Data. In *Proceedings of ICMR '17, June 6–9, 2017, Bucharest, Romania*, , 5 pages.
DOI: http://dx.doi.org/10.1145/3078971.3079009

1 INTRODUCTION

In recent years, time series data have become increasingly critical in organizational awareness, prediction, and decision making. Applications that require time series search and analysis include healthcare [8], surveillance [11], and motion and gesture recognition [16] (Figure 1). When comparing two sequences or time series, exact alignment is not required in most applications. Instead, whether two sequences are to be treated as matching or not depends on the amount of difference, quantified through *distance* measures[7] (see Section 1.1). Edit-distance measures quantify the minimum number (or cost) of symbol *insertions*, *deletions*, and *substitutions* needed to convert one sequence to the other [12]. *Dynamic time warping (DTW)* distance [3, 6], used commonly when comparing *continuous sequences* or time series (especially in scenarios where the sequences carry similar underlying patterns, but are different from each other due to temporal deformations, such as shifts and stretches), is a related distance measure.

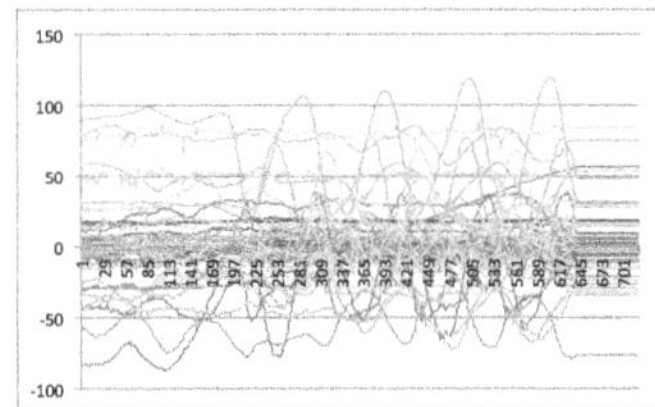

(a) Sample motion data

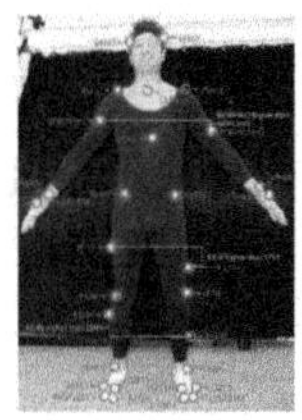

(b) Sensors

Figure 1: A sample multi-variate time series, tracking 62 sensors, created by body motion capture [1]

1.1 Related Work

Euclidean distance and, more generally $L_p - norm$ measures, were among the first used to determine the similarity between two time series. Euclidean distance requires that the time series being compared are of *same temporal length* and, since it assumes a strict synchrony among time series, it is not suitable when two time series can have different speeds or are offset in time [6]. Other measures that require equal length and perfect synchrony across time series include cosine and correlation similarity [14].

In the 1970s, Sakoe [13] and in the 1990s, Berndt [3] proposed an edit distance like dynamic time warping (DTW) technique to find an optimal alignment between two given (time-dependent) sequences under certain restrictions. Intuitively, DTW considers all possible warping paths that can warp (or transform) one series into the other, and picks the warping path that has the lowest cost. DTW has found wide acceptance, and the last two decades have seen several innovations [4, 6]. For example, while the original DTW is not metric (does not satisfy the triangular inequality), [4] proposed an extended version of DTW that does satisfy the triangular inequality. [10] proposed a SAX representation of input

*Both authors have equal contribution. This work is done under the supervision of Prof. K Selçuk Candan (candan@asu.edu) and Prof. Maria Luisa Sapino (mlsapino@di.unito.it). This work is supported by NSF Grant # 1339835 "E-SDMS", and NSF Grant # 1318788 "Data Mgmt. for Real-Time Data Driven Epidemic Spread Simulation".

ICMR '17, June 6–9, 2017, Bucharest, Romania
© 2017 ACM. ACM ISBN 978-1-4503-4701-3/17/06...$15.00
DOI: http://dx.doi.org/10.1145/3078971.3079009

sequences, which divides them into fixed-sized "frames", thus transforming the sequences into a reduce space where distance can be computed efficiently.

An alternative approach to the above techniques is to extract *features* from the given time series and use these features to compute similarity/distance instead of the original series. [5] proposed a feature-extraction algorithm that extracts minimal distinguishing subsequences that can be used as features. [16] proposed to extract and use SIFT-like robust multi-variate temporal features to determine similarity between multi-variate time series. In contrast, edit distance [9] measures aim to determine the minimum sequence of *edit* operations that are required to measure similarity.

1.2 Comparing Multi-Variate Time Series

Naive extensions of the uni-variate measures discussed above might not always work, as we may need to take into account (a) asynchrony among variates, (b) varying scales and importance of the different variates, as well as (c) dependency among the various variates that constitute a multi-variate time series . For example, nearby sensors in a sensor network may observe similar values, or sensors located on a human limb may be constrained to move together, except for some local variations. In this paper, we present, discuss, and evaluate several approaches to computing distances among multi-variate time series.

2 DISTANCE MEASURES FOR MULTI-VARIATE TIME SERIES

In this section, we start by formally defining uni-variate and multi-variate time series.

Definition 2.1 (Uni-Variate Time Series). *A uni-variate time series, $T = (d_1, d_2, ..., d_N)$, is a finite sequence of data values. Here, N denotes the length of the time series; and $d_i \in \mathbb{R}$.*

Multi-variate time series extend the uni-variate time series definition above by encapsulating multiple uni-variate series:

Definition 2.2 (Multi-Variate Time Series). *A multi-variate time series, $\mathbb{T}$, is an ordered set of equi-length time series; that record different observations (or* variates*):*

$$\mathbb{T} = [T_1, T_2, ..., T_v].$$

Here, $v > 1$ is the number of variates for time series, $\mathbb{T}$.

2.1 Metadata-Enriched Multi-Variate Series

Following [16], we define metadata-enriched multi-variate time seriesas follows:

Definition 2.3. *(Metadata-Enriched Multi-Variate Time Series) A* metadata-enriched multi-variate time series, *$\mathbb{T}_R$, is a multi-variate time series annotated with a data structure, R, that encodes the relationships among the variates; i.e. $\mathbb{T}_R = [\mathbb{T}, R]$.*

While in general the metadata R can be complex, here we assume that R is encoded in the form of a relationship matrix:

Definition 2.4 (Relationship Matrix). *A $v \times v$* relationship matrix, *R, encodes the pairwise relationships among the variates; i.e.,*

$$\forall_{1 \leq i,j \leq v} \ R[i,j] = \rho(T_i, T_j)$$

where $\rho()$ is an application-specific function to determine the relationship between a given pair of variates.

Example 2.1 (Encoding Spatial Relationships). Let us consider a set, $\mathbb{S}$, of in-situ sensors distributed in a spatial area, and let us assume that we can compute the spatial distance, Δ_{sp}, between any given pair of sensors. Under the assumption that two nearby sensors are likely to observe more similar processes than sensors that are far apart from each other, we can encode a spatial relationship matrix, R_{sp}, as follows:

$$\forall_{s_i, s_j \in S} \ R_{sp}[i,j] = \max_{s_h, s_k \in \mathbb{S}} \left(\Delta_{sp}(h,k)\right) - \Delta_{sp}(i,j).$$

Intuitively, the difference operation above converts distances to proximities, such that the larger values in the relationship matrix correspond to more-related sensor pairs.

2.2 Synchronized Distance Measures

Dynamic time warping (DTW)[3, 6] is a common technique for comparing sequences or time series by searching for optimal alignments, described in terms of *warp paths*. Recently, various extensions of DTW have been proposed for *multi*-dimensional time series [15]. The most prevalent of these are the *vectorized* and *independent* extensions. In the *vectorized* approach, a multi-variate time series is considered as a sequence of vectors, where the length of a vector is equal to number of variates in the time series. The DTW algorithm is then applied using the distances among these vectors, instead of differences in signal amplitude. In the *independent* approach, however, each variate is treated independently from the others and DTW is applied separately to each; finally, these independent distances are added to compute the overall distance between the given pair of multi-variate time series.

2.2.1 Independent DTW. Given two sequences, $\mathbb{X}$ and $\mathbb{Y}$, each with v variates, the independent DTW measure is computed by treating each variate separately from the others:

$$I\_DTW = \sum_{i=1}^{v} DTW(\mathbb{X}_i, \mathbb{Y}_i).$$

2.2.2 Vectorized DTW. In contrast, vectorized DTW considers $\mathbb{X}$ and $\mathbb{Y}$ as sequences of vectors, where the length of a vector is equal to the number of variates in the time series; i.e, $\mathbb{X} = (\vec{x}_1, \vec{x}_2, \ldots, \vec{x}_N)$ and $\mathbb{Y} = (\vec{y}_1, \vec{y}_2, \ldots, \vec{y}_M)$, such that each $\vec{x}_*$ and $\vec{y}_*$ is a v-dimensional vector. The DTW algorithm is then applied considering the differences among these vectors; i.e.,

$$V\_DTW = DTW_v(\mathbb{X}, \mathbb{Y}),$$

2.2.3 SAX based DTW. SAX [10] transforms a sequence of length n into a string of a length determined by the size of window w. At the same time, SAX can transform two sequences to strings of equal length, thus allowing linear comparison between them. A *uni-variate time series*, $T = (d_1, d_2, ..., d_N)$, can be written as $T_S = \langle C_1, ..., C_m \rangle$ where m is the number of words extracted using aggregation. Similar to the independent DTW, DTW measure between two sequences in SAX representation, $\mathbb{X}_\mathbb{S}$ and $\mathbb{Y}_\mathbb{S}$, each with v variates, can be computed as follows:

$$SAX\_DTW = \sum_{i=1}^{v} DTW(\mathbb{X}_{\mathbb{S}i}, \mathbb{Y}_{\mathbb{S}i}).$$

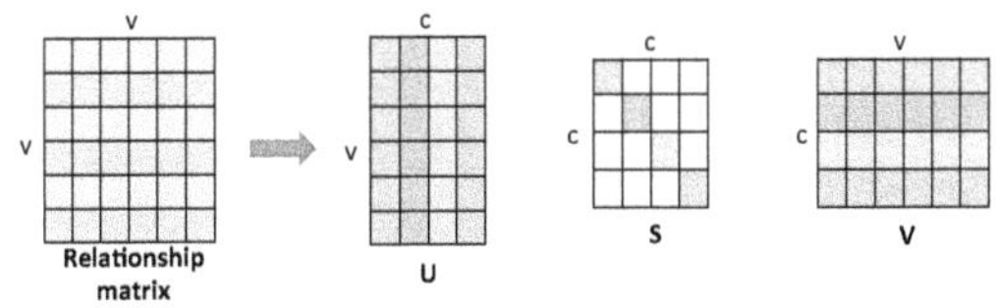

(a) Eigen-decomposition of the relationship matrix

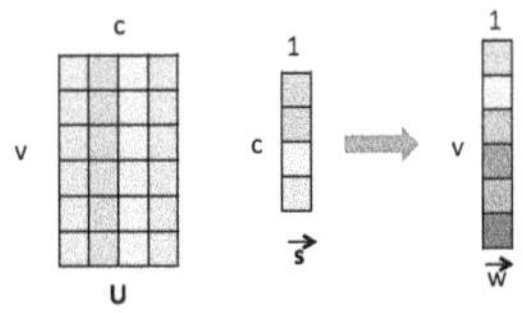

(b) Weight extraction

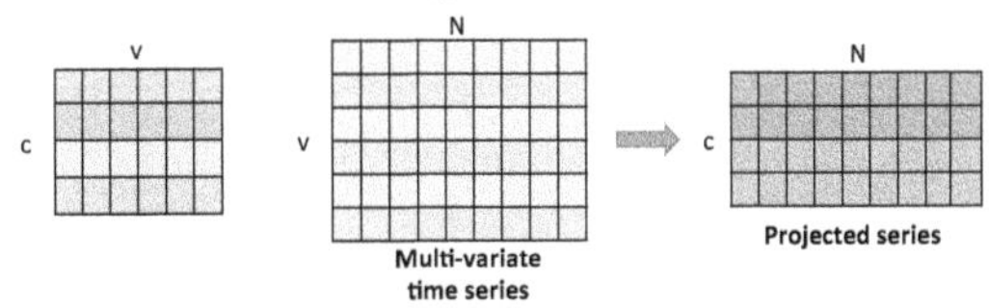

(c) Projecting time series onto orthogonal variates

Figure 2: Weight extraction and projection of a multi-variate time series onto an orthogonal variate basis using relationship matrix *R*.

2.3 Metadata-Driven Distance Measures

In this section, we discuss two approaches to account for the contextual relationships among the variates:

- metadata-driven weighting, and
- orthogonal latent variates.

2.3.1 Metadata-Driven Weights. Given a relationship matrix $R \rightarrow v \times v$, representing the contextual relationship between the variates, we can leverage eigen-decomposition to extract the patterns encoded in R,

$$[U^R, S^R, V^R] = eigen(R),$$

where the $c \times c$ diagonal matrix S^R and the $V \times c$ matrix U^R encode the strengths of pattern and the participation of the variates to these patterns.

Given this, we can calculate variate weights, $\vec{w}_R$, by combining the pattern membership degrees of the variates encoded in U^R with the pattern strengths scores encoded in S^R. In particular, we consider both positive and negative weights:

$$\vec{w}_R^+ = U^R * \vec{s}_R,$$
$$\vec{w}_R^- = U^R * 1/\vec{s}_R,$$

where the vector $\vec{s}_R = diag(S^R)$ encodes the strengths of the latent patterns in the relationship matrix R. Once these weights are extracted, we can adapt uni-variate similarity and distance (such as DTW) measures to account for metadata-driven weights; e.g.,

$$weighted\_DTW = \sum_{i=1}^{v} \vec{w}[i] \times DTW(\mathbb{X}_i, \mathbb{Y}_i).$$

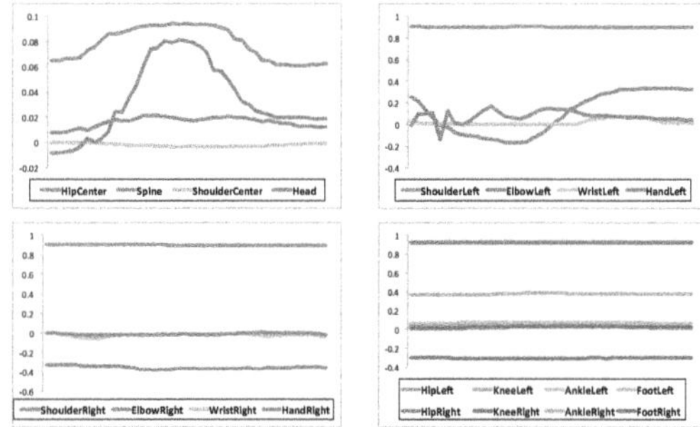

Figure 3: A sample gesture from the Kaggle data set and the corresponding structural groupings of the body sensors [2]

2.3.2 Orthogonal Latent Variates. As discussed in Section 1.1, a major difficulty with existing multi-variate distance/similarity measures is that they assume either that (a) the different variates in the data are completely independent from each other, or that (b) the variates move in perfectly synchronized lock-step fashion.

Here, we note that one way to leverage groupings of variates is to map (or project) the given time series onto an alternative set of latent, orthogonal variates. Intuitively, since each orthogonal variate would correspond to a different structural grouping of the original variates, assuming that these groupings reflect the way temporal observations of the variates vary together, we expect that the observations mapped on to these latent variates would be independent from each other. We can achieve this goal by relying on orthogonal variate bases obtained through eigen-decompositions of the relationship matrix[1]. More specifically, given a relationship matrix, R, we first obtain its eigen-decomposition as before:

$$[U^R,\ S^R,\ V^R] = eigen(R).$$

However, instead of relying on U^R and S^R to assign weights to the existing variates, we leverage the $c \times v$ matrix V^R to help project the two time series, $\mathbb{X}$ and $\mathbb{Y}$, onto a set of orthogonal latent variates:

$$\mathbb{X}^\dagger = V^R\, \mathbb{X} \text{ and } \mathbb{Y}^\dagger = V^R\, \mathbb{Y}.$$

This process is visualized in Figure 2. The resulting time series, $\mathbb{X}^\dagger$ and $\mathbb{Y}^\dagger$, can now be used as inputs to any independent or synchronized multi-variate distance/similarity measure, as discussed in Section 2.2. While evaluating the proposed approach, we will consider orthogonal projection-based independent and vectorized approaches.

3 EXPERIMENTAL EVALUATION

In this section, we evaluate the presented approaches on two human action datasets, Mocap[1] and Kaggle[2] and assess their effectiveness in similarity search. While both record human motion, the Mocap and Kaggle data sets are very different from each other: as we see in Figure 1, the variates in the Mocap data all record varying degrees of repeated motion; in contrast, as Figure 3 illustrates, the motions in Kaggle show significant degrees of variate localization (with only a few sensors recording active motion during a gesture)

[1] In this case, eigen-decompositions of the input time series are not useful, as individually decomposing the two time series would project them onto different orthogonal bases.

Algorithms	Top-5 % Accuracy	Class Tightness
	Original Data Space	
V-DTW	87.83	1.62
V-SAX	67.83	1.38
I-DTW	95.43	1.91
I-SAX	71.74	1.49
MW-DTW(w_R^+)	95.33	1.91
MW-DTW(w_R^-)	**95.87**	**1.93**
MW-SAX(w_R^+)	72.28	1.49
MW-SAX(w_R^-)	71.52	1.48
	Orthogonal Latent Space	
V-DTW	72.07	1.43
V-SAX	71.41	1.41
I-DTW	77.72	1.57
I-SAX	65.98	1.26
MW-DTW(S^R)	69.46	1.56
MW-DTW($1/S^R$)	**81.74**	**1.92**
MW-SAX(S^R)	56.20	1.23
MW-SAX($1/S^R$)	63.80	1.27

Table 1: Percent retrieval accuracy & class tightness for Mocap data set for DTW & SAX (window size =20) measures.

Algorithms	Top-5 % Accuracy	Class Tightness
	Original Data Space	
V-DTW	**44.63**	1.30
V-SAX	35.78	1.31
I-DTW	41.78	1.32
I-SAX	32.81	1.32
MW-DTW(w_R^+)	41.49	**1.35**
MW-DTW(w_R^-)	41.81	1.32
MW-SAX(w_R^+)	22.44	1.34
MW-SAX(w_R^-)	33.16	**1.35**
	Orthogonal Latent Space	
V-DTW	23.65	1.12
V-SAX	**27.88**	1.18
I-DTW	21.85	1.15
I-SAX	24.91	1.22
MW-DTW(S^R)	21.85	1.15
MW-DTW($1/S^R$)	21.84	1.15
MW-SAX(S^R)	18.15	**1.25**
MW-SAX($1/S^R$)	21.90	1.20

Table 2: Percent retrieval accuracy & class tightness for Kaggle data set for DTW & SAX (window size =2) measures.

and do not include repeated patterns. These differences among the motion data sets enable us to study the various algorithms within different contexts. As metadata, we use the sensors' spatial relationship; for latent-space approaches, we preserve 100% energy (variance). For this experiment, to generate SAX representations, we use window size 20 and 2 for Mocap and Kaggle respectively.

3.1 Evaluation Criteria

To assess the effectiveness of the algorithms, we considered two main criteria: *retrieval accuracy* and *class tightness.*

Retrieval Accuracy (ACC). To quantify retrieval accuracy provided by a given distance function, Δ, we execute k-nearest neighbor ($k - NN$) queries (for varying k, excluding itself) and measure accuracy as

$$ACC(k, \Delta) = \underset{C \in Classes}{AVG} \; \underset{s_i \in C}{AVG} \left(\frac{\#match(s_i, k, \Delta, C)}{k} \right),$$

Class Tightness (CT). Given a distance function, Δ, we consider a set of classes *tight* if the following measure is proportionately large:

$$CT(\Delta) = \underset{C \in Classes}{AVG} \frac{avg\_inter\_dist(C, \Delta)}{avg\_intra\_dist(C, \Delta)}.$$

where,

$$avg\_inter\_dist(C, \Delta) = \underset{s_i \in C}{AVG} \left(\underset{s_j \notin C}{AVG} \left(\Delta(s_i, s_j) \right) \right)$$

$$avg\_intra\_dist(C, \Delta) = \underset{s_i \in C}{AVG} \left(\underset{s_j (\neq s_i) \in C}{AVG} \left(\Delta(s_i, s_j) \right) \right).$$

3.2 Results

Mocap dataset: Table 1 presents the results. It can be seen that metadata adds more discriminatory power to the distance measure, which in turn leads to a better retrieval accuracy and class tightness as compared to the naive extensions of both DTW and SAX. While latent space mappings overall result in reduced accuracy, we see that metadata support again provides a significant boost.

Kaggle dataset: Table 2 presents the results. Note that for this data set, retrieval is more difficult, and vectorized approaches, which assume full synchrony, provide an overall better retrieval accuracy. Yet, once again, metadata weighting helps improve the separation between classes, both in original and latent spaces.

4 CONCLUSIONS AND FUTURE WORK

As seen in Section 3, overall we observe a positive impact from the use of metadata, which describes contextual relationships, in computing distances among multi-variate time series.

Naturally, the impact of the use of metadata depends on the type of series we consider, the degree of inherent synchrony/asynchrony amongst the variates in the data, and the quality of metadata representation used to capture the relationships among the variates. Therefore, significant research needs to be done on automated mechanisms to characterize multi-variate data and extract informative metadata. We also note that the degree of synchrony/asynchrony may be different for different groupings of sensors; therefore, we may also seek to identify and leverage sub-groupings of relatively synchronous sensors to improve accuracy.

Another challenge is that, while here we assume that the metadata is common to all series, it is possible that in practice, each individual series will have its own metadata (e.g., each user has their own body shape), and the alignment of these metadata needs to be considered while measuring the similarities and differences among the corresponding multi-variate time series.

In this paper we disregarded (a) feature-based approaches to multi-variate time series comparison, (b) use of distance measures for searching for multi-variate motifs, (c) metadata-supported dynamic topic modeling and deep learning over multi-variate time series, and (d) execution time issues and other performance optimizations. These constitute our future work.

REFERENCES

[1] CMU graphics lab motion capture database, 2015.
[2] Kaggle gesture dataset, 2015.
[3] Donald J Berndt and James Clifford. Using dynamic time warping to find patterns in time series. In *KDD workshop*, volume 10, pages 359–370. Seattle, WA, 1994.
[4] Lei Chen and Raymond Ng. On the marriage of lp-norms and edit distance. In *Proceedings of the Thirtieth international conference on Very large data bases-Volume 30*, pages 792–803. VLDB Endowment, 2004.
[5] Xiaonan Ji, James Bailey, and Guozhu Dong. Mining minimal distinguishing subsequence patterns with gap constraints. *Knowledge and Information Systems*, 11(3):259–286, 2007.
[6] Eamonn Keogh. Exact indexing of dynamic time warping. In *Proceedings of the 28th international conference on Very Large Data Bases*, pages 406–417. VLDB Endowment, 2002.
[7] Eamonn Keogh. Data mining and information retrieval in time series/multimedia databases. In *Proceedings of the 14th ACM international conference on Multimedia*, pages 10–10. ACM, 2006.
[8] Duk-Jin Kim and Balakrishnan Prabhakaran. Multimedia aspects in health care. In *Proceedings of the 17th ACM international conference on Multimedia*, pages 921–922. ACM, 2009.
[9] Joseph B Kruskal. An overview of sequence comparison: Time warps, string edits, and macromolecules. *SIAM review*, 25(2):201–237, 1983.
[10] Jessica Lin, Eamonn Keogh, Stefano Lonardi, and Bill Chiu. A symbolic representation of time series, with implications for streaming algorithms. In *Proceedings of the 8th ACM SIGMOD workshop on Research issues in data mining and knowledge discovery*, pages 2–11. ACM, 2003.
[11] Yang Liu, Feng Zhou, Wei Liu, Fernando De la Torre, and Yan Liu. Unsupervised summarization of rushes videos. In *Proceedings of the 18th ACM international conference on Multimedia*, pages 751–754. ACM, 2010.
[12] Gonzalo Navarro. A guided tour to approximate string matching. *ACM computing surveys (CSUR)*, 33(1):31–88, 2001.
[13] Hiroaki Sakoe and Seibi Chiba. Dynamic programming algorithm optimization for spoken word recognition. *IEEE transactions on acoustics, speech, and signal processing*, 26(1):43–49, 1978.
[14] Gerard Salton and Michael J McGill. Introduction to modern information retrieval. 1986.
[15] Parinya Sanguansat. Multiple multidimensional sequence alignment using generalized dynamic time warping. *WSEAS Transactions on Mathematics*, 11(8):668–678, 2012.
[16] Xiaolan Wang, K Selçuk Candan, and Maria Luisa Sapino. Leveraging metadata for identifying local, robust multi-variate temporal (RMT) features. In *Data Engineering (ICDE), 2014 IEEE 30th International Conference on*, pages 388–399. IEEE, 2014.

Classification of sMRI for Alzheimer's disease Diagnosis with CNN: Single Siamese Networks with 2D+ε Approach and Fusion on ADNI

Karim Aderghal
LaBRI UMR 5800, University of Bordeaux
Cours de la Liberation, 33405 Talence Cedex, FRANCE
karim.aderghal@u-bordeaux.fr

Jenny Benois-Pineau
LaBRI UMR 5800, University of Bordeaux
Cours de la Liberation, 33405 Talence Cedex, FRANCE
jenny.benois-pineau@u-bordeaux.fr

Karim Afdel
LabSIV, Department of Computer Science, Faculty of Sciences
University Ibn Zohr, B.P 8106, City Dakhla, Agadir, MOROCCO
k.afdel@uiz.ac.ma

ABSTRACT

The methods of Content-Based visual information indexing and retrieval penetrate into Healthcare and become popular in Computer–Aided Diagnostics. The PhD research[1] we have started 13 months ago is devoted to the multimodal classification of MRI brain scans for Alzheimer Disease diagnostics. We use the winner classifier, such as CNN. We first proposed an original 2D+ ε approach. It avoids heavy volumetric computations and uses domain knowledge on Alzheimer biomarkers. We study discriminative power of different brain projections. Three binary classification tasks are considered separating Alzheimer Disease (AD) patients from Mild Cognitive Impairment (MCI) and Normal Control subject (NC). Two fusion methods on FC – layer and on the single-projection CNN output show better performances, up to 91% of accuracy is achieved. The results are competitive with the SOA which uses heavier algorithmic chain.

KEYWORDS

Alzheimer's disease (AD); Convolutional Neural Network (CNN); structural MRI (sMRI); Hippocampus; Deep Learning; Fusion of multiple sources.

1 INTRODUCTION

Development of digital image analysis and of machine learning in the field of research on Computer Aided Diagnostics is one of the fields of high priority. With the elder-ling population in the world, the age-related diseases are becoming a major health problem. Alzheimer's disease (AD) is the most prevalent neurodegenerative brain disease affecting the elders, its prevalence is estimated to be around 5% after 65 years old and is staggering 30% for the more than 85 years old in developed countries [1]. From now to 2050 it is estimated that 0.64 Billion of persons will be diagnosed with AD [1]. It requires non-invasive and reliable diagnostics, due to which the adapted therapeutic re-education can prolongate the period for the patient to be maintained at home. This reduces the inherent costs for the families and for public health. The computer – assisted analysis of MRI scans of screened population is one of the promising directions for development of such non-invasive methods. This is why the research in this field is very intensive and competitive, e.g. [2 - 3]. A large variety of methods have been developed using biomarkers of the Alzheimer disease in 3D MRI scans for classification of instantaneous state of the patients and prediction of Alzheimer Conversion. Amongst such biomarkers the most studied one is the shrinkage phenomenon of the Hippocampal region. Hence a variety of methods have been developed for classification of MRI scans in screening of population on the basis of Hippocampal and other biomarkers in the brain. In this work we maintain our claim we first formulated in [4]: a precise segmentation of the brain volume is not needed. Only a rough selection of the biomarker region, using alignment of individual brain and atlas-based selection of the region-of-interest (ROI) are necessary [4]. Then we can work with the selected ROI with common multimedia indexing methods, be it feature-based visual signature of the ROI on the basis of "engineered features", or the winners in classification of visual and multimedia data, that is CNNs. Furthermore, early or late fusion techniques developed for different media such as e.g. image, motion, sound, have to be adapted for Alzheimer classification problem on a single MRI modality (such as three different projections in sMRI) or different modalities, e.g. sMRI and DTI. Thus increasing the classification scores.

2 RELATED WORK

The CNN have become the trend technique in image classification problems. Despite their strong success in Multimedia and Computer vision CNNs are of limited use in AD classification with structural MRI. In the following we present a short overview of recent works using CNNs.

ICMR'17, June 6–9, 2017, Bucharest, Romania.

DOI: http://dx.doi.org/10.1145/3078971.3079010

In [7] the authors have used a two stage approach on the whole MRI brain scans, A sparse auto-encoder has been used to learn filters for the convolution operation, and then they built a 3D CNN whose the first and the only convolution layer uses these learned filters. The 3D CNN architecture was made up of a convolutional layers followed by a max-pooling and a fully-connected layer. Their resulting accuracy in the 3-class classification problem (AD, NC, MCI) is of 89.47%. In case of binary classification problems they have achieved better accuracies AD vs. NC: 95.39%, AD vs. MCI: 86.84%, and NC vs. MCI: 92.11%.

The studies in [2] [3] [8] are focusing on prognosis, the problem here is to classify stable MCI (sMCI) vs. progressive MCI (pMCI), also called MCI converters (cMCI) i.e. MCI subjects that will be diagnosed with AD in a relatively short period of time. In [3] an accuracy of 65% for sMCI vs. pMCI was obtained, 70% in [2], 74% in [8] and 83% accuracy for sMCI vs. cMCI was reported in [9].

In their recent paper [10], the authors use MRI image segmentation into three tissue types of Gray Matter (GM), White Matter (WM), and Cerebrospinal Fluid (CSF). Then they split them into 93 ROIs. Only the GM densities spatially normalized widely used in the AD classification problem are considered in this work. The authors propose an architecture named DeepESRNet containing two convolutional layers and a max-pooling layer, followed by two fully-connected layers. The proposed method achieves for AD vs. NC 91.02%, 92.72%, and 89.94%, and for MCI vs. NC 73.02%, 77.60%, 68.22%, of Accuracy, Sensitivity, and Specificity respectively.

The paper for a doctoral symposium is a synthesis of our achievements up to now and a design of perspectives for the future. Hence we will give an overview of our initial 2D + ε approach that we have developed at the early stage of this research and then move to our previous work [6]. Here we have proposed a fusion approach based on the 2D + ε information from single projections of the 3D MRI scans image.

In [5 - 6], we have focused only on the Hippocampal region, contrarily to the above cited studies where various techniques were used on the whole brain scan mainly.

3 METHODOLOGY AND APPROACHES

3.1 Dataset and its preprocessing

3.1.1 Dataset presentation.

In this work, we use the Alzheimer's disease Neuroimaging Initiative (ADNI) collaborative dataset that is publicly available on their website. We selected the screening MRI set which includes 815 subjects, the images were collected from different acquisition sites with 1.5T MRI, and they are a T1-weighted MRI. The subjects are spilt as 188 Alzheimer's disease (AD), 228 normal control (NC), and 399 mild cognitive impairment (MCI). The Table 1 contains more information about age, gender, and the MMSE which is the value of examination results (Folstein test).

Table 1: Dataset composition.

	Subject	Age[range] /μ(σ)	Gender (M/F)	Age[range] /μ(σ)
AD	188	[55 91]/75.4(± 7.52)	99/89	[18 27]/23.3 (± 2.03)
MCI	399	[55 89]/74.9(± 7.3)	256/143	[23 30]/27 (± 1.78)
NC	228	[60 90]/76(± 5.02)	118/110	[25 30]/29.1 (± 1.0)

3.1.2 Extraction of the Hippocampal region from the MRI images.

Before extracting the region of interest (ROI), the geometric normalization task has been performed on the image dataset, the idea is to align the images with the Montreal Neurological Institute (MNI) template, which represents an average of 152 individual brain scans. The alignment was realized using affine (rigid body) registration, then the voxel intensity normalization has been performed to have similar intensities for similar structures. To select the ROI (Hippocampus), a brain atlas called (AAL) that corresponds to the used MNI template has been used. The process consisted in selecting from the brain volume of a subject, the voxels labeled as Hippocampal region in AAL. Fig. 1 resumes the preprocessing steps, and computing the bounding 3D boxes, these 3D boxes represent a sub-volume of the whole brain which contains the Hippocampal region.

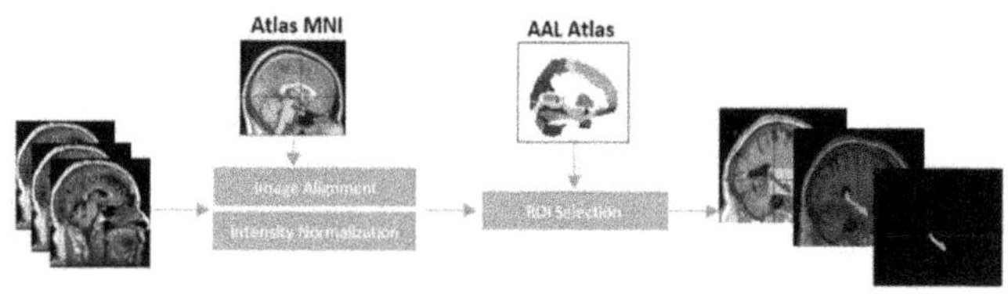

Figure 1: Preprocessing dataset steps.

3.1.3 Data augmentation.

Since the complexity of the Convolutional Neural Networks requires a very large data for the training task, a data augmentation strategy was proposed to increase the size of our dataset. The first method to augment the data, was the blurring technique with three Gaussian filters (3x3, 5x5, and 7x7). The parameter σ (the Standard deviation of the Gaussian distribution) equals to 0.7, 0.7, and 0.6 respectively. The second technique is the translation of the Hippocampal region: we have translated the 3D bounding boxes by ±1 pixel in each of three dimensions. These transformation provides 6 time more data plus the original. Finally, as we know that the brain has two symmetrical Hippocampal regions (left and right), we do flipping technique, by flipping the left Hippocampus to correspond the right one. For training networks we split the dataset as follows: 60% for training, 20% for validation, and 20% for test. Note that for test task we use only the original images.

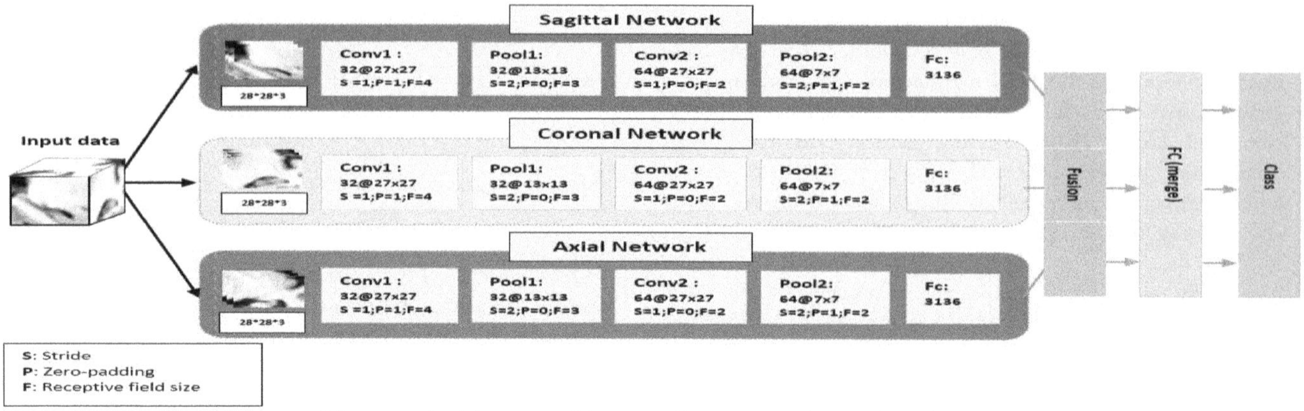

Figure 3: Architecture of intermediate Fusion (on FC layer)

3.2 2D+ ε approach on single projection

In this approach, instead of using one projection slice from the 3D bounding box of the Hippocampal structure, we take three adjacent slices, the median and the two closest neighboring slices as shown in Fig. 2, thus we moved from a 3D volume to three 2D images, and we have called this technique "2D+ ε approach". By the extracting process we got low dimension images of 28x28 pixels size (patches), taking into account that the initial resolution of the original MRI scans was (121x145x121 voxels). And then we use these patches to feed our convolutional neural network. The network was implemented with the publicly available framework Caffe [11]. As illustrated in the Fig. 3 (single projection), the architecture of network consists of two convolutional layers, followed by a max-pooling layer for each one, the ReLU was used as an activation function, and we have a fully connected layer that was connected with the max-pooling 2 layer and gives us two output units. Note that in this network we cannot "go deeper" as this is the trend in computer vision. The MRI scans and many other modalities in medical imaging have low spatial resolution. In our case, ROIs are 28x28 pixels in one slice of a 3D scan. The first convolutional layer uses 32 filters and the second one uses 64 filters. And finally the Softmax function was used as a loss function. The input layer of the network consisted of 28x28*3 units. The parameters and number of layers are depend on the input data, as we have a small patch input (low resolution), this architecture was the best one.

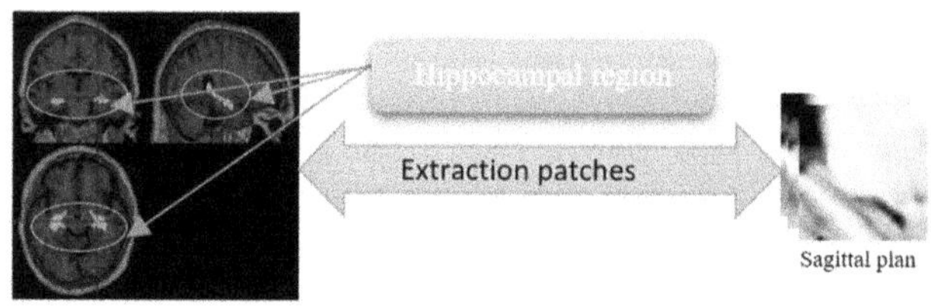

Figure 2: Example of slices extraction on sagittal Projection.

The results we obtained using sagittal projection were promising, AD/NC 82.8%, MCI/NC 66% and AD/MCI 62.5%. Hence in the follow-up of the research we moved in deepening it to identify the most discriminative projection and further apply multimedia techniques of information fusion.

3.3 2D+ ε Fusion approach.

3.3.1 Intermediate fusion.

Since we have a 3D dimension of MRI brain scans, we thought to make an architecture of three single projections, with Axial, Coronal, and Sagittal plans. The networks are completely identical; 2D+ ε, but joint in some layers, "Siamese". The only condition is that three input data images have to be from the same subject's brain, and from the appropriate projection to feed our network. The fusion lies in the last layer precisely in the fully connected layer as depicted in Fig. 3. We insert a concatenation layer that combines the FC layers from each single network.

Table 2: Comparison of single-projection results.

	Sagittal			Coronal			Axial		
	AD vs. MCI	AD vs. NC	NC vs. MCI	AD vs. MCI	AD vs. NC	NC vs. MCI	AD vs. MCI	AD vs. NC	NC vs. MCI
ACC	62,5 %	**82,8 %**	**66,0 %**	**66,4 %**	80,1 %	57,5 %	61,7%	79,7%	61,2 %
SPE	60,0 %	**79,6 %**	**58,7 %**	57,9 %	78,5 %	**58,7 %**	**68,7%**	78,1%	55,0 %
SEN	64,0 %	**85,9 %**	**73,7 %**	**75,0 %**	82,6%	56,3 %	54,6%	81,2%	67,5 %

Table 4: Comparison of late fusion results.

	Max			Mean			Majority Vote		
	AD vs. MCI	AD vs. NC	NC vs. MCI	AD vs. MCI	AD vs. NC	NC vs. MCI	AD vs. MCI	AD vs. NC	NC vs. MCI
ACC	59,38 %	89,06 %	**66,25 %**	63,28 %	89,84 %	**66,25 %**	**69,53 %**	**91,41 %**	65,62 %
SPE	57,81 %	85,94 %	**71,25 %**	64,06 %	85,94 %	68,75 %	67,19 %	**89,06 %**	66,25 %
SEN	60,94 %	92,19 %	61,25 %	62,50 %	**93,75 %**	63,75 %	71,88 %	**93,75 %**	65,00 %

3.3.2 *Late fusion.*

The main idea in this solution, is to make an aggregation operation on the outputs of the last layer of the three networks, as shown in Fig. 4.a. The outputs are real number scores. The other proposed operation Fig. 4.b is the majority vote applied on the three networks decision Softmax results. Note that in this approach, we have firstly trained the three single projection networks separately, and then we applied the fusion operations for each forward input data test step.

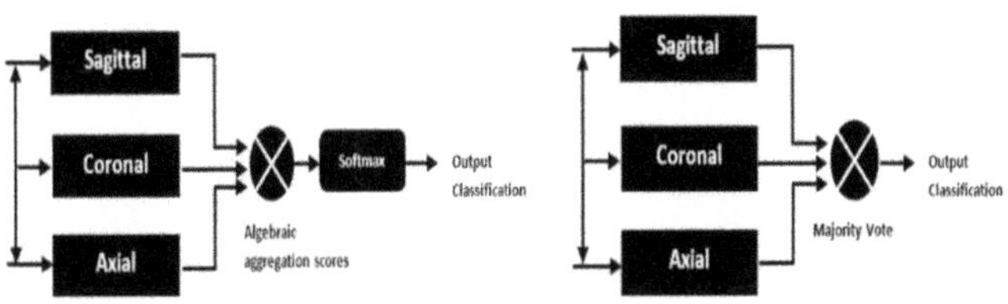

Figure 4: Late Fusion: (a) Algebraic aggregation, (b) Majority vote.

4 EXPERIMENTS AND RESULTS

In our experiments, we split the subjects and reduce the number of scans to get a balanced dataset. The number of original scans was: (188 for AD vs. NC; 228 for MCI vs. NC; and 188 for AD vs. MCI in each binary classification network. The experiments were performed using Caffe framework as mentioned above. The parameters used in the training phase were: 60.000 iterations which gives about 1000 epochs, the Learning rate: 0.0001 and policy: fixed; Momentum: 0.9 Batch-size: 256 (see [11] for definitions).

We present here results we have already submitted for publication. They are quantifying our approach. We state that the sagittal projection is the most discriminative. In fact it yields the best metrics values for AD/NC classification task. In MCI binary classifications there is no consensus on metrics.

Probably they are the most challenging classification tasks as it is difficult to make separation between Mild Cognitive Impairment and already installed Alzheimer disease even for medical experts. The intermediate fusion results presented in Table 3, give us the best scores in all three metrics ACC, SPE, and SEN, in comparison with sagittal single projection. In order to benchmark this intermediate fusion scheme with a classical algebraic operators and other late fusion schemes, we performed three experiments with i) max, ii) mean and iii) a majority vote. The results are presented in Table 4. The max and mean fusion were done on the results of scores before their binarization, and the majority vote was after the binarization of scores. The AD/NC classification gives the best results with majority vote. To position our approach with regard to the literature, we compare it with the most recent work in [10]. Note that a strict comparison is not possible as we use ADNI screening dataset and the authors of [10] do use the baseline dataset. They segment the brain and they parcelate grey matter (GM) into 93 regions. In the AD/NC classification problem we obtain the same figures in accuracy (91.41% vs. 91.02%), better results in sensitivity (93.75% vs. 92.72%) and we are nearly the same in specificity (89.06% vs. 89.94%).The comparison of two other classification tasks is not possible as the authors of [10] are interested in the prediction of conversion of MCI into AD and are not considering AD/MCI and NC/MCI instantaneous classification results. Hence with much more simple method without preliminary fine segmentation we obtain the results which are very close to those in [10].

Table 3: Intermediate Fusion results

	Fusion		
	AD vs. MCI	AD vs. NC	NC vs. MCI
ACC	63.2%	**85.9%**	65.6%
SPE	60.9%	**84.3%**	**66.2%**
SEN	65.6%	**87.5%**	65.0%

Now, we are at one third of PhD research time frame. What are future directions? It is obvious that we have to use more modalities and asses the behavior of fusion approaches on shallow CNNs. Nevertheless, we need a deeper ideas. How to tackle complex classification problems with shallow networks which cannot be deepen.

ACKNOWLEDGMENTS

This work is being supported by French-Morocco Grant PHC TOUBKAL 16/23 AlClass 2016_2018. We thank Dr Pierrick Coupé and Dr Gwënaelle Catheline for fruitful discussions. Data used in the preparation of this article were obtained from the Alzheimer's disease Database Initiative (ADNI) database. A complete listing of ADNI investigators can be found at: http://www.loni.ucla.edu/ADNI/Collaboration/ADNI_Autorship_list.pdf database

REFERENCES

[1] Ramaroson H, Helmer C, Barberger-Gateau P, Letenneur L, Dartigues Jean-François. "Prévalence de la démence et de la maladie d'Alzheimer chez les

personnes de 75 ans et plus: données réactualisées de la cohorte Paquid . Rev Neurol (Paris). 2003; 159:405-411.

[2] Wolz, R., Julkunen, V., Koikkalainen, J., Niskanen, E., Zhang, D. P., Rueckert,D., & Alzheimer's Disease Neuroimaging Initiative. Multi-method analysis of MRIimages in early diagnostics of Alzheimer's disease. 2011; PloS one, 6(10), e25446.

[3] Tong T., Wolz R., Gao Q., Guerrero R., Hajnal J.V., Rueckert D., Multiple instance learning for classification of dementia in brain MRI, Medical Image Analysis, Volume 18, Issue 5, July 2014, Pages 808-818, ISSN 1361-8415, . DOI=http://dx.doi.org/10.1016/j.media.2014.04.006

[4] Ben Ahmed O.,Benois-Pineau J., Allard M., Ben Amar C., Gwénaëlle C.,: Classification of Alzheimer's disease subjects from MRI using hippocampal visual features. Multimedia Tools Appl. 2015; 74(4): 1249-1266

[5] Aderghal K., Boissenin M., Benois-Pineau J., Catheline G., Afdel K., "Classification of sMRI for AD diagnosis with Convolutional Neuronal Networks: a pilot 2-D+epsilon study on ADNI", 23rd International Conference, MMM 2017, Reykjavik, Iceland, January 4-6, 2017.

[6] Aderghal K., Benois-Pineau J., Afdel K., Catheline G., "FuseMe: Classification of sMRI images by fusion of Deep CNNs in 2D+epsilon projections", 15th International Workshop on Content-Based Multimedia Indexing (CBMI2017), submitted.

[7] Payan A., Montana G., "Predicting Alzheimer's disease: a neuroimaging study with 3D convolutional neural networks." 2015; arXiv preprint arXiv: 1502.02506.

[8] Coupé, P., Eskildsen, S. F., Manjón, J. V., Fonov, V. S., Pruessner, J. C., Allard, M., & ADNI. Scoring by nonlocal image patch estimator for early detection of Alzheimer's disease. NeuroImage: clinical, 2012; 1(1), 141-152.

[9] Heung-Il S., Seong-Whan L., Dinggang S., "Latent feature representation with stacked auto-encoder for AD/MCI diagnosis". Brain Structure and Function 2015 Mar; 220(2):841-59. DOI=http//dx.doi.org/10.1007/s00429-013-0687-3. Epub 2013 Dec 22. PubMed PMID: 24363140; PubMed Central PMCID: PMC4065852.

[10] Heung-Il S., Seong-Whan L., Dinggang S., for the Alzheimer's Disease Neuroimaging Initiative, "Deep ensemble learning of sparse regression models for brain disease diagnosis", Medical Image Analysis, Volume 37, April 2017.

[11] Yangqing J., Shelhamer E., Donahue J., Karayev S., Long J., Girshick R., Guadarrama S., Darrell T., "Caffe: Convolutional Architecture for Fast Feature Embedding", In Proceedings of the 22nd ACM international conference on Multimedia.

With 5G Approaching, How will Audio/Video Technology that Serves 800 Million QQ Users Bring Forth New Ideas *

Keynote Talk Abstract†

Xiaozheng Huang
Tencent, China
zenhuang@tencent.com

ABSTRACT

Back to 1999[1], a popular IM QQ in China, stilled called OICQ at that time, released a new version, which included the functionality of audio call for the first time. Not much time later, video call was also enabled. After 18 years of fast growing, QQ has 800 million monthly active users.QQ users spend 1.2 billion minutes for audio and video call every single day.

With QQ's fast growing, the audio and video technology behind it also evolves tremendously. We build our own audio/video technology center, which grows to Tencent Audio/Video Lab, and develops our own SDK when OEM cannot meet our needs. The new generation of audio/video communication engine "SPEAR", developed by our own, serves 800 million QQ users today. Our web broadcasting solution serves China's 10 top web broadcasting platforms, with 200 million user base and 70% market share of China. With 5G approaching, how will audio/video technology that serves 800 million QQ users bring forth new ideas?

In this presentation, I will firstly introduce how the audio/video technology develops in Tencent Audio/Video Lab while internet transferring from PC to mobile. Secondly, I will explain the capability of our technology in the field of audio/video web communication, web broadcasting and image/audio/video processing. Thirdly, I will present our new research results and how they are used in our products and services. Then, I will talk a little about our future plan.

CCS CONCEPTS

• **Applied computing** →Internet telephony; **Information systems** →Multimedia streaming; Web conferencing;

KEYWORDS

multimedia communication; web broadcasting; image/audio/video processing

---

ICMR'17, June 6–9, 2017, Bucharest, Romania.
ACM ISBN 978-1-4503-4701-3/17/06.
DOI: http://dx.doi.org/10.1145/3078971.3081369

BIOGRAPHY

Xiaozheng Huang is a senior scholar and engineer from Tencent Audio/Video Lab. He obtained his bachelor degree from Zhejiang University, China in 2007 and M.A.Sc degree from Simon Fraser University, Canada in 2011. His work is mainly focused on multimedia communication research and application development. Before he joined Tencent, he is core member of audio/video development team in the Skype devision of Microsoft in Redmond, US. He actively participated in the developmen of moduls of video codec, video call and screen sharing for Skype, Microsoft Office Lync and Windows. As a tech lead in Tencent Audio/Video Lab, his work includes SDK of image/video procesing/compression and audio/video communication, which is used in shipped products and services of 800 million user base. He made many outstanding achievements like "Key Tech Breakthrough Award" and "Excellent Operation Award" in Tencent. He also filed several patents, which is adopted by the national standard.

Information Retrieval from Multi-Sensor Data for Enriching Location Services at HERE Technologies

Keynote Talk Abstract

Matei Stroila
HERE Technologies
Chicago, USA
matei.stroila@here.com

ABSTRACT

HERE Technologies provides real-time location services that enable people, enterprises, and cities around the world to harness the power of location and create innovative solutions for a safer and more efficient living. Multimedia retrieval techniques and sensor fusion approaches are essential for enriching location services and for keeping the underlying map up to date.

In this talk, I will give an overview of some of the work we do in the CTO Research group to support existing location services and enable future ones. We aim to automatically extract useful information from massive collections of images, LiDAR point clouds, car sensor data and open web data. I will present work related to image recognition for map making purposes, information retrieval for points of interest enrichment, and work related to creating a highly accurate map of the roads and cities for the future autonomous navigation services.

CCS CONCEPTS

• Information systems ~ Sensor networks • Information systems ~ Image search • Information systems ~ Location based services

KEYWORDS

Information retrieval; multi-sensor data

BIOGRAPHY

Matei Stroila is a Senior Manager of Research at HERE Technologies, currently leading a team of researchers focused on developing innovative solutions for map making techniques and map experiences. He has been with HERE (former NAVTEQ/NOKIA) for more than 10 years, both in individual contributor and managerial roles in Research and Development. During this time, he contributed numerous issued patents and scientific papers in location services relevant areas. In the past, he held research roles in academia, including a research professorship at the University of Virginia, where he worked on medical imaging and computer visualization techniques for brain surgery, and a postdoctoral position at the University of Illinois at Urbana-Champaign, working on shape modeling and vector graphics rendering techniques.

He holds a Ph.D. degree in Mathematics from the University of Southern California and an MS degree in Computer Science from the University of Illinois at Urbana-Champaign.

ICMR '17, June 06-09, 2017, Bucharest, Romania

ACM ISBN 978-1-4503-4701-3/17/06.
http://dx.doi.org/10.1145/3078971.3081370

Intelligently Connecting People with Information

Changhu Wang
Toutiao AI Lab
Beijing, China
wangchanghu@toutiao.com

ABSTRACT

How to effectively connect people with information is a fundamental problem in human society. We are now in the era of mobile first, and everything is digitally connected. With the advent of diverse social contents, information feeds have become a new way to connect people with information. Thus, there is a pretty good opportunity for artificial intelligence (AI) to make innovations in this direction. AI can make more efficient and intelligent the creation, moderation, dissemination, searching, consumption, and interaction of information and contents. [1]

As an industry leader in the product platform and service of information feeds, Toutiao takes the lead to develop and leverage diverse machine learning techniques to efficiently process, analyze, mine, understand, and organize a large amount of multimedia data. Meanwhile, owning to its rich application scenarios and active users all over the world, we have accumulated huge amount of training data, which makes the machine learning system form a closed feedback loop and thus can continually improve and evolve itself. This closed-loop system enables Toutiao to develop core AI technologies in large-scale machine learning, text analysis, natural language processing, computer vision, and data mining.

In this talk, I will share some personal opinions to the development prospects of AI in this fundamental area, including my understanding to AI, important research progress in recent years, the influence of AI to the software industry, and how to build the core competence strategy of AI in a company. Moreover, I will also introduce some research progress of Toutiao AI Lab.

CCS CONCEPTS

• Information systems → Recommender systems; • Computing methodologies → Computer Vision

KEYWORDS

Information feeds; artificial intelligence; machine learning

ICMR '17, June 06-09, 2017, Bucharest, Romania

ACM ISBN 978-1-4503-4701-3/17/06.
http://dx.doi.org/10.1145/3078971.3081371

Short Biography

Changhu Wang is currently Technical Director of Toutiao AI Lab, Beijing, China. He received B.E. and Ph.D. degrees from the University of Science and Technology of China, in 2004 and 2009, respectively. Before joining Toutiao AI Lab, he worked as a lead researcher in Microsoft Research from 2009 to 2017. He worked as a research engineer at the department of Electrical and Computer Engineering in National University of Singapore in 2008.

His current research interests include computer vision, multimedia analysis, and machine learning. In particular, he is interested in applying the techniques from these areas to a broad range of multimedia and vision applications, such as image/video understanding, sketch visual analysis, multimedia search, and deep learning.

Changhu has authored or co-authored over 50 papers in high-quality journals and conferences. He has shipped multiple technologies to Microsoft products, such as Bing, Office, XiaoIce, etc. He holds 9 U.S. granted patents. He also served as program committee member and reviewer for 20+ high-quality conferences and journals. He built one of the first million-level sketch-based image search systems, as well as the first billion-level system in the world. He also built one of the first general sketch recognition systems. He was awarded Microsoft Gold Star Award in 2011, in the recognition of his important contribution to Microsoft's success. He received a Best Demo Award in ACM International Conference on Multimedia 2010 in the recognition of MindFinder system. He was awarded Microsoft Fellowship in 2007.

Homepage: http://chw.azurewebsites.net/

Author Index

www.ingramcontent.com/pod-product-compliance
Ingram Content Group UK Ltd.
Pitfield, Milton Keynes, MK11 3LW, UK
UKHW051415290926
15471UKWH00009B/1614

9 781450 356008